District of Columbia Foreign Deaths

1888-1923

Wesley E. Pippenger

HERITAGE BOOKS
2008

HERITAGE BOOKS
AN IMPRINT OF HERITAGE BOOKS, INC.

Books, CDs, and more—Worldwide

For our listing of thousands of titles see our website
at
www.HeritageBooks.com

Published 2008 by
HERITAGE BOOKS, INC.
Publishing Division
100 Railroad Ave. #104
Westminster, Maryland 21157

Copyright © 2004 Wesley E. Pippenger

All rights reserved. No part of this book may be reproduced or transmitted in any form or by any means, electronic or mechanical, including photocopying, recording or by any information storage and retrieval system without written permission from the author, except for the inclusion of brief quotations in a review.

International Standard Book Numbers
Paperbound: 978-0-7884-3186-9
Clothbound: 978-0-7884-7274-9

DISTRICT OF COLUMBIA
Foreign Death Records
1888 - 1923

Introduction

Death records for the District of Columbia are held at two locations. Original certificates of death starting August 1, 1874[1] and prior to 1932 are maintained at the D.C. Office of Public Records (commonly called the "D.C. Archives"). Death certificates after 1932 are maintained by the D.C. Department of Human Services, Vital Records Division.

Before the District issued individual death certificates, records were kept in a journal inscribed "Interments," which covered the period February 1, 1855 to July 30, 1874. The journal notes that there were no records kept between August 1, 1862 and January 1, 1866. The journal is in the custody of the Vital Records Division and cannot be readily accessed because of its deteriorating condition. Its contents as well as an index can be found on microfilm reels #1994617 and #1994618 that are available through the LDS Church.[2]

In addition to the above, the District of Columbia maintained a somewhat unique type of death record, called "foreign deaths," as indexed here. Perhaps a misleading title— the records were kept for instances where the remains were handled by a District of Columbia undertaker or the remains were in other ways associated with a District of Columbia burying ground. For instance, the "foreign" death records cover situations like:
— if undertaker Francis Gasch made arrangements to bury in Harmony Cemetery the remains of someone who died in New York City,
— if undertaker Joseph F. Birch moved remains from a burying ground in Fairfax County, Virginia to Congressional Cemetery in Washington, D.C.,
— if a person died outside of the District of Columbia and was buried outside the District, yet a D.C. undertaker was involved in the arrangements, or
— sometimes, if the person died in a District of Columbia hospital or public institution, i.e. Providence Hospital, St. Elizabeth's Hospital, jail, D.C. workhouse, or poor house.

One will typically not find records in this group for removals *from* the District. The record group years of 1888-1923 indicates when the action was performed and NOT necessarily when the person died. In most cases removals from one cemetery to another are for persons long dead, in some cases over 75 years!

A "foreign" death record typically shows the name of deceased, age, race, color, place of death, date of interment and undertaker in charge. The various forms used contain blanks for additional information but they were often not filled in. A record often has attached to it a transit permit which shows how the remains were transferred, i.e. by wagon, train or boat, and any paperwork used at the origination. Often one will find attached to the District of Columbia record a transcript of a death record from the jurisdiction where the person died. For remains from Maryland or Virginia, the attached information is typically brief. If a person died aboard a ship, the name of the ship is often given. For this index the compiler has used the term "At Sea" for these instances.

On occasion one will find oddities where body parts were being transferred for burial. Certificate #1959 shows us that only the heart of Preston Adams Ames, who died October 23, 1892, age 37, was transferred in a tin box from Buenos Aires, Brazil to Rock Creek Cemetery. The record includes several foreign letters which give gruesome details. Another record documents that only a leg was buried.

Maryland did not keep early public death records. Although Virginia had a lapse in law requiring the keeping of public death records from 1896 to 1912, one will often find here for that period a local death record in the form of a transfer permit, physician's permit, coroner's certificate, or funeral director's and baggage agent's certificate. These types of records frequently give genealogical information. When space permits, the maiden name of married females or the name of the father of others is inserted in parentheses when found among multiple papers in the record.

In the present index, data has been typed from microfilm copies that were provided by the LDS Church, and, when necessary, cross-checked with the original records at the D.C. Archives. LDS film reels used:

        2116145, nos. 1-1700, 1888-1895
        2116239, nos. 1701-3300, 1895-1900
        2116240, nos. 4200-4299 filmed after 4399; 4000-4199 filmed after 4299, 1900-1904

---

[1] Also see Wesley E. Pippenger, District of Columbia Death Records, August 1, 1874 to July 31, 1879 (Westminster, Md.: Family Line Publications, 1997).
[2] Also see Wesley E. Pippenger, District of Columbia Interments (Index to Deaths), January 1, 1855 to July 31, 1874 (Westminster, Md.: Willow Bend Books, 1999).

2116241, nos. 4601-6000, 1904-1907
2116291, nos. 6001-7300; re-filming of misc., 1907-1909
2116292, nos. 7301-7399, 7600-7699, 7400-7499, 7700-8700, 1909-1912
2116478, nos. 8701-8899, 9000-9199, (numbering change) 11800-12900, 1912-1915
2116479, nos. 12901-14300, 1915-1917
2116480, nos. 14301-15700, 1917-1919
2116605, nos. 15701-17200, 1919-1921
2116606, nos. 17201-17320, 17322-17324, 17430-17452, 17647-17768, 17770-17772, 17779-18600, 1921-1923; several gaps due to poor filming

The following certificates have not been located: 586, 1313, 1327, 2525, 2546, 2868, 3595, 3806, 4084, 5296, 5426, 6714, 7375, 8384, 14826, 15133, 16599, and 16600.

Every effort has been made to correctly interpret the sometimes illegible and frequently difficult handwriting that is found in the original records. The compiler was often suspicious that the record creator could not spell, or did not in some way obtain correct and/or complete information about the decedent. In many cases the compiler compared death certificate information with that available from extant cemetery records or monuments. Also, information that is missing or questionable on the certificate that was created in the District of Columbia can often be found on a source document submitted by the jurisdiction where the death occurred.

Finally, the compiler suggests that this work be used as a finding aid for researchers and not as a replacement for original records.

Wesley E. Pippenger
Arlington, Virginia
Summer 2004

Abbreviations

Common Abbreviations Used

Brig.	Brigadier	M.C.	Member of Congress
C	Colored	min	Minute(s)
Col.	Colonel	N.	North
d	Day	Pk.	Park
D	East Indian	Rev.	Reverend
d/o	Daughter of	S.	South
E.	East	s/o	Son of
G	Mongolian	Sgt.	Sergeant
Gen.	General	Spgs.	Springs
H	Chinese	w/o	Wife of
h	Hour(s)	w	Week(s)
hp.	Hospital	W	White
Hts.	Heights	W.	West
I	American Indian	X	Mexican
J	Japanese	y	Year(s)
Lt.	Lieutenant	Z	Brazilian
m	Month(s)		

Modern postal codes have been used for states, i.e. PA for Pennsylvania or MD for Maryland. Foreign locations are abbreviated as space requires, i.e. Fra. for France or Eng. for England. Occasionally one finds territories or other foreign locations such as C.Z. for the Canal Zone or P.I. for the Philippine Islands.

Local place names are sometimes abbreviated because of space; i.e. Mt. Hope Retreat, Baltimore County, Maryland, is found as "Mt. Hope MD," or Takoma Park (later Washington) Sanatarium, Montgomery County, Maryland, is found as "Takoma Park MD," or the Tuberculosis Hospital of D.C. is found as "T.B. DC." Also, one will find a place of burial as Arlington, Arlington Va. and Arlington National Cemetery. It is not known how many of those without "National Cemetery" actually refer to that location or whether burial was in one of the other burying grounds in Arlington or Alexandria County, Virginia. Because the primary use of the "Place of Burial" column is a burying ground, I have used "Arlington" when the certificate shows Arlington National Cemetery.

Foreign

CERTIFICATE OF DEATH.
DISTRICT OF COLUMBIA.

No. of Record: 5636

FULL INSTRUCTIONS FOR THE GUIDANCE OF THOSE USING THIS BLANK, AND SPACE FOR REMARKS MAY BE FOUND ON THE OTHER SIDE.

1. Date of this Death: July 7, 1906
2. Full Name of Deceased: William B. McIntyre
3. Sex: Male
4. Age: 81 Years
5. Color: White
6. Conjugal Condition: Widower

Under sex, color and conjugal condition, strike out the words not applicable.
Under color, the term "colored" includes all of African descent, whether of pure or mixed blood.

7. Occupation: Merchant
8. Birthplace of Deceased: Scotland
9. Birthplace of Father: "
10. Birthplace of Mother: "
11. Duration of Residence in this District:
12. Place of Death: Nantucket Mass
13. Cause of Death
    PRIMARY: Valv Cardiac _____
    IMMEDIATE:
14. If Death Occurred in an Institution, give:
    NAME OF INSTITUTION:
    LENGTH OF TIME DECEASED WAS AN INMATE:
15. If Deceased did not Die at his or her Residence, give:
    PLACE OF RESIDENCE:

I hereby certify that I attended the deceased professionally during _____ last illness.
_____ M. D.
Address:

TO BE FILLED OUT AND SIGNED BY THE UNDERTAKER:
PLACE OF BURIAL: Oak Hill Cemetery   DATE OF BURIAL: July 11, 1906
IF BODY IS TO BE BURIED OUTSIDE OF THE DISTRICT, STATE:
ROUTE OF TRANSPORTATION: _____   DATE OF REMOVAL: _____ 190__
SIGNATURE: W. H. Spease, Undertaker
Address: 9__ __ N W

THIS SPACE RESERVED FOR BINDING.

Figure 1 - Certificate of Death, for foreign deaths, Style A

CERTIFICATE OF DEATH.
DISTRICT OF COLUMBIA.

No. of Record K 76535

FULL INSTRUCTIONS FOR THE GUIDANCE OF THOSE USING THIS BLANK AND SPACE FOR REMARKS MAY BE FOUND ON THE OTHER SIDE

1 PLACE OF DEATH Alabama Pa

Name of Hospital _____ Duration of residence therein _____

2 FULL NAME Ida Barnes Hagen

(a) Residence No. Herama Pa

PERSONAL AND STATISTICAL PARTICULARS

3 SEX Female **4 COLOR OR RACE** White **5** Married

5A HUSBAND of (or) WIFE of — Ernest L Hagen

6 DATE OF BIRTH 1 9 1868

7 AGE Years 51 Months 5 Days 20

8 OCCUPATION OF DECEASED Housewife

9 BIRTHPLACE D.C.

10 NAME OF FATHER Genn W Barnes

11 BIRTHPLACE OF FATHER D.C.

12 MAIDEN NAME OF MOTHER Martha C DeLay

13 BIRTHPLACE OF MOTHER Md

14 Above information furnished by Mrs George Hagen
(Address) 142 a _____

15 Relation of informant to decedent _____ cousin

MEDICAL CERTIFICATE OF DEATH

16 DATE OF DEATH 6/13 19 20

17 I HEREBY CERTIFY, That I attended deceased from _____

The CAUSE OF DEATH was as follows: _____

CONTRIBUTORY (SECONDARY) _____

19 PLACE OF BURIAL, CREMATION, OR REMOVAL Congressional
DATE 6/15 19 20

INSTRUCTIONS RELATIVE TO THE ISSUANCE OF DEATH CERTIFICATES

1. Certificates should be filled out with ink, and should, as far as possible, contain all information called for.
2. Certificates which bear evidence of unauthorized alterations, or which are in any other manner materially defective, cannot be admitted to record.
3. When death has occurred without the attendance of a physician, or when it is believed or known to have been due to other than natural causes, or when either the cause of death or the identity of the deceased is unknown, the death certificate must be signed by the coroner before a burial permit can be issued.
4. When death has occurred from a communicable disease information should be furnished, if possible, relative to the place where such disease was contracted, if it was contracted elsewhere than at the place of death.
5. Remarks, if any, may be written in the space below, and should be dated and signed by the party responsible for them.
6. Precise statement of occupation is very important, so that the relative healthfulness of various pursuits can be known. The question applies to each and every person, irrespective of age. For many occupations a single word or term on the first line will be sufficient, e. g., *Farmer* or *Planter*, *Physician*, *Compositor*, *Architect*, *Locomotive engineer*, *Civil engineer*, *Stationary fireman*, etc. But in many cases, especially in industrial employments, it is necessary to know (a) the kind of work and also (b) the nature of the business or industry, and therefore an additional line is provided for the latter statement; it should be used only when needed. As examples: (a) *Spinner*, (b) *Cotton mill*; (a) *Salesman*, (b) *Grocery*; (a) *Foreman*, (b) *Automobile factory*. The material worked on may form part of the second statement. Never return "Laborer," "Foreman," "Manager," "Dealer," etc., without more precise specification, as *Day laborer*, *Farm laborer*, *Laborer—Coal mine*, etc. Women at home, who are engaged in the duties of the household only (not paid *Housekeepers* who receive a definite salary), may be entered as *Housewife*, *Housework*, or *At home*, and children, not gainfully employed, as *At school* or *At home*. Care should be taken to report specifically the occupations of persons engaged in domestic service for wages, as *Servant*, *Cook*, *Housemaid*, etc. If the occupation has been changed or given up on account of the DISEASE CAUSING DEATH, state occupation at beginning of illness. If retired from business, that fact may be indicated thus: *Farmer (retired, 6 yrs.)*. For persons who have no occupation whatever, write *None*.
7. Name, FIRST, the DISEASE CAUSING DEATH (the primary affection with respect to time and causation), using always the same accepted term for the same disease. Examples: *Cerebrospinal fever* (the only definite synonym is "Epidemic cerebrospinal meningitis"); *Diphtheria* (avoid use of "Croup"); *Typhoid fever* (never report "Typhoid pneumonia"); *Lobar pneumonia*; *Bronchopneumonia* ("Pneumonia", unqualified, is indefinite); *Tuberculosis of lungs, meninges, peritoneum*, etc., *Carcinoma*, *Sarcoma*, etc., of..........(name origin; "Cancer" is less definite; avoid use of "Tumor" for malignant neoplasms); *Measles*; *Whooping cough*; *Chronic valvular heart disease*; *Chronic interstitial nephritis*, etc. The contributory (secondary or intercurrent) affection need not be stated unless important. Example: *Measles* (disease causing death), 20 ds.; *Bronchopneumonia* (secondary), 10 ds. Never report mere symptoms or terminal conditions, such as "Asthenia," "Anemia" (merely symptomatic), "Atrophy," "Collapse," "Coma," "Convulsions," "Debility," "Congenital," "Senile," etc.), "Dropsy," "Exhaustion," "Heart failure," "Hemorrhage," "Inanition," "Marasmus," "Old age," "Shock," "Uremia," "Weakness," etc., when a definite disease can be ascertained as the cause. Always qualify all diseases resulting from childbirth or miscarriage, as "PUERPERAL *septicemia*," "PUERPERAL *peritonitis*," etc. State cause for which surgical operation was undertaken. For VIOLENT DEATHS state MEANS OF INJURY and qualify as ACCIDENTAL, SUICIDAL, or HOMICIDAL, or as *probably such*, if impossible to determine definitely. Examples: *Accidental drowning*; *Struck by railway train—accident*; *Revolver wound of head—homicide*; *Poisoned by carbolic acid—probably suicide*. The nature of the injury, as fracture of skull, and consequences (e. g., *sepsis*, *tetanus*) may be stated under the head of "Contributory." (Recommendations on statement of cause of death approved by Committee on Nomenclature of the American Medical Association.)

WM. C. FOWLER, M.D., *Health Officer*.

REMARKS

Extracts from "The Code of Law for the District of Columbia, enacted March 3, 1901, amended by the Act approved June 30, 1902, relating to Cemeteries and the Disposal of Dead Bodies."

SEC. 675. That no dead body of any human being, or any part of such body, shall in said District be removed from place to place, interred, disinterred, or in any manner disposed of without a permit for such removal, interment, disinterment, or disposal granted by the health officer of said District, nor otherwise than in accordance with the terms of said permit; permits for the removal, interment, or disposal to be issued upon the presentation of a proper death certificate, signed by a physician registered at the health department of said District, who has attended the deceased during his or her last illness, or by the coroner of said District or his deputy, or by the proper municipal, county or State authorities at the place where the death occurred.

SEC. 677. That it shall be the duty of any person or persons having custody or control of the dead body of any human being, or any part of such body, to report in writing, or cause to be reported in writing, to the health officer of said District within forty-eight hours after the death of the deceased, the name of said deceased and the location of the body or part thereof.

SEC. 683. That it shall be unlawful for any person or persons to cremate or otherwise destroy the dead body, or part of the dead body, of any human being in said District before the issue of the burial permit by the health officer of said District, and then only when said permit is countersigned by the coroner of said District authorizing such cremation or destruction. It shall be unlawful for any person or persons to embalm, inject, or, by any similar method preserve the dead body or part of the dead body of any human being in said District within four hours after death or before the issue of the death certificate; and in case the death is believed to be due to other than natural causes, or the cause thereof is unknown, such embalming, injecting, or preserving shall at no time be done unless such death certificate has been signed or approved by the coroner of said District.

OFFICE HOURS.—The health department is open for the issuance of burial permits, the receipt of complaints, and the transaction of any urgent business, from nine o'clock a. m. until eleven o'clock p. m., daily.

Figure 3 - Certificate of Death, Style B, reverse, instructions

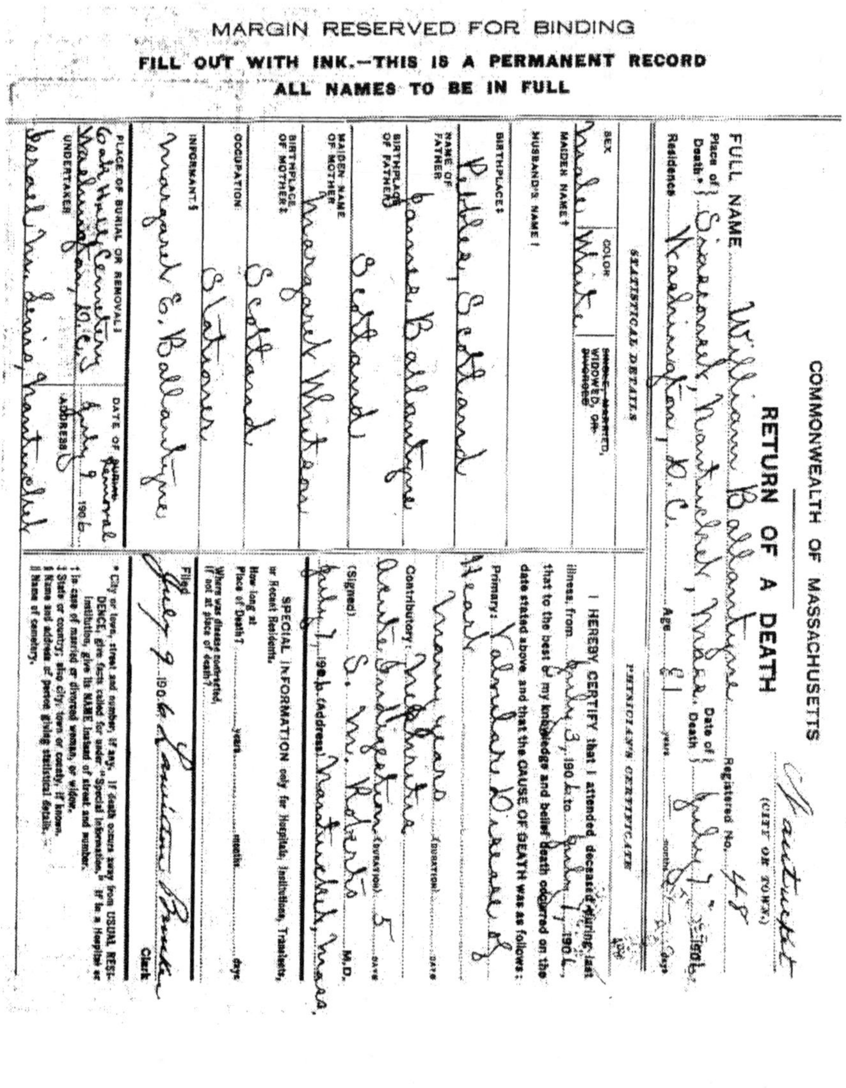
MARGIN RESERVED FOR BINDING
FILL OUT WITH INK.—THIS IS A PERMANENT RECORD
ALL NAMES TO BE IN FULL
COMMONWEALTH OF MASSACHUSETTS
Nantucket
(CITY OR TOWN.)
RETURN OF A DEATH
Registered No. 48
FULL NAME William Ballantyne
Place of Death* Siasconset, Nantucket, Mass. Date of Death July 7, 1906
Residence Washington, D.C. Age 81 years 5 months days

STATISTICAL DETAILS
SEX Male COLOR White SINGLE, MARRIED, WIDOWED, OR DIVORCED
MAIDEN NAME†
HUSBAND'S NAME†
BIRTHPLACE‡ Peebles, Scotland
NAME OF FATHER James Ballantyne
BIRTHPLACE OF FATHER‡ Scotland
MAIDEN NAME OF MOTHER Margaret Whitson
BIRTHPLACE OF MOTHER‡ Scotland
OCCUPATION Stationer
INFORMANT§ Margaret E. Ballantyne
PLACE OF BURIAL OR REMOVAL|| Oak Hill Cemetery, Washington, D.C. DATE OF Removal July 9 1906
UNDERTAKER ADDRESS Nantucket

PHYSICIAN'S CERTIFICATE
I HEREBY CERTIFY that I attended deceased during last illness, from July 3, 1906 to July 7, 1906, that to the best of my knowledge and belief death occurred on the date stated above and that the CAUSE OF DEATH was as follows:
Primary: Valvular Disease of Heart many years (DURATION) DAYS
Contributory: Nephritis Acute Indigestion (DURATION) 5 DAYS
(Signed) S. M. Roberts M.D.
July 7, 1906 (Address) Nantucket, Mass.

SPECIAL INFORMATION only for Hospitals, Institutions, Transients, or Recent Residents.
How long at Place of Death? years months days
Where was disease contracted, if not at place of death?
Filed July 9 1906 Clerk

* City or town, street and number, if any. If death occurs away from USUAL RESIDENCE, give facts called for under "Special Information." If in a Hospital or institution, give its NAME instead of street and number.
† In case of married or divorced woman, or widow.
‡ State or country; also city, town or county, if known.
§ Name and address of person giving statistical details.
|| Name of cemetery.

Figure 4 - Certificate of Death, for foreign deaths, sample attachment

DISTRICT OF COLUMBIA
Foreign Death Records
1888 - 1923

No.	Name	Age	Race	Death Date	Place of Death	Burial Place
A						
13785	Abbe, Cleveland	77y	W	28 OCT 1916	Chevy Chase MD	Rock Creek
04531	Abbot, Ellen J.	89y	W	3 DEC 1903	Bedford Co. VA	Oak Hill
00530	Abbott, Catherine	81y	W	20 APR 1887	Baltimore MD	Rock Creek
00531	Abbott, Edwin A.	65y	W	20 JAN 1876	Baltimore MD	Rock Creek
02623	Abbott, Lizzie	55y	W	7 OCT 1898	Bowie MD	Oak Hill
15480	Abbott, Sidney Ernest	25y	W	20 DEC 1918	Newport News VA	Cremated
01108	Abel, Samuel	61y	C	8 JUN 1892	Huntersville VA	Hillsdale
04336	Abert, S. Thayer	67y	W	11 AUG 1903	Garrett Co. MD	Rock Creek
12609	Abrams, George B.	79y	W	10 NOV 1914	Takoma Park MD	Congressional
09108	Abrams, William D.	43y	W	5 MAR 1913	Northampton PA	Rock Creek
18259	Acee, Wallace Livingston	53y	W	11 JAN 1923	Silver Spring MD	Columbus GA
04409	Ackenbaugh, Ester G.	22y	W	26 JUL 1903	Wash. Grove MD	Glenwood
08080	Acker, Charles A.	80y	W	23 APR 1911	Hyattsville MD	Congressional
18040	Acker, Marjorie E.	25y	W	30 AUG 1922	Memphis TN	Glenwood
04710	Ackerman, Elizabeth B.	6y	W	23 MAR 1904	San Diego CA	Rock Creek
02286	Ackerman, Mary	44y	W	2 DEC 1897	Canfield OH	Prospect Hill
14180	Acton, Wallace Guy	33y	W	18 JUN 1917	Detroit MI	Congressional
05378	Acton, William	35y	W	24 NOV 1905	Baltimore MD	Rock Creek
07921	Adams, Alice H.	55y	W	12 JAN 1911	New York NY	Glenwood
16783	Adams, Alice Moody	79y	W	27 OCT 1920	Silver Spring MD	Congressional
01109	Adams, Annah Eliz. N.B.	45y	W	5 APR 1892	St. Augustine FL	Rock Creek
03036	Adams, Annie G.	32y	W	10 DEC 1899	Starke FL	Rock Creek
04805	Adams, Beulah V.	25y	W	16 JUL 1904	Elizabeth NJ	Oak Hill
05795	Adams, Charles H.	70y	W	28 OCT 1906	Winthrop MA	Arlington
12110	Adams, Cora Y.	32y	W	28 NOV 1913	Saranac Lake NY	Glenwood
06754	Adams, Cornelious, s/o C.	57y	C	1 OCT 1908	Manassas VA	Harmony
14771	Adams, Earl	17y	W	22 APR 1918	Camp McClel. AL	Arlington
15172	Adams, Edward	27y	W	13 OCT 1918	Ft. Oglethorpe GA	Glenwood
05251	Adams, Edward J., Jr.	30y	W	17 AUG 1905	Norfolk VA	Rock Creek
08484	Adams, Emma C.	72y	W	18 JAN 1912	Dominion Hts. VA	Glenwood
15612	Adams, George S.	54y	C	11 FEB 1919	Pittsburgh PA	Harmony
08240	Adams, Hamilton, s/o John	52y	W	4 AUG 1911	Atlantic City NJ	Glenwood
17759	Adams, Helen Root (West)	97y	W	20 MAR 1922	Norfolk VA	Cremated
03715	Adams, Joseph	38y	C	21 NOV 1901	Philadelphia PA	Arlington
17905	Adams, Kate Martha	74y	W	14 JUN 1922	Takoma MD	Congressional
07253	Adams, Mary	40y	C	29 OCT 1909	Rosaryville MD	Mt. Olivet
01012	Adams, Mary A.	74y	W	12 FEB 1893	Ballston VA	Glenwood
15885	Adams, Mary E.	73y	W	19 JUL 1919	Mt. Ranier MD	Rock Creek
08487	Adams, Mary G.	52y	W	19 JAN 1912	New York NY	Oak Hill
07233	Adams, Minnie C.	49y	W	7 OCT 1909	Elizabeth NJ	Oak Hill
06984	Adams, Norval Wilson	60y	W	14 APR 1909	Sligo Mill Rd. MD	Congressional
06721	Adams, Paul	1y	W	9 SEP 1908	Arlington VA	Holyrood
01013	Adams, Robert	30y	C	19 MAR 1893	New York NY	Harmony
07785	Adams, Robert	35y	C	10 OCT 1910	Philadelphia PA	Payne's
13875	Adams, Sarah	77y	C	20 DEC 1916	Riverdale MD	Occoquan VA
03383	Adams, Sarah	39y	C	1 JAN 1901	New York NY	Woodlawn
13939	Adams, Sarah A.	78y	W	21 JAN 1917	Landover MD	Glenwood
00916	Adams, Thomas Jacob	56y	W	9 JUN 1893	Ballston VA	Glenwood
14459	Adams, William Clinton	63y	W	12 NOV 1917	Landover MD	Rock Creek
06870	Adams, William E.	34y	C	24 DEC 1908	Atlantic City NJ	Sidgar MD

District of Columbia Foreign Death Records, 1888-1923

No.	Name of Deceased	Age	Race	Death Date	Place of Death	Place of Burial
14756	Adams, William H.	65y	W	14 APR 1918	Baltimore MD	Glenwood
00385	Adams, William H.	58y	W	4 AUG 1890	Elizabeth NJ	Oak Hill
07483	Adams, William H.	36y	W	27 MAR 1910	Mt. Ranier MD	Rock Creek
13064	Adams, William Henry	75y	W	19 AUG 1915	Oxon Hill MD	Congressional
01014	Adams, William J.	16y	C	31 MAR 1893	Philadelphia PA	Graceland
00445	Adamson, Sophia	78y	W	1 DEC 1890	Friendship MD	Tenallytown
12055	Addison, Edmond Brice, Dr.	82y	W	14 FEB 1853	Alexandria VA	Rock Creek
03609	Addison, Maria Eliason	65y	W	9 AUG 1901	Boerne TX	Oak Hill
06690	Addison, Mary E.	38y	C	14 AUG 1908	Asbury Park NJ	Harmony
12054	Addison, William Bowie	21y	W	2 AUG 1853	Alexandria VA	Rock Creek
03464	Adee, Amelia K.	52y	W	9 SEP 1864	Stamford CN	Oak Hill
03465	Adee, Augustus A., Dr.	41y	W	22 FEB 1844	New York NY	Oak Hill
07307	Ader, Albert	59y	W	1 DEC 1909	Pr. Geo. Co. MD	Rock Creek
01957	Aderer, Edith	1y	W	6 AUG 1896	Berkeley Sp. WV	Wash. Hebrew
06874	Adison, Infant of W.H.	SB	C	30 DEC 1908	Fairmont Hts. MD	Payne's
08684	Adolphus, Amanda	50y	C	24 JUN 1912	Tivoli NY	Payne's
01465	Ager, Elsie L.	9m	W	19 AUG 1894	Hyattsville MD	Rock Creek
01958	Ager, George H.	8m	W	1 JUL 1896	Hyattsville MD	Rock Creek
07868	Ager, India	43y	W	13 DEC 1910	Chillum MD	Rock Creek
05851	Ager, Joseph B.	73y	W	6 DEC 1906	Hyattsville MD	Rock Creek
03362	Ahem, George, plumber	c.35y	W	7 DEC 1900	Weberton MD	Mt. Olivet
06112	Ahern, Mary A.	51y	W	16 JUN 1907	Baltimore MD	Mt. Olivet
14007	Aiers, Florence F.	57y	W	21 FEB 1917	Wichita Falls TX	Congressional
07779	Aiken, Jane	50y	W	7 OCT 1910	Riverdale MD	Rock Creek
16681	Aiken, Mary I.	73y	W	c.24 AUG 1920	Silver Hill MD	Mt. Olivet
16697	Aiken, William J.	29y	W	6 SEP 1920	Saranac Lake NY	Rock Creek
13378	Ainsworth, Mary	64y	W	24 FEB 1916	Alex. Co. VA	Congressional
08732	Akerby, Laura Meigs	79y	W	25 JUL 1912	Takoma Park MD	Delhi NY
01849	Akin, Eliza	28y	W	20 FEB 1847	New York NY	Oak Hill
17987	Albee, Christiania	27y	W	31 JUL 1922	Cherrydale VA	Bath ME
11804	Albomez, Georginia	8y	W	7 MAY 1913	Takoma Park MD	New York NY
13348	Albrecht, Henrietta	82y	W	11 FEB 1916	Takoma Park MD	Chicago IL
13895	Albright, Florine A.	60y	W	30 DEC 1916	New York NY	Rock Creek
13756	Albright, Mollie (Welch)	28y	W	9 AUG 1916	Culpeper Co. VA	Rock Creek
16899	Alden, Ellen I.	40y	W	6 JAN 1921	Asheville NC	Cremated
17573	Alden, Fannie E.	66y	W	7 DEC 1921	Seat Pleasant MD	Ft. Lincoln
17513	Alden, Lydia M.	85y	W	10 NOV 1921	Silver Spring MD	Mt. Vernon IA
17254	Alden, Mary Louise	11m	—	24 JUN 1921	Silver Spring MD	Glenwood
09104	Alden, Thomas	76y	W	2 MAR 1913	Seat Pleasant MD	Glenwood
16229	Aldrich, George Fay	67y	W	19 JAN 1920	Alexandria VA	Congressional
03500	Aldridge, Frank T.	38y	W	6 MAY 1901	Asheville NC	Mt. Olivet
14469	Aldridge, Minnie I.	42y	W	18 NOV 1917	Mt. Ranier MD	Congressional
17748	Alexander, Cassie (Stuart)	76y	W	15 MAR 1922	Colonial Bea. VA	Mt. Olivet
02148	Alexander, Catherine F.	70y	W	27 NOV 1847	Alex. Co. VA	Oak Hill[1]
03512	Alexander, Columbus S.	58y	W	15 MAY 1901	Baltimore MD	Oak Hill
13295	Alexander, David, s/o Simon	29y	W	12 JAN 1916	Atlantic City NJ	Wash. Hebrew
05808	Alexander, Douglas B.	26y	W	5 NOV 1906	Baltimore MD	Oak Hill
07511	Alexander, Eva N.	57y	C	22 APR 1910	Cleveland OH	Harmony
17588	Alexander, Gertrude	59y	W	15 DEC 1921	Takoma Park MD	Wheeling WV
17070	Alexander, Helen R.	30y	W	27 MAR 1921	Mt. Vernon NY	Wash. Hebrew
02360	Alexander, Henry Hay	50y	W	29 SEP 1898	Smithville S. LI	Oak Hill
14364	Alexander, Kate B.	62y	W	12 SEP 1917	Seattle WA	Glenwood
14831	Alexander, Rachel J.	65y	C	14 MAY 1918	St. Paul MN	Harmony
12968	Alexander, Sarah	73y	W	22 MAY 1915	Philadelphia PA	Mt. Olivet
15748	Alexander, Thomson H.	70y	W	21 APR 1919	New York NY	Oak Hill
02149	Alexander, Walter S.	65y	W	9 MAR 1856	Alex. Co. VA	Oak Hill

[1] Note that the Alexander family graves were removed from the Vincent farm, Va.

District of Columbia Foreign Death Records, 1888-1923

No.	Name of Deceased	Age	Race	Death Date	Place of Death	Place of Burial
05154	Alexander, William D.	39y	W	4 JUN 1905	Saranac Lake NY	Oak Hill
07676	Alexander, William K.	4y	W	6 AUG 1910	Mt. Ranier MD	Congressional
00359	Alexandria, Matilda	45y	C	12 JUL 1890	Montg. Co. MD	Graceland
05413	Alleger, Charles W.	22y	W	30 DEC 1905	Loudoun Park[1]	Quantico VA
05787	Alleman, Hiram C.	75y	W	22 OCT 1906	New York NY	Oak Hill
13037	Allen, Abby S.	64y	W	2 AUG 1915	Lakeside ME	Oak Hill
07457	Allen, Aletha A.	34y	W	4 MAR 1880	Pr. Geo. Co. MD	Congressional
02579	Allen, Anne R.H.	75y	W	24 AUG 1898	New York NY	Oak Hill
05311	Allen, Benjamin	53y	W	8 OCT 1905	Lanham MD	Mt. Olivet
18051	Allen, Caroline	75y	C	4 SEP 1922	Fairmont Hts. MD	Mt. Olivet
18360	Allen, Carrie	19y	W	18 FEB 1923	Philadelphia PA	Clarendon VA
04939	Allen, Edgar	62y	W	28 OCT 1904	Richmond VA	Glenwood
18321	Allen, Edgar W., in jail	20y	C	2 FEB 1923	Atlanta GA	Harmony
14355	Allen, Edward Gray, s/o Henry	70y	W	11 SEP 1917	Grantwood NJ	Arlington
06279	Allen, Edwin Ernest	4m	W	21 OCT 1907	Rosslyn VA	Holyrood
02741	Allen, Eliza Brice Clagett	63y	W	8 FEB 1899	New York NY	Rock Creek
07608	Allen, Elizabeth	2y	W	1 JUL 1910	Brentwood MD	Congressional
12849	Allen, Emma	54y	C	27 MAR 1915	New York NY	Harmony
08420	Allen, Ethan	80y	W	7 DEC 1911	New York NY	New York NY
07849	Allen, Florence Ann	33y	W	3 DEC 1910	Chevy Chase MD	Glenwood
07594	Allen, Francis L.	64y	W	24 JUN 1910	Cleveland OH	Bell's Meeting H.
13727	Allen, Frank	34y	C	17 SEP 1916	New York NY	Harmony
16807	Allen, Frank B.	66y	W	13 NOV 1920	Philadelphia PA	Woodlawn
06551	Allen, George W.	35y	W	8 NOV 1907	Ft. Bayard NM	Rock Creek
12708	Allen, Harriett	48y	C	8 JAN 1915	New York NY	Payne's
15969	Allen, Harry	63y	W	31 AUG 1919	Takoma Park MD	Glenwood
17752	Allen, Harry H.	55y	W	14 MAR 1922	Phoenix AZ	Rock Creek
08160	Allen, Irene	28y	C	17 JUN 1911	New York NY	Mt. Zion West
04912	Allen, Jacob S.	68y	W	6 OCT 1904	Germantown PA	Prospect Hill
12872	Allen, Joseph Milton	23y	W	11 APR 1915	Alex. Co. VA	Mt. Olivet
00192	Allen, Katherine	58y	C	8 MAR 1889	Pr. Geo. Co. MD	Dean's Family
12566	Allen, Lile	43y	C	13 OCT 1914	Dupont Hts. MD	Woodlawn
18229	Allen, Luman	36y	W	27 DEC 1922	Lancaster PA	Glenwood
07792	Allen, Maud May Wootson	32y	C	17 OCT 1910	Atlantic City NJ	Harmony
17886	Allen, Mildred	66y	C	2 JUN 1922	Pelham NY	Payne's
08656	Allen, Robert	45y	W	2 JUN 1912	New York NY	Oak Hill
03654	Allen, Sarah A.	17y	C	20 SEP 1901	Lanham Sta. MD	Mt. Olivet
03547	Allen, Sarah J.	62y	W	19 JUN 1901	Takoma Park MD	Glenwood
14759	Allen, Thomas T.	72y	W	7 FEB 1906	Oxon Hill MD	Glenwood
12231	Allen, William T.	22y	W	15 FEB 1914	W. Palm Bea. FL	Glenwood
15602	Alling, Cordelia B.	73y	W	7 FEB 1919	Colchester VA	Rock Creek
14034	Allison, Grace	2y	C	14 MAR 1917	Brentwood MD	Cremated
14652	Allison, Harriett A.	72y	W	19 FEB 1918	FL	Arlington
00193	Allison, J.W.	36y	W	15 JAN 1849	Fairfax Co. VA	Congressional
17470	Allman, Margaret, Sister	24y	W	17 OCT 1921	Brunswick MD	Mt. Olivet
06304	Allwine, Infant of Daniel	SB	W	11 NOV 1906	Ballston VA	Congressional
06304	Allwine, Infant of Daniel T.	SB	W	11 NOV 1906	Brick Haven VA	Congressional
01110	Allwine, Rosie Virginia	1y	W	3 NOV 1892	Alexandria VA	Congressional
01111	Allwine, Rosie Virginia	1y	W	3 NOV 1892	Alexandria VA	Congressional
13789	Almarr, Catherine G.	56y	W	28 OCT 1916	Beltsville MD	Mt. Olivet
14375	Almsted, Emma E.	63y	W	25 SEP 1917	Hyattsville MD	Grand Rapids MI
17879	Alpert, Joseph	46y	W	24 MAY 1922	Denver CO	Elesavetgrad
11979	Altdorfer, William L.	40y	W	29 AUG 1913	Chevy Chase MD	Congressional
06966	Altemus, Sarah Ann	36y	W	27 AUG 1854	Damascus OH	Congressional[2]
05922	Alton, Ann	93y	W	31 JAN 1907	New York NY	Rock Creek

[1] Removal from Loudon Park Cemetery, Baltimore MD.
[2] Removed from the old Baptist cemetery in Salem, Ohio, in APR 1909.

No.	Name of Deceased	Age	Race	Death Date	Place of Death	Place of Burial
05205	Altscher, John Henry	29y	W	8 JUL 1905	St. Louis Co. MO	Oak Hill
07713	Alvey, Edna May	6y	W	25 AUG 1910	Capitol Hts. MD	Mt. Olivet
12639	Aman, Joseph Andrew	87y	W	2 DEC 1914	Hyattsville MD	Mt. Olivet
06794	Aman, Katharine Barbara	74y	W	30 OCT 1908	Hyattsville MD	Mt. Olivet
12198	Aman, William J., s/o Seb.	38y	W	2 FEB 1914	Lewisetta VA	Glenwood
09133	Amateis, Louis	57y	W	16 MAR 1913	Falls Church VA	Capital Cem. MD
07040	Amberg, Christopher	51y	W	10 SEP 1891	Baltimore MD	Prospect Hill
07041	Amberg, Edward William	26y	W	15 MAR 1898	Baltimore MD	Prospect Hill
07038	Amberg, Louis C.	13y	W	8 AUG 1883	Baltimore MD	Prospect Hill
07039	Amberg, Richard Oscar	20y	W	28 FEB 1903	Baltimore MD	Prospect Hill
15625	Ambler, Samuel T.	50y	C	14 FEB 1919	Chicago IL	Woodlawn
05381	Ambrogi, Raffaello	64y	W	3 DEC 1905	Baltimore MD	Mt. Olivet
07512	Ambush, Mary	90y	C	17 APR 1910	Philadelphia PA	Harmony
02654	America, Josie Bell	3y	W	11 NOV 1898	Berwyn MD	Congressional
16711	Ames, Anganette G.	28y	W	9 SEP 1920	Longmont CO	Arlington
04850	Ames, Elizabeth Delano	65y	W	17 AUG 1904	Braddock Hts. MD	Rock Creek
03473	Ames, Infant of John G.	3d	W	JAN 1866	Mt. Vernon OH	Rock Creek
03291	Ames, John	70y	C	23 SEP 1900	Hampton VA	Arlington VA
14570	Ames, Lovanda A.	81y	W	13 JAN 1918	Mt. Ranier MD	Glenwood
01959	Ames, Preston Adams (heart)	37y	W	23 OCT 1892	Buenos Aires, Br.	Rock Creek
17200	Ames, Stanley M.	—	W	28 MAY 1921	Walter Reed Hp.	Arlington
03408	Amiss, Maria S.	86y	W	4 FEB 1901	Westminster MD	Oak Hill
06565	Amos, Helen M.	22y	W	25 MAY 1908	Gaithersburg MD	Rock Creek
09001	Amos, James	50y	W	24 DEC 1912	New York NY	Glenwood
03977	Amos, John B.	12y	W	9 AUG 1902	Leesburg VA	Alexandria VA
00063	Anderson, Adna	62y	W	15 MAY 1889	Philadelphia PA	Oak Hill
12947	Anderson, Albert	51y	C	27 MAY 1915	New York NY	Harmony
03723	Anderson, Alexander D.	58y	W	c.24 NOV 1901	Marshall Hall MD	Oak Hill
13704	Anderson, Alphonsus John	20y	W	30 AUG 1916	Santo Domingo	Philadelphia PA
13640	Anderson, Amanda M.	76y	W	5 AUG 1916	Hyattsville MD	Rock Creek
15784	Anderson, Anna Lena	63y	W	18 MAY 1919	Glen Echo MD	Glenwood
06146	Anderson, Benjamin Franklin	58y	W	19 JUL 1907	Kenilworth MD	Rock Creek
12269	Anderson, Birdy	23y	W	25 MAR 1914	Newport News VA	Potomac MD
16347	Anderson, Blanche C.	44y	W	27 FEB 1920	Takoma Park MD	Congressional
17901	Anderson, Charles	45y	C	11 JUN 1922	Baltimore MD	Harmony
12809	Anderson, Charles B.	64y	W	11 MAR 1915	Williamsburg VA	Glenwood
13431	Anderson, Christian	27y	W	26 MAR 1916	So. Bridge MA	Congressional
02232	Anderson, Clarina A.	9m	W	23 JUL 1897	Harpers Ferry WV	Glenwood
16554	Anderson, Cora Collins	48y	W	23 JUN 1920	Greensboro NC	Arlington
15893	Anderson, Earl T.	29y	W	29 JUL 1919	Alexandria VA	Congressional
01388	Anderson, Eliza	72y	W	26 APR 1894	Philadelphia PA	Oak Hill
07445	Anderson, George B.	62y	W	2 MAR 1910	Weekankin NJ	Rock Creek
16334	Anderson, George Ross	51y	W	23 FEB 1920	Saranac Lake NY	Rock Creek
06132	Anderson, Gillespie	57y	W	7 JUL 1907	Jersey City NJ	Harmony
06060	Anderson, Harper, in jail	30y	C	3 MAY 1907	Cape May Co. NJ	Gomset Bea. VA
14325	Anderson, Harry L.	36y	W	25 AUG 1917	Newport RI	Arlington
14536	Anderson, Henry	40y	C	29 DEC 1917	Baltimore MD	Payne's
09175	Anderson, Jane	55y	C	15 APR 1913	New York NY	Mt. Zion East
01612	Anderson, Joseph	66y	W	9 APR 1895	Boston MA	Oak Hill
12753	Anderson, Louise A.	21y	W	6 FEB 1915	Bluemont VA	Rock Creek
13221	Anderson, Lucius	60y	C	25 NOV 1915	Dupont Hts. MD	Payne's
00194	Anderson, Martha R.	79y	W	3 FEB 1890	Macon MS	Mt. Olivet
17829	Anderson, Mary	—	—	7 MAR 1922	Gloversville NY	Harmony
08869	Anderson, Mary A.	65 or 70y	W	2 OCT 1912	Sykesville MD	Mt. Olivet
11860	Anderson, Mrs. Norman C.	26y	W	13 FEB 1913	Ancon, Can. Zone	Rock Creek
06610	Anderson, Oscar P., Jr.	16m	W	25 JUN 1908	Mt. Ranier MD	Glenwood
07135	Anderson, Raymond Adelbert	8m	W	26 JUL 1909	Edwardsville VA	Congressional
07570	Anderson, Rosie Bell	4m	C	15 JUN 1910	Arlington VA	Moore's
03517	Anderson, Samuel	63y	W	19 MAY 1901	Hyattsville MD	Rock Creek

District of Columbia Foreign Death Records, 1888-1923

No.	Name of Deceased	Age	Race	Death Date	Place of Death	Place of Burial
18020	Anderson, Susan	90y	W	19 AUG 1922	Kensington MD	Oak Hill
13745	Anderson, Thomas Henry	69y	W	30 SEP 1916	Denver CO	Rock Creek
07934	Anderson, Virginia	6m	W	21 NOV 1910	Atlanta GA	Glenwood
17641	Anderson, Waverly	40y	C	18 JAN 1922	Philadelphia PA	Arlington
05841	Anderson, William	45y	C	30 NOV 1906	Philadelphia PA	Harmony
15879	Anderson, William A.	74y	W	14 JUL 1919	Richmond VA	Glenwood
07237	Anderson, William E.	83y	W	16 OCT 1909	W. Livingston	Methodist
16631	Andresen, Louise R.	66y	W	28 JUL 1920	Norfolk VA	Cremated
00195	Andrews, Albert Slocum	44y	W	20 MAY 1890	Baltimore Co. MD	Rock Creek
08722	Andrews, Alma Ruth	1y	W	19 JUL 1912	Maryland Pk. MD	Mt. Olivet
16949	Andrews, Caroline E.	82y	W	30 JAN 1921	Philadelphia PA	Rock Creek
13012	Andrews, Edwin J.	15y	W	19 JUL 1915	Takoma Park MD	Rock Creek
00805	Andrews, Frances	7m	W	8 AUG 1892	Rockville MD	Glenwood
01663	Andrews, Frances V.	61y	W	17 SEP 1896	Homer NY	Rock Creek
01112	Andrews, Gardner Kortwright	69y	W	25 SEP 1892	Bowie MD	Glenwood
03492	Andrews, Helen J.	62y	W	29 APR 1901	Round Hill VA	Rock Creek
16098	Andrews, Joseph Thomas	3y	C	9 NOV 1919	Fairmont Hts. MD	Payne's
17067	Andrews, Lossie	25y	C	24 MAR 1921	Fairmont Hts. MD	Payne's
17946	Andrews, Mira McCoy	58y	W	9 JUL 1922	Atlantic City NJ	Hastings NE
04137	Andrews, Robert	64y	W	15 JAN 1903	Gaithersburg MD	Rock Creek
15532	Andrews, Robert	29y	W	6 JAN 1918	Philadelphia PA	Rock Creek
18345	Andrews, Ruth	21y	C	10 FEB 1923	New York NY	Payne's
06224	Andrews, William T.	10m	W	10 SEP 1907	Forestville MD	St. Mary's
05767	Antisell, Margaret	70y	W	9 OCT 1906	Middletown MD	Congressional
05946	Antisell, Mary	80y	W	20 FEB 1907	Frederick MD	Congressional
01664	Aplin, Dorothy	4y	W	2 JUL 1895	Brunswick MD	Mt. Olivet
02497	Aplin, Stephen A.	63y	W	25 JUL 1898	Harpers Ferry WV	Providence RI
07550	Appel, Charles A., s/o John	74y	W	20 MAY 1910	Middletown CN	Arlington
00917	Appelby, Frank L.	31y	W	24 AUG 1893	Baltimore MD	Oak Hill
07313	Appelby, Mary A.	79y	W	9 DEC 1909	Martinsburg WV	Glenwood
05748	Apple, Andrew G.	27y	W	21 SEP 1906	Rochester NY	Rock Creek
15100	Appleby, George Franklin	28y	W	2 OCT 1918	Jacksonville FL	Oak Hill
04663	Appleby, George W.	74y	W	7 APR 1904	Martinsburg WV	Glenwood
17180	Appleby, Walter F.	76y	W	23 MAY 1921	Brookville MD	Arlington
12288	Appleton, John	33y	W	2 APR 1914	Laurel MD	Bangor ME
00532	Applewhaite, Kate Carter	33y	W	8 JUN 1891	Baltimore MD	Oak Hill
15022	Applewhite, Benjamin W.	66y	W	16 SEP 1918	Takoma MD	Wilmington NC
14129	Aratta, Angelo	56y	W	8 MAY 1917	Seat Pleasant MD	St. Mary's
01273	Arbola, Pasquelo	96y	W	24 DEC 1893	Ardwick Sta. MD	Mt. Olivet
15375	Archer, Dorothy	24y	W	22 NOV 1918	New York NY	Congressional[1]
01211	Archer, Helen Hart	56w	W	15 NOV 1893	New York NY	Rock Creek
18042	Archer, Infant of M. & E.	1d	W	31 AUG 1922	Memphis TN	Glenwood
06419	Archer, John B.	78y	W	6 FEB 1908	Catonsville MD	Rock Creek
13904	Archer, Statira A.	81y	W	2 JAN 1917	Chicago IL	Rock Creek
02645	Archibald, Alice	16y	W	5 NOV 1898	Rockville MD	Glenwood
14067	Argabrite, Elizabeth Virginia	65y	W	1 APR 1917	Vienna VA	Glenwood
14033	Argabrite, Henry Ribble	64y	W	14 MAR 1917	Vienna VA	Glenwood
03324	Armond, William F.	16y	W	21 SEP 1900	Manila, P.I.	Congressional
12885	Armor, Samuel W.	65y	W	20 APR 1915	Takoma Park MD	Pittsburgh PA
08252	Armor, William J.	39y	W	11 AUG 1911	Takoma Park MD	Glenwood
16268	Armour, Edwin F.	39y	W	30 JAN 1920	Greenville SC	Rock Creek
13528	Armour, Julia R.	78y	W	1 JUN 1916	Riverdale MD	Holyrood
03246	Arms, Demaris D.	75y	W	27 JUL 1900	Tarpon Spgs. FL	Rock Creek
12017	Arms, John R.	93y	W	23 SEP 1913	Eaton CO	Rock Creek
08872	Arms, John Taylor	66y	W	3 OCT 1912	Dartmouth MA	Rock Creek
02906	Arms, Kate C.	56y	W	5 AUG 1904	New Bedford MA	Rock Creek

[1] Filmed out of sequence after #15378f.

No.	Name of Deceased	Age	Race	Death Date	Place of Death	Place of Burial
04686	Armstead, George	35y	C	21 APR 1904	Pittsburgh PA	Harmony
08752	Armstead, James H.	47y	C	2 AUG 1912	Pittsburgh PA	Harmony
16687	Armstrong, Albert C.	76y	W	30 AUG 1920	Elizabeth City VA	Arlington
07194	Armstrong, Frank C.	74y	W	8 SEP 1909	Bar Harbor ME	Rock Creek
05689	Armstrong, George	20y	C	12 AUG 1906	Monmouth NJ	Woodlawn
18107	Armstrong, Gordon Stuart	1y	W	26 SEP 1907	Ridgefield CN	Rock Creek
06940	Armstrong, Infant of J.F.	5d	C	8 MAR 1909	Fairmont Hts. MD	Payne's
05596	Armstrong, Infant of Jos.	SB	W	13 JUN 1906	Mt. Ranier MD	Mt. Olivet
07980	Armstrong, Israel, s/o Isaac G.	57y	C	20 FEB 1911	Halls Hill VA	Harmony
06355	Armstrong, John	2y	W	21 DEC 1907	Ft. Myer Hts. VA	Rock Creek
06576	Armstrong, Joseph	2y	W	6 JUN 1908	Hyattsville MD	Mt. Olivet
14977	Armstrong, Luther K., s/o Wm.	62y	W	15 AUG 1918	Charlottesville VA	Culpeper VA
04196	Armstrong, Mary J.	75y	W	31 MAR 1903	Baltimore MD	Rock Creek
17613	Armstrong, Mary R.	65y	W	27 DEC 1921	Takoma Park MD	Mt. Olivet
06609	Armstrong, Michael J.	2m	W	26 JUN 1908	Mt. Ranier MD	Mt. Olivet
01289	Arnett, Charles D.	44y	C	18 JAN 1894	Bladensburg MD	Graceland
06502	Arnold, Conway H.	36y	W	6 APR 1908	Denver CO	Oak Hill
14236	Arnold, Conway H.	68y	W	16 JUL 1917	New York NY	Oak Hill
13592	Arnold, Edwin T.	68y	W	8 JUL 1916	Potomac VA	Cremated
00564	Arnold, George L.	57y	W	28 AUG 1891	Forestville MD	Congressional
18413	Arnold, Harriet B.	83y	W	12 MAR 1923	Takoma Park MD	Boston MA
01787	Arnold, Jos. W., farmer	64y	W	29 OCT 1895	Surratts Hill MD	Congressional
12759	Arnold, Madaline T.	38y	W	10 FEB 1915	Philadelphia PA	Mt. Olivet
05518	Arnold, Margaret	57y	W	3 APR 1906	Philadelphia PA	Congressional
02351	Arnold, William Wood	21y	W	29 DEC 1897	Montclair NJ	Oak Hill
15475	Arrick, Harry	23y	W	23 DEC 1918	Harrisburg PA	Glenwood
17041	Arrington, George	35y	W	12 MAR 1921	Baltimore MD	Oak Hill
08428	Arrington, Martha F. (Frazier)	49y	W	17 DEC 1911	Dominion Hts. VA	Oak Hill
00918	Arthur, Frances	6m	W	21 JUN 1893	Oxon Hill MD	Rock Creek
02641	Arundell, Melinda A.	83y	W	22 OCT 1898	Tryon NC	Oak Hill
01523	Ash, George R., policeman	35y	W	2 MAR 1895	Jacksonville FL	Delaplane VA
05515	Ash, Howard Painter, Lt.	31y	W	17 MAR 1906	Guant. Bay, Cuba	Arlington
00675	Ash, Thomas F.	27y	W	c.JAN 1892	Denison TX	Mt. Olivet
07309	Ash, William M.	64y	W	26 JAN 1910	Woodside MD	Arlington
09196	Ashby, John P.	18y	W	1 MAY 1913	Clarendon VA	Oak Hill
02147	Ashby, John W.M.	45y	W	8 APR 1897	Chicago IL	Glenwood
07060	Ashby, Presley Earnest	6m	W	14 JUN 1909	Maryland Pk. MD	Congressional
07954	Ashby, Richard Edward	—	—	29 JAN 1911	Maryland Pk. MD	Congressional
12070	Ashford, Infant of John	4d	W	2 NOV 1913	Rosslyn VA	Methodist
01960	Ashley, Eugene	15y	W	3 AUG 1896	Elmwood NJ	Glenwood
14517	Ashton, Clarence	33y	W	21 DEC 1917	Richmond VA	Rock Creek
12113	Ashton, Ella	44y	C	3 DEC 1910	Fairmont Hts. MD	Woodlawn
12843	Ashton, George W., plumber	46y	W	29 MAR 1915	Middleburg VA	Congressional
05692	Ashton, Hannah R. (Wakeman)	60y	W	17 AUG 1906	New Hartford CN	Oak Hill
14070	Ashton, L.L.	45y	C	31 MAR 1917	New Castle DE	Harmony
01522	Ashton, Louisa	83y	W	16 DEC 1894	Philadelphia PA	Congressional
04138	Ashton, Patsey	29y	C	13 JAN 1903	New York NY	Harmony
02972	Aspinwall, Ethel	6m	C	5 OCT 1899	Petersburg VA	Payne's
16557	Aspinwall, Martha Humphrey	71y	W	15 JUN 1920	Takoma Park MD	Cremated
00361	Athey, Marian S.	2m	W	17 JUL 1890	Wash. Grove MD	Oak Hill
17618	Atkin, Florence E.	63y	W	28 DEC 1921	N. Bergen NJ	Oak Hill
09180	Atkin, Richard T.	67y	W	19 APR 1913	N. Bergen NJ	Oak Hill
13390	Atkins, Martha	55y	W	28 FEB 1916	Baltimore MD	Payne's
08330	Atkinson, Andrew	63y	W	8 NOV 1825	Philadelphia PA	Congressional
13748	Atkinson, Aulrick, s/o Edward	42y	C	2 OCT 1916	Atlantic City NJ	Harmony
13373	Atkinson, Dorothy Willard	21y	W	23 FEB 1916	Norfolk VA	Cedar Hill
17675	Atkinson, George B. McClellan	60y	W	4 FEB 1922	Auburn NY	Rock Creek
12941	Atkinson, Joseph	39y	W	25 MAY 1915	Chicago IL	Rock Creek
06951	Atkinson, Marianne Eunice	3m	W	20 MAR 1909	Hyattsville MD	Glenwood

No.	Name of Deceased	Age	Race	Death Date	Place of Death	Place of Burial
06089	Atwell, James W.	45y	W	3 JUN 1907	Brentwood MD	Congressional
08327	Atwell, William P.	66y	W	28 JUL 1911	Ghent, Belgium	Arlington
06763	Atwill, William Warren	30y	W	9 OCT 1908	Williamsburg VA	Kinsale VA
03767	Atz, Ellen A.	80y	W	23 JAN 1902	Germantown MD	Glenwood
04319	Aubright, Allison	32y	W	14 JUN 1902	New Orleans LA	Rock Creek
16081	Auckland, John F.	3m	W	28 OCT 1919	PA	Glenwood
07532	Auerbach, Carl, s/o Jonas	66y	W	9 MAY 1910	Atlantic City NJ	Wash. Hebrew
05845	Aufdenbrinke, Walter	30y	W	1 DEC 1906	Pittsburgh PA	Arlington
04450	Augenstein, Julius J.	—	W	6 MAY 1903	Philippine Isl.	Wash. Hebrew
17305	Augenstein, Melvin M., Capt.	—	—	16 OCT 1918	France	Wash. Hebrew
03824	August, Frances Burkhardt	23y	W	20 MAR 1902	Boston MA	Rock Creek
16906	August, James A.	46y	W	8 JAN 1921	Loudoun Co. VA	Rock Creek
08360	August, Lucy Alice, d/o J.A.	7m	W	JUN 1876	Hot Springs VA	Rock Creek
03066	Augustrofer, Thomas M.	23y	W	10 JAN 1900	King Geo. Co. VA	Glenwood
02233	Aulick, Richmond O.	30y	W	16 JUL 1897	Trenton NJ	Congressional
17412	Ault, Ruth Miriam	1y	W	5 OCT 1920	Washington KS	Ft. Lincoln[1]
00806	Austin, Amy	2m	W	19 FEB 1892	Woodside NY	Congressional
14302	Austin, Earnest	28y	C	13 AUG 1917	Montreal, Can.	Woodlawn
15026	Austin, Eugene H.	23y	W	16 SEP 1918	Brooklyn NY	Arlington
14583	Austin, James Beemer	72y	W	15 JAN 1918	St. Thomas, Ont.	Glenwood
18474	Austin, John Walton	65y	W	12 APR 1923	Chevy Chase MD	Rock Creek
01850	Austin, Joseph	40y	W	17 APR 1840	New York NY	Oak Hill
07972	Austin, Manville A.	70y	W	14 FEB 1911	Hamlin KS	Congressional
04726	Austin, William E.	36y	W	21 AUG 1903	Seattle WA	Oak Hill
17927	Auth, J. George	45y	W	29 JUN 1922	Laurel MD	St. Mary's
08492	Avant, Archibald H.	40y	W	25 JAN 1912	Philadelphia PA	Glenwood
05998	Avant, Hugh R.	38y	W	26 MAR 1907	Philadelphia PA	Glenwood
14400	Averett, Ida	29y	C	4 OCT 1917	Philadelphia PA	Woodlawn
18104	Averill, Belle H.	56y	W	6 OCT 1922	Wilkinsburg PA	Herndon VA
01390	Avery, William B., clerk	84y	W	24 APR 1894	Martinsburg WV	Congressional
16736	Ayers, Benjamin	82y	C	2 OCT 1920	Philadelphia PA	Harmony
14092	Ayers, Frank	42y	C	16 APR 1917	Philadelphia PA	Harmony
15860	Ayers, Mary	65y	C	1 JUL 1919	Fairmont Hts. MD	Woodlawn
14901	Ayers, Mary S.	67y	W	7 JUL 1918	Baltimore MD	Arlington
13796	Ayers, William	21y	C	29 OCT 1916	Leavenworth KS	Mt. Olivet
08641	Ayling, Grace, d/o Arthur P.	24y	W	19 MAY 1912	Springfield MD	Cremated
00002	Ayres, Edith J.	10m	W	12 JAN 1889	Kings Co. NY	Arlington
04231	Aytes, Mary S.	28y	C	23 FEB 1903	New York NY	Harmony
13753	Azpell, Bertha V.	46y	W	29 SEP 1909	Denver CO	Oak Hill
13752	Azpell, Sarah V.	65y	W	12 AUG 1907	Denver CO	Oak Hill

[1] Note that after being in the vault at Glenwood Cemetery, the remains were removed 15 NOV 1921 to Ft. Lincoln Cemetery.

No.	Name of Deceased	Age	Race	Death Date	Place of Death	Place of Burial

B

No.	Name of Deceased	Age	Race	Death Date	Place of Death	Place of Burial
14151	Baar, Pauline	80y	W	26 MAY 1917	Toledo OH	Wash. Hebrew
15324	Babbington, Joseph A.	24y	W	3 NOV 1918	Montgomery AL	Mt. Olivet
14578	Babbington, Myrtle D.	23y	W	14 JAN 1918	Saranac Lake NY	Mt. Olivet
15000	Babcock, Ellis B.	21y	W	30 AUG 1918	Wichita Falls TX	Arlington
15456	Babcock, Herbert	1m	W	17 DEC 1918	Niagara Falls NY	Glenwood
07405	Babcock, James H.	60y	W	4 FEB 1910	Capitol Hts. MD	Glenwood
06346	Babcock, Lillian M.	46y	W	8 DEC 1907	Takoma Park MD	Rock Creek
12088	Bacaigaluppi, Francis	57y	W	12 NOV 1913	Seat Pleasant MD	St. Mary's
15566	Bach, John P.	36y	W	17 JAN 1919	Takoma Park MD	Cremated
08335	Bachelder, David M.	50y	W	1 OCT 1911	Bladensburg MD	Glenwood
08307	Bachelder, Sarah M.	8m	W	11 SEP 1911	Bladensburg MD	Glenwood
08661	Bacigallipi, John	61y	W	7 JUN 1912	Seat Pleasant MD	St. Mary's
02038	Bacigaluppi, Infant of John	SB	W	7 JAN 1897	Forestville MD	St. Mary's
04412	Bacigaluppi, John Joseph	12y	W	29 JUL 1903	Forestville MD	St. Mary's
16175	Bacon, Annie W.	51y	W	27 DEC 1919	New York NY	Glenwood
16673	Bacon, Edwin Booth	66y	W	22 AUG 1920	Takoma Park MD	Louisville KY
16417	Bacon, Emily Eliz. Taggart	33y	W	25 MAR 1920	San Diego CA	Mt. Olivet
12913	Bacon, Emma Whitehead Levi	78y	W	6 MAY 1915	Brookline MA	Congressional[1]
16127	Bacon, Frank W.	52y	W	27 NOV 1919	Cumberland MD	Rock Creek
15272	Bacon, Jane R.	74y	W	22 OCT 1918	Hackensack NJ	Glenwood
01113	Bacon, Mary Sweetser Ashby	27y	W	8 DEC 1892	Dorchester MA	Congressional
13143	Bacron, Rebecca	41y	C	5 OCT 1915	New York NY	Harmony
00017	Baden, Frank W.	30y	W	17 FEB 1889	Baltimore MD	Congressional
04193	Baden, Thaddeus	55y	W	30 MAR 1903	Potomac River	Mt. Olivet
05420	Badger, John	74y	C	5 JAN 1906	Kensington MD	Harmony
06532	Badger, Margaret Matilda	78y	W	4 MAY 1908	Annapolis MD	Oak Hill[2]
02856	Badger, Oscar Chas., U.S.N.	76y	W	20 JUN 1899	Concord MA	Oak Hill[3]
15346	Badley, Lena T.	59y	W	10 NOV 1918	Philadelphia PA	Glenwood
18159	Baer, David W.	14y	W	14 NOV 1922	Takoma MD	Waynesboro PA
05818	Baeschlin, Frederick A.	74y	W	14 NOV 1906	Berwyn MD	Mt. Olivet
01665	Bagger, Andrew Louis	49y	W	23 MAY 1895	Ocean Grove NJ	Congressional
00197	Bagley, John B.	50y	W	18 MAR 1890	Baltimore MD	Rock Creek
12899	Bailey, Andrew	66y	W	27 APR 1915	Riggs Mill MD	Rock Creek
13060	Bailey, Beatrice C.	24y	C	16 AUG 1915	Newport RI	Mt. Zion East
07195	Bailey, Carrie	46y	C	10 SEP 1909	New York NY	Woodlawn
04967	Bailey, Charles L.	35y	W	24 NOV 1904	Milford MA	Rock Creek
08571	Bailey, Columbus B.	58y	W	28 MAR 1912	Baltimore MD	Mt. Olivet
15765	Bailey, Edson A.	23y	W	5 MAY 1919	Ft. McHenry MD	Arlington
03257	Bailey, Edward	49y	W	10 AUG 1900	Baltimore MD	Rock Creek
07299	Bailey, Eliza E.	87y	W	16 MAR 1909	Washington DC	Rock Creek
01788	Bailey, Emily A.	27y	W	9 NOV 1895	Hyattsville MD	Oak Hill
15489	Bailey, Emma	35y	W	25 DEC 1918	Washington DC	Congressional
06197	Bailey, Esther	25y	C	23 AUG 1907	Philadelphia PA	Occoquan VA
07298	Bailey, George	58y	W	15 JUL 1906	Riggs Mill MD	Rock Creek
07297	Bailey, George K.	85y	W	8 JAN 1909	Riggs Mill MD	Rock Creek
05994	Bailey, George W.	48y	W	20 MAR 1907	New York NJ	Congressional
04689	Bailey, James A.	40y	W	25 APR 1904	Baltimore MD	Arlington VA
13355	Bailey, John W.	77y	W	14 FEB 1916	Silver Spring MD	Rock Creek
04820	Bailey, Joseph H.	6m	C	28 JUL 1904	Riggs Mill MD	Mt. Olivet
13354	Bailey, Lydia W.	75y	W	14 FEB 1916	Silver Spring MD	Rock Creek
01216	Bailey, Mary Ellen	17y	C	11 SEP 1893	Riggs Farm MD	Mt. Olivet
13454	Bailey, Milo V.	65y	W	27 JAN 1907	Washington DC	Rock Creek
13017	Bailey, Orvilla E.B.	40y	W	18 JUL 1915	Philadelphia PA	Oak Hill

---

[1] Disinterment permit #8535 on 26 JAN 1916 for removal to Rock Creek Cemetery.
[2] Disinterment permit #8442 for removal on 7 OCT 1915 to Arlington National Cemetery.
[3] Note for disinterment permit #8441 for removal 7 OCT 1918 to Arlington National Cemetery.

District of Columbia Foreign Death Records, 1888-1923

No.	Name of Deceased	Age	Race	Death Date	Place of Death	Place of Burial
12966	Bailey, Paul A.	4y	W	19 JUN 1915	Riverdale MD	Mt. Olivet
15696	Bailey, Ray Thompson	30y	W	30 MAR 1919	Takoma Park MD	Glenwood
04904	Bailey, Regehina	18y	C	28 SEP 1904	Riggs Mill MD	Mt. Olivet
00091	Bailey, Robert	50y	C	28 JUL 1889	Riggs Farm MD	Mt. Olivet
09078	Bailey, Theodora	79y	W	14 FEB 1913	White Plains NY	Oak Hill
16885	Bailey, Vincent P.	66y	W	30 DEC 1920	Riverdale MD	Mt. Olivet
15891	Bailey, William C.	63y	W	24 JUL 1919	Park Lane VA	Congressional
00004	Bailey, William E.	26y	W	15 JAN 1889	Nashville TN	Oak Hill
01851	Bailey, William F.	35y	W	26 JAN 1896	Philadelphia PA	Congressional
01666	Bailey, William L.	89y	W	12 AUG 1895	Baltimore MD	Congressional
15302	Bailley, Phillip M.	17y	W	27 OCT 1918	Ramsey MN	Arlington
16645	Bailor, Ellen	11h	C	8 AUG 1920	Seat Pleasant MD	Payne's
05573	Baily, John T.	58y	C	8 MAY 1906	Steelton PA	Bailey's Xrds. VA
01114	Baily, Mary E.	44y	W	13 JUN 1892	Lynchburg VA	Glenwood
08417	Bain, John J., laborer	68y	W	7 DEC 1911	Hampton VA	Arlington
05132	Bair, Elizabeth	77y	W	17 MAY 1905	Landover MD	Rock Creek
05169	Baird, Absolom, Brig. Gen.	80y	W	14 JUN 1905	St. Denis MD	Arlington
14775	Baird, Alfred S.	53y	W	28 APR 1918	Takoma MD	Rock Creek
11862	Baird, Lucy H.	65y	W	19 JUN 1913	Philadelphia PA	Oak Hill
07693	Baker, Benjamin P., s/o P.	18y	W	16 AUG 1910	Colonial Bea. VA	Glenwood
17309	Baker, Blanch	54y	W	20 JUL 1921	Olney MD	Glenwood
07967	Baker, Catherine	85y	W	14 FEB 1911	Riverdale MD	Mt. Olivet
14921	Baker, Charles	8y	W	10 JUL 1918	Seattle WA	King Geo. Co. VA
17781	Baker, Charles Henry	39y	W	3 APR 1922	Atlanta GA	Congressional
01422	Baker, Charles T.M., cooper	69y	W	2 JUL 1894	Rosslyn VA	Oak Hill
15931	Baker, Dorthy	11y	C	16 AUG 1919	Fairmont Hts. MD	Payne's
04359	Baker, Elizabeth	70y	W	24 JUN 1903	Falls Church VA	Congressional
00199	Baker, Elizabeth Hallowell	8y	W	1 DEC 1889	Fairfax Co. VA	Oak Hill
04446	Baker, Eveline S.	85y	W	9 FEB 1903	New York NY	Oak Hill
11937	Baker, Florence Brian	40y	W	5 AUG 1913	Bayville NY	Glenwood
00198	Baker, Frank	6y	W	6 DEC 1889	Fairfax Co. VA	Oak Hill
14802	Baker, George	78y	W	7 MAY 1918	Richmond VA	Rock Creek
07651	Baker, Henry	83y	W	25 JUL 1910	Chatangua NY	Oak Hill
18251	Baker, John Lee	39y	W	6 JAN 1923	Pittsburgh PA	Glenwood
00200	Baker, Josephine	11y	W	7 DEC 1889	Fairfax Co. VA	Oak Hill
03124	Baker, Julia	47y	C	9 MAR 1900	Atlantic City NJ	Woodlawn
03033	Baker, Julia C.	60y	W	5 DEC 1899	Boston MA	Rock Creek
07666	Baker, Karl M., s/o Charles	9y	W	2 AUG 1910	Ft. Myer Hts. VA	Rock Creek
15286	Baker, Laura V.	35y	W	24 OCT 1918	Marshall Hall MD	Glenwood
17816	Baker, Mary Talks	85y	W	24 APR 1922	Silver Spring MD	Glenwood
04382	Baker, Mathew	29y	C	7 JUL 1903	Rockfish VA	Payne's
02417	Baker, Nelson R.	65y	W	1 APR 1898	Bethesda MD	Oak Hill
15791	Baker, Priscilla	56y	C	23 MAY 1919	Cedar Hts. MD	Belvoir VA
07749	Baker, Roswell E.	35y	W	18 SEP 1910	Chesa. Bea. MD	Rock Creek
15669	Baker, Sarah	30y	C	4 MAR 1919	Philadelphia PA	Mt. Zion West
05874	Baker, Sarah Elizabeth	79y	W	30 DEC 1906	Bethesda MD	Oak Hill
18119	Baker, Sybella R.	57y	W	19 OCT 1922	Akron OH	Glenwood
06555	Baker, Thomas B., s/o Thos.	71y	W	19 MAY 1908	Fairfax VA	Glenwood
18330	Baker, Thomas R.	86y	W	6 FEB 1923	Silver Spring MD	Glenwood
04171	Baker, Walter R.	77y	W	13 FEB 1903	Baltimore MD	Glenwood
15018	Balderston, Frances P.	65y	W	14 SEP 1918	Friendship H. MD	Mt. Olivet
14262	Baldic, John	c.28y	W	30 JUL 1917	Camp Meade MD	Hamilton NY
02039	Baldwin, Brenton Lashbrook	40y	W	16 OCT 1896	Brighton NY	Rock Creek
07342	Baldwin, Cornelia A. Gilman	78y	W	23 DEC 1909	Clarendon VA	Congressional
02643	Baldwin, Daisy H.	23y	W	25 OCT 1898	New York NY	Alexandria VA
08457	Baldwin, Edgar	71y	W	3 JAN 1912	Brentwood MD	Congressional
02290	Baldwin, Ernest P., lawyer	46y	W	20 SEP 1897	Atlantic City NJ	Rock Creek
16265	Baldwin, George E.	48y	W	30 JAN 1920	Philadelphia PA	Rock Creek
00201	Baldwin, Harriett	65y	W	20 JUN 1890	Manassas VA	Congressional

No.	Name of Deceased	Age	Race	Death Date	Place of Death	Place of Burial
03732	Baldwin, James M.	62y	W	13 DEC 1901	Spots. Co. VA	Arlington VA
16188	Baldwin, Julian P.	70y	W	6 JAN 1920	Ballston VA	Congressional
11808	Baldwin, Sarah F.	78y	W	12 MAY 1913	Montclair NJ	Congressional
08544	Bales, Henry A.	67y	W	3 MAR 1912	Alex. Co. VA	Oak Hill
06943	Balinger, George William	74y	W	14 MAR 1909	Upton Hill VA	Oak Hill
0202	Balinger, Susan	65y	W	2 MAY 1890	Bailey's Xrds. VA	Tenallytown
14148	Baliny, Edward	28y	C	23 MAY 1917	Oxon Hill MD	Edgemont VA
08194	Ball, Chester W.	18y	C	10 JUL 1911	Philadelphia PA	Harmony
06303	Ball, Fannie W., d/o Thos.	71y	W	29 NOV 1907	Buckland VA	Baltimore MD
01015	Ball, Frances H.	73y	W	1 APR 1893	Stonington MD	Glenwood
13220	Ball, Georgiana	44y	C	24 NOV 1915	Cedar Hts. MD	Harmony
00446	Ball, Richard L.	63y	W	2 DEC 1809	Ball's Farm MD	Tenallytown
05636	Ballantyne, William, s/o Jas.	81y	W	7 JUL 1906	Nantucket MA	Oak Hill
08573	Ballard, C.J.	42y	C	28 MAR 1912	Ocean NJ	Harmony
12772	Ballard, Frederick E.	61y	W	20 FEB 1915	Railroad	New York NY
17074	Ballard, Infant of John	7h	W	28 MAR 1921	Hyattsville MD	Prospect Hill
17753	Ballard, Josephine E.	6m	W	19 MAR 1922	Hyattsville MD	Prospect Hill
04148	Ballard, Josephine W.	60y	W	20 JAN 1903	Birmingham AL	Cremated
14581	Ballard, Melvin A.	11d	W	16 JAN 1919	Hyattsville MD	Prospect Hill
12534	Ballard, William Chester	5m	W	18 SEP 1914	Seat Pleasant MD	Glenwood
06159	Ballard, William O., s/o John	36y	W	27 JUL 1907	Shipman VA	Glenwood
06395	Ballinger, Mary V.	70y	W	19 JAN 1908	Upton Hill VA	Oak Hill
11812	Ballock, Catharine Jane	77y	W	14 MAY 1913	S. Orange NJ	Oak Hill
12023	Ballock, Elizabeth Ann Koones	81y	W	30 SEP 1913	Leesburg VA	Rock Creek
01212	Ballock, James	69y	W	10 NOV 1893	Gaithersburg MD	Oak Hill
06413	Ballock, Robert Alder	76y	W	3 FEB 1908	Alexandria VA	Rock Creek
00676	Balmain, Amy E.	75y	W	17 JAN 1892	Clifton VA	Congressional
01491	Balmain, William H.	45y	W	16 SEP 1894	Clifton VA	Congressional
03994	Baltimore, Archie	63y	C	14 AUG 1902	Hampton VA	Harmony
05204	Baltzell, Charles A.	7m	W	8 JUL 1905	Philadelphia PA	Prospect Hill
13635	Baltzell, Ida	8y	W	30 JUL 1916	Philadelphia PA	Prospect Hill
02684	Banes, Mary Watkins	90y	W	21 DEC 1898	Hyattsville MD	Congressional
05163	Banes, Oscar Howard	1y	C	7 JUN 1905	Alexandria VA	Payne's
04235	Banes, William	70y	W	23 FEB 1903	Hyattsville MD	Congressional
01667	Bangs, Amanda	60y	W	16 MAY 1895	Philadelphia PA	Oak Hill
05422	Bangs, Charles	76y	W	8 JAN 1906	Baltimore MD	Oak Hill
02750	Bangs, Ellen C.	61y	W	23 FEB 1899	Baltimore Co. MD	Oak Hill
17132	Bangs, Harriet Elizabeth	33y	W	29 APR 1921	Silver Spring MD	Glenwood
05366	Bangs, Rebecca	67y	W	16 NOV 1905	Baltimore MD	Oak Hill
05017	Banitz, Augusta D.	74y	W	2 FEB 1905	Takoma Park MD	Glenwood
10300	Bankel, Bress	00y	C	1 MAR 1923	Brentwood MD	Harmony
08403	Bankhager, Frederick E.	74y	W	27 NOV 1911	Portland MD	Rock Creek
13948	Banks, Catherine	68y	C	26 JAN 1917	Huntsville MD	Mt. Olivet
00566	Banks, Charlotte M.L.	16y	C	23 JAN 1891	Providence RI	Mt. Zion
05681	Banks, Clifton W.	33y	W	8 AUG 1906	Asbury Park NJ	Congressional
00565	Banks, Fanny E.	18y	C	18 SEP 1885	Providence RI	Mt. Zion
03485	Banks, Infant of Robert C.G.	1m	C	24 APR 1901	Brick Haven VA	Payne's
03638	Banks, James	20y	C	3 SEP 1901	Potomac River	Harmony
17000	Banks, John	23y	C	25 FEB 1921	Baltimore MD	Harmony
02954	Banks, John C.	32y	W	23 SEP 1899	Wallace WV	Tenallytown
16190	Bankston, Troy Asher, Jr.	8m	W	7 JAN 1920	Chevy Chase MD	Rock Creek
08853	Bantz, Harold	19y	W	18 SEP 1912	Luna NM	Rock Creek
06996	Barber, Amzi Lorenzo	65y	W	17 APR 1909	Livingston NY	Oak Hill
15247	Barber, Cecelia	32y	C	19 OCT 1918	Wilmington DE	Woodlawn
00092	Barber, Dana Chase	30y	W	1 JUN 1889	Knowles Sta. MD	Epping NH
05136	Barber, DeDroiet Langdon	31y	W	19 MAY 1905	Long Branch NJ	Rock Creek
13553	Barber, Estelle	39y	C	6 JUN 1916	New York NY	Harmony
15363	Barber, George N.	32y	W	17 NOV 1918	LaPlata MD	Rock Creek
05333	Barber, John A.	67y	W	24 OCT 1905	Budd's Creek MD	Oak Hill

District of Columbia Foreign Death Records, 1888-1923

No.	Name of Deceased	Age	Race	Death Date	Place of Death	Place of Burial
15843	Barber, Mary Roche	56y	W	21 JUN 1919	Bethel CN	Glenwood
05551	Barber, Merritt	67y	W	19 APR 1906	Albany Co. NY	Arlington
15369	Barbour, Clara C.	31y	W	20 NOV 1918	LaPlata MD	Rock Creek
13109	Barbour, Edward L.	50y	W	14 SEP 1915	Chicago IL	Mt. Olivet
05427	Barcharding, Augusta	88y	W	14 JAN 1906	Suitland MD	Prospect Hill
16434	Barchit, Sarah June	49y	W	11 APR 1920	Annapolis MD	Rock Creek
04648	Barchtel, Esther	66y	W	28 MAR 1904	Hagerstown MD	Cremated
12396	Barclay, Carrie E.	73y	W	10 JUN 1914	Atlantic City NJ	Glenwood
14267	Barcroft, John W.	79y	W	29 JUL 1917	Bel Air MD	Cremated
12393	Barghausen, Lawrence P.	16d	W	9 JUN 1914	Bethesda MD	Methodist
14502	Barghausen, Margaret	37y	W	11 DEC 1917	Wilkinsburg PA	Mt. Olivet
02040	Barkely, Lottie	27y	C	26 OCT 1896	Alexandria VA	Payne's
00920	Barker, Blanch	60y	W	2 JUN 1893	Mapleton IA	Congressional
03687	Barker, Carrie	35y	C	17 OCT 1901	New York NY	Harmony
07907	Barker, Charles Anderson	22y	W	2 JAN 1911	Fulton MO	Glenwood
01527	Barker, Charles F.	42y	W	18 DEC 1894	Chicago IL	Oak Hill
04404	Barker, George O.	58y	W	21 JUL 1903	Boston MA	Glenwood
01213	Barker, Harriett	14y	W	5 SEP 1893	Baltimore MD	Glenwood
08314	Barker, James, laborer	78y	W	16 SEP 1911	Hampton VA	Congressional
00203	Barker, Julia A.	49y	W	30 NOV 1889	Rome NY	Congressional
17645	Barker, Lucy E.	76y	W	19 JAN 1922	Newton MA	Glenwood
02479	Barker, Taylor	49y	W	1 AUG 1898	Glen Echo MD	Holyrood
14941	Barkes, William	59y	W	28 JUL 1918	Ft. Myer Hts. VA	Congressional
18297	Barks, Barbara J.	35y	W	25 JAN 1923	Arlington Co. VA	Congressional
02676	Barlow, Hesser M.	54y	W	8 DEC 1898	New York NY	Arlington VA
05094	Barnaclo, Infant of James K.	1d	W	23 APR 1905	Columbia Pk. MD	Mt. Olivet
03634	Barnaclo, Johanna E.	11m	W	30 AUG 1901	Columbia Pk. MD	Mt. Olivet
18008	Barnaclo, Walter E.	25y	W	12 AUG 1922	Columbia Pk. MD	Mt. Olivet
02491	Barnard, Alexander F.	38y	W	28 JUL 1898	Rosslyn VA	Congressional
16049	Barnard, Edward	66y	W	14 OCT 1919	Brentwood MD	Glenwood
04058	Barnard, Edwin E.	12y	W	17 OCT 1902	Rosslyn VA	Rock Creek
05542	Barnard, Haywood	76y	W	15 APR 1906	Avenel MD	Congressional
02502	Barnard, John W.	21m	W	24 JUL 1898	Pr. Geo. Co. MD	Congressional
12694	Barnard, Lawrence	79y	W	28 DEC 1914	Hotchkiss CO	Oak Hill
08280	Barnard, Lolieta	4y	W	28 AUG 1911	Bethlehem PA	Rock Creek
07217	Barnard, Nettie M.	3y	W	29 SEP 1909	Brentwood MD	Glenwood
14507	Barneclo, Frank J.	54y	W	17 DEC 1917	Sykesville MD	Rock Creek
02966	Barneclo, Richard W.	69y	W	26 SEP 1899	Evansville IN	Oak Hill
01274	Barnes, Benjamin F.	21y	W	18 DEC 1893	Montg. Co. MD	Rock Creek
11856	Barnes, Charles	47y	W	17 JUN 1913	Whitcomb WV	Congressional
16054	Barnes, Charles A.	37y	W	16 OCT 1919	Washington DC	Rock Creek
14804	Barnes, Cora	48y	C	6 MAY 1918	Washington DC	Payne's
13968	Barnes, Cornelia A.	61y	W	5 FEB 1917	Silver Spring MD	Rock Creek
16574	Barnes, Edith (Seufferle)	54y	W	3 JUL 1920	Philadelphia PA	Congressional
07661	Barnes, Elizabeth L.	61y	W	29 JUL 1910	Relay MD	Rock Creek
13063	Barnes, Ernest Vincent	28y	W	17 AUG 1915	Potomac River	Congressional
18065	Barnes, Ethel	29y	C	12 SEP 1922	Takoma Park MD	Louisa Co. VA
01290	Barnes, George Henry	18y	W	11 FEB 1894	Ellicott City MD	Oak Hill
00807	Barnes, Harry	27y	W	18 MAY 1892	Philadelphia PA	Congressional
08467	Barnes, Hattie C.	51y	C	9 JAN 1912	Fairmont Hts. MD	Payne's
02363	Barnes, Hettie	78y	C	11 JAN 1898	Hyattsville MD	Mt. Olivet
08881	Barnes, Infant of B.C.	SB	W	22 AUG 1912	Dubuque IA	Congressional
01511	Barnes, John Thomas	62y	W	17 OCT 1894	Chillum MD	Rock Creek
12447	Barnes, Joseph C.	78y	W	20 JUL 1914	Memphis TN	Glenwood
07276	Barnes, Joshua	66y	C	14 NOV 1909	Fairmont Hts. MD	Payne's
17896	Barnes, Laura L. (Wilson)	74y	W	9 JUN 1922	Sandy Spring MD	Congressional
16108	Barnes, Lemuel	75y	W	17 NOV 1919	Hyattsville MD	Congressional
08407	Barnes, Lewis, s/o Lewis	59y	C	1 DEC 1911	Rosslyn VA	Mt. Zion West
15680	Barnes, Lottie, c/o Bruce	25y	C	18 MAR 1919	Phoebus VA	Harmony

No.	Name of Deceased	Age	Race	Death Date	Place of Death	Place of Burial
18057	Barnes, Louise	11m	C	8 SEP 1922	Takoma Park MD	Mt. Zion West
01526	Barnes, Marcellus	8m	W	2 AUG 1857	Montg. Co. MD	Rock Creek[1]
06971	Barnes, Martha	34y	C	31 MAR 1909	New York NY	Harmony
01525	Barnes, Martha E.	32y	W	3 FEB 1864	Montg. Co. MD	Rock Creek[2]
07420	Barnes, Mary	84y	C	16 FEB 1910	Tuxedo MD	Payne's
18103	Barnes, Morton	20y	C	4 OCT 1922	Johnstown PA	Glymont MD
13506	Barnes, Orena H.	81y	W	14 MAY 1916	Woodmont MD	Rock Creek
09090	Barnes, Pauline	24y	C	23 FEB 1913	Charles Co. MD	Harmony
08569	Barnes, Raymond F.	51y	W	25 MAR 1912	New York NY	Glenwood
15836	Barnes, Samuel A., painter	26y	W	17 JUN 1919	Alexandria VA	Rock Creek
05575	Barnes, Sarah A.	64y	C	11 MAY 1906	New York NY	Harmony
05377	Barnes, Sarah P.	70y	W	16 NOV 1905	Seattle WA	Glenwood
06207	Barnes, Wallace	20y	W	28 AUG 1907	High Point NC	Wash. Hebrew
05330	Barnes, William H.	53y	C	22 OCT 1905	New York NY	Harmony
03065	Barnett, Aaron	39y	W	9 JAN 1900	West Point NE	Adas Israel
01789	Barnett, George	31y	C	28 DEC 1895	Chicago IL	Payne's
00204	Barnett, Mary	57y	W	23 FEB 1890	Philadelphia PA	Mt. Olivet
06770	Barnett, Morris	59y	W	5 OCT 1908	Los Angeles CA	Adas Israel
06241	Barnette, Maud A.	31y	W	23 SEP 1907	Seat Pleasant MD	Glenwood
05986	Barnhardt, George E.	81y	W	16 MAR 1907	Hampton VA	Mt. Olivet
07182	Barnholt, Henry N.	24y	W	16 MAY 1905	Portville NY	Glenwood
07250	Barnsley, George T.	45y	W	23 OCT 1909	Pittsburgh PA	Rock Creek
04482	Barnsley, Joseph M.	3y	W	15 MAR 1902	Oakmont PA	Rock Creek
03328	Barnum, Phebe C.	61y	W	10 NOV 1900	Montclair NJ	Rock Creek
14405	Barnwell, Robertson Grant	75y	W	10 OCT 1917	Atlantic City NJ	Rock Creek
04495	Barr, Charles	71y	W	29 OCT 1903	Soldier's Home	Congressional
08101	Barr, Gertrude, d/o John F.	20y	W	5 MAY 1911	Falls Church VA	Congressional
08027	Barr, Harriett Cornelius	77y	W	25 MAR 1911	Everett PA	Glenwood
02362	Barr, Jane A.	85y	W	26 JAN 1898	Hyattsville MD	Congressional
00447	Barr, M.P.	34y	W	4 AUG 1889	Houston TX	Glenwood
08322	Barr, Rodger H.	5y	W	23 SEP 1911	New York NY	Mt. Olivet
03353	Barr, William Thomas	83y	W	28 NOV 1900	Hyattsville MD	Congressional
04970	Barrett, Bridget	72y	W	18 JUL 1903	Baltimore MD	Mt. Olivet
00679	Barrett, Horace S.	21y	W	4 APR 1892	Jeffersonville IN	Oak Hill
08739	Barrett, Infant of Robert A.	SB	W	29 JUL 1912	Hyattsville MD	Mt. Olivet
03628	Barrett, James	50y	C	21 AUG 1901	Marietta PA	Potters Field
07759	Barrett, Johanna	1m	W	23 SEP 1910	Hyattsville MD	Mt. Olivet
12542	Barrett, Laura	63y	C	20 SEP 1914	Modella FL	Harmony
00567	Barrett, Marion H.	44y	W	20 JUL 1891	Jeffersonville IN	Oak Hill
14550	Barrett, Mollie A.	56y	W	2 JAN 1918	Baltimore MD	Mt. Olivet
16861	Barrett, Rebecca	68y	W	18 DEC 1920	Alexandria VA	Prospect Hill
05224	Barrett, Sallie C.	75y	W	28 MAR 1905	Paris, France	Congressional
09087	Barrick, Charles A., chef	35y	W	21 FEB 1913	Norfolk VA	Mt. Olivet
02361	Barrick, Charles Henry	68y	W	11 JAN 1898	Creagerstown MD	Congressional
18093	Barrick, John A.	72y	W	27 SEP 1922	Broad Creek MD	Mt. Olivet
05882	Barriger, John Walker	75y	W	31 DEC 1906	Asbury Park NJ	Arlington
12094	Barringer, Paul, s/o John F.	16y	C	14 NOV 1913	Occoquan VA	Payne's
08605	Barrington, Caroline C.	81y	W	20 APR 1912	Philadelphia PA	Oak Hill
07642	Barrington, Philip F.	50y	W	20 JUL 1910	Montclair NJ	Oak Hill
08318	Barrington, William H.	55y	W	20 JUL 1911	Manila, P.I.	Oak Hill
13313	Barron, Catherine R.	76y	W	21 JAN 1916	Yonkers NY	Glenwood
13216	Barron, Frederick B.	51y	C	20 NOV 1915	Frederick MD	Harmony
04983	Barron, Noel J.	—	W	20 OCT 1904	Iloilo, P.I.	Arlington
14020	Barry, Bernard M.	31y	W	3 MAR 1917	Steubensville OH	Mt. Olivet

[1] Note from Rockville, Md., 17 DEC 1894, that the late Marcellus Barnes was removed from the graveyard of St. John's Church at Forest Glen, Montgomery Co., Md.
[2] Note from Rockville, Md., 17 DEC 1894, that the late Martha E. Barnes was removed from the graveyard of St. John's Church at Forest Glen, Montgomery Co., Md.

District of Columbia Foreign Death Records, 1888-1923

No.	Name of Deceased	Age	Race	Death Date	Place of Death	Place of Burial
12150	Barry, Geo. D., s/o William	49y	W	8 JAN 1914	Occoquan VA	Congressional
07561	Barry, John N., Jr.	41y	W	22 MAY 1910	Cristobal, C.Z.	Rock Creek
02777	Barry, Mary	53y	W	9 MAR 1899	Chicago IL	Mt. Olivet
02234	Barry, Mary A.	26y	W	23 AUG 1897	New York NY	Mt. Olivet
00919	Barry, Norah	45y	W	23 AUG 1893	Philadelphia PA	Mt. Olivet
00678	Barry, Susan E.	74y	W	12 FEB 1892	St. Louis MO	Mt. Olivet
05550	Barry, Thomas P.	26y	W	21 APR 1906	Dickerson MD	Mt. Olivet
07899	Barry, William J., farmer	74y	W	29 DEC 1910	Colvin Run VA	Soldier's Home
15054	Barssock, Morris Robert	20y	W	25 SEP 1918	Newport RI	Arlington
01336	Barstow, Maria Bedinger P.	51y	W	3 MAR 1894	Wiesbaden, Ger.	Congressional
07310	Bart, Louis R.	49y	W	25 OCT 1909	Mobile AL	Oak Hill
05829	Bart, Robert C.	7y	W	28 NOV 1906	Hyattsville MD	Mt. Olivet
11985	Bartle, Randolph T.	44y	W	15 MAY 1913	Lackawana NY	Mt. Olivet
02125	Bartlett, Daisy	20y	W	10 FEB 1897	Baltimore MD	Rock Creek
08683	Bartlett, David W., s/o John	84y	W	24 JUN 1912	West Haven CN	Oak Hill
17250	Bartlett, Florence Riddle	75y	W	23 JUN 1921	Olney MD	Rock Creek
13093	Bartlett, Frank	78y	W	29 AUG 1915	Bryant Pond ME	Rock Creek
12492	Bartlett, Julia M. (Painter)	80y	W	21 AUG 1914	West Haven CN	Oak Hill
13309	Bartlett, Maurice S.	69y	W	9 JAN 1916	Superior WS	Rock Creek
06564	Bartlett, Wallace A.	63y	W	25 MAY 1908	Brentwood MD	Rock Creek
16423	Bartolucci, Luigi Dundas	32y	W	1 APR 1920	Baltimore MD	Arlington
00677	Barton, Charles H.	33y	C	15 JAN 1892	Trenton NJ	Mt. Olivet
03678	Barton, Emily	22y	W	27 NOV 1859	Philadelphia PA	Oak Hill[1]
18595	Barton, Philomena C.	40y	C	10 JUN 1923	Monessen PA	Mt. Olivet
15867	Bartsch, Henry	88y	W	6 JUL 1919	Sligo MD	Glenwood
03855	Bass, William	36y	W	10 APR 1902	Denver CO	Rock Creek
09098	Bassett, Harry	20y	W	28 FEB 1913	Riverdale MD	Rock Creek
14229	Bassett, Howard W., s/o Geo.	55y	W	15 JUL 1917	Richmond VA	Cremated
15718	Bassett, Rice	19y	W	9 OCT 1918	Brooklyn NY	Oak Hill
03831	Bassford, Richard A.	72y	W	25 MAR 1902	Hampton VA	Rock Creek
03431	Bassil, Belle, dress-maker	40y	C	25 FEB 1901	New York NY	Payne's
14048	Baston, Charles G.	44y	W	23 MAR 1917	Chillum MD	Glenwood
17203	Batchelder, Amos G.	—	W	28 MAY 1921	Walter Reed Hp.	Buffalo NY
00448	Batchelor, Lucretia A.	67y	W	14 APR 1891	Montg. Co. MD	Rock Creek
04757	Bateman, James J.	34y	W	6 JUN 1904	Baltimore MD	Glenwood
14208	Bateman, Joseph F.	72y	W	4 JUL 1917	Annapolis Jct. MD	Holyrood
03385	Bateman, Mary	4y	W	2 JAN 1901	Newark NJ	Holyrood
07644	Bateman, Mary E.	53y	W	21 JUL 1910	Seat Pleasant MD	Glenwood
01524	Bates, Amelia Frances	50y	W	30 JAN 1895	Alexandria VA	Oak Hill
03727	Bates, Caroline W.	50y	W	10 DEC 1901	Hyattsville MD	Congressional
05337	Bates, Charles M.	10y	W	13 DEC 1903	Allentown PA	Rock Creek
08603	Bates, Charlotte	42y	W	17 APR 1912	Leavenworth KS	Arlington
04075	Bates, Earnest Raymond J.	13m	W	21 JUN 1902	Hyattsville MD	Congressional
07471	Bates, Edgar H.	92y	W	16 MAR 1910	New York NY	Glenwood
16650	Bates, Elizabeth	21y	C	9 AUG 1920	New York NY	Payne's
16238	Bates, Emory Hank	60y	W	22 JAN 1920	Beltsville MD	Glenwood
02975	Bates, Gertrude	24y	C	10 OCT 1899	Baltimore MD	Payne's
08029	Bates, Helen	3y	W	26 MAR 1911	Brentwood MD	Glenwood
15078	Bates, John	17y	C	4 OCT 1918	Philadelphia PA	Guinea VA
00074	Bates, John E., Rev.	73y	W	2 JUN 1889	Hyattsville MD	Congressional
04885	Bates, Mary C.	68y	W	10 SEP 1904	Westminster MD	Arlington VA
13045	Bates, Mary O.	57y	W	6 AUG 1915	Bellevue PA	Glenwood
00680	Bates, Mary P.	32y	W	19 JAN 1892	Portland ME	Oak Hill
06160	Bates, Matilda M.	70y	W	28 JUL 1907	Atlantic City NJ	Rock Creek
02808	Bates, Nathaniel	35y	C	3 APR 1899	Montg. Co. MD	Christian
16476	Bates, Norval Edward	76y	W	6 MAY 1920	Brooklyn NY	Glenwood

---

[1] Note dated 8 OCT 1901, of Philadelphia, Pa., for removal from Laurel Hill Cemetery.

No.	Name of Deceased	Age	Race	Death Date	Place of Death	Place of Burial
02838	Bates, Rebecca	52y	W	24 MAY 1899	New York NY	Glenwood
08685	Bates, Sarah Elizabeth	89y	W	25 JUN 1912	Newton NJ	Glenwood
06364	Battey, Sally	29y	C	26 DEC 1907	Jersey City NJ	Harmony
05926	Batton, George M.	21y	W	6 FEB 1907	Baltimore MD	Woodlawn
02785	Bauchages, Sallie W.	54y	W	26 MAR 1899	Hyattsville MD	Oak Hill
00568	Bauer, Amy Mary	11m	W	23 JUL 1891	Atlantic City NJ	Oak Hill
04410	Bauer, Benjamin F.	2m	W	27 JUL 1903	Takoma Park MD	Rock Creek
06157	Bauer, Bernedetta Louise	9m	W	28 JUL 1907	Bethesda MD	St. Mary's
13464	Bauerlein, Max M.	60y	W	18 APR 1916	Takoma Park MD	Souderton PA
05904	Bauf, George	47y	W	23 NOV 1906	Washington DC	Prospect Hill
04239½	Baugester, Infant	SB	W	20 FEB 1903	Montg. Co. MD	Rock Creek
13399	Bauman, August F.	64y	W	5 MAR 1916	Pindell MD	Prospect Hill
08071	Bauman, Augusta (Housdorf)	67y	W	18 APR 1911	Chesterbrook VA	Prospect Hill
16942	Bauman, Elizabeth V.	48y	W	29 JAN 1921	Baltimore MD	Mt. Olivet
15423	Bauman, Mary	32y	W	9 DEC 1918	Baltimore MD	Congressional
16798	Bauman, Mary	60y	W	6 NOV 1920	Forestville MD	Prospect Hill
06053	Baumann, Hannah	76y	W	1 MAY 1907	Pindell MD	Prospect Hill
07853	Bause, John	40y	W	3 DEC 1910	Marcus Hook PA	Rock Creek
01337	Baxter, Alice K.	11y	W	12 APR 1894	Kensington MD	Congressional
12139	Baxter, Charles L.	34y	W	24 DEC 1913	Jackson Spgs. NC	Cremated
01528	Baxter, Douglass	10m	W	28 FEB 1895	Norfolk VA	Glenwood
02041	Baxter, Emory	56y	W	10 NOV 1896	Kensington MD	Congressional
00119	Baxter, Palmyre M.	28y	W	11 AUG 1889	Profit VA	Mt. Olivet
12293	Baxter, Richard	34y	C	2 APR 1914	Philadelphia PA	Mt. Olivet
11969	Bayard, Albert F.	67y	W	19 AUG 1913	Niagara Falls NY	Rock Creek
13735	Bayley, Lloyd	21y	C	24 SEP 1916	Detroit MI	Harmony
18058	Baylie, Jennie	78y	W	9 SEP 1922	New York NY	Glenwood
00205	Bayliss, James E.	21y	W	3 APR 1890	Eliz. City Co. VA	Congressional
05847	Baylor, John G.	34y	W	3 DEC 1906	Pittsford VT	Arlington
05786	Baylord, Louisa E.	67y	W	21 OCT 1906	Platsburgh NY	Arlington VA
14994	Bayly, Emma R.	50y	W	29 AUG 1918	Hyattsville MD	Delaplane VA
01338	Bayly, H.B., Dr.	37y	W	19 JAN 1894	Tacoma WA	Tacoma WA
14003	Bayly, Harry T.	38y	W	23 FEB 1917	Philadelphia PA	Rock Creek
07106	Bayly, John	24y	W	13 JUL 1909	Takoma Park MD	Congressional
00206	Bayne, Adelia I.	43y	W	30 NOV 1889	Shepherdstn. WV	Mt. Olivet
12682	Bayne, James Edward, s/o J.	50y	C	26 DEC 1914	Asbury Park NJ	Harmony
15527	Bayne, Julia A.	42y	C	1 JAN 1919	New York NY	Harmony
13463	Bays, Lorenzo Lafayette	57y	W	15 APR 1916	Black Mtn. NC	Cremated
13481	Beach, Oliver	47y	W	10 APR 1916	At Sea	Glenwood
00533	Beacham, Mary Jane	62y	W	8 JUN 1891	Portsmouth VA	Congressional
02107	Beadle, John H.	57y	W	15 JAN 1897	Rockville MD	Arlington
17670	Beadle, Mary A.	87y	W	2 FEB 1922	Hyattsville MD	Mt. Olivet
00681	Beal, Mary	84y	C	12 JAN 1891	Harpers Ferry WV	Harmony
08704	Beale, George N.	82y	W	5 JUL 1912	Takoma Park MD	Congressional
14685	Beale, Helen M.	68y	W	15 MAR 1918	Hyattsville MD	Oak Hill
16308	Beale, Margaret Elizabeth	34y	W	11 FEB 1920	MD	Mt. Olivet
12387	Beall, Evan T.	61y	W	4 JUN 1914	Seat Pleasant MD	Mt. Olivet
06078	Beall, Infant of George H.	7m	W	24 MAY 1907	Oakmont PA	Glenwood
16845	Beall, James W.	72y	W	5 DEC 1920	Ardwick MD	Mt. Olivet
03395	Beall, John E.	44y	W	19 JAN 1891	Hagerstown MD	Oak Hill
13040	Beall, John H., Jr.	SB	W	6 AUG 1915	Chillum MD	Glenwood
16046	Beall, Joseph E.	4y	W	14 OCT 1919	Landover MD	Mt. Olivet
02042	Beall, Martha Addison	70y	W	25 DEC 1896	Leeland MD	Oak Hill
01291	Beall, Martha Louise	81y	W	27 FEB 1894	Chicago IL	Oak Hill
02150	Beall, Robert N.	70y	W	10 APR 1897	Burnt Mills MD	Rock Creek
02908	Beall, Seward	37y	W	11 AUG 1899	Hyattsville MD	Glenwood
18167	Beall, Warren Hamilton	63y	W	16 NOV 1922	Catlett VA	Ft. Lincoln
12770	Bealor, Samuel K., Sr.	55y	W	17 FEB 1915	Atlantic City NJ	Rock Creek
04539	Beaman, John W.	56y	W	13 DEC 1903	Greensboro NC	Rock Creek

District of Columbia Foreign Death Records, 1888-1923

No.	Name of Deceased	Age	Race	Death Date	Place of Death	Place of Burial
17704	Beamer, Andrew J.	52y	W	19 FEB 1922	New York NY	Glenwood
00808	Bean, Helen C.	39y	W	29 AUG 1892	Bethesda MD	Holyrood
07826	Bean, Infant of John W.	1½d	W	15 NOV 1910	Rosslyn VA	Methodist
15835	Bean, James Delmore	32y	W	16 JUN 1919	Saranac Lake NY	Glenwood
16438	Bean, Marion	25y	W	14 APR 1920	Pittsburgh PA	Glenwood
06547	Bean, Mary A.	74y	W	10 MAY 1908	Bethesda MD	Holyrood
01339	Bean, Samuel	26y	C	18 MAR 1894	Albany NY	Mt. Olivet
13897	Bean, Tarleton H.	70y	W	28 DEC 1916	Albany NY	Congressional
01397	Bearans, Margaret	45y	W	20 JUN 1894	Bladensburg MD	Mt. Olivet
15505	Bearce, Louis Merrill	8y	W	30 DEC 1918	Chevy Chase MD	Rock Creek[1]
00569	Beard, Harriet V.	7y	W	6 SEP 1891	Rockville MD	Oak Hill
04508	Beardslee, Lester A.	68y	W	10 NOV 1903	Summerville GA	Cremated
02817	Beardsley, Mamie J.	25y	W	29 APR 1899	New York NY	Glenwood
06826	Beare, Eliza J.	82y	W	21 NOV 1908	New York NY	Congressional
15614	Beasley, Arthur F.	39y	C	10 FEB 1919	Pittsburgh PA	Harmony
13628	Beason, Arrabella L.	38y	C	28 JUL 1916	Jessup MD	Mt. Zion West
13179	Beaton, Edwin, s/o Edwin	15m	W	4 NOV 1915	Richmond VA	Glenwood
16624	Beattie, Mary D.	74y	W	24 JUL 1920	Cherrydale VA	Glenwood
15481	Beattie, Susan Annetta	38y	W	25 DEC 1918	McLean VA	Oak Hill
17378	Beauverd, George Alfred	64y	W	31 AUG 1921	Columbia Pk. MD	Gettysburg PA
16922	Beavers, Frank	50y	W	13 JAN 1921	Scranton PA	Glenwood
13386	Beavers, Thomas R.	48y	W	26 FEB 1916	Miami FL	Rock Creek
06386	Beazley, Mattie J. (Chew)	36y	C	10 JAN 1908	High View VA	Payne's
05796	Beazley, Phebe	9m	C	30 OCT 1906	Arlington VA	Payne's
05213	Beck, Catherine J.	1m	W	21 JUL 1905	Baltimore MD	St. Mary's
08837	Beck, Infant of Edward	1h	W	16 SEP 1912	Brentwood MD	Glenwood
07745	Beck, Josephine	37y	W	10 SEP 1910	New York NY	Mt. Olivet
03233	Beck, Louisa	11m	W	10 JUL 1900	Silver Spring MD	St. Mary's
07107	Beck, Margaret	8m	W	12 JUL 1909	Bethesda MD	Cremated
00534	Beckenbaugh, Margaret	66y	W	16 MAY 1891	New York NY	Mt. Olivet
04684	Becker, Frederick	89y	W	28 SEP 1890	Baltimore MD	Rock Creek
16311	Becker, Mary Francis	43y	W	14 FEB 1920	Alexandria VA	Mt. Olivet
06166	Becker, Mary Virginia	31y	W	2 AUG 1907	Alexandria VA	Rock Creek
15965	Becker, Robert A.	23y	W	30 AUG 1919	Annapolis MD	Arlington
08182	Becker, William Mathias	11m	W	7 JUL 1911	Mt. Ida VA	Mt. Olivet
17944	Beckert, Bertha L.	17y	W	8 JUL 1922	Cherrydale VA	Glenwood
03676	Beckert, Charles A., Capt.	72y	W	4 OCT 1901	Anniston AL	Arlington
03306	Beckert, Harriett A.	79y	W	18 OCT 1900	Berwyn MD	Oak Hill
01790	Becket, Jeannette	1y	C	1 DEC 1895	New York NY	Mt. Zion
08891	Beckett, Eli E.	71y	C	16 OCT 1912	Baltimore MD	Mt. Zion East
03682	Beckett, Ferdinand	34y	C	12 OCT 1901	New York NY	Mt. Zion
17950	Beckett, George H.	70y	C	9 JUL 1922	Atlantic City NJ	Harmony
15253	Beckett, Henrietta	14y	C	18 OCT 1918	Rosslyn VA	Mt. Zion West
18083	Beckett, Thaddeus	42y	C	18 SEP 1922	Burkeville VA	Harmony
04566	Beckett, William A.	25y	C	12 JAN 1904	Wheeling WV	Harmony
15779	Beckford, Georgie Anna	28y	C	13 MAY 1919	Henderson NC	Payne's
11899	Beckley, Alice	27y	C	14 JUL 1913	Brentwood MD	Harmony
17702	Beckman, Helen T.	53y	W	19 FEB 1922	Montg. Co. MD	Cedar Hill
06895	Beckman, Paul	16y	W	18 JAN 1909	Irvington MD	Richmond VA
04864	Beckwith, G.H.	12y	W	23 AUG 1904	Chevy Chase MD	Congressional
12058	Beckwith, Sadie E.	88y	W	22 OCT 1913	Halls Hill VA	Woodlawn
18241	Beech, Eugene Lancelot	67y	W	2 JAN 1923	Chevy Chase MD	Rock Creek
00150	Beefils, Emily [Belfield]	38y	W	15 SEP 1889	Riggs Farm MD	Holyrood
00392	Beers, Alice	23y	W	25 AUG 1890	Halls Hill VA	Elmira NY
00390	Beers, Mable	2y	W	20 AUG 1890	Halls Hill VA	Elmira NY
03356	Beggs, Agnes H.	34y	W	1 DEC 1900	Ebensburg PA	Holyrood

[1] Disinterment permit #10067 on 30 JUN 1919 for removal to Hebron ME.

No.	Name of Deceased	Age	Race	Death Date	Place of Death	Place of Burial
12581	Behrand, Samuel K., s/o P.K.	57y	W	20 OCT 1914	Boise ID	Glenwood
14480	Behrend, Elon	88y	W	28 NOV 1917	Seat Pleasant MD	Wash. Hebrew
02526	Behrens, Albert	40y	W	2 JUL 1898	Highlands MD	Prospect Hill
01493	Behrle, Milton	7m	W	22 SEP 1894	Philadelphia PA	Prospect Hill
17711	Beinley, Elizabeth	85y	C	22 FEB 1922	Dupont Hts. MD	Payne's
13593	Beiss, Sarah P.	75y	W	9 JUL 1916	Takoma Park MD	Glenwood
03314	Belcher, Edwin	38y	C	7 JAN 1883	Augusta GA	Arlington
14273	Belden, Howard H.	41y	W	3 AUG 1917	Baltimore MD	Arlington
18179	Belden, W. Scott	87y	W	24 NOV 1922	Edgewood PA	Arlington
04247	Belknap, George E.	71y	W	7 APR 1903	Key West FL	Arlington VA
14088	Bell, Annie	75y	W	14 APR 1917	Vienna VA	Congressional
13855	Bell, Bessie	25y	C	7 DEC 1916	Baltimore MD	Mt. Zion West
03545	Bell, Charles Howard	28y	W	17 JUN 1901	Baltimore MD	Oak Hill
16226	Bell, Christine	32y	C	17 JAN 1920	New York NY	Harmony
04248	Bell, Clarance	6y	C	19 APR 1903	Phoebus VA	Payne's
08803	Bell, Gardiner H.	23y	W	2 SEP 1912	Boston MA	Rock Creek
03971	Bell, Hattie	19y	C	28 AUG 1902	Baltimore MD	Harmony
16520	Bell, Helen R.E.	2d	W	3 JUN 1920	Maryland Pk. MD	Manassas VA
04890	Bell, Henry E.	67y	W	1 AUG 1904	Baltimore MD	Oak Hill
16289	Bell, Ida T.	37y	C	3 FEB 1920	Seat Pleasant MD	Payne's
04227	Bell, John T.	62y	C	21 FEB 1903	Philadelphia PA	Arlington VA
12157	Bell, Joseph, s/o John	38y	C	10 JAN 1914	Eliz. City Co. VA	Payne's
18242	Bell, Mabel G.	65y	W	3 JAN 1923	Chevy Chase MD	Cremated
17046	Bell, Margaret M. (Killian)	72y	W	14 MAR 1921	Atlantic City NJ	Prospect Hill
07533	Bell, Mark	64y	C	9 MAY 1910	Fairmont Hts. MD	Harmony
06816	Bell, Pearl Leona	19y	W	12 NOV 1908	Polk PA	St. Barnabas MD
02693	Bell, Raymond C.	4m	W	2 JAN 1899	Fredericksburg VA	Glenwood
08302	Bell, Richard B.	38y	W	3 SEP 1911	Santa Maria CA	Congressional
09046	Bell, Richard, s/o Richard	20y	C	22 JAN 1913	Long Branch NJ	Woodlawn
02043	Bell, Richard T.	19y	C	19 DEC 1896	Seat Pleasant MD	Jones' Chapel
05480	Bell, Robert Francis	2m	W	1 MAR 1906	Pr. Geo. Co. MD	Rock Creek
01114a	Bell, Robert M.	28y	W	12 OCT 1892	Peebles OH	Congressional
02398	Bell, Thomas	25y	C	6 MAR 1898	Philadelphia PA	Moore's
06847	Bell, Virginia	46y	C	6 DEC 1908	Evanston IL	Harmony
01115	Bell, Walter	21y	C	8 JUN 1892	Richmond VA	Graceland
12306	Bell, Wesley	22y	W	5 APR 1914	Railroad	Georgia Sta. VT
07767	Bell, William D.	47y	W	28 SEP 1910	New York NY	Congressional
01668	Bellew, Hannah A.	82y	W	20 AUG 1895	Alexandria VA	Congressional
15712	Bellew, Mary A.	76y	W	5 APR 1919	New Haven CN	Mt. Olivet
16122	Bellinger, Jacob B.	91y	W	21 NOV 1919	Ridgefield Pk. NJ	Glenwood
15585	Bellis, Eva C.	42y	W	26 JAN 1919	Takoma Park MD	Rock Creek
14248	Bellis, Roger	77y	W	25 JUL 1917	Hyattsville MD	Glenwood
17353	Bellmore, Abe	30y	W	c.3 AUG 1921	France	Adas Israel
08098	Belote, A.S.	c.40y	W	30 APR 1911	Miami FL	Rock Creek
06149	Belote, Sidney A.	19y	W	21 JUL 1907	Poolesville MD	Rock Creek
00075	Belt, Ann	80y	C	24 JUN 1889	Arlington VA	Holyrood
12901	Belt, Charles	20y	W	27 APR 1915	Baltimore MD	Glenwood
07598	Belt, Etta	25y	C	22 JUN 1910	Mt. Alto PA	Payne's
11917	Belt, Robert	26y	W	26 JUL 1913	Railroad	Mt. Olivet
02963	Belt, William Middleton, printer	77y	W	23 SEP 1899	Red Rock NM	Oak Hill
04167	Bender, Charles	65y	W	3 FEB 1903	Hyattsville MD	Prospect Hill
08057	Bender, Minnie C.	19y	W	10 APR 1911	Takoma Park MD	Prospect Hill
04589	Benedict, Arria S.	85y	W	3 FEB 1904	New York NY	Oak Hill
04688	Benedict, James T.	86y	W	23 APR 1904	New York NY	Oak Hill
06658	Benedict, William S.	65y	W	1 FEB 1908	New Orleans LA	Cremated
05238	Benham, Andrew E.W.	73y	W	11 AUG 1905	Putnam Co. NY	Arlington
12702	Benham, Eliz. Ann McNeil	94y	W	4 JAN 1915	New York NY	Congressional
08018	Benham, Henry Hall, Maj.	53y	W	21 MAR 1911	New York NY	Congressional
04666	Benham, Henry Kennady	36y	W	8 APR 1904	Key West FL	Arlington VA

District of Columbia Foreign Death Records, 1888-1923

No.	Name of Deceased	Age	Race	Death Date	Place of Death	Place of Burial
03082	Benner, Walter	60y	W	20 FEB 1900	Hampton VA	Congressional
15104	Bennetson, Iver C.	32y	W	5 OCT 1918	Riverdale MD	Glenwood
06729	Bennett, Frank V.	55y	W	12 SEP 1908	New York NY	Rock Creek
15639	Bennett, Harrison Monroe, Dr.	76y	W	25 FEB 1919	Takoma Park MD	Glenwood
17364	Bennett, Howard Abel	18y	W	19 AUG 1921	Norfolk VA	Arlington
06238	Bennett, Jos. B.	36y	W	22 SEP 1907	Salisbury NC	Oak Hill
18362	Bennett, Lida J.	72y	W	19 FEB 1923	Chicago IL	Glenwood
01496	Bennett, Michael	28y	W	20 SEP 1894	Waverly VA	Mt. Olivet
16710	Bennetts, William J.	55y	W	14 SEP 1920	Takoma Park MD	Rock Creek
15249	Benson, Harry	22y	C	19 OCT 1918	Camp Jacks. SC	Arlington
14263	Benson, James	75y	C	29 JUL 1917	Forestville MD	Harmony
03168	Benson, Julia A.T.	73y	W	17 APR 1900	Wash. Grove MD	Rock Creek
13881	Benson, Margaret F.	17y	W	25 DEC 1916	Berwyn MD	Rock Creek
13287	Bent, Annie E.	49y	W	6 JAN 1916	Freeport IL	Glenwood
06657	Bentley, Alexander J.	81y	W	25 JUL 1908	Brooklin ME	Oak Hill
00380	Bentley, Marrian	47y	W	4 AUG 1890	Charlestown WV	Oak Hill
01499	Benton, Edward Vermitya	39y	W	28 SEP 1894	Stafford Co. VA	Glenwood
00207	Bentz, Frederick	39y	W	10 FEB 1890	Baltimore MD	Prospect Hill
05645	Beraus, John	70y	W	15 JUL 1906	Garrett Park MD	Congressional
07465	Beresford, Lillie C.	34y	W	11 MAR 1910	Philadelphia PA	Prospect Hill
14112	Beresford, Randolph	20y	W	26 APR 1917	Evanston IL	Prospect Hill
02726	Bergdorf, Augustus J.	18y	W	28 JAN 1899	Lexington VA	Congressional
08426	Berger, Frederick G., Jr.	29y	W	14 DEC 1911	Saranac Lake NY	Rock Creek
02235	Berger, Martha J.	33y	W	12 JUL 1897	Cherrydale VA	Glenwood
12141	Bergman, Frederick W.	69y	W	27 DEC 1913	Relay MD	Prospect Hill
06860	Bergman, James Ernest	27y	W	14 DEC 1908	Ft. Stanton NM	Rock Creek
12021	Bergmann, Margaret A.	61y	W	30 SEP 1913	Suitland MD	Mt. Olivet
05757	Bergmann, Minnie F.	50y	W	3 OCT 1906	Philadelphia PA	Prospect Hill
06123	Berkeley, Carrie Annie P.	22y	W	1 JUL 1907	Portsmouth VA	Arlington
06953	Berkeley, Emma E.	49y	W	24 MAR 1909	Laurel MD	Congressional
13168	Berkeley, William A.	24y	W	25 OCT 1915	Lowell MA	Glenwood
05837	Berkely, Edmund	58y	W	29 NOV 1906	Philadelphia PA	Haymarket VA
16022	Berlin, Max	23y	W	30 SEP 1919	Baltimore MD	Elesavetgrad
13733	Bermann, Rufus Rhodes	23y	W	14 SEP 1916	New York NY	Rock Creek
17402	Bernard, Ester	71y	W	15 SEP 1921	Baltimore MD	Wash. Hebrew
16037	Bernton, Ruth E.	1y	W	9 OCT 1919	Newport RI	Wash. Hebrew
02755	Berret, Julius B.	86y	W	1 MAR 1899	Freedom MD	Congressional
03724	Berret, Ruth A.	82y	W	1 DEC 1901	Freedom MD	Congressional
14023	Berrett, Mary E., d/o Jos. S.	69y	W	6 MAR 1917	Norfolk VA	Congressional
05370	Berrett, Nancy B.	84y	W	15 NOV 1905	Morristown NJ	Congressional
14599	Berry, Clifford C.	30y	C	22 JAN 1918	Philadelphia PA	Payne's
08489	Berry, George R.	54y	W	24 JAN 1912	Baltimore MD	Congressional
03200	Berry, George T.	41y	W	30 MAY 1900	Phoenix AZ	Oak Hill
08198	Berry, Hilliard	59y	C	11 JUL 1911	Alex. Bay NY	Harmony
14189	Berry, James T.	78y	W	23 JUN 1917	Laurel MD	Milton Mills NH
00120	Berry, Jane	60y	W	3 AUG 1889	Wilmington DE	Mt. Zion
08851	Berry, John	57y	C	22 SEP 1912	Cedar Hts. MD	Payne's
01293	Berry, John H.	18y	W	4 MAR 1894	Aiken SC	Oak Hill
03019	Berry, Maria	75y	C	27 NOV 1899	Pr. Geo. Co. MD	Payne's
14751	Berry, Robert A., s/o Robert	56y	C	11 APR 1918	Racoon Ford VA	Moore's
17728	Berry, Samuel	48y	C	4 MAR 1922	Baltimore MD	Woodlawn
08726	Berry, Samuel T.	42y	C	21 JUL 1912	Arlington VA	—
12696	Berry, William	40y	C	31 DEC 1914	Philadelphia PA	Harmony
05857	Bertinatti, Eugenia	80y	W	9 DEC 1906	Nashville TN	Oak Hill
11935	Best, George R.	37y	C	2 AUG 1913	Ft. Myer VA	Harmony
14622	Best, John T.	71y	W	3 FEB 1918	Darnestown MD	Prospect Hill
07901	Bestor, Selina	88y	W	1 JAN 1911	Asheville NC	Oak Hill
12469	Betts, Edwin J.	79y	W	28 JUL 1914	Dayton OH	Arlington
06773	Bevans, Thomas H.	71y	W	14 OCT 1908	Oxon Hill MD	Congressional

No.	Name of Deceased	Age	Race	Death Date	Place of Death	Place of Burial
05669	Beveridge, Susan J.	65y	W	31 JUL 1906	Franklin Co. PA	Oak Hill
08525	Beverley, William R.	c.50y	C	25 FEB 1912	Petersburg VA	Woodlawn
05064	Beverly, Elizabeth J.	29y	C	22 MAR 1905	Jersey City NJ	Woodlawn
15800	Beverly, Richard	47y	C	28 MAY 1919	Halls Hill VA	Payne's
15705	Bey, Adbul Hak Hussein	44y	W	29 FEB 1919	Atlantic City NJ	Rock Creek
14567	Beyer, Eva	88y	W	11 JAN 1918	Rock Hill VA	Prospect Hill
14856	Beyer, Samuel Bernard	30y	W	7 JUN 1918	Annapolis MD	Arlington VA
05565	Beymer, Albert	54y	W	4 MAY 1906	Potomac MD	Glenwood
04420	Beymer, Alice J.	6m	W	3 AUG 1903	Takoma Park MD	Glenwood
08716	Beymer, Webster	66y	W	12 JUL 1912	Potomac MD	Glenwood
01116	Beynon, Levi H.	68y	W	15 DEC 1892	Colonial Bea. VA	Mt. Olivet
03005	Bias, Charles	47y	W	14 NOV 1899	Cleveland OH	Payne's
13324	Bias, Murry	65y	C	26 JAN 1916	Rosslyn VA	Mt. Zion West
03640	Bias, Sarah H.	1y	C	12 SEP 1901	Rosslyn VA	Mt. Zion
03647	Bias, William Henry	30y	C	16 SEP 1901	Rosslyn VA	Mt. Zion
00535	Bibb, John C.	8y	W	15 MAY 1890	Staunton VA	Congressional
17708	Bibby, Amanda	77y	W	22 FEB 1922	Philadelphia PA	Congressional
05374	Bibby, John G.S.	39y	W	5 NOV 1905	Manitoba, Can.	Iron Sides MD
16553	Bickerton, Dandonia R.	52y	W	24 JUN 1920	Seat Pleasant MD	Mt. Olivet
12162	Bickford, Edwin	60y	W	8 JAN 1914	El Paso TX	Arlington
02556	Bickford, George K.	15y	W	8 AUG 1898	Colonial Bea. VA	Rock Creek
06435	Bickley, John L.	35y	C	17 FEB 1908	New York NY	Harmony
16459	Biddle, Celia M.	64y	W	1 MAY 1920	Mt. Ranier MD	Glenwood
06059	Biddle, Ephraim	45y	C	6 MAY 1907	New York NY	Harmony
07565	Biddle, James	78y	W	9 JUN 1910	Berkeley Sp. WV	Arlington
13043	Biddle, John A., s/o John	47y	W	6 AUG 1915	Atlantic City NJ	Soldier's Home
05243	Bidgell, Julia C.	53y	C	11 AUG 1905	Jersey City NJ	Mt. Zion East
16613	Bidwell, Frances F.	65y	W	19 JUL 1920	Olney MD	Buffalo NY
17808	Bieber, Samuel	78y	W	18 APR 1922	Atlantic City NJ	Wash. Hebrew
17418	Bieg, Valentine N.	31y	W	24 AUG 1921	Hall, Eng.	Arlington
13214	Biehl, David C.	53y	W	15 NOV 1915	Ft. Bayard NM	Arlington
15251	Biehl, Lloyd C.	16y	W	22 OCT 1918	Baltimore MD	Arlington
16766	Bielaski, Oscar	45y	W	16 OCT 1920	Cherrydale VA	Holyrood
07321	Bielsford, Frederick A.	38y	W	11 DEC 1909	Camden NJ	Rock Creek
18185	Bierlein, George M.	80y	W	27 NOV 1922	Clarendon VA	Prospect Hill
08192	Bigelow, Agnes E.	65y	W	11 JUL 1911	Takoma Park MD	Indiana PA
16771	Bigelow, Helen C.	53y	W	20 OCT 1920	Manhattan NY	Congressional
01481	Bigelow, John P.	53y	W	2 AUG 1892	London, Eng.	Oak Hill
15726	Bigelow, Otis	78y	W	15 APR 1919	Silver Spring MD	Rock Creek
18452	Bigley, Harry A.	56y	W	1 APR 1923	Atlantic City NJ	Glenwood
09012	Bilfield, John	62y	W	1 JAN 1913	Philadelphia PA	Mt. Olivet
14582	Billings, Laura E.	—	—	16 JAN 1918	Baltimore MD	Arlington VA
16903	Billings, Luther G., Adm.	80y	W	30 DEC 1920	Eagle Rock CA	Arlington[1]
16833	Billings, Minerva F.	57y	W	1 DEC 1920	Woodside MD	Dayton OH
12720	Billingsley, Anna E.	64y	C	14 JAN 1915	Camden NJ	Woodlawn
17608	Billingsley, Charles M.	48y	W	23 DEC 1921	Mechanicsville VA	Glenwood
02293	Bilyer, Helen M.	19y	W	29 NOV 1897	Philadelphia PA	Rock Creek
12748	Binger, Elizabeth	68y	W	1 FEB 1915	Springfield MA	Prospect Hill
17597	Bingham, Benjamin F.	79y	W	17 DEC 1921	St. Louis MO	Arlington
05000	Bingham, Gilbert E.	78y	W	3 JUL 1903	Arlington VA	Hospital
07374	Binnix, Samuel	67y	W	16 JAN 1910	Baltimore MD	Cremated
00121	Birch, Jane Eliza	72y	W	10 AUG 1889	Falls Church VA	Rock Creek
00682	Birch, Mary F.	62y	W	26 JAN 1892	Arlington VA	Oak Hill
00683	Birch, Pamelia A.	59y	W	17 NOV 1891	Baltimore MD	Oak Hill
04375	Birch, Peter T.	63y	W	6 JUL 1903	Ballston VA	Oak Hill
02697	Birch, Randolph, farmer	74y	W	9 JAN 1899	Ballston VA	Oak Hill

[1] The certificate gives year 1921 in error, and is correctly 1920 based on numerical sequence and source document.

District of Columbia Foreign Death Records, 1888-1923

No.	Name of Deceased	Age	Race	Death Date	Place of Death	Place of Burial
14976	Birch, Rosa	82y	W	13 AUG 1918	Scranton PA	Glenwood
06867	Bird, Florence T.	23y	W	22 DEC 1908	Ft. Wash. MD	Mt. Olivet
11947	Bird, Frank	21y	W	6 AUG 1913	Boston MA	Congressional
12273	Bird, Frank W.	60y	W	27 AMR 1914	Cincinnati OH	Cremated
01117	Bird, Georgiana C.	53y	W	18 JUN 1892	Brooklyn NY	Glenwood
09105	Bird, James H.	65y	C	2 MAR 1913	Newark NJ	Harmony
18549	Bird, Mary C.	72y	W	18 MAY 1923	W. Palm Bea. FL	Congressional
12611	Birdsong, Elizabeth Key	31y	W	12 NOV 1914	Warrenton VA	Oak Hill
15611	Birgfield, Clara Louise	34y	W	11 FEB 1919	Atlanta GA	Glenwood
15679	Birkle, Arthur E.	27y	W	29 MAR 1919	Brooklyn NY	Ft. Myer
06354	Birney, Alice McLellan	49y	W	20 DEC 1907	Chevy Chase MD	Oak Hill
02858	Birney, Arthur A.	16y	W	22 JUL 1899	Ocean City MD	Rock Creek
13695	Birney, Arthur A.	64y	W	4 SEP 1916	Summit VA	Rock Creek
02859	Birney, James G.	14y	W	22 JUL 1899	Ocean City MD	Rock Creek
06180	Birney, William	88y	W	14 AUG 1907	Forest Glen MD	Cremated
14085	Birney, William M.	30y	W	13 APR 1917	Youngstown OH	Rock Creek
02044	Bischof, John A.	57y	W	24 OCT 1896	Alex. Co. VA	St. Mary's
05973	Biscoe, Cornelia Hunt	74y	W	2 MAR 1907	New Orleans LA	Oak Hill
05076	Biscoe, Henry Lawson	63y	W	5 APR 1905	Pensacola FL	Rock Creek
14951	Bishop, Margaret	77y	W	3 AUG 1918	Baltimore MD	Mt. Olivet
06829	Bishop, Nancy S.	39y	W	25 NOV 1908	New York NY	Rock Creek
02418	Bissell, Sarah M.	87y	W	26 MAR 1898	Glen Echo MD	Holyrood
04421	Bisset, Florence	2y	W	2 AUG 1903	Rockville MD	Glenwood
00122	Bittinger, Edmund C.	71y	W	2 AUG 1889	Philadelphia PA	Oak Hill
14002	Bixler, John Wesley	74y	W	22 FEB 1917	Kitlingby CN	Arlington
15312	Black, Henry G.	29y	W	31 OCT 1918	Hyattsville MD	Glenwood
03525	Black, John	51y	W	25 MAY 1901	Chicago IL	Harmony
12315	Black, Philis	51y	C	12 APR 1914	Poughkeepsie NY	Payne's
15463	Blackburn, Harry	28y	C	15 DEC 1918	Camp Sevier SC	Harmony
05621	Blackfair, Margaret	66y	W	29 JUN 1906	Newton MA	Glenwood
08532	Blackford, Hulda W.	77y	W	27 FEB 1912	Birmingham AL	Oak Hill
16621	Blackley, Bassett	32y	W	21 JUL 1920	Staunton VA	Rock Creek
16591	Blackston, John Ralph	42y	C	8 JUL 1920	Providence RI	Mt. Olivet
08451	Blackstone, Maria	c.60y	C	30 DEC 1911	Takoma Park MD	Payne's
03020	Blackville, Julia	60y	C	26 NOV 1899	Jersey City NJ	Harmony
17275	Blackwell, Alice Elizabeth	55y	C	29 JUN 1921	Fairmont Hts. MD	Chesterfield VA
02816	Blackwell, Lily L.G.	24y	W	25 MAR 1899	Phoenix AZ	Oak Hill
00208	Blackwell, Sarah M. Campbell	34y	W	1 FEB 1890	Baltimore MD	Oak Hill
17229	Blackwood, Charles W.	55y	W	8 JUN 1921	Denver CO	Ft. Lincoln
00093	Bladen, Arthur	2y	W	24 JUL 1889	Pr. Geo. Co. MD	Rock Creek
14744	Bladen, Charles A., Jr.	6m	W	10 APR 1918	College Park MD	Rock Creek
00229	Bladen, Jane Elizabeth	33y	W	6 MAY 1890	Pr. Geo. Co. MD	Rock Creek
01512	Bladen, Sarah	10min	W	18 OCT 1894	Pr. Geo. Co. MD	Rock Creek
00076	Bladen, William T.	3y	C	22 JUN 1889	Pr. Geo. Co. MD	Rock Creek
15548	Blades, James	64y	W	10 JAN 1919	New London CN	Congressional
04750	Blades, John H.	59y	W	30 MAY 1904	Hampton VA	Arlington VA
01529	Blagburn, Mary V.	28y	C	2 FEB 1895	New York NY	Harmony
06404	Blagden, Laura S.	88y	W	21 JAN 1908	Saranac Inn NY	Congressional
06313	Blagden, Silliman	61y	W	25 NOV 1907	Boston MA	Congressional
01118	Blagdon, Mary D.	50y	W	23 NOV 1892	Philadelphia PA	Congressional
03031	Blaine, Elizabeth L.	50y	W	9 DEC 1899	Anne Arundel Co.	Glenwood
04395	Blaine, Harriet Stanwood	75y	W	16 JUL 1903	Augusta ME	Oak Hill
17751	Blaine, Robert G.	44y	W	17 MAR 1922	Baltimore MD	Congressional
02399	Blaine, Stephen W.	47y	W	9 MAR 1898	Sharpsburg MD	Glenwood
17299	Blair, Catherine	67y	C	9 JUL 1921	Ft. Foote MD	Mt. Olivet
04929	Blair, Fannie J.B.	50y	W	20 OCT 1904	Cambridge MA	Rock Creek
16253	Blair, Mary Richards	79y	W	30 JAN 1920	Takoma Park MD	Rock Creek
07489	Blair, Robert	35y	C	29 MAR 1910	Newark NJ	Payne's
12289	Blake, Charles G.	26y	W	1 APR 1914	Pittsburgh PA	Oak Hill

No.	Name of Deceased	Age	Race	Death Date	Place of Death	Place of Burial
03757	Blake, Charles W.	59y	W	12 JAN 1902	Baltimore MD	Glenwood
00422	Blake, Ebenezer Tucker	c.60y	W	16 OCT 1890	Baltimore Co. MD	Oak Hill
15115	Blake, Edith Louise	31y	W	9 OCT 1918	Silver Spring MD	Rock Creek
02844	Blake, Eliza J.	56y	W	12 JUL 1899	Cleveland OH	Glenwood
02680	Blake, George W.	65y	W	20 DEC 1898	Kensington MD	Congressional
12584	Blake, Gertrude E.	2m	W	26 OCT 1914	Arlington VA	Holyrood
03350	Blake, Margaret	78y	W	15 SEP 1900	Seabright NJ	Congressional
16359	Blake, Robert C.	31y	W	26 FEB 1920	Madison GA	Glenwood
07553	Blakeley, James	27y	W	29 MAY 1910	Philadelphia PA	Mt. Olivet
04768	Blakeney, Emma	4m	W	19 JUN 1904	Colonial Bea. VA	Glenwood
01292	Blanchard, Charles	42y	W	28 JAN 1894	Mamaronick NY	Congressional
04943	Blanchard, Clarence A.	51y	W	31 OCT 1904	Baltimore MD	Congressional
01669	Blanchard, Ella V.	70y	W	18 JUN 1895	Marshall Hall MD	Congressional
15871	Blanchard, Laura	20y	W	7 JUL 1919	Ellicott City MD	Congressional
00684	Blanck, Mary	29y	W	19 FEB 1892	Baldwinsville NY	Congressional
13439	Bland, John William, Jr.	22y	C	2 APR 1916	Atlantic City NJ	Mt. Zion West
13898	Blandy, Harry A.	44y	W	31 DEC 1916	Cherrydale VA	Rock Creek
01016	Blankman, Annie U.	50y	W	4 MAY 1893	New York NY	Glenwood
14090	Blaubock, Carl	57y	W	24 FEB 1917	Dranesville VA	Prospect Hill
15280	Bleistein, William H.	29y	W	17 OCT 1918	Linda Vista CA	Arlington
02045	Blenkinshop, Peter J., S.J.	78y	W	5 NOV 1896	Philadelphia PA	College
17566	Bless, Melanda	31y	W	30 NOV 1921	Roanoke VA	Prospect Hill
06396	Blick, Hattie	23y	C	13 JAN 1908	Philadelphia PA	Harmony
05217	Bligh, John	50y	W	18 JUL 1905	Philadelphia PA	Mt. Olivet
15089	Bligh, John A.	30y	W	3 OCT 1918	Ft. Harrison IN	Mt. Olivet
15327	Blincoe, Joseph T.	65y	W	2 NOV 1918	Chicago IL	Methodist
02906	Bliss, Charles B.	27y	W	9 AUG 1899	Ocean City MD	Congressional
15761	Bliss, Martha Nancy	78y	W	2 MAY 1919	Cranston RI	Arlington
17562	Bliss, Melande	31y	W	30 NOV 1921	Roanoke VA	Mt. Ranier MD
00685	Blodgett, Edith Rae	1y	W	20 MAR 1892	Mineral Spring MD	Rock Creek
18489	Blodgett, Nettie D.	65y	W	16 APR 1923	Takoma Park MD	Glenwood
06424	Blodgett, William H., s/o Wm.	53y	W	6 FEB 1908	Hartford CN	Rock Creek
16659	Blondel, Mercer D.	49y	W	12 AUG 1920	Bridgeport CN	Rock Creek
16494	Bloom, William F.	68y	W	19 MAY 1920	Jersey City NJ	Rock Creek
18244	Bloss, Christine	63y	W	3 JAN 1923	Cherrydale VA	Prospect Hill
07894	Bloss, Joseph B., s/o John B.	43y	W	25 DEC 1910	Ballston VA	Glenwood
15111	Blosser, Ida May	21y	W	8 OCT 1918	Takoma Park MD	Stanley VA
00420	Blowden, Joseph	42y	C	14 OCT 1890	Riggs Mill MD	Mt. Olivet
16484	Bloxton, Robert Vinton	80y	W	12 MAY 1920	Takoma Park MD	Rock Creek
14063	Blumenkranz, Justus	74y	W	30 MAR 1917	Lanham MD	Prospect Hill
17199	Blumenkranz, Richard C.	—	W	28 MAY 1921	Walter Reed Hp.	Arlington
03561	Blumer, Benjamin Franklin	25y	W	4 JUL 1901	Ballston VA	Congressional
01670	Blundon, J. Waters	13y	W	27 JUL 1895	Riverdale MD	Mt. Olivet
07157	Blundon, Joseph Gawler	65y	W	11 AUG 1909	Riverdale MD	Mt. Olivet
04224	Blundon, Sarah E.	77y	W	28 FEB 1903	Somerset Hts. MD	Oak Hill
14909	Blunt, Evelina	65y	W	9 JUL 1918	Saranac Lake NY	Arlington
02784	Boag, Elenor M.	87y	W	22 MAR 1899	Glen Echo MD	Rock Creek
08737	Boags, Joycie	47y	C	28 JUL 1912	Fairmont Hts. MD	Harmony
13108	Boales, William H.	63y	W	9 SEP 1915	Minneapolis MN	Rock Creek
05304	Boals, Elmira C. (Roy)	56y	W	15 AUG 1905	New Haven CN	Rock Creek
17111	Boardman, Angie Ford	79y	W	22 FEB 1921	Clearwater FL	Cremated
07246	Boardman, Catherine Maria	76y	W	22 OCT 1909	Baltimore MD	—
03243	Boardman, Elijah G.	32y	W	21 JUL 1900	Cleveland OH	Rock Creek
17794	Boardman, Thomas V.	51y	W	10 APR 1922	Baltimore MD	Rock Creek
16610	Boarman, Emily Elizabeth	57y	W	19 JUL 1920	Somerset MD	Oak Hill
04239	Boarman, Mary H.	60y	W	18 FEB 1903	Lander MD	Baltimore MD
02189	Bobbitt, Harry	6m	W	25 JUN 1897	Wilton NC	Congressional
15637	Bocigaluppi, Mary U.	4m	W	24 FEB 1919	Seat Pleasant MD	St. Mary's
05844	Bock, Henry C.	47y	W	24 SEP 1906	Presidio, S.F. CA	Congressional

District of Columbia Foreign Death Records, 1888-1923

No.	Name of Deceased	Age	Race	Death Date	Place of Death	Place of Burial
02536	Bock, Margaret E.	76y	W	21 JUN 1898	Glen Echo MD	St. Albans
18170	Bode, Charles	69y	W	15 NOV 1922	St. Petersburg FL	Rock Creek
05059	Bode, Helen Gertrude	25y	W	16 MAR 1905	Saranac Lake NY	Rock Creek
04618	Bode, Oscar F.	51y	W	29 FEB 1904	New York NY	Glenwood
02852	Bode, William F.	6y	W	7 JUN 1899	New York NY	Glenwood
02190	Bodell, Anna J.	50y	W	18 MAY 1897	Hampton VA	Oak Hill
02818	Bodemer, Alfred	30y	W	15 OCT 1898	Philadelphia PA	Prospect Hill
01791	Boehmer, George H., scientist	53y	W	20 NOV 1895	Gaithersburg MD	Congressional
03331	Boesser, Annie J.N.	11y	W	15 JAN 1883	Baltimore MD	Rock Creek
03332	Boesser, Jennie A.	4y	W	1 MAR 1870	Baltimore MD	Rock Creek
03334	Boesser, John W.	37y	W	28 FEB 1873	Baltimore MD	Rock Creek
03330	Boesser, John W., Jr.	SB	W	21 MAR 1869	Baltimore MD	Rock Creek[1]
03333	Boesser, Katie	2y	W	21 MAR 1865	Baltimore MD	Rock Creek
00921	Boettke, August	29y	W	6 AUG 1893	Colonial Bea. VA	Prospect Hill
05266	Bogan, Janet	29y	W	30 AUG 1905	Montreal, Can.	Oak Hill
16267	Bogert, Charles Peter	42y	W	1 FEB 1920	Clarendon VA	Congressional
05627	Boggins, Irene C.	22y	C	2 JUL 1906	Atlantic City NJ	Harmony
03513	Boggs, Earl	3d	W	18 MAY 1901	Ritchie MD	Rock Creek
14867	Boggs, Elizabeth P.	54y	W	13 JUN 1918	Hushing NY	Arlington
03511	Boggs, Elvin	3d	W	16 MAY 1901	Ritchie MD	Rock Creek
16446	Boggs, Jennie	69y	W	11 APR 1920	Philadelphia PA	Congressional
07567	Boggs, Julius O.	46y	W	9 JUN 1910	Syracuse NY	Mt. Olivet
11936	Bogle, Infant of Jackson	SB	C	13 AUG 1913	Fairmont Hts. MD	Payne's
06399	Bogue, Mary Sewell	21y	W	22 JAN 1908	Glen Echo MD	Rock Creek
02567	Bohrer, B.F., Dr.	78y	W	12 AUG 1898	Kensington MD	Rock Creek
03274	Bohrer, John J.	84y	W	20 AUG 1900	Montg. Co. MD	Oak Hill
00171	Bohrer, Lucinda A.	52y	W	24 OCT 1889	New York NY	St. John's MD
01611	Bohrer, Margaret C.	68y	W	7 FEB 1895	Bethesda MD	Oak Hill
01471	Bohrer, William H.	56y	W	22 AUG 1894	Morgantown NC	Oak Hill
08259	Bois, George	55y	W	18 NOV 1885	Pr. Geo. Co. MD	Congressional
07540	Bolac, Joseph, s/o Henry	41y	W	13 MAY 1910	Crum Lynne PA	Mt. Olivet
12520	Bolac, Josephine	26y	W	5 SEP 1914	Salt Lake City UT	Mt. Olivet
02498	Bolden, Mrs. Martin	43y	W	25 JUL 1898	Rileyville VA	Mt. Olivet
05019	Bolden, R.J.	38y	C	2 FEB 1905	Moundsville WV	Harmony
16612	Bolden, Samuel Amos	20y	C	18 JUL 1920	Arlington VA	Mt. Zion West
14382	Bolden, Thomas	65y	C	27 SEP 1917	Cedar Hts. MD	Payne's
08225	Boles, George Arthur	4m	W	28 JUL 1911	Capitol Hts. MD	Glenwood
17909	Bolger, Maria	64y	W	19 JUN 1922	Dover DE	Mt. Olivet
12484	Bolles, Caroline A.C.	72y	W	13 AUG 1914	Portland ME	Oak Hill
04655	Bolling, Elizabeth N.	7m	W	4 APR 1904	Brentwood MD	Mt. Olivet
03633	Bollman, Thomas W.	61y	W	2 SEP 1901	Indian Head MD	Annapolis MD
06509	Bolstridge, Chester C.	—	W	14 JUN 1907	Camp C., Cuba	Presque Isle ME
16769	Bolton, Harlan K.	45y	W	19 OCT 1920	Chicago IL	Oak Hill
17260	Bond, George	79y	W	24 JUN 1921	Atlantic City NJ	Arlington
04593	Bond, Gerald	7y	W	8 FEB 1904	Baltimore MD	Oak Hill
05155	Bond, Jennie S.	63y	W	5 JUN 1905	Clarks Summit PA	Glenwood
04610	Bond, Paul Thomas	4m	W	24 FEB 1904	Baltimore MD	Oak Hill
05529	Bond, Robert C.	35y	W	11 APR 1906	New Bruns. NJ	Mt. Olivet
05553	Bond, Samuel K.	76y	W	19 FEB 1899	Kinsale MD	Congressional
16787	Bonde, Robert G.	51y	W	30 OCT 1920	Baltimore MD	Cedar Hill
05702	Boney, Jackson	38y	C	23 AUG 1906	Alex. Co. VA	Payne's
16994	Bonifant, Laura C.	73y	W	22 FEB 1921	Great Falls MD	Rock Creek
12051	Bonifant, Marguerit T.	3y	W	21 OCT 1913	Takoma Park MD	Powhatan VA
02287	Bonini, Mary E.	69y	W	8 SEP 1897	Oxon Hill MD	Congressional
13255	Bonner, Edwin Percy, s/o S.	48y	W	18 DEC 1915	Round Hill VA	Cremated
04337	Bonner, Eliza	35y	C	6 AUG 1903	Atlantic City NJ	Payne's

[1] Transit Permit, undated, notes removal of Boesser graves from Western Cemetery, Baltimore, Md.

No.	Name of Deceased	Age	Race	Death Date	Place of Death	Place of Burial
14883	Bonner, Herbert W., s/o Gord.	67y	W	25 JUN 1918	Richmond VA	Cremated
00809	Bonner, Margaret R.	47y	C	23 APR 1892	Boston MA	Harmony
08238	Bonnet, Maria Dorothea	74y	W	3 AUG 1911	Berwyn MD	Prospect Hill
08514	Bonneville, Columbus J., Capt.	72y	W	12 FEB 1912	Hampton VA	Oak Hill
13911	Bonscarew, Mary Elizabeth	11m	W	6 JAN 1917	Hyattsville MD	Congressional
18186	Boogher, Alice	74y	—	25 NOV 1922	St. Louis MO	Rock Creek
03496	Booker, Annie	26y	C	2 MAY 1901	Neelsville MD	Harmony
07476	Booker, Jane C.	52y	C	16 MAR 1910	Denver CO	Harmony
02236	Booth, Arthur Edgar	5m	W	30 AUG 1897	Bowie MD	Mt. Olivet
01671	Booth, Edward Hallaran	35y	W	10 AUG 1895	Takoma Park MD	Rock Creek
01672	Booth, Florence Lockwood	41y	W	3 JUN 1895	Omaha NE	Rock Creek
03287	Booth, Joseph S., farmer	40y	W	12 SEP 1900	Railroad	Mt. Olivet
13812	Booth, Osborne	7y	C	11 NOV 1916	Fairmont Hts. MD	Payne's
01444	Booze, Lizzie, cook	42y	C	24 JUL 1894	Newport RI	Graceland
15825	Boozer, Laura C.	57y	C	10 JUN 1919	New York NY	Harmony
06563	Borden, Thomas S.	36y	W	15 MAY 1908	Silver City NM	Arlington
08340	Bordley, Alice	53y	C	2 OCT 1911	Atlantic City NJ	Harmony
03935	Borelli, Francis V.	38y	W	7 JUL 1902	Augusta GA	Cremated
02126	Borland, John Andrew	62y	W	17 FEB 1897	New York NY	Oak Hill
14260	Borland, Katherine M.	68y	W	29 JUL 1917	Forest Glen MD	Harrisburg PA
12723	Borland, Mary J.	76y	W	14 JAN 1915	Coronia NY	Oak Hill
15725	Borland, William P., M.C.	c.51y	W	21 FEB 1919	Coblenz, Ger.	Kansas City MO
18144	Borzi, Antonio	25y	W	1 NOV 1922	Winston-Sal. NC	Mt. Olivet
05176	Bosenberg, Emma Catherine	37y	W	19 JUN 1905	Baltimore MD	Prospect Hill
03799	Bosley, George	50y	C	18 FEB 1902	Pottsville PA	Harmony
02188	Boss, Charles	26y	C	3 MAY 1897	Philadelphia PA	Mt. Zion
02127	Boss, James N., builder	79y	W	23 FEB 1897	Catonsville MD	Congressional
05289	Boss, Rosanna	60y	W	16 SEP 1905	New York NY	Mt. Zion East
17426	Bosse, Harry V.	44y	W	6 AUG 1921	Romangne, Fra.	Glenwood
06433	Bostick, E.D.	54y	W	15 FEB 1908	Leonardtown MD	Arlington
14412	Boston, Henrietta	55y	C	10 OCT 1917	Cranston RI	Payne's
16223	Boston, Josephine	18y	C	17 JAN 1920	Philadelphia PA	Mt. Olivet
14660	Bostrom, Carl Augustus	39y	W	26 FEB 1918	Hampton Rds. VA	Glenwood
17739	Bostrom, Christina	72y	W	7 MAR 1922	San Diego CA	Glenwood
05843	Boswell, Benjamin Lee	38y	C	29 NOV 1906	Lawyer VA	Harmony
15364	Boswell, Bernard	39y	W	13 NOV 1918	Pittsburgh PA	Congressional
13199	Boswell, Clarence	c.24y	W	11 NOV 1915	Ashland VA	Congressional
14465	Boswell, Leslie Melville	8y	W	17 NOV 1917	Chillum MD	Glenwood
07225	Boswell, Raymond M.	5y	W	3 OCT 1909	Brentwood MD	Rock Creek
12431	Boswell, Susan	85y	C	10 JUL 1914	Bladensburg MD	Woodlawn
03357	Boteler, Andrew J.	2y	W	3 DEC 1900	Forestville MD	Congressional
00536	Boteler, Catherine	67y	W	25 JUN 1891	Baltimore MD	Glenwood
06480	Boteler, Henrietta A.	70y	W	20 MAR 1908	Hyattsville MD	Glenwood
07404	Boteler, James E.	72y	W	4 FEB 1910	Hyattsville MD	Glenwood
04927	Boteler, Margaret	69y	W	20 OCT 1904	Branchville MD	Rock Creek
14897	Boteler, Susan H.	86y	W	4 JUL 1918	Cedar Falls IA	Congressional
04232	Boteler, T. Howard	40y	W	25 FEB 1903	Baltimore Co. MD	Glenwood
06043	Boteler, Theophilus A.	90y	W	23 APR 1907	Berwyn MD	Rock Creek
14437	Boteler, William Hazen	21y	W	3 NOV 1917	Babylon NY	Glenwood
03677	Botts, Pearle V.	24y	C	7 OCT 1901	Canfield OH	Harmony
03637	Boude, John Knox	68y	W	7 SEP 1901	Ocean City NJ	Rock Creek
01119	Boughton, Charles West	78y	W	2 NOV 1892	Linden MD	Rock Creek
12504	Boughton, Daniel H.	55y	W	24 AUG 1914	Ft. Hauchuca AZ	Arlington
03049	Boughton, Jerushia	73y	W	22 DEC 1899	LaGrange IL	Rock Creek
04113	Boughton, Wilford E.	49y	W	26 DEC 1902	Elzria OH	Rock Creek
16968	Boulden, Odessa	1y	C	10 FEB 1921	Arlington	Mt. Zion West
13013	Bourdean, Augustine S.	40y	W	19 JUL 1915	Takoma Park MD	Rock Creek
08193	Bourne, Caleb P.	53y	W	19 MAY 1909	Seattle WA	Glenwood
03083	Bournes, William H.	59y	W	7 FEB 1900	Pomfret MD	Congressional

District of Columbia Foreign Death Records, 1888-1923

No.	Name of Deceased	Age	Race	Death Date	Place of Death	Place of Burial
17027	Bouscaren, Leah	7y	W	8 MAR 1921	Falls Church VA	Congressional
18442	Boushee, Britt	1y	W	27 AMR 1923	Vienna VA	Congressional
12825	Boushee, Kate McLaurin	55y	W	18 MAR 1915	Vienna VA	Congressional
16746	Bowbeer, Matilda	94y	W	6 OCT 1920	Sykesville MD	Rock Creek
12936	Bowdoin, Stephen	45y	W	21 MAY 1915	Baltimore MD	Glenwood
06648	Bowe, Cora	25y	C	20 JUL 1908	Somerset Bea. VA	Payne's
06649	Bowe, William	30y	C	20 JUL 1908	Somerset Bea. VA	Payne's
14150	Bowen, Almeda M.	73y	W	27 MAY 1917	Takoma MD	Congressional
01673	Bowen, Casander C.	82y	W	11 MAY 1895	Baltimore MD	Glenwood
03451	Bowen, Charles H.	65y	W	13 MAR 1901	Hampton VA	Glenwood
12751	Bowen, Erasmus M.	60y	W	6 FEB 1915	Lanham MD	Congressional
11968	Bowen, Francis C.	58y	W	18 AUG 1913	Morristown NJ	Glenwood
16803	Bowen, Harriet	51y	C	11 NOV 1920	Rosslyn VA	Mt. Zion East
01120	Bowen, Harrison S.	68y	W	24 JAN 1893	Hyattsville MD	Rock Creek
04928	Bowen, Johnson W.	64y	W	20 OCT 1904	Takoma Park MD	Congressional
18210	Bowen, Kate	c.63y	W	7 DEC 1922	St. Petersburg FL	Cremated
13696	Bowen, Mary	50y	C	5 SEP 1916	Monmouth Co. NJ	Payne's
08485	Bowen, Mary J.	78y	W	19 JAN 1912	Hyattsville MD	Rock Creek
16937	Bowen, Wilmer E.	60y	W	22 JAN 1921	Brooklyn NY	Glenwood
03379	Bowen, Zelphia	41y	W	7 OCT 1893	Shrewsbury NJ	Congressional
03460	Bower, Fannie	62y	W	27 MAR 1901	Buffalo NY	Wash. Hebrew
08723	Bowers, John H.	41y	W	17 JUL 1912	El Paso TX	Mt. Olivet
18261	Bowers, Ophie	23y	W	9 JAN 1923	Rosslyn VA	Glenwood
01121	Bowersox, Child, s/o David M.	7y	W	1852	Baltimore MD	Glenwood
01121	Bowersox, David M.	27y	W	1851	Baltimore MD	Glenwood
12299	Bowersox, Philip B.	28y	W	7 APR 1914	Baltimore MD	Glenwood
17819	Bowes, John I.	48y	W	26 APR 1922	Vineland NJ	Glenwood
15394	Bowie, Agnes M.G.	73y	W	1 DEC 1918	Philadelphia PA	Rock Creek
07624	Bowie, Albert B.	60y	W	11 JUL 1910	Baltimore MD	Congressional
05474	Bowie, Alice	30y	W	18 FEB 1906	Alexandria VA	Mt. Olivet
00003	Bowie, Clarence L.	56y	W	4 JAN 1889	Baltimore MD	Congressional
01616	Bowie, Duncan M., M.D.	73y	W	6 MAY 1895	Petersburg VA	Glenwood
03514	Bowie, Elizabeth A.	61y	W	16 MAY 1901	Baltimore MD	Congressional
00210	Bowie, Ella B.	32y	W	26 NOV 1889	Upper Marl. MD	Oak Hill
01946	Bowie, George	27y	C	30 MAY 1896	New Rochelle NY	Moore's
06489	Bowie, Henrietta D.	73y	W	2 APR 1908	Forest Glen MD	Congressional
13566	Bowie, Henry	32y	C	19 JUN 1916	New York NY	Woodlawn
07864	Bowie, James	40y	C	9 DEC 1910	New York NY	Harmony
08306	Bowie, John R., Jr.	4m	W	14 SEP 1911	Hyattsville MD	Rock Creek
15507	Bowie, Louis	35y	W	22 DEC 1918	Bridgeville PA	Glenwood
13094	Bowie, Mary Jane	74y	W	9 SEP 1915	Baltimore MD	Rock Creek
01374	Bowie, Melvina H.	80y	W	21 MAY 1894	Baltimore MD	Congressional
00537	Bowie, Phyllis	c.70y	C	23 MAY 1891	Alexandria VA	Graceland
13631	Bowie, Richard	40y	W	28 JUL 1916	Occoquan VA	Mt. Olivet
00077	Bowie, Richmond V.	8m	W	17 JUN 1889	Upper Marl. MD	Oak Hill
14987	Bowie, Victoria A.	68y	W	24 AUG 1918	Baltimore MD	Congressional
01017	Bowie, Virginia	44y	W	18 APR 1893	Baltimore MD	Congressional
05823	Bowie, Virginia E.	4y	W	16 NOV 1906	Eureka Spgs. AR	Rock Creek
14144	Bowler, Leonard	5m	W	18 MAY 1917	Ashton MD	Rock Creek
17517	Bowles, Scoot	41y	C	12 NOV 1921	Silver Hill MD	Payne's
13164	Bowling, Ada Wilson	38y	W	25 OCT 1915	Railroad	New Orleans LA
07318	Bowling, Infant of K.H.	1d	W	11 DEC 1909	Pr. Geo. Co. MD	Mt. Olivet
05188	Bowling, Louise F.	1y	W	30 JUN 1905	Berwyn MD	Mt. Olivet
01961	Bowman, Albert	3m	W	2 JUL 1896	Rosslyn VA	Oak Hill
04273	Bowman, Amie	78y	W	22 APR 1903	Philadelphia PA	Mt. Zion
01458	Bowman, Anna	55y	C	13 AUG 1894	Alex. Co. VA	Holyrood
16808	Bowman, Henrietta	57y	C	15 NOV 1920	Brooklyn NY	Payne's
02961	Bowman, Lottie	12y	W	25 SEP 1899	Pittsburgh PA	Payne's
01018	Bowman, Mary	18y	C	28 MAR 1893	Arlington VA	Holyrood

No.	Name of Deceased	Age	Race	Death Date	Place of Death	Place of Burial
03469	Bowman, Mary	25y	C	31 MAR 1901	Dutchess Co. NY	Woodlawn
15609	Bowman, Mary E.	75y	C	6 FEB 1919	Pomonkey MD	Harmony
04049	Bowman, Philip	42y	C	9 OCT 1902	Atlantic City NJ	Payne's
06198	Bowman, Richard	18y	C	22 AUG 1907	Winston VA	Harmony
17660	Bowman, William H.	44y	W	25 JAN 1922	Coney Island NY	Mt. Olivet
16949	Bowman, William Jackson	60y	W	1 FEB 1921	Wheaton MD	Rock Creek
06110	Bowne, James H., Jr.	23y	W	15 JUN 1907	Charlestown WV	Glenwood
15941	Boxall, Henry	32y	W	17 AUG 1919	Cleveland OH	Prospect Hill
17395	Boxsley, Elizabeth	44y	C	11 SEP 1921	Fairmont Hts. NY	Mt. Olivet
15328	Boxwell, Margaret A.	9m	W	5 NOV 1918	Wilmington DE	Mt. Olivet
05385	Boyce, Isaac D.	61y	W	17 MAY 1882	Hyattsville MD	Congressional
14332	Boyce, James	63y	W	30 AUG 1917	Boston MA	Arlington
05908	Boyce, William, s/o Edward	47y	W	22 JAN 1907	Winchester VA	Oak Hill
06278	Boyd, Almira B.	74y	W	21 OCT 1907	Goshen NY	Rock Creek
01674	Boyd, Annie E.	58y	W	7 JUL 1895	Asbury Park NJ	Oak Hill
13140	Boyd, Delia E.	40y	W	5 OCT 1915	Alexandria VA	Mt. Olivet
05105	Boyd, Ella Moore	50y	W	26 APR 1905	Vienna VA	Congressional
17833	Boyd, James D.	51y	W	5 MAY 1922	Alexandria VA	Glenwood
14300	Boyd, Julia Ann Watson	77y	W	14 AUG 1917	Hector NY	Rock Creek
06918	Boyd, Julia Maria (Spear)	46y	W	6 FEB 1909	Taguache CO	Glenwood
09079	Boyd, Katherine, d/o W.G.	5m	W	15 FEB 1913	Newark NJ	Rock Creek
17861	Boyd, Mary E.	50y	W	13 MAY 1922	Alexandria VA	Glenwood
07710	Boyd, Mary Ellen	7y	W	24 AUG 1910	Woodside MD	Mt. Olivet
03952	Boyd, Samuel J.	26y	W	8 JUL 1902	Railroad	Congressional
17682	Boyd, Virgil M.	65y	W	4 FEB 1922	Norfolk VA	Congressional
05746	Boyden, Almeda F., of Me.	74y	W	21 SEP 1906	Falls Church VA	Glenwood
06269	Boyden, Stephen A.	77y	W	14 OCT 1907	Falls Church VA	Glenwood
13550	Boyer, Courtland	80y	W	7 JUN 1916	Westfield NJ	Rock Creek
03895	Boyer, Marcel	32y	W	10 JUN 1902	Greensboro SC	Mt. Olivet
05202	Boyer, Maria Jane	85y	W	7 JUL 1905	Hyattsville MD	Congressional
17338	Boyer, Ulysses L.	56y	W	1 AUG 1921	Scotch Plains NJ	Rock Creek
11857	Boykin, Edwin T.	33y	W	19 JUN 1913	Philadelphia PA	Arlington
08602	Boyle, Caroline Morsell	46y	W	18 APR 1912	College Park MD	Veitch Family
13711	Boyle, John	79y	W	11 SEP 1916	Silver Spring MD	Rock Creek
15944	Boyle, Mary Dawson Morison	82y	W	19 AUG 1919	Silver Spring MD	Rock Creek
08382	Boyle, Robert M.	42y	W	4 NOV 1911	Laurel MD	Rock Creek
05156	Boynton, Henry Van Ness	70y	W	3 JUN 1905	Atlantic City NJ	Arlington
09093	Boynton, Robert P.	7m	W	26 FEB 1913	Kensington MD	Rock Creek
02568	Brachman, Sarah Ellen	80y	W	14 AUG 1898	Silver Spring MD	Rock Creek
13208	Bracken, Jesse Bobbs	45y	W	14 NOV 1915	Jacksonville FL	Arlington
04252	Brackett, Foster E.	21y	W	10 MAY 1903	Palo Alto CA	Glenwood
13853	Bradbury, Susan E.	77y	W	7 DEC 1916	Boston MA	Rock Creek
06496	Bradford, Harriet Knight	65y	W	6 APR 1908	Woodside MD	Rock Creek
18068	Bradford, Harriet Stanhope	74y	W	12 SEP 1922	Turner ME	Arlington
12357	Bradford, Horatio K.	38y	W	4 MAY 1914	Ft. Bayard NM	Arlington
12133	Bradford, James Henry	77y	W	22 DEC 1913	Rockville MD	Arlington
11983	Bradford, Joseph Edward	71y	W	2 SEP 1913	Woodside MD	Rock Creek
02237	Bradford, Lolita	3y	W	23 JUL 1897	Gaithersburg MD	Oak Hill
05765	Bradford, Mary D.	94y	W	9 OCT 1906	Harrington Pk. NJ	Congressional
00449	Bradford, May G.	45y	W	10 APR 1881	Baltimore Co. MD	Congressional
12472	Bradford, Royal Bird	70y	W	4 AUG 1914	Chelsea MA	Arlington
08185	Bradley, Allen	21y	W	7 JUL 1911	Philadelphia PA	Arlington
01394	Bradley, Charles	25y	W	1 MAY 1894	Potomac River	Glenwood
00922	Bradley, Earnest Carlton	12m	W	11 AUG 1893	Hampton VA	Congressional
02364	Bradley, Fannie B.	30y	C	14 JAN 1898	Philadelphia PA	Harmony
06412	Bradley, Guy M.	36y	W	1 FEB 1908	Walkers Chap. VA	Oak Hill
00570	Bradley, Guy W.	1y	W	7 OCT 1891	Hampton VA	Congressional
15117	Bradley, Henry	63y	C	9 OCT 1918	Rosslyn VA	Mt. Zion East
13945	Bradley, J.W.	75y	W	21 JAN 1917	Conshohocken PA	Rock Creek

District of Columbia Foreign Death Records, 1888-1923

No.	Name of Deceased	Age	Race	Death Date	Place of Death	Place of Burial
17210	Bradley, John	c.72y	C	2 JUN 1921	Forestville MD	Mt. Zion West
03695	Bradley, John T.	24y	C	13 OCT 1901	Presidio, S.F. CA	Arlington
07635	Bradley, Joseph H., Jr.	6y	W	16 JUL 1910	Rosemont Farm	Oak Hill
04194	Bradley, Laura E.	32y	W	31 MAR 1903	Linden NY	Oak Hill
14154	Bradley, Minnie R.	65y	W	29 MAY 1917	Auburn NY	Rock Creek
12749	Bradley, Sarah	51y	C	2 FEB 1915	Fairmont Hts. MD	Woodlawn
02964	Bradley, Virginia G.	23y	C	29 SEP 1899	Seat Pleasant MD	Mt. Olivet
00078	Bradley, William H.	4y	W	22 JUN 1889	Hampton VA	Congressional
16587	Bradley, William Lee	42y	W	8 JUL 1920	Ballston VA	Glenwood
00212	Bradley, William, Rev.	86y	W	27 MAR 1890	Arapahoe Co. CO	Oak Hill
16103	Bradshaw, John	64y	W	12 NOV 1919	Johnson City TN	Congressional
13159	Bradshaw, Leonard Paul	57y	W	21 OCT 1915	Chevy Chase MD	Congressional
07138	Bradt, Alberta	33y	W	27 JUL 1909	Black Mtn. NC	Oak Hill
08627	Bradt, Orlando W.	56y	W	1 MAY 1912	Los Angeles CA	Fairfax C.H. VA
14526	Brady, Alvin	5y	W	26 DEC 1917	Silver Spring MD	Rock Creek
01022	Brady, Daniel E.	48y	W	17 FEB 1893	Roanoke VA	Glenwood
14115	Brady, Emma H.	65y	W	27 APR 1917	Colonial Bea. VA	Congressional
04448	Brady, Frederick L.	30y	W	24 DEC 1902	New York NY	Glenwood
01214	Brady, Jasper E.	75y	W	26 JAN 1871	Washington DC	Rock Creek
01019	Brady, Luther Bruen	60y	W	20 APR 1893	Dobb's Ferry NY	Glenwood
01852	Brady, Mathew B., photog.	72y	W	15 JAN 1896	New York NY	Congressional
14816	Brady, Ora	59y	W	17 MAY 1918	Takoma Park MD	Glenwood
03365	Brady, Thomas Ford	1m	W	14 DEC 1900	Brooklyn NY	Mt. Olivet
03911	Brady, Thomas G.	55y	W	9 JUN 1902	Pittsburgh PA	Arlington
16005	Brady, William Leonard	47y	W	22 SEP 1919	Hyattsville MD	Glenwood
01020	Brady, Winfield Scott	6y	W	13 APR 1893	Forestville MD	Congressional
13410	Bragaw, Charles Lewis	40y	W	8 MAR 1916	Cliff NM	Glenwood
17445	Brager, Sarah	75y	W	2 OCT 1921	Charlottesville VA	K. Israel, Geo.
17836	Bragg, Thomas L.	29y	W	5 MAY 1922	Baltimore MD	Congressional
07204	Brainerd, Clifford	18y	W	15 SEP 1909	Grace ID	Rock Creek
13905	Branch, Margaret	65y	W	3 JAN 1917	Laurel MD	Petersburg VA
15400	Branch, Rosser	33y	C	23 NOV 1918	Camp Merritt NJ	Harmony
12098	Brand, Charles A., s/o Christ.	45y	W	17 OCT 1913	Colchester CN	Arlington
13686	Brand, Mary E.	52y	W	30 AUG 1916	Berkeley Sp. WV	Oak Hill
08859	Brandes, Marie Caceilie	88y	W	30 SEP 1912	Seat Pleasant MD	Prospect Hill
06482	Brando, Charlottie Craig	30y	W	23 MAR 1908	Takoma Park MD	New Brighton PA
14287	Brandon, Lottie May	22y	W	8 AUG 1917	Annapolis MD	Glenwood
06781	Brandon, W.O.	38y	C	22 MAR 1908	Charlotte NC	Harmony
17358	Brandt, Adam	65y	W	17 AUG 1921	Vienna VA	Congressional
11867	Brandt, George, s/o Louis	30y	W	26 JUN 1913	Colonial Bea. VA	Prospect Hill
15322	Brandt, Guy E.	26y	W	1 NOV 1918	Hoboken NJ	Arlington
07113	Brandt, Minnie (Mrs. Louis)	52y	W	17 JUL 1909	Colonial Bea. VA	Prospect Hill
06617	Brandt, Nellie	50y	C	27 JUN 1908	Eliz. City Co. VA	Payne's
14538	Branham, Etta	29y	C	27 DEC 1917	Pittsburgh PA	Moore's
06172	Branham, Jane	67y	C	8 AUG 1907	Philadelphia PA	Harmony
00213	Branham, Lorenzo	60y	C		1889 Philadelphia PA	Harmony
13343	Branham, Mary, d/o William	22y	C	6 FEB 1916	Newark NJ	Harmony
14447	Brannan, Frederick Hixon	18y	W	5 NOV 1917	Laurel MD	Mt. Olivet
04608	Bransom, Gustavus B.	42y	W	24 FEB 1904	Hyattsville MD	Glenwood
13180	Bransom, Walker M.	25y	W	5 NOV 1915	Hyattsville MD	Glenwood
02587	Bransom, Walker S.	31y	W	1 SEP 1898	Hyattsville MD	Glenwood
07734	Branson, James P.	23y	C	6 SEP 1910	New York NY	Harmony
06361	Branson, Lucinda	79y	C	23 DEC 1907	Baltimore MD	Mt. Zion East
12705	Branson, Mary Ruth	74y	W	9 JAN 1915	Chevy Chase MD	Rock Creek
18542	Branson, Philip H.	83y	W	12 MAY 1923	Chevy Chase MD	Rock Creek
00211	Branson, Sarah	26y	C	20 DEC 1889	New York NY	Graceland
04095	Brashers, Leroy	29y	W	6 NOV 1902	Denver CO	Mt. Olivet
16765	Braun, Pauline L.	41y	W	15 OCT 1920	Norristown PA	Prospect Hill
12994	Braund, William H.	86y	W	4 JUL 1915	Hampton VA	Glenwood

No.	Name of Deceased	Age	Race	Death Date	Place of Death	Place of Burial
03608	Brawner, Emily B.	65y	W	9 AUG 1901	Southampton NY	Mt. Olivet
17898	Brawner, Francis Thomas	56y	C	9 JUN 1922	Arlington VA	Mt. Olivet
06719	Brawner, John	55y	W	7 SEP 1908	Moundsville WV	Congressional
02613	Brawner, John F.	21y	W	22 SEP 1898	Jeff. Barr. MO	Mt. Olivet
15510	Braxton, Ella	23y	C	31 DEC 1918	Fairmont Hts. MD	Woodlawn
17828	Braxton, John	c.55y	C	2 MAY 1922	Louisville KY	Harmony
12544	Braxton, Washington	53y	C	24 SEP 1914	Fairmont Hts. MD	Woodlawn
12591	Bray, John	62y	W	7 OCT 1913	Knoxville TN	Congressional[1]
14905	Bray, Mack, Capt.	42y	W	9 JUL 1918	New York NY	Arlington
17431	Bray, Margia A.	82y	W	23 SEP 1921	Capitol Hts. MD	Ft. Lincoln
17488	Bray, Ralph E.	60y	W	26 OCT 1921	Cabin John MD	Cremated
17729	Bray, Sarah E.	53y	C	5 MAR 1922	Poughkeepsie NY	Woodlawn
15334	Brayton, Carrie E.	80y	W	7 NOV 1918	Colonial Bea. VA	Glenwood
13608	Bredon, Ralph V.	SB	W	19 JUL 1916	Chevy Chase MD	Rock Creek
01396	Breen, Thomas	57y	W	15 MAY 1894	Hot Springs AR	Mt. Olivet
08127	Breitbarth, Lillie S.	52y	W	24 MAY 1911	New York NY	Congressional
13134	Bremerman, J. Schaffer	68y	W	3 OCT 1915	Georgetown DC	Rock Creek
15573	Bremermann, Frederick H.	2y	W	4 JAN 1919	Charlotte NC	Oak Hill
15572	Bremermann, Helen M.	8y	W	3 JAN 1919	Charlotte NC	Oak Hill
15574	Bremermann, John H., s/o C.F.	10m	W	10 JAN 1919	Charlotte NC	Oak Hill
16355	Brenelet, Louis	26y	W	4 NOV 1917	Alex. Co. VA	Marseilles, Fra.
01439	Brennan, James	33y	W	12 JUL 1894	Philadelphia PA	Mt. Olivet
06239	Brennan, John	76y	W	20 SEP 1907	Hampton VA	Mt. Olivet
15151	Brennan, John Francis	21y	W	12 OCT 1918	Hampton Rds. VA	Mt. Olivet
14354	Brennan, Joseph A.	28y	W	11 SEP 1917	Baltimore MD	Mt. Olivet
00923	Brennan, Martin P.	22y	W	29 AUG 1893	Hyattsville MD	Mt. Olivet
07155	Brennan, Patrick J.	40y	W	10 AUG 1909	Hyattsville MD	Mt. Olivet
01340	Brennan, William	5y	W	8 APR 1894	New York NY	Mt. Olivet
04219	Brenner, William F.	34y	W	4 MAR 1903	Mays Landing NJ	Middleburg VA
01675	Brent, Arthur	24y	C	4 OCT 1895	Albany NY	Harmony
00151	Brent, Caroline	53y	W	26 SEP 1889	Mt. Hope MD	Carroll Chapel
18505	Brent, Elsworth	62y	C	22 APR 1923	Newark NJ	Harmony
14858	Brent, Emma J.	70y	C	7 JUN 1918	Boyds MD	Payne's
02783	Brent, George	72y	W	21 MAR 1899	Mt. Hope MD	Carroll Chapel
11800	Brent, Hugh, s/o Lafayette	68y	W	5 MAY 1913	The Plains VA	Cremated
13803	Brent, Landonia C.	32y	C	3 NOV 1916	Asheville NC	Harmony
01021	Brent, Martha	45y	C	10 MAY 1893	Sligo MD	Harmony
16858	Brent, Norma L.	28y	W	16 DEC 1920	Alexandria VA	Arlington VA
02292	Brereton, Anna Porter	27y	W	1 NOV 1897	Bridgeport CN	Congressional
13411	Brereton, Georgianna	60y	W	13 MAR 1916	Takoma Park MD	Rock Creek
01294	Brereton, William Henry	68y	W	17 FEB 1894	Omaha NE	Rock Creek
13032	Breslan, Ray	37y	W	3 AUG 1915	Baltimore MD	Wash. Hebrew
05072	Breslin, Anna	86y	W	10 MAR 1905	Harrison Co. WV	Congressional
08857	Bresnahan, Catherine	18y	W	26 SEP 1912	New York NY	Mt. Olivet
01914	Bresnahan, Hugh	45y	W	26 APR 1896	Colonial Bea. VA	Mt. Olivet
13797	Bresnahan, John	45y	W	31 OCT 1916	Youngstown OH	Mt. Olivet
14832	Bresnahan, Maurice F.	64y	W	20 MAY 1918	Hyattsville MD	Mt. Olivet
04203	Bresnahan, William	46y	W	c.24 FEB 1903	Norfolk VA	Mt. Olivet
17750	Brestman, Bessie	66y	W	17 MAR 1922	Baltimore MD	Nat. Cap. Hebrew
12761	Breuninger, Louise Josephine	76y	W	12 FEB 1915	Baltimore MD	Congressional
12527	Brewer, Annie Susanna	73y	W	12 SEP 1914	Clarendon VA	Congressional
15153	Brewer, Charles J., s/o Jno. W.	21y	W	11 OCT 1918	Hampton Rds. VA	Glenwood
16666	Brewer, Daniel O.	40y	C	11 AUG 1920	Denver CO	Mt. Olivet
05221	Brewer, Flora Coombs	21y	W	27 JUL 1905	Laurenburg NC	Glenwood
17873	Brewer, Henry F.	68y	W	23 MAY 1922	Bethesda MD	Tenallytown M.
05634	Brewer, John W.	93y	W	9 JUL 1906	Montg. Co. MD	Tenallytown M.E.

[1] Reinterred in Ft. Lincoln Cemetery, November 1932.

District of Columbia Foreign Death Records, 1888-1923

No.	Name of Deceased	Age	Race	Death Date	Place of Death	Place of Burial
08062	Brewer, Kinsey	28y	W	10 APR 1911	Bethesda MD	Tenallytown M.
16880	Brewer, Milford	22y	C	27 DEC 1920	Chester PA	Harmony
13901	Brewer, Wallace A.	73y	W	31 DEC 1916	Brentwood MD	Mt. Olivet
14880	Brewster, Charles E.	60y	W	23 JUN 1918	Takoma Park MD	Creamted
04340	Brewster, Francis	2y	W	19 MAY 1862	Brooklyn NY	Congressional
04339	Brewster, William F.	2y	W	9 MAY 1860	Brooklyn NY	Congressional
06685	Breze, Colman	42y	W	12 AUG 1908	Calvert Co. MD	Ohev Sholom
02985	Brice, Sophia	50y	C	19 OCT 1899	Baltimore MD	Moore's
04125	Brick, William	30y	W	9 DEC 1902	Denver CO	Mt. Olivet
05505	Bricker, Lena	9y	W	20 MAR 1906	Media PA	Prospect Hill
09171	Bricker, Terry Louis	23y	W	2 MAR 1912	Havana, Cuba	Ohev Sholom
07519	Bricker, William H.	72y	W	26 APR 1910	Carlisle PA	Arlington
15479	Bride, Cotter T.	72y	W	25 DEC 1918	Takoma Park MD	Glenwood
02365	Bridges, Levertt	5y	W	16 OCT 1897	Guthrie OK	Holyrood
04521	Bridges, Lucius Leverett	64y	W	26 NOV 1903	Hyattsville MD	Holyrood
12008	Briggs, Alfred J.	30y	W	20 SEP 1913	Mt. Ranier MD	Mt. Olivet
17680	Briggs, Emily S. (Stine)	62y	W	7 FEB 1922	Cox's Creek KY	Glenwood
00538	Briggs, Leonora J.	32y	W	28 MAY 1891	Lakeland FL	Glenwood
12155	Briggs, Michael C.	29y	W	10 JAN 1914	Mt. Ranier MD	Mt. Olivet
08717	Briggs, Rebecca W.	50y	W	13 JUL 1912	Boston MA	Congressional
16668	Briggs, Robert	1y	C	18 AUG 1920	Rosslyn VA	Mt. Zion West
16092	Briggs, Robert	23y	C	3 NOV 1919	Germantown PA	Payne's
06512	Briggs, Virginia	35y	W	16 APR 1908	New York NY	Alexandria VA
12664	Bright, Annie	37y	C	18 DEC 1914	Landover MD	Woodlawn
08436	Bright, James W.	42y	W	24 DEC 1911	Brooklyn NY	Glenwood
16343	Bright, Walter Ellis	42y	W	22 FEB 1920	Miami AZ	Glenwood
07067	Brigman, Dorothea W.	3y	W	19 JUN 1909	Mt. Ranier MD	Glenwood
12028	Brimson, Frances (Drake)	61y	W	5 OCT 1913	Atlantic City NJ	Rock Creek
03670	Brinkerhoff, Joseph Warren	20y	W	30 SEP 1901	Lynchburg VA	Rock Creek
18333	Brinkley, Hugh G.	36y	W	6 FEB 1923	Tucson AZ	Congressional
07846	Brinkley, Marion (Mrs. James)	83y	W	19 NOV 1910	Weston WV	Glenwood
12466	Brinkley, Thomas H.	24y	W	1 AUG 1914	Va. Beach VA	Mt. Olivet
07183	Brinkman, August	64y	W	6 SEP 1909	New York NY	Prospect Hill
07698	Brinkman, John H.	40y	W	20 AUG 1910	New York NY	Rock Creek
15558	Brisbine, John Milton	70y	W	14 JAN 1919	Barcroft VA	Glenwood
16389	Briscoe, Hanson	33y	C	14 MAR 1920	Detroit MI	Payne's
16472	Briscoe, Julia C.	32y	C	5 MAY 1920	Harrisburg PA	Harmony
06613	Briscoe, Lindon	19y	C	26 JUN 1908	Lakeland MD	Harmony
18295	Briscoe, Maria J.	83y	W	25 JAN 1923	Laurel MD	Mt. Olivet
17643	Briscoe, Martha	51y	C	17 JAN 1922	Martinsburg WV	Harmony
01923	Briscoe, Walter C., Dr.	58y	W	16 MAY 1896	Hopeworth RI	Mt. Olivet
03238	Brisson, Margaret Howard	3m	W	17 JUL 1900	Kensington MD	Rock Creek
16991	Bristol, Baby	SB	W	21 FEB 1921	Philadelphia PA	Arlington
16992	Bristol, Gertrude L.	25y	W	21 FEB 1921	Philadelphia PA	Arlington
12505	Bristow, Pierson H., s/o John	68y	W	28 AUG 1914	Spring Lake NJ	Arlington
06593	Britney, Robert W.	35y	W	17 JUN 1908	Monessen PA	Rock Creek
16979	Britt, Frances	54y	C	9 FEB 1921	Jacksonville FL	Mt. Zion East
06116	Britt, Francis M.	48y	W	24 JUN 1907	Hyattsville MD	Rock Creek
00444	Britten, Harriett	43y	M	22 NOV 1890	Tarrytown NY	Mt. Olivet
08272	Britton, Fanney	39y	C	23 AUG 1911	Atlantic City NJ	Harmony
13576	Britton, George W.	69y	W	25 JUN 1916	Bangor MI	Rock Creek
05650	Britton, Guss	40y	C	18 JUL 1906	Raleigh NC	Harmony
04149	Britton, Rebecca Millard	95y	W	18 JAN 1903	Baltimore MD	Rock Creek
03248	Broadus, Frank James	50y	C	30 JUL 1900	Pittsburgh PA	Payne's
15880	Broas, Helen B.	23y	W	13 JUL 1919	Chestertown MD	Rock Creek
07764	Brock, William H.	68y	W	22 SEP 1910	Colo. Spgs. CO	Glenwood
00810	Brock, William Shepherd	37y	W	26 JUL 1892	Rectortown VA	Glenwood
13721	Brockwell, William N.	57y	W	15 SEP 1916	Glen Echo MD	Mt. Olivet
13525	Broderick, Daniel	34y	W	27 MAY 1916	Saranac Lake NY	Mt. Olivet

No.	Name of Deceased	Age	Race	Death Date	Place of Death	Place of Burial
03664	Broderick, John J.	25y	W	24 SEP 1901	Kittery ME	Mt. Olivet
13728	Broderick, William	27y	W	19 SEP 1916	Baltimore MD	Mt. Olivet
03084	Brodhead, Mary Josephine	c.92y	W	13 FEB 1900	Newfields NH	Congressional
02289	Brodie, Eunice Louise	1y	C	14 SEP 1897	Barnesville MD	Woodlawn
04453	Brodie, William C.	22y	W	20 SEP 1903	Contee MD	Rock Creek
03562	Brols, Luccusall	23y	C	3 JUL 1901	Harrisburg PA	Mt. Zion
08012	Bromwell, Alice Brockenbr.	71y	W	15 MAR 1911	Takoma Park MD	Cremated
17147	Bronson, Anna R.	30y	W	8 MAY 1921	New York NY	Mt. Olivet
13807	Bronson, Clarence King	28y	W	8 NOV 1916	Indian Head MD	Arlington
15218	Bronson, Martha K.	79y	W	17 OCT 1918	Takoma Park MD	Rock Creek
14049	Brook, Edward	—	C	21 MAR 1917	Oxon Hill MD	Owen Sta. MD
02860	Brook, George Theodore	17m	W	27 JUL 1899	Oxon Hill MD	Prospect Hill
18358	Brooke, Gwendolyn	33y	W	18 FEB 1923	New York NY	Glenwood
02791	Brooke, Jane	80y	C	24 APR 1899	Montg. Co. MD	Christian
12967	Brooke, Mary B.	58y	W	18 JUN 1915	Hyattsville MD	Mt. Olivet
14146	Brooke, Rita Virginia	1y	W	23 MAY 1917	New York NY	Congressional
17644	Brooke, Walter B.	47y	W	18 JAN 1922	Elizabeth NJ	Mt. Olivet
15015	Brooke, William J.	22y	W	10 SEP 1918	Camp Logan TX	Rockville MD
07943	Brookes, Harriet E.	21y	C	25 JAN 1911	Hyattsville MD	Mt. Olivet
17921	Brookins, Laura	42y	C	21 JUN 1922	New York NY	Mt. Zion East
13650	Brooks, Anna	54y	C	7 AUG 1916	Atlantic City NJ	Harmony
02548	Brooks, Blanche Stewart	23y	W	17 AUG 1898	Garrett Park MD	Rock Creek
03155	Brooks, Cathrine	50y	C	1 APR 1900	Lakeland MD	Mt. Olivet
16284	Brooks, Clara	31y	C	5 FEB 1920	Freedman's Hp.	Woodlawn
17424	Brooks, Clinton	43y	C	20 SEP 1921	Arlington Co. VA	Harmony
13057	Brooks, Dorothea A.	54y	W	14 AUG 1915	Newport RI	Mt. Zion M.E.
12164	Brooks, Edward	30y	C	12 JAN 1914	New York NY	Mt. Zion West
03876	Brooks, Edwin F.	65y	W	24 JAN 1902	Pasadena CA	Rock Creek
01341	Brooks, Ellen	45y	C	31 MAR 1894	Pr. Geo. Co. MD	Graceland
11861	Brooks, Estella, a.k.a.	19y	C	20 JUN 1913	Philadelphia PA	Payne's
13570	Brooks, Floyd V., M.D.	59y	W	25 JUN 1916	Laurel MD	Rock Creek
14125	Brooks, Grace	18y	C	4 MAY 1917	Atlantic City NJ	Harmony
15122	Brooks, Harold F.	28y	W	6 OCT 1918	Norfolk VA	Rock Creek
00398	Brooks, Henry W.	60y	C	4 SEP 1890	Pr. Geo. Co. MD	Mt. Olivet
13610	Brooks, Herbert	23y	C	17 JUL 1916	Philadelphia PA	Harmony
02046	Brooks, Huldah Victoria	63y	W	4 NOV 1896	Claybank VA	Rock Creek
13940	Brooks, Isabella B.	36y	C	18 JAN 1917	Birmingham AL	Mt. Zion West
13894	Brooks, James	35y	C	28 DEC 1916	Rosslyn VA	Oak Grove VA
01676	Brooks, James J.	70y	W	11 OCT 1895	Pittsburgh PA	Rock Creek
14626	Brooks, John	46y	C	5 FEB 1918	Jefferson VA	Harmony
01473	Brooks, Julia M.	11y	C	26 AUG 1894	Seat Pleasant MD	Scaggs
13231	Brooks, Margaret	72y	W	5 DEC 1915	Arlington MD	Oxon Hill MD
13734	Brooks, Margaret Josephine	1y	W	24 SEP 1916	Garrett Park MD	Glenwood
12432	Brooks, Mary	37y	C	10 JUL 1914	Rosslyn VA	Mt. Zion West
14701	Brooks, Maurice	18y	C	18 MAR 1918	Newark NJ	Harmony[1]
04107	Brooks, Nathaniel Boyd	69y	W	5 DEC 1902	Ashland VA	Rock Creek
05271	Brooks, Percival Drayton	32y	C	5 SEP 1905	Vienna VA	Harmony
01462	Brooks, Ray	4m	C	16 AUG 1894	Seat Pleasant MD	Scaggs
15440	Brooks, Ruth E.	6m	C	15 APR 1920	Fairmont Hts. MD	Payne's
14322	Brooks, Serene	14y	C	26 AUG 1917	Marlboro MD	Croome MD
12668	Brooks, Stephen A.	33y	W	18 DEC 1914	Seattle WA	Congressional
13472	Brooks, Susanna Estelle	35y	C	23 APR 1916	Clarendon VA	Mt. Olivet
16958	Brooks, Walter David	2m	C	6 FEB 1921	Garrett Park MD	Rock Creek
14301	Brooks, Walter John	66y	W	16 AUG 1917	Garrett Park MD	Rock Creek
01613	Brooks, William	60y	C	24 MAR 1895	Montg. Co. MD	Christian
08398	Brooks, William	34y	C	17 NOV 1911	Philadelphia PA	Mt. Olivet

[1] Disinterment permit #9386 for removal on 3 APR 1918 to Ash Grove, Va.

District of Columbia Foreign Death Records, 1888-1923

No.	Name of Deceased	Age	Race	Death Date	Place of Death	Place of Burial
18518	Brooks, William	42y	C	30 APR 1923	Baltimore MD	Mt. Zion West
05290	Brooks, William J.	30y	C	18 SEP 1905	Lakeland MD	Mt. Olivet
08239	Brooks, William, s/o William	11y	C	4 AUG 1911	Rosslyn VA	Mt. Zion West
00925	Brosnan, John	8m	W	25 JUL 1893	Lynn MA	Mt. Olivet
00215	Broughton, Lyman	73y	W	4 FEB 1889	Fairfax Co. VA	Glenwood
15461	Brouner, Catherine M.	49y	W	20 DEC 1918	Laurel MD	Prospect Hill
15695	Brower, Edgar Allen	8m	W	28 MAR 1919	Hyattsville MD	Glenwood
12194	Brown, Adelaide J.	87y	W	26 JAN 1914	Los Angeles CA	Oak Hill
03321	Brown, Albert	23y	C	3 NOV 1900	Berryburg WV	Payne's
12390	Brown, Alice	42y	C	6 JUN 1914	Largo MD	Mt. Olivet
00451	Brown, Ambrose M.	23y	W	15 DEC 1890	Albany NY	Congressional
04947	Brown, Andrew J., Sr.	76y	W	1 NOV 1904	Trimble Farm MD	Congressional
13081	Brown, Annie	53y	C	27 AUG 1915	Catonsville MD	Mt. Zion West
02191	Brown, Annie E.	39y	W	20 JUN 1897	Falls Church VA	Glenwood
14633	Brown, Annie E.	55y	C	8 FEB 1918	Baltimore MD	Harmony
01215	Brown, Arthur H.	40y	W	10 SEP 1893	Baltimore MD	Graceland
01962	Brown, B. Peyton, Rev.	66y	W	26 AUG 1896	Baltimore MD	Oak Hill
12620	Brown, Barbara A.	64y	W	13 NOV 1914	Wichita KS	Rock Creek
02288	Brown, Bedford, M.D.	74y	W	13 SEP 1897	Alexandria VA	Rock Creek
06723	Brown, Benjamin H.	35y	C	14 JUL 1908	New York NY	Woodlawn
05088	Brown, Bessie	24y	C	18 APR 1905	New York NY	Harmony
05014	Brown, Carl Elmo	3y	W	1 FEB 1905	Lakeland MD	Rock Creek
12969	Brown, Carl O.C.	39y	W	19 JUN 1915	Alexandria VA	Glenwood
18112	Brown, Carrie	34y	C	12 OCT 1922	New York NY	Mt. Olivet
14535	Brown, Catherine	71y	W	27 DEC 1917	Brooklyn NY	Congressional
02504	Brown, Cathrine	18y	C	21 JUL 1898	Chester PA	Payne's
03526	Brown, Charles	46y	W	29 MAY 1901	Takoma Park MD	Rock Creek
01924	Brown, Charles A.	19y	W	20 MAY 1896	Moundsville WV	Congressional
02861	Brown, Charles Henry	63y	W	16 JUL 1899	Pittsfield MA	Arlington VA
15386	Brown, Charles M.	28y	W	26 NOV 1918	Ft. Sill OK	Arlington
18567	Brown, Charles Warner	75y	W	29 MAY 1923	Montg. Co. MD	Glenwood
14632	Brown, Charlotte	75y	C	10 FEB 1918	Philadelphia PA	Payne's
00216	Brown, Clark	28y	C	16 APR 1890	Pittsburgh PA	Harmony
09113	Brown, Cordelia	54y	W	9 MAR 1913	Alex. Co. VA	Methodist
16534	Brown, Daniel	44y	C	11 JUN 1920	New York NY	Mt. Zion East
00450	Brown, David	63y	W	4 DEC 1890	Baltimore MD	Congressional
06713	Brown, David	51y	W	3 SEP 1908	Lakeland MD	Rock Creek
06739	Brown, Dora N.	63y	W	19 SEP 1908	Tioga NY	Glenwood
15248	Brown, Douglas M.	27y	C	18 OCT 1918	Greenville SC	Harmony
16246	Brown, Edmonia L.	45y	W	26 JAN 1920	Chevy Chase MD	Lexington VA
04966	Brown, Edward	24y	W	20 NOV 1904	Cincinnati OH	Harmony
02951	Brown, Edward	24y	W	15 SEP 1899	Pittsburgh PA	Harmony
08154	Brown, Edward Floyd	9m	W	20 JUN 1911	Mt. Ranier MD	Mt. Olivet
03632	Brown, Edward J.	45y	C	1 SEP 1901	Hudson NJ	Harmony
16887	Brown, Edward Russel	23d	W	31 DEC 1920	Rosslyn VA	Holyrood
05342	Brown, Edwin	2y	W	3 NOV 1905	Beltsville MD	Rock Creek
03338	Brown, Eliza	54y	C	13 NOV 1900	Glen Echo MD	Payne's
03343	Brown, Elizabeth A.	89y	W	20 NOV 1900	Alex. Co. VA	Oak Hill
17501	Brown, Elizabeth E.	42y	C	26 OCT 1921	Boston MA	Woodlawn
14052	Brown, Elizabeth S.	72y	W	20 MAR 1917	Yuma AZ	Congressional
08701	Brown, Ella	29y	C	30 JUN 1912	Caroline Co. VA	Payne's
05720	Brown, Ellen S.L.	80y	W	31 AUG 1906	Savage MD	Glenwood
05192	Brown, Ellis W., teacher	40y	C	4 JUL 1905	White S. Sp. VA	Harmony
16721	Brown, Elsie M.	19y	W	22 SEP 1920	Garfield Hosp.	Prospect Hill
12741	Brown, Emma Francis	70y	W	31 JAN 1915	Sykesville MD	Congressional
06523	Brown, Estelle	31y	C	23 APR 1908	Philadelphia PA	Harmony
11861	Brown, Estelle, a.k.a.	19y	C	20 JUN 1913	Philadelphia PA	Payne's
07670	Brown, Esther	8m	C	4 AUG 1910	Landover MD	Mt. Olivet
01369	Brown, Etta May	3m	W	25 MAY 1894	Pr. Geo. Co. MD	Congressional

No.	Name of Deceased	Age	Race	Death Date	Place of Death	Place of Burial
08228	Brown, Eugene V.	10m	W	30 JUL 1911	Mt. Ranier MD	Mt. Olivet
11940	Brown, Fannie	65y	C	3 AUG 1913	Ellsworth ME	Harmony
08378	Brown, Felix R.	29y	C	28 OCT 1911	Fairmont Hts. MD	Mt. Olivet
18267	Brown, Florence	29y	C	13 JAN 1923	New York NY	Harmony
06130	Brown, Florence D.	35y	W	3 JUL 1907	Omaha NE	Oak Hill
14123	Brown, Frances E.	72y	W	2 MAY 1917	Philadelphia PA	Arlington
04596	Brown, Frances M.	23y	W	9 FEB 1904	Waterloo VA	Glenwood
07100	Brown, Francis G.	42d	W	8 JUL 1909	Williamsburg WV	Rock Creek
12373	Brown, Frank	68y	W	20 MAY 1914	Staunton VA	Cremated
08738	Brown, Frank Wilson	55y	W	22 JUL 1912	San Jose CA	Oak Hill
12072	Brown, Frankie Waits	13y	C	1 NOV 1913	Pittsburgh PA	Harmony
15773	Brown, Frederick	42y	C	7 MAY 1919	Philadelphia PA	Payne's
15408	Brown, George E.	44y	C	1 DEC 1918	Atlantic City NJ	Harmony
15955	Brown, George R.	37y	W	25 AUG 1919	Baltimore MD	Glenwood
00217	Brown, George Robert	71y	W	24 MAY 1890	Pr. Geo. Co. MD	Rock Creek
03339	Brown, George T.	40y	W	15 NOV 1900	St. Louis MO	Rock Creek
16518	Brown, Grace	25y	C	31 MAY 1920	Winding Gulf WV	Payne's
01677	Brown, Guy	15y	W	27 JUL 1895	Riverdale MD	Mt. Olivet
00051	Brown, Harriet	26y	C	12 APR 1889	Bowie Sta. MD	Graceland
14317	Brown, Harriet C.	79y	W	26 AUG 1917	Baltimore MD	Oak Hill
16696	Brown, Harry	c.47y	C	4 SEP 1920	Philadelphia PA	Woodlawn
04087	Brown, Hawley	62y	W	15 NOV 1902	New York NY	Congressional
01295	Brown, Henrietta	27y	W	27 FEB 1894	Pr. Geo. Co. MD	Congressional
01792	Brown, Henry	45y	C	11 DEC 1895	Alex. Co. VA	Christian
04873	Brown, Henry	70y	C	2 SEP 1904	Hyattsville MD	Mt. Olivet
13141	Brown, Hoffman	26y	C	2 OCT 1915	Franklin Co. PA	Wellington VA
12068	Brown, Infant of Charles H.	3d	W	1 NOV 1913	Baltimore MD	Congressional
08818	Brown, Infant of Preston	13m	C	7 JAN 186	Hyattsville MD	Harmony
08310	Brown, Isabella (Parker)	52y	C	14 SEP 1911	Rosslyn VA	Holyrood
07171	Brown, James	5y	C	25 AUG 1909	Cabin John MD	Christian
16310	Brown, James	4m	C	12 FEB 1920	Fairmont Hts. MD	Harmony
07834	Brown, James L.	40y	W	19 NOV 1910	Indian Head MD	Congressional
15215	Brown, James R.	29y	C	16 OCT 1918	Ft. Myer VA	Mt. Olivet
13969	Brown, James Wesley	70y	W	5 FEB 1917	Takoma Park MD	Rock Creek
13513	Brown, Jane	42y	C	19 MAY 1916	Bladensburg MD	Mt. Olivet
16420	Brown, Jane Reilly	86y	W	5 APR 1920	Rockville MD	Congressional
02047	Brown, Jeannie D.	48y	W	3 DEC 1896	Baltimore MD	Congressional
00571	Brown, John	22y	C	13 OCT 1891	Niagara Falls NY	Harmony
08711	Brown, John	6m	C	9 JUL 1912	Bladensburg MD	Mt. Olivet
06188	Brown, John	2h	W	19 AUG 1907	Mt. Ranier MD	Mt. Olivet
16193	Brown, John H.	71y	C	7 JAN 1920	Suitland MD	Cremated
16178	Brown, John H.	39y	C	27 DEC 1919	Baltimore MD	Harmony
15841	Brown, John H.	74y	W	20 JUN 1919	Takoma Park MD	Mt. Olivet
04427	Brown, John H.	36y	C	30 AUG 1903	Potomac River	Woodlawn
00214½	Brown, John L.	64y	W	– FEB 1887	Eureka KS	Rock Creek
08308	Brown, Joseph Delaney	62y	C	15 SEP 1911	Seat Pleasant MD	Mt. Olivet
06122	Brown, Joseph F.	5m	C	1 JUL 1907	Landover MD	Mt. Olivet
04517	Brown, Julia V., teacher	28y	C	18 NOV 1903	Pr. Geo. Co. MD	Woodlawn
06463	Brown, Juliette W.	95y	W	7 JAN 1901	Hyattsville MD	Congressional
14693	Brown, Larnon J.	24y	C	11 DEC 1917	Ft. Houston TX	Oxon Hill MD
08136	Brown, Leda Gano	88y	W	2 JUN 1911	Monmouth ME	Arlington
03975	Brown, Lena E.	15y	W	10 AUG 1902	Lakeland MD	Rock Creek
14390	Brown, Leonard C.	42y	W	29 SEP 1917	Pittsburgh PA	Glenwood
15529	Brown, Leroy	1m	C	7 JAN 1919	Chevy Chase MD	Mt. Zion West
06877	Brown, Lillian F.	7m	C	3 JAN 1909	Landover MD	Mt. Olivet
13630	Brown, Lillian Jones	35y	C	26 JUL 1916	Boston MA	Harmony
07694	Brown, Loretta	6m	W	16 AUG 1910	Relieve VA	Mt. Olivet
17621	Brown, Louis E.	47y	C	1 JAN 1922	Knoxville TN	Harmony
13005	Brown, Lucy	55y	C	14 JUL 1915	Seat Pleasant MD	Mt. Olivet

District of Columbia Foreign Death Records, 1888-1923

No.	Name of Deceased	Age	Race	Death Date	Place of Death	Place of Burial
02834	Brown, Lue R.	47y	W	27 MAY 1899	Asheville NC	Oak Hill
08812	Brown, Mabel	19y	C	15 OCT 1900	Hyattsville MD	Harmony
17892	Brown, Mabel, d/o James	25y	C	6 JUN 1922	Moundsville WV	Payne's
01900	Brown, Margaret A.	53y	C	3 APR 1896	Jersey City NJ	Harmony
17300	Brown, Marie	21y	C	12 JUL 1921	Orange NJ	Mt. Zion West
07781	Brown, Martha	38y	C	7 OCT 1910	Newport RI	Norbeck MD
16007	Brown, Mary	60y	C	22 SEP 1919	Falls Church VA	Harmony
16161	Brown, Mary	c.45y	C	21 DEC 1919	McKeesport PA	Mt. Olivet
05723	Brown, Mary	26y	W	3 SEP 1906	Piscataway MD	Mt. Olivet
05722	Brown, Mary	60y	C	1 SEP 1906	St. Mary's Co. MD	Woodlawn
13622	Brown, Mary A.	20y	C	27 JUL 1916	Pittsburgh PA	Hyattsville MD
13624	Brown, Mary A.	20y	C	27 JUL 1916	Pittsburgh PA	Mt. Olivet
15659	Brown, Mary Alexandra	6y	W	4 MAR 1919	Chicago IL	Rock Creek
06262	Brown, Mary Elizabeth	80y	W	6 OCT 1907	Alexandria VA	Rock Creek
17609	Brown, Mary Elizabeth	58y	W	26 DEC 1921	Takoma MD	Rock Creek
02935	Brown, Mary Jane	24y	C	4 SEP 1899	Glen Echo MD	Christian
06833	Brown, Mary L.	65y	C	29 NOV 1908	New York NY	Harmony
14096	Brown, Milton E.	25y	C	14 APR 1917	St. Johns Run WV	Mt. Zion East
07281	Brown, Mintern Stanley	61y	W	22 NOV 1909	Takoma Park MD	Cremated
14937	Brown, Moses	2m	C	23 JUL 1918	MD	Cremated
05781	Brown, Naomi	3m	W	19 OCT 1906	Rosslyn VA	Holyrood
04316	Brown, Nicholis J.	61y	W	10 JUN 1903	Mill Point WV	Oak Hill
15530	Brown, Norman	1y	C	7 JAN 1919	Chevy Chase MD	Mt. Zion West
15713	Brown, Oliver	31y	C	3 APR 1919	Camp Lee VA	Arlington
07557	Brown, Olney O.	80y	W	5 JAN 1910	Wichita KS	Rock Creek
05655	Brown, Oscar N.	41y	C	23 JUL 1906	Westborough MA	Barboursville VA
01530	Brown, Palmyra B.	57y	W	7 DEC 1894	Salisbury MD	Oak Hill
07607	Brown, Patrick J.	40y	W	29 JUN 1910	Highland NY	Mt. Olivet
05975	Brown, Perry	58y	W	5 MAR 1907	Albany NY	Glenwood
04853	Brown, Peter	3y	W	19 AUG 1904	Landover MD	Mt. Olivet
08042	Brown, Philip	43y	C	27 MAR 1911	Baltimore MD	Harmony
12999	Brown, Philip	32y	C	8 JUL 1915	Baltimore MD	Mt. Zion East
12924	Brown, Philip S.	49y	W	15 MAY 1915	New York NY	Arlington
08809	Brown, Preston	29y	C	9 AUG 1887	Hyattsville MD	Harmony
07630	Brown, Rachel, d/o G.T.	1m	W	13 JUL 1910	St. Elmo VA	Congressional
15306	Brown, Ralph	21y	C	27 OCT 1918	Fairfax Co. VA	Harmony
14788	Brown, Rebecca M.	66y	W	1 MAY 1918	Millsville MD	Arlington
03337	Brown, Richard S.L.	1y	W	15 NOV 1900	Indian Head MD	Congressional
02048	Brown, Richard T.	47y	W	7 OCT 1896	Funkstown MD	Oak Hill
04597	Brown, Richard Vernon	24y	W	9 FEB 1904	Waterloo VA	Glenwood
04595	Brown, Richard Vernon, Jr.	1y	W	9 FEB 1904	Waterloo VA	Glenwood
05741	Brown, Rosa	37y	C	16 SEP 1906	New York NY	Harmony
07515	Brown, Rose	c.60y	C	22 APR 1910	Grayton MD	Harmony
06226	Brown, Rosie May	24y	C	15 SEP 1907	Takoma MD	Rock Creek
09169	Brown, Ruth	19y	C	12 APR 1913	Boston MA	Oxon Hill MD
14496	Brown, Ruth F.	87y	W	10 DEC 1917	Laurel MD	Glenwood
16120	Brown, Samuel	74y	C	19 NOV 1919	New York NY	Harmony
16088	Brown, Samuel	78y	C	31 OCT 1919	Chicago IL	Woodlawn
06486	Brown, Samuel K.	69y	W	23 MAR 1908	Lemon City FL	Glenwood
07909	Brown, Sarah	62y	W	6 JAN 1911	Maryland Pk. MD	Rock Creek
04978	Brown, Sarah J.	67y	W	17 DEC 1904	Baltimore MD	Congressional
00214	Brown, Stanley	25y	W	– DEC 1868	Washington DC	Rock Creek
04533	Brown, Stith	33y	C	3 DEC 1903	Cambridge MA	Stony Creek VA
14948	Brown, Suzanne W.	62y	W	1 AUG 1918	Allegheny Co. PA	Rock Creek
00924	Brown, Thomas	45y	C	7 JUN 1893	Ft. Wash. MD	Graceland
14531	Brown, Thomas	45y	C	27 DEC 1917	Phillipi WV	Harmony
07884	Brown, Thomas C.	c.55y	C	19 DEC 1910	Ridgeland SC	Brooklyn NY
15003	Brown, Thomas H.	—	C	3 SEP 1918	Havre de Grace	Harmony
13047	Brown, Thomas N.	70y	C	9 AUG 1915	Capitol Hts. MD	Hampton VA

No.	Name of Deceased	Age	Race	Death Date	Place of Death	Place of Burial
03927	Brown, Tresa	50y	C	20 JUL 1902	Cabin John MD	Christian
08822	Brown, Triplets of Preston	3d	C	1883	Hyattsville MD	Harmony
14183	Brown, Viola	16y	C	21 JUN 1917	Cedar Hts. MD	Payne's
16032	Brown, Waite E.	34y	W	16 AUG 1892	Hyattsville MD	St. Mary's[1]
09040	Brown, William	62y	C	14 JAN 1913	Detroit MI	Arlington VA
07373	Brown, William	56y	W	15 JAN 1910	Rochester NY	Congressional
03311	Brown, William Edwin	4m	W	23 OCT 1900	Kensington MD	Rock Creek
04048	Brown, William H.	30y	C	5 OCT 1902	Beverly WV	Harmony
17890	Brown, William H.	58y	C	5 JUN 1922	New York NY	Harmony
13438	Brown, William H.	54y	W	2 APR 1916	Newark NJ	Mt. Olivet
06462	Brown, William J.	74y	W	11 MAR 1908	Hyattsville MD	Congressional
00363	Brown, William Oliver	1y	W	19 JUL 1890	College Sta. MD	Rock Creek
12433	Brown, William Van Horn	64y	W	4 JUL 1914	Los Angeles CA	Oak Hill
01793	Browne, Emilie J.	58y	W	24 NOV 1895	Santa Fe NM	Rock Creek
16704	Browne, Evans	39y	W	9 SEP 1920	Bethesda MD	Rock Creek
17150	Browne, Gertrude W. (White)	62y	W	10 MAY 1921	Milwaukee WI	Rock Creek
11835	Browne, Helen	24y	C	26 MAY 1913	New York NY	Woodlawn
12739	Browne, Jessie Delahay	26y	W	30 JAN 1915	Providence RI	Rock Creek
12754	Browne, Mary Jeanette	23y	W	8 FEB 1915	Alliance OH	Congressional
06788	Browne, Randolph Corey	2y	W	21 JUL 1892	Roanoke VA	Rock Creek
16580	Browne, Sidney	69y	W	3 JUL 1920	New York NY	Glenwood
03289	Browne, William Henry	72y	W	15 SEP 1900	Charlestown WV	Arlington VA
08320	Browne, Wilmer M.	36y	W	19 MAR 1911	Manila, P.I.	Glenwood
13228	Brownell, William V.	30y	W	1 DEC 1916	Mifflentown PA	Congressional
08138	Browning, Bond	37y	W	7 JUN 1911	Seat Pleasant MD	Arlington
03660	Browning, Frank Temple	49y	W	23 SEP 1901	Forest Glen MD	Congressional
08087	Browning, Henry C.	71y	W	27 APR 1911	Riverdale MD	Congressional
17832	Browning, Henry Clay	59y	W	27 APR 1922	Los Angeles CA	Cremated
06377	Browning, Horace	47y	W	4 JAN 1908	Baltimore MD	Congressional
08814	Browning, Margaret Elizabeth	32y	W	1 SEP 1912	Atlantic City NJ	Mt. Olivet
03345	Browning, Perry Warfield	29y	W	21 NOV 1900	Pr. Geo. Co. MD	Rock Creek
02238	Browning, Ringgold W.	55y	W	15 JUL 1897	Riverdale MD	Congressional
17432	Browning, Theodore F.	40y	W	24 SEP 1921	Riverdale MD	Oak Hill
12671	Browning, Virginia E.	31y	W	25 DEC 1914	Waynesboro PA	Oak Hill
17877	Browning, William Silas	71y	W	28 MAY 1922	Takoma Park MD	Glenwood
08375	Brownley, Agnes Meriwether	27y	C	25 OCT 1911	Charlestown WV	Woodlawn
17025	Brownley, Blanch C.H.	34y	W	16 JAN 1921	Columbia Hp. DC	Congressional
01615	Brubaker, Eli	30y	W	30 APR 1895	Cumberland MD	Congressional
00152	Brubaker, Jonas Martin	41y	W	8 SEP 1889	Fairfax Co. VA	Congressional
14611	Bruce, Charles H.	85y	W	29 JAN 1918	Philadelphia PA	Harmony
02917	Bruce, Claude	27y	C	14 AUG 1899	Little Rock AR	Harmony
14191	Bruce, Edward M.	63y	C	25 JUN 1917	New York NY	Harmony
00811	Bruce, Hannah	77y	C	14 AUG 1892	Hamilton VA	Harmony
00559	Bruce, John A.	38y	W	23 APR 1891	Hyattsville MD	Glenwood
18351	Bruce, Josephine Bealle	69y	C	15 FEB 1923	Kimball WV	Woodlawn
16577	Bruce, Lloyd	18y	C	1 JUL 1920	Camp Custer MI	Harmony
05186	Bruce, Robert O.	39y	W	25 JUN 1905	Potomac River	Alexandria VA
05185	Bruce, Robert O.	39y	W	25 JUN 1905	Potomac River	Alexandria VA
06528	Bruce, William	47y	C	29 APR 1908	Harrisburg PA	Payne's
15621	Bruehl, Emil G.	68y	W	17 FEB 1919	Hyattsville MD	Prospect Hill
14608	Brumbaugh, Basil Floyd	21y	W	20 JAN 1918	At Sea	Arlington
04182	Brumfield, Florence V.	54y	W	16 FEB 1903	Godding Croft MD	Glenwood
17268	Brumger, Charles Andrew	26y	W	25 JUN 1921	Jersey City NJ	Glenwood
07224	Brundige, Isabel	61y	W	2 OCT 1909	Baltimore MD	Glenwood
14736	Brunger, Percival A.	21y	W	31 MAR 1918	Tucson AZ	Glenwood
15388	Brunner, Catherine J.	87	W	30 NOV 1918	Falls Church VA	Oak Hill

---

[1] Disinterment permit of 9 OCT 1919 to Gasch for removal from Beltsville MD.

District of Columbia Foreign Death Records, 1888-1923

No.	Name of Deceased	Age	Race	Death Date	Place of Death	Place of Burial
07987	Brunner, James G.W.	80y	W	26 FEB 1911	Falls Church VA	Oak Hill
13326	Brunner, John	49y	W	28 JAN 1916	Bowie MD	Congressional
12985	Brunner, Raymond	20y	W	20 JUN 1915	Edgemere NY	Glenwood
04347	Bruno, Loretta A.	41y	W	8 AUG 1903	Glendale MD	Mt. Olivet
07193	Brush, Harmon M.	67y	W	9 SEP 1909	Buffalo NY	Rock Creek
12582	Brush, Mary M. (Slosson)	—	W	23 OCT 1914	Fairfax VA	Rock Creek
12583	Brush, William M.	32y	W	25 OCT 1914	Fairfax VA	Rock Creek
17425	Bryan, Edward	75y	W	23 SEP 1921	Capitol Hts. MD	Arlington
13933	Bryan, Grace M.	36y	W	14 JAN 1917	Philadelphia PA	Congressional
02419	Bryan, Jennie Byrd	68y	W	26 MAR 1898	Elmhurst IL	Oak Hill
04133	Bryan, Richard	27y	W	29 JAN 1903	Pittsburgh PA	Rock Creek
07490	Bryan, Samuel M.	56y	W	1 APR 1910	Baltimore MD	Congressional
04146	Bryan, Samuel Magill	55y	W	23 JAN 1903	Ruxton MD	Rock Creek
14560	Bryan, Sarah A.	89y	W	7 JAN 1918	Somerville MA	Glenwood
04875	Bryan, Susan C.	71y	W	3 SEP 1904	Brunswick MD	Rock Creek
17996	Bryan, Susan Louise	92y	W	7 AUG 1922	Montrose MD	Akron OH
06899	Bryan, William	78y	W	23 JAN 1909	Somerville MA	Glenwood
00353	Bryan, Winifred Marie	7y	W	30 JUN 1890	Albemarle Co. VA	Mt. Olivet
03983	Bryant, Charles	37y	C	2 AUG 1902	New York NY	Harmony
00424	Bryant, Estelle	2y	W	25 OCT 1890	Green Co. NY	Oak Hill
06310	Bryant, George	23y	C	13 SEP 1907	New York NY	Payne's
15595	Bryant, Isaac H.	69y	W	2 FEB 1919	High Bridge MD	Glenwood
05165	Bryant, Lula	29y	C	10 JUN 1905	Atlantic City NJ	Mt. Zion East
18379	Bucca, Rafiele	63y	W	28 FEB 1923	Capitol Hts. MD	St. Mary's
11866	Bucce, Arthur	3m	W	26 JUN 1913	Tuxedo MD	Mt. Olivet
15105	Buchalter, Victor	27y	W	5 OCT 1918	Camp Meade MD	Ohev Sholom
15252	Buchanan, Albert William	23y	W	20 OCT 1918	Indian Head MD	Bakerfield CA
06370	Buchanan, Beverly R.	2y	W	26 FEB 1907	Brooklyn NY	Holyrood
01794	Buchanan, Infant of Jas.	1d	W	7 MAY 1895	Trenton NJ	Congressional
02291	Buchanan, J.W.	35y	W	22 SEP 1897	Layton Sta. PA	Rock Creek
13917	Buchanan, James W.	70y	W	8 JAN 1917	Philadelphia PA	Rock Creek
01023	Buchanan, Martha E.	17y	W	20 FEB 1893	Pittsburgh PA	Congressional
15700	Buchanan, Mrs. Roberdeau	70y	W	28 MAR 1919	Columbia SC	Oak Hill
14722	Bucher, Solomon J.	75y	W	25 MAR 1918	Canton OH	Arlington VA
00452	Buchhanan, Sallie M.	65y	W	10 JAN 1891	Baltimore MD	Rock Creek
04152	Buchly, Emma Jane	64y	W	27 JAN 1903	Arlington VA	Congressional
05301	Buck, Alonza M.	79y	W	30 SEP 1905	Hyattsville MD	Congressional
06972	Buck, Augustine	4y	W	17 JUL 1849	Baltimore MD	Rock Creek
06975	Buck, Benjamin A.	—	W	5 NOV 1857	Philadelphia PA	Rock Creek
06973	Buck, John D.	40y	W	16 JUL 1849	Baltimore MD	Rock Creek
05599	Buck, Kate	36y	W	14 JUN 1906	Ft. McPherson GA	Arlington
06976	Buck, Margaret	—	W	1857	Philadelphia PA	Rock Creek
05428	Buck, Marian Douglas	67y	W	16 JAN 1906	Hyattsville MD	Congressional
06974	Buck, Susan A.	20y	W	23 SEP 1844	Hancock MD	Rock Creek
06977	Buck, Upton R.	—	W	12 FEB 1862	Washington DC	Rock Creek
12111	Buckey, Charles M.	57y	W	27 NOV 1913	Forestville MD	Congressional
15379	Buckey, Frances B.	39y	W	25 NOV 1918	Brentwood MD	Congressional
05432	Buckingham, Benj. Hoar, s/o E.	57y	W	16 JAN 1906	Carolla NC	Philadelphia PA
01531	Buckingham, Harry Mortimer	37y	W	13 NOV 1894	Baltimore MD	Congressional
13719	Buckingham, Thomas	2y	W	15 SEP 1916	Riverdale MD	Glenwood
03493	Buckler, Edward	27y	W	29 APR 1901	Norfolk VA	Hughesville MD
01532	Buckler, Katie J.	24y	W	12 DEC 1894	Baltimore MD	Prospect Hill
15392	Buckley, Donald	31y	W	29 NOV 1918	York PA	Glenwood
01024	Buckley, Grassie G.	25y	W	18 MAR 1893	Danville PA	Congressional
02538	Buckley, John, Rev.	46y	W	15 JUN 1898	Philadelphia PA	College
04440	Buckley, Kate T.	55y	W	5 SEP 1903	At Sea	Mt. Olivet
16150	Buckley, Mary J.	11m	W	14 DEC 1919	Baltimore MD	Mt. Olivet
17679	Buckley, Robert Wells	58y	W	6 FEB 1922	W. Palm Bea. FL	Rock Creek
17580	Buckley, Sarah F.	61y	W	9 DEC 1921	Cherrydale VA	Rock Creek

No.	Name of Deceased	Age	Race	Death Date	Place of Death	Place of Burial
01122	Buckley, Thomas	31y	W	14 NOV 1892	Chicago IL	Mt. Olivet
03474	Buckman, Albert	43y	C	7 APR 1901	Johnstown PA	Harmony
12608	Buckman, John T.	58y	C	6 NOV 1914	Middletown PA	Harmony
14964	Buckman, William Davis	39y	W	9 AUG 1918	Riverdale MD	W. Newton MA
15808	Buckner, Annette	26y	W	1 JUN 1919	Thurmont MD	Talmud Torah
17559	Buckner, Bertha L.	64y	C	28 NOV 1921	Highland Falls NY	Woodlawn
08069	Buckner, Blanche	17y	C	15 APR 1911	Baltimore MD	Harmony
06217	Buckner, Willis	64y	C	2 SEP 1907	Philipstown NY	Woodlawn
12862	Budd, Frank, s/o Samuel	22y	C	25 MAR 1915	Ancora NJ	Woodlawn
17692	Budd, Joseph	—	W	26 SEP 1918	France	Ohev Sholom
08207	Budlong, Oaphius H.	57y	W	20 JUL 1911	Hyattsville MD	Rock Creek
16918	Buehler, Catherine	68y	W	14 JAN 1921	Chevy Chase MD	Glenwood
18138	Buell, Joseph W.	56y	W	31 OCT 1922	Railroad	Ft. Lincoln
08493	Buell, Perze Barnum	78y	W	24 JAN 1912	Herndon VA	Cremated
05125	Buell, William B.	75y	W	12 MAY 1905	Ocean City MD	Rock Creek
08477	Buersey, Albert	70y	W	15 JAN 1912	Philadelphia PA	Congressional
15819	Buete, George P.	64y	W	8 JUN 1919	Brooklyn NY	St. Mary's
14785	Buford, Charlotte	76y	W	2 MAY 1918	Takoma MD	Rock Island IL
07364	Buford, Grace Bowers	78y	W	10 JAN 1910	Ft. Myer VA	Rock Island IL
00079	Bugher, Aaron Hamilton	58y	W	26 JUN 1889	Long Beach LI	Oak Hill
15997	Buhler, Hector	60y	W	28 NOV 1918	Lawton OK	Oak Hill
14781	Buhman, Alfred	8m	W	30 APR 1918	Chevy Chase MD	Glenwood
01505	Buker, William Spencer	16y	W	6 SEP 1894	Boston MA	Rock Creek
17320	Bukey, Cecilia Agnes	84y	W	22 JUL 1921	Parkersburg WV	Arlington
12811	Buley, Anna	56y	C	10 MAR 1915	New York NY	Harmony
02128	Buley, Jane	62y	C	2 FEB 1897	New York NY	Harmony
04147	Bulger, Clara	28y	W	23 JAN 1903	Philadelphia PA	Chicago IL
16896	Bulger, Mary E.	c.70y	W	4 JAN 1921	Mt. Hope MD	Lockport NY
03702	Bulkley, Daisy	25y	W	9 NOV 1901	Falls Church VA	Rock Creek
07479	Bull, Jessie Williams	41y	W	22 MAR 1910	Orangeburg SC	Cremated
13116	Bullard, Nellie	50y	W	21 SEP 1915	Takoma MD	Tarrytown NY
12980	Bullock, George W.	19y	W	24 JUN 1915	Port Arthur TX	Glenwood
17630	Bullough, Frederick A.	9m	W	12 JAN 1922	Baltimore MD	Congressional
15960	Bulmer, Roscoe C., Capt.	44y	W	5 AUG 1919	Kirkwall, Scot.	Arlington
15972	Bumby, Edward, in jail	33y	C	2 SEP 1919	Philadelphia PA	Moore's
01296	Bunce, Mary	30y	W	10 JAN 1894	Alex. Co. VA	Glenwood
12187	Bundy, George	35y	C	26 JAN 1914	Philadelphia PA	Payne's[1]
14135	Bundy, Mary	28y	C	10 MAY 1917	Bay View MD	Woodlawn
18356	Bunn, Dora P.	53y	C	14 FEB 1923	Cedar Grove NJ	Payne's
01335	Bunnon, Catharine F.	22y	W	4 APR 1894	Charlton Hts. MD	Mt. Olivet
03436	Burbank, E.A.	72y	W	21 FEB 1901	Los Angeles CA	Oak Hill
03879	Burbridge, Elizabeth	83y	W	12 MAY 1902	Baltimore MD	Oak Hill
01533	Burbridge, Stephen Gano	63y	W	30 NOV 1894	Brooklyn NY	Arlington
13239	Burch, Blanche E. (Moore)	31y	W	8 DEC 1915	Norfolk VA	Congressional
05675	Burch, Geo. Colton, s/o Jas.	15y	W	5 AUG 1906	Colonial Bea. VA	Congressional
03056	Burch, Joseph R.	84y	W	31 DEC 1899	Landover MD	Mt. Olivet
05070	Burch, Mary E.	84y	W	30 MAR 1905	Adamstown MD	Glenwood
13887	Burchell, Edward	61y	W	28 DEC 1916	Clarendon VA	Oak Hill
00005	Burden, W.F.	21y	W	23 JAN 1889	So. Beth. PA	Rock Creek
15711	Burdett, George F.	23y	W	4 APR 1919	Silver Spring MD	Rock Creek
04676	Burdette, Horace H.	31y	W	16 APR 1904	Buffalo NY	Oak Hill
17151	Burdette, Marian Henrietta	51y	W	11 MAY 1921	Silver Spring MD	Rock Creek
02947	Burgdorf, Mary A.L.	65y	W	14 SEP 1899	Minneapolis MN	Glenwood
13406	Burgess, Christine	84y	W	12 MAR 1916	Seat Pleasant MD	Mt. Olivet
15430	Burgess, Herman E.	25y	W	8 DEC 1918	Hicks TX	Glenwood
07022	Burgess, John Henry, s/o Wm.	6y	W	13 MAY 1909	Clarendon VA	Mt. Zion West

[1] Reinterred in Woodlawn Cemetery, 25 OCT 1926, permit #8787; and again 28 NOV 1938 to Lincoln Memorial Cem.

District of Columbia Foreign Death Records, 1888-1923

No.	Name of Deceased	Age	Race	Death Date	Place of Death	Place of Burial
06540	Burgess, Kate	62y	C	6 MAY 1908	Montclair NJ	Mt. Olivet
09136	Burgess, Mildred C.	16d	W	20 MAR 913	Hyattsville MD	Glenwood
02696	Burgess, Richard W.	80y	W	8 JAN 1899	Greensburg PA	Oak Hill
07695	Burgess, Wilhelmina F.	62y	W	13 AUG 1910	El Paso TX	Glenwood
06385	Burgess, William H., s/o Wm.	43y	C	9 JAN 1908	Clarendon VA	Mt. Zion West
09071	Burgess, William Samuel	78y	W	12 FEB 1913	Seat Pleasant MD	Mt. Olivet
01956	Burk, Joseph	19y	C	13 JUN 1896	Philadelphia PA	Payne's
16700	Burkart, Caroline	79y	W	8 SEP 1920	Chevy Chase MD	St. Mary's
13960	Burkart, John L.	55y	W	29 JAN 1917	Batavia NY	St. Mary's
14928	Burke, Alice J.	62y	C	20 JUL 1918	Philadelphia PA	Harmony
13364	Burke, Anna G.	58y	W	17 FEB 1916	Buffalo NY	Mt. Olivet
09000	Burke, Annie	75y	W	25 DEC 1912	Baltimore MD	Mt. Olivet
00686	Burke, Catherine	80y	W	21 NOV 1891	Philadelphia PA	Mt. Olivet
12309	Burke, Charles B.	39y	W	11 APR 1914	Friendship H. MD	Mt. Olivet
05552	Burke, Charles Grant	9m	W	22 APR 1906	Chevy Chase MD	Glenwood
17768	Burke, Edward Eugene	2y	W	29 MAR 1922	Clarendon VA	Mt. Olivet
01025	Burke, Eliza	75y	W	25 MAR 1893	Philadelphia PA	Mt. Olivet
17458	Burke, Eugene R.	2d	W	9 OCT 1921	Hyattsville MD	Glenwood
08898	Burke, Frank Fuss	36y	W	21 OCT 1912	Chevy Chase MD	Glenwood
15898	Burke, George A.	27y	W	30 JUL 1919	Ballston VA	Glenwood
16546	Burke, Helen M.	22y	W	16 JUN 1920	Akron OH	Mt. Olivet
03429	Burke, Jane McLean	78y	W	23 FEB 1901	The Plains VA	Oak Hill
11847	Burke, Margaret J.	67y	W	7 JUN 1913	Friendship H. MD	Mt. Olivet
13996	Burke, Margaret V.	62y	C	16 FEB 1917	New York NY	Mt. Zion East
07844	Burke, Mary	67y	C	26 NOV 1910	Newton MA	Harmony
00052	Burke, Nelson Thomas	50y	C	9 APR 1889	Arlington VA	Harmony
01534	Burke, Thomas	31y	W	17 JAN 1895	Rosslyn VA	Mt. Olivet
16447	Burke, William M.	34y	W	23 APR 1920	Allentown PA	Mt. Olivet
15192	Burke, Winnie Harriet	32y	C	15 OCT 1918	Bladensburg MD	Harmony
08396	Burkett, Lincoln W.	48y	W	20 NOV 1911	Pittsburgh PA	Rock Creek
01795	Burkhardt, Mary E.l	38y	W	7 DEC 1895	Philadelphia PA	Mt. Olivet
00218	Burkhart, Joseph W.	56y	W	20 DEC 1889	Hampton VA	St. Mary's
09144	Burkley, Augustus E.	70y	W	28 MAR 1913	Riverdale MD	Mt. Olivet
18207	Burkley, Mary	29y	W	12 DEC 1922	Landover MD	Prospect Hill
02294	Burks, James William	16y	C	5 DEC 1897	College MD	Mt. Olivet
18208	Burks, Margaret Leah	54y	W	13 DEC 1922	Chevy Chase MD	Rock Creek
13084	Burl, Joseph	37y	C	31 AUG 1915	Brentwood MD	Harmony
02781	Burleigh, Willis C.	32y	W	4 AUG 1898	Wash. Barr. DC	Broome Co. NY
02707	Burley, Mary	60y	C	13 JAN 1899	Montg. Co. MD	Christian
02239	Burlingame, Frederick H.	8y	W	30 AUG 1897	Potomac River	Congressional
04419	Burlingham, Justus S.	29y	W	26 JUL 1903	Tucson AZ	Rock Creek
07240	Burman, Virginia	60y	W	19 OCT 1909	Riverdale MD	Rock Creek
18203	Burn, Leon L.	43y	W	7 DEC 1922	Baltimore MD	Ft. Lincoln
07000	Burnell, George C., Capt.	40y	W	22 APR 1909	Laurel MD	Arlington
13301	Burnell, William B., s/o Wm.	34y	W	14 JAN 1916	Westport CN	Congressional
16678	Burner, Lemuel Travel	71y	W	23 AUG 1920	Annapolis MD	Rock Creek
15518	Burnett, Ralph	36y	W	2 JAN 1919	Philadelphia PA	Glenwood
04804	Burnham, Carolina Augustus	80y	W	17 JUL 1904	Laurel MD	Glenwood
06791	Burnham, Elgie L.	52y	W	28 OCT 1908	Chicago IL	Glenwood
02129	Burnham, Eliphalet J.	74y	W	6 MAR 1897	Laurel MD	Glenwood
14725	Burns, Aida	43y	W	31 MAR 1918	Chicago IL	Ohev Sholom
08546	Burns, Arabella Elizabeth	70y	W	8 MAR 1912	Takoma Park MD	Glenwood
12078	Burns, Christina	73y	C	4 NOV 1913	Suitland MD	Mt. Zion West
06240	Burns, James Edward	9m	W	24 SEP 1907	Alexandria VA	Mt. Olivet
12442	Burns, Jennie	29y	W	13 JUL 1914	Albany NY	Mt. Olivet
15458	Burns, John Irving	28y	W	24 OCT 1918	Liverpool, Eng.	Mt. Olivet
13883	Burns, Laura V.	49y	W	26 DEC 1916	Alexandria VA	Mt. Olivet
13681	Burns, Louise	33y	C	25 AUG 1916	New York NY	Mt. Olivet
01614	Burns, Mary	12y	W	15 APR 1895	Delaware Co. PA	Mt. Olivet

No.	Name of Deceased	Age	Race	Death Date	Place of Death	Place of Burial
08650	Burnside, Clarence N.	32y	C	27 MAY 1912	Baltimore MD	Harmony
07317	Burnside, Drusilla A.A.	24y	C	8 DEC 1909	Baltimore MD	Harmony
08888	Burnside, Harry G., s/o John	30y	W	12 OCT 1912	Sideburn VA	Glenwood
06156	Burnside, James B.	51y	W	25 JUL 1907	Hyattsville MD	Rock Creek
11994	Burnside, John, s/o John	80y	W	7 SEP 1913	Sideburn VA	Glenwood
00539	Burnside, Marie	32y	W	10 MAY 1891	Hyattsville MD	Rock Creek
00572	Burnside, Mary Seay	2y	W	15 JUL 1891	Hyattsville MD	Rock Creek
05318	Burnside, William	75y	C	16 OCT 1905	Baltimore MD	Harmony
03251	Burnstein, Solomon H.	9m	W	6 AUG 1900	Colonial Bea. VA	Wash. Hebrew
17119	Burnz, Anna W.	58y	W	20 APR 1921	Brooklyn NY	Oak Hill
06131	Burr, Clara	51y	W	5 JUL 1907	Natick MA	Oak Hill
00540	Burr, David A.	53y	W	21 MAY 1891	Montclair NJ	Oak Hill
17296	Burr, Louise A.	78y	W	10 JUL 1921	Belmont MA	Oak Hill
07091	Burr, Martha J.	30y	W	2 JUL 1909	Plattsburgh NY	Rock Creek
17397	Burrell, Delilah	66y	C	10 SEP 1921	New York NY	Harmony
12831	Burrell, Ella	27y	C	20 MAR 1915	Bay View MD	Hughesville MD
15139	Burrell, Emmett	29y	C	11 OCT 1918	Takoma Park MD	Payne's
05350	Burrell, Samuel	29y	C	7 NOV 1905	Philadelphia PA	Moore's
06957	Burrell, Samuel	71y	C	24 MAR 1909	Philadelphia PA	Moore's
00687	Burrell, William H.	37y	C	7 FEB 1892	New York NY	Mt. Zion
13079	Burrhus, Harold	24y	W	25 AUG 1915	Dayton KY	Riverdale MD
15432	Burri, Leila Jordon	25y	W	9 DEC 1918	Laramie WY	Glenwood
02366	Burrill, Harry K.	23y	C	4 JAN 1898	Baltimore MD	Woodlawn
05947	Burris, Catherine	42y	C	19 FEB 1907	Pittsburgh PA	Harmony
04738	Burris, Elliott	55y	W	27 MAY 1904	Morristown NJ	Glenwood
03955	Burris, Grover C.	19y	W	22 JUL 1902	Ft. Wash. MD	Geyer OH
18575	Burris, James	49y	C	3 JUN 1923	Oxon Hill MD	Harmony
12547	Burritt, Carol F.	43y	W	30 SEP 1914	Wash. Grove MD	Mt. Olivet
01853	Burroughs, Frank N.	27y	W	19 DEC 1895	Washington DC	Congressional
15675	Burroughs, J. Harry	45y	W	5 NOV 1918	Staunton VA	Rock Creek
01679	Burroughs, Mary B.	5m	W	22 JUL 1895	Long Branch NJ	Congressional
02240	Burroughs, Ruth Mulford	8m	W	8 JUL 1897	Ocean Grove NJ	Oak Hill
02770	Burroughs, Stewart	8m	W	14 MAR 1899	New York NY	Congressional
16012	Burruss, Genevieve Munson	38y	W	23 SEP 1919	Hendersonv. NC	Glenwood
07615	Bursch, Ellen	45y	W	5 JUL 1910	Vienna VA	Mt. Olivet
17601	Bursch, John J.	56y	W	21 DEC 1921	Dun Loring VA	Mt. Olivet
01678	Bursley, Ruth W.	19y	W	19 AUG 1895	Potomac River	Congressional
07696	Burson, John William	70y	W	19 AUG 1910	Alexandria VA	Rock Creek
08113	Burton, Bertie	17y	W	12 MAY 1911	Wash. Grove MD	Capitol Cem. MD
15470	Burton, Helen Hazel	19y	W	22 DEC 1918	Silver Spring MD	Mt. Olivet
14600	Burton, Ida E.	4y	W	26 JAN 1918	Hyattsville MD	Rock Creek
17920	Burton, Jessie B. Krogstad	30y	W	28 MAY 1922	Paris, France	Rock Creek
04592	Burton, John F.	75y	W	9 FEB 1904	Laurel MD	Cremated
05699	Burton, William Stansell	57y	W	20 AUG 1906	Hume VA	Congressional
12452	Burwell, Weston	32y	W	23 JUL 1914	Mexico	Rock Creek
00053	Bury, William Robert	9y	W	15 NOV 1888	Norfolk VA	Congressional
02941	Busch, Rozalia E.	53y	C	7 SEP 1899	Cambridge MA	Harmony
18009	Busch, Wendelin	84y	W	12 AUG 1922	Chevy Chase MD	Glenwood
08031	Buscuvilla, William	50y	W	24 MAR 1911	Rockwood PA	Payne's
15486	Busey, Clara Jane	3y	W	27 DEC 1918	Takoma Park MD	Glenwood
15487	Busey, Katherine	8y	W	26 DEC 1918	Takoma Park MD	Glenwood
18014	Bush, Daniel	36y	C	15 AUG 1922	Hughesville MD	Payne's
16522	Bush, Edward	53y	C	2 JUN 1920	Freedman's Hp.	Payne's
07363	Bush, Eliza	68y	C	9 JAN 1910	Philadelphia PA	Mt. Olivet
03114	Bush, Henry	37y	W	4 MAR 1900	Mt. Hope MD	Adas Israel
07372	Bush, Isaac	28y	C	15 JAN 1910	Baltimore MD	Oxon Hill MD
00454	Bush, James H.	46y	W	3 FEB 1891	Boston MA	Mt. Olivet
03150	Bush, John	13y	C	20 MAR 1900	Lakeland MD	Mt. Olivet
04381	Bush, Joseph C. [Clinton]	45y	C	5 JUL 1903	Arundel Bay MD	Woodlawn

District of Columbia Foreign Death Records, 1888-1923

No.	Name of Deceased	Age	Race	Death Date	Place of Death	Place of Burial
15798	Bush, Marcena	1m	C	28 MAY 1919	Fairmont Hts. MD	Payne's
12444	Bush, Marian Cecelia	11m	C	16 JUL 1914	Lakeland MD	Mt. Olivet
06174	Bush, Winfrey N.	6m	C	9 AUG 1907	Port Tobacco MD	Mt. Olivet
05713	Bushby, Lucia E.	71y	W	28 AUG 1906	Wash. Grove MD	Glenwood
17514	Bushby, William Rosser	68y	W	12 NOV 1921	Laurel MD	Rock Creek
15081	Bushee, Mattie	22y	W	4 OCT 1918	Ross Co. OH	Congressional
04435	Busher, George	31y	W	4 SEP 1903	Hyattsville MD	Rock Creek
00688	Busher, James M.	66y	W	18 FEB 1892	Branchville MD	—
04717	Bushnell, Edith Taber J.B.	24y	W	17 MAY 1904	Pittsburgh PA	Rock Creek
03227	Bushnell, Mary F.	80y	W	4 JUL 1900	Baltimore MD	Mt. Olivet
08158	Bushrod, Benjamin	29y	C	18 JUN 1911	Trenton NJ	Payne's
04874	Bussey, Ellen K.	40y	W	20 JAN 1878	Keokuk IA	Arlington
00812	Butcher, Albert G.	7y	C	28 APR 1892	Rosslyn VA	Baptist
13106	Butcher, Harry	4m	C	15 SEP 1915	Brentwood MD	Glenwood
13104	Butcher, John F.	4m	W	13 SEP 1915	Brentwood MD	Glenwood
12631	Butler, Alice Johnson	42y	W	25 NOV 1914	New York NY	Oak Hill
15131	Butler, Alphonso	21y	C	8 OCT 1918	Camp Dix NJ	Harmony
08381	Butler, Ann	66y	C	31 OCT 1911	Ft. Myer VA	Holyrood
03085	Butler, Ann E.	1y	W	18 FEB 1900	Arlington VA	Holyrood
16984	Butler, Bridget	64y	W	17 FEB 1921	Cottage City MD	Mt. Olivet
15933	Butler, Calbraith	12y	W	15 AUG 1919	Nashville TN	Arlington
04783	Butler, Cora	24y	C	6 JUL 1904	Pittsburgh PA	Bailey's Xrds. VA
13966	Butler, David J.	54y	C	30 JAN 1917	Philadelphia PA	Harmony
16779	Butler, Ella	39y	C	23 OCT 1920	Baltimore MD	Payne's
17843	Butler, Eva	44y	C	7 MAY 1922	New York NY	Mt. Olivet
06531	Butler, Frances DeSales	24y	W	3 MAY 1908	Franconia VA	Mt. Olivet
08518	Butler, Francesca S.	—	W	4 JAN 1912	Manila, P.I.	Rock Creek
05738	Butler, Grace M.	13y	C	9 SEP 1906	Philadelphia PA	Mt. Olivet
05012	Butler, Harriett Ann	73y	C	27 JAN 1905	Alexandria VA	Harmony
12666	Butler, Harry L.	42y	C	22 DEC 1914	Fairmont Hts. MD	Payne's
11817	Butler, Henry M.	57y	W	16 MAY 1913	Takoma Park MD	Columbus OH
14528	Butler, Hiram Pitts	28y	W	26 DEC 1917	Saranac Lake NY	Cremated
15783	Butler, Isaac	41y	C	18 MAY 1919	Baltimore MD	Mt. Hope MD
06328	Butler, Jennie	22y	C	8 DEC 1907	Philadelphia PA	Harmony
18181	Butler, John F.	46y	W	25 NOV 1922	Mt. Ranier MD	Mt. Olivet
01482	Butler, John, in jail	19y	C	3 SEP 1894	Philadelphia PA	Harmony
17391	Butler, John J.B.	32y	W	8 SEP 1921	Capitol Hts. MD	Mt. Olivet
07573	Butler, John Medford	1m	W	15 JUN 1910	Arundel on Bay	Glenwood
16556	Butler, Julia	65y	C	22 JUN 1920	Boston MA	Woodlawn
03934	Butler, Lemuel	29y	C	6 JUL 1902	Falls Church VA	Payne's
01535	Butler, Louisa	38y	C	15 JAN 1895	Philadelphia PA	Mt. Olivet
04246	Butler, Lydia S.	68y	W	10 APR 1903	Colesville MD	Oak Hill
13200	Butler, Margaret L.	15y	C	11 NOV 1915	Plainfield NJ	Mt. Olivet
17146	Butler, Martha	31y	C	4 MAY 1921	New York NY	Holyrood
13856	Butler, Mary	38y	C	8 DEC 1916	Chillum MD	Woodlawn
08043	Butler, Mary Sabina	41y	W	30 MAR 1911	Alexandria VA	Mt. Olivet
04624	Butler, Maud E.	24y	W	5 MAR 1904	Pittsburgh PA	Oak Hill
00541	Butler, Scott	6m	C	28 MAY 1891	Bethesda MD	Mt. Zion
06980	Butler, William H.	87y	C	11 APR 1909	Arlington VA	Holyrood
01680	Butt, Anna R.	68y	W	17 JUN 1895	Fairfax Co. VA	Rock Creek
03349	Butt, Samuel	79y	W	26 NOV 1900	Fairfax Co. VA	Rock Creek
16735	Butterfield, Francis	57y	W	21 OCT 1920	Palmers MD	Congressional
16386	Butterfield, Hart	50y	W	15 MAR 1920	Washington DC	Rock Creek
05924	Butterfield, Samuel J.	64y	W	1 FEB 1907	Forest Glen MD	Frederick MD
02367	Butterworth, Benjamin	60y	W	15 JAN 1898	Thomasville GA	Oak Hill
15361	Butterworth, Benjamin, Jr.	39y	W	18 FEB 1907	Washington DC	Rock Creek[1]

---

[1] Transportation premit from the village of Maineville, Warren Co. OH, dated 16 NOV 1918.

No.	Name of Deceased	Age	Race	Death Date	Place of Death	Place of Burial
15362	Butterworth, Benjamin, Sr.	61y	W	16 JAN 1898	Washington DC	Rock Creek[1]
12599	Butterworth, Mary V.	36y	W	6 NOV 1914	New York NY	Rock Creek
03836	Butts, Joseph W.	24y	W	27 MAR 1902	New York NY	Rock Creek
14639	Butts, Julius	49y	C	13 FEB 1918	Rosslyn VA	Mt. Zion East
14675	Butts, Margaret	45y	C	8 MAR 1918	Rosslyn VA	Mt. Zion East
12805	Buxmeyer, Nicholas	65y	W	8 MAR 1915	Brooklyn NY	Mt. Olivet
05906	Buyer, Frederick	79y	W	24 JAN 1907	Alex. Co. VA	Prospect Hill
00453	Buynitzky, Caroline, w/o S.N.	36y	W	22 FEB 1891	Takoma Park MD	Prospect Hill
01217	Byas, Frank	47y	C	19 SEP 1893	Rosslyn VA	Mt. Zion
02661	Byers, James F.	71y	W	22 NOV 1898	Baltimore MD	Congressional
12526	Byers, Mary A.	74y	W	11 SEP 1914	Baltimore MD	Congressional
13893	Byes, James	60y	C	26 DEC 1916	Newark NJ	Harmony
01681	Byk, Servia	65y	W	26 SEP 1895	Cleveland OH	Wash. Hebrew
06883	Byram, Elizabeth N. (Reed)	66y	W	5 JAN 1909	Gainesville VA	Rock Creek
12580	Byrd, Adeline	16y	C	23 OCT 1914	New York NY	Harmony
14222	Byrd, James	43y	C	8 JUL 1917	Detroit MI	Harmony
06477	Byrd, John H., s/o William	81y	W	19 MAR 1908	Onancock VA	Glenwood
13387	Byrd, Thomas	35y	C	27 FEB 1916	Rochester NY	Harmony
17164	Byrne, Ann Patricia	5m	W	16 MAY 1921	Cottage City MD	Mt. Olivet
12350	Byrne, Charles E.	49y	W	2 MAY 1914	Los Animas CO	Congressional
13739	Byrne, Charles F.	50y	W	29 SEP 1916	Roanoke VA	Mt. Olivet
18296	Byrne, Daniel Jameson	83y	W	25 JAN 1923	Takoma Park MD	Rock Creek
06695	Byrne, Ernest E.	16y	W	17 AUG 1908	Palmer MD	Auburn NY
17023	Byrne, Peter David	19y	W	6 MAR 1921	Halethorpe MD	Chicago IL
15393	Byrne, Theodore A., s/o Geo.	45y	W	29 NOV 1918	Charleston WV	Mt. Olivet
11934	Byrnes, Eugene A.	51y	W	1 AUG 1913	Brooklin ME	Glenwood
00573	Byrnes, James	32y	W	5 SEP 1891	Baltimore MD	Mt. Olivet
03424	Byrnes, James P.	36y	W	21 FEB 1901	Cabin John MD	Mt. Olivet
12537	Byrnes, William F.	67y	W	19 SEP 1914	Ware MA	Rock Creek
04162	Byron, James, merchant	60y	W	1 FEB 1903	Fredericksburg VA	Congressional

---

[1] Transportation premit from the village of Maineville, Warren Co. OH, dated 16 NOV 1918.

District of Columbia Foreign Death Records, 1888-1923

No.	Name of Deceased	Age	Race	Death Date	Place of Death	Place of Burial
C						
09015	Caball, Flora B.	80y	W	30 DEC 1912	Quincy IL	Quincy IL
13285	Cabaniss, Alberta (Nugent)	41y	C	5 JAN 1916	Jersey City NJ	Harmony
04387	Cabell, Bessie	28y	C	11 JUL 1903	Philadelphia PA	Harmony
17697	Caddington, Margaret Eliz.	2m	W	16 FEB 1922	Silver Spring MD	Congressional
05931	Cadle, Edward A.	63y	W	9 FEB 1907	Silver Spring MD	Rock Creek
16691	Cady, Infant of Benj. J.	SB	W	2 SEP 1920	Seat Pleasant MD	Mt. Olivet
00219	Cady, Lucinda	79y	W	15 JUN 1890	Shickshinney PA	Rock Creek
12193	Cady, Martin T.	—	W	30 JAN 1914	Portsmouth VA	Mt. Olivet
12282	Cady, Thomas P.	41y	W	28 MAR 1914	Baltimore MD	Holyrood
07832	Caffee, Arthur Gill	27y	W	19 NOV 1910	Indian Head MD	Arlington
03277	Cahill, Infant of Blanche	7m	W	28 AUG 1900	Leesburg VA	Mt. Olivet
01617	Cahill, James C., U.S. Marines	31y	W	8 MAR 1895	Kittery ME	Congressional
05773	Cahill, Nellie	40y	W	15 OCT 1906	Baltimore MD	Congressional
13235	Cahill, Patrick Francis	25y	W	5 DEC 1915	Indian Head MD	Worcester MA
05774	Cahill, Thomas F.	35y	W	15 SEP 1906	Portland OR	Mt. Olivet
16667	Cahoon, Clara H.	38y	W	17 AUG 1920	Seat Pleasant MD	Cedar Hill
00689	Cahoone, William James	58y	W	28 NOV 1891	Chicago IL	Oak Hill
08299	Cain, G. Russell, s/o J. Fendall	32y	W	5 SEP 1911	Sterling VA	Mt. Olivet
00220	Cain, John	29y	W	26 DEC 1889	Baltimore MD	Mt. Olivet
15536	Cala, Angelina	47y	W	8 JAN 1919	Hyattsville MD	Mt. Olivet
16509	Cala, Joseph	52y	W	30 MAY 1920	Hyattsville MD	Mt. Olivet
17519	Calburn, Rallison	78y	W	14 NOV 1921	Takoma Park MD	Rock Creek
09190	Calder, Ellen Maria O'Connor	83y	W	23 APR 1913	Providence RI	Oak Hill
01463	Caldwell, Alexander G.	48y	W	14 AUG 1894	Swan Creek MD	Tecumseh MI
02296	Caldwell, Cealyea A.	6m	W	3 JUL 1897	Falls Church VA	Rock Creek
17731	Caldwell, George Kearsley	42y	W	8 MAR 1922	Montclair NJ	Oak Hill
05297	Caldwell, Jesse B.	60y	W	23 AUG 1905	Palmyra WI	Rock Creek
01963	Caldwell, John W.	24y	W	23 AUG 1896	Baltimore MD	Congressional
04937	Caldwell, Mary Rose C.	47y	W	25 OCT 1904	Cambridge MA	Oak Hill
13965	Caldwell, Samuel Dion	69y	W	30 JAN 1917	Palm Beach FL	Oak Hill
04936	Caldwell, William M.	83y	W	20 OCT 1904	Belmont MA	Oak Hill
18036	Calhoon, Frank L.	52y	W	26 AUG 1922	Wash. Grove MD	Rock Creek
13652	Calhoun, Charles	2m	W	12 AUG 1916	Montg. Co. MD	Cremated
03719	Calhoun, Cornelia T.	74y	W	28 NOV 1901	Kensington MD	Rock Creek
07775	Calhoun, Phebe Halsey	63y	W	28 SEP 1910	Ellenville NY	Arlington
05606	Call, Caroline T.	50y	W	25 JUN 1906	New York NY	Oak Hill
11889	Call, Loren H.	25y	W	8 JUL 1913	Texas City TX	Arlington
02862	Callaghan, Honora	74y	W	14 JUL 1899	Chevy Chase MD	Carroll Chapel
01123	Callaghan, Margaret	60y	W	9 JAN 1893	Boston MA	Mt. Olivet
00018	Callan, Charles C.	47y	W	15 FEB 1889	New York NY	Mt. Olivet
07760	Callan, James	38y	W	22 SEP 1910	Newark NJ	Mt. Olivet
13292	Callan, Mathew	37y	W	9 JAN 1916	Connellsville PA	Mt. Olivet
00455	Callan, Nicholas	40y	W	4 APR 1891	New York NY	Mt. Olivet
06222	Calley, Abbet	5m	W	9 SEP 1907	Atlantic City NJ	Congressional
00574	Callinan, John M.	36y	W	18 OCT 1891	Norfolk VA	Mt. Olivet
17546	Callingback, Julia	65y	C	23 NOV 1921	Fairmont Hts. MD	Croome Sta. MD
16824	Callisher, Henry	55y	W	23 NOV 1920	New York NY	Wash. Hebrew
03576	Calloway, Ruth	7m	C	13 JUL 1901	Harpers Ferry WV	Cremated
14424	Callum, Robert G.	62y	W	22 OCT 1917	Baltimore MD	Oak Hill
03468	Calver, James V.	61y	W	2 APR 1901	Orlando FL	Rock Creek
04334	Calver, W. Irving	35y	W	10 AUG 1903	Denver CO	Rock Creek
16045	Calvert, Ada	25y	W	12 OCT 1919	Washington DC	Glenwood
14539	Calvert, Annie T.	72y	W	31 DEC 1917	Bridgeport CN	Rock Creek
05715	Calvert, Charles Baltimore	63y	W	31 AUG 1906	Mackalpine MD	Rock Creek
13606	Calvert, Charles P., Jr.	15y	W	19 AUG 1915	Ogden UT	Rock Creek
15964	Calvert, Donna Wynona	21y	W	24 AUG 1919	Ogden UT	Rock Creek
14026	Calvert, Jennie G.	42y	W	5 MAR 1917	Ogden UT	Rock Creek
13625	Calvert, Josephine	1y	W	23 JUL 1916	Chevy Chase MD	Cremated

No.	Name of Deceased	Age	Race	Death Date	Place of Death	Place of Burial
02108	Calvert, Margaret F.	70y	W	17 JAN 1897	Brentsville MD	Glenwood
16000	Calvert, Mary Virginia	14h	W	21 SEP 1919	Mt. Ranier MD	Glenwood
01026	Cameron, Eugene	42y	W	6 FEB 1893	Wheeling WV	Glenwood
07394	Cameron, John	52y	W	29 JAN 1910	Huntsville MD	Glenwood
07963	Cameron, Robert Allen	18m	W	23 AUG 1897	Seat Pleasant MD	Glenwood
05269	Camp, Elizabeth J.	80y	W	4 SEP 1905	Arlington VA	Rock Creek
08673	Camp, Richard W.	66y	W	14 JUN 1912	Crossette AR	Rock Creek
12559	Camp, Susie Filmore	41y	W	6 OCT 1914	Chevy Chase MD	Rock Creek
18492	Campagna, Iony	27d	W	20 APR 1923	Capitol Hts. MD	Mt. Olivet
13085	Campbell, Adelaide A.	62y	W	31 AUG 1915	Laurel MD	Glenwood
13555	Campbell, Agnes Stevens	37y	W	12 JUN 1916	E. Woodford VA	Oak Hill
05320	Campbell, Alexander	75y	W	19 OCT 1905	Pittsburgh PA	Soldier's Home
15391	Campbell, Benedict F.	40y	W	26 NOV 1918	Denver CO	Rock Creek
07646	Campbell, Bertha	30y	C	19 JUL 1910	Philadelphia PA	Payne's
08826	Campbell, Bessie C.	39y	W	5 SEP 1912	Chicago IL	Arlington VA
00927	Campbell, Charles E.	22y	W	23 APR 1874	Laurel MD	Rock Creek
12616	Campbell, Edward Lee	3y	W	14 NOV 1914	New York NY	Prospect Hill
13273	Campbell, Estella	45y	C	26 DEC 1915	Pittsburgh PA	Harmony
07351	Campbell, Eugene	32y	C	31 DEC 1909	Hyattsville MD	Harmony
16594	Campbell, Frances R.	23y	W	12 JUL 1920	Chesnut Hill PA	Rock Creek
03551	Campbell, Harry	22y	C	24 JUN 1901	Philadelphia PA	Harmony
04217	Campbell, Hugh A.	33y	W	10 MAR 1903	Catonsville MD	Glenwood
16562	Campbell, Lillian	37y	C	25 JUN 1920	Saranac Lake NY	Harmony
00929	Campbell, Louis	21y	W	NOV 1878	Laurel MD	Rock Creek
00928	Campbell, Louise E.	42y	W	15 APR 1873	Laurel MD	Rock Creek
14927	Campbell, Mary	58y	W	20 JUL 1918	Philadelphia PA	Rock Creek
17860	Campbell, Mary A.	63y	W	15 MAY 1922	Potomac VA	Mt. Olivet
06677	Campbell, Mary J.	54y	W	7 AUG 1908	New York NY	Mt. Olivet
01373	Campbell, Mary Jane	23y	W	23 MAY 1894	Ft. Foote MD	Glenwood
00456	Campbell, Patrick	38y	W	24 DEC 1890	Durango CO	Mt. Olivet
00926	Campbell, Rebecca Jane	70y	W	17 AUG 1893	Brooklyn NY	Mt. Olivet
16206	Campbell, Ruth	35y	W	10 JAN 1920	Atlantic City NJ	Rock Creek
03520	Campbell, Sarah Penniman	58y	W	24 MAY 1901	Takoma Park MD	Glenwood
02629	Campbell, Sarah R.	67y	W	13 OCT 1898	Philadelphia PA	Congressional
05822	Campbell, Sophia (McCann)	73y	W	17 NOV 1906	Cherrydale VA	Congressional
16797	Campbell, Thomas	21y	C	5 NOV 1920	Wilmington DE	Colonial Bea. VA
14894	Campbell, Thomas	49y	W	2 JUL 1918	New York NY	Mt. Olivet
18437	Campbell, Winifred M.	48y	—	21 MAR 1921	Newark NJ	Glenwood
04920	Camper, Georgia	38y	C	13 OCT 1904	Newark NJ	Harmony
06545	Canada, Van B.	49y	W	MAY 1908	Glymont MD	Culpeper VA
14695	Canady, Henry	55y	C	18 MAR 1918	Silver Hill MD	Payne's
15095	Canboer, Peter B. [Caanboer]	44y	W	4 OCT 1918	Schenectady NY	Arlington
07176	Candler, Bettie Elizabeth	70y	W	27 AUG 1909	Cherrydale VA	Congressional
08433	Candler, George Vinton, s/o W.	48y	W	21 DEC 1911	Cherrydale VA	Congressional
15144	Candora, Lewis	33y	W	11 OCT 1918	Capitol Hts. MD	Mt. Olivet
06405	Candy, Sarah M.	76y	W	24 JAN 1908	Dayton OH	Arlington
15551	Canning, Lawrence	27y	W	13 JAN 1919	At Sea	Philadelphia PA
07417	Cannon, Emily Jane (Beach)	71y	W	11 FEB 1910	Colchester VA	Congressional
14406	Cannon, Julia	75y	W	13 OCT 1917	Mt. Ranier MD	Norfolk VA
14904	Cannon, Patrick T.	34y	W	6 JUL 1918	Springfield IL	Mt. Olivet
02807	Cannon, William Minor	85y	W	24 APR 1899	Sideburn VA	Congressional
14873	Canter, Mary F.	7m	W	21 JUN 1918	Brown's Sta. MD	Mt. Olivet
04275	Canty, John	45y	W	19 APR 1903	Mingo OH	Mt. Olivet
04982	Capehart, B. Ashbourne	39y	W	20 DEC 1904	New York NY	Oak Hill
01796	Capehart, Henry	70y	W	15 APR 1895	Minneapolis MN	Arlington
12884	Caperton, Hugh	60y	W	18 APR 1915	Baltimore MD	Holyrood
05256	Caperton, James M.	61y	W	22 AUG 1905	Baltimore MD	Holyrood
17940	Capner, Harriett Ella	59y	W	6 JUL 1922	Ballston VA	Glenwood
02494	Capron, Allyn	27y	W	24 JUN 1898	Siboney, Cuba	Arlington

District of Columbia Foreign Death Records, 1888-1923

No.	Name of Deceased	Age	Race	Death Date	Place of Death	Place of Burial
00930	Capron, George	13y	W	15 JUN 1893	Ft. Sheridan IL	Oak Hill
02151	Capron, James	22y	W	12 MAR 1897	Plattsburgh NY	Oak Hill
14501	Caputo, Joseph	3y	W	13 DEC 1917	Hyattsville MD	Mt. Olivet
18422	Caranfa, Diana	30y	W	22 MAY 1922	Darby PA	Mt. Olivet
09092	Carbo, Luis Felipe	53y	W	25 FEB 1913	New York NY	Rock Creek
18438	Cardoza, Laura J.W.	83y	C	22 MAR 1923	Fairmont Hts. MD	Woodlawn
17878	Carey, Albert	49y	C	18 MAY 1922	Pittsburgh PA	Payne's
11807	Carey, Arthur	28y	C	6 MAY 1913	Philadelphia PA	Gum Springs VA
16739	Carey, Eleanor Cubert	53y	W	5 OCT 1920	College Park MD	Rock Creek
07524	Carey, Henry	22y	C	2 MAY 1910	New York NY	Payne's
02968	Carey, Isabella	3y	C	5 OCT 1899	Rosslyn VA	Mt. Zion
06453	Carey, Isabella	34y	C	29 FEB 1908	New York NY	Payne's
06699	Carey, John W.	10y	C	16 AUG 1908	Columbus OH	Mt. Zion West
12508	Carey, Walter Holmes	1m	W	1 SEP 1914	Chevy Chase MD	Mt. Olivet
07813	Carl, Mary Ellen	57y	W	1 NOV 1910	Capitol Hts. MD	Glenwood
06717	Carlin, Elizabeth	4h	W	7 SEP 1908	Baltimore MD	Mt. Olivet
03217	Carlin, Harvey	8m	W	28 JUN 1900	Colonial Bea. VA	Mt. Olivet
03434	Carlin, William H.F.	75y	W	28 FEB 1901	Glen Carlin VA	Oak Hill
03649	Carlisle, Calderon	49y	W	16 SEP 1901	Asheville NC	Rock Creek
12362	Carlisle, Frederick W.	46y	W	15 MAY 1914	Elizabeth NJ	Rock Creek
07664	Carlisle, John G.	74y	W	31 JUL 1910	New York NY	Rock Creek
06620	Carlisle, Mary Catherine	28y	W	29 JUN 1908	Takoma Park MD	Mt. Olivet
00457	Carlton, Anne W.	—	W	2 APR 1891	Easton MD	Oak Hill
13629	Carman, Ada S. (Salmon)	78y	W	22 JUL 1916	Los Angeles CA	Arlington
11898	Carman, Leo	1y	W	15 JUL 1913	Brentwood MD	Mt. Olivet
17434	Carmick, Melvina Grandin	72y	W	27 SEP 1921	Lansborough NY	Glenwood
05971	Carmine, Joseph W.	30y	C	3 MAR 1907	Philadelphia PA	Harmony
17107	Carmody, Francis S.	82y	W	15 APR 1921	Providence Hosp.	Mt. Olivet
14032	Carmody, John R.	73y	W	17 MAR 1917	Palham NY	Arlington
06562	Carmody, Mary E.	58y	W	24 MAY 1908	Atlantic City NJ	Arlington
06866	Carmody, Thomas	49y	W	21 DEC 1908	Denver CO	Mt. Olivet
04628	Carnahan, Earl Clark	—	W	26 JUL 1902	Dagupan, P.I.	Arlington
07304	Carnes, John H.	50y	W	3 DEC 1909	Baltimore Co. MD	St. Mary's
18047	Caroso, Antonio A.	64y	W	3 SEP 1922	Capitol Hts. MD	St. Mary's
02193	Carothers, Eleanor Ann	78y	W	24 FEB 1897	Sacra. Co. CA	Oak Hill
12468	Carozzi, G. Napoleon	73y	W	19 DEC 1913	Washington DC	Mt. Olivet
02675	Carpenter, Albert	31y	C	11 DEC 1898	Burrsville MD	Woodlawn
18382	Carpenter, Elizabeth	31y	W	3 MAR 1923	Chevy Chase MD	Rock Creek
16298	Carpenter, Ida S.	44y	W	8 FEB 1920	Baltimore MD	Rock Creek
01536	Carpenter, Margaret D.M.	76y	—	21 JAN 1895	Baltimore MD	—
12200	Carpenter, Rachel J.	71y	W	4 FEB 1914	Poolesville MD	Congressional
14766	Carpenter, Robert J.	35y	C	19 APR 1918	Philadelphia PA	Woodlawn
04444	Carpenter, Rufus Daniel	58y	W	9 SEP 1903	Atlanta GA	Rock Creek
15878	Carr, Catherine Frances	56y	W	12 JUL 1919	Bloomfield NJ	Mt. Olivet
15402	Carr, Charles F.	47y	W	4 DEC 1918	Hyattsville MD	Congressional
09138	Carr, Edward	64y	W	20 MAR 1913	Baltimore MD	Congressional
02863	Carr, Elizabeth	84y	W	18 JUL 1899	Westminster MD	Oak Hill
17887	Carr, F. James	22y	C	2 JUN 1922	Philadelphia PA	Harmony
17821	Carr, Francis Quigley	26y	W	7 OCT 1918	France	Mt. Olivet
15604	Carr, George W., s/o John	65y	W	6 FEB 1919	Smyrna GA	Arlington
01429	Carr, J.L. Don. M.	13y	W	9 JUL 1894	Piney Point MD	Mt. Olivet
14164	Carr, Mable M.	22y	C	8 JUN 1917	Charlotte NC	Woodlawn
04346	Carr, Margaret L.	51y	W	8 AUG 1903	Harrisonburg VA	Glenwood
07068	Carr, Mary E.	71y	W	19 JUN 1909	Baltimore MD	Congressional
01398	Carr, Nelson C., plumber	45y	W	19 JUN 1894	Arlington VA	Rock Creek
16320	Carr, Robert Ellingworth	51y	W	15 FEB 1920	Mt. Dora FL	Glenwood
00575	Carr, Rosa Lee Zoda	15y	C	28 SEP 1891	Brooklyn NY	Harmony
12634	Carr, Ruth R.J. (Fisher)	59y	C	26 NOV 1914	Danville VA	Harmony
16422	Carr, Thomas	43y	W	4 APR 1920	Johnson City TN	Holyrood

No.	Name of Deceased	Age	Race	Death Date	Place of Death	Place of Burial
04504	Carr, William H.	67y	W	9 NOV 1903	Clarendon VA	Glenwood
17450	Carrado, Mincio	6m	W	4 OCT 1921	Brentwood MD	Mt. Olivet
04215	Carrall, J.	—	W	—	New Orleans LA	Glenwood
14414	Carrick, Charles I., Rev.	25y	W	16 OCT 1917	Plainfield NJ	Mt. Olivet
08770	Carrick, Edmund	75y	C	17 AUG 1912	New York NY	Mt. Zion East
17292	Carrick, Mary	22y	W	6 JUL 1921	Geo. Wash. Hp.	Mt. Olivet
03175	Carrigan, Mary A.	27y	W	29 APR 1900	New York NY	Congressional
14750	Carrigan, Peter	28y	W	12 APR 1918	New Castle PA	Prospect Hill
01854	Carrington, Marie Antoinette	66y	W	26 JAN 1896	Charlton Hts. MD	Rock Creek
04491	Carrol, Benjamin	27y	C	28 OCT 1903	Bladensburg MD	Mt. Olivet
02152	Carrol, Ella	18y	W	15 APR 1897	Lancaster PA	Congressional
08065	Carrol, Thomas	68y	C	13 APR 1911	Bladensburg MD	Harmony
12897	Carroll, Ada	31y	W	23 APR 1915	Cincinnati OH	Glenwood
04403	Carroll, Ann	65y	C	22 JUL 1903	Bladensburg MD	Woodlawn
12644	Carroll, Catherine	11y	C	4 DEC 1914	Markham VA	Woodlawn
03360	Carroll, Charles O.	82y	W	6 DEC 1900	College Park MD	Glenwood
14716	Carroll, David	51y	C	24 MAR 1918	Philadelphia PA	Woodlawn
07156	Carroll, Dennis	23y	C	8 AUG 1909	Philadelphia PA	Mt. Zion East
07680	Carroll, Ethel	16y	C	8 AUG 1910	Baltimore MD	Harmony
07919	Carroll, Flora	69y	C	10 JAN 1911	New York NY	Harmony
17363	Carroll, Francis deSales	54y	W	21 AUG 1921	Takoma Park MD	Mt. Olivet
14161	Carroll, Guy L.	2m	W	6 JUN 1917	Hyattsville MD	Mt. Olivet
03002	Carroll, J. Jerome	35y	W	5 NOV 1899	New York NY	Mt. Olivet
13029	Carroll, Kate	47y	W	1 AUG 1915	Clinton MD	Congressional
00153	Carroll, Margarett	50y	W	22 SEP 1889	Montg. Co. MD	Rock Creek
11818	Carroll, Martha	46y	C	13 MAY 1913	Pittsburgh PA	Harmony
08081	Carroll, Martha A.	74y	W	25 APR 1911	Gaithersburg MD	Oak Hill
18151	Carroll, Mary	31y	C	6 NOV 1922	Crownsville MD	Cremated
14668	Carroll, Mary	74y	W	4 MAR 1918	Baltimore MD	Mt. Olivet
16123	Carroll, Mary	64y	C	20 NOV 1919	Takoma Park MD	Payne's
16126	Carroll, Mary E.	32y	C	24 NOV 1919	New York NY	Mt. Olivet
07435	Carroll, Mary L.	31y	W	28 DEC 1909	New York NY	Mt. Olivet
13260	Carroll, Odean	12y	C	19 DEC 1915	Baltiomre MD	Payne's
09009	Carroll, Owen C.	33y	W	1 JAN 1913	Baltimore MD	Mt. Olivet
05905	Carroll, Philip	49y	W	14 DEC 1907	Manzanillo, Mex.	Arlington
15036	Carroll, Samual	16y	C	21 SEP 1918	Alex. Co. VA	Harmony
03681	Carroll, Samuel C.	57y	C	10 OCT 1901	Pittsburgh PA	Harmony
03366	Carroll, Susan H.	67y	W	2 FEB 1889	Riverdale MD	Glenwood
09123	Carroll, William Henry	16d	W	11 MAR 1913	Arlington VA	Holyrood
04724	Carry, Amanda	29y	W	7 MAY 1904	Baltimore MD	Congressional
01027	Carry, John	2y	W	25 AUG 1881	Cincinnati OH	Mt. Olivel
01028	Carry, Pauline	5y	W	20 AUG 1881	Cincinnati OH	Mt. Olivet
17572	Carson, Ellen	64y	W	5 DEC 1921	New York NY	Glenwood
08858	Carson, John M.	74y	W	29 SEP 1912	Philadelphia PA	Arlington
03212	Carson, John Miller	1y	W	7 MAY 1900	Denver CO	Rock Creek
02853	Carson, Sarah J.	67y	W	15 JUN 1899	Burke's Sta. VA	Rock Creek
17862	Carstens, Nicholas K.	32y	W	14 MAY 1922	Benedict MD	Arlington
12510	Cart, Margaret	56y	W	2 SEP 1914	Mt. Hope MD	Mt. Olivet
05440	Carter, Amanda	58y	C	24 JAN 1906	Chicago IL	Harmony
16234	Carter, Channing	19y	W	20 JAN 1920	Swarthmore PA	Rock Creek
07541	Carter, Charles	28y	C	11 MAY 1910	Philadelphia PA	Mt. Olivet
07804	Carter, Charley, s/o Abraham	9y	C	27 OCT 1810	Ft. Runyon VA	Harmony
08120	Carter, Charlotte F.	24y	C	12 MAY 1911	Newark NJ	Mt. Olivet
13010	Carter, Cordelia Stansbury	73y	W	16 JUL 1915	Perth Amboy NJ	Oak Hill
17826	Carter, Dorsey	23y	C	31 APR 1922	Baltimore MD	Arlington
15076	Carter, Edward	26y	C	30 SEP 1918	Camp Lee VA	Mt. Zion East
16775	Carter, Edward L.	34y	W	22 OCT 1920	Saranac Lake NY	Rock Creek
14165	Carter, Edward T.	40y	W	9 JUN 1917	Philadelphia PA	Glenwood
07995	Carter, Elizabeth	41y	C	3 MAR 1911	Rock Spring MD	Baptist

District of Columbia Foreign Death Records, 1888-1923   43

No.	Name of Deceased	Age	Race	Death Date	Place of Death	Place of Burial
13918	Carter, Ellen	69y	C	9 JAN 1917	Rosslyn VA	Union Baptist
15154	Carter, Ethel E.	34y	W	12 OCT 1918	Maywood VA	Rock Creek
16999	Carter, Eugene	6m	C	26 FEB 1921	Cedar Hts. MD	Payne's
17784	Carter, Forence	42y	C	4 APR 1922	New York NY	Mt. Olivet
12962	Carter, Frances A.	24y	C	11 JUN 1915	Philadelphia PA	Mt. Olivet
00327	Carter, Frank	2y	W	20 MAY 1890	Montg. Co. MD	Washington DC
07911	Carter, George	22y	C	5 JAN 1911	Philadelphia PA	Mt. Zion West
14305	Carter, George W.	28y	C	16 AUG 1917	Mattawoman MD	Woodlawn
04733	Carter, Georgiana	50y	C	24 MAY 1904	Brick Haven VA	Woodlawn
07111	Carter, Grace	37y	C	15 JUL 1909	New York NY	Woodlawn
02754	Carter, Hattie	26y	C	28 FEB 1899	Philadelphia PA	Woodlawn
08771	Carter, Helen	27y	W	18 AUG 1912	New York NY	Alexandria VA
14299	Carter, Helen C. Hunter	29y	W	12 AUG 1917	Albuquerque NM	Arlington
14241	Carter, Helen E.	1y	C	20 JUL 1917	Hyattsville MD	Bushwood MD
03308	Carter, Henry	27y	C	18 OCT 1900	Baltimore MD	Harmony
04402	Carter, Henry L.	37y	W	21 JUL 1903	New York NY	Oak Hill
12061	Carter, Isabella	54y	C	23 OCT 1913	Philadelphia PA	Mt. Zion East
06799	Carter, Isabelle	4m	C	2 NOV 1098	Fairmont Hts. MD	Harmony
07019	Carter, Jessie E. (Anderson)	40y	W	9 MAY 1909	Alex. Co. VA	Rock Creek
07592	Carter, John	31y	C	23 JUN 1910	Front Royal VA	Harmony
13762	Carter, John F., Jr.	28y	W	11 OCT 1916	W. Palm Bea. FL	Glenwood
07478	Carter, John W.	48y	C	19 MAR 1910	Utica NY	Harmony
14573	Carter, Joseph	78y	W	13 JAN 1918	Knoxville PA	Mt. Olivet
13967	Carter, Lavania	59y	C	3 FEB 1917	Cartersville VA	Mt. Zion West
06212	Carter, Leigh H.	22y	W	27 AUG 1907	Urbana IL	Arlington VA
02769	Carter, Lucy	67y	C	15 MAR 1899	Richmond VA	Harmony
08536	Carter, Lucy A.	35y	C	27 FEB 1912	Boston MA	Woodlawn
03179	Carter, Luke	86y	C	1 MAY 1900	Arlington VA	Mt. Zion
16485	Carter, Mary	60y	C	13 MAY 1920	Arlington VA	Harmony
00931	Carter, Mary E.	62y	C	7 JUN 1893	Brooklyn NY	Harmony
05855	Carter, Mary M.	66y	W	7 DEC 1906	Leland FL	Arlington
07300	Carter, Mary Pitman	44y	W	15 MAY 1909	Washington DC	Congressional
14949	Carter, Nathaniel	35y	C	1 AUG 1918	Occoquan VA	Payne's
15175	Carter, Nellie S.	26y	C	13 OCT 1918	Cumberland MD	Harmony
02633	Carter, Rachael	70-80y	C	15 OCT 1898	Alex. Co. VA	Mt. Olivet
00813	Carter, Richard	40y	C	21 SEP 1892	Alexandria VA	Harmony
00393	Carter, Richard	6m	—	24 AUG 1890	Atlantic City NJ	Washington DC
16644	Carter, Richard	65y	W	6 AUG 1920	Arlington Co. VA	Woodlawn
00221	Carter, Richard R.	33y	C	1 NOV 1889	Buffalo NY	Harmony
08010	Carter, Silas	38y	C	13 MAR 1911	New York NY	Mt. Olivet
18491	Carter, William Golden	53y	W	19 APR 1923	Chevy Chase MD	Rock Creek
09027	Carter, William H.	22y	W	30 DEC 1912	Chicago IL	Payne's
12208	Carter, William H., s/o Jos.	29y	C	3 FEB 1914	Occoquan VA	Payne's
05916	Carter, William J.	39y	W	27 JAN 1907	Asheville NC	Congressional
18424	Carter, William S.	64y	W	15 MAR 1923	Baltimore MD	Glenwood
15403	Cartmell, Emma Eliza	51y	W	4 DEC 1918	Takoma MD	Springfield OH
03232	Cartwright, Levin T.	69y	W	9 JUL 1900	College Park MD	Oak Hill
02192	Cartwright, Lucy	75y	W	—	St. Mary's Co. MD	Rock Creek
06693	Cartwright, Sarah M.	54y	W	16 AUG 1908	Takoma Park MD	Rock Creek
04303	Cartwright, William A.	27y	W	15 MAR 1900	San Antonio TX	Glenwood
12129	Caruthers, Bertha Surgey	37y	W	17 DEC 1913	Riverdale MD	Congressional
14347	Caruthers, Hannah	58y	C	8 SEP 1917	Branchville MD	Harmony
07082	Carver, Joseph C.	5½m	W	26 JUN 1909	Mt. Ranier MD	Mt. Olivet
17080	Carver, Wilburn R.	61y	W	29 MAR 1921	Takoma Park MD	Oak Hill
03974	Cary, Charles C.	22y	W	12 AUG 1902	Ft. Myer VA	Baltimore MD
03034	Case, Ada B.	21y	W	11 DEC 1899	Baltimore MD	Congressional
06842	Case, Ida L.	65y	W	3 DEC 1908	Denver CO	Congressional
08187	Case, Willis W.	66y	W	5 JUL 1911	Denver CO	Congressional
16819	Casey, Anastasia	49y	W	21 NOV 1920	Hoboken NY	Mt. Olivet

No.	Name of Deceased	Age	Race	Death Date	Place of Death	Place of Burial
08409	Casey, Edward	72y	W	3 DEC 1911	Kensington MD	Soldier's Home
14903	Casey, Frank, s/o John	39y	W	5 JUL 1918	Atlantic City NJ	Congressional
12894	Casey, Hannah	35y	W	24 APR 1915	Camp Springs MD	Mt. Olivet
02297	Casey, J.D.	60y	W	30 SEP 1897	Bladensburg MD	Mt. Olivet
05778	Casey, John J.	70y	W	17 OCT 1906	Hoboken NJ	Mt. Olivet
01964	Casey, Mary	60y	W	6 AUG 1896	Jersey City NJ	Mt. Olivet
12025	Casey, Silas	71y	W	14 AUG 1913	Hot Springs VA	Arlington VA
18000	Casey, Sophia Gray Heberton	79y	W	8 AUG 1922	Warm Spgs. VA	Arlington
01342	Casey, Stephen	26y	W	27 MAR 1894	Baltimore MD	Mt. Olivet
08756	Casilear, George W., s/o F.A.	87y	W	7 AUG 1912	Charlottesville VA	Oak Hill
13701	Casilear, Jane C. (Carmichael)	77y	W	6 SEP 1916	Charlottesville VA	Oak Hill
13465	Casinadri, Lena	1y	W	18 APR 1916	Seat Pleasant MD	Mt. Olivet
15385	Caskey, Gardner L.	32y	W	2 NOV 1918	Bereford, Ire.	Arlington
16379	Caskey, Henrietta Hydrick	37y	W	12 MAR 1920	Columbia SC	Arlington
15468	Cason, Susan Mary	73y	W	21 DEC 1918	Chevy Chase MD	Rock Creek
04851	Caspar, John	45y	W	15 AUG 1904	Chicago IL	Mt. Olivet
16432	Cassell, Broders A.	1m	W	12 APR 1920	Mt. Ranier MD	Mt. Olivet
06572	Cassidy, Inez	40y	W	30 MAY 1908	New York NY	Oak Hill
07419	Cassidy, Vesta Harvey	48y	W	14 FEB 1910	Boston MA	Rock Creek
08572	Cassidy, Wm. C., s/o Chas. P.	9m	W	28 MAR 1912	Burke VA	Rock Creek
15578	Cassin, E. Schley	55y	W	23 JAN 1919	Laurel MD	Frederick MD
12887	Castell, George C.	72y	W	20 APR 1915	Fairfax C.H. VA	Mt. Olivet
04026	Castell, John H.	56y	W	26 SEP 1902	Richmond VA	Congressional
15956	Castle, Guy Wilkinson Stuart	40y	W	10 AUG 1919	At Sea	Arlington
06243	Castle, Marion F.	30y	W	23 SEP 1907	Atlantic City NJ	Glenwood
00272	Castleman, Henrietta B.	35y	—	18 JAN 1890	Alexandria VA	Oak Hill
11900	Castleman, Stephen D.	47y	W	15 JUL 1913	Hyattsville MD	Oak Hill
00814	Caswell, Annie	21y	W	20 JUN 1891	Horse Head MD	Congressional
13415	Cate, Clara	81y	W	15 MAR 1916	Peru NY	Rock Creek
01297	Cate, F. Cortez	67y	W	3 AUG 1893	Peru NY	Graceland
08734	Cater, Joseph T.	75y	W	25 JUL 1912	Martinsville IN	Rock Creek
13787	Cathcart, Amy E.	57y	W	28 OCT 1916	Ballston VA	Glenwood
12892	Cathcart, Annie R.	86y	W	22 APR 1915	Ballston VA	Glenwood
03807	Cathcart, Ethel May	14y	W	28 FEB 1902	Philadelphia PA	Glenwood
14681	Cathcart, Ophelia	28y	C	11 MAR 1918	New York NY	Harmony
06767	Catlett, Walter	27y	C	9 OCT 1908	Philadelphia PA	Payne's
02242	Catlette, Edward	20y	C	28 JUL 1897	Bucks Co. PA	Payne's
16615	Catlin, Mary E.	88y	W	19 JUL 1920	Franklin NH	Rock Creek
18450	Catlin, Mary S.	83y	W	30 MAR 1923	New York NY	Soldier's Home
04958	Caton, George W.	34y	W	15 NOV 1904	Rosslyn VA	Glenwood
09044	Caton, Ruth E.	78y	W	20 JAN 1913	Rosslyn VA	Glenwood
00154	Caton, Susie B.	20y	W	17 SEP 1889	Purcellville VA	Rock Creek
00123	Caton, Virginia C.	24y	W	17 AUG 1889	Avenel MD	Patterson's Cr. VA
02241	Cattaggini, Tullier	13y	W	18 AUG 1897	Baltimore Co. MD	Mt. Olivet
16210	Catts, Jennie M.	45y	W	12 JAN 1920	Georgetown DC	Mt. Olivet
14625	Catts, John S.	75y	W	4 FEB 1918	Capitol Hts. MD	Congressional
15060	Cauffman, Joel F., s/o Lewis	74y	W	1 OCT 1918	Colonial Bea. VA	Congressional
07398	Caughy, Walker S.	54y	W	2 FEB 1910	Baltimore MD	Baltimore MD
12555	Cavanagh, Michael I.	40y	W	6 OCT 1914	Woodhaven, L.I.	Mt. Olivet
04432	Cavanaugh, Aloysius T.	26y	W	2 SEP 1903	Baltimore MD	Mt. Olivet
05572	Cavanaugh, Francis M.	23y	W	10 MAY 1906	Wash. Grove MD	Mt. Olivet
07234	Cavanaugh, Josephine	45y	W	14 OCT 1909	Frostburg MD	Mt. Olivet
15887	Cavenaugh, Harry G., Col.	75y	W	18 JUL 1919	Wilmington DE	Arlington
07503	Cavenaugh, Leo	30y	W	15 APR 1910	Santa Fe NM	Mt. Olivet
09101	Caverly, Edward	68y	W	1 MAR 1913	Orange NJ	Rock Creek
03626	Cavers, Adam	70y	W	11 MAY 1901	Bournem'th, Eng.	Oak Hill
16338	Cavis, Sarah A.	79y	W	23 FEB 1920	Nyack NY	Glenwood
06072	Caynor, Alice E.	60y	W	18 MAY 1907	Baltimore MD	Glenwood
06321	Cephas, Baylus H.	25y	C	21 NOV 1907	Alexandria VA	Harmony

District of Columbia Foreign Death Records, 1888-1923

No.	Name of Deceased	Age	Race	Death Date	Place of Death	Place of Burial
13016	Cephas, Carrie E.	39y	C	17 JUL 1915	Boston MA	Harmony
02490	Cephas, Daniel D.	6m	C	31 JUL 1898	Alex. Co. VA	Baptist
12449	Cerrone, Flora	9m	W	19 JUL 1914	Mt. Ranier MD	St. Mary's
16523	Cevola, Gabriel	1y	W	30 MAY 1920	New York NY	St. Mary's
12845	Chadrey, Helen C.	73y	W	30 MAR 1915	Railroad	Rochester NY
12600	Chaffee, Adna R.	72y	W	1 NOV 1914	Los Angeles CA	Arlington
04366	Chaffel, Della	76y	W	26 JUN 1903	Philadelphia PA	Rock Creek
06856	Chamberlain, David W.	62y	W	17 DEC 1908	Riverdale MD	Glenwood
06341	Chamberlain, Georgianna Fr.	58y	W	4 DEC 1907	Hyattsville MD	Rock Creek
15546	Chamberlain, Henry C., s/o J.	46y	W	11 JAN 1919	Richmond VA	Rock Creek
15410	Chamberlain, John A.	32y	W	5 DEC 1918	Camp Meade MD	Mt. Olivet
14914	Chamberlain, Mason	14y	W	13 JUL 1918	Burnt Mills MD	Bethesda MD
07724	Chamberlain, Patrick	75y	W	30 AUG 1910	Chicago IL	Mt. Olivet
14888	Chamberlain, Ryland L.	16y	W	28 JUN 1918	Friendship H. MD	Prospect Hill
03667	Chamberlin, Edward H.	59y	W	23 SEP 1891	Phoenix AZ	Rock Creek
18317	Chamberlin, George Rich.	48y	W	30 JAN 1923	Albuquerque NM	Rock Creek
06862	Chambers, Benjamin, s/o Benj.	67y	W	19 DEC 1908	Lodge VA	Oak Hill
06204	Chambers, Emmet B.	72y	W	14 AUG 1907	Los Angeles CA	Arlington VA
15868	Chambers, Hester Ann	68y	C	6 JUL 1919	Fairmont Hts. MD	Woodlawn
05167	Chambers, Manerva	82y	W	12 JUN 1905	Anne Arundel Co.	Congressional
02608	Chambers, Nellie	30y	C	27 SEP 1898	Norfolk VA	Mt. Zion
02369	Chambers, Walter B.	33y	W	8 JAN 1898	Baltimore MD	Oak Hill
16897	Chambers, William H.	48y	W	18 DEC 1920	France	Baltimore MD
00815	Chamblan, Minor Fur	36y	W	5 AUG 1892	Falls Church VA	Glenwood
13418	Champion, Mary D.	43y	W	18 MAR 1916	Hunter's Sta. VA	Congressional
00576	Chandlee, John F.	27y	W	27 JUL 1891	York PA	Glenwood
12548	Chaney, James	72y	W	30 SEP 1914	Mt. Ranier MD	Arlington
00250	Chaney, Leona M.	43y	W	26 DEC 1889	Takoma Park MD	Rock Creek
13396	Chaney, Richard	55y	C	2 MAR 1916	Laurel MD	Mt. Zion West
14452	Chapin, Byron A.	64y	W	11 NOV 1917	Kensington MD	Glenwood
15029	Chapin, Nellie	59y	W	16 SEP 1918	New York NY	Glenwood
05228	Chapin, Stephen E.	52y	W	4 AUG 1905	Thoroughfare Gap	Congressional
00932	Chapman, Annie R.	22y	W	29 JUL 1893	Stanardsv. VA	Mt. Olivet
05864	Chapman, Augusta F.	48y	W	23 NOV 1906	Philadelphia PA	Glenwood
09152	Chapman, Camillas	35y	C	1 APR 1913	Bethesda MD	Mt. Olivet
02850	Chapman, Charles Lewis	40y	W	14 APR 1866	Baltimore MD	Mt. Olivet
03917	Chapman, Clarence F.	35y	W	15 JUN 1902	Clarksburg WV	Mt. Olivet
14046	Chapman, George H.	49y	C	21 MAR 1917	York PA	Harmony
08047	Chapman, Katherine	76y	W	31 MAR 1911	Roslyn NY	Mt. Olivet
14636	Chapman, Martha	32y	C	10 FEB 1918	Philadelphia PA	Harmony
11859	Chapman, Nellie A.H.	38y	W	21 JUN 1913	Gaithersburg MD	Glenwood
16205	Chapman, Robert H.	51y	W	11 JAN 1920	Manhattan NY	Arlington
03760	Chapman, Spotswood	61y	C	17 JAN 1902	Williamsport PA	Payne's
13066	Chapman, Theodore	25y	C	18 AUG 1915	Arlington VA	Harmony
12498	Chapman, Thomas E.	42y	W	25 AUG 1914	Pittsburgh PA	Mt. Olivet
16269	Chapman, William J.	74y	W	1 FEB 1920	Rockville MD	Glenwood
13441	Chappel, Charles	63y	W	4 APR 1916	Baltimore MD	Rock Creek
04484	Chappel, Fannie M.	29y	W	22 OCT 1903	Baltimore MD	Rock Creek
06369	Chappel, Loring	84y	W	2 JAN 1908	Batavia NY	Rock Creek
04753	Chappelear, Sarah E.	76y	W	4 JUN 1904	Ballston VA	Oak Hill
07126	Chappelear, William H.	81y	W	23 JUL 1909	Ballston VA	Oak Hill
15657	Chappell, Alice Marie	2y	W	4 MAR 1919	Hampton VA	Rock Creek
01298	Chappell, Edward F.	27y	W	7 FEB 1894	River Rd. nr. DC	Tenallytown
06220	Chappell, John E.	87y	W	8 SEP 1907	Glendale NY	Methodist
14076	Chapple, William	38y	W	19 MAR 1917	Beaver Co. PA	Congressional
06427	Charles, Albert E.	78y	W	10 FEB 1908	Hyattsville MD	Rock Creek
00124	Charles, Albert L.	5m	W	4 AUG 1889	Piney Point MD	Rock Creek
01797	Charles, Margaret	55y	W	13 NOV 1895	Pr. Geo. Co. MD	Rock Creek
15520	Charles, Mary E.	33y	W	3 JAN 1919	Avenel MD	Rock Creek

No.	Name of Deceased	Age	Race	Death Date	Place of Death	Place of Burial
09120	Charles, Mary Pasley	71y	W	8 MAR 1913	Glen Echo Ht. MD	Congressional
15942	Charlton, Eleanor Margaret	26y	W	20 AUG 1919	New York NY	Congressional
06633	Charlton, William H.	65y	W	4 JUL 1908	Baltimore MD	Congressional
04172	Chase, Bertha	45y	W	14 FEB 1903	Baltimore MD	Congressional
13857	Chase, Calvin	32y	C	8 DEC 1916	Occoquan VA	Harmony
05368	Chase, Elizabeth S.	75y	W	18 NOV 1905	Drummond MD	Rock Creek
17990	Chase, Emanuel	28y	C	29 JUL 1922	New York NY	Harmony
14249	Chase, Frederick Cotton	55y	W	25 JUL 1917	Glen Carlin VA	Prospect Hill
04294	Chase, Isaac McKim	66y	W	7 JUN 1903	Atlantic City NJ	Cremated
16674	Chase, James H.	3m	C	22 AUG 1920	Landover MD	Mt. Olivet
15474	Chase, Joseph	4m	C	23 DEC 1918	Landover MD	Mt. Olivet
06596	Chase, Julia Elizabeth	7m	W	20 JUN 1908	Brentwood MD	Congressional
15471	Chase, Mignona	18y	C	21 DEC 1918	Ridley Park PA	Payne's
16172	Chase, Sarah L.	39y	W	27 DEC 1919	Cottage City MD	Congressional
04209	Chase, Thomas B.	60y	W	31 JAN 1903	Uxbridge MA	Congressional
06804	Chase, William, butcher	79y	W	7 NOV 1908	Cherrydale VA	Rock Creek
16714	Chase, William W.	83y	W	13 SEP 1920	Dayton KY	Glenwood
07555	Chase, Winfield S.	74y	W	3 JUN 1910	Chevy Chase MD	Rock Creek
00253	Chasley, Yelda E.	8y	C	18 DEC 1889	Albany NY	Mt. Olivet
02563	Chauncey, Ida Virginia	39y	W	15 AUG 1898	Charles Co. MD	Congressional
15869	Chauncey, Laura Vinton	77y	W	8 JUL 1919	Clarendon VA	Glenwood
03683	Cheatham, Annie	33y	C	14 OCT 1901	Rosslyn VA	Baptist
03849	Cheatham, James	1y	C	12 APR 1902	Rosslyn VA	Baptist
08511	Check, Harold, s/o Clarence	3y	W	11 FEB 1912	Falls Church VA	Congressional
00577	Chedal, William Walter	16y	W	16 JUL 1891	MD	Glenwood
14188	Cheek, George	28y	W	22 JUN 1917	Pittsburgh PA	Rock Creek
02810	Cheek, Martha	24y	C	30 MAR 1899	New York NY	Payne's
03190	Cheeks, Robert M.	43y	C	19 MAY 1900	Columbus OH	Harmony
03522	Chelini, Elie	79y	W	24 MAY 1901	Columbia Pk. MD	Mt. Olivet
17713	Cheney, Helen L.	64y	W	23 FEB 1922	Orlando MD	Cremated
01030	Cherry, James	26y	W	12 MAR 1893	Baltimore MD	Graceland
13660	Cheshire, Alice	52y	C	13 AUG 1916	Wilmington DE	Harmony
17939	Cheslom, Ceaza	52y	C	4 JUL 1922	Baltimore MD	Payne's
18069	Chester, Bessie D.	68y	W	15 SEP 1922	New York NY	Oak Hill
13333	Chevalier, Thomas F.	43y	W	2 FEB 1916	Wash. Grove MD	Philadelphia PA
07572	Chew, Christopher C.	75y	W	14 JUN 1910	Hyattsville MD	Rock Creek
02457	Chew, Frank	65y	W	24 MAY 1898	Riggs Rd. MD	Glenwood
01218	Chew, John	92y	C	1 NOV 1893	Seat Pleasant MD	Harmony
01029	Chew, Lillian Coffey	27y	W	22 JUL 1892	Marienbad, Aus.	Oak Hill
05549	Chew, Marian S.	62y	W	22 APR 1906	Ft. Wadsworth NY	Oak Hill
04606	Chew, Mary J.	65y	W	20 FEB 1904	Riggs MD	Rock Creek
02458	Chew, Roberta	70y	W	26 MAY 1898	Pr. Geo. Co. MD	Glenwood
04526	Chew, Spencer	22y	W	27 NOV 1903	Tuxedo MD	Mullikin MD
03086	Chew, Walter S.	59y	W	18 FEB 1900	Boston MA	Oak Hill
12686	Childers, Hickman P.	37y	W	30 DEC 1914	Falls Church VA	Cremated
11883	Childers, John M.	10y	W	9 JUL 1913	Falls Church VA	Cremated
15072	Childress, Edward	47y	W	3 OCT 1918	Mt. Ranier MD	Glenwood
11963	Childress, Mary (Donahue)	42y	W	17 AUG 1913	New Haven CN	Mt. Olivet
02733	Childs, Annie	—	—	1868	Pottstown PA	Congressional
17764	Childs, Edward	42y	C	22 MAR 1922	Baltimore MD	Payne's
02732	Childs, Emma	—	—	1849	Pottstown PA	Congressional[1]
12325	Childs, Jane L.	84y	W	20 APR 1914	Atlantic City NJ	Rock Creek
00933	Childs, Mildred	56y	C	11 JUL 1893	Alex. Co. VA	Harmony
02734	Childs, Robert	—	—	1856	Pottstown PA	Congressional
12259	Childs, Thomas S., Rev.	89y	W	21 MAR 1914	Chevy Chase MD	Rock Creek
06697	Chilson, Inita E.	1y	W	19 AUG 1908	Takoma Park MD	Rock Creek

[1] Note of 30 JAN 1899, Pottstown, Pa., for disinterment of three Childs graves from Edgewood Cemetery to Washington, D.C.

District of Columbia Foreign Death Records, 1888-1923

No.	Name of Deceased	Age	Race	Death Date	Place of Death	Place of Burial
03377	Chilton, Martha Matilda	58y	W	24 DEC 1900	Rockville MD	Oak Hill
17339	Chilton, Mary V.	87y	W	2 AUG 1921	Atlantic City NJ	Forest Glen MD
14542	Chinn, Edwin H.	23y	W	30 DEC 1917	Atlanta GA	Rockville MD
04047	Chinn, Emily M.	31y	C	12 OCT 1902	Hyattsville MD	Harmony
17639	Chisholm, Esther M. Whaley	74y	W	17 JAN 1922	Charleston SC	Creamted
06786	Chisholm, Virginia F.	35y	W	23 OCT 1908	Buffalo NY	Glenwood
16905	Chisley, James	24y	C	9 JAN 1921	West Haven CN	Arlington
01507	Chism, Fanny	32y	C	6 OCT 1894	Chicago IL	Harmony
15255	Chiswell, Henry Ball, s/o W.T.	50y	W	21 OCT 1918	Alexandria VA	Rock Creek
07721	Chittains, Mathias	5m	C	28 AUG 1910	Landover MD	Mt. Olivet
06608	Chittams, Nathaniel	4m	C	25 JUN 1908	Landover MD	Mt. Olivet
12963	Choha, Frank	57y	W	9 JUN 1915	Ruskin FL	Cremated
05609	Chrismond, Francis Aloysius	2m	W	25 JUN 1906	Brentwood MD	Mt. Olivet
08284	Chrismond, Infant of Aloysius	SB	W	1 SEP 1911	Mt. Ranier MD	—
04854	Chrismond, Roccofort B.	1y	W	13 AUG 1904	Brentwood MD	Mt. Olivet
04836	Christian, Emeline M.	27y	C	7 AUG 1904	Alexandria VA	Harmony
07885	Christiani, A. DeSilver	59y	W	20 DEC 1910	Philadelphia PA	Rock Creek
03798	Christie, Elizabeth A.	79y	W	18 FEB 1902	New York NY	Oak Hill
01798	Christine, Albert B., actor	40y	W	19 DEC 1895	Boston MA	Congressional
15686	Christman, Philip H.	78y	W	22 MAR 1919	Atlantic City NJ	Oak Hill
07463	Christopher, Infant of Alex.	SB	C	13 MAR 1910	New York NY	Harmony
07462	Christopher, Lena T.	34y	C	9 MAR 1910	New York NY	Harmony
06926	Christy, Cornelia B.	76y	W	19 FEB 1909	Omaha NE	Glenwood
05704	Christy, James	29y	W	24 AUG 1906	Baltimore Co. MD	Mt. Olivet
09195	Chubb, Charles St.J.	58y	W	27 APR 1913	Galveston TX	Arlington
00578	Church, Amanda	78y	W	16 SEP 1891	College Park MD	Rock Creek
05896	Church, Andrew J., Rev.	78y	W	15 JAN 1907	Lancaster PA	Glenwood
03928	Church, Kilborn Durant	7y	W	20 JUL 1902	Ocean City MD	Oak Hill
02670	Church, Louisa	71y	C	3 DEC 1898	Gaithersburg MD	Harmony
04197	Church, Lovina Drew Smith	74y	W	30 MAR 1903	Baltimore MD	Glenwood
01682	Church, Mary E.	94y	W	12 OCT 1895	Newport News VA	Glenwood
01275	Church, William H.	51y	W	26 DEC 1893	College Park MD	Rock Creek
03070	Churchill, Alice Dow	64y	W	13 JAN 1900	Newport RI	Oak Hill
06460	Churchill, Charles C.	82y	W	6 MAR 1908	Newport RI	Oak Hill
00064	Churchill, Franklin Hunter	66y	W	24 MAY 1889	Newport RI	Oak Hill
18319	Churchill, Hazel	24y	W	2 FEB 1923	Asheville NC	Arlington
18581	Cicivelli, John (Igitto)	42y	W	4 JUN 1923	Takoma Park MD	Mt. Olivet
15284	Cioffi, Maria	7y	W	22 OCT 1918	Lewiston PA	St. Mary's
16378	Cissel, Agnes C.	73y	W	11 MAR 1920	Baltimore MD	Oak Hill
17712	Cissel, Agnes D.	75y	W	28 FEB 1922	Laurel MD	Oak Hill
16430	Cissel, Henry H.	21y	W	10 APR 1920	Ithaca NY	Mt. Olivet
12575	Cissel, John F.	4m	W	21 OCT 1914	Baltimore MD	St. Mary's
03462	Cissel, Miranda S.	23y	W	28 MAR 1901	Richmond VA	Glenwood
14799	Cissel, Susan W.	73y	W	6 MAY 1918	Four Corners MD	Oak Hill
06674	Cissell, Elizabeth	2y	W	20 JUN 1908	Berwyn MD	Mt. Olivet
00369	Cissell, Perry	—	W	21 JUL 1890	Wash. Grove MD	Glenwood
08371	Clabaugh, William Cissel	59y	W	22 OCT 1911	Cleveland OH	Oak Hill
03230	Claflin, Edward E.	19y	W	22 JUN 1900	London, Eng.	Rock Creek
01031	Clagett, Henry B.	81y	W	27 JAN 1893	Boston MA	Congressional
03236	Clagett, Maurice	67y	W	13 JUL 1900	Richmond VA	Rock Creek
06273	Claggett, Montgomery	65y	W	15 OCT 1907	Waynesville OH	Rockville MD
16297	Clapp, Abigail Jane	86y	W	7 FEB 1920	Mt. Vernon VA	Cremated
08262	Clapp, Edward Eugene	36y	W	18 AUG 1911	Atlanta GA	Glenwood
02719	Clare, Malvina	46y	W	18 JAN 1899	Phoebus VA	Congressional
12595	Clare, Mary	64y	C	30 OCT 1914	Norfolk VA	Woodlawn
14061	Clark, Albert E.	50y	W	29 MAR 1917	Beltsville MD	Rock Creek
13233	Clark, Albert R.	55y	W	4 DEC 1915	Hyattsville MD	Glenwood
05590	Clark, Anna T.	44y	W	6 JUN 1906	Pittsburgh PA	Mt. Olivet
01127	Clark, Anne M.	77y	W	30 OCT 1891	Baltimore MD	Congressional

No.	Name of Deceased	Age	Race	Death Date	Place of Death	Place of Burial
00094	Clark, Annie [Amy]	23y	C	24 JUL 1889	Frederick MD	Harmony
17687	Clark, Bernard S.	73y	W	11 FEB 1922	Beaufort SC	Rock Creek
13445	Clark, Caroline Augusta	84y	W	9 FEB 1916	Sierra Madre CA	Glenwood
05872	Clark, Catharine M.	74y	W	26 DEC 1906	Liberty MO	Congressional
15083	Clark, Charles E.	25y	W	2 OCT 1918	Syracuse NY	Congressional
01220	Clark, David B.	17y	W	19 SEP 1893	Halethorpe MD	Mt. Olivet
13130	Clark, Elizabeth Lester	73y	W	30 SEP 1915	Baltimore MD	Mt. Olivet
14356	Clark, Ellen Adel	49y	C	11 SEP 1917	Atlantic City NJ	Harmony
07353	Clark, Elmer E.	41y	W	31 DEC 1909	Laurel MD	Congressional
18303	Clark, Esther May	2y	C	26 JAN 1923	Cedar Hts. MD	Payne's
17992	Clark, Eugene Bradley	73y	W	3 AUG 1922	Bethany Bea. DE	Glenwood
08362	Clark, F.A.P.	27y	W	15 OCT 1911	Santa Fe NM	Oak Hill
00458	Clark, Franklin	5y	C	7 MAR 1891	Bladensburg MD	Mt. Olivet
15818	Clark, George L.	35y	C	31 MAY 1919	Grant Co. NM	Arlington
01219	Clark, George L.	38y	C	5 SEP 1893	Philadelphia PA	Harmony
14875	Clark, Halford	22y	W	20 JUN 1918	Montgomery AL	Arlington
11875	Clark, Hamilton	22y	C	2 JUL 1913	Mt. Airy NC	Harmony
07628	Clark, Hamilton Erastus	39y	W	12 JUL 1910	Chillum MD	Rock Creek
13906	Clark, Hannah	57y	W	3 JAN 1917	New York NY	Wash. Hebrew
14604	Clark, Harold E.	24d	W	28 JAN 1918	Hyattsville MD	Congressional
13621	Clark, Harold V.	30y	W	20 JUL 1916	Phoenix AZ	Congressional
18194	Clark, Henrietta	45y	C	2 DEC 1922	Atlantic City NJ	Harmony
00934	Clark, Henry E.	71y	W	13 JUL 1893	Pr. Geo. Co. MD	Rock Creek
14075	Clark, Ira S.	76y	W	6 APR 1917	Broad Creek MD	Cremated
01459	Clark, Irvin P.	2y	C	13 AUG 1894	Keswick VA	Harmony
02049	Clark, James E.	57y	W	3 OCT 1896	W. Chester PA	Rock Creek
18304	Clark, James Edward	1y	C	26 JAN 1923	Cedar Hts. MD	Payne's
03059	Clark, James G.	28y	W	2 JAN 1900	New York NY	Rock Creek
04540	Clark, James R.	33y	W	15 DEC 1903	Jersey City NJ	Mt. Olivet
06745	Clark, John A.	3m	W	23 SEP 1908	Chillum MD	Rock Creek
18001	Clark, John Blake	65y	W	9 AUG 1922	Boone IA	Mt. Olivet
00579	Clark, John F.	28y	W	14 AUG 1891	Alex. Co. VA	Congressional
14755	Clark, John W.	77y	W	14 APR 1918	Georgetown DC	Rock Creek
14841	Clark, John William	36y	W	26 OCT 1917	Laurel MD	Glenwood
02842	Clark, Julia L.	26y	W	7 JUN 1899	Montg. Co. MD	Rock Creek
04751	Clark, Kate	53y	C	3 JUN 1904	Hyattsville MD	Mt. Olivet
15281	Clark, Katherine	27y	W	23 OCT 1918	Bluemont VA	St. Mary's
05766	Clark, Lucretia (Sister Mary J.)	65y	W	11 OCT 1906	Mt. Hope MD	Convent
18501	Clark, Margarete	9m	W	22 APR 1923	LaSalle NY	Glenwood
08011	Clark, Mary E.	17y	C	14 MAR 1911	Capitol Hts. MD	Payne's
14116	Clark, Mary Estelle Herron	43y	W	28 APR 1917	Chevy Chase MD	Congressional
07365	Clark, Mary L.	45y	C	9 JAN 1910	Hyattsville MD	Harmony
13690	Clark, Mary M.	56y	W	2 SEP 1916	Boston MA	Congressional
08797	Clark, Miranda Plummer	60y	W	4 MAR 1905	Bladensburg MD	Harmony
14694	Clark, Owen A.	21y	C	17 MAR 1918	Occoquan VA	Moore's
12365	Clark, Rachel Jane Floyd	62y	W	17 MAY 1914	New York NY	Congressional
01486	Clark, Reuben B.	76y	W	8 SEP 1894	Providence RI	Oak Hill
13984	Clark, Richard H.	64y	C	12 FEB 1917	Hyattsville MD	Harmony
11962	Clark, Rosanna Wolring	75y	W	16 AUG 1913	Washington PA	Rock Creek
07626	Clark, Rose A.	16y	W	11 JUL 1910	Round Hill VA	Glenwood
08459	Clark, Samuel, machinist	48y	W	4 JAN 1912	Waterloo VA	Baltimore MD
01683	Clark, Sara R.	40y	W	4 JUL 1895	Blue Ridge S. PA	Oak Hill
15539	Clark, Sarah A.	65y	W	11 JAN 1919	Seat Pleasant MD	Glenwood
05102	Clark, Sarah A.	57y	W	25 APR 1905	New York NY	Rock Creek
14709	Clark, Thomas P.	42y	W	21 MAR 1918	Alleghany PA	Mt. Olivet
01128	Clark, Tobias Fisher	32y	W	29 SEP 1892	Hagerstown MD	Mt. Olivet
01684	Clark, William E.	60y	W	12 JUL 1895	Hayfield Farm VA	Rock Creek
05317	Clark, William T.	74y	W	12 OCT 1905	New York NY	Arlington
13230	Clarke, A.R.	c.55y	C	4 DEC 1915	Hyattsville MD	Hyattsville MD

District of Columbia Foreign Death Records, 1888-1923

No.	Name of Deceased	Age	Race	Death Date	Place of Death	Place of Burial
04059	Clarke, Agnes	40y	W	16 OCT 1902	Catonsville MD	Mt. Olivet
07210	Clarke, Bertha	6y	C	16 SEP 1909	Atlantic City NJ	Harmony
18136	Clarke, Edith Regan	54y	W	27 OCT 1922	St. Mary's Co. MD	Glenwood
00388	Clarke, Eliza W.	67y	W	12 AUG 1890	Boston MA	Oak Hill
06710	Clarke, John	—	W	1864	Washington DC	Oak Hill[1]
17845	Clarke, Mary Rebecca	17y	W	5 MAY 1922	Chesa. Bea. MD	Congressional
06710	Clarke, Mollie	—	W	1860	Washington DC	Oak Hill
06710	Clarke, Patrick	—	W	1863	Washington DC	Oak Hill
16921	Clarke, Peter J.	71y	W	14 JAN 1921	Binghampton NY	Mt. Olivet
05045	Clarke, Robert	89y	W	26 FEB 1905	Erie PA	Congressional
07996	Clarke, William	33y	W	8 MAR 1911	Wash. Grove MD	Lewinsville VA
13840	Clarke, William J.	68y	W	3 DEC 1916	Woodside MD	Rock Creek
17385	Clarks, James H.	93y	C	2 SEP 1921	Chesterbrook VA	Arlington
14110	Clarkson, Anna	42y	W	25 APR 1917	New York NY	Harmony
08676	Clarkson, Hugh Thompson	19m	W	18 JUN 1912	Railroad	Haymarket VA
04512	Clarkson, James	78y	W	16 NOV 1903	Alexandria VA	Glenwood
16174	Clarridge, Mary Washington	67y	W	28 DEC 1919	Mt. Ranier MD	Glenwood
03309	Clarridge, William H.	52y	W	19 OCT 1900	Seabrook MD	Congressional
14103	Clarvoe, Annie C.	51y	W	24 APR 1917	Philadelphia PA	Glenwood
13150	Clary, Clara	88y	W	13 OCT 1915	Falls Church VA	Glenwood
01126	Clary, John	32y	W	31 DEC 1892	Baltimore MD	Alexandria VA
02295	Claude, Dorothy R.	2y	W	16 SEP 1897	Oakland MD	Mt. Olivet
18192	Clay, Anna Wood	80y	W	1 DEC 1922	Harrison NY	Arlington
07257	Clay, Cornelia	40y	W	1 NOV 1909	Philadelphia PA	Arlington
15929	Clayton, Ella M.	50y	W	14 AUG 1919	Takoma Park MD	Richmond IN
18157	Clayton, Hermes Douglas	30y	W	8 NOV 1922	Cherrydale VA	Arlington
13899	Clayton, Powell, Maj., U.S.A.	45y	W	27 DEC 1916	Houston TX	Arlington
17802	Clear, Charles Mercer	40y	W	14 APR 1922	Groton MA	Congressional
07761	Cleborne, Jane Eliz. Emma	73y	W	23 SEP 1910	Atlanta GA	Arlington
02955	Clem, Nannie	47y	W	15 SEP 1899	New Castle DE	Rock Creek
12576	Clemens, George	35y	C	20 OCT 1914	Detroit MI	Raleigh NC
13816	Clement, Blanch R.	43y	W	15 NOV 1916	Brevard NC	Cremated
14312	Clement, Josephine A.	49y	W	22 AUG 1917	Scarboro ME	Glenwood
00033	Clements, Fannie Sypherd	33y	W	22 MAR 1889	Arlington VA	Oak Hill
04189	Clements, George	50y	C	3 APR 1903	Berwyn MD	Mt. Zion
16489	Clements, Guy C., s/o C.C.	38y	W	16 MAY 1920	Asheville NC	Glenwood
14043	Clements, Irene	33y	C	19 MAR 1917	Middletown NY	Harmony
04506	Clements, Jessie E.	23y	W	8 NOV 1903	Trenton NJ	Holyrood
11801	Clements, Joseph C.	77y	W	4 MAY 1913	Montg. Co. OH	Glenwood
03087	Clements, Louise	28y	W	21 FEB 1900	Fairfax Co. VA	Oak Hill
07131	Clements, Marion Irene McE.	84y	W	23 JUL 1909	Kenilworth IL	Congressional
18125	Clements, Mary J.	67y	W	19 OCT 1922	Otero Co. CO	Glenwood
15348	Clements, Nellie Estelle	32y	W	12 NOV 1918	Linden MD	Glenwood
01495	Clementson, Jennie Eunice	21y	W	23 SEP 1894	Boyds MD	Glenwood
01372	Clemmons, Annie B.	89y	W	24 MAY 1894	Wilmington DE	Congressional
08019	Clemons, James E.	18y	C	22 MAR 1911	Pittsburgh PA	Payne's
12792	Clemons, Jennie C.	62y	W	3 MAR 1915	Fairmont Hts. MD	Woodlawn
13981	Clemons, Robert A.	61y	W	10 FEB 1917	Fairmont Hts. MD	Payne's
00034	Clendenin, William	52y	W	5 MAR 1889	Union Co. NJ	Glenwood
04552	Cleveland, Charles H.	61y	W	24 DEC 1903	At Sea	Arlington VA
12531	Cleveland, Ester A.	62y	W	12 SEP 1914	Northampton MA	Arlington
06104	Cleveland, Melvin L.	19y	W	26 NOV 1906	Palmer's MD	New Britain CN
06169	Clifford, Charles H.	65y	W	6 AUG 1907	Colonial Bea. MD	Glenwood
08279	Clifford, Lillian M.	43y	W	26 AUG 1911	New York NY	Congressional
00690	Clifford, Thomas	37y	C	16 JAN 1892	New York NY	Graceland
15360	Clifton, Bertha Boiseau	45y	W	16 NOV 1918	Atlanta GA	Rock Creek

[1] Removals of the Clarke and Jackson families to Balimore, Md., in August 1908.

No.	Name of Deceased	Age	Race	Death Date	Place of Death	Place of Burial
12149	Clifton, Norman E.	3y	W	7 JAN 1914	Baltimore MD	St. Barnabas MD
15148	Clifton, Randall, s/o Wm. C.	45y	W	11 OCT 1918	Atlanta GA	Oak Hill
03987	Clinton, Boyd	24y	C	24 AUG 1902	Atlantic City NJ	Mt. Zion
07778	Clinton, Edward	73y	W	5 OCT 1910	Laurel MD	Arlington
12543	Clinton, Helene M.	79y	W	23 SEP 1914	Norwich NY	Arlington
04199	Clipper, Edwin W.	20y	W	11 AUG 1885	Baltimore MD	Rock Creek
04855	Clock, Elizabeth	69y	W	19 AUG 1904	Forestville MD	Woodlawn
13986	Clokey, S. Blanche	c.40y	W	13 FEB 1917	Baltimore MD	Rock Creek
01538	Closs, Lawrence M., lawyer	78y	W	29 JAN 1895	New York NY	Congressional
16058	Clover, Richardson	73y	W	14 OCT 1919	Cheyenne WY	Arlington
04258	Clymer, W.B. Shubrick	48y	W	9 MAY 1903	Cambridge MA	Oak Hill
07028	Coady, John	57y	W	16 MAY 1909	Baltimore MD	Congressional
00314	Coates, Edward F.	20y	C	19 APR 1890	Brooklyn NY	Graceland
15508	Coates, Ella Elizabeth	9y	W	1 JAN 1919	Mt. Ranier MD	Glenwood
08373	Coates, Eva M.	38y	W	25 OCT 1911	Relee VA	Glenwood
16282	Coates, Henry	30y	C	3 FEB 1920	Cedar Hts. MD	Payne's
07623	Coates, Jame	25y	C	9 JUL 1910	Washington DC	Baptist
16774	Coates, Joseph H. [or James]	37y	C	10 OCT 1920	New York NY	Harmony
08830	Coates, William	57y	W	7 SEP 1912	Runion NJ	Mt. Olivet
12523	Coats, Exebenna	14y	C	10 SEP 1914	Annapolis MD	Moore's
08867	Coats, Lewis	24y	C	2 OCT 1912	Bowie MD	Payne's
16280	Cobb, Delia B.	50y	W	4 FEB 1920	Takoma MD	Glenwood
15245	Coberth, Anna Almetta	64y	W	20 OCT 1918	Fairfax C.H. VA	Glenwood
03583	Coburn, Sarah	85y	W	19 JUL 1901	Adamstown PA	Oak Hill
07083	Cochran, Alex.	60y	W	16 SEP 1871	Campbell Co. VA	Glenwood
06567	Cochran, Henry D.	38y	W	20 MAY 1908	Rawhide NV	Glenwood
04699	Cochran, Katharine Sadler M.	51y	W	26 APR 1903	Jacksonville FL	Arlington
04698	Cochran, Melville Augustis	68y	W	3 MAY 1904	Jacksonville FL	Arlington
02153	Cochrane, Ellen Manning	82y	W	13 MAR 1897	Ashton MD	Mt. Olivet
13755	Cockerell, Andrew J.	41y	W	8 OCT 1916	Baltimore MD	Mt. Olivet
13288	Cockley, Cecilia	70y	C	6 JAN 1916	Alex. Co. VA	Holyrood
11924	Cockrell, Allen Vardeman	33y	W	28 JUL 1913	Bluemont VA	St. Louis MO
00581	Cockrell, John H., Jr.	18y	W	13 JUL 1891	Norfolk VA	Mt. Olivet
00580	Cockrell, John H., Jr.	18y	W	13 JUL 1891	Norfolk VA	Mt. Olivet
06394	Coddington, Harriet S.	77y	W	16 JAN 1908	Baltimore MD	Glenwood
13088	Coddington, William C.	56y	W	2 SEP 1915	Baltimore MD	Glenwood
07456	Cody, Cecilila A.	67y	W	7 MAR 1910	Baltimore MD	Holyrood
16676	Coe, Bernard N.	36y	W	22 AUG 1920	Potomac River	Glenwood
03790	Coe, William A.	44y	W	13 FEB 1902	Mt. Hope MD	Rock Creek
00691	Coe, William H.	47y	W	7 DEC 1891	Forest Glen MD	Rock Creek
12451	Cofer, Nathan P., librarian	71y	W	22 JUL 1914	Chevy Chase MD	Richmond VA
04044	Coffee, Alfred	26y	C	9 OCT 1902	Reading PA	Holyrood
15020	Coffee, Rebecca A.	71y	W	15 SEP 1918	Cottage City MD	Glenwood
00430	Coffey, Harry Kerr	33y	W	18 AUG 1889	London, Eng.	Oak Hill
03323	Coffin, George William	53y	W	15 JUN 1899	Yokohama, Jap.	Oak Hill
02050	Coffin, John H.C.	47y	W	4 JAN 1897	Ft. Hamilton NY	Oak Hill
18305	Coffin, William B.	73y	W	28 JAN 1923	Savannah GA	Cremated
08750	Coffin, William H., Col.	60y	W	2 AUG 1912	Rochester MN	Oak Hill
12709	Coffinar, Nicholai	30y	W	10 JAN 1915	Alex. Co. VA	Woodlawn
13987	Cogan, Loretta F.	—	W	13 FEB 1917	Berryville VA	Arlington
06884	Cogdell, Anna	46y	C	1 JAN 1909	Beltsville MD	Harmony
01685	Coggens, Estella	1y	W	11 SEP 1895	Cherrydale VA	Congressional
04183	Coggins, Florence L.	6y	W	15 FEB 1903	Baltimore MD	Congressional
05316	Coghlan, Thomas F.	33y	W	12 OCT 1905	Harrisburg PA	Arlington
06701	Cogsdell, Rebecca	27y	C	20 AUG 1908	Philadelphia PA	Harmony
00816	Cogswell, Susan M.	66y	W	28 JUL 1892	Plainfield NJ	Rock Creek
17496	Cogswell, Winterton J.	34y	W	1 NOV 1921	Brook Park MD	Glenwood
05478	Cohan, John	35y	W	27 FEB 1906	Downingtown PA	Holyrood
15688	Cohen, Aaron	89y	W	23 MAR 1919	Pittsburgh PA	Adas Israel

District of Columbia Foreign Death Records, 1888-1923

No.	Name of Deceased	Age	Race	Death Date	Place of Death	Place of Burial
05976	Cohen, Fannie	48y	W	2 MAR 1907	New York NY	Adas Israel
14738	Cohen, Fannie	63y	W	8 APR 1918	Baltimore MD	Adas Israel
14896	Cohen, Jerry, s/o Solomon	30y	W	5 JUL 1918	Asbury Park NJ	Adas Israel
03698	Cohen, John W.	52y	W	31 OCT 1901	Bailey's Xrds. VA	Glenwood
15039	Cohen, Mabel	35y	W	24 SEP 1918	Baltimore MD	Wash. Hebrew
16584	Cohen, Marjorie W.	23y	W	6 JUL 1920	Saranac Lake NY	Wash. Hebrew
17419	Cohen, Max, s/o Edward	75y	W	19 SEP 1921	Henrico Co. VA	Wash. Hebrew
04204	Cohen, Monroe	22y	W	21 MAR 1903	Kingston NY	Wash. Hebrew
13247	Cohen, Morris	10m	W	12 DEC 1915	Alex. Co. VA	Ohev Sholom
01925	Cohen, Morris	65y	W	22 MAY 1896	Baltimore MD	Wash. Hebrew
01539	Coit, James B., lawyer	58y	W	8 DEC 1894	Norwich CN	Arlington VA
07464	Coit, Lucia Blair	78y	W	12 MAR 1910	Forest Glen MD	Cheraw SC
13958	Colavecchio, Phillip	9y	W	30 JAN 1917	Falls Church VA	St. Mary's
16780	Colbert, George Walter	38y	C	24 OCT 1920	Hot Springs VA	Mt. Olivet
15256	Colbert, Howard Richard	27y	C	2 OCT 1918	At Sea	Arlington
12878	Colbert, John	34y	W	14 APR 1915	Occoquan VA	Mt. Olivet
07306	Colbert, Mary	48y	C	1 DEC 1909	Pittsburgh PA	Payne's
12000	Colbert, Rachal (Cranford)	52y	C	10 SEP 1913	Asbury Park NJ	Mt. Olivet
02154	Colburn, Martha A.	72y	W	27 MAR 1897	Pasadena CA	Rock Creek
01033	Colburn, W. Bradley	46y	W	14 FEB 1893	So. Pines NC	Oak Hill
11958	Colby, John C.S.	76y	W	12 AUG 1913	Hampton VA	Arlington
01540	Cole, Amanda M.	43y	W	25 FEB 1895	Hyattsville MD	Rock Creek
13128	Cole, Elizabeth	1y	W	30 SEP 1915	Baltmore MD	Mt. Olivet
04257	Cole, Emma E.	39y	C	9 MAY 1903	Hartford CN	Payne's
18142	Cole, Frederick A.	6m	W	2 NOV 1922	Mt. Ranier MD	Glenwood
17761	Cole, Ivie Ethel	32y	W	26 MAR 1922	Richmond VA	Glenwood
08615	Cole, James T.	4y	W	28 APR 1912	Dent's Wharf MD	Congressional
16356	Cole, John C.	58y	C	28 FEB 1920	Forestville MD	Payne's
01492	Cole, John P.	48y	W	8 SEP 1894	Ft. Worth TX	Mt. Olivet
08708	Cole, Major	1y	C	6 JUL 1912	Oxon Hill MD	Moore's
16402	Cole, Margaret C.	79y	W	8 FEB 1920	Boston MA	Rock Creek
12907	Cole, Nettie M.	25y	W	27 APR 1915	Jersey City NJ	Payne's
11845	Cole, Sadie	48y	C	4 JUN 1913	Pittsburgh PA	Harmony
06181	Cole, Samuel J.	72y	W	15 AUG 1907	Bethesda MD	Glenwood
03596	Cole, Sarah Ann	70y	W	29 JUL 1901	Silver Spring MD	Glenwood
03829	Cole, Thos. Walter	76y	W	25 MAR 1902	Inverness MD	Rock Creek
04012	Cole, William	26y	C	11 SEP 1902	Philadelphia PA	Harmony
18313	Cole, William	60y	C	30 JAN 1923	Fairmont Hts. MD	Payne's
12981	Coleman, Anna	28y	C	26 JUN 1915	PA	Harmony
06876	Coleman, Carrie	23y	C	29 DEC 1908	New York NY	Payne's
17343	Coleman, Cathrine	49y	C	2 AUG 1921	Pittsburgh PA	Harmony
09005	Coleman, Charles C.	45y	C	24 DEC 1912	Philadelphia PA	Payne's
02194	Coleman, Charles E.	3m	W	30 JUN 1897	Newark NJ	Mt. Olivet
07013	Coleman, Charles K.	42y	W	1 MAR 1909	Panama Zone	Mt. Olivet
03813	Coleman, Eliza	26y	C	12 MAR 1902	New York NY	Harmony
12712	Coleman, Elizabeth	75y	C	11 JAN 1915	Forestville MD	Harmony
04025	Coleman, James	29y	C	28 SEP 1902	Philadelphia PA	Arlington VA
14368	Coleman, James	70y	W	17 SEP 1917	Baltimore MD	Woodlawn
18172	Coleman, Jessie L.	65y	W	19 NOV 1922	Troy OH	Arlington
02540	Coleman, Katie	32y	C	8 JUN 1898	Baltimore MD	Payne's
13666	Coleman, Lawrence	22y	C	17 AUG 1916	Pittsburgh PA	Harmony
01032	Coleman, Marie L.	65y	W	8 JUL 1892	Paris, France	Convent
03483	Coleman, Mary	43y	C	18 APR 1901	Philadelphia PA	Woodlawn
05346	Coleman, Mary C.	61y	C	1 NOV 1905	Buffalo NY	Harmony
15028	Coleman, Max L., soldier	22y	W	18 SEP 1918	Camp Lee VA	Wash. Hebrew
12516	Coleman, Reuben Lindsay	23y	W	10 AUG 1914	Newport RI	Orange VA
18373	Coleman, Ruth Tilden	55y	W	27 FEB 1923	Georgetown Hp.	Prospect Hill
13947	Coleman, Spencer	102y	C	25 JAN 1917	Alex. Co. VA	Harmony
13522	Coler, Hobart	18y	C	24 MAY 1916	Montg. Co. PA	Payne's

No.	Name of Deceased	Age	Race	Death Date	Place of Death	Place of Burial
13219	Colerider, Marion Hayes	17y	W	7 DEC 1900	Grafton WV	Prospect Hill
04599	Coles, Hattie	35y	C	12 FEB 1904	New York NY	Mt. Zion
05813	Coles, Jane	37y	C	8 NOV 1906	Allegheny PA	Harmony
08649	Coles, Martha	40y	C	28 MAY 1912	Philadelphia PA	Harmony
01221	Colgrove, James B., Jr.	24y	W	16 SEP 1893	New Windsor MD	Rock Creek
15892	Colhoun, J. Ross	72y	W	24 JUL 1919	Bowie MD	Arlington
00006	Colignon, Frederick C.	17y	W	13 DEC 1888	Zanesville OH	Prospect Hill
12210	Colison, Charles A.	53y	W	4 FEB 1914	Alamosa CO	Glenwood
14498	Collegman, Edith Mary	27y	W	4 DEC 1917	Denver CO	Congressional
01124	Colley, Edward	35y	W	24 SEP 1892	Baltimore MD	Oak Hill
00095	Colley, James H.	38y	W	24 JUL 1889	West Point VA	Oak Hill
04581	Collier, Edna L.	10y	W	28 JAN 1904	Hyattsville MD	Rock Creek
12945	Collier, Gilla L.	69y	W	27 MAY 1915	Riverdale MD	Rock Creek
06813	Collier, Nellie B.	39y	W	9 NOV 1908	New York NY	Glenwood
05794	Collier, Walter	7y	W	31 OCT 1906	Hyattsville MD	Rock Creek
03194	Collings, Howard P., Jr.	5m	W	26 MAY 1900	Hot Springs AR	Rock Creek
17789	Collins, Anna Catherine	7y	W	10 APR 1922	Mt. Ranier MD	Mt. Olivet
08575	Collins, Anna M.	72y	W	28 MAR 1912	Chicago IL	Arlington
01222	Collins, Benjamin Perry	19y	W	10 DEC 1893	St. Louis MO	Mt. Olivet
17209	Collins, C. Andrew	24y	C	27 SEP 1918	France	Mt. Olivet
08455	Collins, Elizabeth	86y	W	3 JAN 1912	Takoma Park MD	Rock Creek
06286	Collins, James L.	65y	W	24 OCT 1907	Philadelphia PA	Arlington VA
08707	Collins, James Marion	62y	W	5 JUL 1912	Silver Spring MD	Rock Creek
00080	Collins, James Randolph	12d	W	28 JUN 1889	Randolph MD	Holyrood
01619	Collins, James S.	28y	W	25 MAR 1895	New York NY	Mt. Olivet
04300	Collins, Janie A.	8y	C	2 JUN 1903	New York NY	Harmony
05453	Collins, John Wilkie	59y	W	2 FEB 1906	Amityville NY	Arlington
14242	Collins, Kate Hayden	69y	W	20 JUL 1917	Takoma Park MD	Oak Hill
07658	Collins, Katie	46y	W	27 JUL 1910	Philadelphia PA	Mt. Olivet
12419	Collins, Lillian G.	46y	W	29 JUN 1914	E. Haddam CN	Congressional
04669	Collins, Michael	22y	W	12 APR 1904	Philadelphia PA	Mt. Olivet
03425	Collins, Mikle	41y	W	21 FEB 1901	Allegheny PA	Mt. Olivet
16870	Collins, Rebecca	74y	C	19 DEC 1920	Welch WV	Harmony
02155	Collins, Samuel W., U.S.A.	24y	W	14 AUG 1896	Leavenworth KS	Shoemaker Farm
13349	Collins, Sarah L.	69y	W	11 FEB 1916	Ballston VA	Methodist
00389	Collins, W.B.	64y	W	17 AUG 1890	Portsmouth VA	Oak Hill
14892	Collison, George Washington	74y	W	1 JUL 1918	Takoma Park MD	Glenwood
12305	Colman, Rose	53y	W	9 APR 1914	Catonsville MD	Wash. Hebrew
17175	Cologne, Newton S.	64y	W	19 MAY 1921	Seat Pleasant MD	Glenwood
12353	Colona, Fannie Virginia	57y	W	11 MAY 1914	Hyattsville MD	Oak Hill
16180	Colquitt, Mel Redmond	73y	W	1 JAN 1920	Takoma Park MD	Augusta GA
17152	Colston, Roscoe	35y	C	6 MAY 1921	Philadelphia PA	Arlington
13900	Colt, William D.	82y	W	30 DEC 1916	Chevy Chase MD	Oak Hill
01686	Colter, Thomas P.	16y	W	14 AUG 1895	Alexandria VA	Holyrood
08405	Coltman, Mary Jane	70y	W	24 NOV 1911	LaJunta CO	Glenwood
07802	Coltman, Robert	70y	W	22 OCT 1910	LaJunta CO	Glenwood
04022	Colton, Annie Culbertson S.	57y	W	2 JUL 1901	Stresa, Italy	Oak Hill
02051	Colton, Henry	84y	W	30 JUN 1896	Corona LI	Congressional
17507	Colvin, Miranda M. (Chipley)	72y	W	4 AUG 1921	Fowler CO	Alexandria VA
08264	Colvin, Thomas L., s/o John	c.22y	W	17 AUG 1911	Norfolk VA	Congressional
03690	Combs, Robert Manning	22y	W	14 OCT 1901	Phoenix AZ	Congressional
02052	Comer, George W.	61y	W	6 DEC 1896	New York NY	Congressional
14108	Comerel, Jeremiah	54y	W	22 APR 1917	Chicago IL	Mt. Olivet
04703	Comsey, Albert	63y	W	8 MAY 1904	Baltimore MD	Congressional
07793	Conboye, William	6h	W	19 OCT 1910	Maryland Pk. MD	Mt. Olivet
01223	Condict, Henry Ford, Dr.	89y	W	31 OCT 1893	Sligo MD	Rock Creek
05513	Condry, Fannie M.	48y	W	30 MAR 1906	Hyattsville MD	Mt. Olivet
08533	Cone, Roscoe Heitt	1m	W	28 FEB 1912	Hyattsville MD	Glenwood
12114	Conger, Mary A.	85y	W	4 DEC 1913	Edenton NC	Arlington

District of Columbia Foreign Death Records, 1888-1923

No.	Name of Deceased	Age	Race	Death Date	Place of Death	Place of Burial
02518	Conger, Omar B.	80y	W	11 JUL 1898	Ocean City NJ	Port Huron MI
08464	Conklin, Charles B., s/o Geo.	62y	W	9 JAN 1912	Purcellville VA	Glenwood
02594	Conklin, John	52y	W	8 JUN 1881	Bradford PA	Oak Hill
17633	Conklin, Joseph B.	52y	W	10 JAN 1922	Wash. Asylum	Arlington
04922	Conkling, Frank	25y	W	13 OCT 1904	Hot Springs AR	Rock Creek
05185	Connell, Charles F.	23y	W	26 JUN 1905	Chelsea MA	Mt. Olivet
06287	Connell, Ellen	68y	W	22 OCT 1907	Cranston RI	Mt. Olivet
04413	Connell, George E.	56y	W	27 JUL 1903	Erwin VA	Glenwood
08196	Connell, James B.	13y	W	11 JUL 1911	Vineland NJ	Mt. Olivet
13602	Connell, John D.	40y	W	11 JUL 1916	Detroit MI	Mt. Olivet
03575	Connell, Lawrence J.	28y	W	23 JUN 1901	Spike Buck CO	Mt. Olivet
13036	Connell, Margaret A.	63y	W	4 AUG 1915	Atlantic City NJ	Mt. Olivet
06020	Connell, Thomas J.O.	—	W	16 JAN 1907	Cranston RI	Mt. Olivet
12789	Connelly, Fred, a.k.a.	27y	C	3 MAR 1915	Muirkirk MD	Hyattsville MD
04762	Connelly, Margaret	37y	W	12 JUN 1904	San Antonio TX	Holyrood
05927	Conner, Mary A.	70y	W	5 FEB 1907	Takoma Park MD	Rock Creek
13385	Connolly, Agnes G. (Gibbons)	42y	W	18 FEB 1916	Monterey CA	Arlington
08482	Connolly, Francis R.	50y	W	16 JAN 1912	E. St. Louis IL	Mt. Olivet
17884	Connolly, Frank	46y	W	1 JUN 1922	New York NY	Mt. Olivet
13384	Connolly, Infant of George	SB	W	18 FEB 1916	Monterey CA	Arlington
07336	Connolly, James W.	44y	W	20 DEC 1909	Baltimore MD	Holyrood
18444	Connolly, Josephine Blanche	39y	W	21 MAR 1923	Redondo Bea. CA	Mt. Olivet
04660	Connolly, Mary Katherine	1d	W	5 APR 1904	Ft. McHenry MD	Holyrood
17195	Connolly, Maurice	—	W	28 MAY 1921	Walter Reed Hp.	Dubuque IA
13844	Connolly, William H.	48y	W	4 DEC 1916	Hilldale MD	Mt. Olivet
15019	Connor, Charles	50y	W	14 SEP 1918	Baltimore MD	Mt. Olivet
17455	Connor, Charles D.	24y	W	6 OCT 1921	Saranac Lake NY	Mt. Olivet
07850	Connor, Elizabeth C.	30y	—	5 DEC 1910	Catonsville MD	Mt. Olivet
01399	Connor, Helan G.	3m	W	14 JUN 1894	Hyattsville MD	Mt. Olivet
04852	Connor, Henry N.	38y	C	15 AUG 1904	Atlantic City NJ	Harmony
13022	Connor, Mary P.	11m	W	23 JUL 1915	Capitol Hts. MD	Congressional
07822	Connor, Thos. A.	24y	W	4 NOV 1910	Denver CO	Mt. Olivet
07045	Connor, William J.	62y	W	31 MAY 1909	Alexandria VA	Congressional
15182	Connors, John J.	24y	W	13 OCT 1918	Saltsville VA	Arlington
13115	Connors, Rose Bell	23y	W	16 SEP 1915	Penrose VA	Congressional
17700	Conolly, Marguerite W.	33y	W	19 FEB 1922	Takoma Park MD	Cremated
15425	Conrad, Fannie T.	66y	W	9 DEC 1918	Front Royal VA	Congressional
13362	Conrad, Preston L.	32y	W	12 FEB 1916	Havre MT	Congressional
03390	Conradis, Henry	65y	W	12 JAN 1901	Baltimore MD	Rock Creek
09162	Conroy, Frank, s/o Charles	38y	W	8 APR 1913	Burke's Sta. VA	Mt. Olivet
17144	Conroy, Patrick	60y	W	6 MAY 1921	Manchester NH	Ft. Lincoln
02299	Conroy, Patrick J.	45y	W	15 OCT 1897	Chicago IL	Holyrood[1]
13486	Conroy, Paul	3m	C	30 APR 1916	Fairmont Hts. MD	Union
00935	Conroy, Theodosia L.	3y	W	23 JUL 1893	Farmwell VA	Holyrood
07466	Constantini, Pompeo	32y	W	11 MAR 1910	Allegheny PA	Arlington VA
00692	Conte, Phelim	55y	C	17 DEC 1891	Arlington VA	Holyrood
02298	Conte, Phoenix	5m	C	8 OCT 1897	Tuxedo MD	Mt. Olivet
05649	Contee, Frederick	26y	C	16 JUL 1906	Pittsburgh PA	Payne's
12242	Contee, John L.	45y	C	23 FEB 1914	Philadelphia PA	Payne's
02109	Contee, Mabel	17y	C	24 JAN 1897	Takoma Park MD	Harmony
18315	Contee, Maggie	43y	C	31 JAN 1923	Berry Sta. MD	Mt. Olivet
17284	Conway, Al. P.	60y	W	3 JUL 1921	Dayton OH	Rock Creek
17667	Conway, Beulah A.	89y	W	31 JAN 1922	Baltimore MD	Rock Creek
03281	Conway, James C.	62y	W	1 SEP 1900	Knoxville TN	Rock Creek
08494	Conway, Julia	14y	C	24 JAN 1912	Philadelphia PA	Macedonia
12789	Conway, Shadrach, a.k.a.	27y	C	3 MAR 1915	Muirkirk MD	Hyattsville MD

[1] Note 29 OCT 1904 by Mrs. Patrick J. Conroy to remove remains to Mt. Olivet cemetery.

No.	Name of Deceased	Age	Race	Death Date	Place of Death	Place of Burial
18528	Conway, William A.	59y	W	6 MAY 1923	Baltimore MD	Rock Creek
15666	Cook, C.F.	34y	W	11 MAR 1919	Alexandria VA	Boston MA
07705	Cook, Charles	41y	C	21 AUG 1910	Cape May Co. NJ	Harmony
08480	Cook, Corona L.	28y	C	16 JAN 1912	Baltimore MD	Harmony
03501	Cook, Edward	4y	W	5 MAY 1901	Baltimore MD	Mt. Olivet
00298	Cook, George	50y	W	26 MAR 1890	Rockville MD	Glenwood
12867	Cook, George	52y	W	8 APR 1915	Brooklyn NY	Rock Creek
01799	Cook, Harriett M.	58y	C	12 NOV 1895	Pittsburgh PA	Harmony
08873	Cook, Harvey	19y	W	4 OCT 1912	Potomac MD	Glenwood
01911	Cook, James E.	8y	W	4 MAR 1876	Pottsville PA	Rock Creek
01911½	Cook, John	1y	W	23 JUL 1871	Pottsville PA	Rock Creek
01898	Cook, Joseph	50y	C	21 MAR 1896	Reno NV	Harmony
14638	Cook, Josephine	26y	C	13 FEB 1918	Oxon Hill MD	Moore's
12205	Cook, Lewis	50y	C	5 FEB 1914	Bladensburg MD	Payne's
17106	Cook, Margaret	45y	W	12 APR 1921	Cleveland OH	Mt. Olivet
17622	Cook, Marie Bontz	34y	W	31 DEC 1921	Denver CO	Rock Creek
14765	Cook, Mary E.	55y	W	20 APR 1918	Natick MA	Glenwood
06234	Cook, May A.	52y	W	19 SEP 1907	Ocean City MD	Congressional
04795	Cook, Nellie	31y	W	14 JUL 1904	Bealeton VA	Mt. Olivet
01224	Cook, Sadie	15y	W	27 SEP 1893	Highridge MD	Rock Creek
05306	Cook, Stewart	33y	W	2 OCT 1905	Piscataway C. MD	Westm. Co. VA
02572	Cook, Winifred	27y	W	23 AUG 1898	Monson MA	Mt. Olivet
08231	Cooke, Albert E.	77y	W	30 JUL 1911	Hyattsville MD	Glenwood
14404	Cooke, Alberta M.	69y	W	10 OCT 1917	Hyattsville MD	Glenwood
04830	Cooke, Ann Virginia	79y	W	2 AUG 1904	Baltimore MD	Congressional
17204	Cooke, Donald Williams	26y	W	27 MAY 1921	Oakland CA	Glenwood
12565	Cooke, Henry D.	64y	W	9 OCT 1914	New York NY	Oak Hill
07732	Cooke, Laura O.	1m	C	5 SEP 1910	New York NY	Woodlawn
04872	Cooke, Laura S.H.	73y	W	3 SEP 1904	Atlantic City NJ	Oak Hill
13345	Cooke, Philip Henry	56y	W	9 FEB 1916	Hampton VA	Prospect Hill
00081	Cooksey, Charles L.	20y	W	3 JUN 1889	Ft. Wash. MD	Congressional
13468	Cooksey, Joshua I.	89y	W	18 APR 1916	Baltimore MD	Congressional
13532	Cool, Arthur B.	14y	W	3 JUN 1916	Takoma MD	Rock Creek
17361	Coombs, John Leslie	5y	W	19 AUG 1921	Takoma Park MD	Glenwood
16732	Coomes, Sarah A.	64y	W	1 OCT 1920	Baltimore MD	Congressional
00459	Coon, R.F.	21y	W	22 MAR 1891	Pittsburgh PA	Oak Hill
04120	Coons, Alice	23y	W	8 DEC 1902	Chicago IL	Rock Creek
13778	Cooper, Cecelia	66y	C	22 OCT 1916	Pittsburgh PA	Woodlawn
03710	Cooper, E. Marie	18y	W	20 NOV 1901	Philadelphia PA	Glenwood
01965	Cooper, Edmond Mason	64y	W	9 JUL 1896	Oakland CA	Oak Hill
04806	Cooper, Eleanor Jane	76y	W	19 JUL 1904	Elmira NY	Oak Hill
02647	Cooper, Helen H.	36y	W	4 NOV 1898	Baltimore MD	Glenwood
08591	Cooper, Infant of Jacob	SB	W	8 APR 1912	Cass WV	Adas Israel
15186	Cooper, James A.	26y	C	10 OCT 1918	Camp Lee VA	Arlington
06612	Cooper, John William	49y	W	26 JUN 1908	Alexandria VA	Congressional
18428	Cooper, Marion S.	59y	W	21 MAR 1922	Takoma Park MD	Ft. Lincoln
00270	Cooper, Mary Florida	51y	W	11 JAN 1890	Oakland CA	Oak Hill
14019	Cooper, Sarah	37y	C	2 MAR 1917	Brooks Hill MD	Mt. Zion East
16702	Copeland, Mary T. (Brightwell)	56y	W	5 SEP 1920	Denver CO	Congressional
03900	Copeley, Lillian Effie	28y	W	19 JUN 1902	Baltimore MD	Mt. Olivet
18132	Copenhaven, Elmira C.	72y	W	27 OCT 1922	Takoma Park MD	Glenwood
02747	Copenhaver, Margaret Ann	70y	W	21 FEB 1899	Pittsburgh PA	Glenwood
13706	Copius, Walter	22y	W	29 AUG 1916	At Sea	Hempstead NY
08601	Copkins, Bessie F.	16y	W	1896	Baltimore MD	Holyrood
08253	Copland, James H.	65y	W	12 AUG 1911	Arlington VA	Congressional
09172	Copley, Esther	23y	W	17 APR 1903	New York NY	Glenwood
03528	Copperthite, Annie	16y	W	30 MAY 1901	Fairfax Co. VA	Oak Hill
16083	Copperthite, Dennis	40y	W	1 NOV 1919	Petersburg VA	Oak Hill
16683	Coppinger, Mary	23y	W	27 AUG 1920	Glen Echo MD	St. Louis MO

District of Columbia Foreign Death Records, 1888-1923

No.	Name of Deceased	Age	Race	Death Date	Place of Death	Place of Burial
13537	Corbett, Elizabeth W.	83y	W	4 JUN 1916	Takoma MD	Cremated
04037	Corbett, Mary Howard	29y	W	31 OCT 1876	Arlington VA	Oak Hill
04486	Corbett, Sarah J.	52y	W	23 OCT 1903	Philadelphia PA	Oak Hill
07191	Corbin, Henry Clark	67y	W	8 SEP 1909	New York NY	Arlington
09165	Corby, Steven Henderson	58y	W	12 APR 1913	Falls Church VA	Glenwood
18196	Corcoran, Edward D.	86y	W	4 DEC 1922	New York NY	Mt. Olivet
04714	Corcoran, Emmert E.	35y	W	14 MAY 1904	Aiken SC	Mt. Olivet
00436	Corcoran, William M.	57y	W	12 NOV 1890	Morgantown WV	Oak Hill
13919	Cord, Isabel H.	70y	W	9 JAN 1917	Pittsburgh PA	Arlington
15985	Corey, Hattie	58y	W	9 SEP 1919	Rutland VT	Arlington
03441	Corey, Phebe A.	100y	W	3 MAR 1901	Brentsville MD	Rock Creek
08856	Corington, William H.	72y	W	27 SEP 1912	Atlantic City NJ	Rock Creek
12424	Corkey, Timothy J.	21y	W	18 JUN 1914	Arlington Hts. VA	Mt. Olivet
16296	Corley, Joseph E.	75y	W	6 FEB 1920	New Haven CN	Rock Creek
02543	Cornelius, Horace W.	43y	W	9 JUN 1898	Cambridge MD	Oak Hill
03381	Cornelius, John Edwin	36y	W	31 DEC 1900	Baltimore MD	Oak Hill
00693	Cornelius, Martha S.	2m	W	1 JAN 1892	Baltimore MD	Oak Hill
00035	Cornelius, Samuel W.	7m	—	12 MAR 1889	Baltimore MD	Oak Hill
04808	Cornelius, Virginia C.	76y	W	21 JUL 1904	Bowie MD	Oak Hill
16036	Corneliuson, Thomas	54y	W	6 OCT 1919	Bellevill WI	Glenwood
05602	Cornell, Alberta M.	10m	W	19 JUN 1906	Brentwood MD	Congressional
03063	Cornell, Frank M.	28y	W	7 JAN 1900	New York NY	Oak Hill
13244	Corner, Frances Hart	31y	W	10 DEC 1915	Fairfax Co. VA	Muncy PA
15937	Cornish, Rachel May	31y	C	17 AUG 1919	Jersey City NJ	Harmony
14257	Cornwall, Infant of Ernest	SB	W	29 JUL 1917	Bladensburg MD	Congressional
03358	Cornwall, Richard W.	35y	W	28 NOV 1900	Canon City CO	Congressional
17225	Cornwall, Sarah A.	56y	W	10 JUN 1921	Bridgeton NJ	Congressional
06165	Cornwell, Alton W.	38y	W	31 JUL 1907	Kensington MD	Congressional
18147	Cornwell, Charles E.	1y	W	1892	Pr. Wm. Co. VA	Congressional
03979	Cornwell, G. Raymond	3y	W	7 AUG 1902	Kensington MD	Congressional
02892	Cornwell, Infant of Newton	SB	W	21 JUL 1899	Silver Hill MD	Congressional
17283	Cornwell, Jane	63y	W	4 JUL 1921	Silver Hill MD	Congressional
18147	Cornwell, Richard H.	54y	W	1897	Pr. Wm. Co. VA	Congressional
04154	Cornwell, Ruth Abigail	7y	W	12 JAN 1903	Kensington MD	Congressional
13989	Corothers, James D.	48y	C	12 FEB 1917	West Chester PA	Harmony
15075	Corrick, Helen G.	48y	W	3 OCT 1918	Kensington MD	Oak Hill
01125	Corrick, Nettie L.	30y	W	25 JUN 1892	Kensington MD	Oak Hill
12813	Corrick, William Joshua	23y	W	12 MAR 1915	Kensington MD	Rock Creek
06118	Corridon, Phillip	43y	W	24 JUN 1907	Schenectady NY	Mt. Olivet
15319	Corrigan, Jerry	25y	W	31 OCT 1918	Rochester NY	Congressional
08760	Corson, Helen V.	59y	W	10 AUG 1912	Takoma Park MD	Williamsport PA
06797	Coryousky, Maurice	18y	W	31 OCT 1908	Berwyn MD	Adas Israel
14277	Cosby, Fanny Bell	67y	W	6 AUG 1917	Spring Lake NJ	Congressional
18469	Costagginni, Nina Marie	49y	W	8 APR 1923	Dallas TX	Mt. Olivet
04672	Costagino, Felippo	66y	W	13 APR 1904	Baltimore MD	Mt. Olivet
02771	Costello, Blanche C.	30y	W	13 MAR 1899	Omaha NE	Mt. Olivet
15188	Costello, Leo M.	32y	W	15 OCT 1918	Wilmington DE	Mt. Olivet
00694	Costello, Michael	53y	W	21 FEB 1892	Garrett IN	Glenwood
12249	Costello, Rosa	5y	W	8 MAR 1914	Rosslyn VA	Glenwood
06035	Costolow, Christ., s/o John	74y	W	18 APR 1907	Cherrydale VA	Holyrood
06068	Costolow, Elizabeth	58y	W	26 MAR 1900	Cherrydale VA	Holyrood[1]
05556	Couden, Henry C.	28y	W	16 APR 1906	Ft. Lawton WA	Arlington
03052	Coues, Elliott, scientist	57y	W	25 DEC 1899	Baltimore MD	Rock Creek
01687	Cough, Celia	65y	W	6 AUG 1895	New York NY	Mt. Olivet
14383	Coughlan, John D.	60y	W	27 SEP 1917	Sligo MD	Mt. Olivet
05733	Coughlin, Margaret M.	4y	W	8 AUG 1905	Woodside MD	Mt. Olivet

[1] Removed from St. James Catholic Cemetery, Falls Church, Va., where she was buried 28 MAR 1900.

No.	Name of Deceased	Age	Race	Death Date	Place of Death	Place of Burial
15951	Coughlin, Robert E., Jr.	6m	W	25 AUG 1919	Baltimore MD	Rock Creek
14445	Coulter, Annie E.	64y	W	5 NOV 1917	Baltimore MD	Glenwood
14319	Coulton, Mary	70y	W	27 AUG 1917	Takoma Park MD	Cleveland OH
02243	Coumbe, Effa H.	28y	W	12 AUG 1897	Dorchest. Co. MD	Congressional
01485	Countee, Frederick	70y	C	4 SEP 1894	Arlington VA	Holyrood
01129	Countee, Joseph	12y	C	9 DEC 1892	Arlington VA	Holyrood
14874	Coursen, Eva May	3m	W	21 JUN 1918	Takoma Park MD	Vineland NJ
00155	Courtney, Bales	35y	C	9 SEP 1889	Ardwick Sta. MD	Payne's
07215	Courtney, Mamie	32y	W	27 SEP 1909	Mt. Ranier MD	Glenwood
12326	Courts, Andrew J.	57y	W	21 APR 1914	Baltimore MD	Congressional
13724	Courts, James Carson	61y	W	17 SEP 1916	Arundel Bay MD	Rock Creek
02013	Coutier, Walter	27y	C	7 AUG 1896	Wheeling WV	Harmony
17982	Couzens, Bettie	79y	C	27 JUL 1922	Halls Hill VA	Harmony
14926	Covert, Nellie D.	63y	W	20 JUL 1918	Hampton VA	Cremated
08199	Covert, William E.	65y	W	13 JUL 1911	Laurel MD	Congressional
07288	Cowan, William L.	71y	W	24 NOV 1909	New York NY	Congressional
14120	Cowell, Ella M.	35y	W	2 MAY 1917	Silver Spring MD	Rock Creek
18233	Cowell, Jessie Paterson	72y	W	31 DEC 1922	Hyattsville MD	Glenwood
13921	Cowie, Margaret E., d/o Geo.	64y	W	10 JAN 1917	Martinsburg WV	Oak Hill
01800	Cowl, Marian Page	26y	W	18 DEC 1895	Takoma Park MD	Rock Creek
01542	Cowles, Alfred	3y	W	4 DEC 1894	Baltimore MD	Glenwood
01688	Cowles, Annie Adamson	36y	W	18 AUG 1895	Mt. Hope MD	Glenwood
01541	Cowles, Elizabeth	2y	W	4 JAN 1895	Baltimore MD	Glenwood
12590	Cowles, Lucy G. (Gilmore)	81y	W	29 OCT 1914	Oakland WS	Arlington
02934	Cowling, Dorothy B.	1y	W	4 SEP 1899	Ballston VA	Glenwood
07981	Cowling, Edward O.	30y	W	20 FEB 1911	Oklahoma City OK	Glenwood
08090	Cowling, Mary J.	73y	W	30 APR 1911	Gaithersburg MD	Oak Hill
12465	Cowsill, Ada M.	43y	W	1 AUG 1914	Newark DE	Rock Creek
13052	Cox, Addie Brown	25y	C	11 AUG 1915	Annapolis MD	Mt. Olivet
01689	Cox, Ben. Johnston	13m	W	23 JUL 1895	Hyattsville MD	Rock Creek
07649	Cox, Benjamin W.	79y	W	22 JUL 1910	Atlantic City NJ	Congressional
00582	Cox, Caroline	84y	W	6 AUG 1891	Alexandria VA	Congressional
00937	Cox, Elfrida	63y	W	9 AUG 1893	—	Glenwood
16781	Cox, Ethel Jeannette	9m	C	20 OCT 1920	Bealeton VA	Harmony
07788	Cox, George	16y	W	14 OCT 1910	Washington DC	Mt. Olivet
00936	Cox, Isabel S.	1y	W	13 JUL 1893	Gale Hill VA	Rock Creek
00396	Cox, John B.	62y	M	2 SEP 1890	Cumberland MD	Harmony
15923	Cox, John H.	53y	W	9 AUG 1919	Ashtabula OH	Congressional
16279	Cox, Lawrence M.	68y	W	31 JAN 1920	Macon GA	Oak Hill
03481	Cox, Lewis B.	45y	W	11 APR 1901	Portland OR	Rock Creek
04861	Cox, Margaret E.	29y	W	21 AUG 1904	Bristersburg VA	Mt. Olivet
01389	Cox, Patrick	40y	W	26 APR 1894	Pittsburgh PA	Mt. Olivet
08612	Cox, Walter Dunlop	34y	W	27 APR 1912	Vineland NJ	Oak Hill
08813	Cox, William E.	47y	W	5 SEP 1912	Riggs Farm MD	Oak Hill
12798	Cox, William Sherman	48y	W	6 MAR 1915	Tuxedo MD	Congressional
15758	Coxe, Frances Matilda	71y	W	28 APR 1919	Silver Spring MD	Glenwood
03953a	Coyle, Anna McNeir	70y	W	3 JUL 1902	Yonkers NY	Congressional
07036	Coyle, Edward Emory	35y	W	20 MAY 1909	Towson MD	Congressional
00339	Coyle, Emma B.	11y	W	5 JUN 1890	Bridgeton NJ	Oak Hill
07330	Coyle, Frank D.	57y	W	17 DEC 1909	New York NY	Mt. Olivet
06730	Coyle, Hugh	65y	W	13 SEP 1908	Chicago IL	Arlington
03077	Coyle, Mary Ann	73y	W	25 JAN 1900	Inswood PA	Oak Hill
12545	Coyle, Samuel C.	1y	W	28 SEP 1914	Walkers Chap. VA	Holyrood
15601	Coyne, Sarah L.	68y	W	5 FEB 1919	Bethesda MD	Mt. Olivet
15815	Cozzens, Jessie C.	49y	W	7 JUN 1919	Cherrydale VA	Congressional
00817	Cr___, Elizabeth	28y	C	21 MAY 1892	Pr. Geo. Co. MD	Mt. Olivet
06213	Crabbs, Ernest L.	14y	W	2 SEP 1907	Marshall Hall MD	Congressional
07118	Cragen, Harry Wilton, s/o A.	60y	W	19 JUL 1909	Skyland VA	Cremated
13185	Crager, Cuna Parker, Jr.	1y	W	8 NOV 1915	Takoma Park MD	Philadelphia PA

District of Columbia Foreign Death Records, 1888-1923

No.	Name of Deceased	Age	Race	Death Date	Place of Death	Place of Burial
13251	Cragin, Charles I.	72y	W	15 DEC 1915	Philadelphia PA	Rock Creek
00583	Craig, Hattie J.	28y	W	20 JUL 1891	Chicago IL	Glenwood
13452	Craig, John William, Sr.	73y	W	11 APR 1916	Indianapolis IN	Glenwood
00417	Craig, Joseph H.	26y	C	9 OCT 1890	New York NY	Graceland
07239	Craig, Mary Jane	74y	W	16 OCT 1909	Meadows MD	Congressional
04009	Craig, Mary M.	58y	W	7 SEP 1902	Mt. Sterling KY	Glenwood
14214	Craig, Robert	74y	W	4 JUL 1917	Pittsburgh PA	Oak Hill
07461	Craig, Thomas	45y	C	10 MAR 1910	Nomini VA	Payne's
01690	Cragg, William	40y	C	30 MAY 1895	Bethlehem PA	Woodlawn
18370	Craighead, Ida	42y	C	23 FEB 1923	Philadelphia PA	Mt. Olivet[1]
01967	Craighead, James M.	75y	W	2 AUG 1896	Brunswick MD	W. Elizabeth PA
12680	Craine, Dennis I.	2y	W	28 DEC 1914	Seat Pleasant MD	Mt. Olivet
16881	Cralle, Caroline H. (Graham)	39y	W	19 FEB 1908	Colo. Spgs. CO	Rock Creek
16398	Cralley, Sallie	68y	W	17 MAR 1920	Philadelphia PA	Payne's
17221	Cramer, Edward T.	28y	W	5 OCT 1918	France	Glenwood
01618	Cramer, Elizabeth C.	88y	W	20 MAR 1895	Fairmont WV	Oak Hill
05446	Crampsey, Mary L.	30y	W	28 JAN 1906	Baltimore MD	Oak Hill
00435	Crampton, Creinemma	3y	C	12 NOV 1890	Newark NJ	Jones' Chapel
14430	Crandall, Clara	65y	W	23 AUG 1909	Greenville PA	Alexandria VA
02653	Crandall, Martha Lillie	62y	W	9 NOV 1898	Annandale VA	Glenwood
18028	Crandell, Isabel	75y	W	21 AUG 1922	E. Orange NJ	Glenwood
12752	Crandell, Richard A.	77y	W	6 FEB 1915	Hyattsville MD	Rock Creek
12577	Crane, Aaron M.	75y	W	22 OCT 1914	Norfolk VA	Cremated
17405	Crane, Augustus	55y	W	11 SEP 1921	Omaha NE	Glenwood
12151	Crane, James Martin	65y	W	8 JAN 1914	Wilmington NC	Rock Creek
11882	Crane, Lida D. (Flint)	66y	W	7 JUL 1913	Norfolk VA	Cremated
12868	Craven, James	50y	W	7 APR 1915	Cleveland OH	Mt. Olivet
06853	Crawford, A.H., a.k.a.	34y	W	12 DEC 1908	Catonsville MD	Rock Creek
00542	Crawford, Abraham	28y	C	7 MAR 1891	Pr. Geo. Co. MD	Mt. Olivet
02368	Crawford, Anna	109y	C	3 FEB 1898	Pr. Geo. Co. MD	Mt. Olivet
15646	Crawford, Caroline	55y	W	27 FEB 1919	Brentwood MD	Harmony
07586	Crawford, Cora R.	43y	W	20 JUN 1910	So. Pines NC	Mt. Olivet
11886	Crawford, Emily	65y	C	9 JUL 1913	Forestville MD	Payne's
08488	Crawford, Emma	17y	W	22 JAN 1912	Baltimore MD	Congressional
02560	Crawford, George W.	41y	W	15 AUG 1898	Hampton VA	Congressional
16209	Crawford, Harold Lee	29y	W	10 JAN 1920	Ft. Lyon CO	Arlington
03241	Crawford, James	70y	W	20 JUL 1900	Montg. Co. MD	Rock Creek
08804	Crawford, Lydia B.	75y	W	3 SEP 1912	Chevy Chase MD	Glenwood
15229	Crawford, Maggie E.	48y	C	15 OCT 1918	Atlantic City NJ	Harmony
02156	Crawford, Mary	50y	C	25 APR 1897	Brightseat MD	Mt. Olivet
12715	Crawford, Nathaniel	83y	C	12 JAN 1915	Glen Arden MD	Mt. Olivet
00460	Crawford, Newton	81y	W	14 DEC 1890	Hyattsville MD	Congressional
03505	Crawford, Rachael	57y	C	8 MAY 1901	Alex. Co. VA	Mt. Olivet
14597	Crawford, Raymond L.	21y	W	20 JAN 1918	Portsmouth VA	Glenwood
07530	Crawford, Robert	24y	W	1 MAY 1910	Hathead Co. MT	Glenwood
16301	Crawford, William H.	52y	W	8 FEB 1920	Ft. Worth TX	Congressional
02994	Creary, William E.	56y	W	29 JUL 1899	Frederick Co. VA	Arlington VA
17247	Crebo, Florence Marie	27y	W	17 JUN 1921	Ft. Lyon CO	Congressional
05209	Credic, Margaret	9m	C	11 JUL 1905	Glen Echo MD	Harmony
02431	Credway, Louis	22y	W	30 APR 1898	Hyattsville MD	Glenwood
07154	Creecy, Charles Eaton	61y	W	9 AUG 1909	Atlantic City NJ	Mt. Olivet
14893	Creek, Clarence L.	9m	C	30 JUN 1918	Bladensburg MD	Payne's
01299	Creighton, Samuel E.	83y	W	2 MAR 1894	St. Mary's Co. MD	Congressional
12818	Creighton, Sarah E.	60y	W	15 MAR 1915	Glen Echo MD	Edenburgh VA
16713	Cremin, Margaret	83y	W	15 SEP 1920	Baltimore MD	Mt. Olivet
17218	Cresson, William Henry, Rev.	74y	W	7 JUN 1921	Charleston SC	Rock Creek

---

[1] Certificate in error gives month as March, as source document gives February which corresponds to numbering sequence.

No.	Name of Deceased	Age	Race	Death Date	Place of Death	Place of Burial
07220	Crews, William P.H.	66y	W	30 SEP 1909	Laurel MD	Rock Creek
03275	Criddle, Henry Fletcher	35y	W	23 AUG 1900	Swansboro VA	Glenwood
12237	Cridler, Thomas W.	63y	W	23 FEB 1914	New York NY	Rock Creek
15074	Crilly, John	21y	W	28 SEP 1918	N. Sidney, N.S.	Mt. Olivet
01130	Crimmins, John	76y	W	15 NOV 1892	Falls Church VA	Mt. Olivet
00818	Crippen, Frank E.	c.40y	W	5 AUG 1892	Newark OH	Tarrington CN
12661	Cripps, Lydia B.	75y	W	17 DEC 1914	Philadelphia PA	Congressional
04021	Crist, Fowler Raymond	2y	W	2 SEP 1902	Nantucket MA	Glenwood
08048	Crist, George R.	32y	W	3 APR 1911	Baltimore MD	Mt. Olivet
05276	Crittenden, Thomas Turpin	79y	W	6 SEP 1905	Gloucester MA	Rock Creek
04896	Crocker, Anna D.B.	44y	W	13 SEP 1904	Philadelphia PA	St. Mary's
08438	Crocker, Ellen V. (Carpenter)	65y	W	26 DEC 1911	Jewell VA	Rock Creek
02552	Crocker, Frances W.	8y	W	11 AUG 1898	Laurel MD	Glenwood
12104	Crocker, William C.	34y	W	22 NOV 1913	Pittsburgh PA	Congressional
16376	Crockett, Sally Boyd	81y	W	12 FEB 1920	Valdez AK	Oak Hill
15715	Crockett, Sydney	66y	C	4 APR 1919	Camden NJ	Harmony
12757	Crockett, Warren E.	50y	W	7 FEB 1915	Marietta GA	Arlington VA
13332	Croggan, August B.	21y	W	30 JAN 1916	Baltimore MD	Glenwood
06724	Croggan, Charles	35y	W	11 SEP 1908	Jersey City NJ	Mt. Olivet
03833	Croghan, Bridget	63y	W	25 MAR 1902	Baltimore MD	Mt. Olivet
07756	Croghan, John	66y	W	22 SEP 1910	Lynchburg VA	Cremated
01691	Cromelin, Ada	2m	W	5 OCT 1895	Atlantic City NJ	Mt. Olivet
04104	Cromelin, Roland F.	45y	W	20 DEC 1902	New York NY	Mt. Olivet
13879	Cromer, Presley Julian	28y	C	22 DEC 1916	Lynchburg VA	Harmony
05082	Crompton, Emma	38y	C	13 APR 1905	Orange NJ	Payne's
14190	Cromwell, Bartlett J.	79y	W	24 JUN 1917	Montrose PA	Arlington
08212	Cronin, Catherine	84y	W	22 JUL 1911	Berkeley Sp. WV	Holyrood
04358	Cronkite, James W.	62y	W	16 JUN 1903	Plainfield NJ	Arlington
06175	Crook, Charles	11m	W	9 AUG 1907	Bethesda MD	Holyrood
08610	Cropley, Arthur B.	67y	W	23 APR 1912	Baltimore MD	Oak Hill
02400	Cropley, William S.	87y	W	3 MAR 1898	Montg. Co. MD	Rock Creek
16281	Cropper, Jane M.	58y	C	4 FEB 1920	Fairmont Hts. MD	Mt. Olivet
05646	Crosby, Henry T.	63y	W	13 JUL 1906	Baltimore MD	Arlington
16066	Crosman, Alice Hildreth	52y	W	21 OCT 1919	Riverdale MD	Glenwood
17970	Croson, Robert, s/o Henry	52y	W	21 JUL 1922	Asheville NC	Clarendon VA
00938	Cross, Charles L.	7d	W	5 JUN 1893	Carlin Spgs. VA	Congressional
01034	Cross, Charles W.	35y	W	13 APR 1893	Seneca MD	Oak Hill
00096	Cross, Claude	8y	W	9 JUL 1889	Four Mile Run VA	Graceland
13160	Cross, Ella E.	56y	W	21 OCT 1915	New York NY	Congressional
09072	Cross, Harry H.	47y	W	c.12 FEB 1913	Berkley Co. WV	Congressional
17638	Cross, Jay Edgar	49y	W	15 JAN 1922	Takoma Park MD	Rock Creek
02864	Cross, Margaret Frances	8m	W	2 JUL 1899	Hyattsville MD	Mt. Olivet
02401	Cross, Mary	38y	C	20 MAR 1898	New York NY	Harmony
08570	Cross, Millard F.	60y	W	26 MAR 1912	Newark NJ	Congressional
03938	Cross, Morell	1y	W	25 JUL 1902	Ballston VA	Congressional
01543	Cross, Randall T., brakeman	42y	W	17 JAN 1895	Chicago IL	Glenwood
11805	Cross, Samuel	74y	W	8 MAY 1913	Atlantic City NJ	Arlington
01400	Cross, Trueman B.B.	65y	W	23 JUN 1894	Hyattsville MD	Congressional
00095	Cross, William	c.35y	C	4 JAN 1892	Muirkirk MD	Graceland
14612	Crossfield, Florence N.	39y	W	31 JAN 1918	Riverdale MD	Glenwood
14945	Crossfield, Jeheil	79y	W	30 JUL 1918	Riverdale MD	Glenwood
00082	Crossier, Emma R.	69y	W	27 JUN 1889	Suitland MD	North Adams MA
17066	Crouch, Edwin D.	83y	W	25 MAR 1921	Pr. Geo. Co. MD	Congressional
16186	Crounse, Amos	84y	W	5 JAN 1920	Takoma Park MD	Arlington
14274	Crouse, Louise	69y	W	4 AUG 1917	Tuckahoe VA	Cremated
16365	Crovo, Mary Ann	78y	W	7 MAR 1920	Alex. Co. VA	St. Mary's
14778	Crowder, Oliver L.	45y	W	28 APR 1918	Atlantic City NJ	Glenwood
14899	Crowley, Johanna	70y	W	6 JUL 1918	Bethesda MD	Holyrood
13502	Crowley, John	73y	W	12 MAY 1916	Columbia Pk. MD	Mt. Olivet

District of Columbia Foreign Death Records, 1888-1923

No.	Name of Deceased	Age	Race	Death Date	Place of Death	Place of Burial
16617	Crowley, John	53y	W	21 JUL 1920	Rockaway B. NY	Mt. Olivet
15562	Crowley, Josephine	62y	W	18 JAN 1919	Alexandria VA	St. Mary's
07857	Crowley, Thomas F.	35y	W	8 DEC 1910	Landover MD	Mt. Olivet
13527	Crown, Charles R.L.	90y	W	31 MAY 1916	Baltimore MD	Congressional
15129	Crown, Cora	38y	C	10 OCT 1918	Philadelphia PA	Woodlawn
17021	Crown, Maud Juanita	41y	W	6 MAR 1921	Cherrydale VA	Congressional
08097	Crown, Sarah E.	82y	W	2 MAY 1911	Brentwood MD	Congressional
06568	Crowninshield, Arent S.	65y	W	27 MAY 1908	Philadelphia PA	Arlington
12046	Crowninshield, Mary Bradford	69y	W	14 OCT 1913	Stoneham MA	Arlington
04700	Cruikshank, Mary D.	34y	W	5 MAY 1904	New York NY	Congressional
03014	Cruit, Infant of W.W.	10d	W	28 NOV 1899	Takoma Park MD	Oak Hill
15207	Cruit, Marjory	18y	W	17 OCT 1918	Takoma Park MD	Oak Hill
12851	Cruit, Mary	73y	W	30 MAR 1915	Takoma Park MD	Oak Hill
00437	Crumbaugh, Annie Mabel	9y	W	15 NOV 1890	Montg. Co. MD	Holyrood
06409	Crummer, Mary	48y	C	29 JAN 1908	Chevy Chase MD	Crum Sta. MD
02187	Crump, Frank Howard, Jr.	6y	W	10 MAR 1897	Hyattsville MD	Glenwood
18110	Crump, Laura	35y	C	10 OCT 1922	Cedar Hts. MD	Harmony
12735	Crump, Walter A.	36y	W	27 JAN 1915	Mt. Ranier MD	Glenwood
06144	Cruse, James T.	19y	W	19 JUL 1907	Chelsea MA	Arlington VA
03133	Cruse, Madeline	57y	W	18 MAR 1900	Catonsville MD	Prospect Hill
08066	Crusoe, Arthur J.	42y	C	14 APR 1911	Hot Springs VA	Woodlawn
07783	Crutchet, Charles Wesley	26y	W	15 APR 1910	Hannibal OH	Mt. Olivet
05020	Crutchett, Catherine	52y	W	5 FEB 1905	Falls Church VA	Mt. Olivet
04045	Crutchfield, Irene	18y	C	1 OCT 1902	Long Branch NJ	Harmony
07974	Crutchfield, John	38y	C	14 FEB 1911	Baltimore MD	Fredericksburg VA
17834	Crutchfield, Novella	10y	C	3 MAY 1922	Baltimore MD	Mt. Zion West
00414	Cryer, Lucinda A.	53y	C	8 OCT 1890	Philadelphia PA	Harmony
04535	Cryer, William Ford	10m	W	12 AUG 1903	Arlington VA	Congressional
03684	Cudmore, Peter	30y	W	17 JUN 1901	Pittsburgh PA	Mt. Olivet
14059	Cuffy, Edna (Miller)	27y	C	26 MAR 1917	Hampton VA	Woodlawn
00584	Cullen, Georgina	11y	W	29 AUG 1891	New York NY	Mt. Olivet
04384	Cullen, Margaret Mary	4m	W	11 JUL 1903	Falls Church VA	Mt. Olivet
06990	Culley, Theodore	52y	W	16 APR 1909	Takoma Park MD	Rock Creek
03944	Culligan, Patrick William	24y	W	9 JUL 1902	Portsmouth VA	Mt. Olivet
06853	Cullin, Orlan Clyde, a.k.a.	34y	W	12 DEC 1908	Catonsville MD	Rock Creek
18343	Cullinan, Elizabeth	89y	W	10 FEB 1923	Chevy Chase MD	Congressional
01801	Cullinan, James A.	28y	W	3 NOV 1895	Ryan, Ind. Ter.	Mt. Olivet
01300	Cullinane, Annie C.	3y	W	11 JAN 1894	Brooklyn NY	Mt. Olivet
15676	Cullinane, Jeremiah L.	1y	W	18 MAR 1919	Friendship H. MD	Mt. Olivet
15983	Cullinane, John F.	10y	W	8 SEP 1919	New York NY	Rock Creek
07078	Culver, Abraham	53y	W	23 JUN 1909	Baltimore MD	Arlington
04062	Culver, Frank E.	42y	W	9 OCT 1902	Cap. View Pk. MD	Rock Creek
11901	Culver, Gertrude E.	48y	W	15 JUL 1913	Mecklenburg NY	Rock Creek
02865	Culver, Leonora	1y	W	20 JUL 1899	Cap. View Pk. MD	Rock Creek
07810	Cumberland, Frank	26y	W	26 JUN 1910	Gettysburg PA	Congressional
00819	Cumberland, James A.	29y	W	16 JUL 1892	Hyattsville MD	Oak Hill
15763	Cumberland, Mary C.	83y	W	4 MAY 1919	Occoquan VA	Mt. Olivet
03147	Cummings, Alexander B.	50y	W	25 MAR 1900	Philadelphia PA	Philadelphia PA
00585	Cummings, Ann	48y	W	1 SEP 1891	Mt. Hope MD	—
00065	Cummings, James	75y	W	24 MAY 1889	Montg. Co. MD	Holyrood
18076	Cummings, Marian B.	9m	W	21 SEP 1922	Deal NJ	—
07652	Cummings, Mary Ellen	76y	W	26 JUL 1910	Chevy Chase MD	Holyrood
04068	Cummings, Tony	35y	W	3 NOV 1902	New York NY	Mt. Olivet
01468	Cummins, Mary	68y	W	23 AUG 1894	Hyattsville MD	Rock Creek
17740	Cumor, Mary	64y	W	12 MAR 1922	Baltimore MD	St. Mary's
01035	Cuney, Joseph	17y	C	23 APR 1893	Boston MA	Harmony
00461	Cunningham, Charles Aug.	10y	W	30 JUN 1890	Heathsville VA	Mt. Olivet
07699	Cunningham, Charles M.	2m	W	20 AUG 1910	Bethesda MD	Rock Creek
01132	Cunningham, Elizabeth	58y	W	6 JAN 1893	Great Falls MT	Congressional

No.	Name of Deceased	Age	Race	Death Date	Place of Death	Place of Burial
17208	Cunningham, Josephine A.	71y	W	2 JUN 1921	Dominion Hts. VA	Glenwood
08653	Cunningham, Lillie G.	44y	W	26 MAY 1912	Los Angeles CA	Rock Creek
12163	Cunningham, Logan M.	26y	W	14 JAN 1914	Cherrydale VA	Glenwood
14227	Cunningham, Mary	59y	W	14 JUL 1917	Catonsville MD	Rock Creek
17370	Cunningham, Maurice B.	43y	W	25 AUG 1921	Arlington Co. VA	Oak Hill
07758	Cunningham, Richard William	4m	W	24 SEP 1910	Woodmont MD	Rock Creek
01131	Cunningham, Robert E.	4y	W	26 NOV 1892	Rosslyn VA	Oak Hill
18467	Cupid, John C.	55y	C	8 APR 1923	Philadelphia PA	Alexandria VA
08839	Cupollini, Angelo	18y	W	14 SEP 1912	Muirkirk MD	Mt. Olivet
17949	Curley, James	35y	W	8 JUL 1922	Pittsburgh PA	Glenwood
16810	Curran, Clara M.	77y	W	15 NOV 1920	Whitney Point NY	Rock Creek
13245	Curran, Francis M.	47y	W	11 DEC 1915	Ellicott City MD	Glenwood
15992	Curran, Frank W.	47y	W	14 SEP 1919	College Park MD	Mt. Olivet
08073	Curren, Annie Christian	19y	W	17 APR 1911	Hyattsville MD	Holyrood
14225	Curren, William E.	55y	W	11 JUL 1917	Hyattsville MD	Mt. Olivet
17612	Curriden, Samuel W.	71y	W	26 DEC 1921	Miami FL	Rock Creek
05578	Curry, Edward, s/o F.A.	8m	W	18 MAY 1906	Campbell Co. VA	Mt. Olivet
07612	Curry, Florence R.	34y	W	4 JUL 1910	Saranac Lake NY	Prospect Hill
17575	Curry, Frank	70y	W	8 DEC 1921	Clarendon VA	Glenwood
01968	Curry, Hannah Singer	68y	W	14 SEP 1896	Oak Crest MD	Rock Creek
05419	Curry, Henry F.	23y	W	4 JAN 1906	Severn MD	Newport News VA
03818	Curry, Kate Anna Bristow	8m	W	14 MAR 1902	Hyattsville MD	Oak Hill
01802	Curry, Mary	25y	C	25 DEC 1895	Richmond VA	Harmony
08055	Curtain, Joseph	42y	W	5 APR 1911	Occoquan VA	Mt. Olivet
16163	Curtin, Ethel S.	14y	W	25 DEC 1919	Saranac Lake NY	Congressional
00588	Curtin, Mary A.	53y	W	7 AUG 1891	Fairfax Co. VA	Mt. Olivet
12192	Curtis, Alvin G.	4y	W	31 JAN 1914	Chevy Chase MD	Rock Creek
08735	Curtis, Arthur D.	29y	W	20 JUL 1912	Patton CA	Glenwood
18284	Curtis, Carmel (Meehan)	21y	W	20 JAN 1923	Saranac Lake NY	Arlington
04824	Curtis, Caroline Farnham	59y	W	1 AUG 1904	Woodside MD	Glenwood
00587	Curtis, Catharine	75y	C	23 AUG 1891	Harpers Ferry WV	Mt. Zion
15969	Curtis, Celestine	35y	C	30 AUG 1919	Arlington VA	Payne's
18281	Curtis, Edward	6h	W	14 JAN 1923	Saranac Lake NY	Arlington
12084	Curtis, Henry A.	72y	W	11 NOV 1913	Takoma Park MD	Rock Creek
13864	Curtis, James M.	75y	W	12 DEC 1916	Hampton VA	Arlington
12233	Curtis, Maggie	32y	C	20 FEB 1914	Alexandria VA	Payne's
09077	Curtis, Melissa Pattie	90y	W	16 FEB 1913	Laurel MD	Cremated
07951	Curtis, Owen B.	39y	W	25 JAN 1911	Bozeman MT	Glenwood
00696	Curtis, Patrick	71y	W	7 JAN 1892	Petersburg VA	Mt. Olivet
00227	Curtis, Robert F.	19y	W	6 NOV 1889	Baltimore Co. MD	Glenwood
12202	Curtis, Walter	26y	C	3 FEB 1914	New York NY	Payne's
08343	Curtis, William E.	60y	W	5 OCT 1911	Philadelphia PA	Rock Creek
04848	Curtiss, Wright	64y	W	17 AUG 1904	Woodside MD	Glenwood
02898	Cusack, Annie	62y	W	10 JUL 1899	Ponse, P.R.	Mt. Olivet
01301	Cusack, John P.	22y	W	12 MAY 1889	Ft. Niobrara NE	Mt. Olivet
12786	Cusack, Virginia M.F.	78y	W	1 MAR 1915	Chevy Chase MD	Glenwood
00299	Cusbert, William M.	23y	C	27 MAR 1890	Braddock PA	Baptist
13516	Cushman, Belinda B.	85y	W	20 MAR 1913	Rockville MD	Rock Creek
06251	Cushman, Edwin Charles	39y	W	27 SEP 1907	Cedarville VA	Cremated
03165	Cushman, G.W.	91y	W	14 APR 1900	Rockville MD	Rock Creek
08621	Cushman, Ruth Dansbel	22y	W	7 MAY 1912	Vienna VA	Cremated
18486	Cushman, Wayman C., Dr.	58y	W	14 APR 1923	Hagerstown MD	Cremated
04557	Cusick, Kate	46y	W	31 DEC 1903	Baltimore MD	Mt. Olivet
16164	Custard, John Harry, painter	26y	W	25 DEC 1919	Cherrydale VA	Holyrood
13181	Custis, James B.G.	60y	W	4 NOV 1915	Clayton NY	Rock Creek
01036	Cuthbert, James H., Rev.	68y	W	6 MAY 1893	Aiken SC	Oak Hill
15519	Cutter, Cora F.	51y	W	2 JAN 1919	New York NY	Rock Creek
06002	Cutter, Edwin Kendall	35y	W	19 MAR 1907	Paris, France	Glenwood
01544	Cutts, Martha Jefferson	70y	W	17 FEB 1895	Boston MA	Oak Hill

District of Columbia Foreign Death Records, 1888-1923

No.	Name of Deceased	Age	Race	Death Date	Place of Death	Place of Burial
17707	Cyrus, Marie	28y	C	20 FEB 1922	Pittsburgh PA	Woodlawn

No.	Name of Deceased	Age	Race	Death Date	Place of Death	Place of Burial
	D					
01803	Dabney, Eddie	16y	C	21 OCT 1895	New York NY	Mt. Olivet
05492	Dabney, William B.	26y	W	1 MAR 1906	Eusley AL	Rock Creek
17090	Dade, Walter H.	54y	W	26 DEC 1920	Norfolk VA	Cremated
07683	Daffer, Carl H.	29y	W	10 AUG 1910	Princeton MN	Glenwood
13480	Daffer, Frederick	75y	W	26 APR 1916	Hampton VA	Arlington
16473	Daffer, Hugh Taylor	73y	W	7 MAY 1920	Clarendon VA	Glenwood
02915	Dahlgren, John V.	31y	W	11 AUG 1899	Colo. Spgs. CO	College
00589	Dahlgren, Joseph Drexel	1y	W	26 JUL 1891	Narragansett RI	College
17605	Dahlman, Gastaf	41y	W	23 DEC 1921	Laurel MD	Arlington
16525	Dailey, Elizabeth M.K.	80y	W	1 MAY 1920	St. Augustine FL	Congressional
11973	Dailey, Ethel E.	15y	C	24 AUG 1913	Bladensburg MD	Mt. Olivet
00466	Dailey, James H.	59y	W	19 FEB 1891	Montg. Co. MD	Holyrood
18550	Dailey, Robert W.	56y	W	20 MAY 1923	Philadelphia PA	Congressional
08876	Daily, John H.	65y	C	4 OCT 1912	Bladensburg MD	Harmony
01855	Daily, Olive, Dr.	60y	W	4 JAN 1896	Independence MO	Congressional
12347	Daley, Mike	42y	W	30 APR 1914	Newport AR	Mt. Olivet
01434	Daley, Philip	9m	W	13 JUL 1894	Frederick Co. MD	Mt. Olivet
17929	Dalrymple, James A.D.	76y	W	2 JUL 1922	Ardmore MD	Congressional
06546	Dalrymple, Virginia	19y	W	9 MAY 1908	Liberty NY	Rock Creek
04883	Dalton, Francis W.	1y	W	9 SEP 1904	Buenavista PA	Congressional
03943	Dalton, Gertrude E.	1y	W	12 JUL 1902	Hyattsville MD	Congressional
01804	Dalton, William N., agent	c.54y	W	26 NOV 1895	Del Ray VA	Glenwood
02305	Daly, Alice	28y	W	29 SEP 1897	Hampton VA	Mt. Olivet
02420	Daly, B.M.	21y	W	10 MAR 1898	Norfolk MD	Harpers Ferry WV
16128	Daly, E., Mr.	69y	W	28 NOV 1919	Orlando FL	Cremated
15137	Daly, Edward	38y	W	11 OCT 1918	Maryland Pk. MD	Mt. Olivet
04502	Daly, James A.	35y	W	5 NOV 1903	Alexandria VA	Holyrood
04590	Daly, John M.	74y	W	4 FEB 1904	Broad Creek VA	Prospect Hill
07715	Daly, Mary A.	50y	W	28 AUG 1910	Rockville MD	Mt. Olivet
04787	Daly, Timothy D.	68y	W	8 JUL 1904	Hot Springs VA	Mt. Olivet
06148	Daly, William C.	17y	W	21 JUL 1907	Jefferson Co. WV	Holyrood
06639	Dalzell, Hettie	67y	W	12 JUL 1908	Philadelphia PA	Glenwood
08815	Dame, Anna Mae	30y	W	4 SEP 1912	Detroit MI	Rock Creek
16566	Dame, Anna S.	72y	W	27 JUN 1920	Detroit MI	Rock Creek
12624	Dampman, Paul E., Jr.	2y	W	18 NOV 1914	Boston MA	Arlington VA
14268	Dandelet, Rachel V.	3y	W	2 AUG 1917	Chesa. Bea. MD	Glenwood
13891	Dandrich, William, s/o Bird	53y	C	26 DEC 1916	Newark NJ	Payne's
12303	Dandridges, Charles	60y	C	7 APR 1914	Asbury Park NJ	Payne's
01460	Danenhower, James R. Smoot	1y	W	26 JUL 1894	Alexandria VA	Rock Creek
08626	Danforth, John T.D.	1y	W	31 DEC 1881	Washington DC	Glenwood
15600	Danforth, M.E.	57y	W	1 FEB 1919	Canton OH	Oak Hill
07316	Dangerfield, Earnest	22y	C	5 DEC 1909	Atlantic City NJ	Payne's
17312	Dangerfield, Thomas A.	43y	C	19 JUL 1921	Baltimore MD	Harmony
13903	Danhakl, Anton	45y	W	30 DEC 1916	Wilmington DE	St. Mary's
12607	Daniel, Henry M.	24y	C	9 NOV 1914	Boston MA	Woodlawn
07674	Daniel, Simms C.	24y	C	4 AUG 1910	Indian Head MD	Norfolk VA
17467	Daniels, Charles S.	58y	C	13 OCT 1921	Brentwood MD	Harmony
17280	Daniels, Francis B.	19y	W	2 JUL 1921	Falls Church VA	Mt. Olivet
16638	Daniels, Joseph J.	35y	W	2 AUG 1920	Saratoga Spg. NY	Arlington
18293	Daniels, Miranda	96y	W	23 JAN 1923	Cottage City MD	Congressional
07139	Daniels, Ruth A.	58y	C	27 JUL 1909	Brentwood MD	Harmony
12513	Danner, Glover C.	29y	W	22 AUG 1914	Omaha NE	Rock Creek
02130	Dant, Katie V.	37y	C	2 MAR 1897	Philadelphia PA	Harmony
02244	Dant, William H.	40y	C	6 AUG 1897	Asbury Park NJ	Mt. Olivet
13278	Daphney, William	75y	C	30 DEC 1915	Hampton VA	Arlington
03192	Darby, Edward	57y	W	22 MAY 1900	Falls Church VA	Oak Hill
02779	Darby, Edward, farmer	94y	W	20 MAR 1899	Laytonsville MD	Oak Hill

No.	Name of Deceased	Age	Race	Death Date	Place of Death	Place of Burial
05452	Darby, Rufus H.	52y	W	2 FEB 1906	Upton Hill VA	Oak Hill
02302	Darden, Thomas	51y	W	11 NOV 1897	Baltimore MD	Glenwood
00697	Darling, Andrew J.	27y	W	7 NOV 1891	River Rd. MD	Holyrood
07537	Darling, Flora A.	70y	W	6 JAN 1910	New York NY	Congressional
05740	Darling, George A.	64y	W	17 SEP 1906	Takoma MD	Arlington
01692	Darlington, Charlotte G.	76y	W	4 JUL 1895	Due West SC	Oak Hill
00140	Darne, Elmer	9m	W	30 AUG 1889	Fairfax Co. VA	Holyrood
02916	Darneille, Louise Riggs	10m	W	17 AUG 1899	Mt. Lake Pk. MD	Rock Creek
08166	Darneille, Margaret Stewart	43y	W	27 JUN 1911	Wash. Grove MD	Oak Hill
06227	Darneille, Philip A.	71y	W	13 SEP 1907	Gloucester MA	Oak Hill
17436	Darnell, Laura I.	80y	W	27 SEP 1921	Silver Spring MD	Rock Creek
01693	Darnielle, John H.	31y	W	28 MAY 1895	Philadelphia PA	Oak Hill
08321	Darr, Catherine Armstrong	88y	W	21 SEP 1911	Cincinnati OH	Arlington
00141	Darr, John F.	30y	W	11 AUG 1889	Paris, France	Glenwood
04716	Darrach, Charles M.	10y	W	4 APR 1904	Chicago IL	Glenwood
04214	Darrall, C.B.	—	W	–	New Orleans LA	Glenwood
03792	Darrall, Elizabeth	—	W	12 FEB 1902	Falls Church VA	Glenwood
16831	Darrall, Frances C.	81y	W	27 NOV 1920	Oklahoma City OK	Glenwood
12532	Darrall, John S.	84y	W	16 SEP 1914	Laurel MD	Glenwood
18005	Darrell, Benjamin	73y	W	11 AUG 1922	Atlantic City NJ	Cremated
17844	Darrell, Rose B.	76y	W	10 MAY 1922	Chevy Chase MD	Rock Creek
12215	Darris, Rosie T.	54y	C	8 FEB 1914	Philadelphia PA	Harmony
12136	Dasch, Frederick Arthur	10y	W	24 DEC 1913	Stone Mtn. VA	Baltimore MD
02753	Dasenbrock, John J.	3y	W	8 JUN 1898	Allegheny PA	Mt. Olivet
16748	Daskin, Eugene B.	79y	W	10 OCT 1920	Chevy Chase MD	Rock Creek
17651	Daugherty, Maria Louise	77y	W	JAN 1922	Takoma Park MD	Congressional
05023	Daughton, Martha A.	58y	W	8 FEB 1905	Berwyn MD	Oak Hill
06839	Davenport, Charles	48y	C	3 DEC 1908	New York NY	Harmony
17273	Davenport, Ella Annette	74y	W	28 JUN 1921	Falls Church VA	Rock Creek
00820	Davenport, Isaac W.	45y	C	4 SEP 1892	Newark NJ	Mt. Zion
08385	Davenport, James	79y	C	2 NOV 1911	Shepherdstn. WV	Mt. Zion West
12287	Davenport, James L.	69y	W	2 APR 1914	Falls Church VA	Rock Creek
02973	Davenport, Sophia L.	3m	W	8 OCT 1899	Norfolk VA	Rock Creek
16052	Davenport, Willard Goss, Rev.	76y	W	14 OCT 1919	Detroit MI	Brandon VT
05949	Davidge, John H.	1y	W	22 FEB 1907	Bladensburg MD	Mt. Olivet
05424	Davidge, Sarah E.	28y	C	10 JAN 1906	Bladensburg MD	Mt. Olivet
00590	Davidson, Agnes Drum	8m	W	10 JUL 1891	Montrose MD	Oak Hill
00698	Davidson, Charles	24y	W	11 NOV 1891	Baltimore MD	Graceland
16166	Davidson, Edwin Marulles	48y	W	9 DEC 1919	Jefferson Co. CO	Mt. Olivet
12372	Davidson, Elizabeth	74y	W	20 MAY 1914	Nashville TN	Glenwood
04639	Davidson, Francis S.	59y	W	19 MAR 1904	Washington DC	Rock Creek
02157	Davidson, Henrietta M.	81y	W	18 APR 1897	Elizabeth NJ	Congressional
15066	Davidson, John A.	62y	W	3 OCT 1918	Takoma MD	Milwaukee WI
12952	Davidson, John F.	60y	W	3 JUN 1915	Baltimore MD	Mt. Olivet
16786	Davidson, John Henry	51y	W	29 OCT 1920	Takoma Park MD	Mt. Olivet
13596	Davidson, Margaret W.	80y	W	10 JUL 1916	Hyattsville MD	Oak Hill
15032	Davidson, Robert Grant	92y	W	19 SEP 1918	Potomac MD	Oak Hill
04195	Davidson, William H.	57y	W	2 APR 1903	Silver Spring MD	Rock Creek
03302	Davies, Irving	20y	W	3 OCT 1900	Phoenix AZ	Cedar Hill
01621	Davies, Walter	5y	W	8 MAR 1895	Cherrydale VA	Holyrood
03406	Davis, Agnes M.L.	16m	C	30 JAN 1901	Brentwood MD	Mt. Olivet
17855	Davis, Alexander H.	57y	W	6 FEB 1922	Duluth MN	Rock Creek
06601	Davis, Alford Edward	30y	W	21 JUN 1908	Colgate Creek MD	Rock Creek
07918	Davis, Alice L.	5y	W	12 JAN 1911	Mt. Ranier MD	Glenwood
03255	Davis, Alice S.	39y	C	7 AUG 1900	Battle Creek MI	Woodlawn
15033	Davis, Alvin E.	24y	W	19 SEP 1918	Chelsea MA	Glenwood
13403	Davis, Annie	79y	W	6 MAR 1916	Elmwood MD	Newport RI
15771	Davis, Annie	73y	C	9 MAY 1919	Cedar Hts. MD	Woodlawn
07006	Davis, Archibald H., Jr.	6d	W	27 SEP 1908	Philadelphia PA	Oak Hill

No.	Name of Deceased	Age	Race	Death Date	Place of Death	Place of Burial
06656	Davis, Arthur Fairfax	31y	W	24 JUL 1908	Takoma Park MD	Arlington
12977	Davis, Augustus, Jr.	59y	W	24 JUN 1915	Ballston VA	Glenwood
02421	Davis, Benjamin, farmer	79y	W	12 MAR 1898	Sligo Hts. MD	Rock Creek
00173	Davis, Caroline Augusta	78y	W	24 OCT 1889	Wheaton MD	Glenwood
08848	Davis, Carrie Spaulding	53y	C	21 SEP 1912	Chevy Chase MD	Harmony
05141	Davis, Charles T., Sr.	49y	W	22 MAY 1905	Mathewson NY	Glenwood
17442	Davis, Charles Wesley	76y	W	28 SEP 1921	Berwyn MD	Rock Creek
07998	Davis, Clara R.	66y	W	7 MAR 1911	New York NY	Oak Hill
12615	Davis, Clara Young	38y	W	14 NOV 1914	Jacksonville FL	Rock Creek
03688	Davis, Cushman Kellog	62y	W	27 NOV 1900	St. Paul MN	Arlington VA
01969	Davis, David M.	54y	W	27 JUL 1896	Warrenton VA	Rock Creek
16487	Davis, Edwin	38y	W	13 MAY 1920	Liberty NY	Mt. Olivet
07477	Davis, Eldred G., s/o William	72y	W	22 MAR 1910	Atlantic City NJ	Oak Hill
03163	Davis, Eliza	68y	W	12 APR 1900	Atlantic City NJ	Glenwood
00462	Davis, Elizabeth L.	c.80y	W	13 MAR 1891	Wheaton MD	Mt. Olivet
13346	Davis, Elnora D.	34y	C	9 FEB 1916	Wilberforce OH	Woodlawn
04328	Davis, Emmeline	72y	W	20 AUG 1903	Alex. Co. VA	Congressional
14868	Davis, Ermina McCormick	50y	W	15 JUN 1918	Westfield NJ	Glenwood
07208	Davis, Fannie	12y	W	23 SEP 1909	Falls Church VA	Congressional
09145	Davis, Flora M., d/o Henry F.	19y	W	28 NOV 1886	Waterbury CN	Rock Creek
16634	Davis, Frances T.	84y	W	30 JUL 1920	New York NY	Rock Creek
05409	Davis, George	31y	C	23 DEC 1905	Philadelphia PA	Harmony
00371	Davis, George E.	42y	W	27 JUL 1890	Pr. Geo. Co. MD	Congressional
01343	Davis, George W.	36y	W	8 MAR 1894	Baltimore MD	Congressional
07500	Davis, George William	2m	W	29 MAR 1910	Marietta OH	Mt. Olivet
15732	Davis, Georgia F.	43y	W	16 APR 1919	Mt. Ranier MD	Glenwood
15371	Davis, Harry G.	25y	W	19 NOV 1918	Philadelphia PA	Congressional[1]
01344	Davis, Harry S.	18y	W	13 APR 1894	Raleigh NC	Oak Hill
03610	Davis, Hattie	32y	W	11 AUG 1901	Clifton Sta. VA	Rock Creek
01474	Davis, Henrietta	67y	W	25 AUG 1894	N. Keys MD	Congressional
06803	Davis, Henrietta Morrison	34y	W	6 NOV 1908	Linden MD	Glenwood
15863	Davis, Henry	1y	C	4 JUL 1919	Seat Pleasant MD	Woodlawn
14620	Davis, Henry C.	71y	W	3 FEB 1918	Baltimore MD	Alexandria VA
14152	Davis, Henry F.	80y	W	27 MAY 1917	Torrington CN	Rock Creek
14737	Davis, Hugh M.	26y	W	5 APR 1918	Ft. Houston TX	Arlington
05329	Davis, Hunter A.	29y	W	21 OCT 1905	Denver CO	Rock Creek
09146	Davis, Infant of Alex. H.	SB	W	22 JAN 1891	Waterbury CN	Rock Creek
13962	Davis, Infant of Max	SB	W	30 JAN 1917	Leesburg VA	Elesavetgrad
05391	Davis, James	65y	C	8 DEC 1905	Nonesuch MD	Moore's
08497	Davis, James	84y	W	31 JAN 1912	Takoma Park MD	Rock Creek
15440	Davis, James P.	62y	W	12 DEC 1918	Berlin MD	Rock Creek
12383	Davis, James William	28y	W	28 JUN 1915	Alex. Co. VA	Occuquan VA
02866	Davis, Jane	82y	W	23 JUL 1899	Montg. Co. MD	Rock Creek
07425	Davis, John	c.65y	C	18 FEB 1910	Baltimore MD	Harmony
07569	Davis, John C.B.	33y	W	11 JUN 1910	New York NY	Rock Creek
16495	Davis, John Moore Kelson	76y	W	20 MAY 1920	Hartford CN	Arlington
13950	Davis, John T.	78y	W	28 JAN 1917	Clarendon VA	Congressional
05471	Davis, Joseph B.	38y	C	13 FEB 1906	Philadelphia PA	Harmony
01133	Davis, Joseph S.	33y	C	6 DEC 1892	Baltimore MD	Graceland
17256	Davis, Lawrence W.	20y	W	23 JUN 1921	Ft. Wash. MD	Wichita KS
07458	Davis, Leslie M.	27y	W	4 MAR 1910	Lake OH	Glenwood
07706	Davis, Letrew	11m	C	21 AUG 1910	Pomfret MD	Payne's
03822	Davis, Lewis	23y	C	30 MAY 1902	Potomac River	Westm. Co. VA
00097	Davis, Lillian Edna	1y	C	18 JUL 1889	Manassas VA	Graceland
08051	Davis, Llewellen	33y	W	2 APR 1911	Williamsport PA	Congressional
04860	Davis, Mable Josephine	4m	W	22 AUG 1904	College Park MD	Mt. Olivet

---

[1] Disinterment permit #9850 issued 18 FEB 1919 for removal to Fredericksburg VA.

District of Columbia Foreign Death Records, 1888-1923

No.	Name of Deceased	Age	Race	Death Date	Place of Death	Place of Burial
13680	Davis, Margaret J.	4m	W	25 AUG 1916	Arlington VA	Mt. Olivet
04834	Davis, Maria C.	64y	W	5 AUG 1904	Big Moose NY	Arlington VA
06526	Davis, Martha Ellen	64y	W	26 APR 1908	Raleigh NC	Glenwood
17725	Davis, Martha Thompson	50y	W	5 MAR 1922	New York NY	Oak Hill
05363	Davis, Mary A.	37y	W	15 NOV 1905	Bladensburg MD	Mt. Olivet
08423	Davis, Mary Ann	60y	C	11 DEC 1911	Charlotte NC	Harmony
07177	Davis, Mary Ellen	83y	W	29 AUG 1909	Alexandria VA	Rock Creek
17233	Davis, Mary G.	55y	W	9 JUN 1921	Philadelphia PA	Oak Hill
14204	Davis, Mary R.	72y	W	2 JUL 1917	Clarendon VA	Congressional
17141	Davis, Mary Wilson	52y	W	28 APR 1921	Issaquah WA	Oak Hill
13962	Davis, Maud	9y	C	30 JAN 1917	Huntsville MD	Mt. Olivet
06824	Davis, Noble L.	21y	W	19 NOV 1908	Brentwood MD	Alexandria VA
04546	Davis, Nora Ninette	52y	W	20 DEC 1903	Winchester MA	Rock Creek
03558	Davis, Orva	8y	W	28 JAN 1901	Berwyn MD	Glenwood
17710	Davis, Rena A.	52y	W	24 FEB 1922	Clarendon VA	Rock Creek
07898	Davis, Richard	37y	C	28 DEC 1910	Philadelphia PA	Woodlawn
12794	Davis, Robert	77y	W	3 MAR 1915	Orlando FL	Rock Creek[1]
09131	Davis, Robert S.	34y	W	16 MAR 1913	Indian Head MD	Arlington VA
17091	Davis, Samuel	56y	C	2 APR 1921	Philadelphia PA	Payne's
12618	Davis, Samuel Todd, s/o Jas.	70y	W	16 NOV 1914	Bridgeport CN	Oak Hill
15190	Davis, Sarah E.	78y	W	16 OCT 1918	Jefferson VA	Woodlawn
05755	Davis, Sarah V. (Waites)	49y	C	2 OCT 1906	Halls Hill VA	Harmony
15834	Davis, Stafford	23y	C	14 JUN 1919	West Haven CN	Arlington
06805	Davis, Theodore	9y	W	7 NOV 1908	Takoma Park MD	Rock Creek
12170	Davis, Turner	40y	C	12 JAN 1914	Doc Gulley MD	Payne's
08443	Davis, Walter S., s/o Lewis	27y	C	26 DEC 1911	Eliz. City Co. VA	Harmony
13320	Davis, Willard H.	44y	W	26 JAN 1916	Jacksonville FL	Rock Creek
00156	Davis, William B.	3y	M	16 SEP 1889	VA	NY
07829	Davis, William E.	23y	W	16 NOV 1910	Altamont MD	Mt. Olivet
08652	Davis, William Leonard	66y	—	25 MAY 1912	Tucson AZ	Oak Hill
12650	Davis, William M.	85y	W	10 DEC 1914	Rockville MD	Congressional
03387	Davis, William Randolph	1y	W	4 JAN 1901	Takoma Park MD	Rock Creek
14758	Davison, Harry	22y	W	6 APR 1918	Seattle WA	Glenwood
17943	Dawes, Alice Masters	68y	W	8 JUL 1922	Takoma Park MD	Montrose CO
01037	Dawes, George A.	60y	W	12 FEB 1893	Piney Point MD	Glenwood
00054	Dawes, Lucinda	85y	W	3 APR 1889	Takoma Park MD	Rock Creek
17334	Dawkins, Eva	48y	C	28 JUL 1921	Takoma Park MD	Harmony
14160	Dawson, Clarence E.	47y	W	5 JUN 1917	Chevy Chase MD	Cremated
04365	Dawson, Claude M.	25y	W	28 JUN 1903	Cape May NJ	Rock Creek
02053	Dawson, Elizabeth	75y	W	8 JAN 1897	Rosslyn VA	Oak Hill
04560	Dawson, Katherine	49y	W	9 JAN 1904	Buena Vista VA	Oak Hill
15925	Dawson, Rosa (Irving)	59y	C	8 AUG 1919	Fairmont Hts. MD	Harmony
01694	Dawson, Thomas B., farmer	79y	W	4 JUN 1895	Alex. Co. VA	Oak Hill
13197	Day, Andrew R.	31y	C	9 NOV 1915	Philadelphia PA	Harmony
00699	Day, Annie (Mrs. R.F.)	45y	W	13 FEB 1892	Findlay OH	Mt. Olivet
07223	Day, Ella V.	40y	C	30 SEP 1909	Atlantic City NJ	Falls Church VA
16647	Day, Ellen Louisa (Whiting)	76y	W	7 AUG 1920	Carteret Co. NC	Cremated
04451	Day, John	15y	W	30 AUG 1903	Hawkins Point MD	Rock Creek
04092	Day, John A.	33y	W	17 NOV 1902	Garrett Park MD	Rock Creek
16061	Day, Joseph T., Jr.	1m	W	19 OCT 1918	Cambridge MA	Glenwood
16168	Day, Mary L.	9y	W	26 DEC 1919	Capitol Hts. MD	Mt. Olivet
04057	Day, Norris C.	24y	W	17 OCT 1902	Philadelphia PA	Forestville MD
17895	Day, Susan C.	69y	W	9 JUN 1922	Euclid OH	Oak Hill
02515	Dayhoff, Frank McGhee	31y	W	10 JUL 1898	Baltimore MD	Glenwood
08528	Deaborn, Sarah H.	84y	W	27 FEB 1912	Linden MD	Tilton NH
06653	Deakins, Louis Thomas	24y	W	23 JUL 1908	Riverdale MD	Mt. Olivet

[1] Disinterment permit #8544 for reinterment in Woodlawn Cemetery, New York NY, 7 FEB 1916.

No.	Name of Deceased	Age	Race	Death Date	Place of Death	Place of Burial
05745	Deakins, Mrs. W.F.	45y	W	1892	Ft. Pendleton MD	Rock Creek
07585	Deale, George	11y	W	19 JUL 1910	C. River VA	Congressional
12603	Dean, Addie M.	17y	W	7 NOV 1914	University Pk. MD	Methodist
05683	Dean, Amanda M.	67y	W	11 AUG 1906	Lake Placid NY	Rock Creek
12446	Dean, Annie S.	52y	W	17 JUL 1914	University Pk. MD	Methodist
16971	Dean, Byron L.	76y	W	7 FEB 1921	Orlando FL	Cremated
05321	Dean, Charles	31y	C	18 OCT 1905	Allegheny PA	Harmony
12330	Dean, Charles A.	22y	W	26 APR 1914	Montg. Co. MD	Methodist
00463	Dean, E.C.	80y	W	23 DEC 1890	St. Louis MN	Rock Creek
14718	Dean, Eliza Byron	76y	W	26 MAR 1918	Sandwich MA	Rock Creek
05028	Dean, John William	20y	W	10 FEB 1905	Baltimore MD	Barnaby MD
03161	Dean, John Wright	69y	W	8 APR 1900	Pantucket RI	Glenwood
14930	Dean, Maud A.	23y	W	21 JUL 1918	Benedict MD	Mt. Olivet
08195	Dean, Nat. C.	45y	W	12 JUL 1911	Laurel MD	Glenwood
12332	Dean, Rachel	7m	W	11 MAR 1900	—	Eldbrooke
12331	Dean, Thomas	1y	W	2 MAY 1903	Tenleytown DC	Eldbrooke
05347	Dean, Walker	40y	C	2 NOV 1905	Roseton NY	Payne's
09026	Dean, William	33y	C	6 JAN 1913	Calgary, Can.	Harmony
00700	Deane, Louisa E.	c.80y	W	23 MAR 1892	Kensington MD	Congressional
05651	Deanell, Alice	4m	W	22 JUL 1906	Frostburg MD	Glenwood
07325	Dear, Richard B.	59y	W	12 DEC 1909	Superior WS	Glenwood
00939	Deavers, Albert S.	25y	W	15 JUL 1893	Seabrook MD	Accotink VA
17974	Deavers, George William	33y	W	25 JUL 1922	Seat Pleasant MD	Congressional
13061	DeCaindry, William A.	73y	W	17 AUG 1915	Plymouth Mtg. PA	Rock Creek
06105	DeCamp, Allie	47y	W	13 JUN 1907	Sykesville MD	Glenwood
00404	DeCamp, Eliza E.	65y	W	18 APR 1890	Baltimore MD	Glenwood
00543	DeCamp, Henry	88y	W	14 JUL 1891	Baltimore MD	Glenwood
02300	DeCamp, Mary J.	82y	W	29 OCT 1897	Baltimore MD	Glenwood
07529	Deck, Laura V.	45y	W	7 MAY 1910	Capitol Hts. MD	Glenwood
00591	Decker, John A.	7m	W	30 JUN 1891	Strausburgh VA	Oak Hill
08296	Dedman, Florence Maud	6m	W	5 SEP 1911	Maryland Pk. MD	Congressional
08319	Dedman, Henrietta May	7m	W	21 SEP 1911	Maryland Pk. MD	Congressional
04569	Dee, William J.	4y	W	13 JAN 1904	New York NY	Mt. Olivet
09161	Deeck, Bartholomew J.	32y	W	9 APR 1913	Berwyn MD	Mt. Olivet
08342	Deeck, Margaret B.	57y	W	4 OCT 1911	Berwyn MD	Mt. Olivet
07241	Deffer, Philip A.	44y	W	6 OCT 1909	At Sea	Glenwood
01622	DeFord, Sarah R.R.	61y	W	7 MAR 1895	Los Angeles CA	Rock Creek
05322	DeForrest, Charles	50y	W	18 OCT 1905	Jersey City NJ	Mt. Olivet
15150	DeGaw, Edward	23y	W	10 OCT 1918	Camp McClel. AL	Arlington VA
17758	Degenhart, Clara D.	69y	W	21 MAR 1922	Nantucket MA	Congressional
14869	DeGeorge, Infant of Lewis	SB	W	23 MAY 1918	Capitol Hts. MD	St. Mary's
13953	DeGeorge, Lina Annunyiata	3y	W	28 JAN 1917	Capitol Hts. MD	St. Mary's
15663	DeGodoy, Paulo, diplomat	28y	Z	3 MAR 1919	Tokyo, Japan	Oak Hill
04935	DeGrain, Edward R.S.	26y	W	25 OCT 1904	Garrett IN	St. Mary's
02054	DeHass, Amanda M.H.	82y	W	26 DEC 1896	Gaithersburg MD	Glenwood
01970	Deis, Nina Anna	20y	W	10 AUG 1896	Clarington OH	Oak Hill
09176	Delacroix, Louis	55y	W	18 APR 1913	Oxford NC	Cremated
06855	DeLacy, Francis Clare	15h	W	17 DEC 1908	Chevy Chase MD	Mt. Olivet
02867	Delaney, Cassius	49y	C	20 JUL 1899	Pr. Geo. Co. MD	Moore's
14139	Delaney, Eliza Dora	58y	W	16 MAY 1917	Chevy Chase MD	Arlington
12879	Delaney, John C.	66y	W	14 APR 1915	Chevy Chase MD	Arlington VA
08370	Delaney, Minnie	66y	W	23 OCT 1911	Mt. Ranier MD	Glenwood
00464	Delany, John	71y	W	4 FEB 1891	Philadelphia PA	Holyrood
02131	deLeon, Edmund Rodolph	12y	W	6 MAR 1897	Haddonfield NJ	Oak Hill
17994	Deloe, Child of C.E.	SB	W	7 AUG 1922	Cherrydale VA	Glenwood
11996	Deloe, Infant of Charles	4h	W	8 SEP 1913	Harrisburg PA	Glenwood
14285	DeLoffie, Fannie E.	67y	W	5 AUG 1917	Laramie Co. WY	Arlington
02942	DeLoffre, Augustus A.	53y	W	4 SEP 1899	San Antonio TX	Arlington VA
15365	DeLord, William	25y	W	10 OCT 1918	Alex. Co. VA	Alchafalaya AL

District of Columbia Foreign Death Records, 1888-1923

No.	Name of Deceased	Age	Race	Death Date	Place of Death	Place of Burial
14783	deLuca, Mildred M.	24y	W	30 APR 1918	Asheville NC	Glenwood
15921	DeLyons, Thaddeus Clarance	65y	C	6 AUG 1919	Itchester MD	Harmony
14818	Demar, Burns	39y	W	15 MAY 1918	Harwood MD	Arlington
13813	DeMarr, William	3y	W	13 NOV 1916	Mt. Ranier MD	Congressional
01225	deMendonca, Maria Amelia	25y	W	26 SEP 1893	Norwalk CN	Mt. Olivet
00701	Dement, James P.	45y	W	20 MAR 1892	Hampton VA	Woodlawn
07860	DeMontreville, Mary M.	72y	W	7 DEC 1910	New York NY	Glenwood
15086	Demopulos, Nicholas	25y	W	3 OCT 1918	Camp Meade MD	Arlington
18137	Dempsey, John William	4m	W	30 OCT 1922	Lignum VA	Mt. Olivet
02819	Dempsey, Katie Gertrude	25y	W	30 APR 1899	Columbia Pk. MD	Mt. Olivet
16451	Demshock, John	3d	W	26 APR 1920	Alex. Co. VA	Congressional
17988	DeNeal, Robert	c.51y	C	31 JUL 1922	Baltimore MD	Mt. Zion East
04865	DeNeane, Joseph W.	68y	W	26 AUG 1904	Takoma Park MD	Glenwood
06909	Denell, Mary E.	2y	W	5 FEB 1909	Glen Echo MD	Methodist
04579	deNemegyei, Felix	78y	W	24 JAN 1904	Charlestown WV	Congressional
04461	Dengle, James	50y	W	25 SEP 1903	E. St. Louis IL	Mt. Olivet
15269	Denham, Garnett	50y	W	18 OCT 1918	New York NY	Oak Hill
16956	Denison, Georgia I.	79y	W	3 FEB 1921	Winter Haven FL	Glenwood
02578	Denman, Mary Young	61y	W	25 AUG 1898	Eaglesmere PA	Mt. Olivet
13885	Dennerson, Samuel	74y	C	22 DEC 1916	Hampton VA	Arlington
12257	Denney, Harry	33y	W	13 MAR 1914	New York NY	Mt. Olivet
04170	Denney, William H.	55y	W	5 FEB 1903	Richmond IN	Congressional
06569	Dennie, Bertha A.	21y	W	28 MAY 1908	Takoma Park MD	Mt. Olivet
13496	Dennie, Elizabeth (McIntyre)	30y	W	9 MAY 1916	Richmond VA	Holyrood
00702	Dennison, Joseph E.	39y	W	4 APR 1892	Wilmington DE	Congressional
04612	Dennison, Lewis E.	27y	W	24 FEB 1904	Clinton MD	Congressional
16228	Denny, Eleanor	71y	W	18 JAN 1920	Newark NJ	Arlington
01623	Denny, Palmer	1y	W	16 MAR 1895	Chevy Chase MD	Oak Hill
03021	Denny, Sarah E.	43y	W	30 NOV 1899	Mt. Hope MD	Congressional
04416	Denny, William B.	53y	W	29 JUL 1903	Baltimore MD	Soldier's Home
12626	Densey, Leon E.	27y	W	23 NOV 1914	Detroit MI	Vienna VA
04938	Dent, Annie	25y	C	25 OCT 1904	Falls Church VA	Harmony
02986	Dent, Edward L.	39y	W	19 OCT 1899	Wilkinsburg PA	Oak Hill
06225	Dent, Edwin Harris	16y	W	7 SEP 1907	Denver CO	Rock Creek
09055	Dent, Eliza	60y	C	3 FEB 1913	New York NY	Harmony
17179	Dent, Fanny E.	64y	W	20 MAY 1921	New Orleans LA	Cremated
14579	Dent, James Arthur	32y	C	16 JAN 1918	Forestville MD	Mt. Olivet
05298	Dent, John W.	23y	C	25 SEP 1905	Falls Church VA	Harmony
02992	Dent, Josiah	82y	W	28 OCT 1899	Berkeley Sp. WV	Oak Hill
14456	Denty, Joseph S.	48y	W	11 NOV 1917	Washington DC	Holyrood
16450	DeOtte, Marion C.	12y	W	23 APR 1920	Brooklyn NY	Oak Hill
00592	Depue, Hazen	4m	W	21 JUL 1891	Takoma Park MD	Oak Hill
14627	DePue, George Morrison	67y	W	5 FEB 1918	Chevy Chase MD	Rock Creek
01545	Derby, James G.	73y	W	6 JAN 1895	Chicago IL	Glenwood
15372	Derene, William Francis	20y	W	22 NOV 1918	Mt. Ranier MD	Mt. Olivet
12909	DeRichey, Maude	43y	W	30 APR 1915	Central Islip NY	Glenwood[1]
02489	deRomero, Lucrecia Allen	47y	W	29 JUL 1898	Atlantic City NJ	Mt. Olivet
01134	Derrick, Ann P.	85y	W	20 DEC 1892	Charlottesville VA	Congressional
07847	Derrick, Arthur	42y	W	1 DEC 1910	New York NY	Prospect Hill
07095	DeShields, Jennie A.	53y	W	12 FEB 1909	Cumberland MD	Oak Hill
12146	DeSilver, Joseph Francis	37y	W	1 JAN 1914	Atlantic City NJ	Rock Creek
13046	Deskins, Amanda	60y	C	8 AUG 1915	Fairfax Co. VA	Holyrood
15703	Deskins, William H.	56y	W	29 MAR 1919	Philadelphia PA	Ashgrove VA
12216	Desmond, Clifford C.	36y	W	11 FEB 1914	Baltimore MD	Harmony
00125	Desmond, Jeremiah	45y	W	1 AUG 1889	Lawton's Sta. VA	Alexandria VA
06288	Desmond, Jeremiah J.	25y	W	26 OCT 1907	Staunton VA	Mt. Olivet

[1] Disinterment permit #8644 on 5 MAY 1916 for removal to Rock Creek Cemetery.

No.	Name of Deceased	Age	Race	Death Date	Place of Death	Place of Burial
03371	Desmond, Timothy	88y	W	19 DEC 1900	Fairfax Co. VA	Mt. Olivet
16521	DeSynek, Marie	44y	W	29 MAY 1920	San Antonio TX	Prospect Hill
15114	Dettinger, David	27y	W	7 OCT 1918	Camp Meade MD	Wash. Hebrew
17579	Dettmers, Anna	—	W	7 DEC 1921	Sarasota FL	Ft. Lincoln
02776	Detweiler, Emma	21y	W	11 MAR 1899	Hayes Farm MD	Rock Creek
02758	Detweiler, Margaret Agnes	9d	W	3 MAR 1899	Pr. Geo. Co. MD	Rock Creek
07015	DeVan, Susan D.	74y	W	7 MAY 1909	Leamington, Ont.	Rock Creek
02924	Devaughn, George	23y	W	23 AUG 1899	Forestville MD	Glenwood
07992	DeVaughn, Charles J.	68y	W	28 FEB 1911	Forestville MD	Glenwood
13428	DeVaughn, Curtis, s/o Horace	33y	W	23 MAR 1916	Dumfries VA	Congressional
14343	DeVaughn, Harry W.	1m	W	7 SEP 1917	Brentwood MD	Mt. Olivet
03891	deVecchi, Alice	49y	W	29 MAY 1902	New York NY	Arlington VA
13822	Deven, Charles H.	60y	W	23 NOV 1916	Baltimore MD	Glenwood
03924	Dever, James Robertson	52y	W	19 JUL 1902	Riverdale MD	Cremated
02519	DeVere, Lucy (Mrs. Schile)	64y	W	9 JUL 1898	Charlottesville VA	Rock Creek
17724	Devereux, Frances C.	31y	W	2 MAR 1922	Omaha NE	Rock Creek
17269	DeVilling, Charles F.	80y	W	14 JAN 1923	Zanesville OH	Glenwood
16017	Devine, Patrick J.	80y	W	24 SEP 1919	Johnson City TN	Arlington
13670	Deviny, Margaret	26y	W	20 AUG 1916	Dormont PA	Mt. Olivet
03755	Devlin, Anna D.	12y	W	11 JAN 1902	Falls Church VA	Mt. Olivet
18378	Devlin, Edward	58y	W	27 FEB 1923	Hyattsville MD	Congressional
07722	DeVolin, Ellen A.	67y	W	29 AUG 1910	Clifton Spgs. NY	Arlington
07789	DeWalt, Frank H., s/o W.H.	36y	W	11 OCT 1910	Williamsburg VA	Rock Creek
00465	DeWandelair, John A.	56y	W	9 APR 1891	Adamstown MD	Arlington
02869	Dewey, Silas J.	68y	W	30 JUL 1899	Shortsville NY	Congressional
13430	DeWhitt, George	36y	W	24 MAR 1916	Baltimore MD	Prospect Hill
06716	DeWitt, Calvin	68y	W	2 SEP 1908	Yellowstone WY	Arlington
18478	DeWitt, Gasherie	63y	W	13 APR 1923	Syracuse NY	Rock Creek
03305	DeWitt, Helen	38y	W	12 OCT 1900	Brockville, Ont.	Rock Creek
08468	DeWolfe, Desiderius C.	71y	W	11 JAN 1912	Baltimore MD	Mt. Olivet
18476	DeWolfe, Louise V.	51y	C	13 APR 1923	Newport RI	Woodlawn
17483	Dews, Ferdanand	59y	C	21 OCT 1921	Halls Hill VA	Payne's
01345	Dexter, Janette P.	24y	W	16 MAR 1894	Philadelphia PA	Congressional
17772	DiCarlo, Angelo	18y	W	2 APR 1922	Takoma Park MD	St. Mary's
03890	Dice, Julia	20y	C	30 MAY 1902	Philadelphia PA	Payne's
03577	Dick, Ewell Alexander	3m	W	13 JUL 1901	Berwyn MD	Glenwood
01226	Dick, George H.	21y	W	31 OCT 1893	Pasadena CA	Glenwood
17472	Dickens, Beatrice E.	24y	C	16 OCT 1921	Philadelphia PA	Harmony
14478	Dickens, Charles Forrest	56y	W	23 NOV 1917	Laurel MD	Rock Creek
13597	Dickenson, Junius	c.23y		9 JUL 1916	Jamestown VA	Woodlawn
01856	Dickenson, Susie	33y	C	27 JAN 1896	Baltimore MD	Woodlawn
06903	Dickerson, Albert	24y	C	8 OCT 1908	At Sea	Woodlawn
12086	Dickerson, Mamie	27y	C	10 NOV 1913	Philadelphia PA	Mt. Olivet
13466	Dickerson, Mary Virginia	46y	C	17 APR 1916	Wilberforce OH	Woodlawn
11919	Dickerson, Thomas	35y	C	24 JUL 1913	Philadelphia PA	Woodlawn
17993	Dickhaut, Henry E.	61y	W	3 AUG 1922	Colonial Bea. VA	Congressional
07746	Dickins, Francis W.	65y	W	15 SEP 1910	New York NY	Arlington
17629	Dickinson, Elizabeth W.	43y	W	11 JAN 1922	Flushing NY	Ft. Lincoln
07070	Dickinson, Mamie L.	31y	W	17 JUN 1909	Denver CO	Rock Creek
01695	Dickinson, Mary Millard	1y	W	21 AUG 1895	Chevy Chase MD	Rock Creek
12617	Dicksaon, Charles Henry	70y	W	11 NOV 1914	Los Angeles CA	Rock Creek
07912	Dickson, Allen M.	44y	C	7 JAN 1911	New York NY	Mt. Zion East
03235	Dickson, Archibald George	10m	W	13 JUL 1900	Woodside MD	Congressional
06268	Dickson, Henry	69y	W	22 SEP 1907	London, Eng.	Oak Hill
16107	Dickson, Jessie M.	51y	W	15 NOV 1919	Baltimore MD	Glenwood
07279	Dickson, Sarah L.G.	38y	C	18 NOV 1909	Sugar Land MD	Mt. Zion West
06473	Diedrich, Elizabeth	2y	W	11 JAN 1901	Alex. Co. VA	Congressional
06472	Diedrich, Herman C.	13y	W	19 NOV 1905	Washington DC	Congressional
07062	Diehl, Samuel N.B.	57y	W	15 JUN 1909	New York NY	Arlington

District of Columbia Foreign Death Records, 1888-1923

No.	Name of Deceased	Age	Race	Death Date	Place of Death	Place of Burial
17850	Diesrud, Einar	28y	W	12 MAY 1922	Minneapolis MN	Glenwood
12820	Dieter, Joseph J.	c.58y	W	17 MAR 1915	Norfolk VA	Baltimore MD
15805	Dietz, Christina	70y	W	31 MAY 1919	Mt. Ranier MD	Prospect Hill
03293	Dietz, Lewis Henry	59y	W	2 OCT 1900	Severn MD	Congressional
17422	Digges, James F.	—	W	12 JUN 1918	France	Mt. Olivet
14010	Diggins, Bartholomew	73y	W	24 FEB 1917	Key West FL	Arlington VA
02848	Diggins, William	24y	W	14 JUN 1899	Christiana MD	Mt. Olivet
01135	Diggs, Charles	c.55y	C	18 JUN 1892	Pr. Geo. Co. MD	Mt. Olivet
14206	Diggs, Charles Edw.	1y	W	3 JUL 1917	Elkridge MD	Mt. Olivet
17999	Diggs, Frances Martin	5m	C	8 AUG 1922	Fairmont Hts. MD	Mt. Olivet
03278	Diggs, Infant of Daniel	2d	C	30 AUG 1900	Tuxedo MD	Payne's
07399	Diggs, Lucinda	71y	C	2 FEB 1910	Bethesda MD	Baptist
16374	Dikeman, Henry K.	78y	W	9 MAR 1920	Petersburg FL	Arlington
06764	Dilger, Edward	32y	W	9 OCT 1908	Front Royal VA	Cremated
14331	Dilger, Ellen (Burke)	67y	W	26 AUG 1917	Taft CA	Mt. Olivet
08118	Dilger, Hubert, Sr., s/o Edward	75y	W	14 MAY 1911	Front Royal VA	Cremated
00434	Dilger, Lorenz	66y	W	13 NOV 1890	Suitland MD	St. Mary's
14680	Dillard, Frederick	51y	C	12 MAR 1918	Mt. Winans MD	Harmony
16973	Dillard, John James	83y	W	13 FEB 1921	Silver Spring MD	Tye River VA
01504	Diller, Infant of Walter C.	SB	W	8 OCT 1894	Romney WV	Mt. Olivet
13323	Dilli, Katherine M., d/o George	55y	W	23 JAN 1916	Denver CO	Rock Creek
04003	Dimmick, Robert A.	70y	W	17 SEP 1902	Bath NY	Arlington VA
04083	Dimmick, Robert A.	70y	W	17 SEP 1902	Bath NY	Arlington VA
04101	Dinges, Roy W.	—	W	2 JUL 1902	Santa Cruz CA	Arlington
15909	Dishman, Edgar Cline	27y	W	3 JUL 1919	Norfolk VA	Glenwood
17914	Dismer, Jacob J.	43y	W	18 JUN 1922	Penns Grove NJ	Mt. Olivet
18101	Dismon, Fannie	53y	W	OCT 1922	Takoma Park MD	Elesavetgrad
01696	Disney, Elizabeth A.	69y	W	23 AUG 1895	Pr. Geo. Co. MD	Elkridge MD
16342	Dissel, Alice B.	46y	W	24 FEB 1920	Nyack NY	Philadelphia PA
13978	Dittman, Charles F.	25y	W	8 FEB 1917	Chester PA	Glenwood
18191	Divine, Estelle	60y	W	1 DEC 1922	Hagerstown MD	Holyrood
13788	Divine, John	74y	W	28 OCT 1916	Ballston VA	Rock Creek
18067	Divine, Lizzie R.	51y	W	14 SEP 1922	Ballston VA	Rock Creek
01971	Dix, Roy Elwood	2y	W	25 AUG 1896	Germantown MD	Congressional
18352	Dixen, Lucy Ellen	63y	C	15 FEB 1923	Wallkill NY	Harmony
14545	Dixon, Charles S.	43y	C	31 DEC 1917	Mt. Vernon NY	Harmony
09179	Dixon, Clara Sibyl	50y	W	18 APR 1913	Montreat NC	Congressional
14862	Dixon, Clarita May	4y	W	6 JAN 1880	Keokuk IA	Rock Creek[1]
12984	Dixon, D. Randolph, s/o Henry	42y	W	29 JUN 1915	Petersburg VA	Congressional
14863	Dixon, Howard Wilcox	3y	W	9 JAN 1880	Keokuk IA	Rock Creek
14825	Dixon, Ida M.	2y	W	18 NOV 1884	Butte MT	Rock Creek
08148	Dixon, Irene E., d/o Wm. P.	42y	W	13 JUN 1911	Columbia CN	Cremated
18025	Dixon, Laura	60y	W	20 AUG 1922	New York NY	Payne's
14827	Dixon, William W.	22y	W	21 MAR 1900	Butte MT	Rock Creek
08016	Dixon, William Wirt	75y	W	13 NOV 1911	Los Angeles CA	Rock Creek
05161	Dixson, James A.	30y	W	2 JUN 1905	Paterson NJ	Mt. Olivet
00821	Doan, Elbert Sherman	2m	W	13 JUL 1892	Wash. Grove MD	Glenwood
08346	Dobson, Henry	5y	W	7 OCT 1911	Kensington MD	Cremated
02595	Dobson, Henry A., soldier	20y	W	11 SEP 1898	New York NY	Arlington
12777	Dock, Paul R.	2y	C	22 FEB 1915	Brentwood MD	Mt. Olivet
13794	Dockett, Jeremiah	36y	C	25 OCT 1916	Pittsburgh PA	Moore's
02452	Dodd, Harriet A.	74y	W	22 APR 1898	Hyattsville MD	Congressional
08890	Dodd, Lavenia	74y	W	15 OCT 1912	Waterfall VA	Oak Hill
07380	Dode, Richard H.	56y	C	18 JAN 1910	Brentwood MD	Payne's
08714	Dodge, Cornelia Jane, d/o Rev.	55y	W	12 JUL 1912	Roanoke VA	Rock Creek
16892	Dodge, Elizabeth	61y	W	4 JAN 1921	Hempstead NY	Oak Hill

---

[1] Iowa disinterment permit notes buried in Oakland Cemetery of Keokuk, Iowa, cause of death diphtheria.

No.	Name of Deceased	Age	Race	Death Date	Place of Death	Place of Burial
00703	Dodge, Elizabeth G.	62y	W	11 APR 1892	New York NY	Oak Hill
01040	Dodge, Emily E.	7y	W	10 FEB 1893	Bethesda MD	Oak Hill
06003	Dodge, Emma Morton	36y	W	31 MAR 1907	Boston MA	Glenwood
15567	Dodge, Frederick D.	45y	W	18 JAN 1919	Baltimore MD	Congressional
06626	Dodge, H.C.	35y	W	1 JUL 1908	Staunton VA	—
02637	Dodge, Henry Henley, broker	63y	W	20 OCT 1898	Baltimore MD	Oak Hill
03228	Dodge, James H.	66y	W	2 JUL 1900	Danville IL	Arlington VA
14505	Dodge, James Heath	72y	W	16 DEC 1917	Bethesda MD	Oak Hill
12943	Dodge, Jennie M.	42y	W	27 MAY 1915	Hanover OH	Rock Creek
01038	Dodge, Katherine Dulany	4y	W	31 MAR 1893	Heathcote MD	Oak Hill
05223	Dodge, Laura	62y	W	29 JUL 1905	Mt. Clemens MI	Arlington
06575	Dodge, Mary C.	62y	W	3 JUN 1908	Bethesda MD	Oak Hill
16323	Dodge, Mary H.	77y	W	16 FEB 1920	New York NY	Oak Hill
12251	Dodge, Richard D.	74y	W	5 MAR 1914	New York NY	Oak Hill
03446	Dodge, Robert Heath	29y	W	11 MAR 1901	Bethesda MD	Oak Hill
07331	Dodge, Theodore A.	67y	W	25 OCT 1909	Roziers, France	Arlington
01039	Dodge, William Allen	12y	W	6 APR 1893	Heathcote MD	Oak Hill
04620	Dodge, Ysidora B.M.	56y	W	28 FEB 1904	Philadelphia PA	Oak Hill
03011	Dodson, Ellen	65y	C	21 NOV 1899	New York NY	Harmony
00940	Dodson, Harriett W.	72y	W	22 JUL 1893	Warrenton VA	Congressional
07385	Dodson, James	44y	C	7 JAN 1910	Boston MA	Harmony
07753	Doe, Edna B.	32y	W	20 SEP 1910	Kilbuck PA	Arlington
12781	Doe, Sarah A.B.	71y	W	23 FEB 1915	Yonkers NY	Arlington
07079	Doggett, Roberta M.	17y	C	23 JUN 1909	Rosslyn VA	Mt. Zion East
16993	Doherty, Catherine J.	77y	W	22 FEB 1921	New York NY	Arlington
02158	Doherty, Edward P.	56y	W	2 APR 1897	New York NY	Arlington VA
05807	Doherty, Minnie	50y	W	3 NOV 1906	Chattanooga TN	Glenwood
16851	Dohoney, John E.	74y	W	8 DEC 1920	Cincinnati OH	Mt. Olivet
13627	Dohoney, Marie	78y	W	28 JUL 1916	Laurel MD	Mt. Olivet
02110	Dolan, Mary A.	57y	W	22 JAN 1897	Baltimore MD	Mt. Olivet
13173	Dolan, Patrick V., Dr., s/o T.	56y	W	30 OCT 1915	Norfolk VA	Mt. Olivet
00941	Dolan, Thomas A.	28y	W	13 AUG 1893	Wolf Summit WV	Mt. Olivet
00822	Doll, Mary E.	24y	W	12 SEP 1892	Harpers Ferry WV	Congressional
17487	Doll, Sherman M.	53y	W	24 OCT 1921	Philadelphia PA	Ft. Lincoln
06348	Domeincin, Guiseppe D.	23y	W	16 DEC 1907	Landover MD	Mt. Olivet
00942	Donaghue, Joseph	26y	W	27 JUN 1893	St. Louis MO	Holyrood
05801	Donaghy, Harry James	44y	W	31 OCT 1906	Takoma Park MD	Rock Creek
15398	Donahue, D.B.	23y	W	29 NOV 1918	Chesa. Bea. MD	Cambridge MA
05604	Donaldson, Alonzo	43y	W	23 JUN 1906	Ft. Myer VA	Glenwood
13097	Donaldson, Beulah Winter	27y	W	11 SEP 1915	Maywood VA	Oak Hill
12318	Donaldson, Emma	72y	W	18 APR 1914	Ft. Myer VA	Glenwood
13970	Donaldson, George G.	64y	W	5 FEB 1917	Baltimore MD	Mt. Olivet
05220	Donaldson, Gracie	1m	W	29 JUL 1905	Ft. Myer VA	Glenwood
04187	Donaldson, Hattie	14y	C	4 APR 1903	Rosslyn VA	Baptist
14512	Donaldson, James Herbert	33y	W	17 DEC 1917	Norfolk VA	Falls Church VA
04178	Donaldson, Jane	10y	C	17 FEB 1903	Rosslyn VA	Baptist
04692	Donaldson, Maria Irene S.	17y	W	7 NOV 1900	Puerto Plata, S.D.	Oak Hill
04693	Donaldson, Marie Irene S.	43y	W	26 OCT 1900	Puerto Plata, S.D.	Oak Hill
13225	Donaldson, Mary A.	51y	W	27 NOV 1915	Massillon OH	Glenwood
13272	Donaldson, Mary L.	76y	W	28 DEC 1915	Norbeck MD	Oak Hill
04067	Donaldson, Raymond S.	13y	W	2 OCT 1902	Sligo MD	Mt. Olivet
04649	Donaldson, Sarah F.	83y	W	29 MAR 1904	Chesterbrook VA	Oak Hill
01947	Donalson, Samuel	61y	W	7 JUN 1896	Rosslyn VA	Glenwood
08391	Donath, William H.	43y	W	13 NOV 1911	Bellevue PA	Rock Creek
15191	Donavan, Thomas E.	31y	W	14 OCT 1918	Camp Meade MD	Mt. Olivet
03763	Donavan, William	12y	W	20 JAN 1902	Baltimore MD	Mt. Olivet
08874	Donehoo, Henry M.	63y	W	2 JUL 1898	Dayton OH	Arlington
01041	Donelan, Michael	36y	W	1 FEB 1893	Baltimore MD	Mt. Olivet
05711	Donelle, Bendena L.	34y	W	25 AUG 1906	Philadelphia PA	Rock Creek

District of Columbia Foreign Death Records, 1888-1923

No.	Name of Deceased	Age	Race	Death Date	Place of Death	Place of Burial
05849	Donn, Alonza	40y	W	5 DEC 1906	Allegheny PA	Rock Creek
12858	Donn, Edward W.	68y	W	3 APR 1915	Relay MD	Rock Creek
17495	Donn, Elizabeth M.	73y	W	30 OCT 1921	Baltimore MD	Glenwood
07571	Donn, Eugene	39y	W	15 JUN 1910	Brentwood MD	Glenwood
12652	Donn, Oliver A.	72y	W	10 DEC 1914	Brentwood MD	Glenwood
05749	Donn, Wilton C.	56y	W	18 SEP 1906	New York NY	Oak Hill
14757	Donnally, Juliet	63y	W	16 APR 1918	Takoma Park MD	Cremated
04372	Donnel, Marguerite Gander	81y	W	3 JUL 1903	Kensington MD	Glenwood
18209	Donnelly, Earl	25y	W	11 DEC 1922	Colo. Spgs. CO	Mt. Olivet
12494	Donnelly, Edith L.	31y	W	15 AUG 1914	Ancon, Can. Zone	Oak Hill
04464	Donnelly, Elizabeth S.	23y	W	28 SEP 1903	New York NY	Rock Creek
02159	Donnelly, Johanna	57y	W	6 MAY 1897	Chicago IL	Mt. Olivet
15797	Donnelly, Mary E.	49y	W	27 MAY 1919	Philadelphia PA	Mt. Olivet
01136	Donnelly, Richard T.	32y	W	17 OCT 1892	Baltimore MD	Mt. Olivet
16436	Donnelly, Thomas E.	46y	W	13 APR 1920	Huntsville MD	Mt. Olivet
00467	Donnelly, William T.	34y	W	1 APR 1891	New York NY	Oak Hill
00019	Donoghue, James O.	38y	W	22 FEB 1889	Philadelphia PA	Mt. Olivet
17093	Donoghue, Mary Ann	76y	W	6 APR 1921	Charleroi PA	Holyrood
12364	Donoho, Amelia Cooper	78y	W	16 MAY 1914	Wheaton MD	Glenwood
06988	Donoho, William H.	80y	W	16 APR 1909	Wheaton MD	Glenwood
02607	Donohoe, Hugh	76y	W	28 SEP 1898	Wheaton MD	Mt. Olivet
14508	Donohue, Alice H.	80y	W	17 DEC 1917	Jersey City NJ	Oak Hill
04741	Donohue, Florence Wise	10m	W	27 MAY 1904	Jersey City NJ	Oak Hill
09021	Donohue, Francis	71y	W	8 JAN 1913	Seat Pleasant MD	Mt. Olivet
01620	Donohue, Joseph Francis	40y	W	6 MAR 1895	Highland MD	Mt. Olivet
02751	Donohue, Mary A.	76y	W	19 FEB 1899	New York NY	Mt. Olivet
00055	Donohue, Walter Ambrose	1y	W	12 APR 1889	Pr. Geo. Co. MD	Mt. Olivet
08787	Donovan, Catherine T.	70y	W	27 AUG 1912	Newport RI	Mt. Olivet
00379	Donovan, Frank	10m	W	1 AUG 1890	Parham VA	Mt. Olivet
06223	Donovan, H.J.	29y	W	29 AUG 1907	El Paso TX	Mt. Olivet
00368	Donovan, Jeremiah	3m	W	24 JUL 1890	New York NY	Mt. Olivet
16632	Donovan, John P.	65y	W	30 JUL 1920	Newport RI	Congressional
08237	Donovan, Paul	9m	W	3 AUG 1911	E. Riverdale MD	Holyrood
06000	Donovan, Richard	65y	W	27 MAR 1907	Newport RI	Mt. Olivet
14131	Donovan, Richard James	38y	W	5 MAY 1917	Gravenhurst, Can.	Mt. Olivet
03693	Dooley, Everett Farron	8m	C	25 OCT 1901	Rosslyn VA	Mt. Zion
15035	Dooley, John C.	20y	W	21 SEP 1918	Brookline MA	Rock Creek
06421	Doolittle, Lucy Salisbury	75y	W	6 FEB 1908	Linden MD	Rock Creek
11870	Doolittle, Myrick Hascall	83y	W	27 JUN 1913	Linden MD	Rock Creek
04923	Doolittle, William H.	60y	W	17 OCT 1904	Sherburne NY	Oak Hill
14185	Doran, John, carpenter	77y	W	21 JUN 1917	Hampton VA	Mt. Olivet
13843	Doran, John F.	42y	W	6 DEC 1916	Fairfax Co. VA	Mt. Olivet
12733	Doran, Mary Ann	82y	W	25 JAN 1915	Fairfax VA	Mt. Olivet
16795	Doran, Thomas J.	35y	W	2 FEB 1919	Gievres, Fra.	Congressional
17699	Doremus, Estelle	66y	W	16 FEB 1922	Barcroft VA	Nyack NY
15106	Dorian, Haviland	33y	W	7 OCT 1918	New York NY	Glenwood
16712	Dorian, Margaret	61y	W	15 SEP 1920	Arlington VA	Glenwood
01972	Dorman, Ellen	10m	W	17 AUG 1896	Hyattsville MD	Mt. Olivet
04704	Dorman, Katherine	26y	W	7 MAY 1904	Pr. Anne Co. VA	Rock Creek
17451	Dornico, Titto	77y	W	2 OCT 1921	Capitol Hts. MD	Glenwood
04803	Dorr, Aloysius, butcher	35y	W	12 JUL 1904	St. Louis MO	St. Mary's
03990	Dorsett, Josias Hawkins	71y	W	26 AUG 1902	Baltimore MD	Oak Hill
07261	Dorsett, Kate A.	71y	W	4 NOV 1909	Brentwood MD	Congressional
18073	Dorsett, Mary Catherine	82y	W	18 SEP 1922	Westminster MD	Oak Hill
17043	Dorsey, Allene S. (Barnum)	64y	W	13 MAR 1921	New York NY	Glenwood
15130	Dorsey, Aloysius	22y	C	9 OCT 1918	Camp Dix NJ	Mt. Zion East
17963	Dorsey, George	c.50y	C	17 JUL 1922	Townsend GA	Woodlawn
13144	Dorsey, Harriet Ann	71y	C	6 OCT 1915	Yonkers NY	Woodlawn
04207	Dorsey, Harry W.	71y	W	21 MAR 1903	Hyattsville MD	Rock Creek

No.	Name of Deceased	Age	Race	Death Date	Place of Death	Place of Burial
01805	Dorsey, John F.	40y	C	17 DEC 1895	Montg. Co. MD	Mt. Zion
18547	Dorsey, Joseph	22y	C	16 MAY 1923	Hudson NY	Cedar Hts. MD
18548	Dorsey, Joseph	19y	C	16 MAY 1923	Hudson NY	Payne's
08564	Dorsey, Joseph O.	1y	C	19 MAR 1912	New York NY	Woodlawn
02055	Dorsey, Josephine A.	66y	W	12 NOV 1896	Baltimore MD	Congressional
16895	Dorsey, Katherine H.	41y	W	5 JAN 1921	Clarksville MD	Rock Creek
12736	Dorsey, Mary E.	1y	C	26 JAN 1915	Fulton NY	Woodlawn
02533	Dorsey, Robert J.	15y	C	23 JUN 1898	Clayton DE	Mt. Olivet
02111	Dorsey, Thomas	70y	C	24 JAN 1897	Forest Glen MD	Moore's
01624	Dorsey, William	70y	W	9 APR 1895	Baltimore MD	Congressional
16270	Dorsey, William	1y	C	2 FEB 1920	Capitol Hts. MD	Payne's
13131	Dorsey, William	36y	C	29 SEP 1915	Philadelphia PA	Woodlawn
07841	Dorsey, William J.	37y	C	24 NOV 1910	Rockingham NH	Arlington
15031	Dorster, Edwin F.	38y	C	18 SEP 1918	Bridgeport CN	Harmony
01423	Dotey, Harriet	45y	C	2 JUL 1894	Takoma Park MD	Harmony
15651	Dotson, Charles	21y	C	22 FEB 1919	Norristown PA	Lanham MD
09050	Dotson, Harry L.	28y	C	27 JAN 1913	Philadelphia PA	Woodlawn
17617	Dotts, James E.	27y	W	27 DEC 1921	Asheville NC	Arlington
05466	Dotts, Madge	26y	C	10 FEB 1906	Philadelphia PA	Harmony
01697	Dougal, William H.	73y	W	17 OCT 1895	Jersey City NJ	Oak Hill
13777	Dougherty, Ann H.	34y	W	23 OCT 1916	Lynchburg VA	Congressional
04226	Dougherty, Edward D.	56y	W	25 FEB 1903	Philadelphia PA	Glenwood
13227	Dougherty, Edward Plowden	38y	W	1 DEC 1915	Maywood VA	Mt. Olivet
00275	Dougherty, Frank W.	27y	W	25 JAN 1890	St. Louis MO	Mt. Olivet
14370	Dougherty, George H.	74y	W	18 SEP 1917	Hampton VA	Glenwood
03885	Dougherty, Henry L.	31y	W	21 MAY 1902	Kings Park NY	Congressional
02056	Dougherty, John Joseph	43y	W	29 NOV 1896	Cullman AL	Mt. Olivet
01546	Dougherty, Mary A.	78y	W	25 JAN 1895	Chester PA	Glenwood
03118	Dougherty, William A.	41y	W	5 MAR 1900	Hyattsville MD	Mt. Olivet
04394	Dougherty, William E.	56y	W	19 JUL 1903	Kensington MD	Mt. Olivet
08579	Doughty, Mary	66y	W	2 APR 1912	Baltimore MD	Oak Hill
13188	Douglas, Adelaide, s/o Sandy	c.51y	C	5 NOV 1915	Plainfield NJ	Harmony
12232	Douglas, Albert Post	82y	W	21 FEB 1914	Ballston VA	Glenwood
14030	Douglas, Anna J.	53y	W	16 MAR 1917	Philadelphia PA	Rock Creek
07601	Douglas, August	69y	W	27 APR 1894	Baltimore MD	Rock Creek
13175	Douglas, August B.	49y	W	29 OCT 1915	Syracuse NY	Rock Creek
15802	Douglas, Ethel	24y	C	28 MAY 1919	New York NY	Harmony
00403	Douglas, Gertrude	18y	W	19 SEP 1890	New Windsor MD	Rock Creek
03838	Douglas, Howard Grey	40y	W	26 MAY 1902	Baltimore MD	Glenwood
17286	Douglas, Howard T.	—	W	22 JUN 1921	Walter Reed Hp.	Azusa CA
05856	Douglas, Jane	42y	W	11 DEC 1906	Baltimore MD	Glenwood
08004	Douglas, John B.	60y	C	14 MAR 1911	Centerville MD	Harmony
07166	Douglas, John W., s/o Jos. M.	81y	W	21 AUG 1909	Kent CN	Oak Hill
03364	Douglas, Laura V.	71y	W	12 DEC 1900	Ballston VA	Glenwood
16778	Douglas, Lenora	77y	C	21 OCT 1920	Philadelphia PA	Cedar Hill
18508	Douglas, Loys	5m	C	25 APR 1923	New York NY	Woodlawn
06650	Douglas, Mary Virginia	73y	W	21 JUL 1908	Harpers Ferry WV	Rock Creek
07600	Douglas, Mary Virginia C.	5y	W	6 JAN 1877	Baltimore MD	Rock Creek
04773	Douglass, Ann P.	11m	W	23 JUN 1904	Martinsburg WV	Congressional
09031	Douglass, Charles	39y	C	13 JAN 1913	Pittsburgh PA	Harmony
14982	Douglass, Eliza	75y	C	17 AUG 1918	New Rochelle NY	Mt. Olivet
13876	Douglass, John	42y	C	18 DEC 1916	Pittsburgh PA	Harmony
06733	Douglass, John Wesley	46y	W	17 SEP 1908	Ripton VT	Rock Creek
07514	Douglass, Margaretta L.	80y	W	24 APR 1910	Catonsville MD	Oak Hill
12482	Douglass, Martha	53y	C	9 AUG 1914	Philadelphia PA	Harmony
07520	Douglass, Robert	24y	C	27 APR 1910	New York NY	Harmony
18384	Douglass, Robert	26y	C	1 MAR 1923	Philadelphia PA	Harmony
15244	Doup, Fannie M.	34y	W	19 OCT 1918	Hagerstown MD	Congressional
17827	Dove, Elizabeth Ann	65y	W	2 MAY 1922	Hyattsville MD	Glenwood

District of Columbia Foreign Death Records, 1888-1923

No.	Name of Deceased	Age	Race	Death Date	Place of Death	Place of Burial
14898	Dove, George	20y	W	1 JUL 1918	Dearborn MI	Mt. Olivet
16093	Dove, Infant of Maury, Jr.	SB	W	6 NOV 1919	Bethesda MD	Rock Creek
04976	Dove, William E., Capt.	—	W	28 MAY 1864	Ft. Niagara NY	Arlington
00593	Dove, William T.	4m	W	22 JUL 1891	Bethesda MD	Rock Creek
16018	Dover, Katherine	72y	C	27 SEP 1919	Rockville MD	Holyrood
17153	Dowd, Geraldine Rita	8m	W	12 MAY 1921	Somerset MD	Mt. Olivet
01497	Dowden, Doras V.D.	23y	W	21 SEP 1894	Washington DC	Rock Creek
13842	Dowden, Nellie Elizabeth	42y	W	3 DEC 1916	Hampton VA	Mt. Olivet
05815	Dowe, Samuel	21y	C	7 NOV 1906	Asheville NC	Payne's
02913	Dowell, William	64y	W	13 AUG 1899	Stuart Wharf VA	Congressional
05703	Dowling, Catherine	45y	W	24 AUG 1906	Brentwood MD	Mt. Olivet
00157	Dowling, George	5m	W	3 SEP 1889	Montg. Co. MD	Holyrood
07551	Dowling, Mary E.	22y	W	24 MAY 1910	Mt. Ranier MD	Mt. Olivet
00823	Dowling, Thomas J.	3m	W	19 JUL 1892	Cabin John MD	Oak Hill
08034	Down, Susan V.	66y	W	27 MAR 1911	Brentwood MD	Glenwood
01137	Downer, Lewis	35y	W	19 JAN 1893	Hyattsville MD	Mt. Olivet
08657	Downey, Horace H., s/o Thos.	69y	W	3 JUN 1912	Prospect Hill VA	Congressional
12670	Downey, Infant of Charles	SB	W	27 DEC 1914	Mt. Ranier MD	Mt. Olivet
06282	Downey, John F.	25y	W	22 OCT 1907	Boonsboro MD	Mt. Olivet
16307	Downey, John Patrick	18y	W	12 FEB 1920	Hampton Rds. VA	Mt. Olivet
00468	Downey, Mary	45y	W	31 MAR 1891	Philadelphia PA	Mt. Olivet
05997	Downie, William	42y	W	25 MAR 1907	Baltimore MD	Mt. Olivet
02679	Downie, William Edward	3y	W	17 DEC 1898	Rosslyn VA	Mt. Olivet
15821	Downing, Eva	27y	C	5 JUN 1919	Camden NJ	Payne's
02507	Downing, Linnie M.	19y	W	18 JUL 1898	Garrisonville VA	Congressional
00020	Downman, J.B.	—	W	13 JUL 1889	Nogales AZ	Oak Hill
04664	Downs, Ellen Harmon	46y	W	10 APR 1904	Mt. Hope MD	Mt. Olivet
17135	Downs, Florence V.	26y	W	29 APR 1921	Wilmington DE	Rock Creek
17047	Downs, James H.	55y	W	14 MAR 1921	Wilmington DE	Rock Creek
03539	Downs, John A.	58y	W	11 JUN 1901	Potomac River	Congressional
02820	Downs, John B.	45y	W	13 MAY 1892	Temple TX	Mt. Olivet
16493	Downs, Leonard Mitchell	26y	W	18 MAY 1920	Asheville NC	Leonardtown MD
03630	Downs, P.T.	—	W	30 AUG 1901	Flathead Co. MT	Mt. Olivet
05036	Downtain, John G.	63y	W	20 FEB 1905	Lakeland FL	Cremated
02432	Doxon, Marie C.	9y	W	19 JAN 1898	Brooklyn NY	Oak Hill
13889	Doyle, Ethel H.	1y	W	27 DEC 1916	Bayonne NJ	Mt. Olivet
01228	Doyle, Frank F.	30y	W	30 SEP 1893	Laurel MD	Lewiston ME
01227	Doyle, Frank H.	2m	W	16 SEP 1893	Annapolis MD	Glenwood
02301	Doyle, Frederick S.	28y	W	3 OCT 1897	Philadelphia PA	Rock Creek
15042	Doyle, John A.	25y	W	24 SEP 1918	New Haven CN	Mt. Olivet
03563	Doyle, John P.	4m	W	5 JUL 1901	Columbia Pk. MD	Mt. Olivet
06042	Doyle, Peter G.	59y	W	19 APR 1907	Philadelphia PA	Congressional
01698	Dozier, Susan F.	65y	W	9 OCT 1895	Baltimore MD	Oak Hill
16640	Draeger, Gardner	9y	W	6 AUG 1920	Baltimore MD	Glenwood
13051	Drain, Francis	19y	C	11 AUG 1915	Philadelphia PA	Moore's
17776	Drain, John	60y	W	2 APR 1922	New York NY	Mt. Olivet
15187	Drake, Albert S.	23y	W	12 OCT 1918	Jacksonville FL	Arlington
13961	Drake, Ellen P.	92y	W	30 JAN 1917	Wilmington DE	Oak Hill
03622	Drake, Francis	1y	W	23 AUG 1901	Passadena MD	Congressional
14998	Drake, Otis B.	36y	W	29 AUG 1918	Connersville IN	Glenwood
05548	Drake, Robert A.	80y	W	20 FEB 1906	Esterly PA	Oak Hill
17118	Drake, Ruth Chapman	73y	W	22 APR 1921	Friendship H. MD	Watkins NY
13661	Drane, Samuel Dade	49y	W	15 AUG 1916	New York NY	Rock Creek
07338	Draper, Florence D.	39y	W	21 DEC 1909	Wash. Grove MD	Congressional
04490	Drawbaugh, Gertrude	27y	W	25 OCT 1903	Liberty NY	Congressional
02459	Drawbaugh, John A., Dr.	34y	W	27 MAY 1898	Asheville NC	Congressional
13529	Dreher, Estelle	17y	W	1 JUN 1916	T.B. DC	Prospect Hill
05411	Drescher, Frederick William	58y	W	29 DEC 1905	Chase City VA	Glenwood
16825	Dressel, Minnie	44y	W	22 NOV 1920	New York NY	Mt. Olivet

No.	Name of Deceased	Age	Race	Death Date	Place of Death	Place of Burial
00391	Drew, Andrew Francis	30y	W	18 AUG 1890	Chicago IL	Mt. Olivet
04326	Drew, Bernard	73y	W	26 AUG 1903	Alexandria VA	Mt. Olivet
17780	Drew, Henry Frames	5d	W	5 APR 1922	Asheville NC	Mt. Olivet
02738	Drew, Isac N.	56y	W	JAN 1899	Richmond VA	Philadelphia PA
01973	Drewitz, Lena	46y	W	1 SEP 1896	Baltimore MD	Prospect Hill
00943	Drinkgrave, B.H., Mrs.	—	W	1 APR 1878	Winchester VA	Congressional
08268	Drinkhouse, Angeline	75y	W	21 AUG 1911	Colonial Bea. VA	Oak Hill
04282	Drinkhouse, Edward J., Dr.	73y	W	18 APR 1903	Baltimore MD	Oak Hill
00243	Driscoll, Bridget	52y	W	14 DEC 1889	Chicago IL	Mt. Olivet
17464	Driscoll, Cornelius A.	—	W	4 NOV 1918	France	Mt. Olivet
00304	Driscoll, James	52y	W	2 APR 1890	Chicago IL	Mt. Olivet
15656	Driscoll, John A.	57y	W	4 MAR 1919	Mt. Ranier MD	Holyrood
14686	Driver, George W.	80y	W	7 MAR 1918	San Francisco CA	Glenwood
12904	Dronenburg, Mary E.	54y	W	29 APR 1915	Kansas City MO	Oak Hill
13615	Droz, Therese	40y	W	23 JUL 1916	Beverly MA	Mt. Olivet
07238	Drum, Richard Coulter	84y	W	15 OCT 1909	Bethesda MD	Arlington
02195	Drummond, William M.	2y	C	10 JUN 1897	Montg. Co. MD	Christian
08088	Drury, Ada	38y	W	26 APR 1911	Baltimore MD	Mt. Olivet
17820	Drury, Teresa V.	79y	W	28 APR 1922	Beltsville MD	Mt. Olivet
18576	Duane, David	37y	W	22 MAY 1923	San Diego CA	Arlington
12886	Dubant, Susan L.	83y	W	20 APR 1915	Baltimore MD	Rock Creek
04628	DuBois, George J.	69y	W	18 MAR 1904	Norfolk VA	Williamsport PA
03972	DuBois, Nicholi	56y	W	14 AUG 1879	Clarksville MO/IA	Rock Creek
18165	DuBrau, Herman	57y	W	17 NOV 1922	Cumberland MD	Cremated
08244	Duc, Marie Damala	74y	W	7 AUG 1911	Takoma Park MD	Charleston SC
09112	Ducat, Arthur Charles	58y	W	8 MAR 1913	New York NY	Arlington
03981	Ducket, Eliza	50y	W	5 AUG 1902	Forestville MD	Moore's
15113	Duckett, Allen B.	27y	W	8 OCT 1918	Bladensburg MD	Rock Creek
13845	Duckett, Gabriella A.	59y	W	5 DEC 1916	Bladensburg MD	Rock Creek
01926	Duckett, Ruth Catherine	61y	W	29 AY 1896	Woodmoore MD	Congressional
04019	Duckett, Ruth E.	4m	W	3 SEP 1902	Seat Pleasant MD	Congressional
18434	Dudley, Arthur H.	71y	W	21 MAR 1923	Hot Springs AR	Columbia Gardens
13689	Dudley, Audley F.	35y	W	4 SEP 1916	Saranac Lake NY	Rock Creek
06752	Dudley, Charles	30y	W	30 SEP 1908	Liberty NY	Oak Hill
07143	Duehring, Margaret	21y	W	28 JUL 1909	San Antonio TX	Prospect Hill
05033	Duff, Kennedy	62y	W	12 FEB 1905	Downingtown PA	Rock Creek
03220	Duff, Walter C.	41y	W	4 JUL 1900	Lambertville NJ	Rock Creek
18074	Duffee, George W.	78y	W	17 SEP 1922	New York NY	Oak Hill
13781	Duffie, Joseph James	74y	W	26 OCT 1916	Seat Pleasant MD	Mt. Olivet
13467	Duffield, Louise Ladue	84y	W	17 APR 1916	Harlan KY	Arlington
05143	Duffield, Ulysses J.	39y	C	22 MAY 1905	New York NY	Woodlawn
00704	Dufour, Oliver	72y	W	4 NOV 1891	Hyattsville MD	Rock Creek
01974	Dugan, Caroline C.	57y	W	27 AUG 1896	Frederick MD	Glenwood
14679	Dugan, John	29y	W	12 MAR 1918	Camden NJ	Congressional
15396	Dugan, Wilfred A.	33y	W	2 DEC 1918	Wilkes Barre PA	Mt. Olivet
17231	Duke, Edith R. (Slaughter)	57y	W	11 JUN 1921	Charlottesville VA	Cremated
06915	Duke, Hattie M.	30y	W	12 FEB 1909	Brentwood MD	Congressional
03137	Duke, John M.	31y	W	11 FEB 1900	Mare Island CA	Lanham MD
13804	Dulaney, Henry	40y	C	2 NOV 1916	Baltimore MD	Woodlawn
00705	Dulaney, Samuel	15d	C	28 FEB 1892	Alexandria VA	Harmony
00126	Dulany, Infant of Thomas E.	2d	C	9 AUG 1889	Alexandria VA	Mt. Pleasant
01138	Dulany, Martha	4m	C	6 JUN 1892	Alexandria VA	Harmony
01547	Dulany, Mary M.	14m	C	20 DEC 1894	Alexandria VA	Harmony
00001	Dulany, Thomas	18y	M	20 DEC 1888	Alexandria VA	Harmony
00241	Dulin, Henry M.	—	W		1814	Fairfax Co. VA	Congressional
00241	Dulin, John	—	W		1842	Fairfax Co. VA	Congressional
00241	Dulin, John E.	—	W		1835	Fairfax Co. VA	Congressional

District of Columbia Foreign Death Records, 1888-1923

No.	Name of Deceased	Age	Race	Death Date	Place of Death	Place of Burial
00241	Dulin, Lemuel M.	—	W	1811	Fairfax Co. VA	Congressional[1]
00241	Dulin, Mary	—	W	1840	Fairfax Co. VA	Congressional
03843	Dulin, Natalie E.	2y	W	6 APR 1902	Kensington MD	Oak Hill
17287	Duling, William H.	67y	W	6 JUL 1921	Mt. Ranier MD	Glenwood
16709	Dumaine, Pierre Romain	75y	W	14 SEP 1920	Fairfax Co. VA	Congressional
15576	Dunavant, Archie	54y	W	21 JAN 1919	Mt. Ranier MD	Congressional
01449	Dunbar, Agnes	69y	W	31 JUL 1894	Philadelphia PA	Congressional
16065	Dunbar, Nathen H., s/o Daniel	8y	W	28 AUG 1919	Vallejo CA	Glenwood
06986	Duncan, Eliza L.	73y	W	16 APR 1909	Orange NJ	Oak Hill
05990	Duncan, Malinda	40y	C	1887	Culpeper VA	Payne's
06038	Duncan, Margraetta L.S.	79y	W	20 APR 1907	Bethesda MD	Oak Hill
14086	Duncan, Maria L.	88y	W	12 APR 1917	Pelham Manor NY	Oak Hill
06561	Duncan, Stephen	76y	W	23 MAY 1908	Berryville VA	Oak Hill
15329	Duncan, Thomas, Rev., s/o S.	91y	W	4 NOV 1918	Pelham Manor NY	Oak Hill
17849	Dundas, William M.	11y	W	1880	Philadelphia PA	Mt. Olivet
14005	Dungan, Elizabeth	66y	W	25 FEB 1917	Laurel MD	Glenwood
16480	Dunham, Samuel C.	65y	W	10 MAY 1920	Baltimore MD	Glenwood
17187	Dunkin, Frank Edward	28y	W	28 OCT 1918	Vitele, Fra.	Arlington
18145	Dunkinson, David Bauman	74y	W	3 NOV 1922	Takoma Park MD	Chambersburg PA
12311	Dunlap, Andrew, Jr.	19y	W	31 AUG 1902	Buffalo NY	Arlington
16324	Dunlap, Margaret (Corcoran)	40y	W	15 FEB 1920	Jefferson Co. PA	Mt. Olivet
00706	Dunlap, Robert A.	12y	W	23 NOV 1872	Greenville OH	Glenwood
16302	Dunlop, Emily R. (Kerr)	74y	W	9 FEB 1920	Petersburg VA	Oak Hill
06205	Dunlop, Fanny Ayler	41y	W	27 AUG 1907	Chevy Chase MD	Rock Creek
08517	Dunlop, George	73y	W	18 FEB 1912	Chevy Chase MD	Rock Creek
02709	Dunlop, Margaret B.	40y	W	14 JAN 1899	Chevy Chase MD	Oak Hill
12745	Dunlop, Mary S.	78y	W	2 FEB 1915	Palm Beach FL	Glenwood
07671	Dunn, Bernardine G.	11m	W	5 AUG 1910	Mt. Ranier MD	Mt. Olivet
03707	Dunn, Emma Jane	41y	W	17 NOV 1901	Alex. Co. VA	Mt. Olivet
05701	Dunn, George Graham	17d	W	24 AUG 1906	Drummond MD	Mt. Olivet
14568	Dunn, John Rustic	2m	W	11 JAN 1918	New York NY	St. Mary's
12986	Dunn, Lanier, s/o Wm. McK.	63y	W	1 JUL 1915	Hot Springs VA	Oak Hill
13059	Dunn, Rosa E.	47y	W	18 AUG 1915	Hyattsville MD	Congressional
04732	Dunn, Thomas J.	32y	W	21 MAY 1904	Pittsburgh PA	Mt. Olivet
00594	Dunn, William McKee	48y	W	30 SEP 1891	Portland ME	Oak Hill
17889	Dunning, Jane S.	87y	W	7 JUN 1922	Falls Church VA	Plainfield NJ
14774	Dunnington, Ida James	47y	C	27 APR 1918	Hyattsville MD	Harmony
18048	Durcumb, Maggie D.	49y	C	3 SEP 1922	Asbury Park NJ	Payne's
15341	Durham, Adeline M.	23y	C	9 NOV 1918	Alexandria VA	Dover DE
12323	Durnbaugh, Thomas J.	2m	W	20 APR 1914	Capitol Hts. MD	Glenwood
16119	Durney, Daniel J.	62y	W	20 NOV 1919	Huntington WV	Mt. Olivet
00595	Durno, George C.	61y	W	1 SEP 1891	Pr. Geo. Co. MD	Rock Creek
05447	Dury, George	60y	W	30 JAN 1906	Silver Spring MD	Soldier's Home
12589	Duryee, Mary E.	53y	W	30 OCT 1914	New York NY	Oak Hill
02370	Dushay, Katheine	4m	W	22 JAN 1898	Kensington MD	Oak Hill
08574	Dutch, Malina	83y	C	28 MAR 1912	Halls Hill VA	Harmony
16573	Dutcher, William	74y	W	1 JUL 1920	Chevy Chase MD	Plainfield NJ
00469	Dutrow, James Q.	35y	W	26 DEC 1890	New York NY	Congressional
16151	Dutrow, Maria S. (Shepperd)	80y	W	16 DEC 1919	Richmond VA	Glenwood
06255	Dutton, Ellenor J.	75y	W	29 SEP 1907	Hyattsville MD	Rock Creek
17766	Dutton, Helen	45y	C	26 MAR 1922	Chester PA	Rosemont
04295	Dutton, Infant of Walter/Helen	2d	W	1 JUN 1903	Hyattsville MD	Mt. Olivet
05458	Dutton, Mary L.	62y	W	7 FEB 1906	Bladensburg MD	Congressional
13258	Dutton, Thomas H.	86y	W	20 DEC 1915	Hyattsville MD	Rock Creek
08710	Dutton, William H.	71y	W	9 JUL 1912	Hyattsville MD	Rock Creek
01806	Duutton, William A.J.	60y	W	8 NOV 1895	Bladensburg MD	Mt. Olivet

[1] The Dulins and Wrenn were all on one permit issued 16 DEC 1889 to C.E. Hine, real estate, for removal to Congressional.

No.	Name of Deceased	Age	Race	Death Date	Place of Death	Place of Burial
01139	Duval, Eli	55y	W	26 AUG 1892	Lynchburg VA	Oak Hill
03766	Duval, Sarah E.	87y	W	20 DEC 1901	Philadelphia PA	Oak Hill
17485	Duvall, Alice Carey	80y	W	24 OCT 1921	Laurel MD	Oak Hill
05287	Duvall, Andrew B.	58y	W	12 SEP 1905	At Sea	Congressional
11986	Duvall, Charles Roger	5y	W	10 DEC 1911	Lanham MD	Oak Hill
12643	Duvall, Clarence Gillette	19y	W	4 DEC 1914	Princeton NJ	Congressional
02196	Duvall, Edmond B., blacksmith	70y	W	30 MAY 1897	Baltimore MD	Congressional
01455	Duvall, Eliza B.	76y	W	6 AUG 1894	Rutherford NJ	Congressional
14728	Duvall, Frank H.	1m	W	3 APR 1918	Brentwood MD	Mt. Olivet
01548	Duvall, Henry C., farmer	69y	W	28 JAN 1895	Odenton MD	Glenwood
09124	Duvall, J. Albert	55y	W	11 MAR 1913	Rutherford NJ	Congressional
01433	Duvall, Jonathan C.	22m	W	12 JUL 1894	Pr. Geo. Co. MD	Oak Hill
00824	Duvall, Mabel Moore	3y	W	13 AUG 1892	Boyds MD	Congressional
16401	Duvall, Mary A.	53y	W	20 MAR 1920	Bladensburg MD	Glenwood
07878	Duvall, Mrs. T.A.	78y	W	16 DEC 1910	Round Mtn. WV	Holyrood
08454	Duvall, Nancy	91y	W	1 JAN 1912	Albany NY	Glenwood
11911	Duvall, Ruth	9y	W	19 JUL 1913	Collingswood NJ	Oak Hill
16569	Duvall, William S.	56y	W	25 JUN 1920	Chicago IL	Oak Hill
17958	Dux, Bertha Lederman	78y	W	14 JUL 1922	Newport News VA	Wash. Hebrew
03015	Duxbury, Charles H.	43y	W	24 NOV 1899	Cedar Rapids IA	Rock Creek
05037	Dwyer, Hannah C.	83y	W	21 FEB 1905	Hyattsville MD	Mt. Olivet
05867	Dwyer, Thomas B.	80y	W	21 DEC 1906	Hyattsville MD	Mt. Olivet
04844	Dwyer, William	28y	W	12 AUG 1904	Baltimore MD	Mt. Olivet
04056	Dye, Clarence	24y	W	19 OCT 1902	Grafton WV	Fredericksburg VA
03459	Dye, Denny	36y	C	24 MAR 1901	New York NY	Mt. Olivet
08220	Dyer, Albert Polls	77y	W	28 JUL 1911	Takoma Park MD	Cremated
01927	Dyer, Bessie	12y	C	12 MAY 1896	Charlottesville VA	Woodlawn
06099	Dyer, Harry L.	47y	W	18 MAY 1903	Chicago IL	Oak Hill
01367	Dyer, John C., merchant	49y	W	19 APR 1894	Rawlins WY	Mt. Olivet
12511	Dyer, Joseph I.	34y	W	1 SEP 1914	Cherrydale VA	Holyrood
08444	Dyer, Joseph T.	61y	W	28 DEC 1911	Hyattsville MD	Mt. Olivet
04081	Dyer, Louisa	22y	C	4 SEP 1902	Staunton VA	Mt. Olivet
00260	Dyer, Paul Danford	30y	W	6 JAN 1890	Santa Fe NM	Oak Hill
12337	Dyer, Robert T.	57y	W	15 OCT 1913	San Francisco CA	Holyrood
18122	Dyer, Susan H.	41y	W	21 OCT 1922	New York NY	Arlington
16990	Dyer, Susan H.P.	67y	W	20 FEB 1921	Winter Park FL	Arlington
16742	Dykes, Florence M.	28y	C	5 OCT 1920	Takoma Park MD	Woodlawn
13305	Dykes, Mabel	32y	W	19 JAN 1916	Laurel MD	Methodist
08519	Dyson, J. Robert	c.39y	C	17 FEB 1912	Buffalo NY	Harmony

District of Columbia Foreign Death Records, 1888-1923

No.	Name of Deceased	Age	Race	Death Date	Place of Death	Place of Burial
E						
12435	Eacritt, Mary A.	64y	W	8 JUL 1914	Minatare NE	Arlington
18564	Eads, Dora G.	46y	W	23 NOV 1922	—	Mt. Olivet
08766	Eakle, Edward H.	52y	W	15 AUG 1912	Wash. Grove MD	Congressional
06021	Ealer, Eulalie	83y	W	8 APR 1907	Kensington MD	Glenwood
01401	Eames, Charles Campbell	44y	W	9 JUN 1894	Providence RI	Congressional
00321	Eames, Fanny	71y	W	29 APR 1890	Sykesville MD	Congressional
02516	Earl, Charles	61y	W	13 JUL 1898	Riverdale MD	Oak Hill
11925	Earl, David	1y	W	28 JUL 1913	Baltimore MD	Congressional
13925	Earl, Katherine	87y	W	12 JAN 1917	Kew Garden NY	Oak Hill
17294	Earle, Phillip M.	78y	W	21 JUN 1921	Hampton VA	Glenwood
01456	Earle, William E.	57y	W	13 AUG 1894	Portland ME	Greenville SC
02648	Earley, Mary E.	25y	C	3 NOV 1898	Newark NJ	Mt. Zion
01858	Earll, R. Edward	42y	W	19 MAR 1896	Chevy Chase MD	Glenwood
03354	Easby, Elizabeth Barton	77y	W	28 NOV 1900	New York NY	Congressional
18531	Easby, Thomas Barton	63y	W	6 MAY 1923	Poughkeepsie NY	Glenwood
15155	Easterday, Mary E.	84y	W	11 OCT 1918	Newark NJ	Glenwood
04555	Eastlake, R. Elizabeth	66y	W	27 DEC 1903	Paoli PA	Oak Hill
13000	Eastman, Albert Preston	73y	W	13 JUL 1915	Falls Church VA	Oak Hill
06037	Eastman, Janie M.	38y	C	18 APR 1907	New York	Payne's
14711	Eastman, Mary A.L.	74y	W	24 MAR 1918	Penscaola FL	Oak Hill
01549	Easton, Abby	40y	C	13 DEC 1894	Philadelphia PA	Mt. Zion
04005	Easton, Harry B.	39y	W	15 SEP 1902	Alexandria VA	Oak Hill
08589	Easton, Laura Jane Wallis	68y	W	8 APR 1912	Riverdale MD	Glenwood
15701	Easton, Samuel J.	36y	C	27 MAR 1919	Baltimore MD	Glymont MD
03135	Eastwood, Louis L., soldier	—	—	16 DEC 1899	Manila, P.I.	Arlington VA
03536	Eatman, George	30y	C	5 JUN 1901	Conneaut La. PA	Harmony
13311	Eaton, Bernard R.	28y	W	18 DEC 1915	Montreal, Can.	Congressional
00825	Eaton, Fanny Webster	64y	W	13 SEP 1892	Northampton MA	Glenwood
17628	Eberbach, Zachary T.	73y	W	11 JAN 1922	Newark NJ	Glenwood
12102	Eberhardt, Maud	37y	C	18 NOV 1913	Philadelphia PA	Woodlawn
16758	Eberly, Harry W.	26y	W	14 OCT 1920	Dover NJ	Mt. Olivet
12250	Eckel, Rebecca	75y	W	7 MAR 1914	Forestville MD	Tremont PA
05538	Eckhardt, Annie Laura	41y	W	14 APR 1906	Kensington MD	Glenwood
12457	Eckloff, Randolph J.	53y	W	20 JUL 1914	Montpelier ID	Rock Creek
04267	Eckloff, William Frederick	5y	W	1 MAY 1903	Silver Spring MD	Rock Creek
17499	Eckman, Eva	89y	W	3 NOV 1921	Rockville MD	Loudon Pk. MD
04397	Edds, Mary Elizabeth	74y	W	20 JUL 1903	Brentwood MD	Congressional
18586	Edelen, Elizabeth J.	66y	W	4 JUN 1923	Sykesville MD	Oxon Hill MD
04953	Edelin, Alberta	14y	C	8 NOV 1904	Silver Hill MD	Moore's
07858	Edelin, Belle	52y	W	2 DEC 1910	Pasadena CA	Congressional
15189	Edelin, George R.	—	W	15 OCT 1918	Opelita AL	Congressional
02713	Edelin, Robley D.	48y	W	13 JAN 1899	Philadelphia PA	Glenwood
03786	Edelin, Thomas Boyd	67y	W	8 FEB 1902	Culpeper VA	Congressional
05079	Edes, Margaret	70y	W	9 APR 1905	Atlantic City NJ	Oak Hill
14801	Edeson, Theodore	47y	W	17 NOV 1870	Rock Island IL	Glenwood
15239	Edgley, Edward, in jail	22y	C	19 OCT 1918	Lorton VA	Payne's
14830	Edie, Caroline H.	42y	W	13 APR 1918	Marseille, Fra.	Oak Hill
15823	Edington, Alice Newell	8m	W	10 JUN 1919	Markham VA	Glenwood
13124	Edlin, Joseph E.	26y	C	25 SEP 1915	New York NY	Mt. Olivet
02616	Edmond, Sarah Huntington	84y	W	19 SEP 1898	Boston MA	Oak Hill
16643	Edmonds, John R.	74y	W	5 AUG 1920	Memphis TN	Rock Creek
12824	Edmonds, Lucy	53y	C	16 MAR 1815	New York NY	Harmony
13991	Edmonds, Mary E.	70y	W	16 FEB 1917	Chicago IL	Oak Hill
14740	Edmonston, Eleanora F.	86y	W	8 APR 1918	New Market MD	Glenwood
05950	Edmonston, George D.	61y	W	2 JUN 1895	Pittsburgh PA	Glenwood
06642	Edmonston, George Henry J.	38y	W	12 JUL 1908	Irwin PA	Glenwood
12245	Edmonston, Infant of Archibald	8h	W	3 MAR 1914	Chevy Chase MD	Glenwood
04330	Edmonston, Katherine	24y	W	20 AUG 1903	Gloucester MA	Oak Hill

No.	Name of Deceased	Age	Race	Death Date	Place of Death	Place of Burial
17587	Edmonston, Mark Frazier	29y	W	11 DEC 1921	Brentwood MD	Rock Creek
05756	Edmonston, Mary O.	40y	W	2 OCT 1906	Irwin PA	Glenwood
02668	Edmunds, Aaron	29y	C	28 NOV 1898	Philadelphia PA	—
07218	Edmunds, Catherine Fornance	62y	W	27 SEP 1909	Lake George NY	Arlington
15336	Edmunds, Robert Lindsay	20y	W	9 NOV 1918	Hampton Rds. VA	Rockville MD
17522	Edson, John Joy, Jr.	50y	W	15 NOV 1921	Pittsburgh PA	Arlington
03384	Edson, Mary L.	57y	W	2 JAN 1901	Chevy Chase MD	Glenwood
14558	Edwards, Alice B.	53y	W	6 JAN 1918	Mt. Ranier MD	Glenwood
15158	Edwards, Bessie Porter	21y	W	13 OCT 1918	Camp Meade MD	Arlington
15051	Edwards, Charles	c.30y	W	25 SEP 1918	Syracuse NY	Arlington
18190	Edwards, Daniel A.	59y	W	2 DEC 1922	Baltimore MD	Congressional
14511	Edwards, Delia R.	73y	W	17 DEC 1917	Chevy Chase MD	Rock Creek
13623	Edwards, Eaton Albert	71y	W	26 JUL 1916	S. Milford, N.S.	Arlington
13571	Edwards, Elsie	28y	C	22 JUN 1916	Brooklyn NY	Woodlawn[1]
03160	Edwards, George	27y	W	9 APR 1900	New York NY	St. Mary's
02197	Edwards, George K., Dr.	31y	W	4 JUN 1897	Princeton NJ	Oak Hill
05292	Edwards, J. Alex	42y	W	15 SEP 1905	Albuquerque NM	Mt. Olivet
05323	Edwards, James	61y	W	19 OCT 1905	Dranesville VA	Cremated
15237	Edwards, James C.	34y	W	20 OCT 1918	Brentwood MD	Mt. Olivet
07357	Edwards, James H.	36y	C	3 JAN 1910	New York NY	Woodlawn
03574	Edwards, James S.	59y	W	10 JUL 1901	Atlantic City NJ	Rock Creek
04657	Edwards, John W.	28y	W	15 DEC 1903	Patuxent Sta. MD	Congressional
12447½	Edwards, Mary W.	75y	W	18 JUL 1914	Sykesville MD	Glenwood
05357	Edwards, Mrs. Thomas	—	W	—	Cadillac MI	Mt. Olivet
06931	Edwards, Robert W.	46y	W	10 DEC 1908	New York NY	Glenwood
04908	Edwards, Sophia L.	80y	W	3 OCT 1904	Brentwood MD	Rock Creek
05714	Edwards, Susan W.	44y	W	27 AUG 1906	Baltimore MD	Oak Hill
00229	Edwards, Susan W.	69y	W	9 NOV 1889	Baltimore MD	Oak Hill
01928	Egbert, George A.	25y	W	18 MAY 1896	Glen Echo MD	Congressional
02821	Egbert, Harry C.	—	W	9 APR 1899	Philippine Isl.	Arlington VA
11841	Egbert, Nelly Y.	70y	W	2 JUN 1913	Newport RI	Arlington VA
14553	Egerton, John George	27y	W	5 JAN 1918	Philadelphia PA	Arlington
07346	Eglen, Mary L.	46y	C	24 DEC 1909	Cambridge MA	Payne's
00597	Eglin, Alice E.	1y	W	17 JAN 1881	Langley VA	Mt. Olivet
02895	Eglin, Anna	49y	C	3 AUG 1899	New York NY	Mt. Olivet
00596	Eglin, Samuel E.	1y	W	26 FEB 1888	Canal Rd. DC	Mt. Olivet
16820	Egloff, John W.E.	35y	W	23 NOV 1920	Brentwood MD	Congressional
15829	Ehlers, Sena	59y	W	13 JUN 1919	Forest Glen MD	Prospect Hill
18273	Ehrmantrout, Bernard	33y	W	16 JAN 1923	Alexandria VA	Mt. Olivet
08425	Ehrmantrout, Infant of Jos.	SB	W	14 DEC 1911	Rock Spring MD	Holyrood
07407	Eichelberger, George F.	66y	W	6 FEB 1910	Pikesville MD	Charlestown WV
14360	Eichelberger, J.E.	48y	W	13 SEP 1917	Mattapoisett MA	Congressional
17509	Eichholtz, Bettie C.	69y	W	9 NOV 1921	Bethesda MA	Cremated
06890	Eiker, Agnes A.	52y	W	11 JAN 1909	Chevy Chase MD	Rock Creek
13545	Eilbacher, Charles L.	19y	W	25 SEP 1901	Baltimore MD	Mt. Olivet
04661	Eills, Hetty	78y	W	5 APR 1904	Niagara Falls NY	Rock Creek
15232	Eisbey, John	26y	C	16 OCT 1918	Newark NJ	Mt. Zion East
01975	Eisel, Benjamin N.	5y	W	4 SEP 1896	Baltimore MD	Cremated
14615	Eisenmann, David	63y	W	1 FEB 1918	New York NY	Wash. Hebrew
17024	Elbert, Mary	82y	W	6 MAR 1921	Norristown PA	Mt. Olivet
03000	Eldridge, Bogardus	42y	W	2 OCT 1899	Pacoor, P. Isl.	Arlington VA
16363	Eldridge, Cathleen A.S.	1y	W	5 MAR 1920	Takoma Park MD	Glenwood
04399	Eldridge, Charles W.	63y	W	21 JUL 1903	Garrett Park MD	Rock Creek
13993	Eldridge, Ellery W., Capt.	c.74y	W	15 FEB 1917	Newport News VA	Rock Creek
04308	Eldridge, Glen	6m	W	18 APR 1903	Knoxville TN	Rock Creek
05799	Elgin, J. Edward	26y	W	1 NOV 1906	Hume VA	Congressional

[1] Disinterment permit #8702 on 29 JUN 1916 for removal to Payne's Cemetery.

District of Columbia Foreign Death Records, 1888-1923

No.	Name of Deceased	Age	Race	Death Date	Place of Death	Place of Burial
18525	Eliason, Ann M.	78y	W	4 MAY 1923	New York NY	Oak Hill
15502	Ellegood, Gertrude	67y	W	30 DEC 1918	Canton OH	Glenwood
00376	Eller, Maggie	13y	W	28 JUL 1890	Baltimore MD	Prospect Hill
00544	Ellerbrook, George Henry, Jr.	5m	W	21 JUN 1891	Accokeek MD	Congressional
14650	Ellicott, Lidie Dyre	53y	W	20 FEB 1918	Bridgeport CN	Rock Creek
05324	Ellin, Infant of Benj. A.	SB	W	21 OCT 1905	Chillum MD	Rock Creek
18497	Ellinger, Lucretia Morton	59y	W	21 APR 1923	Silver Spring MD	Glenwood
06323	Elliott, Annie C.	58y	W	27 NOV 1907	Shen. A. Spgs. VA	Rock Creek
15528	Elliott, Arthur R.	29y	W	5 JAN 1919	Philadelphia PA	Glenwood
14138	Elliott, Bessie L. (Shoemaker)	32y	C	15 MAY 1917	Fredericksburg VA	Wellington VA
02593	Elliott, Emily	47y	W	27 AUG 1898	Bowie MD	Congressional
02590	Elliott, George	21y	W	29 AUG 1898	Philadelphia PA	Oak Hill
05543	Elliott, Henry R.	56y	W	17 APR 1906	New York NY	Glenwood
14109	Elliott, Ida W.	38y	W	26 APR 1917	Sarasota FL	Rock Creek
06959	Elliott, Maria L.	65y	W	27 MAR 1909	Baltimore MD	Rock Creek
07952	Elliott, Marian V.	53y	W	29 JAN 1911	Chevy Chase MD	Oak Hill
04559	Elliott, Mary A.	44y	W	7 JAN 1904	Chevy Chase MD	Holyrood
00598	Elliott, Mary Cath. Jones	72y	W	30 JUL 1891	Alum Springs VA	Rock Creek
14346	Elliott, William	68y	W	6 SEP 1917	Baltimore MD	Congressional
00707	Ellis, Ann Maria	50y	W	29 FEB 1892	Alexandria VA	Oak Hill
12459	Ellis, Byron E.	4m	W	26 JUL 1914	Cherrydale VA	Rock Creek
04984	Ellis, Dora V.	14y	C	22 DEC 1904	Glen Echo MD	Christian
05277	Ellis, Fay	1y	W	6 SEP 1905	Riderville AL	Congressional
02870	Ellis, James Everette	21y	W	5 JUL 1899	New York NY	Glenwood
03409	Ellis, Jennie	28y	C	2 FEB 1901	Asheville NC	Payne's
00329	Ellis, John A.	38y	W	21 MAY 1890	Jersey City NJ	Glenwood
00293	Ellis, John S.	39y	W	18 MAR 1890	Newark NJ	Oak Hill
01807	Ellis, Joshua, pilot	52y	W	26 OCT 1895	Fairfax Co. VA	Oak Hill
08104	Ellis, Mary A.	40y	W	7 MAY 1911	Baltimore MD	Glenwood
08133	Ellis, Richard C., s/o Rich. C.	1y	W	30 MAY 1911	Clarendon VA	Holyrood
01469	Ellis, Sadie	3y	W	21 AUG 1894	Chilton Co. AL	Congressional
12922	Ellis, Sadie	39y	C	10 MAY 1915	Philadelphia PA	Harmony
17096	Ellis, Sarah Fish	68y	W	8 APR 1921	Silver Spring MD	Northport NY
08521	Ellis, Sarah H.	68y	W	3 FEB 1912	San Francisco CA	Rock Creek
06067	Ellis, William	52y	C	15 MAY 1907	Baltimore Co. MD	Fredericksburg VA
00233	Ellis, William M.	54y	C	25 NOV 1889	Washington DC	Graceland
02371	Elloms, Joseph	48y	W	4 FEB 1898	King Geo. Co. VA	Mt. Olivet
16454	Ellsworth, Frances E.	63y	W	26 APR 1920	Milwaukee WI	Rock Creek
18419	Ellsworth, Martha R.	88y	W	13 MAR 1923	Takoma Park MD	Congressional
03894	Ellwood, Harry	19y	C	10 JUN 1902	Baltimore MD	Mt. Olivet
16717	Ellworth, Worth B.	20y	W	16 SEP 1920	New York NY	Glenwood
07438	Ellyson, Onan, Rev.	84y	W	21 FEB 1910	Lynchburg VA	Cremated
15628	Elmer, Francis E.	67y	W	20 FEB 1919	Takoma MD	Toledo OH
17565	Elmer, Ida T.	73y	W	30 NOV 1921	Jersey City NJ	Glenwood
13234	Elmer, Lavenia G.	91y	W	4 DEC 1915	Jersey City NJ	Glenwood
06948	Elmer, Luther S.	49y	W	15 MAR 1909	Jersey City NJ	Glenwood
01387	Elms, James	75y	W	1 MAY 1894	Unity MD	Mt. Olivet
07716	Elsworth, Joseph P.	7m	C	27 AUG 1910	Seat Pleasant MD	Mt. Olivet
16806	Elterich, Augusta W.	72y	W	14 NOV 1920	Pittsburgh PA	Prospect Hill
05941	Ely, George	48y	W	15 FEB 1907	St. Paul MN	Cremated
15540	Embrey, James D.	27y	W	11 JAN 1919	Washington DC	Glenwood
17919	Embrey, Samantha E. (Colbert)	72y	W	24 JUN 1922	Fredericksburg VA	Arlington
16552	Emch, Leonora A.	31y	W	24 JUN 1920	Takoma Park MD	Ft. Recovery OH
14723	Emerick, Henrietta C.	64y	W	30 MAR 1918	Hyattsville MD	Oak Hill
15795	Emerson, Mattie	36y	C	24 MAY 1919	Baltimore MD	Woodlawn
16588	Emerson, William R.	69y	W	8 JUL 1920	Atlantic City NJ	Rock Creek
13033	Emery, Agnes H.	46y	W	4 AUG 1915	Chevy Chase MD	Rock Creek
12195	Emery, Amanda	60y	W	1 FEB 1914	New York NY	Oak Hill
15077	Emery, Ernest William	21y	W	30 SEP 1918	Hampton Rds. VA	Baltimore MD

No.	Name of Deceased	Age	Race	Death Date	Place of Death	Place of Burial
16153	Emery, Harriet Elizabeth	76y	W	17 DEC 1919	Medford MA	Rock Creek
13722	Emery, Samuel, s/o Samuel	65y	W	14 SEP 1916	Long Branch NJ	Oak Hill
13770	Emi, Helene M.	39y	W	16 OCT 1916	Islip NY	Glenwood
17835	Emmons, Addie M.	57y	W	4 MAY 1922	Brooklyn NY	Congressional
06162	Emmons, Catherine	53y	W	30 JUL 1907	Sykesville MD	Congressional
02792	Emmons, Edward J.	66y	W	14 FEB 1899	Alexandria VA	Oak Hill
01976	Emmons, Sophia M.	48y	W	19 JUN 1896	Atlantic City NJ	Rock Creek
03533	Emory, Hannah D.	67y	W	1 JUN 1901	Town Hill PA	Glenwood
00708	Emory, Harriet L.	—	W	1846	Baltimore MD	Rock Creek
18412	Emory, Jerome	30y	W	9 MAR 1923	New Orleans LA	Mt. Olivet
00708	Emory, Sallie A.	—	W	1862	Baltimore MD	Rock Creek
14234	Emory, William H.	70y	W	15 JUL 1917	Newport RI	Arlington
09117	Enderle, Joseph W., s/o J.L.	42y	W	8 MAR 1913	New York NY	Rock Creek
17590	Endicott, Catherine C.	43y	W	15 DEC 1921	Columbus GA	Arlington
06163	Endicott, John	26y	W	26 JUL 1907	Colo. Spgs. CO	May's Landing NY
16021	Engel, George H.	65y	W	27 SEP 1919	Birmingham AL	Annapolis MD
13982	England, Charles H.	69y	W	2 FEB 1917	Philadelphia PA	Arlington
00709	Engle, James M., Jr.	4y	W	23 JAN 1892	Forest Glen MD	Congressional
07008	Englehart, Robert F.	38y	W	28 APR 1909	Denver CO	Holyrood
14968	English, Alexandria	6m	W	11 AUG 1918	Bethesda MD	Cremated
13195	English, James	3m	W	10 NOV 1915	Capitol Hts. MD	Mt. Olivet
14969	Ennis, Frank	c.30y	W	11 AUG 1918	MD	New York NY
16285	Ennis, George J.	67y	W	5 FEB 1920	Capitol Hts. MD	Glenwood
03455	Ennis, Henrietta	65y	C	17 MAR 1901	New York NY	Woodlawn
06878	Ennis, John	28y	C	2 JAN 1909	Brooklyn NY	Woodlawn
16801	Ennis, Thomas	55y	C	8 NOV 1920	Fairmont Hts. MD	Payne's
07186	Enthoffer, Elizabeth A.	73y	W	6 SEP 1909	Black Mtn. NC	Rock Creek
00944	Erb, Jennie E.	5y	W	1 AUG 1893	New York NY	Congressional
05839	Erdman, Charles	17y	W	17 JUL 1906	Ocean City NJ	Mt. Olivet
01978	Ergood, Addie B.	46y	W	23 AUG 1896	Harpers Ferry WV	Congressional
15103	Erhardt, Irene E.	29y	W	7 OCT 1918	Takoma Park MD	Rome NY
11988	Erly, Pamelia M.	68y	W	2 SEP 1913	Pelham NY	Mt. Olivet
17108	Ernest, Emma Louisa	76y	W	15 APR 1921	Kensington MD	Tenallytown M.
01140	Ernest, Herbert S.	1y	W	17 JUN 1892	Montg. Co. MD	Tenallytown
14425	Erni, Mary	84y	W	23 OCT 1917	Bronx NY	Glenwood
04052	Ernst, Elizabeth M.	5m	W	7 SEP 1902	Forest Glen MD	Prospect Hill
18087	Ervin, Marion H.	72y	W	24 SEP 1922	Sykesville MD	Rock Creek
01954	Ervin, Raymond Wells	13y	W	18 JAN 1896	Hyattsville MD	Rock Creek
15101	Eschenfee, Earnest C.	37y	W	5 OCT 1918	Capitol Hts. MD	Prospect Hill
08119	Eschner, Herbert P., s/o Paul J.	1y	W	16 MAY 1911	Pearce Sta. VA	Cremated
04862	Escoffney, Josephine	15d	C	22 AUG 1904	Atlantic City NJ	Harmony
14787	Eskridge, Edna Louise	18y	C	30 APR 1918	Crownsville MD	Mt. Olivet
09121	Eskridge, George	39y	C	6 MAR 1913	Philadelphia PA	Harmony
05203	Eslin, John C.	21y	W	10 JUL 1905	Mt. Ranier MD	St. Mary's
05566	Eslin, Julia P.	41y	W	5 MAY 1906	Saranac Lake NY	Glenwood
01699	Espey, Logan B.	9m	W	18 JUN 1895	Winchester VA	Mt. Olivet
13888	Espey, Mina G.	65y	W	28 DEC 1916	Hyattsville MD	Mt. Olivet
15859	Esputa, Ethel R.	18y	W	5 JUL 1919	Rockville MD	Mt. Olivet
00945	Esputa, Hinton A.C.	4m	W	13 JUN 1893	Alex. Co. VA	Mt. Olivet
0083	Esputa, Josephine	2y	W	28 JUN 1889	Newport MD	Mt. Olivet
17345	Esser, Joseph H.	27y	W	5 AUG 1921	Saranac Lake NY	Mt. Olivet
18002	Essig, Elizabeth	63y	W	10 AUG 1922	Sykesville MD	Prospect Hill
08049	Essig, Gottlieb	59y	W	3 APR 1911	Forestville MD	Prospect Hill
12143	Estam, Andrew J.	58y	W	2 JAN 1914	Baltimore MD	Prospect Hill
15626	Ester, John	70y	W	17 FEB 1919	Hyattsville MD	Prospect Hill
07396	Estes, Charles	29y	W	1 FEB 1910	Bay View J. MD	Glenwood
14996	Estes, Eva Catherine	1y	W	30 AUG 1918	Alex. Co. VA	Glenwood
12882	Estes, Luther Russell	2y	W	17 APR 1915	Buffalo NY	Glenwood
14258	Estes, Richard W.	2y	W	JUL 1917	Ballston VA	Glenwood

District of Columbia Foreign Death Records, 1888-1923

No.	Name of Deceased	Age	Race	Death Date	Place of Death	Place of Burial
13716	Etheridge, Caroline F.	52y	W	15 SEP 1916	Chevy Chase MD	Rock Creek
01550	Ettinger, A.J.	31y	W	23 FEB 1895	Cowans VA	Glenwood
03213	Eubank, Ethel May	1y	W	23 JUN 1900	Hagerstown MD	Rock Creek
16369	Euchelberger, W.L.	c.45y	W	3 MAR 1920	El Paso TX	Congressional
15913	Europe, Ida	38y	C	26 JUL 1919	New York NY	Harmony
15776	Europe, James Reese	38y	C	9 MAY 1919	Boston MA	Arlington
01700	Eustis, Joseph, soldier	52y	W	24 SEP 1895	—	Soldier's Home
17545	Eustis, William Corcoran	60y	W	24 NOV 1921	New York NY	Oak Hill
18578	Evans, Alice F.	71y	W	23 APR 1923	Panama Canal	Glenwood
07752	Evans, Alice M.	44y	W	18 SEP 1910	Baltimore MD	Mt. Olivet
07518	Evans, Andrew Bunyon	33y	W	24 APR 1910	Colo. Spgs. CO	Richmond VA
02896	Evans, Annie H.	58y	W	5 AUG 1899	Baltimore MD	Congressional
15435	Evans, Claudia C.	5m	C	9 OCT 1918	Cape May Co. NJ	Harmony
02198	Evans, Eliza	72y	W	21 MAY 1897	Indian Head MD	Congressional
13277	Evans, Elizabeth	23y	C	29 DEC 1915	Pittsburgh PA	Harmony
14794	Evans, Elizabeth J.	66y	W	4 MAY 1918	Front Royal VA	Rock Creek
13942	Evans, Emma A.	66y	C	21 JAN 1917	Albany NY	Woodlawn
01977	Evans, George Washington	54y	W	11 AUG 1896	Baltimore MD	Congressional
14705	Evans, Harry	19y	C	19 MAR 1918	Cameron Co. PA	Payne's
06828	Evans, Henry C.	79y	W	24 NOV 1908	Pikesville MD	Oak Hill
15318	Evans, Hilda A.	30y	W	2 NOV 1918	Takoma MD	Cumberland MD
15278	Evans, Infant of Elmer E.	SB	W	25 OCT 1918	Takoma Park MD	Rock Creek
14145	Evans, James	11y	C	21 MAY 1917	Fairmont Hts. MD	Payne's
13224	Evans, Mary	28y	C	25 NOV 1915	New York NY	Payne's
06936	Evans, Mary J.	81y	W	4 MAR 1909	Fairfax Co. VA	Glenwood
04691	Evans, Olivia M.	54y	W	29 APR 1904	Chevy Chase MD	Rock Creek
17481	Evans, Regina Jacobs	31y	W	14 OCT 1921	Baker OR	Glenwood
13504	Evans, Robert	6y	W	13 MAY 1916	Fairmont Hts. MD	Payne's
03910	Evans, Robert F., brickmaker	63y	W	17 JUN 1902	Alex. Co. VA	Congressional
04763	Evans, Rudolph Henry	90y	W	14 JUN 1904	Chevy Chase MD	Rock Creek
01857	Evans, Ruth L.	1y	W	25 FEB 1896	Brooklyn NY	Glenwood
06627	Evans, Seff Allin	9m	W	2 JUL 1908	Mt. Ranier MD	Glenwood
18579	Evans, W. Warrington	80y	W	4 JUN 1923	Ivandale VA	Rock Creek
02372	Evans, Walter Dorsey	25y	W	14 FEB 1898	El Paso TX	Oak Hill
02524	Evans, William	28y	W	3 JUL 1898	Chicago IL	Glenwood
03419	Evarts, Truman	82y	W	16 FEB 1901	Hyattsville MD	Glenwood
08001	Everett, Florence	37y	W	10 MAR 1911	Mt. Clemens MI	Congressional
11895	Everett, Otis	10m	W	13 JUL 1913	Relee VA	Mt. Olivet
08666	Everett, William H.	65y	W	10 JUN 1912	Newport RI	Arlington
18440	Everhart, John W.	47y	W	22 MAR 1923	Weverton MD	Glenwood
17071	Everhart, Mary A. (Vance)	61y	W	25 MAR 1921	Clinton IA	Rock Creek
15353	Ewald, Kate	71y	W	14 NOV 1918	Alexandria VA	Prospect Hill
12090	Ewan, Brubenia	70y	W	10 OCT 1913	Stresa, Italy	Rock Creek
12087	Ewan, John W., Rev.	59y	W	29 DEC 1890	Front Royal VA	Rock Creek
06057	Ewell, Annie	63y	C	7 MAY 1907	Hartford CN	Payne's
14369	Ewell, Lawson	27y	C	19 SEP 1917	Hyattsville MD	Mt. Olivet
14664	Ewing, Charles Beverley	59y	W	1 MAR 1918	Rochester MN	Arlington
15001	Ewing, Laura E.	28y	W	31 AUG 1918	Silverside DE	Cedar Hill MD
15299	Exel, Elizabeth	70y	W	29 OCT 1918	Lakeland MD	Prospect Hill
16471	Eyler, John I.	50y	W	5 MAY 1920	Chester PA	Glenwood
12328	Eyler, Samuel Q.	61y	W	6 OCT 1899	Lewistown MD	Glenwood
17304	Eynon, Edward B.	68y	W	17 JUL 1921	Chevy Chase MD	Tamagua PA
05278	Eyster, Caroline	88y	W	9 SEP 1905	Vienna VA	Oak Hill

No.	Name of Deceased	Age	Race	Death Date	Place of Death	Place of Burial
F						
17214	Fabean, Samuel Monroe	63y	W	5 JUN 1921	Accotink VA	Cremated
18010	Fabrizio, Agnes L.	11y	W	13 AUG 1922	Chesa. Bea. MD	St. Mary's
13050	Fagan, Charles S.	35y	W	11 AUG 1915	Alta Vista MD	Oak Hill
15377	Fagan, Frank T.	27y	W	22 NOV 1918	Niagara Falls NY	Mt. Olivet
01859	Fagan, John	71y	W	9 MAR 1896	Bowie MD	Mt. Olivet
01487	Fagan, Maggie E.	36y	W	9 SEP 1894	Bowie MD	Mt. Olivet
06026	Fagan, Mary Elizabeth	58y	W	11 APR 1907	Bethesda MD	Oak Hill
00599	Fagne, Annie	6m	W	8 AUG 1891	Brandywine MD	Glenwood
02245	Fague, Thomas W., Jr.	11m	W	25 JUL 1897	Rowlesburg WV	Glenwood
02246	Faherty, Joseph D.	32y	W	6 JUL 1897	Piedmont WV	Mt. Olivet
04742	Fahey, Pearl	26y	W	30 MAY 1904	Riverdale MD	Oak Hill
09102	Fahey, William E.	40y	W	1 MAR 1913	Philadelphia PA	Mt. Olivet
11880	Fahooey, Adeeb	15y	W	6 JUL 1913	Bladensburg MD	Glenwood
15274	Fainman, Abraham J.	24y	W	17 OCT 1918	Ft. Oglethorpe GA	Elesavetgrad
12308	Fainter, John C.	79y	W	11 APR 1914	Hyattsville MD	Mt. Olivet
03617	Fainter, Josephine	1y	W	18 AUG 1901	Hyattsville MD	Mt. Olivet
15236	Fair, Ella (Jaeger)	25y	W	19 OCT 1918	Detroit MI	Glenwood
16421	Fairchild, Charles	4h	W	6 JAN 1906	Pelham NY	Rock Creek
16435	Fairchild, Mary E.	49y	W	12 APR 1920	Mt. Vernon NY	Rock Creek
17598	Fairchild, Salome C.	66y	W	20 DEC 1921	Takoma Park MD	Rock Creek
17388	Fairclough, Flora	51y	W	6 SEP 1921	Takoma Park MD	Greenwood NY
13507	Fairfax, Florence	25y	C	14 MAY 1916	Philadelphia PA	Mt. Zion East
03292	Fairfax, John Contee	70y	W	28 SEP 1900	Northampton MD	Rock Creek
08557	Fairfax, Mary Kirby	74y	W	13 MAR 1912	New York NY	Rock Creek
17647	Fairfax, Turner	85y	C	19 JAN 1922	Fairmont Hts. MD	Woodlawn
03204	Fairlamb, Marian K.	57y	W	6 JUN 1900	New York NY	Oak Hill
12400	Falbush, Mary K.	78y	W	13 JUN 1914	Landover MD	Mt. Olivet
07798	Falkner, Lizzie H.	79y	W	24 OCT 1910	Richmond VA	Cremated
02795	Falks, Charles R.	36y	W	19 APR 1899	Hyattsville MD	Glenwood
15753	Fallon, Daniel J.	33y	W	28 APR 1919	Havre de Grace	Mt. Olivet
06142	Fallon, John	79y	W	15 JUL 1907	Hampton VA	Mt. Olivet
01376	Fallon, John F.	18y	W	22 MAY 1894	Baltimore MD	Mt. Olivet
17243	Fallon, John H.	2y	W	17 JUN 1921	Boston MA	Mt. Olivet
12124	Fanning, Carrie C.B.	75y	W	11 DEC 1913	Elmira NY	Congressional
16437	Fanning, Charles E.	66y	W	11 APR 1920	Omaha NE	Congressional
07128	Fanning, Frank	44y	W	22 JUL 1909	Columbus OH	Mt. Olivet
07994	Fanning, Mary E.	57y	W	1 MAR 1911	Omaha NE	Congressional
05244	Fant, Josephine Hellen	73y	W	12 AUG 1905	Elkridge MD	Mt. Olivet
02998	Fant, Lucy J.	71y	W	1 SEP 1893	Culpeper VA	Congressional
09062	Fant, William T.	26y	W	7 FEB 1913	Middleton PA	Congressional
02542	Fantleroy, Georgia Louise	8m	C	10 JUN 1898	Washington DC	Harmony
15634	Fanvell, Virginia S.	36y	W	20 FEB 1919	New York NY	Arlington VA
12148	Faris, Emmerella	70y	W	5 JAN 1914	Hyattsville MD	Rock Creek
01625	Farlee, Fred L.	23y	W	5 MAY 1895	Augusta GA	Oak Hill
12160	Farlee, William A.	44y	W	13 JAN 1914	New York NY	Oak Hill
14544	Farley, Ray	23y	I	2 JAN 1918	New York NY	Harmony
00545	Farmer, Arthur	2y	C	21 JUN 1891	Arlington VA	Mt. Olivet
16607	Farmer, Edward J., Rev.	59y	W	15 JUL 1920	Newark NJ	Mt. Olivet
01143	Farmer, Florine	9y	C	19 DEC 1892	Alex. Co. VA	Mt. Olivet
17415	Farmer, George W.	23y	W	8 OCT 1918	France	Hyattsville MD
18298	Farmer, Hiram B.	80y	W	24 JAN 1923	So. Pines NC	Rock Creek
17671	Farmer, Mary E.	61y	W	2 FEB 1922	Baltimore MD	Glenwood
13944	Farnham, Edwin D.	71y	W	23 JAN 1917	Mt. Dora FL	Glenwood
12778	Farnham, Robert	71y	W	23 FEB 1915	Railroad	Glenwood
07108	Farquhar, Addie W. (Pope)	65y	W	13 JUL 1909	Provincetown MA	Arlington
14477	Farquhar, Charles, s/o Wm.	79y	W	22 NOV 1917	Manassas VA	Arlington VA
00710	Farquhar, Emily	84y	W	28 FEB 1892	Dunkirk Farm MD	Oak Hill

District of Columbia Foreign Death Records, 1888-1923

No.	Name of Deceased	Age	Race	Death Date	Place of Death	Place of Burial
06128	Farquhar, Norman Von H.	67y	W	3 JUL 1907	Jamestown RI	Arlington
01979	Farr, M.B.	70y	W	15 SEP 1896	Delaplane VA	Glenwood
01701	Farr, Nimrod, farmer	35y	W	9 OCT 1865	Benning Rd.	Glenwood[1]
00826	Farr, Thomas E.	9y	W	28 AUG 1892	Manassas VA	Oak Hill
01702	Farrar, William Watson	45y	W	28 MAY 1895	Chevy Chase MD	Rock Creek
00470	Farre, William A.	60y	W	15 DEC 1890	Hyattsville MD	Oak Hill
05671	Farrell, Edward G.	45y	W	1 AUG 1906	Rectortown VA	Mt. Olivet
12830	Farrell, James	75y	W	22 MAR 1815	Emmitsburg MD	Mt. Olivet
15088	Farrell, Thomas W.	30y	W	5 OCT 1918	Camp Hump. VA	New York NY
08427	Farrill, Anna	53y	W	12 DEC 1911	Chicago IL	Rock Creek
03009	Farrington, Ross B.	34y	W	20 NOV 1899	Railroad	Newark NJ
13599	Faught, Isaac Wilson	26y	W	11 JUL 1916	Ballston VA	Linvells Depot VA
04766	Faulkner, Mollie	65y	W	17 JUN 1904	Woodstock VA	Congressional
00471	Faulkner, William H.	37y	W	19 FEB 1891	Douglas Co. WA	Congressional
15870	Faulkner, William S.	33y	W	28 JUN 1919	Ft. Stanton NM	Prospect Hill
09003	Faunce, Christian	80y	W	27 DEC 1912	Va. Highlands VA	Congressional
07604	Faunce, Hazel M., d/o David	15y	W	28 JUN 1910	Meter VA	Congressional
01929	Faunce, John B.	50y	W	10 APR 1896	Virginia Bea. VA	Congressional
01901	Faunce, Percy M.	18y	W	10 APR 1896	Virginia Bea. VA	Congressional
04598	Fauntleroy, Robert Powell	46y	W	5 FEB 1904	Frederick MD	Rock Creek
13896	Fauntroy, Matilda	52y	C	29 DEC 1916	New York NY	Woodlawn
02307	Fauth, Earl Philip	2y	W	22 FEB 1887	Owosso MI	Rock Creek
15330	Fauth, Infant of Frank	SB	W	7 NOV 1918	Mt. Ranier MD	Prospect Hill
00172	Fay, Laura V.	37y	W	22 OCT 1889	New York NY	Prospect Hill
08855	Fay, Lawrence B.	28y	W	17 SEP 1912	Canal Zone	Oak Hill
03265	Fay, Victor B. [D.]	23y	W	6 AUG 1900	Pine Bluff AR	Oak Hill
14981	Fealy, Joseph A.	38y	W	16 AUG 1918	New York NY	Mt. Olivet
13552	Fealy, Thomas F.	39y	W	4 JUN 1916	Delaware River	Mt. Olivet
03656	Fearson, Christopher C. (jail)	70y	W	22 SEP 1901	Mercer Co. NJ	Rock Creek
15409	Fearson, James Thacker	57y	W	7 DEC 1918	Ballston VA	Rock Creek
06017	Fearson, Mary E. (Thecker)	78y	W	7 APR 1877	Ballston VA	Holyrood
00946	Febrey, Ernest F.	5m	W	18 AUG 1893	Bailey's Xrds. VA	Glenwood
06366	Fedell, Paul	35y	W	27 DEC 1907	New York NY	Glenwood
13577	Federline, Elizabeth	73y	W	28 JUN 1916	Brentwood MD	Forest Glen MD
12826	Fee, Joseph C.	36y	W	20 MAR 1915	Warrenton VA	Rock Creek
05791	Feeney, Michael	40y	W	29 OCT 1906	Jersey City NJ	Mt. Olivet
02762	Felger, George E.	17y	W	3 MAR 1899	Grand Haven MI	Congressional
03871	Felka, Augusta	66y	W	3 MAY 1902	Sykesville MD	Cremated
12521	Felka, Marion O.	42y	W	10 SEP 1914	Baltimore MD	Rockville MD
05340	Fellows, August	64y	W	31 OCT 1905	Pugh's Farm VA	Arlington VA
18033	Fellows, Sarah A. (Alden)	72y	W	16 AUG 1922	Los Angeles CA	Glenwood
05111	Fells, Peter	24y	C	1 MAY 1905	Philadelphia PA	Harmony
02660	Felt, David N.	73y	W	17 NOV 1898	Engleside VA	Oak Hill
06221	Felt, Infant of Wells J.	SB	W	17 JUN 1907	Arlington VA	Oak Hill
06625	Felt, Infant of Wells J.	SB	W	1 JUL 1908	Rosslyn VA	Oak Hill
06221	Felt, Infant of Wells J.	SB	W	16 JUN 1906	Rosslyn VA	Oak Hill
05047	Felt, Mary Jane	74y	W	1 MAR 1905	Ingleside VA	Oak Hill
07395	Feltner, Mrs. Dick H.	30y	W	31 JAN 1910	Clarksburg WV	Glenwood
02402	Fendall, Reginald	53y	W	22 FEB 1898	New York NY	Oak Hill
01551	Fendner, Henry	31y	W	4 JAN 1895	Pittsburgh PA	Glenwood
15692	Fendner, William J.	87y	W	25 MAR 1919	Pittsburgh PA	Glenwood
09091	Fennell, Joseph Wheatley	4y	W	25 FEB 1913	Beltsville MD	Mt. Olivet
16916	Fenning, Annie E.	79y	W	13 JAN 1921	Cleveland OH	Rock Creek
00600	Fenton, Bessie O.	11m	W	10 AUG 1891	Colonial Bea. VA	Congressional
08474	Fenton, Helen (Smith)	46y	W	13 JAN 1912	Ballston VA	Rock Creek
07428	Fenton, Lillian	31y	W	18 FEB 1910	San Antonio TX	Rock Creek

---

[1] Note of 31 JUL 1895 that Nimrod Farr was for some thirty years buried at Addison's Chapel.

No.	Name of Deceased	Age	Race	Death Date	Place of Death	Place of Burial
02793	Fenton, Patrick	29y	W	19 APR 1899	Chicago IL	Mt. Olivet
15198	Fenton, Rachel Annie	31y	W	16 OCT 1918	Rosslyn VA	Rock Creek
12398	Fenton, Susie	75y	W	12 JUN 1914	Takoma Park MD	Glenwood
13425	Fenton, Theo. C.	53y	W	23 MAR 1916	Philadelphia PA	Arlington
15211	Fentress, John E.	31y	W	17 OCT 1918	Bladensburg MD	Prospect Hill
06210	Fenwick, Albert J.	33y	W	30 AUG 1907	Hagerstown MD	Mt. Olivet
17578	Fenwick, Alice Herbert	79y	W	24 FEB 1921	Leonardtown MD	Mt. Olivet
17077	Fenwick, Bernard Smith	21y	W	28 MAR 1921	Chicago IL	Rock Creek
03025	Fenwick, Charles E., Dr.	56y	W	DEC 1899	Atlanta GA	Mt. Olivet
17158	Fenwick, Francis L., Rev., S.J.	36y	W	14 MAY 1921	Frederick MD	College
07121	Fenwick, John T.	75y	W	20 JUL 1909	Buffalo NY	Mt. Olivet
01704	Fenwick, Thomas	46y	W	16 OCT 1895	Highlands MD	Mt. Olivet
17205	Fenwick, William D.	—	C	2 AUG 1918	France	Mt. Olivet
08864	Ferguson, Charles	47y	C	27 SEP 1912	Atlantic City NJ	Harmony
00158	Ferguson, J.E.	33y	W	24 SEP 1889	Sioux Falls SD	Mt. Olivet
04544	Ferguson, John C.	41y	C	5 JUL 1887	Richmond VA	Harmony
14296	Ferguson, Leota	44y	W	12 AUG 1917	Laurel MD	Cadiz OH
08017	Ferguson, Mahala (Clark)	88y	W	21 MAR 1911	Crewe VA	Jamestown NY
04458	Ferguson, Paul	3y	W	18 JUL 1901	Hagerstown MD	Rock Creek
14942	Ferguson, Rupert D.	42y	W	27 JUL 1918	Amityville NY	Oak Hill
06481	Fergusson, Arthur Walsh	49y	W	30 JAN 1908	Manila, P.I.	Oak Hill
00947	Fericour, Charles U.	48y	W	24 JUN 1893	Baltimore MD	Glenwood
16884	Fernald, Charles H.	53y	W	31 DEC 1920	New York NY	Congressional
15008	Fernald, George W.	78y	W	8 SEP 1918	Newberg MD	Arlington
02699	Ferraro, Vincent	6m	W	7 JAN 1899	Ft. Myer VA	Mt. Olivet
02591	Ferrer, Newton H.	22y	W	27 AUG 1898	Montauk NY	Arlington
06654	Ferretti, Natalina E. (Pavarina)	30y	W	22 JUL 1908	Newport RI	St. Mary's
18590	Ferrigan, Edwin Newell	9m	W	7 JUN 1923	Glendale MD	Cedar Hill
15645	Fersinger, Jacob	78y	W	26 FEB 1919	Carey OH	Arlington
06611	Fessenden, Joshua A., s/o S.	67y	W	26 JUN 1908	Stamford CN	Arlington
00827	Festitits, Charles Albert	51y	W	4 DEC 1891	Jersey City NJ	Oak Hill
15014	Fey, John F.	53y	W	10 SEP 1918	Baltimore MD	Cedar Hill MD
06995	Ffoulk, Charles M.	67y	W	14 APR 1909	New York NY	Rock Creek
04262	Ffoulk, Horace Cushing	26y	W	2 MAY 1903	Silver City NM	Rock Creek
06150	Ficklin, Lou	26y	W	20 JUL 1907	Hyattsville MD	Rock Creek
15260	Fickling, Frederick	24y	C	20 OCT 1918	Camp Meade MD	Woodlawn
08277	Fickling, William, Jr.	7w	W	28 AUG 1911	Philadelphia PA	Rock Creek
17177	Fidler, Fannie Barnett	62y	W	22 MAY 1921	Sligo MD	Rock Creek
14463	Field, John C.	51y	W	18 NOV 1917	Takoma Park MD	Baltimore MD
03652	Field, Sue Virginia	66y	W	24 AUG 1901	Oakland CA	Rock Creek
14628	Fields, Jessy E.	36y	C	5 FEB 1918	Pittsburgh PA	Orange VA
00473	Fields, Julia A.	27y	C	27 MAR 1891	Philadelphia PA	Harmony
17242	Fields, Martha Jane	50y	C	15 JUN 1921	Ridgeway OH	Odd Fellows VA
17461	Fierney, Milton H.	25y	W	11 OCT 1921	Chelsea MA	Cedar Hill
05900	Fife, Eva	5y	C	21 JAN 1907	Atlantic City NJ	Harmony
02057	Figgins, Letitia A.	56y	W	1 JUN 1894	Falls Church VA	Glenwood
01346	Fillebrown, Marion Sumner	11m	W	8 JAN 1894	Lambertville NJ	Oak Hill
07416	Fillmore, George Millard	67y	W	12 FEB 1910	Suffolk VA	Glenwood
12898	Fillmore, Lottie A.	64y	W	27 APR 1915	Laurel MD	Glenwood
18591	Fina, Joseph	47y	W	5 JUN 1923	Philadelphia PA	St. Mary's
11879	Finch, Arthur T.	26y	W	8 MAY 1913	Birmingham AL	Arlington VA
09143	Finch, Ferris	84y	W	24 MAR 1913	Ozona FL	Glenwood
13183	Finch, Helen Lee	78y	W	5 NOV 1915	Cincinnati OH	Glenwood
01705	Finch, S.P., Dr.	60y	W	26 AUG 1895	Wheeling WV	Glenwood
13014	Fincher, Henry	74y	W	17 JUL 1915	Hampton VA	Arlington
00828	Finckel, DeVin	22y	W	20 AUG 1892	W. Mansfield OH	Rock Creek
06863	Findling, Louis	42y	W	21 DEC 1908	Baltimore MD	Soldier's Home
07392	Finegan, Margaret M.	22y	W	27 JAN 1910	Baltimore MD	Mt. Olivet
12837	Fineran, Thomas J.	30y	W	24 MAR 1915	Jacksonville FL	Mt. Olivet

District of Columbia Foreign Death Records, 1888-1923

No.	Name of Deceased	Age	Race	Death Date	Place of Death	Place of Burial
16529	Finger, Herman	20y	W	9 JUN 1920	Potomac River	Nat. Cap. Hebrew
01141	Fingles, Alice	1y	W	4 JUN 1892	Baltimore MD	Mt. Olivet
12321	Fingley, Joseph C.	28y	W	19 APR 1914	Baltimore MD	Holyrood
06864	Fink, Jacob J.	76y	W	22 DEC 1908	Berwyn MD	Oak Hill
13442	Finley, Grace Marie	50y	W	4 APR 1916	New York NY	Rock Creek
15277	Finn, John J.	6y	W	23 OCT 1918	Lanham MD	Mt. Olivet
12598	Finnegan, Kathryne A.	23y	W	6 NOV 1914	New York NY	Mt. Olivet
15416	Finnell, Virginia G., d/o Montg.	27y	W	6 DEC 1918	Denver CO	Mt. Olivet
05724	Finney, John T., florist	45y	W	4 SEP 1906	Belair VA	Rock Creek
03245	Finney, Lewis Harvie, Jr.	33y	W	29 JUL 1900	Warm Spgs. VA	Oak Hill
03672	Finney, William	38y	C	28 SEP 1901	Philadelphia PA	Harmony*
11893	Finotti, Rose	5m	W	12 JUL 1913	South River MD	Congressional
14315	Firestone, Jewles	c.32y	W	24 AUG 1917	Camp Meade MD	Kokomo IN
03370	Fischer, Bertha	67y	W	8 AUG 1900	Frankfurt, Ger.	Rock Creek
08694	Fischer, Catherine E.	2m	W	29 JUN 1912	Seat Pleasant MD	Glenwood
02638	Fischer, Christina	69y	W	20 OCT 1898	Branchville MD	Prospect Hill
13261	Fischer, Julia Frances	60y	W	21 DEC 1915	Baltimore MD	Rock Creek
04455	Fiscus, William W., Jr.	—	W	2 JAN 1902	Bohal, P.I.	Arlington
02484	Fisher, Adam	79y	W	24 JUL 1898	Colton's Pt. MD	Arlington VA
06582	Fisher, Adelaide J.	SB	W	7 JUN 1908	Brownville NY	Oak Hill
14361	Fisher, Arthur	45y	W	14 SEP 1917	Philadelphia PA	Glenwood
18162	Fisher, Charles F.	62y	W	14 NOV 1922	Alexandria VA	Glenwood
12075	Fisher, Charles H.	57y	W	2 NOV 1913	Riverdale MD	Cremated
15162	Fisher, Fannie (Sulivan)	75y	C	12 OCT 1918	Pr. Geo. Co. MD	Payne's
08292	Fisher, Fannie T.	70y	W	3 SEP 1911	Gaithersburg MD	Congressional
01552	Fisher, John	50y	W	7 NOV 1894	Hampton VA	Arlington
07296	Fisher, John	50y	C	29 NOV 1909	Potomac River	Payne's
14989	Fisher, Margaret L.	59y	W	25 AUG 1918	Takoma Park MD	Glenwood
13381	Fisher, Martha C.M.	94y	W	27 FEB 1916	Clarendon VA	Glenwood
00947½	Fisher, Susan R.	72y	W	22 JUN 1893	Staunton VA	Glenwood
04160	Fisher, Theresa	58y	W	10 JAN 1903	Baltimore MD	St. Mary's
00056	Fiske, Frederick William	19y	W	6 APR 1889	Worcester MA	Glenwood
12660	Fitch, James E.	80y	W	18 DEC 1914	Haverford PA	Oak Hill
17947	Fitch, Mary E.	81y	W	10 JUL 1922	Olney MD	Glenwood
15335	Fitch, Walter F.	25y	W	1 NOV 1918	Camp Lewis WA	Arlington
14091	Fitzgerald, Annie Agnes	7m	W	15 APR 1917	Capitol Hts. MD	Mt. Olivet
04680	Fitzgerald, Eliza M.	82y	W	20 APR 1904	Mt. Hope MD	Glenwood
01302	Fitzgerald, James C.	30y	W	14 FEB 1894	Eliz. City Co. VA	Mt. Olivet
00474	Fitzgerald, Lawrence	31y	W	18 JAN 1891	Johnstown PA	Mt. Olivet
07090	Fitzgerald, Margaret	75y	W	29 JUN 1909	Philadelphia PA	Mt. Olivet
13080	Fitzgerald, Margaret E.	45y	W	25 AUG 1915	Baltimore MD	Mt. Olivet
02305a	Fitzgerald, Maria A.	29y	W	1 OCT 1897	Norfolk VA	Mt. Olivet
00378	Fitzgerald, Mary W.	70y	W	1 AUG 1890	Mt. Hope MD	Glenwood
05734	Fitzgerald, Mrs. Sams	70y	W	7 SEP 1906	Saratoga Spg. NY	Holyrood
04472	Fitzgerald, Robert E.	23y	W	7 OCT 1903	Baltimore MD	Mt. Olivet
06859	Fitzgerald, Wm. H., s/o David	45y	W	20 DEC 1908	Cherrydale VA	Mt. Olivet
13759	Fitzhugh, Annie	49y	C	10 OCT 1916	Philadelphia PA	Harmony
05063	Fitzhugh, George T.	4y	W	7 JUN 1873	Pittsburgh PA	Arlington
17377	Fitzhugh, John B.	77y	W	30 AUG 1921	Landover MD	Mt. Olivet
06843	Fitzhugh, Lilly Keech	70y	W	28 NOV 1908	Alameda CA	Beltsville MD
12815	Fitzhugh, Mary B.	71y	W	13 MAR 1915	Landover MD	Mt. Olivet
13027	Fitzhugh, Mary E.	43y	C	30 JUL 1915	New Rochelle NY	Payne's
18188	Fitzhugh, Mattie Porter	48y	W	30 NOV 1922	Roanoke VA	Glenwood
13416	Fitzpatrick, Andrew P.	47y	W	15 MAR 1916	Portsmouth VA	Mt. Olivet
11955	Fitzpatrick, John Francis	56y	W	12 AUG 1913	Landover MD	Cremated
08303	Fitzsimmons, Sarah Ellen	68y	W	9 SEP 1911	Capitol Hts. MD	Glenwood
05303	Fitzsimons, Isabelle	24y	W	30 SEP 1905	Saranac Lake NY	Mt. Olivet
00351	Flaegler, Mrs.	80y	W	28 JUN 1890	Charlottesville VA	Congressional
02803	Flagler, Daniel W.	63y	W	19 MAR 1899	Ft. Monroe VA	Arlington VA

No.	Name of Deceased	Age	Race	Death Date	Place of Death	Place of Burial
01142	Flannagan, Joseph	17y	W	28 NOV 1892	Glenbrook VA	Mt. Olivet
03499	Flannery, Bernard	3m	W	6 MAY 1901	Riverdale MD	Mt. Olivet
15907	Flannigan, Joseph E.	33y	W	1 AUG 1919	Potomac River	Chicago IL
05469	Fleet, Bellini D.	45y	C	15 FEB 1906	New York NY	Harmony
12368	Fleet, Ella	30y	C	18 MAY 1914	Alex. Co. VA	Mt. Zion West
02715	Fleet, Hermione C.	70y	C	15 JAN 1899	New York NY	Harmony
13634	Fleet, Lucy	31y	C	31 JUL 1916	Capitol Hts. MD	Woodlawn
08331	Fleet, Osborne J.	29y	C	28 SEP 1811	Capitol Hts. MD	Woodlawn
13257	Fleet, Thomas	19y	C	17 DEC 1915	Baltimore MD	Camp Springs MD
08878	Fleharty, Duanna E.	35y	W	29 SEP 1912	San Jose CA	Congressional
06678	Fleishman, Mary	23y	W	9 AUG 1908	Dunn NC	Baltimore MD
15789	Flemer, Martha	91y	W	21 MAY 1919	Springfield NJ	Glenwood
08662	Fleming, Artie L.	23y	C	6 JUN 1912	Newark NJ	Harmony
14635	Fleming, Elizabeth Yancey	61y	W	11 FEB 1918	Richmond VA	Cremated
18111	Fleming, John Syme	80y	W	12 OCT 1922	Jetersville VA	Cremated
05069	Fleming, Patrick	24y	W	21 MAR 1905	Tucson AZ	Mt. Olivet
15037	Fleming, William B.	76y	W	24 SEP 1918	Takoma MD	Louisville KY
04707	Fleming, William Henry	21y	C	10 MAY 1904	New York NY	Woodlawn
05618	Flemming, Mrs. Augustus	73y	W	1 JUL 1906	Buckhall VA	Glenwood
04466	Flemming, Rachel J.	72y	W	2 OCT 1903	Philadelphia PA	Congressional
17262	Flemons, Annette	9m	C	25 JUN 1921	Bethesda MD	Mt. Zion West
12007	Fletcher, Corine V.	20y	C	16 SEP 1913	Youngstown OH	Payne's
14731	Fletcher, Dora A.	7m	W	5 APR 1918	Kensington MD	Glenwood
15254	Fletcher, Franklin E.	23y	W	19 OCT 1918	New York NY	Rock Creek
14569	Fletcher, George Alexander	34y	C	4 JAN 1918	Pittsburgh PA	Harmony
13019	Fletcher, Gertrude I.	24y	C	2 JUL 1915	Suffern NY	Woodlawn
07958	Fletcher, Lillian	19y	C	29 JAN 1911	New York NY	Harmony
08061	Fletcher, Louis C.	54y	W	6 APR 1911	Tucson AZ	Glenwood
00021	Fletcher, Maria	60y	C	24 FEB 1889	Bladensburg MD	Mt. Olivet
11921	Fletcher, Mary	47y	W	27 JUL 1913	Altoona PA	Glenwood
07871	Fletcher, Mary	41y	C	13 DEC 1910	Asbury Park NJ	Harmony
17677	Fletcher, Sallie G.	60y	C	6 FEB 1922	Philadelphia PA	Mt. Olivet
05890	Fletcher, Twin Infants	1d	C	8 JAN 1907	Philadelphia PA	Mt. Olivet
15794	Fletcher, William H.	32y	C	22 MAY 1919	New York NY	Arlington
00711	Flint, Charles W.	69y	W	15 DEC 1891	Westville IN	Oak Hill
05769	Flodstrom, Elizabeth	58y	W	23 AUG 1906	Narragansett RI	Rock Creek
17915	Floegel, Lizzie	61y	W	20 JUN 1922	Colonial Hts. VA	Prospect Hill
03140	Flood, Ada	35y	C	18 MAR 1900	Philadelphia PA	Woodlawn
00084	Flood, Richard T.	11m	W	25 JUN 1889	St. Mary's Co. MD	Mt. Olivet
14398	Florshiem, Henry	72y	W	6 OCT 1917	Railroad	Shreveport LA
18154	Floyd, George W.	78y	W	9 NOV 1922	Capitol Hts. MD	Arlington
15598	Floyd, Lena R.	31y	W	3 FEB 1919	Merchantsville NJ	Medley's Neck MD
00601	Fluery, Margaret	58y	W	4 SEP 1891	Ft. Wash. MD	Congressional
05002	Fluhrer, Jos. Anthony	78y	W	14 JAN 1905	Hyattsville MD	St. Mary's
06907	Flynn, Bridget	3m	W	31 JAN 1909	Mt. Ranier MD	Mt. Olivet
03509	Foley, Anna F.	52y	W	13 MAY 1901	New York NY	Mt. Olivet
05667	Foley, Ethel	20y	W	30 JUL 1906	Gaithersburg MD	Mt. Olivet
16782	Foley, James F.	62y	W	23 OCT 1920	Chicago IL	Mt. Olivet
16728	Foley, Mary A.	75y	W	26 SEP 1920	Mt. Hope MD	Mt. Olivet
02766	Foley, Michael P., soldier	39y	W	8 MAR 1899	Florence SC	Rock Creek
06192	Foley, Michael W.	26y	W	18 AUG 1907	Denver CO	Mt. Olivet
05663	Follanbee, George S.	67y	W	24 JUL 1906	Boston MA	Arlington VA
05684	Foller, John	59y	W	13 AUG 1906	Baltimore MD	St. Mary's
07641	Folliard, Katharyne Marie	3m	W	20 JUL 1910	Bluemont VA	Mt. Olivet
15310	Follin, Charles E.	21y	W	31 OCT 1918	Capitol Hts. MD	Congressional
18291	Follin, Ella W. (Offutt)	38y	W	23 JAN 1923	Clarendon VA	Mt. Olivet
01902	Follin, Leslie E.	21y	W	3 APR 1896	Scranton PA	Glenwood
00313	Folliott, Margaret	87y	W	19 APR 1890	Pr. Geo. Co. MD	Congressional
07001	Folsom, Mary E.	28y	W	24 APR 1909	Somerset MD	Glenwood

District of Columbia Foreign Death Records, 1888-1923

No.	Name of Deceased	Age	Race	Death Date	Place of Death	Place of Burial
15636	Folsome, William Chester	2m	W	23 FEB 1919	Silver Spring MD	Glenwood
04011	Foltzer, Bridget	50y	W	10 SEP 1902	Baltimore MD	Mt. Olivet
15571	Foltzer, Leonard	68y	W	18 JAN 1919	Baltimore MD	Mt. Olivet
03901	Foltzer, Margaret Ellen	23y	W	6 JUN 1902	Baltimore MD	Mt. Olivet
08352	Fonda, Charles Bradford	56y	W	11 OCT 1911	Takoma Park MD	Glenwood
04962	Foote, Henrietta M.	94y	C	19 NOV 1904	Cuyahoga Co. OH	Harmony
05119	Foote, William D.	27y	W	2 MAY 1905	Goldfield NV	Arlington
17685	Forbes, Elizabeth	75y	C	5 FEB 1922	Suitland MD	Mt. Olivet
18515	Forbes, George A.	64y	W	30 APR 1923	Alexandria VA	Glenwood
18290	Ford, Alberta S.	c.36y	C	21 JAN 1923	Moorestown NJ	Harmony
17182	Ford, Annie	53y	W	22 MAY 1921	Capitol Hts. MD	Mt. Olivet
06676	Ford, Benjamin	65y	C	7 AUG 1908	Tuxedo MD	Payne's
14580	Ford, Catherine	8y	C	13 JAN 1918	Dublin GA	Harmony
08889	Ford, Charles A.	39y	C	13 OCT 1912	Tuxedo MD	Payne's
03318	Ford, Charles M.	4y	W	1 NOV 1900	New York NY	Congressional
08842	Ford, Edwin R.	54y	W	18 SEP 1912	Rosslyn VA	Glenwood
08281	Ford, Elizabeth	90y	C	29 AUG 1911	Philadelphia PA	Mt. Olivet
02460	Ford, Elizabeth F.	54y	W	29 MAY 1898	Takoma Park MD	Rock Creek
07812	Ford, Estella	16y	C	30 OCT 1910	Tuxedo MD	Payne's
03294	Ford, Henry	40y	W	28 SEP 1900	Ft. Meade SD	Arlington VA
08875	Ford, Ives M.	39y	W	6 OCT 1912	Seabrook MD	Congressional
00602	Ford, James M.	5y	W	18 AUG 1891	Forest Glen MD	Glenwood
12348	Ford, John Francis	53y	W	4 MAY 1914	Mt. Ranier MD	Glenwood
06324	Ford, John M.	33y	W	28 NOV 1907	Baltimore MD	Mt. Olivet
04881	Ford, Joseph	35y	C	8 SEP 1904	Landover MD	Mt. Olivet
12060	Ford, Josie	52y	C	23 OCT 1913	New York NY	Mt. Olivet
01144	Ford, Julia	52y	W	10 OCT 1892	New York NY	Rock Creek
06636	Ford, Julia A.	65y	W	7 JUL 1908	Ocean Grove NJ	Rock Creek
02531	Ford, Julia F.	82y	W	28 JUN 1898	Fairfax VA	Oak Hill
08300	Ford, Luther F.	46d	W	9 SEP 1911	Brentwood MD	Glenwood
17045	Ford, Maria	64y	W	12 MAR 1921	Takoma Park MD	Harmony
08747	Ford, Mary	65y	W	3 AUG 1912	Takoma Park MD	Rock Creek
18600	Ford, Mattie	56y	C	11 JUN 1923	Seat Pleasant MD	Rosemont
14845	Ford, Nellie	58y	C	27 MAY 1918	Tuxedo MD	Payne's
07014	Ford, Priscilla	97y	C	5 MAY 1909	Dupont Hts. MD	Mt. Zion West
06529	Ford, Richard	46y	C	1 MAY 1908	Philadelphia PA	Mt. Olivet
13880	Ford, Sandy	36y	C	24 DEC 1916	Tuxedo MD	Payne's
04814	Ford, Sarah F.	24y	C	24 JUL 1904	New York NY	Harmony
15070	Ford, Thomas Bartlett	36y	W	3 OCT 1918	Chevy Chase MD	Glenwood[1]
01229	Ford, Vanna R.	39y	W	23 OCT 1893	Forest Glen MD	Glenwood
04695	Ford, Virginia G.	49y	W	29 APR 1904	Philadelphia PA	Congressional
12248	Ford, William L.	46y	W	26 FEB 1914	Albuquerque NM	Mt. Olivet
17216	Fordan, Edward Wines	33y	W	JUN 1921	Phoenix AZ	Prospect Hill
01706	Fordan, Marshall	1y	W	25 AUG 1895	Stafford Co. VA	Prospect Hill
07197	Forest, Anna F.	34y	W	8 AUG 1905	Vernal UT	Oak Hill
13878	Forest, George F.	38y	W	22 DEC 1916	Berwyn MD	Glenwood
07179	Forrest, Catharine S.	75y	W	1 SEP 1909	Lewes DE	Oak Hill
00829	Forrest, Catherine	61y	C	16 MAY 1892	Philadelphia PA	—
03872	Forrest, Douglas F.	63y	W	3 MAY 1902	Ashland VA	Congressional
06600	Forrest, George, s/o Henry	20y	C	20 JUN 1908	Leesburg VA	Harmony
07199	Forrest, Norman, s/o Wm.	23y	W	13 SEP 1909	Jasper AL	Congressional
18425	Forrest, William H.	62y	W	16 MAR 1923	Berwyn MD	Glenwood
14646	Forrester, Charles E.	4y	W	14 FEB 1918	Railroad	Nokesville VA
03906	Forrester, Elizabeth C.	59y	W	23 JUN 1902	Forest Glen MD	Rock Creek
04646	Forster, Charles E.	40y	W	27 MAR 1904	Kensington MD	Rock Creek
04645	Forster, Elizabeth	37y	W	27 MAR 1904	Kensington MD	Rock Creek

[1] Disinterment permit #9715 issued 11 NOV 1918 to remove remains to Laramie WY.

No.	Name of Deceased	Age	Race	Death Date	Place of Death	Place of Burial
16023	Forster, Justine	79y	W	30 SEP 1919	Laurel MD	Rock Creek
17547	Forster, Mina	c.84y	W	25 NOV 1921	Norfolk VA	Prospect Hill
08430	Forsyth, Emma J.	57y	W	19 DEC 1911	Baltimore MD	Glenwood
13039	Forsyth, James McQueen	73y	W	3 AUG 1915	Shamokin PA	Arlington
04028	Forsyth, Lewis Cass	69y	W	25 SEP 1902	S.C. Spgs. VA	Oak Hill
01303	Forsyth, Mary	7d	W	1 FEB 1894	Brightseat MD	Mt. Olivet
04065	Forsyth, William	30y	W	3 OCT 1902	Berwyn MD	Mt. Olivet
13699	Forsythe, John F.	68y	W	7 SEP 1916	Seat Pleasant MD	Mt. Olivet
04139	Forsythe, Nellie	27y	W	17 JAN 1903	Falls Church VA	Baltimore MD
04807	Forsythe, William H.	1y	W	19 JUL 1904	Avenel MD	Mt. Olivet
08448	Fort, Rachel C.	55y	W	29 DEC 1912	Baltimore MD	Congressional
18079	Forti, Infant	SB	W	22 SEP 1922	Baltimore MD	St. Mary's
18080	Forti, Infant of Alphonso	SB	W	22 SEP 1922	Baltimore MD	St. Mary's
18078	Forti, Mary	18y	W	21 SEP 1922	Baltimore MD	St. Mary's
01703	Fosburg, Annie	42y	W	18 OCT 1895	Hanover PA	Rock Creek
17567	Foskey, Isabel	61y	C	29 NOV 1921	Cleveland OH	Payne's
06298	Fossett, Emma	78y	W	5 NOV 1907	Suitland MD	Congressional
16888	Fossett, Montague	57y	W	31 DEC 1920	Chicago IL	Rock Creek
13369	Foster, Anna Johnson	65y	W	19 FEB 1916	Sherborn MA	Rock Creek
00292	Foster, Anna M.	2y	W	18 MAR 1890	Newark NJ	Glenwood
07429	Foster, Arthur B.	—	W	18 DEC 1909	Manila, P.I.	Arlington
17589	Foster, Edna A.	5y	W	15 DEC 1921	Mt. Ranier MD	Prospect Hill
00066	Foster, Eliza	18y	M	17 APR 1889	Pr. Geo. Co. MD	Harmony
00159	Foster, Hannah A.	60y	W	14 SEP 1889	Mt. Hope MD	Rock Creek
02247	Foster, Jane E.	59y	W	30 JUL 1897	Baltimore MD	Congressional
12006	Foster, Lucy A.	56y	C	20 SEP 1913	Baltimore MD	Warrenton VA
06711	Foster, Margaret E.	79y	W	2 SEP 1908	Cumberland MD	Oak Hill
05825	Foster, Marguerita W.	6m	W	20 NOV 1906	Beale PA	Glenwood
06683	Foster, Theodulis H.	36y	W	10 AUG 1908	Tuxedo MD	Loudon Park MD
06265	Foster, William J.	—	W	8 OCT 1907	Baltimore Co. MD	Congressional
06338	Fought, Joseph, s/o Jos.	62y	W	2 DEC 1907	Falls Church VA	Rock Creek
01808	Fouke, Marry Ethal	2y	W	14 DEC 1895	New York NY	Glenwood
17258	Fountain, Charles	22y	C	24 JUN 1921	Detroit MI	Union Baptist
07984	Fountain, Silas A., s/o Charles	2m	C	23 FEB 1911	Arlington VA	Baptist
05081	Fouse, George	67y	W	26 MAR 1905	Newport RI	Arlington
14673	Fowke, Mary	67y	W	6 MAR 1918	Takoma Park MD	Casanova VA
06516	Fowker, Ellen E.	87y	W	17 APR 1908	Pr. Wm. Co. VA	Congressional
04519	Fowle, James J.	2y	W	20 NOV 1903	Kensington MD	Rock Creek
04518	Fowle, John Dorsey	8m	W	21 NOV 1903	Kensington MD	Rock Creek
17441	Fowler, Clara E.	63y	W	28 SEP 1921	Chicago IL	Prospect Hill
14367	Fowler, Donald	2m	W	19 SEP 1917	Cherrydale VA	Prospect Hill
03912	Fowler, Edwin Clarkson	64y	W	12 JUN 1902	Riverdale MD	Mt. Olivet
05936	Fowler, Elizabeth G.	67y	W	10 FEB 1907	Riverdale MD	Mt. Olivet
03448	Fowler, Elizabeth S.	83y	W	11 MAR 1901	Camp Springs MD	Rock Creek
06371	Fowler, Emma	65y	W	3 JAN 1908	Roanoke VA	Oak Hill
09002	Fowler, Enoch Sanford	60y	W	17 DEC 1912	Seattle WA	Oak Hill
00365	Fowler, Eva Louise	22m	W	21 JUL 1890	Martinsburg MD	Rock Creek
05601	Fowler, Gilbert J., s/o Wm. R.	c.58y	W	17 JUN 1876	Waterford VA	Oak Hill
05013	Fowler, Henry B.	33y	W	31 JAN 1905	Baltimore MD	Glenwood
16099	Fowler, Ida A.	53y	W	5 NOV 1919	Providence RI	Congressional
02744	Fowler, Leo	8y	W	15 FEB 1899	Pr. Geo. Co. MD	Mt. Olivet
09099	Fowler, Lorenzo D.	58y	W	27 FEB 1913	Newark NJ	Cremated
14703	Fowler, Marian E.	73y	W	22 MAR 1918	Danville PA	Oak Hill
02132	Fowler, Nannie M.	24y	W	8 MAR 1897	Riverdale Pk. MD	Glenwood
17911	Fowler, Sarah Elizabeth	69y	W	19 JUN 1922	Leesburg VA	Oak Hill
01553	Fowler, Solomon	72y	W	10 JAN 1895	Friendship MD	Rock Creek
04285	Fowler, Virginia	64y	W	15 APR 1903	Baltimore MD	Oak Hill
04333	Fowler, Virginia L.	35y	W	13 AUG 1903	Urbana MD	Glenwood
01230	Fowler, William R.	1y	W	12 NOV 1893	Friendship MD	Rock Creek

District of Columbia Foreign Death Records, 1888-1923

No.	Name of Deceased	Age	Race	Death Date	Place of Death	Place of Burial
17438	Fox, Abraham B.	21y	W	21 SEP 1921	Towson MD	Adas Israel
04401	Fox, Elizabeth A.	82y	W	21 JUL 1903	Pepperell MA	Oak Hill
00127	Fox, Frederick A.	28y	W	4 AUG 1889	Charlottesville VA	Glenwood
12629	Fox, George A.	43y	W	21 NOV 1914	Mt. Ranier MD	Glenwood
11990	Fox, Gilbert D.	32y	W	3 SEP 1913	Bellvale NY	Glenwood
06755	Fox, Gilbert D.	59y	W	4 OCT 1908	Hyattsville MD	Glenwood
04580	Fox, Grace	40y	C	23 JAN 1904	New York NY	Woodlawn
16250	Fox, Grace L.	1y	W	28 JAN 1920	Mt. Ranier MD	Glenwood
06111	Fox, Helen	40y	C	16 JUN 1907	Philadelphia PA	Harmony
14213	Fox, Helen S.	23y	W	2 JUL 1917	El Paso TX	Arlington
03589	Fox, Jacob	4m	W	24 JUL 1901	Glenmont MD	Ohev Sholom
14411	Fox, Mary Virginia	51y	W	15 OCT 1917	Takoma Park MD	Rock Creek
00603	Fox, Robert C.	56y	W	18 JUL 1891	Dansville NY	Oak Hill
14658	Foxwell, Alice M. (Davis)	78y	W	24 FEB 1918	Norfolk VA	Glenwood
04176	Fraber, Lydia	81y	W	10 FEB 1903	Ballston VA	Rock Creek
12123	Fractious, William	53y	C	9 DEC 1913	Baltimore MD	Moore's
12100	Fragerser, John Adam	49y	W	18 NOV 1913	Silver Spring MD	Glenwood
16287	Fralick, Sarah E.	84y	W	6 FEB 1920	Chevy Chase MD	Glenwood
04961	France, Beatrice	10m	W	20 NOV 1904	Woodcliff NJ	Wash. Hebrew
08863	France, James A.	34y	C	28 SEP 1912	New York NY	Payne's
08759	France, Mary E.	62y	W	8 AUG 1912	Ocean Grove NJ	Baltimore MD
18173	France, Mizpah	4y	W	21 NOV 1922	Takoma Park MD	Cedar Hill
09042	France, Winona	35y	W	19 JAN 1913	Baltimore MD	Congressional
06187	Francefort, Michel	62y	W	17 AUG 1907	Charleston SC	Cremated
01707	Frances, Thomas Benedict	1y	W	27 JUL 1895	Long Branch NJ	Congressional
08145	Francis, Dorothy	11m	W	12 JUN 1911	Fairmont Hts. MD	Mt. Olivet
13774	Francis, John R.	30y	W	23 OCT 1916	Perrymand MD	Scottsburg VA
07504	Francis, Mama M. (Burrows)	45y	C	18 APR 1910	Atlantic City NJ	Harmony
16101	Francis, Thomas	54y	W	10 NOV 1919	Chevy Chase MD	Glenwood
02433	Francisco, Bryan S.	55y	W	23 APR 1898	Bradfield PA	Arlington VA
12819	Frank, Babette	90y	W	14 MAR 1915	Boston MA	Wash. Hebrew
06810	Frank, Edward	37y	W	9 NOV 1908	Loudoun Co. VA	Prospect Hill
17875	Frank, Frances Chapman	c.65y	W	26 MAY 1922	Ballston VA	Mt. Olivet
01385	Frank, Julius Augustus	72y	W	3 MAY 1894	Chicago IL	Rock Creek
05127	Frank, Norton F.	20y	W	6 MAY 1905	San Francisco CA	Wash. Hebrew
17694	Frank, Pauline Alfred	65y	W	15 FEB 1922	Takoma Park MD	Baltimore MD
14212	Franke, Frances M.	11m	W	4 JUL 1917	Hyattsville MD	Rock Creek
03380	Frankland, Harry G.	41y	W	26 DEC 1900	Springfield IL	Congressional
05782	Franklin, Alexander	24y	W	14 OCT 1906	Dallas TX	Glenwood
15674	Franklin, Alice	73y	C	16 MAR 1919	Fairmont Hts. MD	Payne's
18214	Franklin, James	74y	W	12 DEC 1922	St. Augustine FL	Arlington
16891	Franklin, James	78y	C	2 JAN 1921	Cabin John MD	Mt. Zion East
11868	Franklin, Jennie J.	70y	W	25 JUN 1913	Frostburg MD	Glenwood
05404	Franklin, Sophia	39y	C	20 DEC 1905	N. Adams MA	Mt. Olivet
06390	Franks, Etta M.	44y	W	13 JAN 1908	Germantown PA	Rock Creek[1]
14789	Frantz, Marie Antoinette	73y	W	2 MAY 1918	New York NY	Glenwood
06402	Fraser, Frances B.	87y	W	24 JAN 1908	Binghampton NY	Rock Creek
15345	Fraser, Lemuel A.	25y	W	10 NOV 1918	Donora PA	Cremated
06759	Frawley, William	24y	W	7 OCT 1908	Laurel MD	Mt. Olivet
06457	Frazer, William B.	29y	W	28 FEB 1908	El Paso TX	Congressional
03490	Frazier, Arthur	27y	C	27 APR 1901	Ridgeville MD	Payne's
12320	Frazier, Robert T.	51y	W	19 APR 1914	Baltimore MD	Rock Creek
00475	Frazier, Thomas Campbell	30y	W	18 MAR 1891	Hyattsville MD	Glenwood
04568	Freas, Charles Johnson	1m	W	15 JAN 1904	Sligo MD	Rock Creek
01554	Freas, Katherine	75y	W	2 JAN 1895	Sligo MD	Rock Creek
04159	Freas, L.S.	7d	W	9 JAN 1903	Sligo MD	Rock Creek

[1] Removed 25 AUG 1908 to Lownesville, S.C.

No.	Name of Deceased	Age	Race	Death Date	Place of Death	Place of Burial
12359	Frederick, Catherine M.	45y	C	14 MAY 1914	Darby PA	Mt. Olivet
06513	Freeh, Elizabeth	42y	W	15 APR 1908	Youngstown OH	Congressional
00949	Freeland, John	38y	W	1854	—	Congressional
00948	Freeland, Josias	3y	W	1855	—	Congressional
06445	Freelander, Henry	60y	W	25 FEB 1908	Baltimore Co. MD	Wash. Hebrew
15219	Freeman, Alice	22y	W	6 OCT 1918	Pensacola FL	Glenwood
03531	Freeman, Benjamin H., Rev.	62y	C	2 JUN 1901	Avondale PA	Harmony
08235	Freeman, Carrie, d/o Henry	29y	C	30 JUL 1911	Norfolk VA	Harmony
14972	Freeman, Charles P.	77y	W	12 AUG 1918	Hampton VA	Arlington
18560	Freeman, Clara F.	59y	C	24 MAY 1923	New York NY	Woodlawn
12001	Freeman, Columbus	c.65y	C	6 SEP 1913	St. Louis MO	Harmony
06628	Freeman, Emma B.	56y	W	2 JUL 1908	Baltimore MD	Glenwood
18226	Freeman, Gladys	28y	C	26 DEC 1922	Louisville KY	Harmony
14415	Freeman, J.E.	50y	W	19 OCT 1917	Perryville MD	Alexandria VA
08434	Freeman, James M.	72y	W	21 DEC 1911	Silver Hill MD	LaPlata MD
15235	Freeman, Josephine	24y	C	16 OCT 1918	Baltimore MD	Odd Fellows VA
02720	Freeman, Mabel V.	13y	W	20 JAN 1899	Norfolk VA	Congressional
12835	Freeman, Mary Anna	42y	W	22 MAR 1915	Blue Ridge S. PA	Rock Creek
02681	Freeman, Samuel	25y	C	20 DEC 1898	Baltimore MD	Payne's
03088	Freeman, William	38y	C	8 JAN 1900	Philadelphia PA	Harmony
16382	Freeman, William	44y	C	10 MAR 1920	Pittsburgh PA	Harmony
16919	Freer, Hulda A. (Evans)	71y	W	14 JAN 1921	Dunbar WV	Congressional
01809	Freer, William H., carpenter	75y	W	24 DEC 1895	Baltimore MD	Congressional
11981	Freewalt, Infant of John A.	SB	W	30 AUG 1913	Brentwood MD	Glenwood
00950	French, Benjamin B.	1y	W	3 FEB 1873	New York NY	Congressional
03061	French, Calrence	44y	W	4 JAN 1900	Alexandria VA	Mt. Olivet
01380	French, Clarence Preston	2y	W	16 MAY 1894	Alexandria VA	Mt. Olivet
01042	French, F.O.	55y	W	26 FEB 1893	Tuxedo Park NY	Congressional
01403	French, G.E.B.	75y	W	7 JUN 1894	Afton VA	Mt. Olivet
04027	French, Harry F.	53y	W	24 SEP 1902	Philadelphia PA	Congressional
07830	French, Mary A.	18y	W	18 AUG 1889	Pittsburgh PA	Rock Creek
04158	French, Rosa C.	74y	W	7 JAN 1903	Ammendale MD	Mt. Olivet
02058	French, Susan B.	75y	W	11 DEC 1896	Baltimore MD	Oak Hill
00476	French, Thomas H., Capt.	—	W	28 MAR 1891	Leavenworth KS	Holyrood
18328	Frere, Clara	65y	W	5 FEB 1923	Potomac VA	Mt. Olivet
01980	Frere, Constance	2m	W	10 JUL 1896	Charles Co. MD	Congressional
02304	Freund, Frederick	57y	W	5 SEP 1897	Atlantic City NJ	Rock Creek
17057	Frey, Infant of Brice A.	SB	W	20 MAR 1921	Manhattan NY	Oak Hill
06199	Frey, John Benton	1y	W	24 AUG 1907	Beltsville MD	Rock Creek
16158	Frey, Levin S.	69y	W	21 DEC 1919	Baltimore MD	Oak Hill
00830	Frey, Louis A.	24y	W	24 AUG 1892	Norbeck MD	Rock Creek
00604	Frey, Mary E.	10m	W	30 JUL 1891	Manassas VA	Oak Hill
17078	Frick, Carl Gastin	29y	W	30 MAR 1921	Philadelphia PA	Arlington
02199	Frick, Cathrine	76y	W	18 JUN 1897	Canfield OH	Prospect Hill
08895	Frick, Eugene Bernard	2y	W	18 OCT 1912	Baltimore MD	Mt. Olivet
08232	Frick, John J.	5m	W	30 JUL 1911	Baltimore MD	Mt. Olivet
15978	Frick, Joseph P.	5m	W	6 SEP 1919	Baltimore MD	Mt. Olivet
13172	Frick, Mrs. Joseph O.	48y	W	14 OCT 1915	Salisbury NC	St. Mary's
06511	Friday, Dorah E.	66y	W	15 APR 1908	Riverdale MD	Glenwood
06423	Friday, William F.	79y	W	7 FEB 1908	Riverdale MD	Glenwood
04278	Friebus, Frederick H.	25y	W	22 APR 1903	Elwyn PA	Glenwood
08478	Friebus, Gustav	68y	W	17 JAN 1912	Norfolk VA	Rock Creek
12551	Friedlander, Harry	53y	W	5 OCT 1914	New York NY	Wash. Hebrew
02920	Friedman, Sarah	74y	W	21 AUG 1899	Baltimore MD	Adas Israel
00036	Frieh, Adam	79y	W	11 MAR 1889	Middleton NY	Prospect Hill
17349	Friend, Harvey M.	61y	W	6 JUL 1921	Atlantic City NJ	Glenwood
07362	Frisard, Alice Lohma	11m	W	9 JAN 1910	Brentwood MD	Prospect Hill
06893	Frisard, Louise	8h	W	14 JAN 1909	Brentwood MD	Prospect Hill
17654	Frisbie, Jean D.	91y	W	24 JAN 1922	Friendship H. MD	Oak Hill

District of Columbia Foreign Death Records, 1888-1923

No.	Name of Deceased	Age	Race	Death Date	Place of Death	Place of Burial
17285	Frisbie, William R.	84y	W	3 JUL 1921	Forest Glen MD	Arlington
06952	Fritter, Cecelia	49y	W	22 MAR 1909	Newark NJ	Prospect Hill
02871	Fritts, James Carroll	20m	W	28 JUN 1899	Berwyn MD	Congressional
17307	Fritts, William T.	20y	W	19 JUL 1921	Falls Church VA	Congressional
04916	Fritze, Catherine	72y	W	10 OCT 1904	Suitland MD	Congressional
13847	Frizzell, John W., s/o Robert	53y	W	5 DEC 1916	Bolton MS	Rock Creek
12041	Frost, Allan F.	24y	W	7 OCT 1913	Portland OR	Rock Creek
05239	Frost, Edmund K.	12y	W	10 AUG 1905	Falls Church VA	Glenwood
15052	Fry, Della E.	38y	W	27 SEP 1918	Laurel MD	Glenwood
06088	Fry, George	76y	W	1 JUN 1907	Cabin John MD	Christian
02306	Fry, Luther	48y	W	1 OCT 1897	Seat Pleasant MD	Gunston VA
16531	Frye, Caroline	23y	C	8 JUN 1920	Philadelphia PA	Harmony
15389	Frye, Clarence F.	c.30y	W	29 NOV 1918	Baltimore MD	Congressional
18310	Frye, James Henry	78y	W	29 JAN 1923	Seat Pleasant MD	Prospect Hill
12700	Frye, John	54y	C	5 JAN 1915	Occoquan VA	Moore's
07639	Frye, Lena	8y	C	18 JUL 1910	Cabin John MD	Christian
13105	Ftizzell, Joseph Man., s/o Jas.	58y	W	14 SEP 1915	Vienna VA	Oak Hill
16582	Fudetani, Nakag	23y	J	3 JUL 1920	Norfolk VA	Cremated
02496	Fudge, Mary Frances	33y	W	25 JUL 1898	Pr. Geo. Co. MD	Glenwood
08404	Fugitt, Elizabeth D.	65y	W	29 NOV 1911	Buck Lodge MD	Rock Creek
12344	Fugitt, Mary Elizabeth	69y	W	1 MAY 1914	Statesville NC	Oak Hill
01432	Fugitt, N. Evans	25y	W	9 JUL 1894	Great Falls MD	Rock Creek
14288	Fuller, Almina Martha	59y	W	7 AUG 1917	Takoma Park MD	Glenwood
06191	Fuller, Charles F.	—	W	12 AUG 1907	Oil City PA	Rock Creek
06868	Fuller, Charles J.	37y	W	25 DEC 1908	Mt. Ranier MD	Glenwood
14864	Fuller, Cornelia A.	50y	W	15 JUN 1918	Baltimore MD	Oak Hill
08397	Fuller, Edward S.	52y	W	22 NOV 1911	Mt. Ranier MD	Cremated
07735	Fuller, Elizabeth S.	79y	W	9 SEP 1910	Long Beach NY	Glenwood
03286	Fuller, Eugene E.	56y	W	7 SEP 1900	Hampton VA	Arlington VA
13127	Fuller, Evelyn Schuyler	18y	W	22 SEP 1915	San Jose CA	Oak Hill
14239	Fuller, George A.	41y	W	12 JUL 1917	Seattle WA	Glenwood
08355	Fuller, Harry W.	69y	W	12 OCT 1911	Chevy Chase MD	Rock Creek
04076	Fuller, Miles, attorney	44y	W	2 JUN 1902	Somerset MD	Glenwood
13376	Fuller, Nellie P.	65y	W	23 FEB 1916	Camden NJ	Congressional
07704	Fuller, Sarah	73y	W	22 AUG 1910	Northampton MA	Rock Creek
01276	Fuller, Sarah M.	20y	W	14 DEC 1893	Baltimore MD	Oak Hill
05812	Fuller, William E.	42y	W	11 NOV 1906	St. Asaph VA	Congressional
00831	Fuller, William H.	52y	W	8 AUG 1892	Hyattsville MD	Glenwood
16492	Fullerton, Daniel	27y	W	28 FEB 1920	Pr. Wm. Co. VA	Arlington
18337	Fulton, Creed M.	60y	W	11 FEB 1923	Boston MA	Oak Hill
17779	Fulton, Etna Clifford	36y	W	3 APR 1922	College Park GA	Congressional
15804	Fulton, Robert Burwell	70y	W	29 MAY 1919	New York NY	Rock Creek
05438	Fulton, W., alias Furlong	35y	W	23 JAN 1906	Princess Anne MD	Congressional
14107	Funk, Isaac M.	46y	W	25 APR 1917	Seat Pleasant MD	Arlington
03797	Furay, Clarence M.	5y	W	19 FEB 1902	Columbus OH	Arlington VA
05512	Furbee, Nettie	36y	C	27 MAR 1906	New York NY	Harmony
05884	Furbershaw, Evelyn	27y	W	3 JAN 1907	Scranton PA	Mt. Olivet
01393	Furguson, Joseph	19y	C	17 APR 1894	Albany NY	Graceland
04722	Furley, Eleanor J.	68y	W	20 MAY 1904	Brooklyn NY	Rock Creek
05438	Furling, Wm. H., a.k.a. Fulton	35y	W	23 JAN 1906	Princess Anne MD	Congressional
13909	Furry, Adline	32y	C	3 JAN 1917	Brentwood MD	Payne's
07472	Furtner, Elizabeth C.	50y	W	18 MAR 1910	Catonsville MD	Glenwood
02544	Fussell, Richard Thomas	48y	W	4 JUN 1898	Alexandria VA	Oak Hill

No.	Name of Deceased	Age	Race	Death Date	Place of Death	Place of Burial
G						
01043	Gadke, C.A., Mrs.	46y	W	1 APR 1893	Staunton VA	Wash. Hebrew
02575	Gaegler, Laura	11m	W	27 AUG 1898	New York NY	Mt. Olivet
13163	Gaeng, Esther May	46y	W	23 OCT 1915	Baltimore MD	Mt. Olivet
18277	Gaff, Thomas T.	67y	W	17 JAN 1923	Boston MA	Rock Creek
00712	Gaffney, James	84y	W	24 JAN 1892	Alexandria VA	Holyrood
00318	Gage, Mary E.	70y	W	23 APR 1890	Saratoga NY	Rock Creek
02589	Gaillard, Joseph D.	65y	W	22 FEB 1898	Baltimore MD	Paris, France
13534	Gaines, Charles P.	44y	C	2 JUN 1916	Pittsburgh PA	Harmony
05049	Gaines, Julia A.	62y	C	7 MAR 1905	Rosslyn VA	Baptist
03896	Gaines, Mary F.	31y	C	11 JUN 1902	Baltimore MD	Harmony
13990	Gains, John	32y	C	14 FEB 1917	New York NY	Payne's
12241	Gaisberg, Emma K.	60y	W	4 FEB 1914	London, Eng.	Rock Creek
02373	Gaisdorff, Emily	63y	W	11 JAN 1898	Philadelphia PA	Rock Creek
14714	Gaither, Albert R.	24y	C	23 MAR 1918	Pittsburgh PA	Baptist in MD
02461	Gaither, John	9m	C	15 MAY 1898	Highland MD	Harmony
04601	Gaither, Rosa Lee	3y	C	13 FEB 1904	Bladensburg MD	Mt. Olivet
05395	Gaither, Samuel	59y	W	13 DEC 1905	Silver Spring MD	Frederick MD
16932	Galbraith, Bessie M. (Mitchell)	64y	W	20 JAN 1921	Asheville NC	Glenwood
04914	Galetzer, Frederick	67y	W	1 OCT 1904	Colonial Bea. VA	Prospect Hill
06742	Gall, Margarett	7m	W	21 SEP 1908	Gaithersburg MD	Glenwood
04390	Gallagher, Edward	77y	W	13 JUL 1903	Pittsburgh PA	Mt. Olivet
03072	Gallagher, Farrell	39y	W	19 JAN 1900	New York NY	Mt. Olivet
03746	Gallagher, George H.	36y	W	28 DEC 1901	Houston TX	Mt. Olivet
12928	Gallagher, Jeremiah H.	48y	W	16 MAY 1915	Seat Pleasant MD	Lima OH
17293	Gallagher, Lewis E.	39y	C	8 JUL 1921	Nauck VA	Harmony
07744	Gallagher, M.J.	27y	W	14 SEP 1910	Maryland Pk. MD	Mt. Olivet
03187	Gallagher, Patrick	52y	W	8 MAY 1900	Adams Co. PA	Mt. Olivet
15378	Gallagher, Raymond King	32y	W	25 NOV 1918	Takoma Park MD	Congressional
11938	Gallant, Francis C.	43y	W	10 AUG 1913	Beltsville MD	Mt. Olivet
03601	Gallant, Mary E.	60y	W	3 AUG 1901	Pr. Geo. Co. MD	Mt. Olivet
00174	Gallant, Mary Jane	21y	W	16 OCT 1889	Pr. Geo. Co. MD	Mt. Olivet
03271	Gallant, Thomas	22y	W	22 AUG 1900	Hyattsville MD	Mt. Olivet
11997	Gallatin, William Albert	36y	W	8 SEP 1913	Baltimore MD	Congressional
17688	Gallaway, Clarisa A.	83y	W	12 FEB 1922	Silver Spring MD	Cremated
04376	Gallery, Catharine	17y	C	2 JUL 1903	Rosslyn VA	Baptist
15814	Gallery, Luvinia	82y	C	6 JUN 1919	Rosslyn VA	Union Baptist
03887	Gallery, Moses	69y	C	21 MAY 1902	Rosslyn VA	Baptist
03219	Galliher, Francis Ewing	11m	W	4 JUL 1900	Herndon VA	Rock Creek
15589	Gallion, Emmett D.	67y	W	27 JAN 1919	Fairland MD	Glenwood
05677	Gallon, John C.	47y	W	5 AUG 1906	Philadelphia PA	Mt. Olivet
14187	Gallon, Vyetta B.	18y	C	19 JUN 1917	Long Branch NJ	Harmony
15949	Galloway, Sheridan Baker	69y	W	22 AUG 1919	Takoma Park MD	Congressional
15970	Galotta, Joseph	34y	W	1 SEP 1919	Colonial Bea. VA	St. Mary's
02112	Galt, Harriet Va. Wingerd	26y	W	17 JAN 1897	New York NY	Oak Hill
18228	Galt, Sterling	57y	W	28 DEC 1922	Emmitsburg MD	Oak Hill
13886	Gamble, Margaret L.	62y	W	27 DEC 1916	Takoma Park MD	Mt. Union PA
18443	Gambrill, Haddie G.	53y	W	27 MAR 1923	Baltimore MD	Oak Hill
11923	Ganbin, Mary	75y	W	28 JUL 1913	Brentwood MD	Glenwood
12495	Gancy, Daniel F.	31y	W	24 AUG 1914	Alexandria VA	Mt. Olivet
14727	Ganes, Anna E.	82y	W	2 APR 1918	Philadelphia PA	Rockville MD
12812	Gangewer, Ida	60y	W	12 MAR 1915	Rockville MD	Rock Creek
03202	Gannen, Salley Anne	20y	W	7 JUL 1900	MD	Mt. Olivet
14036	Gannon, Gilbert J.	42y	W	17 AMR 1917	Montgomery AL	Holyrood
07968	Gant, Charles A.	36y	C	13 FEB 1911	Atlantic City NJ	Arlington
16106	Gant, Ila May	21y	W	17 NOV 1919	Takoma Park MD	Glenwood
08440	Gant, Jane	85y	C	26 DEC 1911	Suitland MD	Mt. Olivet
02059	Gantley, John	65y	W	20 SEP 1896	Hampton VA	Mt. Olivet

District of Columbia Foreign Death Records, 1888-1923

No.	Name of Deceased	Age	Race	Death Date	Place of Death	Place of Burial
00832	Gantner, Jennie	81y	W	30 AUG 1892	Summit Pt. WV	Rock Creek
17852	Gantt, William E.	55y	W	12 MAY 1922	Berlin MD	Lewinsville VA
15770	Gapen, Fannie Nelson	74y	W	8 MAY 1919	Cleveland OH	Rock Creek
08600	Gapen, Nelson, Jr.	1d	W	14 MAR 1912	Hot Springs AR	Congressional
08648	Garden, Henry	35y	C	25 MAY 1912	Danville VA	Cuba AL
06817	Garder, Addin May	9y	C	11 NOV 1908	Forestville MD	Harmony
07969	Gardette, Eulalie J.	76y	W	14 FEB 1911	Rockville MD	Oak Hill
06846	Gardiner, J.A.	55y	W	6 DEC 1908	Clarksburg WV	Congressional
06344	Gardiner, Sarah Eliza	83y	W	5 DEC 1907	Burnt Mills MD	Glenwood
04439	Gardiner, Walter F.	26y	W	2 SEP 1903	Egg Harbor NJ	Mt. Olivet
14577	Gardner, A.P.	53y	W	14 JAN 1918	Macon GA	Arlington
06637	Gardner, Bernice V. (Brown)	35y	W	10 JUL 1908	Goode VA	Rock Creek
08038	Gardner, Carrie E.	44y	C	25 MAR 1911	Philadelphia PA	Harmony
01810	Gardner, Clara P.	22y	W	20 NOV 1895	Chicago IL	Mt. Olivet
12997	Gardner, Clifford G.	27y	W	6 JUL 1915	Montreal, Can.	Rock Creek
14340	Gardner, Edna Lucinda M.	36y	W	4 SEP 1917	Berwyn MD	Glenwood
04846	Gardner, George Clinton	73y	W	12 AUG 1904	Richmond Hill LI	Congressional
15979	Gardner, Harry August	45y	W	7 SEP 1919	Cottage City MD	Prospect Hill
15741	Gardner, Helen A.	82y	W	8 APR 1919	Daytona FL	Cremated
13382	Gardner, James Edward	45y	W	26 FEB 1916	Formosa FL	Leesburg VA
13368	Gardner, Merideth	70y	C	16 FEB 1916	Alexandria VA	Harmony
17161	Gardner, Philip S.	5y	W	15 MAY 1921	Atlantic City NJ	Rock Creek
03173	Gardner, Rosa M.	77y	W	28 APR 1900	Baltimore MD	Mt. Olivet
08524	Gardner, Roynett M.	50y	W	25 FEB 1912	Occoquan VA	Rock Creek
06663	Gardner, Sarah A.	64y	W	30 JUL 1908	Kensington MD	Glenwood
01145	Gardner, William L.	67y	W	22 JAN 1893	Baltimore MD	Congressional
15787	Garfield, Edmund Dana	50y	W	19 NOV 1916	Washington DC	Rock Creek
03756	Garfield, Julian Leland	18y	W	10 JAN 1902	Miami FL	Pittsburgh PA
05193	Garges, Eugene Boyle	21y	W	4 JUL 1905	Battle Creek MI	Mt. Olivet
13189	Garges, George Washington	40y	W	6 NOV 1915	New York NY	Arlington
05736	Garges, Margaret	53y	W	10 SEP 1906	New York NY	Mt. Olivet
16466	Garges, Mary	71y	W	2 MAY 1920	Buffalo NY	Mt. Olivet
13835	Garhardt, Julius I.	60y	W	1 DEC 1916	Brentwood MD	St. Mary's
02604	Garland, Mary	38y	C	5 SEP 1898	Washington DC	Wirt's Wharf MD
17980	Garner, Amanda Lee	52y	C	27 JUL 1922	Fairmont Hts. MD	Payne's
08447	Garner, Annie	60y	C	27 DEC 1911	Fairmont Hts. MD	Moore's
02200	Garner, Arthur	—	W	4 JUN 1897	Denver CO	Congressional
18346	Garner, Elton, in jail	32y	C	FEB 1923	Fulton Co. GA	Mt. Zion West
12816	Garner, Georgiana	37y	C	12 MAR 1915	New York NY	Holyrood
08150	Garner, Infant of George	SB	W	15 JUN 1911	Columbia Pk. MD	Mt. Olivet
03452	Garner, James E.	26y	C	10 MAR 1901	New York NY	Harmony
09178	Garner, Lee	61y	C	18 APR 1913	Fairmont Hts. MD	Moore's
05273	Garner, Patrick	58y	C	4 SEP 1905	New York NY	Mt. Olivet
05747	Garner, Virnie	26y	W	20 SEP 1906	Baden MD	Glenwood
02248	Garnett, Henry Wise	48y	W	10 JUL 1897	Clifton Spgs. NY	Rock Creek
16109	Garrard, Emily L.	68y	W	14 NOV 1919	Laurel MD	Arlington
17492	Garrard, Samuel C.	76y	W	21 OCT 1921	Los Angeles CA	Arlington
02974	Garratt, Simeon, carpenter	74y	W	10 OCT 1899	Pr. Geo. Co. MD	Congressional
03172	Garren, Marion F.	8m	W	29 FEB 1900	Erie PA	Rock Creek
01811	Garret, Harriet	52y	W	12 JAN 1896	Chain Bridge VA	Holyrood
13860	Garrett, Amanda E.	c.72y	W	12 DEC 1916	Takoma Park MD	Rock Creek
08174	Garrett, Charles F.	67y	W	2 JUL 1911	Coney Island NY	Arlington
16954	Garrett, John Randolph Tucker	57y	W	4 FEB 1921	Clarendon VA	Congressional
17913	Garrett, Mary E.	58y	W	20 JUN 1922	Baltimore MD	Congressional
03268	Garrett, Rachel A.	52y	W	14 AUG 1900	Franklin Co. NY	Congressional
08442	Garrett, William	41y	C	25 DEC 1911	Cleveland OH	Harmony
00713	Garriott, Edna	4m	W	9 NOV 1891	Hyattsville MD	Glenwood
16837	Garrison, Annie T.	63y	W	1 DEC 1920	Falls Church VA	Glenwood
12456	Garrison, Florence E.	9m	C	22 JUL 1914	Newark NJ	Payne's

No.	Name of Deceased	Age	Race	Death Date	Place of Death	Place of Burial
03571	Garrison, Hester A.	58y	W	10 JUL 1901	Sligo MD	Rock Creek
0160	Garrity, James	60y	W	24 SEP 1889	Montg. Co. MD	Holyrood
03351	Gartner, Daisy E.	33y	W	17 FEB 1900	New York NY	Oak Hill
05249	Gartrell, Thomas S.	67y	W	17 AUG 1905	Kensington MD	Oak Hill
05964	Garvey, William H.	41y	W	28 FEB 1907	Buffalo NY	Mt. Olivet
06334	Garwood, Elizabeth H.	50y	W	4 DEC 1873	Alexandria VA	Rock Creek
06335	Garwood, Emma D.	55y	W	18 APR 1901	Washington DC	Rock Creek
06333	Garwood, Franklin P.	10y	W	11 AUG 1863	Alexandria VA	Rock Creek
06336	Garwood, Samuel N.	83y	W	22 JAN 1904	Alexandria VA	Rock Creek
06332	Garwood, Theodore C., s/o S.	8m	W	25 NOV 1864	Alexandria VA	Rock Creek
05911	Gary, Edwin F.	67y	W	26 JAN 1907	Columbia SC	Rock Creek
07170	Gary, Infant of Lawrence	1h	W	23 AUG 1909	Dominion Hts. VA	Rock Creek
04895	Gary, Kate N.	36y	W	NOV 1887	Columbia SC	Rock Creek
05087	Gasaway, Charles	28y	C	17 APR 1905	Crawford NJ	Bladensburg MD
12488	Gaskin, Walter	45y	C	15 AUG 1914	Colebrook PA	Harmony
01860	Gaskins, Mary	24y	C	22 JAN 1896	Leesburg VA	Mt. Zion
16983	Gaskins, Mary J.	27y	C	15 FEB 1921	Alexandria VA	Woodlawn
17475	Gass, William H.	61y	W	18 OCT 1921	Baltimore MD	Rock Creek
05932	Gassaway, Infant of John H.	½h	W	9 FEB 1907	Germantown MD	Oak Hill
04369	Gassaway, John	21m	W	30 JUN 1903	Rockville MD	Oak Hill
01981	Gatchel, Howard	3m	W	22 AUG 1896	Boyds MD	Glenwood
08139	Gatchell, J. Fred	42y	W	8 JUN 1911	Laurel MD	Glenwood
14529	Gately, Nellie	57y	W	28 DEC 1917	Takoma MD	Red Bank NJ
01437	Gates, Frank E.	19y	W	14 JUL 1894	Colonial Bea. VA	Mt. Olivet
11931	Gates, George A.	47y	W	31 JUL 1913	Mt. Wash. MD	Congressional
16882	Gates, Harry V.	47y	W	29 DEC 1920	Hyattsville MD	Mt. Olivet
05593	Gates, John	62y	W	11 JUN 1906	Baltimore MD	Shelby OH
05279	Gates, Lemuel A.	76y	W	8 SEP 1905	Baltimore Co. MD	Congressional
12919	Gates, Sarah C.	81y	W	11 MAY 1915	Ft. Wash. MD	Congressional
03913	Gather, Charles	40y	W	23 SEP 1903	Tuxedo MD	Mt. Olivet
14158	Gathman, Louis	73y	W	3 JUN 1917	Cherrydale VA	Glenwood
12132	Gathright, Enoch M.	31y	W	14 DEC 1913	Phoenix AZ	Rock Creek
01708	Gatley, Mable	10m	W	23 AUG 1895	Knoxville TN	Glenwood[1]
04392	Gatley, William A.	59y	W	14 JUL 1903	El Paso TX	Rock Creek
05679	Gatto, Dominico, s/o Mariano	73y	W	6 AUG 1906	Colonial Bea. VA	St. Mary's
15554	Gaul, Elmer	23y	W	12 JAN 1919	At Sea	Philadelphia PA
16449	Gause, Isaac	76y	W	23 APR 1920	Johnson City TN	Arlington
07443	Gautier, Charles	63y	W	1 MAR 1910	New York NY	Mt. Olivet
15697	Gavin, Thomas L.	38y	W	22 MAR 1919	Albuquerque NM	Mt. Olivet
08486	Gawen, Alice Jefferson	54y	W	21 JAN 1912	Wash. Grove MD	Glenwood
01950	Gawler, Charles	42y	W	JAN 1835	Alexandria VA	Oak Hill
07050	Gawler, Joseph, Jr.	58y	W	7 JUN 1909	Relay MD	Oak Hill
01949	Gawler, Sarah	33y	W	JUN 1833	Alexandria VA	Oak Hill
01709	Gay, James W.	37y	M	1 OCT 1895	Bryn Mawr PA	Mt. Olivet
13148	Gay, Laura Ellis	25y	W	11 OCT 1915	Salisbury MD	Congressional
17695	Gayle, Matilda C.	76y	W	15 FEB 1922	Silver Spring MD	Glenwood
00605	Gaylor, Joseph LeRoy Brooke	2m	W	31 JUL 1891	Chesapeake VA	Mt. Olivet
07697	Gearhart, Pauline A.	3m	W	20 AUG 1910	Mt. Ranier MD	Mt. Olivet
04408	Geary, Daniel	50y	W	24 JUL 1903	Jersey City NJ	Mt. Olivet
14655	Geary, Eugene	50y	W	22 FEB 1918	Capitol Hts. MD	Mt. Olivet
05835	Geary, Hattie J.	32y	C	26 NOV 1906	Barnesville MD	Harmony
07423	Geary, Thomas	84y	W	19 FEB 1910	Oxon Hill MD	Mt. Olivet
01982	Gebieke, Louis	41y	W	10 SEP 1896	Montg. Co. MD	Congressional
07879	Geddes, Florence B.	51y	W	16 DEC 1910	New York NY	Arlington
17196	Geddes, James Wilkie	26y	W	6 OCT 1918	France	Glenwood
01555	Gedney, Walter Scott, artist	26y	W	14 FEB 1895	Philadelphia PA	Congressional

[1] Disinterment permit #9746 to remove remains 3 DEC 1918 to Rock Creek cemetery.

District of Columbia Foreign Death Records, 1888-1923

No.	Name of Deceased	Age	Race	Death Date	Place of Death	Place of Burial
14381	Gee, Mary L.	61y	C	26 SEP 1917	Rosslyn VA	Mt. Zion West
18514	Geesling, James J.	77y	W	29 APR 1923	Arlington Co. VA	Mt. Olivet
05089	Geib, Adam	61y	W	20 APR 1905	Hyattsville MD	Congressional
14631	Geiger, Stefanie Fredovinne	53y	W	9 FEB 1918	Forest Glen MD	Cremated
15342	Geigor, Infant of Maurice	1d	W	9 NOV 1918	Washington DC	Congressional
18592	Geisler, Rudolph	55y	W	5 JUN 1923	At Sea	Prospect Hill
03127	Gelray, Joseph W.	63y	W	10 MAR 1900	Boston MA	Arlington VA
00606	Genella, Leo Hammett	4m	W	11 JUL 1891	Falls Church VA	Mt. Olivet
07032	Genella, William G., Jr.	24y	W	17 MAY 1909	Indianapolis IN	Mt. Olivet
01304	Geneste, Leon D.	29y	W	21 JAN 1894	Denver CO	Congressional
14733	Gennari, Frank	32y	W	6 APR 1918	Alexandria VA	Glenwood
05312	Gensler, Adeline E.	55y	W	30 JUL 1905	Yonkers NY	Mt. Olivet
12906	Gensler, Donald Eugene	30y	W	2 MAY 1915	Bennington VT	Mt. Olivet
16533	Gensler, Marion E. (Oliver)	45y	W	11 JUN 1920	Fredericksburg VA	Glenwood
17717	Gentry, Kathleen	71y	W	2 MAR 1922	Takoma Park MD	Charleston WV
03008	Geofroy, Louis Francois H. de	75y	W	5 OCT 1899	Cannes, France	Mt. Olivet
06147	Geoghegan, James A.	66y	W	20 JUL 1907	Baltimore MD	Rock Creek
04286	George, Andrew P.	25y	W	17 APR 1903	Baltimore MD	Glenwood
14532	Georghegan, Rosalie	71y	W	26 DEC 1917	New Bedford MA	Rock Creek
08460	Gephart, Margaret H.	32y	W	1 JAN 1912	Quincy IL	Leesburg VA
00951	Gerard, Alfred	65y	W	15 JUL 1893	Westm. Co. VA	Glenwood
02922	Gerbert, Virginia Alice	69y	W	21 AUG 1899	Temple. Xrds. VA	Rock Creek
16477	Gerdine, Frances Bishop	37y	W	10 MAY 1920	Chevy Chase MD	Mt. Olivet
04290	Gerhardt, Dorothea	69y	W	16 MAY 1903	New York NY	Prospect Hill
17744	Gerhardt, Joseph J.	67y	W	11 MAR 1922	Middletown NY	Prospect Hill
03240	Gerhardt, Milton Osman	6m	W	18 JUL 1900	Garrett Park MD	Prospect Hill
01710	Gering, Conrad, carpenter	70y	W	21 OCT 1895	Indian Head MD	Baltimore MD
15590	German, Norman Talbert	1m	W	28 JAN 1919	Ballston VA	Congressional
05706	Germann, Beatrice	2y	W	28 AUG 1906	Chillum MD	Rock Creek
14047	Germann, George F., Jr.	26y	W	23 MAR 1917	Chillum MD	Rock Creek
01861	Germann, Howard	1m	W	18 JAN 1896	Takoma Park MD	Rock Creek
03053	Germann, J. Irving	1m	W	28 DEC 1899	Chillum MD	Rock Creek
17669	Gersdorff, Albert L. Francis	30y	W	29 JAN 1922	Hominy OK	Prospect Hill
01862	Gersdorff, Augustus, merchant	65y	W	28 FEB 1896	Philadelphia PA	Rock Creek
12876	Gervis, Francis Earl	—	C	14 APR 1915	Seat Pleasant MD	Woodlawn
02656	Geslester, John H.	8y	W	11 NOV 1898	Baltimore MD	Congressional
08218	Gessford, James E., druggist	42y	W	24 JUL 1911	Savannah GA	Congressional
00128	Gessford, William T.	32y	W	10 AUG 1889	Patuxent Br. MD	Congressional
13279	Getz, James	26y	C	31 DEC 1915	Philadelphia PA	Woodlawn
14616	Getzendanner, Maria M.	68y	W	2 FEB 1918	Oxon Hill MD	Congressional
03584	Ghants, Joseph	17y	W	29 JUL 1900	Manila, P.I.	Arlington
06827	Gheen, Benedict W.	34y	W	17 NOV 1908	Nampa ID	Rock Creek
08523	Ghio, Agnes	44y	W	21 FEB 1912	New York NY	Mt. Olivet
00833	Gibbons, Catharine	4y	W	29 AUG 1892	Syracuse NY	Holyrood
12159	Gibbons, John P.	50y	W	11 JAN 1914	Chicago IL	Mt. Olivet
00834	Gibbons, Mary A.	6y	W	29 AUG 1892	Syracuse NY	Holyrood
06055	Gibbons, William	33y	W	5 MAY 1907	Minneapolis MN	Holyrood
01556	Gibbs, Elizabeth	70y	W	8 JAN 1895	Philadelphia PA	Rock Creek
12217	Gibbs, Elizabeth L.	70y	W	9 FEB 1914	Philadelphia PA	Rock Creek
12475	Gibbs, Ethel	1m	W	7 AUG 1914	Capitol Hts. MD	Congressional
16468	Gibbs, Frank M.	70y	W	2 MAY 1920	Philadelphia PA	Rock Creek
16031	Gibbs, James L.	73y	W	6 OCT 1919	Philadelphia PA	Rock Creek
01626	Gibbs, Margarette E.	34y	W	3 APR 1895	Denver CO	Glenwood
05929	Gibbs, Randolph H., s/o Thos.	44y	W	7 FEB 1907	New Haven CN	Arlington
08672	Gibson, Amy	24y	C	13 JUN 1912	Philadelphia PA	Harmony
00022	Gibson, Charles Compt.	7d	W	24 FEB 1889	Hyattsville MD	Congressional
0267	Gibson, Emma	28y	C	14 JAN 1890	Baltimore MD	Mt. Zion
16691	Gibson, Harry	33y	C	2 SEP 1920	Philadelphia PA	Harmony
03739	Gibson, James R.	32y	W	21 DEC 1901	Jacksonville FL	Mt. Olivet

No.	Name of Deceased	Age	Race	Death Date	Place of Death	Place of Burial
00952	Gibson, John	27y	W	4 JUL 1893	Alex. Co. VA	Congressional
08671	Gibson, John	2d	C	12 JUN 1912	Philadelphia PA	Harmony
16547	Gibson, Lillian Susan	28y	C	19 JUN 1920	Capitol Hts. MD	Woodlawn
17557	Gibson, Mary L.	38y	C	26 NOV 1921	Newark NJ	Harmony
08854	Gibson, Samuel H., s/o Wm.	67y	W	24 SEP 1912	Atlantic City NJ	Arlington
04640	Gibson, Sarah E.	64y	W	23 MAR 1904	Baltimore MD	Oak Hill
03860	Gibson, Susan Isabelle	83y	W	22 APR 1902	Landover MD	Mt. Olivet
05399	Gibson, William E.	26y	C	14 DEC 1905	Sideburn VA	Harmony
00607	Gibson, William Henry	44y	W	30 JUL 1891	Marshall VA	Glenwood
16131	Giddings, Bridget	91y	W	1 DEC 1919	Baltimore MD	Oak Hill
04168	Giddings, Charlotte Webster	76y	W	3 FEB 1903	Indian Head MD	Congressional
17010	Giddings, Joseph D.	38y	W	28 FEB 1921	Pittsburgh PA	Glenwood
07104	Gideon, Catharine C.	92y	W	11 JUL 1909	Chevy Chase MD	Oak Hill
13132	Gideon, Hetty A.	33y	W	3 OCT 1915	Ballston VA	Glenwood
13133	Gideon, Infant of Clyde	SB	W	3 OCT 1915	Ballston VA	Glenwood
01557	Gifford, George August	11d	W	28 DEC 1894	Bladensburg MD	Rock Creek
07349	Gifford, Henry Judson	73y	W	29 DEC 1909	Norfolk VA	Arlington VA
04781	Gifford, Mary F.	68y	W	5 JUL 1904	Norfolk VA	Arlington VA
14764	Gifford, Wendell P.	64y	W	17 APR 1918	Jacksonville FL	Cremated
02767	Gilbert, Fannie A.	50y	W	17 MAR 1899	Oak Lodge FL	Glenwood
18221	Gilbert, Helen (Washington)	27y	C	21 DEC 1922	Flint MI	Payne's
03283	Gilbert, John Willett	53y	W	2 NOV 1900	Pr. Geo. Co. MD	Rock Creek
17868	Gilbert, Worthington	c.40y	C	17 MAY 1922	Railroad	Woodlawn
18512	Gilchrist, Henry	42y	C	26 APR 1923	Newark NJ	Harmony
06248	Gilday, Thomas	48y	W	24 SEP 1907	Philadelphia PA	Mt. Olivet
07523	Giles, Ada Pyron	50y	C	29 APR 1910	Vigo IN	Harmony
06398	Giles, Claudius	16y	C	19 JAN 1908	Quincy IL	Harmony
12385	Giles, Mamie	32y	C	29 MAY 1914	Philadelphia PA	Harmony
15200	Giles, William	26y	C	13 OCT 1918	Camp Meade MD	Arlington VA
15648	Giles, William T.	19y	W	26 FEB 1919	Lawton OK	Arlington
08835	Gilkey, Arthur B.	30y	W	13 SEP 1912	Saranac Lake NY	Congressional
02926	Gill, Albert, merchant	47y	W	24 AUG 1899	Montg. Co. MD	Congressional
18459	Gill, Anna E.	56y	W	4 APR 1923	Peoria IL	Glenwood
02621	Gill, Charles A.	22y	W	6 OCT 1898	Sternberg H. GA	Congressional
15024	Gill, Charles F.	53y	W	16 SEP 1918	Alex. Co. VA	Glenwood
14806	Gill, Emma J.	50y	W	9 MAY 1918	Philadelphia PA	Glenwood
00714	Gill, Infant of DeLancy & Rose	1y	W	25 MAR 1892	New York NY	Rock Creek
09153	Gill, Irving	5y	W	1 APR 1913	Riverside NY	Glenwood
05616	Gill, James E., s/o Edward C.	6m	W	2 JUL 1906	Arlington VA	Glenwood
17803	Gill, Mary M.	c.85y	W	14 APR 1922	Baltimore MD	Arlington
14423	Gill, Monita W.	61y	W	22 OCT 1917	Alta Vista MD	Oak Hill
15367	Gill, Mrs. N.H.	40y	W	20 NOV 1918	Charlotte NC	Glenwood
15135	Gill, William A., Adm.	59y	W	10 OCT 1918	Bridgeport CN	Arlington
14902	Gillespie, Frank	c.25y	W	7 JUL 1918	Glen Echo MD	Arlington
15257	Gillespie, Noble	317	C	23 OCT 1918	Fredericksburg VA	Harmony
16761	Gillett, Alfred S.	94y	W	8 DEC 1912	Washington DC	Rock Creek
16488	Gillick, Rose Catherine	21y	W	c.4 APR 1920	Potomac River	West Point NY
14684	Gilliken, Anna S.	26y	W	10 MAR 1918	Denver CO	Congressional
02822	Gilliland, James C.	52y	W	3 MAY 1899	Chevy Chase MD	Rock Creek
12338	Gilliland, Roy B.	30y	W	17 APR 1914	Baltimore MD	Glenwood
06383	Gillingham, James W.	69y	W	9 JAN 1908	Columbia Pk. MD	Glenwood
04964	Gillingham, Roxey Bent	64y	W	26 NOV 1904	Columbia Pk. MD	Glenwood
07855	Gillis, James Henry	79y	W	2 DEC 1910	Melbourn Bea. FL	Arlington
15644	Gillman, Fern Hoskins	39y	W	26 FEB 1919	Saranac Lake NY	Rock Creek
01442	Gillman, Louise Webb	11m	W	23 JUL 1894	Bolivar WV	Glenwood
13726	Gillum, Edward	c.70y	C	18 SEP 1916	Elkins WV	Mt. Olivet
05016	Gillum, Lucius	38y	C	31 JAN 1905	Pittsburgh PA	Harmony
03959	Gillum, Mary	16y	C	31 JUL 1902	Elkins WV	Mt. Olivet
02403	Gilman, Emma N.	67y	W	14 MAR 1898	Newburgh NY	Congressional

District of Columbia Foreign Death Records, 1888-1923

No.	Name of Deceased	Age	Race	Death Date	Place of Death	Place of Burial
12167	Gilmore, James	27y	C	14 JAN 1914	Pittsburgh PA	Woodlawn
16793	Gilmore, Leona M.	9m	W	1 NOV 1920	Mt. Ranier MD	Rock Creek
05959	Gilmour, Allan, s/o Mathew	71y	W	26 FEB 1907	Atlantic City NJ	Rock Creek
14708	Gilott, Clarence M.	38y	W	25 MAR 1918	Occoquan VA	Congressional
02249	Gilroy, John N.	21y	W	4 AUG 1897	Norfolk VA	Mt. Olivet
16262	Ginder, Maud Carlotta	45y	W	31 JAN 1920	Hyattsville MD	Cremated
01984	Gingell, B.M.	5m	W	8 JUL 1896	Bethesda MD	Holyrood
15769	Gingell, Infant of Reginald	SB	W	8 MAY 1919	Fairfax Co. VA	Tenallytown M.
00953	Gingell, Joseph A.	66y	W	16 JUN 1893	Bethesda MD	Holyrood
06095	Gingle, Catherine R. (Ward)	55y	W	4 JUN 1877	Alex. Co. VA	Methodist
03089	Gingle, Mary M.	22y	W	3 FEB 1900	Folsom PA	Holyrood
00954	Ginnaty, Maude Marie	11m	W	8 JUL 1893	Hyattsville MD	Mt. Olivet
16823	Ginnis, Sidney E.	9m	C	22 NOV 1920	Bowie MD	Payne's
14420	Giovannoni, Joseph A., Jr.	7y	W	20 OCT 1917	Charlotte NC	St. Mary's
14575	Giovannoni, Mattie	46y	W	13 JAN 1918	Baltimore MD	Holyrood
04711	Gittings, Ann Virginia	84y	W	13 MAY 1904	Bethesda MD	Glenwood
07506	Gittings, James F.	31y	W	21 APR 1910	Brown's Sta. MD	Glenwood
03249	Gittings, Joel H.	50y	W	3 AUG 1900	New York NY	Congressional
01231	Gittings, Samuel R.	44y	W	2 DEC 1893	Excelsior Sp. MO	Glenwood
18034	Giusta, William	78y	W	25 AUG 1922	Hyattsville MD	Mt. Olivet
14237	Given, John F.	c.55y	W	18 JUL 1917	Lima OH	Sidney OH
12412	Givens, Alice	2d	C	24 JUN 1914	Cedar Hts. MD	Woodlawn
15297	Givens, Harman	22d	C	28 OCT 1918	Fairmont Hts. MD	Woodlawn
17034	Givens, Louisa	8m	C	10 MAR 1921	Fairmont Hts. MD	Woodlawn
14196	Gladden, Ella	27y	C	26 JUN 1917	Philadelphia PA	Payne's
15110	Gladden, James Wilson	38y	W	8 OCT 1918	Mt. Ranier MD	Hiland MD
12512	Gladdish, Leslie	12y	C	31 AUG 1914	Atlantic City NJ	Payne's
05451	Glading, Margaret	14d	W	1 FEB 1906	Takoma MD	Rock Creek
17393	Glancy, John F.	22y	W	2 SEP 1921	Baltimore MD	Bruce Mines, Can.
16847	Glascoe, Joseph H.	40y	C	6 DEC 1920	New York NY	Harmony
16408	Glaser, Elsie	23y	W	25 MAR 1920	Rochester NY	Wash. Hebrew
05760	Glaser, Samuel	11y	W	3 OCT 1906	Delaware Co. PA	Wash. Hebrew
16860	Glaser, Samuel J.	52y	W	18 DEC 1920	Rochester NY	Wash. Hebrew
15080	Glass, Roy Chester	41y	W	3 OCT 1918	Dayton OH	Rock Creek
06684	Gleason, H. Elizabeth	43y	W	11 AUG 1908	Liberty NY	Glenwood
16505	Gleason, James Henry	79y	W	28 MAY 1920	Chillum MD	Rock Creek
01711	Gleason, John J.	42y	W	9 OCT 1895	Philadelphia PA	Oak Hill
01146	Gleason, Madeline Estelle	9y	W	7 JAN 1893	Pr. Geo. Co. MD	Rock Creek
00366	Gleason, Mary	3m	W	21 JUL 1890	Occoquan VA	Glenwood
04725	Gleason, Sarah E.	63y	W	23 MAY 1904	Chillum MD	Rock Creek
06301	Gleaves, Richard H.	65y	C	8 NOV 1907	Philadelphia PA	Harmony
08435	Gleed, Mattie	39y	C	29 DEC 1911	Philadelphia PA	Payne's
16068	Gleeson, James K.P.	75y	W	23 OCT 1919	Takoma Park MD	Rock Creek
14371	Gleeson, Joseph Michael	56y	W	21 SEP 1917	Loudoun Co. VA	Cremated
05113	Gleeson, Vincent	25y	W	4 MAY 1905	New York NY	Congressional
06594	Glick, William A.	27y	W	16 JUN 1908	Tucumcare NM	Glenwood
14916	Gloetzner, Arnulf Anthony	28y	W	15 JUL 1918	Louisville KY	St. Mary's
08421	Glover, William	64y	W	10 DEC 1911	Arlington Jct. VA	Glenwood
07583	Gluckauf, Gustave	37y	W	13 APOR 1910	Walter Reed Hp.	Cremated
06517	Goble, Mary G.	70y	W	18 APR 1908	Fairmont Hts. MD	Congressional
07252	Goddard, Arthur C.	26y	W	24 OCT 1909	Columbus OH	Glenwood
14004	Goddard, Ella V.	46y	W	23 FEB 1917	College Park MD	Glenwood
00608	Goddard, William H.	63y	W	3 JUL 1891	Karlsbad, Ger.	Rock Creek
04990	Godden, Frank W., reporter	24y	W	24 DEC 1904	Tucson AZ	Rock Creek
00835	Godey, Catharine	8y	W	24 SEP 1892	Capon Spgs. WV	Oak Hill
03279	Godey, Cornelia V.	69y	W	1 SEP 1900	Berwyn MD	Oak Hill
00244	Godey, Edward	33y	W	16 DEC 1889	Baltimore Co. MD	Oak Hill
05863	Godfrey, Ira	61y	W	14 DEC 1906	New York NY	Rock Creek
00342	Godfrey, Ralph S.	11y	W	13 JUN 1890	Denver CO	Rock Creek

No.	Name of Deceased	Age	Race	Death Date	Place of Death	Place of Burial
18302	Godson, Mary (Saunders)	48y	C	23 JAN 1923	New York NY	Harmony
03153	Godwin, Henry P.	43y	W	30 MAR 1900	Bridgeport CN	Rock Creek
05629	Godwin, Thomas J.	50y	W	29 JUN 1906	Clay Center KS	Rock Creek
05041	Godwin, Walter G., s/o Thos.	36y	W	24 FEB 1905	Richmond VA	Rock Creek
05733	Goebel, Wm. Allouis, s/o Thos.	14d	W	10 SEP 1906	Vienna VA	Prospect Hill
06274	Goeins, Kate	48y	C	14 OCT 1907	Chambersburg PA	Harmony
15180	Goettelman, Fernend Camille	43y	W	14 OCT 1918	Hyattsville MD	Mt. Olivet
08258	Goetz, Frank	61y	W	16 AUG 1911	Baltimore MD	Prospect Hill
01404	Goetz, Louisa K.	33y	W	2 JUL 1894	Colonial Bea. VA	Prospect Hill
18062	Goetzinger, Walter	—	W	12 SEP 1922	Baltimore MD	St. Mary's
18187	Goetzman, George Alfred	2m	W	29 NOV 1922	Arlington Co. VA	St. Mary's
07733	Goff, William N.	59y	W	3 SEP 1910	Norfolk VA	Rock Creek
04744	Goffney, Randolph	4m	C	29 MAY 1904	Halls Hill VA	Mt. Zion
00098	Goggin, Robert W.	69y	W	17 JUL 1889	Brooklyn NY	Glenwood
07508	Goggins, Mamie L.	30y	C	19 APR 1910	Pittsburgh PA	Woodlawn
13533	Goheen, Infant of John W.	SB	W	3 JUN 1916	Mt. Ranier MD	Mt. Olivet
08033	Goheen, Martha	4h	W	27 MAR 1911	Mt. Ranier MD	Mt. Olivet
08044	Goheen, Mary	3d	W	30 MAR 1911	Mt. Ranier MD	Mt. Olivet
08748	Goines, William Henry	52y	C	2 AUG 1912	Arundel Bay MD	Harmony
12496	Goldberg, Harry	14h	W	24 AUG 1914	Capitol Hts. MD	Nat. Cap. Hebrew
08880	Golden, Charles J.	23y	W	10 OCT 1912	Hunterdon Co. NJ	Congressional
01558	Golden, Jane	87y	W	25 DEC 1894	New York NY	Glenwood
16564	Golden, Julia C.	78y	W	27 JUN 1920	Sykesville MD	Congressional
07726	Golden, Maria E.	76y	W	2 SEP 1910	Paeonian Sp. VA	Congressional
01863	Golden, William	4y	W	18 MAR 1896	New York NY	Mt. Olivet
07941	Goldsborough, Fitzhugh C.	31y	W	23 JAN 1911	New York NY	Cremated
05687	Goldsborough, John McCullen	1y	W	14 AUG 1906	Walkersville MD	Rock Creek
01447	Goldsborough, Mary H.	1y	W	27 JUL 1894	Buena Vista MD	Oak Hill
15618	Goldsmith, Bertha	68y	W	16 FEB 1919	Central Islip NY	Ohev Sholom
15313	Goldsmith, Harry M.	34y	W	29 OCT 1918	Windsor PA	Mt. Olivet
05785	Goldsmith, Zachariah Hebb	83y	W	21 OCT 1906	Vienna VA	Glenwood
17502	Goldstein, Henry	68y	W	10 JAN 1921	Delaware Co. PA	Wash. Hebrew
08563	Gonter, Hannah J.	80y	W	18 MAR 1912	Altoona PA	Congressional
02422	Gonter, Samuel M.	74y	W	29 MAR 1898	Altoona PA	Congressional
01864	Gooch, Charles, painter	74y	W	10 MAR 1896	Wash. Grove MD	Rock Creek
07910	Gooch, Emma J.	74y	W	8 JAN 1911	Wash. Grove MD	Rock Creek
02113	Gooch, Henry, farmer	68y	W	20 JAN 1897	Wash. Grove MD	Rock Creek
18117	Gooch, James	91y	W	17 OCT 1922	Baltimore MD	Rock Creek
08740	Good, Ada	68y	W	30 JUL 1912	Hagerstown MD	Oak Hill
01983	Good, Jane	92y	W	30 JUN 1896	Montg. Co. MD	Oak Hill
15017	Goodall, Julia R.	45y	W	11 SEP 1918	Littleton NH	Rock Creek
05983	Goodall, Marian L.P.	81y	W	15 MAR 1907	New York NY	Congressional
04315	Goode, Richard Urquhart	44y	W	9 JUN 1903	Rockville MD	Rock Creek
17126	Goode, Sarah Judd	67y	W	24 APR 1921	Tallahassee FL	Oak Hill
02562	Goodhart, George	28y	W	18 AUG 1898	—	Leesburg VA
06897	Gooding, Clarence A.	23y	W	15 JAN 1909	Deturo CO	Rock Creek
07328	Gooding, Eliza C.	55y	W	16 DEC 1909	Kensington MD	Glenwood
12298	Gooding, Infant of Charles B.	6m	W	7 APR 1914	Wheaton MD	Glenwood
14935	Gooding, Joseph	27y	W	23 jUL 1918	Quantico VA	Glenwood
13096	Gooding, Lizzie M.	56y	W	11 SEP 1915	Rockville MD	Rock Creek
08202	Goodloe, Franklin	14y	C	15 JUL 1911	Youngstown OH	Harmony
13530	Goodman, Edmond, in prison	28y	C	28 MAY 1916	Leavenworth KS	Payne's
15875	Goodman, Kader	55y	C	7 JUL 1919	Indian Head MD	Woodlawn
17274	Goodman, Maxine Elizabeth	36y	W	29 JUN 1921	Norfolk VA	Glenwood
16813	Goodman, Nathan	51y	W	18 NOV 1920	New York NY	Wash. Hebrew
01812	Goodrich, Charles	45y	W	14 DEC 1895	Fairfax VA	Glenwood
15061	Goodwin, Eugenia Holmes	76y	W	2 OCT 1918	Chevy Chase MD	Cremated
04617	Goodwin, S. Guy	20y	W	22 FEB 1904	Phoenix AZ	Methodist
01147	Goolerick, Jemima E.	77y	W	7 OCT 1892	Herndon VA	Congressional

District of Columbia Foreign Death Records, 1888-1923

No.	Name of Deceased	Age	Race	Death Date	Place of Death	Place of Burial
14275	Goorskey, Norman John	24y	W	5 AUG 1917	Glen Echo MD	Chicago IL
14072	Gorden, Phoebe E.	5y	W	1 APR 1917	Massillon OH	Congressional
09116	Gordon, Dinah	8y	W	9 MAR 1913	Mt. Zion MD	Ohev Sholom
16124	Gordon, Elsie	35y	C	16 NOV 1919	New York NY	Woodlawn
03645	Gordon, George Dent	4m	W	14 SEP 1901	Laurel MD	Oak Hill
12949	Gordon, Harriet	—	C	31 MAY 1915	Fairmont Hts. MD	Payne's
05253	Gordon, James	54y	W	17 AUG 1905	Asbury Park NJ	Rock Creek
01930	Gordon, John	27y	W	18 MAY 1896	Pr. Geo. Co. MD	Congressional
14546	Gordon, John Mitchell	29y	W	3 JAN 1918	Asheville NC	Cremated
05853	Gordon, Joseph H.	67y	W	8 DEC 1906	Alexandria VA	Arlington VA
04487	Gordon, Loretta	28y	W	23 OCT 1903	New York NY	Congressional
14947	Gordon, Martha Jane	18y	W	1 AUG 1918	Sligo MD	Congressional
08359	Gordon, Mary Taylor Gillman	79y	W	14 OCT 1911	Takoma Park MD	Exeter NH
08456	Gordon, Millie	59y	C	3 JAN 1912	Catonsville MD	Harmony
16139	Gordon, Samuel	30y	C	4 DEC 1919	Baltimore MD	Mt. Zion East
06727	Gordon, Stuart C.	37y	W	4 SEP 1908	Silver City NM	Arlington VA
04436	Gordon, Thomas	68y	C	3 SEP 1903	Arlington VA	Mt. Olivet
14971	Gordon, Virginia May	2m	W	13 AUG 1918	Morgantown MD	Congressional
13771	Gordon, William	49y	C	16 OCT 1916	Pittsburgh PA	Woodlawn
17678	Gore, Albert Eager	41y	W	9 FEB 1922	Takoma Park MD	Knoxville TN
12062	Gore, Lillian	47y	W	13 OCT 1913	Paris, France	Oak Hill
17140	Gorham, Effie Bassett	73y	W	3 MAY 1921	Swarthmore PA	Rock Creek
06300	Gorham, James	31y	C	4 NOV 1907	New York NY	Harmony
00716	Gorham, Mary Eunice	1y	W	2 JUN 1853	Falls Church VA	Prospect Hill
05359	Gorham, Susan	32y	C	11 NOV 1905	New York NY	Harmony
00715	Gorham, Talmon Sanford	14y	W	20 JAN 1866	Falls Church VA	Prospect Hill
02651	Goritz, John H.	65y	W	28 OCT 1898	Chicago IL	Prospect Hill
05498	Gorman, Annie V.	54y	W	10 MAR 1906	Baltimore MD	Mt. Olivet
15975	Gorman, Arthur P.	46y	W	3 SEP 1919	Baltimore MD	Oak Hill
00609	Gorman, Samuel E.	30y	W	27 AUG 1891	Statesville NC	Mt. Olivet
16077	Gormley, Herbert S.	45y	W	29 OCT 1919	Branchville MD	Glenwood
07613	Gosling, Adolph Herman L.	50y	W	3 JUL 1910	St. Davids PA	Oak Hill
02250	Gosom, Esther	4m	W	17 AUG 1897	Takoma Park MD	Rock Creek
04063	Gosom, Infant of T.H. & H.B.	2m	W	9 OCT 1902	Montg. Co. MD	Rock Creek
17154	Goss, Albert	—	—	31 OCT 1918	Belgium	Mt. Olivet
11840	Goss, Alice Louise	26y	W	2 JUN 1913	Takoma Park MD	Congressional
16340	Goss, Edna	28y	C	FEB 1920	Philadelphia PA	Mt. Olivet
08364	Gotta, Robert C.	50y	W	18 OCT 1911	Harrisburg PA	Rock Creek
13042	Gotthardt, Frederick M.	54y	W	30 JUL 1915	Anaconda MT	Rock Creek
02060	Gotthilf, Jacob	79y	W	11 OCT 1896	Baltimore MD	Rock Creek
15096	Gottlieb, Everett W.	19y	W	6 OCT 1918	Chevy Chase MD	Glenwood
01903	Gottlief, Amelia	60y	W	12 APR 1896	Baltimore MD	Rock Creek
13738	Gough, Emma J. (Johnson)	69y	W	28 SEP 1916	Tisbury MA	Glenwood
17640	Gough, James T.	31y	W	18 JAN 1922	Alexandria VA	Congressional
04064	Gould, Charles E.	20y	W	7 OCT 1902	Ft. Wright NY	Arlington VA
12687	Gould, Harold Clemens	26y	W	28 DEC 1914	Bethesda MD	Rock Creek
15855	Gould, Harry Lewis	43y	W	25 JUN 1919	Winfield KS	Glenwood
04564	Gould, Margaret Gray	39y	W	12 JAN 1904	Takoma Park MD	Rock Creek
03234	Gould, Martha	10m	W	13 JUL 1900	Takoma Park MD	Rock Creek
02201	Gould, William W.	55y	W	20 MAY 1897	Manassas VA	Glenwood
03045	Goun, Eva May	1y	C	21 DEC 1899	Philadelphia PA	Mt. Olivet
16383	Gover, William Elmer	26y	W	12 MAR 1920	Upper Marl. MD	Congressional
06664	Goward, Gustavus	61y	W	31 JUL 1908	Laurel MD	Newton MA
17642	Grace, J. Agnes	46y	W	19 JAN 1922	Mt. Hope MD	Mt. Olivet
17420	Grace, James	70y	W	20 SEP 1921	Hunts Sta. MD	Brooklyn NY
04659	Grace, Lula J.	23y	W	15 FEB 1892	Fairfax Co. VA	Prospect Hill
02352	Gradwohl, Fred	28y	W	26 DEC 1897	Frankfort IN	Wash. Hebrew
06179	Grady, Charles S.	33y	C	11 AUG 1907	New York NY	Woodlawn
00431	Grady, Margaret	68y	W	9 NOV 1890	Bladensburg MD	Mt. Olivet

No.	Name of Deceased	Age	Race	Death Date	Place of Death	Place of Burial
04434	Grady, Mary E.	—	—	1 JUL 1902	Spencerville MD	Rock Creek
07181	Graeme, Hattie H.	51y	W	2 SEP 1909	Brownsville MD	Rock Creek
00837	Graeves, August Lewis	40y	W	26 JUL 1892	Sligo MD	Rock Creek
00610	Graff, William S.	75y	W	18 JUL 1891	Alexandria VA	Congressional
16585	Grafton, Thomas Edw.	49y	W	7 JUL 1920	Rome GA	Oak Hill
04825	Graham, Annie	54y	C	30 JUL 1904	New York NY	Bailey's Xrds. VA
14777	Graham, Annie Katherine	56y	W	26 APR 1918	Lynchburg VA	Rock Creek
12153	Graham, Charles	75y	C	6 JAN 1914	Philadelphia PA	Payne's
17477	Graham, Chauncey Gilbert	78y	W	18 OCT 1921	Chevy Chase MD	Glenwood
08233	Graham, Christopher Col.	80y	W	31 JUL 1911	Wash. Grove MD	Glenwood
07044	Graham, David O.	25y	C	26 MAY 1909	Saranac Lake NY	Harmony
07957	Graham, Edmund H.	59y	W	31 JAN 1911	Kensington MD	Rock Creek
15653	Graham, Emily	62y	C	28 FEB 1919	Philadelphia PA	Payne's
18463	Graham, Estell	39y	C	4 APR 1923	Philadelphia PA	Rosemont
14838	Graham, Euphemia	75y	W	21 MAY 1918	Nevada MO	Congressional
02585	Graham, Hannah M.	78y	W	2 SEP 1898	Arlington VA	Congressional
07938	Graham, Harriet A. Southgate	68y	W	23 JAN 1911	Falls Church VA	Rock Creek
16199	Graham, Harvey	22y	C	7 JAN 1920	Philadelphia PA	Payne's
12806	Graham, Howard A.	47y	W	9 MAR 1915	Philadelphia PA	Glenwood
07977	Graham, Isaac T., s/o John	90y	W	20 FEB 1911	Grand View VA	Congressional
06815	Graham, James O.	62y	W	11 NOV 1908	Suitland MD	Congressional
04391	Graham, Julia Hutchinson	88y	W	18 JUL 1903	Mtn. Lake Pk. MD	Arlington
18521	Graham, Lucy A.	32y	W	4 OCT 1890	Gordonsville VA	Glenwood
13678	Graham, Neil Duncan	41y	W	25 AUG 1916	Falls Church VA	Rock Creek
14743	Graham, William	40y	W	4 APR 1918	Nogales AZ	Congressional
13303	Graham, William Montrose	81y	W	17 JAN 1916	Wardour MD	Congressional
07791	Graham, William Richard	10y	W	17 OCT 1910	Suitland MD	Congressional
17904	Grahame, Mary Branston	79y	W	14 JUN 1922	Annapolis MD	Congressional
01904	Gramlich, Francis Joseph	56y	W	2 APR 1896	Hyattsville MD	Congressional
13972	Granador, Angelina	16d	W	7 FEB 1917	Mt. Ranier MD	Mt. Olivet
14911	Graninger, Mary	76y	W	12 JUL 1918	Baltimore MD	St. Mary's
07251	Grant, Arthur	25y	C	23 OCT 1909	Pittsburgh PA	Payne's
13030	Grant, Blanche Johnson	33y	C	1 AUG 1915	Atlantic City NJ	Payne's
15455	Grant, Caroline Adelaide	79y	W	18 DEC 1918	Takoma Park MD	Rock Creek
13271	Grant, Fanny M.	75y	W	29 DEC 1915	Radnor Hts. VA	Center C. NH
14291	Grant, Isabelle H.	38y	C	9 AUG 1917	Hackensack NJ	Payne's
13328	Grant, Julia E.	52y	C	28 JAN 1916	Brentwood MD	Mt. Zion West
04715	Grant, Peter	50y	C	12 MAY 1904	Beckley WV	Potters Field
08758	Grant, Richard	36y	C	6 AUG 1912	Ocean Grove NJ	Harmony
12446½	Grant, William C.	67y	C	19 JUL 1914	Colonial Bea. MD	Congressional
17005	Grantt, Alexandria	78y	C	27 FEB 1921	Arlington VA	Payne's
15780	Grass, William M.	29y	C	14 MAY 1919	Spartanburg SC	Chapel Hill NC
08401	Grau, William E., s/o John	69y	W	24 NOV 1911	Occoquan VA	Prospect Hill
17797	Gravatt, Charles U., Hon.	70y	W	14 APR 1922	Richmond VA	Cremated
13980	Gravatt, Florence Marshall	51y	W	11 FEB 1917	Richmond VA	Cremated
18108	Gravatt, James D., s/o Ellis	68y	W	15 JUN 1905	Bowling Green VA	Glenwood
08611	Graveley, John	11m	W	23 APR 1912	Columbia SC	Rock Creek
13447	Graves, Barah T.	30y	W	6 APR 1916	Gaithersburg MD	Glenwood
08109	Graves, Bennie	60y	C	12 MAY 1911	Dupont Hts. MD	Harmony
07819	Graves, Edward, s/o Banner	66y	W	6 NOV 1910	Atlantic City NJ	Rock Creek
04123	Graves, George B.	20y	—	4 DEC 1902	Chicago IL	—
15961	Graves, Herbert C.	50y	W	28 JUL 1919	England	Alexandria VA
01985	Graves, James Porterfield	2m	W	2 JUL 1896	Cherokee NC	Congressional
12810	Graves, Minnie H.	25y	C	9 MAR 1915	Philadelphia PA	Payne's
04837	Gray, Benjamin	48y	W	9 AUG 1904	Sussex Co. DE	Moore's
00477	Gray, Cassie	46y	C	1881	—	Graceland
13491	Gray, Charity	80y	C	3 MAY 1916	Philadelphia PA	Moore's
06534	Gray, Daniel	50y	C	13 APR 1908	Rock Spring MD	Christian
03908	Gray, Ernest W.	33y	W	29 JUN 1902	Cripple Creek CO	Oak Hill

District of Columbia Foreign Death Records, 1888-1923

No.	Name of Deceased	Age	Race	Death Date	Place of Death	Place of Burial
03480	Gray, Frederick	30y	W	15 APR 1901	Baltimore MD	Oak Hill
14576	Gray, George H.	27y	W	13 JAN 1918	Charlotte NC	Mt. Olivet
14584	Gray, Harry, a.k.a. Johnson	21y	C	8 JAN 1918	Philadelphia PA	Payne's
15660	Gray, Irene	29y	C	4 MAR 1919	Philadelhpia PA	Mt. Zion West
11991	Gray, Jay C.	41y	C	3 SEP 1913	Boston MA	Harmony
07295	Gray, John	42y	C	26 SEP 1909	Pittsburgh PA	Harmony
15143	Gray, John Richard	51y	W	11 OCT 1918	Capitol Hts. MD	Congressional
00099	Gray, Julia	28y	C	7 JUL 1889	Asbury Park NJ	Mt. Pleasant
16010	Gray, Julian C.	c.52y	W	21 SEP 1919	Chicago IL	Congressional
12156	Gray, Lenvinia	17y	C	11 JAN 1914	Bennings MD	Mt. Olivet
17775	Gray, Lizzie	52y	C	29 MAR 1922	Philadelphia PA	Woodlawn
01232	Gray, Maria T.	48y	W	29 OCT 1893	London, Eng.	Oak Hill
07808	Gray, Marion B.	53y	W	29 OCT 1910	Tuxedo MD	St. Mary's
07809	Gray, Mary L.	40y	W	29 OCT 1910	Tuxedo MD	St. Mary's
06025	Gray, Mary Viola	17y	C	9 APR 1907	Philadelphia PA	Woodlawn
00836	Gray, Maurice A.	17y	W	16 AUG 1892	Calvert Co. MD	Oak Hill
13703	Gray, Pendleton B.	69y	W	6 SEP 1916	Brooklyn NY	Oak Hill
00717	Gray, Robert	49y	M	10 MAR 1892	Fairfax Co. VA	Graceland
16073	Gray, Robert S.	47y	C	25 OCT 1919	Chillum MD	Brandywine MD
12076	Gray, Roy Preston	1y	W	4 NOV 1913	Baltimore MD	Rock Creek
03679	Gray, Vernon Compton	8y	C	5 OCT 1901	Pr. Geo. Co. MD	Payne's
18322	Gray, Virginia L.	87y	W	3 FEB 1923	Riverdale MD	Glenwood
01044	Graybill, George T.	27y	W	6 FEB 1893	Denver CO	Congressional
01148	Grayson, Harriett	83y	C	13 JAN 1893	Alexandria VA	Harmony
18392	Grayson, Mayme	28y	C	4 MAR 1923	Chillum MD	Payne's
17178	Greeley, Ellen S.	35y	C	19 MAY 1921	Pittsburgh PA	Harmony
11834	Greemert, Richard M.	45y	W	25 MAY 1913	Union Bridge MD	Soldier's Home
00085	Green, Albert	45y	W	27 JUN 1889	Brooklyn NY	Oak Hill
13582	Green, Albertina	50y	C	29 JUN 1916	New York NY	Harmony
03933	Green, Alex W.	20y	W	17 JUL 1902	Notley Hall MD	Arlington
00546	Green, Alonzo M.	26y	C	4 MAR 1891	Philadelphia PA	Mt. Olivet
01233	Green, Ann	65y	C	24 OCT 1893	Montg. Co. MD	Holyrood
18473	Green, Annie M.	81y	C	10 APR 1923	Queens NY	Harmony
17595	Green, Annie Pratt	56y	C	15 DEC 1921	Philadelphia PA	Woodlawn
02705	Green, Benjamin	25y	C	11 JAN 1899	Annapolis MD	Harmony
05939	Green, Benjamin	75y	C	11 FEB 1907	Rosslyn VA	Holyrood
13089	Green, Bessie Jane	3m	C	3 SEP 1915	Takoma Park MD	Payne's
08644	Green, Carrie P.	49y	W	21 MAY 1912	E. Orange NJ	Oak Hill
03386	Green, Catherine E.	86y	W	3 JAN 1901	Alexandria VA	Oak Hill
17511	Green, Cecelia P.	39y	C	8 NOV 1921	Philadelphia PA	Union
00838	Green, Charles	88y	C	26 JUL 1892	Seabrook MD	Mt. Olivet
00008	Green, Clarinda N.	46y	W	– DEC 1888	Philadelphia PA	Oak Hill
05842	Green, Dennis	34y	W	27 NOV 1906	Fredericksburg VA	Congressional
14648	Green, Edward C.	57y	C	18 FEB 1918	Suitland MD	Payne's
17874	Green, Eliza Story	80y	W	26 MAY 1922	Clarendon VA	Oak Hill
06276	Green, Elizabeth	1y	C	17 OCT 1907	Seat Pleasant MD	Mt. Olivet
01461	Green, Ellen	40y	C	14 AUG 1894	Lanham Sta. MD	Mt. Olivet
12647	Green, Emma	73y	C	7 DEC 1914	Chicago IL	Woodlawn
18064	Green, Estelle	29y	C	9 SEP 1922	New York NY	Mt. Zion West
05066	Green, Fielder	1y	C	23 MAR 1895	Baltimore MD	Harmony
06314	Green, Francis	16y	W	17 NOV 1907	College Park MD	Congressional
16510	Green, Francis E.	44y	W	29 MAY 1920	Brentwood MD	Glenwood
02160	Green, George Forrest	2y	W	22 MAR 1897	Chicago IL	Holyrood
05676	Green, Hazel Lucrene	6m	W	6 AUG 1906	Cumberland MD	Rock Creek
0287	Green, Henrietta	24y	M	7 MAR 1890	New York NY	Mt. Zion
00286	Green, Henry	31y	C	8 MAR 1890	Montg. Co. MD	Holyrood
07632	Green, Henry	60y	C	12 JUL 1910	Baltimore MD	Payne's
06208	Green, Henry D., s/o Chas. A.	60y	W	28 AUG 1907	Ballston VA	Oak Hill
00175	Green, James	63y	W	– SEP 1889	Lewinsville VA	Glenwood

No.	Name of Deceased	Age	Race	Death Date	Place of Death	Place of Burial
07446	Green, James Garfield	29y	C	1 MAR 1910	Blassboro NJ	Payne's
15914	Green, James I.	32y	W	1 AUG 1919	New York NY	Holyrood
13829	Green, James, in jail	64y	C	23 NOV 1916	Baltimore MD	Harmony
12346	Green, James W.	47y	C	27 FEB 1914	Baltimore MD	Harmony
13186	Green, Jeremiah J.	2y	C	6 NOV 1915	Upper Marl. MD	Woodlawn
05545	Green, John	60y	C	19 APR 1906	Passaic Co. NJ	Mt. Olivet
15090	Green, John A.	24y	W	3 OCT 1918	Camp Meade MD	Mt. Olivet
09164	Green, Joseph A.	4y	C	9 APR 1913	Chevy Chase MD	Mt. Olivet
17428	Green, Kirt	c.34y	W	2 NOV 1918	France	Arlington
14960	Green, Lucy	19y	C	6 AUG 1918	Philadelphia PA	Woodlawn
16527	Green, Mamie	28y	W	9 JUN 1920	Falls Church VA	Petersburg VA
17237	Green, Margaret N.	58y	W	13 JUN 1921	Alexandria VA	Cremated
02796	Green, Marion D.	2y	W	17 APR 1899	Chicago IL	Holyrood
13654	Green, Mary	1y	C	10 AUG 1916	Baltimore MD	Mt. Zion West
16463	Green, Maurice N.	32y	C	28 APR 1920	Columbus NM	Arlington
14318	Green, Mintrell E.	16y	C	25 AUG 1917	Takoma Park MD	Harmony
18369	Green, Preston J.	1m	C	24 FEB 1923	Rosslyn VA	Mt. Zion West
04993	Green, Richmond D.	56y	C	7 JAN 1905	Glen Echo MD	Baptist
12262	Green, Rose	65y	W	20 MAR 1914	Rosslyn VA	Holyrood
05300	Green, Sarah	37y	C	27 SEP 1905	Waterloo VA	Payne's
00161	Green, Susanna Rosena	62y	W	9 SEP 1889	New York NY	Oak Hill
14012	Green, Waverly H.	16y	W	23 FEB 1917	Asheville NC	Holyrood
16263	Greenapple, Sylvan	35y	W	26 JAN 1920	Phoenix AZ	Adas Israel
02980	Greene, Albert E.S.	27y	W	14 OCT 1899	Loudoun Co. VA	Oak Hill
17167	Greene, Francis V.	70y	W	15 MAY 1921	New York NY	Arlington
12229	Greene, Francis Wallace	4y	W	17 FEB 1914	Trinidad CO	Rock Creek
03519	Greene, Harriet Ann	68y	W	21 MAY 1901	Brooklyn NY	Glenwood
13262	Greene, Henry F.	56y	W	20 DEC 1915	Duluth MN	Rock Creek
13389	Greene, Richard	c.23y	C	26 FEB 1916	Baltimore MD	Arlington VA
04603	Greene, William H.	70y	W	20 FEB 1904	New York NY	Glenwood
04567	Greeney, Catherine M.	40y	W	8 JAN 1904	Elmira NY	Congressional
08009	Greenfield, Walter B.	28y	W	16 MAR 1911	Sykesville MD	Bethesda MD
15786	Greenleaf, Norman	55y	C	18 MAY 1919	Baltimore MD	Moore's
08788	Greenough, George, Brig. Gen.	67y	W	27 JUN 1912	Charleston SC	Congressional
15464	Greenwell, Robert Combs	34y	W	19 DEC 1918	Portsmouth VA	Congressional
18114	Greenwell, William Gustavus	54y	W	13 OCT 1922	Cherrydale VA	Mt. Olivet
15431	Greer, Florence Simpson	27y	W	9 DEC 1918	Highland Park IL	Rock Creek
17745	Greer, Frank	3y	W	13 MAR 1922	Ft. Houston TX	Congressional
18257	Greer, Howard	42y	W	9 JAN 1923	Sykesville MD	Rock Creek
07275	Greer, Joseph H.	26y	W	11 DEC 1909	Kenilworth NC	Rock Creek
13988	Greer, Margaret	68y	W	13 FEB 1917	Chicago IL	Mt. Olivet
08588	Greever, Roberta	44y	W	5 APR 1912	Ft. Hunt VA	Tazewell VA
00478	Gregg, David	c.50y	W	8 JAN 1891	Augusta GA	Congressional
13049	Gregg, Susan Amanda	76y	W	10 AUG 1915	Oakland MD	Rock Creek
00954½	Gregory, Alice Josephine	2m	W	21 JUL 1893	Pr. Geo. Co. MD	Congressional
00440	Gregory, Eliza	55y	W	23 NOV 1890	Moravin NY	Congressional
16059	Gregory, Florence E.	57y	W	18 OCT 1919	Barcroft VA	Oak Hill
13254	Gregory, James W.	66y	W	17 DEC 1915	Baltimore MD	Cambridge MA
17330	Gregory, Musette Brooks	44y	C	26 JUL 1921	Saratoga Sp. NY	Woodlawn
18500	Gregory, Ola	24y	W	22 APR 1923	Dodge Park MD	Greensboro NC
16699	Gregory, Sarah A. (Howell)	87y	W	8 SEP 1920	Westm. Co. VA	Congressional
15118	Gremes, Allen T.	29y	C	6 OCT 1918	Camp Meade MD	Mathias VA
08315	Grenleaf, Charles Ravenscroft	73y	W	2 SEP 1911	San Jose CA	Arlington
02462	Grenling, Charles	62y	W	2 JUN 1898	Great Falls MD	Prospect Hill
08002	Grenling, Herman H., s/o Carl	36y	W	11 MAR 1911	Great Falls VA	Cremated
07740	Gresom, Frances	67y	C	11 SEP 1910	Delaware Co. PA	Harmony
08832	Greve, Otto C.J.	47y	W	11 SEP 1912	Ft. Myer VA	Congressional
13994	Grey, William	30y	C	11 FEB 1917	Baltimore MD	Woodlawn
13226	Grieshaber, Mary T.	8m	W	1 DEC 1915	Brentwood MD	Mt. Olivet

District of Columbia Foreign Death Records, 1888-1923

No.	Name of Deceased	Age	Race	Death Date	Place of Death	Place of Burial
12212	Griff, Rose	39y	W	6 FEB 1914	Ardmore MD	Woodlawn
16410	Griffin, Dollie	35y	C	25 MAR 1920	Philadelphia PA	Harmony
03090	Griffin, Elizabeth	79y	W	7 FEB 1900	Hyattsville	Congressional
04779	Griffin, Frank A.	9y	C	3 JUL 1904	Columbia Pike VA	Harmony
18217	Griffin, George M.	62y	W	20 DEC 1922	Kensington MD	Oak Hill
12677	Griffin, Hugh F.	50y	W	26 DEC 1914	Shamokin PA	Holyrood
12791	Griffin, Maggie Bell	28y	C	3 MAR 1915	Abington MD	Payne's
04634	Griffin, Margaret Mitchell	40y	W	14 MAR 1904	New York NY	Rock Creek
04674	Griffin, Sarah E.	62y	W	14 APR 1904	Atlantic City NJ	Congressional
00142	Griffith, Alice G.	20y	W	29 AUG 1889	Round Hill VA	Glenwood
01499½	Griffith, Anna Viola	13d	W	17 SEP 1894	Pr. Geo. Co. MD	Congressional
16441	Griffith, Annie E.	75y	W	17 APR 1920	Baltimore MD	Congressional
06084	Griffith, Bertha M.	26y	W	28 MAY 1907	Allegheny PA	Congressional
04924	Griffith, Celia E.	55y	W	17 OCT 1904	Baltimore MD	Oak Hill
12179	Griffith, Charles T.	77y	W	21 JAN 1914	Round Hill VA	Glenwood
18218	Griffith, Ella M.	70y	W	20 DEC 1922	New York NY	Mt. Olivet
02597	Griffith, Frank R.	21y	W	7 SEP 1898	Montauk NY	Arlington
06602	Griffith, Harriet Powell	31y	W	22 JUN 1908	Centreville PA	Rock Creek
05444	Griffith, John F.	29y	W	8 JUN 1905	Catonsville MD	Holyrood
13207	Griffith, Katharine A.	32y	W	14 NOV 1915	Harrisburg PA	Prospect Hill
07017	Griffith, Martha A.	81y	W	7 MAY 1909	Baltimore Co. MD	Congressional
01986	Griffith, Mildred T.	5y	W	3 JUL 1896	Chevy Chase MD	Mt. Olivet
01149	Griffith, Robert K.	34y	W	29 DEC 1892	Philadelphia PA	Oak Hill
14654	Griffith, Robert Ridgley	21y	W	16 FEB 1918	Norfolk VA	Arlington VA
06005	Griffith, Walter Scott	60y	W	2 APR 1907	Fairfax Co. VA	Hagerstown MD
17563	Griffith, William R.	69y	W	1 DEC 1921	Laytonsville MD	Rock Creek
07273	Grigg, John	42y	W	12 NOV 1909	Philadelphia PA	Alexandria VA
08476	Grigsby, Hart Preston	52y	W	17 JAN 1912	Kensington MD	Lexington KY
05934	Grigsby, Robert E.L.	41y	W	8 FEB 1907	Baltimore MD	Congressional
13119	Grimes, Francis J.	64y	W	24 SEP 1915	Brooklyn NY	Holyrood
17553	Grimes, Herbert Robert	38y	W	27 NOV 1921	Baltimore MD	Mt. Olivet
04963	Grimes, J. Owen	28y	W	20 NOV 1904	Biltmore NC	St. Barnabas MD
06705	Grimes, John	31y	C	23 AUG 1908	Fayette Co. PA	Arlington
07381	Grimes, John F.	28y	W	15 JAN 1910	Philadelphia PA	Holyrood
17251	Grimes, Louis A., Dr.	81y	W	21 JUN 1921	Concord KY	Rock Creek
01234	Grimes, Martha J.	49y	W	22 SEP 1893	Adamstown MD	Oak Hill
14078	Grimes, Mary John M.	—	W	28 AUG 1916	Concord KY	Rock Creek
09016	Grimes, Robert Sands	1y	W	5 JAN 1913	Catonsville MD	Oak Hill
07835	Grimes, Roy	7m	C	19 NOV 1910	Arlington Jct. VA	Harmony
02667	Grimes, William C.	—	W	—	Charles Co. MD	—
00419	Grimes, William L.	77y	W	10 OCT 1890	Little Rock AR	Congressional
06670	Grimes, William M.	53y	W	3 AUG 1908	Takoma Park MD	Mt. Olivet
12833	Grimke, John	62y	C	21 MAR 1915	New York NY	Harmony
16816	Grimm, Edgar R.	26y	W	21 NOV 1920	New York NY	Oak Hill
00839	Grimm, Frederick, Jr.	2y	W	10 AUG 1892	Lewisburgh PA	Oak Hill
01150	Grimm, Leopold	28y	W	22 NOV 1892	Nauck Sta. VA	Prospect Hill
00611	Grimshaw, Grace M.	2m	C	6 AUG 1891	Brooklyn NY	Graceland
08041	Grinage, Louise	67y	C	29 MAR 1911	Philadelphia PA	Harmony
02950	Grinder, Alice	3h	W	14 SEP 1899	Rosslyn VA	Congressional
02949	Grinder, Dollie Ann	31y	W	14 SEP 1899	Rosslyn VA	Congressional
06422	Grinder, Infant of Richard	SB	W	7 FEB 1908	Grinder VA	Congressional
05364	Grinnell, David	64y	W	15 NOV 1905	Alexandria VA	Soldier's Home
16692	Grinnell, Henry A., Admr.	75y	W	2 SEP 1920	St. Augustine FL	Arlington
07575	Grinnell, Theo. S.	15y	C	15 JUN 1910	Philadelphia PA	Mt. Olivet
16768	Grinstead, Laura M.	45y	W	20 OCT 1920	Norfolk VA	Arlington
16033	Grissom, Albert	22y	W	7 OCT 1919	Stony Run MD	Glenwood
17574	Griswold, George A.	79y	W	8 DEC 1921	New York NY	Rock Creek
06590	Groce, Susan M.	58y	W	13 JUN 1908	Fall River MA	Rock Creek
17548	Groener, Kate	76y	W	25 NOV 1921	Annapolis MD	Prospect Hill

No.	Name of Deceased	Age	Race	Death Date	Place of Death	Place of Burial
01151	Groome, Charles Edwin	1y	W	22 JUN 1892	Charlton Hts. MD	Mt. Olivet
15613	Groot, William C.	65y	W	11 FEB 1919	Philadelphia PA	Oak Hill
12552	Grose, Harriet E.	51y	W	6 OCT 1914	New York NY	Ivy Hill, Alex. VA
04098	Grosh, Almira	69y	W	6 NOV 1902	Fostoria VA	Baltimore MD
18055	Gross, Alice	27y	C	6 SEP 1922	Philadelphia PA	Harmony
11810	Gross, John W.	29y	W	14 MAY 1913	Baltimore MD	Congressional
02686	Gross, Mary	20y	C	27 DEC 1898	Atlantic City NJ	Mt. Olivet
09063	Gross, Mary J.	77y	W	6 FEB 1913	New York NY	Rock Creek
12863	Gross, Matthew	20y	C	1 APR 1915	Atlanta GA	Woodlawn
18006	Gross, Thelma	5m	C	12 AUG 1922	Cedar Hts. MD	Mt. Olivet
16873	Grossell, Bessie B.	41y	W	26 DEC 1920	Somerset MD	Prospect Hill
00840	Grossman, Albert A.	76y	W	7 MAR 1892	New York NY	Rock Creek
05153	Grossmann, Infant of A. & L.	2d	W	4 JUN 1905	Baltimore MD	Prospect Hill
00718	Grossmann, Rosalind	70y	W	24 NOV 1891	New York NY	Rock Creek
08251	Grove, Charles E.	30y	W	10 AUG 1911	Welch OK	Glenwood
05390	Grove, George W.	38y	C	8 DEC 1905	Landover MD	Payne's
11846	Grove, John T.	56y	W	7 JUN 1913	Edgemore DE	Loudon Park
17956	Grover, Estelle (Keene)	21y	W	7 JUL 1922	Los Angeles CA	Arlington
01405	Groves, Joseph A., architect	36y	W	22 JUN 1894	Selma AL	Oak Hill
15760	Grundle, Joseph Maurice	42y	W	29 APR 1919	Salt Lake City UT	Glenwood
12059	Grunwell, Alfred Butterfield	79y	W	23 OCT 1913	Bellevue VA	Arlington
18227	Grunwell, Jane E.	78y	W	25 DEC 1922	Punta Gorda FL	Arlington
03374	Grunwell, Nellie	42y	W	23 DEC 1900	Baltimore MD	Mt. Olivet
18282	Gude, Lehanna W.	69y	W	21 JAN 1923	Chillum MD	Rock Creek
07609	Gude, Obe, d/o Hans	56y	W	1 JUL 1910	W.S. Spgs. WV	Baltimore MD
00841	Gude, William Alexander	11m	W	29 JUL 1892	St. Mary's Co. MD	Congressional
03936	Guest, David P.	35y	W	4 JUL 1902	Philadelphia PA	Rock Creek
02547	Guffin, Charles	25y	W	4 AUG 1898	Camp Thomas TN	Arlington
01712	Guilford, Alice G.	42y	W	15 OCT 1895	St. Elmo VA	Glenwood
03415	Guilford, Eugene F.	50y	W	10 FEB 1901	Yonkers NY	Glenwood
13580	Guilford, Nathan Lewis	44y	W	30 JUN 1916	Columbus OH	Glenwood
14610	Guiliam, James	31y	W	31 JAN 1918	Philadelphia PA	Mt. Olivet
04433	Guiney, Michael F.	26y	W	2 SEP 1903	Baltimore MD	Mt. Olivet
05880	Guista, Joseph	33y	W	25 DEC 1906	Albuquerque NM	Oak Hill
17626	Guista, Margaret R.	80y	W	12 JAN 1922	Hyattsville MD	Mt. Olivet
02944	Gulick, George	40y	W	11 SEP 1899	Montclair NJ	Oak Hill
04671	Gulick, Infant of John Henry	SB	W	23 FEB 1904	Pittsfield MA	Oak Hill
04670	Gulick, Madeline R. (Fisher)	31y	W	23 FEB 1904	Pittsfield MA	Oak Hill
14038	Gulick, Mary K.	67y	W	20 MAR 1917	Takoma Park MD	Congressional
06504	Gullick, Mary E.	45y	W	10 APR 1908	Tryon NC	Oak Hill
07818	Gunn, Sarah	36y	C	6 NOV 1910	Westfield NJ	Harmony
14824	Gunnell, Fanny Baltzer	65y	W	18 MAY 1918	Falls Church VA	Oak Hill
08896	Gunnell, George W.	66y	W	18 OCT 1912	Falls Church VA	Oak Hill
05933	Gunnell, James Samuel, Dr.	77y	W	9 FEB 1907	Bush Hill VA	Oak Hill
06081	Gunnerman, Mary F.	40y	W	16 MAY 1907	Fairfax Co. VA	St. Mary's
03183	Gunther, Sophia H.	26y	W	11 MAY 1900	Rosslyn VA	Prospect Hill
05605	Gunto, Franklin	7m	W	25 JUN 1906	Brentwood MD	Rock Creek
12758	Gurley, William B.	71y	W	10 FEB 1915	Germantown PA	Oak Hill
04760	Gustafson, Augustus	33y	W	13 JUN 1904	Tuscarora MD	Congressional
16514	Gustin, G. Ausley	51y	W	31 MAY 1920	Baltimore MD	Rock Creek
08502	Guthrie, Sophia W.	81y	W	3 FEB 1912	Chevy Chase MD	Oak Hill
05652	Guverman, William Leonard	9m	W	24 JUL 1906	Glen Echo MD	Mt. Olivet
03996	Guy, Clara	7m	W	23 AUG 1902	Mechanicsbg. PA	Glenwood
00009	Guy, John	21d	W	1 JAN 1889	VA	Glenwood
04378	Guy, Precilla	19y	W	7 JUL 1903	Shenandoah PA	Glenwood
03491	Guy, Rachel	5m	W	27 APR 1901	Sch. Co. PA	Glenwood
03504	Guzman, Horatio	49y	W	23 APR 1901	Washington DC	New York NY
12764	Gwindon, Wilfred	43y	W	20 FEB 1899	Bay City MI	Mt. Olivet
07123	Gwynn, Ella P.	49y	W	21 JUL 1909	Pittsburgh PA	Mt. Olivet

District of Columbia Foreign Death Records, 1888-1923

No.	Name of Deceased	Age	Race	Death Date	Place of Death	Place of Burial
14292	Gwynn, Raphael	61y	W	12 AUG 1917	Pittsburgh PA	Mt. Olivet

District of Columbia Foreign Death Records, 1888-1923

No.	Name of Deceased	Age	Race	Death Date	Place of Death	Place of Burial
H						
14678	Haag, Alfred Hoover	7y	W	8 MAR 1918	Kecutan VA	Rock Creek
05569	Haas, Elmira M.	25y	W	5 MAY 1906	Philadelphia PA	Congressional
06322	Haas, Helena K.	41y	W	23 NOV 1907	Mt. Ranier MD	St. Mary's
04188	Haas, Lottie Elizabeth	27y	W	8 JAN 1903	San Francisco CA	Oak Hill
07388	Haas, Wills de	92y	W	24 JAN 1910	Pittsburgh PA	Glenwood
13435	Haber, Mary C.	53y	W	29 MAR 1916	Hyattsville MD	Mt. Olivet
03915	Habercom, Louis W.	68y	W	12 JUN 1902	Berkeley Sp. WV	Cremated
07469	Hack, Earl R.	24y	W	13 MAR 1910	Brunswick MD	Rock Creek
14066	Hackett, Rose	37y	W	29 MAR 1917	New York NY	Mt. Olivet
15962	Hackley, William	41y	C	23 AUG 1919	Philadelphia PA	Woodlawn
07377	Hackney, Susan S.	89y	W	18 JAN 1910	Moorefield WV	Rock Creek
15140	Hadad, Pete	25y	W	OCT 1918	Camp Hump. VA	Glenwood
06756	Hadaway, John	56y	W	4 OCT 1908	Baltimore MD	Congressional
13923	Hadaway, Mary	44y	W	11 JAN 1917	Baltimore MD	Congressional
05764	Haddaway, John Q.A.	50y	W	5 JUN 1878	New York NY	Rock Creek
16827	Hadden, James	85y	W	25 NOV 1920	Capitol Hts. MD	Glenwood
06571	Haddex, Nancy E.	60y	W	31 MAY 1908	Takoma Park MD	Grafton WV
00955	Hadfield, Paul	1m	W	1 JUL 1893	Baltimore MD	Mt. Olivet
16985	Hadley, Lydia E.	85y	W	17 FEB 1921	Falls Church VA	Glenwood
04696	Haffer, Louise	45y	W	1 MAY 1904	Tuxedo MD	St. Mary's
14829	Haga, Claud H.	15y	W	19 MAY 1918	Panman MD	Glenwood
12185	Hagan, Thomas Patrick	31y	W	25 JAN 1914	Big Stone Gap VA	Mt. Olivet
07986	Hagar, Florence May	1y	W	25 FEB 1911	Wilmington DE	Congressional
00276	Hagemeyer, Amelia D.	31y	W	28 JAN 1890	Baltimore MD	Prospect Hill
16535	Hagen, Ida Barnes, d/o G.W.	51y	W	13 JUN 1920	Elrama PA	Congressional
01713	Hagner, Sarah Ann	64y	W	13 JUN 1895	Virginia Bea. VA	Oak Hill
13688	Hahn, Francis G.	35y	W	31 AUG 1916	Wappinger NY	Cremated
07468	Hahn, Mary F.	32y	W	14 MAR 1910	Wash. Grove MD	Mt. Olivet
08668	Hahn, William	58y	W	12 JUN 1912	Atlantic City NJ	Wash. Hebrew
04302	Haight, A.W.	35y	W	1 JUN 1903	New Martinsville	Rock Creek
05984	Haight, Henry	81y	W	16 MAR 1907	Linden MD	Rock Creek
14106	Haight, William G.	35y	W	26 APR 1917	Takoma Park MD	Glenwood
04198	Hailer, Catherine	38y	W	29 MAR 1903	Baltimore MD	Prospect Hill
02782	Hain, John G.	70y	W	18 MAR 1899	Philadelphia PA	Prospect Hill
08614	Haines, Anna A.	61y	W	28 APR 1912	Takoma Park MD	Cremated
16788	Haines, Catherine Elvia	4y	W	2 NOV 1920	Chevy Chase MD	Cremated
02786	Haines, Charles Augustis	59y	W	28 MAR 1899	Danville VA	New York NY
16743	Haines, George Jackson	86y	W	6 OCT 1920	Accotink VA	Congressional
08110	Haines, John Taylor	47y	W	11 MAY 1911	San Antonio TX	Arlington
01559	Haines, Mary Edward	51y	W	10 FEB 1895	Accotink VA	Congressional
04756	Haines, Susie F.	46y	C	6 JUN 1904	Baltimore MD	Harmony
17323	Hainsworth, Charles George	55y	W	23 JUL 1921	New York NY	Glenwood
11897	Hainsworth, Rosette	73y	W	15 JUL 1913	Jersey City NJ	Glenwood
18357	Haislup, Wilton C.	78y	W	17 FEB 1923	Arlington Co. VA	Glenwood
06744	Halderman, John A.	75y	W	21 SEP 1908	Atlantic City NJ	Arlington
16570	Hale, Eugene	14y	W	30 JUN 1920	Concord NH	Rock Creek
04524	Hale, Madge	40y	W	24 NOV 1903	Brentmar MD	Marietta OH
18126	Haley, Katherine	65y	W	24 OCT 1922	Silver Spring MD	Mt. Olivet
18050	Haley, Lola C.	72y	W	4 SEP 1922	Atlantic City NJ	Oak Hill
12137	Halfpap, Augusta	66y	W	23 DEC 1913	Capitol Hts. MD	Prospect Hill
06432	Haliday, Sarah J.	63y	W	12 FEB 1908	San Antonio TX	Glenwood
04254	Hall, Allie	2m	C	14 MAY 1903	Rosslyn VA	Baptist
17261	Hall, Anna M.	76y	W	25 JUN 1921	Lower Merion PA	Rock Creek
06101	Hall, Charles	67y	C	7 JUN 1907	Newton Hook NY	Harmony
03950	Hall, Charles C.	15y	W	20 JUL 1902	St. Elmo VA	Congressional
17627	Hall, Charles E.	55y	W	11 JAN 1922	Baltimore MD	Wallingford CN
04457	Hall, Clifford M., Mrs.	22y	W	27 FEB 1902	Cairo, Egypt	Rock Creek
18414	Hall, Elexener	77y	W	13 MAR 1923	Mt. Ranier MD	Congressional

District of Columbia Foreign Death Records, 1888-1923

No.	Name of Deceased	Age	Race	Death Date	Place of Death	Place of Burial
14309	Hall, Francis R.	49y	W	22 AUG 1917	Baltimore MD	Congressional
09030	Hall, Francis R.	19y	W	12 JAN 1913	Denver CO	Mt. Olivet
01472	Hall, Frank	9m	C	25 AUG 1894	Brandy Sta. MD	Harmony
04809	Hall, Fred A.	48y	W	19 JUL 1904	Mackinac Is. MI	Glenwood
07662	Hall, George J.	2y	W	31 JUL 1910	Hyattsville MD	Mt. Olivet
05763	Hall, George W.	28y	C	6 OCT 1906	New York NY	Harmony
14037	Hall, Harry	23y	C	14 MAR 1917	Philadelphia PA	Moore's
06806	Hall, Ida May	53y	W	6 NOV 1908	Newburgh NY	Congressional
02700	Hall, Irene Preble	4y	W	10 JAN 1899	New York NY	Arlington VA
12927	Hall, Isabella	71y	W	18 MAY 1915	Alexandria VA	Congressional
13872	Hall, J.M., Dr.	61y	C	17 DEC 1916	Richmond VA	Harmony[1]
04520½	Hall, James	81y	W	24 NOV 1903	Hampton VA	Glenwood
16469	Hall, John	61y	C	2 MAY 1920	PA	Harmony
14250	Hall, John	57y	C	24 JUL 1917	Philadelphia PA	Payne's
02308	Hall, John T., farmer	76y	W	29 OCT 1897	Laurel MD	Glenwood
02061	Hall, Josie	1y	C	16 OCT 1896	Rosslyn VA	Baptist
16352	Hall, Mabel Alexenia	27y	W	29 FEB 1920	Clarendon VA	Glenwood
13252	Hall, Margaret A.	42y	W	18 DEC 1915	Union NJ	Mt. Olivet
11950	Hall, Margaret V.	7m	W	10 AUG 1913	Brown's Sta. MD	Norfolk VA
15412	Hall, Marguerite	4y	W	7 DEC 1918	Washington DC	Glenwood
04607	Hall, Martha Ellsworth	56y	W	21 FEB 1904	Portsmouth VA	Arlington
06137	Hall, Mary A.	62y	W	15 JUL 1907	New York NY	Congressional
04449	Hall, Mary C.	50y	W	11 SEP 1903	Atlantic City NJ	Harmony
12085	Hall, Mary Jane	70y	C	11 NOV 1913	Oxon Hill MD	Moore's
12814	Hall, Mary Josephine	23y	C	13 MAR 1915	Seat Pleasant MD	Mt. Olivet
17094	Hall, Mary L.	85y	W	7 APR 1921	Baltimore MD	Oak Hill
01912	Hall, Mary P.	54y	C	14 APR 1896	New York NY	Harmony
00547	Hall, Maud G.	29y	W	20 MAY 1891	Bladensburg MD	Mt. Olivet
03075	Hall, Maurice R.	7y	C	22 JAN 1900	Rosslyn VA	Baptist
02251	Hall, Melissa Frances	1y	C	12 AUG 1897	Pr. Geo. Co. MD	Woodlawn
07935	Hall, Merle Euola	8y	W	22 JAN 1911	Chillum MD	Congressional
13469	Hall, Nellie	28y	C	20 APR 1916	PA	Harmony
12803	Hall, Ruth A.	10m	C	10 MAR 1915	Seat Pleasant MD	Mt. Olivet
08808	Hall, Sallie	18y	C	AUG 1875	Hyattsville MD	Harmony
08584	Hall, Townley	60y	C	3 APR 1912	Oxon Hill MD	Moore's
05430	Hall, Vesta	19y	C	11th JAN 1906	Philadelphia PA	Moore's
04632	Hall, William C.	62y	W	3 FEB 1904	New Castle PA	Congressional
08263	Hall, William G.	69y	C	18 AUG 1911	Atlantic City NJ	Harmony
01714	Halleck, Millard Tillmon, atty.	38y	W	5 JUN 1895	Takoma Park MD	Rock Creek
12478	Haller, Grace	14d	W	9 AUG 1914	Capitol Hts. MD	Congressional
02463	Haller, Julia E.	18y	W	27 MAY 1898	Tuxedo MD	Glenwood
1045	Hallett, Fanny	54y	W	2 JAN 1893	Rome, Italy	Oak Hill
14357	Halliday, Laura Stow	70y	W	5 SEP 1917	Cheyenne WY	Arlington
03211	Hallinan, James J.	28y	W	11 APR 1900	Manila, P.I.	Mt. Olivet
15698	Hallinberger, Hellen Frances	11m	W	29 MAR 1919	Capitol Hts. MD	Congressional
01991	Hallon, Frederick M.	6d	W	17 JUL 1896	Baltimore MD	Congressional
03846	Halloran, James, Capt.	58y	W	12 APR 1902	Ft. Niobrara NE	Arlington
12354	Halloway, Harold P.	45y	W	6 MAY 1914	Galveston TX	Glenwood
14058	Hallyburton, James Gaul	25y	W	26 MAR 1917	At Sea	Biltmore NC
00479	Halsted, Kate C.	30y	W	10 FEB 1891	Brookline MA	Oak Hill
05418	Ham, Judith C.	8m	W	2 JAN 1906	Philadelphia PA	Mt. Olivet
04845	Hamacher, Walter D.	26y	W	14 AUG 1904	Colonial Bea. VA	Glenwood
16609	Hamamoto, Taidie	c.26y	J	16 JUL 1920	Newport News VA	Cremated
17063	Hambright, Mildred McElwain	58y	W	26 MAR 1921	Takoma Park MD	E. Liberty PA
07207	Hamerdenger, Robert E.	32y	W	21 SEP 1909	Philadelphia PA	Congressional
07900	Hamersly, Lewis Randolph	63y	W	31 DEC 1910	Annapolis MD	Oak Hill
12844	Hamil, Reginald J.E.	36y	W	28 MAR 1915	Riverdale MD	Mt. Olivet

[1] Disinterment permit on 23 JUL 1959 for removal to Lincoln Memorial Cemetery, Suitland MD.

No.	Name of Deceased	Age	Race	Death Date	Place of Death	Place of Burial
06641	Hamill, Terence Joseph	35y	W	1 JUL 1908	San Juan, P.R.	Arlington
08705	Hamilton, Abbie S. (Browning)	66y	W	4 JUL 1912	Lynn MA	Arlington
03174	Hamilton, Elizabeth	65y	C	28 APR 1900	Steelton PA	Harmony
05909	Hamilton, Frank	22y	C	20 JAN 1907	Philadelphia PA	Harmony
07105	Hamilton, George H.	4y	W	11 JUL 1909	Huntsville MD	Payne's
17924	Hamilton, George W., Capt.	29y	W	26 JUN 1922	Gettysburg PA	Arlington
14768	Hamilton, Ida M.	58y	W	23 APR 1918	Groveland NY	Rock Creek
03989	Hamilton, J.F., Rev.	44y	C	24 AUG 1902	Warrenton VA	Harmony
01715	Hamilton, John	32y	W	31 AUG 1895	Philadelphia PA	Congressional
02752	Hamilton, John B.	51y	W	24 DEC 1898	Elgin IL	Arlington
08634	Hamilton, Louise	35y	W	16 MAY 1912	Arlington VA	Congressional
05809	Hamilton, Mary	36y	C	7 NOV 1906	Stormville NY	Harmony
14962	Hamilton, Mary C.	69y	W	8 AUG 1918	Chevy Chase MD	Rock Creek
18184	Hamilton, Mary E.	80y	W	26 NOV 1922	Brentwood MD	Mt. Olivet
14218	Hamilton, William	39y	C	4 JUL 1917	Philadelphia PA	Harmony
14220	Hamilton, William M.	51y	W	9 JUL 1917	Hyattsville MD	Rock Creek
07434	Hamlet, Byron D.	33y	W	24 FEB 1910	Landover MD	Cremated
13776	Hamlin, Frances Bacon	70y	W	23 OCT 1916	New York NY	Rock Creek
06036	Hamlin, Junius S., Rev.	59y	W	17 APR 1907	New York NY	Rock Creek
16874	Hamlink, Derrick F.	77y	W	22 DEC 1920	Chicago IL	Oak Hill
04317	Hamlink, Ellen	59y	W	7 JUN 1903	Chicago IL	Oak Hill
16917	Hamm, Sarah	65y	W	10 JAN 1921	Falls Church VA	Moore's
05558	Hammer, John H.	19y	W	30 APR 1906	Gaithersburg MD	Prospect Hill
12509	Hammer, John J.	35y	W	1 SEP 1914	Railroad	Mt. Olivet
17648	Hammer, Rosa C.	59y	W	JAN 1922	Glen Echo MD	Kansas City MO
14431	Hammerli, John R.	9y	W	29 OCT 1917	Chevy Chase MD	Prospect Hill
17038	Hammersly, Julia A.	67y	W	10 MAR 1921	Salisbury MD	Rock Creek
18084	Hammett, Charles A.	49y	W	22 SEP 1922	Cheboygan MI	Ft. Lincoln
16102	Hammett, Charles N.	62y	W	17 NOV 1919	Capitol Hts. MD	Mt. Olivet
13510	Hammond, Anna Stone	54y	W	18 MAY 1916	Baltimore MD	Glenwood
04220	Hammond, Bertha L.	22y	W	6 MAR 1903	Cumberland MD	Rock Creek
04876	Hammond, Charles	48y	W	5 SEP 1904	Atlantic City NJ	Glenwood
08500	Hammond, Daisy Beall	35y	W	31 JAN 1912	Cumberland MD	Rock Creek
02374	Hammond, Mary C.	53y	W	3 JAN 1898	San Francisco CA	Oak Hill
01046	Hammond, Minnie O.	47y	W	1 APR 1893	Cumberland MD	Rock Creek
14543	Hammond, William A.	54y	W	2 JAN 1918	Baltimore MD	Glenwood
00023	Hammond, William T.	94y	W	22 FEB 1889	Falls Church VA	Hampstead MD
07020	Hamner, Marie Barbra	47y	W	8 MAY 1909	Philadelphia PA	Prospect Hill
17279	Hamoney, John E.	70y	C	30 JUN 1921	Baltimore MD	Holyrood
16850	Hamrick, Barbra	24y	W	DEC 1920	Shawnee KS	Glenwood
16926	Hancock, Augusta S.	78y	W	17 JAN 1921	Amityville NY	Oak Hill
08503	Hancock, Marcia M.	35y	—	1 FEB 1912	Newcastle NH	—
13531	Hand, Harry H.	57y	W	2 JUN 1916	Cherrydale VA	Mt. Olivet
03651	Handiboe, John	25y	W	17 SEP 1901	Memphis TN	Mt. Olivet
09061	Handlen, Ellen	74y	W	6 FEB 1913	Fairmont Hts. MD	Mt. Olivet
07408	Handler, Frank A., s/o Frank	63y	W	6 FEB 1910	Vienna VA	Holyrood
05705	Handley, Joseph A.	71y	W	23 AUG 1906	Bath NY	Glenwood
16057	Handley, William White	47y	W	27 SEP 1919	Lima, Peru	Glenwood
17028	Handlon, Eva Izetta	55y	W	8 MAR 1921	Clarendon VA	Glenwood
14100	Handy, Barbara A.	32y	W	21 APR 1917	Hyattsville MD	Mt. Olivet
14666	Handy, Charles W.	66y	W	3 MAR 1918	Hyattsville MD	Mt. Olivet
00143	Handy, Charles W., Jr.	11m	W	3 AUG 1889	Oakland MD	Mt. Olivet
08470	Handy, Frederick A.G., s/o I.	70y	W	12 JAN 1912	Barcroft VA	Oak Hill
03784	Handy, Isobel	79y	W	9 FEB 1902	Hyattsville MD	Congressional
05640	Handy, Rachel	76y	C	9 JUL 1906	Linden MD	Harmony
15606	Handy, Robert Breckenridge	3y	W	20 OCT 1918	San Diego CA	Congressional
00719	Haneke, Mary E.	17y	W	27 OCT 1891	Marlboro NJ	Holyrood
04752	Hanford, Francis	—	W	5 JUN 1904	Arlington VA	Rock Creek
17837	Hanford, Hopkins J.	62y	W	4 MAY 1922	Milwaukee WI	Rock Creek

District of Columbia Foreign Death Records, 1888-1923

No.	Name of Deceased	Age	Race	Death Date	Place of Death	Place of Burial
18272	Hanford, Mamie (O'Conner)	58y	W	14 JAN 1923	Kenosha WI	Rock Creek
15832	Hanger, James Edward	77y	W	15 JUN 1919	Takoma MD	Glenwood
15288	Hanger, Jeanan Francis	1y	W	26 OCT 1918	Berwyn MD	Glenwood
02376	Hanley, John J.	16m	W	8 FEB 1898	Ft. Defiance NM	Mt. Olivet
15550	Hanlon, Timothy	35y	W	10 JAN 1919	Dennison OH	Mt. Olivet
03521	Hanly, Edmund	71y	W	23 MAY 1901	Roseville NJ	Oak Hill
13647	Hann, Elmar, s/o F.E.	15y	W	7 AUG 1916	Norfolk VA	Glenwood
12425	Hanna, Ruth D.	6y	W	6 JUL 1914	Bowie MD	Congressional
00548	Hannegan, Edward A.	21y	W	12 JUN 1891	Ft. Monroe VA	Mt. Olivet
05871	Hanor, Erie Hall	45y	W	25 DEC 1906	Lafayette IN	Congressional
16117	Hanrahan, Florence E.	21y	W	21 NOV 1919	Cherrydale VA	Mt. Olivet
05638	Hanshew, Bessie	4m	W	11 JUL 1906	Germantown MD	Oak Hill
05670	Hanshew, Edward W.	1y	W	2 AUG 1906	Germantown MD	Oak Hill
03701	Hanson, George	44y	C	8 NOV 1901	Philadelphia PA	Harmony
17331	Hanson, Harry	17y	W	28 JUL 1921	Mt. Vernon VA	Glenwood
06768	Hanson, Lars Gustav	42y	W	10 OCT 1908	Newark NJ	Methodist
01561	Hanson, Lucy Ann	98y	C	29 JAN 1895	Alexandria VA	Harmony
01386	Hanson, Maria	29y	W	2 MAY 1894	Chevy Chase MD	Tenallytown
00612	Hanson, Mountjoy Barry	25y	W	9 OCT 1891	Dansville NY	Congressional
05771	Hanson, Raymond H.	23y	W	13 OCT 1906	Wilmington DE	Congressional
18263	Happersett, Cornelia W.	46y	W	5 JAN 1923	Lock Haven PA	Arlington
01236	Happy, Alida Berryhill	—	W	17 SEP 1893	Philadelphia PA	Rock Creek
04116	Harban, Catherine	21y	W	1869	Dayton MD	Glenwood
04119	Harban, James	78y	W	NOV 1890	Dayton MD	Glenwood
13306	Harbaugh, Edgar G.	65y	W	17 JAN 1916	Silver Spring MD	Glenwood
15943	Harbin, George F.	80y	W	21 AUG 1919	Baltimore MD	Mt. Olivet[1]
14503	Hardell, John, s/o Robert C.	28y	W	10 DEC 1917	Newark NJ	Glenwood
06406	Hardenburg, J.F.	70y	W	25 JAN 1908	Jacksonville FL	Arlington
15276	Hardesty, Eustica B.	20y	W	22 OCT 1918	Norbeck MD	Rock Creek
00613	Hardesty, Thomas	47y	C	16 JUL 1891	Bethesda MD	Chappell's Farm
00480	Harding, Ann E.	88y	W	6 MAR 1891	Harrisonburg VA	Oak Hill
01865	Harding, Catherine	81y	W	28 JAN 1896	Stafford Co. VA	Glenwood
15920	Harding, Frank	57y	W	4 AUG 1919	New York NY	Methodist
05470	Harding, Frank	56y	W	16 FEB 1906	Woodside MD	Rock Creek
12142	Harding, Frank R.	49y	W	28 DEC 1913	Jacksonville FL	Glenwood
01305	Harding, Josiah	76y	W	25 JAN 1894	Woodside MD	Rock Creek
08639	Harding, Mary Virginia	87y	W	18 MAY 1912	Woodside MD	Rock Creek
03018	Hardisty, William L.	22y	W	28 NOV 1899	Baltimore MD	Glenwood
05953	Hardon, Annie	63y	W	22 FEB 1907	Silver Spring MD	Rock Creek
18240	Hardt, Antone	83y	W	3 JAN 1923	Takoma Park MD	Wellsboro PA
04447	Hardy, Catherine	81y	W	1861	Dayton MD	Glenwood
08899	Hardy, Susan M. (Oxley)	87y	W	22 OCT 1912	Martinsburg MD	Glenwood
02062	Hardy, William	76y	W	2 OCT 1896	Hampton VA	Congressional
08845	Hardy, William T.	37y	C	17 SEP 1912	Danville VA	Harmony
06725	Hargrove, J. Harry	35y	C	11 SEP 1908	Gordonsville VA	Zanesville OH
13190	Hargrove, John E.	1d	C	7 NOV 1915	Arlington VA	Harmony
15429	Harkins, Minnie Belle	48y	W	12 DEC 1918	Washington DC	Glenwood[2]
08288	Harlan, Dorris Lucile	10d	W	3 SEP 1911	Takoma Park MD	Rock Creek
18594	Harlan, Ralph W.	51y	W	9 JUN 1923	Philadelphia PA	Rock Creek
12729	Harlebaus, George W.	48y	W	22 JAN 1915	New York NY	Prospect Hill
07327	Harlow, George P.	70y	W	11 NOV 1909	Worcester MA	Glenwood
16154	Harman, Arline Newell Engart	30y	W	31 DEC 1918	Lynchburg VA	Rock Creek
15781	Harmon, John O.	73y	W	15 MAY 1919	Sligo MD	Glenwood
08628	Harmon, Matilda	63y	W	8 MAY 1912	Anne Arundel Co.	Congressional
12014	Harmon, Phillip	64y	W	25 SEP 1913	Takoma Park MD	Carlisle PA
02939	Harmon, Sarah L.	73y	W	5 SEP 1899	Atlantic City NJ	Rock Creek

[1] Certificate number written is 19543.
[2] Disinterment date from Cedar Hill Cemetery in Md., once resided at 706 N St., N.W., Washington DC.

No.	Name of Deceased	Age	Race	Death Date	Place of Death	Place of Burial
13930	Harne, Mary Jane	71y	W	14 JAN 1917	Philadelphia PA	Congressional
01453	Harnedy, Timothy	34y	W	3 AUG 1894	Brooklyn NY	Holyrood
15599	Harner, Amanda	64y	W	4 FEB 1919	Pittsburgh PA	Congressional
08386	Harner, Roberta	61y	W	7 NOV 1911	Boston MA	Oak Hill
08126	Harney, Helen F.	77y	W	23 MAY 1911	Philadelphia PA	Oak Hill
06284	Harney, Mary Elizabeth	81y	W	22 OCT 1907	Orlando FL	Arlington
13433	Harnisk, Benjamin F.	57y	W	31 MAR 1916	Railroad	Belvidere IL
04480	Harold, James	37y	W	17 OCT 1903	Baltimore MD	Mt. Olivet
18032	Harper, Abraham	63y	W	24 AUG 1922	Baltimore MD	Woodlawn
04706	Harper, Carrie	8y	W	9 MAY 1904	Fairfax Co. VA	Methodist
16078	Harper, Charles E.	34y	W	30 SEP 1919	Philadelphia PA	Mt. Olivet
07074	Harper, Daniel	26y	C	22 JUN 1909	Rosslyn VA	Mt. Zion East
14687	Harper, Edward P.	50y	C	16 MAR 1918	Hampton VA	Harmony
01815	Harper, Etta M.	38y	W	6 DEC 1895	Ballston VA	Oak Hill
08205	Harper, Francis, d/o Henry	7m	C	19 JUL 1911	Rosslyn VA	Mt. Zion East
15861	Harper, Harrison	77y	W	4 JUL 1919	Laurel MD	Leesburg VA
16295	Harper, Infant of John W.	SB	W	c.9 FEB 1920	Rosslyn VA	Rock Creek
06299	Harper, Infant of Robert	SB	W	7 NOV 1907	Riverside VA	Methodist
05739	Harper, Infant of Robert	SB	W	16 SEP 1906	Ft. Hunt VA	Methodist
02254	Harper, Ira R.	7y	W	17 AUG 1897	Ft. Sheridan VA	Tenallytown
01987	Harper, James	45y	C	18 JUN 1896	Philadelphia PA	Smith
01521	Harper, James C.	28y	C	27 OCT 1894	Colo. Spgs. CO	Harmony
02728	Harper, James E.	82y	C	30 JAN 1899	Cabin John MD	Christian
04621	Harper, Lilly M.	18y	C	3 MAR 1904	Cabin John MD	Christian
02872	Harper, Lucy	53y	C	10 JUL 1899	Paw Paw WV	Payne's
04702	Harper, Mabel	13y	W	9 MAY 1904	Alexandria VA	Methodist
15279	Harper, Neal Anthony, Jr.	1h	W	23 OCT 1918	Takoma Park MD	Rock Creek
04701	Harper, Robert	2y	W	9 MAY 1904	Fairfax Co. VA	Methodist
16062	Harper, Walter A.	36y	W	18 OCT 1919	New York NY	Rock Creek
12991	Harper, William	35y	C	30 JUN 1915	Atlanta GA	Moore's
17386	Harper, William M.	6y	W	3 SEP 1921	Irvington VA	Congressional
17142	Harried, Frances	1y	C	4 MAY 1921	Cedar Hts. MD	Payne's
14464	Harrigan, Ella F.	53y	W	16 NOV 1917	Baltimore MD	Mt. Olivet
14506	Harrigan, Ethel	11y	W	14 DEC 1917	Washington DC	Mt. Olivet
01813	Harrigan, John L.	43y	W	24 OCT 1895	Baltimore MD	Mt. Olivet
01153	Harrington, Daniel	75y	W	6 NOV 1892	Wilmington DE	Mt. Olivet
05516	Harrington, Francis Henry	61y	W	1 APR 1906	New Orleans LA	Oak Hill
01155	Harrington, George	76y	W	5 DEC 1892	At Sea	Oak Hill
03024	Harrington, John F.	25y	W	1 DEC 1899	Haywood NC	Oak Hill
00356	Harrington, Sophia M.	47y	W	9 JUL 1890	Pr. Geo. Co. MD	Congressional
02202	Harrington, W.C.	55y	W	14 MAR 1897	Stoneg. TN	Cremated
15091	Harris, Aloysius	22y	C	29 SEP 1918	Camp Lee VA	Arlington
12804	Harris, Annie S.	43y	W	9 MAR 1915	Capitol Hts. MD	Congressional
16242	Harris, Benjamin	27y	C	24 JAN 1920	Philadelphia PA	Mt. Zion East
18354	Harris, Bessie	50y	C	14 FEB 1923	Atlantic City NJ	Union Baptist
04553	Harris, Carrie Jenkins	56y	W	27 DEC 1903	Rockville MD	Williamsboro NC
06061	Harris, Charles W.	68y	W	9 MAY 1907	Capitol Hts. MD	Congressional
12120	Harris, Edward Killian	78y	W	9 DEC 1913	Takoma Park MD	Boston MA
06492	Harris, Elizabeth	74y	W	4 APR 1908	Capitol Hts. MD	Congressional
18573	Harris, Ellen Elizabeth	c.70y	W	1 JUN 1923	Takoma Park MD	Rock Creek
05423	Harris, Fred	21y	C	6 JAN 1906	New Bruns. NJ	Mt. Zion West
15736	Harris, Fred J.	37y	W	15 DEC 1918	Plano FL	Rock Creek
08083	Harris, George, a.k.a.	65y	W	14 MAR 1911	Norfolk VA	Mt. Olivet[1]
02434	Harris, George H.	28y	C	11 APR 1898	Pittsburgh PA	Payne's
06605	Harris, Gwynn	75y	W	22 JUN 1908	Hyattsville MD	Mt. Olivet
13437	Harris, Helen	26y	C	29 MAR 1916	Philadelphia PA	Mt. Zion West

[1] Note in the file that the "remains of one George Harris whose remains were interred in this city, in Elmwood Cemetery, on March 14th, 1911, were in fact the remains of Joseph E. Iardella."

District of Columbia Foreign Death Records, 1888-1923

No.	Name of Deceased	Age	Race	Death Date	Place of Death	Place of Burial
03801	Harris, Henry S.	2m	C	22 FEB 1902	Kings Hwy. LI	Harmony
05116	Harris, Ida E.	31y	C	5 MAY 1905	New York NY	Harmony
14810	Harris, Ida Elizabeth	57y	W	11 MAY 1918	Norfolk VA	Rock Creek
16225	Harris, Jane	76y	C	16 JAN 1920	Philadelphia PA	Harmony
02746	Harris, John F., Rev.	34y	W	16 FEB 1899	Danville VA	Oak Hill
15724	Harris, Joseph F.	9m	W	14 APR 1919	Capitol Hts. MD	Mt. Olivet
06382	Harris, Leanna	48y	C	9 JAN 1908	Long Branch NJ	Harmony
05574	Harris, Loretta	2y	C	11 MAY 1906	Baltimore MD	Woodlawn
13283	Harris, Mary	42y	C	31 DEC 1915	Media PA	Mt. Zion East
17782	Harris, Mary	65y	C	2 APR 1922	New York NY	Union
18013	Harris, Mary Daisy	36y	C	15 AUG 1922	Rock Spring MD	Woodlawn
05387	Harris, Mary J.	101y	C	25 NOV 1905	New Rochelle NY	Christian
12261	Harris, Merrett W.	47y	W	20 MAR 1914	Baltimore MD	Rock Creek
01869	Harris, Noble	37y	C	6 FEB 1896	Philadelphia PA	Harmony
05520	Harris, Patrick	71y	C	5 APR 1906	Hyattsville MD	Mt. Olivet
12614	Harris, Rosanna	42y	C	11 NOV 1914	Arlington VA	Woodlawn
14992	Harris, Samuel H.	53y	C	23 AUG 1918	Pittsburgh PA	Payne's
16763	Harris, Samuel R.	24y	C	17 OCT 1920	Las Animos CO	Arlington
16380	Harris, Susan A.	83y	W	14 MAR 1920	Hyattsville MD	Mt. Olivet
16025	Harris, Susie	39y	C	4 OCT 1919	Arlington VA	Union
07741	Harris, Thomas Edward	55y	C	11 SEP 1910	Richmond VA	Harmony
03721	Harrison, Beatrice	32y	W	29 NOV 1901	Columbia SC	Cremated
07827	Harrison, Benjamin	39y	C	11 NOV 1910	Philadelphia PA	Mt. Olivet
13581	Harrison, Bertha E.	19y	C	2 JUL 1916	Brightseat MD	Mt. Olivet
01154	Harrison, Carrie	39y	C	13 OCT 1892	Rosslyn VA	Harmony
02760	Harrison, Charles Shirley	56y	W	18 FEB 1899	Brandon VA	Rock Creek
02761	Harrison, Charles Shirley	56y	W	18 FEB 1899	Brandon VA	Rock Creek
01867	Harrison, Daniel C.	50y	W	28 FEB 1896	Allegheny PA	Congressional
12057	Harrison, Ezra B.	5y	W	24 OCT 1913	Takoma Park MD	Rock Creek
02506	Harrison, George B.	54y	W	19 JUL 1898	Cape May NJ	Rock Creek
00549	Harrison, Guy Plumley	16y	W	18 APR 1891	Cedar Hill VA	Oak Hill
03557	Harrison, Hannah	10m	W	30 JUN 1901	Winston NC	Adas Israel
05460	Harrison, Infant of J.	14d	W	5 FEB 1906	Suitland MD	Glenwood
03126	Harrison, James	60y	W	7 MAR 1900	Frenchtown NJ	Glenwood
01717	Harrison, John	c.50y	C	18 FEB 1895	Hyattsville MD	Mt. Olivet
17392	Harrison, John M.	52y	W	8 SEP 1921	Staunton VA	Falls Church VA
07360	Harrison, Luvenia	74y	C	7 JAN 1910	Halls Hill VA	Amherst VA
05923	Harrison, Margaret	17m	W	1 FEB 1907	New York NY	Oak Hill
05803	Harrison, Margaret R.	79y	W	4 NOV 1906	Baltimore MD	Glenwood
14143	Harrison, Marguerite V.	9y	W	17 MAY 1917	Mt. Vernon NY	Oak Hill
02485	Harrison, Mary	12y	W	24 JUL 1898	Waterbury CN	Glenwood
06016	Harrison, Mary E.	3m	C	7 APR 1907	Hyattsville MD	Mt. Olivet
08273	Harrison, May Agnes	16y	W	25 AUG 1911	Brentwood MD	Mt. Olivet
17062	Harrison, Mollie Martin	84y	W	24 MAR 1921	Arlington Co. VA	Oak Hill
01866	Harrison, Peter C.	65y	W	6 MAR 1896	Cabin John MD	Holyrood
00426	Harrison, Phoebe	1y	W	22 OCT 1890	Catonsville MD	Glenwood
15544	Harrison, R. Bruce	46y	W	10 JAN 1919	Dominion Hts. VA	Glenwood
13971	Harrison, Valley	73y	W	1 FEB 1917	Racine OH	Glenwood
07821	Harrison, William Evelyn	33y	W	7 NOV 1910	Waverly MA	Rock Creek
04242	Harriss, Clara	44y	C	11 APR 1903	Alex. Co. VA	Baptist
14621	Harriss, J. Cleveland	33y	W	1 FEB 1918	Rockville MD	Tenallytown M.
15556	Harriss, Lincoln E.	55y	W	14 JAN 1919	Takoma Park MD	DuQuoin IL
02003	Harriss, Mary C.	24y	C	27 MAY 1897	Philadelphia PA	Mt. Olivet
12902	Harriss, Montgomery	37y	W	28 APR 1915	Bethesda MD	Rockville MD
16008	Harrod, Christina	50y	C	21 SEP 1919	Philadelphia PA	Moore's
03591	Harrod, Julius	19y	C	23 JUL 1901	Conduit Rd. MD	Baptist
17796	Harrod, Morris T.	2y	C	13 APR 1922	Huntsville MD	Mt. Olivet
01716	Harrod, William H.	22y	C	14 AUG 1895	Albany NY	Mt. Zion
01868	Harry, Leora M.	11m	W	13 FEB 1896	Chevy Chase MD	Tenallytown

No.	Name of Deceased	Age	Race	Death Date	Place of Death	Place of Burial
01560	Harry, Lillian A.	7m	W	21 NOV 1894	Chevy Chase MD	Tenallytown
15691	Hart, Edward F.	47y	W	23 MAR 1919	New York NY	Rock Creek
07516	Hart, F.W.	38y	W	12 APR 1910	Canal Zone	Wash. Hebrew
02253	Hart, Frederick	38y	W	27 AUG 1897	Philadelphia PA	Rock Creek
13714	Hart, Gilbert T., butcher	56y	C	10 SEP 1916	Cape May NJ	Harmony
12801	Hart, Harriet	57y	W	6 MAR 1915	Philadelphia PA	Payne's
04541	Hart, Infant of James W.	SB	W	19 DEC 1903	Ft. Hunt VA	Rock Creek
06171	Hart, Jennie May, d/o Wm. H.H.	1y	W	8 AUG 1907	Harpers Ferry WV	Harmony
01152	Hart, Joseph S.	76y	W	30 DEC 1892	Ryland PA	Rock Creek
00844	Hart, Josepha	1y	C	18 JUL 18892	Arlington VA	Harmony
00845	Hart, Michael	72y	W	19 APR 1892	—	Congressional
12722	Hart, Morgan Ott	42y	W	17 JAN 1915	Laurel MD	Wheeling WV
17232	Hart, Virginia C.	1y	W	9 JUN 1921	Alamagordo NM	Mt. Olivet
14373	Hartenstine, Annie	60y	W	24 SEP 1917	Baltimore MD	Mt. Olivet
15178	Harter, Gwendolin Rose	8m	W	16 OCT 1918	Takoma Park MD	Rock Creek
14782	Hartgrove, William B.	34y	C	24 APR 1918	Albuquerque NM	Woodlawn
01347	Hartigan, J. French	51y	W	16 FEB 1894	Trieste, Aus.	Arlington
05472	Hartley, James	76y	W	15 FEB 1906	Mt. Ranier MD	Arlington
01047	Hartley, John Billings	9m	W	4 MAR 1893	Mountclair NJ	Oak Hill
02721	Hartley, Joseph W.	33y	W	19 JAN 1899	Philadelphia PA	Rock Creek
15006	Hartley, Lee Bruce, printer	54y	W	5 SEP 1918	Baltimore MD	Glenwood
01306	Hartley, Nellie	43y	W	27 JAN 1894	Chicago IL	Congressional
07145	Hartman, Alfred E., lightning	20y	W	28 JUN 1909	Westm. Co. VA	Rock Creek
07145	Hartman, Alfred E., s/o Edw.	20y	W	28 JUN 1909	Westm. Co. VA	Rock Creek
13815	Hartman, Clarence	42y	W	12 NOV 1916	St. Louis MO	Cremated
07453	Hartnett, Lawrence	68y	W	5 MAR 1910	Philadelphia PA	Mt. Olivet
13922	Hartrick, Edward	72y	W	11 JAN 1917	Baltimore MD	Mt. Olivet
00614	Hartwell, Fleming	30y	C	8 AUG 1891	Findlay OH	Harmony
12140	Harvey, Andrew Robinson	74y	C	28 DEC 1913	Seat Pleasant MD	Payne's
12266	Harvey, Charles W.	83y	W	24 MAR 1914	Mt. Ranier MD	Glenwood
14618	Harvey, Dorothy E.	1y	W	3 FEB 1918	Chevy Chase MD	Rock Creek
15373	Harvey, Eliza	54y	W	23 NOV 1918	Bethesda MD	Prospect Hill
00843	Harvey, George F.	31y	W	30 JUL 1892	Kansas City MO	Glenwood
12914	Harvey, Grace Abbie	4y	W	9 MAY 1886	St. Johnsburg VT	Rock Creek
00842	Harvey, Helen Holman	9m	W	10 AUG 1892	Hamilton VA	Oak Hill
01454	Harvey, John T.	9m	W	5 AUG 1894	Baltimore MD	Mt. Olivet
02067	Harvey, Joseph W.	65y	W	12 NOV 1896	Norfolk VA	Tenallytown
15650	Harvey, Josephine J.	31y	W	1 MAR 1919	Norfolk VA	Mt. Olivet
02603	Harvey, Mary E.	1y	W	7 SEP 1898	Baltimore MD	Mt. Olivet
15152	Harvey, Morgan	28y	W	11 OCT 1918	Camp Meade MD	Mt. Olivet
15045	Harvey, Ruby B.	55y	W	26 SEP 1918	Baltimore MD	Richmond VA
01951	Harvey, Thomas H.	2m	W	12 JUN 1896	Baltimore MD	Mt. Olivet
03674	Harvey, William E.	23y	W	27 JUL 1901	Manila, P.I.	Mt. Olivet
17631	Harvey, William Edwin	50y	W	13 JAN 1922	Takoma Park MD	Arlington
17362	Harwell, Grant	28y	C	12 AUG 1921	Ft. Bayard NM	Arlington
06967	Haskins, Frederick B.	35y	W	1 APR 1909	Baltimore MD	Rock Creek
13561	Haskins, Hannah E.	69y	W	19 JUN 1916	Baltimore MD	Rock Creek
03978	Hasler, Laura	1m	W	8 AUG 1902	Silver Hill MD	Congressional
13761	Hasler, Sarah Jane	61y	W	13 OCT 1916	Mt. Vernon VA	Prospect Hill
00481	Haslup, Susan	63y	W	16 MAR 1891	Laurel MD	Oak Hill
05173	Hassliff, Leon N., teacher	c.60y	W	16 JUN 1905	Henrico Co. VA	Cremated
13673	Hastings, Charles H.	21y	W	22 AUG 1916	Chicago IL	Addison Chapel
03848	Hastings, Edgar E.	53y	W	9 FEB 1901	Carlisle PA	Mt. Olivet
04829	Hastings, Edward	60y	W	4 AUG 1904	Bethesda MD	Arlington VA
15851	Hatch, Adelaide G.	93y	W	27 JUN 1919	Manhattan NY	Arlington
03479	Hatch, John P.	79y	W	13 APR 1901	New York NY	Arlington VA
12604	Hatch, Mark B.	60y	W	31 OCT 1914	At Sea	Cremated
05691	Hatch, Sarah H.	50y	W	11 AUG 1906	San Juan, P.R.	Oak Hill
00328	Hatfield, Susan	8m	W	21 MAY 1890	Lincoln VA	Mt. Olivet

District of Columbia Foreign Death Records, 1888-1923

No.	Name of Deceased	Age	Race	Death Date	Place of Death	Place of Burial
03344	Hatten, Bertha	24y	C	16 NOV 1900	New York NY	Harmony
15877	Hatten, Delia H.	80y	C	9 JUL 1919	Bladensburg MD	Harmony
17171	Hatton, Isaiah Trueman	33y	C	17 MAY 1921	Buena Vista MD	Cremated
15683	Hatton, Rosie	26y	W	21 MAR 1919	Alexandria VA	Glenwood
12040	Hauer, Infant of Wilbur	6d	W	13 OCT 1913	Wash. Grove MD	Mt. Olivet
02313	Hauf, John Francis	28y	W	28 NOV 1897	Alexandria VA	Congressional
14540	Haughawout, P.B.	69y	W	30 DEC 1917	Bedford VA	Cremated
03428	Haupthan, John E.	1d	W	24 FEB 1901	Hyattsville MD	Mt. Olivet
01988	Hauptman, Mary M.	10m	W	24 JUL 1896	Wash. Grove MD	Rock Creek
02423	Hause, William F.	76y	W	28 MAR 1898	New York NY	Baltimore MD
18089	Hausenfluck, J.W.	74y	W	26 SEP 1922	Harrisonburg VA	Glenwood
08450	Hauser, Florida Amelia	25y	W	31 DEC 1911	Wash. Grove MD	Congressional
17774	Hauser, Mary Estella, Dr.	54y	W	2 APR 1922	Takoma Park MD	Rock Creek
07591	Havelos, Charlie	26y	W	24 JUN 1910	Fayetteville NC	Glenwood
07493	Haviland, Sarah S.	88y	W	5 APR 1910	Ypsilanti MI	Rock Creek
06102	Hawes, Abbie L.	88y	W	10 JUN 1907	Hyattsville MD	Congressional
15266	Hawk, Eldon George	21y	W	21 OCT 1918	Indian Head MD	Charleston WV
07086	Hawkins, Addie	57y	C	29 JUN 1909	Atlantic City NJ	Mt. Zion West
07460	Hawkins, Arthur, s/o Alfred	15y	C	9 MAR 1910	Somerset VA	Woodlawn
01562	Hawkins, Bessie E.	11y	M	7 JAN 1895	Upper Marl. MD	Harmony
02650	Hawkins, C.F.H.	48y	W	29 OCT 1898	Wheeling WV	Glenwood
07777	Hawkins, Charles Edward	73y	W	2 OCT 1910	Middletown CN	Glenwood
07593	Hawkins, Cristine C.	11m	C	25 JUN 1910	College Park MD	Mt. Olivet
14244	Hawkins, Edward	67y	C	22 JUL 1917	Brentwood MD	Mt. Olivet
13936	Hawkins, Etta	41y	C	14 JAN 1917	New York NY	LaPlata MD
08677	Hawkins, Flora S.	34y	W	18 JUN 1912	Mt. Ranier MD	Glenwood
16619	Hawkins, Francis	62y	C	21 JUL 1920	Harpers Ferry WV	Payne's
09064	Hawkins, Francis Elizabeth	15y	C	4 FEB 1913	Arlington VA	Harmony
06964	Hawkins, Gasway	92y	C	31 MAR 1909	Brentwood MD	Harmony
16980	Hawkins, Grant	49y	C	11 FEB 1921	Philadelphia PA	Woodlawn
07485	Hawkins, H.S., Gen.	75y	W	27 MAR 1910	Watkins NY	West Point NY
14877	Hawkins, Henry	48y	C	21 JUN 1918	Fairmont Hts. MD	Payne's
01814	Hawkins, Henry	10d	C	19 NOV 1895	Pr. Geo. Co. MD	Payne's
15553	Hawkins, Howard F., in jail	26y	W	11 JAN 1919	Atlanta GA	Glenwood
12236	Hawkins, Ivory E.	1y	C	24 FEB 1914	Fairmont Hts. MD	Mt. Olivet
07574	Hawkins, James	1y	C	16 JUN 1910	Bladensburg MD	Mt. Olivet
05688	Hawkins, James E.	25y	C	12 AUG 1906	New Haven CN	Sligo MD
18199	Hawkins, James W.	54y	C	3 DEC 1922	New York NY	Harmony
02620	Hawkins, Jennie	20y	C	6 OCT 1898	Chester PA	Harmony
07053	Hawkins, Johnnie	21y	C	4 JUN 1909	Philadelphia PA	Payne's
15588	Hawkins, Laura Gertrude	26y	W	27 JAN 1919	Falls Church VA	Mt. Olivet
16548	Hawkins, Louise	27y	C	18 JUN 1920	Philadelphia PA	Fairfax VA
12940	Hawkins, Lucy	51y	C	26 MAY 1915	Saratoga Spg. NY	T.B. MD
17948	Hawkins, Maggie A.	c.40y	C	8 JUL 1922	Baltimore MD	Woodlawn
01426	Hawkins, Mary	37y	C	2 JUL 1894	New York NY	Mt. Zion
03110	Hawkins, Mary E.	30y	C	1 MAR 1900	Boston MA	Mt. Zion
08282	Hawkins, Mary Elizabeth	9d	C	30 AUG 1911	Bladensburg MD	Mt. Olivet
12024	Hawkins, Nancy	68y	C	1 OCT 1913	Brentwood MD	Harmony
11922	Hawkins, Rebecca	59y	C	24 JUL 1913	Chicago IL	Harmony
11873	Hawkins, Robert	22y	C	23 JUN 1913	Stillwater MN	Mt. Olivet
17212	Hawkins, Walter, s/o Fredk.	52y	W	4 JUN 1921	Fredericksburg VA	Glenwood
08473	Hawkins, Willard A.	8m	W	15 JAN 1912	Mt. Ranier MD	Glenwood
18421	Hawkins, William	40y	C	16 MAR 1923	Pittsburgh PA	Hyattsville MD
08003	Hawkins, William H.	64y	W	15 MAR 1911	Seat Pleasant MD	Mt. Vernon VA
04318	Hawks, Olivia	31y	W	10 JUN 1903	Summit NJ	Mt. Olivet
04784	Hawksworth, Darnley	23y	C	9 JUL 1904	Altoona PA	Harmony
13514	Hawley, Frederick T.	74y	W	19 MAY 1916	Brookline MA	Arlington
16118	Hayden, Annie	80y	W	22 NOV 1919	Rockville MD	Glenwood
14513	Hayden, Emma L.	71y	W	19 DEC 1917	Bel Alton MD	Mt. Olivet

No.	Name of Deceased	Age	Race	Death Date	Place of Death	Place of Burial
14488	Hayden, John	64y	W	30 NOV 1917	New York NY	Mt. Olivet
04096	Hayden, Joseph	65y	W	7 NOV 1902	Catonsville MD	Rock Creek
14674	Hayden, Kate Bull	75y	W	6 MAR 1918	Lakewood OH	Rock Creek
15667	Hayden, Katherine Agnes	57y	W	10 MAR 1919	Indian Head MD	Mt. Olivet
16114	Hayden, Lucien Henry	80y	W	17 NOV 1919	New York NY	Oak Hill
01498	Hayden, May A.	67y	C	26 SEP 1894	Alexandria VA	Baptist
01870	Hayden, Nehemiah R.	85y	W	17 JAN 1896	Kensington MD	Rock Creek
17637	Hayes, Alice E.	46y	C	14 JAN 1922	Trenton NJ	Woodlawn
17530	Hayes, Anna	28y	C	17 NOV 1921	Philadelphia PA	Prospect Hill
05315	Hayes, Annie M.	59y	W	12 OCT 1905	Belair VA	Oak Hill
15321	Hayes, Bessie M.	44y	W	3 SEP 1918	Los Angeles CA	Mt. Olivet
08116	Hayes, Bridget H.	28y	W	1860	Brooklyn NY	Mt. Olivet
18130	Hayes, Clara L.S.	42y	W	24 OCT 1922	Boston MA	Oak Hill
01156	Hayes, Doris Adelaide	14m	W	8 JUN 1892	Minneapolis MN	Congressional
08767	Hayes, E.M.	70y	W	15 AUG 1912	Morgantown NC	Arlington
06675	Hayes, Hannah	4y	W	3 AUG 1908	Tuftonboro NH	Rock Creek
08116	Hayes, Infant of Bridget H.	3m	W	1860	Brooklyn NY	Mt. Olivet
04529	Hayes, Jane A.	88y	W	8 APR 1903	New Orleans LA	Oak Hill
06662	Hayes, John	27y	W	29 JUL 1908	Mt. Hope MD	Mt. Olivet
06275	Hayes, John W.	77y	W	16 OCT 1907	Hampton VA	Congressional
00037	Hayes, Julia	58y	W	1 MAR 1889	Hampton VA	Mt. Olivet
05349	Hayes, Katherine	45y	W	5 NOV 1905	Camden NJ	Mt. Olivet
15620	Hayes, Lillie Blanche	36y	W	17 FEB 1919	Capitol Hts. MD	Forestville MD
17291	Hayes, Lucy Ann	79y	W	7 JUL 1921	Montclair NJ	Oak Hill
00720	Hayes, Maria B.	80y	W	7 JAN 1892	Rock Island IL	Glenwood
02063	Hayes, Mary A.	74y	W	3 DEC 1896	Baltimore MD	Glenwood
04840	Hayes, Mary Wilhelmina	3m	W	11 AUG 1904	Belair VA	Oak Hill
05511	Hayes, Oliver	51y	W	26 MAR 1906	Jacksonville FL	Rock Creek
06896	Hayes, Rebecca	25y	W	9 JAN 1909	New York NY	Harmony
13877	Hayhoe, George W.	52y	W	20 DEC 1916	Mt. Ranier MD	Rock Creek
00261	Haymond, Margaret R.	84y	W	10 JAN 1890	Fairmont WV	Oak Hill
03215	Haynes, Benjamin F.	42y	C	18 JUN 1900	Potomac River	Harmony
00482	Haynes, David A.	30y	W	8 DEC 1890	New York NY	Oak Hill
18253	Haynie, Willard H.	26y	W	6 JAN 1923	Asheville NC	Rock Creek
13560	Hays, Rosalie E.	17y	W	19 JUN 1916	Hyattsville MD	Glenwood
18097	Hays, William E.	44y	W	1 OCT 1922	Baltimore MD	Congressional
15768	Hays, William T.	24y	W	4 MAY 1919	Phillipsburg NJ	Congressional
12254	Haywood, Edward	76y	W	10 MAR 1914	Gaithersburg MD	Oak Hill
05876	Haywood, William	43y	W	19 DEC 1906	Ft. Bayard NM	Rock Creek
16465	Hazard, Frank H., Jr.	21y	W	3 MAY 1920	Takoma Park MD	Rock Creek
13540	Hazard, H. Harvey	70y	W	4 JUN 1916	Middlesex Co. MA	Congressional
17611	Hazard, Olive Perry	37y	W	26 DEC 1921	Hartford CN	Ft. Lincoln
03967	Hazart, Josiah	75y	W	3 AUG 1902	Takoma Park MD	Fredericksburg VA
03206	Hazel, Lewis V.	17y	W	11 JUN 1900	Chesa. Bea. MD	Mt. Olivet
05685	Hazell, Amanda	21y	C	12 AUG 1906	New York NY	Danville VA
08831	Hazelton, Simeon Cole	46y	W	6 SEP 1912	Mill Creek UT	Rock Creek
17148	Hazen, Daniel Webster	65y	W	3 MAY 1921	Camp Meade MD	Soldier's Home
01368	Hazen, Mary C.	42y	W	27 MAY 1894	Highlands MD	Oak Hill
08026	Head, Frederick A.	65y	W	19 MAR 1911	Boynton FL	Arlington
01237	Headley, Silas	45y	W	18 OCT 1893	Occoquan VA	Congressional
02911	Headly, Frank	45y	W	11 AUG 1899	Philadelphia PA	Congressional
03738	Healey, John	60y	W	19 DEC 1901	Alexandria VA	Soldier's Home
08894	Healey, Peter S., s/o M.	34y	W	17 OCT 1912	Clifton Forge VA	Mt. Olivet
13985	Healy, Maurice D.	31y	W	14 FEB 1917	Indian Head MD	Mt. Olivet
00129	Heap, Bessie Beale	36y	W	31 JUL 1889	New Brighton NY	Congressional
01718	Heap, Porter	18y	W	27 JUL 1895	Portland ME	Congressional
05643	Heard, George C.	58y	W	30 JUN 1906	Skagway AK	Glenwood
16027	Hearn, William F.	32y	W	3 OCT 1919	Baltimore MD	Glenwood
15723	Hearne, Harold	40y	W	11 APR 1919	New York NY	Rock Creek

District of Columbia Foreign Death Records, 1888-1923

No.	Name of Deceased	Age	Race	Death Date	Place of Death	Place of Burial
11863	Heasley, Emma	45y	C	21 JUN 1913	Fairmont Hts. MD	Payne's
02841	Heath, Anna	45y	W	18 MAY 1899	Philadelphia PA	Oak Hill
15853	Heath, Hattie	23y	W	29 JUN 1919	Baltimore MD	Glenwood
14537	Heath, Mary	52y	W	29 DEC 1917	Long Island NY	Glenwood
07719	Heath, William	57y	W	28 AUG 1910	Highlandtown MD	Mt. Olivet
06795	Heaton, Frank M.	74y	W	30 OCT 1908	Chevy Chase MD	Glenwood
04186	Heaven, Charles	47y	C	7 APR 1903	Landover MD	Mt. Olivet
04605	Hebb, Caroline Penn	87y	W	18 FEB 1904	Wilmington DE	Oak Hill
01477	Hebb, Gertrude A.	18y	W	29 AUG 1894	Matamoras PA	Congressional
15084	Hebbard, Carl Bradford	29y	W	3 OCT 1918	Rochester MN	Congressional
18102	Hebner, Annie	73y	W	4 OCT 1922	Clarendon VA	Cremated
17113	Hechinger, Jonas Wolfe	67y	W	20 APR 1921	Baltimore MD	Wash. Hebrew
05633	Heck, George J.	40y	W	4 JUL 1906	Williston ND	Mt. Olivet
04201	Hedges, Mary Ann	71y	W	25 MAR 1903	Norristown PA	Mt. Olivet
16202	Heffernan, Paul	2y	W	10 JAN 1920	Richmond NY	Holyrood
02907	Heffner, Rose A.	38y	W	10 AUG 1889	Bethesda MD	Holyrood
05424	Hefner, Christian	70y	W	13 JAN 1906	Cloppers MD	St. Mary's
05255	Hefner, Henry W.	32y	W	21 AUG 1905	Cloppers MD	St. Mary's
15497	Heger, Caroline Jennings	79y	W	28 DEC 1918	Somerville NJ	Arlington
03029	Heid, John H.	46y	W	20 SEP 1899	Baltimore MD	Mt. Olivet
16019	Heider, Charles F.	19y	W	21 SEP 1919	Chesapeake Bay	Prospect Hill
00721	Heider, Charlotte	65y	W	6 NOV 1891	Pr. Geo. Co. MD	Oak Hill
02851	Heider, Infant of William J.	SB	W	13 JUN 1889	MD	Prospect Hill
14039	Heidke, Emily	38y	W	20 MAR 1917	Chicago IL	Glenwood
08271	Heil, Lillian Cecelia	6m	W	23 AUG 1911	Piney Point MD	Congressional
07633	Heil, Wm. Ambrose, s/o Geo.	9m	W	15 JUL 1910	Clarendon VA	Congressional
06190	Heilmes, John, s/o William	36y	W	17 AUG 1907	Colonial Bea. VA	Glenwood
13020	Heim, Herman	40y	W	12 JUL 1915	Alex. Co. VA	Milwaukee WI
02255	Heimer, Georgie	1y	W	4 AUG 1897	Keswick VA	Congressional
18133	Heine, Joseph A.	47y	W	29 OCT 1922	Mitchelville MD	Prospect Hill
01466	Heinecke, May F.S.	12y	W	18 AUG 1894	Anne Arundel Co.	Oak Hill
13110	Heiner, Helen Gordon	63y	W	16 SEP 1915	Annapolis MD	Arlington
03930	Heintzelman, Emily L.	46y	W	18 JUL 1902	Warren Co. NY	Arlington
05674	Heise, John E.	60y	W	4 AUG 1906	Columbia SC	Cremated
12602	Heiskell, Edith	44y	W	9 NOV 1914	Baltimore MD	Oxon Hill MD
07484	Heiskell, John C.B.	13y	W	28 MAR 1910	Georgetown DC	Mt. Olivet
13605	Heiss, Mary A.	56y	W	16 JUL 1916	Staunton VA	Holyrood
14264	Heiss, Michael E., farmer	63y	W	29 JUL 1917	Staunton VA	Holyrood
04184	Heistand, Claude J.	35y	W	7 APR 1903	Annapolis Jct. MD	Prospect Hill
07771	Heiston, Walter, Jr.	1y	W	29 SEP 1910	Baltimore MD	Rock Creek
01048	Heitmiller, Dora Lydia	11m	W	15 APR 1893	Hyattsville MD	Glenwood
12029	Heitmuller, Charles Gustave	52y	W	6 OCT 1913	Queen Chapel MD	Glenwood
16028	Heitmuller, Ferdinand A.	61y	W	5 OCT 1919	Wheaton MD	Glenwood
12679	Heitt, Sallie Ann	58y	W	27 DEC 1914	W. Riverdale MD	Glenwood
00615	Hellen, Joseph J.	32y	W	3 JUL 1891	Silver Spring MD	Glenwood
13331	Heller, A. Sidney	53y	W	31 JAN 1916	Baltimore MD	Wash. Hebrew
07891	Heller, Charles M.	51y	W	24 DEC 1910	Harpers Ferry WV	Wash. Hebrew
17923	Heller, Sarah	87y	W	26 JUN 1922	Baltimore MD	Wash. Hebrew
02064	Hellinger, Albert	73y	W	4 JAN 1897	Wheeling WV	St. Mary's
16116	Hellmuth, Frank	37y	W	19 NOV 1919	Asheville NC	St. Mary's
03616	Hellwig, Francis Earles	6y	W	17 AUG 1901	Alex. Co. VA	Congressional
02662	Helmas, William A.	30y	W	20 NOV 1898	Glen Echo MD	Glenwood
09083	Helmsen, Henry H.	94y	W	20 FEB 1913	Bethesda MD	Congressional
05226	Helmsen, Henry Macleod	22y	W	2 AUG 1905	Riverdale MD	Congressional
01719	Helmsey, Arthur W., engraver	24y	W	3 OCT 1895	Alex. Co. VA	Congressional
02114	Helmuth, Nellie	1d	W	20 JAN 1897	Highland MD	St. Mary's
17847	Heltzel, Sarah	73y	W	12 MAY 1922	Silver Spring MD	Arlington
13044	Helwig, Kate Irene	55y	W	5 AUG 1915	Doylestown PA	Rock Creek
01720	Hemingway, Blanch J.	21y	W	10 SEP 1895	Greenwood MS	Congressional

No.	Name of Deceased	Age	Race	Death Date	Place of Death	Place of Burial
16004	Hemmick, Lucy (Smith)	65y	W	22 SEP 1919	Atlantic City NJ	Rock Creek
17042	Hemmick, Roland Joseph	69y	W	12 MAR 1921	Atlantic City NJ	Rock Creek
06467	Henberger, Albertina H.	29y	W	14 MAR 1908	Gaithersburg MD	Cleveland OH
08793	Henderson, Elmar	33y	C	27 AUG 1912	Ft. Bayard NM	Arlington VA
17335	Henderson, Ernest E.	3d	C	29 JUL 1921	Cedar Hts. MD	Payne's
07595	Henderson, Georgiana	54y	W	3 SEP 1907	Woodside MD	Rock Creek
14886	Henderson, Herbert	55y	W	23 JUN 1918	Bethesda MD	Cremated
07596	Henderson, James Thomas	70y	W	18 JUL 1907	Woodside MD	Rock Creek
09167	Henderson, John Brooks	87y	W	12 APR 1913	Takoma Park MD	Rock Creek
02846	Henderson, John N.	51y	W	4 JUN 1899	Philadelphia PA	Glenwood
07129	Henderson, Mary J.	42y	C	22 JUL 1909	Bar Harbor ME	Woodlawn
16936	Henderson, Mary Raylor	31y	W	20 JAN 1921	Takoma Park MD	Rock Creek[1]
14056	Henderson, Nannie	60y	C	23 MAR 1917	Philadelphia PA	Woodlawn
02309	Henderson, Octavius Cazenove	58y	W	2 SEP 1897	Alexandria VA	Congressional
13256	Henderson, Rosa Proctor	25y	C	17 DEC 1915	Muncie IN	Woodlawn
04788	Henderson, William C.	63y	W	9 JUL 1904	Paterson NJ	Congressional
05398	Henderson, Winfred	24y	C	13 DEC 1905	Alex. Co. VA	Occoquan VA
04006	Hendley, Josephine Albert	1y	W	18 SEP 1902	Railroad	Congressional
05630	Hendricks, Arthur W.	34y	W	8 JUL 1906	Kensington MD	Glenwood
13400	Henkel, Alice	47y	W	8 MAR 1916	Chevy Chase MD	Rock Creek
02835	Henkel, Phillip	91y	W	29 MAY 1899	Baltimore MD	Congressional
16718	Henley, Lucy A.	81y	W	17 SEP 1920	Silver Spring MD	Waynesville OH
05336	Henley, Thomas B.	62y	W	27 OCT 1905	Allegheny PA	West Point VA
13736	Hennage, Cornelia	71y	W	27 SEP 1916	Bethesda MD	Deep Point VA
09076	Hennegan, Andrew	76y	W	14 FEB 1913	Jessup MD	Glenwood
07088	Henner, Ann V.	81y	W	30 JUN 1909	Philadelphia PA	Glenwood
00960	Hennessey, Maurice	3m	W	18 JUN 1893	Nottoway Co. VA	Mt. Olivet
04727	Hennike, Peter J.	72y	W	23 MAY 1904	Hampton VA	Mt. Olivet
05660	Henning, John C.	29y	W	25 JUL 1906	Annapolis MD	Glenwood
09089	Henning, Rebecca (Curley)	64y	W	24 FEB 1913	Portsmouth VA	Congressional
03284	Henning, Susanna A.	70y	W	1 SEP 1900	S.W. Harbor ME	Congressional
06558	Henning, William Henry	73y	W	19 MAY 1908	Norfolk Co. VA	Congressional
02065	Henry, Charles	56y	W	24 NOV 1896	Chevy Chase MD	Oak Hill
00616	Henry, Elizabeth F.	69y	W	20 SEP 1891	Pomona FL	Rock Creek
17163	Henry, Mary A.	—	W	10 APR 1903	Seville, Spain	Oak Hill
11811	Henry, Peter	60y	C	13 MAY 1913	Central Islip NY	Harmony
12219	Henry, Richard J.	2y	W	13 FEB 1914	Chevy Chase MD	Mt. Olivet
12270	Henry, William D.	58y	W	25 MAR 1914	Chevy Chase MD	Glenwood
17266	Henry, William E.	60y	C	25 JUN 1921	Baltimore MD	Mt. Zion West
16201	Hensey, Alexander Thomas	58y	W	5 JAN 1920	Pasadena CA	Oak Hill
00957	Hensey, Chester A.	1y	W	14 JUL 1883	Washington DC	Rock Creek
00959	Hensey, Eugene Rose	9m	W	26 JUL 1866	Brooklyn NY	Rock Creek
00956	Hensey, Royal W.	4m	W	23 JUL 1867	Brooklyn NY	Rock Creek
00958	Hensey, Sidney St. John	4m	W	4 JUN 1867	Brooklyn NY	Rock Creek
04297	Henshaw, Caroline D.	81y	W	29 MAY 1903	Camden NJ	Congressional
12896	Henson, Eliza	58y	C	25 APR 1915	Baltimore MD	Payne's
02840	Henson, Frederick	21y	W	19 MAY 1899	Baltimore MD	Mt. Olivet
15762	Henson, Hester	77y	C	3 MAY 1919	Macomb IL	Harmony
06347	Henson, John	42y	W	4 DEC 1907	New Rochelle NY	Harmony
17550	Hepburn, Agnes I.	51y	W	27 NOV 1921	Hyattsville MD	Congressional
05098	Hepburn, Elizabeth V.	58y	W	11 MAR 1905	Philippine Isl.	Arlington
05099	Hepburn, Infant of John B.	1h	W	11 MAR 1905	Manila, P.I.	Arlington
05861	Hepburn, Loretta	6y	C	13 DEC 1906	Landover MD	Mt. Olivet
06096	Herbert, Charles E.	36y	W	2 JUL 1907	Columbia SC	Glenwood
05913	Herbert, Francis	24y	W	20 JAN 1907	Jersey City NJ	Woodlawn
14955	Herbert, Freddie B.	5m	C	7 AUG 1918	Takoma Park MD	Mt. Zion West
12866	Herbert, Frederick	48y	W	7 APR 1915	Atlantic City NJ	Prospect Hill

[1] Middle name of the deceased corrected from Greiner, on the back of the certificate, 11 NOV 1927.

District of Columbia Foreign Death Records, 1888-1923

No.	Name of Deceased	Age	Race	Death Date	Place of Death	Place of Burial
06425	Herbert, George Albert	32y	C	8 FEB 1908	Philadelphia PA	Mt. Zion East
06945	Herbert, Henrietta	48y	C	13 MAR 1909	Philadelphia PA	Mt. Olivet
01915	Herbert, Henry	56y	C	28 APR 1896	Alex. Co. VA	Harmony
04823	Herbert, Leonard J.	54y	C	1 AUG 1904	Glendale MD	Mt. Olivet
18285	Herbert, Louise	84y	C	20 JAN 1923	Glenarden MD	Mt. Olivet
13764	Herbert, Martha	45y	C	14 OCT 1916	Washington DC	Harmony
16805	Herbert, Mary C.	43y	W	13 NOV 1920	Fairfax Co. VA	Bethesda MD
14097	Herbert, William Joseph	60y	C	18 APR 1917	Elmira NY	Mt. Olivet
01516	Hercus, Beulah M.	1y	W	14 MAR 1879	Richmond VA	Rock Creek
15225	Hercus, George Clifton	37y	W	17 OCT 1918	Middletown PA	Rock Creek
01517	Hercus, Hiram R.	7m	W	27 AUG 1879	Richmond VA	Rock Creek
15852	Herilig, Augustus M.	86y	W	29 JUN 1919	Camp Springs MD	Glenwood
02161	Herman, John H.	60y	W	26 APR 1897	Baltimore MD	Soldier's Home
05214	Hermann, Abraham	62y	W	21 JUL 1905	Kensington MD	Wash. Hebrew
06356	Hern, Mrs. John F.	28y	W	5 NOV 1907	Canal Zone	Glenwood
14852	Herndon, William S.	48y	W	6 DEC 1917	Albuquerque NM	Rock Creek
13371	Herold, Madeline L.	54y	W	22 FEB 1916	Bethesda MD	Rock Creek
12578	Herr, Fannie W.	63y	W	21 OCT 1914	Ridley Park PA	Oak Hill
01563	Herr, Narcissa V.	2y	W	14 JAN 1895	Jersey City NJ	Oak Hill
00722	Herr, Philip Hoffman	4y	W	4 JAN 1891	Jersey City NJ	Oak Hill
03748	Herrick, Harriett M.	83y	W	2 JAN 1902	Aquasco MD	Oak Hill
09039	Herriott, Daniel W.	61y	W	18 JAN 1913	Rochester MN	Rock Creek
08585	Herriott, Hallie Irene	31y	W	2 APR 1912	Tucson AZ	Rock Creek
07047	Herrmann, Charles J.	58y	W	3 JUN 1909	Takoma Park MD	Antigo WS
15384	Hershey, Mary E.F.	78y	W	26 NOV 1918	Baltimore MD	Oak Hill
17315	Hershey, Ruth	22y	W	22 JUL 1921	Takoma Park MD	Glenwood
04094	Herzog, James	12d	W	9 NOV 1902	Ft. Myer VA	Holyrood
15670	Herzog, Joseph	78y	W	12 MAR 1919	Augusta GA	Wash. Hebrew
05860	Hess, Edna L.	33y	W	12 DEC 1906	New York NY	Glenwood
15511	Hess, Elizabeth H. (Smith)	72y	W	29 DEC 1918	Newport News VA	Congressional
04437	Hess, James A.	26y	W	3 SEP 1903	Philadelphia PA	Congressional
15915	Hess, Lewis	74y	W	3 AUG 1919	Herndon VA	Oak Hill
03146	Hess, Mary	50y	W	23 MAR 1900	Marion VA	Congressional
04385	Hesse, Ellenor Louise	1y	W	11 JUL 1903	Erie PA	Congressional
01721	Hesse, Margaret Marie	2y	W	18 AUG 1895	Ocean Grove NJ	Congressional
04088	Hessler, Frank J., Jr.	31y	W	29 NOV 1902	Alexandria VA	Mt. Olivet
08181	Hessler, Katherine T.	1y	W	6 JUL 1911	Hyattsville MD	Glenwood
18350	Hester, Margaret Reese	48y	W	14 FEB 1923	Clarendon VA	Glenwood
12539	Hester, Mary E.	71y	W	22 SEP 1914	Newark NJ	Rock Creek
16589	Hester, Michael W.	66y	W	8 JUL 1920	Railroad	Greenville SC
00724	Heues, Elizabeth Ann	51y	W	16 JAN 1892	Landover MD	Rock Creek
02682	Hevner, Peter	78y	W	5 SEP 1898	Philadelphia PA	Glenwood
07454	Hevner, Sallie M.	45y	W	5 MAR 1910	Philadelphia PA	Glenwood
15354	Hewey, Rea Goodwin, d/o H.	24y	W	15 NOV 1918	Langley VA	Cremated
17460	Hewey, Rodger F.	18y	W	11 OCT 1921	Langley VA	Cremated
05031	Hewitt, Lendall	22y	W	13 FEB 1905	Ft. Wash. MD	Rock Creek
14451	Hewitt, Virginia E.	55y	C	7 NOV 1917	New York NY	Harmony
03635	Hewlett, Dangerfield O.	45y	W	31 AUG 1901	Auburn VA	Rock Creek
00136	Hews, Matilda	75y	C	16 AUG 1889	Suitland MD	Mt. Olivet
08163	Hexter, Isaac	57y	W	22 JUN 1911	Galesburg IL	Wash. Hebrew
13618	Heydon, Henry Colonna	2y	W	26 JUL 1916	Norfolk VA	Glenwood
17955	Heydon, Laura Augusta	42y	W	12 JUL 1922	Saranac Lake NY	Glenwood
16864	Heyl, John K.	54y	W	18 DEC 1920	Pittsburgh PA	Cremated
17088	Heyle, Eliza, d/o Christian	89y	W	2 APR 1921	Charlottesville VA	Glenwood
12773	Heyliger, Ada	35y	C	17 FEB 1917	Boston MA	Woodlawn
16829	Heyman, Sidney, s/o Joseph	1y	W	28 NOV 1920	Alexandria VA	Ohev Sholom
01307	Hibbert, Susan E.	42y	W	29 DEC 1893	New York NY	Oak Hill
08278	Hibbs, David R.P., s/o Samuel	74y	W	24 AUG 1911	Minneapolis MN	Arlington
11830	Hibbs, John H.	77y	W	24 MAY 1913	Ann Arbor MI	Rock Creek

No.	Name of Deceased	Age	Race	Death Date	Place of Death	Place of Burial
17048	Hibbs, Katherine	21y	W	16 MAR 1921	White Haven PA	Congressional
15136	Hibbs, William L.	27y	W	13 OCT 1918	Camp Sherm. OH	Arlington
17017	Hickey, David A.	31y	W	5 MAR 1921	Mt. Hope MD	Mt. Olivet
12632	Hickey, Frank	42y	W	25 NOV 1914	New York NY	Arlington
17012	Hickey, John F.	78y	W	3 MAR 1921	Hyattsville MD	Mt. Olivet
17375	Hickey, Louise C.	1m	W	30 AUG 1921	Hyattsville MD	Mt. Olivet
11802	Hickey, Nannie C.	64y	W	6 MAY 1913	Hyattsville MD	Mt. Olivet
14975	Hickey, William J.	45y	W	13 AUG 1918	Hyattsville MD	Mt. Olivet
18091	Hickman, George R.	48y	C	27 SEP 1922	Silver Hill MD	Harmony
00176	Hickman, Louisa	45y	C	4 OCT 1889	Elkins MD	Mt. Pleasant
14432	Hickman, Martha	40y	C	30 OCT 1917	Philadelphia PA	Woodlawn
12854	Hickox, Charles K.	29y	W	31 MAR 1915	Boston MA	Rock Creek
07440	Hicks, Dolly	35y	C	28 FEB 1910	New York NY	Mt. Olivet
12699	Hiden, Philip B., s/o Jos.	72y	W	7 JAN 1915	Newport News VA	Rock Creek
06830	Hieston, Alice Va. Knowles	62y	W	27 NOV 1908	Milford PA	Rock Creek
12297	Hiett, Lula V.	31y	W	7 APR 1914	W. Riverdale MD	Glenwood
06519	Higbee, John Henley	66y	W	18 APR 1908	Buffalo NY	Arlington
17806	Higbee, Mary M.	42y	W	16 APR 1922	Takoma Park MD	Glenwood
00846	Higdon, Andrew	62y	W	28 JUL 1892	Lakeland MD	Mt. Olivet
13237	Higgins, Eliza Virginia	82y	W	7 DEC 1915	Rockville MD	Glenwood
00961	Higgins, Letitia	75y	W	1 AUG 1893	Bayonne NJ	Oak Hill
00483	Higgins, Mary	79y	W	29 DEC 1890	Pr. Geo. Co. MD	Mt. Olivet
13766	Higgins, R.C.	23y	W	9 OCT 1916	St. Louis Co. MN	Prospect Hill
03548	Higgins, Thomas F.	28y	W	18 JUN 1901	Elizabeth NJ	Mt. Olivet
06107	Highbarger, Nathan	80y	W	13 JUN 1907	Sharpsburg MD	Mt. Olivet
02649	Hildebrand, Leila Ada	38y	W	30 OCT 1898	Church Hill MD	Glenwood
01989	Hildebrand, Margaret	6m	W	10 AUG 1896	Middleburg VA	Glenwood
14376	Hilderbrand, Frances	5y	W	24 SEP 1917	Mt. Ranier MD	Glenwood
17570	Hill, Albert	19y	W	30 NOV 1921	Aldrick AL	Ft. Lincoln
08779	Hill, Alice C.	58y	C	21 AUG 1912	Brooklyn NY	Mt. Olivet
17272	Hill, Andrew G.	34y	W	14 JUN 1921	Cristobal, C.Z.	Arlington VA
13198	Hill, Anna M.	4y	W	12 NOV 1915	Cherrydale VA	Holyrood
07634	Hill, Benjamin	61y	W	15 JUL 1910	Chillum MD	Harmony
09198	Hill, Bertha	27y	C	1 MAY 1913	New York NY	Harmony
17478	Hill, Edith Thompson	45y	W	18 OCT 1921	Takoma Park MD	Rock Creek
17917	Hill, Edward E.	65y	W	22 JUN 1922	Seat Pleasant MD	Mt. Olivet
04786	Hill, Eliza A.	72y	W	9 JUL 1904	Springfield MD	Mt. Olivet
00847	Hill, Ellen C.	16y	W	28 AUG 1892	Philadelphia PA	Oak Hill
14476	Hill, Fannie E.	75y	W	22 NOV 1917	Pittsburgh PA	Oak Hill
17586	Hill, Francis	7m	C	13 DEC 1921	Hyattsville MD	Mt. Olivet
15799	Hill, George Chaffee, U.S.N.	25y	W	28 MAY 1919	Norfolk VA	Arlington
06631	Hill, George F.	1m	W	6 JUL 1908	Bladensburg MD	Mt. Olivet
12280	Hill, George William	58y	W	30 MAR 1914	Franklin VA	Mt. Olivet
14127	Hill, Georgina F.	88y	W	6 MAY 1917	Livingston Hts. VA	Oak Hill
05623	Hill, Grace	19y	C	30 JUN 1906	Chillum MD	Harmony
18314	Hill, Harry	27y	W	1 FEB 1923	Capitol Hts. MD	Congressional
08736	Hill, Ida Johnson, d/o James	30y	C	25 JUL 1912	King Wm. Co. VA	Harmony
03661	Hill, Infant of Edward E.	SB	W	10 SEP 1901	Seat Pleasant MD	Mt. Olivet
05942	Hill, Isaiah	27y	C	10 FEB 1907	Providence RI	Payne's
01931	Hill, James	25y	C	20 MAY 1896	Rosslyn VA	Baptist
16986	Hill, Jeanette	56y	W	16 FEB 1921	Capitol Hts. MD	Congressional
04790	Hill, John J.	25y	W	1 JUL 1904	San Francisco CA	Glenwood
14199	Hill, Louise Carson	34y	W	29 JUN 1917	Roanoke VA	Rock Creek
15788	Hill, Louise Davis	25y	C	20 MAY 1919	Takoma MD	Harmony
01871	Hill, Lucy F.L.	31y	W	10 FEB 1896	Chicago IL	Mt. Olivet
17543	Hill, Maggie Jones	32y	C	19 NOV 1921	Philadelphia PA	Payne's
04393	Hill, Martha	5m	C	19 JUL 1903	Chillum MD	Harmony
03079	Hill, Mary K.	1y	W	28 JAN 1900	Pittsburgh PA	Mt. Olivet
05989	Hill, Richard W.	16y	C	20 MAR 1907	Chillum MD	Harmony

District of Columbia Foreign Death Records, 1888-1923

No.	Name of Deceased	Age	Race	Death Date	Place of Death	Place of Burial
01402	Hill, Sarah	4y	C	21 JUN 1894	Pr. Geo. Co. MD	Harmony
03881	Hill, William B.	35y	W	15 MAY 1902	Baltimore MD	Glenwood
00402	Hill, William C.	43y	W	30 AUG 1890	Seattle WA	Rock Creek
16960	Hill, William C.	49y	C	3 FEB 1921	Columbia SC	Woodlawn
01430	Hill, William W., farmer	86y	W	11 JUL 1894	Landover MD	Mt. Olivet
12934	Hillary, Charles E., s/o Jacob	60y	C	18 MAY 1915	Petersburg VA	Fonsville MD
02982	Hilleary, Carl G.	22y	W	19 OCT 1899	Rosslyn VA	Holyrood
04425	Hilleary, Etta R.	7y	W	30 AUG 1903	Rosslyn VA	Holyrood
05054	Hilleary, Lula	11m	W	9 MAR 1905	Rosslyn VA	Holyrood
06584	Hilleary, Theodore	28y	W	8 JUN 1908	Rosslyn VA	Holyrood
04213	Hilleary, Walter L.	29y	W	15 AMR 1903	Rosslyn VA	Holyrood
18041	Hillegerst, Hermine	c.59y		AUG 1922	Bright Seat MD	Baltimore MD
01391	Hillery, Maggie	35y	C	20 APR 1894	Philadelphia PA	Harmony
11869	Hillman, Anna E.	79y	W	26 JUN 1913	South Bend IN	Rock Creek
13914	Hillman, Grace Ann	78y	C	5 JAN 1917	New York NY	Mt. Olivet
13170	Hillman, Lavinia	27y	C	25 OCT 1915	Philadelphia PA	Harmony
05128	Hills, Wallace H.	c.55y	W	10 MAY 1905	Carrizozo NM	Rock Creek
13458	Hillyer, Angeline	82y	W	13 APR 1916	Chevy Chase MD	Oak Hill
05678	Hillyer, Curtis J.	78y	W	5 AUG 1906	Jersey City NJ	Oak Hill
00325	Hillyer, Munson C.	64y	W	12 MAY 1890	New York NY	Oak Hill
08495	Hilner, Lewis C.	62y	W	25 JAN 1912	New York NY	Arlington
16330	Hilton, Emma L.	57y	W	20 FEB 1920	Sligo MD	Darby PA
13137	Hilton, Harry C.	43y	W	4 OCT 1915	Topeka KS	Glenwood
17989	Hilton, Sarah E.	90y	W	31 JUL 1922	Baltimore MD	Glenwood
03410	Himmell, Charles B.	1m	C	4 FEB 1901	Hackensack NJ	Payne's
15443	Hinckley, Thomas	30y	W	6 NOV 1918	London, Eng.	Rock Creek
12013	Hinds, Sarah Barnum	80y	W	24 SEP 1913	Lincolnia VA	Rock Creek
08067	Hine, Charles L.	49y	W	16 APR 1911	Somers WS	Rock Creek
12173	Hine, Lemon G.	82y	W	19 JAN 1914	Battle Creek MI	Rock Creek
01277	Hines, Caroline E.	73y	W	25 DEC 1893	Bethesda MD	Tenallytown
16001	Hines, Georgie	21y	C	19 SEP 1919	New York NY	Payne's
01238	Hines, Kate T.	62y	W	6 DEC 1893	Bethesda MD	Tenallytown
17036	Hinman, Sarah M.E.	78y	W	10 MAR 1921	Pittsburgh PA	Arlington
13572	Hinton, Catherine	32y	C	26 JUN 1916	Brentwood MD	Harmony
17068	Hinton, Dennie	50y	C	24 MAR 1921	Berkeley Sp. WV	Woodlawn
04745	Hinton, Richard J.	72y	W	21 DEC 1904	London, Eng.	Arlington VA
15699	Hipp, Herman	46y	W	17 MAR 1919	Brooklyn NY	Soldier's Home
12522	Hipsley, Somerset R.	44y	W	10 SEP 1914	Tuxedo MD	Congressional
15352	Hirrlinger, John	58y	W	14 NOV 1918	Bladensburg MD	Prospect Hill
16405	Hirsch, John W., s/o Joseph	55y	W	23 MAR 1920	Baltimore MD	Mt. Olivet
13083	Hirsh, Morris	63y	W	29 AUG 1915	Takoma Park MD	Adas Israel
15366	Hirsh, Samuel	35y	W	21 NOV 1918	Takoma Park MD	Adas Israel
18386	Hirst, Bertha	62y	W	4 MAR 1923	Takoma Park MD	Adas Israel
11964	Hirst, Homer Torrence, s/o Wm.	70y	W	17 AUG 1913	Urbana City VA	Glenwood
06812	Hirst, Virginia Crawford	14d	W	30 OCT 1908	Indianapolis IN	Glenwood
14051	Hise, Margaret C.	28y	W	23 MAR 1917	Georgetown DC	Congressional
07092	Hiser, Catherine	3m	W	4 JUL 1909	E. Hyattsville MD	Prospect Hill
01488	Hitchcock, James H.	59y	W	10 SEP 1894	Parisville NY	Congressional
01049	Hitz, George W.	56y	W	2 FEB 1893	Baltimore MD	Congressional
15940	Hitz, Mary Barnard	74y	W	18 AUG 1919	Milwaukee WI	Oak Hill
07534	Hoagland, Henry W.	31y	W	11 MAY 1910	Pittsburgh PA	Rock Creek
08724	Hoake, Elizabeth Hinton	63y	W	2 JUL 1912	Atlantic City NJ	Congressional
15184	Hoban, Elizabeth	14y	W	14 OCT 1918	Falls Church VA	Baltimore MD
18153	Hoban, James	9y	W	8 NOV 1922	Baltimore MD	Mt. Olivet
00429	Hoban, Marion B.	77y	W	4 NOV 1890	Annandale MD	Mt. Olivet
02404	Hobbie, Julianne	90y	W	6 MAR 1898	Westminster MD	Congressional
00484	Hobbs, Florence	29y	W	27 MAR 1891	New York NY	Mt. Olivet
17520	Hobbs, Helen Marilla (Ellis)	79y	W	12 NOV 1921	Linden MD	Cremated
14384	Hobbs, Marion S.	23y	W	28 SEP 1917	Bluemont VA	Congressional

No.	Name of Deceased	Age	Race	Death Date	Place of Death	Place of Burial
07799	Hoben, Emma M.	26y	W	26 OCT 1910	Berwyn MD	Mt. Olivet
07800	Hoben, Infant of John C.	6h	W	26 OCT 1910	Berwyn MD	Mt. Olivet
14297	Hobgood, Jennie T.	76y	W	14 AUG 1917	Chattanooga TN	Oak Hill
14253	Hobine, Louis	38y	W	27 JUL 1917	Annapolis MD	Prospect Hill
13299	Hoblitzell, Eleanor (Simmons)	50y	W	5 JAN 1916	Ohio River	Glenwood
13603	Hoblitzell, John D., s/o W.L.	23y	W	5 JAN 1916	Washington WV	Glenwood
13296	Hoblitzell, Myrtle	23y	W	5 JAN 1916	Ohio River	Glenwood
13315	Hoblitzell, W.L.	43y	W	5 JAN 1916	Ohio River	Glenwood
13536	Hoblitzell, William, Jr.	28y	W	5 JAN 1916	Wood Co. WV	Glenwood
07685	Hock, Mary T.	66y	W	9 AUG 1910	Baltimore MD	Rock Creek
00231	Hockstader, Jennie	21y	W	21 NOV 1889	Philadelphia PA	Glenwood
17831	Hodge, Alonzo	45y	C	3 MAY 1922	Ontario, Can.	Rockville MD
05309	Hodge, Charles	66y	C	4 OCT 1905	Great Falls MD	Harmony
02314	Hodge, Elizabeth	50y	C	2 DEC 1897	Baltimore MD	Mt. Olivet
16515	Hodge, Elizabeth H.	42y	W	1 JUN 1920	Ocean Twp. NJ	Mt. Olivet
08741	Hodge, Robert Ferdinand	3m	C	29 JUL 1912	Tibbets MD	Moore's
04583	Hodgen, Mary S.	7m	W	27 JAN 1904	Baltimore MD	Oak Hill
14018	Hodges, Ambrosea	87y	W	2 FEB 1917	Chevy Chase MD	Rock Creek
09057	Hodges, Emma	72y	W	5 FEB 1913	Takoma Park MD	Rock Creek
15522	Hodges, Francis Lurine	6m	W	1 JAN 1919	Beaufort Co. NC	Mt. Olivet
17238	Hodges, Grace	40y	W	11 JAN 1920	Huntington WV	Rock Creek
13266	Hodges, James	75y	W	23 DEC 1915	Philadelphia PA	Rock Creek
12836	Hodgeson, Robert J.	10y	W	25 MAR 1915	Linden MD	Rock Creek
05103	Hodgkin, Henry Morgan	19y	W	27 APR 1905	Ballston VA	Congressional
13450	Hodgkin, James B., s/o Robt.	78y	W	10 APR 1916	Wilmington NC	Falls Church VA
14549	Hodgkins, Mary J.	75y	W	5 JAN 1918	Baltimore MD	Glenwood[1]
02312	Hodgkins, William	31y	W	11 SEP 1897	New York NY	Glenwood
16443	Hodgson, Charles Stuart	63y	W	15 APR 1920	Passaic NJ	Mt. Olivet
15082	Hodgson, Maron L.	20y	W	3 OCT 1918	Chelsea MA	Arlington
17930	Hoeft, Mary G.	41y	W	17 FEB 1922	Coblenz, Ger.	Mt. Olivet
17690	Hoehling, Wilfrid Carrington	3y	W	14 FEB 1922	Chevy Chase MD	Oak Hill
02066	Hoff, A. Henry, Dr.	54y	W	19 AUG 1896	Poughkeepsie NY	Arlington
01503	Hoff, Johanna	62y	W	5 OCT 1894	Baltimore MD	Prospect Hill
17117	Hoff, John J.	76y	W	20 APR 1921	Bedford VA	Cremated
03852	Hoffman, Georgene	18y	W	13 APR 1902	New York NY	Rock Creek
12900	Hoffman, Gustave A.	36y	W	27 APR 1915	Alex. Co. VA	Rock Creek
13436	Hoffman, Jacob Joshua	85y	W	29 MAR 1916	Chicago IL	Congressional
01722	Hoffman, Leonard	6m	W	25 AUG 1895	Colvin Run VA	Congressional
15469	Hoffman, Marie A.	39y	W	22 DEC 1918	Brentwood MD	Mt. Olivet
00100	Hoffman, Mary A.	43y	W	27 OCT 1888	New York NY	Glenwood
14717	Hoffman, Mary F.	36y	W	26 MAR 1918	Washington DC	Mt. Olivet
03001	Hoffman, W., Dr.	53y	W	8 NOV 1899	Reading PA	Congressional
09119	Hoffman, William H.L.	69y	W	8 MAR 1913	Newark NJ	Glenwood
09028	Hoffmann, George P.T.	61y	W	12 JAN 1913	Rosslyn VA	Oak Hill
02583	Hofman, Edward Bowen	21y	W	5 SEP 1898	Surry C.H. VA	Congressional
02584	Hofman, John	c.61y	W	6 SEP 1898	Surry C.H. VA	Congressional
12207	Hogan, Annie	56y	W	7 FEB 1914	Brentwood MD	Mt. Olivet
06293	Hogan, H.W.	25y	W	25 OCT 1907	El Paso TX	Congressional
07229	Hogan, John	34y	W	10 SEP 1909	Kankakee IL	Mt. Olivet
00723	Hogan, Michael	56y	W	26 FEB 1892	Elk Garden WV	Holyrood
15569	Hogan, Roul L.	43y	W	19 JAN 1919	Falls Church VA	Mt. Olivet
04376	Hogan, Thomas L.	16y	C	4 JUL 1903	Oxon Hill MD	Mt. Olivet
09058	Hogan, Thomas, s/o William	52y	W	3 FEB 1913	Huntington VA	Mt. Olivet
16663	Hoge, William S.	71y	W	15 AUG 1920	Buck Hill Falls PA	Rock Creek
17193	Hogg, William S., Com.	66y	W	28 MAY 1921	Middleburg VA	Arlington
08186	Hogue, George Wesley	11m	W	8 JUL 1911	Capitol Hts. MD	Congressional
14619	Hoile, Henry Columbus	27y	W	31 JAN 1918	Pulaski Co. VA	Congressional

[1] Certificate in error gives year 1917, but originating document is dated 1918.

No.	Name of Deceased	Age	Race	Death Date	Place of Death	Place of Burial
13147	Hoile, Rachel C.	81y	W	11 OCT 1915	Pr. Geo. Co. MD	Congressional
05956	Holbrook, Anna Stanley	42y	W	25 FEB 1907	Chester PA	Soldier's Home
15457	Holbrook, Florence V.	22y	W	17 DEC 1918	Takoma MD	Holyrood
04940	Holbrook, John	80y	W	29 OCT 1904	Hampton VA	Arlington
15311	Holcer, E.F.	42y	W	28 OCT 1918	Memphis TN	St. Mary's
02873	Holden, Catherine	3y	W	27 JUL 1899	Hyattsville MD	Rock Creek
08773	Holden, Elizabeth A.	66y	W	21 AUG 1912	Ocean City MD	Arlington VA
07421	Holden, Ellen F.	80y	W	18 FEB 1910	Hyattsville MD	Rock Creek
03549	Holden, Louis Smith	8m	W	25 JUN 1901	Cape May NJ	Oak Hill
06911	Holeman, Paul	49y	W	21 JAN 1909	London, Eng.	Oak Hill
12834	Holivee, Lucy	60y	C	19 MAR 1915	Baltimore MD	Woodlawn
05737	Holl, Eugene A.	56y	W	9 SEP 1906	Philadelphia PA	Cremated
16219	Hollan, Marie H.	18y	W	17 JAN 1920	Danial's Park MD	Mt. Olivet
08669	Holland, Albert Julian	7m	W	13 JUN 1912	Oakmont Hts. MD	Glenwood
06045	Holland, Andrew	25y	C	24 APR 1907	Moundsville WV	Mt. Zion West
07543	Holland, Milton M.	65y	W	15 MAY 1910	Silver Spring MD	Harmony
15908	Holland, Richard	53y	C	31 JUL 1919	New York NY	Bladensburg MD
07736	Hollander, Monroe E.	23y	W	8 SEP 1910	Prescott AZ	Wash. Hebrew
04054	Holleran, James	46y	W	17 OCT 1902	Helena MT	Holyrood
02162	Holliday, Ruth B.	22y	W	22 APR 1897	Baltimore MD	Congressional
17777	Hollidge, Annie Crawford	64y	W	3 APR 1922	Baltimore MD	Glenwood
09094	Hollidge, Isaac S.	66y	W	26 FEB 1913	Milton MA	Glenwood
02375	Hollidge, Martha A.	54y	W	9 FEB 1898	Occoquan VA	Glenwood
01564	Hollingsworth, Virginia	70y	W	28 FEB 1895	Baltimore MD	Oak Hill
00067	Hollister, Clifford L.	21y	W	3 MAY 1889	Friendship MD	Fairfax VA
02948	Hollister, Frederick A.	45y	W	17 SEP 1899	St. Denis MD	Rock Creek
16694	Hollister, Georgiana	72y	W	3 SEP 1920	Springfield NH	Rock Creek
00851	Hollister, John Jay	43y	W	19 MAY 1892	New York NY	Rock Creek
08221	Holloran, Edward	50y	W	20 JUL 1911	San Pasqual AZ	Holyrood
00848	Holloran, John J.	27y	W	15 SEP 1892	Arlington VA	Holyrood
17584	Holloran, Thomas A.	41y	W	11 DEC 1921	Somerset MD	Mt. Olivet
07510	Holly, S.A.	58y	W	8 SEP 1885	Darnestown MD	Glenwood
11972	Hollyday, John Wilson	59y	W	24 AUG 1913	Winthrop MA	Congressional
12479	Holmead, Charles H.	79y	W	7 AUG 1914	Wilmington DE	Rock Creek
08085	Holmead, Infant	SB	W	28 APR 1911	Bright Seat MD	Rock Creek
07606	Holmes, Alfred Willard	8y	W	30 JUN 1910	Seat Pleasant MD	Congressional
00850	Holmes, Clement	39y	C	16 AUG 1892	New York NY	Graceland
09067	Holmes, Eliza	56y	C	8 FEB 1913	New York NY	Harmony
00413	Holmes, Ella	6y	C	8 OCT 1890	Washington PA	Graceland
02310	Holmes, Frederick W.	27y	W	2 SEP 1897	Potomac River	Arlington
03388	Holmes, George	57y	W	7 JAN 1901	Landover MD	Rock Creek
17174	Holmes, Gilmore D.	48y	W	21 MAY 1921	Clarendon VA	Congressional
00962	Holmes, Jennie	25y	C	2 AUG 1893	Landover MD	Rock Creek
16641	Holmes, John W.	31y	W	6 AUG 1920	Philadelphia PA	Congressional
12454	Holmes, Joseph	27y	C	22 JUL 1914	Fairmont Hts. MD	Payne's
13006	Holmes, Joseph Austin	55y	W	13 JUL 1915	Denver CO	Rock Creek
07581	Holmes, Lillian B., s/o Jos.	33y	C	18 JUN 1910	Asbury Park NJ	Harmony
16462	Holmes, Lucinda	75y	W	2 MAY 1920	Takoma Park MD	Rock Creek
06019	Holmes, Lula	57y	W	7 APR 1907	Baltimore MD	Prospect Hill
15238	Holsinger, Mabel J.	26y	W	20 OCT 1918	Riverdale MD	Glenwood
14500	Holstein, Milton M.	40y	W	11 DEC 1917	Arlington MD	Glenwood
05920	Holt, Charles D.	62y	W	30 JAN 1907	Suitland MD	Rock Creek
04099	Holt, Henry R.	57y	W	13 NOV 1902	Suitland MD	Rock Creek
16277	Holt, Jennie L.	46y	C	2 FEB 1920	Philadelphia PA	Harmony
14630	Holt, John H.	44y	W	7 FEB 1918	Takoma MD	Montgomery AL
14770	Holton, Catharine	50y	C	23 APR 1918	Atlantic City NJ	Mt. Olivet
04241	Holton, Margaret Farley	68y	W	9 APR 1903	Hyattsville MD	Congressional
06438	Holton, Seth A.	79y	W	18 FEB 1908	Carthage IL	Congressional
00849	Holtzclaw, Emma J.	34y	W	3 SEP 1892	Hampton VA	Congressional

District of Columbia Foreign Death Records, 1888-1923

No.	Name of Deceased	Age	Race	Death Date	Place of Death	Place of Burial
15643	Holtzclaw, Fannie	67y	W	27 FEB 1919	Colesville MD	Rock Creek
05044	Holz, Caroline	64y	W	27 FEB 1905	Baltimore MD	Prospect Hill
03478	Holzenstine, Andrew	2y	C	14 APR 1901	Suitland MD	Mt. Olivet
06994	Holzer, William H.	59y	W	26 JAN 1909	—	Rock Creek
13558	Homer, Walter	28y	W	14 JUN 1916	Middletown MD	Arlington VA
00348	Homiller, William	80y	W	25 JUN 1890	Spring Mills VA	Holyrood
06373	Hood, Anna E.	69y	W	4 JAN 1908	Muirkirk MD	Glenwood
02311	Hood, Rollin M.	15y	W	3 SEP 1897	Boyds MD	Rock Creek
07897	Hooe, James Cecil, s/o J.R.	43y	W	28 DEC 1910	Bluemont VA	Oak Hill
03669	Hooe, Rice W.	88y	W	29 SEP 1901	Manassas VA	Congressional
12333	Hooker, Catharine	21y	W	25 APR 1914	Fox Station VA	St. Mary's
05216	Hooker, Elizabeth Stewart	8m	W	24 JUL 1905	Berkeley Sp. WV	Rock Creek
08730	Hooker, Frank	5m	W	25 JUL 1912	Capitol Hts. MD	Woodlawn
15421	Hooker, Mary C. Smith	42y	W	10 DEC 1918	Quantico VA	Rock Creek
17746	Hooker, Robert M.	8d	W	17 MAR 1922	Arlington Co. VA	Glenwood
06337	Hooper, Elsie	6y	W	30 NOV 1907	Falls Church VA	Congressional
03819	Hoover, Charles P.	49y	W	14 MAR 1902	Indianapolis IN	Oak Hill
07148	Hoover, David S.	51y	W	6 AUG 1909	Fairfax Co. VA	Glenwood
11838	Hoover, Edward E.	1y	W	1 JUN 1913	Capitol Hts. MD	Glenwood
18300	Hoover, George M.	70y	W	26 JAN 1923	Baltimore MD	Rock Creek
16661	Hoover, Infant of Eli	SB	W	14 AUG 1920	Alex. Co. VA	Glenwood
14534	Hoover, John	25y	W	28 DEC 1917	E. Riverdale MD	Mt. Olivet
01565	Hoover, Margarite L.	42y	W	20 DEC 1894	Portsmouth NH	Oak Hill
12546	Hoover, Mary E.	47y	W	30 SEP 1914	Takoma Park MD	Frederick MD
05187	Hoover, Robert	51y	W	29 JUN 1905	Mt. Hope MD	Rock Creek
00963	Hoover, Sadie M.	3y	W	2 AUG 1893	Atlantic City NJ	Congressional
08840	Hopkins, Benjamin V.	75y	W	15 SEP 1912	Frederick MD	Glenwood
06292	Hopkins, Catherine A.	61y	W	29 OCT 1907	Erie PA	Glenwood
18265	Hopkins, Daniel H.	75y	W	13 JAN 1923	Silver Spring MD	Orange NJ
03947	Hopkins, Edgar W.	42y	W	9 JUL 1902	Hyattsville MD	Glenwood
12152	Hopkins, Francis A.	48y	W	3 JAN 1914	Loma Linda CA	Glenwood
04769	Hopkins, James	72y	W	17 JUN 1904	N. Hatley, Can.	Oak Hill
17552	Hopkins, James H.	44y	W	25 NOV 1921	New York NY	Oak Hill
05133	Hopkins, John	43y	W	17 MAY 1905	New York NY	Rock Creek
05015	Hopkins, Mary A.	66y	W	31 JAN 1905	Baltimore MD	Oak Hill
16792	Hopkins, Nannie	65y	C	30 OCT 1920	Philadelphia PA	Harmony
08462	Hopkins, Oscar	72y	W	1 JAN 1912	Havana, Cuba	Glenwood
12556	Hopkins, Sallie Frances	57y	W	8 OCT 1914	Takoma Park MD	Glenwood
17801	Hopkins, William, Col.	c.40y	W	14 APR 1922	Saranac Lake NY	Arlington
00235	Hopp, Nicholas	76y	W	26 NOV 1889	Pr. Geo. Co. MD	St. Mary's
16240	Hoppersett, Louisa W.	51y	W	23 JAN 1920	Lock Haven PA	Arlington
13363	Horan, Effie L.	19y	W	18 FEB 1916	Washington DC	Glenwood
14934	Horan, Katherine	16y	W	21 JUL 1918	Benedict MD	Glenwood
07497	Horgan, Edmund, s/o Michael	58y	W	8 APR 1910	Fairfax Sta. VA	Mt. Olivet
16796	Horgan, Frank Vincent	32y	W	5 NOV 1920	Cherrydale VA	Mt. Olivet
15167	Horgan, Margaret Erwin	25y	W	13 OCT 1918	Petersburg VA	Mt. Olivet
16371	Horigan, Margaret	54y	W	10 MAR 1920	Mt. Hope MD	Holyrood
08354	Horigan, Mary F.	65y	W	13 OCT 1911	Mt. Ranier MD	Glenwood
16914	Horn, Theodore	84y	W	11 JAN 1921	New York NY	Oak Hill
02918	Hornsby, Isham H.	76y	W	19 AUG 1899	York Harbor ME	Rock Creek
12861	Horrigan, Cornelius	69y	W	4 APR 1915	Mt. Ranier MD	Glenwood
04166	Horsey, Emma J.	60y	W	6 FEB 1903	Brentwood MD	Glenwood
17663	Horstkamp, William N.	79y	W	25 JAN 1922	Baltimore MD	St. Mary's
14272	Horton, George H.	53y	C	1 AUG 1917	Providence RI	Woodlawn
17456	Horton, Mildred	22y	W	7 OCT 1921	Black Mtn. NC	Glenwood
08582	Horton, Sterling N.	27y	C	2 APR 1912	New York NY	Mt. Zion East
17240	Hoskins, Harry Martin	52y	W	16 JUN 1921	Mt. Ranier MD	Glenwood
12828	Hoskins, Ralph Benjamin	3y	W	22 MAR 1915	Ballston VA	Glenwood
14394	Hoskins, Ralph W.	1y	W	15 MAY 1883	St. Louis MN	Rock Creek

No.	Name of Deceased	Age	Race	Death Date	Place of Death	Place of Burial
06379	Hosley, Harry H.	55y	W	6 JAN 1908	New York NY	Arlington VA
03780	Hosmer, Addison A.	69y	W	1 FEB 1902	New York NY	Arlington VA
06196	Hosmer, Amanda Sturgis	68y	W	21 AUG 1907	Sea Bright NJ	Arlington
17351	Hosmer, Edward S.	56y	W	9 AUG 1921	Morris Planes NJ	Arlington
16375	Hosmer, Louis H.	45y	W	29 DEC 1919	New York NY	Arlington
00433	Hossman, Sarah Jane	64y	W	12 NOV 1890	Hyattsville MD	Glenwood
13584	Hotzfeld, Joseph	33y	W	30 JUN 1916	Philadelphia PA	St. Mary's
12477	Houchen, John W., Jr.	7y	W	8 AUG 1914	Fairfax Co. VA	Mt. Olivet
14922	Houchen, John W., Jr.	6m	W	20 JUL 1918	Seat Pleasant MD	Mt. Olivet
17197	Houchen, Samuel	35y	W	29 MAY 1921	Manhattan NY	Arlington
14965	Houck, Barbara A.	58y	W	9 AUG 1918	Washington DC	St. Mary's
16167	Hough, A. Lincoln	53y	W	25 DEC 1919	Falls Church VA	Rock Creek
15340	Hough, Frank Pennybacker W.	34y	W	27 OCT 1918	At Sea	Arlington
09186	Hough, Henry H.	73y	W	25 APR 1913	Forest Glen MD	Rock Creek
00964	Hough, Mary E.	62y	W	27 AUG 1893	Baltimore MD	Congressional
13259	Hough, Robert I.	65y	W	20 DEC 1915	Balls Hill VA	Hillsboro OH
18189	Hough, Thurza Frances Ellen	78y	W	1 DEC 1922	Forest Glen MD	Rock Creek
02678	Houghton, Allen J.	35y	W	16 DEC 1898	Asheville NC	Rock Creek
04556	Houghton, David Wilson	69y	W	1 JAN 1904	Glen Echo MD	Arlington
13544	Hounold, Mary	31y	W	12 AUG 1886	Baltimore MD	Mt. Olivet
16804	Housel, Oscar L.	47y	W	19 AUG 1918	France	Arlington
15995	Houser, Gideon	76y	W	15 SEP 1919	Brentwood MD	Glenwood
12571	Houser, James O.	46y	W	19 OCT 1914	Brentwood MD	Glenwood
11976	Housman, E.L.	50y	W	25 AUG 1913	Miami FL	Prospect Hill
05124	Houston, Agnes Crane	70y	W	12 MAY 1905	Wyoming OH	Congressional
09130	Houston, Helen Middleton	72y	W	14 MAR 1913	Kinderhook NY	Oak Hill
15499	Houston, Henry C.	75y	W	30 DEC 1918	Takoma Park MD	Princeville IL
04304	Houston, James Buchanan	64y	W	28 MAY 1903	New York NY	Oak Hill
07134	Houston, Percilla E.H.	1y	W	24 JUL 1909	Rock Point MD	Congressional
07784	Houston, William, s/o Jas. H.	24y	W	9 OCT 1910	New Alexa. VA	Congressional
17103	Houtz, Rebecca C.	75y	W	12 APR 1921	Spring Hill VA	Cremated
00401	Hover, Sarah F.	30y	W	6 SEP 1890	Baltimore MD	Oak Hill
14217	Howard, Alma Bernice, d/o C.	13y	W	7 JUL 1917	Fredericksburg VA	Cremated
00725	Howard, Amelia J.	27y	C	22 JAN 1882	Pr. Geo. Co. MD	Dean's Family
15930	Howard, Anna Teresa	54y	W	15 AUG 1919	New York NY	Rock Creek
18400	Howard, Annie B.	45y	C	8 MAR 1923	Harrisburg PA	Harmony
04071	Howard, Annie E.	51y	W	18 JAN 1902	Washington DC	Oak Hill
15704	Howard, Bernard F.	50y	W	1 APR 1919	Landover MD	Mt. Olivet
17253	Howard, Carrie N.	30y	C	JUN 1921	Highland NY	Mt. Zion West
02163	Howard, Edward	70y	C	18 APR 1897	Pr. Geo. Co. MD	Payne's
01723	Howard, Elizabeth	40y	W	10 MAY 1895	Battle Creek MI	Woodlawn
16479	Howard, Emma	63y	W	10 MAY 1920	Camden NJ	Congressional
09137	Howard, Francis F.	61y	W	20 MAR 1913	Landover MD	Mt. Olivet
03224	Howard, Hannah E.	87y	W	5 JUL 1900	Annapolis MD	Congressional
03299	Howard, Hattie E.	24y	W	3 OCT 1900	Denver CO	Congressional
05562	Howard, Henry	27y	W	1 MAR 1906	St. Paul MN	Congressional
08123	Howard, Hestor W.	33y	C	17 MAY 1911	Suffolk Co. MA	Woodlawn
12697	Howard, Infant of Henry	SB	W	5 JAN 1915	Hyattsville MD	Mt. Olivet
13498	Howard, James	60y	C	6 MAY 1916	New York NY	Payne's
14238	Howard, James H.	60y	C	17 JUL 1917	Rehobeth DE	Alexandria VA
06439	Howard, James H.	45y	C	20 FEB 1908	Brentwood MD	Harmony
18309	Howard, Levi H.	1m	W	31 JAN 1923	Hyattsville MD	Mt. Olivet
08324	Howard, Lewis C.	65y	C	24 SEP 1911	Fairmont Hts. MD	Payne's
18212	Howard, Mary	40y	C	12 DEC 1922	Atlantic City NJ	Harmony
14021	Howard, Mary L.	38y	C	4 MAR 1917	Fairmont Hts. MD	Front Royal VA
17479	Howard, Mildred Frances	8y	C	19 OCT 1921	Chevy Chase MD	Congressional
00485	Howard, Nannie	23y	C	16 MAR 1891	Baltimore MD	Graceland
17414	Howard, Robert C., Jr.	7y	W	17 SEP 1921	Chevy Chase MD	Congressional
06522	Howard, Robert Dyer, Jr.	3y	W	25 APR 1908	Atlantic City NJ	Mt. Olivet

No.	Name of Deceased	Age	Race	Death Date	Place of Death	Place of Burial
11855	Howard, Roberteen F.	35y	W	16 JUN 1913	Ft. Sheridan IL	Congressional
03027	Howard, Robertson	52y	W	1 DEC 1899	St. Paul MN	Congressional
18408	Howard, Silas	27y	C	10 MAR 1923	Atlantic City NJ	Harmony
08794	Howard, Thomas	34y	C	APR 1898	Hyattsville MD	Harmony
05955	Howard, William	39y	W	22 FEB 1907	New York NY	Mt. Olivet
16141	Howard, William S.	73y	W	3 DEC 1919	St. Augustine FL	Leesburg VA
01278	Howd, Mary H.	54y	W	26 DEC 1893	Philadelphia PA	Rock Creek
16975	Howder, Edward A.	5d	W	15 FEB 1921	Clarendon VA	Congressional
13422	Howe, Charles E.	75y	C	20 MAR 1916	Raleigh NC	Harmony
12721	Howe, Charlotte A.	69y	W	12 JAN 1915	El Paso TX	Oak Hill
07350	Howe, Chester	45y	W	1 OCT 1898	Muskogee OK	Congressional
02353	Howe, Frank H.	48y	W	29 DEC 1897	New York NY	Rock Creek
01628	Howe, Freeman W.	52y	W	19 JUL 1891	Coldwater MI	Oak Hill
03181	Howe, Ida	29y	—	3 MAY 1900	Jersey City NJ	Oxon Hill MD
17533	Howe, Infant of Wm.	SB	W	19 NOV 1921	Pr. Geo. Co. MD	Mt. Olivet
06910	Howe, Ivers B.	85y	W	5 FEB 1909	Riverdale MD	Congressional
14194	Howe, Joseph N.	10h	W	29 JUN 1917	Capitol Hts. MD	Mt. Olivet
04841	Howe, Mary E.	68y	W	11 AUG 1904	Baltimore MD	Congressional
06659	Howe, Mary E.	1y	W	27 JUL 1908	Berwyn MD	Mt. Olivet
12586	Howe, Mary Francis	SB	W	28 OCT 1914	Capitol Hts. MD	Mt. Olivet
13489	Howe, Mary Ritta	SB	W	3 MAY 1916	Capitol Hts. MD	Mt. Olivet
15728	Howell, Anna	28y	W	17 APR 1919	Takoma MD	Wilmington DE
06308	Howell, Eliz. Gleason Willard	35y	W	13 NOV 1907	Atlantic City NJ	Oak Hill
07344	Howell, Fannie S.	56y	W	25 DEC 1909	New York NY	Glenwood
07287	Howell, George E.	25y	W	19 NOV 1909	Alberton MD	Arlington VA
04374	Howell, Jean	23y	W	5 JUL 1903	Philadelphia PA	Glenwood
06542	Howell, Noranda Ella	28y	W	8 MAY 1908	Capitol Hts. MD	Flintstone MD
14444	Howell, Oliver F.	48y	W	5 MAY 1892	Camden NJ	Arlington VA
17655	Howell, Ralph Williams	33y	W	24 NOV 1920	Baluchistan, India	Rock Creek
08847	Howenstein, James T.	71y	W	18 SEP 1912	Philadelphia PA	Glenwood
07964	Howenstein, Willis Owen	38y	W	11 FEB 1911	Wash. Grove MD	Glenwood
16444	Howes, Cora Merriam	70y	W	23 APR 1920	Firland MD	Cremated
05265	Howes, Katie	17y	W	1 SEP 1905	Anne Arundel Co.	Mt. Olivet
04965	Howes, William H.	64y	W	21 NOV 1904	Germantown MD	Glenwood
07413	Howgate, Edward	55y	W	3 FEB 1910	Gunnison CO	Rock Creek
18256	Howison, Hannah Johnson	79y	W	8 JAN 1923	Yonkers NY	Oak Hill
12692	Howison, Henry L.	77y	W	31 DEC 1914	Yonkers NY	Oak Hill
13448	Howison, Isabelle B.	79y	W	9 APR 1916	Maryland Pk. MD	Glenwood
03590	Howison, James, s/o James H.	1y	W	23 JUL 1901	St. Mary's Co. MD	Glenwood
13685	Howland, Agnes Monroe	73y	W	31 AUG 1916	Piney Point MD	Glenwood[1]
03839	Howland, Frederica	46y	W	31 MAY 1902	Hot Springs VA	Cremated
07387	Howlett, Charles A.	37y	W	23 JAN 1910	Wheeling WV	Mt. Olivet
17591	Howlett, John H.	83y	W	14 DEC 1921	Hampton VA	Rock Creek
16222	Howorth, Martha A.	67y	W	15 JAN 1920	Manayunk PA	Glenwood
15462	Hoxie, George Elwin	34y	W	19 DEC 1918	Takoma MD	McConnellsv. NY
05159	Hoy, Pearl Irene	20y	W	5 JUN 1905	Alexandria VA	Congressional
00101	Hoyberger, Lucinda	6m	W	7 JUL 1889	Landover Sta. MD	Rock Creek
08885	Hoyle, Sarah Frances	70y	W	9 OCT 1912	Grand Rapids MI	Holyrood
00311	Hoynes, Olive M.	30y	W	18 APR 1890	Branchville MD	Mt. Olivet
15594	Hubbard, Anna G.	52y	C	29 JAN 1919	Meadow Brook PA	Woodlawn
05431	Hubbard, George	72y	W	16 JAN 1906	New York NY	Arlington
07738	Hubbard, Infant of P.H.	SB	W	26 JAN 1907	Copperhill TN	Rock Creek
07739	Hubbard, P.H.	37y	W	12 SEP 1910	Copperhill TN	Rock Creek
04870	Hubbard, Walter L.	36y	C	2 SEP 1904	Colonial Bea. VA	Williamsport PA
05211	Hubbard, William F.	28y	W	17 JUL 1905	Cabin John MD	Oak Hill
05493	Huck, Anna Appolinia	20y	W	7 MAR 1906	Tacoma Park MD	St. Mary's
00726	Huddleson, Viola	2d	W	29 DEC 1891	Montg. Co. MD	Tenallytown

[1] Disinterment permit #8830 on 2 DEC 1916 for removal to Arlington National Cemetery.

District of Columbia Foreign Death Records, 1888-1923

No.	Name of Deceased	Age	Race	Death Date	Place of Death	Place of Burial
06082	Huddleson, William E.	48y	W	27 MAY 1907	Montg. Co. MD	Methodist
00486	Huddleston, Martha Mines	59y	W	14 APR 1891	Rockville MD	Oak Hill
00130	Huddleston, William	70y	W	3 AUG 1889	Montg. Co. MD	Oak Hill
01627	Hudel, Thomas	87y	W	13 MAR 1895	Fenwick MD	Oak Hill
01235	Hudlow, Ella	16y	W	9 NOV 1893	Bowie MD	Congressional
08015	Hudnall, Novella Conway	75y	W	20 MAR 1911	Lilian VA	Glenwood
14336	Hudson, Helen	23y	W	3 SEP 1917	White Haven PA	Rock Creek
03804	Hudson, S.S.	65y	W	24 FEB 1902	Baltimore MD	Congressional
14707	Huebner, Anna	78y	W	23 MAR 1918	Mt. Ranier MD	Cremated
01872	Huffman, James Franklin	1m	W	24 FEB 1896	Kensington MD	Rock Creek
14857	Hughes, Adele Jeanette	81y	W	8 JUN 1918	Lenoir NC	Arlington
05577	Hughes, Alonzo	68y	W	14 MAY 1906	Philadelphia PA	Glenwood
17429	Hughes, Arthur	—	C	23 SEP 1921	Baltimore MD	—
12045	Hughes, Charles E.	44y	W	26 AUG 1913	Aurora IL	Arlington
02435	Hughes, Daniel S.	29y	W	1 MAY 1898	Asheville NC	Mt. Olivet
16931	Hughes, Delia	84y	W	20 JAN 1921	Mt. Ranier MD	Alexandria VA
06500	Hughes, Edward Francis	45y	W	9 APR 1908	Baltimore MD	Mt. Olivet
14433	Hughes, Elizabeth Ann	48y	W	31 OCT 1917	Syracuse NY	Glenwood
17030	Hughes, Eva Sophronia	56y	W	8 FEB 1921	New York NY	Glenwood
07219	Hughes, Frank J.	50y	W	29 SEP 1909	Philadelphia PA	Mt. Olivet
03310	Hughes, John	—	C	21 OCT 1900	Hyndeman PA	Mt. Zion
07430	Hughes, John R.	28y	C	21 FEB 1910	Philadelphia PA	Mt. Olivet
06845	Hughes, Margaret	29y	W	6 DEC 1908	New York NY	Mt. Olivet
14391	Hughes, Marion	65y	W	28 SEP 1917	Middletown DE	Rock Creek
02642	Hughes, Marjorie	6y	W	22 OCT 1898	Wash. Grove MD	Glenwood
08374	Hughes, Mary V.	43y	W	25 OCT 1911	Rosslyn VA	Congressional
07065	Hughes, Paul	32y	W	17 JUN 1909	Atlantic City NJ	Mt. Olivet
13316	Hughes, Phillip P.	73y	C	21 JAN 1916	Baltimore MD	Arlington VA
02204	Hughes, Robert	24y	C	25 JUN 1897	Mt. Vernon NY	Harmony
01157	Hughes, Robert B.	81y	W	24 NOV 1892	Falls Church VA	Glenwood
03112	Hughes, Sarah J.	57y	W	3 MAR 1900	Falls Church VA	Glenwood
13526	Hughes, Susan V.	56y	C	29 MAY 1916	Springfield MA	Harmony
02068	Hughes, William B.	64y	W	22 SEP 1896	Baltimore MD	Arlington VA
03635	Hughlett, Dangerfield O.	45y	W	31 AUG 1901	Auburn VA	Rock Creek
15583	Hughston, Clinton D.	19y	C	22 JAN 1919	Newark NJ	Woodlawn
04954	Huidekofer, Gracie	1d	W	6 JUL 1872	New York NY	Oak Hill
15343	Hulings, Mary B. (Thomas)	80y	W	10 NOV 1918	Louisville KY	Rockville MD
15568	Hulse, George C.	78y	W	18 JAN 1919	Takoma Park MD	Arlington
11992	Hulse, Ida Alice	43y	W	5 SEP 1913	Laconia NH	Glenwood
04594	Humbles, Benj. Edward, in fire	2y	C	8 FEB 1904	Alex. Co. VA	Harmony
13367	Hume, Belle W.	40y	W	19 FEB 1916	Pittsburgh PA	Oak Hill
03741	Hume, Infant of Graham	4h	W	13 OCT 1901	Alex. Co. VA	Oak Hill
12397	Hummelbauer, Siegfried	28y	W	27 MAY 1914	New York NY	Rock Creek
05987	Hummer, Annie M.	18y	C	18 MAR 1907	Rosslyn VA	Baptist
17471	Hummer, Fannie	48y	W	17 OCT 1921	Takoma Park MD	Leesburg VA
07415	Hummer, Infant of Dr. H.R.	6d	W	9 FEB 1910	Lincoln Co. SD	Congressional
09036	Hummer, Norena Guest	8d	W	17 JAN 1913	Lincoln Co. SD	Congressional
15010	Humphrey, Albert Rice	42y	W	8 sEP 1918	Cambridge MA	Cremated
02405	Humphrey, Charles F.	42y	W	3 MAR 1898	Columbia Pk. MD	Congressional
15642	Humphrey, Earnest R.	40y	W	25 FEB 1919	Saranac Lake NY	Glenwood
04388	Humphrey, John	69y	W	12 JUL 1903	Round Hill VA	Rock Creek
12317	Humphrey, Katherine	58y	W	16 APR 1914	Chevy Chase MD	Mt. Olivet
11872	Humphrey, Lizzie	27y	W	23 JUN 1913	Fulton KY	Congressional
16987	Humphreys, Katie Park	73y	W	19 FEB 1921	Philadelphia PA	Congressional
01158	Humphreys, Margaret Rogers	35y	W	1 NOV 1892	Fredericksburg VA	Congressional
15056	Humphreys, Mary C.	—	W	19 SEP 1918	Fredericksburg VA	Congressional
02256	Humphreys, Rebecca H.	78y	W	13 JUL 1897	Concordville PA	Congressional
15002	Hungerford, J.D., Capt. U.S.A.	24y	W	29 AUG 1918	Mogales AZ	Arlington
16890	Hungerford, Katie S.	54y	W	4 JAN 1921	Ft. Foote MD	St. Barnabas

No.	Name of Deceased	Age	Race	Death Date	Place of Death	Place of Burial
17691	Hungerford, Marie J.	87	W	11 FEB 1922	Pomfret MD	Syracuse NY
07356	Hungerford, Mary E.	10d	W	22 NOV 1909	Indianapolis IN	Oak Hill
05086	Hungerford, Virginia	9m	W	16 APR 1905	Milwaukee WI	Oak Hill
05624	Hungerford, Walter John	17y	W	1 JUL 1906	Dedham MA	Oak Hill
14489	Hunnell, Catherine	55y	W	1 DEC 1917	Brooklyn NY	Mt. Olivet
06961	Hunnington, Lawrence D.	74y	W	30 MAR 1909	Railroad	New Rochelle NY
17763	Hunt, Edwin Brendel	26y	W	12 MAR 1921	Washington DC	Ft. Lincoln
15199	Hunt, Eleanor	27y	W	15 OCT 1918	Baltimore MD	Rock Creek
03976	Hunt, Emma L.	82y	W	11 AUG 1902	Winchester VA	Oak Hill
14313	Hunt, Henry	77y	W	23 AUG 1917	Providence VA	Cremated
00443	Hunt, Hugh Jerritt	31y	W	23 NOV 1890	New York NY	Oak Hill
18017	Hunt, Jane Allison	50y	W	c.1912	Robertsdale AL	Glenwood[1]
02874	Hunt, John	35y	W	21 JUL 1899	Portsmouth VA	Arlington VA
16799	Hunt, John, s/o Joel	57y	W	2 NOV 1920	Los Angeles CA	Rock Creek
05519	Hunt, John W.	84y	W	4 APR 1906	Erie PA	Rock Creek
07271	Hunt, John William	33y	W	10 NOV 1909	Palenville NY	Glenwood
14823	Hunt, Mamie	30y	C	16 MAY 1918	Newark NJ	Payne's
03644	Hunt, Mamie	10y	W	14 SEP 1901	Ft. Morgan AL	T.B. MD
17762	Hunt, Paul J., Capt.	28y	W	26 MAR 1922	Camp Vale NJ	Glenwood
07873	Hunt, Presley	39y	W	15 DEC 1910	Baltimore MD	Soldier's Home
16335	Hunt, Samuel	29y	W	23 FEB 1920	Knoxville TN	Cremated
07805	Hunt, Wallace L.	23y	W	27 OCT 1910	Allegany Co. MD	Congressional
12342	Hunt, Walter T.	72y	W	30 APR 1914	Troy NY	Glenwood
03091	Hunter, Alice	28y	C	3 FEB 1900	New York NY	Harmony
01990	Hunter, Beatrice Katherine	1y	W	7 JUL 1896	Alex. Co. VA	Mt. Olivet
07324	Hunter, Bertha L.	6m	W	14 DEC 1909	Capitol Hts. MD	Congressional
15591	Hunter, Chadwick, artist	49y	W	24 JAN 1919	Denver CO	Rock Creek
02436	Hunter, Cornelius	22y	C	22 APR 1989	Jersey City NJ	Harmony
16959	Hunter, Edna T.	43y	C	4 FEB 1921	Boston MA	Harmony
01566	Hunter, Eloise Elbert	21y	C	28 FEB 1895	Washington DC	Harmony
18484	Hunter, Emily A.	26y	W	13 APR 1923	Baltimore MD	Ft. Lincoln
12706	Hunter, Filah A.	56y	W	9 JAN 1915	Rockville MD	Arlington
05859	Hunter, James Thomas	51y	W	13 DEC 1906	Bladensburg MD	Holyrood
07991	Hunter, James W.	83y	W	27 FEB 1911	Bladensburg MD	Holyrood
05754	Hunter, Mary C.	50y	C	1 OCT 1906	Arlington VA	Holyrood
18236	Hunter, Olivia	76y	W	1 JAN 1923	Brooklyn NY	Glenwood
18022	Hunter, Robert B.	61y	W	30 APR 1922	Syracuse NY	Mt. Olivet
13240	Hunter, Robert R.	17y	W	15 NOV 1915	Gaillord Cut, C.Z.	Mt. Olivet
16857	Hunter, Robert W.	51y	W	15 NOV 1920	Guant., Cuba	St. Barnabas
06785	Hunter, Virginia (Biers)	78y	W	24 OCT 1908	Roanoke VA	Alexandria VA
03902	Hunter, William F	23y	W	7 JUN 1902	Denver CO	Congressional
17686	Hunter, William G.	75y	W	12 FEB 1922	Hyattsville MD	Glenwood
15856	Huntington, George A.	45y	W	20 JUN 1919	Baltimore MD	Congressional
06917	Huntley, Elias DeWitt	68y	W	12 FEB 1909	Clifton Spgs. NY	Rockville MD
13155	Huntt, Joseph R.	50y	W	18 OCT 1915	Laurel MD	Rock Creek
12428	Hurd, H. Clarence	44y	W	8 JUL 1914	Chesa. Bea. MD	Glenwood
14491	Hurd, Louis Albert	c.30y	C	26 NOV 1917	Vernon CN	Mt. Olivet
00439	Hurlbert, Clinton H.	21y	W	16 NOV 1809	Roanoke VA	Rock Creek
06738	Hurlbut, Maud M.	39y	W	18 SEP 1908	Cleveland OH	Rock Creek
04261	Hurlebaus, Mary	26y	W	29 APR 1903	Seattle WA	Prospect Hill
04407	Hurley, Ebenezer M.	33y	W	25 JUL 1903	Hyattsville MD	Mt. Olivet
14339	Hurley, Elizabeth	92y	W	3 SEP 1917	Hyattsville MD	Mt. Olivet
03588	Hurley, Eugene Greenbury	10y	W	23 JUL 1901	Kensington MD	Rock Creek
04367	Hurley, Francis W.	31y	W	25 SEP 1902	Woosing, China	Holyrood
00177	Hurley, Frank	19y	W	7 MAY 1888	New York NY	Glenwood
13449	Hurley, Infant of Jas. A.	SB	W	10 APR 1916	Kensington MD	Congressional

[1] Letter of 15 AUG 1922, Bay Minette AL, cites deceased as Elizabeth Hunt who died about 10 years ago, and was buried in Robertsdale Cemetery.

No.	Name of Deceased	Age	Race	Death Date	Place of Death	Place of Burial
15126	Hurley, James W.	21y	W	29 AUG 1918	Santiago, D.R.	Glenwood
06232	Hurley, John	55y	W	17 SEP 1907	Hyattsville MD	Mt. Olivet
00086	Hurley, John A.	57y	W	12 JUN 1889	Cincinnati OH	Mt. Olivet
13347	Hurley, Katherine	28y	C	9 FEB 1916	Fairmont Mts. MD	Payne's
13477	Hurley, Lillian E.	40y	W	25 APR 1916	Montg. Co. MD	Congressional
02921	Hurley, Malvinia Rose	64y	W	21 AUG 1899	Boston MA	Oak Hill
12774	Hurley, Mary	49y	W	20 FEB 1915	Riverdale MD	Mt. Olivet
01406	Hurley, Michael M., justice	63y	W	11 JUN 1894	Bladensburg MD	Mt. Olivet
05010	Hurley, Paul W.	18y	W	25 JAN 1905	Portsmouth VA	Mt. Olivet
01724	Hurley, William H.	10m	W	22 AUG 1895	Hyattsville MD	Mt. Olivet
00487	Hurst, Blanche	—	W	7 DEC 1885	Buffalo NY	Rock Creek
04266	Hurst, John F.	68y	W	4 MAY 1903	Bethesda MD	Rock Creek
16044	Hurst, John L.	59y	W	10 OCT 1919	Denver CO	Rock Creek
12015	Husband, Annie Regina	64y	W	25 SEP 1913	Glen Echo MD	Mt. Olivet
16762	Husband, Morris F.	36y	W	16 OCT 1920	Capitol Hts. MD	Mt. Olivet
14828	Huske, George L.	37y	W	11 MAY 1918	Tucson AZ	Glenwood
04127	Hussey, John B.	55y	W	11 DEC 1902	Railroad	Cremated
18510	Husten, William J.	48y	W	27 APR 1923	Easton PA	Arlington
14749	Huston, Robert T.	69y	W	11 APR 1918	Philadelphia PA	Rock Creek
04734	Hutchington, John M.	50y	W	27 MAY 1904	Baltimore MD	Mt. Olivet
15565	Hutchins, Frank	36y	W	15 JAN 1919	Philadelphia PA	Glenwood
01992	Hutchins, William Irvin	28y	W	7 AUG 1896	Cabin John MD	Oak Hill
16082	Hutchinson, Edward	28y	C	28 OCT 1919	Philadelphia PA	Woodlawn
12890	Hutchinson, Emma	61y	W	20 APR 1915	Allentown PA	Congressional
14081	Hutchinson, Florence M.	19y	W	10 APR 1917	Washington DC	Congressional
12970	Hutchinson, Henry W.	55y	W	18 JUN 1915	Richmond VA	Cremated
06682	Hutchinson, James	55y	W	11 AUG 1908	Forestville MD	Congressional
16828	Hutchinson, Louis S.	52y	C	24 NOV 1920	York PA	Harmony
15850	Hutchinson, Mary E.S.	73y	W	28 JUN 1919	College Park MD	Oak Hill
18597	Hutchinson, Rocha	49y	C	8 JUN 1923	Baltimore MD	Payne's
15672	Hutchinson, William	45y	C	13 MAR 1919	Baltimore MD	Woodlawn
15157	Huth, Harry F.	34y	W	6 OCT 1918	El Paso TX	Arlington
12106	Hutton, George W.	90y	C	22 NOV 1910	Portsmouth VA	Woodlawn
18410	Hutton, Hattie	35y	C	10 MAR 1923	Asbury Park NJ	Woodlawn
07127	Huyck, Jesse Van Ness	71y	W	23 JUL 1909	Marblehead MA	Mt. Olivet
04046	Hyatt, Alpheus	64y	W	18 JUN 1902	Cambridge MA	Congressional
02377	Hyatt, Howard B.	26y	W	8 FEB 1878	Alexandria VA	Congressional
16212	Hyatt, Jesse M.	51y	W	14 JAN 1920	New York NY	Congressional
05972	Hyde, George A., s/o Geo.	58y	W	4 MAR 1907	Remington VA	Oak Hill
03800	Hyde, Richard	40y	W	21 FEB 1902	Hartford CN	Glenwood
06635	Hyde, Sue Tyler	65y	W	9 JUL 1908	Forest Glen MD	Oak Hill
01407	Hyde, Thomas, Jr.	—	W	3 JUN 1894	Leesburg VA	Oak Hill
14095	Hyde, William Herbert	43y	W	15 APR 1917	Scarbro WV	Rock Creek
08782	Hyder, Della Viola	49y	W	26 AUG 1912	Point of Rocks MD	Glenwood
14243	Hyer, Rachael A. (Autrum)	56y	W	20 JUL 1917	Ocean Grove NJ	Rock Creek
06665	Hyland, Eliza Jane	77y	W	30 JUL 1908	Reisterstown MD	Rock Creek
03805	Hyland, Henry A.	47y	W	26 FEB 1902	Baltimore MD	Rock Creek
07236	Hyland, Jennie	40y	C	11 OCT 1909	Philadelphia PA	Harmony
01408	Hyman, Frank B.	7m	W	26 JAN 1894	Falls Church VA	Graceland
03614	Hynes, Thomas	61y	W	13 AUG 1901	Seabrook MD	Arlington

No.	Name of Deceased	Age	Race	Death Date	Place of Death	Place of Burial
	I					
08083	Iardella, Joseph E., a.k.a.	65y	W	14 MAR 1911	Norfolk VA	Mt. Olivet
18195	Ibarra, Felicie	73y	W	4 DEC 1922	Wheaton MD	Mt. Olivet
00727	Iddins, Fredeick	39y	W	18 MAR 1892	Berkeley CA	Congressional
08637	Iddins, Mary E.	71y	W	16 MAY 1912	Baltimore MD	Congressional
13676	Iglehart, Evelyn Alice, d/o Jno.	2y	W	24 AUG 1916	Fredericksburg VA	Mt. Olivet
00408	Ihrie, Jeneatte Jean	3y	W	3 OCT 1890	Hyattsville MD	Congressional
06018	Ijams, Raleigh Brown	48y	W	8 APR 1907	Goldsboro NC	Baltimore MD
11915	Immich, Edith Mildred	26d	W	25 JUL 1913	Takoma Park MD	Rock Creek
16152	Imose, Halekichi	19y	G	17 DEC 1919	Norfolk VA	Cremated
02640	Inch, Philip J.	62y	W	18 OCT 1898	Saratoga Spg. NY	Arlington VA
09084	Ingersoll, Clara K.	62y	W	20 FEB 1913	Chevy Chase MD	Glenwood
04323	Ingersoll, John C.	43y	W	6 JUN 1903	Colon, Columbia	Oak Hill
08548	Ingle, Ellen S.	81y	W	9 MAR 1912	Brookline MA	Congressional
14374	Ingle, Imogen Tayloe	70y	W	23 SEP 1917	Blue Ridge S. PA	Congressional
12418	Ingledove, Edward	28y	W	28 JUN 1914	Occoquan VA	Lynchburg VA
06689	Ingledue, John Harrison	18y	W	14 JUL 1908	Norfolk VA	Arlington VA
13048	Ingley, William Geo.	50y	W	9 AUG 1915	Baltimore MD	Glenwood
02875	Ingling, Marie Louise	3d	W	24 JUN 1899	Ballston VA	Glenwood
00488	Ingraham, Phillis	90y	C	31 JAN 1891	Montg. Co. MD	Harmony
17116	Ingram, Florence	27y	C	18 APR 1921	Baltimore MD	Arlington VA
17354	Ingram, Jane	82y	W	4 AUG 1921	Silver Spring MD	Cincinnati OH
15986	Irey, Elmer L., Jr.	1y	W	10 SEP 1919	Shady Side MD	Prospect Hill
14345	Irvin, Martin F.	50y	W	5 SEP 1917	Baltimore MD	Congressional
16314	Irvine, Walter F., s/o Walter	44y	W	15 FEB 1920	Norfolk VA	Cremated
05610	Irving, Henry	57y	W	28 JUN 1906	Boonsboro MD	Rock Creek
09047	Irving, Robert Alphonso	53y	W	25 JAN 1913	New York NY	Rock Creek
03438	Irwin, David Allison	60y	W	28 FEB 1901	Orchard Lake MI	Arlington VA
11825	Irwin, George Alex.	66y	W	23 MAY 1913	Takoma Park MD	Rock Creek
13694	Irwin, Harvey S.	72y	W	3 SEP 1916	Vienna VA	Rock Creek
15812	Irwin, Nettie (Johnson)	70y	W	31 MAY 1919	St. Helena CA	Rock Creek
18472	Iseman, Morton	33y	W	26 MAR 1923	Los Angeles CA	Wash. Hebrew
05883	Israel, August	73y	W	2 JAN 1907	Garrett Park MD	St. Mary's
11930	Israel, Barbara Shank	76y	W	30 JUL 1913	Sykesville MD	St. Mary's
08333	Israel, E.L. (McGuire)	77y	W	29 SEP 1910	Lexington KY	Rock Creek
03188	Israel, George	26y	W	17 MAY 1900	New York NY	St. Mary's
07580	Israel, Infant of George	SB	W	18 JUN 1910	Kensington MD	Oak Hill
13482	Israel, Robert Otho	29y	W	29 APR 1916	Laurel MD	Oak Hill
05263	Iverson, Eugene	17y	C	31 AUG 1905	Rock Castle VA	Harmony
13330	Ives, Cora Semmes	86y	W	27 JAN 1916	New York NY	Holyrood
03568	Ivins, Wright	79y	W	8 JUL 1901	Montg. Co. MD	Congressional
06153	Iwamote, Moraburo, of Japan	22y	J	20 JUL 1907	Norfolk VA	Cremated

District of Columbia Foreign Death Records, 1888-1923

No.	Name of Deceased	Age	Race	Death Date	Place of Death	Place of Burial
J						
01409	Jack, Edwin H., printer	45y	W	20 JUN 1894	Fairfax Co. VA	Mt. Olivet
13915	Jackman, Leicester H.	26y	W	9 JAN 1917	Asheville NC	Cremated
13293	Jackson, Albert	55y	C	9 JAN 1916	Pittsburgh PA	Woodlawn
03922	Jackson, Alexander	30y	W	19 JUL 1902	Hyattsville MD	Oak Hill
00728	Jackson, Amelia	93y	C	31 DEC 1891	Landover MD	Mt. Olivet
03092	Jackson, Andrew K.	17y	C	3 FEB 1900	Baltimore MD	Woodlawn
08713	Jackson, Annie E.	61y	C	10 JUL 1912	Philadelphia PA	Mt. Zion East
14614	Jackson, Annie T.	—	W	31 JAN 1918	Baltimore MD	Mt. Olivet
17767	Jackson, Barbara	38y	C	26 MAR 1922	Poughkeepsie NY	Harmony
15581	Jackson, Catherine	43y	W	23 JAN 1919	Ballston VA	Congressional
00617	Jackson, Charles A.	6m	C	16 OCT 1891	Arlington VA	Mt. Olivet
03044	Jackson, Charles A.	20y	C	20 DEC 1899	Morgantown WV	Mt. Zion
18222	Jackson, Chesterfield, Rev.	54y	C	25 DEC 1922	Brentwood MD	Harmony
05152	Jackson, Christiana L.	33y	C	3 JUN 1905	New York NY	Harmony
18289	Jackson, Dennis	48y	C	22 JAN 1923	Seat Pleasant MD	Mt. Olivet
13535	Jackson, Edward Parke	29y	W	3 JUN 1916	Ballston VA	Congressional
04284	Jackson, Elisha	37y	C	11 APR 1903	Ft. Bayard NM	Arlington VA
12304	Jackson, Eliza	64y	C	8 APR 1914	Savannah GA	Payne's
06708	Jackson, Elizabeth	—	W	7 AUG 1907	Buffalo NY	Oak Hill
05341	Jackson, Elizia J.	32y	C	30 OCT 1905	Philadelphia PA	Woodlawn
04377	Jackson, Ellen L.	65y	W	27 JUN 1903	Shawnee OK	Rock Creek
08297	Jackson, Elsa Winifred	9m	C	5 SEP 1911	Fairmont Hts. MD	Payne's
18390	Jackson, Emma	60y	C	5 MAR 1923	Fairmont Hts. MD	Woodlawn
08107	Jackson, Ervin J., s/o Luther	19y	C	9 MAY 1911	Rosslyn VA	Mt. Zion West
03816	Jackson, Flora	75y	C	12 MAR 1902	Pittsburgh PA	Mt. Zion
02069	Jackson, Frank W.	24y	W	11 NO 1896	Atlantic City NJ	Mt. Zion
01932	Jackson, Frederick	61y	C	3 MAY 1896	Philadelphia PA	Payne's
05254	Jackson, George B.	17y	C	21 AUG 1905	Riverdale MD	Harmony
15124	Jackson, George, s/o Wm.	27y	C	5 OCT 1918	Camp Eustis VA	Woodlawn
16427	Jackson, Henrietta	90y	W	10 APR 1920	Newark NJ	Wash. Hebrew
16945	Jackson, Henry	31y	C	30 JAN 1921	Occoquan VA	Alexandria VA
00331	Jackson, Henry	25y	C	28 MAY 1890	New York NY	Hillsdale
13715	Jackson, James	67y	C	13 SEP 1916	Occoquan VA	Mt. Zion West
03714	Jackson, James	22y	C	18 NOV 1901	Philadelphia PA	Payne's
16283	Jackson, James Andrew	25y	C	4 FEB 1920	Fairmont Hts. MD	Mt. Zion East
04004	Jackson, James H.	36y	C	14 SEP 1902	Connellsville PA	Mt. Zion
06408	Jackson, Jane	62y	C	28 JAN 1908	Pittsburgh PA	Payne's
04570	Jackson, Jas. Henry Lorenzo	21y	C	14 JAN 1904	Arlington VA	Mt. Olivet
06709	Jackson, Jennie	60y		1896	Washington DC	Oak Hill
03342	Jackson, Joe	35y	C	10 NOV 1900	Berryburg WV	Moore's
03642	Jackson, John Henry	53y	C	12 SEP 1901	Baltimore MD	Payne's
18215	Jackson, John T.	36y	C	21 DEC 1922	Huntsville MD	Mt. Olivet
04331	Jackson, John Thomas	22y	W	17 AUG 1903	Ft. Wayne IN	Kenmore VA
16834	Jackson, Joseph A.	71y	W	1 DEC 1920	Rockville MD	Oak Hill
14865	Jackson, Joseph J.	24y	C	12 JUN 1918	Chilicothe OH	Arlington
06260	Jackson, Joseph Lewis	1m	C	5 OCT 1907	Arlington VA	Holyrood
13028	Jackson, Lewis	60y	C	30 JUL 1915	Arlington VA	Mt. Olivet
02257	Jackson, Lewis	26y	C	21 JUL 1897	Brunswick MD	Payne's
01239	Jackson, Lucy L.	17y	C	1 OCT 1893	Brightseat MD	Mt. Olivet
01725	Jackson, Mary	70y	W	10 OCTG 1895	Hyattsville MD	Oak Hill
00236	Jackson, Michael	65y	C	13 DEC 1889	Pr. Geo. Co. MD	Jones' Chapel
13850	Jackson, Moses J.	45y	W	8 DEC 1916	Baltimore MD	Wash. Hebrew
04396	Jackson, Oliver	25y	C	16 JUL 1903	New York NY	Harmony
04144	Jackson, Pearl E.	4y	C	22 JAN 1903	Philadelphia PA	Woodlawn
12688	Jackson, Rebecca	41y	C	28 DEC 1914	Fairfax Co. VA	Mt. Zion West
16003	Jackson, Reginald H.	41y	W	21 SEP 1919	Lake Como PA	Oak Hill
04069	Jackson, Robert	33y	C	4 NOV 1902	Philadelphia PA	Harmony
07599	Jackson, Robert Leo, s/o L.	23y	C	27 JUN 1910	Arlington VA	Mt. Olivet

No.	Name of Deceased	Age	Race	Death Date	Place of Death	Place of Burial
01816	Jackson, Smith	21y	C	15 SEP 1895	Gainesville VA	Christian
14590	Jackson, Susan	50y	C	19 JAN 1918	Fairmont Hts. MD	Woodlawn
14293	Jackson, Thomas A.	4m	C	12 AUG 1917	Cedar Hts. MD	Mt. Zion West
14879	Jackson, Thomas H.	56y	C	22 JUN 1918	Hyattsville MD	Harmony
02551	Jackson, Thomas P.	36y	C	13 AUG 1898	Philadelphia PA	Woodlawn
06838	Jackson, Walter	27y	C	2 DEC 1908	New York NY	Harmony
08383	Jackson, William	26y	C	31 OCT 1911	Philadelphia PA	Payne's
00087	Jackson, William Palmer	23y	W	17 SEP 1889	Laurel Hts. MD	Rock Creek
02774	Jackson, Willie	4y	C	13 MAR 1899	Rosslyn VA	Baptist
03958	Jacksson, Isabella	47y	C	31 JUL 1902	Hartford NY	Mt. Zion
16597	Jacob, George M.	19y	W	11 JUL 1920	Tuscum. NM	Arlington
07147	Jacobs, Anna J.	1y	W	6 AUG 1909	Tuxedo MD	Mt. Olivet
08883	Jacobs, Hellen B.	38y	C	10 OCT 1912	New York NY	Payne's
14710	Jacobs, Lizzie	45y	C	25 MAR 1918	Morristown PA	Falls Church VA
18342	Jacobs, Maggie	37y	C	9 FEB 1923	Baltimore MD	Odd Fellows VA
12341	Jacobs, Margaret B.	84y	W	30 APR 1914	Munson's Hill VA	Oak Hill
02876	Jacobs, Rosa	38y	W	24 JUL 1899	Philadelphia PA	Congressional
02614	Jacobson, Henry	31y	W	20 SEP 1898	Montauk NY	Arlington VA
08865	Jager, Melvin	4h	W	2 OCT 1912	Hyattsville MD	Glenwood
14795	Jaggert, Ida	27y	W	2 MAY 1918	New York NY	Glenwood
08329	James, Alice	35y	W	27 SEP 1911	Washington DC	Rock Creek
00252	James, Charles	34y	C	29 DEC 1889	Rosslyn VA	Mt. Pleasant Plain
05899	James, Edward	20y	C	20 JAN 1907	Baltimore MD	Harmony
14653	James, Edward W.	44y	W	20 FEB 1918	Branchville MD	Congressional
03205	James, Edwin	64y	W	8 JUN 1900	Pikesville MD	Rock Creek
01629	James, Eliza	79y	C	1 APR 1895	Philadelphia PA	Harmony
07640	James, Elizabeth	68y	C	17 JUL 1910	New York NY	Woodlawn
00618	James, Ellen E.	61y	C	1 OCT 1891	Buckland VA	Harmony
18496	James, Henry H.	55y	W	21 APR 1923	Alexandria VA	Congressional
02558	James, Isabel Jane	32y	W	6 AUG 1898	Quebec, Can.	Glenwood
12636	James, James	41y	C	27 NOV 1914	Philadelphia PA	Harmony
13792	James, Jeanetti	50y	W	29 OCT 1916	Takoma Park MD	Glenwood[1]
02517	James, John T.	77y	W	13 JUL 1898	Gaithersburg MD	Glenwood
17125	James, Louise (Koch)	78y	W	25 APR 1921	Staunton VA	Arlington
13809	James, Matilda V.	76y	W	9 NOV 1916	Hyattsville MD	Congressional
03673	James, Rosie	34y	C	4 OCT 1901	Philadelphia PA	Harmony
17341	James, Rowland C.	31y	W	31 JUL 1921	Ira MI	Congressional
03764	James, W.E.	30y	W	20 JUN 1901	Cuba	Congressional
13407	James, William P.	69y	W	9 MAR 1916	New York NY	Rock Creek
14889	Jameson, Archer LeRoy	38y	W	29 JUN 1918	Alexandria VA	Glenwood
15261	Jamieson, Isabel Wintersteen	26y	W	22 OCT 1918	Alexandria VA	Cremated
06374	Jamison, Caroline Bettinfield	24y	W	3 JAN 1908	Memphis TN	Baltimore MD
08545	Janefer, James Edward	27y	C	4 MAR 1912	Biscayne Bay FL	Woodlawn
15160	Janelli, John Godwin	18y	W	12 OCT 1918	Brentwood MD	Glenwood
12533	Jaquette, Frank	48y	W	12 SEP 1914	Ogden UT	Glenwood
02315	Jardin, Armand, Sr., florist	68y	W	10 SEP 1886	Laurel MD	Mt. Olivet
08112	Jardine, Jane	84y	W	11 MAY 1911	Baltimore MD	Congressional
06108	Jarrell, John	32y	W	14 JUN 1907	Hinton WV	Glenwood
03532	Jarrett, Frank E.	25y	W	2 JUN 1901	Four Mile Run VA	Baltimore MD
08128	Jarrott, J.B., M.D.	74y	W	12 MAR 1913	Florence SC	Cremated
01726	Jarvis, John H., waiter	46y	C	5 AUG 1895	New York NY	Harmony
13034	Jarvis, Melissa Hayes	1y	W	4 AUG 1915	Atlantic City NJ	Rock Creek
03957	Jarvis, Susie E.	46y	W	28 JUL 1902	Takoma Park MD	Rock Creek
15809	Jarvis, William H.	47y	C	30 MAY 1919	New York NY	Woodlawn
13336	Javins, John R.	49y	W	2 FEB 1916	Baltimore MD	Congressional
15575	Jawish, Foziek	28y	W	16 JAN 1919	New York NY	Glenwood
16145	Jay, Ida	30y	C	11 DEC 1919	Coatesville PA	Harmony

[1] Disinterment permit #8864 on 12 JAN 1917 for removal to Norfolk VA.

District of Columbia Foreign Death Records, 1888-1923

No.	Name of Deceased	Age	Race	Death Date	Place of Death	Place of Burial
02849	Jay, Jabez	86y	W	14 JUN 1899	Brooklyn NY	Glenwood
07482	Jay, Leonard B.	52y	W	23 MAR 1910	Johnson City TN	Glenwood
15380	Jayne, Gertrude	36y	W	25 NOV 1918	Rosslyn VA	Holyrood
14663	Jayne, John H.	58y	W	3 MAR 1918	Coraspolis PA	Rock Creek
05508	Jeffers, Hannah Rebecca	25y	W	22 MAR 1906	Falls Church VA	Rock Creek
07717	Jeffers, Mary C.	42y	W	24 AUG 1910	Vernon MI	Glenwood
01567	Jefferson, Annie	33y	C	2 FEB 1895	Pittsburgh PA	Mt. Olivet
15987	Jefferson, Earnest	36y	C	8 SEP 1919	Baltimore MD	Mt. Zion East
15631	Jefferson, Geneava	17y	C	19 FEB 1919	Page WV	Arlington VA
01242	Jefferson, Harry E.	21y	W	21 FEB 1889	Clarendon TX	Mt. Olivet
13668	Jefferson, Lillian	36y	C	19 AUG 1916	Philadelphia PA	Marshall Hall MD
06272	Jefferson, Nancy	80y	C	12 OCT 1907	Atlantic City NJ	Payne's
07566	Jeffrey, William	71y	W	8 JUN 1910	Davin CN	Arlington
07962	Jeffries, Harry	38y	W	6 FEB 1911	Philadelphia PA	Glenwood
12635	Jeffries, Peter W.	56y	W	29 NOV 1914	Baltimore MD	Glenwood
01240	Jekyll, Matilda L.	68y	W	29 JUN 1893	Malden MA	Congressional
01241	Jekyll, Thomas	39y	W	2 NOV 1863	New York NY	Congressional
17466	Jenifer, Henry E.	72y	C	14 OCT 1921	Garson Hp.	Harmony
13395	Jenipher, Earnest	43y	C	28 FEB 1916	Philadelphia PA	Moore's
16395	Jenkins, Alfonzo	31y	C	14 MAR 1920	Philadelphia PA	Payne's
06919	Jenkins, Andrew, s/o Alex.	30y	C	11 FEB 1909	Rosslyn VA	Payne's
05281	Jenkins, Bertha Rebecca	4y	W	10 SEP 1905	Glen Echo MD	Glenwood
07058	Jenkins, Bettie Walker	60y	W	14 JUN 1909	Forest Glen MD	Norfolk VA
09141	Jenkins, Elizabeth, d/o Chas.	12y	C	24 MAR 1913	New Haven CN	Harmony
12719	Jenkins, Francis E.	25y	W	14 JAN 1915	Pittsburgh PA	Mt. Olivet
14174	Jenkins, Francis Thornton, Dr.	55y	W	13 JUN 1917	Milwaukee WI	Arlington
17978	Jenkins, George W.	c.23y	—	27 JUL 1922	Chapel Point MD	Rock Creek
06263	Jenkins, Harry S., Jr.	7y	C	5 OCT 1907	Moorestown NJ	Harmony
08658	Jenkins, Infant of Charles	SB	W	3 JUN 1912	Suitland MD	Congressional
17390	Jenkins, Infant of Ray T.	7h	W	9 SEP 1921	Bethesda MD	Congressional
01727	Jenkins, James A.	44y	W	10 SEP 1895	Pr. Geo. Co. MD	Mt. Olivet
06857	Jenkins, James H.	25y	W	14 DEC 1908	El Paso TX	Congressional
02823	Jenkins, Jemima J.	77y	W	5 MAY 1899	Riverside Pk. VA	Rock Creek
01050	Jenkins, John	33y	W	18 APR 1893	Asheville NC	Congressional
01993	Jenkins, John	11y	W	26 JUL 1896	Colonial Bea. VA	Congressional
01873	Jenkins, John Zadock, farmer	75y	W	20 MAR 1896	Pr. Geo. Co. MD	Mt. Olivet
06510	Jenkins, Laura E.	27y	C	13 APR 1908	Baltimore MD	Payne's
07163	Jenkins, Lula	30y	C	20 AUG 1909	Wilmington DE	Woodlawn
08400	Jenkins, Mary	37y	C	23 NOV 1911	Jersey City NJ	Harmony
02378	Jenkins, Mary D.	71y	W	16 JAN 1898	Surrattsville MD	Mt. Olivet
15506	Jenkins, Mattie	35y	W	31 DEC 1918	Fairfax Co. VA	Rock Creek
05559	Jenkins, Mildred R.	18m	C	29 APR 1906	Moorestown NJ	Harmony
17109	Jenkins, Mollie Fawcett	62y	W	16 APR 1921	Suitland MD	Congressional
07859	Jenkins, William	43y	C	5 DEC 1910	Trenton NJ	Mt. Zion East
12247	Jenks, Winfield	71y	W	1 MAR 1914	Auburndale FL	Rock Creek
16425	Jennings, Anna E.	24y	W	5 APR 1920	Pittsburgh PA	Congressional
01308	Jennings, James Louis	3y	W	6 FEB 1894	Takoma Park MD	Rock Creek
00324	Jennings, Joseph Eugene	29y	W	11 MAY 1890	Pr. Geo. Co. MD	Glenwood
02962	Jennings, Mary D.	44y	W	26 SEP 1899	Saranac Lake NY	Mt. Olivet
06932	Jerrell, Sarah E.	8m	W	27 FEB 1909	Walkers Chap. VA	Spots. Co. VA
17009	Jervey, Eugene Postell	77y	W	2 MAR 1921	Charleston SC	Cremated
17081	Jesup, Julia Clark	79y	W	9 SEP 1919	Naples, Italy	Oak Hill
17350	Jeter, Henry H.	82y	W	8 AUG 1921	Seat Pleasant MD	Glenwood
17149	Jeter, Olivia B.	55y	W	9 MAY 1921	Hillman GA	Cremated
15998	Jett, Edw. E.	43y	W	18 SEP 1919	Baltimore MD	Alexandria VA
03863	Jewel, Margaret	45y	W	24 APR 1902	Philadelphia PA	Rock Creek
18007	Jewell, Wallace, Jr.	22y	C	10 AUG 1922	Pittsburgh PA	Harmony
16074	Jiltan, Caroline W.	49y	W	26 OCT 1919	Cherrydale VA	Congressional
05595	Jiudo, Don, of Italy	18y	W	12 JUN 1906	Kensington MD	St. Mary's

No.	Name of Deceased	Age	Race	Death Date	Place of Death	Place of Burial
12956	Joachim, Robert F.	33y	W	6 JUN 1915	New York NY	St. Mary's
18482	Jochum, Janet Smith	48y	W	18 FEB 1923	Winnetka IL	Oak Hill
14422	Johanson, George Peter	55y	W	21 OCT 1917	Alex. Co. VA	Glenwood
04351	John, Dorethy E.	9m	W	4 AUG 1903	Hyattsville MD	Cremated
17526	Johns, Arthur Shaaf	80y	W	16 NOV 1921	Rockville MD	Congressional
07188	Johns, Emma L.	61y	W	7 SEP 1909	Otterbourne MD	Rock Creek
04898	Johnson, A. Roland	30y	W	14 SEP 1904	Denver CO	Oak Hill
12145	Johnson, Albert S.	39y	W	2 JAN 1914	New York NY	Mt. Olivet
13026	Johnson, Alfred	40y	C	26 JUL 1915	Baltimore MD	Woodlawn
17811	Johnson, Alice	50y	C	18 APR 1922	Philadelphia PA	Payne's
12507	Johnson, Aloysius Ay., s/o Wm.	21y	C	29 AUG 1914	Jersey City NJ	Mt. Olivet
18559	Johnson, Amelia Harris	53y	C	25 MAY 1923	Philadelphia PA	Union
05541	Johnson, Andrew	35y	W	16 APR 1906	Gaithersburg MD	Rock Creek
04169	Johnson, Angie	60y	W	21 FEB 1903	Syracuse NY	Arlington VA
13750	Johnson, Ann B.	40y	W	6 OCT 1916	Barnesville MD	Oak Hill
04942	Johnson, Annie	25y	C	27 OCT 1904	Philadelphia PA	Payne's
12633	Johnson, Annie V.	53y	W	27 NOV 1914	Capitol Hts. MD	Rock Creek
18100	Johnson, Annie Wheeler Holtz	68y	W	3 OCT 1922	Colonial Bea. VA	Congressional
15738	Johnson, Armelia	85y	C	17 APR 1919	Orange NJ	Woodlawn
12750	Johnson, Arnold B.	80y	W	2 FEB 1915	Boston MA	Rock Creek
17369	Johnson, Arthur	38y	C	21 AUG 1921	Leavenworth KS	Payne's
12490	Johnson, Arthur Carl	32y	C	20 AUG 1914	Springfield MA	Payne's
05510	Johnson, Beatris	20y	C	24 MAR 1906	Fairmont Hts. MD	Payne's
00296	Johnson, Benjamin	c.65y	C	23 MAR 1890	Montg. Co. MD	Mt. Pleasant
06267	Johnson, Bertha	16y	C	8 OCT 1907	Randallstown MD	Harmony
15434	Johnson, Bettie	61y	C	12 DEC 1918	Brentwood MD	Harmony
03266	Johnson, Carey	50y	C	15 AUG 1900	Arlington VA	Payne's
01443	Johnson, Catharine J.	72y	C	24 JUL 1894	New York NY	Mt. Zion
12082	Johnson, Celia	24y	C	6 NOV 1913	New York NY	Lexington VA
04754	Johnson, Channie	26y	C	3 JUN 1904	Philadelphia PA	Harmony
01051	Johnson, Charles E.	33y	C	13 JAN 1893	Pittsburgh PA	Harmony
00490	Johnson, Charles H.	28y	C	23 DEC 1890	—	Graceland
03391	Johnson, Charles Oscar	23y	W	11 JAN 1901	Glendale MD	Mt. Olivet
14493	Johnson, Clarence	42y	C	8 DEC 1917	Harrisburg PA	Odd Fellows VA
04130	Johnson, Clayton	17y	C	16 JAN 1903	Philadelphia PA	Harmony
04112	Johnson, Cornelius	25y	C	27 DEC 1902	Moundsville WV	Harmony
13928	Johnson, Curtis R.	4m	W	14 JAN 1917	Colonial Hts. VA	Congressional
16635	Johnson, Daisy	26y	C	31 JUL 1920	New York NY	Harmony
16995	Johnson, Daisy E.	27y	W	22 FEB 1921	Tom's Creek VA	Glenwood
14672	Johnson, Delfine	61y	C	4 MAR 1918	Halls Hill VA	Payne's
03303	Johnson, Dora	13y	W	8 OCT 1900	Pittsburgh PA	Harmony
18312	Johnson, Dudley A.	59y	W	26 JAN 1923	Miami FL	Cremated
01425	Johnson, Edgar	25y	W	17 JUL 1894	Norfolk VA	Congressional
04971	Johnson, Edwin C.	56y	C	26 NOV 1904	New York NY	Harmony
12779	Johnson, Elbert, s/o Ellis C.	29y	W	21 FEB 1915	Logan WV	Rock Creek
03524	Johnson, Eleine J.	9y	C	26 MAY 1901	Pittsburgh PA	Payne's
12119	Johnson, Eliza	60y	W	4 DEC 1914	New York NY	Harmony
03239	Johnson, Eliza	61y	C	16 JUL 1900	Philadelphia PA	Mt. Zion
18021	Johnson, Eliza	55y	C	19 AUG 1922	Atlantic City NJ	Woodlawn
06834	Johnson, Elizabeth	5m	C	1 DEC 1908	Riverdale MD	Mt. Olivet
03916	Johnson, Elizabeth G.	62y	W	14 JUN 1902	New York NY	Congressional
07525	Johnson, Emma Coke	57y	W	2 MAY 1910	Cincinnati OH	Rock Creek
13604	Johnson, Fannie M.	23y	C	14 JUL 1916	Asbury Park NJ	Harmony
08247	Johnson, Frank	2y	W	9 AUG 1911	Berwyn MD	Mt. Olivet
13204	Johnson, Frank Richard	79y	W	14 NOV 1915	Lynchburg VA	Congressional
12493	Johnson, Fred	38y	W	21 AUG 1914	Cincinnati OH	Glenwood
03956	Johnson, Fred R.	17y	W	5 JUL 1902	S. Lake Linden MI	Glenwood
07742	Johnson, George	51y	C	11 SEP 1910	Upland DE	Bailey's Xrds. VA
13667	Johnson, George	5m	W	19 AUG 1916	Montg. Co. MD	Cremated

District of Columbia Foreign Death Records, 1888-1923

No.	Name of Deceased	Age	Race	Death Date	Place of Death	Place of Burial
17817	Johnson, George Roy	28y	C	23 APR 1922	Atlantic City NJ	Harmony
15098	Johnson, George V.	42y	W	5 OCT 1918	Takoma Park MD	Congressional
15890	Johnson, George William	27y	C	24 JUL 1919	Halls Hill VA	Payne's
04801	Johnson, Graham M.	1y	C	14 JUL 1904	Wilmington DE	Harmony
09183	Johnson, Hannah	44y	C	21 APR 1913	Pr. Geo. Co. MD	Payne's
11846	Johnson, Harriett	50y	C	31 MAY 1913	New York NY	Payne's
12693	Johnson, Harry	34y	C	1 JAN 1915	New York NY	Harmony
09140	Johnson, Harry	23y	C	26 MAR 1913	Rochester NY	Harmony
14584	Johnson, Harry, a.k.a. Gray	21y	C	8 JAN 1918	Philadelphia PA	Payne's
17971	Johnson, Harry C.	35y	C	19 JUL 1922	Atlantic City NJ	Payne's
00068	Johnson, Hellen, c/o Joseph	10m	C	14 MAY 1889	Alexandria VA	Harmony
16997	Johnson, Henrietta	23y	C	23 FEB 1921	New York NY	Woodlawn
13684	Johnson, Herbert	18y	W	28 AUG 1916	Baltimore MD	Delaplane VA
17521	Johnson, Holice	4y	C	14 NOV 1921	Pittsburgh PA	Chesterbrook VA
17658	Johnson, Howard E.	32y	W	24 JAN 1922	Asheville NC	Congressional
17738	Johnson, Howard V.	32y	W	12 MAR 1922	Silver Spring MD	Oak Hill
05743	Johnson, Ida	35y	C	15 SEP 1906	Camden NJ	Payne's
07114	Johnson, Infant of H.V.	SB	W	17 JUL 1909	Silver Spring MD	Rock Creek
12065	Johnson, Irene	21y	C	28 OCT 1913	Hyattsville MD	Mt. Olivet
08718	Johnson, Irene (Bland)	65y	C	10 JUL 1912	Potomac River	Payne's
02379	Johnson, Isabel	65y	W	20 JAN 1898	New York NY	Oak Hill
18278	Johnson, James	35y	C	18 JAN 1923	Baltimore MD	Mt. Olivet
12461	Johnson, James	21y	C	21 JUL 1914	Deer Creek NM	Moore's
18475	Johnson, James	22y	C	10 APR 1923	Glenarden MD	Orange VA
18430	Johnson, James J.	41y	C	19 MAR 1923	New York NY	Harmony
14102	Johnson, Jefferson D.	c.50y	C	20 APR 1917	Charleston WV	Mt. Zion West
17593	Johnson, Jennie	47y	C	11 DEC 1921	Philadelphia PA	Louisa Co. VA
07451	Johnson, Jeremiah	36y	C	5 MAR 1910	Randallstown MD	Harmony
12005	Johnson, Jerome B.	35y	W	17 SEP 1913	Pittsburgh PA	Glenwood
16988	Johnson, Jester D.	31y	W	19 FEB 1921	Ridgeville MD	Arlington
14167	Johnson, John	37y	C	5 JUN 1917	Occoquan VA	King Geo. Co. VA
07876	Johnson, John	65y	C	27 NOV 1910	Petersburg VA	King Geo. Co. VA
08491	Johnson, John F., s/o Charles	15y	W	24 JAN 1912	Rosslyn VA	Rock Creek
16041	Johnson, John Henry	48y	C	11 OCT 1919	Brentwood MD	Harmony
02165	Johnson, John W.	40y	C	27 APR 1897	Brooklyn NY	Harmony
04528	Johnson, Joseph	32y	C	25 NOV 1903	Arlington VA	Moore's
17040	Johnson, Joseph T.	75y	W	12 MAR 1921	Cherrydale VA	Rock Creek
16844	Johnson, Josephine M.	68y	W	3 DEC 1920	Phoebus VA	Mt. Olivet
03214	Johnson, Kate O.	29y	C	23 MAR 1900	New York NY	Mt. Zion
11929	Johnson, L.H.	67y	W	26 JUL 1913	Garden City KS	Arlington
09038	Johnson, Leah	61y	C	13 JAN 1913	Cincinnati OH	Harmony
00088	Johnson, Letitia	58y	C	3 JUN 1889	Wilmington DE	Harmony
16177	Johnson, Louise	48y	C	28 DEC 1919	Philadelphia PA	Payne's
12243	Johnson, Lucretia E.C.	69y	W	27 FEB 1914	Chicago IL	Oak Hill
17473	Johnson, Lucy	29y	C	16 OCT 1921	Newark NJ	Moore's
07811	Johnson, Mabel	7y	C	30 OCT 1910	Newark NJ	Harmony
07975	Johnson, Maggie	23y	C	18 FEB 1911	Brentwood MD	Harmony
07247	Johnson, Malcolm D.	3y	C	22 OCT 1909	New York NY	Harmony
04709	Johnson, Margaret	82y	C	29 AUG 1906	Brentwood MD	Harmony
02967	Johnson, Margaret E.	69y	W	30 SEP 1899	Burke's Sta. VA	Congressional
01159	Johnson, Margaret E.	40y	W	17 JAN 1893	New York NY	Glenwood
13327	Johnson, Maria	59y	C	23 JAN 1916	Germantown PA	Harmony
00102	Johnson, Marie Evelyn, c/o E.	1y	W	4 JUL 1889	Harpers Ferry WV	Oak Hill
02958	Johnson, Martha A.	57y	W	26 SEP 1899	New York NY	Rock Creek
07259	Johnson, Mary	1d	W	2 NOV 1909	Burrsville MD	Payne's
03113	Johnson, Mary Anna	7m	W	4 MAR 1900	Atlantic City NJ	Oak Hill
16568	Johnson, Mary C.	c.80y	W	27 JUN 1920	Georgetown DC	Rock Creek
09155	Johnson, Mary E.	45y	C	2 APR 1913	Fairmont Hts. MD	Harmony
12593	Johnson, Mary Geraldine Amici	57y	W	1 NOV 1914	W. Haverstraw NY	Mt. Olivet

No.	Name of Deceased	Age	Race	Death Date	Place of Death	Place of Burial
17527	Johnson, Mary Magdelena	67y	W	2 NOV 1921	Milwaukee WI	Mt. Olivet
05060	Johnson, Mary R.	60y	W	10 MAR 1905	Monterey, Mex.	Rock Creek
16744	Johnson, Mary S.	37y	C	6 OCT 1920	Brentwood MD	Harmony
18325	Johnson, Mason	41y	C	2 FEB 1923	Baltimore MD	Harmony
18037	Johnson, Matilda	49y	C	26 AUG 1922	Lincoln MD	Payne's
07915	Johnson, Mattie	26y	C	11 JAN 1911	New York NY	Payne's
13166	Johnson, Minnie Hall	32y	C	25 OCT 1915	Pomona MD	Harmony
05180	Johnson, Missie	24y	C	18 JUN 1905	Philadelphia PA	Harmony
15559	Johnson, Oleda	26y	C	13 JAN 1919	Philadelphia PA	Harmony
07432	Johnson, Oliver H., Jr.	2m	W	23 FEB 1910	New York NY	Oak Hill
07452	Johnson, Rachel	90y	C	4 MAR 1910	Seat Pleasant MD	Payne's
16872	Johnson, Reed	46y	W	23 DEC 1920	Akron OH	Oak Hill
03696	Johnson, Reginald Fleming	1y	C	26 OCT 1901	New York NY	Harmony
15376	Johnson, Richard A.	47y	W	23 NOV 1918	Savage MD	Oak Hill
06694	Johnson, Robert	29y	C	16 AUG 1908	Tomsburg WV	Payne's
07852	Johnson, Roberta F.	64y	W	4 DEC 1810	Camden NJ	Congressional
13890	Johnson, Rosa	55y	C	28 DEC 1916	E. Liverpool OH	Payne's
01882	Johnson, Ruth	77y	W	30 MAR 1896	Mt. Hope MD	Congressional
02164	Johnson, Sarah A.	59y	C	21 APR 1897	Philadelphia PA	Harmony
11887	Johnson, Sarah Frances	65y	C	8 JUL 1913	Newark NJ	Harmony
06245	Johnson, Savina	28y	C	26 SEP 1907	Yonkers NY	Sandy Spring MD
04658	Johnson, Susie	27y	W	24 FEB 1892	Fairfax Co. VA	Prospect Hill
03544	Johnson, Thomas	43y	C	17 JUN 1901	Baltimore MD	Harmony
03074	Johnson, Thomas	c.20y	C	11 JAN 1900	Railroad	Potters Field
13768	Johnson, Thomas Eugene	34y	C	15 OCT 1916	Jersey City NJ	Mt. Olivet
08821	Johnson, Three Infants of Jer.	5d	C	13 JAN 1910	Hyattsville MD	Harmony
08201	Johnson, Tristam B.	c.35y	W	16 JUL 1911	Chevy Chase MD	Newark NJ
15165	Johnson, Violetta Lee	29y	W	13 OCT 1918	Westerville OH	Rock Creek
00965	Johnson, Walter	23y	W	27 MAY 1893	Pittsburgh PA	Gordonsville VA
14605	Johnson, Wellington W.	1y	C	27 JAN 1918	Brentwood MD	Harmony
14209	Johnson, Wilbur	39y	C	1 JUL 1917	Silver Hill MD	Harmony
07893	Johnson, William	40y	C	19 DEC 1910	Chicago IL	Harmony
00619	Johnson, William	51y	C	13 AUG 1891	Uniontown PA	Harmony
01052	Johnson, William	32y	C	4 MAY 1803	Pr. Geo. Co. MD	Jones' Chapel
07931	Johnson, William	30y	C	19 JAN 1911	Occoquan VA	Payne's
08093	Johnson, William, a.k.a.	46y	C	30 APR 1911	Baltimore MD	Mt. Olivet
06058	Johnson, William H.	40y	W	8 MAY 1907	Portsmouth VA	Congressional
08210	Johnson, William H.	43y	C	20 JUL 1911	Louisville KY	Woodlawn
07198	Johnson, William K.	26y	W	4 MAY 1909	Kandy, Ceylon	Oak Hill
01243	Johnson, William M.	32y	C	15 SEP 1893	Denver CO	Graceland
00620	Johnson, Willis	31y	W	4 SEP 1891	Chicago IL	Harmony
18250	Johnston, Alice Hackney	78y	W	5 JAN 1923	Moorefield WV	Rock Creek
00489	Johnston, Antoinette F.	26y	W	8 MAR 1891	Arlington VA	Glenwood
16838	Johnston, Charles R.	81y	W	1 DEC 1920	Clarendon VA	Glenwood
06779	Johnston, Clifford DeC.	3m	C	20 OCT 1908	New York NY	Harmony
12973	Johnston, Cordelia Alvard	45y	W	22 JUN 1915	Lewinsville VA	Cremated
15731	Johnston, Florence A.	3d	C	16 APR 1919	Glendale MD	Payne's
16532	Johnston, Frances	83y	W	10 JUN 1920	New York NY	Rock Creek
18134	Johnston, Frederick	79y	W	28 OCT 1922	Connelsville PA	Arlington
07448	Johnston, G.W.	29y	W	27 FEB 1910	Fairmont WV	Holy Spgs. MS
14366	Johnston, Henry O.	63y	W	18 SEP 1917	Riverdale MD	Rock Creek
13161	Johnston, Joseph M.	21y	W	22 OCT 1915	Streator IL	Glenwood
06468	Johnston, Margaret A.	71y	W	13 MAR 1908	Aurora IL	Glenwood
16737	Johnston, Mary J.	47y	W	3 OCT 1920	Colonial Bea. VA	Glenwood
02424	Johnston, Milton H.	37y	W	2 APR 1898	Montg. Co. MD	Glenwood
17211	Johnston, Minnie F.	80y	W	20 FEB 1915	Washington DC	Glenwood
12596	Johnston, Mollie	48y	C	5 NOV 1914	Norristown PA	Moore's
06117	Johnston, Richard W., s/o Jno.	51y	W	28 JUN 1907	Arlington VA	Cremated
07577	Johnston, Robert	61y	C	15 JUN 1910	Paris VA	Harmony

District of Columbia Foreign Death Records, 1888-1923

No.	Name of Deceased	Age	Race	Death Date	Place of Death	Place of Burial
06927	Johnston, Thomas T.	52y	W	22 FEB 1909	Evanston IL	Glenwood
03826	Johnston, William W.	59y	W	22 MAR 1902	Atlantic City NJ	Oak Hill
01630	Johnstone, Jennette	67y	W	APR 1874	Baltimore MD	Rock Creek
01994	Jones, A.O.	55y	C	4 FEB 1896	Beaufort SC	Harmony
08622	Jones, Anderson	24y	W	19 SEP 1854	Georgetown DC	Rock Creek
04730	Jones, Ann	60y	W	MAR 1891	Caroline Co. VA	Glenwood
01568	Jones, Ann M.	57y	W	28 FEB 1895	Takoma DC	Carroll Chapel
13834	Jones, Baby	SB	W	30 NOV 1916	Baltimore MD	Mt. Olivet
04633	Jones, Benjamin	35y	W	14 MAR 1904	New York NY	Glenwood
16183	Jones, Catherine	89y	C	31 DEC 1919	Mt. Vernon NY	Ardwick VA
13474	Jones, Catherine H.	56y	W	23 APR 1916	Capitol Hts. MD	Mt. Olivet
13319	Jones, Charles E.	70y	W	22 JAN 1916	Petersburg FL	Cremated
04353	Jones, Cornelia	65y	W	4 AUG 1903	Alexandria VA	Congressional
08715	Jones, Dan	37y	W	3 JUL 1912	Denver CO	Silver Spring MD
00621	Jones, David J.	5m	W	15 JUL 1891	Poolesville MD	Mt. Olivet
18364	Jones, Derry	64y	C	21 FEB 1923	Arlington VA	Fredericksburg VA
18113	Jones, Diana Norton	38y	W	12 OCT 1922	Salisbury MD	Arlington
14388	Jones, Dorsey William	14d	W	30 SEP 1917	Montg. Co. MD	Rock Creek
00729	Jones, Edward	19y	C	13 MAR 1892	Pr. Geo. Co. MD	Payne's
16539	Jones, Edward Dorsey	1y	W	17 JUN 1920	Silver Spring MD	Rock Creek
12935	Jones, Edward W.	50y	W	9 MAR 1908	Atlantic City NJ	Cremated
16208	Jones, Edwin	38y	W	12 JAN 1920	New York NY	Rock Creek
01874	Jones, Edwin H., tinsmith	45y	W	25 MAR 1896	Herndon VA	Congressional
01470	Jones, Eliza Ann	70y	W	22 AUG 1894	Southwick MA	Oak Hill
08624	Jones, Eliza S.	92y	W	26 NOV 1895	Clean Drink. MD	Rock Creek
18355	Jones, Elizabeth	70y	W	17 FEB 1923	Wheaton MD	Rock Creek
06185	Jones, Ellis	28y	W	18 AUG 1907	Anne Arundel Co.	Congressional
01730	Jones, Emma	18y	C	21 JUN 1895	Potomac River	Harmony
16390	Jones, Emma B.	35y	C	12 MAR 1920	Boston MA	Woodlawn
15127	Jones, Eva Lillian (Duke)	32y	W	9 OCT 1918	Roanoke VA	Congressional
09011	Jones, Frank	22y	W	5 DEC 1912	Deal's Island MD	Mt. Olivet
03166	Jones, Frederick	90y	C	14 APR 1900	Vienna VA	Mt. Zion
16519	Jones, George A.	—	W	2 JUN 1920	Hyattsville MD	Congressional
06389	Jones, George A.	60y	W	12 JAN 1908	Philadelphia PA	Glenwood
04364	Jones, George J.	67y	W	27 JUN 1903	Riverdale MD	Glenwood
03182	Jones, George W.	22y	W	10 MAY 1900	Baltimore MD	Mt. Zion
01309	Jones, Georgiana	23y	C	23 JAN 1893	Landover MD	Mt. Olivet
04626	Jones, Gideon S.	37y	W	9 MAR 1904	Columbus OH	Rock Creek
17785	Jones, Grace	48y	C	4 APR 1922	Baltimore MD	Payne's
04622	Jones, Harry	—	—	5 FEB 1902	Iba, P.I.	Arlington
03178	Jones, Hattie	7y	C	30 APR 1900	Chevy Chase MD	Hebron
06362	Jones, Henry	37y	C	21 DEC 1907	Newark NJ	Payne's
04218	Jones, Henry J., Rev.	38y	C	9 MAR 1901	Matame NC	Harmony
11844	Jones, Hilda T. (Tyssowski)	30y	W	1 JUN 1913	Asbury Park NJ	Cremated
13644	Jones, Isaac Baggott, s/o Wm.	78y	W	6 AUG 1916	Atlantic City NJ	Rock Creek
16273	Jones, Isabelle	31y	C	1 FEB 1920	Baltimore MD	Mt. Zion West
05497	Jones, James	17y	C	12 MAR 1906	Hart School MD	Harmony
12659	Jones, James H.	96y	W	18 DEC 1914	Seat Pleasant MD	Congressional
17528	Jones, James K.	54y	W	15 NOV 1921	Hope AR	Rock Creek
16654	Jones, James T.	38y	W	8 AUG 1920	Chicago IL	Woodlawn
13031	Jones, Jennie	35y	C	2 AUG 1915	New York NY	Harmony
14470	Jones, Jesse	53y	C	15 NOV 1917	Falls Church VA	Harmony
05960	Jones, Jno. P.	37y	—	26 FEB 1907	Baltimore MD	—
03458	Jones, John	58y	C	19 MAR 1901	Fairfax Co. VA	Hillsdale
07378	Jones, John B.	55y	W	16 JAN 1910	Chicago IL	Oak Hill
08623	Jones, John C., Capt.	75y	W	16 MAY 1880	Forest Glen MD	Rock Creek
04157	Jones, John Davis	53y	W	5 JAN 1903	Augusta GA	Cincinnati OH
14833	Jones, John Edward	47y	W	20 MAY 1918	Altha Hall VA	Cremated
05888	Jones, Joseph	68y	W	7 JAN 1907	Hampton VA	Arlington

No.	Name of Deceased	Age	Race	Death Date	Place of Death	Place of Burial
01728	Jones, Joseph	19y	C	25 JUN 1895	Wilmington DE	Harmony
06872	Jones, Joseph S.	61y	W	29 DEC 1908	New York NY	Mt. Olivet
17554	Jones, Julia	83y	W	27 NOV 1921	Baltimore MD	Glenwood
13732	Jones, Julia Rush	70y	W	19 AUG 1908	Washington DC	Cremated
12358	Jones, Katharine	21y	C	10 MAY 1914	Philadelphia PA	Bryan's Point MD
03507	Jones, Katie	36y	C	10 MAY 1901	Philadelphia PA	Mt. Olivet
08688	Jones, Lewis H.	30y	C	24 JUN 1912	Potomac River	Payne's
15068	Jones, Lovey H.	62y	W	1 OCT 1918	Guinea VA	Arlington
05560	Jones, Lulu R.	27y	W	1 MAY 1906	Kensington MD	Glenwood
06821	Jones, Mamie	44y	W	17 NOV 1908	Hyattsville MD	Mt. Olivet
13578	Jones, Margaret	70y	C	27 JUN 1916	Philadelphia PA	Harmony
17169	Jones, Maria	87y	C	15 MAY 1921	Philadelphia PA	Mt. Zion West
08643	Jones, Mary A.	59y	W	19 MAY 1912	Hyattsville MD	Mt. Olivet
16503	Jones, Mary Catherine	22y	W	26 MAY 1920	Silver Spring MD	Rock Creek
05406	Jones, Mary Eliza	20y	C	19 DEC 1905	Pittsburgh PA	Woodlawn
01729	Jones, Michael	59y	C	16 AUG 1895	Landover MD	Mt. Olivet
04685	Jones, Nat. K.	21y	W	19 JUL 1891	Washington AR	Rock Creek
08625	Jones, Nicholas E.	71y	W	28 FEB 1911	Clean Drink. MD	Rock Creek
16169	Jones, Nicholas W.	86y	W	26 DEC 1919	Johnstown PA	Congressional
15981	Jones, Page Thompson	4m	W	9 SEP 1919	Kensington MD	Cremated
08261	Jones, Percy A.	14y	C	18 AUG 1911	Brentwood MD	Harmony
04729	Jones, R.S.	65y	W	MAR 1895	Washington DC	Glenwood
17016	Jones, Raymond W.	30y	W	2 MAR 1921	Albuquerque NM	Glenwood
00010	Jones, Roger, Gen., U.S.A.	59y	W	26 JAN 1889	Ft. Monroe VA	Arlington
12316	Jones, Rosanna	45y	C	14 APR 1914	Baltimore MD	Mt. Zion East
14859	Jones, Russell	1y	W	19 MAY 1918	Harrisburg PA	Congressional
13731	Jones, Samuel, Gen. C.S.A.	60y	W	3 AUG 1888	Redford Spgs. PA	Cremated
03686	Jones, Sarah	88y	C	15 OCT 1901	Fairfax Co. VA	Mt. Zion
02569	Jones, Sarah G.	32y	W	14 AUG 1898	Virginia Bea. VA	Rock Creek
04647	Jones, Sarah J.	54y	C	26 MAR 1904	Pittsburgh PA	Woodlawn
07187	Jones, Susan H.	41y	C	20 JUL 1897	Lynchburg VA	Woodlawn
01348	Jones, Thaddeus S.	23y	C	16 MAR 1894	Boyds MD	Harmony
18193	Jones, Thomas	21y	W	3 DEC 1922	Occoquan VA	Nanticoke PA
04034	Jones, Thomas	37y	C	25 OCT 1902	Fairmont WV	Payne's
02316	Jones, W.H.	25y	C	29 OCT 1897	Atlantic City NJ	Harmony
01244	Jones, Wailman	50y	W	29 JAN 1868	Baltimore MD	Rock Creek
04905	Jones, Walter	29y	C	28 SEP 1904	Philadelphia PA	Harmony
02380	Jones, William	5y	W	15 JAN 1898	Washington DC	Payne's
12734	Jones, William	71y	W	26 JAN 1915	Takoma Park MD	Rock Creek
08159	Jordan, Alexander Emmett	60y	C	18 JUN 1911	New York NY	Harmony
03111	Jordan, Edward	34y	C	2 MAR 1900	Philadelphia PA	Woodlawn
05892	Jordan, Edward Lawrence	51y	W	8 JAN 1907	Ballston VA	Glenwood
08512	Jordan, Ella Agnes	48y	W	11 FEB 1912	Ballston VA	Glenwood
17931	Jordan, Ethel	20y	C	1 JUL 1922	New York NY	Harmony
07863	Jordan, Hillary	35y	C	8 DEC 1910	Philadelphia PA	Woodlawn
07675	Jordan, John	27y	C	3 AUG 1910	Yonkers NY	Payne's
05537	Jordan, Marcus T.C.	53y	W	14 APR 1906	Philadelphia PA	Congressional
13836	Jordan, Maria L.	60y	C	29 NOV 1916	Philadelphia PA	Harmony
04240	Jordan, Martha	40y	C	13 FEB 1903	Pittsburgh PA	Harmony
08778	Jordon, Charles Wallace	39y	C	22 AUG 1912	Alexandria VA	Payne's
02258	Jordon, Elsinore	12y	C	28 JUL 1897	Long Bridge VA	Harmony
03231	Jordon, Littleton	1y	C	7 JUL 1900	Philadelphia PA	Woodlawn
15445	Jorss, Hans, s/o August	31y	W	13 DEC 1918	Richmond VA	Glenwood
17241	Joseph, Joseph H.	48y	W	14 JUN 1921	New York NY	Wash. Hebrew
00622	Joseph, Sadie	25y	C	21 SEP 1891	Philadelphia PA	Graceland
16516	Josetti, Luther B.	61y	W	30 MAY 1920	Augusta GA	Prospect Hill
05414	Jost, Frederick Christian	55y	W	18 OCT 1891	Montgomery AL	Arlington
01160	Jost, Lillian	34y	W	2 OCT 1892	Orlando FL	Oak Hill
16257	Jotoku, Keizo	22y	J	26 JAN 1920	Norfolk VA	Cremated

District of Columbia Foreign Death Records, 1888-1923

No.	Name of Deceased	Age	Race	Death Date	Place of Death	Place of Burial
07370	Jouvenal, Aloysius	29y	W	14 JAN 1910	Takoma Park MD	Mt. Olivet
07678	Jouvenal, Mildred	1y	W	9 AUG 1910	Silver Spring MD	Mt. Olivet
01349	Jouy, Pierre Louis	38y	W	22 MAR 1894	Tucson AZ	Oak Hill
02166	Joy, Columbus	65y	W	30 APR 1897	Montg. Co. MD	Rock Creek
17525	Joy, Ida M.	63y	W	16 NOV 1921	Hyattsville MD	Rock Creek
02599	Joy, John	56y	W	7 SEP 1898	Bath NY	Arlington
06552	Joy, Jon	86y	W	16 MAY 1908	Hyattsville MD	Rock Creek
17716	Joy, Otto Kosack	43y	W	1 MAR 1922	Chillum MD	Rock Creek
16392	Joy, Pauline	76y	W	18 MAR 1920	Capitol Hts. MD	Mt. Olivet
03565	Joy, Sarah E.W.	67y	W	5 JUL 1901	Montg. Co. MD	Rock Creek
05295	Joy, Sarah Hedges	76y	W	26 SEP 1905	Hyattsville MD	Rock Creek
02877	Joy, Thomas, gardener	79y	W	26 JUN 1899	Pr. Geo. Co. MD	Rock Creek
16029	Joyce, Catharine M.	78y	W	6 OCT 1919	Brentwood MD	Mt. Olivet
15048	Joyce, Maude MacDonald	46y	W	27 SEP 1918	Takoma Park MD	Mt. Olivet
07556	Joyce, Maurice H.	32y	W	4 JUN 1910	Quantico VA	Oak Hill
15242	Joyce, Thomas F.	26y	W	19 OCT 1918	Camp Sherm. OH	Mt. Olivet
13300	Joyner, Ada J.	68y	W	16 JAN 1916	Berwyn MD	Glenwood
03668	Joyner, Joann Margery	80y	W	29 SEP 1901	Berwyn MD	Glenwood
15846	Judd, Ella P. (Pressentin)	45y	W	22 JUN 1919	Milwaukee WI	Rock Creek
17856	Judd, Oscar Maxwell	65y	W	14 MAY 1922	Takoma Park MD	Rock Creek
06215	Judson, John A.	67y	W	2 SEP 1907	New York NY	Arlington VA
13270	Judson, Lucy	81y	W	25 DEC 1915	Springfield MD	Rock Creek
13854	Judson, Sarah	46y	W	9 DEC 1916	Philadelphia PA	Oak Hill
06525	Juilliard, Louisa Fensier	69y	W	25 APR 1908	Chevy Chase MD	Canton OH
18018	Jules, Foetus	5d	C	17 AUG 1922	Mt. Ranier MD	Payne's
06809	Junkens, Eliza Morison	81y	W	9 NOV 1908	Woodside MD	Congressional
02937	Jurix, William H.	36y	C	4 SEP 1899	Cambridge MA	Mt. Zion
04868	Justice, Leiws Carey	37y	W	28 AUG 1904	College Park MD	Glenwood

No.	Name of Deceased	Age	Race	Death Date	Place of Death	Place of Burial

K

No.	Name of Deceased	Age	Race	Death Date	Place of Death	Place of Burial
14230	Kafka, Karolina	75y	W	13 JUL 1917	Richmond VA	Cremated
17346	Kahlert, Anna Sally	52y	W	5 AUG 1921	Say Hill MD	Oak Hill
16055	Kahlert, Edward T.	50y	W	17 OCT 1919	Glenmont MD	Oak Hill
14726	Kaida, Rinhichi	29y	J	1 APR 1918	Norfolk VA	Cremated
04713	Kain, Cora	30y	W	12 MAY 1904	Philadelphia PA	Holyrood
18372	Kain, Mary Katherine	57y	W	26 FEB 1923	Takoma Park MD	Mt. Olivet
06100	Kaiser, Christine, of Ger.	65y	W	6 JUN 1907	Phoebus VA	Oak Hill
02626	Kaiser, George, soldier	c.30y	W	4 OCT 1898	Elkwood VA	Arlington VA
02878	Kaiser, Laura Matilda	27y	W	28 JUL 1899	Wash. Grove MD	Rock Creek
14408	Kaiser, Minnie M.	32y	W	14 OCT 1917	Baltimore MD	Alexandria VA
16097	Kaku, Yosuda	c.29y	J	3 NOV 1919	Newport News VA	Cremated
02646	Kalbfus, Thomas R.	7y	W	5 NOV 1898	Glendale MD	Glenwood
02381	Kalfaugh, Adam	61y	W	16 FEB 1898	Thomasville GA	Piedmont WV
04863	Kalstrom, Andrew	56y	W	23 AUG 1904	Berwyn MD	Congressional
17394	Kane, Dorothy Adell	4y	W	10 SEP 1921	New York NY	Mt. Olivet
05817	Kane, Samuel	65y	W	15 NOV 1906	Alexandria VA	New York NY
06471	Kane, Theodore F.	67y	W	14 MAR 1908	New York NY	Arlington
15801	Kane, William J., Jr.	1y	W	26 MAY 1919	Phoenix AZ	Mt. Olivet
17742	Kaplan, Lena	24y	W	8 MAR 1922	Duarte CA	Ohev Sholom
15331	Karnes, Mary E. (Breene)	74y	W	3 NOV 1918	Atlantic City NJ	Oak Hill
17252	Karns, Benjamin Franklin	71y	W	24 JUN 1921	Friendship MD	Rock Creek
13388	Karr, Alice D.	25y	W	28 FEB 1916	Cropley MD	Cremated
05488	Kast, Caroline	39y	W	6 MAR 1906	Alexandria VA	Cremated
17222	Kates, Edmund J.	45y	W	8 JUN 1921	Wilmington NC	Lincoln NE
17381	Katzenstein, Clara	65y	W	2 SEP 1921	Pittsburgh PA	Wash. Hebrew
00166	Kauffman, Conrad	64y	W	9 SEP 1889	Mundy's Point VA	Glenwood
12932	Kauffman, George	75y	W	17 MAY 1915	Glen Echo MD	Soldier's Home
08483	Kauffman, Marguerite Eleanor	17y	W	16 JAN 1912	Chevy Chase MD	Mifflin PA
16016	Kauffmann, Alphonse	42y	W	20 SEP 1919	Littleton CO	Mt. Olivet
06629	Kaufman, Benjamin	75y	W	1 JUL 1908	Brookline MA	Wash. Hebrew
00349	Kaufman, Carrel	4m	W	27 JUN 1890	Round Hill VA	Wash. Hebrew
14854	Kaufman, Harry	36y	W	4 JUN 1918	New York NY	Rock Creek
14850	Kaufman, Harry	36y	W	4 JUN 1918	New York NY	Silver Spring MD
15743	Kaufman, Joseph	34y	W	1 FEB 1918	New York NY	Rock Creek[1]
09182	Kaufman, Levi J.	72y	W	21 APR 1913	Rockville MD	Wash. Hebrew
03193	Kaufman, Martha	36y	W	24 MAY 1900	Brookline MA	Wash. Hebrew
05388	Kaufmann, Julius L.	40y	W	29 NOV 1905	Phoenix AZ	Wash. Hebrew
11952	Kautz, Fannie Markoviet	67y	W	11 AUG 1913	Winona NJ	Arlington
01731	Kavanaugh, Dennis	40y	W	19 MAY 1895	Philadelphia PA	Mt. Olivet
17656	Kay, Amelia	23y	W	21 JAN 1922	Denver CO	Ohev Sholom
15132	Kay, David	—	W	9 OCT 1918	Edgewood MD	Ohev Sholom
02773	Kay, James	42y	W	14 MAR 1899	Norfolk VA	Holyrood
13366	Kaye, Infant of Frank B.	1d	W	18 FEB 1916	Bethesda MD	Rock Creek
13365	Kaye, Martha Hampton	27y	W	19 FEB 1916	Bethesda MD	Rock Creek
08377	Keady, Dennis T.	72y	W	29 OCT 1911	Mt. Hope MD	Holyrood
15202	Keady, John J.	24y	W	15 OCT 1918	Auburn Co. AL	Holyrood
15677	Kealey, Daniel Bryson	77y	W	18 MAR 1919	Mt. Ranier MD	Mt. Olivet
14885	Kealy, James Hannibal	68y	W	28 JUN 1918	Mt. Ranier MD	Mt. Olivet
03444	Keane, Cathrine	68y	W	7 MAR 1901	Baltimore MD	Mt. Olivet
14057	Kearney, Abbie K.	26y	W	26 MAR 1917	Riverdale MD	Rock Creek
12130	Kearney, Anne E.	76y	W	17 DEC 1913	Alex. Co. VA	Holyrood[2]
04811	Kearney, Edward	5m	W	23 JUL 1904	Cincinnati OH	Mt. Olivet
11874	Kearney, Henry S.	40y	W	1 JUL 1913	Capitol Hts. MD	Mt. Olivet
14548	Kearney, Joseph L.	35y	W	21 DEC 1917	Denver CO	Mt. Olivet

---

[1] Cremated 20 OCT 1931, ashes taken to Los Angeles CA.
[2] Note that remains were removed to Mt. Olivet on 30 APR 1929.

District of Columbia Foreign Death Records, 1888-1923   139

No.	Name of Deceased	Age	Race	Death Date	Place of Death	Place of Burial
05288	Kearney, Nicholas	64y	W	15 SEP 1905	Baltimore MD	Rock Creek
13253	Kearney, Rosalie C.	74y	W	17 DEC 1915	Tuxedo MD	Congressional
02711	Kearny, Isabella	49y	W	13 JAN 1899	Hyattsville MD	Rock Creek
14649	Kearrick, Patrick	70y	W	21 FEB 1918	Railroad	Somerville MA
17684	Keasley, Shepard	48y	C	10 FEB 1922	Pr. Geo. Co. MD	Payne's
06009	Keating, Lizzie	55y	W	2 APR 1907	New York NY	Mt. Olivet
14853	Keck, Alonzo F.	44y	W	4 JUN 1918	Baltimore MD	Congressional
00373	Kedslie, Jas. G.	54y	W	29 JUL 1890	New York NY	Congressional
03611	Keech, Blanch H.	41y	W	11 AUG 1901	Burnt Mills MD	Rock Creek
03953	Keech, James A.	42y	W	9 JUL 1902	Burnt Mills MD	Rock Creek
07249	Keefer, Alberta	72y	W	23 OCT 1909	Frederick MD	Glenwood
12314	Keefer, Charles F.	76y	W	18 APR 1914	Hyattsville MD	Arlington
01410	Keefer, LeGrand E.	7m	W	23 JUN 1894	Branchville MD	Glenwood
14995	Keegan, Edward	40y	W	29 AUG 1918	Washington DC	Mt. Olivet
03396	Keeler, Anna E.	76y	W	19 JAN 1901	Philadelphia PA	Arlington VA
16848	Keeler, Pauline Adelaide	53y	W	8 DEC 1920	Jewel Sta. VA	Rock Creek
03420	Keeler, William F.	45y	W	10 FEB 1885	Mayport FL	Arlington VA
07312	Keeling, Robert J.	80y	W	9 DEC 1909	New York NY	Oak Hill
08147	Keenan, Josephine	62y	W	13 JUN 1911	Brentwood MD	Rock Creek
07487	Keenan, Martha V.	78y	W	29 MAR 1910	Brentwood MD	Rock Creek
17383	Keenan, William H., Sgt.	—	W	10 OCT 1918	France	Glenwood
12838	Keener, Katie	38y	C	20 MAR 1915	Reading PA	Payne's
15597	Keeney, Joseph	72y	W	3 FEB 1919	Brentwood MD	Rock Creek
08179	Keep, Frederick A.	53y	W	24 JUN 1911	Paris, France	Rock Creek
08860	Keer, Karl Stirling	1m	W	30 SEP 1912	Ft. Myer Hts. VA	Rock Creek
07283	Keese, Sarah E. (Hadley)	65y	W	22 NOV 1909	Colonial Bea. VA	Glenwood
08700	Keesecker, John E.	35y	W	29 JUN 1912	Glen Echo MD	Mt. Olivet
01279	Keim, Ella	32y	W	31 DEC 1893	Kansas City MO	Oak Hill
18038	Keithley, Arthur	49y	W	28 AUG 1922	Cherrydale VA	Congressional
05237	Keithley, Francis N.	7m	W	11 AUG 1905	Fairfax C.H. VA	Congressional
05026	Keithley, George	57y	W	10 FEB 1905	Kensington MD	Congressional
00254	Keithley, Samuel	38y	W	28 DEC 1889	White Sulphur VA	Congressional
08111	Keithley, William E.	9y	W	13 MAY 1911	Findlay OH	Congressional
06818	Kelchner, Beranrd S.	29y	W	16 NOV 1908	Sykesville MD	Congressional
04405	Kelchner, John H.	65y	W	23 JUL 1903	Rockville MD	Congressional
06950	Kelchner, Matheda	70y	W	18 MAR 1909	Rockville MD	Congressional
03794	Kelleher, Michael, Rev.	47y	W	15 FEB 1902	Philadelphia PA	Mt. Olivet
03945	Keller, Charles Henry	64y	W	10 JUL 1902	Falls Church VA	Mt. Olivet
17984	Keller, Henry	87y	W	29 JUL 1922	Harrisonburg VA	Prospect Hill
16069	Keller, Johanna (Colson)	74y	W	24 OCT 1919	Richmond VA	Mt. Olivet
18371	Keller, Mary Eloise T.	68y	W	26 FEB 1923	Friendship H. MD	Congressional
12767	Keller, W.F.	63y	W	17 JAN 1915	Augusta GA	Prospect Hill
17020	Keller, William Perry	27y	W	6 MAR 1921	Mt. Ranier MD	Glenwood
17703	Kellerhouse, Florentia	80y	W	20 FEB 1922	Cabin John MD	Glenwood
00623	Kelley, Benjamin F.	84y	W	16 JUL 1891	Oakland MD	Arlington VA
12109	Kelley, Charles E.	32y	W	29 NOV 1913	Bridwell MD	Congressional
07554	Kelley, Clarence L.	50y	C	28 MAY 1910	Gloucester MA	Woodlawn
11998	Kelley, Emma A.	40y	W	8 SEP 1913	Hyattsville MD	Glenwood
15097	Kelley, Emma M.	56y	W	6 OCT 1918	Takoma Park MD	Rock Creek
15142	Kelley, Frances A.	21y	W	12 OCT 1918	Hyattsville MD	Mt. Olivet
12588	Kelley, Henry	c.42y	C	26 OCT 1914	St. Louis MO	Payne's
15446	Kelley, James Dudley	76y	W	14 DEC 1918	Cherrydale VA	Holyrood
17714	Kelley, Lucretia	73y	C	27 FEB 1922	Philadelphia PA	Harmony
01631	Kelley, Mary E.	75y	W	7 MAR 1895	Chicago IL	Mt. Olivet
17340	Kelley, Matthew Grier	21y	W	27 JUN 1921	At Sea	Arlington
05056	Kelley, Velma M. Mullarkey	14y	W	9 MAR 1905	New York NY	Glenwood
06431	Kelley, W. Maurice	36y	W	9 FEB 1908	Goldfield NV	Rock Creek
13479	Kelley, William F.	51y	W	4 MAR 1916	Rome, Italy	Oak Hill
03744	Kellogg, Clarence H.	32y	W	28 DEC 1901	South. Pines NC	Rock Creek

No.	Name of Deceased	Age	Race	Death Date	Place of Death	Place of Burial
13992	Kellogg, Edgar C.	c.60y	W	16 FEB 1917	Raleigh NC	Glenwood
07513	Kellum, Penelope	71y	W	21 APR 1910	Newport News VA	Congressional
06353	Kelly, Aloysius M.	18y	W	19 DEC 1907	Alex. Co. VA	Mt. Olivet
07547	Kelly, Andrew	37y	W	16 MAY 1910	Hudson Co. NJ	Payne's
12010	Kelly, Charles	35y	W	4 SEP 1913	New York NY	Mt. Olivet
14520	Kelly, Jane	73y	C	20 DEC 1917	Atlantic City NJ	Vienna VA
13639	Kelly, John	77y	W	5 AUG 1916	Hyattsville MD	Mt. Olivet
13281	Kelly, Joseph A.	76y	W	4 JAN 1916	Clarendon VA	Congressional
15635	Kelly, Joseph E.	40y	C	21 FEB 1919	Atlantic City NJ	Woodlawn
07029	Kelly, Laura Isabel, d/o Rd.	22y	W	18 MAY 1909	Colonial Bea. VA	Glenwood
06218	Kelly, Mary	3h	W	8 SEP 1907	Rosslyn VA	Mt. Olivet
00405	Kelly, Mary	30y	W	22 SEP 1890	Philadelphia PA	Mt. Olivet
03731	Kelly, Peter C.	49y	W	13 DEC 1901	New York NY	Mt. Olivet
08007	Kelly, Peter C.	19y	W	15 MAR 1911	New York NY	Mt. Olivet
15687	Kelpy, Anthony	75y	W	20 MAR 1919	Utica NY	Arlington
15259	Kelser, John, s/o Charles	22y	W	22 OCT 1918	Ft. Oglethorpe GA	Congressional
16060	Kelser, William W.	62y	W	18 OCT 1919	Pittsburgh PA	Congressional
04279	Kelsey, Kate L. Patchen	50y	W	20 APR 1903	Chevy Chase MD	Cremated
07315	Kelton, Atlee S.	23y	W	27 NOV 1909	Juneau AK	Rock Creek
12657	Keltz, Allen L.	47y	W	13 DEC 1914	Railroad	Legonier PA
17173	Kemp, Carlton	c.25y	W	20 MAY 1921	McCarthy Sta. MD	Baltimore MD
00491	Kemp, Constantine	57y	W	13 APR 1891	Boston MA	Glenwood
05043	Kempton, Harold B.	25y	W	27 FEB 1905	Somerville NJ	Rock Creek
00550	Kenchel, Anthony	62y	W	26 APR 1891	Bel Air MD	Prospect Hill
12413	Kendall, Charles West	86y	W	25 JUN 1914	Mt. Ranier MD	Congressional
06840	Kendall, John Blake	50y	W	5 DEC 1908	Towson MD	Oak Hill
17382	Kendall, Mary R.	72y	W	31 AUG 1921	San Antonio TX	Arlington
14565	Kendig, Helen Butler	90y	W	10 JAN 1918	Montrose MD	Congressional
05129	Kendrick, George W.	52y	C	25 APR 1905	Jersey City NJ	Harmony
01370	Kenerston, John, coachman	43y	W	25 MAY 1894	New York NY	Glenwood
04798	Kenion, Ada	17y	W	14 JUL 1904	Edgewater VA	Rock Creek
04799	Kenion, Harriet	15y	W	14 JUL 1904	Edgewater VA	Rock Creek
04797	Kenion, Helen	19y	W	14 JUL 1904	Edgewater VA	Rock Creek
06483	Kennedy, Andrew E.	33y	W	25 MAR 1908	Hyattsville MD	Glenwood[1]
13485	Kennedy, Charles	74y	W	29 APR 1916	Riverdale MD	Glenwood
12931	Kennedy, Elinda	76y	W	19 MAY 1915	Takoma Park MD	Rock Creek
03716	Kennedy, Elizabeth Susan	72y	W	25 NOV 1901	Capitol View MD	Oak Hill
00332	Kennedy, Emmett	14y	W	27 MAY 1890	Westminster MD	Congressional
16344	Kennedy, Evelyn	3y	W	28 FEB 1920	Ft. Wash. MD	Brooks Sta. VA
03538	Kennedy, Frank	35y	W	7 JUN 1901	Chicago IL	Mt. Olivet
02756	Kennedy, Hattie	20y	W	28 FEB 1899	Louisville KY	Glenwood
12225	Kennedy, James	54y	W	15 JUL 1914	New York NY	Mt. Olivet
03404	Kennedy, John	55y	W	24 JAN 1901	Darien GA	Mt. Olivet
03518	Kennedy, John	37y	W	—	Peking, China	Mt. Olivet
08091	Kennedy, John Robey	5m	W	29 APR 1911	Tuscaloosa AL	Oak Hill
14436	Kennedy, Joseph	SB	W	1 NOV 1917	Potomac VA	Mt. Olivet
08632	Kennedy, Joseph Aloysius	34y	W	11 MAY 1912	Winthrop MD	Louisville KY
00852	Kennedy, Joseph M.	c.55y	W	9 APR 1892	Alberton MD	Oak Hill
13209	Kennedy, Mary Elizabeth	63y	W	17 NOV 1915	Hyattsville MD	Mt. Olivet
15185	Kennedy, Sarah	76y	W	16 OCT 1918	Riverdale MD	Charleston WV
00966	Kennedy, Sarah A.	27y	W	18 JUN 1893	Brooklyn NY	Glenwood
01732	Kennelly, Mary	36y	W	7 OCT 1895	Mt. Hope MD	Mt. Olivet
13795	Kenner, Solomon R.	36y	C	31 OCT 1916	Lewistown PA	Chesterbrook VA
08780	Kennerly, Edward, s/o Eugene	33y	W	11 AUG 1912	Vallejo CA	Harmony
18441	Kennerly, Maria	65y	C	26 MAR 1923	Cumberland MD	Harmony
04910	Kenney, Gertrude	24y	C	4 OCT 1904	Charlestown WV	Harmony

[1] Disinterment permit #6429 issued 27 NOV 1908 for removal of remains to Richmond, Va.

District of Columbia Foreign Death Records, 1888-1923

No.	Name of Deceased	Age	Race	Death Date	Place of Death	Place of Burial
12726	Kenney, Mary J.	75y	W	SEP 1909	Philadelphia PA	Mt. Olivet[1]
18416	Kenney, Thomas Julian	6y	C	12 MAR 1923	Chillum MD	Payne's
00442a	Kennon, Beverley	62y	W	22 NOV 1890	Brooklyn NY	Congressional
00442	Kennon, Beverley	c.60y	W	21 NOV 1890	Brooklyn NY	Oak Hill
06136	Kennon, Peter S.	56y	W	12 JUL 1907	Brunswick GA	Glenwood
14734	Kennon, Wyatt	36y	W	31 MAR 1918	Los Angeles CA	Rock Creek
05073	Kenny, Wilie Annie Woods	35y	C	26 MAR 1905	Cambridge MA	Woodlawn
03736	Kent, Daniel H.	66y	W	22 DEC 1901	Wilmington DE	Arlington VA
02511	Kent, James B.	53y	C	16 JUL 1898	Bridgeport CN	Mt. Olivet
16841	Kent, Rosella	56y	W	2 DEC 1920	Mt. Ranier MD	Lodge Wharf VA
08640	Ker, Mary A.	68y	W	18 MAY 1912	Delmar MD	Glenwood
09109	Ker, Roberta	30y	W	5 MAR 1913	Highlands NC	Cremated
01161	Ker, Samuel, Jr.	19y	W	3 JUL 1892	Chicago IL	Rock Creek
04913	Kerfoot, Andrew J.	72y	W	7 OCT 1904	Riverdale MD	Glenwood
13174	Kerfoot, Elizabeth S.	79y	W	29 OCT 1915	Riverdale MD	Glenwood
04293	Kern, Isabell	54y	W	7 JUN 1903	Brentwood MD	Glenwood
13003	Kernes, Dorothy V.	5m	W	14 JUL 1915	Takoma MD	Rock Creek
04014	Kernwein, Minty G.	44y	W	12 SEP 1902	Catonsville MD	Glenwood
13955	Kerr, Emilie Knockler	52y	W	29 JAN 1917	Alex. Co. VA	Rock Creek
00853	Kerr, John Spencer	25y	W	10 MAY 1892	Fairfax Sta. VA	Mt. Olivet
03028	Kerr, Lucy S.	71y	W	2 AUG 1899	Berryville VA	Oak Hill
01310	Kerr, Nancy	83y	W	19 JAN 1894	Laurel MD	Glenwood
01569	Kerr, Robert W., Jr.	29y	W	23 JAN 1895	Green Cove S. FL	Graceland
13665	Kerr, Thomas W.	36y	W	18 AUG 1916	Pittsburgh PA	Mt. Olivet
16724	Kessler, Mary T.	5m	W	25 SEP 1920	Mt. Ranier MD	Mt. Olivet
05978	Ketcham, N.F.	78y	—	9 MAR 1907	Harpers Ferry WV	Glenwood
04771	Ketchner, John W.	33y	W	21 JUN 1904	Washington DC	Congressional
14704	Ketchum, Charles Leavenworth	76y	W	21 MAR 1918	New York NY	Rock Creek
03080	Ketner, Edith Blanche	10y	W	29 JAN 1900	Riverdale MD	Mt. Olivet
01733	Kettell, W.W.	28y	W	26 AUG 1895	Pittsburgh PA	Rock Creek
15858	Kettler, Charles H.	68y	W	3 JUL 1919	Chesa. Bea. MD	Rock Creek
03665	Kettley, Margaret A.	25y	W	24 SEP 1901	Ft. Monroe VA	Mt. Olivet
07130	Kettner, Mary (McPherson)	43y	W	24 JUL 1909	Ft. Myer Hts VA	Holyrood
16173	Key, Albert L., Jr.	15y	W	27 DEC 1919	Chattanooga TN	Arlington
12112	Key, Henry, Jr., wagon driver	31y	C	25 NOV 1913	Nashville TN	Harmony
05777	Keyes, Anna May	4y	W	15 OCT 1906	Rosslyn VA	Tenallytown M.E.
13821	Keyes, John W.	71y	W	22 NOV 1916	Statesville NC	Cremated
07323	Keyes, William T.	66y	W	15 DEC 1909	Takoma Park MD	Arlington
16227	Keys, Battle	63y	C	17 JAN 1920	Pittsburgh PA	Woodlawn
12762	Keys, Con	45y	C	12 FEB 1915	Round Hill VA	Mt. Zion West
02740	Keys, Henry Elmo	29y	W	7 FEB 1899	Ardsley NY	Oak Hill
03555	Keys, Ira B.	18y	C	26 JUN 1901	Baltimore MD	Payne's
15857	Keys, Juanita	11y	C	1 JUL 1919	Baltimore MD	Mt. Olivet
14747	Keys, Martha A.	72y	W	13 APR 1918	Kensington MD	Rock Creek
02739	Keys, Mary Ward	27y	W	7 FEB 1899	Ardsley NY	Oak Hill
12918	Keys, Nicholas	38y	W	10 MAY 1915	New York NY	Mt. Olivet
08076	Keys, Robert H.	48y	C	21 APR 1911	Silver Hill MD	Mt. Olivet
01053	Keys, Sarah	30y	C	8 FEB 1893	—	Harmony
05830	Keys, Thomas A.	57y	W	26 NOV 1906	Baltimore MD	Arlington VA
04306	Keys, William	30y	W	25 MAY 1903	New York NY	Congressional
02514	Keyworth, Howard	31y	W	12 JUL 1898	Bladensburg MD	Congressional
02259	Keyworth, John Walter	4m	W	12 JUL 1897	Bladensburg MD	Congressional
03751	Keyworth, Mary Ann	62y	W	3 JAN 1902	Hyattsville MD	Congressional
16500	Kibbey, Blanche	45y	W	22 MAY 1920	Lewisburgh PA	Congressional
16504	Kibbey, Charles	48y	W	27 MAY 1920	Danville PA	Congressional
14566	Kidd, Ella	41y	C	8 JAN 1918	Jefferson VA	Harmony

---

[1] Reinterred 6 APR 1933 in Congressional Cemetery.

No.	Name of Deceased	Age	Race	Death Date	Place of Death	Place of Burial
13236	Kidd, Harry Jarvis	—	W	5 NOV 1914	Orange NJ	Congressional[1]
17865	Kidd, James R.	2m	W	20 MAY 1922	Capitol Hts. MD	Congressional
06469	Kidwell, Cath. A. (Lawrence)	93y	W	12 MAR 1908	Remington VA	Oak Hill
00178	Kidwell, Edward	19y	W	20 OCT 1889	Richmond VA	Congressional
11839	Kidwell, Infant of Morris	SB	W	1 JUN 1913	Alex. Co. VA	Methodist
06646	Kidwell, John Edward	6m	W	16 JUL 1908	Chillum MD	Rock Creek
08827	Kidwell, John Henry	80y	W	7 SEP 1912	Fairmont Hts. MD	Viles Cem. MD
04902	Kidwell, Mary	40y	W	22 SEP 1904	Baltimore MD	Congressional
16397	Kidwell, Mary Catherine	75y	W	17 MAR 1920	Philadelphia PA	Congressional
14662	Kidwell, Owen	28y	W	24 FEB 1918	Philadelphia PA	Bell Family
12993	Kidwell, Samuel W.	56y	W	4 JUL 1915	Great Falls VA	Congressional
02510	Kidwell, William R.	28y	W	16 JUL 1898	Baltimore MD	Oak Hill
08267	Kiebs, Robert R.	1y	W	22 AUG 1911	Brentwood MD	Prospect Hill
01054	Kieckhoefer, Adolph Travers	89y	W	8 MAY 1893	Baltimore MD	Mt. Olivet
04507	Kieckhoefer, Anna M.	81y	W	9 NOV 1903	Baltimore MD	Mt. Olivet
03603	Kiefer, Joseph C.	23y	W	4 AUG 1901	Denver CO	St. Mary's
13720	Kilbourne, Alice G.	60y	W	12 SEP 1916	Ft. Leavenw. KS	Cremated
11993	Kilburn, William	64y	W	4 SEP 1913	Gloucester MA	Arlington
07056	Kilby, G. Rice	64y	W	9 JUN 1909	New York NY	Glenwood
16625	Kilduff, Alice Riddle	59y	W	27 JUL 1920	Olney MD	Rock Creek
12169	Kilgour, Harriet N.	84y	W	18 JAN 1914	Berwyn MD	Congressional
08236	Kilgour, Robert W., farmer	58y	W	2 AUG 1911	Staunton VA	Purcellville VA
13538	Killerman, John	65y	W	3 JUN 1916	Occoquan VA	Mt. Olivet
03004	Killian, Clarence	4y	W	10 NOV 1899	Baltimore MD	Prospect Hill
04459	Kilpatrick, John D.	22y	W	21 SEP 1903	New York NY	Oak Hill
15300	Kilroy, Lillie Agnes	31y	W	26 OCT 1918	Baltimore MD	Mt. Olivet
17192	Kimball, Amos W., Col.	58y	W	25 MAY 1921	Omaha NE	Arlington
03840	Kimball, Charles Carroll	72y	W	2 APR 1902	Forest Glen MD	Glenwood
14560	Kimball, Maude E.	76y	W	19 DEC 1918	Takoma Park MD	Glenwood
00733	Kimball, Sarah R.	72y	W	2 FEB 1892	Berlin, Ger.	Rock Creek
01995	Kimes, James B.	22y	W	1 JUL 1896	Philadelphia PA	Congressional
06330	Kimmell, Alice	23y	W	29 NOV 1907	Azalea NC	Congressional
13848	Kimmell, Ferdinand	39y	W	6 DEC 1916	Cherrydale VA	Congressional
14069	Kimmell, Mary Ann Turner	1y	W	1 APR 1917	Elmira NY	Congressional
16623	Kimmell, William Lambell	74y	W	22 JUL 1920	Del Ray VA	Congressional
12788	Kinard, Clarence R.	5y	C	2 MAR 1915	New York NY	Harmony
03820	Kincheloe, Wildman Wallace	63y	W	15 MAR 1902	Brentsville VA	Glenwood
00731	Kincheloe, William Ramsey	12y	W	c.OCT 1891	Brentsville MD	Glenwood
08654	Kinchloe, Evelyn Louise	20m	W	3 JUN 1912	Woodbridge VA	Glenwood
02425	Kindelberger, Hattie L.	50y	W	3 APR 1898	New York NY	Oak Hill
17072	Kindleberger, David	86y	W	25 MAR 1921	New York NY	Oak Hill
14080	King, Ada V.	57y	W	11 APR 1917	Gaithersburg MD	Rock Creek
01311	King, Alice B.	28y	W	28 JAN 1894	Philadelphia PA	Mt. Olivet
00732	King, Annie V.	4y	W	12 APR 1892	Pr. Geo. Co. MD	Oak Hill
12166	King, Arthur T.	59y	W	15 JAN 1914	Winchester VA	Congressional
07102	King, Benjamin Filmore	24y	W	2 JUL 1909	Vallejo Co. CA	Arlington
05608	King, Bernard L.	4m	C	25 JUN 1906	Landover MD	Mt. Olivet
13562	King, Bessie	35y	W	16 JUN 1916	Grassy Pt. NY	Harmony
12220	King, Charles A.	46y	W	14 FEB 1914	Berwyn MD	Glenwood
13846	King, Charles R.	57y	W	5 DEC 1916	Chevy Chase MD	Rock Creek
06211	King, Claude	19y	W	30 AUG 1907	Orange VA	Congressional
08131	King, Cora H.	51y	W	27 MAY 1911	Worcester MA	Rock Creek
17791	King, Elizabeth	61y	C	8 APR 1922	Philadelphia PA	Mt. Pleasant MD
00319	King, Elizabeth	69y	W	25 APR 1890	Montg. Co. MD	Tenallytown
18232	King, Emma J.	53y	W	30 DEC 1922	Hyattsville MD	Rock Creek
18367	King, Estelle M.	78y	W	23 FEB 1923	New York NY	Oak Hill
14342	King, Francis Raymond	17y	W	3 SEP 1917	Berlin MD	St. Mary's

[1] Disinterment permit on 3 DEC 1915 for removal from Rosedale Cemetery, Orange, Essex Co., N.J.

District of Columbia Foreign Death Records, 1888-1923

No.	Name of Deceased	Age	Race	Death Date	Place of Death	Place of Burial
14402	King, G.M.P., Rev.	85y	W	8 OCT 1917	Cambria VA	Cremated
08882	King, George	38y	C	6 OCT 1912	Martic PA	Woodlawn
17539	King, Gertrude E.	52y	W	20 NOV 1921	Dodge Park MD	Poplar Spgs. MD
16544	King, Hellen H.	6y	W	17 JUN 1920	Falls Church VA	Glenwood
17510	King, Herbert E.	46y	W	9 NOV 1921	Pittsburgh PA	Congressional
14471	King, Herman	49y	W	19 NOV 1917	Curtin's Sta. MD	Rock Creek
08005	King, James	53y	W	6 MAR 1911	San Francisco CA	Oak Hill
16138	King, James	85y	C	4 DEC 1919	Buena Vista MD	Stratford, Can.
03392	King, James J.	52y	W	14 JAN 1901	Wilmington DE	Mt. Olivet
15064	King, James Levin Gibbs	29y	W	1 OCT 1918	Norfolk VA	Rock Creek
02833	King, James Samuel	3m	W	2 JUN 1899	Tuxedo MD	Rock Creek
00730	King, James T.	38y	C	23 NBOV 1891	New York NY	Graceland
03269	King, John	58y	W	17 AUG 1900	Calvert Co. MD	Soldier's Home
17957	King, John H.	83y	W	13 JUL 1922	Rochester NY	Congressional
05475	King, John H., s/o John H.	21d	W	27 FEB 1906	Arlington VA	Congressional
11896	King, John, of William	85y	W	14 JUL 1913	New York NY	Oak Hill
07862	King, John S.	71y	W	9 DEC 1910	Hyattsville MD	Rock Creek
15538	King, Joseph G.	30y	W	9 JAN 1919	Rosslyn VA	Glenwood
02736	King, Lemuel	39y	W	4 FEB 1899	Montg. Co. MD	Tenallytown
15102	King, Maria	27y	C	4 OCT 1918	Philadelphia PA	Harmony
17908	King, Marie E.	24y	W	13 JUN 1922	Portland OR	Congressional
12703	King, Martha	66y	C	6 JAN 1915	Philadelphia PA	Westm. Co. VA
03226	King, Martin P.	69y	W	7 JUL 1900	Mt. Hope MD	Congressional
14157	King, Mary Elizabeth	70y	W	31 MAY 1917	Falls Church VA	Oak Hill
08217	King, Mary M. (McClelland)	73y	W	25 JUL 1911	Park Lane VA	Glenwood
13744	King, Paul, s/o J.W.	12y	W	2 OCT 1916	Lexingotn KY	Glenwood
03999	King, Reuben V.	57y	W	15 AUG 1902	Cape May Co. NJ	Arlington
15990	King, Richard H.	75y	W	12 SEP 1919	Alex. Co. VA	Glenwood
06397	King, Robert J.	63y	W	18 JAN 1908	Hudson Co. NJ	Congressional
04782	King, Ruth	45y	W	7 JUL 1904	Addison VA	Congressional
14574	King, Samuel	56y	W	14 JAN 1918	Chillum MD	Rock Creek
03382	King, Virginia E.	64y	W	30 DEC 1900	New York NY	Arlington VA
15963	King, William Henry	75y	W	30 AUG 1919	Clarendon VA	Rock Creek
02070	King, William S., Col.	75y	W	5 SEP 1895	Philadelphia PA	Arlington VA
13280	King, Wilson	63y	W	2 JAN 1916	Bethesda MD	Methodist
12391	Kinglsey, George	55y	W	2 JUN 1914	Ft. Lauderdale FL	Rock Creek
12423	Kingman, A.J.	—	W	19 JUN 1903	Woodstock IL	Rock Creek
13587	Kingman, Carrol F.	55y	W	1 JUL 1916	Chicago IL	Rock Creek
13814	Kingman, Daniel C., s/o John	64y	W	14 NOV 1916	Atlantic City NJ	Arlington
13248	Kingman, Frederick E., s/o D.	27y	W	12 DEC 1915	Norfolk VA	Arlington
03229	Kingsbury, Henry W.	39y	W	6 JUL 1900	Baltimore MD	Oak Hill
03169	Kingsley, Isaac C.	86y	W	19 APR 1900	Spots. Co. VA	Glenwood
04946	Kingsley, Mary Dubois	33y	W	2 NOV 1904	Falls Church VA	Rock Creek
01996	Kingsley, P.P., Mrs.	75y	W	21 JUL 1896	Courtland VA	Glenwood
06934	Kingsman, Ellen	74y	W	1 MAR 1909	Louisville KY	Glenwood
05806	Kingsman, Thomas	48y	W	5 NOV 1906	Louisville KY	Glenwood
17376	Kingston, Alice Murphy	74y	W	31 AUG 1921	Takoma Park MD	Buffalo NY
15803	Kinkle, Joseph	45y	C	30 MAY 1919	Chester PA	Cropleys MD
12381	Kinkle, Oscar	c.22y	C	28 MAY 1914	Glen Echo MD	Cabin John MD
16129	Kinnard, Thomas	11y	C	29 NOV 1919	New York NY	Harmony
05750	Kinney, Hattie	31y	C	21 SEP 1906	New York NY	Harmony
08025	Kinnison, Charles W., Dr.	44y	W	27 MAR 1911	Railroad	Oak Hill WV
06905	Kinsey, Sarah K.	64y	W	27 JAN 1909	Columbia SC	Rock Creek
06836	Kinslow, George H.	68y	C	1 DEC 1908	Glen Echo MD	Christian
06543	Kinslow, Mary A.	60y	C	7 MAY 1908	Bethesda MD	Tenleytown, C.
15025	Kinsman, William G.	41y	W	14 SEP 1918	Saranac Lake NY	Rock Creek
15021	Kinsman, William George	41y	W	14 SEP 1918	Saranac Lake NY	Arlington
12034	Kipp, Whitney	28y	W	19 AUG 1913	Rye NH	Rock Creek
17138	Kippox, Hargraves	75y	W	30 APR 1921	Cabin John MD	Cremated

No.	Name of Deceased	Age	Race	Death Date	Place of Death	Place of Burial
16064	Kirby, French	31y	W	15 OCT 1919	Castle Rock UT	Arlington
06548	Kirby, James T.	28y	W	12 MAY 1908	Baltimore MD	Mt. Olivet
13009	Kirby, John Lewis	50y	W	17 JUL 1915	Chevy Chase MD	Sioux City IA
08036	Kirby, Maurice B.	35y	W	27 MAR 1911	New York NY	Mt. Olivet
01484	Kirby, Mollie T.	24y	M	5 SEP 1894	Montgomery AL	Harmony
00103	Kirby, Thomas	9m	W	3 JUL 1889	Bethesda MD	Holyrood
02561	Kirk, Delia	2m	W	15 AUG 1898	Ballston VA	Mt. Olivet
16616	Kirk, George Lewis	2m	W	21 JUL 1920	Mt. Ranier MD	Glenwood
02317	Kirk, Maria Anna Louise	5m	W	13 NOV 1897	Arlington Co. VA	Mt. Olivet
13503	Kirkendall, George Br. McC.	53y	W	15 MAY 1916	Takoma Park MD	Mt. Vernon OH
04611	Kirkland, Joseph	22y	W	23 FEB 1904	New York NY	Arlington VA
13672	Kirkley, Charles W.	50y	W	23 AUG 1916	Ballston VA	Congressional
17650	Kirkpatrick, James	80y	W	JAN 1922	E. Orange NJ	Glenwood
08032	Kirkus, Wolham	47y	W	22 AUG 1900	Newport RI	Oak Hill
18225	Kirtland, Florence Juliet	43y	W	26 DEC 1922	Rens. Hts. NY	Glenwood
05261	Kirtland, Virginia Carter	60y	W	27 AUG 1905	Chicago IL	Arlington
05554	Kiske, Emma E.	60y	W	23 APR 1906	Boston MA	Glenwood
06644	Kissner, Ellenora	77y	W	14 JUL 1908	Colonial Bea. VA	St. Mary's
06644	Kissner, Ellenora	77y	W	14 JUL 1908	Colonial Bea. VA	St. Mary's
17452	Kitchen, Ione H.	45y	W	4 OCT 1921	Falls Church VA	Glenwood
09073	Kitchin, Margaret J.	64y	W	14 FB 1913	Tuxedo MD	Glenwood
07983	Kitzmiller, William M., soldier	—	W	7 JAN 1911	Manila, P.I.	Glenwood
08786	Klase, Anna M.	29y	W	29 AUG 1912	Wash. Grove MD	Glenwood
13380	Kleefisch, Margaret	55y	W	26 FEB 1916	Clarendon VA	Prospect Hill
04522	Kleider, Walter F.	32y	W	24 NOV 1903	Youngwood PA	Glenwood
04230	Klein, Louis Carl	6m	W	25 FEB 1903	Bladensburg MD	St. Mary's
01570	Klein, P. Mary	6d	W	15 JAN 1895	Bladensburg MD	St. Mary's
11910	Klein, Philip	57y	W	21 JUL 1913	Chesa. Bea. MD	St. Mary's
08058	Kleiner, John J.	66y	W	8 APR 1911	Takoma Park MD	Rock Creek
05661	Kleppel, Caroline	84y	W	26 JUL 1906	Suitland MD	Prospect Hill
06290	Kline, John H.	4y	W	29 OCT 1907	Bethesda MD	Holyrood
17263	Kline, Roy Kenneth	6m	W	25 JUN 1921	Maryland Pk. MD	Glenwood
16915	Kline, William G.	48y	W	13 JAN 1921	Philadelphia PA	Congressional
14564	Klink, Anna R.	65y	W	10 JAN 1918	Rowland Pk. MD	Oak Hill
06544	Klink, John C.	52y	W	9 MAY 1908	Baltimore MD	Oak Hill
03069	Klock, Ezkiah	76y	W	15 JAN 1900	Seat Pleasant MD	Woodlawn
16560	Klopfer, Jessie H.	61y	W	27 JUN 1920	Kensington MD	Glenwood
12420	Klopfer, Norman W.	27y	W	30 JUN 1914	Allentown PA	Rock Creek
14295	Klophenstein, Marguerite J.	2y	W	13 AUG 1917	Takoma Park MD	Rock Creek
07343	Klotz, George C.	59y	W	27 DEC 1909	Forestville MD	Glenwood
07814	Kluepfel, Philip, s/o Michael	62y	W	8 AUG 1900	Utica NY	Rock Creek
14596	Klusacek, Kate	52y	W	21 JAN 1918	Petersburg VA	Cremated
08846	Knapp, Charles C.	37y	W	18 SEP 1912	New Bern NC	Rock Creek
15629	Knapp, Harry C., s/o John H.	29y	W	20 FEB 1919	Falmouth VA	Glenwood
00492	Kneass, Camilla S.	54y	W	15 JAN 1891	Philadelphia PA	Oak Hill
13826	Knechtle, Emma M.	46y	W	24 NOV 1916	Penrose VA	Prospect Hill
16304	Knight, Emma Izetta	39y	W	11 FEB 1920	Landover MD	Congressional
08368	Knight, Harry Alfred	32y	W	21 OCT 1911	Asheville NC	Oak Hill
07414	Knight, Jane Louise	33y	W	10 FEB 1910	Mt. Hope MD	Holyrood
17160	Knight, Lamanda A.	93y	W	15 MAY 1921	Mt. Ranier MD	Oak Hill
12095	Knight, Lillian Gertrude	17y	C	14 NOV 1913	Fairmont Hts. MD	Harmony
08892	Knight, Lovenia D.	83y	W	16 OCT 1912	Rockville MD	Rock Creek
15535	Knight, Lucy	—	C	JAN 1919	Washington DC	Union Hill NJ
00230	Knight, Margaret A.	69y	W	11 NOV 1889	New York NY	Glenwood
12625	Knight, Mary Ellen	72y	W	23 NOV 1914	Westfield NJ	Oak Hill
17625	Knight, Mrs. F.O.	63y	W	7 JAN 1922	St. Augustine FL	Rock Creek
06420	Knight, Octavius	77y	W	6 FEB 1908	Fanwood NJ	Oak Hill
08596	Knight, Richard Thornton	10d	W	10 APR 1912	New York NY	Congressional
01055	Knight, Samuel F.	40y	W	16 MAR 1893	New York NY	Glenwood

District of Columbia Foreign Death Records, 1888-1923

No.	Name of Deceased	Age	Race	Death Date	Place of Death	Place of Burial
01312	Knight, Samuel N., Dr.	26y	W	31 JAN 1894	Pasadena CA	Oak Hill
13440	Knight, Susan	62y	W	3 APR 1916	New York NY	Mt. Olivet
14175	Knipe, Oscar A.	73y	W	16 JUN 1917	Chevy Chase MD	Rock Creek
06591	Knoblack, Louise	62y	W	16 JUN 1908	Berwyn MD	Prospect Hill
12718	Knoblock, Louise L.	4y	W	14 JAN 1915	Berwyn MD	Prospect Hill
17013	Knoblock, Theresa	67y	W	3 MAR 1921	Seat Pleasant MD	St. Mary's
16740	Knoch, Marie Gasch	86y	W	5 OCT 1920	Halpine MD	Prospect Hill
06041	Knock, John Henry	83y	W	22 APR 1907	Montrose MD	Prospect Hill
14571	Knode, Albon G.	73y	W	11 JAN 1918	Staunton VA	Arlington
14372	Knode, Cordelia, d/o Israel	80y	W	20 SEP 1917	Boonsboro MD	Glenwood
17357	Knode, Thomas	c.40y	W	9 AUG 1921	Granit OK	Oak Hill
05759	Knopf, Karl F.	7y	W	5 OCT 1906	Hyattsville MD	Prospect Hill
11831	Knopp, Lina	33y	W	25 MAY 1913	Philadelphia PA	Rock Creek
16760	Knott, Harry Robert	19y	W	12 OCT 1920	Galveston TX	Arlington
13518	Knott, Margaret O.	21y	W	25 MAY 1916	Wash. Grove MD	Congressional
01875	Knott, Mary D.	72y	W	7 MAR 1896	Laurel MD	Glenwood
15406	Knowles, Clarisa	86y	W	3 DEC 1918	Baltimore MD	Oak Hill
15720	Knowles, Daniel O.	56y	W	12 APR 1919	Mt. Ranier MD	Holyrood
02712	Knowlton, Lucretia Walcott	82y	W	14 JAN 1899	Pine Hurst NC	Congressional
17560	Knowlton, Mary A.	74y	W	30 NOV 1921	Takoma Park MD	Rock Creek
18016	Knox, Caroline E.T.	75y	W	15 AUG 1922	Rumson NJ	Oak Hill
13426	Knox, Florence Niles	36y	W	22 MAR 1916	Lakewood NJ	Oak Hill
03076	Knox, Howard S.	25y	W	23 JAN 1900	Hyattsville MD	Glenwood
13429	Knox, John Jay	36y	W	6 JAN 1913	Colo. Spgs. CO	Oak Hill
00734	Knox, John Knox	63y	W	9 FEB 1892	New York NY	Oak Hill
04791	Knox, Mary F.	73y	W	11 JUL 1904	New York NY	Congressional
16404	Knox, Selden	60y	W	20 MAR 1920	New York NY	Congressional
06491	Knox, William H.	45y	W	3 APR 1908	MD	Baltimore MD
13505	Knox, William S., s/o Geo. W.	53y	W	14 MAY 1916	Atlantic City NJ	Glenwood
14593	Knudson, Christine	27y	W	20 JAN 1918	Takoma MD	Rock Creek
00289	Kober, Emily	23y	W	13 MAR 1890	St. Louis MO	Glenwood
15283	Koch, Ella McClure	33y	W	24 OCT 1918	Radnor PA	Arlington VA
17903	Koch, Manley	c.5y	W	12 JUN 1922	Vienna VA	Cedar Hill
14700	Koch, Sophia	69y	W	16 MAR 1918	Denver CO	Prospect Hill
07737	Koehl, Charles C.	33y	W	13 SEP 1910	Takoma Park MD	Ellicott City MD
18389	Koehler, Rosine Helen	82y	W	5 MAR 1923	Springfield MA	Prospect Hill
12760	Koerper, Mary Waters	39y	W	9 FEB 1915	Texas City TX	Arlington
12329	Koerth, Elizabeth	65y	W	25 APR 1914	Sligo MD	Mt. Olivet
15895	Koeth, Theodore M.	76y	W	28 JUL 1919	Portsmouth VA	Arlington
02925	Kohl, Frank	48y	W	22 AUG 1899	Philadelphia PA	St. Mary's
04925	Kohlenberg, Adela E.	45y	W	18 OCT 1904	Buckeystown MD	Congressional
05034	Kohlhase, Otto	—	W	29 JAN 1905	Panama	Arlington VA
13600	Kohlhausen, Julia	26y	W	12 JUL 1916	Pittsburgh PA	Mt. Olivet
04587	Kolkmeyer, Lucile E.	11y	W	2 FEB 1904	Mt. Wash. MD	Mt. Olivet
13243	Kollock, Betty	8y	W	11 DEC 1915	New York NY	Mt. Olivet
08345	Kondrup, Henry E.R.	46y	W	6 OCT 1911	Laurel MD	Cremated
08412	Koonce, Lucy A.	c.30y	C	22 FEB 1898	Cumberland VA	Harmony
01916	Kooner, Moses	23y	C	24 APR 1896	Boston MA	Harmony
13521	Koones, Albert L.	71y	W	26 MAY 1916	Lexington VA	Arlington
17056	Koones, Victorine	59y	W	20 MAR 1921	Leesburg VA	Rock Creek
07341	Koons, Milan B.	8d	W	23 DEC 1909	Pr. Geo. Co. MD	Glenwood
16104	Koontz, Marcelus P.	60y	W	12 NOV 1919	King Geo. Co. VA	Congressional
14811	Koontz, Thomas L.	58y	W	13 MAY 1918	Wash. Grove MD	Rock Creek
16429	Koppen, Frederick W.	28y	W	9 APR 1920	Philadelphia PA	Prospect Hill
17969	Korff, John Kossuth	71y	W	19 JUL 1922	Arlington VA	Oak Hill
16366	Kosack, Edward	87y	W	6 MAR 1920	Betheda MD	Glenwood
04537	Koss, Frederick W.	26y	W	6 DEC 1903	Los Angeles CA	Glenwood
04536	Kraft, Agatha	67y	W	12 DEC 1903	Roanoke VA	Holyrood
01734	Kraft, Christopher, cigar maker	40y	W	2 JUN 1895	Marshall Hall MD	Glenwood

No.	Name of Deceased	Age	Race	Death Date	Place of Death	Place of Burial
07016	Kraft, George	2d	W	7 MAY 1909	Oakmont MD	Glenwood
05450	Kraft, Laura	20y	W	30 JAN 1906	Kansas City MO	Glenwood
15560	Kraft, Mary E.	77y	W	16 JAN 1919	Seat Pleasant MD	Congressional
15750	Kraft, Minnie A.	54y	W	25 APR 1919	Alex. Co. VA	Rock Creek
16840	Kram, Nellie Bryant	48y	W	2 DEC 1920	Chevy Chase MD	Rock Creek
08045	Krams, Arthur	7m	W	21 AUG 1907	Hyattsville MD	Glenwood
08035	Krams, Peter	30y	W	27 MAR 1911	Hyattsville MD	Glenwood
01817	Kranskopf, Charles G.	51y	W	8 NOV 1895	Baltimore MD	Prospect Hill
17696	Krantz, August A.	45y	W	17 DEC 1911	Walter Reed Hp.	Glenwood
14556	Krantz, Joris Ernest	20y	W	4 JAN 1918	Quantico VA	Arlington
12050	Kratta, Mary (Mrs. Gus)	21y	W	18 OCT 1913	Beaumont TX	St. Mary's
12383	Krause, Leslie	3y	W	14 FEB 1911	New York NY	Mt. Olivet
07655	Krause, William	73y	W	20 JUL 1910	Atlantic City NJ	Arlington
12345	Krause, William	34y	W	3 MAY 1914	New York NY	Mt. Olivet
05039	Kraut, Millard B.	45y	C	21 FEB 1905	Baltimore MD	Druit Ridge
03658	Kretschmar, Helen L.	9y	W	3 JUN 1898	Hyattsville MD	Rock Creek
03657	Kretschmar, William	53y	W	22 SEP 1901	Hyattsville MD	Rock Creek
18592	Kretsinger, Hyatte Joseph	23y	W	1 JUN 1923	Takoma Park MD	Williamsport MD
03992	Kreuttner, Caroline Nowell	4m	W	28 AUG 1902	Berwyn MD	Glenwood
08453	Krickhoefer, Francis J.	61y	W	1 JAN 1912	New York NY	Mt. Olivet
05107	Krieg, Katherine Marie	39y	W	30 APR 1905	New York NY	Mt. Olivet
03007	Kritchelt, William	62y	W	12 NOV 1899	St. Clair NV	Mt. Olivet
01314	Kroeger, Margaret A.	59y	W	30 JAN 1894	Baltimore MD	Prospect Hill
12585	Kroh, Daniel	70y	W	26 OCT 1914	Hampton VA	Arlington
04591	Krohling, Conrade	77y	W	7 FEB 1904	Silver Hill MD	Prospect Hill
08064	Krohr, Raymond	4y	W	13 APR 1911	Philadelphia PA	Mt. Olivet
14970	Kronheimer, Charles	39y	W	10 AUG 1918	Thurmont MD	Wash. Hebrew
13212	Krug, George Anthony	48y	W	20 NOV 1915	Colchester VA	Mt. Olivet
05011	Krug, William H.	35y	W	27 JAN 1905	New York NY	Congressional
13643	Kulle, Henry	49y	W	7 AUG 1916	Hempstead NY	Congressional
05246	Kullman, John P.	66y	W	15 AUG 1905	Baltimore MD	Congressional
06559	Kumashire, Koh	28y	J	20 MAY 1908	Jacksonville FL	Cremated
12181	Kuntz, Richard H.	42y	W	25 JAN 1914	Preston Co. WV	Wash. Hebrew
08117	Kuntzberger, Roy J.	12d	W	15 MAY 1911	Friendship H. MD	Glenwood
15928	Kurtz, Minie A.	30y	W	14 AUG 1919	Hinsdale NY	Glenwood
16855	Kurz, Crispin, Brother	50y	W	13 DEC 1920	New York NY	Mt. St. Sepulchre
12783	Kuster, John Frankland	9h	W	27 FEB 1915	Bethesda MD	Rock Creek
18200	Kuster, Joseph	—	W	5 DEC 1922	University Pk. MD	Rock Creek
04877	Kyle, Edna Rose	11d	W	4 SEP 1904	River View MD	Mt. Olivet
16871	Kyle, Mary A.	75y	W	24 DEC 1920	Takoma Park MD	Wheeling WV
17410	Kyle, William D.	35y	W	15 SEP 1921	Brentwood MD	Sweetwater TX
15177	Kyler, Charles Henry	24y	C	14 OCT 1918	Bennet PA	Woodlawn

District of Columbia Foreign Death Records, 1888-1923

No.	Name of Deceased	Age	Race	Death Date	Place of Death	Place of Burial
L						
03071	Lacca, Benjamin F.	71y	W	19 JAN 1900	Hyattsville MD	Glenwood
03508	Lacey, Georgie	6y	W	11 MAY 1901	Montg. Co. MD	Methodist
00162	Lacey, Henry Olmstead, Rev.	32y	W	27 SEP 1889	Lynchburg VA	Brooklyn NY
15817	Lackaye, James M.	53y	W	7 JUN 1919	New York NY	Mt. Olivet
15557	Lackey, Vincent	39y	W	15 JAN 1919	Mt. Hope MD	Mt. Olivet
18577	Lacy, Beulah Nellina	1y	C	4 JUN 1923	Radio VA	Rosemont
05958	Lacy, Charles E.	43y	W	26 FEB 1907	Cincinnati OH	Mt. Olivet
03940	Lacy, John	35y	W	23 JUL 1902	Esopus NY	Mt. Olivet
08897	Lacy, Virginia	78y	C	18 OCT 1912	Norbeck MD	Mt. Zion East
17235	Ladd, Robert Bernard	2y	W	13 JUN 1921	Maryland Pk. MD	Congressional
01922	Ladson, Alice May	37y	W	24 APR 1896	Hyattsville MD	Rock Creek
01998	Ladson, Edna	23m	W	29 JUN 1896	Hyattsville MD	Rock Creek
15195	Laffey, Leo	24y	W	14 OCT 1918	Adams Co. PA	Arlington
12857	Laffingwell, Effie	42y	W	31 MAR 1915	St. Louis MO	Glenwood
15671	Laignel, William A.	c.32y	W	14 MAR 1919	Baltimore MD	Mt. Olivet
04866	Laing, Margaret A.	26y	W	26 MAR 1900	Baltimore MD	Congressional
00735	Laird, Helen D.	66y	W	12 JAN 1892	Rockville MD	Oak Hill
07098	Laird, Hellen C.	4m	W	9 JUL 1909	Waynesboro PA	Rock Creek
01997	Laird, James	68y	W	8 SEP 1896	Poland Spgs. ME	Oak Hill
00624	Laird, William, Jr.	65y	W	24 AUG 1891	Niagara Falls NY	Oak Hill
00967	Lake, Mary	3y	W	12 AUG 1893	Charlton Hts. MD	Rock Creek
00968	Lake, Willmot, Jr.	1y	W	24 AUG 1893	Charlton Hts. MD	Rock Creek
01280	Lally, Foliot T.	78y	W	3 JAN 1894	High Ridge MD	Oak Hill
17681	Lalor, Leo Milton	43y	W	3 FEB 1922	Booneville AR	Mt. Olivet
13588	Lamasure, Edwin, s/o Edwin	49y	W	4 JUL 1916	Bluemont VA	Rock Creek
14087	Lamb, Bert	35y	W	12 APR 1917	Pittsburgh PA	Glenwood
03985	Lamb, Delilah T.	8m	W	7 AUG 1902	Potomac MD	Oak Hill
08379	Lamb, Florence Emma	22y	W	30 OCT 1911	Ft. McKinley ME	Glenwood
17301	Lamb, Pauline Fischer	60y	W	11 JUL 1921	Minneapolis MN	Rock Creek
17384	Lamb, Serina Marion	45y	W	41 JUN 1921	Panama	Glenwood
14696	Lambert, Carrie	44y	C	19 MAR 1918	Fairmont Hts. MD	Woodlawn
00854	Lambert, Harold J.	9m	W	3 AUG 1892	Shepherdstn. WV	Mt. Olivet
15181	Lambert, John M.	30y	W	12 OCT 1918	Camp Meade MD	Congressional
12681	Lambert, Tallmadge A.	72y	W	28 DEC 1914	Laurel MD	Oak Hill
08168	Lamberton, Eliz. Marshall	61y	W	29 JUN 1911	Atlantic City NJ	Arlington
01056	Lambie, Janet Leah	30y	W	4 FEB 1893	Vicksburg MS	Oak Hill
03040	Lamkin, Cornelia N.	54y	W	18 DEC 1899	Falls Church VA	Glenwood
08089	Lamm, Isaac	50y	W	27 APR 1911	Baltimore MD	Glenwood
12587	Lammond, Virginia Minor	65y	W	28 OCT 1914	Takoma Park MD	Rock Creek
14314	Lamond, Angus, s/o Angus	76y	W	23 AUG 1917	Atlantic City NJ	Rock Creek
14269	LaMontague, Kate (Patterson)	57y	W	1 AUG 1917	Atlantic City NJ	Oak Hill
02319	Lanahan, Infant of William	—	W	25 JUL 1891	Laurel MD	Mt. Olivet
02318	Lanahan, Twins of William	—	W	22 MAY 1889	Laurel MD	Mt. Olivet
02115	Lancaster, Augustus	30y	C	21 JAN 1897	Hyattsville MD	Mt. Olivet
18031	Lancaster, Ermindia	75y	W	28 AUG 1922	Mt. Ranier MD	Cremated
13203	Lancaster, Louise	2y	C	13 NOV 1915	Washington DC	Mt. Olivet
16785	Lancaster, Morris	33y	C	OCT 1920	Martins Ferry OH	Harmony
06331	Landen, Zelma Barnett	4y	W	1 DEC 1907	Silver Spring MD	Rock Creek
04352	Lander, Jean Marg. Davenport	74y	W	2 AUG 1903	Lynn MA	Oak Hill
06231	Landers, Sarah Caroline	53y	C	18 SEP 1907	Fairfax VA	Harmony
03754	Landers, Thomas	60y	W	9 JAN 1902	Hampton VA	Arlington VA
13056	Landes, Frederick G.	30y	W	15 AUG 1915	Chatham NJ	Oak Hill
03164	Landgraf, Christian O. [Charles]	32y	W	10 APR 1900	Denver CO	Prospect Hill
01245	Landigan, John	53y	W	6 OCT 1860	Baltimore MD	Mt. Olivet
02894	Landon, Margaret A.R.	59y	W	31 JUL 1899	Suitland Rd. MD	Rock Creek
06219	Landon, Oliver A.	68y	W	8 SEP 1907	Suitland MD	Rock Creek
04748	Landrick, Elizabeth B.	17y	C	30 MAY 1904	New York NY	Harmony
08122	Landstreet, Mrs. Robert	57y	W	18 MAY 1911	Medley WV	Congressional

No.	Name of Deceased	Age	Race	Death Date	Place of Death	Place of Burial
01438	Lane, Annie	3m	W	16 JUL 1894	Bridgeport CN	Mt. Olivet
16862	Lane, Benjamin G.	71y	W	19 DEC 1920	Mt. Ranier MD	Glenwood
06946	Lane, Elinor Macartney	40y	W	16 MAR 1909	Lynchburg VA	Rock Creek
14284	Lane, Geraldine	10m	C	7 AUG 1917	Bethesda MD	Cremated
08304	Lane, Harriet	81y	W	2 JUL 1880	Aspen Hill VA	Rock Creek
12518	Lane, John Williamson, s/o C.	65y	W	6 SEP 1914	Philadelphia PA	Glenwood
07043	Lane, Joseph	25y	W	19 MAY 1909	Lamvine CA	Mt. Olivet
18589	Lane, Julia C.	31y	W	5 JUN 1923	Philadelphia PA	Mt. Olivet
06640	Lane, Mary	24y	C	10 JUL 1908	Baltimore MD	Payne's
17053	Lane, Mary Elizabeth	67y	W	17 MAR 1921	New York NY	Oak Hill
16181	Lane, Nathan C.	54y	W	31 DEC 1919	St. Petersburg FL	Congressional
18072	Lane, Richard H., Jr.	c.18y	W	15 SEP 1922	Oak Bluffs MA	Valley Forge PA
07896	Lane, Roberta	48y	W	28 DEC 1910	Baltimore MD	Oak Hill
18213	Lane, Sarah	80y	C	15 DEC 1922	Cedar Hts. MD	Harmony
16095	Lang, Emma R.	77y	W	6 NOV 1919	Rockville MD	Glenwood
05980	Lang, Margaret	79y	W	9 MAR 1907	Wheaton MD	St. Mary's
02167	Langdon, Agnes	69y	W	29 MAR 1897	Providence RI	Glenwood
01876	Langdon, Alice W.	52y	W	11 MAR 1896	Buffalo NY	Rock Creek
00237	Langdon, Jerusha S.	80y	W	6 DEC 1889	Buffalo NY	Rock Creek
01818	Langdon, William Chauncey	64y	W	28 OCT 1895	Providence RI	Glenwood
15912	Langford, Mary J.	57y	W	3 AUG 1919	Takoma Park MD	Glenwood
07172	Langhorne, Nannie Taylor	75y	W	25 AUG 1909	Atlantic City NJ	Rock Creek
06922	Langley, Ada C.	1y	W	17 FEB 1909	Arlington VA	Rock Creek
03285	Langley, Blanche E.	4m	W	5 SEP 1900	Trenton MD	Rock Creek
06854	Langley, Cora A. (Baum)	42y	W	14 DEC 1908	Vienna VA	Oak Hill
16403	Langley, Frederick William	62y	W	22 MAR 1920	Takoma Park MD	Rock Creek
01371	Langley, James W., laborer	65y	W	24 MAY 1894	Oxon Hill MD	Congressional
13682	Langley, Mary Graer	5m	W	27 AUG 1916	Clarendon VA	Holyrood
02573	Langley, Maurice	16y	W	26 AUG 1898	Camp Springs MD	Mt. Olivet
04602	Langley, Robert C.	61y	W	19 FEB 1904	Hyattsville MD	Congressional
02321	Langley, Samuel G.	43y	W	28 APR 1869	Manchester NH	Arlington VA
02320	Langley, Samuel G.	2y	W	3 FEB 1869	Manchester NH	Arlington VA
05479	Langley, Samuel Pierpont	71y	W	27 FEB 1906	Acken SC	Boston MA
11902	Langsdale, Annie M.	72y	W	17 JUL 1913	Quantico VA	Glenwood
16559	Langtree, William N.	49y	W	23 JUN 1920	Sioux Falls SD	Rock Creek
17166	Lanham, Alfred E.	66y	W	15 MAY 1921	Landover MD	Glenwood
16622	Lanham, Laura Virginia	59y	W	21 JUL 1920	Landover MD	Glenwood
17039	Lanham, William	51y	W	11 MAR 1921	Baltimore MD	Congressional
07412	Lanhardt, George	79y	W	7 FEB 1910	Hyattsville MD	Rock Creek
05945	Lanhardt, Margaret M.	79y	W	19 FEB 1907	Hyattsville MD	Rock Creek
06726	Lanhart, Margaret A.	12d	W	12 SEP 1908	Hyattsville MD	Rock Creek
14959	Lankford, Donald S.	1m	W	8 AUG 1918	Baltimore MD	Congressional
04243	Lanning, Charles E.	36y	W	8 APR 1903	Columbus GA	Glenwood
14967	Lansdale, Charles A., s/o E.	45y	W	8 AUG 1918	Front Royal VA	Rock Creek
15664	Lantz, William H.	48y	W	7 MAR 1919	Sharon PA	Congressional
05383	Lapham, Mary Agnes	42y	W	3 DEC 1905	Providence RI	Holyrood
04007	LaPorte, Annie E.	3y	W	18 SEP 1902	On Steamer	Glenwood
18426	Lappin, Richard C.	60y	W	18 MAR 1923	Jefferson City MO	Glenwood
18258	LaPreux, Augustus, Jr.	66y	W	10 JAN 1923	Takoma Park MD	Oak Hill
02943	Larcomb, Jane C.	63y	W	11 SEP 1899	Phoebus VA	Congressional
05698	Larcombe, Howard S.	56y	W	21 AUG 1906	Beltsville MD	Rock Creek
05865	Larcombe, J. Howard	86y	W	12 DEC 1906	Beltsville MD	Rock Creek
18493	Largey, Anna E.	66y	W	20 APR 1923	Saranac Lake NY	Glenwood
12351	Larkin, Francis S.	43y	W	7 MAY 1914	Takoma Park MD	Holyrood
11918	Larkin, Mrs. R.D.	68y	W	27 JUL 1913	Bluefield WV	Glenwood
02824	Larkin, William J., Rev.	65y	W	28 APR 1899	Baltimore MD	Mt. Olivet
07099	Larkins, Abraham, Jr.	3m	C	8 JUL 1909	Fairmont Hts. MD	Payne's
07727	Larkins, Elnora	20d	C	4 SEP 1910	Capitol Hts. MD	Payne's
05189	Larkins, Ida	29y	C	26 JUN 1905	New York NY	Harmony

District of Columbia Foreign Death Records, 1888-1923

No.	Name of Deceased	Age	Race	Death Date	Place of Death	Place of Burial
08219	Larman, Ella M. (Lunsford)	33y	W	26 JUL 1911	Hitaffer VA	Oak Hill
07769	Larman, John Q., s/o Jacob	83y	W	29 SEP 1910	Lewinsville VA	Oak Hill
15580	Larman, Mary J.	92y	W	24 JAN 1919	Hitaffer VA	Oak Hill
13859	Larne, Jacob, a.k.a. Lyons	72y	C	9 DEC 1916	Hampton VA	Harmony
01246	Larned, Maria	68y	W	5 DEC 1893	Baltimore MD	Oak Hill
09135	Larowe, Elizabeth F.	74y	W	19 MAR 1913	Staunton VA	Oak Hill
02891	Larrabee, Charles Smith	54y	W	2 JAN 1894	Potomac River	Bath ME
17124	Larrison, Levi, s/o John	83y	W	25 APR 1921	Elmira NY	Arlington
07544	Lascelles, Sidney	54y	W	23 MAY 1902	Asheville NC	Cremated
11814	Lash, Gertrude E.	24y	W	15 MAY 1913	Hyattsville MD	Glenwood
11815	Lash, Isabella Nemo	11m	W	25 NOV 1910	Hyattsville MD	Glenwood
02685	Laskey, Barnard	1m	W	26 DEC 1898	Arlington VA	Mt. Olivet
07361	Laskins, Mary	40y	C	7 JAN 1910	New York NY	Payne's
03899	Latchford, Lawrence A.	34y	W	8 JUN 1902	Charlottesville VA	Mt. Olivet
18570	Latham, Sally Evelyn	75y	W	31 MAY 1923	New Rochelle NY	Rock Creek
15619	Latham, Walter W.	36y	W	15 FEB 1919	Rosslyn VA	Congressional
03109	Latham, Woodville	70y	W	27 FEB 1900	Lynchburg VA	Rock Creek
07063	Lathron, Maria	48y	C	14 JUN 1909	New York NY	Harmony
04225	Lathrop, Adeline E.	84y	W	24 FEB 1903	New York NY	Glenwood
14851	Latimer, Mrs. Guy W. (Sanford)	36y	W	5 JUN 1918	Fredericksburg VA	Rock Creek
16608	Latona, Robert C.	6y	W	18 JUL 1920	Takoma Park MD	Congressional
05788	Lattimer, Georgie	9d	W	25 OCT 1906	Belair VA	Prospect Hill
11858	Lattin, William E.	3y	W	3 FEB 1913	Seoul, Korea	Rock Creek
08866	Lattis, Elsie	69y	W	30 SEP 1912	Norwood OH	Prospect Hill
07926	Laub, Cordelia Va. (Reddall)	90y	W	18 JAN 1911	Braddock Hts. VA	Oak Hill
16220	Lauchheimer, Charles H.	60y	W	14 JAN 1920	Washington DC	Arlington
01057	Laucke, William H.	40y	W	8 MAY 1893	Houston TX	Glenwood
00969	Laughlin, Ellen	6d	W	23 AUG 1893	Carlin Sta. VA	Glenwood
08022	Laughlin, Mathew J.	60y	W	24 MAR 1911	Lindenhurst VA	Mt. Olivet
07597	Laupp, Robert	32y	W	26 JUN 1910	Ram's Horn Inn	Prospect Hill
02557	Laurenson, Julia E.	23y	W	8 AUG 1898	Wash. Grove MD	Congressional
05961	Laurie, J.C.	28y	W	21 FEB 1907	Billings MT	Bainbridge PA
12053	Laursen, Catherine A.	26y	W	21 OCT 1913	Baltimore MD	Mt. Olivet
04909	Lavender, Virginia Odell	1y	W	5 OCT 1904	Hyattsville MD	Rock Creek
01999	Lavine, Infant of Samuel	3d	W	27 JUN 1896	Glendale MD	Russian Hebrew
01877	Law, F.M.	31y	W	18 JAN 1896	Denver CO	Oak Hill
15183	Lawless, William J.	27y	W	13 OCT 1918	Fairfax Co. VA	Arlington VA
03123	Lawrence, Cora M.K.	38y	W	10 MAR 1900	Baltimore MD	Mt. Olivet
17897	Lawrence, Ethel V.	29y	W	4 JUN 1922	Los Angeles CA	Rock Creek
06487	Lawrence, Helen Marie	13y	W	27 MAR 1908	Takoma Park MD	Cremated
02899	Lawrence, Joseph S., Dr.	51y	W	5 AUG 1899	Capon Spgs. WV	Charleston SC
02133	Lawrence, Luada	35y	W	9 MAR 1897	Philadelphia PA	Oak Hill
09080	Lawrence, Sarah	46y	C	15 FEB 1913	Alexandria VA	Harmony
01735	Lawrence, Winifred	39y	C	1 SEP 1895	Providence RI	Mt. Zion
00347	Lawrenson, James	87y	W	23 JUN 1890	Baltimore MD	Glenwood
02688	Laws, Isaac L.	43y	C	29 DEC 1898	Boston MA	Mt. Zion
03827	Laws, Nicholas	26y	C	23 MAR 1902	Charlottesville VA	Harmony
07725	Lawson, Blanch	43y	W	1 SEP 1910	Relay MD	Rock Creek
16964	Lawson, Edmund F.	80y	W	7 FEB 1921	Gainesville FL	Glenwood
01448	Lawson, Ethel	6m	C	27 JUL 1894	Rosslyn VA	Mt. Zion
00551	Lawson, Eugene G.	7y	W	– MAY 1877	Baltimore MD	Congressional
14042	Lawson, Fannia	57y	C	21 MAR 1917	Baltimore MD	Harmony
04977	Lawson, Florence	40y	W	9 DEC 1904	Baltimore MD	Newton MA
18152	Lawson, Herbert D., Jr.	—	W	8 NOV 1922	Takoma Park MD	Glenwood
06143	Lawson, John	55y	C	15 JUL 1907	Schenectady NY	Harmony
11853	Lawson, John Henry	35y	C	14 JUN 1913	Alexandria VA	Harmony
14936	Lawson, Mable	27y	C	25 JUL 1918	Takoma Park MD	Harmony
15145	Lawson, Robert L.	28y	C	9 OCT 1918	Camp Dix NJ	Payne's
14434	Lawton, Albert Bradley	65y	W	2 NOV 1917	Mt. Ranier MD	Congressional

No.	Name of Deceased	Age	Race	Death Date	Place of Death	Place of Burial
08155	Lawton, Mary	33y	W	20 JUN 1911	New York NY	Congressional
06352	Lawver, Mary Va. (Schneider)	55y	W	19 DEC 1907	Gainesville VA	Oak Hill
01632	Lay, Martha E.	59y	W	6 MAR 1895	E. Orange NJ	Congressional
09004	Lay, Thomas Wolcott	75y	W	27 DEC 1912	Roland Park MD	Mt. Olivet
04091	Lay, Walcott	64y	W	29 NOV 1902	Atlanta GA	Congressional
07681	Layer, Howard	11y	W	10 AUG 1910	St. Mary's Co. MD	Philadelphia PA
14483	Leach, Anita	47y	W	25 NOV 1917	New York NY	Oak Hill
06825	Leach, Boynton	26y	W	18 NOV 1908	Milwaukee WI	Oak Hill
13827	Leach, Clarence M.	3d	W	25 NOV 1916	Takoma MD	Rock Creek
02071	Leach, James M.	67y	W	6 NOV 1896	Branchville MD	Oak Hill
16909	Leach, John Milton	58y	W	6 JAN 1921	Florida City FL	Cremated
13409	Leach, Piercy	44y	W	10 MAR 1916	New York NY	Congressional
06052	Leadman, Louis	35y	W	2 MAY 1907	Rosslyn VA	Congressional
00131	Leafley, Lena	2m	W	31 JUL 1889	Pr. Geo. Co. MD	Beallesville MD
13193	Leahy, Catherine	60y	W	9 NOV 1915	Seat Pleasant MD	Mt. Olivet
06888	Leahy, John	23y	W	10 JAN 1909	Baltimore MD	Mt. Olivet
05581	Leahy, Michael A., s/o Richard	64y	W	19 MAY 1906	Newport News VA	Mt. Olivet
05197	Leakin, Pearl M.	6m	W	6 JUL 1905	Hyattsville MD	Congressional
18506	Leaman, Annie E.	39y	W	23 APR 1923	Nashville TN	Glenwood
16094	Leaman, Mary Catherine	40y	W	7 NOV 1919	Beltsville MD	Mt. Olivet
16321	Leames, Emmett	21y	C	16 FEB 1920	Sparrows Pt. MD	Harmony
02426	Leas, Cordalie Louisa	54y	W	21 MAR 1898	Baltimore MD	Congressional
15730	Lease, Carrie E.	46y	W	20 MAY 1916	Baltimore MD	Glenwood
15917	Leavenworth, William C., Dr.	33y	W	4 AUG 1919	Augusta GA	Cremated
09007	Leavy, James	44y	C	29 DEC 1912	Martinsburg WV	Harmony
00969½	Leavy, James T.	54y	W	8 JUL 1893	Harpers Ferry WV	Rock Creek
07564	Lebold, Joseph	34y	W	7 JUN 1910	New York NY	Monastery
16087	Leckie, Adam	51y	W	25 OCT 1919	Mexico City, Mex.	Rock Creek
16136	Leckie, Catherine	68y	W	12 MAR 1906	Shenandoah PA	Rock Creek
16137	Leckie, Samuel	58y	W	–	Shenandoah PA	Rock Creek
04789	Leckron, Thomas Q.	73y	W	10 JUL 1904	Hampton VA	Oak Hill
00374	LeCointe, Adolph	5m	W	21 JUL 1890	Boyds Sta. MD	Oak Hill
07579	LeCompte, Victoria J.	45y	W	17 JUN 1910	Wash. Grove MD	Mt. Olivet
08102	LeConte, Eva Harriet	68y	W	4 MAY 1911	Winchester VA	Oak Hill
06087	LeCuyer, Thomas B.	1y	W	31 MAY 1907	Frostburg MD	Baltimore MD
15976	Ledane, Eliza J.	78y	W	4 SEP 1919	Loudoun Co. VA	Congressional
01819	Lederer, Mary C.	49y	W	14 JAN 1896	Baltimore MD	Holyrood
14255	Ledman, Ellis Edward	42y	W	27 JUL 1917	Springfield VA	Glenwood
17778	Lee, Alfred Henry	33y	C	31 MAR 1922	Philadelphia PA	Woodlawn
03116	Lee, Ann Whitman	77y	W	2 MAR 1900	Plainfield NJ	Rock Creek
05177	Lee, Annie	53y	C	17 JUN 1905	New York NY	Harmony
03510	Lee, Annie	4y	C	14 MAY 1901	Hyattsville MD	Mt. Olivet
12272	Lee, Annie Grace (Shorter)	61y	C	25 MAR 1914	Purcellville VA	Harmony
13184	Lee, Charles	80y	C	6 NOV 1915	Railroad	Arlington
07228	Lee, Charles	60y	C	5 OCT 1909	Scranton PA	Harmony
08053	Lee, Charles	38y	C	2 APR 1911	Baltimore MD	Mt. Zion East
09051	Lee, Clarence F.	17y	W	30 JAN 1913	Asheville NC	Congressional
17952	Lee, David	42y	C	10 JUL 1922	Binghampton NY	Cedar Hill
13863	Lee, Edward	25y	C	10 DEC 1916	Salisbury MD	Payne's
14754	Lee, Emma P.	29y	C	15 APR 1918	Ballston VA	Mt. Zion West
04770	Lee, Francis M.	3m	W	20 JUN 1904	Overlook VA	Holyrood
08687	Lee, Frank, in jail	53y	C	25 JUN 1912	Atlanta GA	Baptist
15217	Lee, Fred	26y	C	12 OCT 1918	Ft. Monroe VA	Woodlawn
04345	Lee, George H.	30y	C	3 AUG 1903	Manchester MA	Potters Field
08135	Lee, George T., s/o Geo. W.	42y	C	3 JUN 1911	Arlington VA	Harmony
07329	Lee, Harry	34y	C	15 DEC 1909	Columbus OH	Harmony
08399	Lee, Howard T.	54y	C	20 NOV 1911	Gloucester NJ	Mt. Zion West
02582	Lee, James	22y	C	3 SEP 1898	Philadelphia PA	Payne's
17011	Lee, James C.	81y	W	3 MAR 1921	Staunton VA	Hyattsville MD

District of Columbia Foreign Death Records, 1888-1923

No.	Name of Deceased	Age	Race	Death Date	Place of Death	Place of Burial
17015	Lee, James C.	81y	W	3 MAR 1921	Staunton VA	Rock Creek
05729	Lee, Jewel May	26y	W	4 SEP 1906	Altoona PA	Mt. Olivet
02260	Lee, John	71y	W	28 JUL 1897	Bristol PA	Arlington
18543	Lee, John H.	70y	C	12 MAY 1923	New York NY	Woodlawn
13569	Lee, John W.	66y	W	25 JUN 1916	Baltimore MD	Glenwood
01571	Lee, John W.	33y	C	16 DEC 1894	Glen Cove NY	Harmony
03923	Lee, John W.M.	20y	W	19 JUL 1902	Ft. Myer VA	Baltimore MD
17583	Lee, Joseph Pryme	89y	W	13 DEC 1921	Silver Spring MD	Cremated
04349	Lee, Laura Ann	50y	C	5 AUG 1903	Silver Hill MD	Mt. Olivet
00736	Lee, Lizzie	17y	C	12 DEC 1891	Atlanta GA	Mt. Zion
07119	Lee, Louis H.	72y	W	18 JUL 1909	Takoma Park MD	Cremated
04719	Lee, Lucy J.	33y	W	24 AUG 1901	Kansas City MO	Rock Creek
00625	Lee, Luvenia Jane	16y	C	25 AUG 1891	Vienna VA	Harmony
16014	Lee, Malachi	30y	C	21 SEP 1919	Camp Meade MD	Arlington VA
18287	Lee, Margaret	60y	C	19 JAN 1923	Jersey City NJ	Harmony
13861	Lee, Margaret J.	68y	C	9 DEC 1916	Philadelphia PA	Harmony
15374	Lee, Mary Custis, d/o Robt. E.	83y	W	21 NOV 1918	Hot Springs VA	Cremated
08463	Lee, Nellie	30y	C	7 JAN 1912	Frederick MD	Harmony
01736	Lee, Reed Hurst	6m	C	3 JUL 1895	Baltimore MD	Harmony
17122	Lee, Richard K.	56y	W	24 APR 1921	Olney MD	Rock Creek
03964	Lee, Robert	40y	W	28 AUG 1902	Garrett Park MD	Payne's
14742	Lee, Robert	35y	C	1 APR 1918	Atlantic City NJ	Union Baptist
07209	Lee, Ruth Ann	74y	W	23 SEP 1909	DeSoto MO	Mt. Olivet
14891	Lee, Sarah	28y	C	29 JUN 1918	Washington DC	Harmony
13798	Lee, Sina	c.55y	C	2 NOV 1916	High View Pk. VA	Mt. Zion West
00042½	Lee, Stephen	25y	C	24 MAR 1889	Pittsburgh PA	Graceland
02909	Lee, Theodore	24y	C	11 JUL 1899	White S. Sp. WV	Harmony
01350	Lee, Theron R. Per	69y	W	20 MAR 1894	Togus ME	Rock Creek
18003	Lee, Thomas S.	81y	W	11 AUG 1922	Burkettsville MD	Baltimore MD
03180	Leech, Edward O.	49y	W	1 MAY 1900	New York NY	Glenwood
13356	Leech, Emma M.	65y	W	14 FEB 1916	New York NY	Glenwood
06083	Leech, Florence V.	31y	W	29 MAY 1907	Baltimore MD	Glenwood
16448	Leech, John F.	69y	W	22 APR 1920	Orlando FL	Oak Hill
12541	Leech, Margaretta Park	63y	W	22 SEP 1914	West Point NY	Oak Hill
05147	Leeke, Arthur Warfield	40y	W	22 MAR 1872	Wittman MD	Glenwood
05148	Leeke, Henry	82y	W	7 DEC 1866	Wittman MD	Glenwood
12099	Leeke, Sarah F.	69y	W	17 NOV 1913	Easton MD	Glenwood
08141	Leer, Charles	34y	W	8 JUN 1911	Johnson City TN	Mt. Olivet
12277	Lees, Matilda R.	45y	W	28 MAR 1914	Mt. Ranier MD	Prospect Hill
05376	Leet, Bessie	24y	W	21 NOV 1905	Asheville NC	Cremated
12529	Leet, Ida Mae	4h	W	14 SEP 1914	Chevy Chase MD	Cremated
15426	Leetch, Frederick H.	40y	W	10 DEC 1918	New York NY	Oak Hill
00855	Leetch, Jennette	59y	W	13 JUL 1892	Staunton VA	Oak Hill
12964	Leetch, John A.	19y	W	14 JUN 1915	Council Bluffs IA	Oak Hill
05434	Lefevre, Caroline E.	62y	W	18 JAN 1906	Philadelphia PA	Rock Creek
08729	LeFevre, Leon Henry	46y	W	23 JUL 1912	Concord MD	Cremated
17757	Leflang, Sarah Gertrude	34y	W	16 MAR 1922	Boise ID	Rock Creek
07851	Leftridge, Robert	38y	C	6 DEC 1910	Philadelphia PA	Woodlawn
05968	Leger, Fannie Lee	37y	W	3 MAR 1907	N. Ches. Bea. MD	Glenwood
17223	LeGros, Annie Reynolds	46y	W	16 JAN 1907	Washington DC	Glenwood[1]
17224	LeGros, Eugene	68y	W	2 MAR 1918	Washington DC	Glenwood
05115	Leh, Periline	26y	W	7 MAY 1905	Ballston VA	Congressional
00265	Lehmann, Annie M.	5y	W	14 JAN 1890	Bowie Sta. MD	St. Mary's
02635	Leiber, Francis	29y	W	10 OCT 1898	Fernandria FL	Arlington VA
11912	Leidy, Susan H.	77y	W	21 JUL 1913	Chevy Chase MD	Rock Creek
16854	Leif, Henry Albert	42y	W	10 DEC 1920	New York NY	Glenwood
14814	Leigh, Ralph	40y	W	15 MAY 1918	Richmond VA	Elkins VA

[1] Removed from Springhill Cemetery, Lynchburg VA, c.11 JUN 1921.

No.	Name of Deceased	Age	Race	Death Date	Place of Death	Place of Burial
13790	Leisenring, Olin D.	59y	W	28 OCT 1916	Arlington VA	Glenwood
04379	Leitch, Charles T.	27y	C	7 JUL 1903	Rockfish VA	Mt. Olivet
05885	Leitch, Robert	62y	W	28 DEC 1906	New York NY	Congressional
00350	Leitch, Walter Clark	6m	W	27 JUN 1890	Loudoun Co. VA	Congressional
16912	Leiter, Joseph, Jr.	10y	W	10 JAN 1921	Cheteau Can. LA	Rock Creek
04761	Leiter, Levi Z.	69y	W	9 JUN 1904	Bar Harbor ME	Rock Creek
12672	LeMat, Morris	65y	W	26 DEC 1914	Baltimore MD	Congressional
02797	Lemke, Gotleb	4y	W	15 APR 1899	Kensington MD	Rock Creek
13509	Lemly, Adelaide	35y	W	16 MAY 1916	Baltimore MD	Arlington
03247	Lemmons, William	20y	C	25 JUL 1900	New York NY	Harmony
08757	Lemoine, William	60y	W	8 AUG 1912	Charleston SC	Mt. Olivet
04662	Lemon, Charles	72y	W	6 APR 1904	Hampton VA	Glenwood
02072	Lemon, George Edwin	53y	W	18 DEC 1896	Coronado Be. CA	Soldier's Home
04216	Lenard, Nicholas	19y	W	10 MAR 1903	Elwyn PA	Mt. Olivet
06937	Lenoir, Charles, s/o Wm. J.	35y	W	4 MAR 1909	Norfolk VA	Glenwood
02382	LeNoir, Kate E.	27y	W	31 JAN 1898	New York NY	Glenwood
16708	Lenovitz, Elizabeth	20y	W	12 SEP 1920	Halpine MD	Adas Israel
16688	Lent, Frederick A.	35y	W	30 AUG 1920	Manhattan NY	Glenwood
16545	Leonard, Edith	10m	W	20 JUN 1920	Capitol Hts. MD	Glenwood
13943	Leonard, Gertrude	26y	C	20 JAN 1917	Newark NJ	Harmony
02073	Leonard, Harris C.	22y	W	1 DEC 1896	Savanac Lake NY	Indianapolis IN
12066	Leonard, Hermenia	50y	C	27 OCT 1913	Jersey City NJ	Harmony
04140	Leonard, John J.	47y	W	26 JAN 1903	Phoebus VA	Mt. Olivet
12182	Leonard, Lewis	60y	C	19 JAN 1914	Jacksonville FL	Harmony
04089	Leonard, Minnie	38y	W	23 NOV 1902	Phoebus VA	Mt. Olivet
17755	Leonard, Robert E.	23y	W	20 MAR 1922	Capitol Hts. MD	Ft. Lincoln
15390	Leonhardt, John Henry	64y	W	29 NOV 1918	Selva VA	Congressional
16056	Leonhardt, Peter	88y	W	16 OCT 1919	Rockville MD	Congressional
17029	LePruex, Roy	28y	W	9 MAR 1921	Oxford PA	Mt. Olivet
03128	LeRoy, Eliza	60y	C	7 MAR 1900	Bismarck ND	Mt. Olivet
04826	Lescalett, Mary A.	40y	W	1 AUG 1904	Seabrook MD	Congressional
05284	Lescallett, Charles F.	1y	W	10 SEP 1905	Baltimore MD	Congressional
13556	Lescallett, Jesse W.	84y	W	12 JUN 1916	Baltimore MD	Congressional
11908	Leslie, Clark Otto	26y	W	19 JUL 1913	Ft. Myer VA	Morocco IN
09139	Lester, Charles S.	65y	W	17 MAR 1913	At Sea	Rock Creek
04245	Lester, William Wharton	75y	W	11 APR 1903	Branchville MD	Glenwood
05241	Letts, Mary E.	62y	W	15 AUG 1905	Forest Glen MD	Starkey Sta. NY
13092	Levering, Phebe R.	85y	W	5 SEP 1915	Maringo OH	Rock Creek
13824	Leverone, Serafina	25y	W	23 NOV 1916	Chevy Chase MD	St. Mary's
02322	Levitt, Lizzie	18h	W	23 NOV 1897	Bladensburg MD	Ohev Sholom
02322	Levitt, Samuel	18h	W	23 NOV 1897	Bladensburg MD	Ohev Sholom
06666	Levy, Rita Estelle	23y	W	31 JUL 1908	Springfield MA	Wash. Hebrew
17976	Levy, William M.	61y	W	26 JUL 1922	Asheville NC	Wash. Hebrew
12307	Lewin, Eleanor	50y	W	11 APR 1914	Greensboro NC	Oak Hill
05708	Lewis, Albert	48y	C	28 AUG 1906	Trenton NJ	Harmony
00737	Lewis, Albert H.	58y	W	3 JAN 1892	Baltimore MD	Rock Creek
03789	Lewis, Amelia Goodrich	67y	W	8 FEB 1902	W. Pt. Plea. NJ	Rock Creek
00970	Lewis, Amelie	29y	C	1 AUG 1893	New York NY	Mt. Olivet
01351	Lewis, Ann Rebecca	67y	C	4 JAN 1894	Whitensville MA	Harmony
01634	Lewis, Annetta	10m	W	9 APR 1895	Linden MD	MN
02074	Lewis, Annie	28y	W	5 OCT 1896	Chevy Chase MD	Glenwood
00626	Lewis, Annie	25y	C	2 OCT 1891	Philadelphia PA	Graceland
00738	Lewis, Arthur H.	34y	W	3 FEB 1892	Asheville NC	Graceland
08286	Lewis, Bessie	2y	W	2 SEP 1911	Berwyn MD	Mt. Olivet
03782	Lewis, Catharine L.	19y	C	5 FEB 1902	Atlantic City NJ	Holyrood
18399	Lewis, Charles Henry	56y	W	9 MAR 1923	Sykesville MD	Glenwood
01163	Lewis, Charles Oscar	54y	W	20 OCT 1892	Bladensburg MD	Glenwood
14762	Lewis, Dorothy A.	2y	W	18 APR 1918	Takoma MD	Ford MD
16685	Lewis, Edith Virginia	58y	W	29 AUG 1920	Hyattsville MD	Glenwood

District of Columbia Foreign Death Records, 1888-1923

No.	Name of Deceased	Age	Race	Death Date	Place of Death	Place of Burial
12891	Lewis, Elizabeth Ann	57y	W	22 APR 1915	Takoma MD	Rock Creek
18363	Lewis, Ella P.	39y	C	19 FEB 1923	Lakeland MD	Harmony
01247	Lewis, Ellen	50y	C	28 NOV 1893	Rosslyn VA	Baptist
11959	Lewis, Emma Rising	56y	W	13 AUG 1913	Lake Taxaway NC	Arlington
07093	Lewis, Emmeline	74y	C	5 JUL 1909	Nauck Sta. VA	Harmony
06819	Lewis, Fielding	42y	W	12 NOV 1908	McAlister OK	Holyrood
06554	Lewis, Florence C.	32y	W	16 MAY 1908	New York NY	Glenwood
00307	Lewis, Frank Edgar	27y	W	4 APR 1890	Pine Ridge SD	Rock Creek
13086	Lewis, Geneve	1y	W	30 AUG 1915	Bethesda MD	Cremated
12560	Lewis, George F.	42y	W	8 OCT 1914	Mt. Ranier MD	Congressional
05901	Lewis, Granville	72y	W	20 JAN 1907	Philadelphia PA	Arlington
12769	Lewis, Hannah K.	97y	W	18 FEB 1915	Takoma Park MD	Congressional
06270	Lewis, Henry	33y	C	12 OCT 1907	Philadelphia PA	Odd Fellows VA
16720	Lewis, James Henry	2d	W	20 SEP 1920	Chevy Chase MD	Cremated
14140	Lewis, James T., s/o John	36y	W	17 MAY 1917	Atlantic City NJ	Arlington
17271	Lewis, Jane	4y	W	28 JUN 1921	Harrisburg PA	Oak Hill
04183	Lewis, Jeremiah	70y	C	15 FEB 1903	Rosslyn VA	Baptist
05561	Lewis, Joe	80y	C	1 MAY 1906	Hyattsville MD	Harmony
01633	Lewis, John	34y	C	4 APR 1895	Philadelphia PA	Harmony
04276	Lewis, John	29y	C	22 APR 1903	Philadelphia PA	Harmony
11821	Lewis, John	21y	C	14 MAY 1913	Stockfort NY	Harmony
14588	Lewis, John E.	35y	W	18 JAN 1918	Savannah GA	Congressional
03176	Lewis, John R.	65y	W	8 FEB 1900	Chicago IL	Arlington VA
04869	Lewis, John T.	92y	W	2 SEP 1904	Philadelphia PA	Rock Creek
08039	Lewis, John Vaughan	75y	W	27 MAR 1911	Radner PA	Rock Creek
11836	Lewis, John W.	73y	W	29 MAY 1913	Danville VA	Arlington
14385	Lewis, Katherine M.	54y	W	29 SEP 1917	Takoma Park MD	Baltimore MD
15745	Lewis, Leon	26y	C	18 APR 1919	Atlanta GA	Harmony
15357	Lewis, Levina L.	10y	C	15 NOV 1918	Highland Falls NY	Mt. Zion East
03093	Lewis, Lidey Elliot	30y	W	23 FEB 1900	King Geo. Co. VA	Holyrood
14094	Lewis, Lillie	28y	C	16 APR 1917	Philadelphia PA	Falls Church VA
11999	Lewis, Linwood Riley	17y	W	7 SEP 1913	Great Falls MD	Methodist
11978	Lewis, Mamie	41y	W	26 AUG 1913	Lodge VA	Glenwood
00358	Lewis, Marian	75y	W	12 JUL 1890	Oakland MD	Glenwood
03554	Lewis, Mary	35y	C	25 JUN 1901	Philadelphia PA	Harmony
07988	Lewis, Mary A.	60y	C	27 FEB 1911	Baltimore MD	Mt. Zion West
07230	Lewis, Mary A. (Conway)	40y	C	8 OCT 1909	Halls Hill VA	Harmony
05164	Lewis, Mildred	59y	W	10 JUN 1905	Atlantic City NJ	Glenwood
01162	Lewis, Mildred W.	35y	C	24 DEC 1892	New York NY	Graceland
12263	Lewis, O.	19y	C	18 MAR 1914	Philadelphia PA	Chapel Hill MD
16512	Lewis, Rebecca W.	16y	W	31 MAY 1920	E. Hyattsville MD	Glenwood
06904	Lewis, Richard	32y	C	26 JAN 1909	Philadelphia PA	Harmony
14984	Lewis, Ruth	12y	C	17 AUG 1918	Baltimore MD	Mt. Zion West
05436	Lewis, Sophronia	26y	C	16 JAN 1906	New York NY	Woodlawn
14551	Lewis, Susie Rivers Stokes	37y	W	1 JAN 1918	Lewisville KY	Rock Creek
13808	Lewis, Thomas	39y	C	5 NOV 1916	Harrisburg PA	Harmony
06071	Lewis, Va. Clarke, d/o Isaac	74y	W	18 MAY 1907	Colonial Bea. VA	Glenwood
17747	Lewis, Vialinda Rebecca	83y	W	14 MAR 1922	Bright Seat MD	Glenwood
03699	Lewis, Virginia O.	61y	C	3 NOV 1901	New York NY	Harmony
16266	Lewis, William A.	63y	W	1 FEB 1920	New York NY	Mt. Olivet
11946	Lewis, William J., s/o William	24y	C	8 AUG 1913	Atlantic City NJ	Harmony
05139	Lewis, William Wheeler	44y	W	21 MAY 1905	Clarksburg MD	Rock Creek
00552	Libbey, Louisa	17y	W	24 MAY 1891	Sandy Spring MD	Oak Hill
16325	Lichty, Martin Weaver	54y	W	16 FEB 1920	Wheeling WV	Oak Hill
01164	Liebermann, Jane A.	46y	W	16 NOV 1892	Baltimore MD	Rock Creek
07054	Lieter, Jon	15½d	W	8 JUN 1909	Chicago IL	Rock Creek
04772	Lietz, Frances Marie	1m	W	23 JUN 1904	Pittsburgh PA	Mt. Olivet
13613	Light, Infant of Clinton G.	SB	W	23 JUL 1916	Capitol Hts. MD	Mt. Olivet
07867	Lightboner, Infant of Millard	20min	W	14 DEC 1910	Mt. Ranier MD	Glenwood

No.	Name of Deceased	Age	Race	Death Date	Place of Death	Place of Burial
08245	Lightbrown, Rose E.	1y	W	8 AUG 1911	Mt. Ranier MD	Glenwood
13862	Lightburn, Richard V.	36y	W	11 DEC 1916	Catonsville MD	Glenwood
00971	Lightfoot, Bettie	30y	C	30 JUL 1893	Milton VA	Graceland
11932	Lightfoot, Georgia C.	77y	W	1 AUG 1913	Takoma Park MD	Culpeper VA
04296	Lightfoot, James H., Jr.	1y	W	3 JUN 1903	Tacoma Park MD	Rock Creek
02714	Lightfoot, Marian Hope	11m	W	15 JAN 1899	Arlington VA	Rock Creek
14027	Lilley, Perie Augustine	32y	W	4 MAR 1917	Denver CO	Rock Creek
03136	Lillie, Charles	—	—	12 OCT 1899	Manila, P.I.	Arlington VA
17037	Lilly, Effie M.	42y	W	11 MAR 1921	Takoma Park MD	Glenwood
03666	Lincoln, Marshall Harrold	4y	W	1 AUG 1857	Albany NY	Glenwood
08347	Lincoln, Martha	76y	W	6 OCT 1911	Pittsburgh PA	Glenwood
01878	Lincoln, Mary L.P.	48y	W	24 JAN 1896	Atlantic City NJ	Arlington VA
18286	Lindemuth, Harry	50y	W	18 JAN 1923	Allentown PA	Glenwood
05293	Lindenkohl, George C.F.	28y	W	18 SEP 1905	Laurel MD	Prospect Hill
06441	Lindenkohl, Paulina	62y	W	24 FEB 1908	Laurel MD	Prospect Hill
04879	Lindquist, Carl A.	49y	W	12 AUG 1904	Port Jervis NY	Rock Creek
09010	Lindsay, Eliza	—	C	30 DEC 1912	Philadelphia PA	Harmony
06295	Lindsay, James C.	35y	C	28 OCT 1907	Albuquerque NM	Harmony
05382	Lindsay, Walter E.	52y	W	30 NOV 1905	Philadelphia PA	Congressional
13589	Lindsey, Elizabeth Wilson	78y	W	6 JUL 1916	Arlington VA	Glenwood
00741	Lindsey, Lillie	25y	W	28 MAR 1892	Dumfries VA	Glenwood
12569	Lindsey, Samuel J.	46y	W	13 OCT 1914	Cleveland OH	Alexandria VA
03259	Lindsey, William	38y	W	11 AUG 1900	Brooklyn NY	Alexandria VA
00739	Lindsley, Bettie	22y	W	DEC 1885	Dumfries VA	Glenwood
00740	Lindsly, Willie	3m		JUN 1890	Dumfries VA	Glenwood
13058	Lineham, Bridget E. (Owens)	47y	W	16 AUG 1915	Portsmouth VA	Mt. Olivet
14919	Lingebach, Walter S.	26y	W	16 JUL 1918	Thurmont MD	Prospect Hill
15228	Lingeback, Margaret A.	8m	W	18 OCT 1918	Brentwood MD	Prospect Hill
01820	Linger, Augustus	43y	W	25 SEP 1863	Powhatan MD	Glenwood
13076	Link, John	74y	W	24 AUG 1915	Brentwood MD	Prospect Hill
13062	Link, Mary	75y	W	19 AUG 1915	Brentwood MD	Prospect Hill
14163	Linkins, William A.	59y	W	5 JUN 1917	Silver Spring MD	Congressional
13246	Linnell, Annia Belle	32y	W	10 DEC 1915	Princeton WV	Rock Creek
03304	Linney, Irving H.	19y	W	10 OCT 1900	Baltimore MD	Congressional
06935	Linthicum, Emily	65y	W	2 MAR 1909	Baltimore MD	Oak Hill
03949	Linthicum, Harman R.	70y	W	17 JUL 1902	Wittman MD	Loudon Park
11842	Linthicum, Rosa Gertrude	23y	W	3 JUN 1913	Laurel MD	Baltimore MD
01737	Linton, Julia M.	68y	W	30 AUG 1895	Anne Arundel Co.	Congressional
04032	Linton, Robert	31y	W	13 OCT 1902	Anne Arundel Co.	Congressional
05212	Lipphard, John F.	53y	W	15 JUL 1905	Columbus OH	Congressional
14235	Lipphard, John H.	64y	W	16 JUL 1917	Colonial Bea. VA	Congressional
00309	Lippincott, Rebecca R.	28y	W	10 APR 1890	Denver CO	Congressional
12178	Lippold, Magaretha	76y	W	21 JAN 1914	Suitland MD	Prospect Hill
02539	Lipscomb, Lamar	4y	W	19 JUN 1898	Ruthcomb VA	Cremated
07701	Lipscomb, Lee M., Capt.	49y	W	19 AUG 1910	Salisbury MD	Arlington VA
18503	Lipscomb, William H., jeweler	89y	W	22 APR 1923	Richmond VA	Cedar Hill
01058	Litchfield, Elizabeth	56y	W	8 APR 1893	Pr. Geo. Co. MD	Congressional
15862	Litster, Joseph	c.55y	W	3 JUL 1919	Railroad	New York NY
07184	Little, Anny Sybella	61y	W	5 SEP 1909	Mt. Ranier MD	Congressional
17004	Little, Emily Gray	79y	W	28 FEB 1921	Silver Spring MD	Chicago IL
17003	Little, Harriet M.	51y	W	26 FEB 1921	Westm. Co. PA	Congressional
17001	Little, Harriet M.	51y	W	26 FEB 1921	Westm. Co. PA	Mt. Ranier MD
01352	Little, John E.	51y	W	13 APR 1894	Kensington MD	Glenwood
00179	Little, Joseph F.	63y	W	27 SEP 1889	Piney Point MD	Congressional
07839	Littlefield, Ella	42y	W	25 NOV 1910	Grafton WV	Congressional
04321	Littlefield, George H.	35y	W	6 JUN 1903	Salt Lake City UT	Oak Hill
03618	Littlehales, Helen	32y	W	18 AUG 1901	Falls Church VA	Rock Creek
18558	Littleton, Helen Virginia	4y	W	16 FEB 1899	Bloomfield VA	Glenwood
12921	Litz, Annie Teresa	43y	W	11 MAY 1915	Capitol Hts. MD	St. Mary's

District of Columbia Foreign Death Records, 1888-1923

No.	Name of Deceased	Age	Race	Death Date	Place of Death	Place of Burial
13424	Litz, Marie Agnes	13y	W	22 MAR 1916	Capitol Hts. MD	St. Mary's
00628	Liverpool, Charles L.	20y	C	21 JUL 1891	Nantucket MA	Harmony
03477	Liverpool, Margaret	59y	C	9 APR 1901	Richmond NY	Congressional
05991	Livingston, James R.	26y	W	15 MAR 1907	Las Vegas NM	Rock Creek
08498	Livingston, Mary Eaton	31y	W	29 JAN 1912	E. Orange NJ	Arlington
00627	Livingstone, Samuel	3y	W	26 JUL 1891	Wheaton MD	Wash. Hebrew
05666	Lloyd, Mary E. (Mahoney)	81y	W	27 JUL 1906	Dunn Loring VA	Mt. Olivet
05389	Lloyd, Maurice D., s/o Thomas	49y	W	18 FEB 1905	Herndon VA	Congressional
16561	Lloyd, Nicholas	48y	W	26 JUN 1920	Norfolk VA	Mt. Olivet
04478	Lloyd, Thomas A.	57y	W	16 OCT 1903	Baltimore MD	Congressional
00222	Lloydum, James T.	59y	W	1 NOV 1889	Baltimore MD	Mt. Olivet
04161	Locke, Elizabeth M.	67y	W	10 JAN 1903	Barnaby MD	Congressional
04549	Locke, Mary F.	48y	W	21 DEC 1903	New York NY	Rock Creek
08481	Locke, Norman P.	18y	W	16 JAN 1912	Chevy Chase MD	Milledgeville GA
07097	Locke, W.R.	45y	W	9 JUL 1909	Charlotte NC	Berryville VA
00228	Locke, William P.	c.45y	W	8 NOV 1889	Summit VA	Congressional
15587	Lockett, Grace	32y	C	24 JAN 1919	Philadelphia PA	Mt. Olivet
00856	Lockett, Robert Alexander	2y	W	8 AUG 1892	Deer Park MD	Rock Creek
17906	Lockrey, Ida	c.65y	W	10 JUN 1922	Atlantic City NJ	Mt. Olivet
12877	Lockwood, Catherine M.	77y	W	8 APR 1815	Stockton CA	Oak Hill
08539	Lockwood, Charles B.	48y	W	19 FEB 1912	Chicago IL	Rock Creek
13567	Lockwood, Edward James	67y	W	25 JUN 1916	Riverdale MD	Glenwood
06133	Lockwood, Elenore C.	42y	W	10 JUL 1907	Gaithersburg MD	Mt. Olivet
12979	Lockwood, Fannie	53y	C	25 JUN 1915	Kings Co. NY	Harmony
18156	Lockwood, Mary Smith	91y	W	9 NOV 1922	Plymouth MA	Rock Creek
05058	Lockwood, Philo J.	58y	W	16 MAR 1905	Buffalo NY	Rock Creek
18243	Lodge, Lee Davis	57y	W	1 JAN 1923	Gaffeney SC	Rockville MD
04070	Lodge, Miranda F.	67y	W	5 NOV 1902	Alex. Co. VA	Rock Creek
09110	Loeb, Carrie	28y	W	6 MAR 1913	Takoma Park MD	Wash. Hebrew
18202	Loeb, Joseph Walter	27y	W	8 DEC 1922	Lincolnton NC	Ohev Sholom
17610	Loeffler, Charles C.M.	63y	W	25 DEC 1921	Philadelphia PA	Glenwood
17259	Loeffler, William J.	10m	W	26 JUN 1921	Bladensburg MD	Mt. Olivet
12089	Loftfield, Hannah	36y	W	13 NOV 1913	Takoma Park MD	Rock Creek
17792	Lofton, Lavenia A.	54y	C	8 APR 1922	New York NY	Mt. Olivet
13612	Loftus, Thomas H.	35y	W	18 JUL 1916	Pittsburgh PA	Arlington
16506	Logan, Florence	45y	C	27 MAY 1920	Alexandria VA	Payne's
12889	Logan, George Wood	46y	W	22 APR 1915	Portsmouth VA	Arlington
00742	Logan, Henry Clay	47y	W	15 JAN 1892	New York NY	Oak Hill
03740	Logan, James	11y	C	20 DEC 1901	New York NY	Woodlawn
00493	Logan, Robert, in jail	39y	C	30 MAR 1891	Albany NY	Harmony
08510	Logan, William Richard	55y	W	7 FEB 1912	Chicago IL	Mt. Olivet
17459	Loggins, Robert Lincoln	59y	C	6 OCT 1921	Meadville PA	Harmony
16412	Lohr, N.A.	c.50y	W	25 MAR 1920	Miami FL	Congressional
17427	Lomas, Carrie B.	62y	W	23 SEP 1921	Baltimore MD	Glenwood
01879	Lomax, Churchill	53y	W	17 FEB 1896	Arlington VA	Harmony
05594	Lomax, Fannie	105y	C	11 JUN 1906	Rosslyn VA	Baptist
08772	Lomax, Jane E.	61y	W	20 AUG 1912	Staunton VA	Oak Hill
17085	Lomax, Mildred	16y	W	1 APR 1921	Tuxedo MD	Harmony
18471	Lomax, Susan E.	18y	C	9 APR 1923	Morristown NJ	Payne's
06291	Lomax, Walter	39y	C	20 APR 1907	Milford VA	Harmony
15050	Lombardi, Henry D.	30y	W	24 SEP 1918	Camp Lee VA	Mt. Olivet
18149	Lonergan, Mrs. James	68y	W	9 OCT 1922	Gordonsville VA	Mt. Olivet
12038	Lonesome, Eliza S.	49y	C	11 OCT 1913	Alexandria VA	Union
12483	Lonesome, Genetta	20y	C	12 AUG 1914	Halls Hill VA	Union
05776	Long, Annie M.	52y	W	15 OCT 1906	Hyattsville MD	Rock Creek
16672	Long, Catherine	43y	W	19 AUG 1920	Lake Placid NY	Glenwood
14053	Long, Charles Chaille, s/o L.	74y	W	24 MAR 1917	Virginia Bea. VA	Arlington
01060	Long, Emma Dyer	34y	W	19 FEB 1893	Takoma Park MD	Rock Creek
12458	Long, Harry	32y	W	21 JUL 1914	Columbus NM	Arlington VA

No.	Name of Deceased	Age	Race	Death Date	Place of Death	Place of Burial
12027	Long, Infant of Alex. B.	SB	W	5 OCT 1913	Park Lane VA	St. Mary's
01572	Long, Jeremiah	c.58y	W	12 JAN 1895	Alexandria VA	Mt. Olivet
04332	Long, John G.	56y	W	28 JUL 1903	Dunbar, Scot.	Rock Creek
17815	Long, John Henry	70y	W	18 APR 1922	Lexington NC	Cremated
02437	Long, T. Ashley	36y	W	22 APR 1898	Chicago IL	Harrisonburg VA
13114	Longley, Abbie King	92y	W	20 SEP 1915	Howard KS	Congressional
17966	Longstreet, James	57y	W	15 JUL 1922	Cheyenne WY	Arlington
12926	Longwood, Thomas W.	50y	C	16 MAY 1915	Pittsburgh PA	Fredericksburg VA
02035	Loockerman, Rachael M.	70y	W	14 JUL 1896	Oakmont MD	Oak Hill
05319	Loomis, Lafayette Charles	81y	W	17 OCT 1905	Frederick MD	Glenwood
06094	Lopez, Moses E.	72y	W	3 JUN 1907	Atlanta GA	Atlanta GA
00972	Lorch, Edmond C.	20y	W	18 AUG 1893	Baltimore MD	Glenwood
04268	Lord, Thomas W.	58y	W	17 APR 1903	Potomac River	Arlington VA
00316	Lord, Walter Scott	33y	W	18 SEP 1890	Honesdale PA	Rock Creek
09126	Lorenz, Frances	89y	W	12 MAR 1913	Tuxedo MD	St. Mary's
17344	Lorenze, Jack Hollingsworth	45y	W	4 AUG 1921	Mt. Clemens MI	Glenwood
08558	Lorillard, Kathleen Leslie	28y	W	16 MAR 1912	New York NY	Oak Hill
16213	Loring, Margaret Gardner	81y	W	4 JAN 1920	Mt. Dora FL	Cremated
00973	Losano, Francisco Ellis	17m	W	10 AUG 1893	Wadesville VA	Glenwood
12011	Losee, Frederick Rideau	43y	W	23 SEP 1913	Staunton VA	Prospect Hill
06778	Lothrop, Caroline N.	20y	W	18 OCT 1908	Brookline MA	Oak Hill
11944	Lothrop, Evelyn D.	27y	W	8 AUG 1913	Takoma Park MD	Rock Creek
01518	Lott, William H.	18y	C	17 OCT 1894	Albany NY	Westm. Co. VA
01059	Lottier, Mary Margarett	46y	W	22 MAR 1893	Richmond VA	Mt. Olivet
07042	Loud, John S.	67y	W	27 MAY 1909	Ft. Snelling MN	Arlington VA
16753	Louden, Mary Ann	69y	W	11 OCT 1920	Mt. Ida VA	Mt. Olivet
13359	Loudon, Nancy	45y	C	15 FEB 1916	Catonsville MD	Harmony
07905	Louft, Clara	4d	W	2 JAN 1911	Capitol Hts. MD	Adas Israel
08366	Loughborough, Hamilton A.	46y	W	20 OCT 1911	Somerset Hts. MD	Oak Hill
17505	Loughborough, James H.	85y	W	9 NOV 1921	Bethesda MD	Oak Hill
17807	Loughborough, Ludwell H.	54y	W	17 APR 1922	Bethesda MD	Oak Hill
04889	Loughborough, Robert C.	26y	W	13 SEP 1904	Harrisburg PA	Oak Hill
11803	Loughlin, Ella J.	58y	W	6 MAY 1913	McLean VA	Mt. Olivet
18460	Loughran, Mary A. (Donnelly)	74y	W	27 MAR 1923	Los Angeles CA	Arlington
14207	Loundes, Dorothea	23y	W	5 JUL 1917	Frederick Co. MD	Cremated
15971	Loussarian, Armen Horenes	42y	W	2 SEP 1919	Takoma MD	Glenwood
15450	Love, Charles K.	75y	W	17 DEC 1918	Brentwood MD	Glenwood
06077	Love, Emma	33y	C	20 MAY 1907	Philadelphia PA	Harmony
16391	Love, Emma J.	53y	W	18 MAR 1920	Lanham MD	Glenwood
14591	Love, Isabelle E.	62y	W	21 JAN 1918	Brentwood MD	Glenwood
08751	Love, Susan E.	22y	W	3 AUG 1912	Seabrook MD	Glenwood
13800	Love, William B.	77y	W	–	Culpeper VA	Rock Creek[1]
12080	Lovee, Louise M.	40y	W	9 NOV 1913	Ft. Myer Hts. VA	Prospect Hill
16251	Lovejoy, Augusta Feree	78y	W	27 JAN 1920	Brooklyn NY	Glenwood
06022	Lovejoy, Guy	31y	W	7 APR 1907	Liberty NY	Glenwood
12990	Lovejoy, Mildred Forsyth	55y	W	3 JUL 1915	Pierce VA	Cremated
02564	Loveless, Earnest	24y	W	15 AUG 1898	Washington DC	Winewater VA
06168	Loveless, Ernest Elwood	7m	W	6 AUG 1907	Oxon Hill MD	Congressional
03046	Loveless, George H.	33y	W	21 DEC 1899	Chicago IL	Congressional
17314	Loveless, Norman A.	—	W	17 OCT 1918	France	Arlington
00432	Lovell, Henry	30y	W	11 NOV 1890	Columbus OH	Glenwood
12274	Lovell, Sarah B.	67y	W	27 MAR 1914	Laurel MD	Arlington
04041	Lovett, Emeline D.B.	66y	W	13 OCT 1902	Cobourg, Can.	Rock Creek
06777	Low, Fred H.	22y	W	11 OCT 1908	Monrovia CA	Congressional
16974	Low, Helen F.	72y	W	13 FEB 1921	Mt. Gilead VA	Paterson NJ
07718	Low, John E.	72y	W	26 AUG 1910	Green Cove FL	Congressional
12091	Lowden, Charles B.	71y	W	14 NOV 1913	Berwyn MD	Soldier's Home

[1] Removal, 4 NOV 1916, date of death not stated.

District of Columbia Foreign Death Records, 1888-1923

No.	Name of Deceased	Age	Race	Death Date	Place of Death	Place of Burial
12183	Lowell, Minnie H.	47y	W	25 JAN 1914	Peekskill NY	Rock Creek
15205	Lowen, Hazel M.	31y	W	16 OCT 1918	Takoma Park MD	Rock Creek
16453	Lowen, Olga Pearl, d/o G.R.	3y	W	28 APR 1920	Albemarle Co. VA	Rock Creek
15204	Lowen, Robert C.	35y	W	14 OCT 1918	Takoma Park MD	Rock Creek
05579	Lowery, Woodbury	53y	W	11 APR 1906	Tawmina NY	Rock Creek
07371	Lowndes, James	65y	W	15 JAN 1910	Augusta GA	Cremated
15523	Lowrey, William B.	35y	W	6 JAN 1919	Elkton MD	Oak Hill
05170	Lowry, Harry Preston	24y	W	14 JUN 1905	Rock Hill VA	Rock Creek
03017	Lowry, Mary J.	72y	W	26 NOV 1899	New York NY	Congressional
04383	Lucas, Frank, bricklayer	34y	C	7 JUL 1903	Hyattsville MD	Harmony
13995	Lucas, Fredie	5y	C	10 FEB 1917	Seat Pleasant MD	Woodlawn
05280	Lucas, George W.	57y	W	11 SEP 1905	Mt. Hope MD	Mt. Olivet
07973	Lucas, Joseph	48y	C	12 FEB 1911	Baltimore MD	Harmony
15842	Lucas, Laura M., d/o Chas.	23y	C	19 JUN 1919	Falls Mill VA	Harmony
05647	Lucas, Margaret	72y	W	16 JUL 1906	Brentwood MD	Mt. Olivet
05481	Lucas, Margaret Fr. (Ogle)	50y	W	1 MAR 1906	Ballston VA	Glenwood
14328	Lucas, Marie U.	38y	C	30 AUG 1917	Philadelphia PA	Odd Fellows VA
12929	Lucas, Martha	38y	C	16 MAY 1915	New York NY	Harmony
13751	Lucas, Mary Hellen	57y	W	7 OCT 1916	Maryland Pk. MD	Glenwood
12959	Lucas, Moses E.	15y	C	7 JUN 1915	Cumberland MD	Macedonia
08746	Lucas, William T., s/o A.	64y	W	2 AUG 1912	Ballston VA	Glenwood
14796	Luce, Henry John	8y	W	6 MAY 1918	Baltimore MD	Mt. Olivet
05999	Luce, Jane E.	75y	W	27 MAR 1907	Philadelphia PA	Oak Hill
01880	Luce, Oscar	28y	W	3 FEB 1896	Baltimore MD	Congressional
04642	Lucke, Christine	71y	W	23 MAR 1904	Seat Pleasant MD	Congressional
13543	Lucke, Mary C.	79y	W	14 NOV 1906	Baltimore MD	Mt. Olivet
08706	Luckett, Ed	30y	W	4 JUL 1912	Atlanta GA	Mt. Olivet
17715	Luckett, Elizabeth G.	75y	C	27 FEB 1922	Halls Hill VA	Gainesville VA
12800	Luckett, Mary E.	34y	W	9 MAR 1915	Silver Spring MD	Rock Creek[1]
07815	Luckett, Susan H., d/o Horace	80y	W	4 NOV 1910	Clarendon VA	Frederick MD
03771	Luddy, Patrick	41y	W	28 JAN 1902	Baltimore MD	Mt. Olivet
07382	Ludington, Harriet Marion	62y	W	22 JAN 1910	Savannah GA	Arlington
06766	Ludlum, Carl	2y	W	11 OCT 1908	Bethesda MD	Rock Creek
15926	Ludlum, Lucy O.	81y	W	13 AUG 1919	Chevy Chase MD	Glenwood
15716	Ludwig, C. Ralph, s/o Conrod	29y	W	7 APR 1919	Richmond VA	Prospect Hill
06822	Ludwig, Conrod	44y	W	16 NOV 1908	Richmond VA	Prospect Hill
06928	Ludwig, Infant of E.F.	SB	W	25 FEB 1909	Cottage City MD	Rock Creek
03144	Luebkert, William C.H.	61y	W	20 MAR 1900	Mt. Vernon NY	Glenwood
08054	Lugenbeel, Sarah F.	74y	W	3 APR 1911	Manassas VA	Oak Hill
01952	Lugenbell, French, Dr.	46y	W	5 JUN 1896	Staunton VA	Oak Hill
14519	Lulley, Anthony, s/o Emanuel	75y	W	22 DEC 1917	Atlantic City NJ	Wash. Hebrew
01382	Lulley, Julius C.	42y	W	5 MAR 1894	New York NY	Wash. Hebrew
13767	Lulley, Mark	59y	W	12 OCT 1916	Nogales AZ	Wash. Hebrew
01821	Lulley, Mattie	33y	W	22 SEP 1893	New York NY	Wash. Hebrew
13182	Lully, John	65y	W	6 NOV 1915	Atlantic City NJ	Wash. Hebrew
06851	Lumly, Clara Estelle Marie	29y	W	10 DEC 1908	Baltimore MD	Congressional
17962	Lund, Hilda M.	22y	W	18 JUL 1922	Mitchelville MD	Prospect Hill
17900	Lundy, Myra Bella	62y	W	12 JUN 1922	Camden NJ	Rock Creek
04016	Lung, Frederick J.	45y	W	14 SEP 1902	Wheeling WV	Rock Creek
07997	Lusby, Elizabeth	32y	W	7 MAR 1911	Germantown MD	Rock Creek
13633	Lusby, Ethel V.	3m	W	31 JUL 1916	Capitol Hts. MD	Glenwood
13656	Lusby, Frances Marguerite	6m	W	13 AUG 1916	Cherrydale VA	Congressional
16698	Lusby, Geneva	75y	W	6 SEP 1920	Jackson MI	Congressional
08132	Lusby, George W.	65y	W	28 MAY 1911	Maryland Pk. MD	Congressional
17249	Lusby, Harriet L.	56y	W	17 JUN 1921	Colesville MD	Rock Creek
07840	Lusby, Infant of James F.	SB	W	27 NOV 1910	Capitol Hts. MD	Congressional
07614	Lusby, James H.	2y	W	5 JUL 1910	Capitol Hts. MD	Congressional

[1] Disinterment permit #8385 for reinterment in Colesville MD, 13 JUL 1915.

No.	Name of Deceased	Age	Race	Death Date	Place of Death	Place of Burial
15684	Lusby, John H.	31y	W	22 MAR 1919	Baltimore MD	Congressional
13973	Lusby, Margaret A.	52y	W	5 FEB 1917	Mt. Hope MD	Mt. Olivet
08134	Lusby, Rachel M.	74y	W	31 MAY 1911	Riggs Mill MD	Rock Creek
03708	Lusby, Violet Bladen	4y	W	19 NOV 1901	Burnt Mills MD	Rock Creek
14918	Lusby, William T.	28y	W	16 JUL 1918	Cumberland PA	Congressional
18262	Lusky, William Howard	38y	W	6 JAN 1923	Houston TX	Ft. Lincoln
05191	Luther, John	28y	W	2 JUL 1905	Berwyn MD	Arlington VA
16660	Luxon, Carrie Marion	32y	W	14 AUG 1920	Hyattsville MD	Rock Creek
01411	Lybrand, George Ranney	22y	W	3 JUN 1894	Gaithersburg MD	Rock Creek
13575	Lyddane, Margaret M.	42y	W	26 JUN 1916	Mt. Hope MD	Holyrood
03570	Lyles, Charles H.	65y	C	9 JUL 1901	Lockport NY	Mt. Zion
18513	Lyman, David Hinckley	45y	W	29 APR 1923	Asheville NC	Congressional
13611	Lyman, Maria S.	77y	W	19 JUL 1916	Laurel MD	Glenwood
01822	Lyman, William G.	30y	W	15 NOV 1895	Phoenix AZ	Rock Creek
03157	Lyman, Wyllys, Lt. Col.	—	—	3 FEB 1900	—	Arlington VA
01738	Lynch, Charles	14y	W	27 JUL 1895	Riverdale MD	Mt. Olivet
03151	Lynch, Charles E.	39y	W	26 MAR 1900	Philadelphia PA	Mt. Olivet
13476	Lynch, Daniel	36y	W	23 APR 1916	Baltimore MD	Mt. Olivet
05042	Lynch, Daniel F.	49y	W	24 FEB 1905	Cheltenham MD	Congressional
00180	Lynch, Gertrude B.	1y	W	17 OCT 1889	Montg. Co. MD	Holyrood
13938	Lynch, Gertrude Mary	25y	W	17 JAN 1917	Brooklyn NY	Arlington
04115	Lynch, Henry Thomas	31y	W	26 DEC 1902	Philadelphia PA	Mt. Olivet
06615	Lynch, Irene	23y	C	26 JUN 1908	McKeesport VA	Harmony
18480	Lynch, John	54y	W	12 APR 1923	Johnson City TN	Congressional
03134	Lynch, John S., soldier	—	—	MAY 1899	Manila, P.I.	Arlington VA
14547	Lynch, Joseph	7y	W	4 JAN 1918	Cabin John MD	Rock Creek
13082	Lynch, Mary	72y	W	28 AUG 1915	Seabrook MD	Congressional
14458	Lynch, Mary E.	60y	W	13 NOV 1917	Darnestown MD	Glenwood
02406	Lynch, Mary Nolan	31y	W	3 MAR 1898	Asheville NC	Mt. Olivet
04774	Lynch, Robert	30y	W	21 JUN 1904	New Orleans LA	Mt. Olivet
11948	Lynch, Robert Emmett	21y	W	8 AUG 1913	Baltimore MD	Mt. Olivet
15582	Lynch, Wenonah L.	25y	W	22 JAN 1919	Philadelphia PA	Glenwood
15633	Lynham, Mary E.	60y	W	23 FEB 1919	Takoma Park MD	Congressional
04985	Lynn, David	69y	W	28 DEC 1904	Hyattsville MD	Glenwood
17705	Lynn, Fielder	65y	W	22 FEB 1922	Rosslyn VA	Rock Creek
07302	Lynn, R.H.	40y	W	3 DEC 1909	Cecil Co. MD	Leesburg VA
16194	Lyon, Anne Ellis	36y	W	8 JAN 1920	Riverdale MD	Glenwood
15570	Lyon, Margarine Lorene	22m	W	19 JAN 1919	New Castle PA	Glenwood
07151	Lyon, Melvin E.	26y	W	5 AUG 1909	Philadelphia PA	Congressional
16146	Lyon, Wallace, Jr.	26y	W	11 DEC 1919	Hyattsville MD	Glenwood
03919	Lyons, Beebe M.	62y	W	18 JUL 1902	Hyattsville MD	Mt. Olivet
00024	Lyons, Catherine S.	71y	W	21 FEB 1889	Boyds Sta. MD	Glenwood
04948	Lyons, Dennis J.A.	65y	W	31 OCT 1904	McKeesport PA	Mt. Olivet
04307	Lyons, Evan	65y	W	19 MAY 1903	Orange NJ	Oak Hill
13859	Lyons, Jacob, a.k.a. Larne	72y	C	9 DEC 1916	Hampton VA	Harmony
15865	Lyons, John Chester	25y	W	4 JUL 1919	Cumberland MD	Arlington
15323	Lyons, Michael	25y	W	2 NOV 1918	Youngstown OH	Mt. Olivet

District of Columbia Foreign Death Records, 1888-1923

No.	Name of Deceased	Age	Race	Death Date	Place of Death	Place of Burial
M						
18326	Mabbey, Marie	1y	C	5 FEB 1923	Takoma Park MD	Harmony
16133	MacArthur, Alexander	90y	W	2 DEC 1919	Chicago IL	Oak Hill
02002	MacArthur, Arthur	81y	W	26 AUG 1896	Atlantic City NJ	Rock Creek
00196	MacArthur, Frank	35y	W	1 DEC 1889	MD	Rock Creek
05992	Macartney, Elizabeth J.	70y	W	21 MAR 1907	Atlantic City NJ	Rock Creek
14417	Macat, Dorothy	29y	W	12 OCT 1917	Duluth MN	Fairfax C.H. VA
14015	Macaw, James P.	58y	W	26 FEB 1917	Cincinnati OH	Rock Creek
14780	MacComas, Eugene	51y	W	29 APR 1918	Takoma Park MD	Chicago IL
04185	MacDaniel, Ezekiel	50y	W	18 APR 1836	Mason City WV	Glenwood
14521	MacDonald, Ada	40y	W	19 DEC 1917	Ft. Meyer FL	Purcellville VA
12436	MacDonald, Burnette S.	81y	W	11 JUL 1914	White H. Sta. NJ	Glenwood
08465	MacDonald, Rhoderick A.	39y	W	8 JAN 1912	Mannington WV	Mt. Olivet
08617	MacDonald, Virginia	33y	W	26 APR 1912	Colo. Spgs. CO	Mt. Olivet
16955	MacDougal, Duglas	11y	W	6 FEB 1921	Bluemont VA	Glenwood
15668	MacDowell, E. Janet (Robert)	47y	W	12 MAR 1919	Charlotte NC	Cremated
04100	MacGowan, Annie Woods	18y	W	24 NOV 1902	Falls Church VA	Oak Hill
05407	MacGowan, Josephine W.	19y	W	23 DEC 1905	Newport News VA	Oak Hill
07549	MacGowan, Marianna W.	59y	W	20 MAY 1910	Millbourne PA	Oak Hill
14245	MacIntyre, Mary A.	87y	W	23 JUL 1917	Bethesda MD	Rock Creek
03262	Mack, Daniel Webster	34y	C	12 AUG 1900	Piney Point MD	Harmony
06254	Mack, Ella	28y	C	28 SEP 1907	Monessen PA	Moore's
13018	Mack, Georgina Mechlin	76y	W	22 JUL 1915	Charlottesville VA	Congressional
11828	Mack, James	29y	C	21 MAY 1913	Philadelphia PA	Harmony
08838	Mack, John Alfred	32y	W	15 SEP 1912	Forestville MD	Congressional
12117	Mack, Maggie L.	44y	W	7 DEC 1913	Brentwood MD	Rock Creek
17614	Mack, Robert J.	4m	W	27 DEC 1921	Wilkes-Barre PA	Prospect Hill
18254	Mackall, Evanina F.	74y	W	8 JAN 1923	Bethlehem PA	Oak Hill
03572	Mackall, Henry C.	10m	W	9 JUL 1901	Waynesville NC	Mt. Olivet
04129	Mackall, Madeline P.	41y	W	27 DEC 1902	London, Eng.	Mt. Olivet
03773	Mackall, Mary Kurtz	44y	W	27 JAN 1902	Moorehead MN	Oak Hill
06660	Mackall, Mary L.	73y	W	28 JUL 1908	Aquasco MD	Oak Hill
12799	Mackay, Catherine	17m	W	7 MAR 1915	Philadelphia PA	Mt. Olivet
05503	Mackay, Edward	36y	W	20 MAR 1906	Riverdale MD	Congressional
14594	MacKeen, Robert Abner	6y	W	21 JAN 1918	Takoma MD	Congressional
14098	MacKenzie, Lillian	19y	W	21 APR 1917	Clarksville MD	Congressional
02003	MacKenzie, William A.	3m	W	11 AUG 1896	Berwyn Hts. MD	Glenwood
16105	Mackesey, James W.	26y	W	14 NOV 1919	Baltimore MD	Mt. Olivet
02001	Mackey, Argyle, Dr.	28y	W	28 AUG 1896	Baltimore MD	Mt. Olivet
13949	Mackey, Jeff	23y	C	23 JAN 1917	Youngstown OH	Payne's
07828	Mackey, Robert W.M.	1y	W	16 NOV 1910	Rock Hill VA	Mt. Olivet
15999	Mackey, Rosena Lloyd	79y	W	18 SEP 1919	Alexandria VA	Mt. Olivet
13165	MacLeod, Euphemia N.	80y	W	24 OCT 1915	Philadelphia PA	Rock Creek
12497	MacNichol, Dorothy M.	19d	W	24 AUG 1914	Highland Park MI	Rock Creek
15491	Macomic, O.M. McMillen	32y	W	27 DEC 1918	Bethesda MD	Rock Creek
02323	MacQueen, David Boyd	27d	W	9 SEP 1897	Capitol View MD	Rock Creek
07072	Madden, Adelaide B.	31y	W	20 JUN 1909	Jacksonville FL	Mt. Olivet
06476	Maddex, Thomas E.	65y	W	18 MAR 1908	Bayonne NJ	Glenwood
16261	Maddox, Frances Gertrude	44y	W	30 JAN 1920	Brentwood MD	Glenwood
16646	Maddox, James A.	31y	W	7 AUG 1920	Cincinnati OH	Mt. Olivet
12793	Maddox, James O.	19y	W	30 OCT 1916	Baltimore MD	Congressional
16843	Maddox, Mary E.	71y	W	3 DEC 1920	Florence SC	Glenwood
02659	Maddox, Samuel L.	—	W	NOV 1898	Chester VA	Glenwood
02596	Maddox, Thomas Clay Sanders	17y	W	7 SEP 1898	Montauk Pt. NY	Arlington
16998	Madigan, Jean Patricia	7m	—	23 FEB 1921	Englewood NJ	Mt. Olivet
03969	Madison, Elizabeth E.	35y	C	3 AUG 1902	Pittsburgh PA	Harmony
08663	Madison, Gertrude P.	26y	W	10 JUN 1912	Wash. Grove MD	Glenwood
04476	Madison, James H.	49y	C	9 OCT 1903	Chicago IL	Harmony
13360	Madison, Thomas	55y	C	15 FEB 1916	Cleveland OH	Harmony

No.	Name of Deceased	Age	Race	Death Date	Place of Death	Place of Burial
12574	Maedel, Otto M.	70y	W	18 OCT 1914	Landover MD	Prospect Hill
15822	Magary, Joseph L.	c.46y	W	8 JUN 1919	Chesa. Bea. MD	Glenwood
14171	Magee, Harriett G.	72y	W	13 JUN 1917	McLean VA	Rock Creek
02938	Magee, Helen	22y	W	4 SEP 1899	Ocean City MD	Oak Hill
16893	Magee, Sarah A.	65y	W	6 JAN 1921	Alexandria VA	Mt. Olivet
00629	Magill, Katherine C.	53y	W	28 SEP 1891	Garrett Park MD	Oak Hill
00406	Maginnis, Anna Maria	76y	W	30 SEP 1890	Jersey City NJ	Mt. Olivet
14524	Magruder, Anna	28y	C	23 DEC 1917	New York NY	Harmony
01739	Magruder, Ellen Livinia	16y	C	5 JUN 1895	Seat Pleasant MD	Jones' Chapel
01165	Magruder, Emma J.	45y	W	10 JAN 1893	Hyattsville MD	Rock Creek
16626	Magruder, Ernest Pendleton	—	W	8 APR 1915	Belgrade, Serb.	Baltimore MD
02464	Magruder, Garfield	16y	W	2 JUN 1898	Seat Pleasant MD	Jones' Chapel
14479	Magruder, James E.	36y	C	23 NOV 1917	Philadelphia PA	Mt. Olivet
14840	Magruder, Jennie	71y	W	24 MAY 1918	New York NY	Glenwood
01061	Magruder, John	70y	W	2 MAR 1893	Addison's Chapel	Jones' Chapel
01823	Magruder, John F.D.	72y	W	3 JAN 1896	Unity MD	Oak Hill
00743	Magruder, John W.	51y	W	1 NOV 1891	Boston MA	Oak Hill
11975	Magruder, Lottie	2y	C	27 AUG 1913	Baltimore MD	Payne's
07189	Magruder, Lucretia	60y	C	7 SEP 1909	Seat Pleasant MD	Payne's
14944	Magruder, M. Blanche	63y	W	28 JUL 1918	Springfield MA	Mt. Olivet
16315	Magruder, Martha Lumsdon	82y	W	15 FEB 1920	Rockville MD	Oak Hill
17050	Magruder, Sam	27y	C	14 MAR 1921	Atlanta GA	Payne's
02478	Magruder, Wallace	19y	W	1 AUG 1898	Hunting Hill MD	Glenwood
02326	Maguani, Charles	36y	W	8 NOV 1897	Richmond VA	St. Mary's
00857	Maguire, Edward	3m	W	3 AUG 1892	Rosslyn VA	Holyrood
07825	Maguire, Frank Z.	51y	W	12 NOV 1910	Baltimore MD	Rock Creek
06882	Maguire, Martha	77y	W	6 JAN 1909	Catonsville MD	Rock Creek
07160	Magunson, Swan Olaf	30y	W	18 AUG 1909	Wash. Grove MD	Prospect Hill
11904	Mahan, Anna L.	7y	W	6 JAN 1875	Abilene KS	Rock Creek
11905	Mahan, Clark	46y	W	18 JUL 1913	Kensington MD	Rock Creek
17403	Mahan, John H.	82y	W	8 SEP 1921	Los Angeles CA	Rock Creek
15414	Mahan, John W.	—	W	28 AUG 1905	Charleston WV	Rock Creek
11906	Mahan, Marian	2y	W	7 AUG 1876	Abilene KS	Rock Creek
07965	Mahan, Patrick	52y	W	11 FEB 1911	Whitney IN	Holyrood
12601	Mahan, Stephen	c.4y	W	6 NOV 1914	Marlborough Rd.	Mt. Olivet
05158	Maher, Jessie R.	39y	W	3 JUN 1905	New York NY	Rock Creek
07795	Maher, Rosie	60y	W	20 OCT 1910	Rockville MD	Mt. Olivet
14170	Mahon, Kate S. (Sanderson)	74y	W	13 JUN 1917	Fairfax VA	Mt. Olivet
05410	Mahon, William	35y	W	25 DEC 1905	Chicago IL	Holyrood
07728	Mahoney, Honora	40y	W	3 SEP 1910	Montg. Co. MD	Mt. Olivet
15381	Mahoney, James Bernard	21y	W	23 OCT 1918	Paris, France	Mt. Olivet
09025	Mahoney, John P.	42y	W	11 JAN 1913	Gallitzen PA	Mt. Olivet
04832	Mahoney, Mary	39y	C	4 AUG 1904	Mayfield VA	Harmony
02580	Mahoney, Mary E.	73y	W	23 AUG 1898	Bladensburg MD	Glenwood
12097	Mahoney, William H.	34y	W	17 NOV 1913	Washington DC	Mt. Olivet
13297	Mahorney, Alphonso	23y	C	11 JAN 1916	Boston MA	Harmony
00340	Maier, James Stewart	5m	W	11 JUN 1890	Surry Co. VA	Congressional
12684	Main, Mary E.	84y	W	29 DEC 1914	Seat Pleasant MD	Congressional
13002	Maio, Mike	23y	W	11 JUL 1915	Alpena MI	Mt. Olivet
15355	Maisel, Nellie M.	26y	W	15 NOV 1918	Silver Spring MD	Congressional
00025	Major, Daniel G.	57y	W	24 FEB 1889	New York NY	Holyrood
01917	Major, Elizabeth Ann	67y	W	22 APR 1896	Providence RI	Rock Creek
00057	Major, John J.	55y	W	31 MAR 1889	New York NY	Holyrood
00274	Major, Mabel	80y	W	26 JAN 1890	New York NY	Holyrood
16653	Major, Mary E.	81y	W	9 AUG 1920	Bloomfield NJ	Oak Hill
05694	Malatesta, John	83y	W	20 AUG 1906	Ardwick MD	St. Mary's
02325	Malcolm, Mary	49y	W	29 OCT 1897	Orange NJ	Vienna VA
05468	Mallon, George	79y	W	14 FEB 1906	Barrington RI	Holyrood
04030	Mallone, Charles E.	71y	W	30 OCT 1902	Hampton VA	Arlington

District of Columbia Foreign Death Records, 1888-1923

No.	Name of Deceased	Age	Race	Death Date	Place of Death	Place of Burial
04131	Mallory, David H.	43y	W	3 JAN 1903	Hyattsville MD	Congressional
05887	Malloy, M.J.	—	W	27 DEC 1906	Rhyolite NV	Mt. Olivet
00344	Malloy, Sarah	36y	W	18 JUN 1890	Detroit MI	Mt. Olivet
06925	Malloy, Virgie, d/o Frank	5y	W	20 FEB 1909	Lodge VA	Prospect Hill
18094	Malone, Bertha Virginia	21y	W	29 SEP 1922	Arlington Co. VA	Glenwood
06050	Maloney, David R.	2y	W	2 MAY 1907	Hyattsville MD	Glenwood
06249	Maloney, Joseph	—	W	24 SEP 1907	Canton OH	Mt. Olivet
08408	Maloney, Mark J.	50y	W	2 DEC 1911	Pottsville PA	Mt. Olivet
05536	Maloney, Nannie B.	46y	W	12 APR 1906	San Antonio TX	Rock Creek
05174	Maloney, Stephen A.	9y	W	19 JUN 1905	Chambersburg PA	Mt. Olivet
08550	Maloy, Eleanor Agnes	45y	W	12 MAR 1912	Mt. Hope MD	Oak Hill
01315	Mandley, Julian	26y	W	28 AUG 1890	Alexandria VA	Glenwood
01316	Mandley, Loyd B.	3y	W	11 SEP 1890	Alexandria VA	Glenwood
00494	Mangan, Katie A.	23y	W	30 DEC 1890	New York NY	Mt. Olivet
16239	Manger, Robert S.	46y	W	21 JAN 1920	Pittsburgh PA	Glenwood
02965	Mangold, Christiana Rebecca	53y	W	3 FEB 1896	Seabrook MD	Congressional
00858	Mangum, Annie Rebecca	5m	W	18 JUL 1892	Silver Spring MD	Rock Creek
03340	Mangum, Frances V.	74y	W	17 NOV 1900	Alex. Co. VA	Congressional
15163	Mangum, Harry	35y	W	9 OCT 1918	PA	Glenwood
04111	Mangum, John G.F., farmer	75y	W	30 DEC 1902	Clifton Park MD	Rock Creek
14763	Mangum, Marie F.	49y	W	11 APR 1918	Chicago IL	Congressional
01881	Mangum, Mary M.	40y	W	28 JAN 1896	Forestville MD	Holyrood
05230	Mangum, Susan	73y	W	4 AUG 1905	Takoma Park MD	Rock Creek
14316	Mangum, Thomas Oates	6m	W	27 AUG 1917	Mt. Ranier MD	Congressional
03997	Mangum, William	42y	W	20 AUG 1902	Takoma Park MD	Rock Creek
14884	Manili, Mary	5m	W	27 JUN 1918	Seat Pleasant MD	St. Mary's
13831	Manilli, Rosia	3m	W	30 NOV 1916	Maryland Pk. MD	St. Mary's
00043	Manion, James Herbert	9m	W	14 MAR 1889	Rockville MD	Oak Hill
08285	Mankin, Charles	50y	W	31 AUG 1911	Wilkinsburg PA	Holyrood
01490	Mankins, Blanche Louisa	7y	W	14 SEP 1894	Ft. Myer VA	Holyrood
01167	Manley, Samuel A.	22y	W	14 JUN 1892	Quantico VA	Glenwood
02946	Mann, Alice	26y	C	14 SEP 1899	New York NY	Woodlawn
17657	Mann, Fannie S.	73y	W	25 JAN 1922	Ballston VA	Glenwood
12463	Mann, Freda C.	53y	W	29 JUL 1914	Atlantic City NJ	Wash. Hebrew
05589	Mann, John H.	26y	W	5 JUN 1906	New York NY	Mt. Olivet
14760	Mann, Kate Ray	57y	W	16 APR 1918	Annapolis MD	Arlington VA
04253	Mann, Mabel	7y	W	14 MAY 1903	FL	Montross VA
17544	Mann, Martin William	82y	W	24 NOV 1921	Hanover Co. VA	Arlington
06921	Mann, Mary E. Lee	64y	W	18 FEB 1909	New York NY	Rock Creek
03298	Manning, Caroline E.	70y	W	8 OCT 1900	Forest Glen MD	Rock Creek
15444	Manning, Donald H.	27y	W	13 DEC 1918	Ft. McPherson GA	Arlington
01248	Manning, Edith Reamer	25y	W	17 SEP 1893	Branchville MD	Glenwood
01166	Manning, Van H.	53y	W	3 NOV 1892	Branchville MD	Glenwood
03770	Manning, William	66y	C	27 JAN 1902	Sycolin VA	Harmony
08406	Mannion, James LeRoy	13y	W	1 DEC 1911	Dranesville VA	Rock Creek
16877	Mansfield, Ed. A.	1y	W	29 DEC 1920	Bladensburg MD	Congressional
12853	Mansfield, Harry	36y	C	30 MAR 1915	Philadelphia PA	Mt. Zion East
07266	Mansfield, William	47y	W	7 NOV 1909	Halls Hill VA	Baptist
01740	Mansing, James J.	13d	W	15 AUG 1895	Hyattsville MD	Holyrood
16431	Manville, Loren R.	34y	W	12 FEB 1920	Yonkers NY	Glenwood
07971	Manville, W.E., Dr.	35y	W	16 FEB 1911	Asheville NC	Glenwood
13780	Marble, Emily M.	75y	W	25 OCT 1916	Canton PA	Arlington VA
02976	Marceron, Eliza Cecelia	9y	W	10 OCT 1899	Landover MD	Mt. Olivet
17155	Marceron, Mary J.	9y	W	12 MAY 1921	Alta Vista MD	Oak Hill
14640	March, Payton C.	21y	W	13 FEB 1918	Camp Bowie TX	Arlington
04418	Marche, Frances E.	75y	W	1 AG 1903	Vienna VA	Congressional
02612	Marche, Thomas B.	62y	W	22 SEP 1898	Vienna VA	Congressional
15919	Marche, William F.	39y	W	5 AUG 1919	Washington DC	Prospect Hill
12033	Marcus, Stanley Boone	1m	W	9 OCT 1913	Montclair NJ	Rock Creek

No.	Name of Deceased	Age	Race	Death Date	Place of Death	Place of Burial
13035	Marcy, William C.	72y	W	2 AUG 1915	Hampton VA	Arlington
08638	Marders, Agustus	26y	W	18 MAY 1912	Laurel MD	Congressional
15226	Mares, Guido	22y	W	16 OCT 1918	Philadelphia PA	Mt. Olivet
15980	Margaretten, Selma	21y	W	6 SEP 1919	Great Falls MD	Los Angeles CA
04644	Marindin, Henry Louis F.	60y	W	25 MAR 1904	Woodside MD	Rock Creek
13779	Marinelli, Mary Louise	60y	W	24 OCT 1916	Chesa. Bea. MD	St. Mary's
05257	Markland, Fanny Dailey	55y	W	22 AUG 1905	Maysville KY	Arlington VA
05826	Markland, Mathew	68y	W	25 NOV 1906	Maysville KY	Arlington VA
13520	Marks, Katherine M.	3h	W	27 MAY 1916	Rosslyn VA	Methodist
16416	Marks, Stanhope G.	35y	W	31 MAR 1920	Tulsa OK	Glenwood
07692	Marks, Thomas, Jr.	1y	W	15 AUG 1910	Lynchburg VA	Rock Creek
18004	Markward, Charles P.	60y	W	11 AUG 1922	Takoma Park MD	Mt. Olivet
08424	Markward, Thomas	9m	W	12 DEC 1911	Mt. Ranier MD	Glenwood
16754	Marlon, Frank	38y	W	10 OCT 1920	Sykesville MD	Addison Chapel
17910	Marlow, Annie E.	81y	W	17 JUN 1922	Dunellen NJ	Glenwood
09033	Marlow, Eliza N.	64y	C	12 JAN 1913	Atlantic City NJ	Harmony
05369	Marlow, Francis B.	45y	W	17 NOV 1905	Chevy Chase MD	Glenwood
13964	Marlow, Martha Anne	81y	W	31 JAN 1917	Silver Spring MD	Glenwood
13393	Marlow, Sarah Elizabeth	83y	W	2 MAR 1916	Drummond MD	Glenwood
01281	Marmaduke, Frances V.	34y	W	23 DEC 1893	Rosslyn VA	Oak Hill
02004	Marmion, Francis DeSales	11m	W	26 JUL 1896	Brown's Sta. MD	Mt. Olivet
12807	Marquhart, Robert C., a.k.a.	6y	W	10 MAR 1915	Glen Carlin VA	Oak Hill
03613	Marr, Alonzo A.	56y	W	13 AUG 1901	New York NY	Oak Hill
08699	Marr, Calhoun	59y	W	1 JUL 1912	Baltimore MD	Oak Hill
01062	Marr, James H.	35y	W	9 APR 1893	Brooklyn NY	Glenwood
06351	Marr, Kate F.	57y	W	19 DEC 1907	New York NY	Mt. Olivet
01577	Marr, Sarah A.	84y	W	12 FEB 1895	Baltimore MD	Mt. Olivet
02000	Marr, Walter S.	50y	W	14 SEP 1896	Baltimore MD	Mt. Olivet
02077	Marr, Walter S.	50y	W	14 SEP 1896	Baltimore MD	Mt. Olivet
06728	Marr, William	64y	W	12 JUL 1908	Bar Harbor ME	Rock Creek
14958	Marr, William F.	69y	W	6 AUG 1918	McLean VA	Glenwood
15062	Marscha, Hazel Marble	28y	W	30 SEP 1918	Fairfax Co. VA	Cremated
16910	Marschen, John C.	59y	W	10 JAN 1921	Alexandria VA	Cremated
05456	Marsden, Bertha, suicide	18y	W	c.5 FEB 1906	Selma AL	Prospect Hill
04072	Marsh, Albert Campbell	7m	W	17 FEB 1902	Hyattsville MD	Glenwood
00553	Marsh, Alonza J.	65y	W	15 MAY 1891	Linden MD	Jamestown NY
07213	Marsh, Charlotte B.	66y	W	26 SEP 1909	Laurel MD	Rock Creek
00258	Marsh, Louisa Libbey	30y	W	8 JAN 1890	New York NY	Oak Hill
15649	Marsh, Margaret Elliott	74y	W	2 MAR 1919	Forest Glen MD	Glenwood
14974	Marsh, Susan	63y	C	12 AUG 1918	Trenton NJ	Payne's
13784	Marsh, Wilbert Melvin	68y	W	22 OCT 1916	Grey Cliff MT	Congressional
12443	Marshall, Adrian	5m	C	15 JUL 1914	Alex. Co. VA	Moore's
17864	Marshall, Alfred Colquitt	6y	W	MAY 1893	Macon GA	Arlington
18417	Marshall, Alice	60y	C	13 MAR 1923	Capitol Hts. MD	LaPlata MD
05531	Marshall, Benjamin Hanson	2m	W	26 OCT 1892	Wash. Grove MD	Oak Hill
07444	Marshall, Charles	39y	C	27 FEB 1910	New York NY	Woodlawn
06091	Marshall, Delia M.	3y	C	1 JUN 1907	New York NY	Moore's
00744	Marshall, Edmonia	22y	W	12 MAR 1892	Pr. Geo. Co. MD	Mt. Olivet
08537	Marshall, Frank	37y	C	26 FEB 1912	Chicago IL	Harmony
05533½	Marshall, Herman Travers	4y	W	26 JAN 1898	Wash. Grove MD	Oak Hill
02354	Marshall, Howard	40y	C	18 DEC 1897	New York NY	Mt. Zion
01741	Marshall, Jane V.	67y	W	24 JUL 1895	Harpers Ferry WV	Congressional
03743	Marshall, John G.	49y	C	26 DEC 1901	Utica NY	Harmony
04150	Marshall, John H.	58y	W	14 JAN 1903	Ft. Wash. MD	Congressional
02355	Marshall, John S.B.	20y	C	27 DEC 1897	New York NY	Harmony
05530	Marshall, Marian May	7y	W	21 OCT 1897	Wash. Grove MD	Oak Hill
12448	Marshall, Mary	76y	C	17 JUL 1914	Norfolk VA	Harmony
15166	Marshall, Minnie	26y	C	12 OCT 1918	Baltimore MD	Payne's
06632	Marshall, Montgomery	10y	W	31 DEC 1897	Wash. Grove MD	Oak Hill

District of Columbia Foreign Death Records, 1888-1923

No.	Name of Deceased	Age	Race	Death Date	Place of Death	Place of Burial
17052	Marshall, Mrs. Lute W.	81y	W	16 MAR 1921	Lexington KY	Congressional[1]
12946	Marshall, Rebecca G. (Bird)	54y	W	27 MAY 1915	Accomac VA	Glenwood
16886	Marshall, Richard	46y	C	1 JAN 1921	Freedman's Hp.	Harmony
05533	Marshall, Richard Henry	6y	W	9 AUG 1897	Wash. Grove MD	Oak Hill
04355	Marshall, Thomas	77y	W	15 JUN 1903	Wash. Grove MD	Oak Hill
05534	Marshall, Thomas H.	22y	W	22 NOV 1905	Wash. Grove MD	Oak Hill
07522	Marshall, Thos. H.	52y	W	1 MAY 1910	Wash. Grove MD	Oak Hill
05800	Marshall, Winnie	88y	C	31 OCT 1906	Alexandria VA	Payne's
15275	Marshall, Zenia M.	33y	W	15 FEB 1885	Laurel MD	Rock Creek
16818	Marsteller, Mariamne C.	76y	W	20 NOV 1920	Gainesville VA	Oak Hill
14669	Martin, Achsah J.	77y	W	1 MAR 1918	Dallas TX	Rock Creek
04755	Martin, Allan S.	28y	W	5 JUN 1904	Baltimore MD	Rock Creek
04008	Martin, Augusta E.	60y	W	16 SEP 1902	Chicago IL	Rock Creek
13283	Martin, Benjamin M.	69y	W	4 JAN 1916	Mt. Ranier MD	Congressional
02206	Martin, Catherine	69y	W	18 JUN 1897	Pr. Geo. Co. MD	Glenwood
11907	Martin, Charles Alfred	41y	W	17 JUL 1913	Atlantic City NJ	Rock Creek
01169	Martin, Eliza	76y	W	3 OCT 1892	Montrose MD	Glenwood
18445	Martin, Elizabeth J.	57y	W	29 MAR 1923	Highland Park VA	Congressional
08075	Martin, Elizabeth J.	46y	W	9 DEC 1910	Baltimore MD	Rock Creek
17186	Martin, Elizabeth J.	86y	W	26 MAY 1921	Takoma Park MD	Rock Creek
06411	Martin, Emma W.	38y	W	31 JAN 1908	Forest Glen MD	Glenwood
02993	Martin, George	39y	W	1 NOV 1899	Savannah GA	Mt. Olivet
12388	Martin, Harriett	98y	C	30 MAY 1914	Atlantic City NJ	Payne's
00357	Martin, Henry Neil	45y	W	10 JUL 1890	Greenwood VA	Glenwood
03788	Martin, Ida C.	48y	W	11 FEB 1902	Pr. Geo. Co. MD	Glenwood
08095	Martin, Irene Gertrude	3m	W	2 MAY 1911	Barcroft VA	Glenwood
00362	Martin, James	66y	W	18 JUL 1890	Knowles MD	Glenwood
01168	Martin, James	67y	W	21 NOV 1892	Pr. Geo. Co. MD	Glenwood
12154	Martin, John S.	92y	W	10 JAN 1914	Vineland NJ	Holyrood
02900	Martin, Josephine Gracien	c.65y	W	6 AUG 1899	The Plains VA	Holyrood
02508	Martin, Kate	55y	W	18 JUL 1898	Baltimore MD	Oak Hill
01824	Martin, Leon Danforth	9y	W	19 NOV 1895	Kensington MD	Glenwood
01249	Martin, Levi Q.	c.82y	W	13 NOV 1893	Montg. Co. MD	Soldier's Home
08551	Martin, Lythia, d/o Grant	15y	C	9 MAR 1912	Trenton NJ	Baptist
08164	Martin, Marie, d/o Grant	16y	C	26 JUN 1911	Rosslyn VA	Baptist
04298	Martin, Mary	73y	C	31 MAY 1903	Hyattsville MD	Harmony
17842	Martin, Mary	c.70y	W	8 MAY 1922	Takoma Park MD	Mt. Olivet
03450	Martin, Mary Ellen	60y	W	12 MAR 1901	Baltimore MD	Rock Creek
17594	Martin, Mary F.	75y	W	19 DEC 1921	Pittsburgh PA	Rock Creek
07820	Martin, Mary S.	58y	W	7 NOV 1910	Takoma Park MD	Prospect Hill
17615	Martin, Reggie	26y	W	28 DEC 1921	Stafford Co. VA	Ft. Lincoln
17454	Martin, Richard T.	84y	W	7 OCT 1921	Baltimore MD	Rock Creek
06350	Martin, Robert C.	49y	C	1 DEC 1907	Kansas City MO	Woodlawn
06350	Martin, Robert C.	49y	C	1 DEC 1907	Kansas City MO	Woodlawn
04994	Martin, Thomas	4d	W	8 JAN 1905	Hyattsville MD	Congressional
05690	Martin, Thomas H.	67y	W	15 AUG 1906	Minneapolis MN	Rock Creek
08577	Martin, William McLain	52y	W	31 MAR 1912	Brandywine MD	Glenwood
15043	Martin, William Penn, Jr.	50y	W	24 SEP 1918	Atlantic City NJ	Rock Creek
03058	Martin, William S.	77y	W	1 JAN 1900	Baltimore MD	Congressional
13265	Martinez, Mary	68y	W	26 DEC 1915	Garrett Park MD	Rock Creek
01170	Martins, Mary F.	54y	W	21 OCT 1892	Baltimore MD	Mt. Olivet
08529	Marvel, Charles H.	39y	W	21 FEB 1912	Tucson AZ	Laurel DE
16038	Marx, Lester F.	31y	W	24 JAN 1919	New York NY	Wash. Hebrew
00105	Masi, Frederick H.	43y	W	1 JUL 1889	Salem VA	Mt. Olivet
12561	Masi, Walter C.	59y	W	9 OCT 1914	New York NY	Mt. Olivet
04445	Maske, Bertha	39y	W	9 FEB 1903	Baltimore MD	Forestville MD
16579	Maskew, Frederick H.	39y	W	3 JUL 1920	Clarendon VA	Glenwood

[1] Records of Congressional Cemetery give the name of the deceased as Lucy W. Marshall.

No.	Name of Deceased	Age	Race	Death Date	Place of Death	Place of Burial
04708	Mason, Carlisle	35y	C	6 MAY 1904	Chicago IL	Harmony
15616	Mason, Crawley	38y	C	13 FEB 1919	Glenarden MD	Mt. Olivet
13648	Mason, Daisy	18y	C	6 AUG 1916	Colonial Bea. VA	Woodlawn
16115	Mason, Elizabeth Aranz	47y	W	19 NOV 1919	Clarendon VA	Cremated
12802	Mason, Eva Lee	35y	W	9 MAR 1915	Boston MA	Rock Creek
04955	Mason, George E.	32y	W	11 NOV 1904	Worcester MA	Rock Creek
15531	Mason, Gordon H.	22y	W	14 DEC 1918	Brooklyn NY	Arlington
05501	Mason, Ida M.	50y	W	14 MAR 1906	Allegheny PA	Congressional
18401	Mason, Infant of William	SB	C	9 MAR 1923	Takoma Park MD	Mt. Zion West
12135	Mason, Jessie R.	56y	W	23 DEC 1913	Youngstown OH	Rock Creek
11826	Mason, Josephine A.B.	79y	W	22 MAY 1913	Holbrook MA	Rock Creek
06942	Mason, Kate	59y	W	14 MAR 1909	Carroll Co. MD	Rock Creek
04222	Mason, Lillian	40y	W	27 FEB 1903	New York NY	Rock Creek
08255	Mason, Mamie	31y	C	14 AUG 1911	Fairmont Hts. MD	Harmony
06634	Mason, Mary	1m	C	8 JUL 1908	Hyattsville MD	Harmony
04780	Mason, Persis Proudfit	26y	W	2 JUL 1904	W. Springfield NH	Falls Church VA
03026	Mason, Samuel M.	49y	C	3 DEC 1899	Baltimore MD	Mt. Zion
03225	Mason, Sarah E.	64y	W	5 JUL 1900	Belmar NJ	Oak Hill
12039	Mason, Scott	33y	C	9 OCT 1913	Camden NJ	Tabytown MD
02554	Mason, Victor, Jr.	1y	W	11 AUG 1898	Afton VA	Glenwood
00860	Mason, Wesley	6m	W	28 JUL 1892	Widewater VA	Congressional
06125	Mason, William	30y	W	3 JUL 1907	New York NY	Oak Hill
04525	Mass, James W.	58y	W	24 NOV 1903	New York NY	Oak Hill
15034	Massey, Charles Frederick	67y	W	17 SEP 1918	Winchester VA	Cremated
12737	Massey, Charlotte	60y	C	28 JAN 1915	New York NY	Mt. Zion East
16684	Massey, Mattie	44y	C	26 AUG 1920	Asbury Park NJ	Harmony
03125	Massoletti, Rosalia	69y	W	9 MAR 1900	Boston MA	Congressional
12047	Masters, James L.	73y	W	15 OCT 1913	Baltimore MD	Mt. Olivet
14041	Masters, Lilla V.	32y	W	23 MAR 1917	Riverdale MD	Rock Creek
02438	Mathews, Arthur M.	23y	C	11 MAY 1897	Alex. Co. VA	Harmony
14065	Mathews, Daniel	36y	C	26 MAR 1917	Cleveland OH	Harmony
01063	Mathews, Eliza H.	88y	W	11 FEB 1893	College Park MD	Glenwood
18268	Mathews, Ella Crystal	56y	W	14 JAN 1923	Johnson City TN	Rock Creek
05006	Mathews, Genevieve	24y	W	19 JAN 1905	Kissinun FL	Glenwood
00862	Mathews, James A.	49y	C	20 AUG 1892	Nomini Creek VA	Harmony
05196	Mathews, James, s/o Peter	38y	W	21 JUN 1905	Phoebus VA	Mt. Olivet
04636	Mathews, Sadie	20y	W	12 MAR 1904	Congress J. AZ	Glenwood
02134	Mathews, Sherman	1y	C	13 FEB 1897	Hyattsville	Mt. Olivet
03814	Mathews, T. Wirton	60y	W	11 MAR 1902	Creedmore VA	Glenwood
13383	Mathewson, Almeda	86y	W	25 FEB 1916	Brooklyn NY	Arlington
16826	Mathiot, Benjamin Frank	65y	W	24 NOV 1920	Beltsville MD	Glenwood
05592	Mathis, Harry G.	35y	W	11 JUN 1906	Wash. Grove MD	Congressional
09129	Mathis, Louisiana A.	74y	W	13 MAR 1913	Gaithersburg MD	Congressional
17194	Mathis, William M.	83y	W	27 MAY 1921	Wash. Grove MD	Arlington
05695	Matsukata, Kingiro	18y	W	19 AUG 1906	Annapolis MD	Rock Creek
15864	Mattera, Michael	28y	W	3 JUL 1919	Capitol Hts. MD	Mt. Olivet
00283	Mattern, Marguerite E.	6m	W	19 FEB 1890	Thomasville GA	Glenwood
14741	Mattern, S. Rollins	26y	W	8 APR 1918	Wilkinsburg PA	Rock Creek
00630	Matthews, Alexander	66y	W	5 OCT 1891	Oxford MD	Oak Hill
03742	Matthews, Ann E.	70y	W	15 OCT 1901	Oxford MD	Oak Hill
17515	Matthews, Elizabeth	58y	C	11 NOV 1921	Brentwood MD	Harmony
02530	Matthews, Elizabeth J.	56y	W	2 JUL 1898	Salem MA	Rock Creek
09069	Matthews, Henry B.	74y	C	8 FEB 1913	Philadelphia PA	Woodlawn
12975	Matthews, Henry H.	70y	W	23 JUN 1915	Pikesville MD	Oak Hill
02078	Matthews, Ida L.	34y	W	3 OCT 1896	College MD	Glenwood
18383	Matthews, Jennie	55y	C	2 MAR 1923	Baltimore MD	Harmony
00863	Matthews, Joshua	32y	C	22 APR 1892	Philadelphia PA	Harmony
06997	Matthews, Lillie	45y	C	20 APR 1909	Marlboro Pike MD	Payne's
06039	Matthews, Mary E.	48y	C	18 APR 1907	New York NY	Mt. Olivet

District of Columbia Foreign Death Records, 1888-1923

No.	Name of Deceased	Age	Race	Death Date	Place of Death	Place of Burial
12785	Matthews, Mary S.	45y	C	27 FEB 1915	Philadelphia PA	Wheaton MD
16715	Matthews, Philip F.	40y	W	15 SEP 1920	Camden NJ	Arlington
07545	Matthews, Rebecca J.D.	81y	W	8 MAY 1910	Oxford MD	Oak Hill
06236	Matthews, Richard	58y	C	21 SEP 1907	Hyattsville MD	Harmony
08642	Matthews, Sarah E.	62y	W	30 MAY 1912	Hyattsville MD	Congressional
03629	Mattice, Fannie B.	45y	W	7 SEP 1901	Waynesboro VA	Glenwood
04180	Mattingly, Elmira	21y	W	15 FEB 1903	Philadelphia PA	Oak Hill
06415	Mattingly, John H.	32y	W	2 FEB 1908	Mt. Ranier MD	Mt. Olivet
13852	Mattingly, Mary F.	73y	W	8 DEC 1916	Hyattsville MD	Mt. Olivet
03883	Mattingly, Mary L., w/o Wm. F.	53y	W	21 MAY 1902	Baltimore MD	Glenwood
00861	Mattingly, Salvina Alice	23y	W	24 AUG 1892	Randolph Sta. MD	Glenwood
00859	Maulsby, Ann M.	72y	W	31 JUL 1892	Philadelphia PA	Rock Creek
02592	Maupin, Socrates, soldier	19y	W	13 AUG 1898	Santiago, Cuba	Arlington
01933	Maurey, George D.	41y	W	15 MAY 1896	Buffalo NY	Rock Creek
12912	Maury, Sallie Fontaine	90y	W	3 MAY 1915	Houston TX	Oak Hill
18402	Maus, Peter	65y	W	8 MAR 1923	Winfield NY	Mt. Olivet
18487	Mauss, Martha Elizabeth	75y	W	14 APR 1923	Orange NJ	Rock Creek
01064	Maxfield, Harriet Ann	52y	C	27 MAR 1871	Hanover Co. VA	Harmony
01065	Maxfield, Herbert	38y	C	18 AUG 1879	Hanover Co. VA	Harmony
13025	Maxim, Alonzo A.	73y	W	25 JUL 1915	Atlantic City NJ	Arlington
00341	Maxson, Constance	1y	W	14 JUN 1890	Wash. Grove MD	Congressional
13583	Maxson, Louis W.	61y	W	2 JUL 1916	Baltimore MD	Congressional
09049	Maxwell, Harlan P.	69y	W	26 JAN 1913	Takoma Park MD	Rock Creek
05401	Maxwell, Lottie	32y	W	10 NOV 1905	Liege, Belgium	Glenwood
04411	Maxwell, Robert B.	22y	W	25 JUL 1903	Albany NY	Rock Creek
01317	Maxwell, Sarah E.	68y	W	13 FEB 1894	Ball's Xrds. VA	Congressional
18403	Maxwell, William Wallace	45y	W	10 MAR 1923	Takoma Park MD	Rock Creek
01318	May, Elizabeth	59y	W	5 FEB 1894	Hampton VA	Holyrood
13229	May, Elizabeth A.	65y	W	1 DEC 1915	Mackey Hill VA	Holyrood
01066	May, Julian	8y	W	25 JAN 1878	New York NY	Rock Creek
04431	May, Maria	60y	C	2 SEP 1903	Ashburn VA	Harmony
02537	May, Mercy K.	71y	W	20 JUN 1898	Cumberland MD	Oak Hill
14834	May, Oscar J., Capt.	39y	W	22 MAY 1918	Takoma Park MD	Chicago IL
03489	May, Peter	69y	W	27 APR 1901	Hampton VA	Holyrood
17400	May, Phillip M.	74y	W	13 SEP 1921	Arlington Co. VA	Holyrood
02694	Mayam, Mortoman	50y	C	5 JAN 1899	Augusta GA	Woodlawn
01412	Mayams, Roskya	56y	W	12 JUN 1894	Rosslyn VA	Graceland
07602	Mayer, Rose Gertrude	22y	W	28 JUN 1910	Braddock MD	Prospect Hill
12570	Mayer, Roy Benton	8y	W	15 OCT 1914	Boston MA	Glenwood
15065	Mayer, Victor	27y	W	1 OCT 1918	Camp Hump. VA	Arlington
07033	Mayes, Morse Orton	33y	W	20 MAY 1909	Gettysburg PA	Arlington
15638	Mayfield, George	29y	W	24 FEB 1919	Capitol Hts. MD	Basic City VA
18420	Maynard, Caroline E.	82y	W	14 MAR 1923	Troy NY	Congressional
15744	Maynard, Elizabeth	30y	C	18 APR 1919	Lanham MD	Mt. Olivet
18465	Maynard, George Willoughby	80y	W	5 APR 1923	New York NY	Congressional
07936	Maynard, John G.	68y	W	20 JAN 1911	St. Cloud FL	Arlington
17006	Maynard, Margueritte	84y	W	1 MAR 1921	Takoma Park MD	Rock Creek
08768	Maynard, Nathan B.	21y	W	16 AUG 1912	Montreal, Can.	Glenwood
13501	Maynard, Pela H. (Barnett)	26y	W	11 MAY 1916	Norfolk VA	Cremated
04828	Maynard, Sarah A.	82y	W	2 AUG 1904	Oswego NY	Rock Creek
02787	Mayo, George	—	C	28 MAR 1899	Montauk Pt. NY	Arlington
14991	Mayo, Sara	62y	W	8 AUG 1918	Chattahoochee FL	Rock Creek
05250	McAboy, Alice B.	46y	W	16 AUG 1905	Chevy Chase MD	Oak Hill
15512	McAboy, James Lynn	41y	W	1 JAN 1919	Annapolis MD	Glenwood
03615	McAdams, Margaret	77y	W	15 AUG 1901	Philadelphia PA	Mt. Olivet
11884	McAdoo, Doris	16y	C	8 JUL 1913	Asheville NC	Harmony
15831	McAdoo, Julia	51y	C	12 JUN 1919	Philadelphia PA	Harmony
13470	McAfee, David Benjamin	SB	W	11 APR 1916	Ft. Riley KS	Arlington
13471	McAfee, Marjorie Deshon	27y	W	APR 1916	Ft. Riley KS	Arlington

No.	Name of Deceased	Age	Race	Death Date	Place of Death	Place of Burial
02488	McAnally, Mary A.	67y	W	28 JUL 1898	Portland ME	Mt. Olivet
06549	McAuliff, Mary K.	53y	W	12 MAY 1908	Braddock PA	Mt. Olivet
01476	McAuliff, Terence H.	45y	W	25 AUG 1894	Pittsburgh PA	Mt. Olivet
03329	McAuliffe, Daniel	21y	W	12 NOV 1900	Keatings Sta. PA	Mt. Olivet
09127	McAuliffe, Infant of John H.	SB	W	13 MAR 1913	Friendship H. MD	Mt. Olivet
16543	McBerry, Mary A.	6y	W	17 JUN 1920	Mt. Ranier MD	Glenwood
04090	McBlain, John F., Capt.	55y	W	22 NOV 1902	Houston TX	Arlington
12860	McBlair, Andrew Jackson	63y	W	30 MAR 1915	Rockland Co. NY	Congressional
06201	McBlair, Charles Ridgely	57y	W	24 AUG 1907	Gloucester MA	Congressional
17220	McBride, Charles H.	54y	W	8 JUN 1921	Wilmington NC	Albany NY
06538	McBride, David, s/o James	3d	W	7 MAY 1908	Del Ray VA	Glenwood
12147	McBride, Joseph Herbert	1y	W	5 JAN 1914	Alex. Co. VA	Glenwood
14487	McBride, Molly	45y	W	1 DEC 1817	Washington DC	Glenwood
06941	McBride, William	88y	W	12 MAR 1909	Mt. Vernon VA	Glenwood
17278	McCabe, Bradley B.	69y	W	30 JUN 1921	Staunton VA	Cremated
17825	McCabe, James	75y	W	30 APR 1922	Canton OH	Arlington
04042	McCabe, John	88y	W	13 OCT 1902	Philadelphia PA	Mt. Olivet
06311	McCabe, Martha	64y	W	16 NOV 1907	McKee's Rock PA	Arlington
14266	McCabe, Thomas	87y	W	30 JUL 1917	Alex. Co. VA	Mt. Olivet
08203	McCafferty, George M.	35y	W	17 JUL 1911	Brentwood MD	Glenwood
14289	McCaffrey, Mary Frances	90y	W	10 AUG 1917	Silver Spring MD	Glenwood
14231	McCahey, John Henry	21y	W	16 JUL 1917	Pr. Wm. Co. VA	Philadelphia PA
17172	McCalahan, Luther Thomas	22y	W	18 MAY 1921	Capitol Hts. MD	Edenburgh VA
06616	McCalip, John A.	22y	W	28 JUN 1908	Potomac River	Crawfordsville IN
06266	McCall, James	23y	C	5 OCT 1907	Baltimore MD	Woodlawn
15495	McCalley, Charles Robert	65y	W	28 DEC 1918	Mt. Vernon VA	Glenwood
18197	McCallny, John	c.60y	W	3 DEC 1922	Colonial Bea. VA	Congressional
15673	McCallum, George C.	55y	W	15 MAR 1919	Buffalo NY	Rock Creek
18526	McCalmont, William Shaw	85y	W	4 MAY 1923	Takoma Park MD	Glenwood
17823	McCammon, Ormsby	49y	W	29 APR 1922	Hot Springs AR	Oak Hill
00273	McCann, Ann E.	83y	W	23 JAN 1890	Baltimore MD	Oak Hill
17089	McCann, Catherine A.	54y	W	3 APR 1921	Hyattsville MD	Mt. Olivet
14348	McCarten, Marie	23y	W	6 SEP 1917	Falls Church VA	Mt. Olivet
01573	McCarthy, Anthony	1m	C	28 NOV 1894	New York NY	Mt. Olivet
00869	McCarthy, Bridget	83y	W	19 JUL 1892	Baltimore MD	Mt. Olivet
18060	McCarthy, Elwood Milton	23y	W	10 SEP 1922	Rock Point MD	Manassas VA
15420	McCarthy, Emma Henrietta H.	32y	W	8 DEC 1918	Davenport IA	Rock Creek
02011	McCarthy, Francis X.	4m	W	27 AUG 1896	Colonial Bea. VA	Mt. Olivet
07776	McCarthy, James H.	65y	W	1 OCT 1910	Elmira NY	Mt. Olivet
01883	McCarthy, Justin P.	42y	W	24 FEB 1896	Norfolk VA	Mt. Olivet
02749	McCarthy, L.J.	36y	W	22 FEB 1899	Pittsburgh PA	Mt. Olivet
16196	McCarthy, Marie C.	73y	W	6 JAN 1920	New Castle NY	Mt. Olivet
07707	McCarthy, Nellie Crosby	49y	W	23 AUG 1910	Silver Spring MD	Oak Hill
16680	McCarthy, Sophronia Goodson	72y	W	24 AUG 1920	Baltimore MD	Congressional
00554	McCarty, Allen Tuscott	8y	W	6 JUN 1891	Passaic City NJ	Glenwood
18517	McCarty, Katherine B.	55y	W	1 MAY 1923	New York NY	Rock Creek
01445	McCarty, Mary Esther	66y	W	26 JUL 1894	Asbury Park NJ	Rock Creek
12480	McCarty, Orleans (Peffer)	70y	W	8 AUG 1914	New York NY	Oak Hill[1]
00310	McCarty, Rufus Holsey	36y	W	12 APR 1890	Key West FL	Oak Hill[2]
15246	McCauley, Aloysius	29y	W	17 OCT 1918	Camp Meade MD	Arlington
14643	McCauley, Bernard	54y	W	16 FEB 1918	Hampton VA	Arlington
14793	McCauley, Charles	35y	C	4 MAY 1918	St. Elizabeth's	Harmony
15201	McCauley, John B.	29y	W	14 OCT 1918	Jacksonville FL	Holyrood
04496	McCauley, John F.	24y	W	22 OCT 1903	Ft. Bayard NM	Congressional
01645	McCauley, Theodore F.	50y	W	8 APR 1895	Rome, Italy	Congressional
15370	McCausland, Cora B.	67y	W	20 NOV 1918	Suffolk MA	Glenwood

[1] Disinterment permit #8857 for removal to Rock Creek Cemetery, 11 JAN 1917.
[2] Reinterred in Rock Creek cemetery, 11 JUN 1917.

District of Columbia Foreign Death Records, 1888-1923

No.	Name of Deceased	Age	Race	Death Date	Place of Death	Place of Burial
09035	McCausland, John S.	60y	W	18 JAN 1913	Ballston VA	Rock Creek
13773	McCeney, Anna S.	86y	W	23 OCT 1916	Burnt Mills MD	Rock Creek
00750	McCeney, Edgar P.	50y	W	22 JAN 1892	Leeland MD	Rock Creek
02704	McCeney, Robert	47y	W	9 DEC 1899	San Francisco CA	Rock Creek
07904	McChesney, Liretta M.	52y	W	2 JAN 1911	Hyattsville MD	Rock Creek
12188	McChesney, Susanna	75y	W	29 JAN 1914	Hyattsville MD	Rock Creek
12592	McChesney, William R.	81y	W	2 NOV 1914	Hyattsville MD	Rock Creek
03870	McChrystal, Leo M.	19y	W	30 APR 1902	Pittsburgh PA	Holyrood
07956	McClary, Conway	30y	W	31 JAN 1911	Catlett VA	Alexandria VA
04915	McCleish, Mary	43y	W	8 OCT 1904	Rosslyn VA	Holyrood
15233	McClellan, Margaret B.	24y	W	19 OCT 1918	Ft. Myer VA	Mt. Olivet
02210	McClellan, Rose Lee	40y	W	10 JUN 1897	Ft. Wadsworth NY	Congressional
00980	McClelland, Clarence	40y	W	26 AUG 1893	Hot Springs VA	Oak Hill
12296	McClellen, James R.	1y	W	6 APR 1914	Mt. Ranier MD	Mt. Olivet
18574	McClosky, Jane H.	7y	W	1 JUN 1923	Cherrydale VA	Mt. Olivet
05866	McClure, Daisy E.	28y	W	15 DEC 1906	Gloucester Co. NJ	Congressional
03929	McClure, Dorthie	1y	W	20 JUL 1902	Bolivar WV	Glenwood
05600	McClure, John B.G.	27y	W	14 JUN 1906	Ft. Monroe VA	Arlington
06655	McClure, Martha E.	66y	W	23 JUL 1908	Chicago IL	Arlington VA
12972	McClure, Theophilus	81y	W	20 JUN 1915	Chicago IL	Arlington VA
14136	McColl, James A.	46y	W	15 MAY 1917	Thurmont MD	Forestville MD
17813	McComas, Mower	28y	W	16 APR 1922	Ft. Bayard NM	Rock Creek
06671	McConnell, Charles Curtis	68y	W	4 AUG 1908	Narragansett RI	Arlington
16846	McConnell, Harriet D.	55y	W	3 DEC 1920	Asheville NC	Cremated
04815	McConnell, James C.	60y	W	25 JUL 1904	Liberty NY	Rock Creek
14362	McCormac, Vincent Charles	11m	W	17 SEP 1917	Bennettsville SC	Mt. Olivet
15596	McCormack, Virginia Corcoran	29y	W	2 FEB 1919	Englewood NJ	Baltimore MD
13071	McCormick, Alexander Hugh	73y	W	21 AUG 1915	Annapolis MD	Congressional
07311	McCormick, Arthur M.	41y	W	8 DEC 1909	Cherrydale VA	Rock Creek
09134	McCormick, Denis M., Rev.	40y	W	16 MAR 1913	Washington DC	Mt. Olivet
00044	McCormick, Elizabeth T.B.	60y	W	22 MAR 1889	Pr. Geo. Co. MD	Sherrif's Farm[1]
18344	McCormick, Frank Ross	67y	W	10 FEB 1923	St. Cath., Ont.	Rock Creek
04132	McCormick, Isabella Howard	60y	W	29 JAN 1903	Annapolis MD	Congressional
08214	McCormick, John R., Sr.	67y	W	25 JUL 1911	Hyattsville MD	Rock Creek
06944	McCormick, Kate B.T.	38y	W	14 MAR 1909	Park Lane VA	Congressional
17809	McCormick, Mabel	24y	W	18 APR 1922	Ballston VA	Mt. Olivet
12766	McCormick, Mary E.	72y	W	16 FEB 1915	Cherrydale VA	Glenwood
04542	McCormick, Michael	33y	W	19 DEC 1903	Bladensburg MD	Mt. Olivet
05134	McCoy, Adel	29y	C	16 MAY 1905	New York NY	Harmony
04981	McCoy, Eliza	60y	C	26 DEC 1904	Hyattsville MD	Mt. Olivet
00751	McCoy, Frank E.	26y	W	19 APR 1891	Salt Lake City UT	Rock Creek
12186	McCoy, John R.	67y	W	27 JAN 1914	Brooklyn NY	Rock Creek
18461	McCrary, Cato W.	1y	C	5 APR 1923	New York NY	Harmony
07096	McCray, Archie	65y	C	3 JUL 1909	Pittsburgh PA	Payne's
05735	McCreery, John L.	70y	W	7 SEP 1906	Duluth MN	Glenwood
01905	McCristal, William W.	32y	W	12 APR 1896	Chicago IL	Glenwood
03932	McCubbin, Charles J.	45y	W	17 JUL 1902	Chevy Chase MD	Rock Creek
08257	McCubbin, George E.	43y	W	15 AUG 1911	Baltimore MD	Congressional
17165	McCuen, Margaret	50y	W	15 MAY 1921	New York NY	Congressional
08604	McCullen, C. Albert	28y	W	19 APR 1912	Hyattsville MD	Rock Creek
16586	McCullen, John W.	33y	W	8 JUL 1920	Frederick Co. MD	Rock Creek
16079	McCullen, Peter C.	64y	W	28 OCT 1919	Hyattsville MD	Rock Creek
05919	McCullen, Rena	43y	C	29 JAN 1907	Mt. Herman VA	Payne's
02483	McCulloch, Susan M.	82y	W	25 JUL 1898	Sparkill NY	Rock Creek
05353	McCullough, Baldwin	3y	W	12 NOV 1905	Laurel MD	Rock Creek
12874	McCullough, Frank Wesley	40y	W	11 APR 1915	New York NY	Glenwood
18023	McCullough, George D., Jr.	68y	W	22 AUG 1922	Baltimore MD	Congressional

[1] Reinterred in Congressional cemetery on 28 OCT 1930.

No.	Name of Deceased	Age	Race	Death Date	Place of Death	Place of Burial
03821	McCullough, Gertrude	22y	W	16 MAR 1902	Laurel MD	Rock Creek
04191	McCullough, Hester M.	47y	C	3 APR 1903	Mannington WV	Payne's
01745	McCullough, Hugh	86y	W	24 MAY 1895	Holly Hills MD	Rock Creek
17536	McCullough, Mary Turner	73y	W	20 NOV 1921	Brentwood MD	Port Deposit MD
01744	McCullough, William W., mer.	49y	W	27 JUN 1895	Highlands MD	Oak Hill
07333	McCullum, John	36y	W	17 DEC 1909	Wilmington DE	Holyrood
00981	McCutchen, Cornelia Mary	3m	W	23 JUN 1893	Highlands MD	Congressional
14656	McDaniel, Charles J.	57y	W	22 FEB 1918	Atlantic City NJ	Holyrood
06407	McDaniel, H.C.	78y	W	27 JAN 1908	Shepherdstn. WV	Glenwood
02718	McDaniel, Martha	65y	W	18 JAN 1899	Mt. Hope MD	Glenwood
00364	McDaniel, Mary Ann	57y	W	19 JUN 1890	Sulphur Spgs. MD	Glenwood
02263	McDermitt, Infant of John Wm.	1y	W	13 JUL 1897	Oakland MD	Mt. Olivet
16216	McDermot, Ferdinand G.	50y	W	8 JAN 1920	Phoenix AZ	Rock Creek
17201	McDermott, Cleveland W.	—	W	28 MAY 1921	Walter Reed Hp.	Syracuse NY
06329	McDermott, John Arthur	46y	W	29 NOV 1907	New York NY	Mt. Olivet
01282	McDermott, Margaretta	8m	W	14 DEC 1893	Hyattsville MD	Mt. Olivet
06478	McDermott, Mary	47y	W	19 MAR 1908	Hyattsville MD	Mt. Olivet
16940	McDermott, Thayer	21y	W	25 JAN 1921	Vineland NJ	Glenwood
05283	McDermott, William	5y	W	8 SEP 1905	Elkins MD	Glenwood
17795	McDevitt, Florence	68y	W	10 APR 1922	Steubensville OH	Glenwood
14817	McDevitt, Harold M.	2d	W	17 MAY 1918	Ft. Myer Hts. VA	Mt. Olivet
03559	McDevitt, Harry	33y	W	29 JUN 1901	Chicago IL	Glenwood
06780	McDevitt, John	32y	W	23 OCT 1908	Homestead PA	Glenwood
00412	McDevitt, Regina R.	15y	W	7 OCT 1890	Ft. Monroe VA	Mt. Olivet
12439	McDevitt, William Sewall	42y	W	13 JUL 1914	Coshocton OH	Glenwood
01640	McDonald, Annie	9y	W	1863	Washington DC	Rock Creek[1]
17529	McDonald, Brodie	26y	C	15 NOV 1921	Washington DC	Harmony
18099	McDonald, Cornelius L.	64y	W	30 SEP 1922	Atlantic City NJ	Rock Creek
17722	McDonald, Frank	35y	W	22 FEB 1922	Los Angeles CA	Mt. Olivet
01643	McDonald, Frederick	9y	W	1876	Washington DC	Rock Creek
01642	McDonald, James	19y	W	1865	Washington DC	Rock Creek
15285	McDonald, James B.	18y	W	23 OCT 1918	Atlantic City NJ	Rock Creek
01644	McDonald, Jessie	14d	W	1881	Washington DC	Rock Creek
15099	McDonald, John T.	26y	W	5 OCT 1918	Baltimore MD	Cedar Hill
15053	McDonald, Joseph Gabriel	27y	W	28 SEP 1918	Hampton Rds. VA	Mt. Olivet
06115	McDonald, Larry	34y	W	19 JUN 1907	Robinson IL	Mt. Olivet
03282	McDonald, Mary Ellen	64y	—	1 SEP 1900	Baltimore MD	Rock Creek
08619	McDonald, Roy S., Lt.	27y	W	2 MAY 1912	Brooklyn NY	Arlington
01641	McDonald, William	23y	W	1876	Washington DC	Rock Creek
04534	McDowell, Clark A.	23y	W	7 DEC 1903	Clarksburg WV	Arlington VA
13523	McDowell, Lafayette	1y	C	28 MAY 1916	Fairmont Hts. MD	Woodlawn
08791	McEaddy, Laura V.	32y	C	28 AUG 1912	New Bern NC	Harmony
06097	McElderry, Mary E.	4y	C	5 JUN 1907	Jessup MD	Harmony
06597	McEldrey, Florence R.	34y	C	20 JUN 1908	Anne Arundel Co.	Harmony
03556	McElfreth, Elizabeth	37y	W	26 JUN 1901	Atlantic City NJ	Glenwood
12322	McElhinney, Charles A.	23y	W	16 APR 1914	Denver CO	Rock Creek
04013	McElroy, Charles B.	39y	W	10 SEP 1902	Detroit MI	Glenwood
14409	McElroy, Elsie P.	88y	W	13 OCT 1917	Fairfax Co. VA	Arlington
04190	McElwee, Henry	59y	W	1 APR 1903	Quincy IL	Congressional
08664	McElwee, Samuel	72y	W	9 JUN 1912	Reading PA	Congressional
13490	McEnally, Susan Ella (Wolcott)	78y	W	3 MAY 1916	Chesterf. Co. VA	Arlington VA
14254	McEnaney, Annie A.	c.34y	W	22 JUN 1916	Olongape, P.I.	Glenwood
03641	McEnany, William A.	6y	W	14 SEP 1901	Chevy Chase MD	Mt. Olivet
05793	McEneary, Joseph P.	38y	W	JUL 1904	Shanghai, China	Mt. Olivet
13884	McEvoy, William R.	69y	W	26 DEC 1916	Baltimore MD	Congressional
13549	McEwen, Clarence H.	64y	W	7 JUN 1916	Berwyn MD	Glenwood
14953	McFadden, Alice R.	62y	W	5 AUG 1918	St. Elizabeth's DC	Congressional

[1] Note that McDonald children were moved 24 APR 1895 from an unidentified cemetery in Baltimore, Md.

District of Columbia Foreign Death Records, 1888-1923

No.	Name of Deceased	Age	Race	Death Date	Place of Death	Place of Burial
01175	McFadden, William H.	38y	W	17 OCT 1892	Central City CO	Congressional
01746	McFarland, Arietta O.	59y	W	24 JUL 1895	Paris, France	Oak Hill
05126	McFarland, Sarah J.	74y	W	11 MAY 1905	Pittsburgh PA	Congressional
00635	McFaul, Felix	50y	W	13 OCT 1891	New York NY	Mt. Olivet
00472	McFaul, John B.	24y	W	28 DEC 1890	New York NY	Mt. Olivet
01176	McFaul, Thomas	30y	W	8 DEC 1892	New York NY	Mt. Olivet
07723	McFee, Charles W.	52y	W	31 AUG 1910	Quebec, Can.	Rock Creek
13554	McGahan, John J.	34y	W	9 JUN 1916	Capitol Hts. MD	Mt. Olivet
13799	McGarry, Julia	48y	W	4 NOV 1916	Seat Pleasant MD	Mt. Olivet
06924	McGee, Adam D.	49y	W	18 FEB 1909	Philadelphia PA	Baltimore MD
12841	McGee, Bridget	80y	W	21 FEB 1913	Baltimore MD	Mt. Olivet
06135	McGee, Elizabeth	67y	W	12 JUL 1907	Riverdale MD	Cremated
00262	McGee, Elizabeth	56y	W	11 JAN 1890	Charles Co. MD	Congressional
12840	McGee, Michael	59y	W	29 APR 1880	Baltimore MD	Mt. Olivet
13098	McGee, Owen, s/o Charles	54y	W	11 SEP 1915	Round Hill VA	Congressional
02010	McGelly, Charles A.	3y	W	7 AUG 1896	Colonial Bea. VA	Congressional
03253	McGeorge, Betsey S.	82y	W	5 AUG 1900	New York NY	Rock Creek
13361	McGeorge, Sarah Ann	43y	W	17 FEB 1916	Alex. Co. VA	Rock Creek
0255	McGill, Catherine A.	42y	W	3 JAN 1890	Mt. Hope MD	Mt. Olivet
13152	McGill, J. Nota	48y	W	16 OCT 1915	Asheville NC	Holyrood
08437	McGill, Kate L.	63y	W	25 DEC 1911	Chevy Chase MD	Valparaiso IN
18292	McGill, Mary C.	70y	W	21 JAN 1923	Louisville KY	Mt. Olivet
14203	McGill, Mary Jane (Nolan)	73y	W	2 JUL 1917	Gainesville VA	Holyrood
07689	McGill, William	33y	W	11 AUG 1910	Philadelphia PA	Arlington
05053	McGill, William C.	47y	W	7 MAR 1905	New York NY	Congressional
12502	McGilton, John	56y	W	26 AUG 1914	Oxon Hill MD	Mt. Olivet
03779	McGilvray, John	70y	W	23 JAN 1902	Denver CO	Arlington VA
03853	McGinggan, Alexander	75y	W	16 APR 1902	Hampton VA	Arlington
02959	McGinnell, Agnes	27y	W	24 SEP 1899	Battle Creek MI	Holyrood
14270	McGinniss, James F., s/o P.	48y	W	2 AUG 1917	Quantico VA	Holyrood
15545	McGinniss, John R.	78y	W	17 DEC 1918	Mt. Clemens MI	Arlington
17646	McGivin, Mary	47y	C	16 JAN 1922	Chicago IL	Harmony
08336	McGlue, Ann R.	67y	W	2 OCT 1911	E. Lansdowne PA	Rock Creek
12438	McGovern, Alexander	34y	W	13 JUL 1914	New York NY	Glenwood
06014	McGovern, Helen J.	6m	W	7 APR 1907	Landover MD	Mt. Olivet
02408	McGowan, Eliza	90y	W	22 MAR 1898	Manchester NH	Oak Hill
03096	McGowan, George	35y	W	5 FEB 1899	Manila, P.I.	Glenwood
17689	McGowan, Margaret J.	69y	W	12 FEB 1922	Watertown MA	Mt. Olivet
15382	McGowan, William C.	44y	W	26 NOV 1918	Philadelphia PA	Rock Creek
12260	McGowen, Jannette	49y	W	22 MAR 1914	Brentwood MD	Glenwood
16286	McGowne, Edith M.	36y	W	6 FEB 1920	Mt. Ranier MD	Mt. Olivet
05032	McGrain, Alfred	40y	W	14 FEB 1905	Bowie MD	Mt. Olivet
14358	McGrath, Alexandria	55y	W	14 SEP 1917	College Park MD	Glenwood
17447	McGrath, Daniel	83y	W	1 OCT 1921	Philadelphia PA	Mt. Olivet
04917	McGrath, Helen B.	4y	W	9 JUN 1895	Ft. Foote MD	Mt. Olivet
13636	McGrath, Henry C.	62y	W	3 AUG 1916	Maryland Pk. MD	Mt. Olivet
03038	McGrath, Hugh J., soldier	—	W	7 NOV 1899	Manila, P.I.	Arlington
07167	McGrath, Margarette E.	11d	W	23 AUG 1909	Maryland Pk. MD	Mt. Olivet
04919	McGrath, Maurice	48y	W	6 DEC 1898	Boston MA	Mt. Olivet
02857	McGrath, Michael	24y	W	20 JUN 1899	Potomac River	Mt. Olivet
05710	McGrath, William	42y	W	20 AUG 1906	New York NY	Mt. Olivet
17367	McGraw, John Seiler	27y	W	22 AUG 1921	Fredericksburg VA	Mt. Olivet
16455	McGraw, John Thomas	64y	W	29 APR 1920	Railroad	Grafton WV
18458	McGraw, Loretta (Fitzgerald)	33y	W	3 APR 1923	New York NY	Mt. Olivet
07052	McGraw, Michael E.	4y	W	7 JUN 1909	Pittsburgh PA	Glenwood
12313	McGregor, Elizabeth	77y	W	14 APR 1914	Philadelphia PA	Congressional
01747	McGrew, Jacob Milton, lawyer	65y	W	10 AUG 1895	Bedford Co. PA	Rock Creek
14448	McGrew, Leonard D.	38y	W	7 NOV 1917	Maywood VA	Glenwood
18332	McGroarty, Charles M., Jr.	39y	W	8 FEB 1923	Laurel MD	Falls Church VA

No.	Name of Deceased	Age	Race	Death Date	Place of Death	Place of Burial
01934	McGrotty, William B.	25y	W	17 MAY 1896	New Orleans LA	Congressional
06426	McGruder, Ellen	65y	C	7 FEB 1908	Asheville NC	Mt. Olivet
14805	McGuigan, Henrietta	71y	W	9 MAY 1918	Mt. Hope MD	Mt. Olivet
07507	McGuinn, George, a.k.a.	31y	C	16 APR 1910	Minneapolis MN	Halls Hill VA
04818	McGuire, Anna Chapman	52y	W	26 JUL 1904	Green Park NC	Rock Creek
01354	McGuire, Elizabeth M.	61y	W	16 MAR 1894	Camden NJ	Glenwood
15206	McGuire, George	61y	W	16 OCT 1918	Glendale VA	Soldier's Home
03991	McGuire, Mary	84y	W	26 AUG 1902	Alex. Co. VA	Holyrood
02625	McHenry, Jessie E.	28y	W	5 OCT 1898	Calverton VA	Mt. Olivet
05225	McHenry, Philip J.	37y	W	28 JUL 1905	Quartzite AZ	—
00636	McHenry, Sallie	16y	W	21 JUL 1891	Baltimore MD	Mt. Olivet
04108	McIlhenney, Mamie	28y	W	31 DEC 1902	Hyattsville MD	Congressional
06164	McInerney, James Morgan	11m	W	31 JUL 1907	Dranesville VA	Mt. Olivet
02467	McIntire, Arthur L.	51y	W	27 MAY 1898	Brooklyn NY	Glenwood
07748	McIntire, Harry N.	40y	W	12 SEP 1910	San Diego CA	Congressional
15839	McIntire, Lettie F.	74y	W	19 JUN 1919	Atlantic City NJ	Rock Creek
15451	McIntosh, Ephraim W.	51y	W	16 DEC 1918	New York NY	Glenwood
13497	McIntosh, John	c.55y	C	7 MAY 1916	Occoquan VA	Woodlawn
05726	McIntosh, Maggie	35y	W	4 SEP 1906	Baltimore MD	Congressional
14809	McIntosh, Warnie V.	27y	W	10 MAY 1918	Columbia SC	Falls Church VA
13023	McIntyre, Infant of R.E.	SB	W	25 JUL 1915	Takoma MD	Rock Creek
11833	McIntyre, Jacob N.	77y	W	24 MAY 1913	New York NY	Glenwood
03216	McIntyre, Norman [McCulysi]	9m	W	27 JUN 1900	Wilmington DE	Mt. Olivet
06589	McKall, Nathan	70y	C	14 JUN 1908	Hyattsville MD	Arlington
03942	McKay, Nathaniel	71y	W	10 JUL 1902	Atlantic City NJ	Rock Creek
13763	McKay, Neal	4y	W	15 OCT 1916	Washington DC	Rock Creek
07355	McKay, William	70y	W	3 JAN 1910	Silver Spring MD	Rock Creek
01906	McKean, Edwin R.	61y	W	11 APR 1896	Eustis FL	Congressional
16042	McKee, John	47y	W	10 OCT 1919	Hartford CN	Congressional
16989	McKee, Mary Cora	71y	W	21 FEB 1921	Camp Dix NJ	Congressional
01827	McKeever, Daniel P.	40y	W	14 JAN 1896	Asheville NC	Baltimore MD
01435	McKeever, Susie	19y	W	14 JUL 1894	Westernport MD	Graceland
15493	McKeever, William	37y	W	27 DEC 1918	Camp Dix NJ	Arlington
01635	McKeever, William	44y	C	20 MAR 1895	Brooklyn NY	Moore's
07929	McKelby, Wolsey Martin	1y	W	28 JUL 1910	Manila, P.I.	Arlington
06661	McKelden, Julia Cox	49y	W	28 JUL 1908	New York NY	Oak Hill
06774	McKelsey, Joseph R.	70y	W	13 OCT 1908	New York NY	Arlington
02075	McKenna, Henry J.	27y	W	19 NOV 1896	Philadelphia PA	Mt. Olivet
16327	McKenna, Infant of Patrick B.	10d	W	17 FEB 1920	City Point VA	Mt. Olivet
12869	McKenna, William A.	42y	W	8 APR 1915	Philadelphia PA	Mt. Olivet
18238	McKenney, Glyds Beatrice	9m	W	2 JAN 1923	Capitol Hts. MD	Congressional
12044	McKenney, James Hall	76y	W	13 OCT 1913	Forest Glen MD	Oak Hill
17311	McKenney, Joseph W.	3m	W	21 JUL 1921	Pr. Geo. Co. MD	Prospect Hill
03830	McKenney, Rose	32y	W	25 MAR 1902	Philadelphia PA	Mt. Olivet
05314	McKenney, William Miller	1y	W	10 OCT 1905	Bethesda MD	Oak Hill
16171	McKenny, Eliza	64y	C	26 DEC 1919	New York NY	Harmony
15541	McKenzie, Edward E.	24y	W	9 JAN 1919	Montgomery AL	Arlington
16415	McKenzie, George R.	19y	C	31 MAR 1920	Brentwood MD	Harmony
08543	McKenzie, George W.	40y	C	3 MAR 1912	Brentwood MD	Harmony
12657	McKermen, Thomas	60y	W	1 DEC 1914	Maryland Pk. MD	Mt. Olivet
16604	McKim, Randolh H.	78y	W	15 JUL 1920	Bedford PA	Baltimore MD
01479	McKim, Wayne Harrison	8m	W	1 SEP 1894	Silver Hill MD	Congressional
17423	McKimmie, William H.	23y	W	5 NOV 1918	France	Rock Creek
07149	McKinley, Lillian	27y	W	6 AUG 1909	Baltimore MD	Holyrood
17848	McKinley, Lydia E.	68y	W	12 MAY 1922	Silver Spring MD	Cedar Hill
05622	McKinley, William E., s/o Jas.	5y	W	1 JUL 1906	Vienna VA	Holyrood
06066	McKinney, Rachel	57y	C	11 MAY 1907	Philadelphia PA	Payne's
18587	McKinstry, George Parnell	45y	W	4 JUN 1923	Americus GA	Cremated
03659	McKnight, A.C.	55y	W	22 SEP 1901	Sandusky OH	Oak Hill

District of Columbia Foreign Death Records, 1888-1923

No.	Name of Deceased	Age	Race	Death Date	Place of Death	Place of Burial
17336	McKnight, James	42y	W	30 JUL 1921	River Bend C. VA	Arlington
00637	McKnight, Lucius L.	55y	W	16 JUL 1891	New York NY	Congressional
00441	McKnight, Ralph B.	10y	W	23 NOV 1890	Brooklyn NY	Oak Hill
05779	McKnight, Thomas	40y	W	12 OCT 1906	Chicago IL	Mt. Olivet
17308	McKnight, William Henry	63y	W	19 JUL 1921	Colonial Bea. VA	Congressional
18085	McLachen, Archibald M.	65y	W	18 SEP 1922	Los Angeles CA	Glenwood
02407	McLain, Ellen Clapp	57y	W	21 MAR 1898	New York NY	Oak Hill
00638	McLain, Mary W.	49y	W	1 SEP 1891	New York NY	Oak Hill
08445	McLain, William R., Jr.	1m	W	27 DEC 1911	Philadelphia PA	Rock Creek
15305	McLanahan, George X.	45y	W	29 OCT 1918	Baltimore MD	Rock Creek
15433	McLane, Arthur E.	40y	W	10 DEC 1918	New York NY	Rock Creek
04430	McLane, James	64y	W	1 SEP 1903	New York NY	Oak Hill
05752	McLaren, Ida L.	48y	W	26 SEP 1906	Baltimore MD	Congressional
17317	McLaren, James	73y	W	21 JUL 1921	Baltimore MD	Congressional
00421	McLaren, Mary Osgodby	36y	W	15 OCT 1890	Calverton VA	Glenwood
01478	McLaughlin, Henry J.	52y	W	29 AUG 1894	Virginia Bea. VA	Mt. Olivet
06837	McLaughlin, John	33y	W	3 DEC 1908	Baltimore MD	Congressional
16629	McLaughlin, Josephine	65y	W	27 JUL 1920	Rochester MN	Arlington
00104	McLaughlin, Mary Jane	75y	W	19 JUL 1889	Newark NJ	Congressional
13055	McLaughlin, Mary R.	70y	W	14 AUG 1915	Atlantic City NJ	Mt. Olivet
02495	McLaughlin, Susan	48y	W	22 JUL 1898	Henepin Co. MN	Rock Creek
15627	McLaughlin, William	70y	W	11 FEB 1919	St. Elizabeth's	Arlington
18541	McLauren, Bessie	26y	C	MAY 1923	New York NY	Harmony
06177	McLean, Allen C.	58y	W	11 AUG 1907	Chesa. Bea. VA	Arlington VA
04510	McLean, Carolyn	1y	W	12 NOV 1903	New York NY	Rock Creek
08833	McLean, Emily Beale	57y	W	9 SEP 1912	Bar Harbor ME	Rock Creek
07944	McLean, Lizzie	70y	W	25 JAN 1911	Richmond VA	Oak Hill
01254	McLean, Martha	60y	W	3 OCT 1893	Baltimore MD	Glenwood
02990	McLean, William R.	45y	W	22 OCT 1899	New York NY	Oak Hill
04078	McLearn, Sarah M.	28y	W	17 AUG 1902	New York NY	Mt. Olivet
04465	McLennon, Donald	21y	W	26 SEP 1903	El Paso TX	Rock Creek
07498	McLeod, Arthur R.	6y	W	12 APR 1910	Baltimore MD	Congressional
08289	McLeod, Christina	61y	W	2 SEP 1911	Hyattsville MD	Congressional
05917	McLeod, Hugh S.	62y	W	29 JAN 1907	Annapolis MD	Congressional
00163	McLeod, Robenia	17y	W	27 SEP 1889	Annapolis MD	Congressional
02135	McLeod, Wilfred, Dr.	54y	W	11 FEB 1897	Poolesville MD	Holyrood
04739	McLoughlin, Charles	45y	W	28 MAY 1904	Baltimore MD	Holyrood
08301	McMahan, Michael	67y	W	5 SEP 1911	Waco TX	Arlington
16272	McMahon, Joel Green	38y	W	2 FEB 1920	Cherrydale VA	Lynchburg VA
17518	McMahon, Johanna Mary	59y	W	13 NOV 1921	Ballston VA	Mt. Olivet
03355	McMahon, John	47y	W	30 NOV 1900	Allegheny Co. PA	Mt. Olivet
16254	McMahon, John Eugene	59y	W	28 JAN 1920	Princeton NJ	Oak Hill
05025	McMahon, John M.	24y	W	5 FEB 1905	Central NM	Arlington
16271	McMahon, Julia	64y	W	3 FEB 1920	Cherrydale VA	Lynchburg VA
16809	McMahon, Mabel Ruth	22y	W	15 NOV 1920	Baltimore Co. MD	Glenwood
14247	McMahon, Margaret	5m	W	24 JUL 1917	Brentwood MD	Mt. Olivet
06599	McMahon, Mary	62y	W	20 JUN 1908	New York NY	Arlington
18024	McMahon, Mary B.	37y	W	21 AUG 1922	Brentwood MD	Mt. Olivet
02978	McMakin, Ellen Handy	63y	W	20 NOV 1898	Wilmington DE	Glenwood
16961	McMaster, Clara	72y	W	8 FEB 1921	Takoma Park MD	Bath NY
01935	McMichael, Eugene H.	49y	W	26 MAY 1896	Alex. Co. VA	Rock Creek
06747	McMichael, Eugene H.	38y	W	19 SEP 1908	Hot Springs AR	Rock Creek
01427	McMillan, Allison E.	14d	W	7 JUL 1894	Riverdale MD	Rock Creek
00416	McMillan, Arthur H.	8y	W	8 SEP 1868	Conesus Ctr. NY	Arlington
00415	McMillan, Baby	1h	W	12 NOV 1860	Conesus Ctr. NY	Arlington
16260	McMillan, Ira C.	65y	W	30 JAN 1920	Oxon Hill MD	Rock Creek
07366	McMillen, Infant of Leventine	SB		12 JAN 1910	Ft. Hamilton NY	Arlington
15751	McMorris, George W.	62y	W	24 APR 1919	Takoma Park MD	Glenwood
02116	McMurray, Frank, gardener	56y	W	13 JAN 1897	Allentown MD	Mt. Olivet

No.	Name of Deceased	Age	Race	Death Date	Place of Death	Place of Burial
15764	McMurtrie, Sarah Ann	75y	W	26 APR 1919	Brattleboro VT	Arlington
11832	McMurtrie, William	62y	W	24 MAY 1913	New York NY	Oak Hill
07347	McNab, Harry	35y	C	16 DEC 1909	Philadelphia PA	Harmony
17841	McNair, Clara Warren	80y	W	2 MAY 1922	Annapolis MD	Arlington
07612	McNair, Sarah Pierson	80y	W	11 JUL 1910	Forest Glen MD	Dansville NY
00226	McNally, John, Rev.	63y	W	7 NOV 1889	Baltimore MD	Mt. Olivet
03729	McNally, May	7d	W	13 DEC 1901	Branchville MD	Mt. Olivet
16868	McNamara, Anna A.	50y	W	21 DEC 1920	Laurel MD	Mt. Olivet
13394	McNamara, Hamilton M.	67y	W	2 MAR 1916	Bethesda MD	Prospect Hill
14475	McNamara, John	21y	W	17 NOV 1917	Baltimore MD	Mt. Olivet
04040	McNamara, John	43y	W	9 OCT 1902	Pittsburgh PA	Mt. Olivet
13113	McNamara, Josephine C.	61y	W	19 SEP 1915	Bethesda MD	Prospect Hill
17313	McNamara, Margaret	35y	W	10 JUL 1921	Sligo MD	Mt. Olivet
14379	McNamara, Thomas M.	25y	W	23 SEP 1917	Craney Pt. NJ	Mt. Olivet
11953	McNamee, Elizabeth	56y	W	11 AUG 1913	Rehobeth DE	St. Mary's
02168	McNeal, Marcus	70y	W	20 MAR 1897	Brooklyn NY	Oak Hill
12276	McNeal, Percy M.	48y	W	28 MAR 1914	Rochester NY	Oak Hill
05150	McNeely, Margaret C.	37y	W	29 MAY 1905	Harpers Ferry WV	Congressional
04849	McNeely, Mary Ellen	62y	W	15 AUG 1904	Markleton PA	Congressional
03443	McNeff, James Henry	—	—	26 OCT 1900	At Sea	Kewana IN
14697	McNeir, George A.R.	82y	W	20 MAR 1918	Takoma Park MD	Glenwood
05096	McNelly, Arthur	84y	W	21 APR 1905	Selby SD	Congressional
15258	McNelly, Charles	35y	W	22 OCT 1918	Hyattsville MD	Mt. Olivet
03984	McNelly, Irma	1y	W	6 AUG 1902	Great Falls VA	Congressional
01918	McNerhany, Eugene	35y	W	24 APR 1896	Clifton VA	Mt. Olivet
15267	McNerney, Regina	26y	W	22 OCT 1918	Falls Church VA	Mt. Olivet
15734	McNicholas, Helen A.	28y	W	17 APR 1919	Simpsonville MD	Mt. Olivet
02211	McNulty, Carrie	23y	W	30 JUN 1897	Knoxville TN	Sligo MD
01574	McPhearson, Ella	2m	W	14 MAR 1874	Jersey City NJ	Oak Hill
08879	McPherson, Donald	24y	W	7 OCT 1912	St. Louis MO	Rock Creek
03466	McPherson, Edna J.	56y	W	29 MAR 1901	New York NY	Oak Hill
02701	McPherson, Elizabeth B.	42y	W	9 JAN 1899	Chicago IL	Glenwood
02076	McPherson, Gregory, lawyer	28y	W	22 OCT 1896	Del. Wat. Gap PA	Oak Hill
01828	McPherson, Henry H.	69y	W	29 NOV 1895	Chicago IL	Glenwood
17476	McPherson, James A.	60y	W	18 OCT 1921	Arlington Co. VA	Rock Creek
02212	McPherson, John, farmer	65y	W	12 JUN 1897	Colesville MD	McPherson
02324	McPherson, John R.	65y	W	8 OCT 1897	Jersey City NJ	Oak Hill
15067	McPherson, Lucy	46y	C	1 OCT 1918	Pittsburgh PA	Odd Fellows VA
04619	McPherson, Margaret T.	49y	W	2 MAR 1904	New York NY	Oak Hill
00555	McPherson, Mary A.	60y	W	6 JUN 1891	Chicago IL	Glenwood
03968	McPherson, Robert A.	50y	W	2 AUG 1902	Takoma Park MD	Glenwood
05823	McPherson, Robert W.	58y	W	14 NOV 1906	Atlantic City NJ	Rock Creek
16575	McQuade, Annie L.	17y	W	5 JUL 1920	Front Royal VA	Mt. Olivet
03593	McQuade, Elizabeth	6m	W	26 JUL 1901	Cabin John MD	Mt. Olivet
16576	McQuade, Louise M.	43y	W	5 JUL 1920	Front Royal VA	Mt. Olivet
16249	McQuin, Catherine M.	71y	W	28 JAN 1920	Hyattsville MD	Cremated
00059	McQuinn, Child of Clara/John	3h	W	8 APR 1889	Alex. Co. VA	Holyrood
00058	McQuinn, Clara A.	30y	W	8 APR 1889	Alex. Co. VA	Holyrood
06970	McQuinn, William	1d	W	1 APR 1909	Ballston VA	Glenwood
08030	McRae, Duncan	21y	W	25 MAR 1911	Glen Echo MD	Macon GA
08367	McRoberts, Charles Gregory	39y	W	20 OCT 1911	Bluff Lake IL	Cremated
07159	McShaw, Harvey DeL.	47y	W	15 AUG 1909	Brooklyn NY	Mt. Olivet
06246	McShea, Infant of William E.	SB	W	28 SEP 1907	Ft. Myer Hts. VA	Oak Hill
01575	McShea, William	53y	W	18 JAN 1895	Philadelphia PA	Rock Creek
00639	McSwain, Leawis [sic]	46y	C	2 SEP 1891	Ocean Grove NJ	Harmony
07920	McSween, William H.	51y	W	12 JAN 1911	Buffalo NY	Falls Church VA
13946	McTernan, John S.	45y	W	25 JAN 1917	Brooklyn NY	Mt. Olivet
17484	McThatter, Winfield S.	60y	W	25 OCT 1921	Berwyn MD	Hyattsville MD
08660	McVeany, Honora	48y	W	7 JUN 1912	Capitol Hts. MD	Mt. Olivet

District of Columbia Foreign Death Records, 1888-1923

No.	Name of Deceased	Age	Race	Death Date	Place of Death	Place of Burial
18427	McWhirt, Mary G. (Goodrick)	78y	W	19 MAR 1923	Fredericksburg VA	Glenwood
04681	McWhirter, Martha	77y	W	20 APR 1904	Colesville MD	Rock Creek
00864	Mead, Annie E.	1y	W	3 SEP 1892	Chesapeake VA	Glenwood
09043	Mead, Frank W., s/o Simeon	74y	W	18 JAN 1913	Vineyard Hav. MA	Arlington
16981	Mead, Joseph Raymond	32y	W	15 FEB 1921	Brentwood MD	St. Mary's
12622	Mead, Julia B.	59y	W	15 NOV 1914	Ardmore PA	Arlington
17267	Mead, Mary Catherine	80y	W	27 JUN 1921	Charmion PA	Arlington
03010	Meade, Willie Malissa	9m	W	10 SEP 1899	Bethesda MD	Rock Creek
15087	Meade, Wilson	27y	C	1 OCT 1918	Camp Sevier SC	Owen Sta.
07375	Meagley, Maria	82y	W	18 JAN 1910	Chevy Chase MD	Binghampton NY
16511	Means, Ruth Hildah	1y	W	21 MAY 1920	Landover MD	Congressional
05603	Meany, Richard	35y	W	18 JUN 1906	Allegheny PA	Mt. Olivet
18109	Mearo, Mrs. James Thomas	37y	W	10 OCT 1922	Colonial Bea. VA	Congressional
18128	Mears, Myrtle W.	28y	W	25 OCT 1922	Silver Spring MD	Glenwood
17297	Mechlin, Frederick Aug. Smith	77y	W	11 JUL 1921	Rockville MD	Oak Hill
01250	Mechlin, Joel R.	64y	W	7 SEP 1893	Washington DC	Oak Hill
06154	Meddaugh, Charlotte	55y	W	21 AUG 1903	Olean NY	Rock Creek
17765	Medford, Laura F. (French)	80y	W	26 MAR 1922	Ashland KY	Glenwood
12032	Medley, John	40y	C	8 OCT 1913	Freedman's Hp.	Payne's
14011	Medley, Oneil O.	20y	C	23 FEB 1917	Clinton Co. PA	Payne's
05386	Meeds, Eleanor Nelson Tindall	67y	W	6 DEC 1905	Melwood MD	Congressional
04907	Meeds, Frank	30y	C	1 OCT 1904	Philadelphia PA	Harmony
14276	Meeds, Sarah Eleanor	18y	W	6 AUG 1917	Takoma Park MD	Congressional
01578	Meehan, Infant of J.H.	1y	W	1 DEC 1894	Richmond VA	Mt. Olivet
09014	Meehan, John J.	27y	W	31 DEC 1912	Cincinnati OH	Mt. Olivet
01579	Meehan, Rose	56y	W	12 NOV 1894	Ansonia CN	Mt. Olivet
06285	Meek, Rhoda Gardner	80y	W	21 OCT 1907	Loudoun Co. VA	Glenwood
16776	Meem, Allen F.	14y	W	22 OCT 1920	Lackawana NY	Clarendon VA
13620	Meem, James	80y	W	27 JUL 1916	Leesburg VA	Oak Hill
13215	Megrath, William A.	53y	W	20 MAY 1915	New York NY	Glenwood
01576	Meier, Russell	4y	W	2 FEB 1895	Baltimore MD	Prospect Hill
16233	Meigs, Jane Perry Rodgers	67y	W	20 JAN 1920	Radnor PA	Rock Creek
11820	Meitzler, Charles	35y	W	14 MAY 1913	Philadelphia PA	Congressional
02609	Meitzler, Henrietta	37y	W	27 SEP 1898	Pr. Geo. Co. MD	Congressional
01647	Mejasky, Francis	—	W	SEP 1882	Matanzas, Cuba	Oak Hill
01646	Mejasky, Maria del Rosario	—	W	22 FEB 1886	Matanzas, Cuba	Oak Hill
14351	Melhorn, Henry Clay	68y	W	9 SEP 1917	Berwyn MD	Glenwood
01638	Meline, Florent M.	7m	W	16 MAR 1895	Philadelphia PA	Rock Creek
07913	Mell, Alverta G. (Davis)	58y	W	10 JAN 1911	Alexandria VA	Glenwood
07993	Mellen, Lavinia Hathaway	1y	W	2 MAR 1911	Takoma Park MD	Rock Creek
12196	Meloy, Samuel Henry	78y	W	3 FEB 1914	Meadows MD	Rock Creek
05294	Meloy, William A.	72y	W	20 SEP 1905	Lanham MD	Rock Creek
17995	Melson, Lewis D.	40y	W	7 AUG 1922	Montrose MD	Glenwood
17556	Melton, B.H., Jr.	11y	W	30 APR 1916	Richmond VA	Glenwood
07486	Memler, Gustavus Adolphus	42y	W	19 MAR 1910	Richmond VA	Rock Creek
17191	Menchan, Martin Joseph	44y	W	26 MAY 1921	Philadelphia PA	Mt. Olivet
12961	Menefee, Mamie B.	30y	W	11 JUN 1915	Pr. Geo. Co. MD	Congressional
02327	Menger, Valentine	73y	W	13 NOV 1897	Brooklyn NY	Prospect Hill
14006	Menker, Jennie	65y	W	24 FEB 1917	Mt. Ranier MD	Glenwood
06652	Menocal, Aniceto G.	71y	W	20 JUL 1908	New York NY	Arlington
16695	Menzel, Paul T.	28y	W	4 SEP 1920	St. Louis MO	Prospect Hill
12514	Mercer, Mary Jane	41y	C	1 SEP 1914	Pittsburgh PA	Payne's
18338	Mercer, Morton	20y	W	4 FEB 1923	Glendale CA	Rock Creek
15733	Mercer, Morton Bartow	39y	W	11 APR 1919	Ft. Bayard NM	Rock Creek
08581	Mercer, Nancy K.	79y	W	3 APR 1912	Rochester NY	Rock Creek
17863	Mercer, Winfield Livingston	36y	W	12 MAY 1922	Tucson AZ	Rock Creek
02439	Merchant, Bolan	22y	W	12 APR 1898	Fairfax VA	Glenwood
18266	Merchant, Francis D.	56y	W	13 JAN 1923	New York NY	Rock Creek
05631	Merchant, Silas	76y	W	9 JUL 1906	New York NY	Rock Creek

No.	Name of Deceased	Age	Race	Death Date	Place of Death	Place of Burial
04974	Merchant, William A., Jr.	7y	W	21 OCT 1904	Portsmouth VA	Holyrood
07535	Meredith, Ellen G.	84y	W	11 MAY 1910	Clinton MD	Congressional
18583	Meredith, Frank Clark	56y	W	2 JUN 1923	Harrisburg PA	Cremated
14211	Meredith, Kate	59y	W	1 JUL 1917	Chicago IL	Congressional
15055	Merriam, Henry L.	16y	W	29 SEP 1918	New York NY	Arlington VA
12822	Merrick, Maria E.	86y	W	17 MAR 1915	Cherrydale VA	Congressional
12871	Merrick, Mary W.	98y	W	10 APR 1915	Pikesville MD	Oak Hill
02005	Merrick, Nannie	29y	W	6 JUL 1896	New York NY	Oak Hill
00865	Merrick, William	3y	W	4 AUG 1892	—	Mt. Olivet
00866	Merrick, William Milton	3y	W	4 AUG 1892	Wash. Co. MD	Mt. Olivet
05360	Merriduth, John H.	80y	W	16 NOV 1905	Clinton MD	Congressional
13171	Merrill, Annie F.	70y	W	29 OCT 1915	Chevy Chase MD	Glenwood
12563	Merrill, Daniel Ford, Jr.	50y	W	9 OCT 1914	Jackson VA	Rock Creek
15214	Merrill, Gertrude	40y	C	13 OCT 1918	Bryn Mawr PA	Harmony
09081	Merrill, Henry Stephen	69y	W	17 FEB 1913	Franklin Park VA	Oak Hill
16331	Merrill, Margaret	30y	W	19 FEB 1920	Minneapolis MN	Glenwood
03495	Merrill, Nellie S.	10y	W	2 MAY 1901	Baltimore Co. MD	Oak Hill
01251	Merrill, Vincent James	7d	W	25 SEP 1893	New York NY	Oak Hill
09170	Merriman, Matilda	75y	W	13 APR 1913	New York NY	Oak Hill
12948	Merritt, Addison	49y	C	27 MAY 1915	Philadelphia PA	Woodlawn
03372	Merritt, Elizabeth Barbara	55y	W	30 DEC 1900	Philadelphia PA	Oak Hill
14128	Merritt, Henry Brashears	6y	W	7 MAY 1917	Summit NJ	Mt. Olivet
18116	Merritt, Lonora	50y	W	16 OCT 1922	Canton OH	Congressional
06184	Merritt, William A.	35y	W	16 AUG 1907	Mtn. Lake Pk. MD	Congressional
02780	Merritt, William M., soldier	—	W	8 JUL 1898	Ft. Myer VA	Arlington
00107	Merry, Grace	11m	W	2 JUL 1889	Fairfax Co. VA	Holyrood
03639	Merryman, Thomas	68y	W	12 SEP 1901	Alexandria VA	Glenwood
03602	Mertens, Mary K.	38y	W	5 AUG 1901	Ballston VA	Oak Hill
13329	Mertins, Hannah	61y	W	29 JAN 1916	Clarendon VA	Oak Hill[1]
03506	Mertz, Victoria B.	24y	W	13 MAY 1901	Philadelphia PA	Glenwood
13290	Mertz, William C.	27y	W	8 JAN 1916	Philadelphia PA	Glenwood
05367	Merwin, Claphira S.	82y	W	17 NOV 1905	Cambridge MA	Glenwood
13483	Messenger, Isaiah	75y	W	28 APR 1916	Philadelphia PA	Prospect Hill
07384	Messenger, Willie	55y	W	24 JAN 1910	New York NY	Oak Hill
08224	Messer, Charlotte M.	53y	W	28 JUL 1911	Jersey City NJ	Congressional
05526	Messer, William	56y	W	9 APR 1906	Dickerson MD	Congressional
16235	Messinger, John	71y	W	22 JAN 1920	Mt. Ranier MD	Glenwood
13153	Metcalf, Herbert	18y	W	18 OCT 1915	Takoma Park MD	Rock Creek
00631	Metcalf, Jennie May	9m	W	19 JUL 1891	Pr. Geo. Co. MD	Glenwood
07970	Metz, John W.	56y	W	16 FEB 1911	Laurel MD	Manassas VA
17581	Metzerott, Frank B.	59y	W	7 DEC 1921	Boulder CO	Oak Hill
06113	Metzler, Adolph H.	38y	W	19 JUN 1907	Mt. Ranier MD	Prospect Hill
02825	Mexia, Hegley	23y	W	8 MAY 1899	St. Louis MO	Rock Creek
16357	Meyer, Clara O.	53y	W	1 MAR 1920	Takoma Park MD	Rock Creek
03873	Meyer, George A., of Denmark	61y	W	1 MAY 1902	Togus ME	Rock Creek
09166	Meyer, Julius	35y	C	11 APR 1913	New York NY	Harmony
01173	Meyers, Charles F.	62y	W	22 DEC 1892	Druid Hill Pk. MD	Congressional
05123	Meyers, Edward F.D., Maj.	74y	W	12 MAY 1905	Richmond VA	Cremated
16900	Meyers, Fannie E.	50y	W	4 JAN 1921	Philadelphia PA	Congressional
05358	Meynes, Charles A.	58y	W	15 MAR 1905	Washington DC	Glenwood
02208	Michael, Eli	11y	W	21 JUN 1897	Falls Church VA	Potters Field
05443	Michaels, Anne T.	48y	W	25 JAN 1906	Chicago IL	Congressional
03062	Michaelson, Sarah	2m	W	5 JAN 1900	Galloways MD	Talmud Torah
11943	Michener, Algernon S.	43y	W	4 AUG 1913	Eldon WA	Rock Creek
14665	Michener, Infant of William	1h	W	2 MAR 1918	Somerset MD	Prospect Hill
04475	Mickens, Selena	24y	—	12 OCT 1903	Baltimore MD	Cormill VA
07505	Mickewitz, Elizabeth	30y	W	15 APR 1910	New York NY	Oak Hill

[1] Disinterment permit on 12 JUL 1927 for removal to Columbia Gardens, Arlington, Va.

District of Columbia Foreign Death Records, 1888-1923

No.	Name of Deceased	Age	Race	Death Date	Place of Death	Place of Burial
16303	Micou, Paul H.	18y	W	11 FEB 1920	Annapolis MD	Rock Creek
07948	Middaugh, Ebenezer N.	71y	W	28 JAN 1911	New York NY	Rock Creek
09125	Middleton, Alice	5y	W	12 MAR 1913	Hillsdale MD	Oak Hill
14304	Middleton, Cora E. Brown	54y	W	16 AUG 1917	Warrenton VA	Oak Hill
01742	Middleton, Ella E.	35y	W	14 OCT 1895	Baltimore MD	Congressional
04673	Middleton, Ellen Ross	84y	W	15 APR 1904	Garrett Park MD	Rock Creek
04530	Middleton, James W.	55y	W	29 NOV 1903	New York NY	Rock Creek
15708	Middleton, Jonas B.	61y	W	5 APR 1919	Falls Church VA	Congressional
01743	Middleton, Leander B.	55y	W	15 SEP 1895	Branchville MD	Glenwood
00306	Middleton, Margaret	54y	W	3 APR 1890	New York NY	Congressional[1]
07473	Middleton, Margaret H.	70y	W	18 MAR 1910	Hyattsville MD	Oak Hill
16067	Middleton, Mary Virginia	90y	W	23 OCT 1919	Garrett Park MD	Rock Creek
04291	Middleton, Samuel E.	68y	W	13 MAY 1903	St. Paul MN	Oak Hill
07521	Middleton, Walter	64y	C	28 APR 1910	Hampton VA	Woodlawn
05486	Milans, Joseph D.	54y	W	4 MAR 1906	St. Denis MD	Congressional
06886	Milburn, Richard C.	1y	W	10 JAN 1909	Riverdale MD	Congressional
08534	Miles, Christiana	84y	C	27 FEB 1912	Philadelphia PA	Payne's
03389	Miles, Columbus	21y	W	11 JAN 1901	Clarksburg WV	Marshall Hall MD
16207	Miles, Emily	34y	W	12 JAN 1920	Philadelphia PA	Rock Creek
05091	Miles, Henry Jerry	5d	C	19 APR 1905	Burrsville MD	Payne's
07888	Miles, Henry R.	82y	W	22 DEC 1910	Laurel MD	Oak Hill
13095	Miles, James	45y	W	7 SEP 1915	Pittsburgh PA	Mt. Olivet
05586	Miles, Jerry	66y	C	29 MAY 1906	Seat Pleasant MD	Payne's
12118	Miles, Kossuth	64y	W	6 DEC 1913	New York NY	Arlington
18468	Miles, Lawrence D.	6y	C	7 APR 1923	Seat Pleasant MD	Mt. Olivet
12939	Miles, Louisa	90y	C	26 MAY 1915	Forestville MD	Mt. Olivet
17022	Miles, Maria	50y	C	6 MAR 1921	Fairmont Hts. MD	Payne's
04831	Miles, Mary Sherman	62y	W	1 AUG 1904	West Point NY	Arlington VA
04835	Miles, Sarah	5m	C	5 AUG 1904	Fairmont Hts. MD	Payne's
17055	Milgar, Richard	26y	W	18 MAR 1921	Takoma Park MD	Arlington
12487	Millan, Frederick P., s/o Wm.	45y	W	18 AUG 1914	Waterbury CN	Rock Creek
02169	Millard, Emily	68y	W	11 MAR 1897	Providence RI	Rock Creek
14008	Miller, Adaline V.	59y	W	25 FEB 1917	Chillum MD	Rock Creek
04894	Miller, Alexander M., Col.	62y	W	14 SEP 1904	Irvington VA	Utica NY
17139	Miller, Alice T.H.	66y	W	3 MAY 1921	New York NY	Arlington
05935	Miller, Amelia E.	2d	W	11 FEB 1907	Chillum MD	Rock Creek
15939	Miller, Anna May	3m	W	21 AUG 1919	Silver Spring MD	Rock Creek
00334	Miller, Annie Elizabeth	16m	W	30 MAY 1890	Pr. Geo. Co. MD	Rock Creek
15894	Miller, Anthony	77y	W	27 JUL 1919	Colonial Bea. VA	Glenwood
17198	Miller, Archie	—	W	28 MAY 1921	Walter Reed Hp.	Arlington
15169	Miller, Arnion A.	30y	W	13 OCT 1918	Cumberland MD	Prospect Hill
02006	Miller, Barbary Ruth	1y	W	8 AUG 1896	Unity MD	Glenwood
13932	Miller, Bettie	48y	C	14 JAN 1917	New York NY	Harmony
08526	Miller, Caroline	51y	W	25 FEB 1912	Lyonhurst VA	Glenwood
16461	Miller, Charles Henry	76y	W	30 APR 1920	Falls Church VA	Oak Hill
02383	Miller, Charles L.	30y	W	19 JAN 1898	Pr. Geo. Co. MD	Mt. Olivet
00974	Miller, Elijah	73y	W	1 AUG 1893	Roanoke VA	Glenwood
08841	Miller, Elizabeth C.	53y	W	17 SEP 1912	Silver Spring MD	Midland VA
16526	Miller, Elizabeth Page	69y	W	6 JUN 1920	Fairfax Co. VA	Congressional
08836	Miller, Elmer	29y	W	12 SEP 1912	Ft. Oglethorpe GA	Rock Creek
07620	Miller, Emily H.	65y	W	9 JUL 1910	New York NY	Harmony
18397	Miller, Frances	44y	C	6 MAR 1923	Philadelphia PA	Harmony
14439	Miller, Francis	24y	C	2 NOV 1917	N. Charleroi PA	Mt. Zion West
03516	Miller, Frank	55y	W	18 MAY 1901	Asbury Park NJ	Arlington VA
04477	Miller, Frank	28y	W	14 OCT 1903	New York NY	Holyrood
11851	Miller, Frederick A., s/o Jacob	34y	W	11 JUN 1913	Richmond VA	Mt. Olivet
02328	Miller, Frederick R.	49y	W	23 NOV 1897	Great Falls MD	Prospect Hill

[1] Disinterment permit #9522 issued to remove remains 14 JUN 1918 to Arlington.

No.	Name of Deceased	Age	Race	Death Date	Place of Death	Place of Burial
07269	Miller, Fredk. A. Abercrombie	67y	W	8 NOV 1909	New York NY	Arlington
17604	Miller, George F., s/o Wm. H.	74y	W	23 DEC 1921	Danville VA	Arlington
07066	Miller, Georgie E.M.	39y	W	19 JUN 1909	Falls Church VA	Glenwood
01353	Miller, Harriet	60y	C	25 MAR 1894	Halls Hill VA	Harmony
03925	Miller, Harriett R.	7m	W	17 JUL 1902	Arlington MD	Glenwood
07708	Miller, Henrietta	50y	C	24 AUG 1910	Fairmont Hts. MD	Payne's
05207	Miller, Henry	80y	C	9 JUL 1905	Tuxedo MD	Woodlawn, rem.
00745	Miller, Henry R.	68y	W	1 DEC 1891	Pr. Geo. Co. MD	St. Mary's
18049	Miller, Henry Wesley	72y	W	5 SEP 1922	Brentwood MD	Hyndman PA
07267	Miller, Henry William	35y	W	8 NOV 1909	Takoma Park MD	Prospect Hill
07892	Miller, Infant of homas	SB		24 DEC 1910	Chillum MD	Rock Creek
18381	Miller, Isadore	60y	C	1 MAR 1923	Philadelphia PA	Harmony
12201	Miller, James	73y	W	3 FEB 1914	Chillum MD	Rock Creek
12610	Miller, James Francis	11y	W	11 NOV 1914	Maplewood VA	Glenwood
17854	Miller, Jennie M.	30y	W	13 MAY 1922	Hume Spgs. VA	Congressional
06933	Miller, John	58y	W	26 FEB 1909	Atlantic City NJ	Congressional
00746	Miller, John	19y	W	21 DEC 1891	San Antonio TX	Congressional
00011	Miller, John	22y	W	17 JAN 1889	St. Paul MN	Congressional
03948	Miller, John	1y	W	10 JUL 1902	Riverdale MD	Rock Creek
07780	Miller, John	73y	W	7 OCT 1910	Pr. Geo. Co. MD	Rock Creek
13318	Miller, John Alexander	21y	W	24 JAN 1916	Takoma MD	Rock Creek
15706	Miller, John B.	45y	C	29 MAR 1919	Philadelphia PA	Payne's
09189	Miller, John F.	54y	W	8 MAR 1886	Washington DC	Arlington
09187	Miller, John F., Jr.	7y	W	30 DEC 1878	San Francisco CA	Arlington
03129	Miller, John J.	60y	W	15 MAR 1900	Ballston VA	Tenallytown
14659	Miller, John O.	62y	W	25 FEB 1918	Baltimore MD	Rock Creek
18593	Miller, John W.	35y	C	31 MAY 1923	New York NY	Harmony
07005	Miller, Joseph N.	72y	W	25 APR 1909	E. Orange NJ	Arlington VA
03907	Miller, Katherine Louise	8m	W	28 JUN 1902	Springfield NH	Oak Hill
02409	Miller, Laura L.	28y	W	22 FEB 1898	Tucson AZ	Congressional
00026	Miller, Lemuel B.S.	71y	W	2 FEB 1889	Salt Lake City UT	Congressional
15291	Miller, Lemuel Bland	24y	W	25 OCT 1918	Newport News VA	Rock Creek
05784	Miller, Margaret S.	56y	W	21 OCT 1906	Lay Hill MD	Rock Creek
00867	Miller, Marie Pauline	4m	W	3 AUG 1892	Riverdale Pk. MD	Mt. Olivet
18139	Miller, Martha Ann	87y	W	2 NOV 1922	Chevy Chase MD	Glenwood
09114	Miller, Martha C.	47y	W	6 MAR 1913	Annapolis MD	Oak Hill
12121	Miller, Mary	71y	W	9 DEC 1913	Chillum MD	Rock Creek
03914	Miller, Mary A.	49y	W	19 JUN 1902	Philadelphia PA	Mt. Olivet
03484	Miller, Mary Annie	75y	W	21 APR 1901	Chillum MD	Rock Creek
17159	Miller, Mary Etta	26y	C	13 MAY 1921	Rosslyn VA	Union
09188	Miller, Mary W.C.	54y	W	6 DEC 1891	Washington DC	Arlington
12859	Miller, Matilda	84y	W	2 APR 1915	Philadelphia PA	Glenwood
16689	Miller, Max	27y	W	1 SEP 1920	Morristown NJ	Glenwood
08868	Miller, Nelson H.	65y	W	2 OCT 1912	McLean VA	Congressional
02801	Miller, Pauline	43y	W	19 APR 1899	Trenton NJ	Prospect Hill
13402	Miller, Rebecca R.	49y	W	8 MAR 1916	Mt. Ranier MD	Ohev Sholom
04694	Miller, Roberta V.	1y	W	30 APR 1904	Riverdale MD	Rock Creek
08559	Miller, Rosa	24y	C	16 MAR 1912	Brentwood MD	Harmony
17540	Miller, Rose M.T.	30y	W	19 NOV 1921	New York NY	Rock Creek
11927	Miller, Rosie L.	1m	W	28 JUL 1913	Mt. Ranier MD	Prospect Hill
15273	Miller, Samuel, Jr.	21y	W	21 OCT 1918	Bayshore LI	Glenwood
13392	Miller, Stephen A.	67y	W	1 MAR 1916	Chillum MD	Rock Creek
18150	Miller, Thomas	76y	W	7 NOV 1922	Lincolnia VA	Cremated
08130	Miller, Walter Austin	32y	W	25 MAY 1911	Richmond VA	Cremated
02261	Miller, William Deeds	78y	W	29 JUL 1897	Lynchburg VA	Glenwood
16670	Miller, William Edward	11d	W	21 AUG 1920	Capitol Hts. MD	Congressional
12079	Miller, William H.	73y	W	1 NOV 1913	St. Louis MO	Arlington VA
12226	Miller, William Kaufman	59y	W	16 FEB 1914	Ammendale MD	Congressional
01580	Millett, Clarence, painter	42y	W	16 JAN 1895	Jackson MS	Oak Hill

District of Columbia Foreign Death Records, 1888-1923

No.	Name of Deceased	Age	Race	Death Date	Place of Death	Place of Burial
05597	Millikin, Hugh Geddes	1m	W	14 JUN 1906	Kensington MD	Glenwood
17183	Millrick, Mary Anne	86y	W	25 MAY 1921	Cherrydale VA	Mt. Olivet
14393	Millrick, Morris	82y	W	1 OCT 1917	Clarendon VA	Glenwood
12302	Mills, Alfred D.	23y	C	8 APR 1914	Pittsburgh PA	Harmony
18029	Mills, Infant of Harry & Eva	SB	C	24 AUG 1922	Arlington VA	Rosemont
14499	Mills, Joseph E.	48y	W	9 DEC 1917	Baltimore MD	Congressional
00495	Mills, Lucy, d/o Frank	SB	W	3 APR 1891	New York NY	Glenwood
14153	Mills, Margaret A.	53y	W	30 MAY 1917	Laurel MD	Mt. Olivet
01457	Mills, Mary A.	82y	W	9 AUG 1894	Chicago IL	Congressional
18288	Mills, Mary Chase	72y	W	20 JAN 1923	Beacon NY	Oak Hill
12394	Mills, Richard	25y	C	8 JUN 1914	Burnt Mills NJ	Camp Springs MD
17100	Mills, Roberta M.	52y	W	10 APR 1921	Baltimore MD	Glenwood
16467	Mills, William F.	31y	W	21 APR 1920	New York NY	Holyrood
12842	Mills, William W.	19y	W	28 MAR 1915	Bradley Rd. MD	Rock Creek
03264	Milton, George L.	72y	W	13 AUG 1900	Kensington MD	Congressional
06607	Milton, Phylis	1m	W	24 JUN 1908	Montg. Co. MD	Rock Creek
16063	Mimmack, Katharine Collins	77y	W	18 OCT 1919	New York NY	Arlington
17437	Minami, Zokuichi	24y	J	25 SEP 1921	Norfolk VA	Cremated
06152	Mindel, George N.	63y	W	20 JUL 1907	New York NY	Arlington
09052	Minder, Mary	10min	W	1 FEB 1913	Mt. Ranier MD	Prospect Hill
15938	Miner, James	46y	C	16 AUG 1919	Pittsburgh PA	Orange VA
18106	Miner, Uzziah Elesavetgrad	33y	C	6 OCT 1922	West Haven CN	Woodlawn
12292	Mines, Rosa B.	25y	C	3 APR 1914	Fairmont Hts. MD	Payne's
06209	Minetree, James Lawrence	28y	W	29 AUG 1907	Railroad	Rock Creek
12944	Minetree, Joseph P.	43y	W	28 MAY 1915	Laurel MD	Greensboro NC
00303	Minick, Katie M.	33y	W	3 APR 1890	Hyattsville MD	Glenwood
08690	Minitree, Louise Warner	27y	W	27 JUN 1912	Baltimore MD	Rock Creek
00976	Miniture, Hanora	47y	W	17 JUN 1893	Baltimore MD	Mt. Olivet
05477	Minkings, John H.	61y	C	27 MAR 1905	Norfolk VA	Harmony
01355	Minnick, Edward	23y	W	14 APR 1894	Baltimore MD	Mt. Olivet
06861	Minnix, James E.	18y	W	16 DEC 1908	Phoenix AZ	Congressional
01413	Minnix, John N., coach builder	68y	W	16 JUN 1894	Temples MD	Congressional
00632	Minor, Amy	32y	C	4 AUG 1891	New York NY	Harmony
13101	Minor, Benjamin	30y	C	7 SEP 1915	Leavenworth KS	Payne's
15290	Minor, Carl Olin	31y	W	23 OCT 1918	Blacksburg VA	Arlington
16322	Minor, Edward	48y	C	13 FEB 1920	Columbus OH	Woodlawn
14045	Minor, Eugene P.	48y	C	21 MAR 1917	New York NY	Harmony
13391	Minor, Frank	34y	C	26 FEB 1916	New York NY	Woodlawn
08508	Minor, Houston	31y	C	7 FEB 1912	New York NY	Payne's
12174	Minor, James E.	43y	C	19 JAN 1913	New York NY	Harmony
06465	Minor, Mary Francis	32y	C	11 MAR 1908	Jersey City NJ	Woodlawn
04156	Miskell, Goldie	19y	W	7 JAN 1903	Asheville NC	Herndon VA
15241	Missini, Antonio	25y	W	18 OCT 1918	Camp Meade MD	Arlington
13601	Mitchell, Albert	22y	W	9 JUL 1916	Miner Co. SD	Marshall VA
16024	Mitchell, Amelia F., d/o Thos.	20y	W	1 OCT 1919	Asheville NC	Glenwood
07244	Mitchell, Arthur H.	—	W	—	Uniontown PA	Rock Creek
12790	Mitchell, Donald B.	14d	W	3 MAR 1915	Takoma Park MD	Rock Creek
14773	Mitchell, Dora L.	60y	W	26 APR 1918	Takoma Park MD	Rock Creek
14399	Mitchell, Elizabeth	67y	W	7 OCT 1917	Hyattsville MD	Glenwood
18324	Mitchell, Ella	c.40y	C	3 FEB 1923	Arlington VA	Mt. Zion West
04136	Mitchell, George	63y	W	2 JAN 1903	New Orleans LA	Rock Creek
08146	Mitchell, Harry W.	32y	W	11 JUN 1911	Rosslyn VA	Rock Creek
00975	Mitchell, Hattie	36y	W	13 AUG 1893	Norfolk VA	Graceland
15264	Mitchell, Henry M.	27y	W	21 OCT 1918	Indian Head MD	Shelter Isl. NY
06989	Mitchell, Infant of Joseph	SB	W	17 APR 1909	Arlington VA	—
12965	Mitchell, James W.	45y	W	18 JUN 1915	Ballston VA	Cremated
02007	Mitchell, Joseph Albert	9m	W	6 AUG 1896	Hagerstown MD	Mt. Olivet
07245	Mitchell, Katie R.	—	W	—	Uniontown PA	Rock Creek
01581	Mitchell, Maria A.	75y	W	24 DEC 1894	Charlton Hts. MD	E. Cambridge MA

No.	Name of Deceased	Age	Race	Death Date	Place of Death	Place of Burial
17872	Mitchell, Mary White	31y	W	21 MAY 1922	Salinda NC	Cremated
13211	Mitchell, Milton C.	67y	W	17 NOV 1915	Salisbury NC	Rock Creek
12701	Mitchell, Oscar V.	69y	W	7 JAN 1915	Hyattsville MD	Soldier's Home
11865	Mitchell, Rachel O.	9y	W	25 JUN 1913	Garrett Park MD	Cremated
13609	Mitchell, Richard	30y	C	16 JUL 1916	New Castle PA	Harmony
05331	Mitchell, Robert W.	60y	W	25 OCT 1905	Bedford VA	Cremated
04565	Mitchell, Samuel	22y	C	9 JAN 1904	New York NY	Harmony
02936	Mitchell, Sarah A.	62y	W	4 SEP 189	Bay Head NJ	Rock Creek
15138	Mitchell, Theo.	25y	C	10 OCT 1918	Warwick Co. VA	Harmony
02482	Mitchell, Thomas	64y	W	29 JUL 1898	Batavia OH	Congressional
14690	Mitchell, Warren M.	38y	W	17 MAR 1918	Baltimore MD	Rock Creek
12221	Mitchell, William J.	69y	W	15 FEB 1914	Hyattsville MD	Mt. Olivet
03400	Mitchelmore, Elizabeth	79y	W	21 JAN 1901	Centreville MD	Rock Creek
01356	Moeleck, Frederick	83y	W	13 JAN 1894	Baltimore MD	Rock Creek
08790	Moffett, Geo. Henry, s/o H.M.	67y	W	29 AUG 1912	Waynesboro VA	Rock Creek
06376	Moffitt, Charles Ansil	48y	W	18 OCT 1877	New Castle PA	Rock Creek
02170	Moffitt, Mary Jane	66y	W	13 APR 1897	Highland MD	Glenwood
05514	Moffitt, Stephen J.	45y	W	30 MAR 1906	Chambersburg PA	Congressional
02634	Mohun, Barry	2y	W	13 OCT 1898	Altoona PA	Oak Hill
03138	Mohun, Lewis W.	c.27y	W	29 NOV 1899	Manila, P.I.	Oak Hill
06651	Mohun, Mary V.	9m	W	22 JUL 1908	Chevy Chase MD	Oak Hill
13001	Mohun, Richard Dorsey	47y	W	13 JUL 1957	Royal Oak MD	Oak Hill
03094	Mohun, William Ward	41y	W	19 NOV 1898	Havana, Cuba	Congressional
03472	Moles, Connie	32y	C	4 APR 1901	Philadelphia PA	Payne's
15592	Molineu, Norman Charles	4m	W	30 JAN 1919	Decatur Hts. MD	Glenwood
03560	Moller, Annie R.	71y	W	3 JUL 1901	Brentwood MD	Glenwood
09065	Momberger, Annie	46y	W	8 FEB 1913	Baltimore MD	Mt. Olivet
01582	Momberger, Louise	61y	W	14 DEC 1894	Baltimore MD	Prospect Hill
16662	Monahan, Deane	83y	W	9 AUG 1920	Denver CO	Arlington Co. VA
12960	Monahan, Harry James	33y	W	7 JUN 1915	Reedville VA	Mt. Olivet
14334	Moncure, J.A., Dr., s/o Henry	73y	W	13 MAR 1917	Stafford Co. VA	Congressional
14623	Monocal, Estes Martin	35y	W	2 FEB 1918	Asheville NC	Mt. Olivet
05993	Monroe, Charles R.	54y	W	17 MAR 1907	Atlanta GA	Congressional
05614	Monroe, Hazel M.	17y	W	30 JUN 1906	Ft. Wash. MD	Parkersburg WV
14876	Monroe, Lucy R.	73y	W	22 JUN 1918	Pr. Geo. Co. MD	Congressional
07806	Monroe, Wm. H., s/o Harrison	63y	W	29 OCT 1910	Franconia VA	Rock Creek
00337	Mont, Julia Estelle	17m	C	6 JUN 1890	Pr. Geo. Co. MD	Harmony
00868	Montague, Imogen Exall	37y	W	23 AUG 1892	Baltimore MD	Oak Hill
14162	Montaniro, Maddalena	1y	W	26 JUN 1917	Capitol Hts. MD	Mt. Olivet
03494	Montegriffe, Augustino, of Italy	81y	W	9 JUL 1900	Washington DC	Mt. Olivet[1]
12612	Montgomery, Elmer F.	33y	W	8 NOV 1914	Sacramento CA	Glenwood
05981	Montgomery, Frank	28y	C	11 MAR 1907	Newark NJ	Harmony
17306	Montgomery, Harry F.	36y	W	18 JUL 1921	Baltimore MD	Rock Creek
05348	Montgomery, Julia	22y	W	5 NOV 1905	Philadelphia PA	Congressional
11949	Montgomery, L.N.	47y	W	5 JUN 1913	Austin TX	Arlington VA
03776	Montgomery, Martha	62y	C	28 JAN 1902	Waterbury CN	Harmony
18462	Montgomery, Otto Lee	45y	W	6 APR 1923	Wilton CN	Rock Creek
17698	Montgomery, Raymond	3m	C	15 FEB 1922	Fairmont Hts. MD	Payne's
13902	Montgomery, William Spence	1y	W	1 JAN 1917	Cherrydale VA	Congressional
12765	Montrose, Mrs. Marshall	31y	W	19 JAN 1915	Santa Fe NM	Glenwood
03145	Monzaro, Henry	35y	C	23 MAR 1900	Norfolk VA	Payne's
01068	Moody, Elizabeth	46y	W	13 FEB 1893	Portsmouth VA	Rock Creek
16160	Moody, Nellie	33y	C	21 DEC 1919	Baltimore MD	Payne's
17934	Moody, Ruth Louise	20y	W	2 JUL 1922	Port Byron IL	Glenwood
07507	Mooney, George, a.k.a.	31y	C	16 APR 1910	Minneapolis MN	Halls Hill VA
08099	Moore, Agnes T.	60y	W	4 MAY 1911	New York NY	Arlington
17408	Moore, Alexander	39y	C	13 SEP 1921	Saratoga Sp. NY	Harmony

[1] Note of 29 APR 1901, Depot Quartermaster's Office, for removal from grave #14059 in Arlington National Cemetery.

District of Columbia Foreign Death Records, 1888-1923

No.	Name of Deceased	Age	Race	Death Date	Place of Death	Place of Burial
07403	Moore, Alexander D.	74y	W	2 FEB 1910	Philadelphia PA	Congressional
14602	Moore, Anna Heller	55y	W	24 JAN 1918	Anderson IN	Glenwood
07883	Moore, Annie L.	64y	W	12 DEC 1910	Los Angeles CA	Arlington VA
15654	Moore, Annie W.	54y	W	3 MAR 1919	Kensington MD	Oak Hill
02826	Moore, Barnard	21y	W	6 MAY 1899	Railroad	Alexandria VA
02171	Moore, Benjamin	83y	W	19 MAR 1895	Newtown NY	Congressional
16933	Moore, Bertha Hill	28y	W	19 JAN 1921	Kansas City MO	Rock Creek
13957	Moore, Caroline A.	82y	W	30 JAN 1917	Mt. Ranier MD	Glenwood
17327	Moore, Carrie	49y	C	24 JUL 1921	Upper Marl. MD	Bridgeport CN
02854	Moore, Catherine Hester	1y	W	19 JUN 1899	Falls Church VA	Holyrood
13238	Moore, Cornelia L.	75y	W	16 DEC 1913	New Orleans LA	Rock Creek
03752	Moore, Douglas	45y	W	4 JAN 1902	Knoxville TN	Glenwood
13456	Moore, Edward A., Jr.	—	W	26 MAR 1916	Guant. Bay, Cuba	Boston MA
08659	Moore, Edward L.	2½h	W	5 JUN 1912	Brentwood MD	Mt. Olivet
17104	Moore, Elizabeth	28y	C	9 APR 1921	Cleveland OH	Forestville MD
06722	Moore, Ella	68y	C	7 SEP 1908	Fauquier Co. VA	Harmony
18329	Moore, Ella Osborne	61y	W	5 FEB 1923	Alexandria VA	Oak Hill
17082	Moore, Emma Ruth	67y	W	2 APR 1921	Woodside MD	London, Can.
13659	Moore, Eugene	24y	W	14 AUG 1916	Maryland Pk. MD	Mt. Olivet
07495	Moore, Florice	4y	C	8 APR 1910	Takoma Park MD	Moore's
07927	Moore, Infant of Walter	2h	W	12 JAN 1911	Brentwood MD	Congressional
01067	Moore, Infant of William B.	9d	W	16 OCT 1866	Washington DC	Oak Hill
05095	Moore, James M.	67y	W	24 APR 1905	Chicago IL	Arlington VA
06667	Moore, Jas. Cochran	4m	W	1 AUG 1908	Silver Spring MD	Rock Creek
04039	Moore, John L.	51y	W	11 JUL 1879	Vienna VA	Congressional
05810	Moore, Katie	44y	C	2 NOV 1906	Toledo OH	Woodlawn
08535	Moore, Lawrence C.	52y	W	27 FEB 1912	Ft. Pierce FL	Congressional
16812	Moore, Lena	38y	C	15 NOV 1920	New York NY	Woodlawn
12018	Moore, Lester D., Sr.	74y	W	27 SEP 1913	New York NY	Glenwood
04038	Moore, Lewis [Louis] E.	18y	W	27 AUG 1873	Vienna VA	Congressional
16889	Moore, Louise B.	—	W	11 MAR 1915	Washington DC	Rock Creek
07094	Moore, Louise E.	10y	W	6 JUL 1909	Kensington MD	Laurel DE
15719	Moore, Marcia	50y	W	11 APR 1919	New York NY	Rock Creek
01913	Moore, Martin	55y	C	15 APR 1896	Pr. Geo. Co. MD	Harmony
18571	Moore, Mary	34y	C	29 MAY 1923	Long Branch NJ	Mt. Olivet
12356	Moore, Mary B.	36y	W	11 MAY 1914	New York NY	Rock Creek
08211	Moore, Mary E.	53y	W	24 JUL 1911	Glen Echo MD	Congressional
02172	Moore, Mary H.	66y	W	29 APR 1889	Newtown NY	Congressional
07838	Moore, Robert	—	W	24 NOV 1910	New York NY	Glenwood
03095	Moore, Sarah B.	69y	W	10 FEB 1900	Cabin John MD	Oak Hill
08216	Moore, Sarah Grant	55y	W	26 JUL 1911	Takoma Park MD	Kokomo IN
01171	Moore, William	52y	W	25 SEP 1892	Baltimore Co. MD	Glenwood
02588	Moore, William Bennett	11m	W	31 AUG 1898	Forest Glen MD	Congressional
15422	Moore, William G.	24y	W	4 DEC 1918	Douglas AZ	Arlington
08742	Moorehead, Lizzie A.	68y	W	30 JUL 1912	Laurel MD	Glenwood
05839	Moorehead, Mamie E.	33y	C	29 NOV 1906	Philadelphia PA	Harmony
01637	Moorhead, W.E.C.	40y	W	28 NOV 1894	Los Angeles CA	Oak Hill
13765	Mopp, Edna Nantisha	1y	C	15 OCT 1916	Alex. Co. VA	Moore's
06229	Morales, Rafael E.	65y	W	2 OCT 1902	Guanabacoa, Cu.	Falls Church VA
08479	Moran, Francis Berger	61y	W	16 JAN 1912	Charlottesville VA	Rock Creek
08124	Moran, Francis S.	23y	W	21 MAY 1911	Wash. Grove MD	Congressional
03781	Moran, Irene Warwick	34y	W	3 FEB 1902	Hyattsville MD	Glenwood
14044	Moran, John, bricklayer	69y	W	22 MAR 1917	Roanoke VA	Rock Creek
02827	Moran, John Milton	45y	W	12 MAY 1899	Leabrook MD	Glenwood
08137	Moran, Kathrine	31y	W	1 JUN 1911	St. Louis MO	Rock Creek
06049	Moran, Lillian J.	6y	W	6 JUN 1906	Coney Island NY	Mt. Olivet
03867	Moran, Mary G.	73y	W	6 SEP 1902	Atlantic City NJ	Rock Creek
18366	Moran, Patrick Thomas	58y	W	22 FEB 1923	Baltimore MD	Mt. Olivet
14435	Moran, Thomas M.	81y	W	3 NOV 1917	Hyattsville MD	Glenwood

No.	Name of Deceased	Age	Race	Death Date	Place of Death	Place of Burial
03946	Moran, William Herman	5m	W	7 JUL 1902	Hyattsville MD	Glenwood
18105	Morce, R.N.	72y	W	30 SEP 1922	Miami FL	Cremated
04272	Mordecai, Alfred	—	W	5 NOV 1899	Seneca CA	Oak Hill
01252	Mordecai, William Maynadier	17y	W	8 SEP 1893	Springfield MA	Oak Hill
07101	Moreland, Elijah M.	34y	W	9 JUL 1909	Athens OH	Congressional
16149	Moreland, Joseph Leon	19y	W	16 DEC 1919	Capitol Hts. MD	Congressional
00496	Moreland, Thomas	45y	W	28 DEC 1890	Baltimore MD	Rock Creek
18276	Moreton, Emma J.	40y	W	17 JAN 1923	Durham NC	Congressional
18274	Moreton, Emma J. (Greenwell)	40y	W	17 JAN 1923	Durham NC	Clarendon VA
02465	Moretz, Harry J.	48y	W	9 MAY 1898	Seattle WA	Glenwood
12370	Morey, Fannie Copley	63y	W	30 MAY 1913	Dieta LA	Congressional
05974	Morey, Gwendolyn	4m	W	7 MAR 1907	New York NY	Rock Creek
07880	Morey, Kenneth	1y	W	19 DEC 1910	New York NY	Rock Creek
13871	Morey, William, s/o William	51y	W	13 DEC 1916	Bangor ME	Rock Creek
00977	Morfit, Catherine Campbell	93y	W	2 AUG 1893	Baltimore MD	Congressional
00305	Morfit, Henrietta S.	66y	W	4 APR 1890	Baltimore MD	Congressional
02009	Morfit, Jane Olivet	51y	W	9 AUG 1896	Baltimore MD	Congressional
06908	Morgan, Ann	78y	W	4 FEB 1909	Summit NJ	Rock Creek
08014	Morgan, Charles	39y	C	16 MAR 1911	Philadelphia PA	Harmony
01583	Morgan, Charles William	67y	W	31 JAN 1895	Woodside MD	Congressional
06801	Morgan, Cornelius, s/o C.	60y	C	3 NOV 1908	Catharpin VA	Arlington
05944	Morgan, David D.	75y	W	17 FEB 1907	Summit NJ	Rock Creek
06902	Morgan, David S.	67y	W	24 JAN 1909	Mt. Ranier MD	Glenwood
15240	Morgan, George	24y	C	20 OCT 1918	Takoma Park MD	Amherst Co. VA
02798	Morgan, Henry	36y	C	15 APR 1899	Philadelphia PA	Mt. Zion
04558	Morgan, James	36y	C	1 JAN 1904	Philadelphia PA	Mt. Zion
16121	Morgan, James Dudley	58y	W	21 NOV 1919	Chevy Chase MD	Rock Creek
05969	Morgan, James Henry	69y	W	2 MAR 1907	Baltimore MD	Rock Creek
07305	Morgan, James M.	49y	C	30 NOV 1909	Pittsburgh PA	Harmony
17549	Morgan, James P.	56y	W	26 NOV 1921	Cincinnati OH	Holyrood
13574	Morgan, Lizzie	67y	W	25 JUN 1916	Brentwood MD	Glenwood
01069	Morgan, Margaret M.	53y	W	8 APR 1893	Bethesda MD	Rock Creek
17060	Morgan, Mary E.	48y	C	22 MAR 1921	Ithaca NY	Harmony
15521	Morgan, Mary Ellen (Talbert)	76y	C	2 JAN 1919	Atlantic City NJ	Harmony
06244	Morgan, Mary L.	2y	W	26 SEP 1907	New York NY	Glenwood
17188	Morgan, Mary Susan	72y	W	27 MAY 1921	Indian Head MD	Glenwood
16878	Morgan, Meta E.	27y	C	28 DEC 1920	Baltimore MD	Payne's
02008	Morgan, Nora Deggie	68y	W	18 AUG 1896	Montclair NJ	Rock Creek
03582	Morgan, Patrick H.	57y	W	17 JUL 1901	Phoebus VA	Mt. Olivet
16507	Morgan, Rebecca	58y	W	26 MAY 1920	Philadelphia PA	Mt. Zion East
04847	Morganweek, Casper	28y	W	16 AUG 1904	Hancock MD	Prospect Hill
04175	Morkriter, Bessie	32y	W	10 FEB 1903	Pittsburgh PA	Mt. Olivet
06852	Morolli, Frank	23y	W	11 DEC 1908	Hyattsville MD	Mt. Olivet
00632½	Morris, Albert H.	32y	W	24 OCT 1891	Mt. Hope MD	Glenwood
03998	Morris, Alice R.	52y	W	14 AUG 1902	Atlantic City NJ	Oak Hill
03043	Morris, Benjamin	76y	W	20 DEC 1899	New York NY	Glenwood
05653	Morris, Charity	53y	C	22 JUL 1906	South River MD	Harmony
02209	Morris, Daniel	45y	C	5 JUN 1897	Railroad	Lynchburg VA
13874	Morris, Eliza	47y	C	17 DEC 1916	Rosslyn VA	Mt. Zion East
08554	Morris, Frank G.	43y	W	12 MAR 1912	Capitol Hts. MD	Mt. Olivet
01825	Morris, Fred	22y	C	21 NOV 1895	Philadelphia PA	Harmony
16657	Morris, Green B.	86y	W	13 AUG 1920	Saratoga Spg. NY	Oak Hill
07922	Morris, John	—	C	12 JAN 1911	Fairmont Hts. MD	Mt. Zion East
06692	Morris, Marie E.	8m	W	16 AUG 1908	Cottage City MD	Rock Creek
02079	Morris, Mary A.	86y	W	7 NOV 1896	Baltimore MD	Mt. Olivet
02080	Morris, Robert Murray	72y	W	7 DEC 1896	Philadelphia PA	Congressional
00747	Morris, Victor	43y	W	AUG 1891	Bell Air OH	Glenwood
17859	Morris, William	48y	W	13 MAY 1922	Philadelphia PA	Prospect Hill
11864	Morris, William H.	48y	W	24 JUN 1913	Cherrydale VA	Holyrood

District of Columbia Foreign Death Records, 1888-1923

No.	Name of Deceased	Age	Race	Death Date	Place of Death	Place of Burial
05940	Morris, William P.	49y	W	14 FEB 1907	Philadelphia PA	Glenwood
14642	Morrisey, Thomas S.	63y	W	14 FEB 1918	St. Petersburg FL	Glenwood
14677	Morrison, Alexander H.	72y	W	11 MAR 1918	Bethesda MD	Glenwood
16966	Morrison, Belvidera	76y	W	9 FEB 1921	Lancaster PA	Rock Creek
01319	Morrison, Bessie M.	24y	W	19 FEB 1894	Hinsdale MD	Oak Hill
01384	Morrison, Charles C., Capt.	45y	W	13 MAY 1894	Governor's Isl. NY	Oak Hill
03300	Morrison, Charles P.	9y	W	8 OCT 1900	Culpeper Co. VA	Oak Hill
01357	Morrison, Henry H.	23y	W	12 MAR 1894	Riverdale MD	Oak Hill
03862	Morrison, James R.	67y	W	24 APR 1902	Riverdale MD	Oak Hill
12403	Morrison, Jennie P.	50y	W	15 JUN 1914	Glendale MO	Arlington
06507	Morrison, Laura H.	32y	C	11 APR 1908	Arlington VA	Payne's
02815	Morrison, Martha Kearsly	45y	W	29 MAR 1899	Hyattsville MD	Oak Hill
17255	Morrison, Mary Ellis, Dr.	68y	W	25 JUN 1921	Newport News VA	Glenwood
06982	Morrison, Robert	34y	W	12 APR 1909	Campbell Co. KY	Laurel MD
03426	Morrison, Walter C.	34y	W	21 FEB 1901	Riverdale MD	Oak Hill
16483	Morrow, Clarence	47y	W	9 MAY 1920	PA	Fairfax VA
12713	Morrow, James P.	66y	W	11 JAN 1915	Seabrook MD	Rock Creek
17099	Morrow, Mary V.	79y	W	9 APR 1921	Falls Church VA	Fairmont WV
08843	Morrow, Virginia A. Travis	62y	W	16 SEP 1912	Ocean View VA	Glenwood
06103	Morse, George E.	35y	W	10 JUN 1907	New York NY	Oak Hill
02669	Morse, John B.	48y	W	30 NOV 1898	Stoneleigh VA	Congressional
14798	Morsell, Infant of H.J.	3h	W	7 MAY 1918	Chevy Chase MD	Glenwood
08305	Morsell, Mary Ellen (Collison)	79y	W	11 SEP 1911	Milwaukee WI	Oak Hill
07231	Morsell, Samuel T.G.	86y	W	8 OCT 1909	Avondale PA	Glenwood
14099	Morton, William A., Jr.	30y	W	21 APR 1917	Hyattsville MD	Glenwood
06889	Mosedale, William H.	2y	W	11 JAN 1909	Baltimore MD	Prospect Hill
12606	Moseley, Mary	24y	C	8 NOV 1914	Philadelphia PA	Moore's
08323	Moses, Edward F.	47y	W	22 SEP 1911	Relay MD	Congressional
00633	Moses, Frank Maloy	3y	W	29 JUN 1891	Morris Plains NJ	Oak Hill
01070	Moses, Guy	79y	W	10 MAR 1893	Palmyra NY	Rock Creek
00438	Moses, Louis B.	21y	W	12 APR 1867	Washington DC	Rock Creek
07175	Moses, Rebecca McK.	69y	W	26 AUG 1909	S. Bristol ME	Oak Hill
01636	Mosey, William	3y	W	25 MAR 1895	Kensington MD	Rock Creek
15605	Moss, Julian	16y	C	8 FEB 1919	Baltimore MD	Meadow MD
02743	Moss, Louis A.	6m	W	14 FEB 1899	Charlottesville VA	Mt. Olivet
05457	Mossell, Cornelia (Ruffin)	60y	C	4 FEB 1906	Norfolk VA	Harmony
13607	Mothershead, Eva H. (Hatch)	39y	W	18 JUL 1916	Mt. Holly VA	Rock Creek
03606	Mothershead, Mary A.	43y	W	8 AUG 1901	Richmond Co. VA	Mt. Olivet
14985	Motley, William L.	71y	C	19 AUG 1918	Petersburg VA	Arlington
17302	Mott, Annie	54y	C	12 JUL 1921	Huntsville MD	Payne's
13264	Moulden, Aquilla F.	76y	W	20 DEC 1915	Louisville KY	Glenwood
00634	Moulton, Annie R.	45y	W	9 JUL 1891	Wash. Grove MD	Glenwood
01584	Moulton, William	45y	C	20 DEC 1894	Boston MA	Mt. Zion
02384	Moultrie, Elizabeth	34y	C	20 JAN 1898	New York NY	Harmony
01172	Mount, James H.	—	W	21 OCT 1892	Hampton VA	Congressional
06010	Mount, Margaret J.	76y	W	2 APR 1907	Livingston Hts. VA	Rock Creek
16433	Mountcastle, Edwin K.	23y	W	12 APR 1920	Mt. Ranier MD	Rock Creek
13241	Mountcastle, George C.	68y	W	9 DEC 1915	Four Corners MD	Rock Creek
08441	Mountegriffe, Anna	71y	W	25 DEC 1911	Chicago IL	Mt. Olivet
16291	Mower, Charles Edward	60y	W	6 FEB 1920	Vienna VA	Oak Hill
03605	Mowrey, William F.	45y	W	3 AUG 1901	Houghton MI	Rock Creek
07809	Moxley, Dora Agnes	30y	W	7 DEC 1909	Chevy Chase MD	Prospect Hill
07112	Moxley, Infant of Henry	11m	W	17 JUL 1909	Kensington MD	Prospect Hill
13959	Moxley, James A.	65y	W	29 JAN 1917	Bethesda MD	Oak Hill
05819	Moxley, Willis S.	17y	W	17 NOV 1906	Annapolis Jct. MD	Rock Creek
03115	Moxon, Amanda B.	77y	W	5 MAR 1900	Vienna VA	Rock Creek
17866	Moyer, Earnest D.	68y	W	20 MAY 1922	Atlantic City NJ	Wash. Hebrew
17867	Moyer, Lottie	2yy	W	22 MAY 1922	Lorton VA	Glenwood
16817	Moyer, Rachael A.	45y	W	21 NOV 1920	Clarendon VA	Glenwood
03703	Moyers, Fannie Follett	65y	W	8 NOV 1901	Phillipsburg KS	Rock Creek

No.	Name of Deceased	Age	Race	Death Date	Place of Death	Place of Burial
03068	Moyers, George D.	6y	W	8 JUL 1866	Memphis TN	Rock Creek
02690	Moynihan, Michael	34y	W	30 DEC 1898	Philadelphia PA	Mt. Olivet
01639	Much, George W., ship carp.	43y	W	20 APR 1895	Baltimore MD	Congressional
08188	Much, Hattie M.	31y	W	8 JUL 1911	Brunswick MD	Congressional
03777	Mudd, Emily C.	23y	W	30 JAN 1902	Hyattsville MD	Mt. Olivet
00978	Mudd, George F.	8y	W	24 MAY 1893	Alexandria VA	Congressional
17018	Mudd, Irene Rosetta	31y	W	5 MAR 1921	Leesburg VA	Harmony
13314	Mudd, Joseph A.	73y	W	21 JAN 1916	Hyattsville MD	Mt. Olivet
09106	Mudd, Josephine	65y	C	2 MAR 1913	Chester PA	Mt. Olivet
05380	Mudd, Virginia Elizabeth	60y	W	26 NOV 1905	Hyattsville MD	Mt. Olivet
06869	Mueller, Annie Mary	73y	W	24 DEC 1908	Capitol Hts. MD	Prospect Hill
08144	Mueller, Carl	60y	W	10 JUN 1911	Atlantic City NJ	Prospect Hill
03569	Mueller, Dorothy	7m	W	8 JUL 1901	Clifton Sta. VA	Rock Creek
07711	Mueller, John Rudolph	73y	W	23 AUG 1910	Capitol Hts. MD	Prospect Hill
03759	Muir, Edla McPherson	28y	W	29 DEC 1901	New York NY	Oak Hill
03244	Muir, Marie	9m	W	28 JUL 1900	Riverdale MD	Mt. Olivet
17105	Muldoon, Francis	3d	W	14 APR 1921	Maryland Pk. MD	Mt. Olivet
03463	Mulholland, John H.	53y	W	29 MAR 1901	Lodge Landing VA	Glenwood
13746	Mull, John F.	43y	W	3 OCT 1916	Dayton OH	Arlington VA
15709	Mullan, Virginia B.	63y	W	4 APR 1919	Washington DC	Mt. Olivet
04489	Mullen, John	25y	W	24 OCT 1903	Philadelphia PA	Mt. Olivet
15662	Mullen, John A.	42y	W	6 MAR 1919	Detroit MI	Congressional
09103	Mullen, Katheryn W.	25y	W	3 MAR 1913	Capitol Hts. MD	Mt. Olivet
12107	Mullen, Katie	27y	W	26 NOV 1913	Capitol Hts. MD	Fredericksburg VA
16537	Mullen, Rachel	49y	C	14 JUN 1920	Forestville MD	Payne's
08357	Mullen, Va. Loreta, d/o Jos.	1y	W	13 OCT 1911	Ballston VA	Congressional
07882	Mullen, William	26y	C	18 DEC 1910	Pr. Geo. Co. MD	Payne's
06835	Mullen, William A., s/o Jos.	4m	W	2 DEC 1908	Ballston VA	Congressional
05439	Muller, F. Henrietta	58y	W	5 JAN 1906	Washington DC	London, Eng.
02932	Muller, Rufus A.	36y	W	4 SEP 1899	Presidio, S.F. CA	Glenwood
02639	Muller, William Oliver	19y	W	18 OCT 1898	Portsmouth VA	Congressional
03418	Mullery, James	57y	W	3 MAR 1900	Washington DC	Mt. Olivet[1]
06257	Mullican, Mary E.	60y	W	2 OCT 1907	Derwood MD	Glenwood
17606	Mulligan, William	29y	W	22 DEC 1921	Asheville NC	Rock Creek
06823	Mullikin, Emily	58y	W	18 NOV 1908	Baltimore MD	Congressional
17881	Mullin, Edward, Sr.	68y	W	30 MAY 1922	Berwyn MD	Congressional
06214	Mulvihill, John Thomas	15y	W	1 SEP 1907	Silver Spring MD	Rock Creek
06170	Muncaster, Harriet E.	75y	W	7 AUG 1907	Rockville MD	Oak Hill
03720	Muncaster, Magruder, Dr.	42y	W	28 NOV 1901	Rockville MD	Oak Hill
03810	Muncaster, Rosalie	27y	W	8 MAR 1902	Washington DC	Oak Hill
15156	Munch, Carl J.	28y	W	10 OCT 1918	Camp Hump. VA	St. Mary's
07494	Munday, Hattie Pauline	13y	W	7 APR 1910	Falls Church VA	Glenwood
05140	Mundheim, Adolph A.K.	35y	W	19 MAY 1905	Brooklyn NY	Wash. Hebrew
08270	Mundheim, Augusta	62y	W	22 AUG 1911	Asbury Park NJ	Wash. Hebrew
13222	Mundheim, Lewis	82y	W	28 NOV 1915	New York NY	Wash. Hebrew
02262	Mundheim, Talaman	14y	W	19 JUL 1897	St. Mary's Co. MD	Wash. Hebrew
00240	Mundy, F.N.	c.45y	W	12 DEC 1889	Bryan's Point MD	Congressional
15478	Munford, Edward S., Jr.	24y	W	24 DEC 1918	Hempstead NY	Richmond VA
17114	Munro, David Munro	61y	W	30 MAY 1921	Dallas TX	Oak Hill
07874	Munroe, Frank	41y	W	7 DEC 1910	Tucson AZ	Arlington VA
05499	Munroe, Infant of J.K.	SB	W	14 MAR 1906	Baltimore MD	Rock Creek
04110	Munson, Annie R.	72y	W	20 DEC 1902	Hyattsville MD	Rock Creek
16198	Munson, Daniel O.	87y	W	7 JAN 1920	Ft. Myer VA	Oak Hill
08651	Munson, Harmon A.	81y	W	31 MAY 1912	Hyattsville MD	Rock Creek
06958	Munson, Ruhamah (Bittinger)	76y	W	26 MAR 1909	Munson's Hill VA	Oak Hill
03965	Murdock, Amelia	74y	W	29 AUG 1902	Rockville MD	Oak Hill
00268	Murdock, Joseph	64y	W	17 JAN 1890	Alexandria VA	Holyrood

[1] Note of 16 FEB 1901, from Arlington National Cemetery, Ft. Meyer, for removal from grave #14021, buried 6 MAR 1900.

District of Columbia Foreign Death Records, 1888-1923

No.	Name of Deceased	Age	Race	Death Date	Place of Death	Place of Burial
01826	Murdock, Margaret	53y	W	1 DEC 1895	Alexandria VA	Holyrood
12594	Murff, David E., Rev.	55y	C	1 NOV 1914	Baltimore MD	Harmony
16578	Murphy, Charles J.	48y	W	4 JUL 1920	Jessup MD	Mt. Olivet
06230	Murphy, Clarence T.	28y	W	18 SEP 1907	Muirkirk MD	Laurel MD
02410	Murphy, Edward J., merchant	60y	W	11 MAR 1898	Lynchburg VA	Glenwood
15883	Murphy, Edward V.	76y	W	16 JUL 1919	Albany NY	Mt. Olivet
02466	Murphy, Elizabeth	84y	W	18 MAY 1898	Chillum MD	Rock Creek
05402	Murphy, Johanna	61y	W	19 DEC 1905	Chicago IL	Mt. Olivet
07979	Murphy, John S.	20y	W	20 FEB 1911	Elmira NY	Mt. Olivet
06849	Murphy, John T.	72y	W	9 DEC 1908	Crum Lynne PA	Mt. Olivet
06530	Murphy, John W., soldier	—	W	29 APR 1907	Philippine Isl.	Fall River MA
14514	Murphy, Louisa	41y	W	17 DEC 1917	New York NY	Glenwood
15555	Murphy, Margaret E.D.	19y	W	12 JAN 1919	Glen Dale MD	Glenwood
05138	Murphy, Mortimer F.	35y	W	19 MAY 1905	St. Dennis MD	Holyrood
00749	Murphy, Owen	9m	W	21 MAY 1891	Alex. Co. VA	Oak Hill
02549	Murphy, Rebecca O.	49y	W	16 AUG 1898	Colonial Bea. VA	Congressional
01253	Murphy, Thomas	23y	W	14 NOV 1893	Orsborne KS	Mt. Olivet
00979	Murphy, Thomas	89y	W	18 JUL 1893	Eureka Hall MD	Rock Creek
03347	Murphy, Thomas P.	18y	W	21 NOV 1900	Milton DE	Mt. Olivet
07320	Murphy, W. Oakes	58y	W	22 AUG 1908	Coronado CA	Rock Creek
02535	Murphy, William, stone cutter	32y	W	20 JUN 1898	Baltimore MD	Mt. Olivet
18081	Murray, Basil E.	66y	W	22 SEP 1922	Sykesville MD	Glenwood
08679	Murray, Clinton J., s/o Wm. H.	17y	C	20 JUN 1912	Rock Castle VA	Woodlawn
05697	Murray, Douglass	26y	W	15 AUG 1906	Colonial Bea. VA	Alexandria VA
02440	Murray, Eli H., Gen.	51y	W	18 NOV 1896	Bowling Green KY	Arlington VA
14035	Murray, Frank E.	24y	W	4 MAR 1917	Marquette MI	Glenwood
07942	Murray, Jennie	31y	W	13 DEC 1910	Baltimore MD	Congressional
00497	Murray, John	55y	W	27 FEB 1891	Baltimore MD	Mt. Olivet
06302	Murray, John	2d	W	10 NOV 1907	Baltimore MD	Rock Creek
13837	Murray, John T.	71y	W	30 NOV 1916	New York NY	Mt. Olivet
14688	Murray, Michael J.	24y	W	14 MAR 1918	Portage NY	Mt. Olivet
14386	Murray, Owen F.	55y	W	28 SEP 1917	Baltimore MD	Mt. Olivet
16734	Murray, Richard	35y	C	29 SEP 1920	Dauphin Co. PA	Falls Church VA
14671	Murray, Roger	31y	W	1 MAR 1918	Pittsburgh PA	Congressional
07480	Murray, Samuel	60y	C	23 MAR 1910	Wilmington DE	Arlington VA
16777	Murray, Sarah Jane	78y	W	24 OCT 1920	Chevy Chase MD	Glenwood
16875	Murray, William F.	30y	W	19 JUL 1919	Italy	Mt. Olivet
00748	Murray, William Henry	1y	C	19 DEC 1891	Annapolis MD	Graceland
04899	Murry, Mabel MM.	27y	W	16 SEP 1904	S. Poland ME	Oak Hill
12138	Musanti, Infant of J. Fred.	2h	W	27 DEC 1913	Capitol Hts. MD	St. Mary's
17619	Mussante, Celestina	72y	W	31 DEC 1921	Seat Pleasant MD	St. Mary's
13413	Musson, George E.	18y	W	16 MAR 1916	Baltimore MD	Rock Creek
02492	Muzzy, Charles Arthur	3y	W	29 JUL 1898	Brooklyn NY	Mt. Olivet
02411	Myer, Henrietta	76y	W	7 MAR 1898	Baltimore MD	Prospect Hill
15838	Myers, Charles C.	81y	W	18 JUN 1919	Potomac MD	Oak Hill
17417	Myers, David Arthur	7h	W	17 SEP 1921	Wash. Grove MD	Rock Creek
09100	Myers, Dorsey B.	49y	W	1 MAR 1913	Warwood WV	Glenwood
07285	Myers, Jane	57y	C	24 NOV 1909	Halls Hill VA	Boyce VA
04654	Myers, Joseph W.	—	—	22 JUN 1903	Ft. Russell WY	Congressional
03785	Myers, Louise Gennet	57y	W	2 FEB 1902	Huron SD	Oak Hill
16876	Myers, Matt F.A.	27y	W	30 SEP 1918	France	Mt. Olivet
01174	Myers, Stella Elmira	25y	W	17 OCT 1892	Montclair NJ	Oak Hill
06630	Myles, Annie	45y	W	4 JUL 1908	Ellicott MD	Sidgar MD
09018	Myles, Edgar P.	1y	C	6 JAN 1912	Fairmont Hts. MD	Mt. Olivet
06570	Myles, Francis A.	1y	C	29 MAY 1908	Pr. Geo. Co. MD	Mt. Olivet
05264	Myner, Harry C.	27y	W	20 AUG 1905	Canal Zone	Glenwood
18504	Myrick, Samuel	c.35y	C	23 APR 1923	New London CN	Arlington
05544	Mytinger, Mary Weems	72y	W	13 APR 1906	Bluefield WV	Glenwood

District of Columbia Foreign Death Records, 1888-1923

No.	Name of Deceased	Age	Race	Death Date	Place of Death	Place of Burial
N						
04010	Nachtigell, Edward F.	51y	W	8 SEP 1902	Harrisburg PA	Prospect Hill
11852	Naecker, Alma	1y	W	13 JUN 1913	Capitol Hts. MD	Congressional
01585	Nagle, Edward	43y	W	27 NOV 1894	Baltimore MD	Rock Creek
16620	Nallace, Maria	76y	C	23 JUL 1920	Takoma Park MD	Mt. Zion East
04816	Nalle, Edward J.	30y	C	24 JUL 1904	Takoma MD	Moore's
07400	Nalley, Catherine L.	68y	W	2 FEB 1910	Brightseat MD	Mt. Olivet
06429	Nalley, Doris Elizabeth	4m	W	11 FEB 1908	Landover MD	Mt. Olivet
15454	Nalley, Eunice G.	28y	W	16 DEC 1918	White Station MD	Mt. Olivet
01748	Nalley, Joseph L., farmer	68y	W	2 JUL 1895	Brightseat MD	Mt. Olivet
02606	Nalley, Levi H.	56y	W	29 SEP 1898	Baltimore MD	Rock Creek
02897	Nalls, Philip	8m	W	4 AUG 1899	Silver Hill MD	Rock Creek
07116	Nally, George G.	49y	W	17 JUL 1909	Hampton VA	Glenwood
15176	Nally, Richard	25y	W	15 OCT 1918	Alex. Co. VA	Mt. Olivet
12209	Nash, Elbert T.	19y	W	7 FEB 1914	Ithaca NY	Glenwood
04151	Nash, John	67y	C	26 JAN 1903	Hampton VA	Arlington VA
07667	Nash, Thomas A.	6m	W	3 AUG 1910	Kensington MD	Glenwood
01586	Nauck, Cora M.	27y	W	27 FEB 1895	Chicago IL	Glenwood
05615	Naumann, Alice J.	10m	W	30 JUN 1906	Riverdale MD	Glenwood
16757	Nayle, George W., Jr.	58y	W	13 OCT 1920	Kensington MD	Glenwood
07766	Naylor, Mary S.	69y	W	26 SEP 1910	Hyattsville MD	Congressional
16627	Naylor, William D.	60y	C	24 JUL 1920	New York NY	Moore's
17244	Neal, Florence N.P.	7m	C	18 JUN 1921	Fairmont Hts. MD	Payne's
15315	Neal, Ringold	40y	C	29 OCT 1918	New Haven CN	Woodlawn
16192	Neal, William F.G.	49y	W	31 DEC 1919	San Francisco CA	Marlboro MD
03412	Neale, Alice Russel	51y	W	5 FEB 1901	Philadelphia PA	Rock Creek
05802	Neale, Mary H.	68y	W	3 NOV 1906	Hyattsville MD	Mt. Olivet
04604	Neary, Elizabeth	7y	W	21 FEB 1904	Roanoke VA	Mt. Olivet
03939	Neary, Mary E.	29y	W	26 JUL 1902	Newport News VA	Mt. Olivet
14473	Needham, F.R.	27y	W	18 NOV 1917	Oklahoma City OK	Rock Creek
00132	Needham, George Francis	73y	W	16 AUG 1889	Chicago IL	Lanham MD
12995	Needham, Henry Beach	43y	W	17 JUN 1915	Versailles, Fra.	Rock Creek
13823	Neeley, Mary E.	73y	W	22 NOV 1916	Bedford PA	Arlington
13568	Neff, Charlotte Frances	75y	W	25 JUN 1916	Gaithersburg MD	Rock Creek
05394	Neff, Robert H.	33y	W	12 DEC 1905	Alexandria VA	New Market VA
15309	Neil, Francis	27y	W	28 OCT 1918	Camp Hump. VA	Mt. Olivet
06881	Neil, Louisa	62y	W	4 JAN 1909	Alexandria VA	Harmony
07449	Neill, Charlotte	35y	C	2 MAR 1910	Hendersonv. NC	Harmony
01378	Neill, George W., painter	44y	W	16 MAY 1894	New York NY	Oak Hill
02814	Neill, Louisa	5y	C	29 MAR 1899	Chillum MD	Harmony
01177	Neillson, Mary Archer	—	W	18 OCT 1892	Philadelphia PA	Oak Hill
14013	Neitzey, John F.	54y	W	25 FEB 1917	Hyattsville MD	Rock Creek
01884	Neitzey, Virginia	27y	W	7 FEB 1896	Riggs Farm MD	Rock Creek
14200	Nelligan, Wm. Henry McCoy	22y	W	1 JUL 1917	Petersburg VA	Mt. Olivet
08681	Nelsion, Lester	72y	W	23 JUN 1912	Edgemont MD	Prospect Hill
04747	Nelson, Albert	18y	W	1 JUN 1904	Falls Church VA	Glenwood
13833	Nelson, Alberta	54y	W	29 NOV 1916	Brentwood MD	Harmony
02914	Nelson, Alice Creighton	3m	W	16 AUG 1899	Brentwood MD	Congressional
14761	Nelson, Dennis	72y	C	15 APR 1918	Louisa Co. VA	Arlington
02757	Nelson, Dollie	32y	C	4 MAR 1898	Baltimore MD	Harmony
02929	Nelson, Eleanor	55y	W	29 AUG 1899	Moorefield VA	Holyrood
15524	Nelson, Helen Hunt	33y	W	5 JAN 1919	Salem VA	Glenwood
05925	Nelson, James E.	21y	C	1 FEB 1907	Brooklyn NY	Arlington
02628	Nelson, Jennie Chute	49y	W	1 OCT 1898	Oxon Hill MD	Congressional
04550	Nelson, John	32y	C	20 DEC 1903	Philadelphia PA	Harmony
18075	Nelson, John C.	52y	W	19 SEP 1922	Braddock Hts. MD	Mt. Olivet
02879	Nelson, Laura	17y	C	20 JUL 1899	Camp Springs MD	Moore's
13249	Nelson, Martin	64y	C	12 DEC 1915	New York NY	Mt. Zion East
14090	Nelson, Mary A.	79y	W	11 APR 1917	Oxford NY	Prospect Hill

District of Columbia Foreign Death Records, 1888-1923

No.	Name of Deceased	Age	Race	Death Date	Place of Death	Place of Burial
12227	Nelson, Parker A.	62y	W	18 FEB 1914	Philadelphia PA	Loudon Park MD
13619	Nelson, Virginia Marie	1y	W	26 JUL 1916	Alex. Co. VA	Glenwood
00225	Nelson, William	22y	C	2 NOV 1889	Montg. Co. MD	Christian
02618	Nelson, William T.	21y	W	15 SEP 1898	Boston MA	Arlington VA
04697	Nesbit, Ellen M.	67y	W	2 MAY 1904	Lowry MO	Rock Creek
01392	Nesbit, Francis P.	54y	W	21 APR 1894	Newport News VA	Rock Creek
03811	Nesbitt, Catherine S.	50y	W	10 MAR 1902	Riverdale MD	Mt. Olivet
14720	Nesmith, Mary E.	73y	W	27 MAR 1918	Flushing NY	Oak Hill
12312	Nestler, William	54y	W	6 NOV 1910	Washington DC	Glenwood
00498	Nestor, Thomas Edward	11m	W	15 DEC 1890	Charlton Hts. MD	Mt. Olivet
01255	Neuenschwander, Paul Victor	25y	W	15 OCT 1893	Magruder's Curve	Graceland
16665	Neuffer, Lawton W.	—	W	28 JUL 1920	Nutley, Eng.	Arlington
00982	Neumeyer, Francis S.	25y	W	23 JUL 1893	Potomac River	Mt. Olivet
06782	Neurich, Eric	3y	W	21 OCT 1908	Philadelphia PA	Glenwood
16842	Nevill, Johanna	87y	W	3 DEC 1920	Capitol Hts. MD	Mt. Olivet
17893	Nevitt, James C.	68y	W	7 JUN 1922	Bel Alton MD	Glenwood
14454	Nevitt, Joseph	21y	W	11 NOV 1917	Baltimore MD	Congressional
17217	Newberry, Milton Bradley	16y	W	7 JUN 1921	Highbridge MD	Cedar Hill
14609	Newbold, Annie E.	70y	W	28 JAN 1918	New York NY	Glenwood
06741	Newbold, C.K.	69y	W	16 SEP 1908	Railroad	Rock Creek
01178	Newbold, William Welch	14y	W	28 SEP 1892	Annapolis Jct. MD	Rock Creek
14603	Newby, James T., Rev.	43y	C	22 JAN 1918	Delaware Co. PA	Harmony
14416	Newcomb, Bryan	10y	W	16 OCT 1917	Falls Church VA	Cedar Hill
08439	Newcomb, George E.	69y	W	19 DEC 1911	Central Panama	Arlington
07075	Newcomb, Helen	7y	W	21 JUN 1909	Saranac Lake NY	Glenwood
01506	Newcomb, Sophie DeWolf	21y	W	10 OCT 1894	Falls Church VA	N. Adams MA
05491	Newhaus, Paul	50y	W	6 MAR 1906	Gaithersburg MD	Glenwood
01256	Newlands, John Cutler	1d	W	7 DEC 1893	Chevy Chase MD	Oak Hill
17228	Newlon, John Manly	68y	W	11 JUN 1921	Vienna VA	Glenwood
07120	Newlon, Mildred R., d/o H.E.	3m	W	20 JUL 1909	Ballston VA	Glenwood
16299	Newlon, William F., s/o Sam.	48y	W	FEB 1920	Winston-Sal. NC	Glenwood
01501	Newman, Augusta	61y	W	2 OCT 1894	Lakeland MD	Rock Creek
07875	Newman, Charles M.	41y	W	16 DEC 1910	Blue Ridge S. PA	Oak Hill
16630	Newman, Hilden Moller	59y	W	31 JUL 1920	Mt. Ranier MD	Glenwood
15332	Newman, Irving T.C.	22y	W	2 NOV 1918	Austin TX	Arlington
00027	Newman, John H.	71y	W	9 FEB 1889	Anne Arundel Co.	Oak Hill
00012	Newman, Joseph P.	35y	W	14 JUL 1888	Elbow Lake MN	Rock Creek
03675	Newman, Louisiana H.	77y	W	7 OCT 1901	Brentwood MD	Glenwood
07872	Newman, Martha E.	55y	C	13 DEC 1910	Bethesda MD	Harmony
15221	Newman, Mary E.	49y	W	17 OCT 1918	Cherrydale VA	Glenwood
14311	Newman, Mary E.	75y	W	22 AUG 1917	Falls Church VA	Oak Hill
05658	Newman, Mary Eva	25d	W	24 JUL 1906	College Park MD	Mt. Olivet
14141	Newman, Nancy	61y	C	16 MAY 1917	Torrington CN	Payne's
16414	Newman, Samuel	77y	W	30 MAR 1920	Bedford VA	Cremated
07064	Newman, Sarah	32y	C	15 JUN 1909	New York NY	Harmony
12572	Newman, Walter E.	56y	W	19 OCT 1914	Wash. Grove MD	Glenwood
02952	Newman, Walter George	8y	W	19 SEP 1899	Madison Co. VA	Rock Creek
02329	Newman, William	14y	W	20 SEP 1897	Berkeley Sp. WV	Glenwood
00870	Newmayer, Lewis R.	30y	W	15 JUL 1892	Riverside CA	Congressional
08774	Newmyer, Anna Pallas	24y	W	21 AUG 1912	Asheville NC	Wash. Hebrew
14797	Newsome, Donnessa	22y	C	5 MAY 1918	New York NY	Harmony
07467	Newton, Francis	70y	C	13 MAR 1910	Frederick Co. MD	Surrattsville MD
08419	Newton, Grace	30y	W	10 DEC 1911	Baltimore MD	Rock Creek
04192	Newton, Harry W.	33y	W	1 APR 1903	Philadelphia PA	Rock Creek
05375	Newton, Henry F.	21y	W	20 NOV 1905	New York NY	Rock Creek
07077	Newton, Herbert	SB	W	21 JUN 1909	New York NY	Congressional
12410	Newton, Jennie	48y	C	19 JUN 1914	Brentwood MD	Harmony
04035	Newton, Jessie M.	55y	W	25 OCT 1902	Brentwood MD	Oak Hill
09020	Newton, John A.	51y	C	4 JAN 1913	Westchester NY	Harmony
14223	Newton, Lillie Graham	66y	W	11 JUL 1917	Asheville NC	Cremated

No.	Name of Deceased	Age	Race	Death Date	Place of Death	Place of Burial
07076	Newton, Mary	31y	W	21 JUN 1909	New York NY	Congressional
07077	Newton, Mary	SB	W	21 JUN 1909	New York NY	Congressional
08586	Newton, Mildred D.	21y	W	5 APR 1912	Falls Church VA	Rock Creek
14397	Newton, Minnie E.	57y	W	4 OCT 1917	Gettysburg PA	Alexandria VA
05372	Newton, Susan	1y	W	19 NOV 1905	Columbus GA	Rock Creek
12910	Nicholas, Willie G.	62y	W	2 MAY 1915	New York NY	Glenwood
04968	Nicholls, Ellen R.	68y	W	21 FEB 1904	Warrenton GA	Oak Hill
12923	Nichols, Amanda	65y	C	12 MAY 1915	Fairmont Hts. MD	Harmony
00247	Nichols, Charles Henry	69y	W	16 DEC 1889	New York NY	Congressional
07531	Nichols, Frank	66y	W	23 DEC 1909	Johnstown PA	Congressional
16770	Nichols, Frank Stewart	51y	W	15 OCT 1920	Houston TX	Congressional
08046	Nichols, Henry E.	67y	W	1 APR 1911	Riverdale MD	Glenwood
03414	Nichols, Hugh H.	44y	C	5 FEB 1901	Philadelphia PA	Woodlawn
09013	Nichols, Indiana J.	68y	W	2 JAN 1912	Brownville NY	Glenwood
15924	Nichols, Pious N.	9y	C	10 AUG 1919	Seat Pleasant MD	Mt. Olivet
05641	Nichols, Richard	11m	C	13 JUL 1906	Seat Pleasant MD	Mt. Olivet
01508	Nichols, William Cameron	20y	W	13 OCT 1894	Worcester MA	Congressional
01071	Nicholson, A. Jesup, Lt.	40y	W	22 MAY 1893	Hamilton VA	Oak Hill
15833	Nicholson, Angie	29y	W	15 JUN 1919	Baltimore MD	Mt. Olivet
17726	Nicholson, Anna A.	18y	W	6 MAR 1922	Baltimore MD	Forestville MD
13500	Nicholson, Blanche	6y	W	11 MAY 1916	Rockville MD	Rock Creek
13649	Nicholson, Carl	1y	W	10 AUG 1916	Montg. Co. MD	Congressional
05160	Nicholson, Caroline	64y	W	6 JUN 1905	Lay Hill MD	Rock Creek
06772	Nicholson, Charlotte G. (Gunn)	46y	W	13 OCT 1908	Hamilton VA	Oak Hill
17534	Nicholson, Edward Hamilton	3m	W	20 NOV 1921	Silver Spring MD	Mt. Olivet
08348	Nicholson, Edward J.H.	3y	W	22 FEB 1909	Tehachapi CA	Congressional
18323	Nicholson, Edward S.	1y	W	5 FEB 1923	Maryland Pk. MD	Mt. Olivet
02213	Nicholson, Hannah M.	68y	W	6 JUN 1897	Poolesville MD	Oak Hill
00354	Nicholson, Reginald Fairfax, Jr.	10y	W	2 JUL 1890	Winchester VA	Oak Hill
15344	Nicholson, Susan C.	74y	W	11 NOV 1918	Rockville MD	Rock Creek
06384	Nicholson, William	67y	W	8 JAN 1908	Burlington NJ	Congressional
12284	Nicholson, William	71y	W	29 MAR 1914	Wilmington DE	Glenwood
02081	Nicholson, William, Dr.	42y	W	3 OCT 1896	Salem MA	Congressional
05915	Nickelson, Henrietta	43y	C	26 JAN 1907	Montg. Co. PA	Payne's
17869	Nickens, Mabel	7y	C	22 MAY 1922	Riverdale MD	Mt. Olivet
08522	Nickens, Oliver, s/o Edwin	26y	C	5 FEB 1912	Waterbury CN	Avalon VA
07475	Nickins, James	70y	C	21 MAR 1910	Fairmont Hts. MD	Warrenton VA
15767	Nickins, Leroy	42y	C	4 MAY 1919	Philadelphia PA	Moore's
08490	Niebold, George W.	30y	W	19 JAN 1912	Colo. Spgs. CO	Rock Creek
16110	Niedfeldt, Henry C.	49y	W	16 NOV 1919	Philadelphia PA	Prospect Hill
04452	Niedfeldt, Herman J.	34y	W	6 MAY 1903	Manila, P.I.	Prospect Hill
15112	Niedomski, Louis A.	26y	W	6 OCT 1918	Fairfax Co. VA	Arlington
17973	Niemeyer, Mary C.	85y	W	21 JUL 1922	Westport CN	Prospect Hill
08745	Niemeyer, William Prince	4h	W	2 AUG 1912	Bethesda MD	Prospect Hill
11939	Nies, Harry	51y	W	7 AUG 1913	Stanton DE	Baltimore MD
07037	Nightingale, Mabel	24y	C	21 MAY 1909	Philadelphia PA	Payne's
06832	Nixdorff, Eliza Parkins	64y	W	29 NOV 1908	Forest Glen MD	Frederick MD
04471	Nixon, Amanda	43y	C	8 OCT 1903	Philadelphia PA	Mt. Olivet
08799	Nixon, Annice D., d/o Rich. B.	25y	W	3 SEP 1912	Colonial Bea. VA	Glenwood
02513	Nixon, John B.	70y	W	14 JUL 1898	Somerset Co. NJ	Arlington VA
06498	Nixon, Julia E.	30y	W	8 APR 1908	Livingston NY	Fairfax C.H. VA
00556	Nixon, L.G., Mrs.	23y	W	10 MAY 1891	Glendale MD	Rock Creek
00752	Nixon, Libbie	18m	W	10 DEC 1891	Glendale MD	Rock Creek
07916	Nixon, Lucinda A.	70y	W	11 JAN 1911	Hyattsville MD	Glenwood
08165	Nixon, Marie J.L.	2y	W	28 JUN 1911	Hyattsville MD	Mt. Olivet
07787	Nixon, Thomas A.	69y	W	14 OCT 1910	Hyattsville MD	Glenwood
01320	Nixon, William A.	68y	W	28 FEB 1894	Granville NY	Rock Creek
01452	Nixson, Charlott	69y	W	2 AUG 1894	Pr. Geo. Co. MD	Rock Creek
00144	Noah, Eliza B.	51y	W	26 AUG 1889	New York NY	Oak Hill
09199	Noble, Alice	63y	W	5 MAY 1913	Philadelphia PA	Oak Hill

District of Columbia Foreign Death Records, 1888-1923   187

No.	Name of Deceased	Age	Race	Death Date	Place of Death	Place of Burial
15196	Noble, Charles	34y	W	15 OCT 1918	Baltimore MD	Rock Creek
15298	Noble, Charles C.	34y	W	11 OCT 1918	Baltimore MD	Rock Creek
14624	Noble, Charles J.	64y	W	3 FEB 1918	Baltimore MD	Rock Creek
13122	Noble, Eliza C. (Brown)	66y	W	25 SEP 1915	Stamford CN	Arlington
04858	Noble, Emma Matilda	67y	W	20 AUG 1904	Falls Church VA	Rock Creek
01648	Noerr, Grace L.	25y	W	23 APR 1895	Asheville NC	Oak Hill
00557	Nokes, George W.	55y	W	20 JUN 1891	Centreville MD	Congressional
15796	Nolan, Catherine Teresa	42y	W	26 MAY 1919	Takoma Park MD	Holyrood
15948	Nolan, Henry F.	43y	W	18 AUG 1919	Norfolk VA	Arlington
17551	Nolan, John J.	53y	W	26 NOV 1921	New York NY	Holyrood
00753	Nolan, Mary	57y	W	15 FEB 1892	Chicago IL	Mt. Olivet
00500	Nolan, Mary Elizabeth	55y	W	15 FEB 1891	Baltimore MD	Mt. Olivet
14344	Nolan, Tarissa	14y	W	6 SEP 1917	Hagerstown MD	Congressional
00182	Nolte, August	77y	W	7 OCT 1889	Cincinnati OH	Glenwood
00499	Nolte, Henry	71y	W	6 MAR 1891	Sligo MD	St. Mary's
03261	Noonan, Ann	68y	W	12 AUG 1900	Warren VA	Holyrood
15073	Noone, James F.	22y	W	1 OCT 1918	Pr. Geo. Co. VA	Holyrood
12732	Noone, Mary	62y	W	23 JAN 1915	Suffolk Co. NY	Holyrood
06749	Noordzy, Henry C.	52y	W	25 SEP 1908	New York NY	Mt. Olivet
07669	Norbeck, Lewis Eugene	53y	W	4 AUG 1910	Columbia PA	Mt. Olivet
17564	Nordlinger, Jane Henrietta	3m	W	1 DEC 1921	Scranton PA	Wash. Hebrew
17799	Nordlinger, Tyler	57y	W	14 APR 1922	New York NY	Wash. Hebrew
04743	Norfleck, Andrew	73y	C	28 MAY 1904	Ballston VA	Baptist
06757	Norfleet, Lavenia	68y	C	5 OCT 1908	Clarendon VA	Baptist
03600	Norgaard, Erik Andreas	10m	W	3 AUG 1901	Norfolk VA	Rock Creek
06318	Norley, Webster, F.	23y	W	8 JAN 1904	Riverdale MD	Glenwood
02117	Norman, Katharine Elizabeth	26y	W	28 JAN 1897	Harrisonburg VA	Oak Hill
01587	Norman, Mary Ellen	54y	C	14 FEB 1895	Shrewsbury NJ	Harmony
12171	Norman, Susan	74y	C	19 JAN 1914	Sterling VA	Payne's
03301	Norment, Samuel	1y	W	19 AUG 1881	Suffolk VA	Glenwood
06574	Normyle, Margaret	65y	W	1 JUN 1908	Staunton VA	Mt. Olivet
03159	Norris, Albert H.	43y	W	6 APR 1900	Baltimore MD	Oak Hill
16593	Norris, Delia L. (Clark)	80y	W	12 JUL 1920	Metuchen NJ	Rock Creek
18431	Norris, Dorothy	8y	W	20 MAR 1923	Falls Church VA	Glenwood
00277	Norris, Hattie B.	1y	C	3 FEB 1890	Alexandria VA	Harmony
13747	Norris, Hiram	77y	C	2 OCT 1916	Hampton VA	Harmony
07390	Norris, John	48y	C	24 JAN 1910	New York NY	Harmony
04283	Norris, Laura	61y	W	19 APR 1903	Oxon Hill MD	Glenwood
14001	Norris, Manning	11y	W	20 FEB 1917	Falls Church VA	Glenwood
03405	Norris, Maria	25y	W	24 JAN 1901	Newark NJ	Mt. Zion
01321	Norris, Mary Elizabeth	2y	C	7 FEB 1894	Garrett Park MD	Congressional
01649	Norris, Precilla	75y	C	26 APR 1895	New York NY	Harmony
02553	Norris, Richard	48y	C	11 AUG 1898	Halls Hill VA	Harmony
17693	Norris, Virginia Kelley	27y	W	13 FEB 1922	Atlanta GA	Mt. Olivet
00330	North, Rachel	63y	C	22 MAY 1890	Atlantic City NJ	Holyrood
03073	Norton, Alice R.	13y	C	20 JAN 1900	Landover MD	Mt. Olivet
16089	Norton, Amos Leonard	15y	W	4 NOV 1919	Mt. Ranier MD	Rock Creek
17741	Norton, Amy R.	84y	W	15 MAR 1922	Arlington Co. VA	Congressional
09168	Norton, Charles A., Sgt.	—	W	—	Manague, Nic.	Arlington
12382	Norton, Chester	c.21y	C	30 MAY 1914	Brentwood MD	Bladensburg MD
12384	Norton, Chester F.A.	17y	C	30 MAY 1914	Brentwood MD	Mt. Olivet
13149	Norton, Ellen	4y	W	14 OCT 1915	Mt. Ranier MD	Prospect Hill
00640	Norton, John H.	22y	C	7 AUG 1891	Harpers Ferry WV	Harmony
00871	Norton, Julia Estelle	9m	W	26 AUG 1892	Hyattsville MD	Mt. Olivet
05068	Norton, Mary E.	72y	W	28 MAR 1905	Brooklyn NY	Arlington
15263	Norton, Nettie	41y	C	23 OCT 1918	Brentwood MD	Mt. Olivet
00271	Norton, Oliver Wilburt	3y	W	19 JAN 1890	Arlington VA	Prospect Hill
03297	Norton, Saml.	20y	C	4 OCT 1900	Tuxedo MD	Mt. Olivet
17002	Norton, Sarah Dorcas	68y	W	26 FEB 1921	Princess Anne MD	Cremated
12376	Norton, Tobin	35y	C	24 APR 1914	Panama, C.Z.	Mt. Olivet

No.	Name of Deceased	Age	Race	Death Date	Place of Death	Place of Burial
16565	Norton, Vivian I.	12y	W	27 JUN 1920	Mt. Ranier MD	Rock Creek
00754	Norton, William B.	1m	C	7 MAR 1892	Pr. Geo. Co. MD	Dean's Family
08749	Norton, William H.	72y	W	2 AUG 1912	Webster NY	Arlington
03646	Norton, William Henry	65y	W	15 SEP 1901	Forest Glen MD	Ithaca NY
12252	Norton, Winnie N.	75y	W	9 MAR 1914	Mt. Ranier MD	Mt. Olivet
08265	Norvell, Stevens T.	76y	W	20 AUG 1911	Ogunquit ME	Arlington
16336	Norwood, Eleanor M.	72y	W	23 FEB 1920	Baltimore MD	Glenwood
06680	Norwood, Thomas	70y	W	9 AUG 1908	Blue Ridge S. PA	Glenwood
14739	Noske, Carl F.	9y	W	8 APR 1918	Brentwood MD	Prospect Hill
14557	Noske, Naomi T.	17y	W	6 JAN 1918	Brentwood MD	Prospect Hill
13192	Nottingham, Julian Randolph	69y	W	8 NOV 1915	New York NY	Congressional
13068	Nottingham, Martena	58y	W	23 AUG 1915	Maywood VA	Congressional
06316	Nourse, Charles J.	57y	W	18 NOV 1907	New York NY	Rock Creek
03795	Nourse, Isabella Lucretia	80y	W	18 FEB 1902	Meadows MD	Congressional
14281	Nourse, James B.	88y	W	2 AUG 1917	Casanova VA	Rock Creek
18405	Novak, Mary	30y	W	10 MAR 1923	Takoma Park MD	Glenwood
05506	Nowell, Sadie Cecelia	22y	W	21 MAR 1906	Frederick MD	Glenwood
13145	Noyes, Clara	72y	W	9 OCT 1915	Annapolis MD	Oak Hill
06446	Noyes, Crosby Stuart	83y	W	21 FEB 1908	Pasadena CA	Rock Creek
06400	Noyes, Edward	24y	W	21 JAN 1908	Chattanooga TN	Mt. Olivet
03808	Noyes, Henry C.	72y	W	4 MAR 1902	Cincinnati OH	Oak Hill
16513	Nubee, Mollie Watson	54y	W	1 JUN 1920	College Park MD	Rock Creek
07401	Nutting, Elizabeth	53y	W	2 FEB 1910	Takoma Park MD	Rock Creek
05313	Nye, Frank Edward	38y	W	6 OCT 1905	Chicago IL	Arlington
16930	Nye, Gloria	8m	W	22 JAN 1921	Baltimore MD	Wash. Hebrew
16224	Nymark, John R.W.	54y	W	19 JAN 1920	Indian Head MD	Prospect Hill
11837	Nymark, Marian	9m	W	30 MAY 1913	Indian Head MD	Prospect Hill

No.	Name of Deceased	Age	Race	Death Date	Place of Death	Place of Burial
O						
02136	O'Brien, Annie	4m	W	26 FEB 1897	Alex. Co. VA	Holyrood
17206	O'Brien, Annie	63y	W	1 JUN 1921	Hyattsville MD	Mt. Olivet
03280	O'Brien, Cornelius W.	16y	W	1 SEP 1900	Branchville MD	Mt. Olivet
05074	O'Brien, Emma Katherine	35y	W	1 APR 1905	Huntington WV	Glenwood
13087	O'Brien, James Lewis	68y	W	2 SEP 1915	Sligo MD	Congressional
04023	O'Brien, Jennie E.	13y	W	6 SEP 1902	Colonial Bea. VA	Mt. Olivet
01829	O'Brien, Julia	2y	W	27 OCT 1895	Ft. Myer Hts. VA	Holyrood
00502	O'Brien, Margaret	44y	W	4 DEC 1890	Brooklyn NY	Holyrood
00259	O'Brien, Mary	76y	W	6 JAN 1890	Pinkney MI	Mt. Olivet
00013	O'Brien, Mary	60y	—	20 JAN 1889	Philadelphia PA	Mt. Olivet
18340	O'Brien, Mary E.	78y	W	11 FEB 1923	Baltimore MD	Glenwood
18394	O'Brien, Mary Loretta	67y	W	7 MAR 1923	Clarendon VA	Arlington
12485	O'Brien, William	19y	W	16 AUG 1914	Oakland MD	Holyrood
00239	O'Brien, William	45y	W	9 DEC 1889	New York NY	Mt. Olivet
12223	O'Brien, William B.	2y	W	18 FEB 1914	Cherrydale VA	St. Mary's
14114	O'Brine, John M.	c.45y	W	28 APR 1917	Dauphin Co. PA	Arlington
04357	O'Connell, Deborah	38y	W	17 JUN 1903	Pittsburgh PA	Mt. Olivet
07491	O'Connell, Eva L.	37y	W	29 MAR 1910	San Francisco CA	Oak Hill
12092	O'Connell, Jeremiah D.	77y	W	13 NOV 1913	Chicago IL	Mt. Olivet
06603	O'Connell, Katie, d/o Daniel	33y	W	23 JUN 1908	Charlottesville VA	Mt. Olivet
07631	O'Connell, Margaret Bouttelier	63y	W	12 JUL 1910	Pittsfield MA	Arlington
13912	O'Connell, Mary Ellen	70y	W	4 JAN 1917	Chicago IL	Mt. Olivet
01072	O'Connell, Michael J.	44y	W	21 MAR 1893	Annapolis MD	Mt. Olivet
00503	O'Connell, Timothy	—	W	5 JAN 1891	Surrattsville MD	Mt. Olivet
12648	O'Conner, John Joseph	32y	W	8 DEC 1914	Norfolk VA	Arlington
07270	O'Conner, Katie	27y	W	10 NOV 1909	Friendship H. MD	Mt. Olivet
02441	O'Conner, Sarah Jane	49y	W	18 JAN 1896	Chicago IL	Rock Creek
04972	O'Connor, Bryan F.	51y	W	29 NOV 1904	New York NY	Mt. Olivet
12401	O'Connor, Caatherine	77y	W	13 JUN 1914	Seat Pleasant MD	Mt. Olivet
08721	O'Connor, Elnora	4m	W	15 JUL 1912	Capitol Hts. MD	Mt. Olivet
15658	O'Connor, Francis Anthony	19y	W	3 MAR 1919	Paris Island SC	Holyrood
06618	O'Connor, George J.	1y	W	28 JUN 1908	Capitol Hts. MD	Mt. Olivet
01358	O'Connor, James F.	30y	W	17 MAY 1894	Tucson AZ	Mt. Olivet
18522	O'Connor, John F.	65y	W	2 MAY 1923	Alexandria VA	Mt. Olivet
15358	O'Connor, John F.	26y	W	13 NOV 1918	Camp Wads. SC	Mt. Olivet
15358	O'Connor, John F.	46y	W	13 NOV 1918	Spart. Co. SC	—[1]
12267	O'Connor, John J.	35y	W	25 MAR 1914	Laurel MD	Mt. Olivet
06277	O'Connor, Kate	51y	W	19 OCT 1907	Mt. Hope MD	Glenwood[2]
08635	O'Connor, Marie M.	25y	W	14 MAY 1912	Capitol Hts. MD	Mt. Olivet
08246	O'Connor, Mary G.	4m	W	10 AUG 1911	Capitol Hts. MD	Mt. Olivet
05400	O'Connor, Mary L.	35y	W	16 DEC 1905	Baltimore Co. MD	Mt. Olivet
04206	O'Connor, Patrick, farmer	71y	W	20 MAR 1903	Annandale VA	Mt. Olivet
15293	O'Connor, Teresa	16y	W	26 OCT 1918	Capitol Hts. MD	Mt. Olivet
08184	O'Connor, Teresa F.	3m	W	8 JUL 1911	Capitol Hts. MD	Mt. Olivet
07196	O'Connor, Thomas, s/o Mich.	82y	W	13 SEP 1909	Fairfax Co. VA	Holyrood
17207	O'Dea, Margaret	65y	W	2 JUN 1921	Montg. Co. MD	Mt. Olivet
02264	O'Donnell, Emma Reinhardt	11m	W	14 AUG 1897	Summit Pt. WV	Mt. Olivet
05648	O'Donnell, Irene	5y	W	18 JUL 1906	Frederick MD	Mt. Olivet
03341	O'Donnell, Thomas A.	35y	W	18 NOV 1900	Baltimore MD	Congressional
12275	O'Donoghue, Cornelius	83y	W	29 MAR 1914	River Rd. MD	Holyrood
00060	O'Donoghue, Mrs. D.	48y	W	21 APR 1889	Charlotte NC	Mt. Olivet
12415	O'Dwyer, Rosena M.	65y	W	26 JUN 1914	New York NY	Rock Creek
06712	O'Grady, James P.	31y	W	1 SEP 1908	Chicago IL	Mt. Olivet
14595	O'Gray, Mary Louise	52y	W	21 JAN 1918	Lanham MD	Congressional

---

[1] Certificate is filed and filmed out of order, behind #15055.
[2] Removed 18 NOV 1907 to Mt. Olivet Cemetery.

No.	Name of Deceased	Age	Race	Death Date	Place of Death	Place of Burial
17907	O'Hagan, Margaret	84y	W	17 JUN 1922	Baltimore MD	Mt. Olivet
16346	O'Hagan, Mary	79y	W	26 FEB 1920	New York NY	Mt. Olivet
04015	O'Hagan, Oswald H.	26y	W	11 SEP 1902	Denver CO	Mt. Olivet
03769	O'Hara, Julia	75y	W	27 JAN 1902	Philadelphia PA	Methodist
07339	O'Hern, Ella	34y	W	21 DEC 1909	Indian Head MD	Mt. Olivet
02083	O'Kane, Simon, Capt.	57y	W	12 OCT 1896	Woodside MD	Arlington VA
03845	O'Leary, Charles P.	1m	W	7 APR 1902	Alexandria VA	Mt. Olivet
02775	O'Leary, Charles Randolph	11d	W	21 JAN 1899	Philadelphia PA	Mt. Olivet
05668	O'Leary, Mary	45y	W	31 JUL 1906	Baltimore MD	Mt. Olivet
02956	O'Leary, Michael	80y	W	24 SEP 1899	Annapolis MD	Mt. Olivet
17497	O'Leary, Timothy Stephen	60y	W	31 OCT 1921	Portsmouth VA	Arlington
08458	O'Neal, Mary	63y	W	4 JAN 1912	Occoquan VA	Mt. Olivet
12689	O'Neal, William C.	57y	W	30 DEC 1914	Carroll Co. MD	Tenallytown M.
15661	O'Neal, William E.	38y	C	6 MAR 1919	Dupont Hts. MD	Payne's
04651	O'Neil, Elizabeth A.	70y	W	31 MAR 1904	Sykesville MD	Tenallytown M.
00181	O'Neil, Hugh J., s/o Bernard	84y	W	18 OCT 1889	Norfolk VA	Mt. Olivet
09048	O'Neil, Owen	68y	W	25 JAN 1913	Hampton VA	Arlington
12238	O'Neill, Elnora	1y	W	24 FEB 1914	Bladensburg MD	Mt. Olivet
15262	O'Neill, Eugene G.	18y	W	23 OCT 1918	Baltimore MD	Mt. Olivet
01750	O'Neill, James	32y	W	22 JUL 1895	Chicago IL	Mt. Olivet
02981	O'Neill, James	78y	W	27 OCT 1899	Burlington NJ	Oak Hill
09024	O'Neill, John Francis	39y	W	9 JAN 1913	Pittsburgh PA	Mt. Olivet
11984	O'Neill, John P.	71y	W	29 AUG 1913	Hampton VA	Arlington
03691	O'Reilly, Philip M.	22y	W	24 OCT 1901	Ft. Monroe VA	Arlington VA
05146	O'Rourke, James W.	52y	W	24 MAY 1905	Cincinnati OH	Mt. Olivet
05354	O'Rourke, John	43y	W	8 NOV 1905	Newark OH	Mt. Olivet
05090	O'Rourke, Morris	40y	W	18 APR 1905	Chicago IL	Mt. Olivet
06771	O'Rourke, Patrick	67y	W	1891	Nanticoke PA	Mt. Olivet
07089	O'Rourke, Patrick T., s/o Pat.	39y	W	30 JUN 1909	Bridgeport CN	Mt. Olivet
08616	Oberholtz, Alma	18y	W	2 MAY 1912	Rockville MD	Mt. Olivet
02799	Oberly, John H.	61y	W	15 APR 1899	Concord NH	Rock Creek
16142	Obert, Hamilton Sousa	4h	W	9 DEC 1919	New York NY	Rock Creek
00501	Oberteuffer, Helen	1y	W	6 FEB 1891	Baltimore MD	Oak Hill
06956	Obold, William Alphonse	1½d	W	1 APR 1909	Tuxedo MD	Mt. Olivet
05587	Ockershausen, August	73y	W	1 JUN 1906	New York NY	Oak Hill
03523	Ockershausen, Caroline	63y	W	24 MAY 1901	Brooklyn NY	Oak Hill
04956	Ockershausen, John	81y	W	13 NOV 1904	Flushing NY	Oak Hill
07807	Ockert, Louise E.	70y	W	29 OCT 1910	Augusta GA	Congressional
14142	Odell, Aaron	55y	C	17 MAY 1917	Alexandria VA	Harmony
15509	Odell, Albert S., s/o William	47y	W	21 DEC 1918	Los Angeles CA	Wash. Hebrew
09034	Oden, Sophia	23y	W	11 JAN 1913	Hot Springs AR	Prospect Hill
01650	Odlun, Catherine	74y	W	12 APR 1895	Boston MA	Mt. Olivet
14040	Oehmann, Sarah	66y	W	21 MAR 1917	Detroit MI	Mt. Olivet
02082	Oertly, Frederick E.	21y	W	28 OCT 1896	Edgefield VA	Oak Hill
16305	Offman, Lena M.	50y	W	10 FEB 1920	Brentwood MD	Glenwood
14453	Offord, Louis Montgomery	46y	C	10 NOV 1917	Elkridge MD	Woodlawn
04429	Offutt, Anna E.D.	24y	W	2 SEP 1903	Ashburn VA	Holyrood
03413	Offutt, Anna M.	75y	W	9 FEB 1901	Bethesda MD	Oak Hill
07914	Offutt, Infant of William L.	SB	W	11 JAN 1911	Chevy Chase MD	Rock Creek
14735	Offutt, Mary A. (Lynch)	68y	W	5 APR 1918	Ridgewood NJ	Mt. Olivet
07433	Offutt, Richard Grafton	19y	W	23 FEB 1910	Bethesda MD	Oak Hill
03995	Offutt, Sarah A.	64y	W	24 AUG 1902	Bowie MD	Holyrood
05672	Offutt, Susana M.	69y	W	3 AUG 1906	Difficult Run VA	Holyrood
04949	Ogawa, Sangi (Japanese)	22y	—	29 AUG 1904	Hampton VA	Cremated
01885	Ogden, Allis W.	64y	W	14 FEB 1896	Riverdale MD	Rock Creek
02173	Ogden, Ann M.	57y	W	17 MAR 1897	Cortland NY	Rock Creek
05476	Ogden, Herbert G.	59y	W	25 FEB 1906	Ft. Monroe VA	Oak Hill
04678	Ogden, Joseph Warren	18y	W	19 APR 1904	Atlantic City NJ	Oak Hill
04269	Ogden, Julian S.	56y	W	27 APR 1903	Philadelphia PA	Arlington
13196	Ogden, Lucy	62y	W	10 NOV 1915	Baltimore MD	Newark NJ

District of Columbia Foreign Death Records, 1888-1923

No.	Name of Deceased	Age	Race	Death Date	Place of Death	Place of Burial
02945	Ogg, Elmer A.	25y	W	12 SEP 1899	Falls Church VA	Rock Creek
05483	Ogle, Herbert S.	21y	W	2 MAR 1906	Glen Echo MD	Holyrood
04223	Ogle, John R.	45y	W	2 MAR 1903	Glen Echo MD	Holyrood
04509	Ogle, Joseph E.B.	32y	W	8 NOV 1903	Portsmouth OH	Rock Creek
07397	Ohl, George Frederick	40y	W	2 FEB 1910	Wash. Grove MD	Prospect Hill
07502	Olcott, Henry A.	89y	W	16 APR 1910	New York NY	Glenwood
01179	Olcott, John B.	73y	W	16 JUN 1892	Carlins VA	Glenwood
16125	Olcott, Mindwell Griswold	71y	W	25 NOV 1919	Glen Carlin VA	Glenwood
01907	Oldfield, Catharine Chase	86y	W	13 APR 1896	Baltimore MD	Oak Hill
05528	Oldfield, James A.	38y	W	9 APR 1906	St. Mary's WV	Oak Hill
08861	Olds, Katherine Sargent	84y	W	30 SEP 1912	New Linden MD	Rock Creek
01073	Olendorf, Nellie M.	19y	W	30 JAN 1893	Riverdale MD	Congressional
01749	Oliphant, Elizabeth C.H.	78y	W	22 SEP 1895	Milwaukee WI	Glenwood
18175	Oliphant, Nathaniel E.	63y	W	19 NOV 1922	Wilwaukee WI	Glenwood
15749	Oliphant, Rose K. (Karr)	58y	W	22 APR 1919	Milwaukee WI	Glenwood
15320	Olive, Mary C.	80y	W	1 NOV 1918	Alex. Co. VA	Congressional
06040	Olive, Winfield S.	63y	W	15 APR 1907	Reno NV	Congressional
08552	Oliver, Annie M.	26y	W	11 MAR 1912	Franklin Park VA	Holyrood
07278	Oliver, Bradshaw	39y	W	17 NOV 1909	Capitol Hts. MD	Congressional
16486	Oliver, Elias L.	83y	W	15 mAY 1920	Martinsburg WV	Glenwood
18435	Oliver, Emma	50y	C	18 MAR 1923	New York NY	Harmony
14392	Oliver, Eugene L.	31y	W	30 SEP 1917	Laurel MD	Rock Creek
07409	Oliver, Helen B.	1m	W	6 FEB 1910	Capitol Hts. MD	Congressional
07059	Oliver, Hester M.	1y	W	13 JUN 1909	Capitol Hts. MD	Congressional
03250	Oliver, John R.	19y	W	4 AUG 1900	Ingleside VA	Holyrood
03903	Oliver, Lillie May	26y	W	4 JUN 1902	Arlington Hts. VA	Holyrood
17365	Oliver, Mary Frances	72y	W	20 AUG 1921	Pikesville MD	Congressional
02977	Olmstead, John F.	57y	W	4 SEP 1899	Saratoga NY	Oak Hill
15094	Olmstead, Lewis L.	10y	W	6 OCT 1918	Pr. Geo. Co. MD	Cedar Hill
15419	Olsen, Helen	12y	W	8 DEC 1918	New York NY	Glenwood
17236	Olson, Carl Godfrey	13y	W	13 JUN 1921	Maryland Pk. MD	Cedar Hill
16396	Olson, Jennie N.	65y	W	16 MAR 1920	Stoneham MA	Rock Creek
12747	Olson, Ole	69y	W	29 JAN 1915	Hinsdale IL	Rock Creek
02522	Oram, Edward L.	10m	C	8 JUL 1898	Kensington MD	Mt. Zion
05106	Ord, James Thompson	44y	W	16 APR 1905	San Diego CA	Arlington
02674	Ord, Jules G.	23y	W	1 JUL 1898	Santiago, Cuba	Arlington
00246	Ordey, Keroly	33y	W	15 DEC 1889	Granitsville SC	Rock Creek
02330	Ordway, Albert	54y	W	21 NOV 1897	New York NY	Arlington
14083	Ordway, Albert	10y	W	14 APR 1917	Baltimore MD	Oak Hill
07714	Ordway, John Enykendall	39y	W	24 AUG 1910	Cherrydale VA	Waterlee IA
01180	Orizah, Robert	60y	W	15 JAN 1893	Hyattsville MD	Glenwood
04878	Orlando, Valentine	56y	W	5 SEP 1904	Baltimore MD	Mt. Olivet
08170	Orme, Mary Amelia	11m	W	1 JUL 1911	Chevy Chase MD	Oak Hill
16278	Orme, Mary Frances	80y	W	3 FEB 1920	Takoma Park MD	Mt. Olivet
15407	Orme, William	36y	W	4 DEC 1918	Chevy Chase MD	Oak Hill
07057	Orme, William, Jr.	15d	W	12 JUN 1909	Chevy Chase MD	Mt. Olivet
16946	Orme, William Stahl	7y	W	31 JAN 1921	Chevy Chase MD	Oak Hill
18011	Orndorf, Charles Edw.	2y	W	14 AUG 1922	Glen Echo MD	Glenwood
16091	Orndorff, Dorie M.	2m	C	5 NOV 1919	Glen Echo MD	Glenwood
17366	Orndorff, Fay Elizabeth	1m	W	22 AUG 1921	Glen Echo MD	Glenwood
17379	Orndorff, Margaret E.	79y	W	31 AUG 1921	Rosslyn VA	Rock Creek
16090	Orndorff, Margaret Elizabeth	2m	W	4 NOV 1919	Glen Echo MD	Glenwood
12190	Orr, Beatrice	31y	W	31 JAN 1914	Takoma Park MD	Rock Creek
06306	Orr, Donald	30y	W	12 NOV 1907	New York NY	Glenwood[1]
13460	Orr, Herbert R.	c.36y	W	14 APR 1916	Conway Sta. MD	Boonville IN
12730	Orr, Katherine O.	61y	W	24 JAN 1915	Falls Church VA	Mt. Olivet
16913	Orsborne, Leo	28y	W	29 JAN 1918	France	Mt. Olivet

---

[1] Removed 2 APR 1909 to New Orleans, La.

No.	Name of Deceased	Age	Race	Death Date	Place of Death	Place of Burial
08254	Orton, Warren S.	49y	W	11 AUG 1911	Oakmont Hts. MD	Glenwood
12673	Osaki, M.	46y	J	23 DEC 1914	Middleburg FL	Cremated
16316	Osborn, Andrew John	47y	W	16 FEB 1920	Capitol Hts. MD	Congressional
18529	Osborn, Harriet Charlton	87y	W	6 MAY 1923	Cabin John MD	Glenwood
15514	Osborn, John L.	80y	W	3 JAN 1919	Alexandria VA	Congressional
16418	Osborne, Annie	24y	C	2 APR 1920	Takoma Park MD	Payne's
02084	Osborne, Arthur	16y	W	16 SEP 1896	Montg. Co. MD	Tenallytown
07263	Osborne, Charles	35y	W	3 NOV 1909	Pittsburgh PA	Congressional
08114	Osborne, Charles D.	4m	W	14 MAY 1911	Mt. Ranier MD	Congressional
16502	Osborne, Edward	53y	W	23 MAY 1920	New York NY	Mt. Olivet
14661	Osborne, Joseph H.	71y	W	28 FEB 1918	Maryland Pk. MD	Congressional
02601	Osburn, William H.	29y	W	23 AUG 1898	Long Island NY	Arlington
05285	Osgood, Alfred	66y	W	6 SEP 1905	Baltimore MD	Glenwood
07603	Osin, Fannie	7m	W	29 JUN 1910	Capitol Hts. MD	Adas Israel
13038	Osker, Abraham	28y	W	4 AUG 1915	Colonial Bea. VA	Nat. Cap.
08079	Ossire, Ida Elizabeth	45y	W	23 APR 1911	Takoma Park MD	Oak Hill
17401	Osthoff, Jannette	44y	W	14 SEP 1921	Sibley Hp.	Rock Creek
07152	Ostrander, William H.	50y	W	8 AUG 1909	Colonial Bea. VA	Rock Creek
01257	Oswalt, Charles	1y	W	27 OCT 1893	Arlington VA	Prospect Hill
18123	Othmer, William	43y	W	22 OCT 1922	Sykesville MD	Cremated
05245	Otis, Genevia P.	53y	W	20 AUG 1894	Baltimore MD	Oak Hill
01322	Ott, Anna	29y	W	28 FEB 1894	Forestville MD	Forestville MD
17933	Ott, Elsie E.	29y	W	1 JUL 1922	Hendersonv. NC	Congressional
03368	Ott, Emma	49y	W	19 DEC 1900	Baltimore MD	Rock Creek
15752	Ott, Juliette	84y	W	6 APR 1919	Daytona FL	Cremated
07687	Otte, Adolph H.	7y	W	11 AUG 1910	Nokesville VA	Prospect Hill
02839	Ottenger, David	40y	W	22 MAY 1899	Wilson NC	Wash. Hebrew
01074	Ottis, John	43y	W	28 JAN 1893	Baltimore MD	Mt. Olivet
16701	Otto, Karl	55y	W	9 SEP 1920	Falls Church VA	Congressional
01181	Ould, Elisha R.	53y	W	2 DEC 1892	New York NY	Oak Hill
00427	Ould, Lancaster	74y	W	28 OCT 1890	Baltimore MD	Oak Hill
06588	Ould, Remus	57y	W	12 JUN 1908	Baltimore MD	Oak Hill
06784	Ould, Susan Britton	48y	W	24 OCT 1908	Roan Mtn. TN	Oak Hill
00183	Ourand, Darlin Codcy	4y	W	11 OCT 1889	Charlton Hts. MD	Oak Hill
03348	Ourdan, Henry A.	1y	W	7 MAR 1863	Brooklyn NY	Oak Hill
12915	Ourdan, Marie T.	24y	W	10 MAY 1915	Baltimore MD	Oak Hill
15685	Over, Virginia E.	64y	C	20 MAR 1919	Hunter VA	Harmony
17793	Overacker, Lillian A.	81y	W	11 APR 1922	Takoma Park MD	Glenwood
18247	Overman, Frank	67y	W	4 JAN 1923	Chicago IL	Congressional
11916	Overton, Alexander	60y	C	24 JUL 1913	Alex. Co. VA	Harmony
18599	Owen, James W.	47y	W	9 JUN 1923	Clayton NJ	Glenwood
00038	Owens, Addie	30y	W	8 MAR 1889	Bennings MD	Congressional
15889	Owens, Charles P.	62y	W	22 JUL 1919	Takoma Park MD	Rock Creek
15058	Owens, Earl Theodore	17y	W	30 SEP 1918	Takoma Park MD	Rock Creek
08206	Owens, Lawrence E.	42y	W	21 JUL 1911	Railroad	Winnsboro SC
13341	Owens, Thomas Irving	23y	W	6 FEB 1916	Bladensburg MD	Congressional
17624	Owens, Webb K.	31y	W	8 JAN 1922	Norfolk VA	King Geo. Co. VA
07865	Owsley, Maria	50y	W	10 DEC 1910	Greenwood VA	Congressional
04667	Oxley, Edwin S.	35y	W	11 APR 1904	Forest Glen MD	Rock Creek
17894	Oxnard, Henry T.	61y	W	8 JUN 1922	New York NY	Mt. Olivet
03162	Oyster, Albert Edward	38y	W	11 APR 1900	Baltimore MD	Oak Hill
17120	Oyster, George M., Jr.	71y	W	24 APR 1921	Atlantic City NJ	Oak Hill

District of Columbia Foreign Death Records, 1888-1923

No.	Name of Deceased	Age	Race	Death Date	Place of Death	Place of Burial
P						
05242	Paddock, May	48y	W	13 AUG 1905	N. Adams MA	Rock Creek
08629	Paddon, George H.	71y	W	7 MAY 1912	Hampton VA	Glenwood
13585	Padgett, Florence E.	29y	W	2 JUL 1916	Oxon Hill MD	Glenwood
15203	Padgett, Jennie	30y	C	17 OCT 1918	Chester PA	Payne's
18385	Padgett, Louise H.	33y	W	5 MAR 1923	Mt. Ranier MD	Lynchburg VA
07426	Page, Catherine L.H.	6y	W	21 FEB 1910	Friendship H. MD	Oak Hill
07254	Page, Charles G.	62y	W	28 OCT 1909	Chicago IL	Oak Hill
18406	Page, Ella V.	65y	W	9 MAR 1923	Chicago IL	Rock Creek
16528	Page, Felix	—	C	7 JUN 1920	Ballston VA	Odd Fellows VA
17215	Page, Florence W.	62y	W	6 JUN 1921	Southborough MA	Oak Hill
09160	Page, Gabriella Crawford	c.59y	W	JUL 1867	New Glasgow VA	Rock Creek
03725	Page, Henrietta L.	55y	W	3 DEC 1901	New York NY	Mt. Olivet
15428	Page, Logan Walter	48y	W	9 DEC 1918	Chicago IL	Rock Creek[1]
16135	Page, Mabel S.	33y	C	3 DEC 1919	Baltimore MD	Harmony
06879	Page, Mary J.	59y	W	2 JAN 1909	New York NY	Oak Hill
06645	Page, Nelson C.	52y	W	11 JUL 1908	Fitzgerald GA	Congressional
06914	Page, Peter	70y	C	8 FEB 1909	Glendale MD	Harmony
02901	Page, Pricella W.	73y	W	7 AUG 1899	Bay Head NJ	Oak Hill
07206	Page, Roger Jones	48y	W	28 JUL 1889	Marion NC	Rock Creek
18141	Page, Thomas Nelson, s/o J.	69y	W	1 NOV 1922	Oakland VA	Rock Creek
07221	Pagels, Edward	67y	W	28 SEP 1909	Worthington OH	Oak Hill
02687	Paine, Sumner C.	50y	W	21 DEC 1898	Asheville NC	Oak Hill
06740	Pairo, Alice	48y	W	1 SEP 1908	Deer Isle ME	Oak Hill
06796	Pairo, Elinor C.	54y	W	1 SEP 1902	Deer Isle ME	Oak Hill
06796	Pairo, Elinor C.	54y	W	1 SEP{ 1908	Deer Isle ME	Oak Hill
02501	Pallas, William	47y	W	24 JUL 1898	Glymont MD	Mt. Olivet
03042	Palmer, Emily	18y	W	21 DEC 1899	Rosslyn VA	Rock Creek
07227	Palmer, Eugene Clide	4m	W	6 OCT 1909	Capitol Hts. MD	Woodlawn
14601	Palmer, George Henry	47y	W	27 JAN 1918	Rives MD	Veitch Family
12864	Palmer, George M.	39y	W	3 APR 1915	Cleveland OH	Glenwood
16353	Palmer, James	65y	C	28 FEB 1920	Arlington VA	Cremated
03980	Palmer, James	24y	C	4 AUG 1902	Arlington VA	Holyrood
09177	Palmer, Joseph	76y	W	19 APR 1913	Alex. Co. VA	Rock Creek
13121	Palmer, Lucy	52y	C	21 SEP 1915	Arlington VA	Holyrood
15793	Palmer, Luella J.	72y	C	25 MAY 1919	Takoma Park MD	Rock Creek
06008	Palmer, Mary A.	78y	W	2 APR 1907	Philadelphia PA	Glenwood
09118	Palmer, Richard E.	38y	W	10 MAR 1913	Riverdale MD	Congressional
09185	Palmer, Virginia B.	42y	W	24 APR 1913	New York NY	Oak Hill
14772	Palmer, Walter W.	48y	W	24 APR 1918	New York NY	Glenwood
17098	Palmer, William	64y	W	8 APR 1921	New York NY	Rock Creek
00108	Palmer, William H.	33y	W	27 JUL 1889	Long Island NY	Glenwood
01359	Palmoni, John W., actor	29y	W	10 APR 1894	New York NY	Rock Creek
12116	Panholzer, Francis A.G.	1y	W	6 DEC 1913	Brentwood MD	St. Mary's
03184	Panitz, Hellen	7m	W	12 MAY 1900	Fayetteville NC	Wash. Hebrew
12501	Pannebaker, Albert G.	7m	W	27 AUG 1914	Berwyn MD	Congressional
05484	Pannill, William W.	28y	W	3 MAR 1906	Baltimore MD	Glenwood
03067	Pansola, Johanna	92y	W	13 JAN 1900	Atlantic City NJ	Prospect Hill
05435	Pansy, Peter	42y	W	20 JAN 1906	Pr. Geo. Co. MD	Woodlawn
08764	Paret, Adelia Vassar	50y	W	10 AUG 1912	Baltimore MD	Rock Creek
13118	Paret, Alice E.B.	61y	W	21 SEP 1915	Sweetwater TX	Rock Creek
11942	Paret, John F.	60y	W	2 AUG 1913	Salt Lake City UT	Rock Creek
00983	Paret, Lilian B.	6y	W	20 JUL 1893	Montg. Co. MD	Rock Creek
02118	Paret, Maria G.	70y	W	1 FEB 1897	Baltimore MD	Rock Creek
07925	Paret, Sarah	58y	W	15 JAN 1911	Baltimore MD	Rock Creek
07928	Paret, William	84y	W	18 JAN 1911	Baltimore MD	Rock Creek

[1] Disinterment permit #9779 issued 19 DEC 1918 for removal to Richmond VA.

No.	Name of Deceased	Age	Race	Death Date	Place of Death	Place of Burial
05547	Parfet, Richard W., Jr.	2h	W	21 APR 1906	University Pk. MD	Methodist
04822	Paris, John	49y	W	30 JUL 1904	Clarendon VA	Prospect Hill
01182	Park, Sarah J.	66y	W	19 NOV 1892	At Sea	Oak Hill
08094	Parker, Addie P.	24y	C	27 APR 1911	Philadelphia PA	Harmony
14946	Parker, Alice	82y	W	30 JUL 1918	Pittsburgh PA	Oak Hill
14265	Parker, Andrew McClean	57y	W	30 JUL 1917	Lincolnton NC	Cremated
02332	Parker, Armand J.	2y	W	8 JAN 1886	Laurel MD	Mt. Olivet
15337	Parker, Bertha	38y	C	5 NOV 1918	New York NY	Harmony
05591	Parker, Christopher	63y	W	8 JUN 1906	Baltimore MD	—
04543	Parker, Eliza	57y	C	22 APR 1887	Richmond VA	Harmony
14730	Parker, Elizabeth	32y	C	29 MAR 1918	Boston MA	Mt. Olivet
05396	Parker, Elsie	23y	C	12 DEC 1905	New York NY	Mt. Zion East
04641	Parker, Estelle	28y	C	21 MAR 1904	Cleveland OH	Harmony
06505	Parker, Fleming	28y	W	10 APR 1908	New York NY	Rock Creek
16934	Parker, Florence W.	55y	W	16 JAN 1921	Helena MT	Glenwood
12036	Parker, Frank M.	70y	W	10 OCT 1913	Johnson City TN	Arlington
14396	Parker, George	31y	C	29 SEP 1917	Philadelphia PA	Harmony
08223	Parker, Henry Eastburn	65y	W	20 JUL 1911	Highlands CA	Falls Church VA
13882	Parker, Herbert W.	35y	W	25 DEC 1916	Washington PA	Cremated
03892	Parker, Infant of John	5d	C	27 MAY 1902	Takoma Park MD	Harmony
16542	Parker, Infant of Willis	SB	C	17 JUN 1920	Fairmont Hts. MD	Payne's
08418	Parker, John Frederick	58y	W	8 DEC 1911	New York NY	Rock Creek
18456	Parker, John H.	58y	C	30 MAR 1923	Philadelphia PA	Harmony
08781	Parker, Julia Young	22y	C	25 AUG 1912	Fairmont Hts. MD	Payne's
06391	Parker, Lilly	30y	C	10 JAN 1908	Baltimore MD	Mt. Zion East
08792	Parker, Lizzie	33y	C	28 AUG 1912	Arlington VA	Harmony
08725	Parker, Marvin Blair	19m	W	21 JUL 1912	Landover MD	Glenwood
00642	Parker, Mary	84y	W	5 OCT 1891	Montg. Co. MD	Rock Creek
05356	Parker, Mary L.	68y	W	9 NOV 1905	West Chester PA	Congressional
12525	Parker, Randolph	54y	C	10 SEP 1914	Cambridge MA	Woodlawn
05582	Parker, Rebecca M.	20y	W	20 MAY 1903	Baltimore MD	Glenwood
01183	Parker, Richard	57y	W	8 JUN 1892	Montg. Co. MD	Rock Creek
04574	Parker, Robert, barber	77y	C	18 JAN 1902	Petersburg VA	Harmony
08008	Parker, Ruth	18y	C	14 MAR 1911	New York NY	Mt. Zion West
07117	Parker, Sadie F. (Collins)	31y	W	18 JUL 1909	Falls Church VA	Glenwood
15806	Parker, Sarah C.	60y	C	28 MAY 1919	Philadelphia PA	Harmony
08040	Parker, Sarah E.	74y	C	26 MAR 1911	Philadelphia PA	Cartersville VA
05482	Parker, Sarah F.	53y	W	28 FEB 1906	Baltimore MD	Mt. Zion East
06069	Parker, Theodore H.	36y	C	14 MAY 1907	Philadelphia PA	Mt. Olivet
01323	Parker, Thomas Gordon	35y	W	19 FEB 1894	Takoma Park MD	Harmony
12462	Parker, Thomas H.	48y	C	28 JUL 1914	Coatesville PA	Moore's
04650	Parker, Thomas J.	62y	W	31 MAR 1904	New York NY	Glenwood
08702	Parker, Thomas J.	52y	W	3 JUL 1912	Takoma Park MD	Rock Creek
14226	Parker, Thomas S.	72y	W	11 JUL 1917	Rochester MN	Cremated
03534	Parker, Walter M.	17y	C	2 JUN 1901	Takoma Park MD	Harmony
03256	Parker, William	35y	C	7 AUG 1900	Atlantic City NJ	Mt. Zion
04656	Parker, William	36y	C	29 MAR 1904	Harrisburg PA	Payne's
06621	Parker, William Henry	51y	W	26 JUN 1908	Deanwood SD	Arlington
12144	Parker, William S.	30y	W	23 DEC 1913	Los Angeles CA	Milford VA
14554	Parker, William W.	55y	W	2 JAN 1918	Dallas TX	Arlington
18164	Parker, Willis Lewis	6m	C	16 NOV 1922	Fairmont Hts. MD	Payne's
06750	Parker, Winship Fowler	11m	W	27 SEP 1908	Anne Arundel Co.	Congressional
05403	Parkhurst, Benjamin	46y	W	19 DEC 1905	Easton PA	Rock Creek
18178	Parkhurst, Eliza E.	75y	W	24 NOV 1922	Clarendon VA	Glenwood
00355	Parkhurst, George A.	53y	W	2 JUL 1890	New York NY	Prospect Hill
04819	Parkins, Alfred	32y	W	28 JUL 1904	Pittsburgh PA	Winchester VA
03394	Parkinson, Joseph	69y	W	17 JAN 1901	Luray VA	Glenwood
14014	Parkinson, Laura Ann	73y	W	28 FEB 1917	Takoma Park MD	Glenwood
02828	Parkman, Robert B.	39y	W	7 MAY 1899	San Gabriel CA	Congressional
17033	Parkman, Samuel S.	50y	W	9 MAR 1921	New York NY	Congressional

District of Columbia Foreign Death Records, 1888-1923

No.	Name of Deceased	Age	Race	Death Date	Place of Death	Place of Burial
16275	Parks, Elizabeth Sabrina	29y	W	2 FEB 1920	Highlands NY	Arlington
12043	Parmelee, Infant of Julius	SB	W	14 OCT 1913	Falls Church VA	Cremated
00558	Parmer, Charles	62y	—	16 MAY 1891	Wheeling WV	Congressional
12674	Parnahan, Catherine Howard	38y	W	24 DEC 1914	Evanston IL	Arlington VA
17997	Parnell, Jennie	12y	C	6 AUG 1922	Sparrows Pt. MD	Payne's
15338	Parsley, Charles J.	32y	W	4 NOV 1918	Flagstaff AZ	Rock Creek
00641	Parsley, Enoch H.	46y	W	31 AUG 1891	Pr. Geo. Co. MD	Rock Creek
16458	Parsons, Alfred W.	23y	W	30 APR 1920	Pr. Anne Co. VA	Rock Creek
13832	Parsons, Charles E.	27y	W	26 NOV 1916	Philadelphia PA	Rock Creek
12503	Parsons, Charles S.	64y	W	27 AUG 1914	New York NY	Congressional
15617	Parsons, James	82y	W	15 FEB 1919	Dayton OH	Glenwood
14197	Parsons, James L.	70y	W	30 JUN 1917	Kensington MD	Congressional
04033	Parsons, Roland D.	22y	W	27 OCT 1902	Las Vegas NM	Congressional
16009	Parsons, Sophia Brock	59y	W	20 SEP 1919	Cocoa FL	Rock Creek
01258	Parsons, Theodore	1y	W	10 AUG 1893	Scranton PA	Rock Creek
03850	Partello, Charlotte V.	81y	W	13 APR 1902	Brooklyn NY	Glenwood
02331	Partells, Agnes M.	53y	W	25 MAY 1897	Sonneburg, Ger.	Glenwood
17145	Partridge, Mary (Hilton)	90y	W	2 MAY 1921	Fauquier Co. VA	Congressional
13998	Pate, Margaret	77y	W	18 FEB 1917	Baltimore MD	Glenwood
07222	Patrick, Hattie E.	53y	W	26 SEP 1909	Denver CO	Cremated
18082	Patrick, Mae	32y	C	22 SEP 1922	Pittsburgh PA	Payne's
06079	Pattee, E.J.	63y	W	24 MAY 1907	Pine Bea. VA	Arlington
03108	Patten, Conrad Magruder	21y	W	27 FEB 1900	Cambridge MA	Oak Hill
04794	Patterson, Charles W.	84y	W	13 JUL 1904	Baltimore MD	Glenwood
06228	Patterson, Clara	25y	C	14 SEP 1907	Baltimore MD	Payne's
08513	Patterson, Daniel W.	53y	W	13 FEB 1912	Baltimore MD	Congressional
13487	Patterson, Ellen	41y	W	30 APR 1916	Washington DC	Rock Creek
03875	Patterson, Gladys	1y	C	6 MAY 1902	Baltimore MD	Mt. Olivet
02991	Patterson, Henry J.	56y	C	18 OCT 1899	Cleveland OH	Harmony
08630	Patterson, Isabella	80y	W	17 DEC 1909	Rensselaer NY	Rock Creek
16943	Patterson, James G., Jr.	2m	C	29 JAN 1921	Newport News VA	Woodlawn
15498	Patterson, Louis, s/o Samuel	17y	C	28 DEC 1918	Fairmont Hts. MD	Croome MD
00643	Patterson, Mary W.	46y	W	31 JUL 1891	Baltimore MD	Oak Hill
17770	Pattison, Mary Jane	68y	W	25 MAR 1922	Chicago IL	Congressional
14752	Patton, John E.	51y	W	14 APR 1918	Seat Pleasant MD	Glenwood
18391	Patton, Mary Bryson	88y	W	5 MAR 1923	Plainfield NJ	Oak Hill
17653	Patton, Ruby Holland	27y	C	23 JAN 1922	Paterson NJ	Woodlawn
06141	Patton, William Penn	63y	W	3 JUL 1907	Stamford CN	Glenwood
05179	Paul, Carrie	44y	W	19 JUN 1905	Baltimore MD	Glenwood
12073	Pavarini, Alexander	75y	W	3 NOV 1913	New York NY	St. Mary's
07959	Pavarini, Rosa	69y	W	2 FEB 1911	New York NY	St. Mary's
05200	Paxton, Frank B.	15y	W	3 JUL 1905	Allegany Co. MD	Congressional
04950	Paxton, J.E.	27y	W	1 SEP 1904	San Diego CA	Congressional
15316	Paxton, Sarah M.	78y	W	29 OCT 1918	Troy NY	Congressional
00644	Paxton, Walter	22y	W	30 JUN 1891	New York NY	Congressional
01848	Payne, Alice	—	C	11 JAN 1896	Denver CO	Harmony
17524	Payne, Charles	47y	C	13 NOV 1921	Crownsville MD	Harmony
06485	Payne, Edward	33y	C	22 MAR 1908	Montreal, Can.	Harmony
14126	Payne, Edward L.	10h	W	7 MAY 1917	Capitol Hts. MD	Congressional
15816	Payne, Elizabeth	57y	W	5 JUN 1919	Petersburg VA	Harmony
08096	Payne, Elizabeth E.	55y	W	2 MAY 1911	Clinton MD	Congressional
04959	Payne, Franklin L.	62y	W	15 NOV 1904	Bailey's Xrds. VA	Glenwood
08777	Payne, George A.	38y	C	21 AUG 1912	New York NY	Harmony
14377	Payne, Hattie	—	C	21 SEP 1917	King Geo. Co. VA	Woodlawn
07700	Payne, Hunter V., s/o Varnell	2y	W	20 AUG 1910	Colonial Bea. VA	Marshall VA
15911	Payne, Jennie Bryan	62y	W	31 JUL 1919	Elmhurst IL	Oak Hill
08727	Payne, Jesse B., d/o R.A.	28y	C	22 JUL 1912	Basic City VA	Woodlawn
06056	Payne, John	27y	C	4 MAY 1907	Philadelphia PA	M. VA
07226	Payne, John A. Logan	1m	W	4 OCT 1909	New York NY	Soldier's Home
04000	Payne, John H.	19y	C	29 JUL 1902	Atlantic City NJ	Harmony

No.	Name of Deceased	Age	Race	Death Date	Place of Death	Place of Burial
04957	Payne, Leonard	19y	C	11 NOV 1904	Philadelphia PA	Mt. Zion
12319	Payne, Lucy Northern	55y	W	19 APR 1914	Takoma Park MD	Rock Creek
04029	Payne, Mary M.	58y	W	21 SEP 1902	Surrattsville MD	Congressional
16244	Payne, Maud	37y	C	24 JAN 1920	Alexandria VA	Mt. Olivet
06345	Payne, Melvin	3y	C	7 DEC 1907	Pr. Geo. Co. MD	Payne's
02085	Payne, Olive	27y	W	28 OCT 1896	St. Mary's MD	Oak Hill
04813	Payne, Priscilla R.	70y	W	23 JUL 1904	Hyattsville MD	Oak Hill
05524	Payne, Randolph	35y	C	5 APR 1906	Allegheny PA	Payne's
18418	Payne, Rebecca Fr. Ran.	23y	W	10 MAR 1923	Roswell NM	Rock Creek
16853	Payne, Virginia F.	93y	W	10 DEC 1920	Baltimore MD	Bluemont VA
15899	Payne, William	72y	C	29 JUL 1919	Lane PA	Harmony
03105	Payne, William	27y	C	28 FEB 1900	Oil City PA	Woodlawn
16076	Payne, Winston D.	41y	C	21 OCT 1919	New York NY	Mt. Zion East
04613	Payton, Isaac	29y	C	22 FEB 1904	Philadelphia PA	Harmony
01830	Pazels, George H.	47y	W	25 NOV 1895	Chilicothe OH	Oak Hill
06392	Peabody, Anna Amelia	72y	W	12 JAN 1908	Doylestown PA	Glenwood
15453	Peabody, Hershie E.	44y	W	18 DEC 1918	Takoma MD	West Valley NY
04800	Peach, Willie M.	72y	W	14 JUL 1904	Philadelphia PA	Congressional
16747	Peachy, William S.	45y	W	6 OCT 1920	Boston MA	Rock Creek
18280	Peacock, Agnes	60y	C	18 JAN 1923	Freedmen's Hp.	Woodlawn
13563	Peake, Charles M.	36y	W	20 JUN 1916	Alexandria VA	Glenwood
08655	Peake, James R.	19y	C	25 MAY 1912	Occoquan VA	Payne's
14943	Pearce, Archebel M.	42y	C	28 JUL 1918	New York NY	Oak Hill
02512	Pearce, Ellen M.J.	50y	W	13 JUL 1898	Evanston IL	Oak Hill
00232	Pearce, Harriett E.	73y	W	24 NOV 1889	Alex. Co. VA	Glenwood
13926	Pearl, Helen Kate	c.60y	W	8 JAN 1917	Miami FL	Rock Creek
04256	Pearley, Fannie A., teacher	65y	W	29 APR 1897	Glen Echo MD	Congressional
06161	Pearson, Burton	49y	W	29 JUL 1907	New York NY	Rock Creek
12253	Pearson, Joseph L.	44y	W	9 MAR 1914	Relay MD	Oak Hill
14182	Pearson, Robert R.	48y	W	19 JUN 1917	Maryland Pk. MD	Congressional
06448	Pearson, Sinah E.	65y	C	26 FEB 1908	N. Adams MA	Woodlawn
02902	Peary, Francini	7m	W	7 AUG 1899	Atlantic City NJ	Congressional
00755	Peaster, Frederick F.	65y	W	8 NOV 1891	Philadelphia PA	Glenwood
04288	Peaster, Mary Jane	70y	W	24 APR 1903	Fairfax C.H. VA	Glenwood
02385	Peck, Bennett	24y	W	21 JAN 1898	Danville VA	Oak Hill
16381	Peck, Bertha S.	36y	W	14 MAR 1920	Laurel MD	Rock Creek
00387	Peck, Charles F.	56y	W	12 AUG 1890	Asheville NC	Oak Hill
13951	Peck, Dorothy M.	46y	W	25 JAN 1917	Brooklyn NY	Oak Hill
07034	Peck, Julia T.	72y	W	19 MAY 1909	Montclair NJ	Oak Hill
12536	Peck, Katharine	54y	W	17 SEP 1914	Seat Pleasant MD	Rock Creek
07174	Peck, Norman	6y	C	24 AUG 1909	Dupont I Its. MD	Mt. Olivet
08834	Peck, Paul	23y	W	12 SEP 1912	Chicago IL	Rockville MD
08103	Peck, Rachel Holbrook	49y	W	5 MAY 1911	Brooklyn NY	Oak Hill
07990	Peck, Sarah P.	38y	W	27 FEB 1911	Wash. Grove MD	Oak Hill
05210	Peck, Walter	22y	C	12 JUL 1905	Cape May NJ	Mt. Olivet
07539	Peckham, Alexander P.	27y	W	15 MAY 1910	Railroad	Boston MA
16085	Peeffe, Mary Canfield	2y	W	1 NOV 1919	Chevy Chase MD	Rock Creek
13053	Peelle, Arabella Canfield	80y	W	13 AUG 1915	Chevy Chase MD	Rock Creek
16749	Pegg, Elizabeth Horner	81y	W	10 OCT 1920	Bethesda MD	Cremated
13730	Peirce, Laura Hartley	83y	W	22 SEP 1916	Bethesda MD	Baltimore MD
00756	Pellew, George	32y	W	18 FEB 1892	New York NY	Oak Hill
13404	Pelouze, Ellen L. (Doolittle)	79y	W	6 MAR 1916	Pasadena CA	Arlington
01514	Pelouze, Louis H.	40y	W	2 JUN 1878	Philadelphia PA	Arlington
17406	Peluzzo, Joseph	—	W	10 OCT 1918	France	St. Mary's
15063	Pendleton, Edw. B.	24y	W	30 SEP 1918	Burlington Co. NJ	Oak Hill
17075	Pendleton, Edward Gray	76y	W	20 DEC 1920	W. Palm Bea. FL	Oak Hill
07902	Pendleton, Emma	65y	W	1 JAN 1911	Roland Park MD	Rock Creek
08208	Pendleton, Martha	60y	C	19 JUL 1911	Ft. Myer VA	Woodlawn
17668	Pendleton, William Henry	3y	C	29 JAN 1922	Arlington VA	Rosemont
01324	Penn, Elizabeth Calder	72y	W	16 FEB 1894	Mt. St. Mary's MD	Oak Hill

District of Columbia Foreign Death Records, 1888-1923

No.	Name of Deceased	Age	Race	Death Date	Place of Death	Place of Burial
0133	Penn, Jane C.	85y	W	7 AUG 1889	Nottingham MD	Rock Creek
12557	Penn, Phoebe (Snowden)	35y	C	3 OCT 1914	Newark NJ	Mt. Zion West
07290	Penn, Robert	26y	C	23 NOV 1909	Philadelphia PA	Payne's
13156	Pennell, Charles	48y	W	17 OCT 1915	Brooklyn NY	Glenwood
02477	Pennell, Edward	1m	W	6 AUG 1898	Oxon Hill MD	Glenwood
17202	Pennewill, John M.	—	W	28 MAY 1921	Walter Reed Hp.	Silver City NM
14933	Pennington, William H.	64y	W	21 JUL 1918	Jarrettsville MD	Congressional
18823	Penny, Irene	71y	C	15 MAR 1915	New York NY	Harmony
03793	Penrose, Thomas W.	66y	W	13 FEB 1902	Philadelphia PA	Arlington
04998	Penrose, W.H., Gen.	72y	W	29 AUG 1903	Salt Lake City UT	Arlington VA
17092	Perdue, Fannie Clifton	—	C	18 JUL 1920	Trenton NJ	Woodlawn[1]
14352	Perine, Clarence, s/o John	65y	W	26 JUN 1917	New York NY	Glenwood
00645	Perkins, Alie L.	6m	W	11 JUL 1891	Pr. Geo. Co. MD	Rock Creek
15265	Perkins, Clifton T.	29y	W	21 OCT 1918	Indian Head MD	Hartsville TN
14917	Perkins, Fidella	59y	C	15 JUL 1918	Rockville MD	Harmony
01887	Perkins, George N.	9m	W	25 FEB 1896	Hyattsville MD	Rock Creek
08597	Perkins, Helen L.	69y	W	6 APR 1912	St. Paul MN	Arlington VA
03909	Perkins, Kate Stephens	47y	W	24 JUN 1902	Chicago IL	Arlington
06029	Perkins, Mary V.	67y	W	13 APR 1907	Cape May NJ	Oak Hill
14882	Perlman, Charlotte May	31y	W	25 JUN 1918	Baltimore MD	Congressional
05761	Perrie, Albert W.	60y	W	4 OCT 1906	Baltimore MD	Oak Hill
04126	Perrie, Lilie C.	53y	W	10 DEC 1902	Towson MD	Oak Hill
05219	Perrigo, Ward E.	31y	W	27 JUL 1905	E. Riverdale MD	Glenwood
16928	Perrin, Esther S.	—	C	16 JAN 1921	New York NY	Harmony
00757	Perry, A.T.	6y	W	21 JUN 1891	Portland OR	Rock Creek
08505	Perry, Agnes (Jackson)	27y	C	3 FEB 1912	Atlantic City NJ	Mt. Olivet
15230	Perry, Alice E.	33y	W	19 OCT 1918	Chevy Chase MD	Oak Hill
08496	Perry, Amanda Elizabeth	78y	W	28 JAN 1912	New York NY	Rock Creek
07772	Perry, Annie Elizabeth	70y	W	29 SEP 1910	Lawrence MA	Congressional
17413	Perry, Bertha E.	53y	W	16 SEP 1921	Gloucester MA	Glenwood
18255	Perry, Campbell	27y	C	7 JAN 1923	Lorton VA	Fredericksburg VA
17281	Perry, Carrie E.	53y	W	2 JUL 1921	Silver Spring MD	Mt. Zion East
07757	Perry, Celestine	38y	C	21 SEP 1910	Atlantic City NJ	Harmony
05657	Perry, Edgar J.	51y	W	24 JUL 1906	Colonial Bea. VA	Rock Creek
18044	Perry, Edith Nelson	38y	W	3 SEP 1922	Orange VA	Cremated
03461	Perry, Ella J.	24y	W	27 MAR 1901	Somerset Hts. MD	Tenallytown
18545	Perry, Frances	74y	W	16 MAY 1923	Takoma Park MD	Hamilton VA
14522	Perry, Frederick C.	66y	W	23 DEC 1917	Riverdale MD	Glenwood
17954	Perry, George W., Jr.	26y	C	10 JUL 1922	Baltimore MD	Arlington
09075	Perry, Gertrude Ann	77y	W	14 FEB 1913	Riverdale MD	Rock Creek
00184	Perry, Henry P.	3y	W	12 OCT 1889	Montg. Co. MD	Oak Hill
18429	Perry, Hudson Crandall	33y	W	21 MAR 1923	Falls Church VA	Lacy's Land. MD
12646	Perry, James H.	65y	W	5 DEC 1914	New York NY	Arlington VA
00646	Perry, Jane H.	62y	W	11 OCT 1891	Falls Church VA	Glenwood
13849	Perry, John	58y	C	6 DEC 1916	Takoma Park MD	Harmony
06497	Perry, Josiah Bradon, Rev.	60y	W	7 APR 1908	Natchez MS	Rock Creek
05172	Perry, Martha (Queen)	52y	C	18 JUN 1905	Arlington VA	Holyrood
06501	Perry, Mary A.	75y	C	9 APR 1908	Baltimore MD	Harmony
06679	Perry, Mary Jane	83y	W	9 AUG 1908	Garrett Park MD	Rock Creek
07546	Perry, Nora C.V.	43y	W	20 MAY 1910	Takoma Park MD	Mt. Olivet
02012	Perry, Richard Humphrey	19y	W	8 AUG 1896	Kensington MD	Oak Hill
03597	Perry, Richard Humphrey W.	76y	W	29 JUL 1901	Kensington MD	Oak Hill
01475	Perry, Sarah Ann	75y	W	27 AUG 1894	Montg. Co. MD	Tenallytown
15982	Perry, Stephen M.B.	61y	W	8 SEP 1919	Sykesville MD	Methodist
17756	Perry, Stephen W.	47y	W	17 MAR 1922	Bradentown FL	Cremated
03411	Perry, Thomas J.	3d	W	5 FEB 1901	Montg. Co. MD	Tenallytown
03361	Perry, Walter S.	46y	W	6 DEC 1900	Towson MD	Rock Creek

[1] NJ disinterment dated 6 APR 1921 for removal from Ewing Cemetery, Mercer Co. NJ.

No.	Name of Deceased	Age	Race	Death Date	Place of Death	Place of Burial
16394	Perry, William	68y	W	17 MAR 1920	Purcellville VA	Rock Creek
03336	Perry, William E.	75y	W	30 MAY 1891	Mt. Holly NJ	Rock Creek
06033	Peschall, Charles J.	62y	W	17 APR 1907	Jersey City NJ	Rock Creek
16221	Peschau, J. Harry	37y	W	14 JAN 1910	Albuquerque NM	Rock Creek
03579	Pessagno, Maria Sylvia	9m	W	14 JUL 1901	Annapolis Jct. MD	Mt. Olivet
18507	Peter, Amadeus C., s/o Edw.	76y	W	24 APR 1923	Knoxville TN	Arlington
08128	Peter, Charlotte B.	20y	W	24 MAY 1911	Chevy Chase MD	Oak Hill
07021	Peter, Eliza Lavinia	78y	W	11 MAY 1909	Rockville MD	Oak Hill
12409	Peter, Elizabeth	76y	W	20 JUN 1914	Bethesda MD	Oak Hill
01325	Peter, George	63y	W	9 AUG 1893	Rockville MD	Oak Hill
01075	Peter, Louisa	63y	W	12 MAR 1893	Chicago IL	Glenwood
06030	Peter, William B.	60y	W	15 APR 1907	Ellicott City MD	Oak Hill
06454	Peters, John G.	26y	W	2 MAR 1908	Philadelphia PA	Oak Hill
18143	Peters, Peter	67y	W	1 NOV 1922	Dodge Park MD	Glenwood
08871	Peters, Walter	30y	C	24 SEP 1912	Raleigh NC	Woodlawn
01377	Peters, William, cigar maker	65y	W	18 MAY 1894	Chicago IL	Glenwood
13743	Peters, William H.	85y	W	4 OCT 1916	Capitol Hts. MD	Arlington
07256	Peterson, Andrew	28y	C	30 OCT 1909	Culpeper VA	Payne's
09056	Peterson, Bessie Fairbanks	30y	W	3 FEB 1913	Arlington VA	Glenwood
08509	Peterson, George L., s/o Lee	33y	C	9 FEB 1912	Occoquan VA	Harmony
12175	Peterson, Sadie E.	49y	W	19 JAN 1914	New York NY	Glenwood
02765	Peterson, W.F.	54y	W	22 APR 1898	New Orleans LA	Prospect Hill
15212	Petrello, Josephine	24y	W	11 OCT 1918	Falls Church VA	St. Mary's
01588	Pettibone, Jane Carroll	67y	W	29 JAN 1895	Montg. Co. MD	Oak Hill
00504	Pettibone, William	77y	W	10 MAR 1891	Linden MD	Oak Hill
17014	Pettis, William Montrose, Rev.	83y	W	1 MAR 1921	Orlando FL	Rock Creek
08645	Pettit, Charles A.	65y	W	21 mAY 1912	Atlantic City NJ	Glenwood
13692	Pettit, Mary A.	76y	W	4 SEP 1916	E. Hyattsville MD	Congressional
08560	Pettit, Warren F.	39y	W	15 MAR 1912	Philadelphia PA	Mt. Olivet
02500	Petty, George K.	54y	W	23 JUL 1898	Brandywine MD	Mt. Olivet
00294	Pettybone, John George	26y	W	19 MAR 1890	Linden MD	Congressional
02499	Petze, John Herman Louis	2m	W	24 JUL 1898	Dawsonville MD	Rock Creek
06539	Peyton, Alice	54y	W	8 MAY 1908	Hyattsville MD	Congressional
03765	Peyton, Pauline L.	43y	W	12 JAN 1902	Denver CO	Congressional
17219	Peyton, Ruth L.	19y	W	4 JUN 1921	Hartford CN	Congressional
03828	Peyton, William J.	18y	W	23 MAR 1902	South Bend IN	Congressional
03003	Pfanmann, Ida	66y	W	11 NOV 1899	Alexandria VA	St. Mary's
07260	Pfeiffer, Augusta Va.	70y	W	4 NOV 1909	Annapolis MD	Oak Hill
17270	Pfeiffer, Louis R.	63y	W	28 JUN 1921	Takoma Park MD	Prospect Hill
03195	Pfeil, Katherina	69y	W	28 MAY 1900	Colonial Bea. VA	Prospect Hill
03541	Pfieffer, Carl	28y	W	8 JUN 1901	Manitou CO	Oak Hill
05635	Pfiel, Rudolph	49y	W	7 JUL 1906	New York NY	Prospect Hill
00407	Pfluzer, John William	28d	W	3 OCT 1890	Hyattsville MD	Prospect Hill
14192	Phan, Thomas E.	32y	W	3 SEP 1916	Washington DC	Glenwood
13191	Phearson, Wm., s/o Emanual	43y	C	4 NOV 1915	Occoquan VA	Moore's
00505	Phelan, James	45y	W	30 JAN 1891	Nassau, N.P.	Oak Hill
14589	Phelps, Abby H.	71y	W	20 JAN 1918	Laurel MD	Rock Creek
17007	Phelps, Anna E.	77y	W	28 FEB 1921	Elizabeth NJ	Mt. Olivet
00089	Phelps, Harriett Dyar	59y	W	3 JUN 1889	Orange NJ	Glenwood
05662	Phelps, James O.	67y	W	25 JUL 1906	Glendale MD	Rock Creek
15197	Phelps, Joseph B.	27y	W	12 OCT 1918	Camp Meade MD	Rock Creek
14956	Phelps, Mary M.	7y	W	7 AUG 1918	N. Andover MA	Glenwood
05775	Phelps, Milton	40y	W	15 OCT 1906	Buffalo NY	Laurel MD
12042	Philip, Gaston Pearson	39y	W	11 OCT 1913	Hudson NY	Oak Hill
01184	Philips, Charles T.	68y	W	25 OCT 1892	Silver Hill MD	Glenwood
08209	Philips, Clara	1y	W	22 JUL 1911	Berwyn MD	Mt. Olivet
17058	Philips, Richard	28y	C	18 MAR 1921	Chester PA	Mt. Zion West
14184	Philips, William Henry	67y	W	20 JUN 1917	Takoma Park MD	Library PA
02695	Phillips, Anna Brian Stabler	49y	W	8 JAN 1899	Laurel MD	Arlington VA
15452	Phillips, Augustus L.	85y	W	14 DEC 1918	Otego NY	Glenwood

District of Columbia Foreign Death Records, 1888-1923

No.	Name of Deceased	Age	Race	Death Date	Place of Death	Place of Burial
08082	Phillips, Cecelia Day	70y	W	25 APR 1911	Kensington MD	Baldwin MD
05583	Phillips, Cecilia	19y	W	21 MAY 1906	Baltimore MD	Mt. Olivet
07153	Phillips, Charles W.	8y	W	9 AUG 1909	Riverside VA	Glenwood
13702	Phillips, Christiana	56y	W	7 SEP 1916	Wilkes Barre PA	Oak Hill
16050	Phillips, Edith Norris	47y	W	15 OCT 1919	Alexandria VA	Oak Hill
14159	Phillips, Edward R.	48y	W	1 JUN 1917	Brooklyn NY	Glenwood
02215	Phillips, Eliza Worthington	51y	W	29 OCT 1896	Claverack NY	Oak Hill
08566	Phillips, Emeline	1h	W	25 MAR 1912	Alexandria VA	Oak Hill
07932	Phillips, Eugene	34y	C	19 JAN 1911	Norfolk VA	Harmony
02087	Phillips, Everett L.	53y	W	15 DEC 1896	Mt. Hope MD	Glenwood
05995	Phillips, George S.	71y	W	23 MAR 1907	Capitol Hts. MD	Arlington VA
06401	Phillips, Harry W.	53y	W	22 JAN 1908	Montg. Co. MD	Rock Creek
06981	Phillips, Helen Sophia	70y	W	10 APR 1909	Capitol Hts. MD	Glenwood
00164	Phillips, Henry K.	34y	W	14 SEP 1889	Pr. Geo. Co. MD	Glenwood
17008	Phillips, Jeanne M. (MacVicar)	21y	W	2 MAR 1921	Saranac Lake NY	Glenwood
08527	Phillips, John A., Jr.	23y	W	5 NOV 1911	Vicques, P.R.	Houston VA
14134	Phillips, John Biggs	62y	W	12 MAY 1917	Silver Hill MD	Glenwood
05898	Phillips, John H.	38y	W	24 MAR 1899	Kansas City MO	Congressional
06798	Phillips, John W.	69y	W	31 OCT 1908	Philadelphia PA	Glenwood
08507	Phillips, Lillie Hasler, d/o Rud.	25y	W	6 FEB 1912	Del Ray VA	Prospect Hill
18120	Phillips, Lillie May	49y	W	19 OCT 1922	Rockville MD	Arlington
03503	Phillips, Louisa Henry	36y	W	8 MAY 1901	Hyattsville MD	Glenwood
04561	Phillips, Margaret	2m	W	9 JAN 1904	Norwood PA	Mt. Olivet
06129	Phillips, Mary E.	78y	W	3 JUL 1907	Dallas PA	Oak Hill
15694	Phillips, Minnie	42y	C	25 MAR 1919	Philadelphia PA	Mt. Zion East
02086	Phillips, Parker Norris	1y	W	12 DEC 1896	Alexandria VA	Oak Hill
18535	Phillips, Richard W.	74y	W	8 MAY 1923	Arlington Co. VA	Congressional
06093	Phillips, Samuel A.	66y	W	4 JUN 1907	Chevy Chase MD	Oak Hill
05181	Phillips, Susan Veronica	85y	W	22 JUN 1905	Rockville MD	Congressional
02214	Phillips, William	44y	W	9 MAY 1897	Potomac River	Savannah GA
13350	Phillips, William A. (or Patrick)	45y	W	12 FEB 1916	Baltimore MD	Mt. Olivet
06127	Phillips, William R.	30y	W	3 JUL 1907	Cincinnati OH	Arlington
06698	Philpitt, Ethel Ruth	4y	W	19 AUG 1908	Philadelphia PA	Glenwood
05965	Philpitt, Lula May	31y	W	2 MAR 1907	Philadelphia PA	Glenwood
12291	Phiollips, Sylvia L.	63y	C	2 APR 1914	New York NY	Woodlawn
00648	Phipps, Jeddeiah	38y	W	2 NOV 1891	Hubbardton VT	Rock Creek
00984	Piason, Edward T.T.	57y	W	27 MAY 1893	Montg. Co. MD	Tenallytown
16745	Picard, Theodore	55y	W	6 OCT 1920	Philadelphia PA	Wash. Hebrew
12230	Pickard, Robert O.	2m	W	9 FEB 1914	Boston MA	Huntington WV
02703	Pickerill, Frank B.	48y	W	7 JAN 1899	Sedalia MO	Rock Creek
12264	Pickrell, A. Cooper	c.67y	W	24 MAR 1914	Mt. Hope MD	Oak Hill
04179	Pickrell, Francis Adelaide	62y	W	17 FEB 1903	Chevy Chase MD	Rock Creek
04810	Pickrell, John H.	63y	W	21 JUL 1904	Chevy Chase MD	Rock Creek
01326	Pickrell, Warren E.	29y	W	4 FEB 1894	Colonial Bea. VA	Oak Hill
15326	Piedmont, Martha	49y	C	1 NOV 1918	Long Branch NJ	Harmony
04020	Pierce, Benjamin F.	73y	W	3 SEP 1902	Bethesda MD	Cremated
17079	Pierce, Charles	25y	C	28 MAR 1921	Baltimore MD	Arlington
05625	Pierce, Clement O., Jr.	9m	W	2 JUL 1906	Takoma Park MD	Glenwood
15844	Pierce, Edward B.	73y	W	25 JUN 1919	Takoma Park MD	Lowell MA
17558	Pierce, Emma Ethel	68y	W	28 NOV 1921	Takoma Park MD	Mt. Olivet
12336	Pierce, Harold	7m	W	29 APR 1914	Silver Spring MD	Glenwood
05325	Pierce, Infant of Clement	28d	W	20 OCT 1905	Montg. Co. MD	Glenwood
08852	Pierce, Judgson	1m	W	24 SEP 1912	Silver Spring MD	Glenwood
14847	Pierce, Julia	60y	W	30 MAY 1918	New York NY	Mt. Olivet
03864	Pierce, Mary E. [Peerce]	55y	W	27 APR 1902	Annandale VA	Rock Creek
06235	Pierce, Mary Louise	28y	W	21 SEP 1907	Brentwood MD	Glenwood
00317	Pierce, Mary W.	49y	C	21 APR 1890	Pittsburgh PA	Harmony
05218	Pierce, Ollin	23y	W	26 JUL 1905	Weston WV	Oak Hill
03423	Pierce, Preston M.	6m	W	22 FEB 1901	Takoma Park MD	Rock Creek
00758	Pierce, Warren	19y	W	23 NOV 1891	Carlisle PA	Oak Hill

No.	Name of Deceased	Age	Race	Death Date	Place of Death	Place of Burial
16719	Pierpont, Albert	68y	W	20 SEP 1920	Hamilton VA	Rock Creek
03653	Pierson, John A.	65y	W	18 SEP 1901	Colonial Bea. VA	Rock Creek
13869	Pierson, Richard Dever	22d	W	16 DEC 1916	Hyattsville MD	Cremated
16377	Pierson, Ruth M.	27y	W	10 MAR 1920	New York NY	Glenwood
06281	Pigg, Clem Hindle	3y	W	22 OCT 1907	Hyattsville MD	Glenwood
01283	Pike, Cassie L.	34y	W	6 JAN 1893	Philadelphia PA	Glenwood
08171	Pike, Mary T.	49y	W	1 JUL 1911	Laurel MD	Rock Creek
14957	Pilche, Margaret	17y	W	6 AUG 1918	Penns Grove NJ	Glenwood
18523	Pilcher, John S.	70y	W	4 MAY 1923	Alberton MD	Culpeper VA
01076	Piles, Eliza A.	67y	W	12 APR 1893	Montg. Co. MD	Rock Creek
04263	Piles, Florence	58y	W	6 MAY 1903	Cabin John MD	Rock Creek
02265	Pilling, Arthur T.	19y	W	20 AUG 1897	Gloucester MA	Oak Hill
01751	Pilling, James C., ethnologist	48y	W	26 JUL 1895	Olney MD	Oak Hill
00346	Pilling, Lois Harper	1y	W	22 JUN 1890	Olney MD	Oak Hill
15561	Pillot, Gertrude H.	36y	W	15 JAN 1919	New York NY	Rock Creek
14848	Pillot, Gertrude M.	9y	W	2 JUN 1918	New York NY	Rock Creek
17504	Pillsbury, Arthur D.	41y	W	3 NOV 1921	Baltimore MD	Congressional
17769	Pillsbury, Herbert P.	74y	W	28 MAR 1922	St. Petersburg FL	Glenwood
07168	Pinchback, Henrietta	50y	C	20 AUG 1909	Collegeville PA	Harmony
15641	Pinckney, Bertha D.	38y	C	25 FEB 1919	New York NY	Harmony
03143	Pindell, Caroline	65y	C	17 FEB 1900	Boston MA	Harmony
00185	Pinkney, Cornelia A.	20y	C	6 OCT 1889	Baltimore MD	Graceland
17723	Pinkney, George	55y	C	28 FEB 1922	Atlantic City NJ	Arlington
08056	Pinkney, Henry	51y	C	5 APR 1911	Fairmont Hts. MD	Woodlawn
00872	Pinkney, Mary	4m	C	20 JUL 1892	Hyattsville MD	Mt. Olivet
15735	Pinn, James S.	62y	C	16 APR 1919	Proctor VT	Harmony
14201	Pinyon, Catherine	67y	C	1 JUL 1917	Philadelphia PA	Harmony
14335	Piozet, Robert Allen	13y	W	1 SEP 1917	Hyattsville MD	Glenwood
05836	Pipenbring, Ameline	—	—	17 AUG 1878	Warrenton VA	Prospect Hill
05833	Pipenbring, Louis	—	—	31 JUN 1873	Warrenton VA	Prospect Hill
05834	Pipenbring, Mary	—	—	5 DEC 1881	Warrenton VA	Prospect Hill
01185	Piper, Elizabeth	74y	W	3 JAN 1893	Saratoga Spg. NY	Rock Creek
18182	Piper, Gertrude	36y	C	23 NOV 1922	Philadelphia PA	Harmony
05122	Piper, Horace L.	60y	W	9 MAY 1905	Atlantic City NJ	Arlington VA
15682	Pirelli, Giovanni, Lt.	—	W	4 FEB 1919	Dayton OH	Genoa, Italy
13335	Pitcher, John W.	73y	W	30 JAN 1916	Stoughton MA	Arlington
01831	Pitcher, L.G., Gen., U.S.A.	70y	W	21 OCT 1895	Ft. Bayard NM	Rock Creek
01502	Pitchlynn, Caroline M.	71y	W	4 OCT 1894	Montg. Co. MD	Congressional
15824	Pitkin, Lucy A.	67y	W	10 JUN 1919	Clarendon VA	Rock Creek
07051	Pitner, Bessie E.	17y	W	9 JUN 1909	Takoma Park MD	Danville PA
07124	Pitner, Hannah B.	88y	W	22 JUL 1909	Takoma Park MD	S. Danville PA
18569	Pittis, Osee Wilson	77y	W	30 MAY 1923	Rockville MD	Rock Creek
04228	Pittman, Willis W.	23y	W	23 FEB 1903	Baltimore MD	Rock Creek
02764	Pitts, Lindsay	27y	C	3 MAR 1899	Philadelphia PA	Woodlawn
12417	Plain, Sue Ballenger	66y	W	22 JUN 1914	Los Angeles CA	Rock Creek
13707	Planck, Walter Lois	30y	W	31 AUG 1916	Santo Domingo	Trenton NJ
01888	Plant, Ambrose A.	20y	W	28 JAN 1896	Bakersfield CA	Alexandria VA
12755	Plant, Andrew C.	76y	W	8 FEB 1915	Paterson NJ	Rock Creek
15537	Plant, Emma F. (Morgan)	74y	W	9 JAN 1919	Ashland NJ	Rock Creek
16839	Plant, Fred	44y	W	30 NOV 1920	Chicago IL	Congressional
00386	Plant, Martha W.	76y	W	11 AUG 1890	Baltimore MD	Mt. Olivet
04460	Plant, Mary Jones	32y	W	22 SEP 1903	Deer River MN	Rock Creek
05365	Plato, Nelson, Col.	72y	W	26 MAY 1905	Iowa City IA	Arlington VA
03515	Platt, Amos R.	59y	W	20 MAY 1901	Kensington MD	Glenwood
01446	Pleasanton, Augustus James	86y	W	26 JUL 1894	Philadelphia PA	Congressional
12938	Plugin, Robert	47y	W	24 MAY 1915	New York NY	Cremated
00759	Plumb, Benjamin M.	47y	W	2 DEC 1891	Brooklyn NY	Glenwood
01753	Plumb, Elizabeth P.L.	51y	W	25 JUL 1895	Brooklyn NY	Glenwood
08795	Plummer, Adam F.	86y	C	13 DEC 1905	Hyattsville MD	Harmony
08811	Plummer, Alfred	22y	C	11 OCT 1904	Hyattsville MD	Harmony

District of Columbia Foreign Death Records, 1888-1923

No.	Name of Deceased	Age	Race	Death Date	Place of Death	Place of Burial
08817	Plummer, Anna Augusta	7y	C	27 DEC 1880	Hyattsville MD	Harmony
03276	Plummer, Annie	53y	C	27 AUG 1900	New York NY	Woodlawn
08820	Plummer, Caswell Thaddeus	2y	C	5 JUN 1871	Hyattsville MD	Harmony
08810	Plummer, Charles	19y	C	4 DEC 1905	Hyattsville MD	Harmony
05384	Plummer, Charles	19y	C	4 DEC 1905	Asheville NC	Hyattsville MD
08816	Plummer, Charles Henry	2y	C	30 DEC 1872	Hyattsville MD	Harmony
06875	Plummer, Charlie	31y	C	1 JAN 1909	Rosslyn VA	Baptist
08806	Plummer, Clara	7y	C	20 DEC 1887	Hyattsville MD	Harmony
04856	Plummer, Dallas	21y	C	18 AUG 1904	Rosslyn VA	Baptist
08798	Plummer, Emily, b. Eng.	60y	W	17 JAN 1876	Hyattsville MD	Harmony
14923	Plummer, Frank Everett	60y	W	19 JUL 1918	Takoma MD	Rock Creek
01589	Plummer, George W.	2y	C	25 DEC 1894	Rosslyn VA	Baptist
08807	Plummer, Grace	13y	C	11 OCT 1904	Hyattsville MD	Harmony
08819	Plummer, Harry V.	3y	C	30 OCT 1882	Hyattsville MD	Harmony
02655	Plummer, Helen Marie	2m	W	12 NOV 1898	Bladensburg MD	Mt. Olivet
08796	Plummer, Henry V.	60y	C	17 JAN 1905	Kansas City KS	Harmony
08823	Plummer, Infant of Robert	1d	C	11 MAY 1896	Hyattsville MD	Harmony
04259	Plummer, Joseph	23y	C	10 MAY 1903	Rosslyn VA	Baptist
17031	Plummer, Josephine	7y	W	9 MAR 1921	New York NY	Congressional
13325	Plummer, Julia	60y	C	28 JAN 1916	Rosslyn VA	Union
12989	Plummer, Laura	37y	W	30 JUN 1915	Duvall Co. FL	Harmony
08226	Plummer, N. Saunders	57y	C	28 JUL 1911	Hyattsville MD	Harmony
08805	Plummer, Nicholas	17y	C	11 JAN 1905	Hyattsville MD	Harmony
08824	Plummer, Two Infants of Nich.	5h	C	30 MAR 1898	Hyattsville MD	Harmony
06577	Plummer, Viola Laura	1y	C	7 JUN 1908	Baltimore MD	Harmony
05248	Poe, Elizabeth	68y	W	16 AUG 1905	Baltimore MD	Oak Hill
01966	Poe, Emma	5m	W	31 JUL 1896	Dunkirk MD	Glenwood
14676	Poe, Isadora Rebecca	55y	W	10 MAR 1918	Takoma Park MD	Gumeville SC
16791	Poe, James	61y	C	30 OCT 1920	Richmond VA	Harmony
13663	Poe, Marium	5m	W	17 AUG 1916	Chevy Chase MD	Woodlawn
00986	Pohler, Christian G.	21y	W	3 SEP 1893	Brooklyn NY	Glenwood
15905	Pohlmann, Marie	59y	W	26 FEB 1897	Alexandria VA	Prospect Hill[1]
15903	Pohlmann, Michael	69y	W	26 APR 1898	Alexandria VA	Prospect Hill[2]
02545	Poindexter, Levi (jail)	22y	C	7 JUN 1898	Baltimore MD	Mt. Olivet
14842	Poindexter, Scott B.	30y	C	24 MAY 1918	Philadelphia PA	Payne's
18306	Poland, Emma A.	73y	W	28 JAN 1923	Seat Pleasant MD	Congressional
11971	Polar, Mary Ann	65y	W	23 AUG 1913	Takoma Park MD	Rock Creek
02790	Poler, John S.	79y	W	28 MAR 1899	Takoma Park MD	Rock Creek
15974	Poler, John Wellington	67y	W	3 SEP 1919	Takoma Park MD	Rock Creek
08416	Polk, Annie Franklin	70y	W	8 DEC 1911	Friendship H. MD	College
00985	Polkinhorn, Mary	21y	W	31 MAY 1893	Philadelphia PA	Oak Hill
04728	Pollard, Julia	59y	C	22 MAY 1904	Monmouth NJ	Payne's
05838	Pollard, William B.	38y	C	29 NOV 1906	Lynchburg VA	Harmony
07009	Polleys, Bessie C.	32y	W	1 MAY 1909	Ridge MD	Cremated
17348	Pollock, James J.	53y	W	4 AUG 1921	Hampton VA	Arlington
03592	Pollock, Louise	68y	W	24 JUL 1901	Luray VA	Rock Creek
04454	Pomeroy, Mary E.	69y	W	20 SEP 1903	New York NY	Decatur GA
00647	Pomeroy, Samuel Clark	75y	W	27 AUG 1891	Northbridge MA	Forest Hill, Boston
02930	Pomeroy, Willis B., Dr.	63y	W	28 AUG 1899	Kent Co. DE	Arlington
06242	Pond, Elizabeth B.	54y	W	22 SEP 1907	Plattsburgh NY	Arlington VA
06320	Pond, George E., Gen.	60y	W	20 NOV 1907	Winston-Sm. NC	Arlington
14232	Ponton, M.M., Dr.	62y	C	12 JUL 1917	Atlanta GA	Harmony
03586	Pool, Alden G.	7m	W	23 JUL 1901	Seat Pleasant MD	Glenwood
12642	Poole, Charles Clarence	58y	W	3 DEC 1914	Winnetka IL	Rock Creek
03497	Poole, Elizabeth	1y	W	3 MAY 1901	Pittsburgh PA	Congressional
05797	Poole, Florence A.	22y	W	30 OCT 1906	Baltimore MD	Oak Hill

---

[1] Removal from Bethel Cemetery, Alexandria VA.
[2] Removal from Bethel Cemetery, Alexandria VA.

No.	Name of Deceased	Age	Race	Death Date	Place of Death	Place of Burial
15123	Poole, Francis	31y	W	8 OCT 1918	Albany NY	Rock Creek
05970	Poole, Mary A.	83y	W	4 MAR 1907	Evanston IL	Rock Creek
08311	Poole, Mary J.	23y	W	15 SEP 1911	Brentwood MD	Mt. Olivet
15526	Poole, Virgal T.	38y	W	7 JAN 1919	Beltsville MD	Rockville MD
17181	Poor, William	40y	W	21 MAY 1921	Sharpsburg MD	Holyrood
13664	Pope, Barbara	c.69y	W	18 AUG 1916	Gunston VA	Rock Creek
07622	Pope, Otto Eugene	4y	W	12 JUL 1910	Meechums River	Prospect Hill
08153	Pope, William	48y	C	18 JUN 1911	Pittsburgh PA	Harmony
12445	Pope, William Henry	60y	W	17 JUL 1914	Chevy Chase MD	Rock Creek
07049	Popper, Lottie	1m	W	8 JUN 1909	Bethesda MD	Rock Creek
03931	Poppers, Sophia	65y	W	1 JUL 1902	New York NY	Adas Israel
05564	Porter, Anna	38y	C	29 APR 1906	Philadelphia PA	Harmony
05397	Porter, David E.	62y	W	13 DEC 1905	Baltimore MD	Arlington
02748	Porter, Elsie	32y	C	21 FEB 1899	Philadelphia PA	Baptist
05903	Porter, Frances E.	61y	W	21 JAN 1907	Lee Center NY	Rock Creek
17607	Porter, Frank J.	45y	C	24 DEC 1921	Baltimore MD	Harmony
13065	Porter, Frederick	30y	W	20 AUG 1915	Rockville MD	Glenwood
13870	Porter, Henry C.	76y	W	17 DEC 1916	Bethesda MD	Glenwood
06449	Porter, Libbie M.	75y	W	24 FEB 1908	Arlington VA	Rock Creek
06114	Porter, Mouina G.	—	W	24 MAY 1907	San Francisco CA	Congressional
03120	Porter, Nancy	25y	C	6 MAR 1900	Pottstown PA	Pomonkey MD
07308	Porter, Richard	30y	W	8 NOV 1909	Reading PA	Rock Creek
13004	Porter, Richard B.	—	W	10 JUL 1915	Ft. Fairfield ME	Arlington
07845	Porterfield, William A.	54y	W	28 NOV 1910	New York NY	Hagerstown MD
17838	Portman, Adeline E.	62y	W	6 MAY 1922	Chevy Chase MD	Cremated
02716	Portner, Clara	10y	W	15 JAN 1899	Atlantic City NJ	Rock Creek
13344	Portner, Herman H.	29y	W	8 FEB 1916	New York NY	Rock Creek
15950	Porton, Isaac	68y	W	24 AUG 1919	Alex. Co. VA	Adas Israel
01441	Ports, Harry A.	19y	W	20 JUL 1894	Baltimore MD	Congressional
00649	Posey, Ann Dant	old	W	1847	Montg. Co. MD	Rock Creek
00873	Posey, Florence B.	1m	C	11 JUL 1892	New York NY	Harmony
02910	Posey, Francis G.	70y	C	8 AUG 1899	New York NY	Harmony
00651	Posey, Margaret E.	9y	W	5 MAY 1841	Montg. Co. MD	Rock Creek
00988	Posey, Marie A.	5y	C	22 JUL 1893	New York NY	Harmony
00987	Posey, Mary F.	36y	C	22 JUL 1893	New York NY	Harmony
08469	Posey, Mary F.	75y	C	11 JAN 1912	New York NY	Harmony
18271	Posey, Sarah E.	78y	W	14 JAN 1923	Riverdale MD	Congressional
00650	Posey, Susan	1m	W	23 FEB 1838	Montg. Co. MD	Rock Creek
12071	Post, Truman Sanford	73y	W	1 NOV 1913	Chevy Chase MD	Arlington
18339	Potter, Catherine E.	79y	W	11 FEB 1923	Brooklyn NY	Congressional
03543	Potter, Fannie	29y	C	15 JUN 1901	Baltimore MD	Charles Co. MD
00760	Potter, Frances McNeil	80y	W	27 MAR 1892	Brooklyn NY	Congressional
05496	Potter, Mary E.	24y	C	3 MAR 1906	Philadelphia PA	Payne's
13473	Potter, Nettie L. (Fitzgerald)	38y	W	21 APR 1916	Richmond VA	Cremated
17945	Potts, Boydamora Gilbert	83y	W	8 JUL 1922	Lawrence NY	Oak Hill
00028	Potts, Catharine Jeannette	43y	W	2 FEB 1889	Newton Co. GA	Glenwood
07169	Potts, Frances G.	55y	W	23 AUG 1909	New York NY	Arlington VA
02970	Potts, Ida S.	45y	W	6 OCT 1899	Brentwood MD	Glenwood
00506	Potts, Louisa Elizabeth	72y	W	22 MAR 1891	Alexandria VA	Oak Hill
17051	Poulos, James	61y	W	10 MAR 1921	Miami FL	Rock Creek
12916	Powderly, Hannah	45y	W	OCT 1901	Scranton PA	Rock Creek
03713	Powell, Alfred	35y	C	23 NOV 1901	Baltimore MD	Harmony
01594	Powell, Amelia Burrell	3y	W	23 NOV 1891	Grove City PA	Oak Hill
18601	Powell, Arthur	26y	C	10 JUN 1923	Chester PA	Mt. Pleasant
17234	Powell, Catharine H.	80y	W	13 JUN 1921	Annapolis MD	Oak Hill
13976	Powell, Elias B.	56y	W	9 FEB 1917	Hyattsville MD	Rock Creek
14137	Powell, James Henry	67y	W	16 MAY 1917	Takoma Park MD	Rock Creek
06280	Powell, Jas. W., Col.	67y	W	20 OCT 1097	Denver Co. CO	Arlington
01651	Powell, John, notary public	90y	W	10 APR 1895	Occoquan VA	Glenwood
04629	Powell, John S.	75y	W	12 MAR 1904	Alexandria VA	Glenwood

District of Columbia Foreign Death Records, 1888-1923

No.	Name of Deceased	Age	Race	Death Date	Place of Death	Place of Burial
08173	Powell, Laura Virginia	75y	W	2 JUL 1911	Occoquan VA	Glenwood
05137	Powell, Philip Pendleton	59y	W	10 MAY 1905	Santa Barbara CA	Arlington
05878	Powell, William W.	63y	W	1 JAN 1907	Philadelphia PA	Arlington
07660	Power, Edmund, s/o Jas. D.	35y	W	30 JUL 1910	Stamford CN	Mt. Olivet
01754	Power, Helen Catherine	7m	W	20 OCT 1895	Hyattsville	Congressional
03476	Power, James D.	57y	W	6 APR 1901	San Francisco CA	Mt. Olivet
06885	Power, John A.	72y	W	9 JAN 1909	Riverdale MD	Oak Hill
04361	Praithar, Ryon, s/o Wesley	53y	C	23 JUN 1903	Camden NJ	Brook Grove MD
18045	Prater, Lula	53y	C	3 SEP 1922	New York NY	Mt. Olivet
12125	Prather, Alen	58y	W	12 DEC 1913	Pr. Geo. Co. MD	Congressional
01590	Prather, Hattie	32y	C	9 NOV 1894	Jersey City NJ	—
12530	Prather, Jessie R.	54y	W	13 SEP 1914	Barberton OH	Glenwood
04675	Prather, John	28y	W	14 APR 1904	Jacksonville FL	Glenwood
13801	Prather, William	39y	C	3 NOV 1916	Philadelphia PA	Mt. Zion East
03222	Pratt, Adam S.	82y	W	1 JUL 1900	Shandaken NJ	Oak Hill
14755	Pratt, Adelaide R.	42y	W	5 JUN 1918	Takoma MD	Rock Creek
16326	Pratt, Ammey	72y	C	15 FEB 1920	Philadelphia PA	Woodlawn
09060	Pratt, Clarence	30y	C	1 FEB 1913	Reading PA	Harmony
08893	Pratt, Edward E.	41y	W	17 OCT 1912	Catonsville MD	Glenwood
04493	Pratt, Isaac	60y	C	25 OCT 1903	Philadelphia PA	Payne's
04785	Pratt, Kenith	16y	W	8 JUL 1904	Lovell Center ME	Rock Creek
12122	Pratt, Louisa A.	70y	W	10 DEC 1913	Hyattsville MD	Oak Hill
05504	Pratt, Martha	46y	C	17 MAR 1906	Philadelphia PA	Payne's
15161	Pratt, Martha Anna	23y	W	15 OCT 1918	Philadelphia PA	Woodlawn
02014	Pratt, Sophia M.	80y	W	3 AUG 1896	Rock Enon S. VA	Oak Hill
05078	Pratt, Susannah	86y	W	7 APR 1905	St. Louis Co. MO	Arlington
18387	Pratt, Susie Arlean	36y	C	4 MAR 1923	Arlington Co. VA	Arlington Co. VA
12905	Pratt, Walter S.	64y	W	2 MAY 1915	Forest Glen MD	Oak Hill
05877	Prattis, Charles H.	39y	C	25 DEC 1906	New York NY	Mt. Zion East
08538	Preissmer, Ida	22y	W	29 FEB 1912	Fredericksburg VA	Cremated
15811	Prender, John, Jr., U.S.N.	25y	W	11 APR 1919	LaHavre, Fra.	Arlington
07280	Prentiss, Charles Appleton	72y	W	2 NOV 1909	Riverdale MD	Rock Creek
01886	Prentiss, Margaret Joanna	52y	W	30 JAN 1896	Baltimore MD	Rock Creek
05873	Prentiss, Nancy R.	90y	W	29 DEC 1906	Chevy Chase MD	Glenwood
06916	Prescott, Edward	33y	W	11 FEB 1909	St. Louis MO	Rock Creek
04362	Pressey, Ethelbert L.	28y	W	27 APR 1893	Denver CO	Rock Creek
05584	Preston, Augusta	20y	C	23 MAY 1906	Philadelphia PA	Mt. Zion East
05568	Preston, Erasmus D.	54y	W	2 MAY 1906	Tucson AZ	Rock Creek
01414	Preston, Henry Johnston	10m	W	30 JUN 1894	Boston MA	Rock Creek
08084	Preston, Infant of John H.	SB	W	27 APR 1911	Mt. Ranier MD	Glenwood
16725	Preston, Selina	1d	C	13 SEP 1920	Suitland MD	Mt. Olivet
11987	Presutte, Leziers	2y	W	3 SEP 1913	Tuxedo MD	Mt. Olivet
15966	Price, Butler D.	74y	W	29 AUG 1919	Jamestown RI	Arlington
04327	Price, Byron A.	13y	W	22 AUG 1903	River View MD	Mt. Olivet
03037	Price, C.E.	60y	W	15 DEC 1899	Ft. Sill OK	Arlington VA
12746	Price, Catherine	67y	W	31 JAN 1915	Atlantic City NJ	Harmony
16481	Price, Charles S.	39y	W	9 MAY 1920	New York NY	Mt. Olivet
14702	Price, Daniel	28y	C	20 MAR 1918	Philadelphia PA	Moore's
13952	Price, George Thomas	80y	W	29 JAN 1917	Takoma Park MD	Arlington VA
02988	Price, Hezekiah	39y	C	21 OCT 1899	Philadelphia PA	Woodlawn
00507	Price, Katie	23y	W	15 JAN 1891	Memphis TN	Oak Hill
01428	Price, Lillian	8m	W	9 JUL 1894	Stafford Co. VA	Congressional
05588	Price, Mamie	31y	C	4 JUN 1906	Atlantic City NJ	Mt. Olivet
08607	Price, Maurice	68y	C	18 APR 1912	New York NY	Woodlawn
05814	Price, Milton M.	69y	W	26 OCT 1906	Paris, France	Arlington
08183	Price, Morris	67y	W	2 JUL 1911	Rochester MN	Wash. Hebrew
02216	Price, William, Rev.	74y	W	26 MAY 1897	Soldier's Home	Arlington
04135	Priddy, William	21y	W	2 JAN 1903	New York N.Y.	Congressional
07264	Pride, Alfred W.	30y	C	4 DEC 1909	Jersey City NJ	Harmony
05886	Pride, Samuel	44y	C	5 JAN 1907	Baltimore MD	Harmony

No.	Name of Deceased	Age	Race	Death Date	Place of Death	Place of Burial
06999	Priest, Mary Estelle Tulloch	62y	W	21 APR 1909	New York NY	Rock Creek
12691	Priest, Stephen B.	66y	W	31 DEC 1914	Hyattsville MD	Glenwood
04901	Prigg, William Benjamin	34y	W	19 SEP 1904	Charlestown WV	Glenwood
08598	Priggs, Elizabeth	70y	W	15 APR 1912	Staunton VA	Glenwood
01832	Priloram, William, merchant	46y	W	13 DEC 1895	Birmingham AL	Wash. Hebrew
12573	Prim, Ford	58y	C	17 OCT 1914	Boston MA	Manassas VA
04494	Prince, Edward Lee	32y	W	29 OCT 1903	Smithfield WV	Manassas VA
02971	Prince, Frederick C.	57y	W	4 OCT 1899	Hampton VA	Arlington
16215	Prince, Howard Lyman	79y	W	15 JAN 1920	Sandy Spring MD	Arlington
02386	Prince, Mary T.	29y	W	16 FEB 1898	Baltimore MD	Mt. Olivet
05854	Prince, Sarah M.	73y	W	7 DEC 1906	Govanstown MD	Glenwood
05938	Prince, William T.	76y	W	10 FEB 1907	Baltimore MD	Glenwood
00238	Pritchard, Benjamin Barnett	44y	W	30 NOV 1889	Accotink VA	Congressional
15173	Pritchard, Newton, s/o Jas. H.	23y	W	12 OCT 1918	Vineland NJ	Rock Creek
03966	Probey, James K.	57y	W	29 AUG 1902	Atlantic City NJ	Oak Hill
11954	Proby, Charlottie	73y	W	12 AUG 1913	Mt. Ranier MD	Rock Creek
02566	Procter, Annie	20y	C	11 AUG 1898	Bogg's twp. PA	Moore's
07605	Procter, Ralph J.	6m	C	30 JUN 1910	Tuxedo MD	Mt. Olivet
07161	Proctor, Elizabeth	SB	C	20 AUG 1909	Berwyn MD	Mt. Olivet
12239	Proctor, Fannie W.	42y	W	24 FEB 1914	New York NY	Rock Creek
16034	Proctor, Frank M.	76y	W	9 OCT 1919	Mt. Ranier MD	Arlington
07924	Proctor, George W.	74y	W	14 JAN 1911	Norfolk VA	Glenwood
06028	Proctor, James C.	7m	C	13 APR 1907	Branchville MD	Mt. Olivet
02468	Proctor, Jane Elizabeth	79y	W	30 MAY 1898	Forest Glen MD	Rock Creek
17126	Proctor, Lawrence M.	25y	C	25 APR 1921	New York NY	Arlington
02442	Proctor, Robert	83y	W	23 APR 1898	Kensington MD	Rock Creek
16144	Proctor, Virginia	65y	C	9 DEC 1919	Philadelphia PA	Mt. Olivet
11977	Proshel, Elizabeth C.	41y	W	28 AUG 1913	Forestville MD	St. Mary's
01483	Prosise, Jesse	5m	W	1 NOV 1894	Linden MD	Glenwood
01284	Prott, Maria Walberger	67y	W	18 DEC 1893	Tronoto CA	St. Mary's
05085	Prout, Mary C.	72y	W	18 APR 1905	Rockville MD	Oak Hill
16191	Province, B. Pearl	32y	W	6 JAN 1920	Fairfax Co. VA	Glenwood
15918	Province, Bernard Jesse	1y	W	26 JUL 1919	Clifton Sta. VA	Glenwood
08661	Prudhomme, Lucien Franklin	77y	W	16 MAR 1912	Philadelphia PA	Arlington
04165	Pruett, Francis M.	33y	W	4 FEB 1903	New York NY	Congressional
13074	Pruitt, Isabelle R.	41y	W	23 AUG 1915	Gaithersburg MD	Congressional
13718	Prummer, Charlotte	9y	W	12 SEP 1916	Great Falls VA	Congressional
02708	Pryor, Carrie D.	30y	W	13 JAN 1899	Somerville MA	Glenwood
05194	Pryor, Epes	22y	W	4 JUL 1905	Yazoo City MI	Rock Creek
04368	Pryor, Howard S.	43y	C	c.29 JUN 1903	Potomac River	Payne's
02412	Pryor, Thomas D.	40y	W	16 MAR 1898	Galveston TX	Congressional
16541	Pugh, Marie Anaise	11y	W	17 JUN 1920	Kensington MD	Mt. Olivet
16399	Pugh, Sarah E.	44y	W	19 MAR 1920	Arlington Co. VA	Congressional
08394	Pugh, Sarah Hunter	81y	W	22 NOV 1911	Chevy Chase MD	Eufaula AL
17329	Pugh, William B.	52y	W	27 JUL 1921	Garfield Hp.	Rock Creek
00165	Pulizzi, Frederick F.	22y	W	21 SEP 1889	New York NY	Congressional
09193	Pullett, Laura	40y	C	26 APR 1913	Bridgeville DE	Harmony
16048	Pulliam, Rebecca Ann	64y	W	15 OCT 1919	Maryland Pk. MD	Rock Creek
14173	Pullin, Mary	77y	W	15 JUN 1917	Clinton MD	Congressional
15593	Pullin, Tyler J.	70y	W	29 JAN 1919	Mt. Vernon VA	Congressional
16236	Pumphrey, Elizabeth	75y	W	21 JAN 1920	New York NY	Glenwood
01652	Pumphrey, Elizabeth C.	77y	W	8 MAY 1895	Upper Marl. MD	Glenwood
07720	Pumphrey, Ethel	11y	W	30 AUG 1910	Takoma Park MD	Rock Creek
01489	Pumphrey, G. Emma	46y	W	13 SEP 1894	Anne Arundel Co.	Congressional
15778	Pumphrey, James L.	62y	W	14 MAY 1919	Upper Marl. MD	Glenwood
00652	Pumphrey, Lloyd W.	52y	W	18 JUN 1891	Baltimore MD	Congressional
14419	Pumphrey, Martha E.	74y	W	20 OCT 1917	West Orange NJ	Holyrood
14929	Pupenbring, Marie	81y	W	22 JUL 1918	Forest Glen MD	Prospect Hill
16428	Purcell, John J.	45y	W	4 APR 1920	Phoenix AZ	Mt. Olivet
15149	Purcell, Ruie L.	25y	C	11 OCT 1918	Denver CO	Congressional

District of Columbia Foreign Death Records, 1888-1923

No.	Name of Deceased	Age	Race	Death Date	Place of Death	Place of Burial
04001	Purcell, William	47y	W	19 JUL 1902	Forestville MD	St. Mary's
05728	Purington, Amelia J.	70y	W	5 SEP 1906	Atlantic City NJ	Oak Hill
02174	Purman, David Gray	61y	W	6 MAY 1897	N. Takoma MD	Arlington VA
17457	Purnell, Louis E.	49y	W	6 OCT 1921	Lakewood OH	Cedar Hill
02444	Pursell, Adda Seliner	26d	W	31 OCT 1872	Fairfax Co. VA	Congressional
02445	Pursell, Harry Lee	5y	W	5 APR 1883	Washington DC	Congressional
03573	Pursell, L.C.	40y	W	5 JUL 1901	Atlanta GA	Cremated
02446	Pursell, Ruth	2y	W	28 MAY 1885	Anacostia DC	Congressional
02443	Pursell, William Thomas	6m	W	20 AUG 1872	Fairfax Co. VA	Congressional
03709	Pusey, Anna M.	60y	W	c.1860	New London PA	Rock Creek
01752	Pyer, George, merchant	59y	W	21 AUG 1895	Montg. Co. MD	Rock Creek
17032	Pyle, Catherine Atnella	25y	W	10 MAR 1921	Takoma Park MD	Mt. Olivet
18158	Pyle, Katherine Austa	1y	W	14 NOV 1922	Takoma Park MD	Mt. Olivet
00109	Pyles, Andrew	9m	W	19 JUL 1889	Montg. Co. MD	Tenallytown
18455	Pyles, Ann Mary	58y	W	3 APR 1923	Takoma Park MD	Ft. Lincoln
02137	Pyles, Anna Elender	64y	W	1 MAR 1897	Bethesda Pk. MD	Tenallytown
18056	Pyles, Charles W.	54y	W	9 SEP 1922	Pomonkey MD	Congressional
18318	Pyles, Dallis M.	1y	W	2 FEB 1923	Bethesda MD	Congressional
06731	Pyles, Richard	98y	W	16 SEP 1908	Glen Echo MD	Rock Creek
12489	Pyles, Richard Henry	67y	W	22 AUG 1914	Glen Echo MD	Rock Creek
12064	Pyles, Robert D.	52y	W	26 OCT 1913	Concord MD	Rock Creek
05751	Pywell, Ann Mariah	85y	W	26 SEP 1906	College Park MD	Rock Creek

No.	Name of Deceased	Age	Race	Death Date	Place of Death	Place of Burial
Q						
06343	Quackenbush, Augusta C.	62y	W	7 DEC 1907	Baltimore MD	Rock Creek
08452	Quackenbush, Cynthia H.	83y	W	31 DEC 1911	Annapolis MD	Oak Hill
13157	Quackenbush, Isaac	80y	W	19 OCT 1915	Cannonsville NY	Glenwood
01955	Quackenbush, Stephen W.	47y	W	3 JUN 1896	Brooklyn NY	Oak Hill
18019	Quaiffe, Alfred R.	85y	W	18 AUG 1922	Sharon CN	Arlington
03920	Qualls, Laura B.	31y	C	22 JUL 1902	New York NY	Woodlawn
16963	Quander, James S.	29y	C	8 FEB 1921	Baltimore MD	Mt. Olivet
07499	Quander, John Thomas	30y	W	12 APR 1910	Brentwood MD	Mt. Olivet
17137	Quander, Margreth	53y	C	30 APR 1921	Waldorf MD	Harmony
07947	Quarles, Mary E.	62y	C	25 JAN 1911	Atlantic City NJ	Harmony
12030	Quarrell, Ernest Harry	31y	W	7 OCT 1913	Tuxedo Park NY	Glenwood
00394	Quarrels, Charles	33y	W	26 AUG 1890	Germantown MD	Baltimore MD
05517	Queen, Ann	45y	C	4 APR 1906	Chesa. Jct. MD	Payne's
17652	Queen, Catherine	79y	C	24 JAN 1922	Warrenton VA	Mt. Olivet
08363	Queen, Edna Geneva	2m	—	19 OCT 1911	Takoma Park MD	Rock Creek
00110	Queen, Emma	28y	C	16 JUL 1889	Seat Pleasant MD	Jones' Chapel
05131	Queen, Frances	75y	C	15 MAY 1905	Newport RI	Woodlawn
06673	Queen, Georgena	50y	C	6 AUG 1908	Seat Pleasant MD	Payne's
02880	Queen, Isabella	35y	C	12 JUL 1899	Seat Pleasant MD	Payne's
05500	Queen, James	35y	C	14 MAR 1906	Baltimore MD	Moore's
05038	Queen, Jessie	1y	C	22 FEB 1905	Seat Pleasant MD	Payne's
15224	Queen, John	32y	C	15 OCT 1918	Atlantic City NJ	Woodlawn
00989	Queen, Lemuel	16y	C	21 JUL 1893	Seat Pleasant MD	Jones' Chapel
04500	Queen, Maggie	17y	C	4 NOV 1903	Seat Pleasant MD	Payne's
02725	Queen, Mary C.	80y	C	29 JAN 1899	Warrenton VA	Mt. Olivet
16337	Queen, Mary F.	11m	C	24 FEB 1920	Hyattsville MD	Mt. Olivet
09184	Queen, Richard	35y	C	21 APR 1913	Williamsburg PA	Harmony
01907	Queen, Roland	7m	C	23 APR 1907	Forestville MD	Mt. Olivet
03926	Queen, Walter	6y	C	20 JUL 1902	Tuxedo MD	Payne's
07010	Queen, William T.	7m	C	20 MAY 1909	Riverdale MD	Mt. Olivet
02015	Quesenbury, E.R., Mrs.	73y	W	13 SEP 1896	Galveston TX	Holyrood
02266	Quick, Susan R.S.	78y	W	5 JUL 1897	Gaithersburg MD	Oak Hill
08693	Quigley, James	36y	W	28 MAR 1912	Manila, P.I.	Mt. Olivet
06064	Quigley, John	15y	W	11 MAY 1907	Alex. Co. VA	Mt. Olivet
03185	Quigley, Sabina	61y	W	13 MAY 1900	New York NY	Mt. Olivet
02664	Quill, John H.	36y	W	1 JAN 1891	Washington DC	Mt. Olivet[1]
12500	Quill, Mary C.	53y	W	25 AUG 1914	Atlantic City NJ	Mt. Olivet
16165	Quillen, Leonard LeRoy	2m	W	26 DEC 1919	Capitol Hts. MD	Prospect Hill
05295	Quiller, James	15m	C	19 SEP 1905	Philadelphia PA	Payne's
14912	Quimby, Emma Sinclair	51y	W	11 JUL 1918	Atlanta GA	Cremated
15873	Quince, Walter S.	50y	C	6 JUL 1919	New York NY	Riverdale MD
16789	Quinn, Augusta Grandin	73y	W	31 OCT 1920	New Rochelle NY	Glenwood
18488	Quinn, Jesse C.	30y	W	16 APR 1923	Salem VA	Cedar Hill MD
04893	Quint, Andrew J.	15y	W	18 DEC 1845	N. Anson ME	Glenwood
04892	Quint, William	72y	W	18 APR 1855	N. Anson ME	Glenwood
08580	Quinter, Ada A.	70y	W	3 APR 1912	Wheaton MD	Rock Creek
08369	Quinter, Mary E.	25y	W	23 OCT 1911	Towson MD	Wheaton MD
06892	Quinter, Thomas J.	72y	W	13 JAN 1909	Wheaton MD	Rock Creek

[1] Note of 22 NOV 1898, from Ellicott City, Md., for removal of John H. Quill to a cemetery in Washington, D.C.

No.	Name of Deceased	Age	Race	Death Date	Place of Death	Place of Burial
R						
08037	Rabbia, F. Sebastian, Rev.	70y	W	27 MAR 1911	Hagerstown MD	Mt. Olivet
12430	Rabbitt, Carrie V.	41y	W	9 JUL 1914	Clarendon VA	Glenwood
08215	Rabbitt, Infant of Julia	SB	W	25 JUL 1911	Capitol Hts. MD	Mt. Olivet
05686	Rabbitt, Samuel E.	78y	W	11 AUG 1906	Riverdale MD	St. Mary's
06751	Raborg, Mary Meade	39y	W	28 SEP 1908	Muirkirk MD	Glenwood
12256	Raborg, William A.	55y	W	29 JAN 1914	Philadelphia PA	Rock Creek
04631	Rachner, Katie	34y	W	11 MAR 1904	Asheville NC	Congressional
15442	Racoosin, Charles, s/o Simon	—	W	12 DEC 1918	Detroit MI	Elesavetgrad
13054	Racoosin, Lewis, s/o Charles	28y	W	14 AUG 1915	Roanoke VA	Elesavetgrad
00300	Radcliff, Joseph	86y	W	29 MAR 1890	Baltimore MD	Glenwood
13267	Radcliffe, Jane E.	71y	W	25 DEC 1915	Woodmont VA	Oak Hill
14900	Radford, Ann	91y	W	7 JUL 1918	Rockville MD	Oak Hill
00990	Radigan, George F.	7y	W	7 AUG 1893	New York NY	Holyrood
13351	Raeburn, James S.	47y	W	12 FEB 1916	Falls Church VA	Glenwood
07627	Raeburn, Wm.Locraft, s/o Jas.	10d	W	12 JUL 1910	McLean VA	Glenwood
17659	Raezer, John W.	19y	W	24 JUN 1918	France	Arlington
14111	Raff, Matilda	65y	W	26 APR 1917	Rockville MD	Wash. Hebrew
01653	Ragan, Andrew J.	67y	W	16 MAR 1895	Wilmington DE	Congressional
08542	Ragan, Charles A.	31y	W	3 MAR 1912	New Orleans LA	Mt. Olivet
07496	Ragan, Daniel	43y	W	26 MAR 1910	Omaha NE	Congressional
17541	Ragan, Margaret	86y	W	18 NOV 1921	Philadelphia PA	Holyrood
05084	Ragland, Lucy	56y	C	13 APR 1905	Medford MA	Harmony
17709	Railey, Jane H.	82y	W	23 FEB 1922	Hyattsville MD	Congressional
17576	Rainey, Charles T.	c.42y	W	24 NOV 1921	San Domingo	Rock Creek
18234	Ralph, Joseph E.	55y	W	30 DEC 1922	New York NY	Mt. Olivet
06381	Ralston, John	59y	W	7 JAN 1908	Louisville KY	Oak Hill[1]
15047	Ralston, Ruth	23y	W	26 SEP 1918	Upper Marl. MD	Piemont NY
02673	Ramsay, Douglas	—	W	21 JUL 1861	Battle of Bull Run	Oak Hill
04871	Ramsay, Gertrude C.	30y	W	1 SEP 1904	Oxford MD	Oak Hill
02745	Ramsay, Joseph Gates	55y	W	13 FEB 1899	Augusta GA	Oak Hill
03447	Ramsay, Samuel	82y	W	10 MAR 1901	Baltimore MD	Rock Creek
05798	Ramsberg, Annie C.	54y	W	31 OCT 1906	Hyattsville MD	Oak Hill
12937	Ramsburg, Cornelius S.	76y	W	20 MAY 1915	Laurel MD	Oak Hill
12204	Ramsey, Annie	53y	C	5 FEB 1914	New York NY	Harmony
03417	Ramsey, John, merchant	64y	W	11 FEB 1901	Jersey City NJ	Arlington VA
04979	Ramsey, Lucie C.	60y	W	17 DEC 1904	Oxford MD	Oak Hill
07690	Ramsmer, Hugh E.	29y	W	25 FEB 1901	Atlanta GA	Glenwood
17673	Rand, William Spaulding	46y	W	3 FEB 1922	Takoma Park MD	Glenwood
02267	Randal, James A.	6m	W	7 JUL 1897	Highland MD	Mt. Olivet
12268	Randall, Bessie Evelyn	4m	C	24 MAR 1914	Cedar Hts. MD	Woodlawn
13772	Randall, D.H.	30y	W	23 OCT 1916	Perryman MD	Catlett VA
01440	Randall, Daniel Goodloe	12h	W	7 FEB 1886	McDonnell Co. NC	Glenwood
05108	Randall, Edward C.	14y	C	29 APR 1905	Brentwood MD	Mt. Olivet
04951	Randall, Edward L., Maj.	68y	W	7 NOV 1904	Atlanta GA	Arlington VA
14365	Randall, Emma	45y	C	16 SEP 1917	Potomac MD	Mt. Zion West
05770	Randall, Emma	24y	C	13 OCT 1906	Seat Pleasant MD	Payne's
13828	Randall, Frederick F.	21y	W	24 NOV 1916	Brentwood MD	Mt. Olivet
16550	Randall, Garnet	17y	C	22 JUN 1920	Seat Pleasant MD	Payne's
00395	Randall, George Henry	54y	W	29 AUG 1890	Forestville MD	Congressional
16975	Randall, Isabella	73y	C	13 FEB 1921	Brentwood MD	Mt. Olivet
16865	Randall, John T.	25y	C	17 DEC 1920	Philadelphia PA	Mt. Zion East
04202	Randall, Joseph	18y	C	27 MAR 1903	Brentwood MD	Mt. Olivet
07889	Randall, Maria A.	73y	W	22 DEC 1910	Laurel MD	Congressional
05393	Randall, W.G.	46y	W	11 DEC 1905	Blowing Rock NC	Glenwood
04320	Randolf, Sarah	20y	C	11 JUN 1903	Philadelphia PA	Arlington VA

---

[1] Removed 18 MAR 1908 to Evandale, Tasmanie, Australia.

No.	Name of Deceased	Age	Race	Death Date	Place of Death	Place of Burial
00559½	Randolph, Ann	1y	W	18 MAY 1891	Alexandria VA	Rock Creek
01186	Randolph, Armstead	32y	W	16 DEC 1892	Baltimore MD	Congressional
04281	Randolph, Arthur	46y	W	31 AUG 1899	Douglaston LI	Rock Creek
14071	Randolph, Cornelia P., d/o Wm.	92y	W	2 APR 1917	Moorefield WV	Oak Hill
15994	Randolph, Georganna E.	68y	W	14 SEP 1919	Philadelphia PA	Congressional
04842	Randolph, Henry P.	77y	W	12 AUG 1904	Bethesda MD	Holyrood
01187	Randolph, Ines	50y	W	28 APR 1892	Baltimore MD	Congressional
01077	Randolph, Richard	60y	W	8 FEB 1893	Baltimore MD	Oak Hill
17634	Randolph, Susan P.	—	—	—	Loudoun Co. VA	Congressional[1]
17635	Randolph, Susan P. Armsted	—	—	—	Loudoun Co. VA	Congressional
14637	Rankin, John M.	56y	W	13 FEB 1918	Muirkirk MD	Rock Creek
02387	Rankins, Estella	14y	C	9 JAN 1898	Richmond VA	Harmony
12562	Ransom, David L.	1y	C	8 OCT 1914	Fairmont Hts. MD	Union
03488	Rapley, Charity S.	67y	W	26 APR 1901	Avenel MD	Oak Hill
17926	Rapley, Randolph Rufus	63y	W	28 JUN 1922	Silver Spring MD	Oak Hill
02730	Rapp, Andrew, Rev.	50y	W	31 JAN 1899	Leonardtown MD	College
13937	Raschal, Samuel Scoville	41y	W	19 JAN 1917	Chevy Chase MD	Oak Hill
16639	Rathburn, Maria Axelina	51y	W	3 AUG 1920	Bluemont VA	Denver CO
04989	Rathgeber, Wilhelmina	60y	W	1 JAN 1905	Ft. Myer VA	Jersey City NJ
06202	Raub, Christina S.	76y	W	24 AUG 1907	New York NY	Congressional
06800	Raub, Jane S.	66y	W	2 NOV 1908	Buffalo NY	Arlington
00761	Raub, Viola A.	11y	W	13 NOV 1891	Hyattsville MD	Glenwood
01078	Raub, Walton B.	31y	W	18 APR 1893	VA	Oak Hill
12361	Raum, Greene B.	51y	W	12 MAY 1914	New York NY	Rock Creek
16243	Rauth, Louise	55y	W	25 JAN 1920	Cherrydale VA	Prospect Hill
14895	Ravenel, William DeC.	21y	W	30 JUN 1918	Hicks TX	Rock Creek
03847	Rawlings, Daniel	22y	C	5 APR 1902	Philadelphia PA	Woodlawn
16043	Rawlings, Emma T. (Hollidge)	67y	W	8 OCT 1919	Milwaukee WI	Rock Creek
12211	Rawlings, Josephine F.	35y	W	7 FEB 1914	Kensington MD	Glenwood
15271	Rawlings, Mary L.	32y	W	19 OCT 1918	New York NY	Mt. Olivet
14481	Rawlins, William Joe	22y	W	22 NOV 1917	Ft. Houston TX	Arlington
04060	Rawson, Edward J.	76y	W	16 OCT 1902	Lincoln VA	Cremated
06176	Rawson, Eliza Finch (Coffin)	76y	W	9 AUG 1907	Lincoln VA	Cremated
01591	Ray, Alfred, farmer	70y	W	5 JAN 1895	Montg. Co. MD	Rock Creek
13999	Ray, Birdie	44y	C	18 FEB 1917	New York NY	Mt. Olivet
02088	Ray, Charles	28y	C	28 NOV 1896	Harrisburg PA	Payne's
16245	Ray, Clarence	28y	C	24 JAN 1920	Ardmore PA	Sligo MD
13374	Ray, Clary	50y	W	24 FEB 1916	New York NY	Oak Hill
03772	Ray, Daniel Anthony	70y	W	17 SEP 1901	Honolulu HI	Oak Hill
08583	Ray, Emma	48y	C	3 APR 1912	Philadelphia PA	Woodlawn
17733	Ray, Gertrude E.	73y	W	10 MAR 1922	Bethesda MD	Glenwood
04102	Ray, Harry	21y	C	22 DEC 1902	Philadelphia PA	Payne's
15325	Ray, James Enos	78y	W	4 NOV 1918	Chillum MD	Glenwood
00874	Ray, John G.	28y	W	14 SEP 1892	Orkney Spgs. VA	Holyrood
05693	Ray, Powell	22y	W	19 AUG 1906	Asbury Park NJ	Woodlawn
06490	Ray, Ruth E.	1y	C	3 APR 1908	Jersey City NJ	Harmony
17824	Ray, Thomas J.	81y	W	30 APR 1922	New York NY	Congressional
05118	Raybold, Marguerite L.	1m	W	8 MAY 1905	Riverdale MD	Rock Creek
17773	Raynor, William	38y	W	1 APR 1922	Brooklyn NY	Congressional
13865	Rayworth, William	72y	W	14 DEC 1916	Fauquier Co. VA	Rock Creek
11809	Rea, Carolyn M.	36y	W	11 MAY 1913	Charleston SC	Cremated
06592	Rea, Mary E.	51y	W	16 NOV 1898	Mt. Pleasant NY	Glenwood
12360	Rea, Thomas F.	78y	W	14 MAY 1914	Bon Air VA	Rock Creek
04341	Reach, Bella V.	21d	W	2 MAY 1874	Brooklyn NY	Congressional
04342	Reach, Leo R.	9m	W	10 JUL 1874	Brooklyn NY	Congressional
14878	Reach, Leslie	42y	W	21 JUN 1918	Morristown PA	Congressional

[1] Removal of remains of Susan P. Randolph, Susan P. Armsted Randolph and Randolph Seaton, 12 JAN 1922, noting that they had all been dead over 50 years.

District of Columbia Foreign Death Records, 1888-1923

No.	Name of Deceased	Age	Race	Death Date	Place of Death	Place of Burial
03758	Read, Anna	20y	W	10 JAN 1902	Philadelphia PA	Rock Creek
14691	Reading, Amy B.	4y	W	16 MAR 1918	Black Mtn. NC	Rockville MD
07584	Ready, Bridget (Collins)	74y	W	17 JUN 1910	Winchester VA	Mt. Olivet
12564	Ready, Margaret	53y	W	9 OCT 1914	Allegheny PA	Mt. Olivet
18553	Ready, Michael J.	44y	W	19 MAY 1923	Laurel MD	Mt. Olivet
05201	Reagan, James S.	42y	W	7 JUL 1905	Asheville NC	Mt. Olivet
13334	Reagan, Robert Allen	78y	W	1 FEB 1916	Park City TN	Arlington
00007	Reamer, Elizabeth De.	85y	W	3 JAN 1889	Herndon VA	Oak Hill
09181	Reaney, Agnes	3½y		c.1898	Huntingdon PA	Rock Creek
16293	Reap, Francis J.	55y	W	5 FEB 1920	Jacksonville FL	Dansville NY
05521	Rearden, Thomas E., Jr.	18y	W	4 APR 1906	Orange VA	Mt. Olivet
06520	Reardon, Ralph	6y	W	19 APR 1908	New York NY	Mt. Olivet
09191	Reardon, Sarah Webb	30y	C	26 APR 1913	Boston MA	Harmony
00875	Reason, William	75y	W	21 APR 1892	Ellicott City MD	Mt. Olivet
16856	Reasoner, Bernice	27y	W	12 DEC 1920	Saginaw MI	Glenwood
18308	Reaves, Martha	76y	C	30 JAN 1923	Fairmont Hts. MD	Payne's
00046	Rebitz, Amelia	78y	W	25 MAR 1889	Baltimore MD	Prospect Hill
01259	Rebsamen, Franz Joseph	c.28y	W	15 OCT 1893	Magruder's Curve	Graceland
08682	Redd, Albert V.	8m	C	25 JUN 1912	Brentwood MD	Harmony
15722	Redden, Mr.	45y	W	13 APR 1919	Camden NJ	Prospect Hill
09032	Reddick, Lula	—	C	14 JAN 1913	Atlantic City NJ	Payne's
13858	Rederick, Harry Thomas	24y	C	7 DEC 1916	St. Albans VT	Payne's
06775	Rederson, May	27y	W	15 OCT 1908	New York NY	Congressional
03888	Redman, Dennis	70y	W	27 MAY 1902	Burnt Mills MD	Mt. Olivet
08260	Redmiles, Benjamin	3m	W	19 AUG 1811	Maryland Pk. MD	Mt. Olivet
18204	Redmon, Richard	49y	W	8 DEC 1922	Miami FL	Cremated
14748	Redmond, Florence M.	40y	W	8 APR 1918	Fallon NV	Congressional
13167	Redmund, James	½h	W	28 OCT 1915	Seat Pleasant MD	Mt. Olivet
14000	Redrick, Anna E., d/o Edward	19y	C	17 FEB 1917	Richmond VA	Payne's
17355	Redrick, Edward	72y	C	11 AUG 1921	St. Albans VT	Payne's
15542	Redway, Loriette C.	84y	W	4 JAN 1919	Chattanooga OK	Rock Creek
05732	Reece, Victoria	38y	C	4 SEP 1906	Chicago IL	Harmony
00251	Reed, Amon	50y	W	26 DEC 1889	Montg. Co. MD	Baltimore MD
01188	Reed, Anna M.	65y	W	4 OCT 1892	Hancock MD	Portland OR
07418	Reed, Annie	56y	C	13 FEB 1910	Bladensburg MD	Payne's
13614	Reed, Carl	19y	W	23 JUL 1916	Piscataway C. MD	Rock Creek
02016	Reed, Catherine A.	47y	W	13 SEP 1896	Baltimore MD	Oak Hill
15121	Reed, Charles Augustus	15y	W	9 OCT 1918	Berwyn MD	Mt. Olivet
05151	Reed, Francis	30y	C	29 MAY 1905	Pittsburgh PA	Harmony
11995	Reed, Henry B.	31y	C	6 SEP 1913	New York NY	Harmony
14510	Reed, Henry C.	43y	C	14 DEC 1917	Philadelphia PA	Mt. Olivet
00045	Reed, Homer L.	18y	W	18 MAR 1873	Alex. Co. VA	Rock Creek
07277	Reed, James	34y	W	16 NOV 1909	Brentwood MD	Mt. Olivet
16572	Reed, Jennie A.	60y	W	2 JUL 1920	Marblehead MA	Charleston SC
07386	Reed, Jennie M., d/o George	37y	W	23 JAN 1910	Trenton NJ	Glenwood
15268	Reed, Joseph	29y	W	20 OCT 1918	Camp Hanc. GA	Nomini Wharf VA
17951	Reed, Martha McDee	59y	W	9 JUL 1922	Takoma Park MD	Pittsburgh PA
01592	Reed, Mary	71y	W	13 JAN 1895	Rosslyn VA	Rock Creek
05612	Reed, Mary Agnes	1y	W	28 JUN 1906	Brentwood MD	Mt. Olivet
16419	Reed, Mary Jane	62y	W	3 APR 1920	Brentwood MD	Mt. Olivet
16852	Reed, Matthew	5m	C	9 DEC 1920	Rosslyn VA	Mt. Zion East
15436	Reed, Richard	37y	C	10 DEC 1918	Occoquan VA	Payne's
14418	Reed, Susie	31y	C	19 OCT 1917	New Rochelle NY	Woodlawn
00186	Reed, Theodore, Rev.	45y	W	20 OCT 1889	Bladensburg MD	Rock Creek
00876	Reed, Thomas J.	37y	W	2 MAY 1892	Great Falls MT	Rock Creek
15027	Reed, William A.	18y	W	16 SEP 1918	Chelsea MA	Arlington
06906	Reed, William M.	43y	W	29 JAN 1909	Harrisburg PA	Glenwood
06006	Reed, William R.	70y	W	30 MAR 1907	Freemont LA	Arlington VA
16147	Reeder, Alverta M.	1y	C	11 DEC 1919	Philadelphia PA	Mt. Zion West
05371	Reeder, Anne	75y	W	17 NOV 1905	Sykesville MD	Mt. Olivet

No.	Name of Deceased	Age	Race	Death Date	Place of Death	Place of Burial
12695	Reeder, Daniel K., s/o John	76y	W	2 JAN 1915	Dover DE	Glenwood
16237	Reeder, Eliza J.	77y	W	21 JAN 1920	Dover DE	Glenwood
06090	Reeder, John	22y	C	3 JUN 1907	Baltimore MD	Mt. Olivet
03170	Reeder, Richard	78y	W	19 APR 1900	Baltimore MD	Mt. Olivet
07647	Reeding, Charles E., s/o Walt.	4y	W	23 JUL 1910	Clarendon VA	Congressional
13151	Reese, Emma S.	75y	W	17 OCT 1915	Derwood MD	Glenwood
00399	Reeside, Agnes A.	8m	W	4 SEP 1890	Baltimore MD	Oak Hill
01509	Reeside, Denison	48y	W	12 OCT 1894	Baltimore MD	Oak Hill
12455	Reeside, Francis	79y	W	23 JUL 1914	Garrett Park MD	Rock Creek
05831	Reeside, John E.	87y	W	27 NOV 1906	Baltimore MD	Oak Hill
04479	Reeve, Nathan	87y	W	16 OCT 1903	Dayton OH	Congressional
04109	Reeves, Archie	44y	C	26 DEC 1902	New York NY	Harmony
05267	Reeves, George W.	63y	W	31 AUG 1905	Hampton VA	Glenwood
14233	Reeves, Isaac Stockton Keeth	66y	W	16 JUL 1917	Fredericksburg VA	Arlington VA
13412	Reeves, John B.	44y	W	13 MAR 1916	Atlantic City NJ	Glenwood
04767	Reeves, John George	67y	W	16 JUN 1904	Ellwood City PA	Rock Creek
14068	Reeves, Rebecca	70y	C	2 APR 1917	Atlantic City NJ	Harmony
06372	Reeves, Samuel	60y	C	2 JAN 1908	Alexandria VA	Harmony
01190	Regan, Benjamin R.R.	9y	—	6 NOV 1892	Sacketts Har. NY	Oak Hill
01755	Regan, Grace	16y	W	21 SEP 1895	Sacketts Har. NY	Oak Hill
15670	Regan, James T.	19y	W	5 MAR 1918	Baltimore MD	Mt. Olivet
01189	Regan, Russell	9y	W	6 NOV 1892	Sacketts Har. NY	Oak Hill
02476	Reh, Henry F.	32y	W	4 AUG 1898	Colonial Bea. VA	Prospect Hill
07030	Reh, Henry F.	62y	W	19 MAY 1909	Hyattsville MD	Rock Creek
03973	Reh, Olza	6m	W	12 AUG 1902	Oil City PA	Glenwood
06793	Reh, Sophia	20y	W	29 OCT 1908	Cottage City MD	Rock Creek
14338	Reibetanz, Marea A.	1y	W	4 SEP 1917	Riverdale MD	Mt. Olivet
16112	Reichard, Charles W.	63y	W	16 NOV 1919	Friendship H. MD	Oak Hill
03700	Reichart, Oscar	55y	W	7 NOV 1901	Evansville MD	Rock Creek
17998	Reickert, Louis G.	48y	W	7 AUG 1922	Norfolk VA	St. Mary's
18260	Reid, Elizabeth	61y	C	10 JAN 1923	Baltimore MD	Mt. Olivet
05921	Reid, Horace P.	23y	W	31 JAN 1907	Cincinnati OH	Glenwood
17404	Reid, James T.	51y	C	12 SEP 1921	Annapolis MD	Wayside MD
01889	Reid, John L., Dr.	41y	W	15 FEB 1896	Nassau, N.P.	Oak Hill
04141	Reid, Mary Catharine	85y	W	25 JAN 1903	Orange NJ	Christian
14607	Reigart, Margaret	78y	W	30 JAN 1918	Newark NJ	Glenwood
00291	Reigart, Thomas	47y	W	12 MAR 1890	Maysville KY	Arlington VA
06700	Reiley, Randolph	26y	C	18 AUG 1908	Monmouth Co. NJ	Mt. Zion West
02644	Reilley, Stephen W.	45y	W	5 NOV 1898	New York NY	Congressional
17433	Reilly, Edward	95y	W	27 SEP 1921	Takoma Park MD	Beltsville MD
00877	Reilly, Jennie Diven	62y	W	29 JUL 1892	Colonial Bea. VA	Mt. Olivet
08562	Reilly, John	45y	W	18 MAR 1912	New York NY	Mt. Olivet
17239	Reilly, Mary	72y	W	14 JUN 1921	Mt. Hope MD	Congressional
04918	Reily, James	67y	W	12 OCT 1904	College Park MD	Rock Creek
05889	Reily, Rebecca A.	82y	W	8 JAN 1907	Baltimore MD	Holyrood
03047	Reinburg, Norman	5d	W	24 DEC 1899	Ballston VA	Congressional
16482	Reiners, Jacob	74y	W	13 MAY 1920	Mt. Ranier MD	Prospect Hill
05546	Reinhardt, Susan H.	2m	W	22 APR 1906	Chevy Chase MD	Prospect Hill
07481	Reintzel, Emily	2m	W	25 MAR 1910	Mt. Ranier MD	Rock Creek
14279	Reintzel, Margaret	85y	W	6 AUG 1917	Philadelphia PA	Oak Hill
05326	Reisinger, Charles H.	30y	W	20 OCT 1905	Denver CO	Prospect Hill
13675	Reisinger, Dorathea	65y	W	23 AUG 1916	Middletown NY	Prospect Hill
04205	Reisinger, Wm. Geo., baker	63y	W	20 MAR 1903	Rockville MD	Prospect Hill
17277	Reiss, Benjamin W.	74y	W	1 JUL 1921	Wash. Grove MD	Congressional
15351	Reitz, Lewis M.	54y	W	12 NOV 1918	The Cedars VA	Rock Creek
02912	Reitz, Lizzie MacNichol	33y	W	12 AUG 1899	Tamworth NJ	Congressional
07960	Rekert, Emile	82y	W	4 DEC 1910	St. Elizabeth's	St. Elizabeth's
06614	Remburg, Louis G.	33y	W	21 JUN 1908	Santa Fe NM	Congressional
04723	Remington, Chancey H.	87y	W	22 MAY 1904	Takoma Park MD	Arlington
01079	Remington, Edith	9y	W	20 FEB 1893	Philadelphia PA	Rock Creek

District of Columbia Foreign Death Records, 1888-1923

No.	Name of Deceased	Age	Race	Death Date	Place of Death	Place of Burial
02722	Remington, Hattie	20y	W	22 JAN 1899	Philadelphia PA	Rock Creek
12881	Remington, Justus D.	65y	W	13 APR 1915	Yonkers NY	Rock Creek
15049	Remler, Frederick T.	30y	W	28 SEP 1918	Camp Hump. VA	Rock Creek
07616	Remond, Louis	31y	W	4 JUL 1910	Osterville MA	Mt. Olivet
05175	Renard, Marie Bertha Catron	41y	W	16 MAR 1905	Fredericksburg VA	Holyrood
16030	Rendall, Caroline	54y	W	6 OCT 1919	Takoma Park MD	Kalamazoo MI
00653	Renfro, George W.	19y	C	3 OCT 1891	Huntsville AL	Woodlawn
04350	Renfro, Georgia	4y	C	4 AUG 1903	Hampton VA	Woodlawn
03167	Renick, Edward J.	50y	W	14 APR 1900	Paris, France	Oak Hill
18206	Renney, Mary Thomas	84y	W	12 DEC 1922	Maryland Pk. MD	Congressional
03060	Rennie, J.H.	59y	W	3 JAN 1900	Bladensburg MD	Glenwood
13099	Renshaw, Elizabeth H.	60y	W	10 SEP 1915	Colonial Bea. VA	Oak Hill
13977	Renshaw, Violet	29y	W	10 FEB 1917	Chillum MD	Rock Creek
14256	Rentz, William	46y	W	26 JUL 1917	Charles Co. MD	Prospect Hill
03834	Repetti, Mary A.	49y	W	25 MAR 1902	Norfolk VA	Mt. Olivet
17916	Repetti, William	56y	W	21 JUN 1922	Scotland MD	Congressional
14261	Reppen, Thomas E.	1y	W	30 JUL 1917	Radio VA	Methodist
00654	Retterhouse, Mary	11m	W	8 AUG 1891	Alexandria VA	Mt. Olivet
03856	Revick, Emil A.H.	43y	W	27 FEB 1902	Lakeland MD	Prospect Hill
11951	Rexford, Carolyn M.	75y	W	9 AUG 1913	Buffalo NY	Arlington
13979	Rey, Barbara	79y	W	10 FEB 1917	Takoma Park MD	St. Mary's
02600	Reyburn, Henry Langford	3y	W	26 AUG 1898	Berwyn MD	Oak Hill
13142	Reynolds, Agnes	9m	C	6 OCT 1915	Seat Pleasant MD	Woodlawn
15837	Reynolds, Alice B.	59y	W	17 JUN 1919	Rochester MN	Arlington
05117	Reynolds, Charles R.	41y	W	28 APR 1905	Vancouver WA	Congressional
09149	Reynolds, Edward	49y	C	31 MAR 1913	Fairmont Hts. MD	Woodlawn
04891	Reynolds, Edward R.	40y	W	13 SEP 1904	Indian Head MD	Oak Hill
06358	Reynolds, Harry S.	26y	W	19 JAN 1906	Springfield MA	Glenwood
03689	Reynolds, Henry W.	40y	W	20 OCT 1901	Rosslyn VA	Glenwood
14561	Reynolds, Infant of Mrs. W.H.	10h	W	4 JAN 1918	Charleston SC	Arlington
01833	Reynolds, John W., Jr.	35y	W	23 DEC 1895	Brooklyn NY	Glenwood
07492	Reynolds, Joseph	50y	W	3 APR 1910	Memphis TN	Oak Hill
02527	Reynolds, Joseph L.	1m	W	3 JUL 1898	Ft. Myer Hts. VA	Oak Hill
08829	Reynolds, Lucy Singleton	62y	W	8 SEP 1912	Luray VA	Baltimore MD
00762	Reynolds, Mamie M.	4y	W	30 MAR 1891	New York NY	Rock Creek
12653	Reynolds, Mary Jane	62y	W	12 DEC 1914	Mt. Ranier MD	Glenwood
02487	Reynolds Mattie	28y	C	27 JUL 1898	Hampton VA	Moore's
14844	Reynolds, Mildred	60y	C	26 MAY 1918	Fairmont Hts. MD	Woodlawn
07691	Reynolds, Minnie Gertrude	46y	W	15 AUG 1910	Loch Lynn MD	Oak Hill
18524	Reynolds, S.A.	19y	W	5 APR 1923	Miami FL	Glenwood
04134	Reynolds, V. Clinton	74y	W	26 JAN 1903	Mt. Hope MD	Holyrood
06403	Reynolds, William B.	51y	W	25 JAN 1908	Charlotte NC	Arlington
02268	Rhebaton, William Warner	18m	C	30 JUL 1897	Graves Hill MD	Christian
12406	Rhett, Edward Lowndes	39y	W	12 DEC 1913	New York NY	Rock Creek
11877	Rhode, Matilda C.	53y	W	4 JUL 1913	Philadelphia PA	Rock Creek
15608	Rhodes, Charles A.	46y	W	9 FEB 1919	Hyattsville MD	Glenwood
06503	Rhodes, Clara A.	23y	W	10 APR 1908	New York NY	Glenwood
15350	Rhodes, Daniel	76y	W	3 NOV 1918	San Diego CA	Rock Creek
13839	Rhodes, Howard N.	39y	W	25 NOV 1916	Topeka KS	Cremated
07703	Rhodes, Lena (Mrs. Alexander)	48y	W	22 AUG 1910	Milledgeville GA	Cremated
16790	Rhodes, Thornton	70y	C	31 OCT 1920	Centreville VA	Mt. Zion East
04002	Rhone, Spencer	33y	C	15 SEP 1902	Philadelphia PA	Woodlawn
02217	Rhubottom, Elizabeth E.	20y	C	11 JUN 1897	Montg. Co. MD	Christian
06074	Rianhard, Julia L.	57y	W	20 MAY 1907	Hyattsville MD	Mt. Olivet
14327	Rice, Augusta	65y	W	30 AUG 1917	Woodside MD	Wash. Hebrew
13866	Rice, Carlton Edwin	54y	W	15 DEC 1916	Chevy Chase MD	Fulton KY
14413	Rice, Charles	63y	W	16 OCT 1917	Norfolk NE	Wash. Hebrew
03553	Rice, Charles E.	25y	W	26 JUN 1901	Baltimore MD	Glenwood
15359	Rice, Elizabeth H.	69y	W	15 NOV 1918	Newport RI	Arlington
14993	Rice, Emma	43y	C	27 AUG 1918	Cedar Hts. MD	Payne's

No.	Name of Deceased	Age	Race	Death Date	Place of Death	Place of Burial
05982	Rice, Homer W.	24y	W	15 MAR 1907	Baltimore MD	Landis NC
12780	Rice, Irene O.	30y	W	23 FEB 1915	Ailerstown MD	Glenwood
16836	Rice, Solomon	70y	W	29 NOV 1920	Chicago IL	Wash. Hebrew
06085	Rich, Abbie C.	55y	W	29 MAY 1907	Sharon MA	Congressional
05067	Rich, Albert	42y	C	25 MAR 1905	Philadelphia PA	Harmony
03832	Rich, Bernard	78y	W	25 MAR 1902	New York NY	Wash. Hebrew
00764	Rich, Fannie	64y	W	13 MAR 1892	Brooklyn NY	Wash. Hebrew
03564	Rich, Norman P.	1y	W	5 JUL 1901	Cape May NJ	Congressional
16071	Rich, Waldo, farmer	84y	W	22 OCT 1919	Bradentown FL	Cremated
12378	Rich, William F.	44y	W	27 MAY 1914	Baltimore MD	Prospect Hill
00763	Richard, Mamie	25y	W	19 MAR 1881	Aquasco MD	Congressional
05952	Richards, A.C., Maj.	77y	W	17 FEB 1907	Eustis FL	Rock Creek
14198	Richards, Benjamin S.	72y	W	29 JUN 1917	Jamestown RI	Arlington
01191	Richards, Catherine	50y	C	14 DEC 1892	Atlanta GA	Graceland
06031	Richards, Clorinda C.	76y	W	16 APR 1907	Vienna VA	Oak Hill
11881	Richards, Edward S.	14y	W	6 JUL 1913	Bladensburg MD	Glenwood
14692	Richards, Eva	30y	C	16 MAR 1918	Baltimore MD	Woodlawn
00508	Richards, George S.	40y	W	25 OCT 1890	Philadelphia PA	Glenwood
02176	Richards, Henrietta	62y	W	16 MAR 1897	Baltimore MD	Congressional
05145	Richards, Ida M. (Atwell)	30y	W	25 MAY 1905	Petersburg PA	Congressional
12108	Richards, Louisa Maria	73y	W	27 NOV 1913	Newport RI	Arlington VA
07144	Richards, Lowndes Randolph	9m		2 AUG 1909	Mtn. Lake Pk. MD	Arlington
02843	Richards, Margaret Georg.	56y	W	7 JUN 1899	Aquasco MD	Congressional
02175	Richards, Mary Ann	66y	W	13 APR 1897	Eustis FL	Rock Creek
15013	Richards, Milton Valentine	60y	W	8 SEP 1918	Atlantic City NJ	Rock Creek
17446	Richards, William	54y	W	1 OCT 1921	Silver Spring MD	Knoxville TN
16497	Richardson, Almyone H.G.	80y	W	21 MAY 1920	Mt. Auburn MD	Cremated
04485	Richardson, Amanda	25y	C	22 OCT 1903	Garrett Lane MD	Baptist
18177	Richardson, Benjamin	30y	C	22 NOV 1922	Clarendon VA	Rosemont
07946	Richardson, Charles D.	26y	W	26 JAN 1911	Westfield MA	Congressional
01415	Richardson, Charles H.	37y	W	1 JUL 1894	Baltimore MD	Congressional
02847	Richardson, Charlotte Anne	68y	W	14 JUN 1899	St. Louis MO	Rock Creek
03307	Richardson, Georgianna	41y	C	18 OCT 1900	Baltimore MD	Harmony
04585	Richardson, Henry	27y	W	1 FEB 1904	New York NY	Addison Chapel
06048	Richardson, James W.	43y	W	30 APR 1907	Asbury Park NJ	Rock Creek
04221	Richardson, John Robert	56y	C	28 FEB 1903	Westch. Co. NY	Woodlawn
01416	Richardson, Judson F., hotel	73y	W	5 JUN 1894	Bladensburg MD	Mt. Olivet
07162	Richardson, Lillian	1y	W	21 AUG 1909	Bethesda MD	Congressional
03319	Richardson, Mary E.	74y	W	4 NOV 1900	Brooklyn NY	Glenwood
15577	Richardson, Montague L.	75y	W	21 JAN 1919	Pikesville MD	Glenwood
04469	Richardson, Samuel S.	65y	W	8 OCT 1903	Cumberland MD	Glenwood
05229	Richardson, Thomas Elsworth	1y	W	3 AUG 1905	Colonial Bea. VA	Congressional
15996	Richardson, William S.	60y	W	15 SEP 1919	Riverdale MD	Glenwood
13069	Richey, Hiram	10y	W	22 AUG 1915	Arlington VA	Congressional
15991	Richey, Minna Blair	68y	W	12 SEP 1919	Jamestown RI	Rock Creek
15044	Richmond, Frank R.	32y	W	24 SEP 1918	Brookline MA	Glenwood
15040	Richmond, Frank R.	32y	W	24 SEP 1918	Brookline MA	Hyattsville MD
16614	Richold, Leopold	84y	W	21 JUL 1920	Atlantic City NJ	Wash. Hebrew
02333	Rick, Anne S.	28y	W	7 SEP 1897	Baltimore MD	Prospect Hill
04117	Rickard, Benj.	21y	W	1887	Dayton MD	Glenwood
14467	Ricker, Gustavus	64y	W	31 OCT 1886	Somersworth NH	Rock Creek
07402	Rickett, Basil N.	40y	W	1 FEB 1910	New York NY	Arlington VA
12954	Ricketts, Mary F.	16y	W	3 JUN 1915	Bethesda MD	Glenwood
02413	Ricketts, Marion M.	58y	W	2 MAR 1898	Baltimore MD	Glenwood
15213	Riddick, James	22y	C	11 OCT 1918	Camp Dix NJ	Mt. Zion East
16362	Riddick, Richard P.	67y	W	5 MAR 1920	Brentwood MD	Glenwood
08609	Riddle, Albert Thomas	53y	W	22 APR 1912	Takoma Park MD	Rock Creek
15395	Ridenour, Mabel	29y	W	2 DEC 1918	Takoma Park MD	Hagerstown MD
04074	Ridgeley, Ella C.	40y	W	21 JUN 1902	Baltimore MD	Springfield IL
01260	Ridgely, Lewis R.	60y	C	4 DEC 1893	Seat Pleasant MD	Jones' Chapel

District of Columbia Foreign Death Records, 1888-1923

No.	Name of Deceased	Age	Race	Death Date	Place of Death	Place of Burial
03430	Ridgway, Audubon W.	24y	W	22 FEB 1901	Chicago IL	Glenwood
14963	Ridgway, Isabella	68y	W	8 AUG 1918	Chevy Chase MD	Oak Hill
00338	Ridgway, Leland	4½m	W	6 JUN 1890	Carlin Spgs. VA	Oak Hill
13136	Ridgway, Sarah E.	70y	W	24 DEC 1914	St. Louis IL	Rock Creek
00655	Ridout, Charles G.	10m	W	7 AUG 1891	Long Branch NJ	Congressional
15427	Ridout, John	68y	W	11 DEC 1918	Baltimore MD	Congressional
05104	Riehl, Lena A.	21y	W	26 APR 1905	Jersey City NJ	Prospect Hill
04249	Riemer, Alice De	30y	W	8 APR 1903	Milwaukee WI	Glenwood
07192	Riggles, Hellen, d/o C.W.	11y	W	10 SEP 1909	Louisa VA	Rock Creek
08313	Riggles, Mary Elizabeth	87y	W	16 SEP 1911	Woodside MD	Oak Hill
07618	Riggs, Elisha Francis, s/o G.W.	58y	W	6 JUL 1910	New London CN	Rock Creek
17337	Riggs, Francis B.	68y	W	11 JUL 1921	Paris, France	Oak Hill
18404	Riggs, Helen Wysong	57y	W	4 MAR 1923	San Francisco CA	Rock Creek
17561	Riggs, Hope Vernelle	36y	W	28 NOV 1921	Denver CO	Glenwood
00656	Riggs, Mary B.	69y	W	16 OCT 1891	New York NY	Oak Hill
13111	Riggs, Medora (Thayer)	62y	W	16 SEP 1915	New London CN	Rock Creek
08393	Riggs, Ransom Edwards	38y	W	18 NOV 1911	Hampton VA	Arlington VA
18115	Riggs, William C.	68y	W	12 OCT 1922	Summit NJ	Oak Hill
01261	Righter, George C.	51y	W	20 NOV 1893	Marriottsville MD	Congressional
16867	Rignery, Joseph	74y	W	20 DEC 1920	Winchester VA	Rock Creek
12658	Rigney, Teresa F.	61y	W	17 DEC 1914	New York NY	Rock Creek
16802	Riker, Ann Eliza	73y	W	10 NOV 1920	Fairfax VA	Prospect Hill
03197	Riley, Catharine	78y	W	31 MAY 1900	New York NY	Mt. Olivet
14462	Riley, Edward	40y	C	13 NOV 1917	Philadelphia PA	Harmony
08411	Riley, Elizabeth King (Reid)	76y	W	7 DEC 1911	Winchester VA	Congressional
15737	Riley, Lloyd	32y	W	17 APR 1919	Baltimore MD	Cedar Hill
07953	Riley, Lousa Gibson	78y	W	30 JAN 1911	Winchester VA	Oak Hill
04514	Riley, Mary A.	67y	W	16 NOV 1903	Fairfax Co. VA	Congressional
07200	Riley, Richard R.	53y	W	29 DEC 1899	Washington DC	Arlington VA
06054	Riley, Rose E.	57y	W	18 APR 1907	Paris, France	Mt. Olivet
05004	Riley, Thomas	30y	W	17 JAN 1905	Chicago IL	Mt. Olivet
00397	Riley, Thomas	55y	W	2 SEP 1890	Fairfax C.H. VA	—
07684	Rinaldi, Dominic	37y	W	10 AUG 1910	New York NY	—
14324	Rines, Clara A. (Stephens)	82y	W	28 AUG 1917	Colonial Bea. VA	Glenwood
01936	Ringgold, Isabella E.	37y	W	2 APR 1896	Baltimore MD	Oak Hill
02388	Ringgold, James T.	46y	W	17 JAN 1898	Baltimore MD	Oak Hill
08013	Ringgold, Mary Elizabeth	58y	W	18 MAR 1911	Mt. Hope MD	Mt. Olivet
16313	Riordan, Carrie V.	41y	W	12 FEB 1920	Philadelphia PA	Congressional
17411	Ripley, Daniel	68y	W	15 SEP 1921	Cromwell CN	Glenwood
13077	Rishell, Phillip	c.32y	W	25 AUG 1915	S. Bethlehem PA	Arlington
02671	Risque, Elizabeth	52y	W	4 DEC 1898	Marthasville MO	Oak Hill
14426	Riston, Laura	76y	W	27 OCT 1917	Mt. Ranier MD	Mt. Olivet
00881	Ritchie, Amelia Walters	10d	W	8 AUG 1885	Upper Marl. MD	Congressional
00878	Ritchie, Annie Ridella	1y	W	23 AUG 1892	Upper Marl. MD	Congressional
00882	Ritchie, Aurelia Pinkney	8y	W	11 MAY 1884	Washington DC	Congressional
08295	Ritchie, Fannie C.	31y	W	4 SEP 1911	Wash. Grove MD	Holyrood
00880	Ritchie, James H.	41y	W	7 JUL 1888	Washington DC	Congressional
00879	Ritchie, James Winfield	8m	W	17 MAY 1880	Upper Marl. MD	Congressional
00882½	Ritchie, Janet Adelia	11y	W	2 MAY 1884	Washington DC	Congressional
17494	Ritchie, Mary Jane	75y	W	30 OCT 1921	Lakewood NJ	Holyrood
16751	Rittenhouse, Sarah Emily	89y	W	10 OCT 1920	Rockville MD	Oak Hill
08784	Ritter, Henrietta F.	69y	W	25 AUG 1912	Wash. Grove MD	Congressional
18301	Riturni, LaRosa C.	30y	W	25 JAN 1923	Baltimore MD	Mt. Olivet
04759	Rivebsam, Earle Scott	12y	W	9 JUN 1904	Evensville MD	Rock Creek
05735	Rivers, Alice V.	22y	C	8 AUG 1905	Montg. Co. MD	Christian
07754	Rivers, R.G.	52y	C	19 SEP 1910	Atlantic City NJ	Harmony
14486	Rives, Blair	19y	W	3 APR 1869	Rives Sta. MD	Congressional
08028	Rives, Isabelle K.	37y	W	26 MAR 1911	Brentwood MD	Glenwood
14484	Rives, John C.	69y	W	10 APR 1864	Rives Sta. MD	Congressional
14485	Rives, Lucy	37y	W	22 NOV 1882	Rives Sta. MD	Congressional

No.	Name of Deceased	Age	Race	Death Date	Place of Death	Place of Burial
14482	Rives, Mary Ann	42y	W	31 MAR 1853	Rives Sta. MD	Congressional[1]
13515	Rives, Wright	78y	W	22 MAY 1916	Rives Sta. MD	Congressional
12784	Rixford, Caroline L.	90y	W	21 FEB 1915	Laurel MD	Glenwood[2]
06716	Roach, Henry N.	63y	W	8 OCT 1908	New York NY	Mt. Olivet
14753	Roach, James	26y	W	13 APR 1918	Falls Church VA	Cremated
04051	Roach, William N.	61y	W	7 SEP 1902	New York NY	Congressional
03904	Roache, Dallas [Bache]	63y	W	2 JUN 1902	San Francisco CA	Arlington
07447	Roan, Howard	29y	C	1 MAR 1910	Philadelphia PA	Mt. Olivet
12301	Roan, John	60y	W	9 APR 1914	Indian Head MD	Congressional
02931	Roane, Edward Bertrand	21y	W	28 AUG 1899	Melrose MA	Glenwood
06195	Robain Emeline Louisa	4d	C	21 AUG 1907	Atlantic City NJ	Harmony
06200	Robain, Louisa	28y	C	23 AUG 1907	Atlantic City NJ	Harmony
08392	Robb, Lucy Walker	32y	C	16 NOV 1911	Boston MA	Harmony
03440	Robbins, Cicero R.	33y	C	26 FEB 1901	Chicago IL	Harmony
13284	Robbins, George B.	70y	W	5 JAN 1916	Takoma Park MD	Melrose MA
06378	Robbins, Mary A.	88y	W	6 JAN 1908	Laurel MD	Oak Hill
12499	Robbins, Nancy M.	23y	W	23 MAR 1851	Newfane VT	Rock Creek
07441	Roberson, Chas. W., butcher	78y	W	11 NOV 1909	Falmouth VA	Glenwood
07442	Roberson, Mary Francis	74y	W	17 AUG 1908	Falmouth VA	Glenwood
08549	Roberson, Silvia A.	2m	C	11 MAR 1912	Brentwood MD	Mt. Olivet
01834	Roberts, Annie J.	32y	W	4 NOV 1895	Chicago IL	Oak Hill
14389	Roberts, Harry	29y	W	1 OCT 1917	Takoma Park MD	Rock Creek
12414	Roberts, Henry H.	61y	W	27 JUN 1914	Takoma Park MD	Rock Creek
05540	Roberts, James R.	35y	W	17 FEB 1906	Alexandria VA	Glenwood
17736	Roberts, Louise Young	59y	W	12 MAR 1922	Takoma Park MD	Rock Creek
02140	Roberts, Margot	50y	W	4 FEB 1897	Limington ME	Oak Hill
06537	Roberts, Milton L.	38y	W	4 MAY 1908	Louisville KY	Glenwood
08754	Roberts, Sophia Ludlow	47y	W	8 AUG 1912	Takoma Park MD	Baltimore MD
14490	Roberts, Teresa	68y	W	6 DEC 1917	Washington DC	St. Mary's
08762	Roberts, Wilbur H.	43y	W	10 AUG 1912	New York NY	Glenwood
17508	Roberts, William A.	83y	W	9 NOV 1921	Hughspire PA	Arlington
14401	Robertson, Emma L.	60y	W	6 OCT 1917	Chicago IL	Glenwood
05291	Robertson, George	37y	W	15 SEP 1905	Potomac River	Arlington
16730	Robertson, Harry J.	49y	W	25 SEP 1920	Hyattsville MD	Glenwood
04061	Robertson, James R.	32y	W	5 OCT 1902	Baltimore MD	Holyrood
11933	Robertson, Jane Matilda	80y	W	2 AUG 1913	Chevy Chase MD	Glenwood
02503	Robertson, John	63y	W	25 JUL 1898	Alexandria VA	Glenwood
18176	Robertson, John	82y	W	21 NOV 1922	Homestead PA	Glenwood
14028	Robertson, John Henry	2d	C	11 MAR 1917	Mt. Vernon NY	McLean VA
01192	Robertson, Mary E.	46y	W	29 SEP 1892	Alexandria VA	Glenwood
04018	Robertson, Samuel	71y	W	6 SEP 1902	Baltimore MD	Glenwood
17449	Robertson, Thomas J.W.	88y	W	3 OCT 1921	Rockville MD	Glenwood
14598	Robey, Georgeiana E.	72y	W	24 JAN 1918	Pomfret MD	Congressional
05286	Robey, John	23y	W	14 SEP 1094	Delaware B. DE	Congressional
06762	Robey, Mary	87y	W	10 OCT 1908	Rockville MD	Congressional
04945	Robinette, Francis	28y	W	23 OCT 1904	Tucson AZ	Glenwood
17157	Robinson, Annie	43y	C	12 MAY 1921	Philadelphia PA	Woodlawn
15387	Robinson, Betty	55y	W	28 NOV 1918	Chester PA	Union B., Geo.
13818	Robinson, Carrie E.	27y	C	17 NOV 1916	Harrisburg PA	Falls Church VA
16411	Robinson, Clara	62y	W	29 MAR 1920	Oakdale MD	Ohev Sholom
12953	Robinson, Cornelia	37y	C	2 JUN 1915	Luzerne Co. PA	Woodlawn
01937	Robinson, Daniel	c.25y	C	20 MAY 1896	Bowie MD	Potters Field
07427	Robinson, Edwin W.	73y	W	22 FEB 1910	Bethesda MD	Oak Hill
09086	Robinson, Eliza	82y	C	23 FEB 1913	Philadelphia PA	Woodlawn
03697	Robinson, Elizabeth A.	55y	W	23 JAN 1882	Frederick MD	Rock Creek

---

[1] Mary Ann Rives, John C. Rives, Lucy Rives, and Blair Rives to be disinterred in NOV 1917 from Rives Cemetery, near Bladensburg, Md., by undertaker Gasch.
[2] Disinterment permit #8448 for reinterment in East Highgate VA, 19 OCT 1915.

District of Columbia Foreign Death Records, 1888-1923

No.	Name of Deceased	Age	Race	Death Date	Place of Death	Place of Burial
00134	Robinson, Emily	59y	C	16 AUG 1889	Stamford CN	Harmony
02119	Robinson, Emma	30y	C	29 JAN 1897	Trenton NJ	Harmony
05195	Robinson, Fannie	38y	C	2 JUL 1905	Newport RI	Harmony
15194	Robinson, George R.	26y	C	14 OCT 1918	Hampton VA	Harmony
15041	Robinson, Harold M., s/o G.W.	21y	W	23 SEP 1918	Camp Lee VA	Arlington
05954	Robinson, Harriet	62y	C	23 FEB 1907	Kensington MD	Christian
15307	Robinson, Harry P.	22y	W	30 OCT 1918	Hyattsville MD	Glenwood
03402	Robinson, Helen D.	37y	W	23 JAN 1901	Middletown NY	Glenwood
06011	Robinson, Henrietta	70y	C	14 JUN 1879	Bethel Cem. VA	Harmony
13138	Robinson, Infant of Vincent	SB	C	6 OCT 1915	Hyattsville MD	Mt. Olivet
04143	Robinson, J.C., Mrs.	49y	W	24 JAN 1903	Dresden OH	Congressional
13125	Robinson, John H.	30y	C	24 SEP 1915	Philadelphia PA	Arlington VA
12234	Robinson, Josephine	27y	W	23 FEB 1914	New York NY	Glenwood
13139	Robinson, Josephine	22y	C	6 OCT 1915	Hyattsville MD	Mt. Olivet
07765	Robinson, Louisa Va. (Conrad)	72y	W	25 SEP 1910	Warpool VA	Oak Hill
14924	Robinson, Margaret	4y	C	20 JUL 1918	Railroad	Cremated
06065	Robinson, Martha	17y	C	11 MAY 1907	New York NY	Harmony
02663	Robinson, Mary	54y	C	22 NOV 1898	Charlestown WV	Payne's
00187	Robinson, Mary G.	2y	W	3 OCT 1889	Hyattsville MD	Glenwood
04173	Robinson, Mary H.	49y	C	12 FEB 1903	Marlboro MD	Harmony
18439	Robinson, Minnie E.	72y	—	22 MAR 1923	Chicago IL	Arlington
13177	Robinson, Mittie	29y	C	31 OCT 1915	New York NY	Harmony
08703	Robinson, Norris, Dr.	30y	W	4 JUL 1912	Martinsburg WV	Glenwood
05171	Robinson, Robinson	50y	C	13 JUN 1905	Jersey City NJ	Harmony
03857	Robinson, Samuel	—	C	13 APR 1902	Rahway NJ	Abbeville SC
08023	Robinson, Sarah	30y	C	23 MAR 1911	Atlantic City NJ	Woodlawn
07027	Robinson, Sarah A.	68y	C	16 MAY 1909	Pittsburgh PA	Harmony
16011	Robinson, Susan C.	37y	C	23 SEP 1919	Brentwood MD	Mt. Olivet
01757	Robinson, William	60y	W	26 SEP 1895	Brooklyn NY	Congressional
03456	Robinson, William	28y	C	15 MAR 1901	Columbus OH	Payne's
15227	Robinson, William	17y	C	15 OCT 1918	Chicago IL	Payne's
15727	Robinson, William H.	35y	C	12 APR 1919	Wilmington DE	Payne's
08290	Robinson, William J.	28y	W	31 AUG 1911	Colo. Spgs. CO	Oak Hill
04720	Robison, Hattie	32y	C	19 MAY 1904	Lewisville VA	Harmony
01756	Robison, Mary C.	47y	C	16 OCT 1895	Pittsburgh PA	Moore's
07526	Roby, Sommerset D.	63y	W	4 MAY 1910	Pomfret MD	Congressional
13769	Roche, Ellen J.	36y	W	16 OCT 1916	Saranac Lake NY	Mt. Olivet
16924	Roche, Hettie J.	65y	W	20 JAN 1921	Mt. Ranier MD	Oak Hill
04737	Roche, James E., bar keeper	38y	W	9 MAY 1904	At Sea	Mt. Olivet
05850	Roche, Joanna E.	80y	W	6 DEC 1906	Baltimore MD	Mt. Olivet
06183	Rock, Alfred M.	29y	W	7 AUG 1907	Asientos, Mex.	Rock Creek
13397	Rock, Fannie L.W.	64y	W	3 MAR 1916	Philadelphia PA	Glenwood
16941	Rock, Joseph C.	74y	W	26 JAN 1921	New York NY	Glenwood
03097	Rock, Rosa M.	53y	W	10 FEB 1900	New York NY	Glenwood
16200	Rockfield, Anna	21y	W	10 JAN 1920	Brooklyn NY	Ohev Sholom
03502	Rockwell, John E., Capt.	—	W	c.1881	Harmony Val. VA	Congressional
02334	Rockwood, Emily F.	63y	W	4 DEC 1897	Milton FL	Rock Creek
13308	Rodarte, Alphonso	26y	I	16 JAN 1916	Toledo IA	Mt. Olivet
02017	Rodbird, John E.	23y	W	15 AUG 1896	Wilmington DE	Mt. Olivet
05966	Rodbird, Julia A.	53y	W	1 MAR 1907	Baltimore MD	Mt. Olivet
08230	Roddy, Patrick	c.35y	W	29 JUL 1911	Alexandria VA	Mt. Olivet
12427	Roderick, Virginia F.	69y	W	7 JUL 1914	Warnersville PA	Arlington
02218	Rodgers, Ann E.	74y	W	9 MAY 1897	At Sea	Oak Hill
08592	Rodgers, Calbraith Perry	32y	W	3 APR 1912	Long Beach CA	Rock Creek
02541	Rodgers, Elizabeth	84y	W	9 JUN 1898	Philadelphia PA	Congressional
14441	Rodgers, Frederick	75y	W	3 NOV 1917	St. James LI	Rock Creek
03599	Rodgers, James W.	30y	W	3 AUG 1901	Baltimore MD	Rock Creek
01835	Rodgers, James W., lawyer	70y	W	3 JAN 1895	Bladensburg MD	Mt. Olivet
08501	Rodgers, Robert Slidell	53y	W	31 JAN 1912	Kansas City MO	Rock Creek
00657	Rodgers, Robert Smith	82y	W	10 JUL 1891	Harford Co. MD	Rock Creek

No.	Name of Deceased	Age	Race	Death Date	Place of Death	Place of Burial
05343	Rodgers, Sara Perry	87y	W	30 OCT 1905	Bethlehem PA	Rock Creek
00509	Rodgers, William P.	70y	W	5 MAR 1891	New York NY	Rock Creek
04503	Rodier, Louis	21y	W	5 NOV 1903	Riverdale MD	Congressional
13817	Rodier, Mary Marmaduke	81y	W	17 NOV 1916	Ossining NY	Oak Hill
16475	Roe, Frances Marie Ant.	75y	W	6 MAY 1920	Port Orange FL	Arlington
17585	Roeber, A. Edward	52y	W	12 DEC 1921	Richmond VA	Cremated
01758	Roeser, Auguste	76y	W	1 JUL 1895	Dranesville VA	Rock Creek
16822	Rogers, Charles Evans	61y	W	19 NOV 1920	Palatka FL	Cremated
03422	Rogers, Cora	74y	W	21 FEB 1901	Hyattsville MD	Mt. Olivet
00765	Rogers, Delia Maria	70y	W	26 DEC 1891	New London CN	Congressional
13594	Rogers, Erskine	1y	W	9 JUL 1916	E. Flat Rock NC	Cremated
00560	Rogers, James	1y	W	1 JUN 1891	Bladensburg MD	Mt. Olivet
02571	Rogers, Joseph S., lawyer	27y	W	20 AUG 1898	Bladensburg MD	Mt. Olivet
17468	Rogers, Mary F.	7m	W	14 OCT 1921	Brentwood MD	Glenwood
05464	Rogers, Pennoe K.B.	25y	W	11 FEB 1906	New York NY	Rock Creek
16741	Rogers, William Addison	76y	W	3 OCT 1920	Atlantic City NJ	Rock Creek
18396	Rogers, William S.	67y	W	8 MAR 1923	Hyattsville MD	Mt. Olivet
06365	Roggenkamp, Alberta	2y	W	28 DEC 1907	Takoma Park MD	Rock Creek
13698	Roggenmoser, Gracie P.	34y	W	5 SEP 1916	Braddock Hts. MD	Congressional
18090	Rohm, Anna Glen Jera	44y	W	27 SEP 1922	Takoma Park MD	Glenwood
12416	Rojas, Pedro Ezequiel	—	W	36 JUN 1914	Atlantic City NJ	Caracas, Venez.
07755	Rolar, Millisa Gilbert	98y	W	22 SEP 1910	Takoma Park MD	Rock Creek
04884	Rollings, John A.	76y	W	10 SEP 1904	Lost City WV	Oak Hill
06327	Rollings, Sylvia	60y	C	25 NOV 1907	New York NY	Harmony
16170	Rollins, Annie P.	71y	W	27 DEC 1919	Falls Church VA	Glenwood
03141	Rollins, Daniel	93y	C	19 MAR 1900	Chicago IL	Woodlawn
18585	Rollins, Frances L.	80y	W	3 JUN 1923	Cambridge MA	Glenwood
12063	Rollins, Frederick	43y	W	26 OCT 1913	Seat Pleasant MD	Congressional
13120	Rollins, Hester J.	69y	W	25 SEP 1915	Asheville NC	Addison Chapel
17932	Rollins, Peter	75y	C	1 JUL 1922	Ansonia CN	Woodlawn
15208	Rollins, William H.	29y	W	15 OCT 1918	Camp Hump. VA	Arlington
05881	Rollins, William H.	30y	C	20 DEC 1906	Asheville NC	Harmony
03263	Romaker, Lillian	23y	W	11 AUG 1900	Chesilhurst NJ	Prospect Hill
15759	Romero, Ivan	35y	C	30 APR 1919	Atlantic City NJ	Harmony
06140	Rood, Leslie R.	23y	W	16 JUL 1907	Harpers Ferry WV	Arlington
03970	Roome, Frances Henrietta	89y	W	31 AUG 1902	Kensington MD	Greenwood NY
15714	Rooney, Roma	50y	W	7 APR 1919	Capitol Hts. MD	Mt. Olivet
06070	Roosevelt, George W.	64y	W	14 APR 1907	Brussels, Belg.	Oak Hill
15840	Root, Arthur W., s/o H.E.	29y	W	20 JUN 1919	Baltimore MD	Greenville TX
04415	Root, Richard	69y	W	28 JUL 1903	Camden ME	Arlington VA
03680	Root, Samuel H.	33y	W	10 OCT 1901	St. Denis MD	Broadway VA
04414	Ropl, Joseph	4m	W	29 JUL 1903	Bladensburg MD	St. Mary's
12579	Rorebeck, Azur Curtis	70y	W	22 OCT 1914	Ft. Myers FL	Arlington
07751	Rorer, James	7d	W	18 SEP 1910	Lebanon PA	Congressional
16445	Rosazza, Eusebio	59y	W	22 APR 1920	Franklin Co. PA	St. Mary's
16738	Rose, Emily Frances	75y	W	3 OCT 1920	Seabrook MD	Rock Creek
13401	Rose, Fred Kent	12d	W	8 MAR 1916	Hyattsville MD	Glenwood
13658	Rose, William L.	50y	W	13 AUG 1916	New York NY	Mt. Olivet
05673	Roseberry, Betty (Campbell)	49y	W	3 AUG 1906	Orkney Spgs. VA	Rock Creek
16452	Roseberry, Michael M.	73y	W	25 APR 1920	Manassas VA	Glenwood
01500	Roseberry, Parmelia P.	47y	W	1 OCT 1894	Brentsville VA	Glenwood
00766	Roseberry, Rachel Y.	72y	W	16 JAN 1892	Brentsville VA	Glenwood
12707	Rosebery, John Young	71y	W	9 JAN 1915	Orange VA	Glenwood
00883	Rosembaum, Deva	43y	W	3 MAY 1892	Roanoke VA	Wash. Hebrew
00767	Rosenbaum, Henrietta	74y	W	6 DEC 1891	Staunton VA	Wash. Hebrew
0069	Rosenbaum, Henry	75y	W	21 MAY 1889	Roanoke VA	Wash. Hebrew
17891	Rosenbaum, William L.	13y	W	5 JUN 1922	Ft. Leavenw. KS	Arlington
05772	Rosenberg, Samuel	25y	W	8 OCT 1906	Tucson AZ	Adas Israel
16370	Rosenblatt, Samuel, butcher	36y	W	4 MAR 1920	Denver CO	Wash. Hebrew
08733	Rosenblot, Child of Louis	SB	W	26 JUL 1912	Alexandria VA	Ohev Sholom

District of Columbia Foreign Death Records, 1888-1923

No.	Name of Deceased	Age	Race	Death Date	Place of Death	Place of Burial
03878	Rosencrans, William Stark	78y	W	11 MAR 1898	Rosencrans CA	Arlington VA
05455	Rosenfill, Abraham	32y	W	5 FEB 1906	Bladensburg MD	Cremated
03662	Rosenkatz, Infant of Lewis	SB	W	21 SEP 1901	Alexandria VA	Adas Israel
17542	Rosenson, Benjamin	46y	W	20 NOV 1921	Pottsville PA	Adas Israel
05092	Rosenthal, Sydney E.	37y	W	21 APR 1905	Linden MD	Wash. Hebrew
04234	Rosillo, Frank M.	25y	W	23 FEB 1903	Philadelphia PA	Oak Hill
09097	Ross, Anna M.A.	18y	W	26 FEB 1913	Pittsburgh PA	Prospect Hill
02617	Ross, Edward J.	25y	W	1 JUL 1898	Santiago, Cuba	Rock Creek
04682	Ross, Eugene P.	31y	C	19 APR 1904	New York NY	Mt. Olivet
04859	Ross, Eva	39y	W	20 AUG 1904	Baltimore MD	Glenwood
16925	Ross, George C.	73y	W	17 JAN 1921	Hampton VA	Arlington
01080	Ross, Ida Wood	28y	W	1887	Alexandria VA	Oak Hill
15754	Ross, John W.	30y	W	15 APR 1919	Brest, Fra.	Arlington
02493	Ross, Lucy	75y	C	27 JUL 1898	Easton MD	Mt. Olivet
13194	Ross, Mollie	57y	C	8 NOV 1915	Takoma Park MD	Payne's
00768	Ross, Richard L.	70y	W	16 DEC 1891	Baltimore MD	Rock Creek
17798	Ross, Rosa Westcott	30y	W	14 APR 1922	Takoma Park MD	Nassawadox VA
03706	Ross, Sarah	40y	C	13 NOV 1901	Atlantic City NJ	Payne's
05879	Ross, Thomas C.	76y	W	22 DEC 1906	Washington DC	Oak Hill
01193	Rossback, Lizzie	35y	W	1 NOV 1892	Jersey City NJ	Mt. Olivet
02389	Rossel, Jane G.	36y	W	28 MAY 189y	Mobile AL	Congressional
16047	Rossell, William Trend	70y	W	11 OCT 1919	Richmond NY	Congressional
14990	Roszel, Dulaney Douglas	19y	W	27 AUG 1918	Potomac River	Alexandria VA
14093	Rotenbury, William R.	46y	W	15 APR 1917	Brooklyn NY	Glenwood
16312	Roth, Jacob	59y	W	13 FEB 1920	Hyattsville MD	St. Mary's
15777	Roth, Mary, d/o Frank L.	6y	W	10 MAY 1919	Newport RI	Mt. Olivet
15849	Rothenbeucher, Henry J.	24y	W	28 JUN 1919	Alexandria VA	Glenwood
18532	Rothschild, Harry	56y	W	6 MAY 1923	Chicago IL	Wash. Hebrew
04740	Rothschild, Theresa	56y	W	28 MAY 1904	Atlantic City NJ	Wash. Hebrew
15399	Rothwell, Fannie	67y	W	29 NOV 1918	El Paso TX	Congressional
03487	Rothwell, Richard Randolph	6m	W	31 MAR 1901	Oxon Hill MD	Congressional
04523	Rouch, James L.	28y	C	24 NOV 1903	Steelton PA	Mt. Zion
06790	Roumay, Joseph C.	69y	W	24 OCT 1908	New York NY	Mt. Olivet
15007	Roussilln, John C.	34y	W	7 SEP 1918	Sykesville MD	Mt. Olivet
16703	Roussillon, Thomas	69y	W	8 SEP 1920	Berwyn MD	Mt. Olivet
08161	Routh, Jennie M. (Bates)	71y	W	19 JUN 1911	Atlantic City NJ	Oak Hill
00320	Rowan, Hamilton	13d	W	27 APR 1890	West Point NY	Oak Hill
12976	Rowe, Edward S.	70y	W	24 JUN 1915	Takoma Park MD	Congressional
02269	Rowe, Elizabeth	78y	W	7 AUG 1897	Indianapolis IN	Congressional
05338	Rowe, Emma Josephine	49y	W	29 OCT 1905	Indianapolis IN	Congressional
09054	Rowe, Harry A.	28y	W	2 FEB 1913	Orangeville MD	Congressional
17102	Rowe, Hattie C.	43y	W	11 APR 1921	Oxon Hill MD	Congressional
07293	Rowe, John	4m	W	12 JUN 1892	Baltimore MD	Congressional
07292	Rowe, Laura A.	34y	W	6 APR 1909	Baltimore MD	Congressional
00269	Rowe, Mary E.	46y	W	11 JAN 1890	Wellsbury MA	Graceland
03692	Rowe, William H.	53y	W	24 OCT 1901	Indianapolis IN	Congressional
02812	Rowell, C.W.	—	W	2 MAY 1898	Cuba	Arlington VA
17044	Rowell, Martha H.	90y	W	14 MAR 1921	Falls Church VA	Rock Creek
01328	Rowland, Isaac H.	48y	W	30 JAN 1894	Pittsburgh PA	Oak Hill
17665	Rowzee, John Porter	54y	W	29 JAN 1922	Glen Echo MD	Oak Hill
17632	Roy, Joshua	41y	C	11 JAN 1922	Chester PA	Woodlawn
06062	Roy, Linwood W., s/o Virgil	19y	W	10 MAY 1907	Richmond VA	Rock Creek
02788	Roy, Mattie	69y	C	26 MAR 1899	Alexandria VA	Payne's
17814	Roy, Rosalind	26y	C	21 APR 1922	Fairmont Hts. MD	Harmony
07026	Royce, Nora	35y	W	16 MAY 1909	New York NY	Mt. Olivet
05907	Rye, George E.	13y	C	21 JAN 1907	Philadelphia PA	Woodlawn
12101	Royer, Benjamin Franklin	83y	W	18 NOV 1913	Takoma Park MD	Bellefontaine OH
05962	Rozell, George F.	57y	W	26 FEB 1907	Ithaca NY	Rock Creek
06880	Rubenacker, George	38y	W	3 JAN 1909	Baltimore MD	Rock Creek
17720	Rubin, Max	41y	W	3 MAR 1922	Philadelphia PA	Ohev Sholom

No.	Name of Deceased	Age	Race	Death Date	Place of Death	Place of Burial
13705	Rud, George William	32y	W	29 AUG 1916	At Sea	Minneapolis MN
00423	Rudd, James N.	69y	W	1 APR 1881	Alexandria VA	Rock Creek
06455	Rudd, Mary	73y	W	2 MAR 1908	Kensington MD	Glenwood
14064	Rudderforth, Daisy Lucille	10m	W	30 MAR 1917	Potomac VA	Glenwood
15405	Rudney, Max	28y	W	4 DEC 1918	Clarksville VA	Talmud Torah
16214	Rudolph, Lena (deWeil)	54y	W	14 JAN 1920	Cherrydale VA	Cremated
14290	Rudolph, Reba	26y	W	11 AUG 1917	New York NY	Ohev Sholom
13268	Rudy, Arthur Whitehill	3m	W	25 DEC 1915	Cherrydale VA	Congressional
16581	Ruff, Albert B.	70y	W	5 JUL 1920	Berryville VA	Rock Creek
08825	Ruffin, Edward F.	78y	W	3 AUG 1912	Washington DC	Congressional
03139	Ruffin, James	—	—	3 OCT 1899	Manila, P.I.	Arlington VA
18353	Ruffin, Lucy A.	73y	C	12 FEB 1923	Philadelphia PA	Payne's
03962	Rugg, Henry Fitz	71y	W	19 JUL 1902	River Springs MD	Arlington
15647	Ruggles, E.S., Maj., s/o Dan.	74y	W	1 MAR 1919	Fredericksburg VA	Cremated
12796	Rule, Mattie F.	53y	W	24 FEB 1915	Hilo HI	Oak Hill
17371	Rumels, Bessie E.	33y	C	25 AUG 1921	E. Aurora NY	Herndon VA
15807	Rumphreys, Ralph E.	25y	W	30 MAY 1919	Newport News VA	Arlington
16920	Rumsey, Frances Amelia	74y	W	13 JAN 1921	Fairfax VA	Cremated
12056	Runion, John Kennedy	30y	W	21 OCT 1913	Pulaski VA	Rock Creek
02018	Runion, Sidney	21y	W	5 AUG 1896	Trenton NJ	Soldier's Home
17749	Runkle, L. Gladys	25y	W	15 MAR 1922	New York NY	Rock Creek
03313	Rush, Laura M.	1y	W	26 OCT 1900	Hyattsville MD	Glenwood
16075	Rush, May L.	30y	W	28 OCT 1919	Hyattsville MD	Mt. Olivet
07180	Rushe, Guy W.	3½m	W	2 SEP 1909	Hyattsville MD	Glenwood
18436	Rushlow, Frank	21y	W	22 MAR 1923	Indian Head MD	Taumton MA
17469	Rusk, Robert C.	—	W	17 OCT 1918	France	Congressional
18239	Russell, Alice Adams	67y	W	2 JAN 1923	Camden SC	Rock Creek
01194	Russell, Arthur	7m	C	6 JUN 1892	Rosslyn VA	Baptist
11891	Russell, Charles	62y	C	12 JUL 1913	Rosslyn VA	Union Baptist
02427	Russell, Cornelia	65y	W	31 MAR 1882	Chicago IL	Oak Hill
06119	Russell, Elizabeth Murphy	35y	W	22 JUN 1907	Clarendon VA	Mt. Olivet
04488	Russell, George B.	60y	W	24 OCT 1903	Columbus OH	Arlington VA
08269	Russell, Jennie A.	58y	W	23 AUG 1911	Laurel MD	Congressional
07638	Russell, John B.	5d	W	19 JUL 1910	Hyattsville MD	Mt. Olivet
02428	Russell, John B.	—	W	3 JAN 1861	Chicago IL	Oak Hill
06848	Russell, John R.	38y	C	11 DEC 1908	Atlantic City NJ	Harmony
00884	Russell, Josephine	4y	C	21 APR 1892	Rosslyn VA	Baptist
05437	Russell, Louisa R.	91y	W	20 JAN 1906	New York NY	Congressional
16664	Russell, Lydia Marion	79y	W	15 AUG 1920	Clarendon VA	Congressional
12203	Russell, Mary F.	1y	W	5 FEB 1914	Capitol View MD	Cremated
00312	Russell, Michael	24y	W	17 APR 1890	Pittsburgh PA	Mt. Olivet
16248	Russell, Minnie	21y	C	25 JAN 1920	New York NY	Payne's
07376	Russell, Pauline	38y	W	17 JAN 1910	New York NY	Charlottesville VA
18502	Russell, Theron	15y	W	25 APR 1923	Falls Church VA	Prospect Hill
04079	Russell, William R.	61y	W	14 AUG 1902	Kensington MD	Congressional
11813	Rust, Albert	34y	W	15 MAY 1913	Laurel MD	Glenwood
03663	Rustin, Amanda	40y	C	22 SEP 1901	Baltimore MD	Moore's
07517	Rustin, John C.	61y	C	23 APR 1910	Baltimore MD	Harmony
05352	Ruston, George	39y	C	8 NOV 1905	Pittsburgh PA	Harmony
16218	Ruthenbrucher, Peter, baker	23y	W	17 JAN 1920	Alexandria VA	St. Mary's
08783	Rutherford, Elizabeth McKean	68y	W	26 AUG 1912	Gaithersburg MD	Arlington
14803	Rutledge, Rose Mary Ann	5h	W	8 MAY 1918	Takoma Park MD	Glenwood
04177	Ryan, Bridget	69y	W	10 FEB 1903	Rosslyn VA	Holyrood
03393	Ryan, Cornelius	67y	W	16 JAN 1901	New Orleans LA	Holyrood
04442	Ryan, Edwin A.	26y	W	14 SEP 1903	Woodside MD	Mt. Olivet
05852	Ryan, Ellen	61y	W	6 DEC 1906	New Orleans LA	Holyrood
16155	Ryan, Ellie May	53y	W	18 DEC 1919	Indian Head MD	Cremated
04260	Ryan, Emma	40y	W	6 MAY 1903	Denver CO	Glenwood
18121	Ryan, James H.	c.50y	W	19 OCT 1922	Detroit MI	Mt. Olivet
08720	Ryan, John	55y	W	12 JUL 1912	Bangor ME	Mt. Olivet

No.	Name of Deceased	Age	Race	Death Date	Place of Death	Place of Burial
06688	Ryan, Mabel V.	15y	W	13 AUG 1908	Cottage City MD	Congressional
12131	Ryan, Martin C.	44y	W	16 DEC 1913	New York NY	Mt. Olivet
02469	Ryan, Mary	40y	W	25 MAY 1898	New York NY	Mt. Olivet
04017	Ryan, Michael	27y	W	30 SEP 1902	Pittsburgh PA	Mt. Olivet
05848	Ryan, Sabina	64y	W	3 DEC 1906	Ardwick MD	Mt. Olivet
17672	Ryan, Sarah J. (Watson)	68y	W	2 FEB 1922	Wytheville VA	Oak Hill
07906	Ryan, Thomas	22y	W	2 JAN 1911	Pittsburgh PA	Mt. Olivet
05762	Ryan, William Keane, s/o Thos.	28y	W	7 OCT 1906	Oakridge VA	Mt. Olivet
16567	Ryan, William Lewis	12y	W	28 JUN 1920	Potomac River	Mt. Olivet
16898	Ryan, Winifred	68y	W	6 JAN 1921	Annapolis MD	Mt. Olivet[1]
16863	Ryder, Elizabeth W.	62y	W	18 DEC 1920	Capitol Hts. MD	Glenwood
07109	Ryder, Francis, s/o James	67y	W	12 JUL 1909	Sterling VA	Mt. Olivet
12683	Ryder, James Patrick	c.35y	W	25 DEC 1914	Raleigh NC	Mt. Olivet
05259	Ryders, William Perry	60y	C	24 AUG 1905	Wheeling WV	Harmony
16583	Ryland, Mary E.	72y	W	8 JUL 1920	Laurel MD	Russellville KY
01593	Rynex, Ada Marie	6d	W	10 JAN 1895	Riverdale MD	Rock Creek
02089	Ryon, John T.	75y	W	7 NOV 1896	Philadelphia PA	Glenwood
00352	Ryon, Kate D.	21y	W	30 JUN 1890	Bowie MD	Oak Hill
14410	Ryon, Lewis P.	30y	W	11 OCT 1917	El Paso TX	Leesburg VA
17959	Ryon, Margaret	59y	W	14 JUL 1922	New York NY	Glenwood
12244	Ryon, Richard N.	48y	W	28 FEB 1914	Cottage City MD	Congressional

[1] The certificate gives year 1920 in error, and is correctly 1921 based on numerical sequence and source document.

No.	Name of Deceased	Age	Race	Death Date	Place of Death	Place of Burial
S						
06047	Sabin, Grace S.	24y	W	20 APR 1907	Minneapolis MN	Rock Creek
05327	Sachs, Jacob	58y	W	22 OCT 1905	Millston MD	Wash. Hebrew
01595	Sacks, Augustus Mason	19m	W	1 DEC 1894	Hancock MD	Wash. Hebrew
15108	Sacks, Edward Davis	17y	W	7 OCT 1918	Bethesda MD	Rock Creek
15167	Sacks, William A.	37y	W	7 OCT 1918	Bethesda MD	Rock Creek
05719	Saerenti, Pietro	26y	W	31 AUG 1906	Silver Spring MD	Mt. Olivet
18557	Saers, Harry J.	c.47y	W	24 MAY 1923	Asheville NC	Rock Creek[1]
12235	Saers, Isabella	62y	W	24 FEB 1914	New York NY	Rock Creek
13782	Saffell, Richard J.	73y	W	25 OCT 1916	Mt. Ranier MD	Mt. Olivet
03132	Saffold, Marion B., soldier	—	—	8 OCT 1900	Manila, P.I.	Arlington VA
14113	Safford, William W.	63y	W	25 APR 1917	Norfolk VA	Rock Creek
03529	Sagrario, Jose Felipe	54y	W	3 NOV 1900	Havana, Cuba	Mt. Olivet
06536	Sailer, Charles C.	77y	W	4 MAY 1908	Woodbury NJ	Oak Hill
16879	Sakata, K., fireman	25y	J	27 DEC 1920	Portsmouth VA	Cremated
13405	Salino, Jeannette	81y	W	11 MAR 1916	Asheville NC	Cremated
05144	Salkeld, John N.	22y	W	6 MAY 1905	Connellsville PA	Congressional
12515	Salmon, Daniel E.	64y	W	30 AUG 1914	Butte MT	Rock Creek
01262	Salmon, Sophia S.	48y	W	25 NOV 1893	Belvidere NJ	Glenwood
11926	Salsbury, Himon LeRoy	75y	W	30 JUL 1913	Harpers Ferry WV	Merrifield VA
12797	Salter, Martha A.	76y	W	5 MAR 1915	Silver Spring MD	Glenwood
01424	Saltzstein, Ferdinand	5m	W	3 JUL 1894	Lakeland MD	Wash. Hebrew
13760	Salzman, Infant of Nathan	SB	W	13 OCT 1916	St. Ignatius MD	Ohev Sholom
07961	Salzman, Infant of William	SB	W	8 FEB 1911	Mt. Ranier MD	Congressional
16524	Samperton, Margaret Elizabeth	1y	W	2 JUN 1920	Olney MD	Mt. Olivet
08410	Sampson, Infant of George	SB	W	6 DEC 1911	Mt. Ranier MD	Prospect Hill
14210	Sampson, Thomas	74y	W	3 JUL 1917	Garrett Park MD	Glenwood
18205	Samson, Gladys Lockwood	36y	W	11 DEC 1922	Takoma Park MD	Cremated
18066	Samuels, Amabile	76y	W	15 SEP 1922	Takoma Park MD	Prospect Hill
13632	Samuels, Charles V.	6y	W	25 JUL 1916	Los Angeles CA	Prospect Hill
16354	Samuels, Grace	24y	C	28 FEB 1920	Arlington VA	Moore's
01195	Sanborn, Alfred Dulany	19y	W	24 SEP 1892	Catskill NY	Glenwood
02270	Sanborn, Francis W.	64y	W	29 AUG 1897	Hampton VA	Glenwood
17937	Sanborn, Randolph	7y	W	5 JUL 1922	Takoma Park MD	Rock Creek
14055	Sanborn, Thornton	46y	W	24 MAR 1917	New York NY	Rock Creek
03055	Sanders, Caroline Eliza	92y	W	28 DEC 1899	Pr. Geo. Co. MD	Rock Creek
17899	Sanders, Charles	61y	W	11 JUN 1922	Riverdale MD	Prospect Hill
17730	Sanders, Fred	44y	W	7 MAR 1922	Frederick Co. MD	Congressional
13908	Sanders, Jacob	29y	W	4 JAN 1917	Baltimore MD	Elesavetgrad
16372	Sanders, John W.	2y	W	10 MAR 1920	New York NY	Congressional
01081	Sanders, Lewis Adolphus	21d	W	26 MAR 1893	Sanders Farm	Rock Creek
03594	Sanders, Mary Jennie	18y	W	25 JUL 1901	Burtonsville MD	Mt. Olivet
13223	Sanders, Morris	58y	W	30 NOV 1915	Railroad	New York NY
18556	Sanderson, Emiline	96y	C	22 MAY 1923	Arlington Co. VA	Harmony
03258	Sanderson, Jane C.	79y	W	11 AUG 1900	Leonardtown MD	Congressional
02881	Sands, Laura V.	6m	W	21 JUL 1899	Wash. Grove MD	Congressional
04470	Sands, Lizzie	35y	W	7 OCT 1903	Atlantic City NJ	Harmony
00257	Sands, Mary	10m	W	7 JAN 1890	Stephens City VA	Mt. Olivet
13021	Sands, Rosa Victoria	44y	W	23 JUL 1915	Montg. Co. MD	New York NY
16951	Sanfilippo, Areangelo	63y	W	1 FEB 1921	Clarendon VA	St. Mary's
00991	Sanford, Bertha M.	21y	W	21 JUN 1893	Highland Sta. MD	Mt. Olivet
05523	Sanford, Helen L.	2m	C	5 APR 1906	Baltimore MD	Harmony
15785	Sanford, Mary C.	81y	W	20 MAY 1919	Berwyn MD	Congressional
07203	Sangstad, Elizabeth Browne	42y	W	20 SEP 1909	Fairfax Co. VA	Rock Creek
04106	Sardo, Albert E.	60y	W	23 DEC 1902	Rumford Falls ME	Oak Hill
14667	Sargent, Elijah D.	25y	W	4 MAR 1918	Silver Spring MD	Rock Creek

[1] Surname is also found Severs and Sears in the same group of records.

District of Columbia Foreign Death Records, 1888-1923

No.	Name of Deceased	Age	Race	Death Date	Place of Death	Place of Burial
13802	Sargent, Hannah Josephine	71y	W	4 NOV 1916	Silver Spring MD	Rock Creek
15640	Sarlat, Mary	50y	C	23 FEB 1919	New York NY	Woodlawn
02602	Sarmiento, Joseph C.	62y	W	7 SEP 1898	Carroll Co. MD	Congressional
16258	Satoh, Toker Jo	27y	J	27 JAN 1920	Norfolk VA	Cremated
02882	Satterlee, Charles B., Capt.	44y	W	10 JUL 1899	Honolulu HI	Columbia SC
13559	Satterlee, Jane L.	76y	W	16 JUN 1916	New York NY	Nat. Cathedral
16130	Sauer, Charles H.	90y	W	1 DEC 1919	Baltimore MD	Prospect Hill
02338	Sauer, Christopher	23y	W	7 SEP 1897	Baltimore MD	Prospect Hill
13786	Sauer, Elizabeth E.	60y	W	28 OCT 1916	Alexandria VA	St. Mary's
14446	Sauer, Emily Frances	47y	W	5 NOV 1917	Laurel MD	Mt. Olivet
01890	Sauer, George Victor	4m	W	21 JAN 1896	Philadelphia PA	Congressional
01657	Sauer, John D.	24y	W	4 MAY 1895	Baltimore MD	Prospect Hill
01082	Sauer, Louisa	27y	W	13 FEB 1893	Baltimore MD	Prospect Hill
02141	Sauers, Evellia	65y	W	5 FEB 1897	Baltimore MD	Prospect Hill
14932	Sauers, John	23y	W	21 JUL 1918	Benedict MD	Mt. Olivet
14449	Saul, W. Lawley	58y	W	8 NOV 1917	Baltimore MD	Rock Creek
01360	Saunders, Albert Neville	6y	W	10 OCT 1877	Washington DC	Rock Creek
16866	Saunders, Alice W.	c.75y	W	19 DEC 1920	Atlantic City NJ	Arlington
03802	Saunders, Alice W.	6y	C	24 FEB 1902	Richmond VA	Harmony
03625	Saunders, Annie	1m	W	23 AUG 1901	Bethesda MD	Mt. Olivet
15171	Saunders, Asley Earl	24y	W	13 OCT 1918	New York NY	Glenwood
15317	Saunders, Carrie	65y	W	1 NOV 1918	Hyattsville MD	Glenwood
17839	Saunders, Frances U.	68y	C	5 MAY 1922	Brentwood MD	Harmony
14682	Saunders, Fred	42y	C	12 MAR 1918	Philadelphia PA	Woodlawn
01360	Saunders, Henrietta Frances	5y	W	10 OCT 1877	Washington DC	Rock Creek
03421	Saunders, Henry H.	10y	W	20 FEB 1901	Norfolk VA	Congressional
05345	Saunders, James W.	27y	C	31 OCT 1905	Pittsburgh PA	Harmony
13931	Saunders, John	55y	W	13 JAN 1917	New York NY	Oak Hill
18235	Saunders, John D.	58y	W	1 JAN 1923	Clarendon VA	Congressional
18168	Saunders, Jon H.	54y	W	17 NOV 1922	Silver Spring MD	Rock Creek
00658	Saunders, Katie M.	1y	C	31 JUL 1891	New York NY	Harmony
01360	Saunders, Minnie V.	4m	W	9 JUN 1879	Washington DC	Rock Creek
13565	Saunders, Miriam McKnight	68y	W	18 JUN 1916	Los Angeles CA	Rock Creek
02019	Saunders, Rebecca	9m	W	12 SEP 1896	Murfreesboro NC	—
18536	Saunders, Samuel Adelaide	62y	W	8 MAY 1923	Charlottesville VA	Congressional
12654	Saunders, Samuel, Rev.	73y	W	12 DEC 1914	Albemarle Co. VA	Congressional
18534	Saunders, Samuel S.	37y	W	7 MAY 1923	Binghampton NY	Congressional
15492	Saunders, Thomas A.	34y	W	27 DEC 1918	Capitol Hts. MD	Congressional
02727	Saunders, Wilbur	20y	C	29 JAN 1899	Merrifield VA	Harmony
17938	Sauter, John C.	76y	W	6 JUL 1922	Baltimore MD	St. Mary's
14719	Savage, Alpheus	29y	C	26 MAR 1918	Baltimore MD	Harmony
13499	Savoy, Joseph F.	1y	C	10 MAY 1916	Bethesda MD	Mt. Olivet
06450	Sawtelle, Charles G., Capt.	38y	W	18 FEB 1908	Ft. Russell WY	Arlington
03035	Sawyer, Charles H.	46y	W	2 DEC 1899	Jefferson Co. CO	Oak Hill
13358	Sayer, Nelle M.	28y	W	15 FEB 1916	E. Hyattsville MD	Glenwood
05979	Sayers, James	54y	W	9 MAR 1907	New York NY	Oak Hill
06428	Sayers, Robert Miles	36y	W	10 FEB 1908	St. Paul MN	Oak Hill
12197	Sayers, William S.	50y	W	3 FEB 1914	New York NY	Oak Hill
12437	Sayles, George H.	24y	C	9 JUL 1914	Rockaway B. NJ	Harmony
16499	Sayles, Grace E.	65y	W	22 MAY 1920	Trenton NJ	Harmony
14815	Sayman, Alford S.	7m	W	15 MAY 1918	Arlington MD	Glenwood
02142	Scaggs, James S.	70y	W	4 FEB 1897	Middletown PA	Glenwood
02470	Scammell, Annie	74y	W	25 MAY 1898	St. Dennis MD	Rock Creek
16400	Scammell, Emilie Hart	54y	W	19 MAR 1920	Chevy Chase MD	Congressional
04312	Scammell, William Currier	83y	W	21 MAY 1903	Chevy Chase MD	Rock Creek
05157	Scanlan, Mary E.	44y	W	4 JUN 1905	Ft. Howard MD	Mt. Olivet
00510	Scannell, John	75y	W	9 APR 1891	Hampton VA	Rock Creek
06737	Schaefer, George	62y	W	19 SEP 1908	Silver Spring MD	Rock Creek
04441	Schaefer, Henry	69y	W	7 SEP 1903	Vienna VA	Prospect Hill
16496	Schaefer, Sue Ellen	37y	W	20 MAY 1920	Malden MA	Mt. Olivet

No.	Name of Deceased	Age	Race	Death Date	Place of Death	Place of Burial
14713	Schaeffer, Bertha M.	65y	W	25 MAR 1918	New York NY	Oak Hill
01515	Schaeffer, John S.	41y	W	17 OCT 1894	Chicago IL	Oak Hill
04960	Schaeffer, Mary Martin	51y	W	16 NOV 1904	Baltimore Co. MD	Oak Hill
02271	Schafer, Cathrine	65y	W	29 JUL 1897	Staunton VA	Mt. Olivet
00769	Schafer, George F.	70y	W	26 FEB 1892	Pasadena CA	Rock Creek
02343	Schafer, Joseph	30y	W	17 NOV 1897	Mineral City VA	Rock Creek
03223	Schafer, Madalin B.	1y	W	4 JUL 1900	Herndon VA	Prospect Hill
06138	Schafner, Morse	38y	W	15 JUL 1907	Liberty NY	Ohev Sholom
18198	Schambra, Matilda W.	76y	W	3 DEC 1922	Wheeling WV	Glenwood
16156	Scharffenberg, Mimi	36y	W	19 DEC 1919	Takoma Park MD	Rock Creek
15168	Schaub, John	30y	W	10 OCT 1918	Dumont NJ	Congressional
12628	Schayer, George F.	79y	W	20 NOV 1914	Yonkers NY	Glenwood
14438	Scheer, Hattie	35y	W	3 NOV 1917	Baltimore MD	Adas Israel
17069	Scheer, Samuel	39y	W	26 MAR 1921	Takoma Park MD	Talmud Torah
15904	Scheffel, Rubin E.	—	W	–	Alexandria VA	Prospect Hill[1]
16159	Scheirer, Rachel F. (McMAster)	73y	W	16 DEC 1919	Los Angeles CA	Arvillo
18086	Schell, Wada Scott	25y	W	24 SEP 1922	Newton MA	Oak Hill
18027	Schellberg, Alice E.	41y	W	23 AUG 1922	Dodge Park MD	Ft. Lincoln
06367	Scheller, George J.	47y	W	22 DEC 1907	Philadelphia PA	Rock Creek
15872	Schenck, Jacob	55y	W	8 JUL 1919	Beltsville MD	Glenwood
16013	Schenck, Katherine	56y	W	25 SEP 1919	N. Beach MD	Cremated
08250	Schencks, Alex., shoemaker	104y	C	9 AUG 1911	Four Mile Run VA	Harmony
17960	Schendorf, Charlotte	c.24y	W	14 JUL 1922	Baltimore MD	Congressional
14890	Schenkel, George	6y	W	28 JUN 1918	Washington DC	Prospect Hill
06417	Scherer, Mary	83y	W	4 FEB 1908	Bean MD	Oak Hill
07011	Scherer, Wm. Frederick, Jr.	2y	W	4 MAY 1909	Mt. Ranier MD	Glenwood
02020	Scherich, Mabel	7d	W	16 JUL 1896	Chillum MD	Rock Creek
01596	Scherrer, Bernard	70y	W	30 NOV 1894	Bethesda MD	Tenallytown
02090	Scherrer, John C.	87y	W	17 DEC 1896	Bean MD	Oak Hill
12846	Scheuerman, Camilla	51y	W	28 MAR 1915	Cherrydale VA	Cremated
05263	Schivier, Henry	87y	W	3 SEP 1905	Bladensburg MD	Prospect Hill
02390	Schlaich, Louisa	59y	W	11 FEB 1898	Winchester VA	Prospect Hill
03030	Schlegel, Beulah H.	1y	W	6 DEC 1899	Philadelphia PA	Glenwood
05050	Schlerf, Allen M.	23y	W	25 FEB 1905	Hot Springs AR	Glenwood
08339	Schley, Winfield Scott	—	W	2 OCT 1911	New York NY	Arlington
03199	Schlosser, Anna Elizabeth	31y	W	31 MAY 1900	Allegheny PA	Rock Creek
12711	Schlosser, Harriet E.	67y	W	10 JAN 1915	Cherrydale VA	Congressional
07048	Schlosser, Robert F.	34y	W	28 MAY 1909	Vallejo CA	Arlington VA
14925	Schluth, Ernest C.	36y	W	27 APR 1918	St. Michael AK	Prospect Hill
00770	Schmid, Lewis	68y	W	22 MAR 1892	Rosslyn VA	Rock Creek
14119	Schmidt, August	69y	W	1 MAY 1917	Washington DC	Prospect Hill
17435	Schmidt, Auguste	73y	W	27 SEP 1921	Maryland Pk. MD	Cremated
15610	Schmidt, Christine	84y	W	11 FEB 1919	Takoma Park MD	Prospect Hill
03363	Schmidt, Ferdinand	42y	W	9 DEC 1900	Saranac Lake NY	Prospect Hill
12911	Schmidt, Walter F.	19y	W	2 MAY 1915	Kansas City MO	Prospect Hill
17965	Schmitzlein, Sabina L.	36y	W	17 JUL 1922	Baltimore MD	Congressional
14421	Schmuck, Roy W.	17y	W	20 OCT 1917	Shenandoah VA	Congressional
16935	Schnabele, Jacob	67y	W	20 JAN 1921	Wheaton MD	Prospect Hill
03196	Schnaeble, Henry	32y	W	27 NOV 1890	Alexandria VA	Prospect Hill
15901	Schnebel, Louis	6m	W	1 JUL 1894	Washington DC	Prospect Hill[2]
15900	Schnebel, Louis, Sr.	37y	W	24 JAN 1905	Washington DC	Prospect Hill[3]
15902	Schnebel, Rudolph	21y	W	20 OCT 1895	Washington DC	Prospect Hill[4]
16464	Schneider, Annie M.	54y	W	2 MAY 1920	Brandywine MD	Congressional
16651	Schneider, Anthony	76y	W	9 AUG 1920	Cincinnati OH	Arlington

[1] Removal from Bethel Cemetery, Alexandria VA.
[2] Removal from Bethel Cemetery, Alexandria VA.
[3] Removal from Bethel Cemetery, Alexandria VA.
[4] Removal from Bethel Cemetery, Alexandria VA.

District of Columbia Foreign Death Records, 1888-1923

No.	Name of Deceased	Age	Race	Death Date	Place of Death	Place of Burial
08753	Schneider, Charles C.	7m	W	6 AUG 1912	Round Hill VA	Glenwood
06814	Schneider, Ellen	53y	W	12 NOV 1908	Berwyn MD	Mt. Olivet
02997	Schneider, Gottlob C.	75y	W	7 NOV 1899	Brooklyn NY	Congressional
01919	Schneider, Howard	24y	W	17 MAR 1893	U.S. Jail	Congressional
06506	Schneider, Joseph Bernard	52y	W	12 APR 1908	Berwyn MD	St. Mary's
15932	Schneider, Mary Osborne	49y	W	10 AUG 1919	San Francisco CA	Rock Creek
04635	Schneiderwind, Peter	80y	W	13 MAR 1904	Dayton OH	St. Mary's
00659	Schnouder, Barbara	74y	W	12 SEP 1891	Albany NY	Washington DC
08068	Schoal, Clarence R.	c.35y	W	18 APR 1911	Harpers Ferry WV	Baltimore MD
15483	Schoenbauer, Agnes	80y	W	26 DEC 1918	Riverdale MD	St. Mary's
08636	Schoenbauer, Louis	37y	W	16 MAY 1912	E. Riverdale MD	St. Mary's
15652	Schoenthal, Julius	74y	W	2 MAR 1919	Selma AL	Wash. Hebrew
12374	Schoepf, Emily	45y	W	22 MAY 1914	Baltimore MD	Congressional
14221	Schofield, Infant of Clarence	SB	W	11 JUL 1917	Takoma MD	Rock Creek
05487	Schofield, John M.	74y	W	4 MAR 1906	St. Augustine FL	Arlington
13586	Schofield, Mary Hazel Sweet	52y	W	4 JUL 1916	Takoma MD	Rock Creek
05052	Scholtzel, Albert Charles	19y	W	7 MAR 1905	Baltimore MD	Prospect Hill
04930	Schooler, Horace	25y	C	5 SEP 1904	Rochester PA	Harmony
14307	Schooler, Richard	43y	C	18 AUG 1917	Pittsburgh PA	Harmony
17810	Schools, Infant of Louis	SB	W	20 APR 1922	Fairmont Hts. MD	Payne's
14205	Schreiber, Ernest O.	28y	W	2 JUL 1917	Laurel MD	Glenwood
17493	Schreiber, Joseph	17d	W	31 OCT 1921	Oxon Hill MD	Mt. Olivet
06186	Schreiner, Annie B.	67y	W	16 AUG 1907	Philadelphia PA	Arlington
05027	Schreiner, Francis M.	54y	W	10 FEB 1905	Asheville NC	Soldier's Home
00278	Schreiner, Mary Elizabeth	49y	W	5 FEB 1890	Sattsburg PA	National
02219	Schreyer, Elizabeth	73y	W	10 JUN 1897	Baltimore MD	Prospect Hill
17359	Schriner, Herman	83y	W	17 AUG 1921	Forest Glen MD	Soldier's Home
06844	Schriner, John H.	64y	W	7 DEC 1908	Williamsport PA	Arlington VA
02759	Schroeder, Flora	21y	W	2 MAR 1899	Chicago IL	Rock Creek
18376	Schroeder, Lucille Margaret	30y	W	26 FEB 1923	Falls Church VA	Joliet IL
16869	Schroeder, Otto	60y	W	14 DEC 1920	Chicago IL	Rock Creek
13444	Schroen, Martin J.	10m	W	6 APR 1916	Seat Pleasant MD	Mt. Olivet
07747	Schronder, Catherine	81y	W	17 SEP 1910	Barcroft VA	Cremated
16339	Schrot, Hannah	72y	W	24 FEB 1920	Philadelphia PA	Adas Israel
00301	Schroth, Jennie G.	30y	W	1 APR 1890	New York NY	Mt. Olivet
03712	Schuckers, Jacob	68y	W	23 NOV 1901	Buffalo NY	Rock Creek
05832	Schudder, Louis T.	22y	W	26 NOV 1906	Sacred Heart OK	Linden MD
03874	Schufildt, Catharine	12y	W	5 MAY 1902	New York NY	Rock Creek
08877	Schuler, Albert W.	20y	W	5 NOV 1888	San Antonio TX	Glenwood
08870	Schuler, William	18y	W	1 SEP 1892	Winfield KS	Glenwood
08157	Schulteis, Mary	72y	W	20 JUN 1911	Baltimore MD	St. Mary's
02615	Schultz, George	—	W	17 AUG 1898	Montauk NY	Congressional
14117	Schultz, John C.	35y	W	30 APR 1917	Hamilton MD	Rock Creek
06086	Schultz, Lewis Albert	39y	W	27 MAY 1907	Odenton MD	Rock Creek
12476	Schultz, Louise	80y	W	8 AUG 1914	Manassas VA	Cremated
13598	Schultze, Henry W.	61y	W	11 JUL 1916	Riggs Mill MD	Glenwood
14504	Schultze, Mary Ann	88y	W	11 DEC 1917	Baltimore MD	Oak Hill
15513	Schulze, Herman F.	31y	W	2 JAN 1919	Martinsburg WV	Prospect Hill
02021	Schumacher, Nanetta	65y	W	2 FEB 1896	Norwich CN	Prospect Hill
16040	Schutt, Elizabeth T.W.	80y	W	11 OCT 1919	Cherrydale VA	Oak Hill
15109	Schutt, Frederick Wallis	18y	W	7 OCT 1918	Hampton Rds. VA	Arlington
15958	Schutt, George F.	60y	W	27 AUG 1919	Parsonsfield ME	Rock Creek
02356	Schutt, Hannah	71y	W	23 DEC 1897	Alex. Co. VA	Rock Creek
02622	Schutt, Ruth V.	1y	W	7 OCT 1898	Alex. Co. VA	Rock Creek
02636	Schwartz, Bertha	77y	W	18 OCT 1898	Baltimore MD	Oak Hill
03442	Schwartz, Caroline	76y	W	4 MAR 1901	Bowie MD	Glenwood
15504	Schwartz, Edward G., s/o Jos.	72y	W	27 DEC 1918	Portland ME	Oak Hill
17491	Schwartz, Herbert Woodworth	63y	W	28 OCT 1921	Takoma Park MD	Syracuse NY
03023	Schwartz, Robert Bernard	78y	W	30 NOV 1899	Bowie MD	Glenwood
15119	Schweinhaut, George	29y	W	8 OCT 1918	Mt. Ranier MD	Glenwood

District of Columbia Foreign Death Records, 1888-1923

No.	Name of Deceased	Age	Race	Death Date	Place of Death	Place of Burial
15012	Schwenhart, Frank	31y	W	7 SEP 1918	Jacksonville FL	Mt. Olivet
12744	Scipio, Arthur, s/o John	33y	C	29 JAN 1915	Philadelphia PA	Woodlawn
06776	Scobell, Ida B.	53y	W	18 SEP 1908	Baltimore MD	Congressional
05275	Scoggins, Catherine	20y	C	3 SEP 1905	Philadelphia PA	Harmony
18163	Scott, Ada J.	56y	C	14 NOV 1922	Bridgeport CN	Harmony
00511	Scott, Albert	70y	W	30 MAR 1891	Cabin John MD	Tenallytown
07322	Scott, Albert W.	60y	W	11 DEC 1909	Philadelphia PA	Rock Creek
05718	Scott, Annetha	22y	C	30 AUG 1906	Atlantic City NJ	Harmony
16276	Scott, Carrie L.	30y	C	1 FEB 1920	Brooklyn NY	Harmony
12486	Scott, Celestine Seymour	32y	C	14 AUG 1914	Asbury Park NJ	Harmony
17430	Scott, Charles	70y	C	21 SEP 1921	Elizabeth VA	Harmony
17569	Scott, Daisy, d/o N.B.	15y	W	1888	Wheeling WV	Rock Creek
12704	Scott, Edmonia	35y	C	6 JAN 1915	Akron OH	Harmony
04036	Scott, Ella L.	31y	C	6 OCT 1902	So. Pines NC	Harmony
16348	Scott, Emily	77y	C	24 FEB 1920	Baltimore MD	Mt. Zion West
15250	Scott, Ernest	24y	C	12 OCT 1918	Philadelphia PA	Harmony
13451	Scott, Ernest K.	31y	C	10 APR 1916	Alex. Co. VA	Harmony
02809	Scott, Fannie F.	25y	C	2 APR 1899	Arlington VA	Harmony
09045	Scott, Florence A.	65y	W	20 JAN 1913	Coboarg, Can.	Arlington
06807	Scott, Frances	53y	W	8 NOV 1908	Jamaica NY	Rock Creek
13547	Scott, Fred	40y	C	1 JUN 1916	Philadelphia PA	Woodlawn
09019	Scott, Georgina	90y	W	6 JAN 1913	Laurel MD	Brooklyn NY
16490	Scott, Henry	—	C	8 MAY 1920	Bartow FL	Bethel, Alex. VA
14849	Scott, Henry	27y	C	31 MAY 1918	Philadelphia PA	Harmony
12645	Scott, Ida May	46y	W	5 DEC 1914	S. Nyack NY	Glenwood
04142	Scott, John B.	65y	W	25 JAN 1903	Atlantic City NJ	Glenwood
13176	Scott, John H.	55y	C	31 OCT 1915	Pittsburgh PA	Woodlawn
03117	Scott, Joseph F.	40y	W	4 MAR 1900	New York NY	Glenwood
03722	Scott, Joseph T.	29y	C	29 NOV 1901	New York NY	Hillsdale
06681	Scott, Josephine	1y	W	10 AUG 1908	Berwyn MD	Mt. Zion
03397	Scott, Josephine Magruder	26y	C	20 JAN 1901	Seat Pleasant MD	Payne's
00512	Scott, Julia A.B.	74y	W	29 DEC 1890	Wilkes Barre PA	Rock Creek
01938	Scott, Julia Hunter	3y	W	12 MAY 1896	Meridan MS	Congressional
06521	Scott, Julia Todd	87y	W	24 APR 1908	Erle PA	Arlington VA
07955	Scott, Laura L.	59y	C	30 JAN 1911	Emory Grove MD	Harmony
13357	Scott, Lawrence	79y	W	15 FEB 1916	Halls Hill VA	Harmony
14156	Scott, Lena	34y	C	30 MAY 1917	Philadelphia PA	Harmony
01361	Scott, Lillie Etta	16y	C	11 APR 1894	Washington DC	Mt. Zion
05727	Scott, Lucinda	60y	C	5 SEP 1906	Atlantic City NJ	Payne's
02414	Scott, Martha	64y	W	14 MAR 1898	Baltimore MD	Congressional
06858	Scott, Martha	64y	W	20 DEC 1908	Parkersburg WV	Glenwood
14721	Scott, Mary A.	66y	W	28 MAR 1918	Baltimore MD	Rock Creek
17568	Scott, Mary Bay	10m	W	1903	Wheeling WV	Rock Creek
15011	Scott, Oliver J.	27y	W	5 SEP 1918	Philadelphia PA	Harmony
02220	Scott, Rebecca B.	83y	W	25 JUN 1897	Narraganset RI	Rock Creek
00047	Scott, Rebecca T.	77y	W	2 MAR 1889	Rockville MD	Annapolis MD
12787	Scott, Susie T.	53y	W	2 MAR 1915	Seat Pleasant MD	Congressional
15490	Scott, Thomas J.	74y	W	28 DEC 1918	Cherrydale VA	Mt. Olivet
07870	Scott, Thomas W.	53y	W	13 DEC 1810	Frederick MD	Congressional
14562	Scott, Virginia	21y	C	6 JAN 1918	Wilmington NC	Payne's
05272	Scott, William A.	69y	C	5 SEP 1905	Emory Grove MD	Harmony
18519	Scriber, Robert	39y	C	29 APR 1923	Philadelphia PA	Payne's
02923	Scriven, Percival R.	9m	W	1 AUG 1899	Rome, Italy	Rock Creek
06985	Scrivener, John D.	83y	W	14 APR 1909	Laurel MD	Glenwood
08499	Scudder, Alice	67y	C	29 JAN 1912	Preston CN	Mt. Zion East
06459	Scuderi, Giuseppi	20y	W	7 MAR 1908	Railroad	Mt. Olivet
01375	Sculley, Emma Lillian	27y	W	21 MAY 1894	Phoebus VA	Congressional
15093	Scully, John	57y	W	1 OCT 1918	Aberdeen MD	Rock Creek
04997	Seager, Rose Dillon	33y	W	2 JAN 1905	Panama	Rock Creek
17512	Seal, Frances I.	61y	W	10 NOV 1921	Brentwood MD	Rock Creek

District of Columbia Foreign Death Records, 1888-1923

No.	Name of Deceased	Age	Race	Death Date	Place of Death	Place of Burial
02559	Seaman, Henrietta LaMerle	75y	W	11 JUL 1898	Sing Sing NY	Glenwood
00992	Sears, Eliza Sterrett	62y	W	20 JUN 1893	Brooklyn NY	Oak Hill
18140	Sears, John H., s/o Thomas	43y	W	30 OCT 1922	Denver CO	Glenwood
05869	Sears, Joseph	47y	W	22 DEC 1906	Newark NJ	Congressional
14606	Seaton, Daniel P.	82y	C	26 JAN 1918	Lincoln MD	Baltimore MD
00885	Seaton, Hanna E.	27y	C	20 AUG 1892	Easton MD	Moore's
03774	Seaton, Josephine	81y	W	29 JAN 1902	Randallstown MD	Congressional
04880	Seaton, Malcolm	75y	W	6 SEP 1904	Marblehead MA	Congressional
17636	Seaton, Randolph	—	—	—	Loudoun Co. VA	Congressional[1]
16972	Seaver, Desire T.	99y	W	24 JAN 1821	Toldeo OH	Glenwood
00513	Seavers, George A.	80y	W	20 JAN 1891	Thoroughfare VA	Rock Creek
07132	Seay, Infant of Richard	SB	W	24 JUL 1909	Seat Pleasant MD	Woodlawn
17616	Seay, John	34y	W	29 DEC 1921	New York NY	Cedar Hill
13484	Seay, Joseph A.	61y	W	30 MAR 1916	Riverdale MD	Glenwood
17912	Seay, Melville T.	29y	W	20 JUN 1922	Columbia SC	Glenwood
13475	Sebastian, Margaret E.	11d	W	24 APR 1916	Clarendon VA	Rock Creek
16039	Sebold, Charles Emily	32y	W	8 OCT 1919	Pensacola FL	Glenwood
02447	Sebring, Margaret A.	60y	W	2 MAY 1898	Minneapolis MN	Glenwood
02091	Sebring, Rachel Regina	75y	W	5 JAN 1897	Mt. Vernon NY	Glenwood
08633	Sechrist, Irvin D.	24y	W	13 MAY 1912	Charles Town WV	Glenwood
08555	Seckendorff, Gertrude H.	38y	W	12 MAR 1912	Newark NJ	Rock Creek
12850	Sedden, Lavenia	79y	C	30 MAR 1915	Olney MD	Midland VA
04520	Seden, Eliza E.	62y	W	24 NOV 1903	Baltimore MD	Congressional
02342	Sedler, Carrie B.	26y	C	7 NOV 1897	Atlantic City NJ	Harmony
07190	Seeger, Gustave	55y	W	7 SEP 1909	Langley VA	Cremated
08775	Seek, Emon E.	35y	W	22 AUG 1912	Takoma Park MD	Rock Creek
17986	Seek, Gilbert	16y	W	31 JUL 1922	Takoma Park MD	Rock Creek
13997	Seek, Olive Sarah	19y	W	18 FEB 1917	Chillum MD	Rock Creek
00167	Seek, Rose	5y	W	11 SEP 1889	Four Corners MD	Rock Creek
17600	Seeley, Katherine F.	65y	W	21 DEC 1921	New York NY	Rock Creek
13916	Seeney, Emma J.	64y	C	7 JAN 1917	Nauck VA	Harmony
04545	Seibel, Mable	27y	W	19 JAN 1904	Asheville NC	Rock Creek
14527	Seiben, George	48y	W	24 DEC 1917	Pittsburgh PA	Rock Creek
00886	Seiffort, Sarah J.	54y	W	8 AUG 1892	Wernersville PA	Rock Creek
11892	Seip, Alta	37y	W	9 JUL 1913	Ogden UT	Middletown MD
15710	Seip, Margaret A.	82y	W	4 APR 1919	Catonsville MD	Congressional
13757	Seitz, Stratton S.	19y	W	9 OCT 1916	Pittsburgh PA	Congressional
13302	Selbie, James	74y	W	13 JAN 1916	Winnipeg, Can.	Glenwood
05893	Selby, Esther Louise	1y	W	9 JAN 1907	Riverdale MD	Congressional
01263	Selden, Florence R.	37y	W	24 SEP 1893	Philadelphia PA	Congressional
08755	Selden, Sarah L.	63y	W	7 AUG 1912	Philadelphia PA	Congressional
07122	Selden, Virginia A.	57y	W	20 JUL 1909	Philadelphia PA	Congressional
00660	Selegson, H.A.	50y	W	18 AUG 1891	Baltimore MD	Arlington VA
06735	Selfridge, Thomas E.	26y	W	17 SEP 1908	Ft. Myer VA	Arlington
01329	Selke, Annie C.	51y	W	28 FEB 1894	Williamsburg VA	Mt. Olivet
13646	Sellers, Jesse	28y	W	6 AUG 1916	Wilmington DE	Glenwood
14587	Sellhausen, Harry A.	45y	W	17 JAN 1918	Brooklyn NY	Glenwood
13927	Sellman, Ella	50y	C	13 JAN 1917	Baltimore MD	Moore's
06237	Sembly, Thomas	43y	C	21 SEP 1907	Baltimore MD	Woodlawn
08024	Semmes, Christopher C.	68y	W	25 MAR 1911	Baltimore MD	Mt. Olivet
02391	Semmes, John H.	74y	W	7 JAN 1898	Chevy Chase MD	Congressional
00514	Semple, Charles E.	35y	W	29 MAR 1891	Philadelphia PA	Congressional
04749	Semple, Elizabeth P.	72y	W	31 MAY 1904	Philadelphia PA	Congressional
02336	Sener, Henry W.T.	1y	W	5 SEP 1897	Baltimore MD	Glenwood
03823	Sener*, Isabella C.	55y	W	19 MAR 1902	Richmond VA	Glenwood
14939	Seraphin, Charles E.	21y	W	25 JUL 1918	Indian Head MD	Philadelphia PA

[1] Removal of remains of Susan P. Randolph, Susan P. Armsted Randolph and Randolph Seaton, 12 JAN 1922, noting that they had all been dead over 50 years.

No.	Name of Deceased	Age	Race	Death Date	Place of Death	Place of Burial
17727	Service, Ann E.	79y	W	7 MAR 1922	Alexandria VA	Oak Hill
05100	Sessford, Susan M.	83y	W	25 APR 1905	Cabin John MD	Glenwood
13337	Seufferle, Ella Elizabeth	54y	W	4 FEB 1916	Takoma Park MD	Congressional
06488	Sevine, Catherine	79y	W	2 APR 1908	Catonsville MD	Prospect Hill
07474	Seward, Emma S.	30y	W	17 MAR 1910	St. Petersburg FL	Cremated
05467	Sewell, George	36y	C	13 FEB 1906	Moundsville WV	Mt. Zion East
14461	Sewell, Rose Lee	5m	C	15 NOV 1917	Pleasant View MD	Payne's
05379	Seyburn, John R.	—	W	22 NOV 1905	Abbeville LA	Arlington VA
01464	Seymore, John G.	15y	W	29 JUL 1894	Jamestown RI	Rock Creek
01451	Seymour, John Guest	15y	W	29 JUL 1894	Jamestown RI	Washington DC
12371	Shackelford, Anna, d/o J.A.	33y	W	20 MAY 1914	Colonial Bea. VA	Congressional
13974	Shackelford, John A.	79y	W	6 FEB 1917	Colonial Bea. VA	Congressional
03791	Shackford, Alice V.	30y	W	10 FEB 1902	Phillipsburg NJ	Rock Creek
02340	Shackleford, Annie	72y	W	16 OCT 1897	Pr. Geo. Co. MD	Congressional
08515	Shackleford, Mary E.	71y	W	13 FEB 1912	Colonial Bea. VA	Congressional
04986	Shafer, Benjamin E.	26y	W	20 DEC 1904	Denver CO	Glenwood
05585	Shaffer, Michael	73y	W	26 MAY 1906	Clinton MD	Congressional
12839	Shaler, Charles	71y	W	26 MAR 1915	Indianapolis IN	Arlington
15116	Shaler, Florence S.	46y	W	9 OCT 1918	Baltimore MD	Arlington
12037	Shambaugh, Charles	73y	W	12 OCT 1913	Hyattsville MD	Prospect Hill
13205	Shane, George B.	48y	W	14 NOV 1915	Collingswood NJ	Rock Creek
17282	Shanholtz, Samuel A.	32y	W	4 JUL 1921	Glen Echo MD	Winchester VA
01891	Shankland, Manning R.	65y	W	26 FEB 1896	Round Hill VA	Rock Creek
12127	Shanklin, Mary	18y	C	9 DEC 1913	Baltimore MD	Woodlawn
12052	Shanks, Thurman E.	39y	W	21 OCT 1913	Cherrydale VA	Oak Hill
16373	Shannon, Anna F.	73y	W	11 MAR 1920	Mt. Ranier MD	Glenwood
17133	Shannon, Ella May (Poole)	46y	W	29 APR 1921	Norfolk VA	Cedar Hill
16551	Shannon, W.	55y	W	19 JUN 1920	Arlington VA	Cedar Hill
18377	Shansey, Mary	29y	W	26 FEB 1923	Brooklyn NY	Mt. Olivet
03252	Shanter, Susan	72y	C	4 AUG 1900	Auburn NY	Mt. Olivet
18095	Shapiro, Joseph	9y	W	29 SEP 1922	Alexandria VA	Elesavetgrad
15179	Shapiro, Sara	85y	W	29 DEC 1919	Baltimore MD	Adas Israel
15525	Sharp, Julia E.E.	72y	W	6 JAN 1919	Friendship H. MD	Los Angeles CA
03445	Sharp, Mary C.	30y	W	8 MAR 1901	Pinehurst NC	Cremated
04988	Sharp, Nellie Dent	76y	W	26 DEC 1904	The Woodley DC	San Francisco CA
04338	Sharp, Robert Shepherd	26y	W	12 AUG 1903	Otterbourne MD	Rock Creek
13091	Sharper, Frank	17y	W	4 SEP 1915	Pr. Geo. Co. MD	Congressional
05730	Sharretts, David E.	44y	W	6 SEP 1906	Boston MA	Rock Creek
05731	Sharretts, Selma B.	40y	W	7 SEP 1906	Boston MA	Rock Creek
02969	Shaw, Annie	64y	W	5 OCT 1899	Charlottesville VA	Glenwood
12481	Shaw, Benjamin, cook	28y	C	8 AUG 1914	Dayton KY	Woodlawn
17818	Shaw, Charles Pierson	72y	W	26 APR 1922	Norfolk VA	Cremated
01083	Shaw, Clark G.	51y	W	11 FEB 1893	Takoma Park MD	Soldier's Home
05637	Shaw, Fannie E.	38y	W	9 JUL 1906	New York NY	Oak Hill
02630	Shaw, George Alvah	55y	W	16 OCT 1898	Gaithersburg MD	Glenwood
13758	Shaw, George F.	49y	W	12 OCT 1916	Bladensburg MD	Rock Creek
03057	Shaw, Issabla W.	55y	W	27 NOV 1873	Woodville VA	Glenwood
15632	Shaw, James A.	79y	X	22 FEB 1919	N. Glenside PA	Harmony
05502	Shaw, Johnson	12h	W	14 MAR 1906	New York NY	Congressional
03312	Shaw, Mary Elizabeth	54y	W	24 OCT 1900	Laurel MD	Congressional
06452	Shaw, Maud J.	32y	W	1 MAR 1908	New York NY	Congressional
17888	Shea, Andrew J.	32y	W	3 JUN 1922	Chicago IL	Glenwood
18359	Shea, Annie E.	67y	W	19 FEB 1923	New York NY	Mt. Olivet
04547	Shea, Daisy G.	5min	W	21 DEC 1903	New York NY	Holyrood
17571	Shea, Jack	2y	W	4 DEC 1921	Chicago IL	Glenwood
13617	Shea, John	30y	W	25 JUL 1916	Riverdale MD	Mt. Olivet
05875	Shea, John F.	58y	W	29 DEC 1906	Mt. Hope MD	Mt. Olivet
16318	Shea, Lena	38y	W	15 FEB 1920	Boston MA	Adas Israel
03064	Shea, Michael	45y	W	11 JAN 1900	Norbeck MD	Mt. Olivet
00515	Shea, Thomas J.	48y	W	17 NOV 1890	Chicago IL	Mt. Olivet

District of Columbia Foreign Death Records, 1888-1923

No.	Name of Deceased	Age	Race	Death Date	Place of Death	Place of Burial
06643	Sheahan, John	66y	W	14 JUL 1908	Colonial Bea. VA	Mt. Olivet
18245	Shear, Joseph, s/o Sam	20y	W	27 DEC 1922	At Sea	Nat. Cap. Hebrew
15465	Shearer, Leo J.	19y	W	21 DEC 1918	Capitol Hts. MD	Mt. Olivet
02272	Shearman, William Pitt	67y	W	20 JUL 1897	Allendale NJ	Oak Hill
17602	Sheckels, William Henry	67y	W	22 DEC 1921	Takoma Park MD	Rock Creek
11850	Sheckles, Mary May Dora	50y	W	29 MAY 1913	London, Eng.	Mt. Olivet
15747	Sheehan, John Dunleavy	49y	W	20 APR 1919	Pueblo CO	Mt. Olivet
08744	Sheehan, Maurice	7y	W	31 JUL 1912	Chesa. Bea. MD	Mt. Olivet
01760	Sheehy, Emma M.	32y	W	24 JUN 1895	Forestville MD	Prospect Hill
12295	Sheehy, Letta G.	26y	W	3 APR 1914	Saranac Lake NY	Mt. Olivet
12278	Sheets, Henrietta H.	69y	W	27 AMR 1914	Louisville KY	Arlington
16965	Sheets, Nancy Maddox	42y	W	10 FEB 1921	Takoma Park MD	Louisville KY
18499	Shegogne, Martha	1y	W	23 APR 1923	Oxon Hill MD	Congressional
08692	Shegogue, Eugene R.	76y	W	28 JUN 1912	Seat Pleasant MD	Cremated
04903	Shehan, Julia Hellen	38y	W	24 SEP 1904	Kensington MD	Mt. Olivet
04443	Sheid, Elizabeth	35y	W	8 SEP 1903	New York NY	Glenwood
16259	Sheina, Rokura	24y	J	29 JAN 1920	Norfolk VA	Cremated
04329	Sheiry, Russell C.	1y	W	21 AUG 1903	Bethesda MD	Glenwood
12294	Shekell, Eugene	20y	W	2 APR 1914	Braddock PA	Mt. Olivet
12776	Shekell, Eugene A.	83y	W	22 FEB 1915	Detroit MI	Oak Hill
17977	Shelander, Alice E.	27y	W	26 JUL 1922	Brunswick GA	Rock Creek
02120	Shelby, Ann M.	52y	C	19 JAN 1897	Albany NY	Harmony
02274	Shelby, Dyse O.	62y	C	15 JUL 1897	Albany NY	Harmony
18169	Shelby, Joseph A., s/o Dyer	46y	W	16 NOV 1922	New York NY	Harmony
03718	Shelding, Infant of Arthur B.	—	W	28 NOV 1901	Wilmington NC	Rock Creek
02093	Sheldon, Elvira Bliss	62y	W	7 JAN 1897	Akron OH	Arlington
14029	Shellenberger, Elizabeth C.	86y	W	15 MAR 1917	New York NY	Oak Hill
01759	Shelley, John	25y	W	20 OCT 1895	Alex. Co. VA	Fordham NY
06015	Shelliga, Stephen	c.30y	W	2 APR 1907	Dickerson MD	Potters Field
09070	Shelly, Mrs. James	29y	W	11 FEB 1913	Chattanooga TN	Arlington
16317	Shelton, Cecelia I.	28y	W	7 FEB 1920	Denver CO	Mt. Olivet
12009	Shelton, Charles William	70y	W	20 SEP 1913	Catonsville MD	Arlington
06436	Shelton, R.W.	46y	W	18 FEB 1908	Cherrydale VA	Congressional
04103	Shelton, William H.	53y	W	24 DEC 1902	Phoebus VA	Congressional
04857	Shepard, Edwin Malcom	60y	W	17 AUG 1904	Jaffrey NJ	Arlington
00111	Shepard, John Summers	2m	W	21 JUL 1889	Annandale VA	Glenwood
01196	Shepard, Mary A.	32y	C	29 JUN 1892	Philadelphia PA	Holyrood
02723	Shepard, Sarah	68y	C	21 JAN 1899	Baltimore MD	Harmony
17290	Shepard, Seth, Jr., lawyer	39y	W	7 JUL 1921	Mystic CN	Rock Creek[1]
02273	Shephard, Edward	53y	W	8 JUL 1897	Pittsburgh PA	Payne's
04609	Shephard, Infant of John A.	15y	W	22 FEB 1904	Highland MD	Glenwood
17463	Shephard, Robert L.	18y	W	1 NOV 1918	France	Arlington
04250	Shepherd, Alexander Roby	67y	W	12 SEP 1902	Batopilas, Mex.	Rock Creek
02448	Shepherd, John	78y	W	26 APR 1898	Old Point VA	Glenwood
05897	Shepherd, Martha (Bankhead)	79y	W	15 JAN 1907	Phoebus VA	Glenwood
04085	Shepley, Harry A.	31y	W	20 NOV 1902	Brooklyn NY	Arlington
02022	Sheppard, Lillin	23y	C	8 AUG 1896	Philadelphia PA	Harmony
16794	Sheppard, Lorraine Drucille	9m	W	1 NOV 1920	Mt. Ranier MD	Cedar Hill
12214	Sheppard, Mrs. Hamilton	45y	W	11 FEB 1914	Wash. Grove MD	Richmond VA
07340	Sherer, Henry Clay	77y	W	22 DEC 1909	Takoma Park MD	Glenwood
08293	Sheridan, Ada B.J.F.	48y	W	3 SEP 1911	Landover MD	Cremated
04053	Sheridan, Edw., amputated leg	—	—	7 OCT 1902	—	—
18118	Sheridan, George W.	52y	W	18 OCT 1922	New York NY	Congressional
06253	Sheridan, Margaret	64y	W	27 SEP 1907	Towson MD	Mt. Olivet
02092	Sheriden, George A.	56y	W	7 OCT 1896	Eliz. City Co. VA	Arlington VA
17882	Sheriff, Jessie R.	45y	W	31 MAY 1922	Wadsworth OH	Rock Creek
01940	Sheriff, John B.	33y	W	26 MAY 1896	Elizabeth NJ	Mt. Olivet

[1] Note that the body was disinterred and reburied at Lake Forrest, Ill. on 25 MAY 1922.

No.	Name of Deceased	Age	Race	Death Date	Place of Death	Place of Burial
03470	Sheriff, John Bealle	3y	W	6 APR 1901	Seat Pleasant MD	Mt. Olivet
01264	Sheriff, Magruder	24y	W	8 NOV 1893	Landover MD	Sheriff Family[1]
06357	Sheriff, Mary A.	79y	W	25 DEC 1907	Hyattsville MD	Mt. Olivet
01953	Sherman, Agnes	6m	W	8 JUN 1896	Del Ray VA	Congressional
05433	Sherman, Alexander, barber	c.55y	C	12 JAN 1906	Alex. Co. VA	Payne's
02341	Sherman, Anna B. Burham	74y	W	15 OCT 1897	Stratford CN	Oak Hill
09157	Sherman, Anna Burnham	64y	W	4 APR 1913	Hartford CN	Oak Hill
08059	Sherman, Annye B.	66y	W	28 FEB 1911	Denver CO	Glenwood
15847	Sherman, Delia	77y	W	24 JUN 1919	Highland Falls NY	Mt. Olivet
03433	Sherman, Ellen Minott	50y	W	23 FEB 1901	Lawrence NY	Oak Hill
03897	Sherman, Hobart	9y	W	17 MAY 1902	Pacasinago, Peru	Oak Hill
03636	Sherman, Infant of Fred. R.	2h	W	28 MAY 1901	Takoma Park MD	Congressional
03177	Sherman, Mozelle	2y	W	29 APR 1900	Manchester VA	Glenwood
01084	Sherrer, John W.	38y	W	5 MAY 1893	Birmingham AL	Oak Hill
01085	Sherrer, Samuel R.	22y	W	19 JUL 1887	Montg. Co. MD	Oak Hill
17883	Sherwood, Hattie E.	82y	W	31 MAY 1922	Richmond VA	Glenwood
12375	Sherwood, James H.	78y	W	21 MAY 1914	Chambersburg PA	Glenwood
07966	Sherwood, Susan L.	67y	W	11 FEB 1911	Wittman MD	Glenwood
15886	Sherwood, Virginia H.	62y	W	21 JUL 1919	Philadelphia PA	Congressional
02883	Shettle, Mary E.	20y	W	29 JUN 1899	Hyattsville MD	Glenwood
16950	Shiba, George	19y	J	31 JAN 1921	Portsmouth VA	Cremated
04311	Shields, A.W.	60y	C	20 MAY 1903	Newton MS	Woodlawn
12434	Shields, Ella V. (Sweeney)	43y	W	11 JUL 1914	Gainesville VA	Mt. Olivet
15828	Shields, Thomas	52y	W	12 JUN 1919	Springfield MA	Arlington
02610	Shilling, George, soldier	19y	W	22 SEP 1898	Montauk NY	Arlington VA
12988	Shinn, Caroline C.	86y	W	2 JUL 1915	Takoma Park MD	Rock Creek
16633	Shinowara, Kuraro	c.29y	J	31 JUL 1920	Newport News VA	Cremated
14333	Shipley, Doris A.	2y	W	2 SEP 1917	Takoma Park MD	Rock Creek
04775	Shipley, Francis L.	70y	W	25 JUN 1904	Chevy Chase MD	Glenwood
14429	Shipley, Hattie Catherine	41y	W	30 OCT 1917	Takoma Park MD	Rock Creek
16096	Shipley, Joseph Lloyd	59y	W	8 NOV 1919	Riverdale MD	Glenwood
17788	Shipley, Lizzie Baldwin	61y	W	9 APR 1922	Edgewater MD	Loudon Park MD
17683	Shipley, Mary Ann	56y	W	10 FEB 1922	Takoma Park MD	Glenwood
08100	Shipley, Mary Hazel	6y	W	5 MAY 1911	Takoma Park MD	Rock Creek
06556	Shipley, Robert E.	22y	W	19 MAY 1908	Daniel's Pk. MD	Rock Creek
03648	Shipley, Sarah	31y	C	13 SEP 1901	Redland MD	Harmony
06075	Shipley, Virginia F.	61y	W	21 MAY 1907	Bladensburg MD	Rock Creek
14179	Shipley, William M.	4d	W	23 APR 1917	New York NY	Rock Creek
13423	Shipman, George W.	72y	W	19 MAR 1916	Corinth MI	Glenwood
00224	Shipman, Marion H.	26y	W	31 OCT 1889	Gallipolis OH	Mt. Olivet
08540	Shire, Giles	61y	W	28 FEB 1912	New York NY	Mt. Olivet
16456	Shoemaker, Abner Claude P.	34y	W	28 APR 1920	Atlantic City NJ	Rock Creek
16962	Shoemaker, Alice C.	47y	W	8 FEB 1921	Brookmont MD	Congressional
13307	Shoemaker, Anna M.	75y	W	20 JAN 1916	Philadelphia PA	Rock Creek
01597	Shoemaker, Charles, farmer	81y	W	14 FEB 1895	Montg. Co. MD	Oak Hill
05539	Shoemaker, Charles, s/o Sam.	23y	W	12 APR 1906	Boston MA	Glenwood
11894	Shoemaker, Chas. F., s/o Wm.	72y	W	11 JUL 1913	Woodstock VA	Arlington
12649	Shoemaker, Della T.	2y	W	8 DEC 1914	Baltimore MD	Methodist
17732	Shoemaker, Edward	82y	W	8 MAR 1922	Brookmont MD	Congressional
05571	Shoemaker, Edward	81y	W	8 MAY 1906	St. Denis MD	Oak Hill
00029	Shoemaker, Frank A.	26y	W	21 FEB 1889	Trappe MD	Oak Hill
04571	Shoemaker, Hannah L.	73y	W	17 JAN 1904	Wilkes-Barre PA	Rock Creek
15689	Shoemaker, Henry P.	47y	W	24 MAR 1919	Glen Echo MD	Congressional
17840	Shoemaker, Isaac W.	60y	W	13 APR 1905	Chesterbrook VA	Glenwood
04577	Shoemaker, Joseph	58y	W	24 JAN 1904	Montg. Co. MD	Oak Hill
08334	Shoemaker, Laura D.	75y	W	30 SEP 1911	Riverdale MD	Rock Creek
13286	Shoemaker, Louis E.	48y	W	6 JAN 1916	Chevy Chase MD	Tenallytown M.

[1] Removed to Rock Creek cemetery on 11 JUN 1930.

District of Columbia Foreign Death Records, 1888-1923

No.	Name of Deceased	Age	Race	Death Date	Place of Death	Place of Burial
03621	Shoemaker, Louis E.	1y	W	22 AUG 1901	Chevy Chase MD	Tenallytown
08599	Shoemaker, Margaret Helen	12d	W	16 APR 1912	Drummond MD	Mt. Olivet
16894	Shoemaker, Mary E.	85y	W	5 JAN 1921	Brookmont MD	Congressional
01761	Shoemaker, Mary E.	57y	W	10 OCT 1895	Montg. Co. MD	Tenallytown
04668	Shoemaker, Mary Elizabeth	78y	W	12 APR 1904	Montg. Co. MD	Oak Hill
07886	Shoemaker, Mattie	29y	W	12 DEC 1910	Phoenix AZ	Rock Creek
00382	Shoemaker, Thomas Floyd	56y	W	23 JUL 1890	Ukiah CA	Rock Creek
13067	Shoemaker, William B.	1y	W	21 AUG 1915	Drummond MD	Mt. Olivet
14657	Shomo, Thomas W.	57y	W	23 FEB 1918	Brentwood MD	Glenwood
16113	Shopland, Alfred Arscott	41y	W	20 NOV 1892	Berryville VA	Prospect Hill
08266	Shork, Henry L.	73y	W	21 AUG 1911	Riverdale MD	Glenwood
06647	Short, Sallie	31y	C	13 JUL 1908	Philadelphia PA	Harmony
02094	Short, Sarah	16y	C	21 OCT 1896	Bladensburg MD	Mt. Olivet
02095	Shorter, Eliza A.	9y	C	1 DEC 1896	Bladensburg MD	Mt. Olivet
05557	Shorter, Elizabeth	61y	C	24 APR 1906	Philadelphia PA	Mt. Olivet
18546	Shorter, Milton	28y	C	13 MAY 1923	Arlington Co. VA	Arlington
04551	Shorts, Alfred	65y	C	26 DEC 1903	E. Hyattsville MD	Mt. Olivet
04077	Shreve, Charles E.	28y	W	16 AUG 1902	Saratoga Spg. NY	Rock Creek
12067	Shreve, Nannie M.	46y	W	31 OCT 1913	Arlington VA	Rock Creek
05065	Shreve, William J.	66y	W	26 MAR 1905	Falls Church VA	Rock Creek
06178	Shrewsbury, A.D., s/o Dick.	39y	W	9 AUG 1907	Cape Henry VA	Rock Creek
02577	Shryock, Susan A.	76y	W	26 AUG 1898	Baltimore MD	Glenwood
00887	Shufeldt, Robert Wilson, 3d	15y	W	11 JUL 1892	Marietta OH	Rock Creek
13041	Shuler, Amanda L.	77y	W	2 AUG 1915	W. Palm Bea. FL	Cremated
02555	Shultz, Henry C.	31y	W	6 AUG 1898	Davenport IA	Prospect Hill
13564	Shumate, George C.	29y	W	22 JUN 1916	Cherrydale VA	Rock Creek
13825	Shumate, Louisa	56y	C	23 NOV 1916	Halls Hill VA	Willington VA
00771	Shuster, Eliza	77y	W	25 DEC 1891	Landover Sta. MD	Glenwood
12717	Shuster, J. Ward	38y	W	12 JAN 1915	Clearwater FL	Oak Hill
00281	Shuster, J.C.	80y	W	19 FEB 1890	Hyattsville MD	Glenwood
02632	Shuttleworth, Harriet B.	64y	W	14 OCT 1898	Glen Echo MD	Rock Creek
11871	Shyrock, Theophilus Y.	54y	W	26 JUN 1913	Hyattsville MD	Rock Creek
05077	Sibert, John M.	58y	W	7 APR 1905	S. Jacksonville FL	New Market VA
02528	Sibley, Albert, engraver	22y	W	2 JUL 1898	Arlington VA	Glenwood
08449	Sibley, Julia	85y	W	31 DEC 1911	Herndon VA	Glenwood
00993	Sibley, William Hanson	67y	W	4 AUG 1893	Dallas TX	Arlington VA
00661	Sickels, Anna Elizabeth	68y	W	18 AUG 1891	Silver Hill MD	Brooklyn NY
08151	Sickles, John E.	84y	W	18 JUN 1911	Takoma Park MD	Alexandria VA
00336	Sickles, Ziporia	46y	W	2 JUN 1890	Bristol RI	Wash. Hebrew
06158	Sidell, Edward Thomas	4m	W	27 JUL 1907	Colonial Bea. VA	Congressional
16288	Sidman, George D.	75y	W	3 FEB 1920	Lakeland FL	Arlington
16367	Sidway, Franklin	85y	W	7 MAR 1920	St. Augustine FL	Buffalo NY
03893	Siebert, Emma	74y	W	11 JUN 1902	Cumberland MD	Cremated
02611	Siebert, Kate R.	40y	W	22 SEP 1898	Cumberland MD	Oak Hill
02177	Siffold, John A., lawyer	52y	W	6 MAY 1897	Chevy Chase MD	Glenwood
18224	Siford, Harry M.	41y	W	21 DEC 1922	Phoenix AZ	Glenwood
04497	Signor, William H.	57y	W	28 OCT 1903	Mound City IL	Arlington
15586	Sigsbee, Charles D.	29y	W	23 JAN 1919	Annapolis MD	Cremated
02957	Sigsbee, Eleanor	13y	W	25 SEP 1899	Rehobeth DE	Annapolis MD
08606	Siioussa, Mary	84y	W	18 APR 1912	Mobile AL	Glenwood
15459	Sikken, Arthur	29y	W	19 DEC 1918	Hyattsville MD	Glenwood
06203	Silbey, Adam	19y	W	25 AUG 1907	Baltimore MD	Glenwood
07383	Silcott, Warren F.	21y	W	19 JAN 1910	Tucson AZ	Glenwood
12870	Silence, Alice Roberta	64y	C	9 APR 1915	Fairmont Hts. MD	Harmony
14450	Silence, Emma Bernice	12y	C	9 NOV 1917	Fairmont Hts. MD	Harmony
16540	Silence, George P.	53y	C	17 JUN 1920	Fairmont Hts. MD	Harmony
15411	Silver, Estella	38y	C	7 DEC 1918	Baltimore MD	Harmony
12971	Silver, Tena	61y	W	21 JUN 1915	New York NY	Wash. Hebrew
14202	Simenton, John Paul	SB	W	3 JUL 1917	Arlington VA	Mt. Olivet
15146	Simmes, Symphronia Bryan	72y	W	10 OCT 1918	Lansdowne PA	Mt. Olivet

No.	Name of Deceased	Age	Race	Death Date	Place of Death	Place of Burial
06013	Simmins, Alice	19y	C	24 JAN 1892	Washington DC	Harmony
07976	Simmons, Elizabeth A.	60y	W	18 FEB 1911	Baltimore MD	Glenwood
16722	Simmons, George R.	59y	W	20 SEP 1920	Capitol Hts. MD	Glenwood
16731	Simmons, Jane	80y	W	1 OCT 1920	Mt. Ranier MD	Congressional
01265	Simmons, John E.	55y	W	26 OCT 1893	Abingdon VA	Rock Creek
07656	Simmons, John F., soldier	74y	W	26 JUL 1910	Hampton VA	Glenwood
07940	Simmons, Julia E.	35y	C	21 JAN 1911	New York NY	Harmony
15134	Simmons, Leo I.	32y	C	9 OCT 1918	Hampton VA	Mt. Olivet
07258	Simmons, Martha E. (Benton)	59y	W	2 NOV 1909	Rosslyn VA	Glenwood
02275	Simmons, Phillip T.	—	C	5 AUG 1897	Helena MT	Harmony
13269	Simms, Emma	70y	C	23 DEC 1915	Newark NJ	Harmony
12081	Simms, Emma	64y	C	8 NOV 1913	Relee VA	Moore's
02023	Simms, Frederick	24y	C	21 JUL 1896	Dickerson MD	Harmony
00889	Simms, Giles Constantine	9y	W	5 AUG 1892	Summit Pt. WV	Mt. Olivet
16478	Simms, John	64y	C	8 MAY 1920	Baltimore MD	Mt. Olivet
07081	Simms, John	25y	C	24 JUN 1909	Stockport NY	Payne's
18035	Simms, Julius	35y	C	26 AUG 1922	Berwyn MD	Payne's
18331	Simms, Leo	4m	C	7 FEB 1923	Fairmont Hts. MD	Mt. Olivet
12821	Simms, Montgomery Ward	—	W	c. MAR 1915	Mexico City, Mex.	Alexandria VA
06012	Simms, Primus	3m	C	APR 1882	Washington DC	Harmony
16413	Simms, Richard Douglas	51y	W	31 MAR 1920	Asheville NC	Oak Hill
00360	Simms, Richard E.	62y	W	15 JUL 1890	Baltimore MD	Mt. Olivet
13642	Simon, Anne C.	47y	W	5 AUG 1916	Colo. Spgs. CO	Rock Creek
07672	Simon, Katharine, d/o Louis	11y	W	5 AUG 1910	Warrenton VA	Rock Creek
05665	Simon, Louise	4y	W	27 JUL 1906	Oakland CA	Rock Creek
02449	Simonds, Helen May	29y	W	9 APR 1898	Riverdale MD	Congressional
16184	Simonds, Justin F.	93y	W	3 JAN 1920	Riverdale MD	Cremated
08298	Simons, Abraham	—	W	7 SEP 1911	Capitol Hts. MD	Talmud Torah
07085	Simons, Hildegarde Eliz.	5m	W	30 JUN 1909	Sandy Spring MD	Rock Creek
15174	Simonton, Lawrence Joseph	28y	W	10 OCT 1918	Cumberland MD	Mt. Olivet
09029	Simpson, Agnes Close Bryant	41y	W	13 JAN 1913	Cuba NY	Rock Creek
00888	Simpson, Alan	19y	W	23 OCT 1892	Cambridge MA	Rock Creek
02768	Simpson, Albert	72y	W	30 JAN 1890	Centerville MD	Rock Creek
07657	Simpson, Albert Jones	4y	W	29 JUL 1910	Chevy Chase MD	Rock Creek
08191	Simpson, Ernest B.	64y	W	9 JUL 1911	River View MD	Rock Creek
12389	Simpson, Flora Andrews	16y	W	6 JUN 1914	Chevy Chase MD	Rock Creek
01197	Simpson, George J.	23y	W	27 DEC 1892	Hampton FL	Rock Creek
01939	Simpson, George L., Dr.	62y	W	10 MAY 1896	New York NY	Rock Creek
07985	Simpson, Harriett H.	79y	W	25 FEB 1911	Forest Glen MD	Rock Creek
02276	Simpson, Helen	1y	W	14 JUL 1897	Waterloo PA	Congressional
07677	Simpson, Isabella Carr, d/o E.	22d	W	8 AUG 1910	Ballston VA	Holyrood
13913	Simpson, Jacob Sleppy	70y	W	6 JAN 1917	Ballston VA	Glenwood
09122	Simpson, Jane R.	70y	W	11 MAR 1913	Suitland MD	Congressional
15896	Simpson, John, Jr.	53y	W	30 JUL 1919	Brentwood MD	Rock Creek
08074	Simpson, John S.	1y	W	19 APR 1911	Livingston Hts. VA	Rock Creek
06004	Simpson, John, Sr.	71y	W	2 APR 1907	Forest Glen MD	Rock Creek
06979	Simpson, Marcus D.	84y	W	7 APR 1909	Riverside IL	Rock Creek
00662	Simpson, Margaret	6m	W	3 AUG 1891	Laurel MD	Holyrood
05408	Simpson, Mary J.	68y	W	23 DEC 1905	Cabin John MD	Congressional
12471	Simpson, Matilda Blair	66y	W	5 AUG 1914	Ballston VA	Glenwood
05870	Simpson, Phillip Anthony	74y	W	25 DEC 1906	Hoadley VA	Mt. Olivet
04118	Simpson, Resin B.	—	W	1870	Dayton MD	Glenwood
15876	Simpson, Sallie Kershaw	83y	W	9 JUL 1919	Willoughby B. VA	Rock Creek
12115	Simpson, Sarah Ann	91y	W	4 DEC 1913	N. Braddock PA	Rock Creek
18304	Simpson, Silas A.	54y	W	17 JAN 1916	Hopewell VA	Harrington DE
05005	Sims, Joseph S.	45y	C	19 JAN 1905	Chicago IL	Mt. Olivet
01086	Sims, William E.	49y	W	26 JUL 1891	Columbia, So. A.	Congressional
11823	Sinclair, Joseph McD.	32y	W	8 MAY 1913	Ancon, Can. Zone	Congressional
14443	Singles, Levenia	61y	W	6 NOV 1917	Silver Spring MD	Philadelphia PA
08325	Singleton, Harry Bell	2m	W	24 SEP 1911	Tiverton RI	Rock Creek

No.	Name of Deceased	Age	Race	Death Date	Place of Death	Place of Burial
06746	Singleton, William	68y	C	22 SEP 1908	Laurel MD	Macedonia
15973	Sinkfield, Samuel	47y	C	1 SEP 1919	Philadelphia PA	Payne's
16611	Sinsheimer, Moses	65y	W	18 JUL 1920	Ambler PA	Wash. Hebrew
03475	Sioussa, Elizabeth A.	66y	W	9 APR 1901	Gaithersburg MD	Glenwood
18180	Sioussant, Merritt	75y	W	25 NOV 1922	Baltimore MD	Oak Hill
17190	Sipe, Hiram M.	93y	W	27 MAY 1921	Woodside MD	Rock Creek
02339	Sipe, Thomas N.	45y	W	28 SEP 1897	Glenwood MD	Glenwood
18348	Siphen, Marie Louise	29y	W	15 FEB 1923	Mt. Ranier MD	Mt. Olivet
13123	Sipperly, Phoebe	89y	W	26 SEP 1915	Jewell VA	Glenwood
14786	Sirowaltky, William	38y	W	30 APR 1918	Baltimore MD	Glenwood
12402	Sisson, Elizabeth	3y	W	14 JUN 1914	Forest Glen MD	Mt. Olivet
12605	Sisson, Eva M., a.k.a. Wilson	28y	W	8 NOV 1914	Richmond VA	Congressional
01836	Sizer, Charles Hines	22m	W	14 NOV 1895	Riverdale MD	Mt. Olivet
02178	Sizer, Dorothy Margaret	4m	W	24 APR 1897	Riverdale MD	Mt. Olivet
02919	Sizer, George Ashby	6m	W	21 AUG 1899	Riverdale MD	Mt. Olivet
03745	Sizer, Ralph Donald	4y	W	29 DEC 1901	Riverdale MD	Mt. Olivet
08350	Skeels, Emily Elizabeth	1y	W	1 AUG 1911	Takoma Park MD	Rock Creek
04975	Skelding, Dorothy Ames	30y	W	6 DEC 1904	Wilmington NC	Rock Creek
14915	Skerrett, Joseph Taylor	56y	W	13 JUL 1918	Philadelphia PA	Congressional
14509	Skillman, Enos Ayres	84y	W	17 DEC 1917	Rockville MD	Oak Hill
18015	Skilman, John B.	26y	W	13 AUG 1922	Dawson Spgs. KY	Arlington
14979	Skinner, Aaron N.	73y	W	14 AUG 1918	Framingham MA	Rock Creek
14349	Skinner, Evelyn	2y	W	8 SEP 1917	Dranesville VA	Methodist
00248	Skinner, George Francis	16y	W	20 DEC 1889	Glendale MD	Mt. Olivet
04124	Skinner, Julia L.	97y	W	7 DEC 1902	Burlington VT	Oak Hill
02534	Skinner, Randall	58y	C	20 JUN 1898	Hampton VA	Arlington VA
02605	Skinner, William E.	60y	W	28 SEP 1898	Battle Creek MI	Rock Creek
04468	Skirving, Caroline H. McEwen	82y	W	5 OCT 1903	Philadelphia PA	Oak Hill
07637	Skirving, Esther M.A.	57y	W	14 JUL 1910	Philadelphia PA	Oak Hill
08177	Skirving, William A.	60y	W	1 JUL 1911	Philadelphia PA	Oak Hill
12424	Slack, John H.	27y	W	4 JUL 1914	Beverly MA	Congressional
14283	Slade, John M.	54y	C	7 AUG 1917	New York NY	Woodlawn
05628	Slarrow, James M.	49y	W	5 JUN 1906	Baltimore MD	Rock Creek
04233	Slater, Edith	50y	W	21 FEB 1903	Catonsville MD	Congressional
06023	Slater, Isaac E.	64y	W	8 APR 1907	Lovettsville VA	Congressional
16555	Slater, William A.	3y	C	24 JUN 1920	Takoma Park MD	Mt. Zion East
15092	Slattery, William Patrick	c.27y	W	5 OCT 1918	Norfolk VA	Mt. Olivet
14732	Slaughter, Amy	114y	C	5 APR 1918	Cedar Hts. MD	Harmony
18279	Slaughter, Annie	33y	C	15 JAN 1923	Philadelphia PA	Payne's
08176	Slaughter, Charles E.	27y	C	6 JUN 1911	Philadelphia PA	Odd Fellows VA
17049	Slaughter, Hugh W.	3y	C	18 MAR 1921	Chillum MD	Fredericksburg VA
18071	Slaughter, Lawrence A., 3rd	1y	W	17 SEP 1922	Up. Saranac NY	Mt. Olivet
00890	Slee, Lydia	59y	W	21 JUL 1892	Salem MA	Congressional
08172	Sleman, John B., Jr.	37y	W	1 JUL 1911	Clifton Spgs. NY	Rock Creek
03272	Sliney, Ruth	19y	W	22 AUG 1900	Montg. Co. MD	Rock Creek
01654	Sloman, Henry O.	75y	W	10 MAR 1895	Baltimore MD	Prospect Hill
05985	Slough, George W.	57y	W	16 MAR 1907	Philadelphia PA	Mt. Olivet
08380	Slough, Martin	51y	W	31 OCT 1911	Baltimore MD	Oak Hill
04511	Slrrell, Infant & Lawrence	SB	W	14 NOV 1903	Brentwood MD	Glenwood
03598	Slye, John Raymond	8m	W	31 JUL 1901	Hampton VA	St. Barnabas MD
05055	Smackum, Helena	14y	W	12 MAR 1905	Baltimore MD	Holyrood
07854	Small, Archibald	48y	W	6 DEC 1910	Providence Farm	Oak Hill
07509	Small, Emma M.	42y	W	30 JAN 1904	Darnestown MD	Glenwood
18155	Small, Holmes B.	19y	W	9 NOV 1922	Hop Bottom PA	Ft. Lincoln
12678	Small, Infant of Harry	SB	W	28 DEC 1914	Capitol Hts. MD	Congressional
16590	Small, Jacob	24y	W	11 JUL 1920	Annapolis MD	Adas Israel
15399	Small, John Henry	63y	W	2 DEC 1918	Takoma Park MD	Rock Creek
12597	Smallwood, Eliza	73y	C	5 NOV 1914	Bladensburg MD	Woodlawn
07431	Smallwood, Elizabeth	75y	C	23 FEB 1910	Baltimore MD	Holyrood
07790	Smallwood, George	55y	W	23 JUN 1910	Peekskill NY	Glenwood

No.	Name of Deceased	Age	Race	Death Date	Place of Death	Place of Burial
07686	Smallwood, George W.	69y	W	12 AUG 1910	Farmington MD	Mt. Olivet
12246	Smallwood, Hattie Belle	27y	C	1 MAR 1914	Uniontown MD	Payne's
12987	Smallwood, James Arthur	34y	C	29 JUN 1915	Pittsburgh PA	Moore's
02277	Smallwood, Martha	14y	C	26 AUG 1897	Philadelphia PA	Harmony
08587	Smallwood, Mary	60y	C	5 APR 1912	Riverdale MD	Mt. Olivet
17168	Smallwood, Mary J.	56y	C	16 MAY 1921	Rockville MD	Harmony
04573	Smallwood, Thomas	66y	C	20 JAN 1904	Bladensburg MD	Woodlawn
00891	Smallwood, William	65y	C	2 MAY 1892	Baltimore MD	Holyrood
05101	Smart, Charles	64y	W	23 APR 1905	St. Augustine FL	Arlington
00663	Smart, Frank T.	33y	W	28 AUG 1891	Albuquerque NM	Oak Hill
13178	Smart, Henry G., w/o R.D.	24y	W	2 NOV 1915	Charlottesville VA	Cremated
05507	Smart, Laura V.	57y	W	22 MAR 1906	Philadelphia PA	Congressional
08070	Smiles, John S.	26y	C	4 APR 1911	Franklin OH	Harmony
07636	Smire, Jean	5y	W	16 JUL 1910	Spring Lake NJ	Glenwood
14215	Smith, A.R.	48y	W	4 JUL 1917	Decatur AL	Mt. Olivet
06900	Smith, Addison B.	78y	W	24 JAN 1909	Laurel MD	Glenwood
12470	Smith, Adle Rosalie	2y	W	6 AUG 1914	Hyattsville MD	Cremated
17661	Smith, Albert	85y	W	26 JAN 1922	Bowie MD	Glenwood
00322	Smith, Alexenia Claudia	52y	W	28 APR 1890	Carter WY	Rock Creek
15884	Smith, Alfred J.	55y	W	17 JUL 1919	Rockville MD	Mt. Olivet
01519	Smith, Alice	40y	C	22 OCT 1894	Burnt Mills MD	Harmony
17444	Smith, Amanda	21y	C	27 SEP 1921	Moundsville WV	Payne's
08243	Smith, Amelia	78y	C	5 AUG 1811	Brentwood MD	Payne's
00517	Smith, Ana M.C.	87y	W	5 DEC 1890	Philadelphia PA	Congressional
17674	Smith, Andrew Thomas	23y	W	4 FEB 1922	Saranac Lake NY	Rocky Mount NC
13070	Smith, Anna	48y	C	20 AUG 1915	Atlantic City NJ	Harmony
01892	Smith, Anna B.	62y	W	20 JAN 1896	Hyattsville MD	Oak Hill
05222	Smith, Annie	1d	W	28 JUL 1905	Brentwood MD	Mt. Olivet
04145	Smith, Annie	27y	C	24 JAN 1903	Philadelphia PA	Payne's
17086	Smith, Annie Eliza	77y	W	3 APR 1921	Takoma Park MD	Rock Creek
18131	Smith, Annie Elizabeth	76y	W	25 OCT 1922	Bronx NY	Oak Hill
11888	Smith, Annie M.	69y	W	9 JUL 1913	Mt. Hope MD	Rock Creek
04931	Smith, Annie M. (Conrad)	67y	W	22 OCT 1904	Centreville VA	Oak Hill
08328	Smith, Arthur C.	22y	W	24 SEP 1911	Fairview MD	Rock Creek
12690	Smith, Augusta S.	77y	W	28 DEC 1914	Mishawaka IN	Rock Creek
14846	Smith, Augustine Jaquelin	61y	W	30 MAY 1918	Alexandria VA	Oak Hill
06668	Smith, Baby	6m	W	2 AUG 1908	Rock Hill SC	Glenwood
08670	Smith, Bayard T.	54y	W	14 JUN 1912	Philadelphia PA	Rock Creek
07645	Smith, Benj. Taylor, s/o A.T.	16y	W	21 JUL 1910	Mt. Holly VA	Rock Creek
12710	Smith, Benjamin Aubrey	46y	W	11 JAN 1915	Philadelphia PA	Congressional
18511	Smith, Carl	29y	C	26 APR 1923	Pittsburgh PA	Harmony
08567	Smith, Caroline R.	43y	W	30 JAN 1876	Philadelphia PA	Rock Creek
13312	Smith, Carrie V.	46y	W	19 JAN 1916	Alexandria IN	Glenwood
13210	Smith, Carrie W.	22y	W	18 NOV 1915	Takoma Park MD	Kendall NY
08229	Smith, Catherine C.	1y	C	29 JUL 1911	Bladensburg MD	Mt. Olivet
03130	Smith, Chandler Price	56y	W	14 MAR 1900	Baltimore MD	Congressional
03750	Smith, Charles	59y	W	4 JAN 1902	Alex. Co. VA	Rock Creek
15210	Smith, Charles L.	c.32y	W	14 OCT 1918	Key West FL	Arlington
06707	Smith, Charles Leroy	11m	W	9 JUN 1908	Canal Zone	Congressional
03210	Smith, Charles M.	22y	W	22 NOV 1899	Manila, P.I.	Arlington VA
03154	Smith, Cora R.	52y	W	29 MAR 1900	New Brunsw. NJ	Oak Hill
07142	Smith, Cornelia F.	64y	W	30 JUL 1909	Bethlehem NH	Congressional
03467	Smith, Daniel	78y	W	2 APR 1901	Baltimore MD	Glenwood
18294	Smith, Daniel	36y	C	22 JAN 1923	Philadelphia PA	Harmony
17347	Smith, Dempster Martin, Jr.	10y	W	7 AUG 1921	Arlington Co. VA	Oak Hill
05828	Smith, E.J.	—	W	27 NOV 1906	Harrisburg PA	Rock Creek
06938	Smith, Edith H.	19y	W	4 MAR 1909	Boston MA	Rock Creek
05682	Smith, Edna	1y	W	11 AUG 1906	E. Riverdale MD	Congressional
03880	Smith, Edward	42y	W	13 MAY 1902	Philadelphia PA	Mt. Olivet
01837	Smith, Edward A., carpenter	63y	W	30 OCT 1895	Baltimore MD	Congressional

District of Columbia Foreign Death Records, 1888-1923

No.	Name of Deceased	Age	Race	Death Date	Place of Death	Place of Burial
13519	Smith, Edward C.	49y	W	27 MAY 1916	Railroad	New York NY
18451	Smith, Edward F.	68y	W	31 MAR 1923	Norfolk VA	Cremated
14843	Smith, Edward J.	22y	W	25 MAY 1918	Camp McClel. AL	Arlington
08050	Smith, Edward O., s/o Edw. A.	56y	W	3 APR 1911	Falls Church VA	Congressional
17603	Smith, Elenora Grace	73y	W	19 DEC 1921	Cincinnati OH	Rock Creek
02586	Smith, Elizabeth	58y	C	31 AUG 1898	Pittsburgh PA	Harmony
05758	Smith, Elizabeth	54y	W	4 OCT 1906	New York NY	Oak Hill
18457	Smith, Ella	49y	C	1 APR 1923	Union Hill NJ	Union Baptist
15005	Smith, Ella D.	39y	W	5 SEP 1918	Philadelphia PA	Payne's
17856	Smith, Ellis	65y	C	11 MAY 1922	Brentwood MD	Woodlawn
15234	Smith, Ethel	7y	W	16 OCT 1918	Mt. Ranier MD	Glenwood
04389	Smith, Fannie C.	67y	W	13 JUL 1903	Takoma Park MD	Rock Creek
16232	Smith, Felix Willouby	48y	W	11 DEC 1919	Battle Creek MI	Congressional
15543	Smith, Fenwick R.	24y	W	9 JAN 1919	Pisgah MD	Glenwood
17787	Smith, Frances A.	50y	W	5 APR 1922	New York NY	Glenwood
02523	Smith, Francis E.	67y	W	6 JUL 1898	Philadelphia PA	Mt. Olivet
05696	Smith, Francis H.	77y	W	14 AUG 1906	Washington CN	Oak Hill
16120	Smith, Francis Marion	32y	W	7 OCT 1918	Hampton Rds. VA	Arlington VA
08140	Smith, Frank	28y	C	5 JUN 1911	New York NY	Harmony
12367	Smith, Frank	63y	C	11 MAY 1914	New Kens. PA	Payne's
12775	Smith, Frank, a.k.a.	39y	W	27 JAN 1915	Philadelphia PA	Arlington
03868	Smith, Frank S.	43y	W	29 APR 1902	Baltimore MD	Congressional
00168	Smith, Gaston D.	66y	W	18 SEP 1889	New York NY	Glenwood
01087	Smith, George	42y	C	7 APR 1893	Brookline MA	Harmony
17830	Smith, George	42y	C	25 APR 1922	Baltimore MD	Mt. Zion West
07332	Smith, George	16y	C	16 DEC 1909	Baltimore MD	Payne's
12002	Smith, George E.	45y	W	13 SEP 1913	Railroad	Glenwood
06963	Smith, George H.	69y	W	30 MAR 1909	Laurel MD	Glenwood
15449	Smith, George Linville	35y	W	15 DEC 1918	Laurel MD	Rock Creek
01655	Smith, George McClelland	34y	W	6 APR 1895	Canon City CO	Glenwood
00516	Smith, George N.	82y	W	29 DEC 1890	Philadelphia PA	Holyrood
01494	Smith, Gertrude	21m	W	23 SEP 1894	Rives MD	Glenwood
17535	Smith, Gilbert Cole	50y	W	21 NOV 1921	Laurel MD	Arlington
12738	Smith, Grant	46y	C	30 JAN 1915	Ballston VA	Payne's
09150	Smith, Grisella	50y	W	30 MAR 1913	Cass Lake MN	Rock Creek
07816	Smith, Hannah V.	38y	C	3 NOV 1910	Philadelphia PA	Purcellville VA
05707	Smith, Harriet Francis	50y	C	25 AUG 1906	N. Wales PA	Harmony
00892	Smith, Harriette M.	78y	W	24 JUL 1892	Falls Church VA	Rock Creek
17482	Smith, Harrison	45y	C	18 OCT 1921	T.B. MD	Mt. Zion West
12395	Smith, Harry Blair, s/o H.H.	40y	W	10 JUN 1914	Atlantic City NJ	Oak Hill
07663	Smith, Harry E.	16m	W	2 AUG 1910	Riverdale MD	Mt. Olivet
05425	Smith, Hause H.	68y	W	12 JAN 1906	Hampton VA	Congressional
16835	Smith, Helen	49y	W	29 NOV 1920	New York NY	Glenwood
05680	Smith, Henrietta (Wilson)	62y	W	7 AUG 1906	Vienna VA	Glenwood
02832	Smith, Henrietta E.	76y	W	11 MAY 1899	Baltimore MD	Rock Creek
00070	Smith, Henry	76y	W	25 MAY 1889	Brooklyn NY	Soldier's Home
04679	Smith, Henry Harrison	60y	W	17 APR 1904	Savannah GA	Oak Hill
04778	Smith, Hezekiah E.	69y	W	30 JUN 1904	Branchville MD	Mt. Olivet
15516	Smith, Hilda A.	21y	W	2 JAN 1919	New York NY	Prospect Hill
06923	Smith, Horatio W.	64y	C	18 FEB 1909	Brentwood MD	Harmony
12865	Smith, Howard Harrison	29y	W	18 MAR 1915	Guan. Bay, Cuba	Mt. Gilead OH
15417	Smith, Hugh	7y	W	8 DEC 1918	Baltimore MD	Mt. Olivet
13907	Smith, Infant of Clarence B.	SB	W	5 JAN 1917	Takoma MD	Rock Creek
17368	Smith, Infant of Harry E.	SB	W	18 JUL 1921	Washington DC	Prospect Hill
05654	Smith, Infant of T.S.	9m	W	21 JUL 1906	York Co. SC	Glenwood
15874	Smith, Isaiah	52y	C	9 JUL 1919	Philadelphia PA	Woodlawn
17407	Smith, Israel	26y	W	3 SEP 1919	Berlin, Ger.	Hebrew
00188	Smith, J. Bayard N.	79y	W	20 AUG 1889	San Francisco CA	Rock Creek
06702	Smith, J. Clement	90y	W	18 JAN 1908	Topeka KS	Oak Hill
06076	Smith, J. Henry	45y	W	13 APR 1907	Florence, Italy	Rock Creek

No.	Name of Deceased	Age	Race	Death Date	Place of Death	Place of Burial
04735	Smith, James	53y	C	25 MAY 1904	Pittsburgh PA	Harmony
15830	Smith, James	46y	C	12 JUN 1919	Baltimore MD	Moore's
09096	Smith, James E.	46y	C	23 FEB 1913	Pittsburgh PA	Harmony
14572	Smith, James R.	19y	C	12 JAN 1918	Harrisburg PA	Harmony
04313	Smith, Jane E.W.	60y	W	20 MAY 1903	Sang. NY	Oak Hill
04481	Smith, Jefferson S.	52y	W	20 OCT 1903	Hyattsville MD	Glenwood
13810	Smith, Jennie	47y	C	11 NOV 1916	Brentwood MD	Woodlawn
13213	Smith, Jeremiah	42y	C	14 NOV 1915	Philadelphia PA	Arlington VA
07590	Smith, John	27y	C	19 JUN 1910	Chicago IL	Colonial Bea. VA
16350	Smith, John	64y	W	27 FEB 1920	Baltimore MD	Ohev Sholom
08862	Smith, John	67y	W	30 SEP 1912	Baltimore MD	Soldier's Home
17440	Smith, John Augustus	59y	C	27 SEP 1921	Boston MA	Harmony
17421	Smith, John B.	58y	W	16 SEP 1921	Philadelphia PA	Ft. Lincoln
13557	Smith, John C.	77y	W	24 MAR 1916	West Fairlee VT	Rock Creek
05902	Smith, John E.	66y	W	23 JAN 1907	New York NY	Oak Hill
17701	Smith, John Edward	6m	W	4 FEB 1922	Port-au-Prince	Rock Creek
04677	Smith, John F.	55y	W	17 APR 1904	Alexandria VA	Rock Creek
01763	Smith, John, farmer	55y	W	17 AUG 1895	Randall Sta. MD	Mt. Olivet
02570	Smith, John L.	15y	C	20 AUG 1898	New York NY	Mt. Olivet
13112	Smith, John Lloyd	52y	C	17 SEP 1915	New York NY	Mt. Olivet
09197	Smith, John M.	83y	W	2 MAY 1913	McGhesport MD	Conover NC
17189	Smith, John R.	36y	W	23 MAY 1921	Chicago IL	Rock Creek
06873	Smith, Joseph	22y	C	26 DEC 1908	Jersey City NJ	Mt. Olivet
06703	Smith, Joseph A., s/o Aug.	40y	C	24 AUG 1908	Clarendon VA	Holyrood
08568	Smith, Joseph E.	4y	W	19 JAN 1866	Philadelphia PA	Rock Creek
16306	Smith, Joseph N.	80y	W	12 FEB 1920	Fairfax Co. VA	Arlington
07379	Smith, Joseph Shotwell	41y	W	19 JAN 1910	Wheeling WV	Rock Creek
06264	Smith, Julia	63y	W	6 OCT 1907	Baltimore MD	Mt. Olivet
07625	Smith, Julia L.	50y	W	11 JUL 1910	Baltimore MD	Congressional
13075	Smith, Julia M.	72y	W	24 AUG 1915	Laurel MD	Rock Creek
03960	Smith, Katherine	56y	C	27 JUL 1902	Atlantic City NJ	Harmony
08395	Smith, Katherine Martin	24y	W	21 NOV 1911	Baltimore MD	Rock Creek
13687	Smith, Leonard	21y	W	31 AUG 1916	Middleton PA	Congressional
14186	Smith, Lester E.	38y	W	21 JUN 1917	Philadelphia PA	Arlington
14746	Smith, Lidia Justine	64y	W	10 APR 1918	Louisville KY	Arlington
08631	Smith, Lillie G.	3y	W	10 MAY 1911	Vallejo CA	Oak Hill
02096	Smith, Lucia D.	85y	W	4 DEC 1896	Baltimore MD	Rock Creek
09085	Smith, Lucy	24y	C	19 FEB 1913	New York NY	Woodlawn
12429	Smith, Mann Page	29y	W	8 JUL 1914	Charleston SC	Mt. Olivet
08129	Smith, Margaret	53y	W	24 MAY 1911	Colonial Bea. VA	Mt. Olivet
04882	Smith, Margaret J.	1y	W	8 SEP 1904	Baltimore MD	Mt. Olivet
16328	Smith, Maria B.	79y	W	18 FEB 1920	Takoma Park MD	Oak Hill
02480	Smith, Marie A.	4y	W	2 AUG 1898	Fenwick Sta. MD	Mt. Olivet
17532	Smith, Marie F.	53y	C	15 NOV 1921	New York NY	Harmony
08287	Smith, Marjorie Ernestine	3m	W	1 SEP 1911	Cherrydale VA	Worcester MA
01599	Smith, Martha A.	75y	W	10 DEC 1894	Glendale MD	Rock Creek
11941	Smith, Mary	63y	W	6 AUG 1913	Atlantic City NJ	Harmony
00409	Smith, Mary	46y	W	17 NOV 1868	Brooklyn NY	Oak Hill
07165	Smith, Mary B. (Bidwell)	36y	W	21 AUG 1909	Kinsale VA	Glenwood
08789	Smith, Mary C.	53y	W	29 AUG 1912	Brentwood MD	Congressional
15882	Smith, Mary C.	80y	W	15 JUL 1919	Philadelphia PA	Congressional
03844	Smith, Mary Calhoun	1d	W	5 APR 1902	Alex. Co. VA	Mt. Olivet
02221	Smith, Mary E.	42y	C	19 JUN 1897	Asbury Park NJ	Harmony
04736	Smith, Mary E.	27y	C	25 MAY 1904	New York NY	Harmony
07284	Smith, Mary E.	6d	W	24 NOV 1909	Takoma Park MD	Rock Creek
05790	Smith, Mary F.	54y	W	28 OCT 1906	Mt. Ranier MD	Glenwood
06155	Smith, Mary G.	35y	W	25 JUL 1907	Relay MD	Rock Creek
13478	Smith, Mary I.	64y	W	25 APR 1916	Arlington VA	Congressional
07563	Smith, Mary J.	20y	C	7 JUN 1910	Riverdale MD	Mt. Olivet
17577	Smith, Mary Lee	61y	W	6 DEC 1921	Saranac Lake NY	Congressional

District of Columbia Foreign Death Records, 1888-1923

No.	Name of Deceased	Age	Race	Death Date	Place of Death	Place of Burial
16197	Smith, Mary Louise	75y	W	8 JAN 1920	Atlantic City NJ	Rock Creek
02144	Smith, Mary M.	23y	C	12 FEB 1897	Loudoun Co. VA	Harmony
08283	Smith, Masie	31y	W	17 DEC 1910	Proiso, Panama	Mt. Olivet
02337	Smith, Matie	1y	W	6 SEP 1897	Odenton MD	Glenwood
18063	Smith, Maude	51y	C	10 SEP 1922	Mayview PA	Harmony
13494	Smith, May A.	52y	W	7 MAY 1916	Takoma Park MD	Glenwood
06783	Smith, Medora	61y	W	8 OCT 1908	Chicago IL	Oak Hill
15810	Smith, Mrs. E.	81y	W	31 MAY 1919	New Orleans LA	Congressional
03986	Smith, Mrs. Geo.	81y	W	4 AUG 1902	Linden VA	Congressional
15301	Smith, Mrs. Geo. A.	30y	W	28 OCT 1918	Goldsboro NC	Rock Creek
06968	Smith, Myrtia A.	30y	W	31 MAR 1909	Philadelphia PA	Rock Creek
06535	Smith, Nannie	29y	C	5 MAY 1908	Philadelphia PA	Harmony
18146	Smith, Oliver	57y	W	1 NOV 1922	Orlando FL	Cremated
06978	Smith, Olivia L.	84y	W	10 APR 1909	Alexandria VA	Congressional
09082	Smith, Peter	40y	C	16 FEB 1913	Baltimore MD	Woodlawn
11909	Smith, Philip, s/o E.J.	63y	W	19 JUL 1913	Haymarket VA	Rock Creek
03898	Smith, Pierce W.	45y	W	3 JUN 1902	Boston MA	Woodlawn
06913	Smith, Priscille	65y	C	8 FEB 1909	Moorefield VA	Harmony
17967	Smith, Rachel Laundry	79y	W	17 JUL 1922	Round Hill VA	Rock Creek
03398	Smith, Ramsay W.	27y	W	17 JAN 1901	Pueblo CO	Rock Creek
00518	Smith, Rebecca G.	c.80y	W	30 DEC 1878	Philadelphia PA	Holyrood
01762	Smith, Richard	25y	W	11 AUG 1895	Garrett Co. MD	Mt. Olivet
07763	Smith, Richard P., w/o Wm. C.	58y	W	26 SEP 1910	Braddock Hts. VA	Rock Creek
02989	Smith, Robert D.O., atty.	67y	W	21 OCT 1899	Mishawaka IN	Rock Creek
07084	Smith, Robert Henry	4m	C	28 JUN 1909	Fairmont Hts. MD	Payne's
15693	Smith, Robert, in jail	19y	W	2 MAR 1919	Atlanta GA	Harmony
07133	Smith, Rosa May	5m	W	24 JUL 1909	Montg. Co. MD	Holyrood
05445	Smith, Samuel A.	50y	W	27 JAN 1906	Baltimore MD	Congressional
02831	Smith, Samuel C.	56y	W	8 MAY 1899	Baltimore MD	Congressional
02186	Smith, Samuel C.	26y	C	28 APR 1897	Rome NY	Jones' Chapel
12756	Smith, Samuel W.	68y	W	10 FEB 1915	Mt. Ranier MD	Congressional
03627	Smith, Sarah E.	63y	W	4 SEP 1901	Forestville MD	Congressional
12731	Smith, Sarah L.	90y	W	22 JAN 1915	Baltimore MD	Glenwood
06581	Smith, Sarah S. Condit	69y	W	7 JUN 1908	Atlantic City NJ	Rock Creek
16255	Smith, Sibert S.	26y	W	23 JAN 1920	Ft. Bayard NM	Rock Creek
11974	Smith, Sterling T.	84y	W	27 AUG 1913	Gaithersburg MD	Columbia PA
14983	Smith, Susanna Duvall	72y	W	19 AUG 1918	Braddock Hts. MD	Oak Hill
06969	Smith, Sylvia E.	SB	W	31 MAR 1909	Philadelphia PA	Rock Creek
00061	Smith, Thomas	25y	C	10 APR 1889	Lorenzo IL	Harmony
16939	Smith, Thomas A.	67y	C	20 JAN 1921	Philadelphia PA	Woodlawn
08108	Smith, Thomas C., Rev.	71y	W	11 DEC 1875	Deer Lodge MT	Oak Hill
08776	Smith, Thomas H.	2d	W	23 AUG 1912	Riverdale MD	Mt. Olivet
18498	Smith, Uhl M.	—	W	21 APR 1923	Dayton OH	Arlington
14629	Smith, Wadsworth Ramsay	53y	W	4 FEB 1918	Burlington VT	Congressional
06743	Smith, Walter Harvey, s/o W.	82y	W	22 SEP 1908	Catlett VA	Rock Creek
15349	Smith, Westor W.	26y	W	6 NOV 1918	Denver CO	Glenwood
00323	Smith, William	23y	C	4 MAY 1890	Philadelphia PA	Graceland
02471	Smith, William	28y	C	20 MAY 1898	Philadelphia PA	Harmony
17734	Smith, William	70y	C	7 MAR 1922	Arlington Co. VA	Mt. Zion West
02903	Smith, William	69y	W	7 AUG 1899	Sea Girt NJ	Rock Creek
14586	Smith, William	31y	C	15 JAN 1918	Philadelphia PA	Woodlawn
17248	Smith, William C.	54y	W	20 JUN 1921	New York NY	Glenwood
12627	Smith, William E.	60y	W	19 NOV 1914	Baltimore MD	Glenwood
01285	Smith, William E.	37y	W	23 DEC 1893	Buffalo NY	Mt. Olivet
08316	Smith, William F.	40y	W	17 SEP 1911	Norfolk VA	St. Mary's
17298	Smith, William F. (or B.)	22y	C	9 JUL 1921	Ft. McHenry MD	Mt. Olivet
02772	Smith, William H.	38y	W	1 JUL 1898	Santiago, Cuba	Arlington
07437	Smith, William H.	43y	C	24 FEB 1910	New York NY	Payne's
17453	Smith, William Hamilton	59y	W	5 OCT 1921	Atlantic City NJ	Congressional
00410	Smith, William Henry	18y	W	29 AUG 1862	Washington DC	Oak Hill

No.	Name of Deceased	Age	Race	Death Date	Place of Death	Place of Burial
18454	Smith, William Russell	80y	W	26 FEB 1896	Washington DC	Mt. Olivet[1]
02143	Smith, William S.	61y	W	7 FEB 1897	Philadelphia PA	Rock Creek
05206	Smith, William, sailor	55y	W	9 JUL 1905	Norfolk VA	Congressional
05190	Smith, Wilton H.	3m	W	2 JUL 1905	Hyattsville MD	Congressional
03631	Smith, Zella	20y	W	29 AUG 1901	Thomasville NC	Rock Creek
17953	Smithers, Mary L.	71y	W	13 JUL 1922	Ft. Myer Hts. VA	Congressional
04575	Smithson, James	64y	W	27 JUN 1829	Genoa, Italy	Smithsonian
02999	Smnith, John H.	37y	W	3 NOV 1899	Atlantic City NJ	Payne's
07212	Smoot, Catharine C.	66y	W	26 SEP 1909	Langley VA	Oak Hill
07552	Smoot, Dora	55y	W	29 MAY 1910	Baltimore MD	Glenwood
03866	Smoot, Emma J.	43y	W	28 APR 1902	Clarendon VA	Glenwood
12641	Smoot, Harriet E.	71y	W	3 DEC 1914	McLean VA	Oak Hill
02884	Smoot, Helen M.	53y	W	24 JUL 1899	Langley VA	Oak Hill
00071	Smoot, Jeanette N.M.	15y	W	17 MAY 1889	Baltimore MD	Glenwood
06808	Smoot, John W.	73y	W	9 NOV 1908	Hyattsville MD	Mt. Olivet
17035	Smoot, Juliana Brawner	7y	W	10 MAR 1921	Chapel Hill NC	Oak Hill
02624	Smoot, Sarah E.	38y	C	4 OCT 1898	Philadelphia PA	Harmony
03081	Smoot, William S.	50y	W	31 JAN 1900	Langley VA	Oak Hill
14329	Smoothers, George	c.43y	C	1 SEP 1917	Seat Pleasant MD	Owen Sta. MD
04208	Smothers, Annie	43y	C	17 MAR 1903	New York NY	Harmony
08063	Smothers, Grace	6y	C	12 APR 1911	Kensington MD	St. Phillips
13427	Smothers, James, s/o John	24y	C	24 MAR 1916	Occoquan VA	Payne's
05046	Smothers, Moses	65y	C	1 MAR 1905	Glen Echo MD	Baptist
06580	Smyth, Fannie E. (Shippen)	55y	C	6 JUN 1908	Richmond VA	Harmony
06715	Smyth, John Henry, Hon.	64y	C	5 SEP 1908	Richmond VA	Harmony
12829	Sneden, Celia A.	69y	W	20 MAR 1915	Hackensack NJ	Rock Creek
00772	Sneeks, Mary S.	73y	W	9 MAR 1892	Lewinsville VA	Harpers Ferry WV
01362	Snelling, Beverly T., carpenter	61y	W	28 MAR 1894	Colonial Bea. VA	Glenwood
17230	Snellings, Milton	52y	W	8 JUN 1921	Denver CO	Fredericksburg VA
08021	Snider, Francis Christ, s/o G.L.	4y	W	24 MAR 1911	W. Cherrydale VA	Mt. Olivet
08189	Snider, Melvin A., s/o John J.	4m	W	9 JUL 1911	Cherrydale VA	Mt. Olivet
08531	Snider, Sophia Kathrine	11y	W	26 FEB 1912	W. Cherrydale VA	Mt. Olivet
11967	Snoots, Henry K.	65y	W	15 AUG 1913	Brewster NY	Rock Creek
16671	Snow, Alpheus Henry	60y	W	19 AUG 1920	Manhattan NY	Indianapolis IN
00048	Snow, Charles Willis	84y	W	22 MAR 1889	Washington DC	Portland ME
18538	Snow, Cornelia Ann	84y	W	9 MAY 1923	Wellesley MA	Rock Creek
00773	Snow, Homer S.	16y	W	26 DEC 1891	Nokesville VA	Oak Hill
00664	Snow, Patrick	44y	W	21 JUL 1891	Ellaville MD	Mt. Olivet
06484	Snowden, Albert E.A.	67y	C	21 MAR 1908	Silver Spring MD	Payne's
00519	Snowden, Annie	62y	C	3 FEB 1891	Burlington NJ	Holyrood
03717	Snowden, Charles	30y	C	23 NOV 1901	Bowie MD	Payne's
13322	Snowden, Charlotte	53y	C	25 JAN 1916	Silver Spring MD	Payne's
08175	Snowden, Eliza Ann	41y	C	2 JUL 1911	Cedar Hts. MD	Woodlawn
00994	Snowden, Fred C.	26y	W	29 AUG 1893	Dear Park MD	Oak Hill
17076	Snowden, Geneve Farnette	2m	C	28 MAR 1921	Fairmont Hts. MD	Mt. Olivet
18539	Snowden, Harriet	88y	C	9 MAY 1923	Glenarden MD	Glenarden MD
11961	Snowden, Rebecca J.	68y	C	12 AUG 1913	Newport RI	Payne's
09023	Snowden, Sarah	64y	C	8 JAN 1913	Cedar Hts. MD	Woodlawn
13493	Snowden, Sarah Holmes	74y	W	7 MAR 1916	Fairfax Co. VA	Oak Hill
08388	Snowden, Spencer	66y	C	11 NOV 1911	Cedar Hts. MD	Woodlawn
12177	Snowden, Stacy H.	83y	W	22 JAN 1914	Snowden VA	Oak Hill
17156	Snowden, Walter H.	45y	C	11 MAY 1921	Fairmont Hts. MD	Harmony
08086	Snyder, Albert F., Jr.	6y	W	27 APR 1911	Clarendon VA	Congressional
02222	Snyder, Benjamin P., banker	62y	W	6 JUN 1897	Collingswood MD	Cremated
02278	Snyder, Clarinda C.	67y	W	4 JUL 1897	Bismark MO	Cremated
17490	Snyder, Clvira E.	85y	W	27 OCT 1921	Annapolis MD	Rock Creek
00112	Snyder, Ella May	5m	W	21 JUL 1889	King Geo. Co. VA	Mt. Olivet

[1] Removed from Greenwood Cemetery, Tuscaloosa AL, by permit of 30 MAR 1923.

District of Columbia Foreign Death Records, 1888-1923

No.	Name of Deceased	Age	Race	Death Date	Place of Death	Place of Burial
05018	Snyder, Frank G.	41y	W	3 FEB 1905	New York NY	Congressional
14950	Snyder, Harry C.	39y	W	13 AUG 1918	Camp Meade MD	Rock Creek[1]
05862	Snyder, Howard T., Jr.	5d	W	14 DEC 1906	Capitol Hts. MD	Mt. Olivet
17941	Snyder, John W.	76y	W	7 JUL 1922	Riverdale MD	Rock Creek
17416	Snyder, Maurice B.	19y	W	9 OCT 1918	France	Hyattsville MD
14729	Snyder, Riley D.	65y	W	31 MAR 1918	Danville IN	Glenwood
06339	Snyder, William	10d	W	12 DEC 1907	Capitol Hts. MD	Mt. Olivet
13725	Solain, Thomas	49y	W	16 SEP 1916	Philadelphia PA	Mt. Olivet
04370	Solar, Margaarite	5m	W	1 JUL 1903	Brentwood MD	Glenwood
12206	Soldano, Veriglio	5m	W	7 FEB 1914	Charlottesville VA	St. Mary's
12519	Soldona, Stanislao	44y	W	8 SEP 1914	Charlottesville VA	St. Mary's
17462	Sollers, William A.	79y	W	10 OCT 1921	Phoebus VA	Arlington
15500	Solomon, Elizabeth	63y	W	29 DEC 1918	Chain Bridge VA	Glenwood
00893	Somerville, Joseph	23y	C	25 JUL 1892	New York NY	Mt. Olivet
18464	Sommerlott, Charles August	84y	W	7 APR 1923	Maryland Pk. MD	Prospect Hill
17858	Sommers, Aaron	65y	W	13 MAY 1922	Atlantic City NJ	Glenwood
18231	Sommers, Rachel Talbott	84y	W	30 DEC 1922	Chevy Chase MD	Cincinnati OH
12651	Sondheimer, Donna Isabel	27y	W	10 DEC 1914	Capitol Hts. MD	Congressional
02205	Songster, Thomas G.	26y	W	23 JUN 1897	Philadelphia PA	Glenwood
00030	Sonnemann, Frank	23y	W	19 FEB 1889	Lewistown PA	Prospect Hill
04802	Sonnemann, Ottmar	79y	W	15 JUL 1904	Chevy Chase MD	Prospect Hill
15439	Sonnemann, Rebecca	84y	W	12 DEC 1918	Chevy Chase MD	Prospect Hill
13011	Sonnemann, William	57y	W	17 JUL 1915	Chevy Chase MD	Prospect Hill
11913	Soper, Thomas	64y	W	23 JUL 1913	Sykesville MD	St. Ignatius MD
06206	Sorrell, Richard	65y	W	27 AUG 1907	Alexandria VA	Holyrood
18375	Sothern, Helen Leola	1m	C	26 FEB 1923	S. Wash. VA	Rosemont
03260	Sothoron, Bettie C.	57y	W	12 AUG 1900	Hughesville MD	Glenwood
17245	Sothoron, Emma E.	70y	W	18 JUN 1921	Brentwood MD	Mt. Olivet
17503	Sothoron, Mary E.	21y	W	3 NOV 1921	Ft. Lyon CO	Bryantown MD
03835	Souder, Albert Godfrey	24y	W	25 MAR 1902	Gwynn's Bridge	Congressional
01330	Souder, Amos	79y	W	21 FEB 1894	Pr. Geo. Co. MD	Rock Creek
08358	Souder, Charles H.	64y	W	14 OCT 1911	Hyattsville MD	Rock Creek
01838	Souder, Fanny Mabel	29d	W	14 NOV 1895	Pr. Geo. Co. MD	Rock Creek
00894	Souder, Margaret Eleanor	5m	W	16 APR 1892	Pr. Geo. Co. MD	Rock Creek
07255	Soule, Jules E.	48y	W	20 OCT 1909	Mt. Vernon NY	Congressional
02735	Soules, Ester Sarah	1y	W	3 FEB 1899	Highlands MD	Glenwood
04066	Soules, Fred Albert	1y	W	1 OCT 1902	Hyattsville MD	Glenwood
14089	Soules, Ida S.	18y	W	16 APR 1917	Capitol Hts. MD	Glenwood
13645	Soules, Jane	47y	W	8 AUG 1916	Hyattsville MD	Glenwood
14808	Sousa, Anthony August	50y	W	8 MAY 1918	Rocky Ford CO	Congressional
16772	Southard, Nellie J.	24y	W	22 OCT 1920	Laurel MD	Congressional
06585	Southard, Theophil	15y	W	9 JUN 1908	Baltimore MD	Congressional
08761	Southwick, Walter	47y	W	10 AUG 1912	Baltimore MD	Congressional
12933	Southworth, James	48y	W	19 MAY 1915	Anne Arundel Co.	Congressional
17389	Sowerbutts, Samuel W., Capt.	—	W	10 NOV 1918	France	Congressional
17026	Sowers, Josephine G.	84y	W	7 MAR 1921	Edgewood PA	Oak Hill
01598	Spaide, Carlton, farmer	53y	W	31 JAN 1895	Burnt Mills MD	Glenwood
02521	Spake, Charles K.	6m	W	10 JUL 1898	Bladensburg MD	Glenwood
01286	Spaks, Mabel M.	2y	W	23 DEC 1893	Bladensburg MD	Evergreen
02121	Spalding, John Dominick	32y	W	23 JAN 1897	Pr. Geo. Co. MD	Mt. Olivet
01088	Spangler, Walter	50y	W	28 APR 1893	Ft. Monroe VA	Arlington
06518	Spanier, Louis	83y	W	18 APR 1908	Laurel MD	Wash. Hebrew
15922	Sparks, Arthur W.	48y	W	5 AUG 1919	Philadelphia PA	Mt. Olivet
06622	Sparks, Clifton	42y	W	28 JUN 1908	New York NY	Glenwood
13232	Sparks, Finley H.	42y	W	5 DEC 1915	Cherrydale VA	Glenwood
14082	Sparks, Richard	33y	W	7 APR 1917	Warrensville OH	Arlington
00135	Sparshott, Emma Jane	39y	W	10 AUG 1889	Rosslyn VA	Glenwood

[1] Disinterment permit #9584 to remove the remains on 8 AUG 1918 to the D.C. crematorium.

No.	Name of Deceased	Age	Race	Death Date	Place of Death	Place of Burial
06560	Sparshott, Nellie	—	W	1876	Philadelphia PA	Glenwood
06560	Sparshott, Samuel J.	—	W	1878	Philadelphia PA	Glenwood
06560	Sparshott, Willie	—	W	1876	Philadelphia PA	Glenwood
00234	Spatis, Mary E.	45y	W	4 FEB 1888	Clarksburg MD	Glenwood
16938	Spaulding, Henry J.	25y	W	22 JAN 1921	Aberdeen MD	Arlington
13657	Spaulding, James J., s/o Patk.	19y	W	13 AUG 1916	Ft. Myer VA	Mt. Olivet
14073	Spear, Ellas	82y	W	3 APR 1917	St. Petersburg FL	Arlington
14326	Specht, Annie M., d/o Henry H.	46y	W	31 AUG 1917	Portsmouth VA	Congressional
11827	Specht, Henry Harrison	72y	W	21 MAY 1913	Hartley PA	Congressional
02179	Speer, Ernest C.	1y	W	17 MAR 1897	Oakton VA	Glenwood
05416	Speer, Kittie	76y	W	1 JAN 1906	Takoma Park MD	Rock Creek
06139	Speer, Myrtle Raub	40y	W	16 JUL 1907	Lovettsville VA	Congressional
18264	Speer, Susan Virginia	40y	W	12 JAN 1923	Langley VA	Glenwood
04721	Speiden, William Robert	77y	W	20 MAY 1904	Hyattsville MD	Congressional
02024	Speir, Annie	73y	W	10 JUL 1896	Hyattsville MD	Congressional
13542	Speiss, Charles	38y	W	3 JUN 1916	New York NY	Mt. Olivet
13443	Spence, Adolph Nichols	59y	W	4 APR 1916	Selma AL	Congressional
16140	Spence, Emma Frances	60y	W	4 DEC 1919	Cherrydale VA	Cremated
12281	Spence, Lena	50y	C	28 MAR 19114	Lexington KY	Woodlawn
01908	Spencer, Fannie	39y	C	31 MAR 1896	New York NY	Harmony
07908	Spencer, Frank Austin	68y	W	6 JAN 1911	Rockville MD	Rock Creek
16563	Spencer, George E.	14y	C	21 JUN 1920	Eliz. City NC	Woodlawn
15988	Spencer, Louisa C.	71y	W	10 SEP 1919	Albany NY	Oak Hill
11966	Spencer, Mabel	11m	W	17 SEP 1876	Columbus IN	Rock Creek
00665	Spencer, Maggie	27y	W	10 JUL 1891	Philmont VA	Mt. Olivet
15820	Spencer, Mary A.	80y	W	8 JUN 1919	Takoma Park MD	Congressional
12883	Spencer, Robert Russell	43y	W	15 APR 1915	New York NY	Glenwood
05840	Spencer, Samuel	59y	W	29 NOV 1906	Lynchburg VA	Oak Hill
17316	Spencer, Sarah Jane	48y	W	20 JUL 1921	Takoma Park MD	Glenwood
08431	Spencer, Stephen O.	74y	W	16 DEC 1911	Bradentown FL	Cremated
15772	Spencer, Tenner	84y	C	6 MAY 1919	Halls Hill VA	Payne's
07178	Spengler, George	46y	W	28 AUG 1909	Maywood IL	Prospect Hill
12714	Sperle, Mary (Kellett)	54y	W	12 JAN 1915	Elizabeth NJ	Glenwood
17184	Sperling, Infant of Max & A.	SB	W	27 MAY 1921	Alexandria VA	Rock Creek
05412	Spicer, Regina R.	71y	W	28 DEC 1905	Philadelphia PA	Congressional
12506	Spicer, Susan M.	87y	W	31 AUG 1914	Takoma Park MD	Rock Creek
06340	Spier, Henry	58y	W	1 DEC 1907	New York NY	Rock Creek
16384	Spier, Olga Marie	61y	W	15 MAR 1920	Chevy Chase MD	Cremated
04428	Spillman, Fannie B.	30y	C	31 AUG 1903	New York NY	Payne's
18361	Spilman, George D.	81y	W	18 FEB 1923	Hampton VA	Glenwood
17846	Spilman, John T.	73y	W	11 MAY 1922	Baltimore MD	Congressional
00774	Spilman, Mary	25y	W	15 JAN 1892	Philadelphia PA	Oak Hill
04237	Spindler, Johanna	78y	W	25 FEB 1903	Cumberland MD	Rock Creek
17134	Splane, Infant of Jose. D.	12h	W	28 APR 1921	Washington DC	Mt. Olivet
06686	Spofford, Ainsworth R.	82y	W	11 AUG 1908	Holderness NH	Cremated
16345	Sprackling, Maud	34y	W	21 FEB 1920	Los Angeles CA	Rock Creek
13321	Sprague, A.V.M., s/o Foster	75y	W	27 JAN 1916	Front Royal VA	Cremated
06586	Sprandel, Mary	56y	W	9 JUN 1908	Laurel MD	Glenwood
03050	Spranger, Gay B.	27y	W	20 JUN 1895	Wright's Sta. CA	Rock Creek
12464	Sprecker, Newton	59y	W	30 JUL 1914	Takoma Park MD	Ephrata PA
03869	Sprigg, Lucy Addison	71y	W	21 JUN 1900	San Antonio TX	Oak Hill
01331	Sprigg, Mamie	12d	C	16 FEB 1894	Landover MD	Mt. Olivet
04973	Sprigg, Maria	38y	C	5 DEC 1904	Landover MD	Mt. Olivet
05753	Sprigg, Mary M.	18y	C	29 SEP 1906	Seat Pleasant MD	Mt. Olivet
15848	Sprigg, William Mercer, Jr.	20y	W	26 JUN 1919	Philadelphia PA	Oak Hill
02335	Spriggs, Amelia	30y	C	25 OCT 1897	Pr. Geo. Co. MD	Mt. Olivet
04210	Spriggs, Arleser	12y	C	14 MAR 1903	New York NY	Harmony
00031	Spriggs, Bernard, s/o Mary	1y	W	28 FEB 1889	Arlington VA	Holyrood
18349	Spriggs, Charles E.	60y	C	15 FEB 1923	Seat Pleasant MD	Mt. Olivet
12407	Spriggs, Daniel	54y	W	20 JUN 1914	Chesa. Jct. MD	Mt. Olivet

District of Columbia Foreign Death Records, 1888-1923   239

No.	Name of Deceased	Age	Race	Death Date	Place of Death	Place of Burial
04400	Spriggs, Hazel	10y	C	19 JUL 1903	New York NY	Payne's
07073	Spriggs, Infant of Eliz.	1d	C	22 JUN 1909	Seat Pleasant MD	Mt. Olivet
01839	Spriggs, John, farmer	85y	C	29 DEC 1895	Landover MD	Mt. Olivet
07303	Spriggs, John P.	55y	C	3 DEC 1909	Hills MD	Mt. Olivet
16693	Spriggs, Joyce Teresa	17y	C	4 SEP 1920	Huntsville MD	Mt. Olivet
07527	Spriggs, Louise	39y	C	6 MAY 1910	New York NY	Payne's
05260	Spriggs, Robert	21y	W	27 AUG 1905	Seat Pleasant MD	Mt. Olivet
05429	Spriggs, Virginia	6m	C	15 JAN 1906	Seat Pleasant MD	Mt. Olivet
00775	Sprightley, J.T.	30y	W	29 DEC 1891	Chicago IL	Mt. Olivet
15547	Sprightly, Patrick S.	62y	W	11 JAN 1919	Baltimore MD	Mt. Olivet
17396	Springler, Henry C.	—	W	5 OCT 1918	Bois deS., Fran.	Arlington
08356	Springman, Frederick	68y	W	11 OCT 1911	Pr. Geo. Co. MD	Congressional
03152	Springman, George	75y	W	30 MAR 1900	Hampton VA	Congressional
12126	Sproesser, Mary Eliz. Cath.	73y	W	13 DEC 1913	Mt. Ranier MD	Prospect Hill
01266	Sprouse, Thos.	21d	W	21 NOV 1893	Gaithersburg MD	Graceland
07729	Sprucebank, Charles Russell	17y	W	4 SEP 1910	Wedderborn VA	Congressional
15466	Squire, Susan J. (Durgan)	73y	W	10 DEC 1918	Los Angeles CA	Oak Hill
05712	Squires, Henry Thompson	1y	W	28 AUG 1906	Baltimore MD	Glenwood
03207	Squires, Mary R.	61y	W	16 JUN 1900	Brandywine MD	Glenwood
12827	Squires, William H.	78y	W	22 MAR 1915	Brandywine MD	Glenwood
06514	St. Clair, Francis O.	69y	W	17 APR 1908	Bethesda MD	Rock Creek
01537	St. Clair, Henrietta	69y	W	7 JAN 1895	Baltimore MD	Congressional
01089	St. Clair, Martha M.	75y	W	27 MAR 1893	Baltimore MD	Congressional
06696	St. Clair, William	44y	W	17 AUG 1908	New York NY	Congressional
17264	St. John, Frederick P.	33y	W	26 JUN 1921	Arlington Co. VA	Holyrood
08389	Stack, Thomas A.	71y	W	12 NOV 1911	Harrisburg PA	Mt. Olivet
13488	Stadkeilis?, F. Anthony	21y	W	2 MAY 1916	Potomac River	Blissville NY
02710	Stafford, George J.	52y	W	13 JAN 1899	Baltimore MD	Mt. Olivet
07617	Stahl, Mary B.W.	43y	W	5 JUL 1910	Philadelphia PA	Oak Hill
06046	Stailey, Samuel A.	85y	W	29 APR 1907	E. Riverdale MD	Congressional
05644	Stainer, Linne	23y	C	14 JUL 1906	Clifton Forge VA	Mt. Zion East
09053	Stallilngs, Maurice E.	51y	W	2 FEB 1913	Mt. Ranier MD	Glenwood
12540	Stalter, Eliza	38y	W	20 SEP 1914	Philadelphia PA	Congressional
11928	Stanback, John W.	16d	W	30 JUL 1913	Oxon Hill MD	Mt. Olivet
04229	Stangier, Peter	48y	W	26 FEB 1903	Philadelphia PA	Glenwood
01656	Stanley, Anna M.	60y	W	23 APR 1895	Baltimore MD	Soldier's Home
17851	Stansbury, Charles Frederick	68y	W	12 MAY 1922	Norfolk VA	Congressional
05522	Stansbury, Irene Hunter	65y	W	4 APR 1906	Summerville SC	Oak Hill
14881	Stansell, Dwight David	33y	W	23 JUN 1918	Norfolk VA	Cedar Hill
13729	Stanton, Winifred	36y	C	20 SEP 1916	Dinwiddie Co. VA	Union Baptist
05362	Staples, Allen	3y	W	1870	Watertown NY	Rock Creek
05361	Staples, Helen	3d	W	1870	Watertown NY	Rock Creek
18129	Staples, Kenneth A.	15y	W	25 OCT 1922	Staunton VA	Congressional
15009	Staples, Orrin G.	81y	W	8 SEP 1918	Alex. Bay NY	Rock Creek
18053	Staples, William R.	58y	W	6 SEP 1922	Centreville VA	Congressional
06442	Stapleton, James, soldier	—	W	22 MAR 1907	Guines, Cuba	Arlington
17516	Stark, Sophia	71y	W	11 NOV 1921	Chesa. Jct. MD	Rock Creek
06841	Starke, Charles L.	23y	W	29 NOV 1908	Patton CA	Holyrood
07949	Starr, Eve Haney (Jones)	44y	W	29 JAN 1911	Herndon VA	Congressional
11982	Starr, Henry M.	72y	W	31 AUG 1913	Laurel MD	Oak Hill
06811	Stasburger, Emma	44y	W	9 NOV 1908	Philadelphia PA	Wash. Hebrew
00014	Statesman, Daniel	33y	—	21 JAN 1889	Philadelphia PA	Mt. Olivet
16811	Stattin, Bettie (Cofield)	52y	C	17 NOV 1920	Tarboro NC	Union
14910	Stead, Cynthia Force	65y	W	12 JUL 1918	Elkridge MD	Oak Hill
01765	Stead, Mary Force	44y	W	6 JUN 1895	Elkridge MD	Oak Hill
06566	Stealey, Elizabeth A.	67y	W	24 MAY 1908	Parkersburg WV	Oak Hill
08765	Stearman, Sarah	68y	W	14 AUG 1912	Silver Spring MD	Ohev Sholom
17443	Stearns, Fred J.	64y	W	28 SEP 1921	Colonial Bea. VA	Arlington
14645	Stebbins, B.	45y	W	14 FEB 1918	Norfolk VA	Cremated
08142	Stebbins, Martha Ellen	1y	W	9 JUN 1911	Capitol Hts. MD	Mt. Olivet

No.	Name of Deceased	Age	Race	Death Date	Place of Death	Place of Burial
05912	Stedman, Hilda B.	41y	W	25 JAN 1907	Allegheny Co. PA	Oak Hill
12550	Steed, Delia M.	43y	W	3 OCT 1914	Baltimore MD	Piscataway MD
02472	Steele, Carrie	27y	W	19 MAY 1898	Wilmington DE	Rock Creek
13250	Steele, Earnest H., s/o Wm. H.	37y	W	15 DEC 1915	Greenville VA	Glenwood
03733	Steele, Ellen	28y	C	17 DEC 1901	Pittsburgh PA	Payne's
17876	Steele, Floyd Thomas, Jr.	8m	W	27 MAY 1922	Arlington Co.	Congressional
04933	Steele, Henry J., s/o Alex.	34y	W	21 OCT 1904	New York NY	Glenwood
16830	Steele, James	45y	W	27 NOV 1920	New York NY	Rock Creek
00776	Steele, John A.	67y	W	12 NOV 1891	Rockville MD	Rock Creek
03327	Steele, Joseph	35y	W	12 NOV 1900	Takoma Park MD	Rock Creek
14813	Steele, Kate	89y	W	JUN 1917	Philadelphia PA	Mt. Olivet[1]
02280	Steele, Marian B.	1y	W	19 AUG 1897	Ocean Grove NJ	Glenwood
03734	Steele, Merle L.	16y	W	19 DEC 1901	Lanham MD	Baltimore MD
05821	Steele, Rush	42y	W	18 SEP 1906	San Francisco CA	Arlington VA
04310	Steer, Edwin	68y	W	23 MAY 1903	Staunton VA	Oak Hill
02731	Steers, Charles Walker, Sr.	46y	W	21 JAN 1899	Takoma Park MD	Glenwood
02665	Steers, Marion S.	7m	W	27 NOV 1898	Takoma Park MD	Glenwood
06619	Steever, Mary E.	57y	W	29 JUN 1908	Hyattsville MD	Rock Creek
01764	Stegmaier, Francis	1y	W	29 AUG 1895	Bladensburg MD	Mt. Olivet
02223	Stegmaier, Lillian M.	6m	W	25 JUN 1897	Bladensburg MD	Mt. Olivet
07289	Steifel, Leo	41y	W	25 NOV 1909	New York NY	Wash. Hebrew
07289	Steifel, Leo	41y	W	25 NOV 1909	New York NY	Wash. Hebrew
13457	Steigauf, Joseph John	19y	C	25 MAR 1916	At Sea	Johnston PA
00666	Steiger, Martha L.	48y	W	22 AUG 1891	Laurel MD	Oak Hill
00049	Steiger, William Tell	38y	W	23 MAR 1889	Laurel MD	Oak Hill
15473	Stein, Hannah C.	39y	W	24 DEC 1918	Riverdale MD	Glenwood
16549	Stein, Julia	59y	W	21 JUN 1920	Laurel MD	Wash. Hebrew
16675	Stein, Paul A.	24y	W	5 OCT 1918	England	Adas Israel
06027	Steinberg, Joseph	24y	W	13 APR 1907	Culpeper VA	New York NY
13590	Steinbraker, Charles Henry	49y	W	7 JUL 1916	Pinecrest VA	Glenwood
00245	Stelle, Adelaide St.H.	78y	W	16 DEC 1889	Brooklyn NY	Congressional
15910	Stelle, Morton B.	71y	W	1 AUG 1919	New York NY	Oak Hill
16368	Stelle, Rosa W.	69y	W	8 MAR 1920	New York NY	Congressional
04709	Stembel, Louise D.	59y	W	10 MAY 1904	Atlantic City NJ	Arlington
17246	Stengel, Simson Carl, Jr.	3y	W	18 JUN 1921	Troy NY	Arlington
07837	Stenz, Carl George, s/o G.F.	27y	W	22 NOV 1910	Luray VA	Rock Creek
07002	Stephens, Daniel Harvey	4y	W	25 APR 1909	Baltimore MD	Glenwood
07012	Stephens, Lillian A.	6y	W	6 MAY 1909	Baltimore MD	Glenwood
01941	Stephens, Louis G.	61y	W	17 MAY 1896	Forestville MD	Glenwood
00995	Stephens, William Albert	26y	W	16 JUL 1893	Quantico VA	Congressional
17805	Stephenson, Ann	6m	W	15 APR 1922	Darby PA	Ft. Lincoln
14321	Stephenson, James A.	40y	W	27 AUG 1917	Washington DC	Congressional
06736	Stephenson, Mary	24y	C	20 SEP 1908	Capitol Hts. MD	Mt. Olivet
03884	Sterling, Edward C.	64y	W	22 MAY 1902	New York NY	Rock Creek
17721	Sterling, Elizabeth	58y	C	28 FEB 1922	Plymouth MA	Payne's
05130	Sterling, James D., s/o Geo.	31y	W	13 MAY 1905	Norfolk VA	Mt. Olivet
14872	Stern, Albert	40y	W	19 JUN 1918	New York NY	Wash. Hebrew
12450	Stern, Milton	34y	W	20 JUL 1914	New York NY	Wash. Hebrew
08415	Sterne, Charles Fague	31y	W	7 DEC 1911	Asheville NC	Glenwood
07861	Sterne, Grace May	17y	W	8 DEC 1910	Alexandria VA	Glenwood
17289	Sterner, Francis A.	10y	W	8 JUL 1921	Maryland Pk. MD	Mt. Olivet
00897	Sterrett, Addie	4y	W	2 APR 1888	Fairbault MN	Springdale
07774	Stettinius, Maria R.	80y	W	2 OCT 1910	Jessup MD	Congressional
03796	Steuart, Edward	44y	C	16 FEB 1902	New York NY	Moore's
13674	Steuart, George	40y	C	19 AUG 1916	New York NY	Kinsale VA
08125	Steuart, William H.	44y	C	17 MAY 1911	Pittsburgh PA	Mt. Olivet
14466	Stevens, .R., Maj., U.S.A.	57y	W	16 NOV 1917	Brunswick GA	Arlington

[1] Disinterment permit dated 11 MAY 1918 for removal from Fernwood Cemetery.

District of Columbia Foreign Death Records, 1888-1923

No.	Name of Deceased	Age	Race	Death Date	Place of Death	Place of Burial
07562	Stevens, Albert Charles	79y	W	6 JUN 1910	Relay MD	Congressional
00996	Stevens, Anna M.	68y	W	17 JUL 1893	Sligo MD	Congressional
02845	Stevens, Caroline McAlister	78y	W	4 JUN 1899	Brooklyn NY	Congressional
06494	Stevens, Durham White	55y	W	25 MAR 1908	San Francisco CA	Oak Hill
00285	Stevens, Ezra L.	68y	W	6 MAR 1890	Asbury Park NJ	Oak Hill
15678	Stevens, James D.	55y	W	20 MAR 1919	Rockville MD	Rock Creek
00015	Stevens, Margaret	88y	W	28 JAN 1889	Frederick Co. MD	Oak Hill
02429	Stevens, Marian Etta E.	8y	W	6 APR 1898	Arlington VA	Congressional
18160	Stevens, Marie Wales	50y	W	13 NOV 1922	Pensacola FL	Cremated
17310	Stevens, Martin V.	—	—	18 JUL 1921	Morristown NJ	Glenwood
14147	Stevens, Mitchel	24y	W	25 MAY 1917	Frederick Co. MD	Mt. Olivet
08728	Stevens, Robert	2y	W	23 JUL 1912	Takoma Park MD	Dunkirk NY
00895	Stevens, Robert Calfus	64y	W	27 JUL 1892	Montg. Co. MD	Congressional
15957	Stevens, Stanly	70y	W	24 AUG 1919	Kansas City MO	Mt. Olivet
14455	Stevenson, Annie	65y	C	11 NOV 1917	New York NY	Harmony
08414	Stevenson, Lena	45y	C	6 DEC 1911	New York NY	Mt. Zion West
12978	Stevenson, Matilda Coxe	65y	W	24 JUN 1915	Rosecroft MD	Rock Creek
13653	Stevenson, Samuel	38y	C	9 AUG 1916	Philadelphia PA	Woodlawn
01766	Stever, Sarah Ann	80y	W	16 MAY 1895	Pr. Geo. Co. MD	Mt. Olivet
12665	Steward, Arthur P.	64y	W	21 DEC 1914	Chevy Chase MD	Rock Creek
13202	Steward, Eleanor M.	63y	W	12 NOV 1915	Chevy Chase MD	Rock Creek
04576	Steward, Julia	24y	W	23 JAN 1904	Wilson NC	Congressional
12888	Steward, Samuel	30y	C	19 APR 1915	Philadelphia PA	Payne's
03778	Steward, Thomas Corwin	61y	W	1 FEB 1902	Albany NY	Columbus OH
06720	Stewart, Agnes	15y	C	8 SEP 1908	Chesa. Jct. MD	Mt. Olivet
12426	Stewart, Alexander	46y	W	28 JUN 1914	Paris, France	Cremated
06553	Stewart, Allen H.	41y	C	16 MAY 1908	Brooklyn NY	Harmony
06732	Stewart, Ann Eliza	78y	W	17 SEP 1908	Louisville KY	Mt. Olivet
12982	Stewart, Arthur Brown	20y	C	27 JUN 1915	Seat Pleasant MD	Mt. Olivet
08578	Stewart, Augustus	50y	C	31 MAR 1912	Seat Pleasant MD	Payne's
16602	Stewart, Charles A., Jr.	19y	W	14 JUL 1920	Camp Owens MA	Falls Church VA
08698	Stewart, Charlotte D.	53y	W	1 JUL 1912	Hyattsville MD	Arlington
13353	Stewart, Charlotte	40y	C	13 FEB 1916	Seat Pleasant MD	Mt. Olivet
02279	Stewart, David S.	68y	W	21 AUG 1897	Mt. Clemens MI	Rock Creek
08227	Stewart, Diana	57y	C	27 JUL 1911	Orange NJ	Payne's
03817	Stewart, Dora	18y	C	11 MAR 1902	Allegheny PA	Harmony
07950	Stewart, Elizabeth	39y	W	30 JAN 1911	Capitol Hts. MD	Rock Creek
12895	Stewart, Elizabeth Sarah	79y	W	24 APR 1915	Chevy Chase MD	Oak Hill
00145	Stewart, Ella	38y	C	31 AUG 1889	Fairfax C.H. VA	Mt. Pleasant
02122	Stewart, Emma	32y	C	18 JAN 1897	Philadelphia PA	Payne's
15314	Stewart, Florance	31y	C	28 OCT 1918	New York NY	Harmony
07610	Stewart, Fred. J.T., Jr.	8m	W	1 JUL 1910	Summit NJ	Mt. Olivet
04270	Stewart, George	38y	W	24 APR 1903	Buffalo NY	Mt. Olivet
09066	Stewart, George F.	29y	W	8 FEB 1913	El Paso TX	Mt. Olivet
05943	Stewart, Henry C.	37y	W	16 FEB 1907	Hampton VA	Glenwood
17474	Stewart, Ida	67y	W	18 OCT 1921	Forest Glen MD	Mt. Olivet
03267	Stewart, Isaac F.	37y	W	12 AUG 1900	Branchville MD	Congressional
05093	Stewart, James	78y	W	19 APR 1905	Ft. Thomas KY	Arlington
05109	Stewart, James	80y	W	30 APR 1905	Germantown MD	Mt. Olivet
04155	Stewart, James A.	56y	W	3 JAN 1903	Baltimore MD	Arlington VA
14997	Stewart, James P.	36y	W	31 AUG 1918	Bel Air MD	Mt. Olivet
04289	Stewart, James S.	58y	W	18 MAY 1903	Riverdale MD	Mt. Olivet
04687	Stewart, Jane	48y	C	23 APR 1904	Ballston VA	Baptist
18432	Stewart, John	26y	C	16 MAR 1923	Gary IN	Mt. Zion West
00896	Stewart, John C.	62y	W	21 APR 1892	Stem. Run MD	Graceland
04348	Stewart, John W., Lt. U.S.N.	50y	W	6 AUG 1903	Savannah GA	Graceland
14706	Stewart, Joseph	24y	W	21 MAR 1918	Camp Meade MD	Mt. Olivet
14769	Stewart, Levin C.	29y	W	22 APR 1918	Philadelphia PA	Glenwood
06993	Stewart, Lillian May	7m	W	18 APR 1909	Capitol Hts. MD	Tenallytown M.
02025	Stewart, Lydia	50y	C	15 AUG 1896	Seat Pleasant MD	Jones' Chapel

No.	Name of Deceased	Age	Race	Death Date	Place of Death	Place of Burial
05149	Stewart, Margaret	29y	C	23 MAY 1905	Philadelphia PA	Payne's
08886	Stewart, Mary E.	69y	W	13 OCT 1912	Hyattsville MD	Mt. Olivet
08541	Stewart, Morgan E.	72y	W	2 MAR 1912	Laurel MD	Arlington
08291	Stewart, Rachel A.	64y	W	1 SEP 1911	Severn MD	Glenwood
14585	Stewart, Raymond Leon	27y	W	10 JAN 1918	Ft. Lyon CO	Arlington
05580	Stewart, Rosa	56y	C	19 MAY 1906	Seat Pleasant MD	Mt. Olivet
14286	Stewart, Rose A.	39y	W	7 AUG 1917	Franklin NJ	Mt. Olivet
16904	Stewart, Ruth A.	8m	W	9 JAN 1921	Hyattsville MD	Rock Creek
15775	Stewart, Sarah Margret	46y	C	7 MAY 1919	Denton MD	Union Ben.
13375	Stewart, William M.	40y	C	21 FEB 1916	KS	Harmony
00520	Stewart, William T.	76y	W	17 JUN 1890	Hampton VA	Glenwood
07291	Stickel, Melvin	2y	W	26 NOV 1909	Brentwood MD	Glenwood
04438	Stickney, Jennie K.	75y	W	29 AUG 1903	Long Beach CA	Oak Hill
04456	Stickney, John B.	50y	W	5 NOV 1882	Washington DC	Rock Creek
14363	Stidham, Alfred D., s/o John	81y	W	18 SEP 1917	Ocean City NJ	Rock Creek
16406	Stiefel, William	46y	W	23 MAR 1920	Mt. Pleasant SC	Prospect Hill
06604	Stien, George W.	53y	W	23 JUN 1908	Berwyn MD	Prospect Hill
15069	Stier, Henry C.	42y	W	2 OCT 1918	Pittsburgh PA	Glenwood
01467	Stiffel, Clara L.	24y	W	19 AUG 1894	Norfolk VA	Congressional
14779	Stiles, Molly	59y	C	26 APR 1918	Philadelphia PA	Harmony
02145	Stillings, S. Vinton	56y	W	24 FEB 1897	Woods Hole MA	Congressional
08471	Stillyard, Marian	53y	C	12 JAN 1912	E. Arlington VA	Harmony
06289	Stimkle, Gay	37y	W	16 OCT 1907	Marshall MI	Glenwood
07158	Stimson, Elisabeth	2y	W	15 AUG 1909	Hyattsville MD	Glenwood
16457	Stinchcomb, Lucretia V.	67y	W	28 APR 1920	Bel Air MD	Mt. Olivet
13754	Stine, George Washington	10m	W	30 JUN 1916	Chicago IL	Congressional
00997	Stinemetz, John R.	5y	W	30 AUG 1893	Brooklyn NY	Oak Hill
02450	Stinemetz, William G.	61y	W	27 APR 1898	Buffalo NY	Glenwood
06317	Stinzing, Rose	30y	W	12 NOV 1907	Denver CO	Mt. Olivet
01198	Stits, John S.	60y	W	1 JUN 1892	Brooklyn NY	Glenwood
08317	Stockard, Thomas W.	56y	W	19 SEP 1911	Takoma Park MD	Glenwood
00561	Stockbridge, Elizabeth R.	29y	W	20 APR 1891	New York NY	Oak Hill
17853	Stockbridge, Laura P.	56y	W	12 MAY 1922	Great Falls VA	Arlington
14407	Stockman, Anna P.	88y	W	14 OCT 1917	Mt. Ranier MD	Glenwood
15339	Stockman, Eileen M.	13d	W	10 NOV 1918	Mt. Ranier MD	Glenwood
06305	Stockman, Ella M.	49y	W	11 NOV 1907	Hyattsville MD	Glenwood
17880	Stockton, Israel C.	75y	W	27 MAY 1922	Fairfax Co. VA	Rock Creek
18327	Stockton, Sarah A.	c.62y	W	3 FEB 1923	Detroit MI	Glenwood
04305	Stoddard, Daniel	42y	C	26 MAY 1903	Pittsburgh PA	Harmony
13941	Stoddard, Josiah Clark	72y	W	21 JAN 1917	Rockville MD	Glenwood
05454	Stoddard, Ulysses L.	40y	W	5 FEB 1906	Gaithersburg MD	Oak Hill
00113	Stoek, Henry	78y	W	29 JUL 1889	Knowles MD	Oak Hill
02098	Stoek, Margaret G.	54y	W	24 NOV 1896	Kensington MD	Oak Hill
16508	Stohlman, Charles P.	53y	W	31 MAY 1920	Laurel MD	Holyrood
12218	Stokes, Alan B.	38y	W	10 FEB 1914	Dallas TX	Rock Creek
04238	Stokes, Allen W.	70y	W	16 FEB 1903	Birmingham AL	Rock Creek
01769	Stokes, Annie E.	49y	W	4 JUL 1895	Keysville VA	Scaggs
13637	Stokes, Catherine	23y	C	31 JUL 1916	New York NY	Woodlawn
11914	Stokes, Fannie	45y	C	23 JUL 1913	Charles Co. MD	Harmony
15756	Stokes, Fred Herbert	50y	W	11 DEC 1917	Kansas City MO	Glenwood
09068	Stokes, Mattie	50y	C	8 fEB 1913	Arlington VA	Harmony
07611	Stoll, Aquila Wilhelmina	63y	W	30 JUN 1910	Staunton VA	Prospect Hill
13749	Stoll, Charles F.	71y	W	4 OCT 1916	Connellsville PA	Prospect Hill
06464	Stommel, Julius	1m	W	11 MAR 1908	Capitol Hts. MD	Woodlawn
07018	Stone, Charles Henry	74y	W	10 MAY 1909	Forest Glen MD	Baltimore MD
16219	Stone, Francis Wayland, Capt.	27y	W	15 JAN 1920	Rockford IL	Rock Creek
01767	Stone, Frank Pelham	1m	W	10 SEP 1895	Cabin John MD	Oak Hill
16948	Stone, Frank Pellam	75y	W	1 FEB 1921	Bethesda MD	Oak Hill
12083	Stone, George H.	78y	W	8 NOV 1913	Corona NY	Arlington
13892	Stone, George Washington	78y	W	28 DEC 1916	Avenel MD	Rock Creek

District of Columbia Foreign Death Records, 1888-1923

No.	Name of Deceased	Age	Race	Death Date	Place of Death	Place of Burial
07087	Stone, Katharine Abagail	4m	W	1 JUL 1909	Chevy Chase MD	Rock Creek
08785	Stone, Mary Frances	83y	W	27 AUG 1912	Earlhurst VA	Rock Creek
03270	Stone, Philip	51y	W	20 AUG 1900	Mtn. Lake MD	Oak Hill
05232	Stone, Roy	69y	W	5 AUG 1905	Mendham NJ	Arlington
04827	Stone, Stephen W., Jr.	2w	W	3 AUG 1904	Cumberland MD	Rock Creek
15193	Stoner, Jessie Edna	31y	W	15 OCT 1918	Baltimore MD	Congressional
16349	Stoops, Newland P.	72y	W	27 FEB 1920	Relay MD	Glenwood
03753	Stoops, William B.	50y	W	7 JAN 1902	New York NY	Mt. Olivet
06939	Storch, E.E.	43y	W	1 MAR 1909	Tucson AZ	Oak Hill
06939	Storch, E.E.	43y	W	1 MAR 1909	Tucson AZ	Oak Hill
01942	Storer, Frederick	15y	W	29 APR 1896	Philadelphia PA	Wash. Hebrew
00377	Storey, Mary E.	—	—	1 AUG 1890	Forest Glen MD	—
01768	Storey, Samuel	63y	W	22 SEP 1895	Hampton VA	Congressional
07391	Storm, Edward H., s/o Tmile	3y	W	28 JAN 1910	Crozet VA	Cremated
02026	Storm, Francis Eugene	55y	W	2 JUL 1896	San Francisco CA	Rock Creek
05120	Storty, John S.	2y	W	8 MAY 1905	Chevy Chase MD	Holyrood
02100	Storty, Lillian	2y	W	3 JAN 1897	Montg. Co. MD	Holyrood
02099	Storty, Richard	6y	W	2 JAN 1897	Montg. Co. MD	Holyrood
11854	Story, Anna Warren	65y	W	13 JUN 1913	Gloucester MA	Rock Creek
07903	Story, Ephrin J.	81y	W	1 JAN 1911	Green Valley VA	Cremated
04114	Story, G.W.	73y	W	24 DEC 1902	Apollo PA	Arlington
07069	Story, J.E.	30y	W	13 JUN 1909	Pueblo CO	Congressional
16072	Stott, Leonora M.	29y	W	18 SEP 1919	Puerto Plata, S.D.	Congressional
07470	Stott, Sallie E. (Lindsay)	24y	W	14 MAR 1910	Bluemont VA	Congressional
08052	Stotts, Harry	31y	C	3 APR 1911	Omaha NE	Arlington VA
08691	Stout, Julia A.	—	W	23 DEC 1863	Florence, Italy	Oak Hill
18248	Stovall, Harry Eldridge	27y	W	31 DEC 1922	Mexico City TX	Arlington
12128	Strachan, George	51y	W	12 DEC 1913	New York NY	Harmony
01480	Strachan, John A.	33y	C	1 SEP 1894	Brooklyn NY	Harmony
01199	Strain, Cornelia	59y	W	23 NOV 1892	Brookville MD	Oak Hill
01600	Straining, John	63y	W	17 DEC 1894	Bowie MD	Prospect Hill
17372	Strait, Berton Anderson	34y	W	25 AUG 1921	Philadelphia PA	Arlington
18166	Strasburger, Henry	82y	W	17 NOV 1922	Augusta GA	Wash. Hebrew
00372	Strasburger, Infant of Meyer	2h	W	28 JUL 1890	Oakland MD	Wash. Hebrew
17985	Strasburger, Joseph	66y	W	30 JUL 1922	Atlantic City NJ	Wash. Hebrew
16162	Strasburger, Zody	76y	W	23 DEC 1919	Boston MA	Wash. Hebrew
07424	Strattan, George William	37y	W	12 FEB 1910	Vancouver, B.C.	—
07150	Stratton, Robert Bell	1y	W	8 AUG 1909	Gapland MD	Rock Creek
08850	Street, Daniel Baen	70y	W	18 SEP 1912	Moose Jaw, Can.	Arlington
03013	Streeter, F. Louisa	22y	W	25 NOV 1899	New Glatz	Rock Creek
08326	Streets, Catherine, laundress	40y	C	21 SEP 1911	Atlantic City NJ	Payne's
16517	Stribling, John N.	23y	W	29 MAY 1920	Liverpool Pt. MD	Arlington
16148	Stricker, Albert Jean	13y	W	14 DEC 1919	Baltimore MD	Prospect Hill
01770	Stricker, Margaret A.	67y	W	2 SEP 1895	Alexandria VA	Congressional
03375	Stricklen, W. Raymond, Rev.	42y	W	19 DEC 1900	Phoenix AZ	Baltimore MD
08402	Strickler, Fannie E.	39y	W	26 NOV 1911	Capitol Hts. MD	Congressional
02657	Strider, Eliza Jane	85y	W	13 NOV 1898	Urvilla WV	Mt. Olivet
17398	Strines, Ida	48y	W	13 SEP 1921	Takoma Park MD	Nat. Cap. Hebrew
14644	Strisby, George W.	22y	W	17 FEB 1918	Camp Sevier SC	Glenwood
18246	Strobel, Harriet W.	24y	W	4 JAN 1923	Baltimore MD	Oak Hill
02811	Strolter, Albert [Stotler]	—	C	1 JUL 1898	Cuba	Fairfax C.H. VA
04406	Strong, Frank	65y	W	25 JUL 1903	Garrett Co. MD	Arlington
14790	Strong, Harry J.	35y	W	28 APR 1918	New York NY	New Orleans LA
12771	Strong, Mary E.	70y	W	18 FEB 1915	Walkersville MD	Arlington
14303	Strong, Viola E. (Chapin)	55y	C	15 AUG 1917	Indianapolis IN	Woodlawn
16426	Strong, William, Jr., s/o W.N.	33y	W	21 DEC 1919	Altadena CA	Arlington
13805	Strother, Allen H.	56y	C	4 NOV 1916	Fairmont Hts. MD	Payne's
00297	Stroughberger, Frederick	50y	W	21 MAR 1890	Flatbush NY	Oak Hill
07211	Stuard, Charles E.	55y	C	27 SEP 1909	Philadelphia PA	Payne's
08241	Stuart, Anna Fairfield	34y	W	4 AUG 1911	Takoma Park MD	Rock Creek

No.	Name of Deceased	Age	Race	Death Date	Place of Death	Place of Burial
02987	Stuart, Bessie M.	47y	W	21 OCT 1899	Philadelphia PA	Congressional
09173	Stuart, Elizsabeth	c.57y	W	15 APR 1913	Morris Plains NJ	Rock Creek
16460	Stuart, Katherine Margaret	3d	W	15 FEB 1920	Guan. Bay, Cuba	Detroit MI
17735	Stubener, Annie M. (Haislip)	47y	W	9 MAR 1922	Benedict MD	Rock Creek
13591	Stubener, Elizabeth Margaret	69y	W	7 JUL 1916	Bladensburg MD	Glenwood
16143	Stubener, Fannie McClellan	56y	W	9 DEC 1919	Brentwood MD	Glenwood
07003	Stubener, Philip J.	14y	W	26 APR 1909	Bladensburg MD	Glenwood
16598	Studds, Robert H.	54y	W	14 JUL 1920	Norfolk VA	Mt. Olivet
00375	Stull, Catherine	6m	W	31 JUL 1890	Fairfax Co. VA	Marlboro MD
00384	Stull, Minnie Bowie	5m	W	4 AUG 1890	Clifton Sta. VA	Marlboro MD
12768	Stull, William R.	39y	W	15 JAN 1915	W. Sul. Spgs. VA	Arlington
12992	Sturbitts, William	c.67y	W	2 JUL 1915	Forestville MD	Glenwood
18447	Sturdavent, Claud	16y	C	28 MAR 1923	Cape Charles VA	Harmony
03054	Sturgeon, David B.	70y	W	26 DEC 1899	Whitesburg PA	Arlington
02652	Sturgis, George W.	c.27y	W	26 OCT 1898	Stiff's Wharf VA	Earmore Sta. VA
18283	Sturtavant, Richard W.	38y	C	18 JAN 1923	Port Norris NJ	Harmony
01771	Sturtivant, Edward Kinsley	25y	W	28 AUG 1895	Brooklyn NY	Rock Creek
04532	Stutz, Louis F.	50y	W	3 DEC 1903	Asheville NC	Glenwood
13317	Stutz, Sophie Amelia	41y	W	24 JAN 1916	N. Franklin PA	Glenwood
07354	Suell, M. Porter, Rev.	70y	W	31 DEC 1909	Newton NJ	Congressional
14105	Sugenheimer, Zerline	68y	W	26 APR 1917	Catonsville MD	Wash. Hebrew
16929	Suit, Arthur Birch	53y	W	18 JAN 1921	St. Augustine FL	Congressional
14836	Sullivan, Adelaide	67y	W	22 MAY 1918	Mt. Ranier MD	Mt. Olivet
06418	Sullivan, Anna	55y	W	4 FEB 1908	Richmond VA	Mt. Olivet
13339	Sullivan, Catherine	80y	W	15 DEC 1907	Austin TX	Holyrood
03963	Sullivan, Charles A., Jr.	1y	W	26 JUL 1902	Baltimore MD	Holyrood
00898	Sullivan, Clara	1y	W	17 AUG 1892	Rock Enon VA	Mt. Olivet
14563	Sullivan, David S., s/o Roger	48y	W	7 JAN 1918	Indianapolis IN	Mt. Olivet
18307	Sullivan, Edward R.	10y	W	30 JAN 1923	Derwood MD	Mt. Olivet
15159	Sullivan, Elizabeth Ada	62y	W	14 OCT 1918	Takoma MD	Dubuque IA
15624	Sullivan, Evelyn R.	34y	W	17 FEB 1919	Baltimore MD	Glenwood
17523	Sullivan, Frances D.	65y	W	15 NOV 1921	Philadelphia PA	Rock Creek
04373	Sullivan, Frank	6m	W	4 JUL 1903	Hyattsville MD	Mt. Olivet
15059	Sullivan, Harry M.	30y	W	30 SEP 1918	New York NY	Arlington
13541	Sullivan, James A.	26y	W	4 JUN 1916	Potomac River	Congressional
01450	Sullivan, James A.	8m	W	31 JUL 1894	Akron OH	Mt. Olivet
03851	Sullivan, James E.	41y	W	13 APR 1902	Jackson City VA	Mt. Olivet
01332	Sullivan, John	c.64y	M	17 JAN 1894	Branchville MD	Harmony
03012	Sullivan, John	42y	W	20 NOV 1899	Baltimore MD	Mt. Olivet
04887	Sullivan, John	50y	W	11 SEP 1904	Hyattsville MD	Mt. Olivet
17538	Sullivan, John Henry	43y	W	21 NOV 1921	Trumbull CN	Mt. Olivet
18446	Sullivan, John J.	c.40y	W	29 MAR 1923	Wilmington DE	Mt. Olivet
11957	Sullivan, Joseph	6m	W	13 AUG 1913	Clarneton VA	Holyrood
07359	Sullivan, Kate	50y	W	6 JAN 1910	Brentwood MD	Mt. Olivet
13340	Sullivan, Michael	59y	W	26 JAN 1916	Houston TX	Holyrood
07335	Sullivan, Michael	50y	W	19 DEC 1909	Baltimore MD	Mt. Olivet
01840	Sullivan, Rebecca	25y	W	26 DEC 1895	Baltimore MD	Mt. Olivet
05231	Sullivan, Robert E., s/o Edw. J.	40y	W	6 AUG 1905	Harrisonburg VA	Mt. Olivet
06466	Sullivan, Thomas C., s/o Saml.	74y	W	11 MAR 1908	Ft. Monroe VA	Arlington
01090	Sullivan, Thomas F.	38y	W	26 FEB 1892	Austin TX	Holyrood
00016	Sullivan, Thos. F.	47y	W	17 JAN 1889	Chicago IL	Holyrood
18237	Sullivan, William A.	50y	W	1 JAN 1923	Derwood MD	Mt. Olivet
15947	Suman, James L.	68y	W	23 AUG 1919	Seabrook MD	Congressional
00381	Sumby, Mary E.	37y	C	1 AUG 1890	Knoxville MD	Harmony
03416	Summerman, Sophia	54y	W	13 FEB 1901	Chillum MD	Rock Creek
06753	Summers, John Edward	86y	W	1 OCT 1908	Atlantic City NJ	Arlington
16026	Summers, Nathan R.	86y	W	4 OCT 1919	Cape Charles VA	Bladensburg MD

District of Columbia Foreign Death Records, 1888-1923

No.	Name of Deceased	Age	Race	Death Date	Place of Death	Place of Burial
05448	Summers, Samuel	38y	W	28 APR 1894	Struthers OH[1]	Glenwood
03905	Summers, William H.	68y	W	23 JUN 1902	Chicago IL	Glenwood
15984	Summy, Catherine J.	58y	W	7 SEP 1919	Pittsburgh PA	Rock Creek
06474	Sumner, Emma J.	40y	W	17 AMR 1908	Camp Springs MD	Rock Creek
07794	Sumner, William H.	57y	C	9 OCT 1910	Ardwick MD	Harmony
07801	Sumwalt, Margaret M.	50y	W	26 OCT 1910	Hyattsville MD	Glenwood
13289	Sumwalt, William James	64y	W	9 JAN 1916	E. Hyattsville MD	Glenwood
12172½	Sunday, George Frederick	48y	W	18 JAN 1914	Takoma Park MD	Rock Creek
00521	Sunderland, Frank Spencer	32y	W	17 JAN 1891	Rye Patch NV	Oak Hill
16648	Supple, Katy Agnes	72y	W	10 AUG 1920	Forest Glen MD	Cremated
16530	Surface, Henry E.	37y	W	9 JUN 1920	Glenville NY	Glenwood
17676	Surgay, Thomas H.	82y	W	4 FEB 1922	New Orleans LA	Congressional
06296	Surratt, Isiac D.	66y	W	3 NOV 1907	Baltimore MD	Mt. Olivet
16189	Suter, Alexander	68y	W	4 JAN 1920	Atlanta GA	Glenwood
01772	Suter, Henderson, Rev.	67y	W	25 AUG 1895	Alexandria VA	Oak Hill
02101	Suter, Mary C.	75y	W	29 DEC 1896	Baltimore MD	Glenwood
11956	Suter, Robert	2y	C	12 AUG 1913	Cumberland MD	Harmony
02392	Suter, Thomas R., farmer	82y	W	9 FEB 1898	Frederick MD	Glenwood
17409	Sutherland, Douglas Martin	38y	W	14 SEP 1921	New York NY	Arlington
08446	Sutherland, Edgar	72y	W	28 DEC 1911	Alexandria VA	Mt. Olivet
17288	Sutherland, Margaret M.	73y	W	8 JUL 1921	Hartford CN	Congressional
02729	Sutton, Clarence B.	26y	W	1 FEB 1899	Nomini Ferry VA	Glenwood
08167	Sutton, Edmond A.	—	W	28 JUN 1911	N. Fork VA	Congressional
02724	Sutton, Ella F.	40y	W	26 JAN 1899	Baltimore MD	Oak Hill[2]
13372	Sutton, Henry S.	60y	W	23 FEB 1916	Laurel MD	Congressional
05166	Sutton, Louis J.	73y	W	11 JUN 1905	Hyattsville MD	Rock Creek
15946	Swain, Benj. J.W.	55y	W	21 AUG 1919	Sykesville MD	Forestville MD
05332	Swain, Mary C.E.	77y	W	23 OCT 1905	Rutherford NJ	Oak Hill
00256	Swain, Robert S.	61y	W	4 JAN 1890	Camp Springs MD	Congressional
00146	Swan, Alfonza C.	79y	W	28 AUG 1889	Seabrook MD	Congressional
05465	Swan, James	30y	C	8 FEB 1906	Carrol WV	Payne's
14193	Swan, Lilly Mae	37y	W	27 JUN 1917	Asheville NC	Rock Creek
08547	Swan, Mamie M.	48y	W	9 MAR 1912	Ft. Myer VA	Rock Creek[3]
07869	Swander, William H., Dr.	75y	W	11 DEC 1910	Hampton VA	Rock Creek
13548	Swank, William H.	33y	W	5 JUN 1916	Saranac Lake NY	Glenwood
00899	Swann, Catherine	38y	C	18 JUL 1892	Leesburg VA	Harmony
14988	Swann, Francis Leroy	28y	W	24 AUG 1918	Elizabeth NJ	Congressional
16595	Swanson, Elizabeth Lyons	49y	W	13 JUL 1920	Bethesda MD	Richmond VA
18566	Swanton, Mary O.	81y	W	30 MAY 1923	Somerset MD	Bath ME
05449	Swartz, Sophronia P.	59y	W	31 JAN 1906	Baltimore Co. MD	Oak Hill
18135	Swayze, Samuel E.	44y	W	30 OCT 1922	Baltimore MD	Rock Creek
06991	Sweeney, Agnes E.	1y	W	17 APR 1909	Capitol Hts. MD	Mt. Olivet
04121	Sweeney, Arthur W.	75y	W	9 DEC 1902	Indian Head MD	Congressional
03317	Sweeney, Bridget	36y	W	14 JUN 1868	Baltimore MD	Mt. Olivet
17662	Sweeney, Bridget E.	69y	W	25 JAN 1922	Baltimore MD	Mt. Olivet
03315	Sweeney, Ellen	50y	W	24 DEC 1866	Baltimore MD	Mt. Olivet[4]
03567	Sweeney, George M.	57y	W	6 JUL 1901	New York NY	Congressional
14017	Sweeney, John A.	27y	W	25 FEB 1917	New Orleans LA	Mt. Olivet
15739	Sweeney, Mattie	46y	W	25 NOV 1918	Minneapolis MN	Mt. Olivet
03316	Sweeney, Thomas	48y	W	5 OCT 1861	Baltimore MD	Mt. Olivet
00242	Sweeney, Timothy	86y	W	15 DEC 1889	VA	Mt. Olivet
03566	Sweeney, William	23y	W	5 JUL 1901	McKeesport PA	Mt. Olivet
15476	Sweeny, Aubray	27y	W	24 DEC 1918	Seat Pleasant MD	Congressional
03156	Sweeny, Eugenia	71y	W	3 APR 1900	Baltimore MD	Mt. Olivet

[1] Removed from Oak Hill Cemetery, Youngstown, Hamoning Co., Ohio
[2] Note for disinterment permit #5673 issued 19 FEB 1906 for removal to Loudon Park Cemetery, Baltimore, Md.
[3] Disinterment permit #9742 issued 29 NOV 1918 for removal to Arlington National Cemetery.
[4] Transit Permit dated 31 OCT 1900 notes Sweeney remains are to be removed from St. Patrick's Cemetery, Baltimore, Md.

No.	Name of Deceased	Age	Race	Death Date	Place of Death	Place of Burial
05963	Sweet, Georgia	93y	W	28 FEB 1907	Westminster MD	Oak Hill
16002	Sweet, Mary Adelaide (Wilson)	82y	W	20 SEP 1919	Roanoke VA	Arlington
00266	Sweet, William E.	45y	W	13 JAN 1890	Denver CO	Glenwood
15438	Swenson, Jeannette	21y	W	14 DEC 1918	Takoma MD	Brooklyn NY
00998	Swift, James H.	c.55y	W	13 JUL 1893	Alex. Co. VA	Arlington VA
07410	Swiggett, June B.	49y	W	5 FEB 1910	Chicago IL	Oak Hill
02789	Swing, Letitia Gilman	72y	W	27 MAR 1899	Somerset Hts. MD	Rock Creek
02451	Switzer, Annie A.	28y	W	29 APR 1898	Philadelphia PA	Congressional
06820	Switzer, Annie E.	52y	W	16 NOV 1908	Catonsville MD	Wash. Hebrew
12405	Sword, Jennie	3y	W	18 JUN 1914	Brentwood MD	Congressional
09022	Swords, Charles Lee	42y	W	8 JAN 1913	New York NY	Glenwood
00777	Swormsteed, Samuel L.	54y	W	5 DEC 1891	Troy NY	Rock Creek
15243	Sykes, Allen	59y	C	21 OCT 1918	Cedar Hts. MD	Woodlawn
13873	Sykes, Tamer	69y	C	17 DEC 1916	New York NY	Payne's
18433	Sylvester, John McFall, Jr.	8y	W	20 MAR 1923	Fountain Hill PA	Rock Creek
05527	Symes, William	55y	C	9 APR 1906	New York NY	Harmony
00900	Symington, Julia J.	44y	W	10 AUG 1892	Chesapeake VA	Mt. Olivet
17771	Syphax, Bertha E.	57y	C	31 MAR 1922	New York NY	Harmony
05121	Sypher, Hale	67y	W	9 MAY 1905	Baltimore MD	Arlington VA
01200	Sypherd, Elizabeth A.I	57y	W	31 MAY 1892	Ballston VA	Oak Hill

District of Columbia Foreign Death Records, 1888-1923

No.	Name of Deceased	Age	Race	Death Date	Place of Death	Place of Burial
	T					
05632	Tabbs, Benjamin	65y	C	9 JUL 1906	E. Riverdale MD	Mt. Olivet
02737	Tabbs, Margaret	55y	C	6 FEB 1899	Hyattsville MD	Mt. Olivet
00295	Taber, Mercy D.	80y	W	20 MAR 1890	Monroe Co. NY	Glenwood
12003	Tabler, Charles H.	3y	W	15 SEP 1913	Ballston VA	Congressional
07654	Tabler, Mary E.	3y	W	27 JUL 1910	Seabrook MD	Congressional
17295	Taff, George	72y	W	10 JUL 1921	New York NY	Oak Hill
06493	Taft, Mary Jane	75y	W	5 APR 1908	Oxon Hill MD	Congressional
00778	Taggart, Catherine A.	63y	W	5 NOV 1891	New Bruns. NJ	Congressional
07712	Taggart, Courtney B.	23y	W	24 AUG 1910	Colonial Bea. VA	Rock Creek
09154	Tailof, Ivan	78y	W	31 MAR 1913	New York NY	Arlington
03099	Tait, William R.	49y	W	4 FEB 1900	Hyattsville MD	Glenwood
13417	Talbert, Annie Eliza	62y	W	18 MAR 1916	Rosecroft MD	Congressional
16883	Talbert, Basil H.	69y	W	1 JAN 1921	Glendale MD	Congressional
07930	Talbert, George Washington	71y	W	19 JAN 1911	Greensboro NC	Congressional
17143	Talbert, Helen Louise, d/o S.	21y	W	6 MAY 1921	Purcellville VA	Rock Creek
17649	Talbert, Jonathan Perkins	73y	W	20 JAN 1922	Oxon Hill MD	Congressional
08506	Talbott, Arthur	2y	W	6 FEB 1912	Burnt Mills MD	Rock Creek
18311	Talbott, Laura Asborn	83y	W	1 FEB 1923	Forest Glen MD	Cremated
18059	Talbutt, Benjamin Early	69y	W	10 SEP 1922	Durham NC	Ft. Lincoln
00114	Talcott, Charles G.	28y	W	25 JUL 1889	Brooklyn NY	Oak Hill
07848	Talcott, Robert Barnard	47y	W	4 DEC 1910	Lutherville MD	Oak Hill
02742	Taliaferro, Mary	45y	C	11 FEB 1899	Cleveland OH	Harmony
0040	Taliaferro, Thomas	35y	C	15 MAR 1889	Englewood IL	Harmony
03098	Tallmadge, Flora M.	31y	W	13 FEB 1900	Falls Church VA	Rock Creek
08695	Talman, Jessica M.	72y	W	29 JUN 1912	Laurel MD	Arlington
04426	Talty, Albert M.	27y	W	29 AUG 1903	Columbia TN	Oak Hill
13129	Talty, David, s/o Marshall	69y	W	30 SEP 1915	Atlantic City NJ	Mt. Olivet
04492	Talty, Infant of A.M.	SB	W	15 OCT 1902	Columbia TN	Oak Hill
14025	Tancil, Isaac	48y	C	8 MAR 1917	Philadelphia PA	Woodlawn
08351	Tanner, Helen J.	67y	W	8 OCT 1911	Brooklyn NY	Rock Creek
04627	Tanner, John	41y	W	6 MAR 1904	New York NY	Mt. Olivet
05626	Tanner, Mrs. James	62y	W	29 JUN 1906	Helena MT	Arlington VA
12873	Tanner, William Jay	39y	W	12 APR 1915	Takoma Park MD	Collingwood NJ
02885	Tappan, Blanche	35d	W	15 JUL 1899	Hyattsville MD	Glenwood
03201	Tappan, Robert	3y	W	19 APR 1859	Brooklyn NY	Rock Creek
14224	Tappe, Marie G.	17y	C	9 JUL 1917	Wilmington DE	Woodlawn
14380	Tappe, William	45y	C	26 SEP 1917	Wilmington DE	Woodlawn
15220	Tappen, Hiram	24y	W	9 OCT 1918	Pensacola FL	Glenwood
03643	Tardy, William	37y	C	13 SEP 1901	New York NY	Payne's
14077	Tasch, Mary	73y	W	10 APR 1917	Loyd's Sta. MD	Evansville MD
05252	Tashof, Jacob	38y	W	20 AUG 1905	Suffolk Co. NY	Adas Israel
16182	Tashof, Sarah	56y	W	1 JAN 1920	Morristown NJ	Adas Israel
18520	Tasker, Augusta Maria	80y	W	2 MAY 1923	Takoma Park MD	Glenwood
05804	Tasker, C.V.	36y	W	3 NOV 1906	Ohio River	Chaney MD
16923	Tate, Ruth	7y	C	14 JAN 1921	Pittsburgh PA	Woodlawn
14403	Taube, Lillian H. (Hart)	68y	W	9 OCT 1917	Richmond VA	Cremated
02180	Tauberschmidt, Leonard	39y	W	10 APR 1897	Scottville MI	Prospect Hill
17352	Taulelle, Auguste Frederick	75y	W	10 AUG 1921	Falls Church VA	Mt. Olivet
05022	Tavenner, Bessie	18y	W	7 FEB 1905	Lancaster PA	Rock Creek
05417	Tavenner, L.E., Mrs.	47y	W	20 SEP 1901	Bainbridge PA	Rock Creek
00326	Taylor, Albertine M.	41y	W	10 MAY 1890	Little Rock AR	Oak Hill
01091	Taylor, Alice E.	51y	W	3 FEB 1893	Baltimore MD	Congressional
12349	Taylor, Allen	11y	W	6 MAY 1914	Baltimore MD	Mt. Olivet
12134	Taylor, Allison R.	33y	C	23 DEC 1913	New York NY	Harmony
07282	Taylor, Andrew Bryson	26y	W	22 NOV 1909	Wilmington DE	Cremated
03815	Taylor, Anna	53y	C	9 MAR 1902	Chicago IL	Harmony
08553	Taylor, Annie	19y	C	1 MAR 1912	Chicago IL	Mt. Zion West
02576	Taylor, Annie	18y	C	26 AUG 1898	Baltimore MD	Payne's

No.	Name of Deceased	Age	Race	Death Date	Place of Death	Place of Burial
02393	Taylor, Annie E.	59y	W	31 JAN 1898	Pr. Geo. Co. MD	Glenwood
11878	Taylor, Arman D.	27y	C	5 JUL 1913	Shade PA	Harmony
01092	Taylor, Asher Clayton	12y	W	7 MAR 1893	Billerica MA	Mt. Olivet
14837	Taylor, Benjamin C.	48y	W	22 MAY 1918	New York NY	Rock Creek
18171	Taylor, Betty Lee	2d	W	21 NOV 1922	Takoma Park MD	Rock Creek
05780	Taylor, Carl W.	23y	W	15 OCT 1906	Liberty NY	Arlington
15757	Taylor, Charles F.	73y	W	28 APR 1919	Laurel MD	Fairfax C.H. VA
06573	Taylor, Charles H.	36y	C	30 MAY 1908	Philadelphia PA	Harmony
15467	Taylor, Christopher C.	72y	C	20 DEC 1918	Baltimore MD	Mt. Olivet
05162	Taylor, Daniel W.	66y	W	6 JUN 1905	New York NY	Rock Creek
06533	Taylor, Ednor	7y	W	4 MAY 1908	Rockville MD	Tenallytown
03242	Taylor, Elizabeth	75y	W	21 JUL 1900	Saratoga Spg. NY	Glenwood
00279	Taylor, Ellen Barry	1m	W	10 FEB 1890	Ft. Warren MA	Mt. Olivet
01510	Taylor, Ellen H.	42y	C	14 OCT 1894	Philadelphia PA	Baptist
05110	Taylor, Emma Pearl	18y	W	2 MAY 1905	Silver Hill MD	Congressional
13740	Taylor, Fanney	60y	C	29 SEP 1916	Dupont Hts. MD	Payne's
03325	Taylor, Frank Walker	4m	W	10 NOV 1900	Baltimore MD	Congressional
07488	Taylor, Frederick McGuire	3y	W	1 APR 1910	Chevy Chase MD	Rock Creek
18223	Taylor, Hannis	71y	W	26 DEC 1922	Takoma MD	Rock Creek
01418	Taylor, Henry	31y	W	11 DEC 1828	W. Springfield MA	Oak Hill
04817	Taylor, Henry Clay	59y	W	26 JUL 1904	Copper Cliffe CA	Arlington VA
04992	Taylor, Hiram C.	36y	W	6 JAN 1905	Allentown PA	Glenwood
16733	Taylor, James	47y	C	28 SEP 1920	Washington DC	Payne's
00999	Taylor, James DeWilton	26y	W	12 AUG 1893	Philadelphia PA	Mt. Olivet
18096	Taylor, James J.	54y	W	30 SEP 1922	Glymont MD	Congressional
15223	Taylor, John H.	24y	W	15 OCT 1918	Camp Jackson SC	Arlington
13158	Taylor, John S.	76y	W	20 OCT 1915	Occuquan VA	Arlington
01417	Taylor, Joseph	7m	W	1 JUL 1894	Manassas VA	Mt. Olivet
17083	Taylor, Joseph E.	19y	W	2 APR 1921	Capitol Hts. MD	Congressional
02344	Taylor, Julia	54y	W	22 OCT 1897	Mt. Vernon NY	Mt. Olivet
18054	Taylor, Julia M.	50y	C	6 SEP 1922	Philadelphia PA	Woodlawn
09006	Taylor, Juliet Watson H.	44y	W	15 DEC 1912	Los Angeles CA	Arlington VA
04886	Taylor, Louis Walls	6m	W	11 SEP 1904	Silver Hill MD	Congressional
16628	Taylor, Louise	40y	C	24 JUL 1920	Dartmouth MA	Harmony
14647	Taylor, Maggie	40y	—	17 FEB 1918	Pittsburgh PA	Orange VA
14359	Taylor, Margaret	49y	W	13 SEP 1917	Staunton VA	Falls Church VA
12022	Taylor, Margaret A.	76y	W	28 SEP 1913	Hutchinson KS	Arlington
05789	Taylor, Martha V.	80y	W	26 OCT 1906	Hyattsville MD	Glenwood
06470	Taylor, Mary	26y	C	14 MAR 1908	New York NY	Payne's
15584	Taylor, Mary E.	63y	W	23 JAN 1919	Cherrydale VA	Congressional
14940	Taylor, Mary E.	59y	W	23 JUL 1918	Wilmington DE	Harmony
13717	Taylor, Mary Eliza	65y	C	12 SEP 1916	Halls Hill VA	Harmony
12663	Taylor, May Ellen	80y	W	18 DEC 1914	Ft. Barrancas FL	Rock Creek
15603	Taylor, Millie	62y	C	5 FEB 1919	New York NY	Leesburg VA
18052	Taylor, Rachel Wick	92y	W	6 SEP 1922	McLean VA	Youngstown OH
16637	Taylor, Samuel A.	44y	W	31 JUL 1920	Johnson City TN	Arlington
00901	Taylor, Samuel W.	60y	W	1 AUG 1892	New York NY	Mt. Olivet
06368	Taylor, Sarah M.	73y	W	31 DEC 1907	Cumberland MD	Congressional
12640	Taylor, Susie	55y	C	30 NOV 1914	Pittsburgh PA	Payne's
05355	Taylor, T.B.	71y	W	10 NOV 1905	Cumberland MD	Congressional
16388	Taylor, Thomas Corwin	c.66y	W	16 MAR 1920	Rockville MD	Cambridge OH
06325	Taylor, Thomas H.	55y	W	24 NOV 1907	Hampton Rds. VA	Congressional
06434	Taylor, Thos. T.	—	W	15 FEB 1908	Lake Charles LA	Arlington
00106	Taylor, Walter	28y	W	15 JUL 1889	Elkton MD	Harmony
14251	Taylor, William A.	49y	W	23 JUL 1917	New York NY	Harmony
12026	Taylor, William D.	15y	C	30 SEP 1913	Cumberland MD	Payne's
16407	Taylor, William M.	25y	W	20 MAR 1920	Adams CO	Congressional
00428	Taylor, William W.	39y	C	31 OCT 1890	Jersey City NJ	Harmony
17110	Taylor, Zebulon Vane	52y	W	18 APR 1921	Railroad	Greensboro NC
08556	Tayman, James H., s/o Sam.	64y	W	14 MAR 1912	Ft. Myer Hts. VA	Rock Creek

No.	Name of Deceased	Age	Race	Death Date	Place of Death	Place of Burial
06579	Teachum, W.B.	10m	W	8 JUN 1908	Cedartown GA	Congressional
02102	Teanor, William John	1y	W	19 SEP 1896	Pottsville PA	Mt. Olivet
01093	Teasdale, Sidney F.	77y	W	23 MAR 1893	Dubois PA	Glenwood
07369	Tebbs, William	40y	C	11 JAN 1910	Philadelphia PA	Payne's
13820	Teiling, Charles J.	72y	W	22 NOV 1916	Roanoke VA	Congressional
02224	Temple, Betram	24y	W	18 MAY 1897	Montreal, Can.	Rock Creek
00779	Temple, Edward	57y	W	1 MAR 1892	Norfolk VA	Congressional
05700	Temple, Gertrude	1y	C	21 AUG 1906	Rosslyn VA	Baptist
13924	Temple, William Chase	54y	W	9 JAN 1917	Winter Park FL	Cremated
07243	Templeton, Charles	17y	C	18 OCT 1909	Philadelphia PA	Rockville MD
07688	Tenley, Charles M.	79y	W	13 AUG 1910	Worcester MA	Glenwood
05563	Tennant, Alexandria	58y	W	2 MAY 1906	E. Hyattsville MD	Holyrood
00667	Tennant, Douglas J.	26y	W	5 JUL 1891	Danville VA	Mt. Olivet
03453	Tenney, Jennie	35y	C	13 MAR 1901	New York NY	Harmony
06216	Tennyson, Rosa Belle	30y	C	3 SEP 1907	Kalamazoo MI	Lynchburg VA
17101	Teraci, Anthony	69y	W	10 APR 1921	Rushville MD	St. Mary's
12172	Terneax, August	50y	W	18 JAN 1914	Norfolk VA	St. Mary's
13462	Terrell, Georgia	31y	C	14 APR 1916	Petersburg VA	Union
04926	Terrell, June Beatrice	5y	C	20 OCT 1904	Rosslyn VA	Baptist
17871	Terrell, Nell Winslow	75y	W	21 MAY 1922	Syracuse NY	Rock Creek
07842	Terrell, Tolliver, s/o Jacob	50y	C	26 NOV 1910	Rosslyn VA	Baptist
12421	Terrill, Elizabteh Loretta	55y	W	3 JUL 1914	Chevy Chase MD	Dayton OH
16773	Terville, Gladys Mayme	38y	W	21 OCT 1920	New York NY	Rock Creek
04085	Tesk, Mamie	1y	W	20 OCT 1902	Chillum MD	Rock Creek
08152	Test, Alice Power	43y	W	19 JUN 1911	Hyattsville MD	Congressional
18030	Test, Julia C. (Ellis)	79y	W	22 AUG 1922	LaPorte IN	Congressional
00411	Thames, Amy	55y	C	4 OCT 1889	Philadelphia PA	Harmony
06252	Tharp, Henry Paul	36y	W	27 SEP 1907	Mt. Clemens MI	Mt. Olivet
03437	Tharp, James	72y	W	27 FEB 1901	Hot Springs AR	Mt. Olivet
01094	Thatcher, J. Markley	2y	W	11 AUG 1855	Philadelphia PA	Oak Hill
04153	Thaw, Charles	65y	W	14 JAN 1903	New York NY	Rock Creek
18423	Thaw, Elizabeth S.	84y	W	14 MAR 1923	Manhattan NY	Rock Creek
17065	Thayer, Mrs. J.G.	40y	W	26 MAR 1921	Hansford WV	Rock Creek
16185	Theikuhl, Gustave	57y	W	2 JAN 1920	New York NY	Prospect Hill
15482	Therin, Robert Symmes	87y	W	27 DEC 1918	Takoma Park MD	Glenwood
15303	Thiebolt, Marie A.	24y	W	29 OCT 1918	Ft. Myer Hts. VA	Mt. Olivet
08608	Thiel, Harry	29y	W	20 APR 1912	Baltimore MD	Prospect Hill
08180	Thomas, Addie, d/o Henry	18y	C	2 JUL 1911	King Geo. Co. VA	Payne's
18483	Thomas, Addie Rebecca A.	17y	C	12 APR 1923	Crownsville MD	Chapel Hill
11849	Thomas, Albert G.	63y	W	8 JUN 1913	Ballston VA	Oak Hill
04538	Thomas, Alfred	87y	W	11 dEC 1903	Chicago IL	Congressional
12077	Thomas, Amanda G.	80y	W	31 OCT 1913	Mason NV	Rock Creek
16729	Thomas, Benjamin	—	C	27 SEP 1920	Fairmont Hts. MD	Woodlawn
02181	Thomas, Catharine	66y	C	8 APR 1897	Chillum MD	Harmony
04356	Thomas, Catharine	40y	C	7 AUG 1903	Philadelphia PA	Payne's
13975	Thomas, Catherine E.	60y	W	7 FEB 1917	Springfield OH	Glenwood
16815	Thomas, Charles	54y	W	17 NOV 1920	Philadelphia PA	Payne's
12621	Thomas, Clarissa	26y	W	16 NOV 1914	Chipley FL	Oakton VA
05535	Thomas, David R.	13m	C	12 APR 1906	Philadelphia PA	Harmony
07782	Thomas, Delia	30y	C	7 OCT 1910	New York NY	Mt. Olivet
14474	Thomas, Denziloe A.	19y	W	21 NOV 1917	Lynchburg VA	Rock Creek
08349	Thomas, Earle D., Jr.	33y	W	8 MAR 1910	Colo. Spgs. CO	Arlington
12549	Thomas, Earnest, s/o Jos.	26y	C	29 SEP 1914	Mt. Holly NJ	Marshall Hall MD
03295	Thomas, Edith B.	32y	W	2 OCT 1900	Georgetown SC	Congressional
00062	Thomas, Edward	71y	W	20 APR 1889	Baltimore MD	Glenwood
13218	Thomas, Eleanor	72y	C	24 NOV 1915	Baltimore MD	Mt. Olivet
04024	Thomas, Elizabeth	50y	W	2 SEP 1902	Laurel MD	Mt. Olivet
17786	Thomas, Elmer P.	8y	C	7 APR 1922	Brentwood MD	Payne's
06687	Thomas, Emma Roslea	38y	C	12 AUG 1908	Del. Wat. Gap PA	Mt. Olivet
15655	Thomas, Evelyn A.	2m	W	4 MAR 1919	Brentwood MD	Glenwood

No.	Name of Deceased	Age	Race	Death Date	Place of Death	Place of Burial
03378	Thomas, Everett R.	26y	W	22 DEC 1900	New York NY	Harmony
01899	Thomas, Francis W.	48y	W	31 MAR 1896	Baltimore MD	Congressional
04299	Thomas, Frank	36y	C	31 MAY 1903	Pittsburgh PA	Mt. Olivet
16442	Thomas, Frank	37y	C	15 APR 1920	Philadelphia PA	Payne's
03580	Thomas, George	30y	W	12 JUL 1901	Philadelphia PA	Payne's
03322	Thomas, George, alias	65y	C	6 NOV 1900	Baltimore MD	Payne's
17356	Thomas, George William	26y	C	12 AUG 1921	Philadelphia PA	Payne's
08222	Thomas, Gwendolyn Wilfred	8m	C	27 JUL 1911	Madison Mills VA	Union Baptist
00783	Thomas, Gwenllian	74y	W	7 DEC 1891	Baltimore MD	Congressional
07314	Thomas, Helen	6m	W	10 DEC 1909	Lanham MD	Mt. Olivet
07334	Thomas, Henry Colesberry	77y	W	13 DEC 1909	Colville WA	Rock Creek
00282	Thomas, Hylerary	56y	C	20 FEB 1890	Pr. Geo. Co. MD	Mt. Olivet
00039	Thomas, Isaac L.	49y	W	4 MAR 1889	Takoma Park MD	Rock Creek
17991	Thomas, J. Edwards	50y	W	30 JUL 1922	Dallas TX	Glenwood
12285	Thomas, Jack C.	28y	W	29 MAR 1914	St. Louis MO	Congressional
00668	Thomas, James B.	32y	W	11 AUG 1891	Laurel MD	Congressional
06706½	Thomas, James E., Jr.	4y	W	30 AUG 1908	R.A. Springs VA	Glenwood
12998	Thomas, James E.L.	20y	C	8 JUL 1915	Alex. Co. VA	Payne's
12228	Thomas, Jane	70y	W	19 FEB 1914	Cherrydale VA	Congressional
17922	Thomas, Jane	68y	C	24 JUN 1922	Brentwood MD	Harmony
17760	Thomas, Jennie	54y	C	22 MAR 1922	Atlantic City NJ	Woodlawn
00522	Thomas, Jennie T.	20y	W	26 FEB 1891	Takoma Park MD	Rock Creek
12848	Thomas, Jessica C.	41y	W	31 MAR 1915	Takoma Park MD	Glenwood
12725	Thomas, John E., s/o Wm. H.	52y	C	17 JAN 1915	Burke VA	Harmony
00902	Thomas, John F.	62y	M	11 AUG 1892	New York NY	Graceland
12467	Thomas, John H.	53y	C	1 AUG 1914	Brentwood MD	Harmony
05827	Thomas, John Harper	19y	W	26 NOV 1906	Pittsburgh PA	Rock Creek
02453	Thomas, John L.	44y	W	28 APR 1898	Baltimore MD	Congressional
13135	Thomas, John Perry	66y	W	2 OCT 1915	Brentwood MD	Harmony
09074	Thomas, Joseph Burk	55y	C	12 FEB 1913	Pittsburgh PA	Harmony
04969	Thomas, Leah W.	24y	W	24 NOV 1904	Atlanta GA	Glenwood
13539	Thomas, Lee A., s/o Christ.	50y	W	3 JUN 1916	Lovettsville VA	Congressional
07881	Thomas, Lizzie	2d	C	19 DEC 1910	Brentwood MD	Payne's
05057	Thomas, Lizzie Jane	37y	W	27 FEB 1907	Baltimore MD	Glenwood
08709	Thomas, Lorenzo	75y	W	7 JUL 1912	Hampton VA	Oak Hill
04097	Thomas, Louisa	52y	C	5 NOV 1902	Suitland MD	Mt. Olivet
12716	Thomas, Lucy Ann	73y	W	13 JAN 1915	Baltimore MD	Soldier's Home
14278	Thomas, Mabel	12y	C	5 AUG 1917	Crownsville MD	Woodlawn
04080	Thomas, Maggie	29y	C	5 SEP 1902	Pomonkey MD	Harmony
16679	Thomas, Mamie E.	33y	C	24 AUG 1920	Brentwood MD	Harmony
07559	Thomas, Margaret	59y	W	3 JUN 1910	Baltimore MD	Congressional
02138	Thomas, Margaret	21y	C	10 FEB 1897	Forestville MD	Mt. Olivet
05744	Thomas, Margret A.	74y	C	18 SEP 1906	Pomonkey MD	Mt. Olivet
00333	Thomas, Maria	32y	C	29 MAY 1890	Montg. Co. MD	Brightwood
08294	Thomas, Maria	34y	C	2 SEP 1911	Philadelphia PA	Woodlawn
00189	Thomas, Mary	16y	C	1 OCT 1889	Montg. Co. MD	Tenallytown
07046	Thomas, Mary Eliza (Fisher)	84y	W	31 MAY 1909	Madison WS	Congressional
02357	Thomas, Mary Francis Ann	40y	C	25 DEC 1897	Seabrook MD	Harmony
00781	Thomas, May A.	40y	W	16 JAN 1892	Baltimore MD	Congressional
00903	Thomas, Nellie	8y	W	28 NOV 1882	New Bedford MA	Rock Creek
07080	Thomas, Richard	35y	C	21 JUN 1909	Akron OH	Harmony
08149	Thomas, Richard	51y	C	13 JUN 1911	Pr. Geo. Co. MD	Mt. Olivet
17961	Thomas, Robert	14d	C	17 JUL 1922	Cedar Hts. MD	Payne's
05168	Thomas, Rosalie P.	39y	W	12 JUN 1905	Laurens Co. SC	Barnesville MD
07833	Thomas, Rowland W.	1y	C	18 NOV 1910	Philadelphia PA	Harmony
01601	Thomas, Sarah	58y	C	10 JAN 1895	Newport RI	Harmony
03078	Thomas, William	80y	W	23 JAN 1900	St. Louis MO	Glenwood
12623	Thomas, William Earl	c.2m	W	17 NOV 1914	Falls Church VA	Glenwood
08769	Thomas, Willie Melvin	5m	W	19 AUG 1912	Capitol Hts. MD	Glenwood
03048	Thomas, Winifred J.	67y	W	24 DEC 1899	Baltimore MD	Glenwood

District of Columbia Foreign Death Records, 1888-1923

No.	Name of Deceased	Age	Race	Death Date	Place of Death	Place of Burial
14031	Thomas, Woodrow Wilson	3m	W	17 MAR 1917	Alex. Co. VA	Glenwood
13169	Thomason, Elizabeth B.	81y	W	27 OCT 1915	St. Cath., Can.	Arlington VA
05555	Thomason, Samuel, of Can.	72y	W	24 APR 1906	Hampton VA	Arlington VA
01909	Thompkins, Augusta R.	58y	W	12 APR 1896	Bethlehem PA	Oak Hill
12675	Thompkins, Daniel D., Jr.	2y	W	22 DEC 1912	Cheyenne WY	Congressional
12676	Thompkins, Margaret Grines	10y	W	23 DEC 1912	Cheyenne WY	Congressional
08060	Thompson, Ada A.	61y	W	7 APR 1911	Lowell MA	Arlington
14195	Thompson, Alberta	23y	C	27 JUN 1917	Baltimore MD	Moore's
16358	Thompson, Alvah M.	89y	W	29 FEB 1920	W. Palm Bea. FL	Glenwood
13723	Thompson, Annie T.	23y	W	14 SEP 1916	Luray VA	Mt. Olivet
01201	Thompson, Benjamin F.	15y	W	16 OCT 1892	Fairfax Co. VA	Oak Hill
15308	Thompson, Bernard	27y	W	29 OCT 1918	Pittsburgh PA	Mt. Olivet
12240	Thompson, Bertha	36y	W	26 FEB 1914	Takoma Park MD	Rock Creek
12300	Thompson, Catherine C.	59y	W	8 APR 1914	Takoma Park MD	Rock Creek
06802	Thompson, Charles	33y	C	4 NOV 1908	Pomonkey MD	Mt. Olivet
16132	Thompson, Charles Newton	53y	W	2 DEC 1919	Takoma Park MD	Hamilton VA
12343	Thompson, Delia A.	45y	W	2 MAY 1914	Takoma Park MD	Rock Creek
05463	Thompson, E.L., Mrs.	62y	W	11 FEB 1906	Baltimore Co. MD	Glenwood
14523	Thompson, Edward Milton	45y	W	23 DEC 1917	Savage MD	Congressional
02996	Thompson, Elizabeth M.F.	48y	W	5 NOV 1899	Remington VA	Oak Hill
01379	Thompson, Ella	29y	W	18 MAY 1894	Philadelphia PA	Congressional
07558	Thompson, Ellen B.	7y	W	4 JUN 1910	New York NY	Rock Creek
15534	Thompson, Emma Key	26y	W	8 MAR 1886	Chattanooga TN	Arlington
01920	Thompson, Emma T.	27y	C	2 MAY 1896	Newark NJ	Harmony
13338	Thompson, Erma L.	10m	W	5 FEB 1916	Takoma MD	Rock Creek
02886	Thompson, Etta	63y	W	5 JUL 1899	Lacona NY	Rock Creek
11920	Thompson, Florence W.	29y	W	27 JUL 1913	Norfolk VA	Fairfax C.H. VA
05895	Thompson, Frances A.C.	78y	W	16 JAN 1907	Chevy Chase MD	Zanesville OH
05768	Thompson, Frank	63y	W	13 OCT 1906	Remington VA	Oak Hill
12339	Thompson, Frederick	48y	W	22 APR 1914	San Diego CA	Oak Hill
11970	Thompson, Harrold K.	30y	W	22 AUG 1913	Terra Alta WV	Glenwood
00782	Thompson, Harry Bearniston	41y	W	6 APR 1892	Patuxent Sta. MD	St. Mary's
18544	Thompson, Helen S.	84y	W	13 MAY 1923	Silver Spring MD	Glenwood
16727	Thompson, Howard B.	10y	W	30 MAR 1898	Hagerstown MD	Congressional
18012	Thompson, Hyman	41y	W	13 AUG 1922	Baltimore MD	Elesavetgrad
07650	Thompson, Ida W.	62y	W	23 JUL 1910	Saranac Lake NY	Rock Creek
16656	Thompson, J. Ford	c.52y	W	11 AUG 1920	Emmitsburg MD	Oak Hill
04462	Thompson, J.L.	35y	W	27 SEP 1903	Danville VA	Congressional
07368	Thompson, James	79y	W	13 JAN 1910	Park Lane VA	Glenwood
02520	Thompson, James	81y	W	9 JUL 1898	Philadelphia PA	Glenwood
03131	Thompson, James M.	85y	W	18 MAR 1900	Hampton VA	Arlington
18584	Thompson, Jefferson	57y	C	4 JUN 1923	Capitol Hts. MD	Harmony
01841	Thompson, John	5m	W	13 NOV 1895	Del Ray VA	Congressional
06051	Thompson, John	40y	C	1 MAY 1907	Whipple WV	Woodlawn
00524	Thompson, John D.	65y	W	18 MAR 1891	Baltimore MD	Oak Hill
07345	Thompson, John H.	69y	W	27 DEC 1909	Ballston VA	Holyrood
01202	Thompson, John Horner	8m	W	16 JUN 1892	Burdett MD	Oak Hill
12951	Thompson, Joseph A.	56y	W	2 JUN 1915	Hyattsville MD	Cremated
02123	Thompson, Leigh A.	21y	W	12 JAN 1897	Baltimore MD	Lynchburg VA
06524	Thompson, Lena P.	55y	W	25 APR 1908	Hyattsville MD	Glenwood
18477	Thompson, LeRoy J.	22y	W	13 APR 1923	Lanham MD	Mt. Olivet
06145	Thompson, Lester G.	65y	W	19 JUL 1907	Hyattsville MD	Glenwood
11843	Thompson, Lucy C.	54y	W	4 JUN 1913	Takoma Park MD	Cremated
01287	Thompson, Margaret	55y	W	8 DEC 1893	Flatbush NY	Mt. Olivet
08828	Thompson, Margaret V.	68y	W	4 SEP 1912	Kansas City MO	Congressional
05247	Thompson, Marian	63y	W	17 AUG 1905	Atlantic City NJ	Oak Hill
06475	Thompson, Martha	50y	C	19 MAR 1908	Emory Grove MD	Harmony
07164	Thompson, Marven, Jr.	13m	W	21 AUG 1909	Monterey PA	Rock Creek
02036	Thompson, Mary	52y	C	13 SEP 1896	Saratoga Spg. NY	Harmony
00523	Thompson, Mary A.	57y	W	9 JAN 1891	Baltimore MD	Congressional

No.	Name of Deceased	Age	Race	Death Date	Place of Death	Place of Burial
14104	Thompson, Mary E.	60y	W	25 APR 1917	Ardmore MD	Glenwood
06182	Thompson, Ora A.	5y	W	15 AUG 1907	Rosslyn VA	Congressional
04812	Thompson, Porter M.	23y	W	24 JUL 1904	Colonial Bea. VA	Congressional
15222	Thompson, Raymond	29y	W	15 OCT 1918	Camp Johnson FL	Oak Hill
14791	Thompson, Robert	20y	C	26 APR 1918	St. Louis MO	Harmony
05030	Thompson, Sarah A.	62y	W	12 FEB 1905	Richmond VA	Colesville MD
13146	Thompson, Smith	54y	W	9 OCT 1915	Toronto, Can.	Rock Creek
13983	Thompson, Susan M.S.	72y	W	11 FEB 1917	Ormond Bea. FL	Congressional
12669	Thompson, Walter	30y	C	21 DEC 1914	UVA Hosp. VA	Baltimore MD
06124	Thompson, Walter Harold	4y	C	1 JUL 1907	Stafford VA	Payne's
02027	Thompson, William	62y	W	23 JUL 1896	Silver Spring MD	Glenwood
15936	Thompson, William B.	80y	W	13 AUG 1919	Brooklin ME	Arlington
12893	Thompson, William M.	45y	W	22 APR 1915	Rosslyn VA	Rock Creek
08413	Thompson, William Mills	64y	W	7 DEC 1911	Hyattsville MD	Rock Creek
06307	Thompson, William P.	86y	W	24 JUN 1907	Orange VA	Congressional
05846	Thompson, William S.	47y	W	3 DEC 1906	Aiken SC	Oak Hill
03186	Thompson, Zachariah	26y	W	13 MAY 1900	New York NY	Harmony
16187	Thomsen, Frederick	62y	W	4 JAN 1920	Hyattsville MD	Cremated
12184	Thomson, Edward F.	75y	W	24 JAN 1914	Clarendon VA	Mt. Olivet
05811	Thomson, Eliza B.	74y	W	9 NOV 1906	Baltimore MD	Oak Hill
00784	Thomson, Joseph	69y	W	25 MAR 1892	Gaithersburg MD	Oak Hill
15607	Thomson, Judith Marie	2m	W	10 FEB 1919	Clarendon VA	Mt. Olivet
00780	Thomson, Louise	78y	W	24 JAN 1892	Baltimore MD	Oak Hill
01419	Thomson, Lucie A.	4m	W	8 JUN 1894	Rosslyn VA	Mt. Olivet
02778	Thomson, Wesley D., Dr.	25y	W	8 MAR 1899	New York NY	Rock Creek
05473	Thorn, Charles W.	29y	C	18 FEB 1906	Atlantic City NJ	Harmony
02028	Thorn, Jos. E.	71y	W	5 AUG 1896	Pr. Geo. Co. MD	Oak Hill
06623	Thorn, Joseph E.	37y	C	30 JUN 1908	Atlantic City NJ	Harmony
01000	Thornburg, Mary E.	22y	W	3 SEP 1893	Saulsbury NC	Glenwood
04474	Thornburgh, George Wash.	3y	W	22 FEB 1876	Ft. Steele WY	Arlington VA
04473	Thornburgh, Thomas Tipton	35y	W	29 SEP 1879	Milk Creek CO	Arlington VA
01267	Thornton, Mathilde N.	69y	C	5 DEC 1893	Brooklyn NY	Baptist
14169	Thornton, Rachel	80y	C	10 JUN 1917	Asbury Park NJ	Woodlawn
05570	Thornton, William H.	45y	W	30 MAY 1881	Alexandria VA	Glenwood
05048	Thorpe, Ruby	16y	C	27 FEB 1905	New York NY	Mt. Zion East
04515	Thrasher, Luther A., Capt.	68y	W	15 NOV 1903	Lynchburg VA	Arlington
17073	Thrift, Benjamin	73y	W	26 MAR 1921	Richmond VA	Arlington
17162	Thrift, William	65y	W	15 MAY 1921	Leesburg VA	Rock Creek
12286	Thrift, William H.	66y	W	30 MAR 1914	Hot Springs AR	Arlington
07743	Through, William H.	20y	W	13 SEP 1910	Ft. Myer VA	Cremated
14440	Thurber, Alfred B.	23y	W	2 NOV 1917	Alex. Co. VA	Congressional
13783	Thurber, Ella May	34y	W	28 OCT 1916	Takoma Park MD	Adrian MI
14516	Thurber, William B.	25y	W	19 DEC 1917	Madison Mts. VA	Congressional
02415	Thurston, Martha Lydia	48y	W	14 MAR 1898	Saquon L.G. CA	Omaha NE
06706	Thwing, Alice	46y	W	27 AUG 1908	Old Orchard ME	Rock Creek
15579	Tibbets, Florence M.	30y	W	22 JAN 1919	Rye NY	Rock Creek
06024	Tibbets, Frank J.	c.50y	W	6 APR 1907	Grand Junct. CO	Oak Hill
08372	Tibbs, J.H.	37y	C	23 OCT 1911	Charleston SC	Arlington
04354	Tibbs, William A.	29y	C	3 AUG 1903	Monmouth Co. NJ	Spots. Co. VA
12517	Tice, Nannie B., d/o Henry K.	58y	W	6 SEP 1914	Roanoke VA	Cremated
18039	Tiepe, Elizabeth Ann	68y	W	30 AUG 1922	Takoma Park MD	Rock Creek
01842	Tiernay, Margaret	4y	W	5 JAN 1896	Springfield OH	Mt. Olivet
14062	Tierney, Annie	56y	W	27 MAR 1917	Philadelphia PA	Mt. Olivet
02207	Tierney, Infant of Matthew	3d	W	13 JUN 1897	Ft. Wayne IN	Mt. Olivet
01948	Tierney, M. Vincent	6y	W	7 JUN 1896	Hyattsville MD	Oak Hill
05208	Tierney, Matthew	46y	W	11 JUL 1905	Hyattsville MD	Mt. Olivet
03882	Tierney, Michael V.	44y	W	20 MAY 1902	Baltimore MD	Mt. Olivet
00904	Tiers, Mary	26y	W	18 AUG 1892	Harpers Ferry WV	Rock Creek
04582	Tiffany, Jennie C.	53y	W	24 JAN 1904	Oneida Castle NY	Rock Creek
13201	Tiffey, Sarah E.	69y	W	13 NOV 1915	Laurel MD	Oak Hill

No.	Name of Deceased	Age	Race	Death Date	Place of Death	Place of Burial
07890	Tignor, Ethel C.	2y	C	23 DEC 1910	Ft. Myer Hts. VA	Harmony
07770	Tignor, Ethel L. (Williams)	25y	C	28 SEP 1910	Ft. Myer Hts. VA	Harmony
18320	Tilford, Cornelis Van Ness	84y	W	2 FEB 1923	Hartford CN	Arlington
05051	Tilghman, Beulah B.	7m	C	6 MAR 1905	Philadelphia PA	Harmony
06550	Tilghman, Charles	73y	C	13 MAY 1908	Pittsburgh PA	Mt. Zion East
01773	Tilghman, Henry E.	45y	C	29 JUN 1895	New York NY	Harmony
06769	Tilghman, Leticia	50y	C	12 OCT 1908	Forestville MD	Mt. Olivet
09111	Tilghman, Michael	92y	C	8 MAR 1913	Suitland MD	Mt. Olivet
17064	Tillett, Mrs. Percy I.	21y	W	25 MAR 1921	Alexandria VA	Congressional
02416	Tilley, Mary Jane	74y	W	24 FEB 1898	Mt. Hope MD	Congressional
07588	Tillman, Charles	39y	C	18 JUN 1910	Philadelphia PA	Harmony
18026	Tillman, Hilleary	21y	C	21 AUG 1922	Atlanta GA	Rosemont
07568	Tillman, James A.	33y	C	10 JUN 1910	Pittsburgh PA	Mt. Olivet
01383	Tilp, Charles, baker	32y	W	12 MAY 1894	Philadelphia PA	Prospect Hill
05112	Tilton, Frances M.	37y	W	2 MAY 1905	Hammonton NJ	Oak Hill
05607	Tilton, Henry R.	70y	W	25 JUN 1906	Sacketts Har. NY	Arlington
03454	Tilton, Katharine	2y	W	25 FEB 1901	Wayne PA	Oak Hill
12855	Tilton, Warren C.	60y	W	30 MAR 1915	Atlantic City NJ	Oak Hill
00785	Timby, Charlotte M.	58y	W	15 MAY 1876	N. Tarrytown NY	Oak Hill
08353	Timby, Theodore R.	90y	W	9 NOV 1909	Brooklyn NY	Oak Hill
14341	Timko, Stanley Lincoln	6m	W	6 SEP 1917	Mt. Ranier MD	Glenwood
17942	Tindall, Helen Rand	71y	W	7 JUL 1922	Boone MD	Cremated
06871	Tinkler, Clara Lewis	50y	W	28 DEC 1908	Colonial Bea. VA	Glenwood
13841	Tinsley, John	49y	C	29 NOV 1916	Baltimore MD	Payne's
12258	Tippett, Edith Louise	4y	W	15 MAR 1914	Baltimore MD	Glenwood
14166	Tippett, Thomas	3y	W	7 JUN 1917	Baltimore MD	Glenwood
03540	Tippetts, Goldie	5m	W	13 JUN 1901	Arlington VA	Congressional
08156	Tisdel, Willard P.	76y	W	21 JUN 1911	Laurel MD	Rock Creek
07055	Tise, George	70y	W	9 JUN 1909	Hyattsville MD	Glenwood
00343	Tise, George	70y	W	17 JUN 1890	Hyattsville MD	Glenwood
17332	Tise, Rachel A.	75y	W	28 JUL 1921	Hyattsville MD	Glenwood
17719	Titcomb, Anna C.E.	37y	W	2 MAR 1922	Mt. Ida VA	Ft. Lincoln
05080	Titus, Ruth L.	1m	W	10 APR 1905	Somerset Hts. MD	Tenallytown
14228	Titus, Susie	39y	C	15 JUL 1917	Winchester VA	Woodlawn
16491	Tobin, Ellen T.	73y	W	17 MAY 1920	Mt. Ranier MD	Holyrood
02933	Tobin, Eugene T.	18m	W	4 SEP 1899	Haymarket VA	Holyrood
03749	Tobin, John W.	11m	W	3 JAN 1902	Riggs Mill MD	Holyrood
06447	Todd, Arabella	60y	W	23 FEB 1908	Chester PA	Rock Creek
00280	Todd, Robert S.	46y	W	8 FEB 1890	Mt. Vernon KY	Rock Creek
06134	Todelinger, Mary E.	26y	W	9 JUL 1907	Durham NC	Payne's
04324	Toense, William	33y	W	11 JUN 1903	Buffalo NY	Prospect Hill
18509	Tokes, Hilda E. Moore	20y	C	25 APR 1923	Ednor MD	Harmony
16677	Tokus, Leonard	26y	C	20 AUG 1920	Cleveland OH	Harmony
08006	Toler, Sarah (Barker)	90y	C	15 MAR 1911	Rosslyn VA	Mt. Zion West
12103	Toliver, Isaac, Rev.	56y	C	17 NOV 1913	Birmingham AL	Harmony
07750	Toliver, Leroy	27y	C	19 SEP 1910	Philadelphia PA	Harmony
07576	Toliver, Mary	45y	C	15 JUN 1910	Harpers Ferry WV	Woodlawn
08000	Tolliver, James	30y	C	9 MAR 1911	Philadelphia PA	Harmony
16084	Tolliver, Rowena	2y	C	30 OCT 1919	Baltimore MD	Union Baptist
15888	Tolliver, Susan	45y	C	21 JUL 1919	New York NY	Mt. Zion West
12327	Tolman, Albert J.	67y	W	22 APR 1914	Barcroft VA	Cremated
03886	Tolson, Ada Speiden	52y	W	23 MAY 1902	Forest Glen MD	Congressional
02893	Tolson, Arthur	62y	W	22 JUL 1899	Bright Seat MD	Congressional
07578	Tolson, Edward C.	8m	C	17 JUN 1910	Dupont Hts. MD	Payne's
01363	Tolson, Francis, farmer	66y	W	29 MAR 1894	Weston Farm MD	Congressional
05198	Tolson, Helen	7m	W	7 JUL 1905	Lavis VA	Congressional
02598	Tolson, Roy S.	20y	W	10 SEP 1898	Baltimore MD	Congressional
12630	Tolson, Virginia C.	75y	W	20 NOV 1914	New York NY	Congressional
13655	Tomlin, Catharine	4m	W	11 AUG 1916	Montg. Co. MD	Cremated
13712	Tomlinson, Edith F. (Larcombe)	39y	W	11 SEP 1916	Atlantic City NJ	Glenwood

No.	Name of Deceased	Age	Race	Death Date	Place of Death	Place of Burial
15016	Tomlinson, John Wilder	23y	W	11 SEP 1918	San Antonio TX	Arlington
01431	Tomlinson, T. Arthur	29y	W	9 JUL 1894	Little Rock AR	Glenwood
18533	Tomlinson, William H.	74y	W	8 MAY 1923	Takoma Park MD	Glenwood
13117	Tompkins, Grace G.	35y	W	18 SEP 1915	San Francisco CA	Congressional
04122	Toner, Edward T.	40y	W	4 DEC 1902	Chicago IL	Congressional
15128	Toney, Henry P.	29y	W	24 SEP 1918	At Sea	Arlington
16501	Tongue, Mary Murray	84y	W	24 MAY 1920	Baltimore MD	Rock Creek
06309	Tonlon, Mathew H.	69y	W	14 NOV 1907	Maryland Pk. MD	Soldier's Home
15294	Toomey, Dennis J.	2y	W	26 OCT 1918	E. Hyattsville MD	Mt. Olivet
16439	Toomey, Florence T.	53y	W	15 APR 1920	Philadelphia PA	Mt. Olivet
15295	Toomey, Nora	4y	W	26 OCT 1918	E. Hyattsville MD	Mt. Olivet
17465	Topoloff, Harry	c.23y	W	4 OCT 1918	France	Talmud Torah
15517	Topp, Josephine	17m	W	4 JAN 1919	Arlington VA	Rock Creek
15989	Toppen, Helen Elizabeth	62y	C	10 SEP 1919	Atlantic City NJ	Harmony
13419	Torbert, Mary Elizabeth	72y	W	20 MAR 1916	Chevy Chase MD	Rock Creek
04483	Torrance, Gabrielle	34y	W	23 OCT 1903	Railroad	Baltimore MD
15826	Torrance, Thomas M.	36y	W	10 JUN 1919	Oteen NC	Arlington
07367	Torrens, Emeline R.	37y	W	4 DEC 1909	Brooklyn NY	Congressional
03730	Torrens, Joseph	30y	W	12 DEC 1901	New York NY	Congressional
03775	Torrey, Hannah M.	77y	W	30 JAN 1902	Weymouth MA	Congressional
01658	Tourney, Francis	46y	W	14 MAR 1895	Asheville NC	Mt. Olivet
07730	Tourney, Leonard S.	20y	C	3 SEP 1910	Clark's Place VA	Holyrood
04932	Toury, Anna E.S.	61y	W	24 OCT 1904	Baltimore MD	Mt. Olivet
05308	Toury, William P.	64y	W	3 OCT 1905	Baltimore MD	Mt. Olivet
16969	Toussaint, O.H.	64y	W	6 FEB 1921	Wichita Falls TX	Cremated
15615	Towers, Agnes Va. (Irving)	81y	W	13 FEB 1919	Passaic NJ	Glenwood
00115	Towers, Blanchard Moore	9m	W	4 JUL 1889	Sligo MD	Oak Hill
12942	Towers, David I.	54y	W	26 MAY 1915	New York NY	Glenwood
02139	Towers, Infant of David J.	3h	W	5 FEB 1897	Chevy Chase MD	Glenwood
07999	Towers, James E.	73y	W	6 MAR 1911	St. Louis MO	Glenwood
15533	Towers, Julia F.	76y	W	8 JAN 1919	Takoma Park MD	Congressional
04888	Towers, William H.	70y	W	11 SEP 1904	Richmond Hill NY	Glenwood
05610	Towles, Mary E.	55y	W	26 JUN 1906	Charlottesville VA	Glenwood
04244	Towles, Susie L.	23y	C	6 APR 1903	Philadelphia PA	Payne's
00786	Towles, Therriett	1y	W	16 APR 1892	Albemarle Co. VA	Glenwood
01268	Towles, William B., Dr.	45y	W	15 SEP 1893	Albemarle Co. VA	Glenwood
05656	Town, Infant of Frederick	SB	W	21 JUL 1906	New York NY	Oak Hill
05996	Town, John B.	72y	W	23 JAN 1907	Pittsburgh PA	Congressional
16176	Towne, Hattie W.	38y	W	29 DEC 1919	Baltimore MD	Congressional
02225	Towne, Herbert L., Dr.	27y	W	3 JUN 1897	Galveston TX	Rock Creek
16538	Townes, Mary	75y	C	15 JUN 1920	New York NY	Harmony
07589	Towns, Williams	60y	C	21 JUN 1910	New York NY	Harmony
02631	Townsend, Mary W.	54y	W	18 JAN 1893	Ft. Leavenw. KS	Arlington VA
03107	Townsend, Rosa	26y	W	25 FEB 1900	Macon GA	Prospect Hill
01001	Townshend, Augusta M.	44y	W	13 JUL 1893	Springfield MA	Rock Creek
05061	Townshend, William J.	45y	W	19 MAR 1905	Philadelphia PA	T.B. MD
02346	Tracy, Cornelia Jenette	65y	W	9 NOV 1897	Lakeland MD	Glenwood
01893	Tracy, H.P.	44y	W	22 MAR 1896	Glendale MD	Congressional
12199	Tracy, John T., s/o William	88y	W	3 FEB 1914	Harrisonburg VA	Oak Hill
11885	Tracy, Margarette R.	1y	W	9 JUL 1913	Clarendon VA	Congressional
12020	Tracy, Mary Ann	—	—	c.1901	—	Oak Hill
12974	Trail, Margaret	24y	W	16 JUN 1915	Roseburg OR	Harpers Ferry WV
16686	Trail, Mary Priscilla	77y	W	30 AUG 1920	Silver Hill MD	Glenwood
16649	Trail, Richard T., s/o Hezekiah	74y	W	9 AUG 1920	Silver Hill MD	Glenwood
07286	Trammell, William T.	35y	W	24 NOV 1909	Sparrows Pt. MD	Arnon Chapel VA
15356	Transtrom, Elizabeth Margret	24h	W	16 NOV 1918	Takoma MD	Rock Creek
12568	Travers, Emily Rebecca	59y	W	15 OCT 1914	Oakland MD	Congressional
01921	Travers, Mary E.	64y	W	26 APR 1896	Laurel MD	Oak Hill
03498	Travers, Sidney	32y	W	5 MAY 1901	Laurel MD	Oak Hill
15289	Travers, William D.	34y	C	24 OCT 1918	Ellwood PA	Moore's

District of Columbia Foreign Death Records, 1888-1923

No.	Name of Deceased	Age	Race	Death Date	Place of Death	Place of Burial
07836	Travis, P.M.B., Maj.	56y	W	18 NOV 1910	Great Bend KS	Arlington VA
12386	Traylor, George A.	62y	W	2 JUN 1914	Philadelphia PA	Congressional
17706	Traynham, Lula Pauline	1m	C	21 FEB 1922	Arlington VA	Rosemont
03650	Treadwell, M.S., Mrs.	29y	W	17 SEP 1901	Atlanta GA	Glenwood
04271	Treadwell, Mary	8m	W	4 APR 1903	Atlanta GA	Glenwood
07629	Treanor, John	68y	W	13 JUL 1910	Las Animos CO	Mt. Olivet
14427	Treanor, Peter E.J.	51y	W	27 OCT 1917	Syracuse NY	Mt. Olivet
06578	Tree, Ellen Fuollerton	69y	W	6 JUN 1908	Atlantic City NJ	Rock Creek
14280	Tree, Frances L.	88y	W	6 AUG 1917	Richmond VA	Glenwood
13697	Tree, Joseph B., s/o Lambert	88y	W	6 SEP 1916	Richmond VA	Glenwood
02763	Trego, John T., hotel prop.	65y	W	9 DEC 1898	Baltimore MD	Rock Creek
08275	Treiber, Fred B.	53y	W	26 AUG 1911	Charlottesville VA	Glenwood
11945	Trenis, Benjamin	64y	W	7 AUG 1913	Raspeburg MD	Glenwood
06034	Trennel, Elizabeth	65y	W	18 APR 1907	Suitland MD	Congressional
16911	Trent, George	43y	C	6 JAN 1921	Roxbury NY	Harmony
18249	Trent, Hillman	33y	C	2 JAN 1923	Philadelphia PA	Woodlawn
13461	Trescot, Thomas C.	57y	W	14 APR 1916	Ballston VA	Rock Creek
03550	Tretler, Charles E.	63y	W	26 JUN 1901	Hyattsville MD	Glenwood
16385	Tretler, Frank	77y	W	15 MAR 1920	Mt. Ranier MD	Glenwood
06894	Trexler, Anna M.	21y	W	17 JAN 1909	Lewinsville VA	Rock Creek
05405	Trice, Annie	54y	C	19 DEC 1905	Brooklyn NY	Mt. Olivet
02473	Trieber, Belle E.	64y	W	11 MAY 1898	Memphis TN	Glenwood
02226	Trieber, Enest F.	47y	W	12 JUN 1897	Baltimore MD	Prospect Hill
17115	Trieber, John W.	56y	W	16 APR 1921	Albuquerque NM	Glenwood
05075	Trigg, Francis	30y	W	5 APR 1905	Baltimore MD	Mt. Olivet
05215	Trimble, Emily J.	68y	W	21 JUL 1905	Pueblo CO	Oak Hill
01894	Trimble, Jane	69y	W	17 SEP 1849	New York NY	Oak Hill
08121	Trimble, Marjorie Smith	21y	W	17 MAY 1911	York PA	Woodlawn
01895	Trimble, Mathew	68y	W	3 DEC 1837	New York NY	Oak Hill
07877	Trimmer, Louise F.	42y	W	17 DEC 1910	Takoma Park MD	Norfolk VA
05021	Triplett, Emma	25y	C	7 FEB 1905	Rosslyn VA	Baptist
08680	Triplett, Martha	c.75y	C	23 JUN 1912	Hyattsville MD	Harmony
18092	Trippe, Mary K.	85y	W	28 SEP 1922	Berwyn MD	Rock Creek
02474	Troth, Carl E.	9m	W	3 JUN 1898	Linden MD	Rock Creek
12724	Troth, Ezra	70y	W	18 JAN 1915	Burnt Mills MD	Oak Hill
07682	Trotter, Ernest S.	c.21y	C	4 AUG 1910	Indian Head MD	Harmony
08646	Trout, John F.	68y	W	23 MAY 1912	Jersey City NJ	Rock Creek
18220	Troutman, Charles E.	79y	W	22 DEC 1922	Johnson City TN	Arlington
00787	Troutman, Julia T.	45y	W	20 NOV 1891	Chester PA	Congressional
05977	Trueworthy, Jessie N.	38y	W	7 MAR 1907	New York NY	Oak Hill
07439	Truitt, Benjamin P., Rev.	45y	W	1 MAR 1910	Baltimore MD	Congressional
07393	Trumbo, J. Herbert	33y	W	30 JAN 1910	Laurel MD	Arlington
00041	Trumbull, Ann Jane	58y	W	19 MAR 1889	Chicago IL	Glenwood
04513	Trussell, John E.L.	21y	W	2 NOV 1903	Mare Island CA	Arlington VA
15287	Tschefelly, Elizabeth W.	68y	W	26 OCT 1918	Boonboro MD	Oak Hill
00905	Tschiffely, F.A.	76y	W	20 JUL 1892	Darnestown MD	Oak Hill
02565	Tschiffely, Lewin Albert	17y	W	14 AUG 1898	Leesburg VA	Oak Hill
05937	Tubbs, Eva B.	30y	W	10 FEB 1907	Richmond VA	Congressional
15845	Tubia, Angelo	2y	W	24 jUN 1919	Colonial Bea. VA	St. Mary's
18127	Tubman, George W.	89y	W	25 OCT 1922	Landover MD	Congressional
03218	Tucker, Clarence Howe	24y	W	8 MAY 1900	Yonkers NY	Glenwood
05305	Tucker, Eliza	70y	C	2 OCT 1905	Orange NJ	Woodlawn
12460	Tucker, Emeline	43y	C	25 JUL 1914	Occoquan VA	Mt. Zion East
05334	Tucker, George Edwin	14y	W	6 AUG 1905	Manila, P.I.	Soldier's Home
06444	Tucker, George H., soldier	—	W	30 DEC 1907	Pinar d. Rio, Cub.	Arlington
02486	Tucker, George W.	21y	W	31 JUL 1898	Saranac Lake NY	Glenwood
05007	Tucker, Lawrence	7m	C	19 JAN 1905	Rosslyn VA	Holyrood
13187	Tucker, Lillian B. (Moffett)	43y	W	6 NOV 1915	Henrico Co. VA	Rock Creek
08432	Tucker, Logan	33y	W	20 DEC 1911	Gwynedd PA	Soldier's Home
15046	Tucker, Martha F.	58y	W	26 SEP 1918	Brentwood MD	Glenwood

No.	Name of Deceased	Age	Race	Death Date	Place of Death	Place of Burial
03367	Tucker, Mary Anne	65y	W	1 DEC 1900	Paris, France	Oak Hill
07560	Tucker, Mary V.	65y	W	5 JUN 1910	Baltimore MD	Congressional
11960	Tucker, May Barbour	36y	W	14 AUG 1913	Atlantic City NJ	Oak Hill
12355	Tucker, Mortimer H.	68y	W	11 MAY 1914	Occoquan VA	Congressional
00302	Tucker, Susie	22y	C	31 MAR 1890	Chicago IL	Mt. Zion
17326	Tucker, William E.	82y	W	26 JUL 1921	Baltimore MD	Congressional
07824	Tudge, Frederick	15y	W	12 NOV 1910	Silver Hill MD	Congressional
07136	Tudge, William	81y	W	27 JUL 1909	Nonesuch MD	Glenwood
18516	Tuigg, Patrick J., s/o Barth.	62y	W	29 APR 1923	Roanoke VA	Mt. Olivet
14252	Tull, Luigi E., Jr.	10m	W	26 JUL 1917	Del Ray VA	Mt. Olivet
16767	Tumelty, Benedict	77y	W	19 OCT 1920	Baltimore MD	Mt. Olivet
12728	Tung, Tsai C.	31y	H	13 DEC 1914	Asheville NC	San Francisco CA
00562	Tunia, Annie T.	47y	C	22 APR 1891	Brookeville MD	Harmony
02794	Tunia, John (jail)	24y	C	18 APR 1889	Baltimore MD	Harmony
03535	Tuohy, Aloysius G.	45y	W	3 JUN 1901	New York NY	Mt. Olivet
07978	Tuohy, Mike	43y	W	21 FEB 1911	Pr. Geo. Co. MD	Mt. Olivet
13103	Tupper, Charles A.	82y	W	12 SEP 1915	Berwyn MD	Congressional
16927	Turnage, Sarah (Bohannan)	65y	C	19 JAN 1921	Hudson NJ	Harmony
08675	Turnbull, Jeannie, d/o Wm.	70y	W	15 JUN 1912	Newport RI	Oak Hill
14724	Turnburke, Frank	28y	W	27 MAR 1918	Camp Meade MD	Glenwood
14132	Turnburke, Katie	52y	W	8 MAY 1917	Capitol Hts. MD	Glenwood
06541	Turner, Albert	34y	C	5 MAY 1908	Norristown PA	Woodlawn
13310	Turner, Albert B.	45y	C	16 JAN 1916	Chicago IL	Woodlawn
13242	Turner, Allen A.	29y	C	6 DEC 1915	Denver CO	Harmony
03288	Turner, Amanda F.	78y	W	16 SEP 1900	Falls Church VA	Congressional
18495	Turner, Annie L.	46y	C	19 APR 1923	Washington PA	Payne's
05135	Turner, Carrie S.	25y	C	15 MAY 1905	Philadelphia PA	Payne's
18201	Turner, Cornelia	40y	C	1 DEC 1922	New York NY	Rosemont
15413	Turner, Edward	37y	C	6 DEC 1918	Landover MD	Mt. Olivet
05485	Turner, Edward, laborer	86y	C	3 MAR 1906	Alex. Co. VA	Baptist
01603	Turner, Elizabeth Lee	2y	W	12 FEB 1895	Omaha NE	Rock Creek
02806	Turner, Ellen	61y	W	23 MAR 1899	Falls Church VA	Glenwood
17227	Turner, Elzie E.	31y	W	17 OCT 1918	France	Mt. Olivet
17226	Turner, Elzie E.	31y	W	17 OCT 1918	France	Seat Pleasant MD
07762	Turner, Eva J.	63y	W	23 SEP 1910	New York NY	Congressional
02666	Turner, Fanny F.	20y	C	27 NOV 1898	Arlington VA	Baptist
03694	Turner, Frederick	9m	C	25 OCT 1901	Ballston VA	Baptist
02481	Turner, George	1y	W	2 AUG 1898	Bladensburg MD	Glenwood
07232	Turner, George, s/o Hayes W.	1m	C	14 OCT 1909	Clarendon VA	Baptist
01910	Turner, Henry	94y	W	2 APR 1896	Falls Church VA	Congressional
03320	Turner, Jacob J.	61y	W	5 NOV 1900	Mt. Hope MD	Glenwood
17061	Turner, Jane Grant	79y	W	28 DEC 1920	St. Petersburg FL	Cremated
16750	Turner, Jasper C.	60y	W	6 OCT 1920	Cleveland OH	Rock Creek
03542	Turner, Joanna Wilhelmina	78y	W	15 JUN 1901	Phoebus VA	Arlington VA
15906	Turner, John A.	75y	W	31 JUL 1919	Seat Pleasant MD	Mt. Olivet
15282	Turner, John C.	50y	C	23 OCT 1918	New York NY	Congressional
01203	Turner, John E.	58y	W	4 OCT 1892	Sligo MD	Rock Creek
02887	Turner, Josephine	55y	W	24 JUN 1889	Buffalo NY	Glenwood
03208	Turner, Lewis	1y	C	20 JUN 1900	Ballston VA	Baptist
13206	Turner, Lola A.	27y	W	14 NOV 1915	Washington DC	Mt. Olivet
03158	Turner, Lora E.	29y	W	5 APR 1900	Baltimore MD	Congressional
08249	Turner, Maggie	40y	C	6 AUG 1911	Pittsburgh PA	Harmony
15993	Turner, Margaret Alice	64y	W	13 SEP 1919	Mt. Ranier MD	Rock Creek
14155	Turner, Marion Ethel	21y	W	29 MAY 1917	Elmira NY	Congressional
02227	Turner, Mary	1y	W	8 JUN 1897	Seat Pleasant MD	Mt. Olivet
12795	Turner, Mary E.G.	65y	W	4 MAR 1915	Baltimore MD	Rock Creek
04287	Turner, Mildred	51y	C	23 APR 1903	Philadelphia PA	Woodlawn
18347	Turner, Nannie E.	35y	W	14 FEB 1923	Takoma Park MD	Glenwood
02103	Turner, Sarah C.	78y	W	6 OCT 1896	Clifton Sps., Can.	Oak Hill
02394	Turner, Susan W.	92y	W	6 JAN 1898	New York NY	Oak Hill

No.	Name of Deceased	Age	Race	Death Date	Place of Death	Place of Burial
15484	Turner, Thomas Addison	16y	W	30 NOV 1918	Atlanta GA	Rock Creek
04718	Turner, Viola	7y	C	18 MAY 1904	Falls Church VA	Harmony
02345	Turner, Virginia J.	37y	W	11 SEP 1897	Newark NJ	Holyrood
02805	Turner, Weston	64y	W	23 MAR 1899	Falls Church VA	Glenwood
03171	Turner, William	70y	W	23 APR 1900	Bladensburg MD	Glenwood
18448	Turner, William	57y	C	30 MAR 1923	Asbury Park NJ	Harmony
17257	Turner, William, in jail	50y	C	24 JUN 1921	Richmond VA	Odd Fellows VA
01602	Turner, William J.	10y	W	6 JUN 1891	Omaha NE	Rock Creek
03369	Turpin, Harriet E.	33y	W	20 DEC 1900	Bowie MD	Glenwood
01604	Tuttle, LeRoy	73y	W	26 NOV 1894	VA	Rock Creek
07673	Twedale, Wilson	21y	W	5 AUG 1910	Baltimore MD	Wash. Jct. MA
00906	Tweddle, William	75y	W	22 AUG 1892	Baltimore MD	Congressional
16814	Twine, Edward	54y	C	15 NOV 1920	Chicago IL	Harmony
04746	Twitchell, Frances Euphrata	34y	W	1 APR 1904	Baltimore MD	Congressional
05071	Twitchell, Paul T.	2y	W	30 MAR 1905	Cumberland MD	Congressional
12105	Twohey, James A.	43y	W	c.20 NOV 1913	Ottawa, Can.	Mt. Olivet
12422	Twyman, Grace	18y	C	1 JUL 1914	Arlington VA	Odd Fellows VA
00345	Tyler, Albert C.	19y	C	29 JUN 1890	Long Branch NJ	Harmony
01002	Tyler, Albert W.	27y	W	25 MAY 1893	Bannock ID	Oak Hill
05009	Tyler, Alice E.	2y	C	25 JAN 1905	Tuxedo MD	Mt. Olivet
06704	Tyler, Andrew	38y	C	25 AUG 1908	Fairfax Co. VA	Payne's
12817	Tyler, Elizabeth Jane	91y	C	13 MAR 1915	Monessen PA	Harmony
05894	Tyler, George Edward	64y	W	14 JAN 1907	Silver Hill MD	Congressional
01095	Tyler, Henry	50y	C	25 FEB 1893	Suitland MD	Moore's
00263	Tyler, Lavinia S.	82y	W	11 JAN 1890	New York NY	Glenwood
12775	Tyler, Lemuel, a.k.a.	39y	W	27 JAN 1915	Philadelphia PA	Arlington
16111	Tyler, Mary E.	49y	C	16 NOV 1919	Philadelphia PA	Harmony
02683	Tyler, Mary Elizabeth	53y	C	22 DEC 1898	Falls Church VA	Payne's
08020	Tyler, Matilda Geneva	35y	C	21 MAR 1911	Providence RI	Harmony
05344	Tyler, Richard B.	50y	W	2 NOV 1905	Decatur AL	Oak Hill
07115	Tyler, Richard W.	67y	W	19 JUL 1909	Pocono PA	Arlington
09163	Tyler, Samuel	65y	W	9 APR 1913	Decatur AL	Oak Hill
00042	Tyler, W. Bowie	42y	W	6 MAR 1889	Somervill SC	Oak Hill
03783	Tylor, Margaret	27y	C	4 FEB 1902	Pittsburgh PA	Harmony
18316	Tyree, Frank L.	59y	W	30 JAN 1923	Huntington WV	Rock Creek
01659	Tyree, Henrietta	55y	W	23 JUL 1884	Millen GA	Rock Creek
17399	Tyree, Nellie A.	23y	C	12 SEP 1921	Fairfax Co. VA	Harmony
03988	Tyree, Samuel	85y	W	25 AUG 1902	Cranston RI	Rock Creek
18411	Tyrell, Richard M.	78y	W	13 MAR 1923	Baltimore MD	Glenwood
00116	Tyrrell, John F.H.	26y	C	9 JUL 1889	St. Joe MI	Mt. Pleasant[1]
12408	Tyson, William	39y	C	19 JUN 1914	Milford VA	Woodlawn
02574	Tyssouski, Mary G.	26y	W	26 AUG 1898	Jordan VA	Glenwood

---

[1] Disinterment permit #6004, dated 11 APR 1907, for removal to Woodlawn cemetery.

No.	Name of Deceased	Age	Race	Death Date	Place of Death	Place of Burial
U						
09088	Uber, Susan Killen	75y	W	23 FEB 1913	Parksley VA	Arlington
05182	Ucker, Robert Seymour	1y	W	24 JUN 1905	Hamilton VA	Mt. Olivet
08461	Udelewitz, Infant of Howard	SB	W	9 JAN 1912	Capitol Hts. MD	Ohev Sholom
03982	Uhthoff, Margaret G.	22y	W	4 AUG 1902	Herndon VA	Rock Creek
00367	Ulke, Carl	15y	W	24 JUL 1890	Franklin Co. PA	Oak Hill
07436	Ulrich, Henry Charles	63y	W	27 FEB 1910	Sligo MD	Soldier's Home
17387	Umberger, Elizabeth	74y	W	6 SEP 1921	Staunton VA	Glenwood
05930	Umberger, Isaac C., s/o John	54y	W	7 FEB 1907	Clarendon VA	Glenwood
08312	Umberger, John C.	36y	W	15 SEP 1911	Magnolia MD	Glenwood
05441	Umphrey, George Clagett	80y	C	23 JAN 1906	Four Corners MD	Harmony
01843	Unden, Mack, farmer	40y	W	6 DEC 1895	Philadelphia PA	Potters Field
01204	Underwood, Eugene H.	20y	W	12 JUN 1892	Alexandria VA	Glenwood
14938	Unknown, adult male bones	—	W	c.19 JUL 1918	Knox's Run MD	Potters Field
14219	Unknown, found	—	—	5 JUL 1917	Alexandria VA	Potters Field
13691	Unknown Infant	10h	W	31 AUG 1916	Bethesda MD	Cremated
15404	Unknown Male	c.50-60y	W	c.15 OCT 1918	Baltimore MD	Potters Field
00788	Unsworth, M.M., Mrs.	74y	W	1 DEC 1891	Brentsville PA	Rock Creek
12880	Upman, Georgeanna W.	35y	W	16 APR 1915	Livingston Hts. VA	Congressional
14310	Upman, Mary C.	80y	W	22 AUG 1917	Livingston Hts. VA	Cremated
17059	Upperman, Charles H.	66y	W	23 MAR 1921	New York NY	Oak Hill
06410	Upperman, Minerva	45y	W	30 JAN 1908	New York NY	Glenwood
17318	Upperman, William A.	70y	—	22 JUL 1921	Silver Spring MD	Glenwood
02702	Upshaw, Alexander B.	48y	W	7 JAN 1899	New York NY	Oak Hill
16752	Upshur, Custis Parke	68y	W	9 OCT 1920	Norfolk VA	Arlington
14699	Upshur, Julia	55y	W	17 MAR 1918	New York NY	Rock Creek
13662	Upton, Mary DeHaas	71y	W	15 AUG 1916	Annapolis MD	Glenwood
02619	Upton, William W.	26y	W	14 SEP 1898	Warren OH	Oak Hill
08092	Urell, Michael Emmett	66y	W	6 SEP 1910	Cork, Ire.	Arlington
15866	Urquhart, Infant of John	2d	W	6 JUL 1919	Riverdale MD	Mt. Olivet
12807	Urquhart, Robert C., a.k.a.	6y	W	10 MAR 1915	Glen Carlin VA	Oak Hill
14515	Urquhart, William R.	2y	W	21 DEC 1917	Riverdale MD	Mt. Olivet
01605	Usher, John	63y	W	22 FEB 1895	Piney Point MD	Glenwood
17084	Utterback, James L.	66y	W	2 APR 1921	Fairfax Co. VA	Glenwood
18395	Utterback, Thomas F.	4m	W	8 MAR 1923	Rosslyn VA	Rock Creek

District of Columbia Foreign Death Records, 1888-1923

No.	Name of Deceased	Age	Race	Death Date	Place of Death	Place of Burial
V						
05057	Vaden, Frank H.	7m	C	14 MAR 1905	Brentwood MD	Harmony
13078	Vaden, George William	9y	W	26 AUG 1915	Riverdale MD	Glenwood
02097	Vail, Alice Creighton Stevens	45y	W	4 OCT 1896	Lenox MA	Oak Hill
15740	Vail, Benjamin	64y	W	19 APR 1919	Baltimore MD	Congressional
12222	Vail, Ellen	60y	W	15 FEB 1914	Birmingham AL	Congressional
14552	Valeteen, William	59y	C	4 JAN 1918	Baltimore MD	Woodlawn
18335	Valk, James R., s/o Wm. E.	54y	W	9 FEB 1923	Atlanta GA	Owensville MD
13546	Van Antwerp, Jane Caroline	67y	W	29 DEC 1901	Pr. Geo. Co. MD	Rock Creek
03439	Van Branlick, Francis Xavier	75y	W	2 MAR 1901	New York NY	Congressional
16361	Van Casteel, Gerald	47y	W	2 MAR 1920	New York NY	Glenwood
06387	Van Clief, Augustus P.	74y	W	11 JAN 1908	Scranton PA	Arlington VA
17373	Van Demark, Ruth N.	c.30y	C	24 AUG 1921	Kingston NY	Moore's
16195	Van Devanter, Hortense D.	26y	W	7 JAN 1920	Hyattsville MD	Rock Creek
02104	Van Doren, Mary Goodwin	52y	W	26 DEC 1896	Columbus MS	Congressional
15552	Van Doren, Rose	33y	C	8 JAN 1919	New Haven CN	Harmony
17555	Van Duzer, Nellie W.	43y	W	28 NOV 1921	Takoma Park MD	Prospect Hill
17664	Van Fleet, Walter	65y	W	26 JAN 1922	Miami FL	Watsontown PA
07856	Van Horn, Harold Patton	2m	W	7 DEC 1910	Takoma Park MD	Rock Creek
07265	Van Horn, John H.	4y	W	3 NOV 1909	Philadelphia PA	Rock Creek
03032	Van Horn, Reba	39y	W	9 DEC 1899	New York NY	Glenwood
13954	Van Horn, Sarah A.	72y	W	29 JAN 1917	Takoma Park MD	Congressional
14121	Van Kirk, D.R.	28y	W	1 MAY 1917	Pensacola FL	Arlington
16274	Van Matie, Hester L.	65y	W	29 JAN 1920	Portland OR	Rock Creek
04944	Van Ness, W.J.	36y	W	31 OCT 1904	Charlotte NC	Cremated
17486	Van Orsdale, John T.	71y	W	18 OCT 1921	Beverly Hills CA	Arlington
02182	Van Riswick, Eugene	48y	W	24 MAR 1897	Baltimore MD	Congressional
13090	Van Sant, Harry	47y	W	4 SEP 1915	Wash. Grove MD	Arlington
14871	Van Sickler, Mary E.	45y	W	20 JUN 1918	Dunn Loring VA	Oak Hill
15827	Van Sickler, Scott	49y	W	14 JUN 1919	McLean VA	Oak Hill
13929	Van Valen, Florence	66y	W	14 JAN 1917	Philadelphia PA	Alexandria VA
13551	Van Vleck, Florence Noyes	55y	W	8 JUN 1916	Linden MD	Glenwood
05717	Van Vlick, Anna	60y	W	13 AUG 1906	Seattle WA	Glenwood
17123	Van Wildinberg, John D., Rev.	58y	W	24 APR 1921	Philadelphia PA	Mt. Olivet
12742	Van Zandt, Jane Henry Mer.	85y	W	2 FEB 1915	Arundel Bay MD	Oak Hill
03191	Van Zant, Nicholas H.	78y	W	21 MAY 1900	Havershaw NY	Oak Hill
03747	VanAntwerp, Jane C.	71y	W	29 DEC 1901	New York NY	St. Barnabas MD
03346	VanBoskerck, Caroline	74y	W	20 NOV 1900	Chicago IL	Congressional
08696	Vance, Ida J.	54y	W	30 JUN 1912	Takoma Park MD	Rock Creek
17599	Vance, Joseph	52y	W	16 DEC 1921	Miami FL	Bladensburg MD
06672	Vance, Milton J.	59y	W	5 AUG 1908	Bladensburg MD	Rock Creek
12908	Vancort, David A.	22y	W	3 MAY 1915	Baltimore MD	Congressional
13511	Vandegrift, J. Redwood	79y	W	16 MAY 1916	Forest Glen MD	Rock Creek
15746	Vandenberg, William	56y	W	22 APR 1919	New York NY	Rock Creek
00907	Vandenburgh, John Vanwert	59y	W	12 AUG 1892	Forest Glen MD	Congressional
14216	Vandercook, George	75y	W	4 JUL 1917	Philadelphia PA	Rock Creek
08849	Vanderhoef, Lorenzo	72y	W	16 SEP 1912	Los Angeles CA	Rock Creek
18043	Vandermark, Helen Evelyn	1y	W	14 JUL 1902	Falls Church VA	Glenwood
01333	Vanderwerken, Gilbert	84y	W	22 JAN 1894	Falls Grove VA	Oak Hill
01395	Vanderwerken, Jane	79y	W	12 MAY 1894	Falls Grove VA	Oak Hill
02905	Vandoren, Infant of Theodore	SB	W	9 AUG 1899	Hyattsville MD	Mt. Olivet
04251	VanDusen, Harry	23y	W	15 MAY 1903	Falls Church VA	Lockport NY
03581	Vangender, Martha	7d	W	15 JUL 1901	Riverdale MD	Congressional
16256	Vangender, Wallace	34y	W	27 JAN 1920	Alexandria VA	Congressional
01606	Vanhorn, Florence Lilian	7m	W	21 DEC 1894	Landover MD	Glenwood
03403	VanHoy, Lillian R.	37y	W	24 JAN 1901	Kensington MD	Glenwood
01774	Vansant, Mary A.A.	52y	W	26 JUN 1895	Baltimore MD	Oak Hill
02037	Vansciver, Mary E.	64y	W	24 SEP 1896	Fairfax Co. VA	Oak Hill
03825	VanSicklin, Rose Ann	23y	W	21 MAR 1902	Hartford CN	Congressional

No.	Name of Deceased	Age	Race	Death Date	Place of Death	Place of Burial
14074	Varcoe, Derious	75y	W	5 APR 1917	Falls Church VA	Rock Creek[1]
06998	Varnell, Raymond Mensuneal	1m	W	22 APR 1909	Capitol Hts. MD	Congressional
04105	Vasant, John, M.D., surgeon	71y	W	12 DEC 1902	Charleston SC	Arlington
12958	Vass, Spencer	55y	C	7 JUN 1915	Niagara Falls NY	Falls Church VA
14428	Vaughan, Henry	72y	W	30 JUN 1917	Boston MA	St. Albans[2]
03121	Vaughan, Walter R., Jr.	30y	W	7 MAR 1900	Kansas City MO	Glenwood
02550	Vaughn, Alicia Anna	17y	W	15 AUG 1898	Brooksville ME	Rock Creek
08106	Vaughn, Bertha	39y	C	8 MAY 1911	Philadelphia PA	Harmony
15717	Vaughn, Perry	50y	W	6 APR 1919	Philadelphia PA	Harmony
12048	Veihmeyer, Albert	39y	W	16 OCT 1913	Dickerson MD	Glenwood
03352	Veiolland, Robert Joseph	2m	W	27 NOV 1900	Brentwood MD	Glenwood
06987	Veirs, Laura V.	52y	W	16 APR 1909	Baltimore MD	Oak Hill
12793	Veise, Elizabeth	35y	W	3 MAR 1915	Baltimore MD	Holyrood
13398	Veitch, Annie H.	71y	W	5 MAR 1916	Rives Sta. MD	Veitch Family
02689	Veitch, Clara J.	80y	W	30 DEC 1898	Bladensburg MD	Veitch Family
03854	Veitch, Fletcher	1y	W	26 MAY 1899	Bladensburg MD	Veitch Family
15079	Veitch, Florence	67y	W	3 OCT 1918	Centreville MD	Veitch Family
08422	Veitch, Infant of Fletcher	SB	W	12 DEC 1911	College Park MD	Veitch Family
12004	Veitch, Isabel C.	87y	W	15 SEP 1913	College Park MD	Veitch Family
02706	Veitch, Margaret	78y	W	12 JAN 1899	Rives Sta. MD	Veitch Family
07272	Veitch, Mary Ann	79y	W	13 NOV 1909	College Park MD	Veitch Family
04031	Venable, Charles E.	41y	W	19 OCT 1902	San Francisco CA	Congressional
03585	Venable, Margaret L.	10m	W	20 JUL 1901	Oakland MD	Rock Creek
07843	Venable, Nancy	46y	C	14 OCT 1910	Marion IN	Payne's
18537	Venerzky, Gussie B.	36y	W	9 MAY 1923	Hyattsville MD	Adas Israel
13838	Veney, Jennie	28y	C	2 DEC 1916	Rosslyn VA	Holyrood
06632	Venn, Henry G.	3d	W	6 JUL 1908	New York NY	Rock Creek
03427	Verdi, Nathalie L.S. deS.	38y	W	1 AUG 1899	Florence, Italy	Oak Hill
12698	Vergi, Antonio	c.49y	W	5 JAN 1915	Hyattsville MD	Mt. Olivet
08390	Verleger, Debora	54y	W	10 NOV 1911	Amsterdam NY	Prospect Hill
05928	Verleger, William F.	56y	W	4 FEB 1907	Johnstown NY	Prospect Hill
14181	Vernell, John J.	34y	W	16 JUN 1917	Chicago IL	Holyrood
04625	Vernon, Maria L.	82y	W	8 MAR 1904	Hasbrouck H. NJ	Oak Hill
08376	Very, Margaret Z.	58y	W	26 OCT 1911	New York NY	Arlington
07242	Vessell, Horace	32y	C	18 OCT 1909	New York NY	Mt. Zion East
03705	Vessels, Jennie	50y	C	7 NOV 1901	Baltimore MD	Mt. Zion
03620	Vicuna, Carlos Morla	58y	W	20 AUG 1901	Buffalo NY	Rock Creek
14698	Vierkorn, Henry	83y	W	19 MAR 1918	St. Elmo VA	Prospect Hill
05716	Vietch, William Boyle	2y	W	31 AUG 1906	College Park MD	Veitch Family
15023	View, Susie	22y	C	16 SEP 1918	Philadelphia PA	Payne's
06440	Viles, Charles P.	71y	W	19 FEB 1908	Methuen MA	Oak Hill
11980	Viles, Hannah E.	76y	W	27 AUG 1913	Methuen MA	Oak Hill
14149	Viles, Pamelia Hart	78y	W	27 MAY 1917	Berwyn MD	Oak Hill
14530	Viller, Elise	50y	W	28 DEC 1917	Cherrydale VA	Holyrood
13935	Viller, Elizabeth (Collins)	79y	W	15 JAN 1917	Cherrydale VA	Holyrood
08590	Vincent, Emily	76y	W	5 APR 1912	Jersey City NJ	Oak Hill
13298	Vincent, Frederick Steele	35y	W	13 JAN 1916	Elkton MD	Oak Hill[3]
00147	Vincent, Margaret W.	62y	W	24 AUG 1889	Dan'ville MD	Oak Hill
12638	Vineberg, Archibald	c.53y	W	2 DEC 1914	Hyattsville MD	Wash. Hebrew
03607	Vinson, Harriet R.F.	83y	W	9 AUG 1901	Boyce VA	Arlington
04163	Vinson, John Thomas	78y	W	7 FEB 1903	Rockville MD	Oak Hill
04643	Vinson, Napoleon B.	83y	W	24 MAR 1904	Rockville MD	Oak Hill
05001	Vinson, Richard Bowie	32y	W	7 JAN 1905	Rapid City SC	Oak Hill
17380	Virgil, Natline DeLoyse Ross	20y	C	1 SEP 1921	Buena Vista MD	Woodlawn
03761	Virginus, Maria	77y	C	20 JAN 1902	Alexandria VA	Woodlawn

[1] Disinterment permit 10 MAY 1917 for removal to PA.
[2] To be interred in the crypt in Bethlehem Chapel, St. Alban's Episcopal Cathedral, Wisconsin and Massachusetts Avenue, D.C.
[3] Disinterment permit #8817 on 22 NOV 1916 for removal to Oak Hill Cemetery.

No.	Name of Deceased	Age	Race	Death Date	Place of Death	Place of Burial
05598	Vitale, Pasquale, of Italy	40y	W	13 JUN 1906	Richmond VA	St. Mary's
13934	Vogel, William	39y	W	15 JAN 1917	Somerset PA	St. Mary's
06173	Vogt, Clifford F.	26y	W	7 AUG 1907	Denver CO	Rock Creek
04277	Voigt, Mary E.	42y	W	30 MAR 1903	W. Chevy Chase	Holyrood
02983	Volk, Francis Oliver	21y	W	15 JUL 1879	Laurel MD	Congressional
06359	Volk, Martha A.	73y	W	26 DEC 1907	Norfolk VA	Congressional
06120	Volker, Harry B.	18y	W	24 JUN 1907	Glymont MD	Glenwood
03449	Volkmar, William J.	53y	W	4 MAR 1901	Pasadena CA	Arlington VA
05335	Von Briesen, Susanna	73y	W	28 OCT 1905	Clifton VA	Rock Creek
13370	Von Entress, Frederick A.	44y	W	21 FEB 1916	Union NJ	Rock Creek
17303	Von Ezdorf, Dorothy Joy (Dunn)	29y	W	14 JUL 1921	Queens NY	Cedar Hill
13710	Von Ezdorf, R.H., Dr.	50y	W	8 SEP 1916	Crouse Sta. NC	Cremated
14784	Von Ezdorf, Robert R.	65y	W	30 APR 1918	Queens NY	Cedar Hill
16241	Vonaka, Frank, wheelwright	31y	W	22 JAN 1920	Glenallen VA	Cremated
03951	VonHerman, Evelyn	75y	W	14 JUL 1902	Raleigh NC	Arlington
12925	Voss, Mary P.	c.75y	W	17 MAY 1915	Forest Glen MD	Oak Hill
15292	Vosslman, Pearl R.	4y	W	26 OCT 1918	Takoma MD	Cedar Hill MD
13737	Vreeland, Charles Edward	64y	W	27 SEP 1916	Atlantic City NJ	Arlington
05307	Vrooman, Charles Carroll	18y	W	4 OCT 1905	Hyattsville MD	Glenwood

W

No.	Name of Deceased	Age	Race	Death Date	Place of Death	Place of Burial
06443	Wacks, Joe, soldier	—	W	28 SEP 1907	Pinar d. Rio, Cub.	Arlington
01609	Waddell, James F.	28y	W	24 FEB 1895	Albany NY	Congressional
16332	Waddy, Gertrude	32y	C	18 FEB 1920	Baltimore MD	Littonsville MD
14592	Wade, Hannah A.	78y	W	20 JAN 1918	Gaithersburg MD	Mt. Olivet
15415	Wade, Infant of Charles T.	5d	—	7 DEC 1918	Richmond VA	Glenwood
15721	Wade, Lottie L.	34y	C	10 APR 1919	Manhattan NY	Harmony
07103	Wade, Thomas S.	35y	W	10 JUL 1909	Saranac Lake NY	Oak Hill
18490	Wadleigh, John Winthrop	43y	W	3 APR 1923	At Sea	Arlington
02677	Wadsworth, Caroline Antoin.	96y	W	14 DEC 1898	New York NY	Mt. Olivet
02717	Wadsworth, John Henry	48y	W	13 JAN 1899	New York NY	Mt. Olivet
02029	Waggaman, George G.	1y	W	29 JUL 1896	New York NY	Mt. Olivet
07173	Waggaman, Henry Elliott E.	30y	W	25 AUG 1909	South River MD	Rock Creek
14822	Waggaman, John Floyd	65y	W	17 MAY 1918	Annapolis MD	Rock Creek
05611	Waggaman, Thomas E.	66y	W	27 UN 1906	South River MD	Mt. Olivet
05178	Wagner, Arthur L.	52y	W	17 JUN 1905	Asheville NC	Arlington
16800	Wagner, Charles W.	46y	W	8 NOV 1920	Brooklyn NY	Prospect Hill
18230	Wagner, David H.	63y	W	30 DEC 1922	Chevy Chase MD	Congressional
18388	Wagner, Emma M.	60y	W	5 MAR 1923	Georgetown Hp.	Congressional
03941	Wagner, John	79y	W	24 JUL 1902	Takoma Park MD	Oak Hill
17097	Wagner, Mary Jane	53y	W	7 APR 1921	St. Petersburg FL	Rockville MD
04941	Wagner, Paulina B.	43y	W	29 OCT 1904	Boston MA	Oak Hill
16944	Wagstaff, Alfred J.	67y	W	30 JAN 1921	Takoma Park MD	Rock Creek
13791	Wailes, Mary Victoria	75y	W	30 OCT 1916	Cornfield Har. MD	Oak Hill
17087	Wailes, Rose L.	76y	W	31 MAR 1921	Philadelphia PA	Glenwood
02183	Wainwright, Ann E.	72y	W	23 MAR 1897	Norfolk VA	Congressional
08743	Waite, Charles T.	3y	W	30 JUL 1912	E. Orange NJ	Glenwood
08802	Waite, Evelyn Gardner	25y	W	3 SEP 1912	Alexandria VA	Oak Hill
18598	Waite, Infant of James F.	SB	W	12 JUN 1923	Mt. Ranier MD	Oak Hill
02105	Waite, Mary A.	70y	W	4 JAN 1897	Delta LA	Congressional
16707	Wakano, Yastematsu	26y	J	8 SEP 1920	Norfolk VA	Cremated
08618	Wake, Virginia Marr	57y	W	3 MAY 1912	New York NY	Oak Hill
17783	Wakefield, Vernon R.	25y	W	22 JAN 1922	France	Vienna VA
01436	Walcott, C.W., Jr.	6m	W	14 JUL 1894	Colonial Bea. VA	Congressional
09158	Walcott, Charles D., Jr.	23y	W	7 APR 1913	Loomis NY	Rock Creek
00790	Walcott, Clina T.	36y	W	19 NOV 1882	Nyack NY	Oak Hill
14980	Walcott, Grace A., d/o F.W.	22y	W	16 AUG 1918	Colonial Bea. VA	Congressional
04174	Walcott, Harriet	65y	W	12 FEB 1903	Colonial Bea. VA	Congressional
08197	Walcott, Helena B. (Stevens)	53y	W	11 JUL 1911	Bridgeport CN	Rock Creek
07679	Walcott, May Maria (MacKay)	34y	W	8 AUG 1910	Colonial Bea. VA	Congressional
01776	Walcott, Mrs. Edward	64y	W	15 AUG 1895	Almo MI	Oak Hill
11903	Walcott, Oliver, s/o Alfred F.	19y	W	18 JUL 1913	Hampton VA	Cremated
17185	Waldman, Leonard	—	—	22 OCT 1918	France	Rock Creek
13595	Waldron, Florence L.	1y	W	11 JUL 1916	Takoma MD	Glenwood
16474	Waldron, Philip H.	78y	W	7 MAY 1920	Hampton VA	Milton PA
18393	Waldron, Robert	68y	W	6 MAR 1923	Takoma Park MD	Glenwood
14240	Waldsaur, Virginia	70y	W	19 JUL 1917	Capitol Hts. MD	Rock Creek
00909	Wales, Mary	c.65y	C	13 SEP 1892	Rosslyn VA	Mt. Zion
05097	Wales, Mary R.	—	W	19 DEC 1904	Philippine Isl.	Arlington
05792	Wales, Philip S.	69y	W	15 SEP 1906	Paris, France	Arlington
02658	Walker, Ann Sophronia	42y	W	16 NOV 1898	Pr. Geo. Co. MD	Glenwood
08504	Walker, Annie M.	76y	W	3 FEB 1912	Hagerstown MD	Cremated
18494	Walker, Beatrice	24y	C	17 APR 1923	Philadelphia PA	Payne's
18596	Walker, Bessie B.	50y	W	9 JUN 1923	Chicago IL	Rock Creek
02505	Walker, Blanch	10y	C	21 JUL 1898	Rosslyn VA	Baptist
06416	Walker, Caroline	88y	C	3 FEB 1908	Cabin John MD	Holyrood
18334	Walker, Catherine	89y	C	7 FEB 1923	Fairmont Hts. MD	Harmony
06992	Walker, Charles Edward	52y	W	17 APR 1909	Forestville MD	Mt Olivet
05373	Walker, Clarence G.	22d	W	22 NOV 1905	Hyattsville MD	Rock Creek

District of Columbia Foreign Death Records, 1888-1923

No.	Name of Deceased	Age	Race	Death Date	Place of Death	Place of Burial
03254	Walker, Edward O.	58y	—	6 AUG 1900	Boston MA	Congressional
00149	Walker, Edwin L.	1y	W	20 AUG 1889	Oakland MD	Mt. Olivet
06557	Walker, Elbert L.	2m	W	20 MAY 1908	Hyattsville MD	Glenwood
16351	Walker, Eliza	73y	W	27 FEB 1920	DeLeon Spgs. FL	Rock Creek
06718	Walker, Elizabeth (Bradley)	44y	W	8 SEP 1908	Del Ray VA	Glenwood
00148	Walker, Elizabeth A.	60y	W	24 AUG 1889	Governor's Isl. NY	Congressional
18470	Walker, Ella Edwards	30y	C	9 APR 1923	Chicago IL	Payne's
00400	Walker, Ethel Josephine	11m	W	6 SEP 1890	Rockville MD	Glenwood
15164	Walker, Francis G.	20y	W	13 OCT 1918	Ballston VA	Glenwood
04821	Walker, Frank	65y	C	28 JUL 1904	Rosslyn VA	Mt. Zion
05062	Walker, Franklin	1y	C	19 MAR 1905	Rosslyn VA	Baptist
12379	Walker, George F.	46y	W	28 MAY 1914	Baltimore MD	Glenwood
13626	Walker, Gertrude	5h	W	26 JUL 1916	Alex. Co. VA	Cremated
14961	Walker, Hall C.	28y	W	3 AUG 1918	Ft. Houston TX	Harrisonburg VA
07803	Walker, Henry B.	49y	W	26 OCT 1910	Port Tampa FL	Kinsale VA
12440	Walker, Jacob B.	53y	C	11 JUL 1914	Bay Head NJ	Woodlawn
14745	Walker, James E.	43y	C	4 APR 1918	Ft. Bayard NM	Arlington
06092	Walker, James H.	50y	C	4 JUN 1907	Deer Park MD	Harmony
13573	Walker, James W.	2y	W	26 JUN 1916	Brooklyn NY	Congressional
17666	Walker, James William	51y	W	28 JAN 1922	Cherrydale VA	Tenallytown
01364	Walker, Jane A.	81y	W	4 APR 1894	Pr. Geo. Co. MD	Glenwood
06233	Walker, John G.	72y	W	15 SEP 1907	York ME	Arlington
14870	Walker, John S.	73y	W	15 APR 1918	Washington DC	Prospect Hill
13579	Walker, Joseph Edw.	4y	W	29 JUN 1916	Brooklyn NY	Congressional
01775	Walker, Julia	66y	W	22 SEP 1895	Baltimore MD	Rock Creek
01003	Walker, Leland	7m	W	7 AUG 1893	Oakland MD	Rock Creek
01096	Walker, Louisa	2d	W	11 MAY 1893	Pr. Geo. Co. MD	Glenwood
02836	Walker, Margaret	1y	W	27 MAY 1899	Atlantic City NJ	Rock Creek
00789	Walker, Maria	24y	C	27 OCT 1891	New York NY	Graceland
06960	Walker, Marion Eliz. (Ross)	72y	W	27 MAR 1909	St. Louis MO	Oak Hill
01004	Walker, Mary	23y	W	30 JUL 1893	Concord NH	Oak Hill
08387	Walker, Mary A.C.	73y	W	6 NOV 1911	Ritchie MD	Congressional
08242	Walker, Mary E.C. (Chase)	49y	W	5 AUG 1911	Bridgeport CN	Glenwood
18415	Walker, Mary J.	59y	W	13 MAR 1923	Philadelphia PA	Oak Hill
16908	Walker, Mary L. (Chamblin)	79y	W	10 JAN 1921	Leesburg VA	Glenwood
04572	Walker, Ralph	14m	W	22 JAN 1904	Hyattsville MD	Glenwood
02228	Walker, Redford Husted	2y	W	22 JUN 1897	Oakland MD	Rock Creek
06954	Walker, Redford W.	68y	W	25 MAR 1909	Pikesville MD	Rock Creek
03604	Walker, Richard B.	54y	W	4 AUG 1901	Chesa. Bea. MD	Oak Hill
02940	Walker, Sabina	59y	C	4 SEP 1899	Culpeper VA	Harmony
06831	Walker, Sadie, d/o John W.	27y	W	28 NOV 1908	Purcellville VA	Glenwood
12955	Walker, Thomas H., s/o Wm.	81y	W	6 JUN 1915	Herndon VA	Congressional
15472	Walker, Vesta	26y	W	23 DEC 1918	Takoma Park MD	Glenwood
16716	Walker, Victoria	36y	C	15 SEP 1920	Seat Pleasant MD	Payne's
16053	Walker, William	7y	W	5 FEB 1921	Covington VA	Ballston VA
16957	Walker, William	7y	W	5 FEB 1921	Covington VA	Glenwood
13851	Walker, William Henry	72y	W	8 DEC 1916	Cherrydale VA	Methodist
01610	Walker, William T.	24y	W	3 DEC 1894	Alex. Co. VA	Alexandria VA
14634	Wall, Adolph	36y	W	11 FEB 1918	Philadelphia PA	Glenwood
14282	Wall, Edward, Rev., s/o Hy.	66y	W	6 AUG 1917	Berryville VA	Rock Creek
12279	Wall, James Henry	72y	W	29 MAR 1914	Relay MD	Arlington
05421	Wall, Joseph E.	58y	W	6 JAN 1906	Ft. Wash. MD	Glenwood
06312	Wall, Kate	52y	W	17 NOV 1907	Atlantic City NJ	Glenwood
06106	Wall, Sarah E., d/o Caleb	82y	W	13 JUN 1907	Colonial Bea. VA	Worcester MA
14954	Wallace, Emma	45y	C	4 AUG 1918	New York NY	Payne's
17800	Wallace, Frank	56y	C	14 APR 1922	Arlington VA	Harmony
07422	Wallace, Grace	—	C	15 FEB 1910	Hudson NY	Payne's
02124	Wallace, James	79y	W	30 JAN 1897	Remington VA	Oak Hill
12224	Wallace, Louisa	47y	C	17 FEB 1914	Philadelphia PA	Payne's
08712	Wallace, Mary D.	52y	C	11 JUL 1912	Lakeland MD	Mt. Olivet

No.	Name of Deceased	Age	Race	Death Date	Place of Death	Place of Burial
04073	Wallace, Noble	21y	C	16 APR 1902	Easton PA	Mt. Olivet
12856	Wallace, Peter	49y	C	28 MAR 1915	Asheville NC	Harmony
12399	Wallace, Rush R.	78y	W	12 JUN 1914	New York NY	Arlington
15916	Wallace, Wilkins T.	71y	W	4 AUG 1919	Silver Spring MD	Glenwood
03552	Wallace, William	80y	C	26 JUN 1901	Lakeland MD	Mt. Olivet
00525	Wallach, Annie E.	57y	W	28 FEB 1891	New York NY	Oak Hill
01777	Wallach, Cuthbert P.	69y	W	19 MAY 1895	New York NY	Oak Hill
01520	Wallach, Ellen	94y	W	28 OCT 1894	Baltimore MD	Congressional
01205	Wallach, Lavinia	73y	W	16 DEC 1892	Laurel MD	Congressional
14330	Wallach, Marshall Brown	54y	W	26 AUG 1917	San Francisco CA	Oak Hill
16264	Wallach, Richard	71y	W	30 JAN 1920	New York NY	Oak Hill
09059	Wallach, Virginia	52y	W	4 FEB 1913	New York NY	Oak Hill
14908	Waller, Edward	29y	C	7 JUL 1918	New York NY	Harmony
14306	Waller, Horace	45y	W	19 AUG 1917	Catonsville MD	Rock Creek
00910	Wallis, Elizabeth Finkle	12d	W	7 AUG 1892	Altoona PA	Congressional
00284	Wallis, Elsie	SB	W	27 FEB 1890	Altoona PA	Congressional
14689	Wallis, Samuel B.	55y	W	13 MAR 1918	Baltimore MD	Congressional
08337	Walls, Jessie, s/o Geo. N.	41y	W	2 OCT 1911	Occoquan VA	Congressional
04683	Walsh, Adele V.	6y	W	21 APR 1904	Mt. Wash. MD	Mt. Olivet
04777	Walsh, Anne T.	19y	W	29 JUN 1904	New York NY	Mt. Olivet
05183	Walsh, E.	—	W	15 DEC 1904	Philippine Isl.	Mt. Olivet
12613	Walsh, James F.	34y	W	12 NOV 1914	Hunting Creek	Arlington VA
15953	Walsh, James L.	4m	W	25 AUG 1919	Buena Vista PA	Arlington
14907	Walsh, Jean	2y	W	11 JUL 1918	Chevy Chase MD	Mt. Olivet
05008	Walsh, John	63y	W	23 JAN 1905	Hyattsville MD	Mt. Olivet
04934	Walsh, Katherine	5y	W	26 OCT 1904	Hyattsville MD	Mt. Olivet
13709	Walsh, Margaret	62y	W	10 SEP 1916	Deer Park MD	Mt. Olivet
01844	Walsh, Mary A.	28y	W	4 JAN 1896	Chicago IL	Mt. Olivet
02395	Walsh, Mary A.	51y	W	5 JAN 1898	New York NY	Mt. Olivet
05114	Walsh, Rose E. (Sullivan)	32y	W	3 MAY 1905	Fairfax Co. VA	Holyrood
06151	Walsh, Susannah	2y	W	22 JUL 1907	Hyattsville MD	Mt. Olivet
05274	Walsh, Vinson F.	17y	W	19 AUG 1905	Newport RI	Rock Creek
09174	Walsh, William	45y	W	15 APR 1913	Philadelphia PA	Mt. Olivet
17981	Walsky, Zachariah	50y	W	28 JUL 1922	Baltimore MD	Wash. Hebrew
18098	Walter, Eleanor Barrett	56y	W	1 OCT 1922	Clark's Gap VA	Oak Hill
07023	Walter, Fannie H.	66y	W	14 MAY 1909	Baltimore MD	Congressional
17737	Walter, Frank J.	37y	W	9 MAR 1922	Denver CO	Mt. Olivet
16784	Walter, Margaret	74y	W	28 OCT 1920	Fairfax VA	Prospect Hill
18270	Walter, Thomas William	69y	W	15 JAN 1923	Silver Spring MD	Luray VA
12453	Walters, Charles F.	30y	W	23 JUL 1914	Jacksonville FL	Lewinsville VA
07024	Walters, Fannie R.	69y	W	15 MAY 1909	Glen Echo MD	Congressional
17439	Walters, Jennie	53y	W	29 SEP 1921	Silver Hill MD	Rockwood MI
16230	Walters, Lucien N.	70y	W	20 JAN 1920	White Plains NY	Lewinsville VA
16333	Walters, Savilda Anna	62y	W	19 FEB 1920	Takoma Park MD	Rock Creek
13414	Walther, Emil	58y	W	17 MAR 1916	Philadelphia PA	Prospect Hill
07887	Walton, Daniel	11m	W	23 DEC 1910	Hyattsville MD	Mt. Olivet
17870	Walton, David S.	76y	W	21 MAY 1922	Baltimore MD	Rock Creek
14460	Walton, Ivan Orloff	31y	W	13 NOV 1917	Petersburg VA	Arlington
14468	Walton, James W., Jr.	2y	W	19 NOV 1917	Baltimore MD	Glenwood
12528	Walton, John Randolph	84y	W	15 SEP 1914	College Park MD	Annapolis MD
00908	Walton, Joseph R.	47y	W	23 SEP 1892	Gaithersburg MD	Oak Hill
06891	Walton, Margaret B.	74y	W	12 JAN 1909	St. Mary's MD	Glenwood
15702	Walz, Joseph B.	53y	W	30 MAR 1919	Bluemont VA	Congressional
07210	Wandel, Alfred	76y	W	26 SEP 1909	Baltimore MD	Glenwood
01269	Wandling, David B.	65y	W	9 DEC 1893	N. Mountain VA	Oak Hill
05918	Wanser, George	34y	C	30 JAN 1907	Philadelphia PA	Woodlawn
01097	Wanstall, Emily L.	72y	W	11 APR 1893	Baltimore MD	Rock Creek
12310	Wanzer, Frank	37y	C	13 APR 1914	Baltimore MD	Woodlawn
03290	Ward, Ann	65y	W	18 SEP 1900	Forestville MD	Mt. Olivet
01944	Ward, Arianna E.	—	W	14 JUL 1893	—	Oak Hill

District of Columbia Foreign Death Records, 1888-1923

No.	Name of Deceased	Age	Race	Death Date	Place of Death	Place of Burial
11890	Ward, Clara E.	18y	W	10 JUL 1913	Glen Echo MD	Mt. Olivet
05868	Ward, Daniel P.	29y	C	19 DEC 1906	Philadelphia PA	Macedonia
03486	Ward, G.S. Luttrell	60y	W	21 APR 1901	New York NY	Arlington VA
01943	Ward, George C.	50y	W	22 MAR 1896	Omaha NE	Oak Hill
07643	Ward, H. Anna, d/o Electus	42y	W	21 JUL 1910	Catlett VA	Rock Creek
12334	Ward, Harmon, Jr.	1y	W	27 FEB 1905	New York NY	Rock Creek
04690	Ward, Helen Isabel	7m	W	24 APR 1904	Pindell MD	Mt. Olivet
12667	Ward, John Melton	6y	W	21 DEC 1914	Railroad	Mt. Olivet
08763	Ward, Levin S.	32y	W	9 AUG 1912	Newark OH	Rock Creek
06456	Ward, Louisa	67y	W	9 FEB 1908	Rome, Italy	Arlington VA
06167	Ward, Maria	53y	C	4 AUG 1907	Randallstown MD	Woodlawn
14952	Ward, Martha Gordon	78y	W	6 AUG 1918	New Windsor MD	Oak Hill
12335	Ward, Mary L.	45y	W	16 APR 1904	New York NY	Rock Creek
03937	Ward, Melvin	8m	W	3 JUL 1902	Rockville MD	Woodlawn
08678	Ward, Robert	47y	C	18 JUN 1912	Marshalsea PA	Harmony
00050	Ward, Sarah A.	82y	W	14 MAR 1889	New London CN	Congressional
00791	Ward, Thomas	69y	W	25 JAN 1892	Occoquan VA	Rock Creek
06247	Ward, Thomas Z.	41y	W	26 SEP 1907	Charlotte Hall MD	Mt. Olivet
01420	Ward, Thos. M.D., D.D.	71y	C	11 JUN 1894	Jacksonville FL	Graceland
16601	Ward, William Clayton	37y	W	15 JUL 1920	Harpers Ferry WV	Glenwood
03803	Ward, William H.	27y	W	21 FEB 1902	Canon City CO	Rock Creek
00370	Ward, William Hanly	3m	W	26 JUL 1890	Montg. Co. MD	Oak Hill
07945	Warde, Maud C.	35y	W	27 JAN 1911	Philadelphia PA	Rock Creek
15030	Warden, Lucy A.	69y	W	19 SEP 1918	New York NY	Oak Hill
01334	Warder, Benjamin H.	69y	W	13 JAN 1894	Cairo, Egypt	Rock Creek
12727	Warder, Clarence W.	24y	W	4 SEP 1914	Jersey City NJ	Congressional
14494	Ware, Annie Rebecca	31y	C	9 DEC 1917	Fairmont Hts. MD	Mt. Olivet
00072	Ware, Battle	60y	C	30 APR 1889	Pittsburgh PA	Harmony
13867	Ware, Catlienne A. [Angelus]	17y	C	13 DEC 1916	Philadelphia PA	Mt. Olivet
05459	Ware, James H.	45y	C	5 FEB 1906	Atlantic City NJ	Woodlawn
12808	Ware, John Edward	66y	W	12 MAR 1915	Pr. Geo. Co. MD	Congressional
09142	Ware, Lawrence, s/o John A.	3y	C	27 MAR 1913	Fairmont Hts. MD	Mt. Olivet
02281	Ware, Loyd	47y	C	5 AUG 1897	Chevy Chase MD	Mt. Zion
05310	Ware, Mildred	57y	W	7 OCT 1905	New Port MD	Congressional
00669	Ware, William	21y	C	24 AUG 1891	Sandy Hook MD	Moore's
15630	Warfield, James Monroe	4m	C	16 FEB 1919	Silver Spring MD	Mt. Zion East
17885	Waring, Alfred Brown	24y	C	31 MAY 1922	Hopkinton MA	Harmony
16292	Waring, Amanda Fitzallen	85y	C	6 FEB 1920	Pittsburgh PA	Arlington
13379	Waring, Mary E.	86y	C	24 FEB 1916	Pomonkey MD	Mt. Olivet
06527	Warman, Frederick C.	36y	W	27 APR 1908	Norfolk VA	Rock Creek
13512	Warner, Brainard H.	68y	W	16 MAY 1916	Chevy Chase MD	Oak Hill
14866	Warner, Elizabeth	40y	W	15 JUN 1918	Buffalo NY	Glenwood
13742	Warner, George S., s/o G.W.	40y	W	3 OCT 1916	Penns Grove NJ	Glenwood[1]
09151	Warner, Hannah	55y	W	2 APR 1913	Relay MD	Glenwood
12411	Warner, Southard P.	—	W	9 MAY 1914	Harbin, China	Oak Hill
02888	Warren, Bates, Jr.	10m	W	27 JUN 1899	Oakland MD	Rock Creek
05142	Warren, Catherine	25y	C	25 MAY 1905	Irvington MD	Prospect Hill
15231	Warren, Earl Harper	33y	W	20 OCT 1918	Laurel MD	Rock Creek
07294	Warren, Ethel	2m	W	24 SEP 1893	Baltimore MD	Congressional
18561	Warren, Grant	48y	C	24 MAY 1923	Pittsburgh PA	Mt. Zion West
14966	Warren, Henry	3m	W	9 AUG 1918	Montg. Co. MD	Cedar Hill
04093	Warren, J. Noble	28y	W	19 NOV 1902	Baltimore MD	Prospect Hill
16832	Warren, J.L.	c.58y	W	29 NOV 1920	Norfolk VA	Congressional
16952	Warren, John L.	47y	W	30 JAN 1921	Columbus GA	Rock Creek
12049	Warren, Mahala, s/o Lloyd	60y	C	18 OCT 1913	New Haven CN	Mt. Olivet
12655	Warrens, Walter	1y	W	12 DEC 1914	Alex. Co. VA	Holyrood
14353	Warrington, James	35y	W	10 SEP 1917	Falls Church VA	Cremated

[1] Disinterment permit #8847 on 30 DEC 1916 for removal to Arlingotn National Cemetery.

No.	Name of Deceased	Age	Race	Death Date	Place of Death	Place of Burial
07348	Wasekesewski, Caroline	55y	W	29 DEC 1909	Capitol Hts. MD	Mt. Olivet
07137	Washburn, Blanche	31y	W	28 JUL 1909	Rockville MD	Rock Creek
06624	Washburn, Julia Morgan	6m	W	2 JUL 1908	Rockville MD	Rock Creek
01270	Washington, Addie	19y	C	20 OCT 1893	Brightseat MD	Mt. Olivet
16319	Washington, Albert	33y	C	14 FEB 1920	Baltimore MD	Payne's
07653	Washington, Alice L.	9m	C	26 JUL 1910	Seat Pleasant MD	Mt. Olivet
05442	Washington, Annie A.	25y	C	22 JAN 1906	Sunberry PA	Harmony
13638	Washington, Benjamin A.	26y	C	4 AUG 1916	Annapolis MD	Harmony
15488	Washington, Catherine	22y	C	22 DEC 1918	New York NY	Harmony
13073	Washington, Dora Ella	57y	C	23 AUG 1915	Fairmont Hts. MD	Woodlawn
00911	Washington, Ella Carter	18y	C	26 AUG 1892	Alex. Co. VA	Harmony
02927	Washington, Erwin West	7m	W	27 AUG 1899	Falls Church VA	Mt. Olivet
13651	Washington, Estelle	16y	W	10 AUG 1916	Baltimore MD	Oak Hill
00169	Washington, Harriet	47y	C	10 SEP 1889	Boston MA	Graceland
04578	Washington, Infant of Albt.	6d	C	23 JAN 1904	Silver Hill MD	Moore's
03322	Washington, Joseph, a.k.a.	65y	C	6 NOV 1900	Baltimore MD	Payne's
00792	Washington, Louise	18y	C	3 MAR 1892	Pr. Geo. Co. MD	Mt. Olivet
16294	Washington, Mary E. (Proctor)	31y	C	6 FEB 1920	Richmond VA	Woodlawn
17500	Washington, Nellie	57y	C	4 NOV 1921	Halls Hill VA	Mt. Zion East
17129	Washington, P.D., hotel kpr.	—	C	27 APR 1921	Baltimore MD	Woodlawn
15782	Washington, Ruben	17y	C	18 MAY 1919	Takoma Park MD	Silver Spring MD
04838	Washington, Thomas	29y	C	7 AUG 1904	New York NY	Harmony
02106	Washington, Thomas	36y	C	6 SEP 1896	Cumberland MD	Payne's
07205	Washington, Virgie	22y	C	21 SEP 1909	Long Branch NJ	Woodlawn
14812	Washington, Walter	29y	C	13 MAY 1918	Brentwood MD	Payne's
16606	Washington, William	18y	C	14 JUIL 1920	Belleville NJ	Woodlawn
06947	Washington, William H.	46y	C	15 MAR 1909	Upper Marl. MD	Harmony
08472	Wasmansdorff, Adelaide A.E.	61y	W	14 JAN 1912	Walkers Chap. VA	Cremated
16393	Wasson, George H.	44y	W	15 MAR 1920	Camp Hump. VA	Congressional
03051	Waterman, Leslie R., soldier	—	W	30 SEP 1899	Japan	Arlington VA
17902	Waters, Brown Morgan	75y	W	13 JUN 1922	Annapolis MD	Glenwood
04584	Waters, Byron E.	45y	W	1 FEB 1904	New York NY	Glenwood
06363	Waters, Charles	46y	C	24 DEC 1907	W. Newton MA	Harmony
01005	Waters, Daniel J.	28y	W	17 JUN 1893	Philadelphia PA	Mt. Olivet
11819	Waters, Elizabeth A.	18y	W	18 MAY 1913	Washington DC	Mt. Olivet
06787	Waters, Elkanah N.	50y	W	26 OCT 1908	Frederick MD	Rock Creek
08169	Waters, Frederick R.B.	24y	W	28 JUN 1911	Vincennes IN	Rock Creek
08530	Waters, James W.L.	55y	W	24 FEB 1912	Brooklyn NY	Congressional
02829	Waters, John P.	36y	C	8 FEB 1899	Boston MA	Harmony
17319	Waters, Louise	58y	C	22 JUL 1921	Fairmont Hts. MD	Woodlawn
14492	Waters, Margaret Jerusha	92y	W	9 DEC 1917	Laytonsville MD	Oak Hill
00290	Waters, Mary Linsey	81y	—	14 MAR 1890	St. Louis MO	Washington DC
13693	Waters, S. Birch, s/o John M.	1y	W	4 SEP 1916	Ocean View VA	Oak Hill
04211	Waters, Sarah Emma	64y	W	16 MAR 1903	Brentwood MD	Glenwood
04867	Waters, Susie	36y	W	24 AUG 1904	Philadelphia PA	Harmony
15622	Waters, Thomas Jackson	74y	W	15 FEB 1919	New York NY	Oak Hill
15954	Wathen, Otis Sterling	20y	W	24 AUG 1919	Atlantic City NJ	Newport MD
12283	Watkins, Anna	75y	W	25 MAR 1914	Dayton OH	Congressional
06375	Watkins, Dicey (Hayes)	62y	C	3 JAN 1908	Richmond VA	Harmony
13342	Watkins, Elizabeth	70y	W	6 FEB 1916	Williamsburg VA	Northd. Co. VA
07202	Watkins, Ernest Elwood	11m	W	19 SEP 1909	Jessup MD	Glenwood
13920	Watkins, Fidelia	72y	W	8 JAN 1917	Detroit MI	Cedar Hill
06587	Watkins, George B.	42y	C	8 JUN 1908	Lewiston NY	Harmony
04343	Watkins, John E.	51y	W	11 AUG 1903	New York NY	Rock Creek
08565	Watkins, Laura E.	49y	C	23 MAR 1912	Fairmont Hts. MD	Woodlawn
12069	Watkins, Norval Archibald	21y	W	1 NOV 1913	Baltimore MD	Congressional
16364	Watkins, Wesley	65y	C	5 MAR 1920	Rosslyn VA	Summit VA
00264	Watmaugh, Matilda Pleasanton	6y	W	13 JAN 1890	Philadelphia PA	Oak Hill
04417	Watson, Carolyn	42y	W	29 JUL 1903	Baltimore MD	Rock Creek
06929	Watson, Charles Emmons	33y	W	23 FEB 1909	Chestnut Hill PA	Glenwood

District of Columbia Foreign Death Records, 1888-1923

No.	Name of Deceased	Age	Race	Death Date	Place of Death	Place of Burial
03809	Watson, David E.	35y	W	4 MAR 1902	Monessen PA	Arlington
04900	Watson, Harry L.	48y	W	12 SEP 1904	Atlanta GA	Glenwood
13459	Watson, Jessie Patterson	c.35y	W	14 APR 1916	Conway Sta. MD	Boonville IN
16652	Watson, Johannas V.	53y	W	9 AUG 1920	Bladensburg MD	Glenwood
00793	Watson, Malbone F., Maj.	52y	W	9 DEC 1891	Dayton OH	Oak Hill
15333	Watson, Martha Westray	66y	W	7 NOV 1918	Norfolk VA	Cremated
04380	Watson, Mary	15y	W	8 JUL 1903	Ocean City MD	Mt. Olivet
06515	Watson, Mary A.	1y	C	19 APR 1908	Pittsburgh PA	Mt. Olivet
05659	Watson, Roderick D.	40y	W	22 JUL 1906	Colonial Bea. VA	Glenwood
06930	Watson, Samuel	26y	C	23 FEB 1909	Glymont MD	Payne's
16571	Watson, Sarah	57y	C	29 JUN 1920	Philadelphia PA	Mt. Zion East
03399	Watson, Susia	19y	W	17 JAN 1901	Boulder MT	Glenwood
00670	Watson, W.C.	53y	W	15 AUG 1891	Wilmington DE	Congressional
12165	Watson, William	69y	W	14 JAN 1914	Baltimore MD	Arlington
16902	Watson, William A.	81y	C	JAN 1921	Pittsburgh PA	Mt. Olivet
13455	Watson, William Stanley	22y	C	27 MAR 1916	At Sea	Jersey City H. NJ
08077	Watt, Jennie McInnis	31y	W	21 APR 1911	Wilmington DE	Glenwood
13107	Watts, Alice	48y	W	16 SEP 1915	Baltimore MD	Congressional
08697	Watts, Anna	52y	C	29 JUN 1912	New York NY	Harmony
15170	Watts, Charles L.	30y	W	13 OCT 1918	New York NY	Mt. Olivet
17596	Watts, Ellen M.	77y	W	18 DEC 1921	Norfolk VA	Mt. Olivet
16859	Watts, George W.	c.30y	C	16 DEC 1920	New Market MD	Hermansville MD
08115	Watts, Grace E.	9y	C	11 MAY 1911	New York NY	Payne's
00911½	Watts, Mac	33y	W	15 JUL 1892	Bethesda MD	Mt. Zion
17128	Watts, Mary A.	c.50y	W	26 APR 1921	College Park MD	Concord TN
18530	Watts, Phyllis Walker	13y	W	5 MAY 1923	Kensington MD	Oak Hill
15477	Watts, Richard H.	60y	W	25 DEC 1918	Seat Pleasant MD	Congressional
15437	Watts, Thomas	44y	C	9 DEC 1918	Atlantic City NJ	Harmony
09192	Watts, William M.	2y	W	JUN 1878	Carlisle PA	Rock Creek
06850	Watzman, Rachael Zetta	6y	W	11 DEC 1908	Arlington VA	Talmud Torah
01778	Waugh, James E.	54y	W	26 MAY 1895	Charlton Hts. MD	Oak Hill
05489	Waugh, John S.	71y	W	6 MAR 1906	Hampton VA	Arlington VA
03728	Waugh, Thaddeus	32y	C	11 DEC 1901	Philadelphia PA	Woodlawn
13420	Wave, Ely	36y	W	19 MAR 1916	Georgetown DC	Prospect Hill
14079	Wayman, William H.	38y	C	7 APR 1917	Philadelphia PA	Mt. Zion East
01006	Wayne, Ada	6m	C	4 SEP 1893	Montg. Co. MD	Baptist
17322	Wayne, William	79y	C	21 JUL 1921	Hampton VA	Arlington
02184	Wayson, Mary A.	77y	W	22 MAR 1897	Grosse Pt. MI	Congressional
08887	Weakley, Elly E.	39y	W	14 OCT 1912	Saranac Lake NY	Congressional
14016	Wear, Ernest E.	45y	W	27 FEB 1917	New York NY	Arlington
17374	Wear, Joseph J.	48y	W	28 AUG 1921	Bethesda MD	Congressional
14022	Wears, Mary F.	81y	C	4 MAR 1917	Philadelphia PA	Harmony
02698	Weaver, Edward, butcher	54y	W	3 JAN 1899	Dublin GA	Congressional
17448	Weaver, Emma V.	67y	W	3 OCT 1921	Silver Spring MD	Elkton VA
15447	Weaver, Fairy E.	36y	W	15 DEC 1918	Alex. Co. VA	Glenwood
09037	Weaver, George A.	69y	W	18 JAN 1913	Alex. Co. VA	Woodlawn
05525	Weaver, Joseph C.	44y	C	5 APR 1906	Newark NJ	Harmony
12366	Weaver, Lula Helen	22y	W	14 MAY 1914	Dallas TX	Glenwood
06920	Weaver, William S.	9y	W	15 FEB 1909	Baltimore MD	Rock Creek
00671	Webb, Bettie D.	49y	W	3 JUL 1891	Baltimore MD	Glenwood
02995	Webb, Francis J. Leake	43y	W	2 NOV 1899	Needham MA	Glenwood
18551	Webb, Frank	27y	C	20 MAY 1923	New York NY	Alexandria VA
04086	Webb, George P.	52y	W	16 NOV 1902	New York NY	Payne's
12189	Webb, Gilbert L.	35y	C	29 JAN 1914	Cumberland MD	Harmony
03203	Webb, Harry Sumner	28y	C	5 JUN 1900	Worcester MA	Payne's
03587	Webb, Hattie	20y	C	21 JUL 1901	Markham VA	Harmony
02904	Webb, Lizzie B.	45y	W	7 AUG 1899	Deal Bea. NJ	Congressional
05024	Webb, Mary	58y	C	8 FEB 1905	Loudoun Co. VA	Mt. Zion
16705	Webb, Maud	21y	C	8 SEP 1920	Baltimore MD	Mt. Zion West
16134	Webb, Theodore	1y	C	2 DEC 1919	New York NY	Mt. Olivet

No.	Name of Deceased	Age	Race	Death Date	Place of Death	Place of Burial
13446	Weber, Augustine J.	23y	W	4 APR 1916	Danvers MA	Rock Creek
06583	Weber, Jean Jaques	84y	W	26 MAY 1908	Washington DC	Glenwood
02802	Weber, Katherine C.	35y	W	25 APR 1899	New York NY	Mt. Olivet
17170	Weber, Margaret E.	20y	W	19 MAY 1921	Columbia Pk. MD	St. Mary's
07542	Weber, Theresa	2y	W	16 MAY 1910	Rosslyn VA	Holyrood
11876	Weber, William C.F.	37y	W	4 APR 1913	Los Angeles CA	Rock Creek
00073	Webster, Addison A.	33y	C	18 MAY 1889	Morriston AL	Harmony
13830	Webster, Armstead	74y	C	26 NOV 1916	New York NY	Mt. Zion West
18407	Webster, Elizabeth	92y	W	12 MAR 1923	Silver Spring MD	Alexandria VA
18174	Webster, Florence Belle	58y	W	20 NOV 1922	Atlantic City NJ	Rock Creek
17121	Webster, Harris, Rear Adm.	78y	W	23 APR 1921	Richmond VA	Arlington
14130	Webster, Lenore Perky	59y	W	3 MAY 1917	Forest Glen MD	Wooster OH
04623	Webster, Mary	73y	W	4 MAR 1904	Hyattsville MD	Congressional
15959	Webster, Mary Hein	73y	W	28 AUG 1919	Richmond VA	Arlington
18161	Webster, Myron E.	34y	W	10 NOV 1922	Maimi FL	Ft. Lincoln
01845	Webster, William, cook	45y	C	23 NOV 1895	Great Falls MD	Harmony
16070	Webster, William F.	30y	W	24 OCT 1919	New York NY	Glenwood
00425	Weech, Sewell	19y	W	23 OCT 1890	Carlisle PA	Oak Hill
01780	Weech, William T.L., Rev.	59y	W	5 SEP 1895	Alexandria VA	Oak Hill
01779	Weed, George W.	61y	W	20 OCT 1895	Hynes Park MD	Arlington
12290	Weedon, Daniel B.	65y	W	2 APR 1914	Takoma Park MD	Rock Creek
00137	Weeks, Clyde	1y	W	13 AUG 1889	Charlestown WV	Congressional
05282	Weeks, Fannie A.	40y	W	4 SEP 1905	Livingston MT	Rock Creek
14807	Weems, John D.	—	—	—	Detroit MI	Oak Hill
03326	Weems, Mary Wharton	88y	W	11 NOV 1900	Catonsville MD	Oak Hill
04200	Wehage, A.J.	24y	W	13 JUN 1887	Baltimore MD	Rock Creek
04200	Wehage, A.J.	24y	W	13 JUN 1887	Baltimore MD	Rock Creek
04398	Weide, Bessie	19y	W	19 JUL 1903	Diana NY	Rock Creek
16970	Weidman, Godfrey F.	51y	W	12 FEB 1921	Cottage City MD	Glenwood
05302	Weigand, Amelia	61y	W	30 SEP 1905	Great Falls MD	Prospect Hill
15270	Weiler, John	70y	W	24 OCT 1918	Mt. Ranier MD	Holyrood
07358	Weinberg, Sarah	63y	W	6 JAN 1910	Chambersburg PA	Talmud Torah
17136	Weinreich, Nathan C.	60y	W	28 APR 1921	Philadelphia PA	Wash. Hebrew
05083	Weir, Constance	25y	W	14 APR 1905	New York NY	Glenwood
01098	Weir, William Jas.	48y	W	6 MAY 1893	Cockeysville MD	Glenwood
00335	Weisel, Daniel	49y	W	30 OCT 1888	Fort Sill, Ind. Ter.	Arlington
08595	Weisenberger, Karl	63y	W	9 APR 1912	Capitol Hts. MD	Cremated
17975	Weisenborn, Albert	48y	W	23 JUL 1922	Philadelphia PA	Prospect Hill
18562	Weiss, Emelia	70y	W	28 MAY 1923	Rockville MD	St. Mary's
08309	Weiss, Jacob, s/o Philip J.	62y	W	16 SEP 1911	Rosslyn VA	Prospect Hill
00170	Weissinger, John T.	23y	W	14 SEP 1889	Baltimore MD	Glenwood
04527	Weissmuller, Elizabeth	62y	W	28 NOV 1903	Hawley Spgs. MD	Congressional
14767	Welborne, Carter Lee	5y	C	23 APR 1918	Bladensburg MD	Payne's
08576	Welborne, Walter	1y	C	31 MAR 1912	Bladensburg MD	Payne's
05567	Welby, John	53y	W	7 MAY 1906	Baltimore MD	Congressional
08665	Welch, Albert L.	31y	W	11 JUN 1912	College Park MD	Adas Israel
16247	Welch, Alexandria William	64y	W	27 JAN 1920	Rosslyn VA	Starkville MS
00308	Welch, Aristides	—	W	10 APR 1890	Philadelphia PA	Oak Hill
04897	Welch, Bridget	47y	W	15 SEP 1904	Portland ME	Holyrood
15216	Welch, Catherine	24y	W	15 OCT 1918	Annapolis MD	Mt. Olivet
14133	Welch, Elizabeth V.	66y	W	9 MAY 1917	Pelham NY	Rock Creek
13126	Welch, Hattie M. (Mulford)	64y	W	28 SEP 1915	Norfolk VA	Oak Hill
00139	Welch, James S.	76y	W	14 AUG 1889	Alex. Co. VA	Oak Hill
01007	Welch, M.O., Mrs.	82y	W	4 SEP 1895	Cumberland MD	Rock Creek
16596	Welch, Rosia W.	75y	W	13 JUL 1920	Norfolk VA	Oak Hill
00418	Welch, Warren Eugene	9m	W	12 OCT 1890	Alex. Co. VA	Oak Hill
01896	Welch, William N.	38y	W	27 FEB 1896	Alex. Co. VA	Oak Hill
07731	Weld, Edward Joseph	50y	W	4 SEP 1910	Meyersdale PA	Oak Hill
06508	Welkins, Annie	60y	C	11 APR 1908	New York NY	Harmony
18368	Weller, Giles Walthan	59y	W	20 FEB 1923	Calfax CA	Rock Creek

No.	Name of Deceased	Age	Race	Death Date	Place of Death	Place of Burial
04424	Weller, William B.	70y	W	28 AUG 1903	Wheaton MD	Rock Creek
04616	Weller, William B., Jr.	25y	W	27 FEB 1904	Wheaton MD	Rock Creek
06760	Wells, Adderson	12y	C	8 OCT 1908	Bladensburg MD	Harmony
04758	Wells, Albert H.	24y	W	6 JUN 1904	St. Louis MO	Glenwood
04764	Wells, Annie V. (Mrs. F.G.)	32y	W	FEB 1888	Fauquier Co. VA	Glenwood
04764½	Wells, Arthur E.	19y	W	JUL 1895	Washington DC	Glenwood
05816	Wells, Cara	21y	C	11 NOV 1906	New York NY	Covington VA
07937	Wells, George	28y	W	23 JAN 1911	Falls Church VA	Rock Creek
13432	Wells, George T.	60y	W	27 MAR 1916	River Rd.	Mt. Olivet
02454	Wells, Harry	55y	W	12 APR 1898	Jacksonville FL	Rock Creek
03100	Wells, Henry H.	76y	W	12 FEB 1900	Palmyra NY	Rock Creek
14308	Wells, Infant of John N.	SB	W	17 AUG 1917	University Pk. MD	Mt. Olivet
08256	Wells, Josephine M.	29y	W	13 AUG 1911	Detroit MI	Oak Hill
15766	Wells, Louisa	52y	C	3 MAY 1919	Philadelphia PA	Mt. Zion West
06430	Wells, Maria	77y	W	12 FEB 1908	New York NY	Mt. Olivet
04765	Wells, Mary B.	7y	W	JUN 1879	Washington DC	Glenwood
06080	Wells, Nathaniel	83y	W	25 MAY 1907	Charleston SC	Glenwood
01008	Wells, Phoebe E.	63y	W	20 JUL 1893	Saratoga Spg. NY	Rock Creek
18341	Wells, Richard, s/o Richard	87y	C	10 FEB 1923	Portsmouth VA	Mt. Olivet
07536	Wells, William	50y	C	10 MAY 1910	Fairmont Hts. MD	Payne's
06073	Welsh, Florence May	24y	W	16 MAY 1907	El Paso TX	Rock Creek
14541	Welsh, Mary Rebecca	89y	W	2 JAN 1918	Hyattsville MD	Glenwood
07268	Welsh, Sallie K.	59y	W	10 NOV 1909	Baltimore MD	Glenwood
17928	Welty, Peony G.	57y	W	1 JUL 1922	Silver Spring MD	E. Liberty OH
07262	Wendell, Mary	88y	W	13 OCT 1909	Poughkeepsie NY	Glenwood
16536	Wendle, Jane E.	96y	W	13 JUN 1920	Baltimore MD	Glenwood
18124	Werlick, Hattie McCenney	66y	W	19 AUG 1922	Paris, France	Oak Hill
07141	Werntz, Infant of Lawrence	4m	W	30 JUL 1909	Mtn. Lake Pk. MD	Bell's Meeting H.
01781	Wernwag, Isaac	78y	W	23 JUN 1895	Hyattsville MD	Glenwood
14821	Werres, John P.	30y	W	10 MAY 1918	Arlington VA	St. Mary's
16020	Wescott, Edward Stewart	72y	W	25 JAN 1919	Arlington VA	Rock Creek
12473	Weser, Mary E.	71y	W	6 AUG 1914	Mt. Ranier MD	Mt. Olivet
07455	Wesley, Catherine	2d	W	8 MAR 1910	Capitol Hts. MD	Mt. Olivet
06194	Wesley, Raymond Frank	10m	W	22 AUG 1907	Hyattsville MD	St. Mary's
13806	Wesley, Thelma L.	1y	W	7 NOV 1916	Capitol Hts. MD	St. Mary's
08800	Wessman, Franklin	22y	W	3 SEP 1912	Colonial Bea. VA	Havana IL
14172	Wesson, Robert Cotton	11m	W	15 JUN 1917	Norfolk VA	Cremated
05951	West, Amanda	55y	C	20 FEB 1907	Williamston MA	Harmony
05805	West, Arthur Joseph	19y	W	5 NOV 1906	Cherrydale VA	Holyrood
06734	West, Bertha	28y	C	17 SEP 1908	Asbury Park NJ	Harmony
04987	West, Elisabeth	73y	W	30 DEC 1904	Black Mtn. NC	Oak Hill
12567	West, Eliza L.	68y	W	12 OCT 1914	Sherborn MA	Glenwood
02229	West, Ellen	94y	C	17 JUN 1897	Forestville MD	Jones' Chapel
12930	West, Francis St. Clair	77y	W	19 MAY 1915	Takoma Park MD	Rock Creek
03006	West, Frank, Dr.	48y	W	18 NOV 1899	Asbury Park NJ	Congressional
16409	West, George Nelson	74y	W	26 MAR 1920	Natick MA	Glenwood
01206	West, James	7m	W	22 JUN 1892	Ballston VA	Holyrood
04164	West, Jerome	21y	W	7 FEB 1903	Toldeo OH	Wash. Hebrew
15881	West, John T.	25y	W	16 JUL 1919	Towson MD	Congressional
03142	West, John T.	37y	W	21 MAR 1900	Asheville NC	Glenwood
05495	West, Julia	14y	C	10 MAR 1906	Wilmington DE	Harmony
04921	West, Lucy	30y	C	7 JUL 1903	Knoxville TN	Harmony
04995	West, Luke	56y	W	4 JAN 1905	Philadelphia PA	Payne's
16300	West, Mamie A.	42y	C	7 FEB 1920	Smithfield VA	Woodlawn[1]
07185	West, Matilda P.	63y	W	7 SEP 1909	Baltimore MD	Congressional
00190	West, Ruth	70y	C	2 OCT 1889	Philadelphia PA	Graceland
12740	West, Sarah	47y	C	1 FEB 1915	Fairmont Hts. MD	Payne's

[1] Out of sequence on film, found after certificate #16336.

No.	Name of Deceased	Age	Race	Death Date	Place of Death	Place of Burial
17936	West, Sue Harris	58y	W	6 JUL 1922	Arlington Co. VA	Cremated
00138	West, Theodore Sterling	49y	W	15 AUG 1889	Asbury Park NJ	Arlington
16907	West, Walter Scott	c.51y	W	10 JAN 1921	Chesa. Bea. MD	Prospect Hill
15707	West, William	41y	C	2 APR 1919	Occoquan VA	Moore's
08078	West, William K.	26y	W	17 APR 1911	Seattle WA	Oak Hill
12213	Westermeyer, Irma M.M.	4m	W	10 FEB 1914	Silver Spring MD	Prospect Hill
18540	Westmoreland, Edgar Pane	2y	C	12 MAY 1923	Baltimore MD	Woodlawn
06032	Westney, Joseph	65y	W	15 APR 1907	Philadelphia PA	Congressional
18409	Weston, Eva Cowling	52y	W	11 MAR 1923	Takoma Park MD	Glenwood
06297	Weston, Harriet A.	74y	W	9 JUN 1906	Manasquan NJ	Rock Creek
07768	Weston, Mary M.	42y	W	29 SEP 1910	Capitol Hts. MD	Occoquan VA
03704	Weston, Sarah Edson	45y	W	20 NOV 1851	Randolph VT	Rock Creek
13811	Weston, Walter M., Jr.	2y	W	11 NOV 1916	Charleston WV	Rock Creek
17269	Wetzel, William O.	63y	W	27 JUN 1921	Bradbury Hts. MD	Glenwood
08072	Whalan, Jennie E.	37y	W	17 APR 1911	New York NY	Falls Church VA
07895	Whalen, James	33y	W	25 DEC 1910	Hyattsville MD	Falls Church VA
08620	Whalen, James Peyton	10d	W	7 MAY 1912	Bethesda MD	Glenwood
03865	Whalen, William Henry	c.30y	C	27 APR 1902	Lakeland MD	Mt. Olivet
16977	Whaley, William Baynard	76y	W	12 FEB 1921	Charleston SC	Cremated
15296	Whaling, James E.	23y	W	25 OCT 1918	Elwyn PA	Mt. Olivet
06259	Whalley, William John	23y	W	28 SEP 1907	Albuquerque NM	Congressional
13291	Whallon, Henry A.	76y	W	9 JAN 1916	Park Lane VA	Glenwood
05576	Whallon, Mary H.	68y	W	14 MAY 1906	Arlington VA	Glenwood
07866	Whealer, Sarah	—	C	11 DEC 1910	Brentwood MD	Mt. Olivet
01607	Wheat, Margaret B.P.	75y	W	16 NOV 1894	Atlanta GA	Congressional
18555	Wheatfield, Lawrence C.	64y	W	23 MAY 1923	Richmond VA	Congressional
08688	Wheatley, Emma L.	4m	W	27 JUN 1912	Hyattsville MD	Mt. Olivet
14931	Wheatley, Etta G.	33y	W	22 JUL 1918	Pomfret MD	Congressional
16035	Wheatley, Hattie Taylor	72y	W	29 JUL 1919	Nill, Fra.	Oak Hill
00249	Wheatley, Mary	57y	W	24 DEC 1889	Knowles Sta. MD	Oak Hill
03198	Wheatley, Samuel Edwin	56y	W	2 JUN 1900	Bethesda MD	Oak Hill
03359	Wheatley, William H.	74y	W	6 DEC 1900	Kensington MD	Oak Hill
14613	Wheatley, William, s/o Chas.	65y	W	29 JAN 1918	Atlanta GA	Oak Hill
15665	Wheaton, Laura J.	74y	W	10 MAR 1919	Hyattsville MD	Glenwood
08719	Wheelan, Florence M.	26y	W	13 JUL 1912	Baltimore MD	Mt. Olivet
05967	Wheelan, Thomas	59y	W	2 MAR 1907	Taunton MA	Mt. Olivet
12255	Wheeler, Anne Bascom	3d	W	12 MAR 1914	Cherrydale VA	Rock Creek
18077	Wheeler, Charles W.	47y	C	20 SEP 1922	Bladensburg MD	Harmony
00795	Wheeler, Creighton	6m	W	17 JUL 1882	Falls Church VA	Congressional
13508	Wheeler, Daniel H.	50y	C	14 MAY 1916	Washington DC	Harmony
08647	Wheeler, George L., s/o John	66y	W	25 MAY 1912	Falmouth VA	Glenwood
15997	Wheeler, Henry	60y	W	28 NOV 1918	Lawton OK	Oak Hill
06765	Wheeler, Ida Lentz	62y	W	5 JUL 1908	Yonkers NY	Glenwood
02984	Wheeler, John B., merchant	28y	W	19 OCT 1899	Reisterstown MD	Glenwood
04796	Wheeler, John H.	50y	C	14 JUL 1904	Hyattsville MD	Mt. Olivet
15368	Wheeler, John W.	34y	W	19 NOV 1918	Camp Merritt NJ	Oak Hill
17531	Wheeler, Joseph Rich., Rev.	93y	W	18 NOV 1921	Baltimore MD	Glenwood
13868	Wheeler, Julia	57y	C	14 DEC 1916	Baltimore MD	Payne's
08162	Wheeler, Julia C.	75y	W	22 JUN 1911	Reisterstown MD	Glenwood
16360	Wheeler, Louisa M.	62y	W	2 MAR 1920	Hyattsville MD	Glenwood
03787	Wheeler, Lucy J.B.	48y	W	4 FEB 1902	New York NY	Rock Creek
04499	Wheeler, Mabella E.	1y	C	3 NOV 1903	Riverdale MD	Harmony
06887	Wheeler, Mary Cornelia	3y	C	10 JAN 1909	Baltimore MD	Mt. Olivet
04839	Wheeler, Mary Julia	44y	W	10 AUG 1904	Reisterstown MD	Glenwood
02030	Wheeler, Morris C.	20y	W	25 AUG 1896	Great Falls MD	Congressional
04630	Wheeler, Mrs. Daniel	59y	C	8 MAR 1904	Hyattsville MD	Harmony
06258	Wheeler, Robert, Rev.	85y	C	2 OCT 1907	Harrisonburg VA	Mt. Zion East
16821	Wheeler, Rudolph	1m	C	22 NOV 1920	Cedar Hts. MD	Payne's
10720	Wheeler, Samuel H.	74y	W	25 SEP 1920	Madison NJ	Oak Hill
07411	Wheelock, Arthur W.	33y	W	3 FEB 1910	Hyattsville MD	Congressional

District of Columbia Foreign Death Records, 1888-1923   271

No.	Name of Deceased	Age	Race	Death Date	Place of Death	Place of Burial
04731	Wheelock, Melissa J.W.	73y	W	25 MAY 1904	New York NY	Glenwood
00526	Whelan, Emma F.	13y	W	19 JAN 1891	Easton MD	Oak Hill
05490	Whelan, Mary	85y	W	7 MAR 1906	Baltimore MD	Mt. Olivet
02581	Whellock, David B.	55y	W	4 SEP 1898	Bladensburg MD	Congressional
14973	Whelpley, James Winnie	83y	W	11 AUG 1918	Albany NY	Congressional
12950	Whinerey, Adelia	72y	W	2 JUN 1915	Hyattsville MD	Glenwood
15790	Whipple, Nancy Williams	35y	W	22 MAY 1919	Roanoke VA	Arlington
03841	Whipple, William D.	76y	W	1 APR 1902	New York NY	Arlington VA
15977	Whipps, Thresa	45y	C	4 SEP 1919	Arlington VA	Mt. Olivet
06126	Whitaker, Grenville A., s/o Eph.	61y	W	30 JUN 1907	Jasper IN	Rock Creek
15729	Whitaker, Joseph G.	26y	W	15 APR 1919	Takoma MD	Anatomical Board
15563	Whitcomb, Helen	25y	W	15 JAN 1919	Toldeo OH	Rock Creek
03041	Whitcraft, Rosa	20y	W	18 DEC 1889	Philadelphia PA	Prospect Hill
05858	White, Alberta	41y	W	12 DEC 1906	Seat Pleasant MD	Congressional
06598	White, Alice A.	62y	W	20 JUN 1908	Baltimore MD	Glenwood
13679	White, Alice V.	59y	W	25 AUG 1916	St. Elmo VA	Barnesville MD
03101	White, Anita Maud	25y	W	24 FEB 1900	Riverdale MD	Glenwood
03407	White, Bridget K.	53y	W	3 FEB 1901	Bethesda MD	Holyrood
07659	White, Charles	5y	W	30 JUL 1910	Mt. Ranier MD	Mt. Olivet
05339	White, Charles	80y	W	1 NOV 1905	Landover MD	Rock Creek
14320	White, Cinderrilla	75y	W	28 AUG 1917	Ardwick MD	Rock Creek
16605	White, Dorothy	22y	C	14 JUL 1920	Baltimore MD	Harmony
15441	White, Edward	—	W	6 DEC 1918	Roanoke Co. VA	Congressional
04309	White, Edwin Albert	4y	W	23 MAY 1903	Baltimore MD	Glenwood
02509	White, Elias E.	70y	W	17 JUL 1898	Baltimore MD	Rock Creek
13162	White, Elizabeth (Steuart)	38y	C	23 OCT 1915	New Haven CN	Harmony
08674	White, Elizabeth A.S.	74y	C	15 JUN 1912	Oxon Hill MD	Mt. Zion East
01271	White, Emma	29y	C	24 AUG 1893	Pittsburgh PA	Payne's
12662	White, Fannie B.	54y	W	19 DEC 1914	Mt. Ranier MD	Congressional
13671	White, Florence	34y	C	17 AUG 1916	Philadelphia PA	Payne's
17276	White, Frances E.	88y	W	1 JUL 1921	Burnt Mills MD	Congressional
15424	White, Frank H.	24y	W	5 DEC 1918	Kansas City MO	Cremated
03149	White, Frank H.	34y	W	26 MAR 1900	Saranac Lake NY	Rock Creek
14820	White, George	50y	W	17 MAY 1918	Landover MD	Rock Creek
03435	White, George F.	31y	W	26 FEB 1901	Elgin IL	Oak Hill
18275	White, Gordon C.	50y	W	16 JAN 1923	Baltimore MD	Cremated
04952	White, H.W.	43y	C	6 NOV 1904	Asheville NC	Harmony
14641	White, Harold A.	1y	W	12 FEB 1918	Hartford CN	Congressional
05824	White, Harriet	41y	W	21 NOV 1906	New York NY	Congressional
06898	White, Hattie, nee White	32y	C	20 JAN 1909	Baltimore MD	Payne's
03877	White, James	27y	C	11 MAY 1902	Baltimore MD	Harmony
16636	White, James L.	84y	C	30 JUL 1920	Pittsfield MA	Payne's
04335	White, James T.	30y	W	14 AUG 1903	Baltimore MD	Mt. Olivet
13956	White, Jemina C.	77y	W	28 JAN 1917	Jersey City NJ	Congressional
06271	White, John M.	36y	C	12 OCT 1907	Falls Church VA	Hamilton VA
12917	White, Joseph C.	15y	C	8 MAY 1915	Bladensburg MD	Mt. Olivet
08516	White, Julia McKee	85y	W	14 FEB 1912	Primos PA	Arlington
14819	White, Katherine	6y	W	17 MAY 1918	Landover MD	Rock Creek
12168	White, M.W., Rev.	46y	C	17 JAN 1914	Easton MD	Harmony
07216	White, Malvin	3y	C	28 SEP 1909	Rome NY	Harmony
03335	White, Mamie	22y	C	13 NOV 1900	Cabin John MD	Christian
07923	White, Manuel	69y	C	14 JAN 1911	Arlington VA	Harmony
08332	White, Margaret	21y	W	29 AUG 1911	Baltimore MD	Congressional
08520	White, Margaret	28y	W	18 FEB 1912	Mt. Hope MD	Mt. Olivet
16006	White, Marion H.	69y	W	22 SEP 1919	Ossining NY	Rock Creek
16231	White, Mary	39y	C	16 JAN 1920	Philadelphia PA	Harmony
03918	White, Mary Aurelia Reynold	27y	W	23 JUL 1902	Alexandria VA	Rock Creek
01099	White, Mary E.	9y	W	9 FEB 1893	Philadelphia PA	Mt. Olivet
04082	White, Mary F.	—	W	14 JUL 1886	Vincennes IN	Arlington
16558	White, Mary H.	21y	W	25 JUN 1920	Mt. Ranier MD	Mt. Olivet

No.	Name of Deceased	Age	Race	Death Date	Place of Death	Place of Burial
15418	White, Mary J.	67y	W	8 DEC 1918	Hyattsville MD	Mt. Olivet
01662	White, Mary O.	7y	C	9 APR 1895	New York NY	Harmony
16290	White, Mattie	47y	W	7 FEB 1920	Takoma Park MD	Mt. Olivet
13708	White, Melva, d/o John	1y	W	7 SEP 1916	Hartford CN	Congressional
05184	White, Pearl Irene	5m	W	29 JUN 1905	Alexandria VA	Mt. Olivet
16967	White, Plymton	25y	W	20 JAN 1921	Port-au-Prince	Arlington
04562	White, Simon P.	63y	W	11 JAN 1904	Baltimore MD	Glenwood
00794	White, Susan	74y	W	25 DEC 1891	Philadelphia PA	Congressional
04563	White, Theodore R.	6m	W	10 JAN 1904	Forestville MD	Mt. Olivet
06912	White, Warren H.	17y	W	8 FEB 1909	Riverdale MD	Glenwood[1]
02672	White, William H.	77y	W	13 DEC 1898	Bailey's Xrds. VA	Oak Hill
14800	White, William L.	19y	W	2 MAY 1918	Philadelphia PA	Congressional
00003½	White, Z.L.	46y	W	31 DEC 1888	Nassau, B.I.	Congressional
15179	Whitehand, Robert	30y	W	13 OCT 1918	Camp Meade MD	Arlington VA
02837	Whitehead, Josephine S.	56y	W	26 MAY 1899	New York NY	Arlington VA
15501	Whiteley, Josephine P.	65y	W	30 DEC 1918	Riverdale MD	Congressional
08276	Whiteley, Richard P.	4d	W	27 AUG 1911	E. Hyattsville MD	Congressional
06789	Whitfield, Mary E.	24y	W	27 OCT 1908	New York NY	—
07326	Whitford, Infant of George L.	SB	W	16 DEC 1909	Chevy Chase MD	Glenwood
04652	Whitford, Onslow Sterns	26y	W	31 MAR 1904	Crownsville MD	Warner NH
14395	Whiting, Clara	33y	C	29 SEP 1917	Philadelphia PA	Harmony
03861	Whiting, Evans Lyons	34y	W	22 APR 1902	Frederick MD	Oak Hill
03858	Whiting, George B.	70y	W	14 APR 1902	Cattarengus NY	Oak Hill
06865	Whiting, Harry	30y	C	20 DEC 1908	Chicago IL	Harmony
05270	Whiting, Harry C.	64y	W	2 APR 1905	Atlantic City NJ	Oak Hill
06495	Whiting, Louis	54y	C	4 APR 1908	Baltimore MD	Harmony
04615	Whiting, Martha E.	83y	W	25 FEB 1904	Baltimore MD	Glenwood
07248	Whitlocke, George Carlile	5y	W	24 OCT 1909	Mt. Ranier MD	Cremated
04653	Whitlow, Frances	72y	C	5 DEC 1903	Jersey City NJ	Harmony
06414	Whitlow, William H.	44y	C	31 JAN 1908	New York NY	Harmony
12832	Whitman, Anthony	21y	W	23 MAR 1915	Trenton NJ	Arlington
03148	Whitman, Charles S.	17y	W	26 MAR 1900	Greenfield MA	Rock Creek
04843	Whitman, Frank H., Capt.	34y	W	7 AUG 1904	Railroad	Arlington VA
09041	Whitmer, Elizabeth J.	63y	W	20 JAN 1913	Takoma Park MD	Culpeper VA
15623	Whitmore, William Titus	48y	W	18 FEB 1919	Railroad	Boonton NJ
06956	Whitney, Charlotte S.	77y	W	18 MAR 1909	Washington DC	Rock Creek
04280	Whitney, Edith S.	45y	W	6 MAY 1899	Westbury LI	Rock Creek
07702	Whitney, Eleanora G.	1m	W	8 MAR 1910	Minneapolis MN	Rock Creek
05613	Whitney, Ellen R.	70y	W	27 JUN 1906	Camden Co. NJ	Glenwood
06669	Whitney, George M.	7y	W	4 AUG 1908	Hyattsville MD	Glenwood
04322	Whitney, Hattie Myrick	42y	W	8 JUN 1803	Ft. Missoula MT	Arlington VA
16669	Whitney, John C.	16y	W	17 AUG 1920	Sterling NY	Rock Creek
07274	Whitney, Sims E.	52y	W	13 NOV 1909	New York NY	Rock Creek
03993	Whitney, Thomas	42y	C	11 AUG 1902	Columbus OH	Payne's
02691	Whitney, William H.	57y	W	10 DEC 1898	Manchester NH	Oak Hill
06748	Whitson, Infant of W.	SB	W	25 SEP 1908	Alexandria VA	Rock Creek
07352	Whittemore, Robert Edward	38y	W	2 JAN 1910	Wash. Grove MD	Norfolk VA
15813	Whitten, Catherine	76y	W	6 JUN 1919	New York NY	Congressional
04264	Whitting, George	43y	W	1 MAY 1903	Anne Arundel Co.	Prospect Hill
07665	Whittlesey, Augusta Patten	75y	W	31 JUL 1910	Waterville NH	Arlington
04360	Whitton, Byrde Denise	4d	W	25 JUN 1903	Bridgeport CN	Mt. Olivet
07061	Whyte, Frederick D.	18y	W	13 jUN 1909	Potomac River	Mt. Olivet
09156	Wibirt, Amelia T.	49y	W	5 APR 1913	Clarendon VA	Mt. Olivet
12996	Wichmann, Henry Othmar	24y	W	7 JUL 1915	Eliz. City VA	Cremated
05783	Wichter, John S.	66y	W	8 JUL 1906	Salt Lake UT	Arlington
15485	Widdecombe, Alice Ann	82y	W	25 DEC 1918	Chicago IL	Arlington
12685	Widmer, Annie M.	48y	W	28 DEC 1914	Capitol Hts. MD	Prospect Hill

[1] Disinterment permit #6520, dated 30 MAR 1909, for removal to St. Paul, Minn.

District of Columbia Foreign Death Records, 1888-1923

No.	Name of Deceased	Age	Race	Death Date	Place of Death	Place of Burial
05199	Wiebking, William Henry	10m	W	7 JUL 1905	Westminster MD	Prospect Hill
04793	Wiggin, Maud	35y	W	10 JUL 1904	St. Louis MO	Congressional
17324	Wiggins, Andrew B.	30y	C	23 JUL 1921	Philadelphia PA	Woodlawn
11806	Wiggins, Annie R.	75y	W	9 MAY 1913	Ft. Myer Hts. VA	Glenwood
04255	Wiggins, Jessie L.	28y	W	12 MAY 1903	New York NY	Oak Hill
07035	Wigginton, John Harvey	44y	C	21 MAY 1909	Brentwood MD	Harmony
16498	Wight, Ellen Cuyler	89y	W	22 MAY 1920	Grander MD	Rock Creek
14124	Wight, Harriet Wilson (Dickins)	73y	W	3 MAY 1917	Fredericksburg VA	Cremated
18449	Wight, John Brewer	70y	W	31 MAR 1923	Montclair NJ	Oak Hill
12441	Wilber, Emery A.	74y	W	13 JUL 1914	W. Springfield MA	Oak Hill
08475	Wilber, Henry	51y	W	14 JAN 1912	New York NY	Mt. Olivet
08689	Wilbur, Eliza Stone C.	78y	W	27 JUN 1912	Sligo MD	Rock Creek
09095	Wilbur, Jeremiah B.	72y	W	27 FEB 1913	Sligo MD	Rock Creek
07301	Wilcox, Daniel	—	W	21 MAY 1887	Marshall MN	Rock Creek
00090	Wilcox, John A.	45y	W	7 FEB 1864	Richmond VA	Oak Hill
11989	Wilcox, John Andrew, s/o C.	84y	W	1 SEP 1913	Atlantic City NJ	Arlington VA
07786	Wilcox, Walter Dwight	8m	W	25 JUL 1910	Banff, Can.	Rock Creek
07831	Wilcoxen, Thos. J.	32y	W	19 NOV 1910	Berwyn MD	Mt. Olivet
02455	Wilcoxon, Hanswon	1y	W	1 JUN 1859	Baltimore MD	Congressional
02455	Wilcoxon, Horace	39y	W	1 JUN 1859	Baltimore MD	Congressional
07319	Wild, Harry W.	30y	W	11 DEC 1909	Philadelphia PA	Rock Creek
02032	Wild, William R.	21y	W	2 AUG 1896	Cedar Point MD	Rock Creek
03432	Wilde, Thomas Edwan	22y	W	23 FEB 1901	New Haven CN	Cremated
18527	Wildman, Marie Icilla	70y	W	5 MAY 1923	Landover MD	Mt. Olivet
12538	Wildman, Theodore	1y	W	22 SEP 1914	Landover MD	Mt. Olivet
07071	Wildman, Thomas	11m	W	22 JUN 1909	Landover MD	Mt. Olivet
05461	Wiley, Charles E.	53y	W	9 FEB 1906	Hillsboro VA	Rock Creek
12265	Wiley, Elizabeth	65y	W	25 MAR 1914	S. Pines NC	Congressional
05040	Wiley, Ellen R.	37y	C	21 FEB 1905	Humboldt TN	Woodlawn
01782	Wiley, Jefferson	40y	C	28 JUN 1895	Hot Springs NC	Woodlawn
05948	Wilfong, Vincent M.	64y	W	20 FEB 1907	Westphalia MD	Arlington VA
14050	Wilgus, Thomas P.	32y	W	17 MAR 1917	Phoenix AZ	Glenwood
07235	Wilhelm, Florence I.	31y	W	9 OCT 1909	Seattle WA	Rock Creek
02034	Wilhorte, William A.	23y	W	11 JUL 1896	Baltimore MD	Mt. Olivet
08594	Wiliams, Quincy T.	64y	W	10 APR 1912	Brooklyn NY	Congressional
03578	Wilkeison, Henrietta W.	60y	W	14 JUL 1901	Branchville MD	Rock Creek
17620	Wilkening, William H.	81y	W	3 JAN 1922	Yonkers NY	Glenwood
15742	Wilkerson, Dorothea (Meyer)	55y	W	18 APR 1919	Baltimore MD	Rock Creek
06691	Wilkes, Eliza, d/o Charles	69y	W	15 AUG 1908	Winchester VA	Oak Hill
00913	Wilkes, Elizabeth E.	39y	W	20 MAY 1892	Lockhart GA	Oak Hill
17360	Wilkes, Jane	92y	W	17 AUG 1921	Wellesley MA	Arlington
04265	Wilkins, Alfred	18y	C	27 JUL 1901	Baltimore MD	Harmony
02830	Wilkins, Charles A.	60y	W	26 APR 1899	Chicago IL	Oak Hill
18299	Wilkins, Ellie B.	57y	W	25 JAN 1923	Lincoln MA	Rock Creek
02185	Wilkins, Fannie G.	5y	W	17 MAR 1872	Philadelphia PA	Rock Creek
01381	Wilkins, Joseph, produce dlr.	58y	W	15 MAR 1894	Philadelphia PA	Rock Creek
03842	Wilkins, Sarah E.	50y	C	2 APR 1902	Philadelphia PA	Harmony
06983	Wilkins, Virginia	55y	C	13 APR 1909	Brentwood MD	Weldon NC
14442	Wilkinson, Berta	62y	W	4 NOV 1917	Silver Spring MD	Rock Creek
13377	Wilkinson, Elizabeth	80y	C	23 FEB 1916	Baltimore MD	Halls Hill VA
13524	Wilkinson, Eve E.	SB	W	30 MAY 1916	Montg. Co. MD	Rock Creek
15945	Wilkinson, Infant of Benj.	SB	W	23 AUG 1919	Takoma Park MD	Rock Creek
18398	Wilkinson, Jennie	20y	W	5 MAR 1923	Winsor PA	Glenwood
13352	Wilkinson, Kathryn Mildred	14y	W	13 FEB 1916	Harrisburg PA	Mt. Olivet
07648	Willard, Alexander D.	74y	W	21 JUL 1910	Farmington ME	Rock Creek
08274	Willard, Louise M.	82y	W	27 AUG 1911	Takoma Park MD	Burlington VT
01272	Willard, Walter Jones	24y	W	5 NOV 1893	Bristol RI	Oak Hill
06063	Willcox, O.B.	84y	W	10 MAY 1907	Cobourg, Can.	Arlington
15854	Willeke, Frank Aloysius	26y	W	12 JUN 1919	Tangier, Morocco	Arlington
14776	Willett, James P.	45y	W	25 APR 1918	Chicago IL	Oak Hill

No.	Name of Deceased	Age	Race	Death Date	Place of Death	Place of Burial
05664	Willett, John T., s/o Jos. F.	18y	W	25 JUL 1906	Manassas VA	Congressional
07025	Willett, Susan M.	78y	W	16 MAY 1909	Bethesda MD	Methodist
05910	Willey, Marion	21y	W	25 JAN 1907	Takoma Park MD	Cambridge MD
03546	Willhoite, Kenneth B.	25y	W	17 JUN 1901	Alexandria VA	Congressional
00563	Williams, Alexander Bodisco	42y	W	20 MAY 1891	Aiken SC	Oak Hill
05258	Williams, Alexander R.	68y	W	24 AUG 1905	Atlantic City NJ	Rock Creek
01100	Williams, Alice B.	56y	W	16 JUL 1892	Baltimore MD	Oak Hill
13276	Williams, Alice Moore	81y	W	2 JAN 1916	Takoma Park MD	Rock Creek
04665	Williams, Andrew J.	35y	W	9 APR 1904	Baltimore MD	Congressional
15057	Williams, Archie W.	20y	W	30 SEP 1918	Philadelphia PA	Cherrydale VA
14792	Williams, Arthur Fisher	23y	W	16 APR 1918	San Juan, P.R.	Rock Creek
08093	Williams, Benjamin, a.k.a.	46y	C	30 APR 1911	Baltimore MD	Mt. Olivet
05227	Williams, Caleb C.	70y	W	3 AUG 1905	Atlantic City NJ	Oak Hill
16086	Williams, Carleton Lemont	5y	W	3 NOV 1919	Clarendon VA	Congressional
02397	Williams, Caroline	63y	W	27 JAN 1898	Baltimore MD	Rock Creek
00223	Williams, Carrie Rives	49y	W	28 OCT 1889	Pr. Geo. Co. MD	Congressional
12363	Williams, Catherine	63y	W	15 MAY 1914	Tuxedo MD	Mt. Olivet
02230	Williams, Charity	26y	C	2 JUN 1897	New London CN	Payne's
14712	Williams, Charles	85y	W	27 MAR 1918	Takoma Park MD	Rock Creek
12031	Williams, Charles	40y	C	5 OCT 1913	Occoquan VA	Woodlawn
14472	Williams, Charles E.	52y	C	19 NOV 1917	New York NY	Harmony
03102	Williams, Charles F., Col.	58y	W	30 JAN 1900	Mare Island CA	Glenwood
02692	Williams, Charles Henry	23y	W	3 JAN 1899	Rosslyn VA	Holyrood
06349	Williams, Delia	40y	W	14 DEC 1907	Mt. Hope MD	Mt. Olivet
16329	Williams, Edgar D.	45y	W	17 FEB 1920	Cleveland OH	Congressional
13641	Williams, Edward H.	c.60y	W	6 AUG 1916	Driver VA	Glenwood[1]
17692	Williams, Eliza Ann	76y	W	13 FEB 1922	Ballston VA	Mt. Olivet
00288	Williams, Ella	22y	M	10 MAR 1890	Alexandria VA	Harmony
12019	Williams, Ephrum W.	67y	W	28 SEP 1913	Malcolm MD	Congressional
16309	Williams, Fannie	60y	C	11 FEB 1920	Pittsburgh PA	Harmony
14525	Williams, Frank	c.40y	W	18 DEC 1917	San Angelo TX	Mt. Olivet
06121	Williams, Frank	27y	C	27 JUN 1907	Baltimore MD	Payne's
13517	Williams, Fred Childs	40y	W	24 MAY 1916	Claremont VA	Cremated
05029	Williams, George W.	73y	W	11 FEB 1905	Hampton VA	Glenwood
00032	Williams, Georgie Eva	1y	W	14 FEB 1889	Bethesda MD	Tenallytown
14323	Williams, Gertrude	14y	C	26 AUG 1917	Pittsburgh PA	Harmony
14337	Williams, Grace P.	54y	W	1 SEP 1917	New York NY	Oak Hill
15125	Williams, Guy	23y	C	7 OCT 1918	Camp Meade MD	Payne's
02529	Williams, Halley L., electrician	26y	W	3 JUL 1898	Glen Echo MD	Glenwood
16387	Williams, Hammond	42y	C	14 MAR 1920	Jersey City NJ	Harmony
17754	Williams, Hannah N.	73y	W	17 MAR 1922	Edgemore MD	Rock Creek
02813	Williams, Hayes	21y	C	20 JUL 1898	Trenton NJ	Harmony
16618	Williams, Helen Margaretta	88y	W	21 JUL 1920	New York NY	Oak Hill
04588	Williams, Henrietta	25y	C	2 FEB 1904	Philadelphia PA	Payne's
16211	Williams, Henry	28y	C	12 JAN 1920	Mansfield OH	Harmony
07796	Williams, Hester Ann	65y	W	20 OCT 1910	Capitol Hts. MD	Congressional
16706	Williams, Horace P.	71y	W	9 SEP 1920	Baltimore MD	Congressional
13453	Williams, Ida	50y	C	11 APR 1916	Baltimore MD	Falls Church VA
04422	Williams, Iola F.	33y	W	12 SEP 1893	Washington DC	Rock Creek
13275	Williams, Irene C.	24y	C	31 DEC 1915	New York NY	Harmony
07548	Williams, James	2y	C	16 MAY 1910	Philadelphia PA	Payne's
00673	Williams, James Berry	24y	W	25 AUG 1891	Wilmington DE	Glenwood
03889	Williams, James H.	25y	W	30 MAY 1902	Four Mile Run VA	Fredericksburg VA
05734	Williams, Jennie C.	82y	W	6 AUG 1905	Wilmington DE	Mt. Zion
18365	Williams, Jennie M.	51y	W	21 FEB 1923	Philadelphia PA	Oak Hill
12920	Williams, Jerry	83y	W	11 MAY 1915	New York NY	Arlington VA
00797	Williams, John	28y	C	13 MAR 1892	Springfield NJ	Payne's

[1] Disinterment permit #8799 on 5 NOV 1918 for removal to Richmond VA.

District of Columbia Foreign Death Records, 1888-1923

No.	Name of Deceased	Age	Race	Death Date	Place of Death	Place of Burial
01897	Williams, John	24y	C	26 FEB 1896	Philadelphia PA	Woodlawn
14378	Williams, John E.	56y	W	24 SEP 1917	Baltimore H. MD	Congressional
03039	Williams, Jorden	38y	C	15 DEC 1899	Boston MA	Woodlawn
03921	Williams, Joseph	63y	W	23 JUL 1902	Pisgah MD	Congressional
15549	Williams, Kate	54y	C	12 JAN 1919	Brentwood MD	Payne's
18582	Williams, Laura E.	48y	C	3 JUN 1923	Pittsburgh PA	Woodlawn
16204	Williams, Laura E. (Peter)	75y	W	11 JAN 1920	Relay MD	Cremated
07989	Williams, Lawrence J.	—	W	25 FEB 1911	Memphis TN	Mt. Olivet
14860	Williams, Lea D.	26y	W	1 JUN 1918	Douglas AZ	Rock Creek
15564	Williams, Leola Dale	27y	C	16 JAN 1919	New York NY	Harmony
08593	Williams, Louisa M.	83y	W	9 APR 1912	Chicago IL	Rock Creek
07587	Williams, Louise	59y	C	19 JUN 1910	Cumberland MD	Harmony
17506	Williams, Mahala	73y	C	6 NOV 1921	Philadelphia PA	Harmony
18568	Williams, Margaret	20yt	C	29 MAY 1923	Cleveland OH	Payne's
04325	Williams, Margret P.	23y	C	16 JUN 1903	Philadelphia PA	Harmony
14999	Williams, Maria	70y	W	22 AUG 1918	Tacoma WA	Congressional
03119	Williams, Maria	38y	W	5 MAR 1900	New York NY	Harmony
16655	Williams, Maria	51y	C	10 AUG 1920	Lynn MA	Mt. Olivet
01660	Williams, Maria Scott Tucker	72y	W	13 MAR 1895	Brooklyn NY	Congressional
03376	Williams, Martha A.	40y	W	23 DEC 1900	Baltimore MD	Oak Hill
01102	Williams, Mary E.	20y	C	7 MAR 1893	Lakeland MD	Mt. Olivet
02282	Williams, Octavia J.	64y	W	13 AUG 1897	Oakdale MD	Glenwood
08341	Williams, Ophelia (Ames)	58y	W	8 FEB 1885	Washington DC	Rock Creek
18216	Williams, Page	37y	C	19 DEC 1922	Johnstown PA	Rosemont
14054	Williams, Philip W.	33y	W	25 MAR 1917	Baltimore MD	Rock Creek
04999	Williams, Precilla	29y	C	9 JAN 1905	Pittsburgh PA	Harmony
01009	Williams, Richard J.	2m	W	29 MAY 1893	Ft. McPherson GA	Mt. Olivet
12535	Williams, Richard T.	31y	W	18 SEP 1914	Elkridge MD	Glenwood
03623	Williams, Robert	73y	W	24 AUG 1901	Plainfield NJ	Arlington VA
16759	Williams, Robert	46y	C	10 OCT 1920	Colo. Spgs. CO	Harmony
04363	Williams, Samuel Thomson	72y	W	25 JUN 1903	New York NY	Rock Creek
14683	Williams, Sarah	36y	C	9 MAR 1918	Braddock PA	Harmony
00796	Williams, Sarah H.	37y	W	3 FEB 1892	Rosslyn VA	Holyrood
11822	Williams, Susan B.	65y	W	15 MAY 1913	South Bend IN	Rock Creek
04637	Williams, T.E.	77y	W	16 MAR 1904	Richmond VA	Barnilo MD
02800	Williams, Thomas	86y	C	8 APR 1899	Fairfax VA	Woodlawn
08234	Williams, Thomas J., s/o Jas.	82y	W	31 JUL 1911	Cherrydale VA	Rock Creek
02031	Williams, Thomas T.	28y	W	8 JUL 1896	Baltimore MD	Glenwood
12161	Williams, Walter J.	43y	W	13 JAN 1914	W. Asheville NC	Mt. Olivet
01208	Williams, Walter W., Rev.	58y	W	29 JUN 1892	Sudbrook MD	Oak Hill
04423	Williams, Watson S.	33y	W	13 OCT 1862	Antietam MD	Rock Creek
14835	Williams, Willard	42y	C	21 MAY 1918	Sunnyside MD	Harmony
07817	Williams, William	48y	C	1 MAR 1910	Alta Vista MD	Payne's
14497	Williams, William E.	90y	W	11 DEC 1917	Takoma Park MD	Warren RI
14518	Williams, William H.	49y	C	21 DEC 1917	Kensington MD	Mt. Olivet
04386	Williams, William H.	49y	W	11 JUL 1903	Maryland Pk. MD	Woodlawn
04301	Williamson, Alexander	90y	W	2 JUN 1903	New York NY	Glenwood
04586	Williamson, Elizabeth M.	75y	W	2 FEB 1904	Brunswick MD	Congressional
00914	Williamson, Hallam Gregory	28y	W	6 AUG 1892	Hot Springs NM	Rock Creek
04050	Williamson, James A.	73y	W	7 SEP 1902	Jamestown RI	Rock Creek
04554	Williamson, James A.	26y	C	25 DEC 1903	Occoquan VA	Woodlawn
17935	Williamson, L. Cabell	68y	W	3 JUL 1922	Wash. Grove MD	Rock Creek
14457	Williamson, Mark	30y	W	23 AUG 1917	Washington DC	Glenwood
16978	Williamson, W. Preston	57y	W	15 FEB 1921	Jacksonville FL	Glenwood
14986	Williamson, William Price	34y	W	17 AUG 1918	At Sea	Arlington
14024	Williamson, Windfield S.	69y	W	10 MAR 1917	Cottage City MD	Glenwood
17130	Willis, Arthur Ross	31y	W	24 APR 1921	Great Falls MD	Springfield OH
12324	Willis, Charles	7y	W	20 APR 1914	Martinsburg WV	Glenwood
11829	Willis, Edward Mott, s/o Henry	70y	W	24 MAY 1913	Atlantic City NJ	Rock Creek
18061	Willis, Eliza E.	56y	C	9 SEP 1922	Hartford CN	Harmony

No.	Name of Deceased	Age	Race	Death Date	Place of Death	Place of Burial
16755	Willis, Hattie E.	55y	C	9 OCT 1920	New York NY	Harmony
03859	Willis, Helen A.	26y	W	19 APR 1902	Saranac Lake NY	Glenwood
17979	Willis, Julia M.	79y	W	25 JUL 1922	Waseca MN	Glenwood
08248	Willis, Laurence	37y	C	11 AUG 1911	Upper Marl. MD	Woodlawn
03961	Willis, Lloyd A.	7m	W	31 JUL 1902	Harpers Ferry WV	Mt. Olivet
08429	Willis, Rodolph	69y	W	18 DEC 1911	Hyattsville MD	Glenwood
03837	Williston, Helen Beatrice	71y	W	25 MAR 1902	San Francisco CA	Glenwood
01661	Willmarth, Austin F.	78y	W	31 MAR 1895	Mt. Hope MD	N. Adams MA
12656	Wills, Mary M.	82y	W	13 DEC 1914	Greensboro NC	Glenwood
14060	Wills, Nisbit	50y	W	27 MAR 1917	Newark NJ	Glenwood
12096	Willson, Clara G.	30y	W	14 NOV 1913	Philadelphia PA	Cremated
07004	Willson, Fred	40y	W	24 APR 1908	Newark NJ	Glenwood
14913	Willson, William H.	58y	W	12 JUL 1918	Chicago IL	Glenwood
07619	Wilmarth, Caroline Coburn	69y	W	8 JUL 1910	Pender VA	Oak Hill
12369	Wilmot, John H.	52y	W	1 MAY 1894	Columbia PA	Rock Creek
14651	Wilsie, Jerome C.	38y	W	21 FEB 1918	Hyattsville MD	Glenwood
13775	Wilsie, Kyes Jerome	65y	W	23 OCT 1916	Hyattsville MD	Glenwood
18088	Wilson, Ada	39y	C	22 SEP 1922	Asbury Park NJ	Harmony
12271	Wilson, Alexander F.	53y	W	26 MAR 1914	Gaithersburg MD	Glenwood
14177	Wilson, Allan Edwin, Sr.	51y	W	17 JUN 1917	Dominion Hts. VA	Glenwood
15004	Wilson, Amanda J.	68y	W	6 SEP 1918	Landover MD	Mt. Olivet
04274	Wilson, Amelia	33y	C	24 APR 1903	Bright Seat MD	Mt. Olivet
03762	Wilson, Andrew, sign painter	34y	W	19 JAN 1902	Norfolk VA	Congressional
13700	Wilson, Annie Edwards	78y	W	5 SEP 1916	Newport RI	Oak Hill
07450	Wilson, Beulah P.	41y	W	4 MAR 1910	New York NY	Rock Creek
02396	Wilson, Bridget	68y	W	23 JAN 1898	Alex. Co. VA	Mt. Olivet
13616	Wilson, Caroline M.	62y	C	23 JUL 1916	Arlington VA	Harmony
07501	Wilson, Charles C.	68y	W	15 APR 1910	Amityville NY	Rock Creek
01207	Wilson, Charles H.	38y	W	17 DEC 1892	Baltimore MD	Congressional
12012	Wilson, Charles J.	76y	W	22 SEP 1913	New York NY	Arlington
09115	Wilson, Chloe Murdock	5y	W	9 MAR 1913	Lynchburg VA	Oak Hill
13015	Wilson, Edward E.	43y	W	19 JUL 1915	Clarendon VA	Rock Creek
02358	Wilson, Edward Hartford	5y	W	13 DEC 1897	Riverdale MD	Oak Hill
12176	Wilson, Edwin Sherwood	41y	W	20 JAN 1914	Roseland VA	Oak Hill
16723	Wilson, Edwin Walter	72y	W	21 SEP 1920	Chevy Chase MD	Rock Creek
13263	Wilson, Eliza J.	89y	W	19 DEC 1915	St. Louis MO	Oak Hill
16642	Wilson, Elizabeth	7y	C	4 AUG 1920	Chicago IL	Payne's
03103	Wilson, Emily Montague	77y	W	14 FEB 1900	Pelham NY	Oak Hill
00798	Wilson, Ephraim King	60y	W	21 FEB 1891	Baltimore MD	Glenwood
12743	Wilson, Estelle P.	2y	W	2 FEB 1915	Clarendon VA	Rock Creek
12605	Wilson, Eva M., a.k.a. Sisson	28y	W	8 NOV 1914	Richmond VA	Congressional
06250	Wilson, Everett	11m	W	27 SEP 1907	Bethesda Pk. MD	Rock Creek
01365	Wilson, Francis	49y	C	12 APR 1894	Alex. Co. VA	Harmony
07823	Wilson, George	80y	W	13 NOV 1910	Sligo MD	Congressional
06007	Wilson, George	61y	C	31 MAR 1907	New York NY	Woodlawn
06007	Wilson, George	61y	C	31 MAR 1907	New York NY	Woodlawn
12377	Wilson, George G.	85y	W	25 MAY 1914	Hampton VA	Glenwood
11816	Wilson, George Robert	56y	W	16 MAY 1913	Newport News VA	Congressional
15085	Wilson, Gertrude	27y	W	5 OCT 1918	Takoma Park MD	Congressional
00672	Wilson, Grace A.	16y	W	17 JUL 1891	Catlett's Sta. VA	Oak Hill
01608	Wilson, Harriett C.	68y	W	31 JAN 1895	New York NY	Congressional
16203	Wilson, Helen	1y	W	11 JAN 1920	Baltimore MD	Oak Hill
06294	Wilson, Henrietta W.	69y	W	29 OCT 1907	Omaha NE	Arlington
03685	Wilson, Hiram Gerry	80y	W	20 AUG 1901	St. Louis MO	Oak Hill
16470	Wilson, J. Thomas	29y	W	5 MAY 1920	Somerset MD	Oak Hill
18046	Wilson, Jack	21y	C	1 SEP 1922	Pittsburgh PA	Arlington
15209	Wilson, John F.	22y	W	10 OCT 1918	Philadelphia PA	Mt. Olivet
00315	Wilson, John H.	63y	W	21 APR 1890	Alexandria VA	Mt. Olivet
17176	Wilson, Joseph	76y	W	20 MAY 1921	Wayne PA	Glenwood
16015	Wilson, Joseph	40y	C	23 SEP 1919	Rockville MD	Payne's

District of Columbia Foreign Death Records, 1888-1923 277

No.	Name of Deceased	Age	Race	Death Date	Place of Death	Place of Burial
09132	Wilson, Joseph F.	56y	W	15 MAR 1913	Hyattsville MD	Congressional
06955	Wilson, Katherine M.	56y	W	20 MAR 1909	Denver CO	Congressional
14118	Wilson, Kathrine	75y	W	1 MAY 1917	Rockville MD	Glenwood
17918	Wilson, Lawrence	79y	W	22 JUN 1922	Mobile AL	Arlington
12782	Wilson, Lillian B.	9y	W	25 FEB 1915	Clarendon VA	Rock Creek
12158	Wilson, Lizzie	26y	C	11 JAN 1914	New York NY	Mt. Olivet
15792	Wilson, Mancil	31y	C	24 MAY 1919	Genesco NY	Harmony
03221	Wilson, Margaret	6m	W	4 JUL 1900	Bel Air MD	Mt. Olivet
17480	Wilson, Marion Elizabeth	18m	W	10 NOV 1910	Seattle WA	Troy PA
17582	Wilson, Mary A.	58y	W	4 DEC 1921	Los Angeles CA	Mt. Olivet
16051	Wilson, Mary E.	43y	C	14 OCT 1919	Huntsville MD	Mt. Olivet
07982	Wilson, Mary E.	71y	W	21 FEB 1911	Philadelphia PA	Mt. Olivet
02889	Wilson, Mary H.	44y	W	10 JUL 1899	Nantucket MA	Oak Hill
18183	Wilson, Merritt, Jr.	1d	C	25 NOV 1922	Arlington VA	Woodlawn
12090½	Wilson, Richard	c.50y	C	12 NOV 1913	Potomac River	Cremated
07773	Wilson, Robert	73y	W	2 OCT 1910	Hyattsville MD	Glenwood
02283	Wilson, Robert	9m	W	31 JUL 1897	Oakland MD	Rock Creek
04236	Wilson, Samuel, s/o Henry	66y	C	21 FEB 1903	Plainfield NJ	Woodlawn
06388	Wilson, Sarah D.	73y	W	15 JAN 1908	Leonardtown MD	Rock Creek
08731	Wilson, Teresa	20m	W	26 JUL 1912	Berwyn MD	Mt. Olivet
18453	Wilson, Thomas	1y	W	2 APR 1923	Hyattsville MD	Mt. Olivet
03527	Wilson, Thomas, Gen.	68y	W	30 MAY 1901	New York NY	Arlington VA
05415	Wilson, Thomas H.	47y	W	25 DEC 1905	Ft. Logan CO	Arlington VA
13102	Wilson, Virginia M.	58y	W	12 SEP 1915	Seat Pleasant MD	Mt. Olivet
18563	Wilson, Virginia M.	87y	W	25 MAY 1923	St. Petersburg FL	Rock Creek
12474	Wilson, Wallace W.	20y	W	5 AUG 1914	Wheeling WV	Glenwood
12852	Wilson, Walter L.	c.43y	W	31 MAR 1915	Norfolk VA	Charlestown WV
00383	Wilson, Whitwell Arnold	6y	W	2 AUG 1890	Montg. Co. MD	Rock Creek
03655	Wilson, Whitwell Hamilton	46y	W	22 SEP 1901	Capitol View MD	Rock Creek
07337	Wilson, William A.	73y	W	19 DEC 1909	Hampton VA	Congressional
17968	Wilson, William H.	87y	W	17 JUL 1922	Laurel MD	Congressional
13408	Wiltberger, Amelia E.	86y	W	9 MAR 1916	Cambridge MA	Rock Creek
12352	Wiltse, Arthur, s/o Gilbert	28y	W	8 MAY 1914	Stamford CN	Oak Hill
01101	Wiltse, Gilbert Cranville	55y	W	26 APR 1893	New York NY	Oak Hill
05721	Wimberly, Nellie	11y	C	31 AUG 1906	Cambridge MD	Harmony
17498	Windham, Annie Kate	69y	W	2 NOV 1921	Colesville MD	Rock Creek
13072	Windham, George Thornton	63y	W	22 AUG 1915	Colesville MD	Rock Creek
15515	Windham, Nellie Martin	32y	W	2 JAN 1919	Colesville MD	Rock Creek
16100	Windham, Roberta LaRoche	1m	W	1 NOV 1919	Finland MD	Rock Creek
12554	Windom, Ellen Town	83y	W	4 OCT 1914	Williamstown MA	Rock Creek
00527	Windom, William	64y	W	29 JAN 1891	New York NY	Rock Creek
12340	Wine, Mary Powell	15y	W	21 APR 1914	Philadelphia PA	Rock Creek
04128	Winebrener, Rebecca	—	W	2 DEC 1902	Frederick MD	Frederick MD
02146	Winfield, Robert	42y	W	7 MAR 1897	New York NY	Harmony
04548	Wingard, Edward, Dr.	45y	W	17 DEC 1903	Leadville CO	Mt. Olivet
02348	Wingate, William	27y	W	23 NOV 1897	Baltimore MD	Oak Hill
17718	Winkfield, Helen	13y	C	2 MAR 1922	Bucks Co. PA	Mt. Olivet
03401	Winkler, John	51y	W	21 JAN 1901	Brooke VA	Mt. Olivet
07140	Winlock, Alice Brown	65y	W	28 JUL 1909	Atlantic City NJ	Congressional
04505	Winn, Robert	10m	C	14 JUN 1903	Boston MA	Harmony
15494	Winslow, Albert	19y	W	27 DEC 1918	Steubensville OH	St. Matthews MD
09147	Winslow, Albert H.	39y	W	29 MAR 1913	Mt. Ranier MD	St. Mary's
06606	Winslow, Francis, s/o Francis	56y	W	22 JUN 1908	Norfolk CN	Arlington
06256	Winslow, Hattie A.	65y	C	30 SEP 1907	Newark NJ	Payne's
07146	Winslow, Martha Ann	67y	C	6 AUG 1909	Asbury Park NJ	Payne's
06380	Winslow, Martha C.	63y	W	6 JAN 1908	Riverdale MD	Oak Hill
06499	Winston, Benjamin	84y	C	9 APR 1908	Arlington VA	Payne's
01513	Winston, Isaac	33y	W	1 MAY 1863	Tuscumbia AL	Congressional
04776	Winston, Mattie S.W.	62y	W	27 JUN 1904	New York NY	Rock Creek
09148	Winston, Olive M.	78y	W	29 MAR 1913	New York NY	Congressional

No.	Name of Deceased	Age	Race	Death Date	Place of Death	Place of Burial
06326	Winston, Samuel	72y	W	24 NOV 1907	New York NY	Rock Creek
09107	Winston, Walker	54y	W	4 MAR 1913	Forrest City AR	Congressional
13421	Winter, Eugene Charles Curtis	66y	W	20 MAR 1916	Dominion Hts. VA	Oak Hill
03296	Winthrop, Alice Worthington	54y	W	2 OCT 1900	New York NY	Rock Creek
02804	Winthrop, William, Col., U.S.A.	67y	W	8 APR 1899	Atlantic City NJ	Oak Hill
14920	Wirt, John D.	22y	W	18 JUL 1918	Elkton MD	Rock Creek
16982	Wise, Annie B.	55y	W	16 FEB 1921	Baltimore MD	Glenwood
18588	Wise, Annie M.	70y	W	5 JUN 1923	Baltimore MD	Mt. Olivet
17925	Wise, John Crupper	73y	W	13 JUN 1922	Arlington VA	Warrenton VA
14298	Wise, Mabel	29y	W	14 AUG 1917	New York NY	Harmony
06360	Wise, Maria	65y	C	23 DEC 1907	Philadelphia PA	Mt. Zion East
15755	Wise, Mary E. Cook	90y	W	27 APR 1919	Baltimore MD	Glenwood
14906	Wiseman, Clarence H.	19y	W	9 JUL 1918	Fairfax Co. VA	Mankato MN
15401	Witham, Annie E.	60y	W	3 DEC 1918	Philadelphia PA	Rock Creek
07709	Withers, Rose L.	38y	W	24 AUG 1910	Chevy Chase MD	Glenwood
12191	Withington, Gertrude	66y	W	29 JAN 1914	Trenton NJ	Rock Creek
04996	Witter, Elizabeth	36y	W	8 JAN 1905	New York NY	Rock Creek
00912	Wittington, William	94y	W	31 AUG 1892	Jackson MI	Rock Creek
01209	Wittmer, Fritz	42y	W	24 JUN 1892	Allegheny PA	Oak Hill
08178	Wofford, Jefferson Llew., Col.	77y	W	4 JUL 1911	Estouliville VA	Cremated
02855	Wohlfarth, Mary E.	12y	W	22 JUN 1899	Glen Echo MD	Rock Creek
03768	Wohlfarth, Nettie F.	38y	W	26 JAN 1902	Glen Echo MD	Rock Creek
06261	Wolcott, Elizabeth W.	—	W	4 OCT 1907	Annapolis MD	Glenwood
16053	Wolf, Abraham B., Rabbi	48y	W	14 OCT 1919	Knoxville TN	Talmud Torah
13713	Wolf, Frederick	39y	W	9 SEP 1916	Saranac Lake NY	Congressional
00799	Wolf, Herbert	6y	W	1875	Philadelphia PA	Wash. Hebrew
06461	Wolf, Leopold	42y	W	10 MAR 1908	N. Takoma MD	Wash. Hebrew
01421	Wolf, Samuel, bookkeeper	37y	W	21 JUN 1894	Burlington IA	Wash. Hebrew
18580	Wolf, Simon, s/o Levi	86y	W	4 JUN 1923	Atlantic City NJ	Wash. Hebrew
13492	Wolf, Stanley L., Jr.	10m	W	5 MAY 1916	Washington DC	Rock Creek
17743	Wolf, William	62y	W	14 MAR 1922	Atlantic City NJ	Adas Israel
07538	Wolfe, Joseph T.	39y	W	6 MAY 1910	Los Angeles CA	Mt. Olivet
16424	Wolford, Henrietta	51y	C	5 APR 1920	Philadelphia PA	Holyrood
12553	Wolford, Henry Claw	43y	W	6 OCT 1914	Chevy Chase MD	Methodist
08667	Wolford, Sarah E.	62y	W	12 JUN 1912	Chevy Chase MD	Methodist
14387	Wollard, Charles F.	67y	W	28 SEP 1917	Washington DC	Glenwood
14715	Wollman, Mary Ebele	54y	W	26 MAR 1918	New York NY	Rock Creek
05509	Wolls, Elizabeth Caroline	81y	W	28 MAR 1906	Chevy Chase MD	Bethlehem PA
01366	Wolz, George C.	3y	W	13 APR 1894	Rosslyn VA	Rock Creek
04043	Wolz, George M.	33y	W	13 OCT 1902	Ft. Myer Hts. VA	Rock Creek
17112	Wolz, Henry	46y	W	18 APR 1921	Hampton VA	Oak Hill
13217	Wolz, Mary C.	26y	W	21 NOV 1915	Rosslyn VA	St. Mary's
13007	Wonderstahl, Charlotte	60y	W	15 JUL 1915	King Geo. Co. VA	Arlington
04292	Wonn, Laura	58y	W	6 JUN 1903	Redland MD	Glenwood
13495	Wonn, William W.	74y	W	5 MAY 1916	Towson MD	Glenwood
14294	Wood, Annie L.	35y	W	13 AUG 1917	Arlington VA	Lewistown PA
16764	Wood, Asabel Frank	84y	W	17 OCT 1920	Silver Spring MD	Rock Creek
14533	Wood, Charles	21y	C	25 DEC 1917	Pittsburgh PA	Woodlawn
07933	Wood, Charles E.	32y	C	20 JAN 1911	Occoquan VA	Payne's
17804	Wood, Clarence	38y	W	15 APR 1922	Camp Hump. VA	Congressional
04212	Wood, Delphane	18y	W	12 MAR 1903	Boston MA	Arlington
08204	Wood, Edgar W.	34y	W	13 JUL 1911	Kansas City MO	Forestville MD
18479	Wood, Edna M.	20y	W	14 APR 1923	N. Bea. MD	Congressional
04911	Wood, Foster P., Capt.	80y	W	6 OCT 1904	Bedford PA	Arlington
03189	Wood, Francis Gregory	36y	W	20 MAY 1900	Utica NY	Oak Hill
06451	Wood, Frank	18y	W	29 FEB 1908	Ft. Wash. MD	Mitchell IN
03016	Wood, George J., Jr.	27y	W	15 APR 1877	Ellington CN	Oak Hill
01785	Wood, Helen J.	64y	W	6 AUG 1895	Baltimore MD	Rock Creek
17489	Wood, Henrietta V.	67y	W	26 OCT 1921	Arlington Co. VA	Glenwood
03711	Wood, Henry	73y	W	23 NOV 1901	Berwyn MD	Arlington

District of Columbia Foreign Death Records, 1888-1923

No.	Name of Deceased	Age	Race	Death Date	Place of Death	Place of Burial
17983	Wood, Ida	28y	C	27 JUL 1922	Asheville NC	Woodlawn
17623	Wood, Jack M.	1y	C	7 JAN 1922	Park Lane VA	Glenwood
09194	Wood, James	24y	W	20 APR 1913	Pocatello ID	Mt. Olivet
05351	Wood, James E.	59y	W	9 NOV 1905	Ft. Myer Hts. VA	Glenwood
17019	Wood, John A.	21y	C	5 MAR 1921	Brentwood MD	Mt. Olivet
08844	Wood, Julia A.	32y	W	16 SEP 1912	New York NY	Oak Hill
14259	Wood, Marie G. (Storch)	45y	W	30 JUL 1917	Atlantic City NJ	Oak Hill
17213	Wood, Matilda	57y	C	4 JUN 1921	Crownsville MD	Harmony
03373	Wood, Montgomery	23y	W	23 DEC 1900	Linden MD	Rock Creek
12016	Wood, Nancy E.	79y	W	25 SEP 1913	Winchester NH	Rock Creek
03812	Wood, Rebecca A.	59y	W	13 MAR 1902	Montg. Co. MD	Rock Creek
18481	Wood, Richard A.	74y	W	11 APR 1923	Tampa FL	Cremated
00117	Wood, Sarah Amanda	54y	W	27 JUL 1889	Forest Glen MD	Glenwood
15347	Wood, Sarah E.	60y	C	10 NOV 1918	Baltimore MD	Harmony
17812	Wood, Sophia L.	47y	C	21 APR 1922	Brentwood MD	Mt. Olivet
14887	Wood, Susan A.	66y	W	28 JUN 1918	Goshen NY	Arlington
07917	Wood, Susan L.	62y	C	10 JAN 1911	Fairmont Hts. MD	Payne's
03122	Wood, Thomas	24y	C	8 MAR 1900	Alex. Co. VA	Baptist
17131	Wood, Victoria M.	54y	W	28 APR 1921	Wilmington DE	Oak Hill
01010	Wood, Viola K.	6y	W	29 AUG 1893	Riggs Rd. MD	Rock Creek
14176	Wood, William E.	36y	W	13 JUN 1917	Glen Echo MD	Rock Creek
12903	Wood, William R.C.	40y	W	29 APR 1915	Baltimore MD	Oak Hill
12847	Woodal, Elizabeth	5d	W	30 MAR 1915	Takoma Park MD	Rock Creek
12180	Woodall, Addie Evelyn	2y	W	23 JAN 1914	Takoma Park MD	Rock Creek
02359	Woodbury, Alice M.	—	W	1 JAN 1898	Middleboro KY	Oak Hill
01945	Woodbury, Catherine R.	76y	W	11 MAY 1896	Middleborough KY	Oak Hill
08338	Woodbury, Thomas C.	61y	W	26 SEP 1911	LaJolla CA	Oak Hill
16341	Woodend, George Kenneth B.	1m	W	26 FEB 1920	Capitol Hts. MD	Congressional
00915	Woodet, John	70y	C	8 SEP 1892	Pr. Geo. Co. MD	Mt. Olivet
03624	Woodfin, P.T., Col.	61y	W	24 AUG 1901	Hampton VA	Arlington VA
17325	Woodhall, Maxwell V.Z.	77y	W	25 JUL 1921	Watkins NY	Oak Hill
01783	Woodhull, Ellen Frances	75y	W	9 SEP 1895	Narragansett RI	Oak Hill
16756	Woodhull, Ellen Marian Eliz.	65y	W	13 OCT 1920	Atlantic City NJ	Oak Hill
17265	Woodland, Clifford	18y	C	25 JUN 1921	Brentwood MD	Harmony
05003	Woodland, Frank	11m	C	15 JAN 1905	Pr. Geo. Co. MD	Harmony
16996	Woodland, Lucille	30y	C	20 FEB 1921	New York NY	Payne's
12957	Woodland, Theodore	6y	W	7 JUN 1915	Brentwood MD	Harmony
01846	Woodroe, Charles	65y	C	7 JUL 1895	Hampton VA	Arlington VA
02350	Woodruff, Dorothy B.	22m	W	10 APR 1897	Ft. Custer MT	Holyrood
06189	Woodruff, George A., Jr.	21y	W	17 AUG 1907	Pittsburgh PA	Rock Creek
03104	Woodruff, Ruth Hop	5m	W	30 JAN 1900	Ft. Riley KS	Holyrood
01103	Woods, Arthur Tannett	34y	W	7 FEB 1893	Chicago IL	Rock Creek
14978	Woods, Elizabeth	c.32y	W	14 AUG 1918	Dodge Park MD	Rock Creek
18554	Woods, Elliott	59y	W	22 mAY 1923	Spring Lake NJ	Cremated
12093	Woods, Howard Thorpe	44y	W	13 NOV 1913	Brooklyn NY	Rock Creek
01784	Woods, William N.	24y	W	16 OCT 1895	Petersburg VA	Congressional
04344	Woodson, Albert E.	63y	W	7 AUG 1903	Paola KS	Arlington
06758	Woodson, Emmett L., s/o A.W.	49y	W	6 OCT 1908	Dranesville VA	Cremated
17333	Woodson, John Henry	38y	C	11 JUN 1918	France	Payne's
14178	Woodson, Lucy	45y	C	17 JUN 1917	Long Branch NJ	Mt. Zion West
17095	Woodward, Alice G.	75y	W	8 APR 1921	Silver Spring MD	Glenwood
17537	Woodward, Beall	18y	W	20 NOV 1921	Chapel Hill NC	Congressional
06283	Woodward, Charles J.	76y	W	22 OCT 1907	Hampton VA	Oak Hill
11965	Woodward, Charlotte F.	70y	W	17 AUG 1913	Franklin Co. PA	Arlington
13819	Woodward, Florence A.	39y	C	19 NOV 1916	Huntsville MD	Mt. Olivet
03106	Woodward, Frank B.	19y	W	5 MAR 1900	W. Palm Bea. FL	Glenwood
12763	Woodward, Frank L.	72y	W	13 FEB 1915	Glen Echo MD	Cremated
15383	Woodward, Infant of Mark R.	SB	W	24 NOV 1918	Allentown PA	Congressional
12380	Woodward, James Savage	59y	W	28 MAY 1914	Roland Park MD	Mt. Olivet
07125	Woodward, Jean	6m	W	22 JUL 1909	Wash. Grove MD	Oak Hill

No.	Name of Deceased	Age	Race	Death Date	Place of Death	Place of Burial
05891	Woodward, Jeffry	55y	C	9 JAN 1906	Landover MD	Mt. Olivet
04498	Woodward, Mary C.	19y	W	1 NOV 1903	Del Ray VA	Mt. Olivet
14495	Woodward, Mary E.	63y	W	11 DEC 1917	Alexandria VA	Mt. Olivet
08801	Woodward, Mary E.	81y	W	13 MAR 1912	Wilkinsburg PA	Oak Hill
02960	Woodward, Mary Elizabeth	70y	W	26 SEP 1899	Annapolis MD	Mt. Olivet
00674	Woodward, Mary Florence	26y	W	20 SEP 1891	Montg. Co. MD	Rock Creek
15690	Woodward, Mary M.	18y	C	22 MAR 1919	Huntsville MD	Mt. Olivet
08466	Woodward, Rebecca	77y	W	9 JAN 1912	Jacksonville FL	Oak Hill
14271	Woodward, Samuel Walter	68y	W	1 AUG 1917	Eden Hill MA	Oak Hill
01210	Woodward, Thomas Carrington	63y	W	14 DEC 1892	Woodside MD	Oak Hill
02475	Woodward, Walter Lothrop	16y	W	3 MAY 1898	Paris, France	Oak Hill
05236	Woodward, William B.	86y	W	7 AUG 1905	Wash. Grove MD	Oak Hill
03457	Woodward, William James	10y	W	19 MAR 1901	Del Ray VA	Mt. Olivet
02532	Woodward, William Redin	44y	W	27 JUN 1898	Wash. Grove MD	Oak Hill
16252	Woody, Louis	35y	C	27 JAN 1920	Baltimore MD	Harmony
07110	Woog, Benjamin Bernard	30y	W	15 JUL 1909	Atlantic City NJ	Wash. Hebrew
07528	Woog, Edmund S.	71y	W	3 MAY 1910	New York NY	Wash. Hebrew
18252	Woolf, Samuel Register	41y	W	4 JAN 1923	Clifton Forge VA	Congressional
00528	Woolley, George A.	48y	W	12 JAN 1891	Chester VT	Congressional
13008	Woolsey, William M.	64y	W	16 JUL 1915	Takoma Park MD	Greenville TN
05988	Wootson, Moses	41y	C	14 MAR 1907	Philadelphia PA	Payne's
05725	Worch, John	73y	W	24 FEB 1905	Boise ID	Glenwood
15448	Worden, Charles H.	76y	W	15 DEC 1918	Baltimore MD	Arlington
02979	Work, Henry Lester	49y	W	12 OCT 1899	Birmingham AL	Glenwood
06962	Work, William J.	52y	W	29 MAR 1909	Maryland Pk. MD	Mt. Olivet
07214	Workman, Infant of Wilford	46h	W	25 SEP 1909	Takoma Park MD	Glenwood
13274	Workman, Richard	37y	W	28 DEC 1915	Hoboken NJ	Mt. Olivet
18485	Works, Catherine Shepard	73y	W	16 APR 1923	Takoma Park MD	Arlington
13669	Wormeley, Sarah E.	49y	C	19 AUG 1916	Bergen NJ	Harmony
13100	Wormley, James A.	49y	C	10 SEP 1915	Newark NJ	Harmony
09159	Wormley, John	c.70y	C	6 APR 1913	Hampton VA	Arlington VA
17822	Wormley, Leonard B.	40y	C	29 APR 1922	Burlington NC	Harmony
15897	Wormley, William Stanton	49y	C	30 JUOL 1919	Ardwick MD	Harmony
08105	Wormly, Clemont H.	33y	C	7 MAY 1911	Detroit MI	Harmony
03237	Worth, Henry A.F.	c.63y	W	16 JUL 1900	Ramsey NJ	Rock Creek
04712	Worth, John C.	55y	W	14 MAY 1904	Ardwick Sta. MD	Newark DE
14839	Worthen, Louise C.	24y	W	25 MAY 1918	Anniston AL	Glenwood
01104	Worthington, Albert, Rev.	86y	W	16 MAY 1893	Ambler PA	Graceland
17790	Worthington, Augustus Storrs	78y	W	9 APR 1922	Chevy Chase MD	Oak Hill
15927	Worthington, Henrietta P.	77y	W	12 AUG 1919	Birmingham AL	Valley Farm MD
00118	Worthmiller, Edward Joseph	22y	W	18 JUL 1889	Montg. Co. MD	Holyrood
01011	Worthmiller, John	59y	W	14 JUN 1893	Bethesda MD	Holyrood
15774	Worthmiller, John H.	56y	W	11 MAY 1919	Bethesda MD	Holyrood
06638	Woster, Giles	38y	W	11 JUL 1908	Middleburg VA	Glenwood
18336	Wracks, Ella	65y	C	9 FEB 1923	Milford CN	Woodlawn
18552	Wrenn, John Lee	50y	W	20 MAY 1923	Silver Spring MD	Glenwood
15147	Wrenn, Stanley	21y	W	12 OCT 1918	Baltimore MD	Congressional
00241	Wrenn, William	—	W	1823	Fairfax Co. VA	Congressional
16592	Wright, Alice S.	65y	W	11 JUL 1920	Forrestville MD	Congressional
14350	Wright, Carrie	77y	W	6 SEP 1917	Long Branch NJ	Arlington
15496	Wright, Charles A.	36y	W	27 DEC 1918	Hyattsville MD	Mt. Olivet
01288	Wright, Christina	37y	W	15 DEC 1893	Baltimore MD	Glenwood
11824	Wright, Eleanor Herdman	82y	W	23 MAY 1913	Forest Glen MD	Rock Creek
00800	Wright, Eliza R.	75y	W	14 MAR 1892	Baltimore MD	Glenwood
08213	Wright, Elizabeth	68y	W	25 JUL 1911	Round Hill VA	Congressional
00529	Wright, Elizabeth E.	15y	W	27 FEB 1891	Marriottsville MD	Mt. Olivet
05742	Wright, Esther J.	77y	W	12 SEP 1906	Bevier KY	Arlington
01106	Wright, Eva M.	6m	W	12 MAR 1893	Baltimore MD	Glenwood
16157	Wright, George L.	63y	C	19 DEC 1919	Mountclair NJ	Harmony
04614	Wright, George Wash. Taylor	72y	W	27 FEB 1904	Kensington MD	Rock Creek

District of Columbia Foreign Death Records, 1888-1923

No.	Name of Deceased	Age	Race	Death Date	Place of Death	Place of Burial
13294	Wright, Georgie Hays	76y	W	12 JAN 1916	Pine Bluff AR	Rock Creek
06393	Wright, Helen B., d/o Lawr.	3m	W	17 JAN 1908	Ballston VA	Methodist
06315	Wright, Henry Clay	59y	W	19 NOV 1907	Catonsville MD	Glenwood
16080	Wright, Infant of Charles A.	12h	W	29 OCT 1919	Mt. Ranier MD	Congressional
01105	Wright, Jonathan	71y	W	19 MAY 1893	Hyattsville MD	Glenwood
03619	Wright, Joseph	40y	W	1 AUG 1901	Canal Fulton OH	Congressional
09017	Wright, Levi Parker, s/o Geo.	88y	W	3 JAN 1912	Bevier KY	Arlington
06458	Wright, Lillian Ellion, d/o Lawr.	3y	W	6 MAR 1908	Ballston VA	Methodist
02456	Wright, Louise T.	9m	W	14 APR 1898	Lincoln MD	Rock Creek
03530	Wright, Marion Helena	45y	W	1 JUN 1901	Mt. Hope MD	Congressional
02284	Wright, Mary E.	70y	C	24 JUL 1897	Bladensburg MD	Mt. Olivet
14168	Wright, Mary Mildred	70y	W	11 JUN 1917	Lorton VA	Congressional
13741	Wright, Roberta D.	22y	W	30 SEP 1916	Thurmont MD	Congressional
02231	Wright, Sallie	51y	W	10 MAY 1897	Dresden, Ger.	Oak Hill
08884	Wright, Sarah	56y	C	10 OCT 1912	Baltimore MD	Woodlawn
05617	Wright, Sarah L.	10m	C	1 JUL 1906	Bethesda MD	Christian
03471	Wright, Stephen	5y	W	4 APR 1901	Newport News VA	Rock Creek
02928	Wright, Susan M.	27y	W	25 AUG 1899	Baltimore MD	Congressional
06001	Wright, Washington S.	86y	W	30 MAR 1907	Forestville MD	Glenwood
05035	Wright, William	28y	W	18 FEB 1905	Allegheny PA	Mt. Zion
08361	Wright, William H.	67y	C	17 OCT 1911	Baltimore MD	Payne's
12619	Wright, William L.	36y	W	14 NOV 1914	Wash. Grove MD	Glenwood
04516	Wright, William Wallace	83y	W	16 NOV 1903	Hamburg NY	Rock Creek
04792	Wrisley, Fanny B.	62y	W	13 JUL 1904	Brooklyn NY	Oak Hill
08613	Wunder, Anna M.	74y	W	28 APR 1912	Livingston Hts. VA	Congressional
06479	Wunder, George O.	78y	W	20 MAR 1908	Livingston Hts. VA	Congressional
05494	Wunderlick, John F.	61y	W	9 MAR 1906	New York NY	Congressional
17342	Wurdeman, Sidney S.	58y	W	1 AUG 1921	Yellowstone WY	Rock Creek
04980	Wurdemann, Charles F.	55y	W	19 DEC 1904	Philadelphia PA	Glenwood
06792	Wurtenberg, Isidor	43y	W	30 OCT 1908	Laurel MD	Wash. Hebrew
15141	Wurtz, Harry L.	19y	W	12 OCT 1918	Mt. Ranier MD	Glenwood
03954	Wyatt, Rose	42y	C	4 JUL 1902	Asbury Park NJ	Harmony
02953	Wyckoff, Mary Jane	60y	W	2 SEP 1899	Glen Echo MD	Arlington VA
01107	Wyckoff, Minnie Amelia	30y	W	19 FEB 1893	Hickory NC	Congressional
07007	Wylie, Annie E.	73y	W	1 MAY 1909	Beltsville MD	Rock Creek
04467	Wylie, James H.	2y	W	4 OCT 1903	Boston MA	Oak Hill
03537	Wylie, William H.	59y	W	9 JUN 1901	Oakdale MD	Rock Creek
00801	Wyman, A.M.	55y	W	1 NOV 1871	Altoona PA	Glenwood
07582	Wyman, Emily M.	92y	W	19 JUN 1910	Ellicott City MD	Oak Hill
18211	Wyman, Margaret T.	75y	W	11 DEC 1922	Cheyenne WY	Oak Hill
17972	Wynn, Howard B.	55y	C	14 JUL 1922	Garrett IN	Payne's
16849	Wynn, John	34y	W	5 DEC 1920	Chicago IL	Cedar Hill
02285	Wynne, Claude	52y	W	7 JUL 1897	Chicago IL	Rock Creek
14555	Wynne, Madiline Yale	70y	W	4 JAN 1918	Asheville NC	Cremated
13154	Wynne, Mary E.	60y	W	14 OCT 1915	Los Angeles CA	Mt. Olivet
16901	Wynne, Minerva S.	89y	W	6 JAN 1921	New York NY	Oak Hill
15934	Wyville, Walter N.	49y	W	15 AUG 1919	Philadelphia PA	Oak Hill

No.	Name of Deceased	Age	Race	Death Date	Place of Death	Place of Burial
X						
02252	Xander, Caroline	51y	W	21 JUL 1897	Harpers Ferry WV	Prospect Hill
15968	Xander, Gottlieb F.	49y	W	31 AUG 1919	Mt. Ranier MD	Prospect Hill
06193	Xander, William C.F.	1y	W	21 AUG 1907	Potomac MD	Prospect Hill

District of Columbia Foreign Death Records, 1888-1923

No.	Name of Deceased	Age	Race	Death Date	Place of Death	Place of Burial
Y						
13683	Yaeger, John Herster	24y	W	27 AUG 1916	Lake Harmony PA	Rock Creek
05262	Yager, Mary V. (Coles)	34y	C	29 AUG 1905	Pittsburgh PA	Harmony
12895	Yager, Thomas Beverly	50y	C	11 APR 1915	Melrose Park PA	Harmony
18565	Yarnell, Carrie J. (Jordan)	50y	W	24 MAY 1923	Los Angeles CA	Rock Creek
12491	Yates, Allen	38y	W	23 AUG 1914	Rosslyn VA	Mt. Zion West
01847	Yates, Annie T.	41y	C	8 JAN 1896	New York NY	Mt. Zion
07939	Yates, Charlotte (Colt), d/o Ja.	47y	W	24 JAN 1911	Park Lane VA	Oak Hill
18304	Yates, Elizabeth	23y	C	26 OCT 1918	Philadelphia PA	Payne's
09008	Yates, Frederick Colt	54y	W	1 JAN 1913	Alex. Co. VA	Oak Hill
00802	Yates, Lucinda	84y	W	9 APR 1892	Chantilly VA	Mt. Olivet
04463	Yates, Mary	58y	C	26 SEP 1903	New York NY	Harmony
08190	Yates, Moyston	28y	W	10 JUL 1911	Arlington VA	Leonardtown MD
00803	Yates, Sophia	76y	C	12 MAR 1892	Bladensburg MD	Harmony
04705	Yates, William	22y	C	5 MAY 1904	Philadelphia PA	Payne's
06109	Yates, William A., s/o Wm. A.	42y	W	15 JUN 1907	Colonial Bea. VA	Congressional
07459	Yates, William N.	—	W	8 MAR 1910	Tampa FL	Glenwood
14246	Yeager, Mary	43y	C	22 JUL 1917	Philadelphia PA	Moore's
03273	Yeates, George S.	38y	W	20 AUG 1900	Cincinnati OH	Glenwood
06437	Yeates, William S.	52y	W	19 FEB 1908	Atlanta GA	Glenwood
05914	Yeatman, Arthur A.	57y	W	27 JAN 1907	Tampa FL	Oak Hill
01786	Yeatman, Edward Clement	22y	W	7 OCT 1895	Charlestown WV	Rock Creek
18219	Yeatman, Marshall H.	80y	W	20 DEC 1922	Wilmington DE	Arlington
00804	Yeatman, Susan	28y	W	16 JAN 1892	Ft. Monroe VA	Oak Hill
03209	Yeatman, Thomas J.	59y	W	14 OCT 1893	Washington DC	Glenwood
03482	Yeatman, William S.	62y	W	20 APR 1901	York PA	Oak Hill
08143	Yerke, Arlene O.	23y	W	9 JUN 1811	Berwyn MD	Glenwood
08365	Yerkes, Orinda E.	70y	W	18 OCT 1911	Rochester NY	Rock Creek
12558	Yoe, Ellen Beall	65y	W	2 AUG 1914	Highland Park IL	Oak Hill
13024	Yoeckel, John Lewis	67y	W	24 JUL 1915	Darnestown MD	Baltimore MD
08200	Yohe, Ida Craigen	40y	W	13 JUL 1911	Cumberland MD	Rock Creek
04991	York, Cath. Ellen	27y	W	4 JAN 1905	Newark NJ	Rock Creek
17328	Yoshikawa, Masanon	25y	J	21 JUL 1921	Leesburg VA	Cremated
14122	Young, Anna M., d/o Edward	60y	W	1 MAY 1917	Thomason GA	Oak Hill
00191	Young, Annie W.	50y	W	12 OCT 1889	Mt. Hope MD	Oak Hill
02890	Young, Bernard J., merchant	32y	W	30 JUL 1899	Norfolk VA	Adas Israel
15935	Young, Charles E., Rev.	70y	W	17 AUG 1919	Takoma Park MD	Harpers Ferry WV
12035	Young, Curtis	23y	C	8 OCT 1913	Pittsburgh PA	Harmony
03671	Young, Florence Edith	58y	W	2 OCT 1901	Spring Hill VA	Mt. Olivet
03726	Young, George W.	62y	W	27 NOV 1901	Englewood NJ	Arlington VA
14617	Young, Herbert D.	7y	W	2 FEB 1918	Alexandria VA	Congressional[1]
16658	Young, Ida Perry	71y	W	13 AUG 1920	Centerville MD	Rock Creek
14559	Young, Infant of Charles	1d	W	27 DEC 1917	Arlington VA	Mt. Zion West
14101	Young, John H.	12y	W	21 APR 1917	Baltimore MD	Congressional
17054	Young, John M.	39y	C	18 MAR 1921	Hyattsville MD	Payne's
15071	Young, John Wesley	74y	W	3 OCT 1918	Chevy Chase MD	Rock Creek
15038	Young, Margaret	36y	W	20 SEP 1918	Philadelphia PA	Woodlawn
02430	Young, Marian E.	61y	W	13 DEC 1897	Jersey City NJ	Oak Hill
06949	Young, Marie	10y	C	14 MAR 1909	Atlantic City NJ	Payne's
04501	Young, Mary	72y	W	4 NOV 1903	Manchester MD	Congressional
06098	Young, Mattie Lee	—	W	5 JUN 1907	Kensington MD	Rock Creek
18374	Young, Oliver	30y	C	26 FEB 1923	Fairmont Hts. MD	Woodlawn
14084	Young, Rachel	54y	C	10 APR 1917	Rosaryville MD	Woodlawn
16682	Young, Ruth	25y	W	27 AUG 1920	Glen Echo MD	Milwaukee WI
03735	Young, Samuel G.	34y	W	20 DEC 1901	Baltimore MD	Rock Creek
12392	Young, Sarah C.	76y	W	7 JUN 1914	New York NY	Congressional

[1] Removed to Alexandria, Va., 20 MAY 1919.

No.	Name of Deceased	Age	Race	Death Date	Place of Death	Place of Burial
13677	Young, Susan Grice	38y	W	25 AUG 1916	Chevy Chase MD	Rock Creek
12524	Young, William A.	55y	W	9 SEP 1914	Atlantic City NJ	Glenwood
03737	Young, William Andrew	61y	W	19 DEC 1901	Arlington VA	Congressional
02349	Young, William H.	55y	C	29 SEP 1897	Batesburg SC	Moore's
06595	Young, William H.	70y	W	19 JUN 1908	Chicago IL	Mt. Olivet
17321	Youngs, Marie Adail	71y	W	22 JUL 1921	Takoma Park MD	Glenwood
05299	Yznago, Martina	28y	W	20 SEP 1905	Vancouver WA	Rock Creek

No.	Name of Deceased	Age	Race	Death Date	Place of Death	Place of Burial

Z

No.	Name of Deceased	Age	Race	Death Date	Place of Death	Place of Burial
13484	Zagos, George K.	c.27y	W	30 APR 1916	Chapel Point MD	Rock Creek
05462	Zanies, Louis, of Italy	23y	W	11 FEB 1906	Norfolk VA	St. Mary's
05328	Zchammer, Julius	73y	W	20 OCT 1905	Newport RI	Soldier's Home
15952	Zegowitz, Frederick J.	54y	W	25 AUG 1919	Mt. Ranier MD	St. Mary's
04314	Zeh, William H., grocer	68y	W	20 MAY 1903	Mt. Hope MD	Prospect Hill
04600	Zell, George R.	50y	W	8 FEB 1904	Troy TN	Mt. Olivet
05642	Zellers, Pauline	1y	W	13 JUL 1906	Brentwood MD	Glenwood
07797	Zellers, Webster Franklin	1y	W	21 OCT 1910	Brentwood MD	Glenwood
02033	Zepp, Aggie E.	—	W	7 JUL 1896	Grafton WV	Rock Creek
07406	Zevely, Elizabeth C.	61y	W	5 FEB 1910	New York NY	Rock Creek
03612	Zevely, Howard	41y	W	5 AUG 1901	New York NY	Rock Creek
06342	Zevely, Mary E., d/o Alex. M.	58y	W	6 DEC 1907	New York NY	Rock Creek
06342	Zevely, Mary E., d/o Alex.	58y	W	6 DEC 1907	New York NY	Rock Creek
03022	Zier, Mary Ellen	61y	W	1 DEC 1899	Hyattsville MD	Prospect Hill
07031	Zimmerman, Edward George	36y	W	20 MAY 1909	E. Hyattsville MD	Mt. Olivet
18070	Zimmerman, Janet	34y	W	15 SEP 1922	Takoma Park MD	Oak Hill
18466	Zinkham, Mary Alice	64y	W	24 JAN 1923	Boonsboro MD	Rock Creek
15503	Zirwes, Milton W.	14y	W	31 DEC 1918	Takoma Park MD	Prospect Hill
15681	Zoellner, Marie	23y	W	17 MAR 1919	Falls Church VA	Prospect Hill
13910	Zucca, Harriett E.	37y	W	4 JAN 1917	Pitman NJ	Rock Creek
06901	Zucca, John	54y	W	1 SEP 1908	Chicago IL	Rock Creek
08344	Zures, Peter	4m	W	6 OCT 1911	Seat Pleasant MD	Mt. Olivet
05240	Zurhorst, Grace Marie	15y	W	10 AUG 1905	Kemptville, N.S.	Congressional
08334	Zych, Andrew	45y	W	30 OCT 1911	Silver City NM	Mt. Olivet
14861	Zytkoskee, Laura T.	31y	W	10 JUN 1918	Takoma Park MD	Rock Creek

ABOUT THE AUTHOR

Wesley E. Pippenger is an active member in a number of historical and genealogical societies in Virginia, and is past-President of the Board of Governors of the Virginia Genealogical Society. He has been employed by the Federal Government for over twenty-seven years, and is a management analyst with the Office of Inspector General, National Aeronautics and Space Administration in Washington, D.C. He resides in Arlington, Virginia.

Mr. Pippenger has been active in genealogical research since 1970. Shortly after moving from Colorado to Virginia in 1982, he began to locate, study, catalog, and have data published about cemeteries in the Alexandria, Virginia area. Subsequent published works, now numbering upwards of sixty items, include abstracts of court records, vital records, acts of the Virginia Assembly, newspapers, land, probate, and legislative petition records, and more. His current landmark project, published in series by the Virginia Genealogical Society, is to inventory all estate-related documents for the period 1800-1865, for the entire state of Virginia.

Other Heritage Books by Wesley E. Pippenger:

Alexandria (Arlington) County, Virginia Death Records, 1853-1896

Alexandria City and Arlington County, Virginia Records Index: Vol. 1

Alexandria City and Arlington County, Virginia Records Index: Vol. 2

Alexandria County, Virginia Marriage Records, 1853-1895

Alexandria Virginia Marriage Index, January 10, 1893 to August 31, 1905

Alexandria, Virginia Marriages, 1870-1892

*Alexandria, Virginia Town Lots, 1749-1801
Together with the Proceedings of the Board of Trustees, 1749-1780*

Alexandria, Virginia Wills, Administrations and Guardianships, 1786-1800

Alexandria, Virginia 1808 Census (Wards 1, 2, 3, and 4)

Alexandria, Virginia Death Records, 1863-1896

Alexandria, Virginia Hustings Court Orders, Volume 1, 1780-1787

*Connections and Separations: Divorce, Name Change and Other
Genealogical Tidbits from the Acts of the Virginia General Assembly*

Daily National Intelligencer *Index to Deaths, 1855-1870*

Daily National Intelligencer, *Washington, District of Columbia
Marriages and Deaths Notices (January 1, 1851 to December 30, 1854)*

*Dead People on the Move: Reconstruction of the Georgetown Presbyterian
Burying Ground, Holmead's (Western) Burying Ground, and
Other Removals in the District of Columbia*

Death Notices from Richmond, Virginia Newspapers, 1841-1853

District of Columbia Ancestors, A Guide to Records of the District of Columbia

District of Columbia Death Records: August 1, 1874-July 31, 1879

District of Columbia Foreign Deaths, 1888-1923

District of Columbia Guardianship Index, 1802-1928

*District of Columbia Interments (Index to Deaths)
January 1, 1855 to July 31, 1874*

District of Columbia Marriage Licenses, Register 1: 1811-1858

District of Columbia Marriage Licenses, Register 2: 1858-1870

*District of Columbia Marriage Records Index
June 28, 1877 to October 19, 1885: Marriage Record Books 11 to 20*
Wesley E. Pippenger and Dorothy S. Provine

*District of Columbia Marriage Records Index
October 20, 1885 to January 20, 1892: Marriage Record Books 21 to 30*

District of Columbia Probate Records, 1801-1852

District of Columbia: Original Land Owners, 1791-1800

Early Church Records of Alexandria City and Fairfax County, Virginia

*Georgetown, District of Columbia 1850 Federal Population Census (Schedule I)
and 1853 Directory of Residents of Georgetown*

Georgetown, District of Columbia Marriage and Death Notices, 1801-1838

*Husbands and Wives Associated with Early Alexandria, Virginia
(and the Surrounding Area), 3rd Edition, Revised*

Index to District of Columbia Estates, 1801-1929

*Index to Virginia Estates, 1800-1865
Volumes 4, 5 and 6*

John Alexander, a Northern Neck Proprietor, His Family, Friends and Kin

Legislative Petitions of Alexandria, 1778-1861

Pippenger and Pittenger Families

Proceedings of the Orphan's Court, Washington County, District of Columbia, 1801-1808

The Georgetown Courier *Marriage and Death Notices:
Georgetown, District of Columbia, November 18, 1865 to May 6, 1876*

*The Georgetown Directory for the Year 1830: to which is appended, a Short Description
of the Churches, Public Institutions, and the Original Charter of Georgetown, and
Extracts of the Laws Pertaining to the Chesapeake and Ohio Canal Company*

The Virginia Gazette and Alexandria Advertiser:
Volume 1, September 3, 1789 to November 11, 1790

The Virginia Journal and Alexandria Advertiser:
Volume I (February 5, 1784 to January 27, 1785)

Volume II (February 3, 1785 to January 26, 1786)

Volume III (March 2, 1786 to January 25, 1787)

Volume IV (February 8, 1787 to May 21, 1789)

The Washington and Georgetown Directory of 1853

Tombstone Inscriptions of Alexandria, Volumes 1-4

www.ingramcontent.com/pod-product-compliance
Lightning Source LLC
Chambersburg PA
CBHW070937230426
43666CB00011B/2475